Black Americans in Congress
1870–2007

PREPARED UNDER THE DIRECTION OF

THE COMMITTEE ON HOUSE ADMINISTRATION OF THE

U.S. HOUSE OF REPRESENTATIVES

ROBERT A. BRADY, CHAIRMAN

VERNON J. EHLERS, RANKING MINORITY MEMBER

BY THE

OFFICE OF HISTORY AND PRESERVATION

OFFICE OF THE CLERK

U.S. HOUSE OF REPRESENTATIVES

U.S. GOVERNMENT PRINTING OFFICE, WASHINGTON, DC, 2008

107th Congress
H. Con. Res. 43
House Document 108-224
U.S. Government Printing Office
Washington, DC: 2008

Library of Congress Cataloging-in-Publication Data

Black Americans in Congress, 1870-2007 / prepared under the direction of the Committee on House Administration of the U.S. House of Representatives, by the Office of History and Preservation, Office of the Clerk, U.S. House of Representatives.
     p. cm.
   Includes bibliographical references and index.
   1.   African American legislators--Biography. 2.   United States. Congress--Biography.   I. United States. Congress. House. Committee on House Administration. II. United States. Congress. House. Office of History and Preservation.
   E185.96.B526 2008
   328.73092'396073--dc22

                                                                    2008010047

For sale by the Superintendent of Documents, U.S. Government Printing Office
Internet: bookstore.gpo.gov Phone: toll free (866) 512-1800;   DC area (202) 512-1800
Fax: (202) 512-2104 Mail: Stop IDCC, Washington, DC 20402-0001
ISBN 978-0-16-080194-5

On the Cover

One of the preeminent African-American politicians of the 19th century, John Mercer Langston of Virginia was the only black Member of Congress to serve in elected office both before and after the Civil War. Langston's career as a proponent of civil rights, which spanned nearly five decades, was capped by his service in the U.S. House (1890–1891).

Langston, John Mercer. *From the Virginia Plantation to the National Capitol*
(Hartford, CT: American Publishing Company, 1894)

HOUSE CONCURRENT RESOLUTION NO. 43

ONE HUNDRED SEVENTH CONGRESS, FIRST SESSION

SUBMITTED BY THE HONORABLE STENY A. HOYER

Resolved by the House of Representatives (the Senate concurring),

SECTION 1. PRINTING OF REVISED VERSION OF "BLACK AMERICANS IN CONGRESS, 1870–1989". An updated version of House Document 101–117, entitled "Black Americans in Congress, 1870–1989" (as revised by the Library of Congress), shall be printed as a House document by the Public Printer, with illustrations and suitable binding, under the direction of the Committee on House Administration of the House of Representatives.

SECTION 2. NUMBER OF COPIES. In addition to the usual number, there shall be printed 30,700 copies of the document referred to in section 1, of which—(1) 25,000 shall be for the use of the Committee on House Administration of the House of Representatives; and (2) 5,700 shall be for the use of the Committee on Rules and Administration of the Senate.

Approved by the House March 21, 2001
Approved by the Senate April 6, 2001

IV

COMPILED AND EDITED UNDER THE DIRECTION
OF THE

COMMITTEE ON HOUSE ADMINISTRATION OF THE

U.S. HOUSE OF REPRESENTATIVES

ROBERT A. BRADY OF PENNSYLVANIA, CHAIRMAN
VERNON J. EHLERS OF MICHIGAN, RANKING MEMBER

ZOE LOFGREN OF CALIFORNIA

DANIEL E. LUNGREN OF CALIFORNIA

MICHAEL E. CAPUANO OF MASSACHUSETTS

KEVIN MCCARTHY OF CALIFORNIA

CHARLES A. GONZALEZ OF TEXAS

SUSAN A. DAVIS OF CALIFORNIA

ARTUR DAVIS OF ALABAMA

LORRAINE C. MILLER, CLERK OF THE U.S. HOUSE OF REPRESENTATIVES

OFFICE OF HISTORY AND PRESERVATION,
OFFICE OF THE CLERK OF THE U.S. HOUSE OF REPRESENTATIVES

MATTHEW A. WASNIEWSKI, *Historian and Editor-in-Chief*
ERIN MARIE-LLOYD HROMADA, *Writer and Researcher*
KATHLEEN JOHNSON, *Writer and Researcher*
TERRANCE RUCKER, *Writer and Researcher*
LAURA K. TURNER, *Writer and Researcher*

Contents

INTRODUCTION 1

PART I: FORMER BLACK MEMBERS OF CONGRESS

    CHAPTER I: "THE FIFTEENTH AMENDMENT IN FLESH AND BLOOD": THE SYMBOLIC GENERATION
    OF BLACK AMERICANS IN CONGRESS, 1870–1887 17

    CHAPTER II: "THE NEGROES' TEMPORARY FAREWELL": JIM CROW AND THE EXCLUSION OF AFRICAN
    AMERICANS FROM CONGRESS, 1887–1929 152

    CHAPTER III: KEEPING THE FAITH: AFRICAN AMERICANS RETURN TO CONGRESS, 1929–1970 234

    CHAPTER IV: PERMANENT INTERESTS: THE EXPANSION, ORGANIZATION, AND RISING INFLUENCE
    OF AFRICAN AMERICANS IN CONGRESS, 1971–2007 368

PART II: CURRENT BLACK MEMBERS OF CONGRESS 669

APPENDICES

    APPENDIX A: FIRST-TERM BLACK-AMERICAN MEMBERS OF THE 110TH CONGRESS 748

    APPENDIX B: BLACK-AMERICAN REPRESENTATIVES AND SENATORS BY CONGRESS,
    1870–2007 751

    APPENDIX C: BLACK-AMERICAN REPRESENTATIVES AND SENATORS BY STATE AND TERRITORY 766

    APPENDIX D: BLACK-AMERICAN MEMBERS' COMMITTEE ASSIGNMENTS (STANDING, JOINT, SELECT)
    IN THE U.S. HOUSE AND SENATE, 1870–2007 769

    APPENDIX E: BLACK AMERICANS WHO HAVE CHAIRED CONGRESSIONAL COMMITTEES,
    1877–2007 780

    APPENDIX F: BLACK-AMERICAN CHAIRS OF SUBCOMMITTEES OF STANDING COMMITTEES
    IN THE U.S. HOUSE AND SENATE, 1885–2007 782

    APPENDIX G: BLACK AMERICANS IN PARTY LEADERSHIP POSITIONS, 1977–2007 787

    APPENDIX H: BLACK-AMERICAN FAMILIAL CONNECTIONS IN CONGRESS 788

    APPENDIX I: CONGRESSIONAL BLACK CAUCUS CHAIRMEN AND CHAIRWOMEN, 1971–2007 789

    APPENDIX J: CONSTITUTIONAL AMENDMENTS AND MAJOR CIVIL RIGHTS ACTS OF CONGRESS
    REFERENCED IN THE TEXT 790

INDEX 795

BLACK AMERICANS IN CONGRESS

An Introduction

The arrival of Senator Hiram Revels of Mississippi and Representative Joseph Rainey of South Carolina on Capitol Hill in 1870 ranks among the great paradoxes in American history; just a decade earlier, these African Americans' congressional seats were held by southern slave owners. Moreover, the U.S. Capitol, where these newest Members of Congress came to work—the center of legislative government, conceived by its creators as the "Temple of Liberty"—had been constructed with the help of enslaved laborers.[1] From this beginning, *Black Americans in Congress, 1870–2007* chronicles African Americans' participation in the federal legislature and their struggle to attain full civil rights.

The institution of Congress, and the careers of the 121 black Members who have served in both its chambers, have undergone extensive changes during this span of nearly 140 years.[2] But while researching and writing this book, we encountered several recurring themes that led us to ask the following questions: What were black Members' legislative priorities? Which legislative styles did African Americans employ to integrate into the institution? How did they react to the political culture of Capitol Hill and how did they overcome institutional racism? Lastly, how did the experiences of these individuals compare to those of other newly enfranchised Americans?

SHARED EXPERIENCES OF BLACK AMERICANS IN CONGRESS

In striking aspects, the history of blacks in Congress mirrors that of other groups that were new to the political system. Throughout African-American history in Congress,

Members viewed themselves as "surrogate" representatives for the black community nationwide rather than just within the borders of their individual districts or states.[3] George White of North Carolina (1897–1901) and Robert Elliott of South Carolina (1871–1874) first embodied these roles, serving as models for 20th-century black Members such as Oscar De Priest of Illinois (1929–1935), Adam Clayton Powell, Jr., of New York (1945–1971), and Shirley Chisholm of New York (1969–1983). Surrogate representation was not limited to black Members of Congress; nearly half a century after blacks entered Congress, woman Members, too, grappled with the added burdens of surrogate representation. In 1917, women throughout the country looked to the first woman to serve in Congress, Representative Jeannette Rankin of Montana, for legislative support. Indeed, Rankin received so many letters she was forced to hire additional secretaries to handle the workload.[4]

Twentieth-century African-American pioneers' experience was similar in some respects to that of women.[5] Known and admired by blacks nationally, Representative De Priest and those who followed him were often sought out by individuals across the country, many of whom expected unfailing receptiveness to the long-neglected needs of the black community. In late 1934, the *Atlanta Daily World* memorialized De Priest, who lost re-election in his Chicago-centered district to Arthur W. Mitchell (1935–1943), the first black Democrat to serve in Congress. De Priest, the editors wrote, lifted his "voice in defense of those forgotten people he represented" in Chicago and nationally. Lionizing De Priest as a "gallant statesman and fearless defender"

An 1867 Harper's Weekly *cover commemorates the first vote cast by African-American men. The passage and ratification of the Reconstruction Amendments (13th, 14th, and 15th) between 1865 and 1870 catapulted former slaves from chattel to voters and candidates for public office.*

of blacks in the North and South, the editors expressed frustration with Mitchell, who explicitly noted during a speech to an Atlanta church congregation that he did not intend to represent "black interests" per se. Mitchell, the editors noted, "dashed the hopes of every Negro who sat within hearing of his voice, most of whom looked to him as their personal representative in the federal government."[6]

Collectively, African Americans in Congress overcame barriers by persevering through three eras of participation that can be classified as pioneering (1870–1901), apprenticeship (1929–1970), and mature integration (1971–2007).[7] These stages were typical of those experienced by other minority groups, such as women, that integrated into the established political system. However, Black Americans were distinct from other groups because they experienced a prolonged period of contraction, decline, and exclusion that resulted from segregation and disfranchisement. After winning the right to participate in the American experiment of self-government, African Americans were systematically and ruthlessly excluded from it: From 1901 to 1929, there were no blacks in the federal legislature.

Under the leadership of Chairman Adam Clayton Powell, Jr., of New York, the Committee on Education and Labor approved more than 50 measures authorizing increases in federal educational programs. Fellow committee members referred to Powell's leadership as the most productive period in then-recent committee history.

IMAGE COURTESY OF LIBRARY OF CONGRESS

While seeking to advance within Congress and adapt to its folkways, each generation of black Members was challenged by racial prejudice, both overt and subtle; exclusion; marginalization; and, because they were so rare, an inability to organize that lasted for many decades. Black Members of Congress also contended with increased expectations from the public and heightened scrutiny by the media. They cultivated legislative strategies that were

common on Capitol Hill, but took on an added dimension in their mission to confront institutional racism and represent the interests of the larger black community. Some, such as Representatives Chisholm and Powell, became symbols for African-American civil rights by adopting the "show horse" style; circumventing prescribed congressional channels, they appealed directly to the public and media. Others pursued an institutionalist, "work horse" strategy; adhering to the prevailing traditions and workways

As the first black politician from west of the Mississippi River elected to the House, Augustus (Gus) Hawkins of California earned the nickname "Silent Warrior" for his persistent work on behalf of minorities and the urban poor.

IMAGE COURTESY OF THE NATIONAL ARCHIVES AND RECORDS ADMINISTRATION

of the House and Senate, they hoped to shape policies by attaining positions of influence on the inside.[8] Representative William Levi Dawson of Illinois (1943–1970), Powell's contemporary, and others like him, such as Augustus (Gus) Hawkins of California (1963–1991) and William H. (Bill) Gray III of Pennsylvania (1979–1991), favored the methodical "work horse" legislative style, diligently immersing themselves in committee work and policy minutiae.[9]

Black Americans in Congress, 1870–2007 follows the contours of this tumultuous, and ultimately triumphant, history. The first section of this volume encompasses the careers of former Members who served from 1870 through 2007. Seventy-nine individuals, grouped into four distinct chapters, or generations (described in the following sections), are profiled in chronological order. Each generation of Members is accompanied by a contextual essay on the congressional history and U.S. social history that shaped its Members' careers. The second section of this book includes profiles of the 38 black incumbent Members who have served two or more terms. The black freshman Members of the 110th Congress (2007–2009) are profiled in Appendix A using a résumé format.

THE SYMBOLIC GENERATION, 1870–1887

This group of 17 black Congressmen symbolized the triumph of the Union and the determination of Radical Republicans to enact reforms that temporarily reshaped the political landscape in the South during Reconstruction. These pioneers were all Republicans elected from southern states. Though their educational, professional, and social backgrounds were diverse, they were all indelibly shaped by the institution of slavery. Eight were enslaved, and their experience under slavery disrupted their early lives. Others, as members of strictly circumscribed southern mulatto, or mixed-race, communities and free black classes, were relatively well-to-do. However, mulatto heritage was a precarious political inheritance; mixed-race Members of Congress were shunned by southern whites and were never fully trusted by freedmen, who often doubted they had blacks' interests at heart.

Though these black Members adopted various legislative strategies, each sought to improve the lives of their African-American constituents. Their agendas invariably included three primary goals: providing education, enforcing political rights, and extending opportunities to enable economic independence. "Place all citizens upon one broad platform. . . .," declared Richard Cain of South Carolina (1877–1879) on the House Floor. "All we ask of this country is to put no barriers between us, to lay no stumbling blocks in our way; to give us freedom to accomplish our destiny."[10]

Despite their distinguished service and their symbolic value for African-American political aspirations, these black Members produced few substantive legislative results. They never accounted for more than 2 percent of the total congressional membership. Their exclusion from the internal power structure of the institution cut them off from influential committee assignments and at times prevented them even from speaking on the House Floor, leaving them little room to maneuver. Most of the key civil rights bills and constitutional amendments were enacted before a single African American served in Congress. The Ku Klux Klan Acts and the Civil Rights Act of 1875, which

embodied black legislative interests, depended solely on the impermanent support of the shifting but uniformly white House leadership. Black Members of Congress often were relegated to the sidelines and to offering testimonials about the malfeasance of racially conservative southerners against freedmen.

On February 27, 1869, John Willis Menard of Louisiana became the first African American to address the U.S. House while it was in session, defending his seat in a contested election. In November 1868, Menard appeared to have won a special election to succeed the late Representative James Mann—a victory that would have made him the first African American to serve in Congress. But his opponent, Caleb Hunt, challenged Menard's right to be seated. The House deemed neither candidate qualified, leaving the seat vacant for the remainder of the final days of the 40th Congress (1867–1869).

IMAGE COURTESY OF LIBRARY OF CONGRESS

After Reconstruction formally ended in 1877, ex-Confederates and their Democratic allies wrested power from Republican-controlled state governments and, through law and custom, gradually built a segregated society during the next several decades, effectively eliminating Black Americans from public office and ending their political participation. As the next group of African-American Members discovered, the federal government reacted impassively to blacks' disfranchisement by the states.

"THE NEGROES' TEMPORARY FAREWELL," 1887–1929

This era was defined by a long war on African-American participation in state and federal politics, waged by means of local southern laws, Jim Crow segregation, and tacit federal assent. Between 1887 and 1901, just five

A U.S. Senator encounters a hanging anti-lynching bill outside the Capitol in this Edmund Duffy cartoon. The Senate's unique parliamentary procedures allowed southern Democrats to kill civil rights and anti-lynching legislation, allowing the upper chamber to act as a bottleneck for measures seeking to overthrow Jim Crow until the mid-20th century.

IMAGE COURTESY OF LIBRARY OF CONGRESS

blacks served in Congress. Black Members of Congress encountered an institution that was often inhospitable to their very presence and their legislative goals. With their middling to lower-tier committee assignments and few connections to the leadership, they were far from the center of power.[11] Moreover, black Members of Congress were so rare that they were incapable of driving a legislative agenda.

Over the years, electing African Americans to Congress grew more difficult. Obstacles included violence, intimidation, and fraud by white supremacists; state and local disfranchisement laws that denied increasing numbers of blacks the right to vote; and contested election challenges in Congress. Moreover, the legislative focus shifted from the idealism of the postwar Radical Republicans to the business interests of a rapidly industrializing nation. Ambivalence toward protecting black civil rights bolstered southern racial conservatives, who sought to roll back the protections that were extended to African Americans during Reconstruction. "I beg all true men to forget party and partisanship and right the great wrongs perpetrated upon humble and

unoffending American citizens," said Representative George W. Murray of South Carolina (1893–1895; 1896–1897). "I declare that no class of people has ever been more misrepresented, slandered, and traduced than the black people of the South."[12]

Though Black Americans were excluded from Congress after 1901, larger social and historical forces portended future political opportunities for African Americans in the northern United States. Southern black political activism transferred northward changing the social and cultural dynamic of established black communities in northern cities, as rural, agrarian African Americans were lured to industrialized cities by jobs and greater political freedoms. Advocacy groups such as the National Association for the Advancement of Colored People (NAACP), founded during this era, lobbied Congress on issues that were important to the black community. Geographical relocation also contributed to the gradual realignment of African Americans from the Republican Party to the ranks of northern Democrats during the mid-20th century.

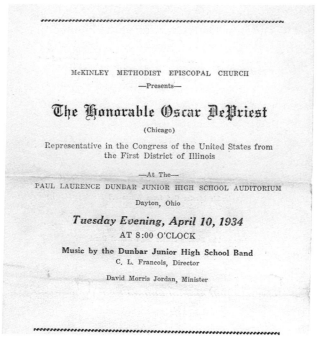

On April 10, 1934, Illinois Representative Oscar De Priest addressed a group of supporters at the Paul Laurence Dunbar Junior High in Dayton, Ohio. The three-term Member broke racial barriers when he became the first African American elected to Congress in nearly three decades. De Priest served as a symbol of hope for African Americans and spoke at venues across the nation.

COLLECTION OF U.S. HOUSE OF REPRESENTATIVES

Without a single black Member to advocate black interests, both major political parties in Congress refused to enact legislation to improve conditions for African Americans. Except for a few stalwart reformers, Congress responded to civil rights measures with ambivalence or outright hostility. During this era, too, a corps of southern racial conservatives was positioned, by virtue of their seniority, to hold a strong grip on the levers of power when Democrats gained control of the chamber in 1931.

The third consecutive African American to serve from a South Chicago district, Representative William Dawson of Illinois participated in an NAACP annual meeting held at the Union Baptist Church in Baltimore, Maryland.

IMAGE COURTESY OF LIBRARY OF CONGRESS

KEEPING THE FAITH: AFRICAN AMERICANS RETURN TO CONGRESS, 1929–1970

In 1929, African Americans' long exile from Congress ended when Oscar De Priest entered the House. All 13 African Americans elected during this era represented northern constituencies, all (except Senator Edward W. Brooke of Massachusetts, 1967–1979) were elected from majority-black, urban districts, and all except De Priest and Brooke were Democrats. By promising fuller participation in American society, the New Deal reactivated black political participation and brought greater numbers of African Americans into the Democratic Party.[13] World War II also rekindled African-American political activism, and black contributions to the war effort helped pave the way for the civil rights movement.

Black Members of Congress embarked on a long institutional apprenticeship in the 1940s, 1950s, and 1960s, attaining more-desirable committee assignments and accruing the requisite seniority to gain leadership positions.[14] Their apprenticeship coincided with the blossoming of the civil rights movement on the streets of the South.[15] Although Martin Luther King, Jr., and his Southern Christian Leadership Conference (SCLC) spearheaded the nonviolent protest movement, everyday

Americans from all walks of life formed the core of the movement, but outside advocacy groups such as the NAACP, and black Members of Congress, also played an important role.

While the SCLC, the NAACP, and black Members of Congress shared the same goals, they often diverged over tactics. Some black Members made substantive legislative achievements. For example, Representative Powell crafted an amendment banning discrimination in federal contracts that was incorporated in the landmark Civil Rights Act of 1964. Other black Members, who preferred to work within the institution of Congress to effect change, or who placed party imperatives ahead of black interests, were chided by civil rights advocates for insufficient commitment.[16] Perhaps the greatest consequence of the civil rights movement for black Members was its decisive effect on the early political development of many who entered the institution after 1970.

Throughout this period, African Americans constituted a small percentage of Congress. Even in the 91st Congress (1969–1971), with a record high 11 black Members, African Americans accounted for just 2 percent of the combined membership of the House and the Senate. But change was underway. Within a decade, the number of

Propelled by the Congressional Black Caucus, African-American Members of Congress steadily gained seniority and power in the House of Representatives. In this late 1970s picture from left to right (standing) are: Louis Stokes of Ohio, Parren Mitchell of Maryland, Charles Rangel of New York, Andrew Young, Jr., of Georgia, Charles Diggs, Jr., of Michigan, Ralph Metcalfe of Illinois, Robert Nix, Sr., of Pennsylvania, Walter Fauntroy of the District of Columbia, Harold Ford, Sr., of Tennessee; seated from left to right: Cardiss Collins of Illinois, Yvonne Brathwaite Burke of California, and Shirley Chisholm of New York.

IMAGE COURTESY OF MOORLAND–SPINGARN RESEARCH CENTER, HOWARD UNIVERSITY

African Americans in Congress doubled. As their numbers increased, their momentum for organizing strengthened.

PERMANENT INTERESTS: THE EXPANSION, ORGANIZATION, AND RISING INFLUENCE OF AFRICAN AMERICANS IN CONGRESS, 1971–2007

This post–civil rights movement generation of lawmakers created a legislative groundswell on Capitol Hill. Civil rights acts of the 1960s and court-ordered redistricting opened new avenues of political participation for millions of African Americans. Consequently, many more blacks were elected to political office, and even to Congress. Eighty-six of the 121 African Americans who have served in congressional history—more than 70 percent—were seated in Congress after 1970. Many of these Members were elected from southern states that had not been represented by blacks in seven decades or more, for example, Representative Andrew Young of Georgia (1973–1977), Barbara Jordan of Texas (1973–1979), and Harold Ford, Sr., of Tennessee (1975–1997). During the 1992 elections alone the total black membership in Congress grew by

Despite the predictions of Jet *magazine and other news media, Shirley Chisholm of New York became the first African-American Congresswoman in 1969. Yvonne Brathwaite Burke of California eventually entered the House of Representatives in January 1973.*

COLLECTION OF U.S. HOUSE OF REPRESENTATIVES

one-third and Carol Moseley-Braun of Illinois (1993–1999) was elected as the first black woman and the first African-American Democrat to serve in the U.S. Senate.

With the ranks of African Americans growing in Congress, the time for formal organization and coordination of black efforts had arrived. In early 1971, 13 African-American Members of Congress led by Charles C. Diggs, Jr., of Michigan (1955–1980), formed the Congressional Black Caucus (CBC) to address "permanent interests" that were important to Black Americans, to advance black Members within the institution, and to push legislation, sometimes with potent results. Among the CBC's notable legislative achievements were the passage of the Humphrey–Hawkins Act of 1978 to promote full employment and a balanced budget, the creation in 1983 of a federal holiday commemorating the birthday of Martin Luther King, Jr., and legislation in 1986 that imposed the first sanctions against South Africa's all-white government for its practice of apartheid. Within Congress, the CBC used its influence as a growing unit within the Democratic Caucus to push party leaders to appoint blacks to better committees and more leadership positions. "Blacks never could rely on somebody in Congress to speak out on racial questions; they can with the caucus," declared Representative Louis Stokes of Ohio (1969–1999), a cofounder of the CBC.[17]

During this era, African-American Members of Congress entered a mature phase of institutional development. This generation had more experience in elective office, particularly in state legislatures. In Congress, blacks held positions on a full cross-section of panels, including the most coveted committees, such as Appropriations, Ways and Means, and Rules. In doing so, they were involved in legislative issues that affected every facet of American life. Representing

Top: Andrew Young of Georgia won election to the U.S. House in 1973, becoming one of the first African Americans to represent a southern state since Reconstruction.

Bottom: North Carolina Representative Eva Clayton became the first African-American woman to represent the state as well as the state's first black Representative since George Henry White left office in 1901.

COLLECTION OF U.S. HOUSE OF REPRESENTATIVES

districts that overall were electorally safe, many African-American Members enjoyed long careers that allowed them to accrue the seniority they needed to move into leadership positions. Fourteen black Members chaired congressional committees between 1971 and the end of the first session of the 110th Congress (2007–2009).[18] And for the first time, black Members rose into the ranks of party leadership, including: Bill Gray, Democratic Majority Whip (1989–1991); J. C. Watts of Oklahoma, Republican Conference Chairman (1999–2003); and James Clyburn of South Carolina, Democratic Majority Whip (elected in 2007).

Nevertheless, African-American Members continued to face new challenges. By the end of the first session of the 110th Congress, the 41 black Representatives and one black Senator represented constituencies whose unique geography and special interests expanded their legislative agendas. Additionally, gender diversity also shaped the bloc of black Members of Congress. After Shirley Chisholm was first elected in 1968, another 25 African-American women were elected to Congress—making them a uniquely influential component of the story of blacks in Congress. Finally, although leadership positions afforded African Americans a more powerful institutional voice and greater legislative leverage, they exposed latent conflicts between party imperatives and perceived black interests.

The Historiography of Black Americans in Congress

The present volume originated with the first edition of *Black Americans in Congress* (H. Con. Res. 182, House Document No. 95–258, 95th Congress, 3 November 1977), which was compiled and published shortly after the U.S. bicentennial. Organized by Representative Corinne (Lindy) Boggs of Louisiana and Senator Brooke, the booklet featured the 45 African Americans who had served in Congress (42 Representatives and three Senators). A résumé-style format included basic biographical information, congressional service dates, party affiliation, committee assignments, and information about Members' other political offices. Entries were arranged chronologically, with one section for Senators and another for Representatives. A thumbnail image accompanied each profile. In a brief introduction, the renowned African-American historian Benjamin Quarles of Morgan State University wrote that black Members on Capitol Hill were "living proof that Blacks could produce an able leadership of their own. Moreover, their presence in the halls of

Congress, made their Black constituents feel that they were more than bystanders—they were participants, however vicariously, in the political process."[19]

The second edition of *Black Americans in Congress, 1870–1989* (H. Con Res. 170, H. Doc. No. 101-117) was authorized by the House and the Senate in the fall of 1989 and was published in 1990. By that point, 66 African Americans (63 Representatives and three Senators) had served in Congress. The volume was dedicated to the memory of Representative George Thomas (Mickey) Leland of Texas (1979–1989) who was killed, as the book went to press, in a plane crash while delivering food to starving Ethiopians. Representative Ronald V. Dellums of California (1971–1998), then the chairman of the CBC, contributed a brief introduction for the volume: "For Black Americans the promise of republican government and democratic participation was delayed well beyond the founding of the federal government in 1789." Dellums also observed, "In this bicentennial year of Congress and the federal government, it is important to recognize that the Constitution we enjoy today evolved over a number of years

George Thomas (Mickey) Leland of Texas poured his energy into raising awareness of hunger and poverty in the United States and around the world. In 1984, Leland successfully persuaded the House to create the Select Committee on Hunger, which he chaired.

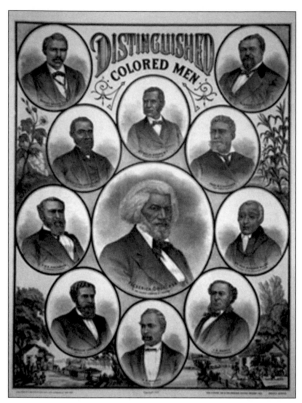

Abolitionist Frederick Douglass anchors an 1883 chromolithograph of "distinguished colored men." Among those featured are Representatives Robert Elliott and Joseph Rainey of South Carolina, John Langston of Virginia, and Senator Blanche Bruce of Mississippi. The image also includes Henry Highland Garnet, minister at Washington's Fifteenth Street Presbyterian Church. He became the first African American to speak in the House Chamber when he addressed a crowd of Sunday worshippers on February 12, 1865.

IMAGE COURTESY OF LIBRARY OF CONGRESS

and did not protect the civil rights of Black Americans until after a Civil War and passage of significant amendments."[20] Created partly to commemorate the bicentennial of Congress in 1989, the volume contained 500- to 1,000- word profiles of Members, with basic biographical information. Suggestions for further reading were provided at the end of each profile. Profiles of former and current Members, arranged alphabetically, were merged into one section and accompanied by larger pictures.

The Present Edition

In the spring of 2001, House Concurrent Resolution 43 was introduced. The resolution, which passed the House on March 21, 2001, and was agreed to by the Senate on April 6, 2001, authorized the Library of Congress to compile "an updated version" of *Black Americans in Congress, 1870–1989.* In late 2001, the Library of Congress transferred the project to the Office of the Clerk of the U.S. House of Representatives. Subsequently, the Office

of History and Preservation (OHP) was created under the Clerk of the House, and OHP staff began work on this publication.

This volume reflects the far-reaching changes that have occurred since the second edition of the book. When the 1990 edition was published during the 101st Congress (1989–1991), 25 black Members served in the House. There were no African-American Senators. But within less than two decades there were a number of unprecedented developments. In 1992 alone, 17 new blacks were elected to Congress, the most ever in any single election and more than in any previous decade in congressional history. From 1991 through the end of 2007, 55 African Americans were elected to Congress—roughly 45 percent of all the blacks who have served in the history of the institution. By the closing of the first session of the 110th Congress, there were 42 African Americans in Congress (41 in the House and one in the Senate).

Moreover, the appreciable gender gap between male and female African-American Members of Congress narrowed during this period. Before 1991, just five black women had been elected to Congress. But in 1992 alone, five new women were elected. Between 1991 and the end of 2007, 20 African-American women were elected to Congress (36 percent of all blacks elected to Congress in that period).

The structure, scope, and content of this edition of *Black Americans in Congress* reflect the dramatic growth, changing characteristics, and increasing influence of African-American Members. Like the first edition, this volume is organized chronologically, to represent more accurately the effects of historical trends on blacks' entry into Congress. In contrast to the Members' profiles in both of the previous editions of *Black Americans in Congress,* the profiles in this edition have been expanded, with more emphasis on elections and congressional service. Additionally, the political and institutional developments affecting African Americans' participation in Congress are analyzed in contextual essays. Appendices include committee assignments, leadership positions (committee, subcommittee, and elected party posts), familial connections in Congress, CBC chairs, and major civil rights acts since 1863. Charts and graphs illustrate historical statistics and trends. Photographs of each Member are also included, as well as an index.

Throughout this book, we use the terms "black" and "African American" interchangeably. The title of this volume, *Black Americans in Congress,* was specified in the print resolution and follows the first two editions of this book. However, since the last edition of this book was published

An illustration in Harper's Weekly, *July 1868, depicts a political meeting of African Americans in the South. Personal campaigns conducted among their neighbors in majority-black districts throughout the South propelled 22 black men into the U.S. Congress between 1870 and 1901.*

IMAGE COURTESY OF LIBRARY OF CONGRESS

in 1990, the term "African American" has become more commonplace in both academic and general usage. Our use of both terms reflects these considerations.

Part I of *Black Americans in Congress* contains profiles of former black Members, averaging 1,500 words; some profiles of Members with longer House and Senate careers exceed 2,500 words. Each profile describes the Member's precongressional career and, when possible, contains a detailed analysis of the subject's first campaign for congressional office as well as information about re-election efforts, committee assignments, leadership, and major legislative initiatives, and a brief summary of the Member's postcongressional career.

Part II contains profiles of current black Members, with information on precongressional careers, first House or Senate campaigns, committee and leadership positions, and legislative achievements. Because these Members' careers are still in progress, comprehensive accounts must await a later date. At approximately 750 words each, the

profiles in Part II are about half as long as those for former Members. These profiles are arranged alphabetically, rather than chronologically.

We hope this volume will serve as a starting point for students and researchers. Accordingly, bibliographic information is provided for former and current Members. When applicable, information about manuscript collections and other repositories with significant holdings (e.g., the transcript of an oral history or extended correspondence) is included at the end of each Member's profile. This information was drawn from the House and Senate records that were used to compile the *Biographical Directory of the U.S. Congress* at http://bioguide.congress.gov.

The literature on African-American history, which has grown into one of the most dynamic fields in the profession, has been created largely since the 1960s. John Hope Franklin, the post–World War II dean of black history, wrote the textbook *From Slavery to Freedom* (first published in 1947; later editions were written with Alfred

A. Moss, Jr.); with eight editions in half a century, this textbook remains an excellent starting point for those who wish to appreciate the breadth of the African-American historical experience. The ample literature on black history is far too complex for a detailed discussion here. As often as possible we have pointed readers, in the endnotes of the essays and profiles of this volume, toward standard works on various aspects of black history and congressional history. However, the following studies proved exceptionally important and deserve mention: Eric Foner, *Reconstruction: America's Unfinished Revolution, 1863–1877* (New York: Harper and Row, 1988), C. Vann Woodward, *The Strange Career of Jim Crow* (New York: Oxford University Press, 1974); J. Morgan Kousser, *The Shaping of Southern Politics: Suffrage Restriction and Establishment of the One-Party South, 1880–1910* (New Haven: Yale University Press, 1974); Robert L. Zangrando, *The NAACP Crusade Against Lynching, 1909–1950* (Philadelphia, PA: Temple University Press, 1980); Carol Swain, *Black Faces, Black Interests: The Representation of African Americans in Congress* (Cambridge, MA: Harvard University Press, 1993); and Robert L. Singh, *The Congressional Black Caucus: Racial Politics in the U.S. Congress* (Thousand Oaks, California: Sage, 1998). We also consulted several general texts that profile black Members of Congress and major politicians: Maurine Christopher, *Black Americans in Congress* (New York: Thomas Y. Crowell and Company, 1976); Stephen Middleton, ed., *Black Congressmen During Reconstruction: A Documentary Sourcebook* (Westport, CT: Praeger, 2002); and Eric Foner, *Freedom's Lawmakers: A Directory of Black Officeholders During Reconstruction*, revised edition (Baton Rouge: Louisiana State University Press, 1996).

Historians now know a great deal more about the lives of early African-American politicians than they did even

Top: Earning a seat in the House of Representatives by special election, Robert Nix of Pennsylvania went on to serve there for 21 years. He was one of the first blacks elected to Congress during the civil rights era, and once commented that he dedicated himself "to ending the oppression of black people."

Right: A former Olympic track star, Illinois Representative Ralph Metcalfe broke ranks with the Chicago political machine to investigate allegations of police brutality in the city. Despite the loss of party support from the machine, Metcalfe successfully won re-election. "There is only one issue," Metcalfe declared. "The right of black people to choose their own public officials and not have them picked from downtown."

<small>COLLECTION OF U.S. HOUSE OF REPRESENTATIVES</small>

a brief generation ago. The civil rights movement of the 1960s renewed black participation in the political process and refocused interest on this long-neglected aspect of history. As the field of African-American history has grown, a number of political biographies have been published on 19th-century black Members of Congress, including Revels, Elliott, White, Murray, Robert Smalls of South Carolina (1875–1879; 1882–1883; 1884–1887), John Mercer Langston of Virginia (1890–1891), and Blanche K. Bruce of Mississippi (1875–1881). The lives of major 20th-century black Members of Congress have been chronicled in recent biographies, including Mitchell, Powell, and Young. But a number of prominent legislators have yet to be studied thoroughly, including 19th-century figures such as Rainey and John Roy Lynch of Mississippi (1873–1877; 1882–1883) and many 20th-century Members, including De Priest, Dawson, Diggs, Hawkins, and Jordan.

Several sources were indispensable starting points in the compilation of this book. Inquiries into Members' congressional careers should begin with the *Biographical Directory of the United States Congress*, http://bioguide.congress.gov. Maintained by the House Office of History and Preservation and the Senate Historical Office, this publication contains basic biographical information about Members, pertinent bibliographic references, and information about manuscript collections. It is easily searchable and updated regularly. In the early phase of research, we also consulted standard reference works such as the *American National Biography*, the *Dictionary of American Biography*, the *Dictionary of American Negro Biography*, and *Current Biography*. We used various editions of the *Almanac of American Politics* (Washington, DC: National Journal Inc.) and *Politics in America* (Washington, DC: Congressional Quarterly Press) as a starting point in our research involving current Members as well as many former Members who served after 1971.

Much of the information was researched using primary sources, particularly published official congressional records and scholarly compilations of congressional statistics. Following is a summary of the sources consulted for information related to congressional elections, committee assignments, legislation, votes, floor debates, news accounts, and images.

Congressional election results for the biennial elections from 1920 onward are available in the Clerk's "Election

In 1977, 15 of the Congressional Black Caucus members posed on the steps of the U.S. Capitol, from left to right: (front row) Barbara Jordan of Texas, Robert Nix, Sr., of Pennsylvania, Ralph Metcalfe of Illinois, Cardiss Collins of Illinois, Parren Mitchell of Maryland, Gus Hawkins of California, Shirley Chisholm of New York; (middle row) John Conyers, Jr., of Michigan, Charles Rangel of New York, Harold Ford, Sr., of Tennessee, Yvonne Brathwaite Burke of California, Walter Fauntroy of the District of Columbia; (back row) Ronald Dellums of California, Louis Stokes of Ohio, and Charles C. Diggs, Jr., of Michigan.

Statistics," published by the Government Printing Office (GPO) and available in PDF/HTML format at http://clerk.house.gov/member_info/electionInfo/index.html. Michael J. Dubin et al., *United States Congressional Elections, 1788–1997* (Jefferson, NC: McFarland and Company, Publishing, Inc., 1998) contains results for both general and special elections. For information on district boundaries and reapportionment, we relied on Kenneth C. Martis's *The Historical Atlas of Political Parties in the United States Congress, 1789–1989* (New York: Macmillan Publishing Company, 1989) and the three-volume work by Stanley B. Parsons et al., *United States Congressional Districts* (New York: Greenwood Press, 1986).

Committee assignments and information about jurisdiction can be found in two indispensable scholarly compilations: David T. Canon, Garrison Nelson, and Charles Stewart III, *Committees in the U.S. Congress, 1789–1946*, four volumes (Washington, DC: Congressional Quarterly Press, 2002) and Garrison Nelson, *Committees in*

the U.S. Congress, 1947–1992, two volumes (Washington, DC: Congressional Quarterly Press, 1994). We also consulted the *Congressional Directory*, a GPO publication that dates back into the 19th century. From the 104th Congress onward, it is available online at GPO; see http://www.gpoaccess.gov/cdirectory/index.html.

Legislation, floor debates, roll call votes, bills, resolutions, and public laws as far back as the 1980s can be searched on the Library of Congress's THOMAS Web site at http://thomas.loc.gov. Two particularly useful print resources that discuss historical acts of Congress are: Steven V. Stathis's *Landmark Legislation, 1774–2002: Major U.S. Acts and Treaties* (Washington, DC: Congressional Quarterly Press, 2002) and Brian K. Landsberg, ed., *Major Acts of Congress*, three volumes (New York: Macmillan Reference, Thompson–Gale, 2004). Floor debates about legislation can be found in the *Congressional Record* (1873 to the present), which is available at the THOMAS Web site from 1989 to the present; an index of the *Record* from

In 1992, Senator Carol Moseley-Braun of Illinois became the first black woman and the fourth African American to win election to the U.S. Senate. Moseley-Braun was one of 17 new African-American Members elected in the 1992 campaign. As a result, the Congressional Black Caucus's numbers increased to a significant voting bloc of 40 members.

IMAGE COURTESY OF THE U.S. SENATE HISTORICAL OFFICE

1983 to the present is available at http://www.gpoaccess. gov/cri/index.html. Electronic copies of the *Congressional Globe* (the predecessor to the *Congressional Record*) are available at "A Century of Lawmaking," part of the Library of Congress's online American Memory Collection. We also consulted the official proceedings in the *House Journal* and the *Senate Journal*. For House roll call votes back to the second session of the 101st Congress, please visit the House History page on the Web site of Clerk of the House at http://clerk.house.gov/art_history/house_history/index. html. For Senate roll call votes back to the 1st session of the 101st Congress, see the following page on the U.S. Senate Web site: http://www.senate.gov/pagelayout/legislative/a_ three_sections_with_teasers/votes.htm. For print copies of the *Congressional Directory*, the *Congressional Record*, the *House Journal*, or the *Senate Journal*, please consult a local federal depository library. A GPO locator for federal depository libraries is accessible at http://catalog.gpo.gov/ fdlpdir/FDLPdir.jsp.

Using an online database, we reviewed key newspapers for major historical time periods covered in this book, including the *New York Times*, the *Washington Post*, the *Los Angeles Times*, the *Christian Science Monitor*, the *Wall Street Journal*, the *Chicago Tribune*, the *Boston Globe*, and

the *Atlanta Constitution.* We also consulted old editions of African-American newspapers, including the *Chicago Defender*, the *Atlanta Daily World*, the *Pittsburgh Courier* and the *New York Amsterdam*. News accounts and feature stories, particularly for Members who served before 1945, helped fill in obscure details. Many of these newspaper citations appear in the notes.

This edition of *Black Americans in Congress* involved a significant amount of photo research. Previous editions of this book included only a head-and-shoulders image of each Member. Individual picture credits were not included in the 1977 edition, though the book contained an acknowledgement page. In the 1990 edition, each picture was accompanied by a photo credit, but many images were credited to Members' offices that no longer exist or to the collection of the House Historian whose office closed in the mid-1990s.

Anticipating that some readers might want to acquire photo reproductions, we strove to provide accurate information for images that are accessible from public, private, and commercial repositories. We used the following photo collections: Prints and Photographs Division of the Library of Congress (Washington, DC); the Still Pictures Branch of the National Archives and Records Administration (College Park, MD); the Moorland–Spingarn Research Center at Howard University (Washington, DC); the Scurlock Studio Records, Archives Center, National Museum of American History, Smithsonian Institution (Washington, DC); the John Mercer Langston Collection, Fisk University Franklin Library (Nashville, TN); the Dwight D. Eisenhower Presidential Library (Abilene, KS); the John F. Kennedy Presidential Library (Boston, MA); the Lyndon Baines Johnson Presidential Library (Austin, TX); the *Philadelphia Inquirer* archives; the Mike Espy Collection at the Congressional and Political Research Center at Mississippi State University (Starkville, MS); and the Texas State Senate Media Services (Austin, TX). Additionally, some images were provided by the Office of the Clerk, U.S. House of Representatives; the Collection of the U.S. House of Representatives; the U.S. House of Representatives Photography Office; the Collection of the U.S. Senate; and the U.S. Senate Historical Office. The images of current Members were provided by their offices, which are the point of contact for persons seeking official images.

ACKNOWLEDGMENTS

Special thanks are due to our colleagues in the field of congressional history, whose comments have greatly improved this volume. The following individuals graciously shared their time and insights: Kenneth Kato of the Center for Legislative Archives at the National Archives and Records Administration; Historian Richard A. Baker, Associate Historian Donald A. Ritchie, and Assistant Historian Betty K. Koed of the Senate Historical Office; and Donald R. Kennon, chief historian of the U.S. Capitol Historical Society. We are also indebted to Professor Alfred A. Moss, Jr., of the University of Maryland at College Park, whose insights as a co-author of the standard textbook on African-American history have improved this book.

We thank the supportive and collegial staff of the Office of Clerk of the House of Representatives. Clerk of the House Lorraine C. Miller and Deputy Clerk Deborah Spriggs provided instrumental support. The Office of Publication Services (OPS) in the Office of the Clerk designed the print version and the Web version of this publication. For their collaboration and enthusiasm, we especially thank OPS Chief Janice Wallace-Hamid, Webmaster Catherine Cooke, copyeditor Marcie Kanakis, and designers David Serota, Angela Rock, Mark Seavey, and Lauren Haman. The courteous and professional staff of the libraries of the U.S. House of Representatives and the U.S. Senate provided timely research assistance.

Lastly, we thank our colleagues in the Office of History and Preservation for providing good cheer and unfailing help. Farar Elliott, Chief of OHP and House Curator, handled the myriad issues involved in producing a volume of this size, allowing us to focus on content. House Archivist Robin Reeder provided information about manuscript collections. Curatorial staff Karen McKinstry and Felicia Wivchar vetted captions and credits related to artifacts from the House Collection, and proofed galleys. Cathcrine Wallace and Joe Wallace worked with the offices of current Members to obtain images. Toni Coverton's masterful administration of correspondence, copyedits, and countless other tasks kept everyone on track. With such support, writing House history is enjoyable and educational.

Matthew Wasniewski
Historian and Editor-in-Chief,
Office of History and Preservation

Erin Marie-Lloyd Hromada, Kathleen Johnson,
Terrance Rucker, and Laura K. Turner
Writers and Researchers,
Office of History and Preservation

NOTES

1 See William C. Allen with a foreword by Richard Baker and Kenneth Kato, *History of Slave Laborers in the Construction of the United States Capitol* (Washington, DC: Architect of the Capitol, 2005), a report commissioned by the U.S. House of Representatives and the U.S. Senate Slave Labor Task Force. Available at http://clerk.house.gov/art_history/art_artifacts/slave_labor_reportl.pdf (accessed 28 February 2008). For a detailed analysis of Congress's management and, often, avoidance of central questions related to the practice of slavery from 1789 to 1860, see Don E. Fehrenbacher, *The Slaveholding Republic: An Account of the United States Government's Relations to Slavery* (New York: Oxford University Press, 2001).

2 The closing date for this volume was December 31, 2007.

3 Jane Mansbridge, "Should Blacks Represent Blacks and Women Represent Women? A Contingent 'Yes,'" *Journal of Politics* 61 (1999): 628–657. See also Carol Swain, *Black Faces, Black Interests: The Representation of African Americans in Congress* (Cambridge, MA: Harvard University Press, 1993): 3–19.

4 Office of History and Preservation, U.S. House of Representatives, *Women in Congress, 1917–2006* (Washington, DC: Government Printing Office, 2007): 26.

5 Charlayne Hunter, "Shirley Chisholm: Willing to Speak Out," 22 May 1970, *New York Times*: 31. For additional perspective, see William L. Clay, *Bill Clay: A Political Voice at the Grass Roots* (St. Louis: Missouri Historical Society Press, 2004): 7.

6 See the *Atlanta Daily World*: "The Battle Royal in the Old First Illinois," 9 November 1934: 4; "Congressman Mitchell," 11 November 1934: 4; and "Congressman Mitchell Speaks," 13 March 1935: 6.

7 See Office of History and Preservation, *Women in Congress, 1917–2006*: 1–5.

8 For the "work horse" versus "show horse" styles, see James L. Payne, "Show Horses and Work Horses in the United States House of Representatives," *Polity* 12 (Spring 1980): 428–456; see also James Q. Wilson, "Two Negro Politicians: An Interpretation," *Midwest Journal of Political Science* 5 (1960): 349–369.

9 For descriptions of these legislative styles in both chambers of Congress, see Payne, "Show Horses and Work Horses in the United States House of Representatives," and Donald R. Matthews, *U.S. Senators and Their World* (Chapel Hill: University of North Carolina Press, 1960), especially the chapter "Folkways of the U.S. Senate."

10 *Congressional Record*, House, 43rd Cong., 1st sess. (3 February 1875): 957.

11 For a discussion of the relative influence and attractiveness of individual House committees during this era, see Charles Steward III, "Committee Hierarchies in the Modernizing House, 1875–1947," *American Journal of Political Science* 36 (1992): 835–856.

12 *Congressional Record*, House, 53rd Cong., 1st sess. (5 October 1893): 2161.

13 Nancy Weiss, *Farewell to the Party of Lincoln: Black Politics in the Age of FDR* (Princeton, NJ: Princeton University Press, 1983): 227. Black voting loyalty underwent a fundamental shift during the 1930s, as voters left the Republican Party and joined the Democratic Party, but this development was multidecadal. Scholars often point to several milestones to map that movement: the promise of the New Deal and the relatively moderate racial policies of the Franklin D. Roosevelt administration; President Harry S. Truman's continuation of racial progressivism, embodied by the desegregation of the military and the creation of the Civil Rights Commission; the appeal of President Truman and northern Democrats versus the racially conservative Dixiecrats in 1948; Barry Goldwater's embrace of racial conservatism during the 1964 presidential campaign; passage of the 1964 Civil Rights Act and 1965 Voting Rights Act; and the trend, beginning in the 1960s and extending for several decades, of old-line white southern Democrats switching their allegiance to the GOP. See also Michael K. Fauntroy, *Republicans and the Black Vote* (Boulder, CO: Lynne Rienner, 2007): 41, 42–55.

14 Office of History and Preservation, *Women in Congress, 1917–2006*: 136–153, 324–343; Irwin Gertzog, *Congressional Women: Their Recruitment, Integration, and Behavior*, 2nd edition (Westport, CT: Praeger, 1995): 254–257.

15 For more on this complex subject, see Taylor Branch's landmark three-volume history, which uses Martin Luther King, Jr., as a lens for viewing the movement and its many factions: *Parting the Waters: America in the King Years, 1954–63* (New York: Simon and Schuster, 1988); *Pillar of Fire: America in the King Years, 1963–65* (New York: Simon and Schuster, 1998); *At Canaan's Edge: America in the King Years, 1965–68* (New York: Simon and Schuster, 2006).

16 Even Powell, who did not shy from publicly confronting racism, had a strained relationship with the movement. According to his chief biographer, the charismatic Harlem Representative viewed civil rights leaders outside Congress as competition for the mantle he had grown accustomed to wearing as the leading spokesperson for black civil rights. See Charles V. Hamilton, *Adam Clayton Powell, Jr.: The Political Biography of an American Dilemma* (New York: Cooper Square Press, 1991): 283–284; see also Branch, *Pillar of Fire*: 45–46, 95–96.

17 Quoted in Robert Singh, *The Congressional Black Caucus: Racial Politics in the U.S. Congress*, (Thousand Oaks, California: Sage, 1998): 105.

18 See Appendix E, Black Americans Who Have Chaired Congressional Committees, 1877–2007.

19 *Black Americans in Congress, 1870–1977* (Washington, DC: Government Printing Office, 1977).

20 *Black Americans in Congress, 1870–1989*, Office of the Historian, U.S. House of Representatives, Bruce A. Ragsdale and Joel D. Treese, eds. (Washington, DC: Government Printing Office, 1990): 1.

Black Americans as a Percentage of Congress, 1870–2009*

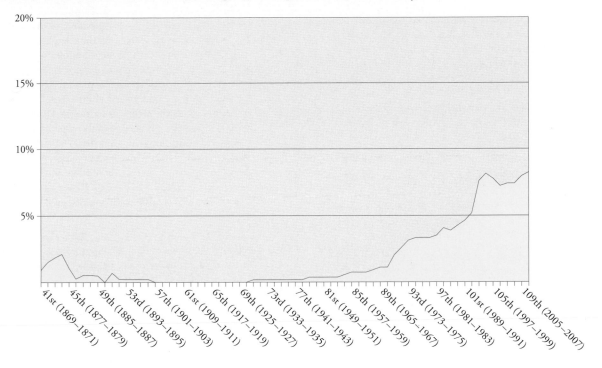

Black Americans in Congress, 1870–2009*

REPRESENTATIVES
SENATORS

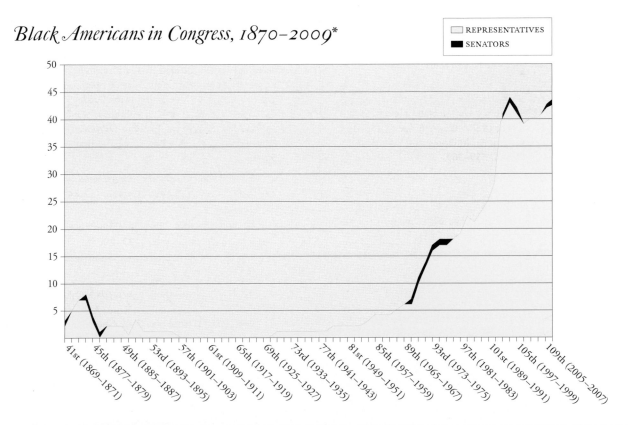

Sources: Appendix B: Black-American Representatives and Senators by Congress, 1870–2007; Office of the Clerk, U.S. House of Representatives; U.S. Senate Historical Office.

*110th Congress (2007–2009) as of December 31, 2007.

★ PART ONE ★

Former Black-American Members

"The Fifteenth Amendment in Flesh and Blood"

THE SYMBOLIC GENERATION OF BLACK AMERICANS IN CONGRESS, 1870–1887

When Senator Hiram Revels of Mississippi—the first African American to serve in Congress—toured the United States in 1871, he was introduced as the "Fifteenth Amendment in flesh and blood."[1] Indeed, the Mississippi-born preacher personified African-American emancipation and enfranchisement. On January 20, 1870, the state legislature chose Revels to briefly occupy a U.S. Senate seat, previously vacated by Albert Brown when Mississippi seceded from the Union in 1861.[2] As Senator Henry Wilson of Massachusetts escorted Revels to the front of the chamber to take his oath on February 25, the *Atlanta Constitution* reported that "the crowded galleries rose almost en masse, and each particular neck was stretched to its uttermost to get a view. . . A curious crowd (colored and white) rushed into the Senate chamber and gazed at the colored senator, some of them congratulating him. A very respectable looking, well dressed company of colored men and women then came up and took Revels captive, and bore him off in glee and triumph."[3] The next day, the *Chicago Tribune* jubilantly declared that "the first letter with the frank of a negro was dropped in the Capitol Post Office."[4] But Revels's triumph was short-lived. When his appoint-

---

Joseph Rainey of South Carolina, the first black Representative in Congress, earned the distinction of also being the first black man to preside over a session of the House, in April 1874.

Oil on canvas, Simmie Knox, 2004, Collection of U.S. House of Representatives

"TIME WORKS WONDERS."

In a print featured in an 1870 Harper's Weekly, *Jefferson Davis's ghost lurked in the Senate Chamber, observing the swearing-in of the first black Senator, Hiram Revels of Mississippi. Revels's importance is given Shakespearean proportions by placing the words of Othello's villainous Iago in Davis's mouth. This print was drawn by artist Thomas Nast, who sympathized with Radical Republicans in Congress.*

IMAGE COURTESY OF LIBRARY OF CONGRESS

Reconstruction:

Refers to both the 12-year period (1865–1877) and political process after the American Civil War in which the former Confederate states were re-admitted to the Union, beginning the nation's long process of readjustment after the end of slavery.

---

ment expired the following year, a leading white Republican, former Confederate general James Alcorn, took his place for a full six-year term.

In many respects, Revels's service foreshadowed that of the black Representatives who succeeded him during Reconstruction—a period of Republican-controlled efforts to reintegrate the South into the Union. They, too, were largely symbols of Union victory in the Civil War and of the triumph of Radical Republican idealism in Congress. "[The African-American Members] have displaced the more noisy 'old masters' of the past," a reporter with the *Chicago Tribune* wrote, "and, in their presence in [Congress], vindicate the safety of the Union which is incident to the broadest freedom in political privileges."[5] The African-American Representatives also symbolized a new democratic order in the United States. These men demonstrated not only courage, but also relentless determination. They often braved elections marred by violence and fraud. With nuance and tact they balanced the needs of black and white constituents in their Southern districts, and they argued passionately for legislation promoting racial equality. However, even in South Carolina, a state that was seemingly dominated by black politicians, African-American Members never achieved the level of power wielded by their white colleagues during Reconstruction. Though pushed to the margins of the institutional power structure, the black Representatives nevertheless believed they had an important role as advocates for the United States's newest citizens.

RECONSTRUCTION'S NEW ORDER

On New Year's Day 1863, Republican President Abraham Lincoln signed the Emancipation Proclamation, freeing slaves in captured portions of the Confederacy, and changing the goal of the two-year-old Civil War from one of suppressing a rebellion and preserving the Union to bringing a new order to the United States.[6] The North's victory in 1865 elated the newly freed slaves, but their freedom also generated new questions about the future economic and political landscape of the South. Sweeping change transformed the former Confederacy in the decade that followed, as the Northern victors in Congress experimented with ways to reconcile with their former enemies.[7]

Radical Republicans were the driving force in Congress in the waning days of the Civil War. Primarily former abolitionists who represented Northern constituencies, these politicians looked to implement in the postwar South their "utopian vision of a nation whose citizens enjoyed equality of civil and political rights, secured by a powerful and beneficent state."[8] They emphasized the political equality of American men, yet with few exceptions, stopped short of calling for the social integration of the races. The venerable Charles Sumner of Massachusetts—a fiery, well-spoken abolitionist who endured an infamous beating from South Carolina Representative Preston Brooks on the Senate Floor in 1856— led the Radical Republicans in the Senate. Pennsylvania Representative Thaddeus Stevens—caustic, brooding, and a brilliant political strategist—led the charge in the House. Sumner and Stevens hoped Democratic President Andrew Johnson, who succeeded the assassinated President Lincoln in April 1865, would be even more harsh than Lincoln in readmitting Confederate states. But Johnson believed in limited federal intervention and did not share the Radical Republicans' sweeping vision of freedmen's rights. The President's plan granted amnesty to repentant former Confederates and turned southern politics over to Union loyalists. The administration and the congressional majority were

Freedmen's Bureau:

From 1865 to 1872, the Bureau of Abandoned Lands, Freedmen, and Refugees (better known as the Freedmen's Bureau) provided resources such as food, clothing, and medical treatment to freed slaves and southern white refugees. The Freedmen's Bureau also interceded with employers to secure economic and civil rights for freed slaves and worked with northern philanthropists to open schools for them.

soon at odds. Of the 29 vetoes issued by Johnson—many involving Reconstruction bills—15 were overridden, more than for any other President.[9]

Unable to circumvent Johnson, Radical Republicans sought to remove him. In January 1867, Republican Representative James M. Ashley of Ohio introduced a resolution, adopted by the House, instructing the Judiciary Committee to "inquire into the conduct of Andrew Johnson," with an eye toward impeaching the President. The committee initially rejected the measure. But in September 1867, after President Johnson attempted to dismiss Secretary of War Edwin Stanton—who opposed Johnson's Reconstruction plan and worked closely with congressional Radicals—the committee recommended impeachment proceedings in a 5 to 4 vote, claiming Johnson had violated the Tenure of Office Act (14 Stat. 430–432). The full House rejected that report, but Johnson was bent on confronting Congress. In February 1868, when the President again tried to dismiss Stanton, congressional retribution was swift. The House voted 126 to 47 to impeach President Johnson, though the Senate later acquitted him by a single vote.

Even in the face of presidential intransigence, the Radical Republicans imposed a bold agenda of strict reforms upon the former Confederacy. Collectively, their push for African-American political rights surpassed any measure ever seen in the United States. The 38th Congress (1863–1865) quickly passed and submitted for ratification the 13th Amendment (13 Stat. 744–775)—outlawing slavery— in 1865. That same year, Congress established the Freedmen's Bureau (13 Stat. 507–509), which was charged with preparing the newly freed slaves for civic life by providing social services and education. In 1866, the 39th Congress (1865–1867) passed the first Civil Rights Bill (14 Stat. 27–30), granting American citizenship to freed slaves, and then expanded upon the legislation by approving the 14th Amendment (14 Stat. 358–359), which enforced the equality of all citizens before the law. On the final day the House met during the 39th Congress, the Radicals divided the former Confederacy into five military districts, each commanded by a U.S. Army general and ruled by military law. The act also provided strict conditions for re-admission to the Union: each of the 10 remaining Confederate states was required to rewrite its constitution at a convention attended by black and white delegates, to guarantee black suffrage, and to ratify the 14th Amendment.[10] In a rare move, the 40th Congress (1867–1869) convened minutes after the 39th Congress adjourned and quickly granted greater authority to the commanders of each military

"THE FREEDMAN'S BUREAU."

This 1868 Currier & Ives print, titled "The Freedman's Bureau," featured a young man dressing for a visit to Congress. An ambivalent image highlighting both the subject's conscientiousness and low economic status, this commercial decorative print reflected the complex attitudes toward African Americans during the period.

IMAGE COURTESY OF LIBRARY OF CONGRESS

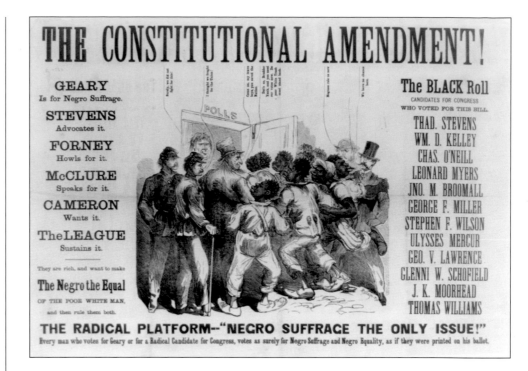

district by vesting them with considerable powers to hold elections and determine
citizens' eligibility to vote. The 15th Amendment (16 Stat. 40–41), which passed
in 1869, enforced the right to vote for eligible African-American men. Thus, in an
effort to achieve their ambitious vision for a racially transformed South, Radical
Republicans drastically changed the status of southern blacks; within the space of
a decade, millions who formerly had been classified as property exercised their new
rights as voters and potential officeholders.[11]

After the ratification of the 15th Amendment, former slaves flocked to the ballot
boxes and the more ambitious sought political office. By 1877 about 2,000 black
men had won local, state, and federal offices in the former Confederate states.[12]
But although black voters formed the bulk of the Republican constituency in the
former Confederacy, black officeholders never achieved significant power within
the GOP ranks. Nor did any southern state elect black officeholders in proportion
to its African-American population. Finally, black politicians never controlled
a government at the state level during the Reconstruction Era even though the
populations in several states were majority black.

PRE-CONGRESSIONAL EXPERIENCE

Slavery

All 17 of the African-American Congressmen elected between 1870 and 1887
came from the new Reconstruction governments in the former Confederacy. All
but two—Representatives Robert Elliott of South Carolina and James O'Hara of
North Carolina—were born in the South and just under half (eight) were born into
bondage. Even the early lives of those who had not been enslaved were profoundly
shaped the by the institution of slavery. Laws restricting the movements and
opportunities of free and enslaved blacks in the South uprooted families and lives.
Before age 25, John Hyman of North Carolina was sold at least eight times. Joseph
Rainey of South Carolina, though free, faced several legal obstacles while traveling to

wed Susan Rainey in Philadelphia in 1859; only with the help of friends did Rainey avoid being charged as a criminal for an unauthorized visit to a free state. When the newlyweds returned to Charleston, they had to circumvent laws disallowing free blacks from returning to the South.

While navigating the antebellum South was difficult for all blacks, skin color affected postbellum African Americans' economic and political opportunities.[13] Regional differences of opinion on racial miscegenation dated back to colonial slavery. Fifteen of the Reconstruction-Era Congressmen hailed from the Lower South, a geographic region stretching southwest from South Carolina. Thirteen were of mixed race heritage. The Lower South adopted a Caribbean plantation system of slavery from its earliest colonization that included three castes: white, "mulatto" (or mixed race), and black.[14] Often, biracial slaves were given less menial tasks, offered more educational opportunities, and treated on better terms than darker slaves, giving them many advantages that prepared them to be leaders in their postbellum communities. Those who were the sons of their white masters or of prominent local white men especially benefited from being light-skinned, both within and outside of the bonds of slavery. Four Reconstruction-Era black Members were likely the offspring of their former slaveowners.

Relative to communities of slaves, free black communities in the antebellum Lower South were small, urban, economically independent, and overwhelmingly of mixed race. These communities developed from the private manumission of favored personal servants or a slaveowner's offspring, as well as free black immigrants during the colonial period. The 1850 Census was the first to include statistics on the mixed race population in the United States. Eighty-six percent of mulatto Americans (350,000) lived south of Maryland. Though only 39 percent of this population lived in the Lower South, 75 percent of them were free and the bulk of them lived in Charleston, South Carolina, New Orleans, Louisiana, and other port cities.[15] Three of the black men who served in Congress in the postbellum years descended from the free, mixed-race elite in the Lower South.

Though mulattos in the Lower South had more opportunities than their darker neighbors, their existence in a racial middle ground presented a unique set of challenges. Before and after the Civil War, mixed-race men and women were fully accepted by none. Colonial and antebellum mulatto aristocrats often looked down on darker-skinned blacks, who frequently resented these elites because of the privileges they enjoyed and the snobbery they sometimes exhibited. Southern whites made fewer distinctions between gradations of skin color, preferring a rigid boundary between black and white.[16] For example, Mississippi Senator Blanche Bruce's black constituents were skeptical about his privileged background, and their concerns intensified when Bruce made his permanent home in Washington, DC, to escape violence in Mississippi. He took his position on civil rights from a distance, regarding the African-American cause as a practical political strategy rather than as a personal issue. Yet, despite his centrist politics, Mississippi whites refused to support his re-election because of the color of his skin.[17]

Education

The educational backgrounds of these 17 men were mixed, though collectively they far exceeded those of most African Americans of the time. From the colonial period on, southern states banned teaching both free and enslaved black children to read and write, largely as a means of social control. Restricting the slaves' education

Mulatto:

The offspring of a European-American and African-American union; also used loosely in the 19th century to describe anyone of mixed race resembling a mulatto.

Antebellum:

The era preceding a war, especially the American Civil War, 1861–1865.

Postbellum:

The period after a war, especially the American Civil War, 1861–1865.

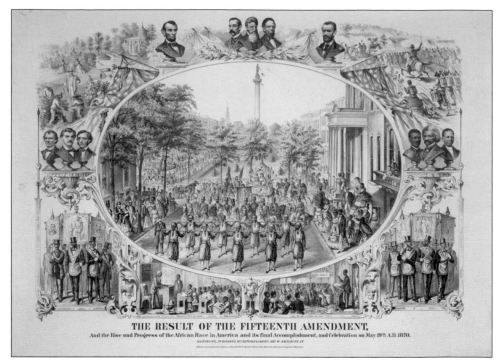

THE RESULT OF THE FIFTEENTH AMENDMENT,
And the Rise and Progress of the African Race in America and its final Accomplishment, and Celebration on May 19th A.D. 1870.

limited their ability to survive apart from their masters. Southern cities afforded the best opportunities to circumvent anti-literacy laws. Ignoring harsh punishment, well-educated free blacks and liberal whites sometimes opened illegal schools to teach urban slaves.[18]

Most of the black Congressmen who were raised in urban areas attained basic skills. The more fortunate—both slave and free—obtained an education as children. Hiram Revels attended one of two schools for black children in Fayetteville, North Carolina. "Together with the other colored youths [I] was fully and successfully instructed by our able and accomplished teacher in all branches of learning," Revels recalled. Advancement beyond the secondary school level, however, was not an option open to any black men in the antebellum South. "While I appreciated the educational advantages I enjoyed in the school and was proud of what I could show in mental culture," Revels admitted, "I had an earnest desire for something more than a mere business education . . . I desired to study for a profession and this prompted me to leave my native state."[19] Revels went on to attend seminary and received a college education in Indiana, Ohio, and Illinois. Others also born in the South acquired educations in the North or in Canada.

Those who were not educated as children—predominantly former slaves— acquired reading and mathematical skills or a trade as adults during and after the Civil War. State and local governments sometimes financed public schools, or normal schools, but the Freedmen's Bureau used federal money to fund educational institutions. By 1870, more than 4,000 schools in the South served nearly a quarter-million students.[20] Having learned the photographer's trade, future Mississippi Representative John Lynch attended a few months of night school in Natchez, Mississippi, after 1865. Lynch improved upon his brief formal education by reading northern newspapers and listening in on lessons at an all-white school adjacent to his photography shop.

Professional Background

In many respects, the professional backgrounds of the 19th-century black Representatives reflected the work experiences of black officeholders in the South generally; however, many were also ambitious entrepreneurs. Most 19th-century black Representatives were educators; seven served as teachers and five worked as school administrators. Others were clergy, farmers, barbers, tailors, hotel managers, steamboat porters, photographers, or store owners.

Many 19th-century political aspirants flocked to the newspaper industry, as these publications were primarily organs for political parties and a time-honored vehicle for advancing one's political career.[21] Black newspapers increased slowly in the 1870s due to widespread illiteracy in the black population, yet these publications increased fivefold in the next decade.[22] Black Representatives used their newspapers to aid their campaigns. Richard Cain of South Carolina bought the *South Carolina Leader* (renamed the *Missionary Record* in 1868) to express the political and theological views of his African Methodist Episcopal (AME) Emanuel Church congregation, which was, one local observer noted, "one of the strongest political organizations in the state."[23] Robert Smalls of South Carolina also started his own newspaper, the *Beaufort Southern Standard*, in 1872. As well, Josiah Walls of Florida bought the *Gainesville New Era* newspaper after losing his re-election bid in 1874, to retain a public presence and to boost his odds of recapturing his seat. Alabama Representative James Rapier worked briefly as a reporter for a northern newspaper. In 1872, after white newspapers refused to print his speeches or acknowledge his candidacy for Congress, he started his own newspaper, the *Republican Sentinel*, in Montgomery, Alabama, and used it to promote his campaign.

Given their relative professional success, it is no surprise that 19th-century black Representatives were affluent relative to the rest of the population. At least seven amassed more than $5,000. The average worth of the first 16 black Members of Congress (first elected before 1876) was $5,825. Forty-one percent of state and local black officeholders, generally, were worth less than $1,000 each.[24] Senator Blanche Bruce, the wealthiest individual, was worth more than $150,000 when he served in the U.S. Senate; he amassed his fortune primarily through real estate.[25] Several South Carolinians participated in the speculative railroad fever that swept across the South during Reconstruction. Four black South Carolina Representatives—Joseph Rainey, Richard Cain, Alonzo Ransier, and Robert Smalls—partnered with seven others to form the Enterprise Railroad Company in 1870. The small, horse-drawn rail service shipped goods from the wharves on the Cooper River in Charleston to stations farther inland that connected to major cities. The business barely weathered the boom-and-bust economy of the early 1870s. It passed to white ownership in 1873 and lasted until the 1880s.[26]

CRAFTING AN IDENTITY

The Republican Party and Black Representation

All of the 19th-century black Representatives were Republicans, recognizing and appreciating the role that the Republican Party played in obtaining their political rights and—for many—their emancipation.[27] Most remained lifelong Republicans and encouraged their black constituents to vote for white GOP candidates as well. "We are not ungrateful or unappreciative people," Robert Smalls said on

E.E. Murray's 1883 print, "From the Plantation to the Senate," illustrated notable black leaders including Joseph Rainey of South Carolina, Hiram Revels of Mississippi, and Josiah Walls of Florida.

IMAGE COURTESY OF LIBRARY OF CONGRESS

African-American Members of Congress were often grouped together in the public imagination. This print, from Speaker James G. Blaine of Maine's memoirs, Twenty Years of Congress from Lincoln to Garfield, *showed, clockwise from upper right: James Rapier of Alabama, John Lynch of Mississippi, Joseph Rainey of South Carolina, and Hiram Revels of Mississippi. Blanche K. Bruce of Mississippi is pictured in the center.*

COLLECTION OF U.S. HOUSE
OF REPRESENTATIVES

Nominating convention:

A meeting of local party officials to select the delegates who eventually designated party nominees for elective office or represented the locality at state or national conventions. Developed in the 1820s and 1830s, the system ensured that only one member would run for an elective position while providing structure and publicity for the party. In the early 20th century the modern primary election replaced nominating conventions as the principal method for selecting congressional candidates.

---

the House Floor. "We can never forget the Moses who led us out of the land of bondage."[28] In 1872, Liberal Republicans ran their own candidate, newspaper editor Horace Greeley, against incumbent President Ulysses S. Grant, testing the black Representatives' loyalty to the GOP. The Liberal platform embraced the enforcement of the Reconstruction Amendments, amnesty for former Confederates, and a laissez-faire economic policy. Prominent advocates for black civil rights, including Senator Charles Sumner, joined the Liberal camp. Despite their agreement with most of the Liberal Republican platform, black Representatives generally allied themselves with the GOP. Jeremiah Haralson of Alabama told a meeting of prominent black New Orleans politicians, "I have been a slave all my life and am free on account of the Republican Party, and if it comes to an issue, I for one am ready to let Charles Sumner fall and let the Republican Party stand."[29] Grant handily defeated Greeley—who also ran as the Democratic candidate.[30]

Factionalism was an even larger problem for the GOP in the South than it was on a national scale. Propped up by military rule under Reconstruction governments, southern Republicans recognized early on that their majorities depended on courting both black and white constituencies—especially as former Confederates regained the right to vote. Various Republican factions disagreed on how best to accomplish this, pivoting on several fulcrums in the Reconstruction South. The foremost was geographic origin, dividing between carpetbaggers and scalawags. Carpetbaggers were white Republicans from the North, who were primarily Union veterans seeking new political and economic opportunities in the South. White GOP partisans native to the South, many of whom were Unionists during the Civil War, were known as scalawags. Initially, scalawags were typically elected on more conservative platforms—they favored leniency toward former Confederates and focused on the economic rehabilitation of the war-torn South. Carpetbaggers tended to run more radical campaigns, advocating forceful civil rights legislation protecting black southerners.[31]

The nominating convention system used to select candidates only exacerbated GOP factionalism. In a practice born in the 1830s, voters elected delegates, who then attended local conventions to elect candidates for Congress as well as for other state and local offices. Delegates elected candidates by voice vote; if a single candidate did not receive a majority of votes, the convention chair would call for another round of voting (or balloting) and continue this practice until a majority was obtained. The convention system initially consolidated party power and allowed party leaders to control the flow of the conventions. However, in the Reconstruction South, party conventions were often contentious, violent, and inconclusive in the face of several factions. Those not officially receiving the party nomination often ran as third-party "Independent Republican" candidates.[32] Race was a second fulcrum on which GOP factions balanced, and white Republicans losing nominations to black candidates frequently ran as Independent Republicans in the general election, effectively splitting the GOP vote.

White Republican leaders were careful to maintain hegemony, even in states with black majorities, such as South Carolina, which had the largest black population (60 percent) concentrated in the low country—coastal areas with pre-war rice and cotton plantations.[33] A series of strong, white Republican governors came to power throughout the Reconstruction period, often bolstered by the large black electorate. Carpetbagger Robert Scott (1868–1872), scalawag Franklin Moses (1872–1874),

and carpetbagger Daniel Chamberlain (1874–1877) all served as
Republican executives.

The Scott and Moses administrations were ridiculed nationwide for their
corruption. A former doctor and Civil War colonel from Ohio, Robert Scott
arrived in South Carolina as an assistant commissioner in the Freedmen's Bureau
in 1866. He soon became a staunch defender of African-American rights in the
South, volunteering his medical services and setting up camps and clinics for
destitute freedmen. Scott's popularity catapulted him to the governor's mansion
just two years later, primarily via the black vote. Yet Scott's administration soon
succumbed to accusations of kickbacks and bribes involving the state's railroad funds
as well as corrupt practices by the State Land Commission, created to purchase
and resell parcels of land to freedmen. Scott left office in 1872 under a cloud of
scrutiny, leaving the state heavily in debt. His successor, South Carolina native
Franklin Moses, followed his predecessor's practices, often steering public money
into projects to pay down his personal debt. When creditors attempted to arrest
him, Moses called in the state militia to defend himself. Thoroughly discredited
by 1874, Moses did not stand for re-election.[34] Alonzo Ransier, who had earned a
reputation for honesty statewide, despite having served as lieutenant governor under
Scott, was particularly critical of the Moses administration. He told an audience
of constituents, "let every man feel that society at large will hold him and the
party accountable for every misdeed in the administration of government, and will
credit him with every honest effort in the interest of the people and . . . of good
government."[35] Generally, however, the black Representatives defended their GOP
state governments against attacks by Democrats on the House Floor. Josiah Walls
noted that, "daily, you hear it loudly proclaimed upon this floor by the enemies of
this Government that 'reconstruction' in the South caused by the enfranchisement of
the Negro 'is a failure.' . . . But they suggest no remedy for evils that are said to exist,
nor do they deny the fact that it is the [white supremacists] banded together for
the very purpose of overthrowing regularly established State governments by force
and fraud."[36]

The relationship between black and white Republicans was the "progeny of a
simple quid pro quo," explains one scholar. "Republicans wanted southern black
votes to secure their burgeoning political dominance, and, in exchange . . . African
Americans wanted protection from discrimination . . . and a greater share of freedom
and equality."[37] African Americans eventually expressed a hope that the freedmen
constituency would have a choice in party loyalty in the future. Representative John
Lynch noted on the House Floor, "I want to see the day come when the colored
people of this county can afford to occupy an independent position in politics.
But that day, in my judgment, will never come so long as there remains a strong,
powerful, intelligent, wealthy organization arrayed against them as a race and
as a class."[38]

Relegated to a single party, black candidates had the overwhelming task of
balancing both factions of the Republican Party. One historian notes that "since
[African-American politicians] could neither leave the party, nor control it, black
Republicans began to operate as a pressure group within it. . . . In this sense,
they were practicing what later became known as ethnic politics. Operating as a
group, they tried to barter votes for offices and benefits."[39] Black officeholders saw
themselves as advocates for their race, not just their constituents—a political strategy

Carpetbagger:

A derogatory term applied by the
popular press to a Northerner who went
to the South during Reconstruction
to pursue economic or political
opportunities. Many of these
Northerners carried their belongings
in carpetbags. This term is also used
by observers of current political affairs
to describe a person who interferes
with the politics of a locality to which
he or she has no permanent or
genuine connection.

Referencing the trend of northerners moving
to southern states to run for elective office,
Harper's Weekly *illustrated the "carpet*
bagger" in another drawing by Radical-
Republican-sympathizing cartoonist
Thomas Nast, its November 9, 1872, issue.

IMAGE COURTESY OF LIBRARY
OF CONGRESS

A.R. Waud portrayed the agents of the Freedmen's Bureau as peacemakers between blacks and whites in this 1868 print.

<small>IMAGE COURTESY OF LIBRARY OF CONGRESS</small>

that was later described as "surrogate" representation.[40] Richard Cain, who served in the 43rd and 45th Congresses (1873–1875; 1877–1879), regularly referred to the "five million people for whom I speak," indicating the total African-American population in the United States at the time.[41]

Elections

Black-majority districts were essential for electing African-American Representatives, especially in South Carolina, which elected relatively large numbers of black Members. Only one man served a district whose population was less than 50 percent black: James Rapier represented, for one term, a southeastern Alabama district whose population was 44 percent black.[42] The rest served districts whose populations were typically at least 60 percent African-American. Reconstruction-Era Republican state legislatures gerrymandered (drew districts that maximized their voting populations) southern states to boost the party's national strength upon their return to the Union. As speaker of the Mississippi state assembly in 1872, John Lynch reapportioned the state's six seats in the U.S. House of Representatives, creating five Republican-dominated districts. Later that year, he won a coastal seat with a majority-black (55 percent) population.

South Carolina was, arguably, the crucible of black congressional experience in the Reconstruction South; six of the 17 Black Americans to serve in Congress during Reconstruction were from the Palmetto State. This number alone, however, fails to convey South Carolina's influence on black service in the Capitol during the 19th century. Only one Congress—the 46th Congress (1879–1881)—did not have a black man in the South Carolina delegation between 1870 and 1887; no black men from any state served in the House during that Congress. In the 42nd Congress (1871–1873), all but one of the state's four congressional districts were represented by black men. Richard Cain's election as an At-Large Representative (representing the entire state) in the following Congress meant five out of six South Carolina Representatives were black.

Several factors account for South Carolina's dominance in black representation. Union forces captured some of the South Carolina Sea Islands as early as 1861, emancipating the large slave populations and introducing them early to the educational and economic benefits of Reconstruction—as well as political organization. Led by a mixed-race elite, black Charlestonians also organized quickly after the war's end. Protesting the Black Codes—a series of restrictive laws dictating black employment, movement, and lifestyle approved by the state legislature in September 1865—black South Carolinians organized a statewide Colored Peoples Convention in November. Several future South Carolina Members of Congress cut their political teeth at the convention, including Joseph Rainey, Robert De Large, Alonzo Ransier, and Richard Cain. Their protest proved successful; in early 1866 the new military commander of South Carolina, Union General Daniel Sickles, nullified the Black Codes. After the 15th Amendment became law, the Republican Party quickly marshaled the large, organized population on the South Carolina coast into a dominant voting bloc.[43] Unlike other states, whose black participation succumbed to white Republicans by the 1870s, black South Carolinians maintained a majority in the state legislature from 1868 to 1876. Black presiding officers reigned in the state house of representatives from 1872 to 1876; Robert Elliott resigned his seat in Congress to take over the state speakership in 1874.

Black candidates still faced monumental electoral obstacles, despite the majority of black and Republican voters in their districts. Violence and intimidation were commonplace during congressional campaigns. A variety of white supremacist groups existed, the most notorious being the Ku Klux Klan (KKK). Red Shirts and Rifle Clubs operated out of South Carolina. White Leagues flourished throughout the South.[44] White supremacists threatened black voters and attacked the candidates during campaigns. The irregularities and confusion resulting from violent campaigns led to an influx of contested elections, and the House Committee on Elections handled an unusually heavy caseload during the Reconstruction Era. Established in the 1st Congress in 1789, the committee was charged with rendering judgments on disputed elections based on evidence and witness testimony. Members of the panel heard each candidate's evidence asserting his right to the seat. The committee voted for its choice candidate and reported its findings to the whole House for a final vote. Usually, the candidate representing the majority party had a distinct advantage because votes within the committee and on the House Floor were often decided along party lines.[45] Sixty percent of cases heard by the committee between 1867 and 1911 were from the former Confederacy—a percentage that is even more impressive given the Confederate states constituted around 25 percent of the House.[46]

Though every southern state experienced violent elections, Alabama was the center of KKK activity. In September of 1868, Klansmen forced James Rapier to flee his home for a Montgomery, Alabama, boarding house where he lived in obscurity for a year. Seeking re-election in 1874 to his southeastern Alabama district, Rapier faced stolen and destroyed ballot boxes, bribery, fraudulent vote counts, armed intimidation, and murder. Frightened black voters stayed home and Rapier lost the election.[47] The inability of his central Alabama neighbor Jeremiah Haralson to garner more than 700 votes in a district whose population was more than 80 percent black led the *New York Times* to observe in 1884, "the Democrats will always win in Alabama, no matter how great the preponderance of the black voting population."[48]

When Mississippi Democrats vowed to recapture the state government in the spring of 1874, Representative John Lynch's re-election campaign nearly succumbed to the pressure. "The Democrats were bold, outspoken, defiant, and

Gerrymander:

The act of dividing a geographic area into districts so as to give one party an unfair advantage during elections. In the early 19th century, the party of Massachusetts Governor Elbridge Gerry redrew the state's congressional districts to favor its candidates. One district resembled a salamander; hence the combination of "Gerry" and "mander."

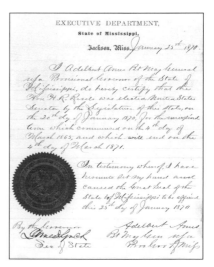

On January 25, 1870, the provisional governor of Mississippi certified that the Mississippi state legislature elected Hiram Revels to the United States Senate.

Hiram Revels's original election certificate, Center for Legislative Archives, National Archives and Records Administration.

At-Large Representative:

A Representative elected to the House in statewide voting when a majority of the state delegation was elected by single-member, geographically defined districts. This method for electing differs from the general ticket, in which an entire delegation is elected statewide. Until the mid-20th century, At-Large Representatives were often elected immediately following decennial apportionment. At-Large elections were abolished by federal law in 1968.

determined," Lynch remarked. "I noticed that I was not received and greeted." Mississippi Democratic clubs were converted into "armed military companies" that raided his Republican meetings.[49] At an evening speech in Vicksburg, lights were extinguished and Lynch was nearly crushed in a riotous stampede.[50] Lynch was the only Republican to survive a Democratic sweep in the polls in Mississippi. "It would be a source of personal pride and congratulation if I could declare upon the floor of the House of Representatives today that mob-law and violence do not exist in any part of the South and are not tolerated by any portion of its citizens," Lynch said. "The circumstances are such that the facts would not sustain me in making this declaration."[51] Senator Blanche Bruce made a similar observation. Having witnessed White League intimidation, Bruce warned his colleagues that "violence so unprovoked . . . is a spectacle not only discreditable to the country, but is dangerous to the integrity of our free institutions."[52]

Contested Elections

Black Representatives in the Reconstruction Era were profoundly affected by contested elections. A contested election prevented the seating of the first black man who won a congressional election. On October 4, 1868, John Willis Menard, an Illinois-born mulatto newspaper editor who had held several GOP patronage positions since 1862, declared his candidacy for a special election to fill a vacant New Orleans, Louisiana, seat in the U.S. House of Representatives. Though he won the special election with 65 percent of the vote, his opponent, Democrat Caleb Hunt, contested the results, and the House Committee on Elections declared the seat vacant. Menard defended his right to take office, becoming the first black man to speak before the House while it was in session, on February 27, 1869. Three other black men—Joseph Rainey, Josiah Walls, and Richard Cain—all lost contested elections. Rainey remained in his seat, despite the ruling of the Committee on Elections, because the House never took up his case for a full vote. Five black Members contested six separate elections they lost. Only John Lynch and Robert Smalls successfully contested their 1880 electoral losses before the majority Republican 47th Congress (1881–1883).[53]

Black Members preoccupied with defending their contested seats lost valuable time needed to introduce legislation or give speeches on the House Floor. As the enormous caseload trickled through the Committee on Elections, the panel often delayed its deliberations until late in the second session. Contested elections and the personal and political turmoil that ensued marred the political career of Josiah Walls. The Ku Klux Klan, entrenched near his northern Florida home, managed to unseat him twice by running ex-Confederate generals against him in contests for an At-Large seat and a district representing eastern Florida. Walls was unable to legislate at all in the 44th Congress (1875–1877), as he was preoccupied defending his seat.

WASHINGTON EXPERIENCE

Black Representatives found one of the country's most expansive black elite communities when they arrived in Washington during the Reconstruction Era. In the postwar years, the country's well-educated and wealthy African-American population escaped the violence of the South and competition from white elites in Boston and Philadelphia to settle in Washington. The "black 400" were drawn to the capital city because of its cultural opportunities, government employment, and relative economic security, and because of the presence of one of the country's premier black colleges: Howard University. They considered themselves socially superior to the rest of the 40,000-plus African Americans in the city, who were primarily former slaves seeking refuge in the city following the Civil War.[54] Black Representatives were well accepted among the black elite. Blanche Bruce's family was among the leading households; he purchased a lavish home near Mount Vernon Square in the District of Columbia and socialized in the highest circles of the "black 400."[55] Several black Representatives lived in the upper-class black neighborhoods near Howard University.

Other black Representatives lived in upscale boarding houses and homes near Lafayette Square and on Capitol Hill.[56] In the 42nd Congress, Benjamin Turner of Alabama and Josiah Walls occupied the same boarding house on 14th Street in the northwest section of the city, near Franklin Park. The two were close neighbors to Joseph Rainey and to prominent Republicans including Speaker James G. Blaine of Maine as well as Senator Sumner and Representatives Benjamin Butler and George Hoar, all of Massachusetts.[57]

Yet African Americans in Congress during the Reconstruction Era also experienced widespread discrimination. In an 1874 newspaper interview, Joseph Rainey documented the second-class treatment he and his colleagues received in Washington. He noted that black Representatives were forced to pay higher rent and higher prices at local restaurants.[58] "Why is it that colored members of Congress cannot enjoy the same immunities that are accorded to white members?" Rainey asked on the House Floor. "We are here enacting laws for the country and casting votes upon important questions; we have been sent here by the suffrages of the people."[59]

A defining feature of the experience of black Congressmen on Capitol Hill in the 19th century was their relative isolation. Only a handful of black Representatives served at any given time, and the two black Senators did not serve together. The apex of black Membership in Congress during the 19th century was, ironically, in the Democrat-controlled House during the 44th Congress. Seven African Americans served in the House and Blanche Bruce kept his seat in the Senate. Because of their small number and because they were a relative novelty, these men were often under the glare of public scrutiny. When the African-American Representatives arrived in Washington, they faced skepticism of their ability to fulfill their duties. "When the first black man took his place in the House of Congress, Americans looked on with wide-opened mouths and eyes, with caustic criticism," Marie Le Baron reported for the *St. Louis Daily Globe* in the opening paragraph of her piece profiling the Members of the 43rd Congress. Skeptics, she continued, held "openly expressed doubts of his ability to retain and fill the place of honor, and creditably to himself and to the white nation."[60]

Black Congressmen typically received high marks for their performance from Republicans, who generally welcomed their colleagues to their respective chambers. Speaker Blaine later praised his black colleagues in his memoirs. "They were as a rule, studious, earnest, ambitious men," wrote Blaine, "whose public conduct . . . would be honorable to any race."[61] Senator Roscoe Conkling of New York escorted Senator Blanche Bruce to his swearing-in, beginning a lifelong friendship. Conkling coached Bruce in Senate procedure and procured him advantageous committee assignments. Bruce named his only child for the New York Senator.

Though floor debate remained civil for the most part, black Congressmen

In a unique case of double contested elections, African-American Pinckney B. S. Pinchback of Louisiana was elected simultaneously to both the Senate and House. Pinchback lost the contested House seat and, citing claims of fraud in the state legislature, the Senate denied him his seat as well. Serving as provisional governor of Louisiana at the time, Pinchback signed his own election certifications.

IMAGE COURTESY OF LIBRARY OF CONGRESS

When the first black Members of Congress arrived in Washington, DC, they found a majestic, marble Capitol with a massive dome completed during the Civil War. "National Capitol," Ballou's Pictorial Weekly Drawing-Room Companion, 1856.

COLLECTION OF U.S. HOUSE OF REPRESENTATIVES

"Heroes of the Colored Race," a print published by J. Hoover of Philadelphia in 1881, pictured Senator Blanche K. Bruce of Mississippi, orator Frederick Douglass, and Senator Hiram Revels of Mississippi. The vignettes depicted scenes from African-American life as well as portraits of other Members of Congress: John Lynch of Mississippi, Joseph Rainey of South Carolina, Charles Nash of Louisiana, and Robert Smalls of South Carolina.

IMAGE COURTESY OF LIBRARY OF CONGRESS

occasionally encountered the patronizing attitude of their opposition. A northern Democrat, New York Representative Samuel Cox was consistently adversarial. Representative Hoar once noted that the black Members had in Cox "the most formidable antagonist, perhaps the most trained and experienced debater in the House."[62] In a memorable run-in with the New York Democrat, Joseph Rainey attempted to interrupt Cox's scathing remarks regarding Republican governments in South Carolina. Cox responded with a patronizing, "Oh honey, sit down," eliciting laughter from the chamber.[63] Chairman of the Committee on Elections in the 44th and 45th Congresses, Virginia Democrat John Harris also harangued the black Representatives. In a floor debate on January 5, 1874, Harris rhetorically asked, "Is there not one gentleman on the floor who can honestly say he really believes that the colored man is created his equal?" Alonzo Ransier quietly replied with a simple, "I can," to which a flustered Harris retorted, "Of course you can; but I am speaking to the white men of the House; and, Mr. Speaker, I do not wish to be interrupted again by him."[64] Another Democrat, John Brown—a young, wealthy, outspoken Member from Kentucky—regularly ignored the black Members and refused to yield to them in debate.[65] Richard Cain made light of the fact that blacks were often treated as inferiors in Congress. "We believe that we are made just like white men," he said. "Look; I stretch out my arms. See; I have two of them, as you have. Look at your ears; I have two of them. I have two eyes, two nostrils, one mouth, two feet. I stand erect like you. I am clothed in humanity like you. I think, I reason, I talk . . . Is there any difference between us? Not so far as our manhood is concerned."[66]

LEGISLATIVE INTERESTS

Committee Assignments

Black Congressmen's committee service underscored their lack of power in the House Chamber. Most black Members had low-ranking committee assignments. Though two men—Richard Cain and Robert Smalls—served on the prestigious Agriculture Committee, their power was limited.[67] Certainly, the brevity of African-American careers during this era contributed to their lack of seniority and influence on committees, but it does not fully explain their inability to secure prominent committee assignments.

Beginning in the 1840s in the Senate and in the post–Civil War era in the House, length of service began to determine the committee hierarchy; the more terms in Congress, the higher the rank. But this process of broad and multidecadal centralization within the House evolved slowly and, until the 1910s, seniority was not the primary determinant of committee hierarchy.[68] Perhaps of greater consequence to black Members during Reconstruction was their relative isolation from the key individuals in the party leadership who had power to procure or assign plum committee posts. Even the longest-serving black Member of the period, Joseph Rainey, had difficulty rising in the ranks in his nine years in Congress. GOP leadership consistently assigned Rainey a rank lower than his seniority permitted. Most blatantly, Rainey was the last-ranking GOP Member on the newly created Select Committee on the Freedmen's Bank in the 44th Congress, even though he had more terms of service than any other Member on the committee.[69] No black Member chaired any House standing committee. Senator Blanche Bruce chaired two select committees: the Select Committee to Investigate the Freedmen's Savings and Trust Company and the Select Committee on Levees of the Mississippi River, which oversaw development of the river's delta region.[70]

The House and Senate Education and Labor committees were the most common assignments for black Congressmen.[71] Senators Hiram Revels and Blanche Bruce served on the Senate panel. Five men took seats on the equivalent House committee. Black Congressmen vocally supported the sale of federally owned land in the South and West to fund public education. But even congressional allies considered such a program controversial. Opponents feared federal funding for schools would impede states' rights and blocked black Members' efforts to enact such legislation. Josiah Walls, one of the most vocal supporters of the program, insisted the national government must provide for education of southern blacks because, left to their own devices, southern state governments would not act. "It is useless to talk about patriotism existing in those states . . . who now and always have believed that it was wrong to educate the Negro and that such offenses should be punishable by death or a lash," Walls chided. "Away with the patriotism that advocates and prefers ignorance to intelligence!" Joseph Rainey was so desperate to fund normal schools, he even supported a $1 poll tax (which would have disfranchised many newly freed slaves) to directly fund public education. "Do you suppose I want my two children hindered in the enjoyment of educational opportunities in this country," Rainey asked, "merely on account of their color when we are taxed to support those schools?"[72]

Absent key committee assignments and leadership positions, the relatively small number of black Members lacked the ability to drive a legislative agenda. Most introduced bills on the House or the Senate Floor only to have them die in committee. The near-universal desire among black Congressmen to reimburse depositors to the Freedmen's Bank illustrates how both the House and the Senate rebuffed black legislators' dogged efforts. Congress established the bank in 1865 to help freedmen manage their money; however, reckless loans and corruption depleted the bank's $57 million in deposits, forcing it to close in 1874. Mismanagement and a lack of resources continued after the bank's failure. Three commissioners were appointed to reimburse depositors, but shortly afterward they were criticized for failing to complete their overwhelming task. The bank's failure had far-reaching

The second African American to serve as a Senator, Blanche K. Bruce of Mississippi later noted that success in the Senate required managing his relationship with all of his colleagues: "The novelty of my position [compels me] to cultivate and exhibit my honorable associates a courtesy that would inspire reciprocal courtesy."

IMAGE COURTESY OF SCURLOCK STUDIO RECORDS, ARCHIVES CENTER, NATIONAL MUSEUM OF AMERICAN HISTORY, SMITHSONIAN INSTITUTION

This famous print titled "The first colored senator and representatives—in the 41st and 42nd Congress of the United States" was published by Currier & Ives in 1872. The group portrait assembled Robert De Large of South Carolina, Jefferson Long of Georgia, Hiram Revels of Mississippi, Benjamin Turner of Alabama, Josiah Walls of Florida, Joseph Rainey of South Carolina, and Robert Elliott of South Carolina.

IMAGE COURTESY OF LIBRARY OF CONGRESS

effects on black businesses that continued well into the late 1890s.[73] Nearly every black Member of Congress sponsored a bill to provide financial relief to African Americans who lost their savings when the Freedmen's Bank failed. However, no one was a greater advocate than Senator Blanche Bruce, who took the reins of the Select Committee to Investigate the Freedmen's Savings and Trust Company in April 1879. Bruce's committee was unable to convince the Senate to reimburse depositors. Yet Bruce used some of his own personal fortune as well as his political clout to raise funds to reimburse a small portion of depositors.[74]

Lacking any qualitative institutional power, African Americans in Congress were relegated for the most part to ancillary, passive support roles for legislation shaped almost entirely by their House and Senate colleagues. Rather than acting as legislative entrepreneurs or public advocates, black Members of Congress were resigned to those roles the institution's leaders tolerated: cheerleading for reform legislation or providing firsthand accounts of civil rights abuses to sway public opinion. Where Congress's true power lay—behind the closed doors of committee meetings and markup sessions—African-American Members had virtually no influence.

Ku Klux Klan and Amnesty Acts

Reconstruction-Era Congresses were preoccupied with curbing racial violence that afflicted the postwar South. Disturbing reports about the activities of the KKK, as well as other white supremacist groups, inspired congressional leaders to pass a series of three Ku Klux Klan Acts (also known as the Force Acts) during the 41st and 42nd Congresses (1869–1873).[75] The first reinforced the 15th Amendment (universal manhood suffrage), the second placed all southern elections under federal control, and the third protected the voter registration and justice system from infiltration and intimidation by Klansmen. The 10 black Members who served in the Congresses voting on these bills universally supported the legislation. Most significantly, their electoral struggles confirmed the need for such measures. "If you cannot protect the loyal men of the South," Robert Elliott warned in April 1871, "then have the loyal people of this great Republic done and suffered much in vain, and your free Constitution is a mockery and a snare."[76]

Yet Congress softened the forceful nature of the Ku Klux Klan legislation by enacting generous pardons for former Confederates. The bill offered near blanket amnesty, excepting former public servants and military personnel who resigned their positions to join the Confederacy. Senator Hiram Revels and Representatives Joseph Rainey, Robert De Large, and Benjamin Turner voted for the bill in their respective chambers. "We are desirous, sir, of being magnanimous," Rainey told his congressional colleagues in May 1872. "We have open and frank hearts toward those who were our former oppressors and taskmasters. We foster no enmity now, and we desire to foster none for their acts in the past to us, nor to the Government we love so well."[77] Rainey was among those who cast a "yea" vote for amnesty provided the Ku Klux Klan Acts remained enforced. Robert De Large pledged his support only if former Confederates swore a formal oath of allegiance to the Union. One of the more conservative black politicians, Turner, expressed no animosity towards former slaveowners—though he had been a slave—and focused on procuring economic aid for his war-torn state. "I have no coals of fiery reproach to heap upon [former Confederates] now," Turner informed his congressional colleagues. "Rather would I extend the olive branch of peace, and say to them, let the past be forgotten."[78] Not

On April 20, 1871, President Ulysses S. Grant, shown with Secretary of the Navy George M. Robeson and presidential advisor General Horace Porter in this Frank Leslie's Illustrated *print, signed the Third Ku Klux Klan Act, which enforced the 14th Amendment by guaranteeing all citizens of the United States the rights afforded by the Constitution and providing legal protection under the law.*

<small>IMAGE COURTESY OF LIBRARY OF CONGRESS</small>

all black Members agreed; Representatives Jefferson Long of Georgia and Robert Elliott voted against the bill, primarily out of their wish to solidify black rights in the South before restoring former Confederates to full political participation.

Civil Rights Bill of 1875

No issue preoccupied black Representatives more than the 1875 Civil Rights Bill (18 Stat. 335–337). Neither the Civil Rights Act of 1866, which guaranteed citizens the right to enter into contracts and to purchase, sell, or lease property, nor the series of Ku Klux Klan Acts, which had incrementally outlawed discrimination in voter registration in local and congressional elections and empowered circuit judges to appoint election supervisors, satisfied ardent reformers, such as Senator Charles Sumner. He introduced legislation on May 13, 1870, that provided the basis for the Civil Rights Bill of 1875.[79] Senator Sumner envisioned a far more sweeping bill that would fully enforce and expand upon the 13th, 14th, and 15th Amendments. The centerpiece of his original bill outlawed racial discrimination in juries, schools, transportation, and public accommodations. However, Illinois Senator Lyman Trumbull, chairman of the powerful Judiciary Committee, disapproved of the bill and trapped it in his panel for more than two years.

On December 2, 1873, the opening day of the 43rd Congress, Sumner dutifully submitted his civil rights bill.[80] On December 18—bolstered by the GOP's 111-Member majority—House Judiciary Committee Chairman Benjamin Butler submitted his own bill, which echoed much of Sumner's language.[81] A former states' rights Democrat, Butler changed his party allegiances and his attitude toward African Americans while serving as a brigadier general in the Civil War. Recalling the deaths of black Union soldiers on the battlefield, Butler declared, "May my right hand forget its cunning and my tongue cleave to the roof of my mouth if I ever fail to defend the rights of these men who have given their blood for me and my country . . . God helping me, I will keep that oath."[82]

Opponents lined up to denounce the bill when it came to the House Floor the following January, railing against the measure's perceived threat to incite "a war of the races, [in which] the black race in this country will be exterminated," in the words of Representative Milton Durham of Kentucky.[83] Democrats stood up one by one, claiming that the Civil Rights Bill attempted to enforce rights beyond the scope of the Constitution, usurped states' power to regulate common (public) schools, and forced the undesired social mixing of the two races. Amendments aimed at killing the Civil Rights Bill soon flooded in at such an alarming rate that Butler was forced to recommit the bill to the House Judiciary Committee on January 7 for consideration.

In the Senate, Sumner's passing breathed new life into his legislative agenda. On his deathbed on March 11, 1874, Sumner allegedly repeated at least three times to Representative George Hoar: "You must take care of the civil rights bill—my bill, the civil rights bill—don't let it fail!"[84] Primarily out of respect for their deceased colleague, Senators passed the bill—29 to 16—two months later.[85] The legislation was referred to the House Judiciary Committee on June 18, leaving the lower chamber to consider both pieces of legislation.[86]

A GOP debacle in the 1874 midterm elections further endangered the Civil Rights Bill. Sixty-two House Republican incumbents failed to win re-election; 43 hailed from northern or western states. The large GOP majority in the House during the 43rd Congress gave way to a 79-Member Democratic advantage in

As chairman of the House Judiciary Committee, Representative and Civil War Brigadier General Benjamin Butler of Massachusetts submitted his own version of the Civil Rights Bill in 1874.

Image courtesy of Library of Congress

Refers to a session of Congress that transpires after congressional elections but before the start of a new Congress. In the 19th century, new Congresses commenced on March 4 (though both Chambers often convened for business at later dates). Thus, after biennial fall elections, a new Congress was not seated for four months. Congress often convened for an additional, or lame duck, session in the intervening weeks in a hurried effort to complete legislative business. Ratification of the 20th Amendment in 1933 set the start date for new Congresses to January 3, drastically reducing the time period in which a lame duck session could transpire. As a result, modern Congresses have rarely held lame duck sessions.

the 44th Congress.[87] A financial panic in 1873 and the resulting depression, as well as multiple charges of corruption in Republican President Ulysses S. Grant's administration, were primarily blamed for the loss.[88] However, growing public disinterest in and frustration with civil rights legislation were also at fault. A top House Republican, James Garfield of Ohio—where GOP electoral losses were especially devastating—noted "a general apathy among the people concerning the war and the negro."[89] James Sener, a scalawag from Virginia, blamed prolonged congressional debate on the Civil Rights Bill for his electoral loss. Noting that he continually opposed the bill during the first session of the 43rd Congress, he claimed his constituents feared that "under the whip and spur of party pressure," Sener might "yield my honest convictions to the will of the majority."[90] Among those who lost their elections was Benjamin Butler, who succumbed to Democrat Charles P. Thompson with 47 percent of the vote as compared to Thompson's 53 percent.[91] However, the electoral loss also rallied Republican Representatives, who returned to the lame duck session in 1875 determined not to leave office without passing some form of civil rights legislation.

The victorious Democrats, however, believed their mandate included scuttling the Civil Rights Bill. They continually halted business by submitting multiple motions to adjourn every time Butler attempted to place the legislation on the House Calendar for debate. A top GOP lieutenant, John Cessna of Pennsylvania, attempted to circumvent Democrats by drastically changing House Rules, disposing of all dilatory motions (those put forward strictly to stall consideration of legislation) for the remainder of the term. The change failed to achieve the two-thirds majority needed to alter House Rules after 15 Republicans defected. But over strong Democratic objections, Cessna worked with Speaker Blaine to broker a compromise, restricting the use of dilatory motions and opening an opportunity to debate civil rights legislation.[92]

During the precarious lead-up to the 1874 elections, few white GOP supporters spoke on the House Floor on behalf of the Civil Rights Bill. Facing some of the former Confederacy's great orators, the black Representatives carried the debate on the measure throughout the 43rd Congress by making some of their most famous and impassioned speeches. The record-breaking seven black men on the House Floor was, in itself, an argument in favor of the bill. As one scholar notes, "their presence demonstrated that equality in politics could work [and] . . . signaled the drastic change that had overtaken the country's political order."[93] The climax of the first session was Robert Elliott's eloquent rebuttal to former Confederate Vice President Alexander Stephens of Georgia on January 6, 1874. Elliott's speech, in which he asserted that the federal government's highest duty was to protect African Americans, received attention and praise from newspapers nationwide.[94] The *Chicago Tribune* —a newspaper typically favorable to black Representatives—delivered a glowing review of the South Carolinian's speech: "Mr. Elliott has demonstrated the real force of the new order of things."[95]

As southern Democrats denied any racial discrimination on the part of southern railroads, hotels, theaters, and restaurants, the black Representatives provided vivid anecdotes of personal experiences with racism and segregation in public accommodations as evidence of the need for a Civil Rights Bill. Joseph Rainey claimed he was unable to procure first-class tickets on some railway lines and pointed out that he could not eat in the first-class dining room on a boat from

Washington to Norfolk. Forced to wait for a table in the servants' dining room, Rainey had shouted, "I'd starve first," and thereafter brought his own meals while traveling. Rainey drilled this injustice into the heads of his colleagues: "Do you think it is right that when I go forth from this capital as an honored member of Congress that I should be subjected to the insults from the lowest fellow in the street if he should happen to feel so inclined?"[96] When traveling from his district to the nation's capital, John Lynch noted, "I am treated, not as an American citizen, but as a brute. Forced to occupy a filthy smoking car both night and day, with drunkards, gamblers, and criminals; and for what? Not that I am unable or unwilling to pay my way; not that I am obnoxious in my personal appearance or disrespectful in my conduct; but simply because I happen to be of a darker complexion."[97] James Rapier pointed out the irony of the second-class treatment he received while traveling though he had a privileged role as a Representative. "Just think that the law recognizes my right upon this floor as a law-maker, but that there is no law to secure me an accommodation whatever while traveling here to discharge my duties as a Representative. . . . Is not this most anomalous and ridiculous?" Rapier reminded his colleagues that, "Every day my life and property are exposed, are left to the mercy of others, and will be so long as every hotel-keeper, railroad conductor, and steamboat captain can refuse me with impunity."[98]

Opponents argued that regulating discrimination in public accommodations and transportation was beyond the scope of the Constitution. The Reconstruction Amendments, which already guaranteed the basic political rights afforded to all male citizens, extended the federal government's power to its limit. "The colored people are now in substantial enjoyment of their full rights and privileges granted by the recent amendments to the Constitution," argued Democrat John Storm of Pennsylvania. "This bill is thrust upon us now for no other purpose than exciting bad feelings." Virginian Thomas Whitehead added "now the colored man is a citizen. He can vote. He can hold office. . . . He can hold property. He can do in my state just what any other man can do. . . . Now, what is the object of this bill?"[99] While the Constitution could provide political equality before the law, southerners argued that it could not enforce social equality. John Harris of Virginia declared that the racial division was "a natural prejudice that God himself placed in the hearts of southern children," adding that a Representative of any race could be "thrust from a particular railroad car when his high position was not known."[100] Representative Whitehead observed that "the Almighty has given [black men] what he cannot get rid of—a black skin! . . . You have not the power to make him white and he will never be satisfied short of that."[101] James Blount of Georgia observed that Black Americans in the South did not care for equal access to theaters, hotels, and streetcars. "These people are poor," he observed, "and these things they care nothing about. . . . They are especially often involved in criminal charges. . . . [Judicial rights] are the rights of most practical value to them."[102]

Many southern Democrats' greatest fear was enforced social mixing between blacks and whites. "There are in the Southern States two races, as distinct in their social feelings and prejudices as in color," declared Representative Blount. "The sooner they are recognized by our rulers the better for both races and the country."[103] Democrat Charles Eldredge of Wisconsin blamed the unrest in the South on the "*unnatural relation* in which two races have been placed to each other," adding, "it is a result . . . which may always be expected when it is attempted to subject men

A six-term Representative from Virginia, John Harris belittled his black congressional colleagues by questioning their right to be called men.

IMAGE COURTESY OF LIBRARY OF CONGRESS

Titled "The shackle broken—by the genius of freedom," this print memorialized a defining moment in South Carolina Representative Robert Elliott's congressional career, his 1874 speech in support of the Civil Rights Act.

IMAGE COURTESY OF LIBRARY OF CONGRESS

By 1880, partisan politics began to divide the black vote, as depicted in this Frank Leslie's Illustrated, *portraying Democrats taunting Republican voters en route to the polls.*

of culture . . . to the domination and rule of brute force."[104] Despite their idealism, most Radical Republicans also believed African Americans belonged to a separate social sphere. Even Benjamin Butler admitted, "We do not propose to legislate to establish any equality." However, he clearly believed that equality did not divide on racial grounds: "Not all men are equal, *but every man has the right to be the equal of every other man if he can.* . . . And all constitutions, all laws, all enactments, all prejudices, all caste, all custom, all contravention of that right is unjust, impolitic, and unchristian."[105]

The African-American Members displayed considerable political pragmatism when addressing the issue of using legislation to compel social equality of the races. Richard Cain noted that "no laws enacted by legislators can compel social equality."[106] James Rapier claimed that the Civil Rights Bill "does not and cannot contemplate any such idea as social equality; nor is there any man upon this floor so silly as to believe that there can be any law enacted or enforced that would compel one man to recognize the other as his equal socially." However, he also rejected segregation as a caste system that prevented social mobility, calling such a method "an anti-republican principle in our free country."[107] John Lynch pointed out the hypocrisy of the argument that social equality divided on racial grounds: "I have never believed for a moment that social equality could be brought about even between persons of the same race. . . . But those who contend that the passage of this bill will have a tendency to bring about social equality between the races virtually and substantially admit that there are no social distinctions among white people, whatsoever."[108] As white southerners made dire predictions about the deleterious effects of the Civil Rights Bill on white southern culture, Richard Cain responded with his characteristic good humor: "I think [that if] so harmless a measure as the civil-rights bill, guaranteeing to every man of the African race equal rights with other men, would bring death to the South, then certainly that noble march of Sherman to the sea would have fixed them long ago."[109]

The sticking point on the final version of the Civil Rights Bill of 1875 became the section providing federal funding for and oversight of public education. Traditionally, states and local municipalities controlled public schools. Throughout the South, local prejudice led to uneven educational opportunities. The most controversial component, however, was the provision to desegregate public schools. Both Southern Democrats and moderate Republicans greatly feared angry white parents would pull their children out of mixed race schools, effectively ending public education in the South. "The great evil this bill has in store for the black man is found in the destruction of the common schools of the South," declared Roger Mills of Texas. "When the common schools are broken up in all the Southern States. . . what is to become of the children of the colored people? Are they to grow up on ignorance and vice?"[110] Milton Durham argued that his white constituents paid the bulk of the taxes and that many took advantage of public schools. "Should this bill pass," Durham warned, "and the children of freedmen demand admission into these schools, I believe the system in Kentucky will be so injured as to become worthless."[111] Moderate Republicans were wary of the education clause as well. Though Barbour Lewis of Tennessee supported the Civil Rights Bill, noting that "the colored people deserve this measure," he argued that integrated schools were unacceptable to all "because people of their own choice . . . simply as a matter of taste, have maintained separate schools."[112]

To move the bill out of the Judiciary Committee in the face of such broad opposition, Butler amended the education clause by inserting language that called for "separate, but equal" public schools.[113] By the time the bill came to a vote on February 4, 1875, three versions existed, each differing only on the education provisions: the amended House bill, calling for "separate, but equal" public schools; the Senate bill, which included the legislation's original intent to desegregate and federally fund common schools; and an amended version offered by Stephen Kellogg of Connecticut, stripping the bill of all references to public education.

Black Members vigorously defended the education clause, preferring almost unanimously the Senate version of the bill.[114] John Lynch contended that increased federal funding for education was the most harmless provision of the bill: "All share its benefits alike," he said.[115] Richard Cain sharply admonished his southern colleagues: "Examine the laws of the South, and you will find that it was a penal offense for anyone to educate the colored people there. . . . You robbed us for two hundred years. During all that time we toiled for you. We have raised your cotton, your rice, and your corn. . . . And yet you upbraid us for being ignorant—call us a horde of barbarians!"[116] Alonzo Ransier had great faith that equal rights and opportunities in education would allow talented black men to earn good standing in their communities and would in turn curb discrimination. "Let the doors of the public school house be thrown open to us alike," he declared, "if you mean to give these people equal rights at all, or to protect them in the exercise of the rights and privileges attaching to all freemen and citizens of our country."[117]

By the time the Civil Rights Bill came to a vote, the measure had been gravely wounded. The bill's last days were filled with desperate pleas from its supporters. "Spare us our liberties; give us peace; give us a chance to live; . . . place no obstruction in our way; give us an equal chance," Richard Cain pleaded. "We ask no more of the American people."[118] James Rapier despaired, "I have no compromise to offer on this subject. . . . After all, this question resolves itself into this: either I am a man or I am not a man."[119] Minutes before the final measure came to a vote in the House, Members passed Kellogg's amendment eliminating all references to public education, 128 to 48. A motion replacing the House version with the Senate bill failed soon afterward, 148 to 114. The battered Civil Rights Bill finally passed 162 to 99. The measure provided no mechanism to regulate public schools, but stipulated equal use of public transportation and accommodations regardless of race. It also prohibited the exclusion of African Americans from jury service. Black Members received the final version of the bill with mixed reactions: Richard Cain, John Lynch, Joseph Rainey, and James Rapier voted in its favor, despite its diluted form, but Alonzo Ransier and Josiah Walls were so disappointed by the elimination of the education clause, they declined to vote.[120] The legislation passed the Senate on February 27. On March 1, President Ulysses S. Grant signed it into law.[121] The fact that Republicans, who within days would be relegated to minority status, managed to steer such a bill through the chamber at the conclusion of a lame duck session represented a considerable legislative victory. But in their desperation to pass the measure, Republicans had left the Civil Rights Act of 1875 in such a weakened state that it did little to impede the creation of a system of segregation in the South. Moreover, the limited protection it did afford would soon be stripped by the courts.

To aid the passage of the 1875 Civil Rights Bill, three-term Representative Stephen Kellogg of Connecticut stripped the bill of all references to education.

Image courtesy of Library of Congress

ROLLING BACK CIVIL RIGHTS

After the passage of the Civil Rights Act of 1875, Congress enacted no further civil rights legislation for more than 80 years. The difficulty passing the weakened legislation indicated that the Radical Republicans' idealistic experiment had come to an end. Moreover, though Republicans made gains in the House in the 1876 elections, the political battle that erupted over disputed presidential returns (and its resolution) effectively ended Reconstruction.

The 1876 presidential contest between Republican candidate Rutherford Hayes and Democratic candidate Samuel Tilden caused an electoral crisis when South Carolina, Florida, and Louisiana submitted a set of electoral votes for each candidate. On January 29, 1877, the House adopted an independent 15-member Electoral Commission consisting of Representatives, Senators, and Supreme Court Justices—apportioned on party divisions in each body—to investigate the disputed electoral returns. The six black Representatives who served in the House during the discussion of the disputed election—three from two of the contested states—were among the minority opposing the establishment of the Electoral Commission. John Lynch made two speeches opposing the commission and later observed in his autobiography that the office of the presidency was too important to be placed in "a game or scheme of luck and chance."[122] Joseph Rainey noted the constitutional quandary of establishing the commission, since the framers had never contemplated such a mechanism. "Once permit the Constitution to be made a mere piece of pottery to fashion as party exigencies seem to demand," he warned his colleagues, "and in that moment we are cut adrift from safe moorings and carried beyond rescue upon tossing billows of the political sea."[123]

The Electoral Commission ruled eight to seven in favor of electing Hayes by one electoral vote over Tilden. Though no black Representative was afforded time to speak on the subject, all voted in favor of the commission's conclusion, supporting the election of a Republican candidate over a Democrat, despite their reservations about the commission's formation.[124] However, Hayes's victory came at the cost of congressional Reconstruction. The new administration pulled federal troops out of the South, unbinding southern Democrats' ambitions to roll back the decade-long experiment in fostering racial equality. The new Republican President did little for black civil rights. A disillusioned John Lynch noted that "the Hayes administration not only completed the destruction of what had been thus accomplished, but made any further progress . . . absolutely impossible."[125]

Without federal protection for southern blacks, the next decade marked a period of "redemption"—the capture and control over local and state governments by white supremacists in the South. Historian C. Vann Woodward notes that the racial interaction during Reconstruction "was strained. It was also temporary, and it was usually self-conscious. It was a product of contrived circumstances."[126] African-American politicians examined anew their loyalty to the Republican Party. From his home in Macon, Georgia, Jefferson Long began encouraging black voters to vote for Independent Democrats if Republican candidates proved unsatisfactory. Long himself campaigned for several Independent candidates in the 1870s and 1880s.[127] Robert De Large noted during his congressional service, "I hold that my race has always been Republican for necessity only."[128] After leaving Congress, he and fellow South Carolinians Richard Cain and Alonzo Ransier allied with Martin Delany— a disillusioned former Republican who had abandoned the party for the Democrats and talked of a third party for African Americans in the South.

A series of Supreme Court decisions throughout the last three decades of the 19th century negated civil rights legislative gains and circumscribed protections for freedmen under the Reconstruction Amendments. The Supreme Court rejected the 1873 *Slaughterhouse Cases*—a set of three lawsuits initiated by Louisiana butchers challenging a state law that centralized the state's slaughterhouses into one private company. The butchers claimed protection under the 14th Amendment against state incursion on "privileges or immunities." The decision limited the ability of the federal government to protect Black Americans by confining its power to influence the states on behalf of individual rights. The *United States v. Cruikshank* and *United States v. Reese* decisions weakened the 15th Amendment's protection of voting rights in March 1876. *Cruikshank* initiated an erosion of the Civil Rights Act of 1875 as the court ruled the act did not guarantee First Amendment Rights. The high court in the *Reese* case opened a Pandora's box with its finding that the 15th Amendment did not confer upon any individual the right to vote, but merely forbade states to give any citizen preferential treatment. In this light, the right to vote derived from states, rather than the federal government—leaving state governments to determine how voters were qualified and under what circumstances voting would be allowed. In *United States v. Harris* (1883), the court determined that federal laws did not apply to private persons, which proved a blow to the Ku Klux Klan Acts. That finding essentially unleashed white supremacists to attack any African American seeking to exercise his political rights.[129]

On October 15, 1883, the rollback of civil rights continued when the Supreme Court struck down the 1875 Civil Rights Bill's weak provisions. Ruling 8 to 1, the court declared the law unconstitutional in the *Civil Rights Cases*. The majority opinion asserted that individuals were relegated to appealing to state governments—which proved unfriendly to Black Americans in the South—to stop such discrimination.[130] The two black Representatives serving at the time, James O'Hara and Robert Smalls, attempted unsuccessfully to revive portions of the Civil

"The Colored Congressman"

The President's dinners now are done,
And over all the bother;
He dined and wined 'em every one,
But not the colored brother.

He took the Congressmen in turn—
There's nothing could be fairer—
But the one whose turn came not at all
Was Congressman O'Hara.

In calling on the President
Of course his rights were stable;
He'd shake with "Chet," but couldn't get
His legs beneath "Chet's" table.

If, scenting for the dinner's fumes,
He pined for pork and "tater,"
His only living chance would be
To ring in as a waiter.

Of crowded off upon that track,
The next most likely switchin'
To hie him round in humbler guise
And chance it in the kitchen.

Which shows that black is hardly yet
The color of the winner
Since good Republicans still draw
The colored line at dinner.

POEM ABOUT REPRESENTATIVE JAMES O'HARA OF NORTH CAROLINA

FROM THE *BOSTON STAR* (REPRINTED IN THE *WASHINGTON POST* APRIL 14, 1884)

This Thomas Nast sketch from an 1877 Harper's Weekly *made note of an African-American man voting for a Democrat. Until that time, the Republican Party was the party of most blacks.*

Rights Bill shortly thereafter. In December 1884, O'Hara offered an amendment to an interstate commerce bill prohibiting discrimination on railroad cars. Joined by Representative Smalls on December 17, the two made arguments echoing those of their predecessors who fought for the Civil Rights Bill. However, O'Hara and Smalls served in a minority and were speaking in a different era. Even many congressional Republicans viewed racial equality as an irreconcilable division between the North and South that should be ignored politely rather than discussed.

CONCLUSION

The 19th-century black Congressmen's inability to rise within the congressional power structure circumscribed their legislative legacy and relegated them to a symbolic representation of the accomplishments of the Civil Rights Amendments and northern victory in the Civil War. Yet they remained forceful advocates for the civil and political rights of their constituents, despite the obstacles they faced in and out of Congress. Their role as surrogate representatives for millions of newly freed African Americans provided a representational blueprint for black Members in future generations. The mantle of advocacy figuratively passed from the pioneer generation when the aged John Lynch—living in Republican Oscar De Priest's Chicago district in 1928—advised the new Member of Congress to place the interests of the African-American community before even partisan loyalty. "We need a man who will have the courage to attack not only his political opponents," he told De Priest, "but those within his own party who fail to fight unfair legislation directed toward people of color."[131]

The Supreme Court's *coup de grâce* to the Civil Rights Bill marked the end of the federal government's role as champion of freedmen. Over time, the government became impassive to the states' diminution of blacks' political and social status. Righteous Republicans excoriated southern Democrats for erecting an architecture of social and legal racial apartheid, while indignant southerners dismissed emblematic Republican racial initiatives as Janus-faced appeals to black voters. Both major parties regularly traded barbs about the "Negro issue" on the House and Senate floors. Thus, Congress shirked substantive legislative action to improve blacks' quality of life, repeatedly refusing to pass additional provisions intended to safeguard their 14th and 15th Amendment rights. Recognizing that a new era had dawned, James O'Hara concluded, "It is too late for the American Congress to legislate on the question of color."[132] What would soon develop was a rigid system of segregation codified in state law and tacitly sanctioned by the federal government.

NOTES

1   Quoted in Maurine Christopher, *Black Americans in Congress* (New York: Thomas Y. Crowell Company, 1976): 9. Revels seems to attribute this quote to Massachusetts journalist Wendell Phillips. See "Autobiography of Hiram Revels," Carter G. Woodson Collection of Negro Papers and Related Documents, box 11, Manuscript Division, Library of Congress, Washington, DC.

2   U.S. Senators were elected by state legislatures until 1913, when the adoption of the 17th Amendment required their direct election. Jefferson Davis, formerly the President of the Confederacy, left his Senate seat at the same time Brown left his. The Union victors in the Civil War were quick to elevate Revels's place in the chamber, representing the state that once selected Davis, as a symbolic moment; they played their message so well that contemporary newspapers and many historians mistakenly place Revels in Davis's former seat. See, for example, *Congressional Globe*, Senate, 41st Cong., 2nd sess. (23 February 1870): 1513; Gath, "Washington," 17 March 1870, *Chicago Tribune*: 2; Maurine Christopher, *Black Americans in Congress* (New York: Thomas Y. Crowell Company, 1976): 5–6; Stephen Middleton, ed., *Black Congressmen During Reconstruction: A Documentary Sourcebook* (Westport, CT: Praeger, 2002): 320.

3   "The Negro United States Senator," 3 March 1870, *Atlanta Constitution*: 3.

4   "Washington," 27 February 1870, *Chicago Tribune*: 1.

5   "The Negro in Congress," 7 March 1871, *Chicago Tribune*: 2.

6   President Lincoln issued a preliminary version of the Emancipation Proclamation on September 22, 1862, after the Civil War battle of Antietam. In his message to the Confederacy, the President announced his intention to free the slaves in the rebellious states; one hundred days later he signed the official proclamation. For more information on the history of both proclamations, see James M. McPherson, *Crossroads of Freedom: Antietam* (New York: Oxford University Press, 2002): 138–146; James M. McPherson, *Battle Cry of Freedom* (New York: Oxford University Press, 1988): 562–563. See also the National Archives and Records Administration's online "Featured Documents" at http://www.archives.gov/exhibits/featured_documents/emancipation_proclamation/ (accessed 13 May 2008).

7   The Confederacy originally included 11 states (South Carolina, Mississippi, Florida, Alabama, Georgia, Louisiana, Texas, Virginia, Arkansas, North Carolina, and Tennessee).

8   Eric Foner, *Reconstruction: America's Unfinished Revolution, 1863–1877* (New York: Harper & Row, 1988): 230.

9   This includes the 21 formal vetoes and eight pocket vetoes issued by Johnson in the 39th and 40th Congresses (1865–1869). Johnson had the second-highest percentage of vetoes overridden (51.7 percent). Franklin Pierce, who had 55.7 percent of his vetoes overridden, issued nine vetoes only to have five overridden by the 33rd and 34th Congresses (1853–1857). See Office of the Clerk, "Presidential Vetoes," available at http://clerk.house.gov/art_history/house_history/vetoes.html.

10 Tennessee, which had rejoined the Union on July 24, 1866, was exempt from the requirements of the Reconstruction Act.

11 See Appendix J, Constitutional Amendments and Major Civil Rights Acts of Congress Referenced in the Text.

12 Eric Foner, *Freedom's Lawmakers: A Directory of Black Officeholders During Reconstruction* (New York: Oxford University Press, 1993): xi.

13 Several historians discuss the impact of skin color on the stratification of free and enslaved black communities in different regions of the South from the colonial to the postbellum periods. Winthrop D. Jordan discusses the colonial period in "American Chiaroscuro: The Status and Definition of Mulattoes in the British Colonies," in Edward Countryman ed., *How Did American Slavery Begin?* (Boston: Bedford/St. Martin's, 1999). Both Eugene D. Genovese and Paul D. Escott discuss stratification within slave communities in the antebellum period: Genovese, *Roll, Jordan, Roll: The World the Slaves Made* (New York: Pantheon Books, 1974) and Escott, *Slavery Remembered: A Record of Twentieth-Century Slave Narratives* (Chapel Hill: University of North Carolina Press, 1979). For a discussion of the racial tensions within the free black communities in the antebellum period, see Ira Berlin, *Slaves Without Masters: The Free Negro in the Antebellum South* (New York: The New Press, 1974). Joel Williamson provides a thorough history of racial miscegenation in the United States in *New People: Miscegenation and Mulattoes in the United States* (New York: The Free Press, 1980). Willard Gatewood examines the effects of skin color on the postbellum elite communities in *Aristocrats of Color: The Black Elite, 1880–1920* (Fayetteville: University of Arkansas Press, 2000).

14 The word "mulatto" first came into English use around 1666 to define those of mixed race. *The Oxford English Dictionary* and most major American dictionaries do not classify "mulatto" as offensive; however, the word's etymology is controversial. See *The Oxford English Dictionary*, 2nd ed., Vol. X., comp. J. A. Simpson and E. S. C. Weiner (Oxford: Clarendon Press, 1989), s.v. "mulatto"; Jordan, "American Chiaroscuro": 102, 107.

15 Williamson, *New People*: 25; Berlin, *Slaves Without Masters*: 179.

16 Berlin, *Slaves Without Masters*: 57, 277, 161–164, 280–281; Gatewood, *Aristocrats of Color*: 160. In popular press accounts, skin tone was a prominent descriptor of Reconstruction-Era black Congressmen. Observers uniformly described Representative Joseph Rainey as having an "olive" or "bright" complexion upon nearly every mention when he was first elected in 1870. In contrast, Representative Robert Elliott, the first non-mulatto elected to Congress, was often described as a "full negro," "purest African," or the "darkest" or "blackest" yet elected. See, for example, "Black Enough," 7 March 1871, *Atlanta Constitution*: 1; "Colored Congressmen," 16 April 1874, *National Republican* (Washington, DC): 6; "Washington," 2 April 1871, *Chicago Tribune*: 2; "How The Colored Members of Congress Look," 16 May 1872, Volume 49, *Zion's Herald*: 235; "South Carolina Congressmen," 14 November 1870, *New York Times*: 2.

17 William C. Harris, "Blanche K. Bruce of Mississippi: Conservative Assimilationist," in Howard Rabinowitz, ed., *Southern Black Leaders of the Reconstruction Era* (Urbana: University of Illinois Press, 1982): 27, 33.

18 Genovese, *Roll, Jordan, Roll*: 561–564; Richard C. Wade, *Slavery in the Cities: The South 1820–1860* (London: Oxford University Press, 1964): 173–176; see, for example, the Virginia law cited in Berlin, *Slaves Without Masters*: 304–305.

19 "Autobiography of Hiram Revels," Carter G. Woodson Collection, Library of Congress.

20 John Hope Franklin and Alfred A. Moss, *From Slavery to Freedom: A History of African Americans*, 8th ed. (New York: Alfred A. Knopf, 2000): 257.

21 In 1860, 74 percent of American newspapers reported a partisan affiliation; this figure jumped to 83 percent in the South. See Richard H. Abbot, *For Free Press and Equal Rights: Republican Newspapers in the Reconstruction South* (Athens: University of Georgia Press, 2004): 2.

22 Newspaper ownership generally skyrocketed in the Reconstruction period—the number of people identifying themselves as "editors," "newsmen," or "reporters," doubled between 1870 and 1880 and doubled again in the next decade. See Alan Bussel, *Bohemians and Professionals: Essays on Nineteenth-Century American Journalism* (Atlanta: Emory University Graduate Institute of the Liberal Arts, 1981): 7, 22.

23 Quoted in Joel Williamson, *After Slavery: The Negro in South Carolina During Reconstruction, 1861–1877* (Chapel Hill: The University of North Carolina Press, 1965): 206.

24 Foner, *Freedom's Lawmakers*: xxii (see Table 13). This is perhaps a low statistic given that 37 percent had unreported wealth. Also, black Congressmen on average were less wealthy than their white counterparts, who were typically worth between $11,000 and $15,000. See Terry L. Seip, *The South Returns to Congress* (Baton Rouge: Louisiana State University Press, 1983): 28 (see Table 4). According to a standard method of calculating the 21st-century value of 19th-century fortunes (taking 1870 as the basis year), the average black Member from the Reconstruction Era would have amassed roughly $92,000 in wealth in 2007 dollars. Senator Bruce's fortune would translate into more than $2.3 million in 2007 dollars. The typical white Member of Congress in that time period had amassed a fortune of between $180,000 and $250,000 in 2007 dollars. These figures are drawn from calculations using the historical Consumer Price Index data. Other methods for making such calculations, including extrapolations based on the Gross Domestic Product, produce sometimes drastically different valuations. For an explanation of the difficulty in accounting for inflation conversion factors and determining the relative value of dollars over long periods of time see Oregon State University's "Inflation Conversion Factors for Dollars, 1774 to Estimated 2018," at http://oregonstate.edu/cla/polisci/faculty-research/sahr?sahr.htm (accessed 14 May 2008).

25 Lawrence Otis Graham, *The Senator and the Socialite: The True Story of America's First Black Dynasty* (New York: HarperCollins, 2006): 5–7.

26 Edward A. Miller, Jr., *Gullah Statesman: Robert Smalls from Slavery to Congress, 1839–1915* (Columbia: University of South Carolina Press, 1995): 58; Bernard E. Powers, Jr., *Black*

Charlestonians, 1822–1885 (Fayetteville: The University of Arkansas Press, 1994): 169–170; Thomas C. Holt, *Black Over White: Negro Political Leadership in South Carolina During Reconstruction* (Urbana: University of Illinois Press, 1977): 164–165; Foner, *Reconstruction*: 361.

27 Some sources note that Jeremiah Haralson of Alabama ran for Congress as a Democrat in the 1868 election. See Loren Schweninger and Alston Fitts, III, "Haralson, Jeremiah," *American National Biography* 10 (New York: Oxford University Press, 1999): 37–38 (hereinafter referred to as *ANB*). Michael Dubin makes no mention of Haralson's candidacy for the 1868 general election; it is possible Haralson failed to win the nomination. See Michael Dubin et al., *U.S. Congressional Elections, 1788–1997* (Jefferson, NC: McFarland & Company, Inc., Publishers, 1998): 213.

28 *Congressional Record*, Appendix, 49th Cong., 1st sess. (30 July 1886): A319.

29 Quoted in Christopher, *Black Americans in Congress*: 133.

30 For more on the Liberal Republican movement, see Andrew L. Slap, *The Doom of Reconstruction: The Liberal Republicans in the Civil War Era* (New York: Fordham University Press, 2006).

31 Michael Perman, *The Road to Redemption: Southern Politics, 1869–1879* (Chapel Hill: University of North Carolina Press, 1984): 22–56.

32 Though the post–Civil War years saw the first interest in popular primaries, the convention system remained in place in the South. For more on this topic, see John F. Reynolds, *The Demise of the American Convention System, 1880–1901* (New York: Cambridge University Press, 2006); Charles Edward Merriam, *Primary Elections* (Chicago: University of Chicago Press, 1908): 1–17.

33 Foner, *Freedom's Lawmakers*: xii.

34 William L. Barney, "Scott, Robert Kingston," 19 *ANB*: 505–507; Christine Doyle, "Moses, Franklin J., Jr.," 15 *ANB*: 971–972.

35 Quoted in Christopher, *Black Americans in Congress*: 103.

36 *Congressional Record*, Appendix, 43rd Cong., 2nd sess. (2 March 1875): A166–169.

37 Michael K. Fauntroy, *Republicans and the Black Vote* (Boulder, CO: Lynne Reinner Publishers, 2007): 34.

38 *Congressional Record*, House, 43rd Cong., 1st sess (13 June 1874): 4955.

39 Perman, *The Road to Redemption*: 38.

40 For a discussion of surrogate representation using modern examples, see Jane Mansbridge, "Should Blacks Represent Blacks and Women Represent Women? A Contingent 'Yes,'" *Journal of Politics* 61 (1999): 628–657.

41 See, for example, *Congressional Record*, House, 43rd Cong., 2nd sess. (3 February 1875): 957.

42 Stanley B. Parsons et al., *United States Congressional Districts, 1843–1883* (New York: Greenwood Press, 1986): 146. Ultimately, Rapier left his seat after one term to run against Representative Jeremiah Haralson in a neighboring black-majority district. Josiah Walls also served as an At-Large Representative in Florida—with a population that was 44 percent black—in the 42nd Congress (1871–1873). See Parsons et al., *United States Congressional Districts, 1843–1883*: 99. Senators Hiram Revels and Blanche Bruce were both elected to the Senate by Republican majority state legislatures in Mississippi, a state whose black population was more than 50 percent black in 1870. See Foner, *Freedom's Lawmakers*: xiii.

43 Okun Edet Uya, *From Slavery to Political Service: Robert Smalls, 1839–1915* (New York: Oxford University Press, 1971): 32–36; Powers, *Black Charlestonians*: 81–85; Williamson, *After Slavery*: 371.

44 For more names and state affiliations of white supremacist groups, see Franklin and Moss, *From Slavery to Freedom*: 275.

45 In response to the growing number of contested elections, the Senate created its Committee on Privileges and Elections on March 10, 1871. See David T. Canon et al., *Committees in the U.S. Congress, 1789 to 1946*, Volume 2 (Washington, DC: Congressional Quarterly Press, 2002): 253–257.

46 Jeffrey A. Jenkins, "Partisanship and Contested Election Cases in the House of Representatives, 1789–1902," *Studies in American Political Development* 18 (Fall 2004): 130.

47 Loren Schweninger, "James T. Rapier of Alabama and the Noble Cause of Reconstruction," in Rabinowitz, ed., *Southern Black Leaders of the Reconstruction Era*: 86; Dubin et al., *U.S. Congressional Elections, 1788–1997*: 230.

48 "The Election in Alabama," 29 November 1884, *New York Times*: 1.

49 John Roy Lynch, *Reminiscences of an Active Life: The Autobiography of John Roy Lynch*, edited with an introduction by John Hope Franklin (Chicago: University of Chicago Press, 1970): 163–166.

50 John Hope Franklin, "John Roy Lynch: Republican Stalwart from Mississippi," in Rabinowitz, ed., *Southern Black Leaders of the Reconstruction Era*: 47.

51 *Congressional Record*, House, 44th Cong., 1st sess. (13 June 1876): 3781–3786.

52 *Congressional Record*, Senate, 44th Cong., 1st sess. (31 March 1876): 2101–2105.

53 Chester H. Rowell, *A Historical and Legal Digest of All the Contested Election Cases* (Washington, DC: Government Printing Office, 1901). Though Rowell offers one of the most comprehensive sources on the activities of the Committee on Elections for this era, his data are incomplete. At least six contested elections cases involving black men are missing from his volume.

54 The *New York Times* reports that, according to the 1870 Census, the total black population of the District of Columbia was 43,404. See "The Census of 1870," 8 July 1871, *New York Times*.

55 Gatewood, *Aristocrats of Color*: 38–68; Graham, *The Senator and the Socialite*: 101.

56 Boarding houses were common lodging for Representatives, who often spent the short sessions in Washington living away from their families. Representatives often depended on one another, as well as their neighbors, as social companions during their months in Washington. See Tom Shroder, "Out of the Mud," 8 December 2002, *Washington Post Magazine*: 20–27, 41–48.

57 *Congressional Directory*, 42nd Cong., 2nd sess. (Washington, DC: Government Printing Office, 1872): 120–125.

58 James Whyte, *The Uncivil War: Washington During the Reconstruction, 1865–1878* (New York: Twayne Publishers, 1958): 242–243.

59 *Congressional Record*, House, 43rd Cong., 1st sess. (19 December 1873): 344.

60 Marie Le Baron, "Colored Congressmen," 12 April 1874, *St. Louis Daily Globe*: 3.

61 James G. Blaine, *Twenty Years of Congress From Lincoln to Garfield*, Volume 2 (Norwich, CT: Henry Bill Publishing Co., 1886): 515.

62 *Congressional Record*, House, 44th Cong., 1st sess. (15 July 1876): 4641–4644.

63 *Congressional Record*, House, 44th Cong., 1st sess. (18 July 1876): 4707.

64 *Congressional Record*, House, 43rd Cong., 1st sess. (5 January 1874): 376.

65 Kirt H. Wilson, *The Reconstruction Desegregation Debate: The Politics of Equality and the Rhetoric of Place, 1870–1875* (East Lansing: Michigan State University Press, 2002): 25.

66 *Congressional Record*, House, 43rd Cong., 1st sess. (24 January 1874): 901–903.

67 Charles Stewart III ranks the House Agriculture Committee as the chamber's eighth most desirable panel for this era. However, no black member of the Agriculture Committee rose above the second-to-last ranking GOP Member. For more information, see Stewart, "Committee Hierarchies in the Modernizing House, 1875–1947," *American Journal of Political Science* 36 (1992): 845–846. See also Canon et al., *Committees in the U.S. Congress, 1789 to 1946*, Volume 3.

68 On the general topic of centralization of power in the House, which gave rise to the hierarchical committee system, see Peter Swenson, "The Influence of Recruitment on the Structure of Power in the U.S. House, 1870–1940," *Legislative Studies Quarterly* VII (February 1982): 7–36. For an analysis of committee seniority see, Michael Aboam and Joseph Cooper, "The Rise of Seniority in the House of Representatives," *Polity* 1 (Fall 1968): 52–84. For an analysis of factors that mitigate seniority as the determining factor in committee hierarchy as well as a discussion of when the seniority system solidified in the House, see Nelson Polsby, Miriam Gallaher, and Barry S. Rundquist, "The Growth of the Seniority System in the U.S. House of Representatives," *American Political Science Review* 63 (September 1969): 787–807.

69 Canon et al., *Committees in the U.S. Congress, 1789 to 1946*, Volume 4: 295.

70 Representative James O'Hara was an unofficial subcommittee chairman on the Committee on Invalid Pensions in the 49th Congress. See Appendix F, Black-American Chairs of Subcommittees of Standing Committees in the U.S. House and Senate, 1885–2007.

71 The names and jurisdictions of these panels changed during the Reconstruction Era. In the House, the Education and Labor Committee was created in 1867 but was terminated in 1883 in favor of a Committee on Education and a Committee on Labor. In the Senate, the Education Committee was established in 1869 and was renamed the Committee on Education and Labor one year later. See Canon et al., *Committees in the U.S. Congress, 1789 to 1946*, Volume 1: 65; ibid., Volume 2: 77.

72 *Congressional Globe*, House, 42nd Cong., 2nd sess. (23 February 1872): 809; quoted in Christopher, *Black Americans in Congress*: 33.

73 For further reading, see Carl R. Osthaus, *Freedmen, Philanthropy, and Fraud: A History of the Freedmen's Savings Bank* (Urbana: University of Illinois Press, 1976).

74 Graham, *The Senator and the Socialite:* 120–121.

75 These were: the Ku Klux Klan Act (16 Stat. 140–146, approved 31 May 1870), sometimes referred to as the Civil Rights Act of 1870; the Ku Klux Klan Act (16 Stat. 433–440, approved 28 February 1871), sometimes referred to as the Civil Rights Act of 1871; and the Third Force Act (17 Stat. 13–15, approved 20 April 1871).

76 *Congressional Globe*, House, 42nd Cong., 1st sess. (1 April 1871): 392.

77 *Congressional Globe*, House, 42nd Cong., 2nd sess. (13 May 1872): 3382.

78 *Congressional Globe*, Appendix, 42nd Cong., 2nd sess. (30 May 1872): A530–531. The *Congressional Globe* was the precursor to the *Congressional Record* as a printed source for congressional debates, the last in a long series of privately published volumes. The increase in legislation and debate during the Civil War eventually overwhelmed the *Globe's* printers. In 1873, Congress transferred authority for publishing the debates to the Government Printing Office (GPO), which publishes them under the title *Congressional Record*. For more on this topic, see Elizabeth Gregory McPherson "The History of Reporting the Debates and Proceedings of Congress" (Ph.D. diss., University of North Carolina, Chapel Hill, 1940).

79 For a concise summary of congressional civil rights legislation in the 19th and 20th centuries, see Donald Bacon et al., *The Encyclopedia of the United States Congress*, Volume 1 (New York: Simon and Schuster, 1995): 354–363. See also Appendix J, Constitutional Amendments and Major Civil Rights Acts of Congress Referenced in the Text

80 See S. No. 1, *Congressional Record*, Senate, 43rd Cong., 1st sess. (2 December 1873): 2.

81 See H.R. 796, *Congressional Record*, House, 43rd Cong., 1st sess. (18 December 1873): 318.

82 *Congressional Record*, House, 43rd Cong., 1st sess. (7 January 1874): 458.

83 *Congressional Record*, House, 43rd Cong., 1st scss. (6 January 1874): 406.

84 Edward L. Pierce, *Memoir and Letters of Charles Sumner*, Volume 4 (New York: Arno Press, 1969): 598.

85 *Congressional Record*, Senate, 43rd Cong., 1st sess. (22 May 1874): 4176.

86 *Congressional Record*, House, 43rd Cong., 1st sess. (18 June 1874): 5162–5163.

87 Office of the Clerk, "Party Divisions," http://clerk.house.gov/art_history/house_history/partyDiv.html.

88 Steven W. Stathis, *Landmark Legislation, 1774–2002: Major U.S. Acts and Treaties* (Washington, DC: Congressional Quarterly Press, 2003): 111.

89 Quoted in Foner, *Reconstruction:* 555.

90 *Congressional Record*, House, 43rd Cong., 1st sess. (4 February 1875): 978.

91 Dubin et al., *U.S. Congressional Elections, 1788–1997*: 231.

92 Asher C. Hinds, *Hinds' Precedents of the House of Representatives*, Volume 4 (Washington, DC: Government Printing Office, 1907): 353–354; Foner, *Reconstruction*: 555; Wilson, *The Reconstruction Desegregation Debate*: 38. Republicans lost some support in the final vote on the Civil Rights Bill because of the rule change. In a speech denouncing the bill, William Phelps of New Jersey noted, "In order to pass this bill we have altered the rules of procedure under which for fifty years this House has transacted its business." See *Congressional Record*, House, 43rd Cong., 2nd sess. (4 February 1875): 1001. Debate was often very contentious, with Butler facing the brunt of the attacks. On February 3, 1875, Butler found himself squaring off in the center aisle of the House Chamber with William McLean of Texas when the latter accused Butler of denigrating

the South. McLean hurled a personal insult at Butler, in violation of House Rules, and later retracted his comment. See *Congressional Record*, House, 43rd Cong., 2nd sess. (3 February 1875): 940–941, 943. The following day, John Brown of Kentucky declared, "If I wished to describe all that was pusillanimous in war, inhuman in peace, forbidden in morals, and infamous in politics, I should call it 'Butlerism.'" Brown was censured for his remarks. See *Congressional Record*, House, 43rd Cong., 2nd sess. (4 February 1875): 985–992. An attempt to strike Butler's words from the *Congressional Record* failed just before the Civil Rights Bill passed. See *Congressional Record*, House, 43rd Cong., 2nd sess. (4 February 1875): 1008. Though they overwhelmingly favored censuring Brown, black Members remained silent during the more heated bickering on the House Floor.

93 Wilson, *The Reconstruction Desegregation Debate:* 25.

94 See, for example, "Congress," 7 January 1874, *New York Times:* 1.

95 "Congressman Elliott's Speech," 8 January 1874, *Chicago Daily Tribune*: 4.

96 Christopher, *Black Americans in Congress:* 32–33.

97 *Congressional Record*, House, 43rd Cong., 2nd sess. (3 February 1875): 945.

98 *Congressional Record*, House, 43rd Cong., 1st sess. (9 June 1874): 4782–4785.

99 *Congressional Record*, House, 43rd Cong., 2nd sess. (3 February 1875): 951, 952–953.

100 *Congressional Record*, House, 43rd Cong., 1st sess. (5 January 1874): 377.

101 *Congressional Record*, House, 43rd Cong., 2nd sess. (3 February 1875): 953.

102 *Congressional Record*, House, 43rd Cong., 2nd sess. (4 February 1875): 978. For further discussion of the constitutional arguments made during Civil Rights Bill debate, see Wilson, *The Reconstruction Desegregation Debate*: 151–181.

103 *Congressional Record*, House, 43rd Cong., 1st sess. (6 January 1874): 411.

104 *Congressional Record*, House, 43rd Cong., 2nd sess. (4 February 1875): 983 (emphasis his).

105 *Congressional Record*, House, 43rd Cong., 1st sess. (7 January 1874): 455–456 (emphasis his).

106 *Congressional Record*, House, 43rd Cong., 1st sess. (10 January 1874): 565–567.

107 *Congressional Record*, House, 43rd Cong., 1st sess. (9 June 1874): 4782–4785.

108 *Congressional Record*, House, 43rd Cong., 2nd sess. (3 February 1875): 944.

109 *Congressional Record*, House, 43rd Cong., 1st sess. (24 January 1874): 901–903. For more on the equality debate in the Civil Rights Bill, see Wilson, *The Reconstruction Desegregation Debate*: 77–120.

110 *Congressional Record*, House, 43rd Cong., 1st sess. (5 January 1874): 385.

111 *Congressional Record*, House, 43rd Cong., 1st sess. (6 January 1874): 406.

112 *Congressional Record*, House, 43rd Cong., 2nd sess. (4 February 1875): 998–999.

113 Wilson, *The Reconstruction Desegregation Debate*: 37.

114 Most black Members preferred the Senate version of the Civil Rights Bill. See, for example, *Congressional Record*, House, 43rd Cong., 2nd sess. (4 February 1875): 1001. Richard Cain expressed lukewarm support for Kellogg's version, probably because of his firm rejection of the compromise "separate, but equal" legislation. See *Congressional Record*, House, 43rd Cong., 2nd sess. (4 February 1875): 982.

115 *Congressional Record*, House, 43rd Cong., 2nd sess. (3 February 1875): 943–947.

116 *Congressional Record*, House, 43rd Cong., 1st sess. (24 January 1874): 901–903.

117 *Congressional Record*, House, 43rd Cong., 1st sess. (7 February 1874): 1314.

118 *Congressional Record*, House, 43rd Cong., 2nd sess. (4 February 1875): 982.

119 Ibid., 1001.

120 Ibid., 1011.

121 *Congressional Record*, Senate, 43rd Cong., 2nd sess. (27 February 1875): 1870; *Congressional Record*, House, 43rd Cong., 2nd sess. (1 March 1875): 2013.

122 Lynch, *Reminiscences of an Active Life: The Autobiography of John Roy Lynch*: 195.

123 *Congressional Record*, Appendix, 44th Cong., 2nd sess. (25 January 1877): A60.

124 *Congressional Record*, House, 44th Cong., 2nd sess. (28 February 1877): 2019–2020.

125 Lynch, *Reminiscences of an Active Life: The Autobiography of John Roy Lynch*: 201.

126 C. Vann Woodward, *The Strange Career of Jim Crow* (New York: Oxford University Press, 1955; reprint 2002): 29.

127 John M. Matthews, "Long, Jefferson Franklin," *ANB* 13 (New York: Oxford University Press, 1999): 875–876.

128 Quoted in Timothy P. McCarthy, "DeLarge, Robert Carlos," *ANB* 6: 383–384; Joel Williamson, *After Slavery*: 359.

129 For more information, see Slaughterhouse Cases 83 U.S. 36 (1873), United States v. Cruikshank 92 U.S. 542 (1876), United States v. Reese 92 U.S. 214 (1876), United States v. Harris 106 U.S. 629 (1883), and Civil Rights Cases 109 U.S. 3 (1883). The various cases are discussed in detail in Kermit L. Hall, ed., *The Oxford Companion to the Supreme Court of the United States* (New York: Oxford University Press, 2002).

130 Robert J. Cottrol, "Civil Rights Cases," in Hall, ed., *The Oxford Companion to the Supreme Court of the United States*: 149.

131 Franklin, "Introduction," in Lynch, *Reminiscences of an Active Life: The Autobiography of John Roy Lynch*: xxx.

132 *Congressional Record*, House, 48th Cong., 2nd sess. (17 December 1884): 317.

Congressional Service for Black Americans First Elected, 1870–1886

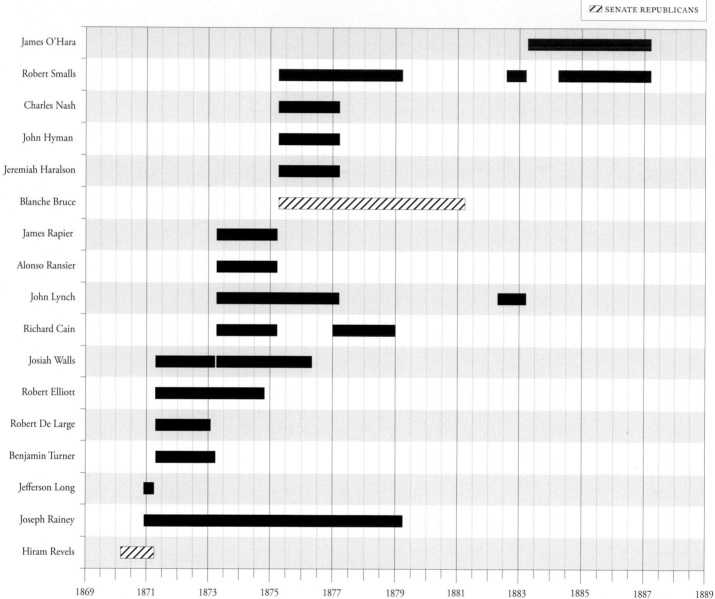

Legend: ■ HOUSE REPUBLICANS ▨ SENATE REPUBLICANS

Source: *Biographical Directory of the United States Congress, 1774–2005* (Washington, DC: Government Printing Office, 2005); also available at http://bioguide.congress.gov.

Party Divisions in the House of Representatives

41st–49th Congresses (1869–1887)*

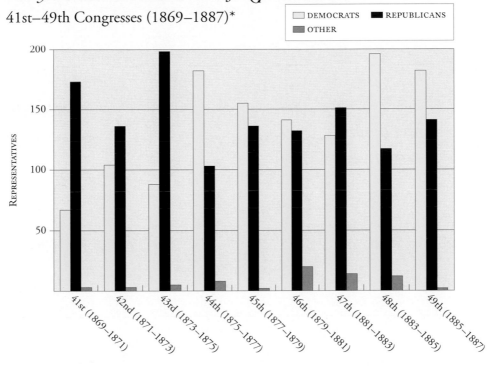

Party Divisions in the Senate

41st–49th Congresses (1869–1887)

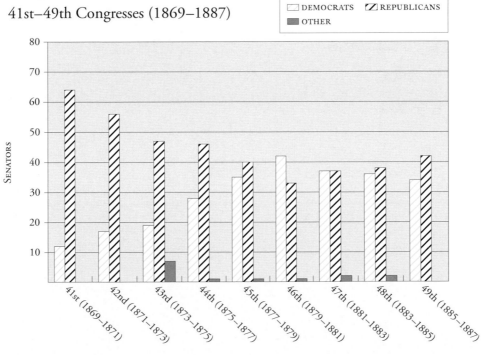

Sources: Office of the Clerk, U.S. House of Representatives; U.S. Senate Historical Office.

*Does not include Delegates or Resident Commissioners.

Contested Election Cases in the U.S. House of Representatives, 1789–1901

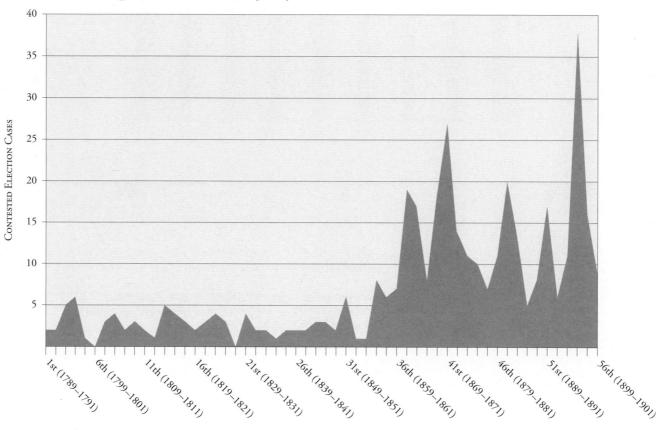

Source: Chester H. Rowell, *A Historical and Legal Digest of All the Contested Election Cases* (Washington, DC: Government Printing Office, 1901).

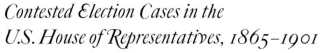

Contested Election Cases in the U.S. House of Representatives, 1865–1901

TOTAL CASES   INVOLVING BLACK CANDIDATES

FROM FORMER CONFEDERATE STATES

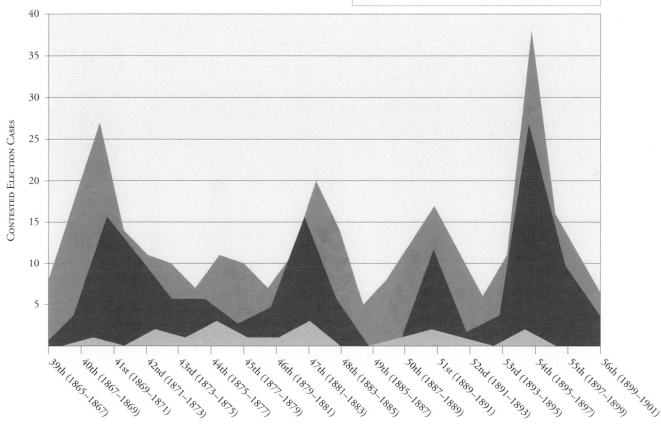

Source: Chester H. Rowell, *A Historical and Legal Digest of All the Contested Election Cases* (Washington, DC: Government Printing Office, 1901).

Hiram Rhodes Revels
1827–1901

UNITED STATES SENATOR ★ 1870–1871
REPUBLICAN FROM MISSISSIPPI

A freedman his entire life, Hiram Rhodes Revels was the first African American to serve in the U.S. Congress. With his moderate political orientation and oratorical skills honed from years as a preacher, Revels filled a vacant seat in the United States Senate in 1870. Just before the Senate agreed to admit a black man to its ranks on February 25, Republican Senator Charles Sumner of Massachusetts sized up the importance of the moment: "All men are created equal, says the great Declaration," Sumner roared, "and now a great act attests this verity. Today we make the Declaration a reality. . . . The Declaration was only half established by Independence. The greatest duty remained behind. In assuring the equal rights of all we complete the work."[1]

Hiram Rhodes Revels was born to free parents in Fayetteville, North Carolina, on September 27, 1827. His father worked as a Baptist preacher, and his mother was of Scottish descent. He claimed his ancestors "as far back as my knowledge extends, were free," and, in addition to his Scottish background, he was rumored to be of mixed African and Croatan Indian lineage.[2] In an era when educating black children was illegal in North Carolina, Revels attended a school taught by a free black woman and worked a few years as a barber. In 1844, he moved north to complete his education. Revels attended the Beech Grove Quaker Seminary in Liberty, Indiana, and the Darke County Seminary for black students, in Ohio. In 1845, Revels was ordained in the African Methodist Episcopal (AME) Church. His first pastorate was likely in Richmond, Indiana, where he was elected an elder to the AME Indiana Conference in 1849.[3] In the early 1850s, Revels married Phoebe A. Bass, a free black woman from Ohio, and they had six daughters.[4]

Revels traveled throughout the country, carrying out religious work and educating fellow African Americans in Indiana, Illinois, Kansas, Kentucky, and Tennessee. Although Missouri forbade free blacks to live in the state for fear they would instigate uprisings, Revels took a pastorate at an AME Church in St. Louis in 1853, noting that the law was "seldom enforced." However, Revels later revealed he had to be careful because of restrictions on his movements. "I sedulously refrained from doing anything that would incite slaves to run away from their masters," he recalled. "It being understood that my object was to preach the gospel to them, and improve their moral and spiritual condition even slave holders were tolerant of me."[5] Despite his cautiousness, Revels was imprisoned for preaching to the black community in 1854. Upon his release, he accepted a position with the Presbyterian Church in Baltimore, Maryland, working alongside his brother, Willis Revels, also an AME pastor. Hiram Revels was the principal of a black school in Baltimore and subsequently attended Knox College in Galesburg, Illinois, graduating in 1857. He was one of the few college-educated black men in the United States.

When the Civil War broke out in 1861, Revels helped recruit two black regiments from Maryland. In 1862, when black soldiers were permitted to fight, he served as the chaplain for a black regiment in campaigns in Vicksburg and Jackson, Mississippi. In 1863, Revels returned to St. Louis, where he established a freedmen's school. At the end of hostilities, Revels served in a church in Leavenworth, Kansas. While traveling in Kansas, Revels and his family were asked to sit in the smoking car rather than the car for first-class ticket holders. Revels protested that the language in the smoking car was too coarse for his wife and children, and the conductor finally relented. Revels served in churches in Louisville, Kentucky, and New Orleans, Louisiana, before settling in Natchez, Mississippi, in 1866.

Before the Civil War, fewer than 1,000 free black Mississippians had access to a basic education. Thus, leadership from freedmen such as Revels became vital to the Republican Party for rallying the new electorate in the postwar years.[6] It was through his work in education that Revels became involved in politics, taking his first elected position as a Natchez alderman in 1868. He entered politics reluctantly, fearing racial friction and interference with his religious work, but he quickly won over blacks and whites with his moderate and compassionate political opinions. In 1869, encouraged to run by a friend, future Representative John Roy Lynch, Revels won a seat in the Mississippi state senate.[7] Under the newly installed Reconstruction government, Revels was one of more than 30 African Americans among the state's 140 legislators.[8] Upon his election, he wrote a friend in Leavenworth, Kansas: "We are in the midst of an exciting canvass. . . . I am working very hard in politics as well as in other matters. We are determined that Mississippi shall be settled on a basis of justice and political and legal equality."[9] A little-known politician, Revels attracted the attention of fellow legislators when he gave a moving prayer on the opening day of the session.

The primary task of the newly elected state senate was to fill U.S. Senate seats. In 1861, Democrat Albert Brown and future Confederate President Jefferson Davis both vacated Mississippi's U.S. Senate seats when the state seceded from the Union.[10] When their terms expired in 1865 and 1863, respectively, their seats were not filled and remained vacant. In 1870, the new Mississippi state legislature wished to elect a black man to fill the remainder of one term, due to expire in 1871 for the seat once held by Brown, but was determined to fill the other unexpired term, ending in 1875, with a white candidate.[11] Black legislators agreed to the deal, believing, as Revels recalled, that an election of one of their own would "be a weakening blow against color line prejudice." The Democratic minority also endorsed the plan, hoping a black Senator would "seriously damage the Republican Party."[12] After three days and seven ballots, on January

20, 1870, the Mississippi state legislature voted 85 to 15 to seat Hiram Revels in Brown's former seat. They chose Union General Adelbert Ames to fill Davis's former seat.

Revels arrived in Washington at the end of January 1870, but could not present his credentials until Mississippi was readmitted to the United States on February 23. Senate Republicans sought to swear in Revels immediately afterwards, but Senate Democrats were determined to block the effort. Led by Senator Garrett Davis of Kentucky and Senator Willard Saulsbury of Delaware, the Democrats claimed Revels's election was null and void, arguing that Mississippi was under military rule and lacked a civil government to confirm his election. Others claimed Revels was not a U.S. citizen until the passage of the 14th Amendment in 1868 and was therefore ineligible to become a U.S. Senator. Senate Republicans rallied to his defense. Though Revels would not fill Davis's seat, the symbolism of a black man's admission to the Senate after the departure of the former President of the Confederacy was not lost on Radical Republicans. Nevada Senator James Nye underlined the significance of this event: "[Jefferson Davis] went out to establish a government whose cornerstone should be the oppression and perpetual enslavement of a race because their skin differed in color from his," Nye declared. "Sir, what a magnificent spectacle of retributive justice is witnessed here today! In the place of that proud, defiant man, who marched out to trample under foot the Constitution and the laws of the country he had sworn to support, comes back one of that humble race whom he would have enslaved forever to take and occupy his seat upon this floor."[13] On the afternoon of February 25, the Senate voted 48 to 8 to seat Revels, who subsequently received assignments to the Committee on Education and Labor and the Committee on the District of Columbia.

Although Revels viewed himself as "a representative of the State, irrespective of color," he also represented freedmen and, as such, received petitions from black men and women from all states.[14] His sense that he represented his entire race was evident in his maiden speech, in which he spoke in favor of reinstating black legislators forced from office in Georgia. In April 1868, Georgia voters had ratified the state's constitution, enfranchising African Americans and thus, under the terms of Congressional Reconstruction, taking a necessary step toward the state's re-admission to the Union. In the same election, Georgians sent 29 black legislators to the state house of representatives and three to the state senate. Yet, when the legislature met in July, moderate white Republicans joined Democrats in both chambers to unseat the black members, arguing that the state constitution did not permit black officeholders. Spurred to action, black Georgians appealed to Congress for federal intervention before Georgia was readmitted to the Union. On March 16, 1870, before a packed chamber and a gallery filled with black men and women, Revels argued that the North and the Republican Party owed Georgian black legislators their support: "I remarked that I rose to plead for protection for the defenseless race that now send their delegation to the seat of Government to sue for that which this Congress alone can secure to them. And here let me say further, that the people of the North owe to the colored race a deep obligation that is no easy matter to fulfill."[15] In his speech, Revels professed his loyalty to and faith in the Republican Party, claiming, "the Republican party is not inflamed, as some would . . . have the country believe, against the white population of the South. Its borders are wide enough for all truly loyal men to find within them some peace and repose from the din and discord of angry faction."[16] The Georgia legislature eventually agreed to a congressional mandate reinstating the legislators as a requirement for re-entry into the Union in July 1870.[17]

Revels also favored universal amnesty for former Confederates, requiring only their sworn loyalty to the Union. "I am in favor of removing the disabilities of those upon whom they are imposed in the South, just as fast as they give evidence of having become loyal and being loyal," Revels declared. "If you can find one man in the South who gives evidence that he is a loyal man, and gives that evidence in the fact that he has ceased to denounce the laws of Congress as unconstitutional, has ceased to oppose them, and respects them and favors the carrying of them out, I am in favor of removing his disabilities."[18] Revels's support for the bill, which eventually passed, solidified his reputation as a political moderate.

Although Revels sided with Radical Republicans in opposing Ohio Senator Allen Thurman's amendment perpetuating segregated schools in the District of Columbia, his views on social integration of blacks and whites were less sanguine than those of his colleagues. Revels clearly rejected legal separation of the races, believing it led to animosity between blacks and whites, but he did not view forced social mixing as desirable or necessary. He cited mixed-race churches in northern cities, where a congregation would worship together on Sundays but part ways for the remainder of the week. In one of his most gripping floor speeches, he said: "I find that the prejudice in this country to color is very great, and I sometimes fear that it is on the increase. . . . If the nation should take a step for the encouragement of this prejudice against the colored race, can they have any grounds upon which to predicate a hope that Heaven will smile upon them and prosper them?"[19] As a former teacher, Revels appreciated the need to educate freed slaves, claiming, "The colored race can be built up and assisted . . . in acquiring property, in becoming intelligent, valuable, useful citizens, without one hair upon the head of any white man being harmed."[20] Revels believed the abolition of segregation statutes would result in less prejudice, saying, "Let lawmakers cease to make the difference, let school trustees and school boards cease to make the difference, and the people will soon forget."[21]

With mixed results, Revels also promoted Black Americans' civil rights by less conventional means. In May 1870, he startled the military establishment when he nominated black candidate Michael Howard to the U.S. Army Military Academy at West Point, long a bastion of southern white gentlemen. Revels knew Howard's parents, former slaves, and Howard's father had served in the state legislature. Critics claimed Revels callously and publicly humiliated the youth, who had little formal education and was not admitted to West Point, and supporters claimed the school administration's prejudice had blocked Howard's entrance.[22] Additionally, Revels successfully appealed to the War Department on behalf of black mechanics from Baltimore who were barred from working at the U.S. Navy Yard in early 1871, an accomplishment he recalled with great pride. [23]

After the expiration of his Senate term on March 3, 1871, Revels declined several patronage positions, offered by President Ulysses S. Grant at the recommendation of Senators Oliver Morton of Indiana and Zachariah Chandler of Michigan. He returned to Mississippi to become the first president of Alcorn University (formerly Oakland College), named for his political ally Governor James Alcorn. Located in Rodney, Mississippi, Alcorn University was the first land-grant school in the United States for black students.[24] Revels took a leave of absence in 1873 to serve as Mississippi's interim secretary of state after the sudden death of his friend James Lynch. During this period, Revels grew more critical of the corruption in the Republican Party, and he resigned from his position

at Alcorn in 1874 to avoid being removed by his political rival and former Senate colleague, then-Mississippi Governor Adelbert Ames. Revels returned to the ministry, taking a pastorate at a church in Holly Springs, Mississippi. In the violent and controversial 1875 election campaign, he supported several Democrats. In 1876, when a U.S. Senate select committee questioned him about the well-documented fraud and violence in the previous year's election, Revels testified that to the best of his knowledge, conditions had been relatively peaceful and he was unaware of any widespread violence. His statement was met with skepticism by many Mississippi black voters. Revels returned to his former position as president of Alcorn University in July 1876. He also edited the *Southwestern Christian Advocate* newspaper, the official organ of the AME Church. Revels retired in 1882 and returned to his former church in Holly Springs. He remained active in the religious community, teaching theology at Shaw University (later Rust College) in Holly Springs, Mississippi, and serving as the AME's district superintendent. He died of a paralytic stroke in Aberdeen, Mississippi, on January 16, 1901, while attending a religious conference.

FOR FURTHER READING

Lawson, Elizabeth. *The Gentleman From Mississippi: Our First Negro Representative, Hiram R. Revels* (New York: privately printed, 1960).

"Revels, Hiram Rhodes," *Biographical Directory of the United States Congress, 1774–Present*, http://bioguide.congress.gov/scripts/biodisplay.pl?index=R000166.

Thompson, Julius E. *Hiram R. Revels, 1827–1901: A Biography* (New York: Arno Press, 1982).

_____. "Hiram Rhodes Revels, 1827–1901: A Reappraisal," *The Journal of Negro History* 79 (Summer 1994): 297–303.

MANUSCRIPT COLLECTIONS

New York Public Library (New York, NY) Schomburg Center for Research in Black Culture. *Papers:* ca. 1870–1948, one linear foot. The Hiram Revels Collection consists principally of a scrapbook of news clippings in addition to biographical articles about Revels. The scrapbook (1870–1893) discusses Revels as a U.S. Senator, pastor of the African Methodist Episcopal Church, and president of Alcorn University. It also describes local events and contains homilies and miscellany as well as some letters to Revels and programs and invitations. The collection includes several letters from Revels to his family (1870–1900); a biographical sketch about Revels written in the first person, apparently by his daughter, Susan; a typescript of an obituary of Revels; and legal papers regarding the settlement of his estate. There also are letters soliciting information about Revels from Hermann R. Muelder of Knox College, who planned to write an article about him. Obituaries of Susan Revels Cayton complete the collection.

Brown University, John Hay Library (Providence, RI). *Papers:* 1870, one item. A letter from Hiram Revels to Mrs. Philip Allen written on March 4, 1870.

Library of Congress (Washington, DC) Manuscript Division. *Papers:* In the Carter G. Woodson Papers, ca. 1736–1974, 21.2 linear feet. Persons represented include Hiram Revels.

Mississippi Department of Archives and History (Jackson, MS) *Papers:* In the Congressmen's Files, 1815–1979, 2003. Persons represented include Hiram Revels.

NOTES

1 *Congressional Globe*, Senate, 41st Cong., 2nd sess. (25 February 1870): 1567.

2 Elizabeth Lawson, *The Gentleman From Mississippi: Our First Negro Representative, Hiram R. Revels* (New York: privately printed, 1960): 8; "Autobiography of Hiram Revels," Carter G. Woodson Collection of Negro Papers and Related Documents, box 11, Manuscript Division, Library of Congress, Washington, DC (hereinafter referred to as LC) Revels's parents' names are not known.

3 Revels's travels took him to as many as eight states before the Civil War. It is difficult to determine in which state he began his ministry. See Kenneth H. Williams, "Revels, Hiram Rhoades," *American National Biography* 18 (New York: Oxford University Press, 1999): 367–369 (hereinafter referred to as *ANB*). Williams is one of the few historians to spell Revels's middle name "Rhoades." In his handwritten autobiography, Revels lists several states where he ministered, Indiana being the first; see "Autobiography of Hiram Revels," Carter G. Woodson Collection, LC.

4 Revels's daughter, Susan—the only one of his children whose name is known—edited a black newspaper in Seattle, Washington.

5 "Autobiography of Hiram Revels," Carter G. Woodson Collection, LC.

6 Julius E. Thompson, "Hiram Rhodes Revels, 1827–1901: A Reappraisal," *The Journal of Negro History* 79 (Summer 1994): 298.

7 "Autobiography of Hiram Revels," Carter G. Woodson Collection, LC.

8 Historians disagree about the number of black Mississippi state senators elected in 1869 (figures range from 34 to 40). See Kenneth Potts, "Hiram Rhoades Revels," in Jessie Carney Smith, ed., *Notable Black American Men* (Farmington Hills, MI: Gale Research, Inc., 1999): 145; Lawson, *The Gentleman From Mississippi*: 14; Williams, "Revels, Hiram Rhoades," *ANB*; Maurine Christopher, *Black Americans in Congress* (New York: Thomas Y. Crowell Company, 1976): 3.

9 Quoted in Lawson, *The Gentleman From Mississippi*: 13.

10 U.S. Senators were selected by state legislatures until 1913, when the adoption of the 17th Amendment required their direct election.

11 For more about the chronological order of United States Senators from Mississippi, see Senate Historical Office, "U.S. Senators from Mississippi," available at http://www.senate.gov/pagelayout/senators/one_item_and_teasers/mississippi.htm (accessed 5 September 2007). See also, *Biographical Directory of the United States Congress, 1774–2005* (Washington, DC: Government Printing Office, 2006): 180.

12 "Autobiography of Hiram Revels," Carter G. Woodson Collection, LC.

13 *Congressional Globe*, Senate, 41st Cong., 2nd sess. (23 February 1870): 1513. The enthusiasm with which Republicans in Congress and the media heralded Revels's admission to the Senate inspired the erroneous story common in the historical record that Revels took Davis's former seat instead of Brown's. See, for example, Gath, "Washington," 17 March 1870, *Chicago Tribune*: 2; Christopher, *Black Americans in Congress*: 5–6; Stephen Middleton, ed., *Black Congressmen During Reconstruction: A Documentary Sourcebook* (Westport, CT: Praeger, 2002): 320.

14 Quoted in Lawson, *The Gentleman From Mississippi*: 16, 22–23.

15 *Congressional Globe*, Senate, 41st Cong., 2nd sess. (16 March 1870): 1986–1988. For an indication of the number of African Americans in the gallery for Revels's maiden speech, see "By Telegraph," 15 March 1870, *Atlanta Constitution*: 2.

16 *Congressional Globe*, Senate, 41st Cong., 2nd sess. (16 March 1870): 1986–1988.

17 John M. Matthews, "Negro Republicans in the Reconstruction of Georgia," in Donald G. Nieman, ed., *The Politics of Freedom: African Americans and the Political Process During Reconstruction* (New York: Garland Publishing, Inc., 1994): 253–268; W. E. B. Du Bois, *Black Reconstruction in America* (New York: Harcourt, Brace, 1935 under the title *Black Reconstruction*; New York: Free Press, 1998): 500–504 (citations are to the Free Press edition).

18 *Congressional Globe*, Senate, 41st Cong., 2nd sess. (17 May 1870): 3520. Revels was so adamant about clarifying his position on amnesty, he reprinted this speech in his unpublished autobiography. See "Autobiography of Hiram Revels," Carter G. Woodson Collection, LC.

19 *Congressional Globe*, Senate, 41st Cong., 3rd sess. (8 February 1871): 1059–1060.

20 Ibid.

21 Quoted in Lawson, *The Gentleman From Mississippi*: 41.

22 Michael Howard was not admitted to West Point because he failed the entrance exam. See Williams, "Revels, Hiram Rhoades," *ANB*. See also, for example, "West Point," 28 May 1870, *New York Times*: 4.

23 See "Autobiography of Hiram Revels," Carter G. Woodson Collection, LC.

24 Revels noted that the state legislature tried to name the school after him, but he insisted it remain named for the governor. See "Autobiography of Hiram Revels," Carter G. Woodson Collection, LC.

As a former teacher, Revels appreciated the need to educate freed slaves, claiming, "The colored race can be built up and assisted . . . in acquiring property, in becoming intelligent, valuable, useful citizens, without one hair upon the head of any white man being harmed."

Joseph Hayne Rainey
1832–1887

UNITED STATES REPRESENTATIVE ★ 1870–1879
REPUBLICAN FROM SOUTH CAROLINA

Born into slavery, Joseph Rainey was the first African American to serve in the U.S. House of Representatives, the first African American to preside over the House, and the longest-serving African American during the tumultuous Reconstruction period. While Rainey's representation—like that of the other black Congressmen of the era—was symbolic, he also demonstrated the political nuance of a seasoned, substantive Representative, balancing his defense of southern blacks' civil rights by extending amnesty to the defeated Confederates. "I tell you that the Negro will never rest until he gets his rights," he said on the House Floor. "We ask [for civil rights] because we know it is proper," Rainey added, "not because we want to deprive any other class of the rights and immunities they enjoy, but because they are granted to us by the law of the land."[1]

Joseph Hayne Rainey was born on June 21, 1832, to Grace and Edward L. Rainey in Georgetown, South Carolina, a seaside town consisting mainly of rice plantations. The Raineys raised at least one other child, Edward, Jr. Grace Rainey was of French descent. Edward Rainey was a barber, and his master permitted him to work independently if he shared some of his profits, as required by law. Rainey used his earnings to buy his family's freedom in the early 1840s, and in 1846 the family moved to Charleston, South Carolina, where Edward became a barber at the exclusive Mills House Hotel. As giving official instruction to black children was illegal, Joseph Rainey received a limited education and his father taught him the barber's trade. By the 1850s, Edward Rainey could afford to buy two male slaves for his family.[2] In 1859, Joseph Rainey traveled to Philadelphia, where he met and married his wife, Susan, also a half-French mulatto, originally from the West Indies. Rainey continued to work as a barber, and the couple had three children: Joseph II, Herbert, and Olivia.

The Confederate Army called Rainey to service when the Civil War broke out in 1861. At first, he dug trenches to fortify the outskirts of Charleston. He later worked as a cook and a steward aboard a blockade runner, a Confederate ship charged with carrying tradable goods through the Union Navy's blockade of the South. In 1862, he and his wife escaped to Bermuda. The self-governed British colony had abolished slavery in 1834, and proved a hospitable home for the Raineys, who took advantage of the thriving economy and growing population that resulted from the lucrative blockade-running business.[3] The Raineys lived in St. George and Hamilton, Bermuda, where Joseph set up a successful barbershop and Susan Rainey opened a dress store.[4] The Raineys were informed about the progress of the Civil War by passing sailors and, after the Union victory, returned to Charleston in 1866.

The wealth Joseph Rainey acquired in Bermuda elevated his status in the community, and looked upon as a leader, he soon became active in the Republican Party. In 1867, Rainey returned to Georgetown, South Carolina, and became the Republican county chairman. When a state constitutional convention was called in 1868, Rainey traveled to Charleston to represent Georgetown. In 1869, he also attended a state labor commission and served as Georgetown's census taker. In the late 1860s, he worked as an agent for the state land commission and was a brigadier general in the state militia. Joseph Rainey was elected to his first public office in 1870 when he won a seat in the state senate, where he immediately became chairman of the finance committee.

In February 1870, Representative Benjamin F. Whittemore resigned his northeastern South Carolina seat, having been charged with selling appointments to U.S. military academies. The Republican Party nominated Rainey for the remainder of Whittemore's term in the 41st

Congress (1869–1871) and for a full term in the 42nd Congress (1871–1873). On October 19, 1870, Rainey won the full term, topping Democrat C. W. Dudley by a substantial majority (63 percent). On November 8, he defeated Dudley once again, garnering more than 86 percent of the vote, in a special election to fill the seat for the remainder of the 41st Congress.[5] Joseph Rainey was sworn in on December 12, 1870, as the first African American to serve in the U.S. House of Representatives. One month later he was joined by the second black Member, Representative Jefferson Long of Georgia. Rainey's moderate policies were met with approval by both African-American and white voters, and he was elected without opposition to the 43rd Congress (1873–1875).

Rainey advocated for his constituents—both black and white. He used his growing political clout to influence the South Carolina state legislature to retain the customs duty on rice, the chief export of the district and the state. He also submitted a petition to improve Charleston Harbor and fought against an appropriations cut for Fort Moultrie and Fort Sumter in Charleston. However, Rainey's committee appointments and policies reflected his desire to defend black civil rights, and his loyalty to the Republican Party. Rainey received seats on three standing committees: Freedmen's Affairs (41st–43rd Congresses), Indian Affairs (43rd Congress), and Invalid Pensions (44th–45th Congresses, 1875–1879). He also served on several select committees, including the Select Committee on the Centennial Celebration and the Proposed National Census of 1875 (44th Congress) and the Committee on the Freedmen's Bank (44th Congress).

Rainey's work on the Committee on Freedmen's Affairs—created in 1865 to handle all legislation concerning newly freed slaves—earned him the most recognition.[6] On April 1, 1871, he delivered his first major speech, arguing for the use of federal troops to protect southern blacks from the recently organized Ku Klux Klan. Enumerating the dangers of returning home to South Carolina on congressional breaks, exposing himself to violence by the Red Shirts—a virulent South Carolina

white supremacist organization—Rainey said, "When myself and my colleagues shall leave these Halls and turn our footsteps toward our southern homes, we know not that the assassin may await our coming, as marked for his vengeance."[7] The Ku Klux Klan Act was signed into law by President Ulysses S. Grant on April 20, 1871, but the bill failed to stop Klan terrorism.[8] After his speech, Rainey received a letter written in red ink instructing him and other advocates of black civil rights to "prepare to meet your God."[9] White southerners virtually ignored the Ku Klux Klan Act, and congressional opponents circumvented its provisions by eliminating funding. In March of 1872, Rainey found himself arguing for the federal appropriations needed to enforce the act.[10]

Rainey also advocated Radical Republican Senator Charles Sumner's Civil Rights Bill of 1875, which outlawed racial discrimination on juries, in schools, on transportation, and in public accommodations. Sumner believed a law passed in 1872 granting amnesty to former Confederates should be conditioned by the passage of his civil rights bill. Although Rainey favored the Amnesty Act, which allowed most former Confederates to regain their political rights, he agreed with Sumner because of personal experience with discrimination in both Washington and South Carolina, ranging from exorbitant charges for drinks at a pub, to more serious violations of his civil rights. Rainey also described widespread segregation on public transportation, including trains and streetcars. Speaking for his black constituents, he declared, "We are earnest in our support of the Government. We were earnest in the house of the nation's perils and dangers; and now, in our country's comparative peace and tranquility, we are earnest for our rights."[11]

Rainey focused on the bill's provisions for desegregation in public schools, an issue that had bedeviled race relations for more than a century. Breaking from fellow Republicans, he was among the minority favoring a $1 poll tax to support public education. Other Republicans successfully argued this would disfranchise most freed slaves. Nonetheless, Rainey continued to advocate education, later arguing that money from the sale of public land should be used to fund public education. Though the Civil Rights Bill passed the House on February 5, 1875, with the Senate quickly concurring, its diluted provisions failed to address desegregation or equality in public schools.

Rainey's fight against discrimination was not limited to prejudice against African Americans. Appointed to the Committee on Indian Affairs, he made history in April 1874 when he took the chair from Speaker James G. Blaine, becoming the first black American to preside over the House of Representatives.[12] He oversaw the debate on an appropriations bill providing for the management of Indian reservations. Rainey also generally opposed legislation restricting the influx of Asian immigrants to the United States.

Throughout his career, Rainey involved himself in the economic issues that affected his race. Established by Congress in 1865, the Freedmen's Savings and Trust Company (Freedmen's Bank) was envisioned as a means to help newly emancipated African Americans build capital through secure savings. Two-thirds of the bank's holdings were originally invested in United States treasury bonds. In 1870, an amendment to the bank's charter allowing half of its deposits to be invested in real estate bonds came to the floor. Recognizing the instability of such an investment, Rainey opposed the amendment and stood behind congressional control over the institution: "I am opposed to any one man holding assets of that bank, having them wholly at his disposal, I do not care who he is, whether he be colored or white, whether he be a German or an Irishman it makes no difference to me. I want no one man to handle the assets of the bank."[13] His position on the Select Committee on the Freedmen's Bank gave him a voice, but he and his colleagues were unable to prevent the bank's failure in 1874.

After an easy re-election in 1872, Rainey's subsequent campaigns were made vulnerable by the growing threat to Congressional Reconstruction in the South. In 1874, Rainey faced Independent Republican Samuel Lee, another African American and a former speaker of the state house of representatives, in a dangerous and close campaign. When Rainey planned to travel to a meeting in Bennettsville, South Carolina, friends warned him that Lee's supporters were planning a violent intervention. Accompanied by a large posse of friends and met by U.S. soldiers upon his arrival, Rainey arrived safely and the meeting was peaceful. Rainey won the election, taking 14,360 votes (52 percent) to Lee's 13,563, but Lee demanded that the House Committee on Elections void some of Rainey's votes due to a spelling error in Rainey's name on some ballots.[14] The committee upheld Rainey's election, with the whole House concurring in May 1876. That same year, Rainey defeated Democrat John S. Richardson for a seat in the 45th Congress, again winning a tight campaign with 52 percent of the vote (18,180 to Richardson's 16,661).[15] Richardson later accused Rainey and the Republican Party of voter intimidation. Noting the presence of federal troops during the election, Richardson also claimed that armed black political clubs and black militia were scaring voters at the polls. Richardson's election had been certified by Democratic South Carolina Governor Wade Hampton, and Rainey maintained that only the South Carolina secretary of state could certify elections. Rainey took his seat, but in May 1878 the Committee on Elections declared the seat vacant, citing irregularities. The House failed to act on the committee report, and Rainey kept his seat for the remainder of his term.

Rainey's final two terms were wracked by setbacks for African-American civil rights in South Carolina and the final blow that virtually ended federal Reconstruction in the South. On the American centennial on July 4, 1876, black militia celebrated by parading through a street in Hamburg, South Carolina. When a group of white men attempted to cross the street, the black soldiers refused to stop. The white men subsequently fired upon and killed several militiamen. Debate over the incident became bitter on the House Floor during Rainey's final term in the 45th Congress. Rainey condemned the murders and exchanged coarse remarks with Democratic Representative Samuel

Cox of New York, who believed the "Hamburg massacre" resulted from poor government by black South Carolina leaders.[16] Bolstered by renewed Democratic control in South Carolina, John S. Richardson defeated Rainey in the 1878 election for the 46th Congress (1879–1881) by more than 8,000 votes.[17] Joseph Rainey retired from the House on March 3, 1879.

Upon his departure from Congress, Rainey was promised that Republicans would nominate him as Clerk of the House of Representatives; however, Democratic control over the 46th Congress precluded Rainey's selection as Clerk. When Republicans regained control of Congress in 1881, Rainey spent time in Washington trying to secure the appointment, but he lost the nomination.[18] In 1879, Rainey was appointed a special agent of the U.S. Treasury Department in South Carolina. After being endorsed by 84 Representatives, including future President James A. Garfield of Ohio, Rainey served two years. In 1881, he started a brokerage and banking business in Washington, but the firm collapsed five years later. For one year, he managed a coal mining operation and a wood yard before returning to Georgetown in ill health. Joseph and Susan Rainey opened a millinery shop shortly before Joseph died of congestive fever on August 1, 1887.

FOR FURTHER READING

Packwood, Cyril Outerbridge. *Detour-Bermuda, Destination-U.S. House of Representatives; The Life of Joseph Rainey* (Hamilton, Bermuda: Baxter's Limited, 1977).

"Rainey, Joseph Hayne," *Biographical Directory of the United States Congress, 1774–Present*, http://bioguide. congress.gov/scripts/biodisplay.pl?index=R000016.

MANUSCRIPT COLLECTION

Columbia University, Rare Book and Manuscript Library (New York, N.Y.) *Papers:* In the L. S. Alexander Gumby Collection of Negroiana, ca. 1800–1981, 88 linear feet. The collection contains one letter from Joseph Hayne Rainey, written on March 29, 1874.

NOTES

1   *Congressional Record*, House, 43rd Cong., 1st sess. (19 December 1873): 344.

2   William C. Hine, "Rainey, Joseph Hayne," *American National Biography* 18 (New York: Oxford University Press, 1999): 78–79 (hereinafter referred to as *ANB*).

3   Cyril Outerbridge Packwood, *Detour-Bermuda, Destination-U.S. House of Representatives; The Life of Joseph Rainey* (Hamilton, Bermuda: Baxter's Limited, 1977): 11.

4   Barber's Alley in St. George, Bermuda, is named for Rainey.

5   Michael J. Dubin et al., *U.S. Congressional Elections, 1788–1997* (Jefferson, NC: McFarland & Company, Inc., Publishers, 1998): 214.

6   For more on the jurisdiction of the Committee on Freedmen's Affairs, see Charles E. Schamel et al., *Guide to the Records of the United States House of Representatives at the National Archives, 1789–1989: Bicentennial Edition* (Washington, DC: Government Printing Office, 1989): 209.

7   Packwood, *Detour-Bermuda, Destination-U.S. House of Representatives*: 25.

8   Act of April 20, 1871, 17 Stat. 13–15.

9   "More Loyal Men Threatened in South Carolina," 18 May 1871, *New York Times*: 1.

10 *Congressional Globe*, House, 42nd Cong., 2nd sess. (5 March 1872): 1439–1443.

11 *Congressional Globe*, House, 42nd Cong., 2nd sess. (13 May 1872): 3383.

12 The date Joseph Rainey was Speaker *pro tempore* is not known. Most sources claim Representative Rainey presided over the House during an Indian appropriations debate in May 1874. See, for example, an early secondary work, Samuel Denny Smith, *The Negro in Congress: 1870–1901* (Port Washington, NY: Kennikat Press, Inc., 1940): 47–48. Most subsequent sources cite Smith. Yet the *New York Herald* published an article reporting that Rainey served as Speaker *pro tempore* on April 29; see "A Liberated Slave in the Speaker's Chair," 30 April 1874, *New York Herald*: 9. Similar accounts exist in the *Baltimore Sun*, the *Charleston News and Courier*, and the African-American newspaper *The New National Era*, though these reports cite April 29 and April 30. There is no mention of Rainey's presiding in the *Congressional Record* or the *House Journal* for either date: *Congressional Record*, House, 43rd Cong., 1st sess. (29–30 April 1874): 3457–3476, 3490–3507; *House Journal*, 43rd Cong., 1st sess. (29–30 April 1874): 877–885.

13 *Congressional Record*, 43rd Cong., 2nd sess. (3 March 1874): 2263.

14 Dubin et al., *U.S. Congressional Elections, 1789–1997*: 233; "Notes from the Capitol," 24 January 1876, *New York Times*: 1; Chester H. Rowell, *A Historical and Legal Digest of All the Contested Election Cases* (Washington, DC: Government Printing Office, 1901): 313.

15 Dubin et al., *U.S. Congressional Elections, 1788–1997*: 240.

16 *Congressional Record*, House, 44th Cong., 1st sess. (18 July 1876): 4707.

17 Dubin et al., *U.S. Congressional Elections, 1788–1997*: 247.

18 "Keifer for Speaker," 4 December 1881, *Washington Post*: 1.

Jefferson Franklin Long
1836–1901

UNITED STATES REPRESENTATIVE ★ 1871
REPUBLICAN FROM GEORGIA

The second African American elected to the U.S. House of Representatives, Jefferson Long served less than three months—the shortest term of any African-American Member—but nevertheless became the first black Member to speak on the House Floor.[1] Speaking against the Amnesty Bill, which restored political rights to most former Confederates, Long pleaded with his colleagues to acknowledge the atrocities being committed by white supremacists in Georgia. "Do we, then, really propose here to-day . . . when loyal men dare not carry the 'stars and stripes' through our streets . . . to relieve from political disability the very men who have committed these Kuklux [sic] outrages?" he declared on the House Floor. "I think that I am doing my duty to my constituents and my duty to my country when I vote against such a proposition."[2]

Jefferson Long was born to a slave mother on March 3, 1836, in Knoxville, a small town in west-central Georgia. Long's father was believed to have been the son of a local white man.[3] Defying the law, Long learned to read and write. Trained as a tailor, he opened a successful business in Macon, Georgia, after his emancipation following the end of the Civil War. Most of his clients were white, as they were the only rural Georgians able to afford custom-made clothing.[4] Shortly after the war, Long married Lucinda Carhart, and they raised seven children. One of Long's sons helped run his business.

Unlike neighboring South Carolina, Georgia did not have a majority-black population, or a large antebellum free black community. As a result, Georgia freedmen often looked to white politicians as leaders after the war. Long was an exception.[5] His prosperous tailor shop catered to politically connected clients and provided him the resources to become involved in Republican politics. Starting in 1866, Long began promoting literacy among African Americans, and in 1867, he became active in the Georgia Educational Association, formed to protect and advance the interests of freedmen. Long also belonged to the Macon Union League, a grass-roots political action group. A dazzling orator, he introduced Georgian freedmen to politics by preaching the virtues of the Republican Party. While traveling the state, organizing local Republican branches, and encouraging black voters to register, Long brought many whites into the Republican fold. In 1869, he served on the Republican state committee and was a leader in the Georgia Labor Convention, which organized black agricultural workers to demand increased wages, better jobs, and improved working conditions.[6]

Congress delayed Georgia's re-entry into the Union because the state legislature refused to ratify the 14th Amendment, and white Republicans and Conservatives expelled 29 legally elected black members from the Georgia legislature in September 1868. Conditions for readmission included reseating the black members and ratification of the 15th Amendment. In July 1870, these terms were agreed to, and a Georgia delegation was permitted to return to Congress. A special election to fill the delegation's seats for the remainder of the 41st Congress (1869–1871) was set for the same day—December 20, 1870—as the election for a full term to the 42nd Congress (1871–1873). The Georgia Republican Party chose black candidates to run for the abbreviated terms, reserving the full term for white candidates. In the state's central district, the party nominated Long for the 41st Congress and state senator Thomas Jefferson Speer for the 42nd Congress. The night before the election, Long gave a series of speeches across the district, encouraging black voters to support the Republican ticket. The following day, he rallied a large number of blacks from Macon and marched with them to the polls. Armed whites were waiting, and a riot broke out. Long was unharmed, but four others were killed, and

most blacks left the polls without voting. The unusual election lasted three days. White politicians accused blacks of voting multiple times and spread rumors that African Americans from South Carolina and Alabama had crossed state lines to vote. But despite the election's inconsistencies, Long defeated his opponent, Democrat Winburn J. Lawton, garnering 12,867 votes (53 percent). However, he was not sworn in until January 16, 1871, because of complications related to Georgia's readmission to the Union.[7] Long took his seat one month after Representative Joseph Rainey of South Carolina was seated in the House.

Long's term was so short he was not assigned to any committees, yet he was determined to fight for the civil rights of freed slaves. On February 1, 1871, he became the first African-American Representative to speak before the House when he disagreed with a bill that exempted former Confederate politicians from swearing allegiance to the Constitution.[8] Long argued against allowing unrepentant Confederates to return to Congress, noting that many belonged to secret societies like the Ku Klux Klan, which intimidated black citizens, and feigned loyalty to rebuild political strength. "If this House removes the disabilities of disloyal men," Long warned, "I venture to prophesy you will again have trouble from the very same men who gave you trouble before."[9] Many major newspapers reported on Long's address, and northern newspapers, especially, commended his oratorical skills. Georgia newspapers described his speech as a malicious attempt to disfranchise whites.[10] Long's efforts were fruitless; the House voted 118 to 90 to grant Confederates amnesty.

One of the few votes Long cast in the House was to seat Thomas P. Beard, a black Republican from northeast Georgia, after his defeat by Democrat Stephen Corker. Led by Massachusetts Republican Benjamin Butler, a few Radical Republicans, Long among them, objected to seating Corker when he presented his credentials on January 24, 1871. (The Beard–Corker election equaled Long's for its violence. Beard testified that large numbers of voters who had intended to vote for him were "shot, beat or otherwise maltreated" by "organized bands of desparadoes [sic]," connected to the Democrats.) Butler's resolution objecting to Corker's credentials was soundly defeated in a 148 to 42 vote.[11] A number of Republicans voted against it on procedural grounds, believing Corker's credentials qualified him to remain seated until the Elections Committee ruled on the case. Beard's case never came before the panel, and Corker served out the term.[12]

Long was the last black Representative elected from Georgia until Representative Andrew Young won a seat in 1972. After leaving Congress on March 3, 1871, Long returned to his tailoring business in Macon. Although he remained active in politics, he never again ran for public office, recognizing that the white-controlled Georgia government had shut blacks out of politics. He campaigned for Republican candidates in 1872 and served as a member of the Southern Republican Convention in 1874 and as a delegate to the Republican National Conventions from 1872 to 1880. Long eventually became frustrated by white Republican leaders' failure to protect black southerners. By the late 1870s, he began encouraging African Americans to vote for Independent Democrats if Republican candidates proved unsatisfactory.[13] Political upheaval and sharp racial division in all the political parties had so disillusioned Long by the mid-1880s that he left politics permanently to focus on his business. However, his reputation as a radical politician eventually cost him his affluent white clientele.[14] Unable to survive on the income from his tailor shop, he started other businesses, including a liquor store and a dry-cleaning shop. He remained self-employed until his death in Macon on February 4, 1901.

FOR FURTHER READING

Drago, Edmund L. *Black Politicians and Reconstruction Georgia: A Splendid Failure*, 2nd edition (Athens: University of Georgia Press, 1992).

"Long, Jefferson Franklin," *Biographical Directory of the United States Congress, 1774–Present*, http://bioguide.congress.gov/scripts/biodisplay.pl?index=L000419.

MANUSCRIPT COLLECTION

Atlanta History Center (Atlanta, GA) *Papers:* In the Long–Rucker–Aiken Family Portraits and Personal Images, dates unknown; approximately 1,117 photographs. Subjects include Jefferson Long.

NOTES

1 John Willis Menard of Louisiana was elected to the House in 1868, but the election was contested, and Menard was unseated upon his arrival. His speech defending his right to his seat marked the first time an African American addressed the U.S. House from the floor.

2 *Congressional Globe*, House, 41st Cong., 3rd sess. (1 February 1871): 882.

3 Maurine Christopher, *Black Americans in Congress* (New York: Thomas Y. Crowell Company, 1976): 27. The names of Long's parents are not known.

4 Eric Foner, *Freedom's Lawmakers: A Directory of Black Officeholders During Reconstruction* (New York: Oxford University Press, 1993): 136.

5 Edmund L. Drago, *Black Politicians and Reconstruction in Georgia: A Splendid Failure* (Athens: University of Georgia Press, 1992): xi–xii.

6 Foner, *Freedom's Lawmakers*: 136.

7 Michael J. Dubin et al., *U.S. Congressional Elections, 1788–1997* (Jefferson, NC: McFarland & Company, Inc., Publishers, 1998): 213–214; *Congressional Globe*, House, 41st Cong., 3rd sess. (16 January 1871): 530.

8 *Congressional Globe*, House, 41st Cong., 3rd sess. (1 February 1871): 881–882.

9 Ibid., 882.

10 Samuel Denny Smith, *The Negro in Congress* (Port Washington, NY: Kennikat Press, Inc., 1940): 73–74.

11 *Congressional Globe*, House, 41st Cong., 3rd sess. (24 January 1871): 703–707.

12 The fact that Beard's case is not recorded in Chester H. Rowell's *A Historical and Legal Digest of All Contested Election Cases* (Washington, DC: GPO, 1901), strongly suggests the Committee on Elections never heard the case. Michael Dubin reports that Corker handily defeated "Simeon W. Beard" with 62 percent of the vote. This is likely a misprint. See Dubin et al., *U.S. Congressional Elections, 1788–1997*: 214. (Simeon Beard was an active black politician in Georgia in the early 1870s. See "Bullock's Last Dodge," 27 March 1870, *Atlanta Constitution*: 1.) It is unclear whether the two Beards were related.

13 John M. Matthews, "Long, Jefferson Franklin," *American National Biography* 13 (New York: Oxford University Press, 1999): 875–876.

14 Foner, *Freedom's Lawmakers*: 136.

Robert Carlos De Large
1842–1874

UNITED STATES REPRESENTATIVE ★ 1871–1873
REPUBLICAN FROM SOUTH CAROLINA

A wealthy resident of Charleston, South Carolina, Robert De Large won election to the U.S. House of Representatives as an ally of the scandal-ridden administration of Republican Governor Robert Scott. Though he maintained a personal political alliance with Scott, De Large was constantly at odds with the state Republican Party and rarely defended the corrupt state government. "I am free to admit," De Large noted on the House Floor while advocating for victims of racial violence in the South, "that neither the Republicans of my State nor the Democrats of that State can shake their garments and say that they had no hand in bringing about this condition of affairs."[1] A protracted contested election, in which De Large's lack of political capital, prickly personality and failing health conspired against him, cut short the young politician's career.

Robert Carlos De Large was born on March 15, 1842, in Aiken, South Carolina. Although some records indicate De Large was born a slave, he likely was the offspring of free mulatto parents. De Large's father was a tailor, and his Haitian mother was a cloak maker.[2] The De Large family owned slaves and, as members of the free mulatto elite, were afforded opportunities denied their darker-skinned neighbors. Robert De Large was educated at a North Carolina primary school and attended Wood High School in Charleston, South Carolina. He later married and had a daughter, Victoria.[3] De Large was a tailor and a farmer before gaining lucrative employment with the Confederate Navy during the Civil War. Perhaps regretting the source of his financial windfall, De Large later donated most of his wartime earnings to the Republican Party.[4] Nevertheless, by 1870 he had amassed a fortune that exceeded $6,500. He moved within Charleston's highest circles and joined the Brown Fellowship Society, an exclusive organization for mulattos.[5]

After the war, De Large worked for the Republican state government as an agent in the Freedmen's Bureau. He became an organizer for the South Carolina Republican Party, serving on important committees at several state conventions. He chaired the credentials committee at the 1865 Colored People's Convention at Charleston's Zion Church. At the 1867 South Carolina Republican Convention, he chaired the platform committee, and he served on the committee on franchise and elections at the state's 1868 constitutional convention. Among African-American politicians of the era, De Large was comparatively conservative. He advocated mandatory literacy testing for voters but opposed compulsory education while supporting state-funded and integrated schools. He did favor some more radical measures, however, arguing that the government should penalize ex-Confederates by retaining their property and disfranchising them. In 1868, De Large won his first elected office, serving in the state house of representatives where he chaired the ways and means committee. He also served on a board for the mentally ill and was a member of the state sinking fund commission. In 1870, seeking a black appointee, the legislature chose De Large as land commissioner. In his quest to help South Carolina's poor, De Large oversaw the sale and transfer of almost 2,000 small tracts of land to be paid for over a maximum of eight years, but his tenure on the land commission was discredited by allegations of fraud. Political opponents suspected that De Large skimmed money from the commission to help finance his congressional campaign, but he was never charged with a crime.[6]

In 1870, De Large set his sights on a congressional district representing Charleston and the southeastern portion of the state. He secured the Republican nomination over incumbent scalawag Christopher Bowen,

a former Confederate soldier and one of Governor Scott's most formidable political enemies.[7] According to a leading historian, De Large maintained a personal friendship with the embattled governor, although he was often at odds with Scott's supporters. De Large refused to defend white South Carolina Republicans against charges of corruption and often publicly chided those connected with Scott's administration for their unscrupulous activities. Yet Scott continued to support De Large throughout his political career, primarily because of their friendship.[8]

Christopher Bowen challenged De Large in the 1870 general election, running as an Independent Republican. Having lost favor with the black majority (68 percent of the district's population) due to the influence of Bowen's allies, De Large was ahead by only a slender margin (fewer than 1,000 votes out of more than 32,000 cast) despite considerable political and financial support from Governor Scott.[9] Bowen challenged the election results, but De Large was sworn in to the 42nd Congress (1871–1873) when it convened on March 4, 1871, and assigned to the Committee on Manufactures.

De Large's legislative agenda as a freshman Member lacked continuity, principally because of the large workload created by Bowen's challenge. Early in his term, De Large unsuccessfully offered an amendment to provide $20,000 to rebuild a Charleston orphanage. He also supported a bill providing amnesty to former Confederates, but felt loyal black and white southerners should be protected from intimidation and terror. Arguing in favor of a bill to curb the activities of the Ku Klux Klan in April 1871, De Large referred to intolerable conditions throughout the South that required action from Congress. "The naked facts stare us in the face, that this condition of affairs does exist, and that it is necessary for the strong arm of the law to interpose and protect the people in their lives, liberty, and property," he noted. However, De Large was emphatic that his Charleston district had no reported cases of "outlawry" but admitted that "until within the last few months no one upon the face of God's earth could have convinced me that a secret organization existed in my

State for the purpose of committing murder, arson, and other outrages."[10]

De Large's unvarnished comments on the House Floor about local party corruption caused him to run afoul of state Republicans. Responding to a speech by Democrat Samuel Cox of New York—in which Cox accused black politicians of fueling the corruption in South Carolina's government—De Large insisted that black South Carolina politicians were guilty only of trusting corrupt white Republicans. "While there may have been extravagance and corruption resulting from the placing of improper men in official positions," De Large declared, "these evils have been brought about by the men identified with the race to which the gentleman from New York belongs, and not by our race."[11] Republicans outside South Carolina praised De Large's speech—the *Chicago Tribune* said it showed "fearlessness and frankness"—but white political leaders inside South Carolina were infuriated by De Large's accusations.[12] White party leadership suspected he was trying to create a political party that would alienate blacks from the Republican Party. De Large had reportedly told a Charleston crowd, "I hold that my race has always been Republican for necessity only," during his 1870 election campaign.[13] Though he denied rumors he planned to change parties, De Large's alliance with black nationalist Martin R. Delany, who had abandoned the Republican Party, fueled such speculation.[14]

De Large participated sparingly in House Floor debate during the second session, as he was occupied defending his seat. The House Committee on Elections began consideration of Christopher Bowen's challenge to his election in December 1871, and De Large took a leave of absence in April 1872 to prepare his defense.

Bowen's sensationalized bigamy trial—his political enemies accused him of marrying a third wife without having legally separated from his first and second wives—focused national attention on the case and damaged Bowen's chances of successfully contesting De Large's election.[15] Nevertheless, Bowen accused De Large supporters of stuffing ballot boxes with false votes and was backed by white South Carolina Republicans. The *Chicago Tribune* observed wryly, "It really seems that the only way a South Carolina politician can keep out of State Prison or in Congress is by proving all the rest to be bigger scoundrels than himself."[16] Despite Bowen's political problems, De Large had few political allies. He had developed a less-than-favorable reputation with his stubborn, elitist, and temperamental antics, including a fistfight in front of the state assembly in 1869. Even fellow black lawmakers offered stinging judgments. South Carolina Representative Robert Elliott derided De Large for his small stature and outsized ego, calling him a "pygmy who is trying to play the part of a giant."[17] Left to mount his own defense, De Large accused Bowen of bribing a lawyer to keep exonerating evidence from the Committee on Elections.[18] The case was further complicated when De Large's health failed in the summer of 1872. Black South Carolina Representative Joseph Rainey pleaded on the House Floor for a delay in the case, but the committee reported that the many abuses and irregularities during the election made determining a victor impossible, and on January 18, 1873, declared the seat vacant for the rest of the 42nd Congress, set to adjourn in March. The full House agreed with the committee's findings.[19]

The rigors of defending his seat in the 42nd Congress took a toll on De Large's fragile health and left him few options other than retirement. Black politician Alonzo Ransier won his seat. De Large returned to the state capital in Columbia and later moved to Charleston after Governor Scott appointed him magistrate of that city. He died of tuberculosis shortly thereafter on February 14, 1874, at the age of 31. Despite De Large's difficult relationship with South Carolina Republicans, city magistrates statewide closed their offices on the day of his funeral to show their respect.

FOR FURTHER READING

"De Large, Robert Carlos," *Biographical Directory of the United States Congress, 1774–Present*, http://bioguide. congress.gov/scripts/biodisplay.pl?index=D000208.

NOTES

1 *Congressional Globe*, Appendix, 42nd Cong., 1st sess. (6 April 1871): A230.

2 Timothy P. McCarthy, "De Large, Robert Carlos," *American National Biography* 6 (New York: Oxford University Press, 1999): 383–384 (hereinafter referred to as *ANB*). De Large's parents' names are not known.

3 De Large's wife's name is not known.

4 McCarthy, "De Large, Robert Carlos," *ANB*; Thomas C. Holt, *Black Over White: Negro Political Leadership in South Carolina During Reconstruction* (Urbana: University of Illinois Press, 1977): 115. Stephen Middleton conjectures that De Large might have initially abhorred the northern invasion of his home because of regional pride. See Stephen Middleton ed., *Black Congressmen During Reconstruction: A Documentary Sourcebook* (Westport, CT: Praeger, 2002): 79.

5 McCarthy, "De Large, Robert Carlos," *ANB*.

6 Ibid; Joel Williamson, *After Slavery: the Negro in South Carolina During Reconstruction, 1861–1877* (Chapel Hill: University of North Carolina Press, 1965): 146.

7 Carol K. Rothrok Bleser, *The Promised Land: The History of the South Carolina Land Commission, 1869–1890* (Columbia: University of South Carolina Press, 1969): 75.

8 Holt, *Black Over White*: 111.

9 Peggy Lamson, *The Glorious Failure: Black Representative Robert Brown Elliott and the Reconstruction in South Carolina* (New York: Norton, 1973): 95; Holt, *Black Over White*: 118–119.

10 *Congressional Globe*, Appendix, 42nd Cong., 1st sess. (6 April 1871): A230–231.

11 Ibid.

12 "Amnesty," 8 April 1871, *Chicago Tribune*: 2.

13 Quoted in McCarthy, "De Large, Robert Carlos," *ANB*; Williamson, *After Slavery*: 359.

14 McCarthy, "De Large, Robert Carlos," *ANB*.

15 "The Case of C. C. Bowen," 15 June 1871, *New York Times*: 4. According to newspaper reports, primarily in the *Chicago Tribune,* Bowen received a presidential pardon after he was convicted of bigamy.

16 [No title], 22 June 1871, *Chicago Tribune*: 2.

17 Williamson, *After Slavery*: 397; Quoted in McCarthy, "De Large, Robert Carlos," *ANB*. However, Elliott helped De Large when the latter was absent from Congress by explaining his colleague's opinion during several votes, indicating that the two worked together. See *Congressional Globe*, House, 42nd Cong., 2nd sess. (28 May 1872): 3931–3932.

18 "Bowen Again," 25 December 1871, *Chicago Tribune*: 4.

19 Chester H. Rowell, *A Historical and Legal Digest of All the Contested Election Cases* (Washington, DC: Government Printing Office, 1901): 282.

"THE NAKED FACTS STARE US
IN THE FACE, THAT THIS
CONDITION OF AFFAIRS DOES
EXIST, AND THAT IT IS NECESSARY
FOR THE STRONG ARM OF THE LAW
TO INTERPOSE AND PROTECT
THE PEOPLE IN THEIR LIVES,
LIBERTY, AND PROPERTY,"
DE LARGE SAID IN SUPPORT OF
A BILL TO CURB KU KLUX KLAN
ACTIVITIES IN THE SOUTH.

Robert Brown Elliott
1842–1884

UNITED STATES REPRESENTATIVE ★ 1871–1874
REPUBLICAN FROM SOUTH CAROLINA

With a legislative style more flamboyant and aggressive than his predecessors', and considerable oratorical skills, young, talented Robert Elliott regularly dazzled audiences. Possessing a strong, clear voice "suggestive of large experience in outdoor speaking," Elliott fought passionately to pass a comprehensive civil rights bill in his two terms in Congress. However, his fealty to the South Carolina Republican Party led him to resign his seat in the U.S. House of Representatives to serve the state government in Columbia.[1] Elliott's classical education, photographic memory, and obsession with politics impressed contemporary observers. "He knew the political condition of every nook and corner throughout the state," Elliott's law partner Daniel Augustus Straker commented. "[Elliott] knew every important person in every county, town or village and the history of the entire state as it related to politics."[2]

Robert Elliott was born on August 11, 1842, likely to West Indian parents in Liverpool, England.[3] He received a public school education in England and learned a typesetter's trade. Elliott served in the British Navy, arriving on a warship in Boston around 1867. Historical records show that in late 1867 Robert Elliott lived in Charleston, South Carolina, where he was an associate editor for the *South Carolina Leader,* a freedmen's newspaper owned by future Representative Richard H. Cain. Elliott married Grace Lee, a free mulatto from Boston or Charleston, sometime before 1870. The couple had no children.[4]

Robert Elliott was intellectually gifted and well-educated. He often quoted classical literature and demonstrated facility with several languages. He quickly dove into Reconstruction-Era Republican politics in his new South Carolina home, emerging as a leading figure at the 1868 state constitutional convention. One of 78 black delegates at the convention, he advocated compulsory public education (although he opposed school integration) and helped defeat the imposition of a poll tax and a literacy test for voters. At the state Republican convention that year, he was nominated for lieutenant governor, but dropped out of the race after finishing third on the first ballot.[5] Later in 1868, while serving as the only black member of the Barnwell County board of commissioners, Elliott was elected to the state house of representatives, where he remained until 1870. He almost was elected speaker—placing second on the balloting—and he went on to receive influential assignments as chairman of the committee on railroads and chairman of the committee on privileges and elections. During his tenure in the state assembly, Elliott used his keen intelligence and ambition to study law and was admitted to the South Carolina bar in September 1868. In 1870, Republican Governor Robert K. Scott appointed Elliott the assistant adjutant general of South Carolina, giving him authority to raise the state militia to protect black citizens from the Ku Klux Klan. Shortly thereafter, Elliott came to believe Scott was using him for his own political advantage, and he resigned later that year. Nevertheless, he served on the South Carolina Republican executive committee throughout his career.

In October 1870, Republicans in a west-central South Carolina congressional district nominated Robert Elliott over incumbent Solomon L. Hoge to run for a seat in the U.S. House of Representatives. The district included the capital, Columbia, and had only a slight black majority. The seat was once held by Representative Preston Brooks, notorious for his caning assault on Senator Charles Sumner in 1856. Elliott faced Union Reform Party candidate John E. Bacon, the son of a prominent, aristocratic, low country family. The election was contentious. Bacon accused Elliott of using his position on the committee on railroads in the state legislature to line his own pockets.[6] Though the

New York Times predicted Bacon's victory, Elliott soundly defeated him with 60 percent of the vote.[7] He was sworn in to the 42nd Congress (1871–1873) on March 4, 1871.

White colleagues received Elliott coolly. His dark skin came as a shock, as the two other African Americans on the floor, Joseph Rainey and Jefferson Long, were light-skinned mulattos. Described as the first "genuine African" in Congress, Elliott seemed to embody the new political opportunities—and southern white apprehensions—ushered in by emancipation. "I shall never forget [my first day in Congress]," Elliott later recalled. "I found myself the center of attraction. Everything was still."[8] Furthermore, his politics were more radical than his African-American colleagues', and his unwavering stance for black civil rights made many Representatives of both parties wary of his intentions. Elliott was given a position on the Committee on Education and Labor, where he served during both of his terms.

The current of suspicion surrounding his arrival did not erode Elliott's natural confidence. He gave his maiden speech just 10 days after his swearing-in, challenging the Amnesty Bill, which re-established the political rights of nearly all former Confederates, and quickly followed that speech with another supporting the Ku Klux Klan Bill, aimed at curbing the terrorist activities of the clandestine organization.

Rising racial violence in his home state stirred Elliott to speak. Just before Christmas 1870, a white whiskey peddler allegedly was killed by a group of drunk, black militiamen in the town of Union Courthouse, South Carolina. Thirteen men were arrested in connection with the crime, but before they were tried, the Ku Klux Klan raided several jails, executing the suspects. The Klansmen subsequently posted a notice on the Union Courthouse jail door justifying the lynchings and warning other African Americans in the state. Elliott argued for a delay in the restoration of political rights to ex-Confederates and pleaded with Congress to protect the rights of African Americans and other loyal southerners from terror organizations. Referring to the violence at Union

Courthouse, Elliott told his colleagues that "to relieve those men of their disabilities at this time would be regarded by the loyal men of the South as an evidence of weakness of this great Government, and of an intention on the part of this Congress to foster the men who today are outraging the good and loyal people of the South."[9] Elliott's arguments against the Amnesty Bill ultimately failed, as the measure passed the following year.

Elliott's efforts to enact legislation to weaken the Klan were more successful. In his April 1 speech, he read the letter posted by the Klansmen at the Union Courthouse jail, following it with words about the prejudice against his race: "It is custom, sir, of Democratic [newspapers] to stigmatize the negroes of the South as being in a semi-barbarous condition; but pray tell me, who is the barbarian here, the murderer or the victim? I fling back in the teeth of those who make it this most false and foul aspersion upon the negro of the southern States."[10] The Third Ku Klux Klan Bill, which reinforced freedmen's voting rights, passed and was signed into law three weeks later. The following October, President Ulysses S. Grant used the powers granted him by the bill to suspend *habeas corpus* in nine southern states, facilitating the prosecution of Klansmen. Elliott felt his life was in danger, and before leaving for Columbia the following day, he wrote his wife with instructions in case of his death.[11] Also in the 42nd Congress, Elliott attempted in May 1872 to gain appropriations to pull South Carolina out of its postwar debt.

In October 1872, Elliott was re-elected practically unopposed, garnering 93 percent of the vote against two weak Democrats, W. H. McCaw and Samuel McGovan.[12] In November, Elliott attempted to become the first African American to win a full term in the U.S. Senate. The state general assembly voted 73 to 27 to elect his opponent, carpetbagger John J. Patterson, but two hours later, Patterson was arrested and charged with bribing a number of state legislators. (Elliott claimed he was offered between $10,000 and $15,000 to drop out of the race.)[13] The corrupt South Carolina government later dropped the charges, and Patterson was duly elected. Elliott returned to his House seat in December 1873 for the opening of the 43rd Congress (1873–1875) and received an additional assignment on the Committee on the Militia.

During his second term, Elliott worked to help pass Massachusetts Senator Charles Sumner's Civil Rights Bill, to eliminate discrimination from public transportation, public accommodations, and schools. Elliott gained national attention for a speech rebuffing opponents of the bill, who argued that federal enforcement of civil rights was unconstitutional. Responding to former Confederate Vice President Alexander Stephens of Georgia, who had been re-elected to the House, Elliott reaffirmed his belief in the right and duty of Congress to legislate against discrimination. He concluded by evoking the sacrifices made during the Civil War and asserting that its true purpose was to obtain civil rights for all Americans, including women, who experienced discrimination. Elliott undoubtedly drew upon a large reserve of personal experience with racism. Like other African-American Representatives, he faced discrimination almost daily, particularly in restaurants and on public transportation.[14] Before a packed House, Elliott stated his universal support for civil rights, "I regret, sir, that the dark hue of my skin may lend a color to the imputation that I am controlled by motives personal to myself in my advocacy of this great measure of national justice. The motive that impels me is restricted to no such boundary, but is as broad as your Constitution. I advocate it because it is right."[15] Elliott's youthful appearance and the "harmony of his delivery" contrasted sharply with those of the elderly Stephens, who, confined to a wheelchair, dryly read a prepared speech.[16] The *Chicago Tribune* published a glowing review, noting that "fair-skinned men in Congress . . . might learn something from this black man."[17]

Elliott returned to South Carolina on February 6, 1874, although Congress was still in session. His well-publicized speeches left him a hero among black constituents, but Elliott realized that the corruption in the state's Republican Party was allowing the Democrats

to gain power and endangering the prospects of black politicians. After the death of Senator Sumner in early March 1874, Elliott delivered a famous eulogy at Boston's Faneuil Hall. Shortly afterward, he returned to South Carolina and resigned his House seat on November 1, 1874. Wishing to remain close to the South Carolina government, Elliott subsequently ran for and won a seat in the state general assembly.[18]

The general assembly elected Elliott speaker of the house, (he succeeded South Carolina's first black speaker, Samuel Lee). After serving in that position until 1876, Elliott was elected state attorney general in a bitter and controversial race; however, the collapse of the state's Reconstruction government the following year and the withdrawal of federal troops forced him out of office in May 1877. After leaving his post, Elliott founded a law practice, but it attracted few customers. In 1879, he accepted an appointment as a special customs inspector for the Treasury Department in Charleston, South Carolina. On a trip to Florida, he contracted malaria, which severely undermined his health for the remainder of his life. Elliott remained active in politics, however, working on Treasury Secretary John Sherman's campaign for President, seconding his nomination and managing his black delegates at the 1880 Republican National Convention. In January 1881, Elliott was part of a black delegation that met with President James Garfield to protest the lack of civil and political rights in the South. In May of that year, the Treasury Department transferred him to New Orleans, uprooting him from his home and causing him great personal anguish. Elliott was dismissed as a Treasury inspector in 1882. Unable to afford to return to South Carolina, he started another law practice in New Orleans. Robert Elliott lapsed into poverty before his death on August 9, 1884.

FOR FURTHER READING

"Elliott, Robert Brown," *Biographical Directory of the U.S. Congress, 1774–Present*, http://bioguide.congress.gov/scripts/biodisplay.pl?index=E000128.

Lamson, Peggy. *The Glorious Failure: Black Congressman Robert Brown Elliott and the Reconstruction in South Carolina* (New York: Norton, 1973).

NOTES

1   "Washington," 2 April 1871, *Chicago Tribune*: 2.

2   Quoted in Eric Foner, *Freedom's Lawmakers: A Directory of Black Officeholders During Reconstruction* (New York: Oxford University Press, 1993): 70. The context of the quote is unclear.

3   The circumstances of Robert Brown Elliott's early life are enigmatic. He claimed he was born in Boston and attended public schools in England, graduating with honors from Britain's prestigious Eton College in 1859. He further asserted that he had worked for a famous London barrister before returning to the United States in 1861 to join the Union Navy. Elliott later attributed a lifelong limp to a battle wound. Other evidence indicates that his parents were originally from South Carolina and that the Elliott family escaped slavery on the Underground Railroad to a northern state. Still other sources suggest Elliott was born in the West Indies and spent his early years there. Elliott's version of his origins cannot be corroborated, and recent scholarship indicates that the bright and ambitious young man may have invented his American citizenship and embellished his credentials in 1867 to establish his eligibility and credibility as a candidate for political office. Elliott's mysterious background is discussed at length by his chief biographer. See Peggy Lamson *The Glorious Failure: Black Representative Robert Brown Elliott and the Reconstruction in South Carolina* (New York: Norton, 1973): 22–33. See also Peggy Lamson "Elliott, Robert Brown," *Dictionary of American Negro Biography* (New York: Norton, 1982): 210–211 (hereinafter referred to as *DANB*). The most recent scholarship accepts Lamson's evidence of Elliott's background. See Stephen Middleton ed., *Black Congressmen During Reconstruction: A Documentary Sourcebook* (Westport, CT: Praeger, 2002): 85–86.

4   The identity of Elliott's wife also is mysterious. Though Elliott addressed Grace L. Elliott in a letter as "my dear wife," other sources indicate Elliott's wife was Nancy Fat. Others conclude that Nancy Fat was Elliott's mistress; see Lamson, *The Glorious Failure*: 31–33.

5   Howard N. Rabinowitz, "Elliott, Robert Brown," *American National Biography* 7 (New York: Oxford University Press, 1999): 434–436.

6   Maurine Christopher, *Black Americans in Congress* (New York: Thomas Y. Crowell Company, 1976): 70.

7   "Political," 18 October 1870, *New York Times*: 5; Michael J. Dubin et al., *U.S. Congressional Elections, 1788–1997* (Jefferson, NC: McFarland & Company, Inc., Publishers, 1998): 220.

8   Quoted in Lamson, *The Glorious Failure*: 122.

9   *Congressional Globe*, House, 42nd Cong., 1st sess. (14 March 1871): 102–103.

10 *Congressional Globe*, House, 42nd Cong., 1st sess. (1 April 1871): 392.

11 Lamson, *The Glorious Failure*: 131–132.

12 Dubin et al., *U.S. Congressional Elections, 1788–1997*: 226.

13 Foner, *Freedom's Lawmakers*: 70; Christopher, *Black Americans in Congress*: 73.

14 Lamson, *The Glorious Failure*: 120–121.

15 *Congressional Globe*, House, 43rd Cong., 1st sess. (6 January 1874): 407–410.

16 Lamson, *The Glorious Failure*: 175–176; "Congress," 7 January 1874, *New York Times*: 1.

17 "Representative Elliott's Speech," 8 January 1874, *Chicago Daily Tribune*: 4.

18 Lamson, "Elliott, Robert Brown," *DANB*.

"I REGRET, SIR, THAT THE DARK HUE OF MY SKIN MAY LEND A COLOR TO THE IMPUTATION THAT I AM CONTROLLED BY MOTIVES PERSONAL TO MYSELF IN MY ADVOCACY OF THIS GREAT MEASURE OF NATIONAL JUSTICE," ELLIOTT SAID OF HIS SUPPORT FOR THE CIVIL RIGHTS BILL OF 1875. "THE MOTIVE THAT IMPELS ME IS RESTRICTED TO NO SUCH BOUNDARY, BUT IS AS BROAD AS YOUR CONSTITUTION. I ADVOCATE IT BECAUSE IT IS RIGHT."

Benjamin Sterling Turner
1825–1894

UNITED STATES REPRESENTATIVE ★ 1871–1873
REPUBLICAN FROM ALABAMA

A former slave and a self-made businessman who lost property during the Civil War, Benjamin Turner focused on restoring peace and repairing economic damage in the war-ravaged South. The first African-American Representative from Alabama, Turner tirelessly promoted the industriousness of his black constituents. "These people have struggled longer and labored harder, and have made more of the raw material than any people in the world," he noted on the House Floor. "Since they have been free they have not slackened in their industry, but materially improved their economy."[1] Turner also struck a conciliatory tone with white constituents, seeking restored political rights for former Confederates before Congress passed laws declaring general amnesty. His political moderation limited his legislative influence in an institution still controlled by Radical Republicans.

Benjamin Sterling Turner was born a slave on March 17, 1825, in Weldon, North Carolina.[2] His widowed owner, Elizabeth Turner, moved to Selma, Alabama, in 1830, taking five-year-old Turner to live with her on the Alabama River. Turner obtained an education, most likely sitting in as a playmate on lessons for the family's white children. He was sold at age 20 to Major W. H. Gee, the husband of Elizabeth Turner's stepdaughter. Gee owned a hotel and a livery stable and permitted Turner to manage the businesses and keep part of the profits. Major Gee's brother, James, inherited Turner upon his brother's death, and Turner managed James Gee's hotel. Turner married a black woman, but a white man purchased her as his mistress. Turner never remarried, but the 1870 Census indicates he cared for a nine-year-old mulatto boy named Osceola.[3]

By the time the Civil War broke out, Turner had enough money to purchase some property. He also looked after his owner's land and businesses when Gee left to serve in the Confederate Army. Selma became a hub for weapons manufacturing and was overrun by the Union cavalry in the spring of 1865. The troops burned two-thirds of the city and, along with his white neighbors, Turner suffered great financial loss. He later sought $8,000 in damages from the Southern Claims Commission, but it is unclear if he received it.[4] Turner continued to work as a merchant and a farmer after the war, replenishing much of his capital. Eager to provide freedmen with the opportunities an education had provided him, he founded a school in Selma in 1865. In 1867, he attended the Republican state convention and attracted the attention of local GOP officials. That same year he was appointed Dallas County tax collector. In 1869, Turner was elected a Selma councilman, but he resigned in protest after being offered compensation because he believed public officials should not be paid when economic conditions were poor.[5]

In 1870, Turner made a bid for a southwestern Alabama seat in the U.S. House of Representatives. Claiming he sold a horse to finance his campaign, Turner noted the lack of support from the numerous white carpetbagger Republicans, who supported more-radical, redemptive candidates. Yet Turner had strong support from the black population, which constituted nearly 52 percent of the district—the second-largest black voting bloc in Alabama.[6] Running on a balanced platform of "Universal Suffrage and Universal Amnesty," he defeated Democrat Samuel J. Cummings with 18,226 votes (58 percent) in the November 8 election, taking his seat in the 42nd Congress (1871–1873).[7]

Having witnessed firsthand the devastation of the Civil War, Turner spent much of his congressional career seeking financial aid for his broken southern state. In one instance, he introduced a bill to eliminate legal and political disabilities imposed on former Confederates. Though the Radical Republicans in the 42nd Congress

denied his request, the 43rd Congress (1873–1875) eventually passed an Amnesty Act, clearing most former Confederates' political restrictions. Turner's charity toward former slave masters did not prevent him from taking a more radical stance on other legislation concerning the injustices of slavery. He advocated racially mixed schools and financial reparation for former slaves; years later, both issues remained controversial.

Turner sought to repair the devastation in his hometown by sponsoring a bill to appropriate $200,000 for the construction of a federal building in Selma and the reconstruction of Selma's St. Paul's Episcopal Church. Continuing his call for amnesty, he claimed that the federal money would help heal wounds from the war. Turner included a plea for the federal reconstruction money in the *Congressional Globe Appendix*—a tactic he often relied upon because Republican leaders denied him time to speak on the floor. "The Government made a display in that unfortunate city of its mighty power and conquered a gallant and high-toned people. They may have sinned wonderfully, but they suffered terribly," Turner wrote on behalf of the Selma appropriation.[8] Although that bill was not passed, Turner was able to help individual Alabamians from his position on the Committee on Invalid Pensions. Turner passed two private pension bills, one of which put a black Civil War veteran on the pension roll at $8 per month.[9]

On February 20, 1872, Turner presented a petition from the Mobile board of trade requesting a refund of the taxes on cotton collected from the southern states from 1866 to 1868. On May 31, he submitted a speech to the *Congressional Globe Appendix*, declaring the tax unconstitutional and decrying its effect on the impoverished cotton workers—a disproportionate number of whom were freedmen. He pleaded "on behalf of the poor people of the South, regardless of caste or color, because this tax had its blighting influence. It cut the jugular vein of our financial system, bled it near unto death. . . . It so crippled every trade and industry that our

suffering has been greater under its influence than under that of the war."[10] In the same speech, Turner called for the government to purchase private land, divide it into tracts of no more than 160 acres, and sell it to freedmen. No action was taken on this proposal, nor did the House consider a refund for the cotton tax.

In 1872, Republicans renominated Turner for his congressional seat, but his popularity had eroded in his Selma district. Turner's relative conservatism, his refusal to make patronage appointments on a partisan basis, and his failure to pass economic revitalization bills roiled voters.[11] Turner's decline also reflected class tensions among local blacks. Prominent African-American leaders noted condescendingly that during his industrious but modest past Turner had been a "barroom owner, livery stable keeper, and a man destitute of education."[12] The black elite—fearing Turner would embarrass them because, they claimed, he lacked the social graces, manners, and experience of the upper class—backed Philip Joseph, a freeborn newspaper editor. Joseph ran as an Independent, splitting the black vote. White candidate Frederick G. Bromberg, running on the Democratic and Liberal Republican ticket, benefited from the split African-American vote, winning the general election with a 44 percent plurality. Turner took 37 percent, and Joseph garnered 19 percent.[13]

After his congressional career, Turner curtailed his political activities, emerging in 1880 to attend the Alabama Labor Union Convention and to serve as a delegate to the Republican National Convention in Chicago. He then returned to his livery stable in Selma. Turner eventually lost his business during a national economic downturn at the end of the 1870s. Resorting to making his living as a farmer, Benjamin Turner died nearly penniless in Selma on March 21, 1894.

FOR FURTHER READING

"Turner, Benjamin Sterling," *Biographical Directory of the United States Congress, 1774–Present*, http://bioguide.congress.gov/scripts/biodisplay.pl?index=T000414.

NOTES

1   *Congressional Globe*, Appendix, 42nd Cong., 2nd sess. (30 May 1872): A530–531.

2   Turner's parents' names are not known.

3   William W. Rogers, "Turner, Benjamin Sterling," *American National Biography* 22 (New York: Oxford University Press, 1999): 9–11 (hereinafter referred to as *ANB*).

4   Rogers, "Turner, Benjamin Sterling," *ANB*.

5   Ibid.

6   Stanley B. Parsons et al., *United States Congressional Districts, 1843–1883* (New York: Greenwood Press, 1986): 93–94.

7   Rogers, "Turner, Benjamin Sterling," *ANB*. See also Michael J. Dubin et al., *U.S. Congressional Elections, 1788–1997* (Jefferson, NC: McFarland and Company, Inc., Publishers, 1998): 217.

8   *Congressional Globe*, Appendix, 42nd Cong., 2nd sess. (30 May 1872): A530–531.

9   Private bills are bills introduced on behalf of an individual, typically a constituent.

10 *Congressional Globe*, Appendix, 42nd Cong., 2nd sess. (31 May 1872): A540–541.

11 Rogers, "Turner, Benjamin Sterling," *ANB*.

12 Quoted in Eric Foner, *Freedom's Lawmakers: A Directory of Black Officeholders During Reconstruction* (New York: Oxford University Press, 1993): 215.

13 Dubin et al., *U.S. Congressional Elections, 1788–1997*: 223.

Josiah Thomas Walls
1842–1905

UNITED STATES REPRESENTATIVE ★ 1871–1873; 1873–1876
REPUBLICAN FROM FLORIDA

Overcoming deep political divisions in the Florida Republican Party, Josiah Walls became the first African American to serve his state in Congress. The only black Representative from Florida until the early 1990s, Walls was unseated twice on the recommendation of the House Committee on Elections. When he was not fiercely defending his seat in Congress, Walls fought for internal improvements for Florida. He also advocated compulsory education and economic opportunity for all races: "We demand that our lives, our liberties, and our property shall be protected by the strong arm of our government, that it gives us the same citizenship that it gives to those who it seems would . . . sink our every hope for peace, prosperity, and happiness into the great sea of oblivion."[1]

Josiah Thomas Walls was born into slavery in Winchester, Virginia, on December 30, 1842.[2] He was suspected to be the son of his master, Dr. John Walls, and maintained contact with him throughout his life.[3] When the Civil War broke out, Walls was forced to be the private servant of a Confederate artilleryman until he was captured by Union soldiers in May 1862. Emancipated by his Union captors, Walls briefly attended the county normal school in Harrisburg, Pennsylvania. By July 1863, Josiah Walls was serving in the Union Army as part of the 3rd Infantry Regiment of United States Colored Troops (USCT) based in Philadelphia. His regiment moved to Union-occupied northern Florida in February 1864. The following June, he transferred to the 35th Regiment USCT, where he served as the first sergeant and artillery instructor. While living in Picolota, Florida, Walls met and married Helen Fergueson, with whom he had one daughter, Nellie. He was discharged in October 1865 but decided to stay in Florida, working at a saw mill on the Suwannee River and, later, as a teacher with the Freedmen's Bureau in Gainesville. By 1868, Walls had saved enough money to buy a 60-acre farm outside the city.

One of the few educated black men in Reconstruction-Era Florida, Walls was drawn to political opportunities available after the war. He began his career by representing north-central Florida's Alachua County in the 1868 Florida constitutional convention. That same year, Walls ran a successful campaign for state assemblyman. The following fall, he was elected to the state senate and took his seat as one of five freedmen in the 24-man chamber in January 1869. Josiah Walls attended the Southern States Convention of Colored Men in 1871 in Columbia, South Carolina.

After gaining traction in 1867, the Florida Republican Party disintegrated into factions controlled by scalawags and carpetbaggers—each group fighting for the loyalty of a large constituency of freedmen. The disorganized GOP faced another grim situation when their nominating convention met in August 1870. The three previous years would be remembered as the apex of anti-black violence in the state, orchestrated by the well-organized Jacksonville branches of the Ku Klux Klan.[4] In the face of such unrestrained intimidation, Florida freedmen were widely expected to avoid the polls on Election Day. Fearing conservative Democrats would capture the election in the absence of the black vote, state GOP party leaders—a group made up entirely of white men from the scalawag and carpetbagger factions—agreed that nominating a black man to the state's lone At-Large seat in the U.S. House of Representatives would renew black voters' courage and faith in the Republican Party. Passing over the incumbent, former Union soldier Representative Charles Hamilton, the state convention delegates advanced the names of their favorite black candidates. Fierce competition between the nominees led to unruly debate as well as attempts to cast fraudulent votes, and almost resulted in rioting. Walls's reputation as an

independent politician who would not fall under the control of a single faction gave him the edge, and the convention selected him for the party's nomination on the 11th ballot. The narrow victory was not encouraging for Walls. In the general election, he would confront not only Democratic opposition but also the doubts of his own party.[5]

Walls faced former slave owner and Confederate veteran Silas L. Niblack in the general election. Niblack immediately attacked Walls's capabilities, arguing that a former slave was not educated enough to serve in Congress. Walls countered these charges by challenging his opponent to a debate and speaking at political rallies throughout northern Florida (the most populous section of the state). The campaign was violent; a would-be assassin's bullet missed Walls by inches at a Gainesville rally, and Election Day was tumultuous. As one Clay County observer noted, Florida had been "turned upside down with politics and the election."[6] Walls emerged victorious, taking just 627 more votes than Niblack out of the more than 24,000 cast.[7] After presenting his credentials on March 4, 1871, he was immediately sworn in to the 42nd Congress (1871–1873) and given a seat on the Committee on the Militia.

Niblack quickly contested the election. He provided solid evidence that the canvassers who rejected Democratic ballots in at least eight counties throughout the state were not legally allowed to do so; their job had been limited to counting votes. Walls claimed that he had lost more votes due to voter intimidation by the Ku Klux Klan in several northeastern counties, but he had little tangible evidence to support this claim.[8] Walls was in office for nearly two years before the House Committee on Elections ruled on his case. The Republican majority declared Niblack the winner on January 29, 1873—a rare case in which the committee decided with the candidate from the minority party.[9] Despite his loss, Walls's congressional career was not over. In November 1872, he had won one of the two Florida At-Large seats in the 43rd Congress (1873–1875).[10] In the four-way race, the top-two vote getters won a seat. Walls was just 34 votes shy of carpetbagger

Republican William Purman. Niblack, running as a Conservative, was third.[11] Walls returned to Congress when it convened in December 1873, receiving an additional assignment: to the Committee on Expenditures in the Navy Department.

Walls spent much of the 42nd and 43rd Congresses advancing the political and economic interests of his Florida constituents. Even Jacksonville's Democratic *Florida Union* praised Walls's efforts on behalf of the state, declaring, "Mr. Walls adds his mite to what has gone before and does it well."[12] He affectionately referred to Florida as "my own sunny state," in an attempt to promote the potential of his new home for tourism and farming.[13] Walls presented resolutions for statewide internal improvements including the construction of telegraph lines, customhouses, courthouses, and post offices. He sought funding to improve Florida's harbors and rivers and to create a land-grant state agricultural college. In an 1872 tariff bill, Walls also fought to protect Florida's orchards from foreign competition. Most of Walls's measures failed to make it out of committee, but he had more success passing private bills (those submitted for the benefit of an individual). He managed to gain pensions for Seminole War veterans who fought several battles against Native Americans in Florida throughout the early 19th century.

Walls feared the cause of public education would languish if it were left to the states. During the 43rd Congress, he enthusiastically supported a measure to establish a national education fund financed by the sale of public land. Walls addressed this issue in his first major floor speech on February 3, 1872: "I believe that the national Government is the guardian of the liberties of all its subjects," Walls said. "Can [African Americans] protect their liberties without education; and can they be educated under the present condition of society in the States where they were when freed? Can this be done without the aid, assistance, and supervision of the General Government? No, sir, it cannot."[14] The bill passed with amendments protecting a state's right to segregated education and granting states greater control over the distribution of federal funds, but the money was never appropriated.[15] Walls's support for education was further frustrated when the Civil Rights Bill—a battered piece of legislation seeking to eliminate discrimination in public accommodations, first introduced in 1870—came to a vote in February 1875. Opponents managed to excise a clause calling for equal educational opportunities just before the measure came to a vote. Walls was so displeased, he abstained from voting on the final bill on February 5, 1875.[16] Submitting a speech to the *Congressional Record Appendix* just one month after the civil rights vote, Walls assessed the future of the South as Reconstruction began to deteriorate: "I reluctantly confess, after so many years of concessions that unless partisan and sectional feeling shall lose more of its rancor in the future than has been experienced in the past, fundamental law will be disregarded, overthrown, and trampled under foot, and a complete reign of terror and anarchy will rule supreme."[17]

For the 1874 campaign, Florida was split into two congressional districts, and Walls ran in a district covering the eastern half of the peninsula. Nearly the entire population of the new district, which was more than half black, lived between Walls's home in north-central Florida and Jacksonville, on the Atlantic Coast.[18] The state Republican Party remained fractured, and an economic depression further endangered its grip on the state government. Walls returned to Florida after the 43rd Congress to maximize his personal wealth and to muster local political strength for the coming election. He succeeded in both goals. Using his congressional salary, Walls purchased a cotton plantation formerly owned by Confederates. That same year, he was admitted to the Florida bar (legal training was not required in some rural states) and bought the Gainesville *New Era* newspaper. Walls used the *New Era* to campaign for his renomination. In his first editorial, Walls promised to focus on internal improvements and to address the "wants and interests of the people of color," loosely defined as education, thrift, and industry.[19] His local popularity soared, and district Republicans nominated him on the first ballot in August 1874.

In the general election, Walls faced Conservative candidate Jesse J. Finley, a Tennessee native and pre-Civil War member of the Whig Party. Voters divided almost entirely along racial lines; Walls topped Finley by a slim margin of 371 votes out of nearly 17,000 cast, taking 51 percent.[20] He was sworn in to the 44th Congress and assigned to the Committee on Mileage.

Once again Walls was confronted by a challenge to his seat. Finley contested the election, claiming that ballots from several precincts where Walls resided in Alachua County had been miscounted. Finley supporters also claimed that other Alachua County votes were illegal because the eligibility oath was executed improperly (Florida law required this oath from voters whose names did not appear on the precinct's list). Finley also accused Walls's black political ally W. U. Saunders of impersonating a federal marshal at one of the polling places to protect and encourage black voters. Furthermore, Finley supporters suspected Walls's votes in one Columbia County precinct had been tampered with by GOP state senate candidate E. G. Johnson.[21] With Democrats now in power in the House, the Committee on Elections reported 8 to 3 against Walls. As the debate moved to the House Floor, Democratic Speaker Michael Kerr of Indiana allocated time to Members during the two-day discussion. Not one of Walls's six black colleagues was allowed to speak, although Walls briefly took the floor in his own defense. On April 19, 1876, the House adopted the committee report, 135 to 84, with 71 abstentions (including Representatives Robert Smalls of South Carolina and Charles Nash of Louisiana). Walls returned to Florida a week later and, in August 1876, Republican Horatio Bisbee defeated his attempt at renomination.

In November 1876, Walls won a seat in the Florida state senate, where he championed his cause of compulsory public education. Ultimately frustrated by the futility of Republican politics after the collapse of Reconstruction, he took a permanent leave of absence in February 1879. The opportunity to face his old foe Bisbee for the Republican nomination to a Florida U.S. House seat lured him back into politics in 1884. He lost and then ran unsuccessfully in the general election as an Independent candidate.[22] In 1890, Walls lost another bid for the state senate. In 1885, his wife, Helen Fergueson Walls, died and Josiah Walls married her young cousin, Ella Angeline Gass. His successful farm was destroyed when his crops froze in February 1895. Walls subsequently took charge of the farm at Florida Normal College (now Florida A&M University), until his death in Tallahassee on May 15, 1905. Josiah Walls had fallen into such obscurity, no Florida newspaper published his obituary.[23]

FOR FURTHER READING

Klingman, Peter D. *Josiah Walls: Florida's Black Congressman of Reconstruction* (Gainesville: University of Florida Press, 1976).

"Walls, Josiah Thomas," *Biographical Directory of the United States Congress, 1774–Present*, http://bioguide.congress.gov/scripts/biodisplay.pl?index=W000093.

NOTES

1 *Congressional Record,* House, 43rd Cong., 2nd sess. (2 March 1875): A166–169.

2 Most evidence indicates Walls was born a slave. Although at one point he claimed his parents were freed in 1842, he also commented that he had never been free until he enlisted in 1863. See Peter D. Klingman, "Race and Faction in the Public Career of Florida's Josiah T. Walls," in Howard Rabinowitz, ed., *Southern Black Leaders of the Reconstruction Era* (Urbana: University of Illinois Press, 1982): 60.

3 There is no information available about Walls's mother or about the existence of any siblings.

4 From 1868 to 1871, the Florida secretary of state estimated that there were 235 Klan-instigated murders in the eight northern Florida counties. See Joe M. Richardson, *The Negro in the Reconstruction of Florida, 1865–1877* (Tallahassee: Florida State University Press, 1965): 172.

5 Peter D. Klingman, *Josiah Walls: Florida's Black Congressman of Reconstruction* (Gainesville: University of Florida Press, 1976): 12–13, 30–37.

6 Quoted in Klingman, *Josiah Walls*: 38.

7 Michael J. Dubin et al., *U.S. Congressional Elections, 1788–1997* (Jefferson, NC: McFarland & Company, Inc., Publishers, 1998): 217.

8 Klingman, *Josiah Walls*: 46–47.

9 Chester H. Rowell, *A Historical and Legal Digest of All the Contested Election Cases* (Washington, DC: Government Printing Office, 1901): 282–283.

10 The second seat was added as a result of apportionment after the 1870 Census.

11 Dubin et al., *U.S. Congressional Elections, 1788–1997*: 223.

12 Klingman, "Race and Faction": 72 (originally quoted in the *Florida Union,* 5 February 1874).

13 Quoted in Maurine Christopher, *Black Americans in Congress* (New York: Thomas Y. Crowell Company, 1976): 82.

14 *Congressional Globe,* House, 42nd Cong., 2nd sess. (23 February 1872): 809.

15 Klingman, *Josiah Walls*: 78.

16 Christopher, *Black Americans in Congress*: 84.

17 *Congressional Record,* Appendix, 43rd Cong., 2nd sess. (2 March 1875): A166–169.

18 See Stanley B. Parsons et al., *United States Congressional Districts, 1843–1883* (New York: Greenwood Press, 1986): 156.

19 Klingman, *Josiah Walls*: 54.

20 Dubin et al., *U.S. Congressional Elections, 1788–1997*: 230.

21 Suspiciously, Johnson was murdered in August 1875, and the questionable Columbia County ballots were destroyed in a fire at the county Clerk's Office. See Klingman, *Josiah Walls*: 64–69.

22 Dubin et al., *U.S. Congressional Elections, 1788–1997*: 265.

23 Klingman, "Race and Faction": 75.

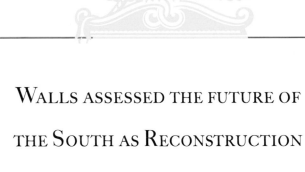

WALLS ASSESSED THE FUTURE OF THE SOUTH AS RECONSTRUCTION BEGAN TO DETERIORATE: "I RELUCTANTLY CONFESS, AFTER SO MANY YEARS OF CONCESSIONS THAT UNLESS PARTISAN AND SECTIONAL FEELING SHALL LOSE MORE OF ITS RANCOR IN THE FUTURE THAN HAS BEEN EXPERIENCED IN THE PAST . . . A COMPLETE REIGN OF TERROR AND ANARCHY WILL RULE SUPREME."

Richard Harvey Cain
1825–1887

UNITED STATES REPRESENTATIVE ★ 1873–1875; 1877–1879
REPUBLICAN FROM SOUTH CAROLINA

Born into freedom, Richard Cain was a pastor, a newspaper editor, and an entrepreneur, making his mark as a writer and a land speculator before being elected to the U.S. House for two nonconsecutive terms. During the 43rd Congress (1873–1875), Cain used his considerable oratorical skills and wit to defend the education clause in the Civil Rights Bill of 1875. He displayed a rich sense of humor, mocking southern white Representatives who pronounced African Americans incapable of learning. Addressing Representative William Robbins of North Carolina, Cain retorted, "The gentleman . . . states that the Negro race is the world's stage actor— the comic dancer all over the land; that he laughs and he dances. . . . Now he dances as an African; then he crouched as a slave."[1] Amid deteriorating conditions for southern blacks at the end of Reconstruction, Cain promoted African-American immigration to the West African colony of Liberia in the 45th Congress (1877–1879).

Richard Harvey Cain was born to free parents on April 12, 1825, in Greenbrier County, Virginia (now West Virginia). His Cherokee mother and black father moved with their son to Gallipolis, Ohio, in 1831. Living in a "free state" afforded Cain an education; he learned to read and write in Sunday school classes. He also worked on steamboats along the Ohio River. In 1844, Cain entered the Methodist ministry; his first assignment was in Hannibal, Missouri. In 1848, frustrated by the Methodists' segregated practices, he transferred to the African Methodist Episcopal (AME) Church. Cain then served as a pastor in Muscatine, Iowa, where he was elected a deacon in 1859. When the Civil War broke out in 1861, he was studying at Wilberforce University in Ohio, one of the first American colleges founded by black men. Cain claimed that he and 115 other Wilberforce students attempted to enlist but were turned away by the Ohio governor.[2]

In 1861, Richard Cain was assigned to serve as pastor at the Bridge Street Church in Brooklyn, New York, where he quickly became involved in politics. As a delegate to a national black convention held in Syracuse, New York, in 1864, he advocated universal manhood suffrage. After the war, the AME Church assigned Cain to the historic Emanuel Church in Charleston, South Carolina. The state government had dissolved the congregation in 1822 because of a slave revolt, but under Cain's leadership the congregation swelled to the largest in the state by 1871. Cain established himself as a writer at the 1865 Charleston Colored People's Convention, penning "Address to the People of South Carolina" in which he set forth some of his lifelong political positions, including his advocacy of land grants for freedmen. To disseminate his views to a larger audience, he founded the *South Carolina Leader* newspaper in 1866 (renamed the *Missionary Record* in 1868). Cain hired future black Representatives Robert Elliott and Alonzo Ransier as associate editors. The exposure he gained from his church and his newspaper helped jump-start Cain's political career. Under Cain, Emanuel's congregation became "one of the strongest political organizations in the state," and its support base grew through the editorial pages of the *Missionary Record*.[3] Cain first served in South Carolina as a delegate to the state constitutional convention in 1868. He was elected to the state senate that same year, heading a commission to investigate South Carolina state senators who voted against the ratification of the 14th Amendment. After an unsuccessful campaign for re-election to the state senate in 1870, Cain was named chair of the party's Charleston branch, and he set his sights on national politics. Known widely as "Daddy Cain," he had firmly established his credentials as a paternal champion of African-American civil rights and social advancement.[4]

While further entrepreneurial endeavors garnered Cain important political connections, they also invited scrutiny and unwanted attention. In 1869, he supported enacting a state land commission and petitioning the U.S. Congress to fund it with a $1 million loan from the Freedmen's Bank.[5] When the commission proved corrupt and ineffective, Cain purchased large tracts of farmland 20 miles outside Charleston in 1871 and attempted to sell them exclusively to freedmen. He established the Ebenezer AME Church on the property, and a new community (Lincolnville) grew out of its congregation.[6] Financiers foreclosed on the project when Cain was unable to meet the mortgage payments. He was later indicted for obtaining money from buyers under false pretenses, but the case never went to trial. His participation in Reconstruction-Era politics was also attended by personal risk; white supremacy groups harassed him, and his daughter would later recall, "We… lived in constant fear at all times."[7]

The 1872 campaign in South Carolina signaled a new reform movement in state politics, particularly following the revelation of corruption on the part of outgoing Governor Robert K. Scott.[8] As a longtime advocate for the removal of corrupt politicians from state government and a cofounder of the Honest Government League, Cain was an attractive candidate for statewide and national office.[9] After failing to obtain the nomination for lieutenant governor, Cain sought an At-Large seat in the U.S. House of Representatives. He defeated his nearest opponent, Independent Democrat Lewis E. Johnson, by more than 38,000 votes, garnering 71 percent of the total in a four-way race.[10]

Upon being sworn into the 43rd Congress, Cain was assigned to the influential Committee on Agriculture as a nod to his state's large farming population. He spent his first term in Congress, however, focusing on the long-awaited Civil Rights Bill. First introduced in 1870, the bill, which called for equal services and accommodations for all races, had been diluted by amendments restricting its scope. Cain, an assertive and entertaining orator, made

two major speeches and on several occasions spoke on the House Floor in support of the legislation. Both of Cain's significant floor speeches, delivered in January 1873, identified the civil rights legislation as the final battle of the Civil War and a fatal blow to slavery, fulfilling "the great mission . . . of giving all the people equal rights."[11] Cain touched on race relations in the South as well as discrimination related to public transportation, hotel accommodations, and education. He attempted to dispel the well-worn argument that civil rights legislation would destroy the possibility of good relations between southern whites and African Americans. On January 10, he said, "Now I am at a loss to see how the friendship of our white friends can be lost to us by simply saying we should be permitted to enjoy the rights enjoyed by other citizens… We do not want any discrimination. I do not ask for any legislation for colored people of this country that is not applied to the white people. All that we ask is equal laws, equal legislation, and equal rights. . . ."[12] Cain also made a case for the contributions of blacks to southern society, observing that black men provided essential labor for the economy and fulfilled many skilled tasks. Cain noted that, "the carpenters, the machinists, the engineers—nearly all the mechanics" in the South were black.[13]

A distilled version of the beleaguered civil rights legislation passed on February 4, 1875, with Cain reluctantly accepting an amendment striking the clause that would have integrated public schools.[14] With the adjournment of the 43rd Congress one month later, Cain's At-Large seat was eliminated due to reapportionment. He did not seek renomination in his home district, which included the large black populations of Charleston, Georgetown, and the Sea Islands, then represented by black Representative Joseph Rainey, but returned to his ministry and local political activity in Charleston.[15]

Cain did not remain out of elective office for long, however. In 1876, he accepted the Republican nomination for a seat in a new district mapped by the Republican state legislature and favorable to the election of its partisans. Cain's new district, which swept from low-country

Charleston to neighboring inland Orangeburg County, was more than 65 percent black.[16] Although Cain defeated his opponent, Michael O'Connor, by more than 8,000 votes (taking 62 percent), that Election Day was one of the most tumultuous in South Carolina history. Violence and corruption wracked the state. The chaos drew national attention when South Carolina, along with two other states, provided two sets of electoral votes for each of the presidential candidates, Republican Rutherford B. Hayes and Democrat Samuel J. Tilden.[17] Citing election irregularities, O'Connor contested Cain's victory. He challenged Cain's credentials, signed by South Carolina Secretary of State Henry E. Hayne, a black man later declared by the state government to be a fugitive from the law. O'Connor also argued that the state canvassers, who had met in secret to count the final votes, were candidates on the Republican ticket along with Cain and thus biased.[18] On October 16, 1877, the second day of the 45th Congress, Cain defended himself against these claims, noting that the secretary who had signed his credentials also had signed those of four other South Carolina Representatives of different races and political parties.[19] That same day the House voted 181 to 89 to seat Cain, and he was assigned to the Committee on Private Claims. O'Connor again tried to unseat him a year later; however, the Elections Committee unanimously supported Cain. The House upheld his election for the second time in an unrecorded vote on May 8, 1878.[20]

The provisions that had been gutted from the Civil Rights Bill of 1875 were at the top of Cain's agenda when he returned to Congress, and he introduced a bill requiring the federal government to set aside monies from the sale of public lands to fund public education. The money would be apportioned to the states based on population. Cain did not use racial or partisan arguments to make his case; providing federal census statistics showing that school attendance was low among the poor of all races and regions, Cain declared, "The education of the nation is paramount, and should not be neglected. We should recognize the absolute necessity of elevating our citizens of whatever class or condition from ignorance, from degradation, from superstition, from pauperism, from crime. It is an accepted axiom, I believe everywhere, that the more intelligent the citizen is the better citizen he is."[21] Although Cain gained the support of several of his colleagues, including Representative Rainey, his proposal never made it out of the Committee on Education and Labor.

Cain's frustration with the collapse of Reconstruction shaped his policy during his second term. He defended the controversial order of South Carolina carpetbagger Governor Daniel Chamberlain to employ military protection for voters in the 1876 election and argued against cutting military budgets, to ensure domestic peace and protect western pioneers from Indian uprisings.[22] Concerned with the erosion of black civil rights in the South, Cain also reconsidered his initial reluctance to support emigration to Liberia.[23] Citing growing black disillusionment in the South, he began to advocate legislation to aid that cause.[24] On March 11, 1878, Cain submitted a bill to establish routes for mail and passenger ships to the West African colony. Although his proposal never left the Committee on Commerce, Cain became a member of the Liberian Exodus Joint Stock Steamship Company in 1877.

Representative Cain's politics became more radical as his term progressed. He joined former black Representatives Robert De Large and Alonso Ransier from South Carolina in supporting the movement of black nationalist Martin Delany to gain power for blacks in the federal government. Cain cooperated with Delany, castigating white Republican leaders who favored light-skinned candidates and scorning mulatto men who endorsed this discrimination. He argued that this practice splintered the Republican Party.[25] He also advocated violent retaliation against the Ku Klux Klan and the like-minded Red Shirts of South Carolina.[26] Such maverick positions cost Cain the Republican nomination in 1878. Instead the party nominated a local white man, Edmund W. M. Mackey, who went on to lose a close election to Cain's former opponent Michael O'Connor.

After leaving Congress, Cain distanced himself from South Carolina politics. In 1880, the AME Church elected Cain to serve as bishop in the Texas–Louisiana Conference. He cofounded Paul Quinn College in Waco, Texas, and served as its president until July 1884. Cain then returned to Washington, DC to serve as bishop of the AME Conference with jurisdiction in the mid-Atlantic and New England states, overseeing his new post from the nation's capital, until he died on January 18, 1887.

FOR FURTHER READING

"Cain, Richard Harvey," *Biographical Directory of the United States Congress, 1774–Present*, http://bioguide. congress.gov/scripts/biodisplay.pl?index=C000022.

Lewis, Ronald L. "Cultural Pluralism and Black Reconstruction: The Public Career of Richard H. Cain," *Crisis* 85 (February 1978): 57–60.

NOTES

1   *Congressional Record*, House, 43rd Cong., 1st sess. (24 January 1874): 901–903.

2   Governor William Dennison likely rejected the black volunteers from Wilberforce. Cain stated that he enlisted in the Union Army when African Americans were permitted to fight, in 1862, but his service cannot be verified. See Maurine Christopher, *Black Americans in Congress* (New York: Thomas Y. Crowell Company, 1976): 88.

3   Quoted in Joel Williamson, *After Slavery: The Negro in South Carolina During Reconstruction, 1861–1877* (Chapel Hill: The University of North Carolina Press, 1965): 206.

4   Peggy Lamson, "Cain, Richard Harvey," *Dictionary of American Negro Biography* (New York: Norton, 1982): 85.

5   Christopher, *Black Americans in Congress*: 88; Thomas C. Holt, *Black Over White: Negro Political Leadership in South Carolina During Reconstruction* (Urbana: University of Illinois Press, 1977): 131.

6   Bo Peterson, "Lincolnville: Church Remains Town's Cornerstone," 22 February 2003, *Charleston Post and Courier*: 1A.

7   Quoted in Eric Foner, *Freedom's Lawmakers: A Directory of Black Officeholders During Reconstruction* (New York: Oxford University Press, 1993): 36. Cain's daughter's name is not known.

8   Williamson, *After Slavery*: 399.

9   C. G. W., "Cain, Richard Harvey," *Dictionary of American Biography* (New York: American Council of Learned Societies, 1973): 404 (hereinafter referred to as *DAB*); Williamson, *After Slavery*: 393.

10 Michael J. Dubin et al., *U.S. Congressional Elections, 1788–1997* (Jefferson, NC: McFarland & Company, Inc., Publishers, 1998): 226. There is no evidence that Cain faced violence or irregularities in his election, as did some of his colleagues.

11 *Congressional Record*, House, 43rd Cong., 1st sess. (10 January 1874): 565–567.

12 Ibid.

13 *Congressional Record*, House, 43rd Cong., 1st sess. (24 January 1874): 901–903.

14 *Congressional Record*, House, 43rd Cong., 1st sess. (3 February 1875): 982.

15 Stanley B. Parsons et al., *United States Congressional Districts, 1843–1883* (New York: Greenwood Press, 1986): 213.

16 Parsons et al., *United States Congressional Districts, 1843–1883*: 213. This percentage was estimated using data provided by Parsons. Though Parsons mentions the redistricting of South Carolina for the 1874 election, he omits a second redistricting for the 1876 election. This second change in district lines eliminated Lexington County from Cain's district. Parsons includes Lexington County, whose population was only 35 percent black, in his calculation. See also Kenneth Martis, *The Historical Atlas of Political Parties in the United States Congress: 1789–1989* (New York: Macmillan, 1989): 128–131.

17 Eric Foner, *Reconstruction: America's Unfinished Revolution, 1863–1877* (New York: Harper and Row Publishers, 1988): 573–575.

18 Christopher, *Black Americans in Congress*: 94.

19 *Congressional Record*, House, 45th Cong., 1st sess. (16 October 1877): 68. Representatives Joseph Rainey and Robert Smalls were black Republicans, and Representatives David Aiken and John Evins were white Democrats.

20 *Congressional Record*, House, 45th Cong., 2nd sess. (8 May 1878): 3274.

21 *Congressional Record*, House, 45th Cong., 3rd sess. (23 January 1879): 684.

22 *Congressional Record*, House, 45th Cong., 2nd sess. (22 May 1878): 3683.

23 *Congressional Record*, House, 43rd Cong., 1st sess. (24 January 1874): 901–903. In this earlier speech on the House Floor Cain declared, "We [Black Americans] feel that we are part and parcel of this great nation; as such, as I said before, we propose to stay here and solve this problem of whether the black race and the white race can live together in this country."

24 Quoted in Foner, *Freedom's Lawmakers*: 36.

25 William C. Hine, "Cain, Richard Harvey," *American National Biography* 4 (New York: Oxford University Press, 1999): 188–189 (hereinafter referred to as *ANB*).

26 C. G. W., "Cain, Richard Harvey," *DAB*; Hine, "Cain, Richard Harvey," *ANB*; Terry L. Seip, *The South Returns to Congress: Men, Economic Measures, and Intersectional Relationships, 1868–1879* (Baton Rouge: Louisiana State University Press, 1983): 76–77.

John Roy Lynch
1847–1939

UNITED STATES REPRESENTATIVE ★ 1873–1877; 1882–1883
REPUBLICAN FROM MISSISSIPPI

The only African-American Representative from Mississippi for a century, following a quick rise in politics at a young age, John Roy Lynch fought to maintain Republican hegemony in his state in the face of violent Democratic opposition. A veteran of the Civil War and, later, the Spanish–American War, Lynch emphasized his rights as an American citizen on the House Floor. "It is certainly known by southern as well as northern men that the colored people of this country are thoroughly American," he declared. "Born and raised upon American soil and under the influence of American institutions; not American citizens by adoption, but by birth."[1] An outspoken advocate for the Civil Rights Bill of 1875 and an active Republican throughout his long life, Lynch later challenged a major school of interpretation that disparaged black political activity during the Reconstruction Era.

John Roy Lynch was born into slavery near Vidalia, Louisiana, on September 10, 1847. His Irish immigrant father, Patrick Lynch, managed the Tacony Plantation, and his mother, Catherine White, was a mulatto slave. He had two older brothers, William and Edward. John Lynch became the personal valet of his owner, Mississippian Alfred W. Davis, until Davis was drafted by the Confederate Army in 1862. Lynch recalled Davis as "reasonable, fair, and considerate."[2] After being emancipated at the end of the war, Lynch worked as a cook for the 49th Illinois Volunteers regiment and performed other odd jobs. He subsequently managed a photographer's studio. Lynch's business prospered, and he invested in local real estate.

Lynch rose rapidly in politics because of the opportunities that were available to black men in Reconstruction-Era Mississippi. He began his political career in 1868 by speaking at the local Republican club in favor of a new Mississippi constitution. The following year, he served as an assistant secretary at the Republican state convention. In April 1869, the local Republican Party selected Lynch to advise Reconstruction Governor Adelbert Ames about various candidates for political positions in Natchez, Mississippi. When the list of appointments was unveiled, Lynch professed to be surprised to find he had been appointed justice of the peace. The local favorite for the appointment, Reverend H. P. Jacobs, accused Lynch of stealing the position.[3] In November 1869, Lynch won his first elected office, serving in the Mississippi state house of representatives. In January 1872, colleagues selected the 24-year-old as speaker.

Lynch sought a U.S. House seat representing coastal Mississippi, a district that he largely created as presiding officer in the state house of representatives. The district encompassed the southern quarter of the state, including his Natchez home. Lynch enjoyed broad support from his district, whose population was 55 percent black.[4] He defeated incumbent Republican Legrand Perce for the nomination, noting his vulnerability to Democratic accusations that he was a carpetbagger. Facing Democratic Judge Hiram Cassidy in the general election, Lynch conducted a strong campaign organized by a trio of influential black politicians: William McCary, Robert Wood, and Robert Fitzhugh. In a quiet election in which both candidates canvassed the state and engaged in joint debates, Lynch defeated Cassidy, taking 15,091 votes (65 percent).[5] When the 43rd Congress (1873–1875) convened, 26-year-old John Lynch was its youngest Member.[6] He received appointments to the Committee on Mines and the Committee on Expenditures in the Interior Department.

Like other African Americans in Congress, Lynch enthusiastically promoted the Civil Rights Bill, which outlawed discrimination on public transportation and in

public accommodations and provided for equal education for the races.[7] Speaking twice before his colleagues on an issue that preoccupied much of the 43rd Congress, Lynch argued that civil rights legislation would help Black Americans achieve political independence, and claimed Democratic opposition to the bill forced freedmen to support the Republican Party. Despite Democrats' tactical attempts to prevent him from speaking, Lynch addressed his colleagues on February 3, 1875, just before the Civil Rights Bill came to a vote. Maintaining that the legislation would not force blacks and whites to mix socially, as southern Democrats feared, Lynch said, "It is not social rights that we desire. We have enough of that already. What we ask for is protection in the enjoyment of public rights—rights that are or should be accorded to every citizen alike."[8] The legislation that came to a final vote on February 4, 1875, was severely weakened by amendments, but Lynch was among the majority supporting the bill.

Lynch returned home to a crisis in Mississippi in the spring of 1875. Democrats sought to seize power by implementing their Mississippi Plan, which involved using economic coercion and violence to exclude black voters and Republican politicians at the state level. Governor Ames asked for federal troops to keep the peace but was rebuffed by the administration of President Ulysses S. Grant. Beginning his campaign for re-election, Lynch was doubtful he would retain his seat in the face of formidable Democratic opposition. Though he was supported by loyal members of his party, many white Republicans who had supported him in 1872 became Democrats in 1874.[9] Facing Democratic candidate Roderick Seal, Lynch traveled throughout his district, despite the threat of being physically attacked by white supremacists.[10] In a violent, confused campaign, he narrowly defended his seat, taking 13,746 votes (51 percent).[11] Lynch was the only Republican in the Mississippi House delegation to survive a Democratic sweep in the polls. Retaining his assignment on the Committee on Mines and Mining, Lynch took his seat in the 44th Congress (1875–1877).

Although a record eight African-American Members

(including Senator Blanche K. Bruce of Mississippi) took the oath of office in December 1875, the Democratic Party controlled the House for the first time since before the Civil War.[12] Lynch spent the remainder of his second term defending Congressional Reconstruction in the South. Throughout 1876, he attacked the violent practices of White Leaguers and pleaded for political parties in the South to cease dividing along racial lines. He called the White League "an organization which has been brought into existence by the bad men of the Democratic Party for the purpose of securing position by the power of the bullet and not by the power of the ballot."[13] Lynch's pleas fell on deaf ears approaching the 1876 election. Traveling home to Mississippi to seek re-election, Lynch faced a hostile campaign against Democrat James R. Chalmers, a former Confederate general and cavalry commander. Having restored a majority in the state legislature, Democrats reconfigured Lynch's district to their advantage. His new district, called the "shoestring district" because it narrowly hugged the Mississippi River, was the only Republican-dominated district. The new boundaries squeezed the majority of the state's GOP voters into one district, almost guaranteeing a Democratic Mississippi delegation.[14] Having secured the Republican nomination without opposition, Lynch made his trademark canvass of the new district. Although he was able to prevent violent riots, which were common in other parts of the state, his stump speeches were often interrupted by jeers and groans from the crowd. Lynch characterized this activity as "harmless" compared with the "riot and bloodshed which had been contemplated."[15] Chalmers defeated Lynch, taking 15,788 votes. Lynch garnered only 12,386 votes (44 percent) and contested the election.[16] The Committee on Elections, dominated by Democrats, who controlled the House, refused to hear his case.

After leaving Congress, Lynch remained active in the Mississippi Republican Party, working with Senator Bruce to maintain party unity in the face of dwindling federal support. However, in 1880, Lynch's interest in national politics was renewed when his former House colleague James Garfield of Ohio ran for President on the Republican ticket. Seeking a seat in the "shoestring district," Lynch gained the support of his old allies and, with the blessing and support of Senator Bruce, barely won the nomination in a four-way race.[17] Riding the statewide strength of the Democratic Party, Chalmers defeated Lynch with 63 percent of the vote, garnering 9,172 votes to Lynch's 5,393.[18] Lynch contested the election. When his case came before the Committee on Elections on April 27, 1882, Lynch argued that in five counties, more than 5,000 of his votes had been counted for Chalmers. He further asserted that several thousand Republican ballots had been thrown out after a secret hearing because of technicalities such as a clerical failure to send a list of names with the returns and the presence of unusual marks on the ballots.[19] Lynch's strongest arguments were based on Chalmers's remarks that Lynch's votes had been thrown out and that he (Chalmers) was "in favor of using every means short of violence to preserve [for] intelligent white people of Mississippi supreme control of political affairs."[20] The committee ruled in Lynch's favor, and on April 29, 1882, the House voted 125 to 83 to seat him; 62 Members abstained. He received positions on the Committee on Education and Labor and the Committee on the Militia.

The legislative agenda of the 47th Congress (1881–1883), unlike Reconstruction-Era Congresses, focused on internal improvements and tariff legislation instead of on conditions in the South and freed slaves. Arriving late in the first session, Lynch concentrated on economic legislation favoring his Mississippi constituents; he requested funds to reimburse an orphanage in Natchez that was damaged in the Civil War, sought appropriations to improve the shoreline of the Mississippi River, and split the state into two judicial districts. On a national level, Lynch submitted legislation to reimburse depositors who lost money when the Freedmen's Savings and Trust Company failed. His colleagues on the Education and Labor Committee reported favorably on the bill, but it died in the House Rules Committee. He also sought appropriations for a National Board of Health, citing

devastation from the 1878 yellow fever epidemic that swept through the South. Based on personal experience, Lynch also appealed to the House to revise the statute limiting reimbursement for losses incurred contesting an election, believing a $2,000 cap would deter all but the wealthy candidates.

Lynch faced Democrat Henry S. Van Eaton, a local judge, for re-election in 1882. A skilled debater aided by the Natchez newspapers' harsh treatment of Lynch during the campaign, Van Eaton defeated Lynch 7,615 votes (53 percent) to 6,706. John Lynch made two more unsuccessful bids for Congress. In 1884, Van Eaton defeated Lynch with 60 percent of the vote. Lynch later lost to Democrat Thomas Stockdale in 1886, polling less than a third of the vote.[21]

After his congressional career, Lynch returned to Mississippi to oversee his real estate, but remained active in politics. He served as a Mississippi member of the Republican National Committee from 1884 to 1889. In 1884, he was a delegate to the Republican National Convention. Lynch served as a temporary chairman and was accorded the honor of delivering a keynote address, making him the only African American to deliver a keynote address at a national political convention until 1968.[22] He returned to the Republican National Convention in 1900 to serve on the committee on platform and resolutions. On December 18, 1884, Lynch married Ella Wickham Somerville, a Creole mulatto woman from a prominent southern family. The couple had one daughter (her name is not known). Lynch was admitted to the Mississippi bar and opened a Washington, DC, law office in 1897, practicing for one year. In 1897, the William McKinley administration appointed him a major in the U.S. Army and paymaster of volunteers in the Spanish–American War. After divorcing his wife in 1900, Lynch spent three years in Cuba. His orders subsequently took him to San Francisco, Hawaii, and the Philippines. Lynch retired as a major in 1911. Upon his return, he married Cora Williamson, and the couple moved to Chicago, where Lynch practiced law.

In reaction to negative literature on the Reconstruction Era, Lynch published *The Facts of Reconstruction* in 1913. In 1917 and 1918, he published two articles in the *Journal of Negro History* challenging historian James Rhodes's attack on Republican governments during the postwar era. The articles were published in 1922 in the book *Some Historical Errors of James Ford Rhodes*. During the 1930s, Lynch began writing his autobiography, *Reminiscences of an Active Life*, which was published in 1970. He was editing the manuscript when he died at age 92 on November 2, 1939, in Chicago.

FOR FURTHER READING

Franklin, John Hope. "John Roy Lynch: Republican Stalwart from Mississippi," in Howard Rabinowitz, ed., *Southern Black Leaders of the Reconstruction Era* (Urbana: University of Illinois Press, 1982).

"Lynch, John Roy," *Biographical Directory of the United States Congress, 1774–Present*, http://bioguide.congress.gov/scripts/biodisplay.pl?index=L000533.

Lynch, John Roy. *The Facts of Reconstruction* (New York: Arno Press, reprint 1968).

_____. *The Late Election in Mississippi* (Washington: Government Printing Office, 1877).

_____. *Reminiscences of an Active Life,* edited and with an introduction by John Hope Franklin (Chicago: The University of Chicago Press, 1970).

_____. *Some Historical Errors of James Ford Rhodes* (Boston: The Cornhill Publishing Co., 1922).

MANUSCRIPT COLLECTIONS

Duke University, Rare Book, Manuscript, and Special Collections Library (Durham, NC) *Papers:* In the George Gifford Papers, 1860–1920, 546 items. Subjects include John Roy Lynch.

Library of Congress, Manuscript Division (Washington, DC) *Microfilm:* In the Robert H. Terrell Papers, ca. 1870–1925, four microfilm reels. Correspondents include John R. Lynch. A finding aid is available in the library. *Microfilm:* In the Carter G. Woodson Collection of Negro Papers and Related Documents, ca. 1803–1936, 10 microfilm reels. Subjects include John Roy Lynch.

Mississippi Department of Archives and History (Jackson, MS) *Papers:* 1873–1877, four items. The papers of John Roy Lynch include a manuscript of his autobiography, a photograph, and three letters.

The Morgan Library, Department of Literary and Historical Manuscripts (New York, NY) *Papers:* 1873, one item. A letter from Adelbert Ames to George H. Williams, Attorney General, written on April 16, 1873. In the letter, Adelbert Ames recommends John Roy Lynch as U.S. Marshal for the Southern District of Mississippi.

NOTES

1   *Congressional Record*, House, 44th Cong., 2nd sess. (12 August 1876): 5540–5543.

2   Lynch became Davis's slave in a roundabout way. Having purchased his family just before his death in April 1849, Patrick Lynch willed them to family friend, William Deal, requesting that they be treated as free people. Deal ignored the request and sold the Lynches to Davis in Natchez, Mississippi. Davis, who also purchased Tacony Plantation, learned of the family's misfortune and allowed Catherine Lynch to hire out her time while looking after his Mississippi home. See John Roy Lynch, *Reminiscences of an Active Life: The Autobiography of John Roy Lynch*, edited with an introduction by John Hope Franklin (Chicago: University of Chicago Press, 1970): 23.

3   Maurine Christopher, *Black Americans in Congress* (New York: Thomas Y. Crowell Company, 1976): 56.

4   Kenneth Martis, *The Historical Atlas of Political Parties in the United States Congress: 1789–1989* (New York: Macmillan, 1989): 126–127; Stanley B. Parsons et al., *United States Congressional Districts, 1843–1883* (New York: Greenwood Press, 1986): 184–185.

5   Michael J. Dubin et al., *U.S. Congressional Elections, 1788–1997* (Jefferson, NC: McFarland & Company, Inc., Publishers, 1998): 224.

6   Lynch remains the youngest African American to date to serve in Congress. Though the 43rd Congress did not convene until December 1, 1873 (after John Lynch's 26th birthday), Lynch's term of service officially commenced on March 3, 1873 (while Lynch was still 25). Harold Ford, Jr. of Tennessee was also 26 when he was elected and sworn in to Congress on January 3, 1997.

7   John Hope Franklin, "John Roy Lynch: Republican Stalwart from Mississippi," Howard Rabinowitz ed., *Southern Black Leaders of the Reconstruction Era* (Urbana: University of Illinois Press, 1982): 46.

8   *Congressional Record*, House, 43rd Cong., 2nd sess. (3 February 1875): 943–947.

9   Franklin, "John Roy Lynch: Republican Stalwart From Mississippi": 46.

10 Ibid., 47.

11 Dubin et al., *U.S. Congressional Elections, 1788–1997*: 234.

12 Office of the Clerk, "Party Divisions," available at http://clerk.house.gov/art_history/house_history/partyDiv.html.

13 *Congressional Record*, House, 44th Cong., 1st sess. (15 June 1876): 3824–3825.

14 Franklin, "John Roy Lynch: Republican Stalwart from Mississippi": 47.

15 Lynch, *Reminiscences of an Active Life*: 185–186.

16 Dubin et al., *U.S. Congressional Elections, 1788–1997*: 238.

17 Lynch, *Reminiscences of an Active Life*: 217–219, 223.

18 Dubin et al., *U.S. Congressional Elections, 1788–1997*: 252.

19 Christopher, *Black Americans in Congress*: 63.

20 *Congressional Record*, House, 47th Cong., 1st sess. (27 April 1882): 3376–3394.

21 Dubin et al., *U.S. Congressional Elections, 1788–1997*: 259, 267, 274.

22 Mississippi Senator Blanche K. Bruce was the first African American to preside over a national political convention (at the 1880 Republican Convention); see Thura Mack, "John Roy Lynch," in Jessie Carney Smith, ed., *Notable Black American Men* (Farmington Hills, MI: Gale Research, Inc., 1999): 145.

Alonzo Jacob Ransier
1834–1882

UNITED STATES REPRESENTATIVE ★ 1873–1875
REPUBLICAN FROM SOUTH CAROLINA

South Carolina's first black lieutenant governor, Alonzo Ransier had a reputation for fighting corruption that helped him win election to the 43rd Congress (1873–1875). An observer on the House Floor described him as "a man of great courage and sagacity," concluding, "Mr. Ransier's political career has been a varied and powerful one, and his strong, tough, active brain makes him an effective and worthy worker in the House."[1]

Alonzo Jacob Ransier was born to free parents—likely Haitian immigrants of mulatto French background—on January 3, 1834, in Charleston, South Carolina.[2] As a free black child, he received a limited education before beginning work as a shipping clerk at age 16. Free African Americans were prohibited by state law from holding jobs other than those involving manual labor, and his employer was brought to trial; however, the law generally often went unenforced, and, in Ransier's case, the judge levied a fine of only one cent plus court costs.[3]

Ransier's prewar freedom provided him the financial security and prominence to establish himself quickly in postwar South Carolina politics. In 1865, the military governor of the Carolinas, General Daniel Sickles, appointed Ransier as register of elections. In October 1865, Ransier participated in a Charleston meeting of the Friends of Equal Rights and was part of a delegation charged with presenting a petition to the U.S. Congress.[4] Ransier's political star rose in 1868. In January, he served as a delegate from Charleston to the South Carolina constitutional convention. The following October, he took over the post of Republican state central committee chairman after Benjamin F. Randolph was assassinated by the Ku Klux Klan.[5] The following November, he served as a South Carolina elector for President Ulysses S. Grant and was elected to the state house of representatives where he served one term.

Although he was not a dominant personality in South Carolina politics, Ransier became a well-recognized and popular leader in Charleston. In 1870, he reached what is widely considered the apex of his political career when he defeated ex-Confederate General M. C. Butler to become South Carolina's first black lieutenant governor, under Governor Robert K. Scott.[6] His position afforded him an opportunity to preside over the state senate as well as the Southern States Convention in Columbia in 1871. Ransier's tenure in South Carolina's executive government was remarkable for his honesty in a notoriously corrupt administration.[7]

In August 1872, Representative Robert De Large declined the renomination for his coastal South Carolina seat in the U.S. House of Representatives, citing poor health. Local Republicans selected Ransier to represent the district, whose population was 70 percent black.[8] Ransier defeated Independent Republican candidate General William Gurney with 20,061 votes (75 percent) in the general election.[9]

When he was sworn in to the 43rd Congress Ransier received De Large's assignment to the Committee on Manufactures.[10] His earnest but conventional attempts to look after the interests of his coastal Carolina constituents in the House were typically ignored. He introduced measures to erect a public building in Beaufort, South Carolina, and to rebuild the war-damaged west wing of the Citadel Academy in Charleston. Ransier also requested $100,000 to improve Charleston Harbor. However, none of these bills passed.

Representative Ransier broke from his understated legislative style to speak passionately on several occasions in 1874 during debate on the Civil Rights Bill. On February 7, Ransier delivered a speech, which was later published and distributed, asserting that African Americans'

resistance to punishing ex-Confederates demonstrated a desire for racial harmony and praising the black soldiers who fought for the Union in the Civil War. He stressed freedmen's overwhelming loyalty to the Republican Party, stating that such fidelity should be rewarded by the passage of the Civil Rights Bill. Ransier also focused on the portion of the bill calling for equal educational opportunities, discussing the advantages of integrated education, and citing mixed-race programs at Oberlin College and at Wilberforce, Harvard, and Yale Universities. Ransier believed equal rights and opportunities in education would allow talented black men to achieve a respectable position in their communities, ultimately curbing discrimination. "Let the doors of the public school house be thrown open to us alike," he declared, "if you mean to give these people equal rights at all, or to protect them in the exercise of the rights and privileges attaching to all free men and citizens of our country."[11] For Ransier, the legislation rose above party politics. He pleaded with opponents not to defeat the bill to spite corrupt Republican state governments: "Because some officials in [the South] have abused the public confidence and prostituted their office should violence be done to a great principle of justice and . . . a race denied therein equal rights in a government like ours? It cannot be. Let justice be done though the heavens fall."[12] When the Civil Rights Bill came to a vote in February 1875, the education clause had been eliminated. Ransier was so disappointed, he declined to vote.[13]

Upon returning to South Carolina in 1874, Ransier was outspoken about his disenchantment with the corruption in scalawag Governor Franklin Moses's administration. The governor's crimes were infamous. Having paid off some of his personal debt with public funds and sold executive pardons to prisoners, Moses resisted arrest by calling the South Carolina militia to defend him. His well-paid allies in the state legislature saved him from impeachment, and Moses carefully placed his friends in key patronage positions to maintain his political control.[14] Ransier aligned himself with a faction in the South Carolina Republican Party calling for statewide reform. Ransier's insubordination cost him the renomination for his congressional seat at the district convention. He lost the bid to Charles W. Buttz (whom Ransier accused of buying the nomination for $4,000). Despite his break with local Republicans, Ransier supported the party ticket in November. Buttz lost the election to Independent Republican Edmund Mackey, who also opposed the Moses administration, but the seat was declared vacant in July 1876 when Buttz contested the election.[15]

Soon after Ransier left Congress, his wife, Louisa Ann Carroll Ransier, died giving birth to their 11th child, whom Ransier named Charles Sumner Ransier for the late Massachusetts Senator.[16] Alonzo Ransier married Mary Louisa McKinlay in 1876. In an effort to provide for his large family, he secured an appointment as U.S. Internal Revenue Service collector in Charleston, despite his abhorrence of corruption and hence, political patronage. He later appealed to Governor Daniel Chamberlain for a position in the South Carolina state government when his tenure as a tax collector came to an end.[17] Ransier did not receive a nomination, but worked instead as a night watchman in a customs house and as a municipal street sweeper. Lapsing into poverty by 1880, he lived in a crowded Charleston boarding house. Ransier died in obscurity on August 17, 1882, at age 48.[18]

FOR FURTHER READING

"Ransier, Alonzo Jacob," *Biographical Directory of the United States Congress, 1774–Present*, http://bioguide.congress.gov/scripts/biodisplay.pl?index=R000060.

MANUSCRIPT COLLECTION

College of Charleston, Avery Research Center for African-American History & Culture (Charleston, SC). *Papers:* In the Lillian Ransier Wright Papers, 1945–1995, 0.25 linear feet. The papers contain information on Reconstruction Era African-American politicians, specifically Alonzo Jacob Ransier.

NOTES

1   Marie La Baron, "Colored Congressmen: How the Enfranchised Race Is Represented in Washington," 12 April 1874, *St. Louis Daily Globe*: 3.

2   The names of Ransier's parents are not known. It also is not known whether Ransier had any siblings.

3   William C. Hine, "Ransier, Alonzo Jacob," *American National Biography* 18 (New York: Oxford University Press, 1999): 151–152 (hereinafter referred to as *ANB*); see also Stephen Middleton, ed., *Black Congressmen During Reconstruction: A Documentary Sourcebook* (Westport, CT: Praeger, 2002): 297.

4   There is no record of the petition in the *House Journal* or the *Congressional Globe* for the 39th Congress.

5   For more information, see Daniel W. Hamilton, "Randolph, Benjamin Franklin," *ANB 18*: 120–121.

6   Thomas Holt, "Ransier, Alonzo Jacob," *Dictionary of American Negro Biography* (New York: Norton, 1982): 511–512. Hine calls the early 1870s the "pinnacle" of Ransier's political career; see Hine, "Ransier, Alonzo Jacob," *ANB*.

7   Maurine Christopher, *Black Americans in Congress* (New York: Thomas Y. Crowell Company, 1976): 101.

8   Stanley B. Parsons et al., *United States Congressional Districts, 1843–1883* (New York: Greenwood Press, 1986): 212–213.

9   Michael J. Dubin et al., *U.S. Congressional Elections, 1788–1997* (Jefferson, NC: McFarland and Company Inc., Publishers, 1998): 226.

10   As Ransier's election as lieutenant governor is considered the pinnacle of his political career, there are no detailed accounts of his first bid for the U.S. House of Representatives.

11   *Congressional Record*, House, 43rd Cong., 1st sess. (7 February 1874): 1314.

12   *Congressional Record*, House, 43rd Cong., 1st sess. (9 June 1874): 4786.

13   *Congressional Record*, House, 43rd Cong., 2nd sess. (4 February 1875): 1011.

14   Christine Doyle, "Moses, Franklin J., Jr.," *ANB* 15: 971–972.

15   Chester H. Rowell, *A Historical and Legal Digest of All the Contested Election Cases* (Washington, DC: Government Printing Office, 1901): 320–321.

16   The names of Ransier's 10 other children are not known.

17   Quoted in Hine, "Ransier, Alonzo Jacob," *ANB* 18.

18   Ibid.

James Thomas Rapier
1837–1883

UNITED STATES REPRESENTATIVE ★ 1873–1875
REPUBLICAN FROM ALABAMA

A freeborn Alabamian educated in Canada, James Thomas Rapier fended off death threats from the Ku Klux Klan, rose to the top of the state Republican Party, and won a seat in the 43rd Congress (1873–1875). Rapier was one of seven black Representatives who fought for the passage of the major Civil Rights Bill of 1875. "Mr. Speaker," he declared on the House Floor, "nothing short of a complete acknowledgement of my manhood will satisfy me."[1]

James Thomas Rapier was born in Florence, Alabama, on November 13, 1837, to John H. and Susan Rapier. He had three older brothers: Richard, John, Jr., and Henry. The Rapiers were wealthy and well established in Florence. John Rapier, Sr., was a freed slave who had a lucrative business as a barber for 40 years.[2] Susan Rapier was a freeborn mulatto from Baltimore, Maryland, who died in 1841 during childbirth.[3] Five-year-old James Rapier and his brother, John, Jr., went to live with their paternal grandmother, Sally Thomas. Supported by his grandmother's work as a cleaning woman, James Rapier attended a secret school for black children from 1854 to 1856 but also spent a great deal of time drinking and gambling on riverboats.[4] Disappointed with his son's behavior, in 1856 John Rapier, Sr., sent him to live with another family member in the experimental black community of Buxton, Ontario, Canada. While living in Buxton, which was inhabited entirely by fugitive slaves, Rapier experienced a religious conversion and decided to devote his life to helping his race. He later attended a normal school in Toronto, earning a teaching certificate in 1863, and returned to Buxton as an instructor.[5] After following the events of the Civil War from Canada, Rapier returned to Nashville in late 1864. There he worked briefly as a reporter for a northern newspaper. With his father's help, he purchased 200 acres of land in Maury County,

Tennessee, and, over time, became a successful cotton planter. A self-described loner, he never married.[6]

The end of the Civil War provided Rapier opportunities in politics. His first political experience was a keynote address at the Tennessee Negro Suffrage Convention in Nashville in 1865. His father's illness and his own disillusionment with the restoration of former Confederates to power in the state government prompted Rapier's return to Florence, where he rented 550 acres along the Tennessee River. His continued success as a planter allowed him to hire black tenant farmers. He also financed sharecroppers with low-interest loans. In March 1867, when freedmen could vote in Alabama, he called a local meeting to elect a black registrar. His father, John Rapier, Sr., won the election, and James Rapier was unanimously chosen to represent the county at the Alabama Republican convention. James Rapier served as the convention's vice chairman and directed the platform committee. Although he sought equality among the races, Rapier emerged as a moderate politician. He did not ignore the fears of white Alabamians, and, consequently, opposed the total disfranchisement of former Confederates and the redistribution of seized land. Rapier recognized that a political alliance between Republican whites and blacks—though fragile—was necessary for the party's success in Alabama.[7] In October 1867, he served as a delegate to the Alabama constitutional convention, where he advanced the Republican platform as the only black man representing his district.

Rapier traveled to Washington, DC, in 1869 to attend the founding convention of the National Negro Labor Union (NNLU). The union organized to protect black laborers, to help sharecroppers, and to improve educational and economic opportunities for freedmen. The NNLU chose Rapier as its vice president in 1870. He opened

IMAGE COURTESY OF MOORLAND–SPINGARN RESEARCH CENTER, HOWARD UNIVERSITY

an Alabama branch in 1871, serving as president and executive chairman, and attended three more national conferences throughout his career. Rapier's increased name recognition allowed him to secure the Republican nomination for secretary of state in 1870. The first black man to run for statewide office in Alabama, he lost the position primarily because white Republicans remained uneasy about a black candidate.[8] Rapier was appointed as a federal internal revenue assessor with the assistance of black Alabama Representative Benjamin Turner.[9] By the early 1870s, Rapier was one of the most powerful black politicians in the state.

In August 1872, Alabama Republican Party leaders determined it would be nearly impossible to persuade native-born white Alabamians to vote for an African American in the upcoming congressional elections.[10] Although constituents from a district representing the state's southeastern corner did not favor carpetbaggers, incumbent Charles Buckley, originally from New York, maintained a strong base among conservatives. Furthermore, Buckley represented a district in which freedmen were a minority, making up 44 percent of the population.[11] Defying party leaders, Rapier sought the district's Republican nomination. He used his recently founded newspaper, the Montgomery *Republican State Sentinel* (the state's first black-owned and -operated news source), to crusade for the Republican Party, freedmen's rights, and the re-election of President Ulysses S. Grant over Liberal Republican Horace Greeley.[12] Rapier hoped his newspaper would improve communication between the races in Alabama and campaigned on the promise that he would represent equally voters in his district, regardless of their race.[13] At a late-summer convention, Rapier easily gained the Republican nomination, receiving 25 delegate votes to Buckley's five.[14]

In the general election, Rapier faced Democrat and Liberal Republican candidate William C. Oates, an ex-Confederate with a debilitating war wound. Rapier tirelessly traversed the district, speaking in 36 towns in as many days. He espoused his equal rights platform before the crowds and promised to support national legislation providing land for tenant farmers.[15] Congressionally enacted federal enforcement acts (the Ku Klux Klan bills) temporarily quelled Klan violence, making for a peaceful election.[16] Rapier defeated Oates with 19,397 votes (55 percent), becoming Alabama's second black Representative in Congress.[17] Heading to Washington, Rapier exuded confidence, declaring, "No man in the state wields more influence than I."[18] Before the 43rd Congress convened in late 1873, he traveled to Vienna, Austria, as Alabama's commissioner to the Fifth International Exposition. Rapier noted that once he stepped onto foreign soil, "distinctions on account of my color ceased."[19]

In the 43rd Congress, Rapier soon earned a reputation as a prudent and diplomatic legislator. Though a forceful and outstanding orator, he rarely embellished his speeches with rhetorical flourishes. An observer in the gallery noted, "Mr. Rapier is an insatiable reader, which does not make him, fortunately, less original in expression of his own ideas. . . . He is a plain, forcible speaker."[20] Rapier's first act as a Representative, on January 5, 1874, was to introduce legislation designating Montgomery, Alabama, a federal customs collection site. The passage of the measure, which would boost the city's economy, was considered Rapier's greatest legislative achievement, and President Grant signed the bill into law on June 20, 1874. Rapier's subsequent attempts to gain federal funding for improvement projects in Alabama were less successful, and he became involved in economic debates that usually divided along sectional lines. Rapier voted in favor of railroad regulation and called for increased currency circulation, promoting economic conditions favorable to the agrarian south and west. These debates signaled a significant split between southern and northern Republicans that proved damaging in future national elections.[21]

Rapier's experience as a teacher and a labor organizer earned him a position on the Committee on Education and Labor, but he focused his first term on advancing the controversial Civil Rights Bill. Rapier hosted strategy meetings in his Washington home in an attempt to pass the longstanding bill, which sought equal accommodations on public transportation and in lodging as well as equal education for blacks and whites. On June 9, 1874, Rapier spoke on the House Floor in favor of the bill, largely recounting his personal experiences with discrimination.[22] Deeply disappointed with the eviscerated final measure that came before the House at the end of the 43rd Congress, Rapier, along with the other Alabama Republicans, voted nevertheless in its favor. The measure passed 162 to 99.[23]

The Civil Rights Bill had not yet come to a vote in July 1874 when Rapier returned to Alabama in anticipation of a close re-election contest. Divisions among southeastern Alabama Republicans were his greatest obstacle. Earlier that year, two factions split over the case of a federal judge credited with enforcing laws against the Ku Klux Klan. Rapier refused to take sides, yet most of his supporters allied themselves with the judge. Meanwhile, emboldened by state and federal ambivalence, the Klan attained new power in Alabama. As the election approached, one conservative Democratic newspaper said, "We will accept no result but that of blood."[24] White Alabama Democrats then proceeded to launch a campaign of economic coercion: Major business owners refused to hire black men or anyone who swore allegiance to the Republican Party.[25] Rapier approached the mounting opposition by running an aggressive campaign. He attempted to assuage white fears about the Civil Rights Bill by maintaining that the legislation did not require integrated schools or social equality but merely gave blacks equal opportunity and funding.[26] He traversed the state in a fashion reminiscent of his 1872 campaign, though threats from the Ku Klux Klan often disrupted his itinerary.[27] Rapier's pleas to federal authorities to ensure a peaceful election, including a personal telegram to U.S. Attorney General George H. Williams, went unanswered.[28] In the chaos that ensued,

more than 100 people were killed and scores of black voters stayed away from the polls.[29] With the freedmen's vote eliminated, Conservative Democrats swept the elections, taking two-thirds of the state offices. Attorney and former Confederate Army Major Jeremiah Williams edged out Rapier, taking 20,180 votes (51 percent) to Rapier's 19,124. Rapier contested the election, without success, in the new Democratic House.[30]

In 1876, Rapier moved to Lowndes County near Montgomery to run for a congressional seat for the only remaining district with a black majority (65 percent) after gerrymandering by the Democratic state legislature.[31] Rapier defeated incumbent black Representative Jeremiah Haralson in the primary election, and Haralson subsequently ran in the general election as an Independent. While both Rapier and Haralson advocated civil rights, voter protection, and increased leadership roles for freedmen, their personalities were drastically different: Haralson was outspoken, brash, and rhetorical, whereas Rapier was prudent and polished.[32] The two men split the black vote—Haralson won 8,675 votes (34 percent) and Rapier won 7,236 (28 percent)—handing the election to white Democrat Charles Shelley, who emerged with 9,655 votes (38 percent).[33]

For his service, the Republican Party rewarded Rapier with an appointment as a collector for the Internal Revenue Service in July 1878. That same year, Rapier transformed the *Republican Sentinel* into the *Haynesville Times* and began a call for black emigration to the West—a movement he supported financially and by testifying before a Senate committee. In 1882 and 1883, Rapier fended off attempts by political enemies to remove him from his post as a collector, but failing health forced him to resign. He was appointed a disbursing officer for a federal building in Montgomery just before he died of pulmonary tuberculosis on May 31, 1883.

FOR FURTHER READING

Feldman, Eugene Pieter Romayn. *Black Power in Old Alabama: The Life and Stirring Times of James T. Rapier, Afro-American Congressman from Alabama, 1839–1883* (Chicago: Museum of African American History, 1968).

"Rapier, James Thomas," *Biographical Directory of the United States Congress, 1774–Present,* http://bioguide. congress.gov/scripts/biodisplay.pl?index=R000064.

Schweninger, Loren. "James T. Rapier of Alabama and the Noble Cause of Reconstruction," in Howard Rabinowitz, ed., *Southern Black Leaders of the Reconstruction Era* (Urbana: University of Illinois Press, 1982).

_____. *James T. Rapier and Reconstruction* (Chicago: University of Chicago Press, 1978).

MANUSCRIPT COLLECTIONS

Alabama Department of Archives and History (Montgomery, AL) *Papers:* In the Eugene Feldman Papers, 1856–1978, 0.66 cubic feet. The papers collected by Eugene Feldman consist of photocopied letters written to the U.S. Department of the Treasury in 1882 in an unsuccessful effort to prevent James T. Rapier's dismissal as an U.S. Revenue Tax Collector in the 2nd District of Alabama. Most of the original letters appear to be in the National Archives in Washington, DC. There is a small collection of letters (photocopies), circa 1856–1857, from James T. Rapier to his brother, John H. Rapier. The papers also contain drafts of an article by Eugene Feldman about James T. Rapier as well as the notes that he took for the article.

Howard University (Washington, DC), Moorland–Spingarn Research Center. *Papers:* In the Rapier Family Papers, 1836–1883, two linear feet. Correspondents include James Thomas Rapier.

NOTES

1   *Congressional Record*, House, 43rd Cong., 1st sess. (9 June 1874): 4782–4785.

2   Loren Schweninger, *James T. Rapier and Reconstruction* (Chicago: The University of Chicago Press, 1978): 16–18.

3   Following his wife's death, John Rapier had a relationship with a local slave named Lucretia. Forbidden by law to marry, the couple had five children, who lived in bondage because of their mother's status. The names of these children are not known.

4   Schweninger, *James T. Rapier and Reconstruction*: 29–31; see also Robert L. Johns, "James T. Rapier," in Jessie Carney Smith, ed., *Notable Black American Men* (Farmington Hills, MI: Gale Research, Inc., 1999): 994.

5   Other sources indicate that Rapier may have attended the University of Glasgow and Franklin College in Nashville during the Civil War, but this is not mentioned in major biographies about him, including Schweninger's *James T. Rapier and Reconstruction*. See also Maurine Christopher, *Black Americans in Congress* (New York: Thomas Y. Crowell Company, 1976): 126.

6   Loren Schweninger, "Rapier, James Thomas," *American National Biography* 18 (New York: Oxford University Press, 1999): 167–168 (hereinafter referred to as *ANB*).

7   Loren Schweninger, "Rapier, James Thomas," *Dictionary of American Negro Biography* (New York: Norton, 1982): 514 (hereinafter referred to as *DANB*). See also Christopher, *Black Americans in Congress*: 123–124.

8   Schweninger, "Rapier, James Thomas," *ANB*.

9   Loren Schweninger, "James T. Rapier of Alabama and the Noble Cause of Reconstruction," in Howard Rabinowitz, ed., *Southern Black Leaders of the Reconstruction Era* (Urbana: University of Illinois Press, 1982): 80.

10   Schweninger, *James T. Rapier and Reconstruction*: 106.

11   Schweninger, "James T. Rapier of Alabama and the Noble Cause of Reconstruction": 82; Stanley B. Parsons et al., *United States Congressional Districts, 1843–1883* (New York: Greenwood Press, 1986): 146.

12   Schweninger, *James T. Rapier and Reconstruction*: 108. Liberal Republicans stood for states' rights, believing local governments were more effective at securing individual liberties. This platform was endorsed by southern Democrats.

13   Christopher, *Black Americans in Congress*: 128; Schweninger, *James T. Rapier and Reconstruction*: 114.

14   Schweninger, "James T. Rapier of Alabama and the Noble Cause of Reconstruction": 81.

15   Ibid.

16   Schweninger, "Rapier, James Thomas," *ANB*.

17   Michael J. Dubin et al., *U.S. Congressional Elections, 1788–1997* (Jefferson, NC: McFarland & Company, Inc., Publishers, 1998): 223.

18   Quoted in Schweninger, "Rapier, James Thomas," *DANB*: 515.

19   Ibid.

20   Marie Le Baron, "Colored Congressmen: How the Enfranchised Race Is Represented in Washington," 12 April 1874, *St. Louis Daily Globe*: 3.

21   Schweninger, *James T. Rapier and Reconstruction*: 123–125.

22   *Congressional Record*, House, 43rd Cong., 1st sess. (9 June 1874): 4782–4785.

23   *Congressional Record*, House, 43rd Cong., 2nd sess. (4 February 1875): 1011.

24   Quoted in Schweninger, "James T. Rapier of Alabama and the Noble Cause of Reconstruction": 84.

25   Schweninger, *James T. Rapier and Reconstruction*: 136.

26   Schweninger, "James T. Rapier of Alabama and the Noble Cause of Reconstruction": 85.

27   Schweninger, *James T. Rapier and Reconstruction*: 143–144.

28   Ibid.

29   Schweninger, "James T. Rapier of Alabama and the Noble Cause of Reconstruction": 86

30   Dubin et al., *U.S. Congressional Elections, 1788–1997*: 230.

31   Schweninger, "James T. Rapier of Alabama and the Noble Cause of Reconstruction": 86; Parsons et al., *United States Congressional Districts, 1843–1883*: 148–149. Parsons notes that a southwestern district also had a black majority, with 53 percent.

32   Schweninger, "Rapier, James Thomas," *ANB*.

33   Dubin et al., *U.S. Congressional Elections, 1788–1997*: 236.

Blanche Kelso Bruce
1841–1898

UNITED STATES SENATOR ★ 1875–1881
REPUBLICAN FROM MISSISSIPPI

A slave who became a successful plantation owner, Blanche Kelso Bruce was the second African American to serve in the United States Senate and the first to be elected to a full term. Though Bruce focused on protecting the rights of freedmen and other minorities, his life of social privilege in the nation's capital insulated him from the deprivations suffered by many of his black constituents. Bruce moved among elite circles of wealthy white politicians, including his close friends Senator Roscoe Conkling of New York and Senator Lucius Q. C. Lamar of Mississippi. "Mr. Bruce's conduct in the senate has been such as not to alienate himself from the Southern people," noted Lamar, who had drafted the Mississippi ordinance of secession, served as a Confederate diplomat, and returned to the U.S. Congress as an unabashed opponent of Reconstruction. "[Bruce] has not joined in the abusive warfare on the South that many of his Republican colleagues in the Senate Chamber have constantly pursued," Lamar added. "He is an intelligent man, and the best representative of his race in public life."[1]

Blanche Bruce was born near Farmville, Virginia, on March 1, 1841. His mother, Polly Bruce, was a slave, and his father, Pettus Perkinson, was his mother's owner and the son-in-law of her deceased former owner, Lemuel Bruce. Bruce's first name was originally "Branch," but he changed it to "Blanche" as a teenager. For unexplained reasons, he later adopted the middle name "Kelso."[2] One of 11 children, Blanche Bruce was a personal servant to his half brother William Perkinson.[3] Even though he was a slave, Bruce was accorded a status nearly equal to the Perkinson children's. Described by contemporaries as an eager learner, he studied with William's private tutor. But despite such benign treatment, Bruce escaped to Kansas during the Civil War and attempted to enlist in the Union Army. His application was refused, and he settled in Lawrence to teach school. Returning to Hannibal, Missouri, near the war's end, he organized the state's first school for black children in 1864. Though he planned to attend Ohio's Oberlin College to study for his divinity degree, he could not afford the tuition.[4] He spent the remainder of the 1860s working as a steamboat porter out of St. Louis on the Mississippi River, moving to Mississippi in 1869 to find more-lucrative opportunities.

Upon his arrival in Mississippi, Blanche Bruce witnessed a stump speech by Republican gubernatorial candidate James Alcorn, which inspired him to enter politics.[5] On an 1870 trip to Jackson, the young, articulate Bruce caught the eye of white Republicans. That same year, the district military commander, General Adelbert Ames, appointed Bruce registrar of voters in Tallahatchie County. When the first postwar Mississippi legislature met in late 1870, Bruce, who was large and imposing, was elected sergeant at arms. In 1871, he was elected to the joint office of sheriff and tax collector of Bolivar County. The following year, the Republican state board of education appointed him county superintendent of education. In a singular achievement, Bruce turned the Bolivar County school system into one of the best in the state, creating a segregated but equally funded system that boasted the support of both blacks and whites.[6] Bruce's wealth also increased. He invested in land, becoming a successful planter by the late 1870s. In 1872, he was named to the board of levee commissioners for a district containing three counties. The commissioners were empowered to raise revenue and build embankments in the Mississippi Delta region.

By the mid-1870s, Blanche K. Bruce was among the best-recognized politicians in the state.[7] However, he faced a difficult decision when the state Republican Party split into two factions. A moderate, primarily white faction, led by then-Senator Alcorn, began ignoring African

OIL ON CANVAS, SIMMIE KNOX, 2001, COLLECTION OF THE U.S. SENATE

Americans' demands for civil rights. Then Alcorn's political rival Governor Ames adopted a more radical stance, abandoning efforts to reach out to conservative whites. Although Bruce disagreed with the Radical Republicans, because he believed that political stability required biracial cooperation, he allied himself nonetheless with the Ames faction so as to support his fellow blacks. Governor Ames offered Bruce the position of lieutenant governor in 1873, but Bruce refused, eyeing the governor's vacant seat in the U.S. Senate.[8] In January 1874, the state legislature met to nominate a U.S. Senator to fill Ames's unexpired term, and to select someone for a full six-year term beginning in the 44th Congress (1875–1877). Unlike Senator Hiram Revels before him, Bruce was selected to serve the full term primarily by black Republican colleagues, taking 52 of the 84 votes in the second ballot over Republican carpetbaggers, Representative George McKee and U.S. District Attorney G. Wiley Wells. The full legislature elected Bruce nearly unanimously on February 4, 1874.[9]

When Bruce arrived in the U.S. Senate Chamber on March 5, 1875, precedent called for his state's senior Senator to escort him to the podium, but Senator Alcorn snubbed the junior Senator because of Bruce's alliance with Governor Ames. Bruce walked up the aisle alone until Republican Senator Roscoe Conkling of New York offered to escort him. Thereafter Bruce had a powerful ally in Conkling, who coached him in Senate procedures and procured him assignments on influential committees, such as the Education and Labor, Manufactures, and Pensions committees.

Bruce remained quiet during the special session of the Senate, and concerned white Republicans feared he would shirk his responsibility to Mississippi by deferring to the Radical Republican leadership; black political leaders doubted Bruce would stand up for freedmen, who faced terrible violence from white supremacists implementing the Mississippi Plan.[10] Bruce may have been following the time-honored tradition that a freshman remains studious and silent during his first few months in the Senate Chamber. He later noted that success in

the Senate required managing diplomacy: "The novelty of my position [compels me] to cultivate and exhibit my honorable associates a courtesy that would inspire reciprocal courtesy."[11]

Bruce finally broke his silence on March 3, 1876, in defense of southern blacks, petitioning his colleagues to seat Pinckney B. S. Pinchback, a black Senator-elect from Louisiana and a personal friend. But Pinchback's political opponents questioned his selection by the state legislature due to corruption charges and despite Bruce's pleas, the Senate narrowly rejected Pinchback's claim to the seat.[12] Bruce followed this speech with a demand for an inquiry into the violent 1875 Mississippi gubernatorial election. The Senate passed a bill to investigate the political conditions in Mississippi during the previous election; however, the Democratic House did not act on the legislation.[13]

Bruce's advocacy for African Americans was most evident in issues affecting black war veterans. He was a staunch defender of black servicemen, promoting integration of the armed forces and fair treatment. On April 10, 1878, he unsuccessfully attempted to desegregate the U.S. Army, citing the U.S. Navy as a precedent.[14] Two years later, Bruce delivered a speech asking the War Department to investigate the brutal hazing of black West Point cadet Johnson C. Whittaker. The following year, he supported legislation that prevented discrimination against the heirs to black soldiers' Civil War pensions.[15] He also submitted a bill in 1879 to distribute money unclaimed by black Civil War soldiers to five African-American colleges. As the bill gained publicity, however, more claimants came forward and depleted the fund. The Senate Committee on Education and Labor eventually reported against the bill.[16]

Senator Bruce also favored the interests of other ethnic and racial minorities. During a debate on the Chinese Exclusion Act, with which he disagreed, Bruce became the first black Senator to preside over a Senate session, on February 14, 1879. Bruce also demanded more-equitable treatment for Native Americans. On April 6, 1880, he railed against federal management of Native

Americans in a Senate Floor speech. "Our Indian policy and administration seem to me to have been inspired and controlled by stern selfishness," Bruce declared. Admonishing those who placed the goal of territorial expansion over honoring treaties, he continued, "We have in the effort to realize a somewhat intangible ideal, to wit, the preservation of Indian liberty and the administration and exercise of national authority. . . . The political system that underlies our Indian policy … is foreign in its character; the individuals and the system of laws are not American."[17]

In April 1879, Bruce was appointed chairman of the Select Committee to Investigate the Freedmen's Savings and Trust Company after its failure in 1874. Comprising three southern Democrats and three Republicans, including Bruce, the committee set out to investigate the more-than 600 pages of testimony and documentation collected at the bank's closure to identify employees who were guilty of fraud and incompetence. The resultant Senate bill to reimburse former customers did not pass, but Bruce and his fellow Republicans succeeded in convincing the federal government to purchase the bank's former Washington, DC, headquarters to provide the company with some capital.[18]

As a landowner, Bruce was interested in the financial health of property owners on the banks of the Mississippi River. He supported many internal improvements and financial incentives, including the creation of a Mississippi Valley railroad and a refund for cotton taxes levied during the Civil War. In the 45th Congress (1877–1879), he served as chairman of the Select Committee on the Mississippi River. In this position, he fought for federal funding to control flooding and advocated the creation of a channel and levee system for parts of the river's edge. Bruce introduced a measure in 1879 to form the Mississippi River Improvement Association, a federally funded organization to control river flooding and protect waterfront property.[19]

Bruce's favor among white conservative voters was not matched among his black constituents. Despite Bruce's political advocacy, Mississippi blacks questioned his commitment to the plight of freedmen in collapsing Reconstruction governments. Bruce's privileged background often alienated him from his poorer constituents.[20] He and his wife, Josephine Beall Wilson of Ohio—the first black teacher in the Cleveland public schools and the daughter of a prominent mulatto dentist— whom he married on June 24, 1878, became fixtures in Washington, DC, high society. As a matter of policy, Bruce hesitated to support the westward migration of Black Americans from the South to Kansas and other Plains states. At the urging of his constituents, he introduced legislation that would assist destitute black farmers in Kansas by encouraging the federal government to issue more western land grants. His bill died in committee; however, he managed to appropriate the distribution of duty-free British cotton clothing to impoverished Kansas communities.[21] Yet these efforts were judged lacking by the black community. Nor did the white establishment look favorably on Bruce. Despite Bruce's moderation and political connections, rising "reform" politicians in power in Mississippi, who wished to recreate a "lily white" government, discounted him because of his race. When the Democratic Mississippi legislature gathered to select a new Senator in January 1880, Bruce did not even attempt a bid for a second term. The legislature chose Democrat James Z. George to succeed him.

After leaving the Senate, Bruce remained active in the Mississippi and national Republican parties.[22] He briefly served as presiding officer at the 1880 Republican National Convention in Chicago, where he received eight votes for the nomination for Vice President. When the convention returned to Chicago in 1888, Bruce received 11 such votes. He also served as superintendent for black achievement at the World's Cotton Exposition in New Orleans from 1884 to 1885 before returning to Washington to seek presidential patronage positions, his only hope of sustaining his political career. Though he rejected an offer to be Minister to Brazil because that country practiced slavery, Bruce received many endorsements for a post in President James Garfield's Cabinet in 1881. Garfield ultimately passed him over, but Bruce obtained a prime position as register of the U.S. Treasury and remained there until 1885. In 1889, President Benjamin Harrison appointed him recorder of deeds for the District of Columbia; however, he left that office in 1893 after receiving an honorary LL.D. and joining the board of trustees at Howard University.[23] Bruce returned to the Treasury post in 1897 after being considered for a Cabinet position in President William McKinley's administration. He continued to reside in Washington until he succumbed to a kidney ailment due to complications from diabetes on March 17, 1898.[24]

FOR FURTHER READING

"Bruce, Blanche Kelso," *Biographical Directory of the United States Congress, 1774–Present*, http://bioguide.congress.gov/scripts/biodisplay.pl?index=B000968.

Graham, Lawrence Otis. *The Senator and the Socialite* (New York: HarperCollins Publishers, 2006).

Harris, William C. "Blanche K. Bruce of Mississippi: Conservative Assimilationist," in Howard Rabinowitz ed., *Southern Black Leaders of the Reconstruction Era* (Urbana: University of Illinois Press, 1982).

MANUSCRIPT COLLECTIONS

Howard University (Washington, DC), Moorland–Spingarn Research Center. *Papers:* 1870–1891, 2.5 linear feet. The papers of Blanche Kelso Bruce consist of research notes, a bibliography, and other documents used by Sadie Daniel St. Clair to write a dissertation about Bruce. Includes correspondence with Bruce's family, constituents, and political allies of the State of Mississippi and letters in support of candidates for appointments and pensions.

Library of Congress, Manuscript Division, Washington, DC *Microfilm:* 1878–1890. The items consist of one letter (18 February l878) from Blanche Bruce to Murat Halstead relating to the emigration of blacks from the southern United States to Liberia, a poem inscribed to Blanche Bruce's infant son, and a volume of news clippings relating chiefly to personal matters, especially to his wife, Josephine Bruce, and to Washington, DC, social life.

NOTES

1 William C. Harris, "Blanche K. Bruce of Mississippi: Conservative Assimilationist," in Howard Rabinowitz ed., *Southern Black Leaders of the Reconstruction Era* (Urbana: University of Illinois Press, 1982): 30.

2 Lawrence Otis Graham, *The Senator and the Socialite: The True Story of America's First Black Dynasty* (New York: HarperCollins, 2006): 11; Grace E. Collins, "Blanche Kelso Bruce," in Jessie Carney Smith ed., *Notable Black American Men* (Farmington Hills, MI: Gale Research, Inc., 1999): 144 (hereinafter referred to as *NBAM*).

3 Bruce's family situation was complicated. His half siblings through his mother and Lemuel Bruce included Sandy, Calvin, James, and Henry and a half sister whose name is not known. His full siblings through his mother and Pettis Perkinson included Howard, Edward, Robert, Eliza, and Mary. See Graham, *The Senator and the Socialite*: 10–11, 16–17.

4 Collins, "Blanche Kelso Bruce," *NBAM*: 144.

5 Ibid.

6 William C. Harris, "Bruce, Blanche Kelso," *American National Biography* 3 (New York: Oxford University Press, 1999): 779–780 (hereinafter referred to as *ANB*).

7 Eric Foner, *Freedom's Lawmakers: A Directory of Black Officeholders During Reconstruction* (New York: Oxford University Press, 1993): 29.

8 Collins, "Blanche Kelso Bruce," *NBAM*: 145.

9 Harris, "Blanche K. Bruce of Mississippi: Conservative Assimilationist": 11–12.

10 Ibid., 15.

11 Graham, *The Senator and the Socialite*: 68–70, 76; quoted in Harris, "Blanche K. Bruce of Mississippi: Conservative Assimilationist": 20.

12 Pinchback had recently been elected an At-Large Representative from Louisiana, and while his election was being contested, he was elected by the state legislature to fill a vacant U.S. Senate seat. His selection for the Senate seat also was contested. He was rejected by both houses on charges of bribery and corruption. See Eric R. Jackson, "Pinchback, P. B. S.," *ANB* 17: 527–529.

13 *Congressional Record*, Senate, 44th Cong., 1st sess. (31 March 1876): 2101–2105; Graham, *The Senator and the Socialite*: 80–81.

14 The Navy had long accepted blacks. Predictably, its race record suffered during the Jim Crow decades. Few blacks secured appointments to the Naval Academy at Annapolis, and none matriculated as officers. In the 1880s, black sailors were routinely denied promotions and assigned to perform menial tasks or labor. See David Osher's essay "Race Relations and War," *The Oxford Companion to American Military History* (New York: Oxford University Press, 1999): 585.

15 *Congressional Record*, Senate, 46th Cong., 3rd sess. (10 February 1881): 1397–1398.

16 See S. 865, 46th Congress, 2nd session.

17 *Congressional Record*, Senate, 46th Cong., 2nd sess. (7 April 1880): 2195–2196. Bruce was supporting a bill selling federal lands to the Ute Indians in Colorado (S. 1509), which passed and was approved by President Rutherford B. Hayes in the 46th Congress (1879–1881).

18 Harris, "Blanche K. Bruce of Mississippi: Conservative Assimilationist": 22.

19 Samuel L. Shapiro, "Bruce, Blanche Kelso," *Dictionary of American Negro Biography* (New York: Norton, 1982): 74–76 (hereinafter referred to as *DANB*).

20 Harris, "Blanche K. Bruce of Mississippi: Conservative Assimilationist": 27, 33. See also Thomas C. Holt, *Black Over White: Negro Political Leadership in South Carolina During Reconstruction* (Urbana: University of Illinois Press, 1977).

21 Graham, *The Senator and the Socialite*: 116.

22 Harris, "Blanche K. Bruce of Mississippi: Conservative Assimilationist": 19.

23 Shapiro, "Bruce, Blanche Kelso," *DANB*.

24 Foner, *Freedom's Lawmakers*: 30. Bruce's family continued his legacy of public service and focus on education. Josephine Bruce was the principal of the Tuskegee Institute and was active in the National Federation of Colored Women's Clubs. Bruce's son, Roscoe Conkling Bruce, and his grandson, Roscoe Bruce, Jr., graduated with honors from Harvard University. The latter was embroiled in controversy when Harvard's president refused to admit him into the dormitories in 1923.

Jeremiah Haralson
1846–1916

UNITED STATES REPRESENTATIVE ★ 1875–1877
REPUBLICAN FROM ALABAMA

Admired by his contemporaries as a natural politician, Jeremiah Haralson made his reputation in Alabama politics as a powerful orator and an adroit debater. Black civil rights advocate Frederick Douglass observed that Haralson spoke "with humor enough in him to supply a half dozen circus clowns."[1] However, a Democratic majority during his single congressional term tempered his public wit; he made no speeches on the House Floor. Haralson's unsuccessful re-election campaign in 1876 set off a series of difficult and fruitless attempts to regain his seat in the Jim Crow South, ending a political career marked by mystery and contradiction.

Jeremiah Haralson was born a slave near Columbus, Georgia, on April 1, 1846. His early life is not well documented. He was sold twice as a child before John Haralson, a lawyer from Selma, Alabama, purchased him in 1859. After winning his freedom in 1865, Jeremiah Haralson taught himself to read and write. He made his living as a farmer and may also have been a clergyman.[2] Haralson married Ellen Norwood in 1870 and had one son, Henry.

Throughout his career, Haralson demonstrated a natural shrewdness and a gift for politics, yet contemporaries described him as forceful, "uncompromising, irritating, and bold."[3] Haralson's party loyalty spanned the political spectrum throughout his early career. Likely drawn to politics because of his oratorical talent, he reportedly became a Democrat in 1867—an unusual move given the Democratic Party's affiliation with former Confederates and slaveholders. Haralson campaigned for Democratic presidential candidate Horatio Seymour in 1868, claiming his allegiance to the Democrats stemmed from loyalty to his former master and from the uncertain future of the Republican Party in the South, then dominated by carpetbaggers and former Union soldiers.[4] However,

Haralson may have acted as a double agent. By some accounts, his speeches backing Seymour were insincere, and he used private conversations afterward to sway listeners to the Republican ticket.[5] Despite being too young to meet the constitutional requirement to serve in the U.S. House, the ambitious Haralson made his first unsuccessful bid for Congress at age 22 in 1868.[6] By 1869, Haralson had formally switched parties. He publicly allied himself with the Republicans, claiming that the Democrats had failed to attract the newly enfranchised freedmen.[7] However, just one year later he successfully ran as an Independent for the state house of representatives, marking the beginning of a trend toward third-party candidacy, to which he would adhere for his entire political career. In 1870, Haralson was chosen to preside over the Republican Party's district convention, at which Benjamin S. Turner—the first African American from Alabama to serve in Congress—was nominated.[8] By 1872, when he was elected a Republican member of the Alabama state senate, Haralson seemed firmly in the GOP camp. After successfully navigating a civil rights bill through the state senate, his political power soared. One local newspaper observed, "He is perhaps feared more than any other colored man in the legislature in Alabama."[9]

The Alabama Republican Party was divided along racial lines throughout the Reconstruction Era, and Haralson was no friend to white carpetbagger Republicans, who were wary of his former Democratic ties and believed he had entered politics strictly for personal gain. White Republicans in the state senate accused him of accepting bribes from railroad officials and of stealing bales of cotton.[10] Haralson often played up his pure African-American heritage in his campaigns. One Alabama newspaper described him as "black as the ace of spades," (most of his African-American opponents were mulatto).[11]

IMAGE COURTESY OF LIBRARY OF CONGRESS

He also stoked the racial fears of his black constituents, noting in 1872 that if Grant were not re-elected, African Americans would be exterminated in a southern race war.[12] In 1874, Haralson won the Republican nomination in the district formerly represented by Representative Turner, which stretched over a swath of western Alabama including Haralson's hometown of Selma and a large chunk of central Alabama "black belt." The district's population was about 50 percent black.[13] Haralson campaigned on a strong civil rights platform, appealing to the district's abundant freedmen. White Republicans and Democrats alike rallied behind incumbent liberal Republican Frederick Bromberg, who had taken advantage of a divided black electorate to defeat Turner and another black candidate two years earlier. Haralson captured 54 percent of the vote to claim victory in the general election.[14]

Bromberg contested Haralson's victory. In delivering the decision of the Committee on Elections on April 18, 1876, Democratic Chairman John Harris of Virginia informed his colleagues that their investigation uncovered "frauds as flagrant and abuses as violent as ever have been committed in this country upon the elective franchise."[15] Harris flailed the district's Republicans for controlling voters with money appropriated for helping freedmen, noting that more "colored voters were intimidated by their own race against voting for [Bromberg]," than were hassled by white supremacists. The committee declared some of Haralson's votes invalid, but the black Representative retained a secure margin over Bromberg. The committee ruled unanimously to reject Bromberg's challenge, a decision sustained by the House.[16] Haralson received a single assignment: to the Committee on Public Expenditures.

Radical Republicans from Haralson's district frowned on his friendships with former Confederate President Jefferson Davis, and southern Democratic Senators Lucius Q. C. Lamar of Mississippi and John Gordon of Georgia. Haralson rebuffed Radical Republican scorn by accusing white members of his own party of conspiring against African-American voters. "We must drive out these hell hounds and go in for peace between the two races in the South," he noted in a January 29, 1876, statement.[17] As the contentious 1876 election promised violence in the South, he broke with the Republican Party by criticizing the use of federal soldiers to police polls and ensure orderly voting. Haralson claimed their presence would hurt the Republican Party, telling a southern Democratic newspaper "every blue jacket sent to the South makes Democratic votes."[18] During his term, he introduced legislation to use the proceeds from the sale of public land for education, although he favored strict segregation of the races, particularly in public schools. He also presented a petition from citizens in Mobile, Alabama, requesting compensation for the use of a medical college and supplies by officers of the Freedmen's Bureau. None of the bills proposed by Haralson passed.

By 1876, the Alabama state legislature had gerrymandered Haralson's district—cutting it nearly in half—so that it encompassed only the west-central Alabama "black belt." The new district had by far the largest black electorate—65 percent—of any district in the state. Yet, despite this advantage, Haralson spent nearly a decade attempting to win back his seat. Former black Representative James Rapier, who had recently purchased a plantation in the newly reconfigured district to avoid running in his former, black-minority district, challenged Haralson in the 1876 primary. When Rapier won, the outraged Haralson entered the general election as an Independent. Haralson and Rapier split the substantial Republican ticket, emerging with 34 and 28 percent of the vote, respectively. Democrat Charles M. Shelley—a former Confederate general, the Selma sheriff, and a stalwart of the local Democratic Party—won the election with a 38 percent plurality.[19] This loss in such a strong Republican district was a blow to the state Republican Party.[20] Haralson determinedly contested the election, claiming Shelley had unfairly selected the inspectors at the polling places. As sheriff, Shelley had assigned illiterate black men as Republican inspectors, putting them at the mercy of their literate white Democratic counterparts. After inspectors threw out many of his votes, Haralson argued that there had been plenty of literate black Republicans available to work as inspectors. In a letter to the editor of the *Washington Post*, he wrote, "Mr. Shelley is no more entitled to the seat in the Forty-fifth Congress than the Sultan of Turkey, and is only here by taking advantage of his own wrong."[21] Haralson submitted his official complaint to the Committee on Elections on April 16, 1878, but the committee never reported back on the issue.[22]

Haralson returned to win the Republican nomination for his former seat in 1878. The *Chicago Daily Tribune*, a newspaper favoring Haralson, noted that racial prejudices in the district were so extreme, white Democrats preferred "to see the Devil himself in Congress rather than Haralson."[23] Shelley's re-election campaign looked promising after a third candidate, white Independent Republican Jonathan Henry, entered the race.[24] Though Henry took only 2 percent of the electorate, Haralson failed to defeat Shelley for a seat in the 46th Congress (1879–1881); Shelley took 55 percent to Haralson's 43 percent.[25] Haralson believed several thousand of his votes were thrown out for no apparent reason and contested the election, but the *Tribune* reported he could not find a local judge who would take affidavits from his witnesses. When Haralson was finally able to procure a judge, Shelley supporters jailed his witnesses and attempted to have Haralson and his lawyer imprisoned under false charges. Moreover, while traveling between Montgomery and Selma, Alabama, Haralson was attacked by an armed mob and ordered to leave the state.[26] Fearing for his life, he fled to the District of Columbia.[27] Haralson stated his case in the contested election in a memorial introduced on the House Floor, to be printed by Republican Representative J. Warren Keifer of Ohio—a Union veteran, a member of the Committee on Elections, and

a future Speaker of the House.[28] A debate ensued as to the necessity of making a special request to print the memorial, since petitions and memorials were routinely reproduced on the House Floor. Opponents disliked the special attention the letter was receiving; they feared it would be printed in the *Congressional Record* and accessible to the public.[29] The House referred the memorial to the Committee on Elections, which printed it but never ruled on Haralson's claim.[30]

After six years Haralson revived his campaign for a central Alabama district. He spent the intervening years in patronage positions, first as a clerk at Baltimore's federal customs house and later as a clerk at the Department of the Interior. He also worked for the Pension Bureau in Washington, DC, from 1882 to 1884. Having failed to receive his party's nomination in 1884, Haralson ran once again as an Independent Republican. He came away with just 683 votes in a four-way contest, even though the district's population was 80 percent black.[31] Democrat Alexander Davidson easily won the election with 14,225 votes (64 percent), garnering twice as many votes as his nearest competitor, Republican George Craig.[32] The lopsided results—relative to the number of registered voters in each party and the racial makeup of the district—led Republican newspapers to question the returns, but there is no record that Haralson officially contested the election.[33]

After Haralson's final bid for Congress, he lived in Louisiana and Arkansas before returning to Selma, Alabama, in 1912. Haralson later wandered through Texas and Oklahoma, finally settling in Colorado, where he became a coal miner. In 1916, he was killed by a wild animal while hunting near Denver. No death certificate was ever filed.[34]

FOR FURTHER READING

"Haralson, Jeremiah," *Biographical Directory of the United States Congress, 1774–Present*, http://bioguide.congress.gov/scripts/biodisplay.pl?index=H000179.

MANUSCRIPT COLLECTIONS

Alabama Department of Archives and History
(Montgomery, AL) *Papers:* In the Reconstruction Era Political Materials, 1868–1878, 0.33 cubic feet. Authors include Jeremiah Haralson.

University of Alabama Libraries, W. S. Hoole Special Collections Library (Tuscaloosa, AL) *Papers:* 1876, one item. A letter from Jeremiah Haralson to the United States Centennial Commission in Philadelphia, Pennsylvania, written on April 27, 1876. In the letter, Haralson requests an invitation for his wife to the opening of the Centennial International Exhibition of Industry.

NOTES

1 Eric Foner, *Freedom's Lawmakers: A Directory of Black Officeholders During Reconstruction* (New York: Oxford University Press, 1993): 95.

2 Maurine Christopher, *Black Americans in Congress* (New York: Thomas Y. Crowell Company, 1976): 132; Stephen Middleton, ed., *Black Congressmen During Reconstruction: A Documentary Sourcebook* (Westport, CT: Praeger, 2002): 115.

3 Quoted in Christopher, *Black Americans in Congress*: 132.

4 Loren Schweninger and Alston Fitts III, "Haralson, Jeremiah," *American National Biography* 10 (New York: Oxford University Press, 1999): 37–38 (hereinafter referred to as *ANB*).

5 Christopher, *Black Americans in Congress*: 132.

6 Bruce A. Ragsdale and Joel D. Treese, *Black Americans in Congress, 1870–1989* (Washington, DC: Government Printing Office, 1990): 63; Christopher, *Black Americans in Congress*: 132; Middleton, ed., *Black Congressmen During Reconstruction*: 166. Article I, Section 2 of the U.S. Constitution states that no one under the age of 25 may be seated in the U.S. House of Representatives. Michael Dubin makes no mention of Haralson's candidacy for the 1868 general election; it is likely that Haralson never received the party nomination. See Michael J. Dubin et al., *U.S. Congressional Elections, 1788–1997* (Jefferson, NC: McFarland & Company, Inc., Publishers, 1998): 213.

7 Schweninger and Fitts, "Haralson, Jeremiah," *ANB*.

8 Christopher, *Black Americans in Congress*: 132–133.

9 Haralson's civil rights bill was subsequently abandoned by the state house of representatives. See Schweninger and Fitts, "Haralson, Jeremiah," *ANB*. Quoted in Christopher, *Black Americans in Congress*: 134, and Middleton, ed., *Black Congressmen During Reconstruction*: 116.

10 Schweninger and Fitts, "Haralson, Jeremiah," *ANB*.

11 Quoted in Foner, *Freedom's Lawmakers*: 95, and Middleton, ed., *Black Congressmen During Reconstruction*: 116.

12 Schweninger and Fitts, "Haralson, Jeremiah," *ANB*.

13 Stanley B. Parsons et al., *United States Congressional Districts, 1843–1883* (New York: Greenwood Press, 1986): 146.

14 Dubin et al., *U.S. Congressional Elections, 1788–1997*: 230.

15 *Congressional Record*, House, 44th Cong., 1st sess. (18 April 1876): 2552.

16 *Congressional Record*, House, 44th Cong., 1st sess. (23 March 1876): 1913; *Congressional Record*, House, 44th Cong., 1st sess. (18 April 1876): 2552; Chester H. Rowell, *A Historical and Legal Digest of All the Contested Election Cases* (Washington, DC: Government Printing Office, 1901): 303.

17 Quoted in Middleton, ed., *Black Congressmen During Reconstruction*: 117.

18 Quoted in Christopher, *Black Americans in Congress*: 135.

19 According to Loren Schweninger's biography of Representative James Rapier, Haralson withdrew from the race before the election. However, Haralson appears in the election results and split the Republican ticket with Rapier. See Loren Schweninger, *James T. Rapier and Reconstruction* (Chicago: University of Chicago Press, 1978); Dubin et al., *U.S. Congressional Elections, 1788–1997*: 236.

20 Schweninger, *James T. Rapier and Reconstruction*: 157.

21 "Jere Haralson's Case: The Colored Statesman Puts a Few Points to the Public," 10 April 1878, *Washington Post*: 2.

22 *Congressional Record*, House, 45th Cong., 2nd sess. (16 April 1878): 2580. This case is not included in Rowell's *A Historical and Legal Digest of All the Contested Election Cases*. There has been considerable discussion among scholars as to the outcome of Haralson's contested election to the 45th Congress (1877–1879). Some sources indicate that the Committee on Elections ruled for Haralson in the 45th Congress but that Congress adjourned before he was seated. See Schweninger and Fitts, "Haralson, Jeremiah," *ANB*; Foner, *Freedom's Lawmakers*: 94. Others confirm that the committee ruled for seating Representative Charles Shelley. See Ragsdale and Treese, *Black Americans in Congress, 1870–1989*:

64. Contemporary accounts, however, suggest the committee never considered or ruled on Haralson's claim; see, for instance, "Wasting Time In Congress," 14 May 1878, *New York Times*: 1. The most likely result of Haralson's election contest can be inferred from congressional sources: The *Congressional Record* notes that Haralson's claim was reported to the Committee on Elections, but there is no mention of a decision. The *Biographical Directory of the United States Congress, 1774–Present* confirms that Representative Charles Shelley was elected fairly to the 45th Congress; see "Shelley, Charles Miller," available at http://bioguide.congress.gov/scripts/biodisplay.pl?index=S000326. Finally, Dubin et al., *U.S. Congressional Elections, 1788–1997*: 236, contains no mention of a successful challenge to Shelley's seat in the 45th Congress.

23 "Alabama," 14 October 1878, *Chicago Tribune*: 2.

24 "Independents in Alabama," 3 November 1878, *New York Times*: 1.

25 Dubin et al., *U.S. Congressional Elections, 1788–1997*: 243.

26 "Washington," 6 June 1876, *New York Times*: 5.

27 "How a Southern Republican Was Cheated Out of His Seat," 2 February 1880, *Chicago Daily Tribune*: 4.

28 *Congressional Record*, House, 46th Cong., 2nd sess. (31 January 1880): 633; "Keifer, Joseph Warren," *Biographical Directory of the United States Congress, 1774–Present*, available at http://bioguide.congress.gov/scripts/biodisplay.pl?index=K000048.

29 *Congressional Record*, House, 46th Cong., 2nd sess. (31 January 1880): 634.

30 The case does not appear in Rowell's, *A Historical and Legal Digest of All the Contested Election Cases*; see also *Congressional Record Index*, 46th Congress, three sessions.

31 Stanley B. Parsons et al., *United States Congressional Districts, 1883–1913* (New York: Greenwood Press, 1990): 3.

32 Dubin et al., *U.S. Congressional Elections, 1788–1997*: 264.

33 See *Congressional Record Index*, 49th Congress, both sessions.

34 Christopher, *Black Americans in Congress*: 136.

John Adams Hyman
1840–1891

UNITED STATES REPRESENTATIVE ★ 1875–1877
REPUBLICAN FROM NORTH CAROLINA

While in bondage, John Adams Hyman repeatedly broke laws prohibiting his education so he could learn to read and write, and as a result, was sold at least eight times. After his emancipation, Hyman sought with equal determination to become the first black U.S. Representative from North Carolina. Though the shy legislator made no speeches on the House Floor, a letter to Senator Charles Sumner of Massachusetts, written in 1872, demonstrated his eloquence. "If [an African American] is a man," Hyman declared, "he is entitled to *all* the rights and privileges of any other man. There can be no grades of citizenship under the American flag."[1]

Born into slavery near Warrenton, North Carolina, on July 23, 1840, John Adams Hyman is believed to have been a child of Jesse Hyman, a slave.[2] Starting in his early twenties, John Hyman was a janitor for a Warrenton jeweler. Hyman later noted that he was treated like "chattel, bought and sold as a brute."[3] When he gained his freedom in March 1865, Hyman returned to Warrenton, where he became a farmer and opened a country store. He also became a trustee of the first public school in his area. Hyman married and had two sons and two daughters. The names of his immediate family members are not known.[4]

Upon his return, Hyman became active in the movement to secure political rights for North Carolina blacks. At age 26, he served on two committees at the state's Freedmen's Convention, including the committee on invitations, an important panel whose purpose was to encourage the attendance of influential politicians and to raise awareness about the convention.[5] Hyman also served as a delegate to the March 1867 Republican State Convention, and as the registrar for northern Warren County, recruiting emancipated voters. In November 1867, Hyman was elected to the Warren County delegation to the North Carolina constitutional convention, which

met in Raleigh the following January. Hyman was one of 15 black delegates in the 133-member body. In 1868, he won election to the state senate where he served for six years. From this seat, Hyman wrote U.S. Senator Charles Sumner in support of his Civil Rights Bill.[6] He also opposed President Andrew Johnson's leniency toward ex-Confederates and strongly advocated requiring states to ratify the 14th Amendment before being readmitted to the Union. Hyman voted against impeaching Republican Governor William Holden in 1872 for ordering the arrest of Ku Klux Klan members suspected of lynching and terrorizing the state's black population. In the senate, which was divided over how to resuscitate North Carolina's postwar economy, Hyman deflected Conservatives' and Democrats' charges that he accepted bribes from railroad lobbyists. Most members of the penitentiary committee, on which Hyman served, were caught up in this scandal.[7]

Hyman's hometown of Warrenton was in the northern section of the "Black Second" district, the only safe Republican district after gerrymandering by the Democratically controlled North Carolina legislature. The "Black Second" stretched from Warren County, adjacent to the Virginia border, and hooked around to coastal Craven County.[8] The earliest reliable census, taken in 1880, showed that the populations of three of the district's 10 counties were more than two-thirds black. All the counties in the district had populations that were at least 45 percent black. In 1872, white Republican Charles R. Thomas, a pre-Civil War Whig, sought a third congressional term in the reapportioned district, but newly powerful African-American politicians in the "Black Second" demanded that a freedman run for Congress. Hyman challenged Thomas for the nomination—embittering many white Republicans and opening racial fissures in the party—but lost at the May 1872 district convention. However, black

voters remained loyal to the party of the emancipators, and Thomas handily defeated his Democratic opponent in the general election.

Yet Thomas's term in the 43rd Congress (1873–1875) was minimally successful and marred by political blunders. Seven candidates, including Hyman and African-American state representative James O'Hara, challenged the weakened incumbent at the 1874 district convention.[9] The early ballots taken at the convention saw the votes split evenly among the candidates—each county cast one vote for its favored contender—but after a series of negotiations among the candidates, Hyman prevailed on the 29th ballot. Realizing their redistricting efforts had opened the door for North Carolina's first black Representative, white supremacist Democrats frantically sought a viable last-minute challenger. The success of their candidate, George W. Blount, depended on the chance that ever-growing racial divisions in the Republican Party would prevent white Republicans from voting for Hyman.[10] Opposition newspapers emphasized that Hyman lacked the support of white Republican leaders, as evidenced by the candidacy of white Independent Republican Garland White. The Democratic press also spread the rumor that white Republicans were bribing Hyman not to run.[11] Yet Hyman emerged victorious, taking 62 percent of the vote.[12] Blount contested Hyman's election. His chief complaint was that the phrase "Republican Congressional Ticket" at the top of Hyman ballots persuaded many voters who were barely literate to vote for him.[13] On August 1, 1876, a Democratic House unanimously agreed that Hyman was entitled to the seat.[14]

Upon his arrival for the 44th Congress (1875–1877), Hyman was assigned to the Committee on Manufactures. For the first time in nearly two decades, the Republicans found themselves in the minority, and Hyman's committee assignment had little significance for his agricultural district. A quiet man who preferred behind-the-scenes politics, Hyman made no speeches on the House Floor. Instead, he submitted private bills and petitions on behalf of the poor in his district and state.[15] He

sponsored a bill authorizing the Treasury Department to build a lighthouse at Gull Rock on North Carolina's Pamlico Sound and introduced legislation to compensate constituents for financial losses incurred during the Civil War. He joined others from the North Carolina delegation in seeking relief for Cherokee Indians resettled in the West. A loyal Republican, he cast a noteworthy "nay" vote against restricting President Ulysses S. Grant to two terms. (Though a formal term limit for Presidents did not yet exist, the resolution determined that a chief executive should step down after two terms based on the precedent established by President George Washington.) Hyman was one of only 18 dissenting Members, as many Republicans defected.[16] Hyman attempted to protect his black constituents by introducing a bill to reimburse the depositors of the failed Freedmen's Bank, but it never made it out of committee.

As racial divisions widened in the state's Republican Party, former North Carolina Reconstruction Governor Curtis Brogden began mustering support to defeat Hyman for the Republican nomination in the spring of 1876. By the following July, Brogden's supporters were so confident he would be nominated, many did not attend the district convention, though Brogden himself arrived at the convention site several days early.[17] Brogden's small but powerful force convinced some of Hyman's lieutenants—white and black—of Brogden's superiority, and the former governor won on the ninth and deciding ballot.[18] Deflecting rumors he would run as a third-party candidate, Hyman threw his support behind his rival. Winning the general election by a wide margin, Brogden took his place as the only Republican in the state's new congressional delegation.[19]

Hyman returned to his farm in Warrenton, where he also ran a grocery and liquor store. He briefly served as a special deputy internal revenue collector for the Rutherford B. Hayes administration, but political pressure from the North Carolina Republican Party kept him from fully assuming his post.[20] In 1878, he again ran for Congress, losing the nomination to James O'Hara. Hyman served as a steward and Sunday school superintendent for the Warrenton Colored Methodist Church. As the temperance movement took hold in North Carolina, he was expelled from the church on charges of selling alcoholic beverages and embezzling Sunday school funds. Hyman left Warrenton, moving to Washington, DC, and later to Richmond, Virginia. In 1887, he returned to Warrenton with renewed political ambitions, but he failed to obtain a congressional nomination in 1888. The winner, black candidate Henry Cheatham, eventually reclaimed the "Black Second." Shortly thereafter, Hyman defected from the Republican Party after agreeing to encourage blacks to vote for district Democrats in exchange for minor political posts.[21] Returning north, Hyman worked as a mail clerk's assistant in Maryland for 10 years before moving back to Washington, DC, in 1889, where he took a position in the Department of Agriculture's seed dispensary.[22] John Hyman died at home of a stroke on September 14, 1891.

FOR FURTHER READING

Anderson, Eric. *Race and Politics in North Carolina, 1872–1901* (Baton Rouge: Louisiana State University Press, 1981).

"Hyman, John Adams," *Biographical Directory of the United States Congress, 1774–Present*, http://bioguide.congress.gov/scripts/biodisplay.pl?index=H001025.

Reid, George W. "Four in Black: North Carolina's Black Congressmen, 1874–1901," *The Journal of Negro History* 64 (Summer 1979): 229–243.

NOTES

1   John Hyman to Charles Sumner, 24 January 1872. Charles Sumner Papers, Houghton Library, Harvard University, Cambridge, MA (emphasis Hyman's).

2   Hyman's parentage has never been confirmed, and it is unclear whether his presumed parent, Jesse Hyman, was his mother or his father. See George W. Reid, "Four in Black: North Carolina's Black Congressmen, 1874–1901," *Journal of Negro History* 64 (Summer 1979): 229.

3   Hyman to Sumner, 24 January 1872. Sumner Papers.

4   The only record of Hyman's family is in his obituary, which does not mention his wife's and children's names. See "Years of Service Ended," 16 September 1891, *Washington Post*: 8.

5   Debi Hamlin, "Hyman, John Adams," *American National Biography* 11 (New York: Oxford University Press, 1999): 617–618 (hereinafter referred to as *ANB*).

6   Eric Foner, *Freedom's Lawmakers: A Directory of Black Officeholders During Reconstruction* (New York: Oxford University Press, 1993): 113.

7   Eric Anderson, *Race and Politics in North Carolina, 1872–1901* (Baton Rouge: Louisiana State University Press, 1981): 37, 43. According to Anderson, Hyman claimed to know nothing about the bribes and was never officially charged with a crime.

8   Anderson, *Race and Politics*: 4; Stanley B. Parsons et al., *United States Congressional Districts, 1843–1883* (New York: Greenwood Press, 1986): 201.

9   O'Hara eventually won election to the "Black Second" district in 1882.

10 Anderson, *Race and Politics*: 39.

11 Maurine Christopher, *Black Americans in Congress* (New York: Thomas Y. Crowell Company, 1976): 150.

12 Michael J. Dubin et al., *U.S. Congressional Elections, 1788–1997* (Jefferson, NC: McFarland & Company, Inc., Publishers, 1998): 232. White's name does not appear in the election results.

13 Anderson, *Race and Politics*: 44.

14 *Congressional Record*, House, 44th Cong., 1st sess. (1 August 1876): 5051.

15 Stephen Middleton, ed., *Black Congressmen During Reconstruction: A Documentary Sourcebook* (Westport, CT: Praeger, 2002): 123.

16 *Congressional Record*, House, 44th Cong., 1st sess. (15 December 1875): 228. The 22nd Amendment, ratified in 1951, restricted Presidents to two terms.

17 Christopher, *Black Americans in Congress*: 151.

18 Ibid.

19 Anderson, *Race and Politics*: 52.

20 Christopher, *Black Americans in Congress*: 152; Anderson, *Race and Politics*: 144. Other sources indicate Hyman obtained the appointment but was later removed because of political pressure. See Foner, *Freedom's Lawmakers*: 113.

21 Foner, *Freedom's Lawmakers*: 113.

22 It is unclear where Hyman served in Maryland since most sources include only the state (Middleton, *Black Congressmen During Reconstruction*: 123; Christopher, *Black Americans in Congress*: 152; Foner, *Freedom's Lawmakers*: 113; Reid, "Four in Black": 230). *ANB* places him in Washington, DC, lending credence to the possibility that his post was near the capital. See Hamlin, "Hyman, John Adams," *ANB*.

"I<small>F</small> [<small>AN</small> A<small>FRICAN</small> A<small>MERICAN</small>] <small>IS</small> <small>A MAN</small>," H<small>YMAN</small> <small>DECLARED</small>, "<small>HE IS ENTITLED TO</small> *ALL* <small>THE</small> <small>RIGHTS AND PRIVILEGES OF ANY</small> <small>OTHER MAN</small>. T<small>HERE CAN BE NO</small> <small>GRADES OF CITIZENSHIP UNDER</small> <small>THE</small> A<small>MERICAN FLAG</small>."

Charles Edmund Nash
1844–1913

UNITED STATES REPRESENTATIVE ★ 1875–1877
REPUBLICAN FROM LOUISIANA

Although Charles E. Nash commanded less national attention than some of his Louisiana contemporaries, his status as a wounded war hero vaulted him to the House of Representatives in the 44th Congress (1875–1877). Louisiana would not elect another black Representative until the late 20th century.[1] In the Democratically controlled House, Nash encountered great difficulty gaining even the right to speak before his colleagues on the House Floor.

Charles Edmund Nash was born to free parents, Richard and Masie Cecile Nash, in Opelousas, St. Landry Parish, Louisiana, on May 23, 1844.[2] Nash attended common (public) schools before becoming a bricklayer in New Orleans. He married Martha Ann Wycoff. Following her death in 1884, he married a French woman, Julia Lucy Montplaisir, in 1905.[3] Union troops occupied New Orleans early in the Civil War, taking the strategic port city in 1862. In July 1863, Nash enlisted as a private in Company A of the 82nd Regiment, United States Volunteers. He was eventually promoted to sergeant major. In a battle at Fort Blakely, Alabama, Nash was severely wounded and lost part of his right leg on April 9, 1865.

Though the injury limited his mobility and affected his health for the rest of his life, Nash's reputation as a hero impressed local Republicans after the war. The Republican Party was well organized and teaming with able men, most of them free mulattos who lived in New Orleans.[4] In 1869, Nash was hired for a federal patronage position as a night inspector in the New Orleans Custom House. His combat record made him an attractive candidate for a U.S. congressional seat in 1874 for the district surrounding Baton Rouge.

Louisiana Republicans faced a precarious situation after the state was re-admitted to the Union and federal military occupation ended. In 1870, black Lieutenant Governor Oscar Dunn split from white incumbent Governor Henry Warmoth at the Republican state convention. With Dunn seizing black support, both men laid claim to the executive office. Dueling state legislatures emerged, and the racially divided Republicans barely held sway over local politics, depending on support from the administration of President Ulysses S. Grant to fend off Democratic challengers. It was during this near-anarchy that Nash was nominated for a congressional seat.[5] Only the presence of federal troops and the support of Louisiana blacks ensured that Nash's election to Congress in 1874 was relatively smooth.[6] He defeated Democrat Joseph B. Moore by a little more than 1,000 votes, taking 52 percent of the vote and becoming Louisiana's first black Representative. His uneventful election contrasted sharply with that of his predecessor John Willis Menard, who was elected in 1868 but never seated, and that of P. B. S. Pinchback—one of Louisiana's most prominent black politicians—who ran unsuccessfully for the U.S. House and Senate two years later.[7]

Nash joined a record number of eight black Congressmen—including Mississippi Republican Blanche K. Bruce in the Senate—in the 44th Congress. Upon his swearing in, the substantial Democratic majority limited him to a single assignment: the Committee on Education and Labor. Nash submitted few pieces of legislation but was eager to voice his views in the House Chamber for the public record. However, the Democrats, who controlled the House Floor, were determined to deny Nash that opportunity. For example, in late May 1876—following a two-hour speech by Louisiana Republican Frank Morey—Nash attempted to express his views on a disputed election in a district just north of his. Democratic Representative John House of Tennessee cut off debate before Nash could speak. When Nash protested, Speaker Michael Kerr of Indiana offered only to print his

speech in the *Congressional Record Appendix*. Nash rejected this offer. The presiding officer ignored Nash's repeated request to speak but subsequently permitted New York Democrat George Beebe to make a lengthy speech on the same subject.[8]

On the evening of June 7, Nash finally made a speech on the House Floor. He chastised the Democratic Party for undermining the status of freedmen and harassing whites who supported black civil rights. Nash also emphasized the importance of supporting public education, noting the discouraging condition of the common schools in the South and "the ignorance of the masses." He then called for strict enforcement of the 13th, 14th, and 15th Amendments, warning "a government which cannot protect its humblest citizens from outrage and injury is unworthy of the name and ought not to command the support of a free people."[9] He ended on an optimistic note, reaffirming his faith that the United States could overcome its racial and political divisions. "For we are not enemies, but brethren," he declared, "America will not die.

As the time demands them great men will appear, and by their combined efforts render liberty and happiness more secure."[10] It was late at night when Nash finally finished his speech.[11]

In 1876, Nash lost his seat to Democrat Edward Robertson, who won with 58 percent of the vote to Nash's 42 percent.[12] Nash's campaign was overshadowed by the presidential electoral crisis: Louisiana and two other states sent two sets of certified electoral votes to Washington—one for Republican candidate Rutherford B. Hayes and the other for Democrat Samuel Tilden. As House Members discussed the crisis, Nash attempted to participate but once again was ignored.[13] Abandoning his political career at the close of the 44th Congress, Nash returned to Louisiana to work as a bricklayer. After injuries and his age forced him to abandon the trade, he served briefly as postmaster in St. Landry Parish in 1882. Nash subsequently made his living as a cigar maker. He died in New Orleans, on June 21, 1913.

FOR FURTHER READING

"Nash, Charles Edmund," *Biographical Directory of the United States Congress, 1774–Present*, http://bioguide. congress.gov/scripts/biodisplay.pl?index=N000008.

NOTES

1   Representative William Jefferson of New Orleans, the next black Member from Louisiana, was sworn in on January 3, 1991. See "Jefferson, William Jennings," *Biographical Directory of the United States Congress 1774–Present*, available at http://bioguide.congress. gov/scripts/biodisplay.pl?index=J000070.

2   Maurine Christopher is the only biographer who claims Nash was a slave; see Christopher, *Black Americans in Congress* (New York: Thomas Y. Crowell Company, 1976): 104. For other accounts, see Chandra Miller, "Nash, Charles Edmund," *American National Biography* 16 (New York: Oxford University Press, 1999): 234–235 (hereinafter referred to as *ANB*); Stephen Middleton, ed., *Black Congressmen During Reconstruction: A Documentary Sourcebook* (Westport, CT: Praeger, 2002): 267; and Thomas Holt, "Nash, Charles Edmund," *Dictionary of American Negro Biography* (New York: Norton, 1982): 471–472.

3   Nash had no children. See Miller, "Nash, Charles Edmund," *ANB*.

4   Christopher, *Black Americans in Congress*: 105.

5   Ibid., 106.

6   Joe Gray Taylor, *Louisiana Reconstructed, 1863–1877* (Baton Rouge: Louisiana State University Press, 1974): 299–300.

7   For more information on these two men, see James Haskins, *The First Black Governor, Pinkney Benton Stewart Pinchback* (Trenton, NJ: Africa World Press, 1996); John Willis Menard, *Lays in Summer Lands*, ed. by Larry E. Rivers et al. (1879; reprint, Tampa, FL: University of Tampa Press, 2002).

8   *Congressional Record*, House, 44th Cong., 1st sess. (31 May 1876): 3437.

9   *Congressional Record*, House, 44th Cong., 1st sess. (7 June 1876): 3667–3668.

10 Ibid., 3669.

11 Christopher, *Black Americans in Congress*: 107.

12 Michael J. Dubin et al., *U.S. Congressional Elections, 1788–1997* (Jefferson, NC: McFarland & Company, Inc., Publishers, 1998): 238.

13 *Congressional Record*, House, 44th Cong., 2nd sess. (15 December 1876): 236.

Robert Smalls
1839–1915

UNITED STATES REPRESENTATIVE ★ 1875–1879; 1882–1883; 1884–1887
REPUBLICAN FROM SOUTH CAROLINA

An escaped slave and a Civil War hero, Robert Smalls served five terms in the U.S. House, representing a South Carolina district described as a "black paradise" because of its abundant political opportunities for freedmen.[1] Overcoming the state Democratic Party's repeated attempts to remove that "blemish" from its goal of white supremacy, Smalls endured violent elections and a short jail term to achieve internal improvements for coastal South Carolina and to fight for his black constituents in the face of growing disfranchisement. "My race needs no special defense, for the past history of them in this country proves them to be equal of any people anywhere," Smalls asserted. "All they need is an equal chance in the battle of life."[2]

Robert Smalls was born a slave on April 5, 1839, in Beaufort, South Carolina. His mother, Lydia Polite, was a slave who worked as a nanny, and the identity of Robert Smalls's father is not known, but Smalls had distinct mulatto features.[3] Owned by John McKee, he worked in his master's house throughout his youth and, in 1851, moved to the McKees' Charleston home. Smalls was hired out on the waterfront as a lamplighter, stevedore foreman, sail maker, rigger, and sailor, and became an expert navigator of the South Carolina and Georgia coasts. In 1856, he married Hannah Jones, a slave who worked as a hotel maid in Charleston. The couple had two daughters: Elizabeth and Sarah. A third child, Robert, Jr., died of smallpox as a toddler.[4] The Smalls lived separately from their owners, but sent their masters most of their income.[5]

During the Civil War, the Confederate Army conscripted Robert Smalls into service aboard the *Planter,* an ammunitions transport ship that had once been a cotton steamer. On May 13, 1862, a black crew captained by Smalls hijacked the well-stocked ship and turned it over to the Union Navy. Smalls became a northern celebrity.[6] His escape was symbolic of the Union cause, and the

publication of his name and former enslaved status in northern propaganda proved demoralizing for the South.[7] Smalls spent the remainder of the war balancing his role as a spokesperson for African Americans with his service in the Union Armed Forces. Piloting both the *Planter,* which was re-outfitted as a troop transport, and later the ironclad *Keokuk,* Smalls used his intimate knowledge of the South Carolina Sea Islands to advance the Union military campaign in nearly 17 engagements.[8]

Smalls's public career began during the war. He joined free black delegates to the 1864 Republican National Convention, the first of seven total conventions he attended as a delegate.[9] While awaiting repairs to the *Planter,* Smalls was removed from an all-white streetcar in Philadelphia on December 30, 1864. In the following months, his celebrity allowed him to lead one of the first mass boycotts of segregated public transportation. A city law finally permitted integrated streetcars in 1867.[10]

At the war's conclusion, Smalls received a commission as brigadier general of the South Carolina militia. He then purchased his former owner's house in Beaufort, but he was generous to the economically devastated McKees.[11] Having received a rudimentary education from private tutors in Philadelphia during the war, Smalls continued his studies after settling in Beaufort.[12] He embarked on business ventures, opening a store and a school for black children in 1867. He also published a newspaper, the Beaufort *Southern Standard,* starting in 1872.[13] Smalls's impressive résumé and his ability to speak the Sea Island Gullah dialect enhanced his local popularity and opened doors in South Carolina politics. He joined other prominent black and white politicians as a delegate to the 1868 South Carolina constitutional convention. Later that year, Smalls won his first elective office: a term in the state house of representatives. From 1870 to 1874, he

served in the state senate, chairing the printing committee.

In 1874, redistricting gave Smalls the opportunity to run for the U.S. Congress in a southeast South Carolina district with a majority-black constituency (68 percent of the population). In Smalls's hometown of Beaufort, African Americans outnumbered whites seven to one.[14] In an uneventful campaign, Smalls defeated Independent nominee J. P. M. Epping—a white man who ran on a "reform" platform opposing the Radical Republican state government—with nearly 80 percent of the vote. Smalls received a position on the Agriculture Committee in his freshman term, a key assignment for his farming constituency and thus a boost to his efforts to prepare for the potentially formidable opposition to his re-election.

Despite the Democratic majority, Smalls's first term was one of his most active and fruitful. For his coastal constituents, he obtained appropriations to improve the Port Royal Harbor that passed with little debate, owing to a letter from the Secretary of War presented as evidence.[15] Smalls also sought other internal improvements, including compensation from the federal government for its use of Charleston's military academy, the Citadel, since 1865.[16]

Smalls spoke openly in defense of his race and his party. In June 1876, he attempted unsuccessfully to add an antidiscrimination amendment to an army reorganization bill. His amendment, which would have integrated army regiments, required that race would no longer affect soldiers' placement. The following month, Smalls addressed a bill to redeploy federal troops in the South to patrol the Texas–Mexican border. Smalls argued against transferring federal troops stationed in his home state, warning that private Red Shirt militias—South Carolina's version of the Ku Klux Klan—would make war on the government and freedmen. Advocates of the troop transfer argued that the corrupt Republican government in South Carolina brought on the violence and that it remained a state issue. Smalls disagreed, noting that the federal presence would help "cut off that rotten part all round South Carolina so as to let the core stand. It is those rotten parts which are troubling us. We are getting along all right ourselves."[17]

While touring the state with Republican Governor Daniel Chamberlain during the 1876 campaign, Smalls attended a rally in Edgefield, South Carolina, where Red Shirt leader and former Confederate General Matthew Butler overran the meeting and threatened Smalls's life. Though the Republican entourage escaped unharmed, a sympathetic observer noted the ease with which Butler and his Red Shirts moved through the town: "Even in Mexico Gen. Butler's command could only be regarded as a revolutionary army, but in South Carolina they are called 'reformers.'" Smalls's opponent, George D. Tillman, who hailed from a prominent Democratic family, exacerbated tensions. The New York Times referred to Tillman as a "Democratic tiger, violent in his treatment of Republicans, incendiary in his language, and advising all sorts of illegal measures to restrain Republicans from voting." During the campaign, Smalls described Tillman as "the personification of red-shirt Democracy" and the "arch enemy of my race."[18] Despite heading the militia to break up a strike in the middle of the campaign, Smalls escaped the Democratic tsunami that swept South Carolina local elections, barely defeating Tillman with 52 percent (19,954 votes).[19] Polling places were spared much of the Red Shirt violence, primarily because Governor Chamberlain requested federal troops to stand guard.[20] Tillman later contested the military presence, hoping a Democratic Congress would rule in his favor. Defending himself in the final session of the 44th Congress, Smalls called Election Day in South Carolina "a carnival of bloodshed and violence."[21]

Smalls arrived in Washington for the 45th Congress (1877–1879) to receive his position on the Committee on the Militia and face Tillman's challenge to his election; however, he was unable to get to work. The following July, the Democratic South Carolina state government charged Smalls with accepting a $5,000 bribe while chairing the printing committee in the state senate. Smalls arrived in Columbia on October 6, 1877, to face trial. On November 26, he was convicted and sentenced to a three-year prison term. Republican newspapers cried foul, accusing Democrats of targeting the "hero of the *Planter*" because of his success as a black Representative.[22] After three days in jail, Smalls was released pending his appeal with the state supreme court. He returned to Washington to face Tillman's contested election challenge before the Democratically controlled Committee on Elections. Though the committee ruled in Tillman's favor, just before the end of the second session on June 20, 1878, Smalls retained his seat because the whole House never considered the findings. Though his triumph over Tillman was a symbolic victory for House Republicans, Smalls's preoccupation with his criminal case and the defense of his seat left him little time to legislate during the short third session.

Smalls's chances in the 1878 election were slim. South Carolina black politicians faced a deadly threat from the white supremacist-controlled government. Sea Island observer Laura Towne noted in her diary: "Political times are simply frightful. Men are shot at, hounded down, trapped and held til certain meetings are over and intimidated in every possible way."[23] The final blow to Smalls's campaign was his unresolved conviction, which Tillman—who returned as his opponent—used to defeat him. Though Smalls received a majority of the black votes in the district, the small number who braved the fierce intimidation were unable to prevent the Democratic sweep.[24] Tillman took 26,409 votes (71 percent) compared to Smalls's 10,664 votes (29 percent).[25]

An 1879 resolution to his criminal case allowed Smalls to concentrate on returning to politics. Although the state supreme court rejected his appeal, Democratic Governor William Simpson pardoned him on April 29, 1879—acting on assurances from the U.S. District Attorney that charges would be dropped against South Carolinians accused of violating election laws in 1878.[26] Smalls, nevertheless, remained optimistic about Republican politics in South Carolina. "Robert S. is very cheerful, and says that the outrageous bulldozing and cheating in this last election is the best thing that could have happened for the Republican Party," observed Laura Towne, "for it has

been so barefaced and open that it cannot be denied."[27] Smalls still controlled the Beaufort Republican Party, and he remained popular among the town's substantial black population. By 1880, Smalls resolved to take back his seat from Tillman. However, his allegiance to the Republican Party made it increasingly difficult for Smalls to rally black voters to his side. Issues that wedded black voters to the GOP—primarily fears of returning to slavery— were fading in light of black disenchantment with local Republican corruption scandals. The state party also was in chaos, as the South Carolina Republican convention was unable to nominate a state ticket. Smalls's attachment to the disorganized and disgraced state party proved to be the strongest point of attack for Democratic opponents. Red Shirt intimidation, which had become routine in recent elections, complicated matters.[28]

Smalls failed to defeat Tillman in a violent campaign, garnering only 15,287 votes, or 40 percent; however, he contested the election, hoping to capitalize on the slim Republican majority in the 47th Congress (1881–1883). His case came before the Committee on Elections on July 18, 1882. Using Edgefield, South Carolina, as a case study, Smalls won the support of the committee by testifying that his supporters had been frightened away from the polls.[29] In an attempt to prevent Smalls from taking the seat, House Democrats sought to avoid a quorum by deserting the House Chamber when his case came to a vote on July 19, 1882. Their plan backfired, however, as the House seated him, 141 to 1 with 144 abstentions.[30] Smalls returned to his appointments on the Agriculture and Militia committees. While his victory was yet another blow to southern Democrats, the curtailed term again left him little time to legislate.

By 1882, South Carolina Democrats had gerry-mandered the state so that only one district retained any hope of electing a black candidate. The new district's lines demonstrated the legislature's intent; completely ignoring county lines, the district contained one-quarter of the state's substantial black population (82 percent of the district's population was black).[31] Smalls sought the nomination but was opposed at the Republican convention by longtime black politician Samuel Lee and Smalls's congressional friend and ally Representative Edmund Mackey. Smalls deferred to Mackey—a sympathetic white man whose wife was mulatto—to maintain unity in the party. However, Mackey died suddenly on January 28, 1884, shortly after defeating Lee—who ran as an Independent candidate—in the general election. Lee had taken a federal patronage position in Alabama, leaving Smalls the best chance at the seat. He won a special election without opposition and took his oath of office on March 18, 1884.[32] Smalls resumed his position on the Committee on the Militia and received an appointment to the Committee on Manufactures.

Smalls continued earlier attempts to secure federal debt relief for South Carolinians who lost their property due to nonpayment of wartime taxes, justifying the relief by pointing to the free services and the welcome federal soldiers had received in places like Port Royal; however, the House rejected his proposal.[33] Smalls was more successful with a bill regulating the manufacture and sale of liquor in the District of Columbia. He offered an amendment that would guarantee the integration of restaurants and other eating facilities in the nation's capital. After parliamentary debate about the germaneness of the amendment, it was added to the bill, which passed the House though it died in the Senate Committee on the District of Columbia.[34] In the 1884 election, Smalls's victory over Democrat William Elliott was unexpectedly easy. Though both candidates expected a violent campaign, the election was relatively quiet, with Sea Island blacks coming out to support their favorite son. Smalls was appointed to the Committee on War Claims in the 49th Congress (1885–1887), made up of a safe Democratic majority. Encouraged by his recent victory, black state senators nominated Smalls for an open seat in the U.S. Senate in December 1884. Although he lost to Democratic Governor Wade Hampton, 31 to 3, his nomination was a symbolic protest of white supremacy.[35]

In his first full term since he was a freshman, Smalls gave one of the more impassioned speeches of his career,

asking Congress to approve a $50 per month pension for Maria Hunter, the widow of General David Hunter. Hunter was one of the first white Union commanders to raise African-American regiments in the Civil War and was known for issuing an order to free slaves in Florida, Georgia, and South Carolina. But, Hunter was also controversial for his slash-and-burn strategy during several Shenandoah Valley campaigns, as well as for his inattention to defendants' rights in the trial of conspirators in President Abraham Lincoln's assassination. Democrats argued against permitting the pension. Smalls admonished his colleagues: "Can it be that there is a secret or sinister motive either personal or political? . . . Can it be that this is your revenge for all his patriotic conduct?"[36] Though the private bill passed both the House and Senate, President Grover Cleveland vetoed the measure, claiming the Widow Hunter's case was best handled by the Pensions Bureau. Smalls also steered through the House a bill that allowed for the redemption of school farmlands outside Beaufort that had been owned by the federal government since the Civil War.[37] He also submitted a resolution requesting relief funds after a flood in 1886 destroyed crops and homes in his district. The House refused to appropriate funds, despite Smalls's appeal that the state government would not furnish relief money until late in the year. Smalls also failed in a bid to make Port Royal a coaling station for the U.S. Navy.[38]

Smalls faced a challenge from within his own party for re-election in 1886. African-American rival Henry Thompson attempted to capitalize on the growing competition within the black community between dark-skinned blacks and mulattos. Thompson's radical position proved less of a threat for the nomination; however, black voters divided in the general election, with the "darker delegation" voting against Smalls.[39] The split in the black vote made Smalls vulnerable to Democratic attack. "Elections," Smalls lamented to the *Washington Post*, "are all in the hands of Democrats."[40] His foe, Democrat William Elliott, returned to defeat him with 56 percent of the vote in an election in which black disfranchisement was routine.[41] Smalls contested his loss. Despite more than 800 pages of testimony and support from powerful Republican Representatives Henry Cabot Lodge of Massachusetts and Robert M. La Follette of Wisconsin, a House weary of handling the South's racial problems declined to seat Smalls, with a vote of 142 to 127 on February 13, 1889.[42] Accepting the inevitability of his loss, Smalls had already stepped aside to allow a younger politician, Thomas Miller, to run for his seat in 1888.

Smalls remained an active and popular politician, managing to win the chairmanship of the Republican state convention in 1890.[43] Although he was favored for the post of sheriff in Beaufort County, Smalls made another bid for the U.S. Senate, but he received only one vote from the state legislature.[44] He also attempted to return to the House in 1892 but lost a four-way race for the Republican nomination, which Representative George W. Murray

secured en route to a general election victory. After his wife Hannah died in 1883, Smalls married Annie Wigg on April 9, 1890. They had one son, William Robert, in 1892, before Annie's death in 1895. Smalls benefited throughout this period from GOP patronage. In 1889, Republican President Benjamin Harrison appointed him the collector at the port of Beaufort. He held the post until Republicans lost the White House in 1892. Smalls regained the appointment in 1898 from Republican President William McKinley. Over time, his duties as collector became more onerous in the face of racism and segregation in Beaufort. He was forced to step down in 1913 after the White House again transferred to a Democrat. Smalls died of natural causes in his Beaufort home on February 22, 1915.

FOR FURTHER READING

Billingsley, Andrew. *Yearning to Breathe Free: Robert Smalls of South Carolina and his Families* (Columbia: University of South Carolina Press, 2007).

Congressman Robert Smalls: A Patriot's Journey From Slavery to Capitol, DVD, produced by Adrena Ifill (Washington, DC: DoubleBack Productions LLC, 2005).

Miller, Edward A. Jr., *Gullah Statesman: Robert Smalls from Slavery to Congress, 1839–1915* (Columbia: University of South Carolina Press, 1995).

"Smalls, Robert," *Biographical Directory of the United States Congress, 1774–Present*, http://bioguide.congress.gov/scripts/biodisplay.pl?index=S000502.

Uya, Okun Edet. *From Slavery to Political Service: Robert Smalls, 1839–1915* (New York: Oxford University Press, 1971).

MANUSCRIPT COLLECTIONS

Library of Congress, Manuscript Division (Washington, DC) *Papers:* In the Frederick Douglass Papers, ca. 1841–1967, 19.4 linear feet. Correspondents include Robert Smalls. *Papers:* In the Rufus and S. Willard Saxton Papers, ca. 1834–1934, 10 linear feet. Subjects include Robert Smalls. *Microfilm:* In the Carter G. Woodson Collection of Negro Papers and Related Documents, ca. 1803–1936, 10 microfilm reels. Persons represented include Robert Smalls.

South Carolina Historical Society (Charleston, SC) *Papers:* In the Steamship *Planter* Records, 1861–1862, one folder. Persons represented include Robert Smalls.

NOTES

1   Okun Edet Uya, *From Slavery to Political Service: Robert Smalls, 1839–1915* (New York: Oxford University Press, 1971): 90.

2   Uya, *From Slavery to Political Service*: vii.

3   Historians debate the identity of Smalls's father. Smalls's descendants claim his father was his owner, John McKee; see Ingrid Irene Sabio, "Robert Smalls," in Jessie Carney Smith, ed., *Notable Black American Men* (Farmington Hills, MI: Gale Research, Inc., 1999): 1071 (hereinafter referred to as *NBAM*). Sabio also suggests that Smalls may have been the son of Moses Goldsmith, a Charleston merchant. Another biographer notes that his father was unknown but suggests John McKee's paternity; see Glenda E. Gilmore, "Smalls, Robert," *American National Biography* 20 (New York: Oxford University Press, 1999): 111–112 (hereinafter referred to as *ANB*). Still others indicate his father was a white manager on the McKee plantation named Patrick Smalls; see Shirley Washington, *Outstanding African Americans of Congress* (Washington, DC: United States Capitol Historical Society, 1998): 8. If he was not Smalls's son, it is unclear how he received his surname, though his chief biographer speculates "Smalls" may have been a pejorative description of his stature. See Edward A. Miller, Jr., *Gullah Statesman: Robert Smalls from Slavery to Congress, 1839–1915* (Columbia: University of South Carolina Press, 1995): 7.

4   Smalls also had two stepdaughters, Clara and Charlotte Jones. See Andrew Billingsley, *Yearning to Breathe Free: Robert Smalls of South Carolina and his Families* (Columbia: University of South Carolina Press, 2007): xxiii.

5   Maurine Christopher, *Black Americans in Congress* (New York: Thomas Y. Crowell Company, 1976): 42; Gilmore, "Smalls, Robert," *ANB*.

6   The U.S. Government never fully compensated Smalls for the value of the *Planter* as a reward for its capture. During the next 30 years, black Members of Congress sought compensation for Smalls equal to the value of the ship. James O'Hara sought compensation for Smalls in the 49th Congress (1885–1887). Henry Cheatham made similar unsuccessful requests in the 51st and 52nd Congresses (1889–1893), and George White failed to pass a resolution reimbursing Smalls in the 55th Congress (1897–1899). The House finally approved a measure submitted by White on May 18, 1900, during the 56th Congress (1899–1901). White originally requested that Smalls receive $20,000. The Committee on War Claims, however, reduced the amount to $5,000. Smalls received this sum after President William McKinley signed the bill into law on June 5, 1900. See *Congressional Record*, House, 56th Cong., 1st sess. (18 May 1900): 5715.

7   Uya, *From Slavery to Political Service*: 16–17.

8   Details on Smalls's military service are unclear because his paperwork was lost. Several sources indicate that Smalls served in the Navy, but others note that he did not have the education to pilot a naval vessel. Therefore, he either received a commission in or worked as a civilian for the Union Army and was frequently detailed to the Navy for service at sea. Smalls was promoted to captain of the *Planter* in 1865, though it is unclear whether he attained that rank in the Navy or the Army. His alleged salary of $150 per month made him one of the highest-paid African-American servicemen in the Civil War. Smalls received his Navy pension after petitioning Congress in 1897. See Christopher, *Black Americans in Congress*: 42; Gilmore, "Smalls, Robert," *ANB*; Sabio, "Robert Smalls," *NBAM*; Eric Foner, *Freedom's Lawmakers: A Directory of Black Officeholders During Reconstruction* (New York: Oxford University Press, 1993): 198; Uya, *From Slavery to Political Service*: 20–22; Miller, *Gullah Statesman*: 12–27; Billingsley, *Yearning to Breathe Free*: 61, 75, 82; Kitt Haley Alexander, "Robert Smalls' Timeline," *Robert Smalls Official Website and Information Center*; see http://www.robertsmalls.org/timeline.htm (accessed 11 October 2007).

9   Foner, *Freedom's Lawmakers*: 198. Smalls was a delegate to the Republican National Conventions in 1864, 1872, and 1876 and the Republican National Conventions from 1884 to 1896.

10 Uya, *From Slavery to Political Service*: 26–27; Miller, *Gullah Statesman*: 23.

11 Rupert Sargent Holland, ed., *Letters and Diary of Laura M. Towne* (New York: Negro Universities Press, 1969): 241; Miller, *Gullah Statesman*: 95. While serving in Congress, he introduced a private bill asking for the relief of the McKee family, but the bill did not pass (see H.R. 2487, 44th Congress, 1st session).

12 Christopher, *Black Americans in Congress*: 42.

13 Foner, *Freedom's Lawmakers*: 198.

14 Uya, *From Slavery to Political Service*: 90.

15 *Congressional Record*, House, 44th Cong., 1st sess. (23 May 1876): 3272–3275; *Congressional Record*, House, 44th Cong., 1st sess. (25 July 1876): 4876.

16 Miller, *Gullah Statesman*: 97. His bill passed the House, but no action was taken in the Senate.

17 *Congressional Record*, House, 44th Cong., 1st sess. (18 July 1876): 4705.

18 "The Rifle Clubs 'Dividing Time,'" 20 October 1876, *New York Times*: 1; "The South Carolina Cheating," 15 December 1880, *New York Times*: 1; "The South Carolina Issue," 31 October 1890, *Washington Post*: 4.

19 Michael J. Dubin et al., *U.S. Congressional Elections, 1788–1997* (Jefferson, NC: McFarland & Company, Inc., Publishers, 1998): 240.

20 Miller, *Gullah Statesman*: 108.

21 *Congressional Record*, Appendix, 44th Cong., 2nd sess. (24 February 1877): A123–136.

22 "Robert Smalls' Trial," 17 December 1877, *New York Times*: 2; Grace Greenwood, "Remember Those in Bonds," 14 January 1878, *New York Times*: 1; "The Persecution of Mr. Smalls," 7 December 1878, *New York Times*: 1.

23 Holland, ed., *Letters and Diary of Laura M. Towne*: 288.

24 Uya, *From Slavery to Political Service*: 111.

25 Dubin et al., *U.S. Congressional Elections, 1788–1997*: 247.

26 Miller, *Gullah Statesman*: 131.

27 Holland, ed., *Letters and Diary of Laura M. Towne*: 293.

28 Uya, *From Slavery to Political Service*: 111–113.

29 *Congressional Record*, Appendix, 47th Cong., 1st sess. (19 July 1882): A634–643.

30 Miller, *Gullah Statesman*: 138.

31 Ibid., 139; Stanley B. Parsons et al., *United States Congressional Districts, 1883–1913* (New York: Greenwood Press, 1990): 136–143.

32 Miller, *Gullah Statesman*: 147.

33 Uya, *From Slavery to Political Service*: 118–119; Miller, *Gullah Statesman*: 147–148.

34 *Congressional Record*, House, 48th Cong., 2nd sess. (23 February 1883): 2057–2059; see H.R. 7556, 48th Congress, 2nd session.

35 See Christopher, *Black Americans in Congress*: 50: Miller, *Gullah Statesman*: 153.

36 *Congressional Record*, Appendix, 49th Cong., 1st sess. (30 July 1886): A319.

37 *Congressional Record*, House, 49th Cong., 1st sess. (6 January 1886): 481.

38 *Congressional Record*, House, 49th Cong., 1st sess. (26 June 1886): 6183.

39 "Congressman Smalls's Canvass," 20 September 1886, *New York Times*: 1.

40 "Why Smalls Was Defeated," 12 December 1886, *Washington Post*: 3.

41 Christopher, *Black Americans in Congress*: 50; Dubin et al., *U.S. Congressional Elections, 1788–1997*: 276.

42 Christopher, *Black Americans in Congress*: 50–51.

43 "Negro Delegates in Control," 18 September 1890, *Washington Post*: 1.

44 "Wade Hampton Losing Votes," 11 December 1890, *New York Times*: 1.

James Edward O'Hara
1844–1905

UNITED STATES REPRESENTATIVE ★ 1883–1887
REPUBLICAN FROM NORTH CAROLINA

A freeborn Irish–West Indian mulatto, James O'Hara was the only black Member on the first day of the 48th Congress (1883–1885), having succeeded on his fourth attempt to win a seat representing North Carolina's "Black Second" district. A resolute legislator, he worked to restore the civil rights stripped from African Americans since the end of Congressional Reconstruction in 1877. "I for one . . . hold that we are all Americans," he told his congressional colleagues. "That no matter whether a man is black or white he is an American citizen, and that the aegis of this great Republic should be held over him regardless of his color."[1] Despite O'Hara's drive to secure a seat in the House and, subsequently, to pass legislation, congressional opponents of black civil rights stymied his efforts.

James Edward O'Hara was born February 26, 1844, in New York City. The illegitimate son of an Irish merchant and a black West Indian mother, he had light skin and red highlights in his curly hair.[2] The historical record first picks up O'Hara in the company of New York-based missionaries in Union-occupied eastern North Carolina in 1862.[3] Well-educated, he taught primary school to free black children in New Bern and Goldsboro, North Carolina.[4] In 1864, O'Hara married Ann Marie Harris, but the couple separated two years later and eventually divorced. They had one son, born after their divorce. O'Hara married Elizabeth Eleanor Harris in 1869.[5] They also had a son, Raphael. O'Hara studied law at Howard University in Washington, DC, but there is no record of his graduation. Admitted to the North Carolina bar in 1873, he established a private practice in Enfield, North Carolina.

North Carolina was a bastion of lucrative patronage positions in the 1870s, and Republican lawmakers clamored for offices. James O'Hara was quick to recognize these benefits and became involved in the local party machine. He first served as a secretary at the freedmen's and Republican Party meetings just after the Civil War, composing reports for newspapers. At the 1868 North Carolina constitutional convention, he served as a delegate and an engrossing clerk. From 1868 to 1869, O'Hara also served in the state house of representatives. In 1873, he was elected chairman of the Halifax County board of commissioners. During his four-year tenure, O'Hara endured multiple Democratic accusations of corruption and extravagance—all of which he initially denied, claiming the charges were politically and racially motivated. However, when he and several other Republican commissioners were indicted, O'Hara and a colleague pleaded no contest and agreed to pay court costs to have the charges dropped.[6] O'Hara faced further difficulty in 1876, when he resigned his post as a presidential elector in the face of threats from local Democrats.[7]

O'Hara began his long quest for a seat in the U.S. Congress in 1874 when he made a bid for North Carolina's northeastern "Black Second" district seat. Centered in the cotton-growing portion of the state, the district acquired its nickname because its population was 58 percent black, the largest of any part of the state.[8] O'Hara lost the Republican nomination to John A. Hyman, who became the first African American to serve North Carolina in the U.S. Congress. Nevertheless, O'Hara remained committed to winning the seat, in part because there were fewer patronage opportunities in the Democratically controlled state at the end of Congressional Reconstruction. Political office remained a viable outlet.

O'Hara made another attempt at the "Black Second" nomination in 1878. He obtained the party endorsement over moderate Republican and former Representative Curtis Brogden, Hyman, and three other candidates. The fight for the nomination lasted 29 ballots at the

IMAGE COURTESY OF MOORLAND–SPINGARN RESEARCH CENTER, HOWARD UNIVERSITY

contentious Republican district convention. In the general election, O'Hara's opponents brought up his past corruption charges and accused him of bigamy, as it was unclear whether he was divorced from his first wife. Dissatisfied with his defenses, state Republican leaders gathered three weeks before Election Day to nominate white candidate James H. Harris to take O'Hara's place. But O'Hara refused to step down and, despite the attacks and the loss of party support, he won the three-way race between the two Republican candidates and Democrat William H. Kitchin, a member of a politically powerful family in North Carolina. Based on technicalities, election canvassers subsequently eliminated enough of O'Hara's votes in three counties to hand Kitchin the victory. O'Hara challenged the results, but evidence in his favor was destroyed when his house suspiciously burned down. O'Hara failed to persuade either the North Carolina state supreme court or the Democratic 46th Congress (1879–1881) to unseat Kitchin. He returned in 1880 to seek the congressional seat but lost a bitter race for the Republican nomination to carpetbagger Orlando Hubbs. [9]

Between congressional bids, O'Hara was active in local and national politics. By 1881, he had aligned himself with a statewide anti-Prohibition campaign and was an architect of a coalition between Liberal Democrats and North Carolina Republicans in 1882. That same year, he made his fourth attempt to gain the "Black Second" seat, bolstered by discontented local black politicians who believed they were being marginalized within the party. [10] At the state Republican convention, two other candidates opposed him: incumbent Hubbs and scalawag Lotte W. Humphrey. Though Democrats accused African-American voters in the "Black Second" of voting only for black candidates, voters were divided. None of the candidates controlled the convention's first ballot, and all three engaged in ruthless attack campaigns, promising patronage to potential supporters. Humphrey eventually bowed to O'Hara, giving the black candidate the majority of delegates. An O'Hara delegate called for his nomination

by voice vote. Though the crowd roared in O'Hara's favor, the convention chairman declared Hubbs's candidacy and quickly adjourned. [11] Both sides claimed victory and, in the following months, Hubbs and O'Hara vigorously sought each other's resignation. Shortly before the election, Hubbs capitulated to pressure from O'Hara forces, who spoke for the majority-black voters in the district when they threatened to abandon the state Republican ticket if their candidate was not on the ballot. Without adequate Democratic opposition, O'Hara was unopposed in the general election. [12] Reapportionment in 1883 changed the borders of O'Hara's district in his favor, increasing the black population with the addition of Bertie County. [13] In 1884, he was easily re-elected over Democrat Frederick A. Woodard, taking 59 percent of the total returns and the most votes ever recorded for an African-American candidate in the "Black Second" district. [14]

As part of the Republican minority in the House, O'Hara received appointments to the Mines and Mining and the Expenditures on Public Buildings committees when he arrived in Washington for the 48th Congress (1883–1885) in December 1883. He later traded his Mines and Mining position for a spot on the Invalid Pensions Committee in the 49th Congress (1885–1887). O'Hara was active on the Invalid Pensions Committee. In the first session, he introduced more than 100 committee reports, serving as an unofficial subcommittee chairman. [15] O'Hara did not take the floor to make long addresses; instead, he delivered concise speeches and put forth bold legislation, often fighting for the rights he and other Black Americans had lost since the end of Reconstruction. [16]

On January 8, 1884, O'Hara boldly proposed a constitutional amendment to ensure equal accommodations for blacks on public transportation. He wanted to reverse a Supreme Court decision delivered in 1883 declaring the 1875 Civil Rights Bill unconstitutional, but the House refused to consider the measure. [17] The following December, O'Hara proposed an amendment to regulate interstate travel and commerce, calling for equal accommodations for all railroad passengers, regardless of color. Under the existing law, when a railroad passed into southern states, first-class black passengers were typically forced to move to a second-class "Jim Crow car." O'Hara capitalized on contemporary arguments favoring federal regulation of interstate commerce, maintaining that if Congress had authority over freight passing between states and could set standards for the treatment of animals, it could regulate how railroads served their customers. O'Hara's amendment passed on the first vote, but Democratic opponents quickly nullified the measure with another allowing railroads to classify passengers at their own discretion. The final bill passed—without O'Hara's vote—in the 49th Congress with language so vague, the railroads continued their discriminatory practices.[18]

In the face of repeated rejections of his civil rights legislation, O'Hara focused on individual instances and locations of discrimination, but he met similar opposition. On January 12, 1885, he offered a bill that would require eating establishments in the nation's capital to charge customers without discriminating based on race, or risk fines up to $100. Referred to the Committee on the District of Columbia, the bill was never reported back.[19] He reiterated his request at the opening of the 49th Congress, but the bill met the same fate.[20] On March 17, a white mob stormed a Carrollton, Mississippi, courthouse where seven white men were charged with assaulting two black men. The mob opened fire on all of the black men present, killing 11 and wounding nine. O'Hara requested that Speaker John G. Carlisle of Kentucky appoint a five-member committee to investigate the incident and issue a report. His original request was rejected before it could be submitted to the Rules Committee, and a renewed request submitted the following month was referred to the committee but never reported.[21]

O'Hara used his legislative persistence to help his constituents, both white and black. Residing in a coastal district, he sought river and harbor appropriations for North Carolina in nearly every session of his congressional service, stressing funding to improve waterways on which cotton was shipped to support his district's cotton-growing industry. Despite his determination, most of O'Hara's amendments were rejected.[22] Recognizing that a great number of his constituents were working-class laborers, he opposed the passage of a labor arbitration bill that allowed a third party to settle disputes between employers and employees. Though he favored arbitration, O'Hara wanted to concentrate on organizing unions to defend labor interests.[23]

Internal feuds among "Black Second" Republicans ended O'Hara's congressional career. Although O'Hara won 75 percent of the nominating convention's vote, his candidacy was weakened by accusations that he was unable to meet the needs of his constituents, that he did not distribute available patronage positions to other black aspirants, and that, as a light-skinned mulatto, he was not a fair representative for his race.[24] Another black Republican, Israel B. Abbott, opposed O'Hara in the 1886 race as an Independent Republican. Abbott had one term in the state legislature to his credit and had served as a delegate to the national Republican convention in 1880, but his most significant advantage was that he was dark-skinned—"a true representative of his race" according to the *Washington Bee*—and "a native of the district," having escaped to New Bern, North Carolina, after Union forces took over in 1861.[25] Nevertheless, O'Hara won most of the black vote from loyal Republican freedmen, taking 40 percent to Abbott's 15 percent. However, Democrat Furnifold Simmons capitalized on the GOP fissure, capturing 45 percent of the vote for victory.[26] Two years later, O'Hara again sought a congressional nomination, but lost to Henry Cheatham, who would reclaim the "Black Second." O'Hara returned to his law practice, partnering with his son, Raphael. He began publishing a newspaper, the Enfield *Progress* shortly before his death in New Bern, North Carolina, on September 15, 1905.

FOR FURTHER READING

Anderson, Eric. "James O'Hara of North Carolina: Black Leadership and Local Government," Howard Rabinowitz, ed., *Southern Black Leaders of the Reconstruction Era* (Urbana: University of Illinois Press, 1982).

_____. *Race and Politics in North Carolina, 1872–1901* (Baton Rouge: Louisiana State University Press, 1981).

"O'Hara, James Edward," *Biographical Directory of the United States Congress, 1774–Present*, http://bioguide. congress.gov/scripts/biodisplay.pl?index=O000054.

Reid, George W. "Four in Black: North Carolina's Black Congressmen, 1874–1901," *The Journal of Negro History* 64 (Summer 1979): 229–243.

MANUSCRIPT COLLECTION

University of Chicago Library (Chicago, IL) Special Collections Research Center. *Papers:* 1866–1970, 1.5 linear feet. The James E. O'Hara Papers consist of miscellaneous materials that document the life and career of one of America's first black Representatives. There are several letters from family and from constituents in North Carolina. In addition, three folders are devoted to photographs of Representative O'Hara, his wife and son, and his associates. An important and detailed resource for the study of the O'Hara family and the social history of the late-19-century South is the biographical sketch of Representative O'Hara and his family written by his granddaughter, Vera Jean O'Hara Rivers, entitled "A Thespian Must Play His Role." Finally, the collection includes some ephemeral material, such as a handbill announcing the establishment of a Canadian newspaper for fugitive slaves, an autograph book and "Register of Documents sent" owned by James E. O'Hara, and a small 20th-century booklet of biographical sketches that includes a brief description of Representative O'Hara. An inventory is available in the repository and online.

NOTES

1 *Congressional Record*, House, 48th Cong., 2nd sess. (17 December 1884): 317.

2 The names of O'Hara's parents are not known.

3 One scholar claims O'Hara was born in the West Indies. See George W. Reid, "Four in Black: North Carolina's Black Congressmen, 1874–1901," *The Journal of Negro History* 64: 3 (Summer 1979): 229–243. O'Hara's childhood is not documented. Most likely, he moved from New York, where he attended public schools, to the West Indies around 1850. See Eric Anderson, "O'Hara, James Edward," *American National Biography* 16 (New York: Oxford University Press, 1999): 649–651 (hereinafter referred to as *ANB*); Thomas Holt, "O'Hara, James Edward," *Dictionary of American Negro Biography* (New York: Norton, 1982): 474–475; Maurine Christopher, *Black Americans in Congress* (New York: Thomas Y. Crowell Company, 1976): 152.

4 Anderson, "O'Hara, James Edward," *ANB*.

5 The name of O'Hara's first son is not known. There is no evidence that Ann Marie Harris and Elizabeth Eleanor Harris were related.

6 Anderson, "O'Hara, James Edward," *ANB*.

7 Eric Anderson, "James O'Hara of North Carolina: Black Leadership and Local Government," in Howard Rabinowitz, ed., *Southern Black Leaders of the Reconstruction Era* (Urbana: University of Illinois Press, 1982): 104.

8 Stanley B. Parsons et al., *United States Congressional Districts, 1843–1883* (New York: Greenwood Press, 1986): 200.

9 Eric Anderson, *Race and Politics in North Carolina, 1872–1901* (Baton Rouge: Louisiana State University Press, 1981): 63–68.

10 Anderson, *Race and Politics*: 98.

11 Anderson, "James O'Hara of North Carolina: Black Leadership and Local Government": 117.

12 Ibid.

13 Anderson, *Race and Politics*: 141; Kenneth Martis, *The Historical Atlas of Political Parties in the United States Congress: 1789–1989* (New York: Macmillan, 1989): 139; Stanley B. Parsons et al., *United States Congressional Districts, 1883–1913* (New York: Greenwood Press, 1990): 97–99.

14 Michael J. Dubin et al., *U.S. Congressional Elections, 1788–1997* (Jefferson, NC: McFarland & Company, Inc., Publishers, 1998): 268; Anderson, *Race and Politics*: 118.

15 Anderson, *Race and Politics*: 124. There were no official subcommittees for the Invalid Pensions Committee, but Members were often assigned leadership roles to consider specific bills or were charged with organizing petitions from specific states. See the Minutes of the Committee on Invalid Pensions, 49th Congress, Records of the United States House of Representatives (RG 233), Center for Legislative Archives, National Archives and Records Administration, Washington, DC

16 Anderson, "O'Hara, James Edward," *ANB*.

17 *Congressional Record*, House, 48th Cong., 1st sess. (10 January 1884): 347.

18 Okun Edet Uya, *From Slavery to Political Service: Robert Smalls, 1839–1915* (New York: Oxford University Press, 1971): 120; a more detailed account is available in Christopher, *Black Americans in Congress*: 153–155. Smalls did vote for the final bill; see *Congressional Record*, House, 48th Cong., 2nd sess. (8 January 1885): 554.

19 *Congressional Record*, House, 48th Cong., 2nd sess. (12 January 1885): 632.

20 *Congressional Record*, House, 49th Cong., 1st sess. (5 January 1886): 438.

21 *Congressional Record*, House, 49th Cong., 1st sess. (29 March 1886): 2897; *Congressional Record*, House, 49th Cong., 1st sess. (2 April 1886): 3123.

22 Although most of O'Hara's requests were rejected, he obtained funding to remove obstructions from a North Carolina stream and to expand another. See *Congressional Record*, House, 48th Cong., 1st sess. (10 June 1884): 4980–4982; *Congressional Record*, House, 48th Cong., 1st sess. (12 June 1884): 5069; *Congressional Record*, House, 48th Cong., 2nd sess. (18 February 1885): 1857; *Congressional Record*, House, 49th Cong., 1st sess. (22 April 1886): 3748; *Congressional Record*, House, 49th Cong., 1st sess. (12 February 1886): 1404.

23 *Congressional Record*, House, 49th Cong., 1st sess. (2 April 1886): 3049.

24 Anderson, "O'Hara, James Edward," *ANB*.

25 Anderson, *Race and Politics*: 135.

26 Dubin et al., *U.S. Congressional Elections, 1788–1997*: 275.

"The Negroes' Temporary Farewell"

JIM CROW AND THE EXCLUSION OF AFRICAN AMERICANS FROM CONGRESS, 1887–1929

On December 5, 1887, for the first time in almost two decades, Congress convened without an African-American Member. "All the men who stood up in awkward squads to be sworn in on Monday had white faces," noted a correspondent for the *Philadelphia Record* of the Members who took the oath of office on the House Floor. "The negro is not only out of Congress, he is practically out of politics."[1] Though three black men served in the next Congress (51st, 1889–1891), the number of African Americans serving on Capitol Hill diminished significantly as the congressional focus on racial equality faded. Only five African Americans were elected to the House in the next decade: Henry Cheatham and George White of North Carolina, Thomas Miller and George Murray of South Carolina, and John M. Langston of Virginia. But despite their isolation, these men sought to represent the interests of all African Americans. Like their predecessors, they confronted violent and contested elections, difficulty procuring desirable committee assignments, and an inability to pass their legislative initiatives. Moreover, these black Members faced further impediments in the form of legalized segregation and disfranchisement, general disinterest in progressive racial legislation, and the increasing power of southern conservatives in Congress.

John M. Langston took his seat in Congress after contesting the election results in his district. One of the first African Americans in the nation elected to public office, he was clerk of the Brownhelm (Ohio) Township in 1855.

JOHN MERCER LANGSTON, *FROM THE VIRGINIA PLANTATION TO THE NATIONAL CAPITOL* (HARTFORD, CT: AMERICAN PUBLISHING COMPANY, 1894)

Thomas Rice created the character "the Jim Crow minstrel" in 1828. The actor was one of the first to don blackface makeup and perform as a racially stereotyped character.
IMAGE COURTESY OF LIBRARY OF CONGRESS

Jim Crow:

The term used to describe the segregation, social control, and political and economic subjugation of African Americans in the South from the late 1800s to the 1960s.

Foreshadowing the struggles of a half-century later, magazines like Puck Illustrated *noted the inequities of Jim Crow transportation as early as 1913.*
IMAGE COURTESY OF LIBRARY OF CONGRESS

In the decade after the 1876 presidential election, the Republican-dominated Reconstruction governments, which had provided the basis for black political participation in the South, slowly disintegrated, leaving the rights of black voters and political aspirants vulnerable to Democratic state governments controlled by former Confederates and their sympathizers. The electoral crisis of 1876 also revealed fissures within the GOP, as many party stalwarts focused on commercial issues rather than on the volatile racial agenda previously pursued by the Republicans. This period marked the beginning of a "multigenerational deterioration" of the relationship between black and white Republicans.[2] By the 1890s, most Black Americans had either been barred from or abandoned electoral politics in frustration. Advocacy for blacks in Congress became substantially more difficult.[3] After Representative White's departure from the House of Representatives in March 1901, no African American served in the U.S. Congress for nearly three decades. The length and persistence of this exile from national politics starkly conveyed the sweeping success of the system of racial segregation imposed upon blacks by law and custom, known widely as "Jim Crow."

JIM CROW

During this era African Americans experienced unique suffering and deprivation. Beginning in the last quarter of the 19th century, blacks—the vast majority of whom still lived in the South—endured a system of racial segregation that circumscribed their political, economic, and social status. Distinguished historian of the South C. Vann Woodward explains that the removal of key "restraints" unleashed widespread, virulent racist social policies. Eroding northern liberal interest in fostering a biracial society in the South after 1877, the failure of southern conservatism to check race baiting politics, and the corresponding capitulation of the southern ruling class to rising white supremacist radicalism, each played a part in fashioning a uniquely American racial apartheid.[4]

Jim Crow, a system of segregation enforced by legal and extralegal means, evolved over several decades.[5] Jim Crow was a popular character in southern minstrel shows—in which white performers in blackface portrayed African Americans. How the term Jim Crow came to be associated with segregation is not clear, but it was eventually used to describe both the formal and the informal manifestations of segregation in the South. Beginning with Tennessee in 1870, every southern state adopted laws against interracial marriage. By the 1880s, most public places and many private businesses had Whites Only and Colored facilities. These included schools, seating areas, drinking fountains, work spaces, government buildings, train stations, hospitals, restaurants, hotels, theaters, barbershops, laundries, and even public restrooms.

Virtually all the political advances afforded freedmen during Reconstruction were rolled back and eradicated during the years after 1890. In the South, the races were separated even more systematically and rigidly than during slavery. Many blacks were reduced to a suppressed citizenship that was repeatedly exploited for political and economic purposes. As C. Vann Woodward writes, Jim Crow laws "did not assign the subordinate group a fixed status in society. They were constantly pushing the Negro farther down."[6]

PRE-CONGRESSIONAL EXPERIENCE

Though they served in Congress during the onset of Jim Crow laws, the five Black Americans elected in the late 19th century benefited from educational, economic, and social opportunities provided by federal intervention in the Reconstruction-Era South. All five men were born in the South and hailed from the former Confederacy. Three were born slaves, but before their 14th birthdays all were freed after the conclusion of the Civil War in 1865.[7] Like their predecessors, most of those elected in the early Jim Crow Era were of mixed race: Four of the five were mulatto; two were their masters' sons. Three of these men hailed primarily from the Upper South, a region encompassing North Carolina and extending northwest through Virginia and Maryland. Compared to the more relaxed views on racial miscegenation prevalent in the Lower South—the region stretching southwest from South Carolina—the Upper South had adopted the early British North American system of slavery in which sharp social lines defined the "white" and "black" races. Denied special legal or social privileges of their counterparts in the Lower South, both mulatto and dark-skinned men from the Upper South saw greater opportunity for advancement only after the end of slavery in 1865.[8]

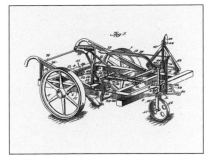

George W. Murray of South Carolina patented several farming inventions before his election to Congress. Patent No. 517,961 was a cultivator and marker to "open furrows for the reception of seeds."
IMAGE COURTESY OF U.S. PATENT AND TRADEMARK OFFICE

These late-19th-century Members also received substantially more formal education than their predecessors. Though their primary and secondary schooling was sporadic, all five attended college—compared with two of the 17 black men who served before them.[9] Their more extensive education allowed Jim Crow-Era black Representatives prestigious careers. Three men practiced law: John Langston, Thomas Miller, and George White. Miller received training at Howard University, but in most rural states, formal legal training was not a requirement for passing the bar, which often consisted of an oral exam administered by local judges and lawyers.[10] Several law schools rejected Langston in the 1850s. Tutored by local professionals, he passed an oral exam in 1854 for admission to the Ohio bar. George White studied law with a local retired judge and former Confederate officer, William John Clarke, in the late 1870s and later served as a district solicitor in his home in New Bern, North Carolina.[11]

Black Representatives in the Jim Crow Era had substantial political résumés before arriving in Congress. John Langston's was the most impressive: He became one of the first blacks in American history to hold elective office when the Brownhelm (Ohio) Township elected him clerk in 1855 and later served as a U.S. diplomat in Haiti and Santo Domingo. As political opportunities diminished after Union troops withdrew from the South in 1877, Black Americans depended on local connections to secure government jobs doled out by elected officials. George Murray, for example, obtained a patronage position as a customs inspector in Charleston Harbor from 1890 to 1893.[12]

SHIFTING REPUBLICAN FOCUS

Black Members of Congress remained loyal Republicans, but their allies at home and in Congress were quickly disappearing. Southern politics in the post-Reconstruction years witnessed the rapid collapse of the states' Radical Republican governments, which had drawn from the ranks of newly freed African-American men. Over time, a cadre of local, state, and national politicians—composed of many former Confederates and Democrats—replaced the Republican regimes and they were determined to end the experiment in multiracialism. In the "redeemed" South, the Democratic Party eventually became synonymous with the codification and formalization of racial segregation.

Though the Republican Party's ideological makeup remained complicated in the late 1880s, two primary factions, dubbed "reformers" and "money men," emerged.

Harper's Weekly *published "Death at the polls, and free from federal interference" in 1879. The cartoon depicted the violence that characterized elections in the post-Reconstruction South.*
IMAGE COURTESY OF LIBRARY OF CONGRESS

In a difficult campaign for the House in 1888, John M. Langston lost to his opponent Edward Venable by 641 votes. However, Langston was seated in the Republican-controlled House after contesting the election results in his Virginia district. This sketch depicts Langston taking the oath of office in the well of the House. Empty seats in the foreground belong to Democrats who left the chamber in protest.

JOHN MERCER LANGSTON, *FROM THE VIRGINIA PLANTATION TO THE NATIONAL CAPITOL* (HARTFORD, CT: AMERICAN PUBLISHING COMPANY, 1894).

Reformers clung to the idealistic plans of postwar Radical Republicans to extend full civil rights to African Americans. Yet they began to lose support in the face of popular demand to lay the problems of the post–Civil War Reconstruction to rest, as well as a growing interest in American commercial power—the stance of the "money men." Consequently, Congress deprioritized racial legislation.[13] Control of the chamber seesawed between unsympathetic Democrats and increasingly ambivalent Republicans in the 1880s and early 1890s. Though one reformer implored Republican colleagues to "never surrender the great principles of human liberty of which [the party] was the born champion," party leaders sensed little opportunity in pushing for black voting rights in the South.[14] One historian explains that the Republicans "harbored some hope that if race was no longer salient in southern politics, other issues might rise to the surface and become the catalyst for a realignment of the parties . . . if the Republican Party in the South was no longer identified with and supported by black voters, it might have the opportunity to redefine itself and become accepted as a legitimate political entity."[15] Black Representatives admonished their party for abandoning the freedmen. "A veritable set of fools a few of our party leaders have been," Thomas Miller said on the House Floor in February 1891. "They will listen to all the cheap sentimentality sounded under the name of negro domination and business prostration, be swerved from a plighted duty to a faithful constituency the country over."[16]

Rapid industrialization brought economic and social changes that displaced race reform on the political agenda and moved it out of the public eye. Between 1869 and 1899, the population of the United States nearly tripled. Railroads extending to the Pacific Ocean allowed cheap transportation of goods around the country; the invention of the telephone in 1876 improved communication; entrepreneurs such as steel magnate Andrew Carnegie amassed fortunes in manufacturing. In 1890, for the first time in American history, industrial workers outnumbered farmers.[17] Emigration from southern Europe had begun to increase, just as the American frontier was declared closed. Journalist and historian Frederick Jackson Turner aptly expressed the belief that the nation was poised at the beginning of a new, uncertain era. "Movement has been . . . [America's] dominant fact," he told an audience at the American Historical Association, gathered for the 1893 World Columbian Exhibition in Chicago. "But never again will such gifts of free land offer themselves. . . . The frontier is gone, and with its going has closed the first period of American history."[18]

Such tectonic social shifts created cultural uncertainty. Historian Robert Wiebe describes late-19th-century America as a "distended society." Industrialization and expansion swept away the familiar rhythms and guideposts of local community life, leaving "a society without a core" and widespread "dislocation and bewilderment."[19] Even long familiar political landmarks were in flux. According to historian Robert Marcus, the issues of race and sectionalism during the Civil War and Reconstruction "[stabilized] political loyalties by keeping eyes focused on a past full of familiar friends and enemies," and "fulfilled some of the need for order." By the 1880s and 1890s, "politicians could only guess at the direction in which the electorate was moving and wonder if the party system they knew was capable of containing the new populations, new pressures, and the new demands that all parts of an increasingly interconnected society made on the political system."[20] The Republican Party recast itself around commercial issues, expressing caution at "waving the bloody shirt" and finding unprecedented success with its new strategy by the mid-1890s.[21]

ELECTIONS

Disfranchisement

Black constituencies in the South were disappearing faster than the western frontier. Through a variety of legal mechanisms, from the rewriting of state constitutions that began in the 1890s to the implementation of a maze of local and statewide electoral devices that went on the books in earnest between 1889 and 1908—including the poll tax, the grandfather clause, and educational tests— southern white Democrats effectively shut blacks and opposition parties out of the political process.[22] Poll taxes, which were widely adopted and hugely successful at excluding blacks, required prospective voters to pay as much as $2 (a considerable sum for most blacks and whites). Additional registration laws required documents many voters did not possess and, to complicate matters, registration was sporadic and often occurred at odd times. Strategies that worked in one state were copied in others. "Each state became in effect a laboratory for testing one device or another. Indeed, the cross-fertilization and coordination between the movements to restrict the suffrage in the Southern states amounted to a public conspiracy."[23] One of the last but most effective devices was the Democratic "white primary" system. By excluding blacks from the process during which party candidates were chosen and strategy was set, the Democratic Party became the *de facto* government in the South.

South Carolina Representatives Thomas Miller and George Murray consistently protested the "eight box" law, an 1882 state law requiring multiple ballot boxes. Voters placed their ballots in boxes designated for specific offices. White voters received instructions for navigating the system, whereas black voters received no instruction, and their votes were disqualified if they dropped their ballots in the wrong box. The effect of the law was dramatic: Whereas turnout in southeastern

Bloody Shirt:

A violent event or controversial political issue used to stir up outrage or partisan support. Typically used during the late 19th century, "wave the bloody shirt" refers to the Republican Party's use of the Civil War as justification for political revenge on former Confederates.

Grandfather Clause:

A constitutional provision that was frequently used in southern states, exempting descendants of men who voted prior to 1866 from suffrage restrictions such as literacy tests, poll taxes, and property requirements. This clause allowed poor, illiterate southern whites to vote while disfranchising blacks, whose slave ancestors had no voting rights.

South Carolina on Election Day had been close to 20 percent in 1880, the number of constituents whose votes counted dropped to less than 10 percent in the decade after the law went into effect for the 1882 election.[24] "I declare to you and the people of America," George Murray said on the House Floor in 1883, "that no gambler nor conjurer has ever planned more meaner tricks and schemes to beat his competitor or victimize his companion than has been used by the sworn officers of the law to deceive American citizens . . . [and] destroy the effectiveness of their votes on election day."[25] When Murray lost his South Carolina seat encompassing the Sea Islands and Charleston in 1894, only 4 percent of the district's eligible population voted.[26]

State constitutional conventions—called to rewrite a state's constitution with the intention of eviscerating the remaining eligible black vote—proved the final disfranchising blow in most southern states. To call such a convention required majorities in both houses of the state legislature. Voters had to approve the proposed convention and then select delegates to act as their representatives. The process typically took several years, from the first call for the convention to the ratification of the new constitution. More of these conventions occurred in the 11 former Confederate states in the late 19th century than in any other period in U.S. history.[27] The first wave of conventions, which took place just after the Civil War, involved a requirement to rejoin the Union: Under Reconstruction law, former Confederate states were required to redraft their constitutions to incorporate elements of the 13th, 14th, and 15th Amendments. Throughout the 1870s, a second wave of constitutional conventions swept southern states to restore former Confederates' political rights. The third wave, between 1890 and 1910, sought to roll back these rights for African Americans.[28]

One of the most notable constitutional conventions took place in South Carolina in 1895. Once the crucible of Reconstruction—owing to the state's large and politically well-organized black population—Democrats held the majority in the state legislature in the early 1890s. In addition, Democrat Benjamin Tillman, a member of one of the most politically prominent families in the state and a vehement white supremacist, held the governor's seat, elevated to power by a potent coalition of white farmers hailing from the western portion of the state.[29] "My Democracy means white supremacy," Tillman declared. Indeed, disfranchising laws and reapportionment had severely hampered the black voting population in South Carolina, which numbered about 31,000 more than the white voting population.[30] However, Tillman also had a near-hysterical fear that his political rivals within the Democratic Party—primarily elite former planters in the state's coastal regions— would ally with black voters to defeat him. "If these people want to warm this black snake into life and join forces with it," Tillman warned in his characteristically colorful language, "we are ready to meet them and give them the worst drubbing they ever had in their lives."[31]

Tillman first suggested calling a constitutional convention in 1894, clearly with the intention of permanently disfranchising the state's black population. He was the driving force throughout the convention, controlling the powerful committee on suffrage. One scholar notes that "in no other state was a single public figure identified so vividly and indisputably with disfranchisement."[32] However, six black delegates with vast political experience—including former Representatives Robert Smalls and Thomas Miller—were elected to the convention, primarily via a voter

An ardent segregationist, Benjamin Tillman of South Carolina served 23 years in the U.S. Senate. He once declared, "My Democracy means white supremacy."

registration drive before the 1894 election that was spearheaded by Representative George Murray as part of his effort to win re-election in his coastal South Carolina congressional seat.[33] Though severely outnumbered and hampered by rules that discouraged their participation, the black delegates were eloquent and determinedly opposed to the proceedings. They drew national attention to South Carolina's convention when they submitted their grievances for publication in the *New York World* in September 1895.[34]

The election laws proposed in the new constitution included a residency requirement for a specific length of time in one county, proof of voter registration six months before the election, and a literacy test or proof of land ownership worth more than $300, all of which had to be certified by a white local elections manager. The new provisions were clearly aimed at the migratory, primarily illiterate, poor black communities of South Carolina. Thomas Miller declared that the election laws "make absolutely certain the placing in operation every form of cheatery and fraud at the elections that has ever been conceived by the most fertile imagination of any man who has been engaged in this class of legislation during the last thirteen years. I see no hope, absolutely no hope, for us in South Carolina to ever have fair and honest elections as long as the men in control see imaginary evils coming through the channels of honest elections."[35] The black delegates' outspokenness prompted Tillman to deliver a scathing speech on October 31, 1895, lobbing personal attacks at them. The convention overwhelmingly (116 to 7) approved the new constitution, including the disfranchising language. Only two white men joined the five black delegates who opposed the new constitution.[36]

Disfranchisement devices dramatically winnowed the number of voters in southern states, disproportionately affecting African Americans. In three states with majority-black populations in the 1880s—Mississippi, South Carolina, and Louisiana—the total number of votes cast in congressional elections plummeted by 55 to 61 percent between 1890 and 1898. In each of these three states in 1898, at least one district with between 160,000 and 200,000 residents elected the sitting white Representative with less than two percent of the voting base.[37] Just three years after Mississippi's 1890 constitutional convention, which was squarely aimed at disfranchising blacks, fewer than 9,000 blacks out of a total population of nearly 748,000 were registered to vote (6 percent of men over age 21). In 1896—before the enactment of Louisiana's literacy, poll tax, and property qualifications—there were approximately 130,000 registered black voters in the state, composing the majority in 26 parishes. Only 5,320 voted in 1900. By 1904, there were little more than 1,300 registered blacks statewide, and they constituted a majority in no parish.[38] Alabama in 1900 counted more than 181,000 black men of voting age. After the state's 1901 constitution went into effect, only 3,000 remained registered.[39]

"Packing" and "Cracking" Black Majority Districts

State legislatures with Democratic majorities also attempted to gerrymander congressional districts so as to restrict the election of African Americans. In a process known as "packing," state legislatures attempted to cluster black and dependably Republican votes into a single district, leaving the remaining districts safely in Democratic hands.[40] These conglomerate districts often contained populations that were overwhelmingly black—60 percent or more. When Democrats took power in the South Carolina legislature in the 1876 election, they packed black votes into

In 1889, Representative-elect Henry Cheatham of North Carolina was the only African American sworn in when the 51st Congress convened. John M. Langston of Virginia and Thomas Miller of South Carolina joined him after successfully contesting the elections in their districts.

IMAGE COURTESY OF LIBRARY OF CONGRESS

a single district. This proved much more difficult with the state's large African-American population, and the new district lines wound haphazardly over county and city boundaries, sometimes leaving "island" pockets of one district enclosed in another.[41] The residents of a winding, narrow east-central South Carolina district known as the "shoestring district" elected two black Representatives—Thomas Miller and George Murray—after the Democrats regained the majority in the state government.

Another significant delegation of Black Americans came to Congress from a "packed" North Carolina district known as the "Black Second." Designed to contain the state's large coastal black population, the district elected black men to Congress from the mid-1870s to the 1890s. Every black North Carolina Representative in the 19th century—John Hyman, James O'Hara, Henry Cheatham, and George White—served the "Black Second" district in one of its gerrymandered forms. Created in 1870, this salamander-shaped district originally stretched from Warren County, along the northeastern border with Virginia, and hooked around to coastal Craven County. More than one-fifth of the state's black population resided in this district. Republican Governor Tod R. Caldwell described the "Black Second" district as "extraordinary, inconvenient, and most grotesque." African-American victories in the "Black Second" district provoked the Democratic Party to wage extreme white supremacy campaigns in the late 1880s. By 1892, the state legislature reversed its policy of consolidating the black vote and "cracked," or removed, heavily black localities from the "Black Second" district, scattering its traditional voting base.[42] Representatives Cheatham and White managed to win the district in 1892, 1896, and 1898, but the reconfigured district required them to capture the ever-dwindling support of white voters to win election.

Fusion

Though the origins of the 20th-century solid South dominated by the Democratic Party began to take shape in the late 19th century, the process was slow. For the last quarter-century after Reconstruction, formidable opposition parties existed in the South—including Republican, Populist, Independent, Greenback, and Readjuster challengers. As one historian notes, despite the efforts of white supremacists allied with Democrats to intimidate blacks and oppositionist whites, this political period in the South was marked by "transition, uncertainty, and fluctuation." In the 1880s, between one-third and one-half of all southern voters supported opposition parties.[43]

Black politicians were able to capitalize on this fluctuation and on the rising popularity of the Populists—a growing national alliance of agricultural advocates. This third party gained traction with poor, white farmers in the South, and a sizable percentage abandoned the Democrats in favor of the Populists. Republicans willing to provide economic aid to farmers and local Populists created temporary coalitions, a practice known as "fusion" and the primary method by which George White and Henry Cheatham won election in what remained of North Carolina's "Black Second" district.[44]

Black Political Rivalries

The consolidation of black votes into single districts led to increased competition between black candidates. African Americans had faced one another in past contests, the most famous being those between Representative Joseph Rainey of South

Carolina and Samuel Lee throughout the 1870s, between James Rapier and Jeremiah Haralson after the former moved to the latter's neighboring Alabama district in 1876, and between James O'Hara and Israel Abbott in the North Carolina "Black Second" in 1886. However, the number of repeat contests between two candidates as well as the bitterness of the rivalries intensified with the decrease in the number of black voters. Moreover, tensions between mulatto and dark-skinned candidates escalated as a result.[45]

Such racial tension was especially prevalent in South Carolina's "shoestring district" where Robert Smalls, Thomas Miller, and George Murray continually battled for the Republican nomination throughout the 1890s. Smalls and Miller were both mulatto. Miller was so fair, he was rumored to be the illegitimate child of a white couple, adopted by free black parents.[46] In 1892, Murray surprisingly won the GOP nomination for the "shoestring district" over the incumbent, Miller. Murray encouraged the use of the names given the candidates by local newspapers; the name "Black Bold Eagle" or "Blackbird" (both evoked strength) was linked to him, in contrast to Miller's weak "Canary."[47] Miller returned to challenge Murray in the 1894 campaign, as did Robert Smalls. Murray described the racial animosity between the candidates, noting that Smalls and Miller "seem more desirous of accomplishing my defeat than even [white supremacist Democrat William] Elliott, [and] are doing everything in their power, foul or fair, to accomplish their work."[48] White supremacists enjoyed the rivalry and even supported it. A newspaper endorsing Tillmanite Democrats teased, "by the time the Canary gets through with the Blackbird, the latter will be willing to shed its feathers." The bitter rivalry came to a head after Murray backed down from contesting South Carolina's electoral votes while serving in Congress during the 1896 election—the first one held after the 1895 state constitution severely hampered black voters. Miller labeled Murray "a heartless traitor" who "cowardly [deserted] them before the battle was on." Murray countered Miller's "malevolent remarks" by calling him a "miserable vampire." He also defended his decision not to challenge the results because he did not want to disrupt GOP candidate William McKinley's certification as the winner of the election.[49]

The political competition between brothers-in-law Henry Cheatham and George White in the North Carolina "Black Second" district also had a "sharp, unpleasant character." Cheatham was refined and quiet and often courted the district's white Republicans, whereas White tended to be outspoken, blunt, and less receptive to his white constituents. After White moved to the district while Cheatham served in Congress in the mid-1890s, the latter observed that White intended to "give me trouble purely on personal grounds."[50] In 1894, both laid claim to the GOP nomination after the district convention "broke up in a row." After local Republican leaders pleaded with the two men to withdraw from the contest so as not to split the GOP vote, Cheatham asked his brother-in-law to "stop his foolishness." A committee of national GOP officials eventually ruled that Cheatham deserved the nomination, though a North Carolina newspaper endorsed White, noting, "Cheatham is said to be a man of excellent character; but we need a man of energy and ability to represent us in Congress."[51] Disgusted with GOP bickering over the two black candidates, the Populists decided to run their own candidate, siphoning off Republican votes. Democrat Frederick Woodard carried the contest; the GOP loss was blamed on the "White–Cheatham mess."[52] Woodard's victory effectively

In 1890, John M. Langston of Virginia ran an unsuccessful campaign for re-election to the 52nd Congress (1891–1893).

IMAGE COURTESY OF JOHN MERCER LANGSTON COLLECTION, SPECIAL COLLECTIONS, FISK UNIVERSITY FRANKLIN LIBRARY

Populism:

A political philosophy and movement that emerged in the agrarian West and South during the late 19th century. Populists advocated greater public participation in government and business to protect individuals from impersonal bureaucracies and financial conglomerates.

A rare example of a campaign song for John M. Langston of Virginia, written by Jesse Lawson and sung to the tune of "Scatter Seeds of Kindness."

IMAGE COURTESY OF JOHN MERCER LANGSTON COLLECTION, SPECIAL COLLECTIONS, FISK UNIVERSITY FRANKLIN LIBRARY

sank Cheatham's political career, though Cheatham eventually supported White's candidacy in the late 1890s.

Contested Elections

The number of contested elections in the House increased dramatically in the late 19th century; the majority originated in the former Confederacy. Several factors accounted for this exponential increase. The United States was nearly evenly divided between the two traditional political parties; congressional majorities flip-flopped five times between 1870 and 1900. One scholar speculates that the partisan competition and southern disfranchisement directly influenced the increased number of contested elections, particularly during GOP-controlled Congresses. When a Republican majority could influence the outcome, the party encouraged its candidates to contest, viewing contested elections as an "institutional equalizer" for electing southern GOP Representatives to the House and maintaining a majority.[53] As loyal Republicans, African-American candidates enjoyed greater success in contesting their Democratic opponents' victories before a GOP-controlled House during this period. John Langston and Thomas Miller won their seats to the 51st Congress by contesting their elections. George Murray successfully contested his opponent's victory in the 54th Congress (1895–1897).[54] However, contesting elections was time-consuming. Murray spent the entire third session of the 53rd Congress (1893–1895) preparing to contest his opponent's election before the House, leaving him little time to legislate as he gathered and submitted a massive amount of testimony to prove election fraud; the paperwork was reported to be nearly a foot thick.[55]

LEGISLATIVE INTERESTS

African Americans had never been elected to Congress in high enough numbers to influence legislation, and their increased isolation in the Jim Crow Era further eroded their ability to reach their legislative goals. They were often denied the opportunity to speak in the well of the House; their prepared remarks were relegated to the *Congressional Record Appendix*, which contained speeches for which no time was allotted on the House Floor. Yet all five black Representatives from this era attempted to defend the diminishing rights of their black constituencies, considering themselves "surrogate" Representatives for the entire U.S. black population.[56] The only African American in Congress from 1897 to 1901, George White elicited laughter from the House Gallery when he said, "I am easily the leader of one thing, and that is the black phalanx on this floor. I have no rival and will not be disturbed in that leadership."[57] Black Members' committee assignments of this era also reflected their relative lack of power. Henry Cheatham and White served on the prestigious Agriculture Committee, ranked by one political scientist as the eighth-most-attractive panel (out of 29) in the House. However, neither achieved the seniority required to set the committee's priorities.[58] Most of the black Members served on middle-ranking committees, including four who served on the Education Committee (ranked 18th).

Monetary, Economic, and Foreign Policy Issues

Black Members were typically relegated to weighing in on the largely commercial legislation that dominated Congress throughout the late 19th century, adjusting their legislative strategies to meet the new GOP focus on economic and foreign policy issues. The five black Members who served during the 1890s joined in debates on the coinage of silver and imperialism, typically voting according to sectional or partisan loyalties. However, they found ways to weave these contemporary issues into a dialogue about the continuing deterioration of civil rights in the South.

When an economic panic gripped the agrarian United States in the late 1880s, rural Members of Congress supported the coinage of silver. Circulating silver would incite inflation and raise commodity prices, creating an economic boon for the agricultural economy. Joined by western Members—whose states provided much of the precious metal—rural southern Representatives of both parties also supported the circulation of silver bullion to weather the boom-and-bust economy. GOP leaders, centered in the industrial northeast and the Midwest, however, typically upheld the gold standard (backing currency entirely with gold bullion), to create a more stable economy. The issue divided Members along sectional, partisan, and rural-versus-urban lines.[59]

Representing primarily rural districts, black Members favored the coinage of silver. Concerned about the failing economy in his North Carolina district, Henry Cheatham broke from the Republican Party and joined with the entire North Carolina delegation in supporting the Sherman Silver Purchase Act in 1890. The law required the federal government to mint 4.5 million ounces of silver bullion each month in exchange for legal tender. Cheatham was one of only eight Republicans in the House to defect; the bill failed, 154 to 136.[60] In 1892, George Murray campaigned in support of the free coinage of silver. However, Murray cleverly turned his defense of silver into a speech advocating civil rights, relating the prejudice against silver coinage to the prejudice against African Americans. "I sincerely trust that the lovers of white metal will hereafter have more sympathy," Murray said, "for human beings . . . suffering and dying under the fell blows of hateful prejudice and discrimination."[61]

In the 1880s and the 1890s, U.S. officials—influenced by business interests and geostrategic arguments advanced by advocates such as Alfred Thayer Mahan—turned their focus to acquiring overseas possessions. Industrialists envied the wealth of natural resources available in the colonized world. Also, Americans wished to guard the "New World" from Europeans, following the Monroe Doctrine of 1823, which stipulated that the United States had compelling reasons to protect the Western Hemisphere from foreign encroachments. However, the acquisition of Hawaii, Cuba, and the Philippines in the late 1890s involved the absorption of eight million residents from these countries, renewing discussions on race. Imperialists' approaches to the "white man's burden" in these new colonies often echoed those of southern segregationists: They believed the white race was inherently superior to colonized peoples and sought to limit their political participation.[62] It can certainly be argued that U.S. racial attitudes were projected abroad onto imperialistic adventures of the era—providing both rhetoric and rationale for empire-building. But efforts to undertake colonizing projects abroad (and internal perceptions of those efforts) also strengthened racist views at home, both in the North and the South.[63]

Serving during the high tide of U.S. colonial acquisitions in the 56th and 57th Congresses (1897–1901), George White—the lone African American in Congress—supported U.S. imperialist acquisitiveness. He endorsed the Spanish–American War and voted to annex Cuba and the Philippines. However, White expressed

In this detail of a print from 1889, Frank Leslie's Illustrated *documented the great interest of African Americans in observing Congress. Although no official segregation laws existed, in practice the visitors' galleries in both the House and Senate were segregated by gender and race.*

COLLECTION OF U.S. HOUSE OF REPRESENTATIVES

In 1898, a segregated group of soldiers prepares for deployment to Santiago, Cuba, to participate in the Spanish–American War.

IMAGE COURTESY OF LIBRARY OF CONGRESS

concern about the treatment of colonized populations. He purposely avoided a vote on the annexation of Hawaii to protest the treatment of Native Hawaiians and later submitted (unsuccessful) legislation for their protection. He also used American paternalism toward colonized peoples to garner support for his ultimately unsuccessful anti-lynching legislation and related the issue of imperialism to inequities at home: "Recognize your citizens at home, recognize those at your door, give them the encouragement, give them rights that they are justly entitled to, and then take hold of the people of Cuba and establish a stable and fixed government there that wisdom predicated, which justice may dictate," White told his House colleagues. "Take hold of the Philippine Islands, take hold of the Hawaiian Islands, there let the Christian civilization go out and magnify and make happy those poor, half-civilized people; and then the black man, the white man—yes, all the riff-raff of the earth that are coming to our shores—will rejoice with you in that we have done God's service and done that which will elevate us in the eyes of the world."[64] White's complex and often contradictory approach to imperialism demonstrated the difficulty of balancing his plea for black civil rights with imperialist goals.

Federal Elections Bill

When Democratic candidate Grover Cleveland won the presidential campaign in 1884, the Republican Party lost control of the White House for the first time since 1860. GOP reformers were quick to blame disfranchisement of black (and mostly Republican) voters in the South for the devastating electoral loss. Republican Senators William Chandler of New Hampshire and John Sherman of Ohio—both staunch reformers with GOP careers predating the Civil War—led an attempt to roll back disfranchisement. Chandler began amassing evidence of election fraud in the South after the 1884 election, which led one African-American committee witness to call him "the greatest man in the United States."[65] Sherman introduced a bill to enact federal control over national elections in January 1889; however, the bill had no chance of passing the 50th Congress (1887–1889). Republicans held a slim, two-person majority in the Senate and Democrats controlled the House. Nevertheless, the Senators captured the attention of other Republicans who, pushed and pulled by the monetary and humanitarian factions of the party, began to realize the political expedience of reasserting federal election law in the South.

In 1888, Republican presidential candidate Benjamin Harrison added election reform to his campaign platform. Born in Ohio and hailing from Indiana, Harrison was a Civil War veteran who had declared in 1876 that the U.S. government had "an obligation solemn as a covenant with God to save [freedmen] from the dastardly outrages that their rebel masters are committing upon them in the South." During his campaign, he refused to "purchase the Presidency by a compact of silence" regarding black voting rights in the South.[66] Riding the coattails of Harrison's victory, the Republican Party gained a majority in both houses for the first time in eight years at the start of the 51st Congress. Led by the influential Massachusetts duo of Representative Henry Cabot Lodge and Senator George Hoar, the GOP made one last attempt at reinforcing the 15th Amendment and combating disfranchisement in the South.

George Hoar had been a leading GOP House Member and an ally to abolitionist-turned-freedmen's advocate Senator Charles Sumner of Massachusetts during the Reconstruction Era. When Senator Chandler fell ill just before the opening of the 51st Congress, Hoar drafted a new bill to place national elections under federal control. Representative Lodge, however, soon convinced Hoar that since the bill affected only the lower chamber (Senators were not directly elected until 1913) the legislation should originate there. A Boston native of Puritan stock, Lodge earned one of the first history Ph.D. degrees awarded by Harvard University. Described as a "self-righteous humanitarian," he was abrasive and blunt with friends and enemies alike.[67] Unlike Hoar, who died in 1904, Lodge enjoyed a long and storied career in the Republican Party well into the 20th century. In 1893, he moved to the Senate, where he remained for more than 30 years, chairing five committees, serving as chairman of the Republican Conference, and becoming a spokesman for the party's foreign policy initiatives.

Lodge submitted the Federal Elections Bill to the House on June 14, 1890. The legislation was a conglomerate of several measures, including Hoar's and those of other House and Senate Members. Exceeding 70 pages, the bill allowed a small number of constituents in any given precinct to petition a federal judge to take charge of a national election rather than leaving the process in the hands of local—and, in the South, usually Democratic—officials. The federal government also would appoint supervisors to oversee all phases of federal elections, from voter registration to the certification of the results. The bill reaffirmed the President's prerogative to send federal troops to monitor violent or chaotic elections. On June 26, Lodge opened the debate to support the bill with what one historian describes as a "racial sermon."[68] "The first step . . . toward the settlement of the negro problem and toward the elevation and protection of the race is to take it out of national party politics," Lodge asserted. "This can be done in but one way. The United States must extend to every citizen equal rights." Addressing southern Representatives' tendency to call forth the specter of "negro domination," he continued, "This bitter appeal to race supremacy, which is always ringing in our ears, is made a convenient stalking horse to defraud white men as well as black men their rights. It is an evil which must be dealt with, and if we fail to deal with it we shall suffer for our failure."[69] Opponents in the South soon labeled the Federal Elections Bill the "Force Bill" and recalled the chaos caused by federal regulation during the Reconstruction Era. "If you could only realize as we do how this measure is destined to retard our progress, destroy confidence, impair development, engender strife, revive bitterness, relegate us to the dark and deplorable conditions of reconstruction, and produce only evil," Representative Samuel Lanham of Texas declared.[70]

The Federal Elections Bill barely passed the House on July 2, 1890, 155 to 149. It then languished in the Senate, where the debate over circulating silver bullion eventually killed it. Western Republicans dismissed the bill, hoping the coinage of silver—a policy beneficial to their mining states—would come before the Senate first. When the Senate finally took up the Federal Elections Bill, angry Silver Republicans joined Democrats in a week-long filibuster that defeated the legislation in February 1891. Most notably, Nevada Senator William Stewart—a principal architect of the 15th Amendment and the floor manager during debate on the Ku Klux Klan bills—joined the filibuster.

In many ways, the GOP reformers' efforts paralleled those of the Radical Republicans, who steered the 1875 Civil Rights Bill through Congress. Both pieces of legislation were carefully whittled into the form that was deemed most palatable to the competing factions of the Republican Party. Both bills were partially blamed for

As a Representative from Massachusetts, Henry Cabot Lodge authored the controversial Federal Elections Bill in 1890. He later served in the Senate as one of the GOP's foreign policy leaders.

IMAGE COURTESY OF LIBRARY OF CONGRESS

and threatened by GOP losses in midterm elections. Much as in the 1874 elections, the Republican Party was devastated in 1890. In the House, the 17-seat majority in the 51st Congress gave way to a whopping 152-seat deficit in the 52nd Congress (1891–1893). Though Senate Republicans maintained their majority, they lost four seats.

Several other obstacles doomed the passage of the Federal Elections Bill. Foremost, it landed low on the congressional priority list. Republican leaders in both chambers saw to it that commercial legislation was dispensed with before taking up the Lodge Bill. Congress spent half of the first session debating the McKinley Tariff—which raised duties on imports almost 50 percent to protect domestic agricultural and industrial products—before taking up the Federal Elections Bill. Once debate commenced, few Members put a human face on the legislation, despite ample evidence of black suffering in the South. Lodge was one of the few supporters of the bill who emphasized African-American rights. In contrast to the debate on the Civil Rights Bill, which was permeated by talk of "equality" and "humanity," debate on the Federal Elections Bill emphasized the need to defend "republicanism"—abstractly defined as the "right to vote."[71]

Finally, in contrast to the firsthand testimony of black Members during the Civil Rights Bill debate in 1874 and 1875, black Representatives had very little input on the 1890 Federal Elections Bill. Henry Cheatham, the only black Member serving in the House while that chamber considered the bill, never gave a speech on the topic. Thomas Miller and John Langston, who joined Cheatham in the next session after winning their contested election cases, could only encourage Senate consideration of the bill. "It does not matter how black we are; it does not matter how ignorant we are; it does not matter what our race may be," Langston declared in January 1891. "The question presented here to-day under our amended Constitution . . . is shall every freeman, shall every American citizen, shall every American elector . . . be permitted to wield a free ballot?"[72] Miller noted that southern blacks lacked necessities whose absence overshadowed their lack of voting rights. "Ah, gentlemen," he lamented, "what we need in this land is not so many [political] offices. Offices are only emblems of what we need and what we ought to have. We need protection at home in our rights, the chiefest of which is the right to live."[73]

Early Congressional Anti-Lynching Campaign

As the lone black Member at the dawn of the 20th century, Representative George White defended the "right to live" in his campaign for anti-lynching legislation. Lynching—public execution by hanging or shooting, sometimes involving torture—was a particularly racially tinged form of violence that had long been a scourge of American society. Lynch mobs consisted of a handful of vigilantes, or sometimes hundreds, ranging from criminals and thugs to the leading citizens and favorite sons of local communities. Occasionally, lynchings were attended by throngs of onlookers. A disproportionate number of the victims were black men. Particularly in the South, they were accused of rape and other sexual offenses against white women (even though the vast majority of victims already under arrest were not charged with any crime of sexual violence).[74] Accurate figures are impossible to obtain, but from 1882, when reliable statistics first became available, to the early 1930s, approximately 3,400 African Americans were lynched.[75]

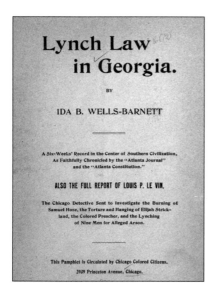

"Lynch Law in Georgia," a pamphlet distributed by the Chicago Colored Citizens group in 1899, presented the findings of journalist and civil rights advocate Ida B. Wells-Barnett who investigated the deaths of 11 men in Georgia.

IMAGE COURTESY OF LIBRARY OF CONGRESS

Representative White called for an end to the barbarism of lynching in the South on January 20, 1900, when he introduced H.R. 6963, the first federal anti-lynching bill "for the protection of all citizens of the United States against mob violence."[76] A month later, during general debate on American territorial expansion in the Caribbean and Pacific, White defended his bill on the House Floor. He provided graphic accounts of lynching atrocities and a stern rebuttal to derogatory comments made on the House and Senate floors against blacks. White noted that his goal in seeking to require lynching cases to be tried in federal courts was "that the National Government may have jurisdiction over this species of crime." But conditions in the South were such that they provoked serious questions not only about regional race relations but also about national and international policy. "Should not a nation be just to all her citizens, protect them alike in all their rights, on every foot of her soil," White asked rhetorically, "in a word, show herself capable of governing all within her domain before she undertakes to exercise sovereign authority over those of a foreign land—with foreign notions and habits not at all in harmony with our American system of government? Or, to be more explicit, should not charity first begin at home?"[77] The legislation garnered no support from the William McKinley administration, stirred little enthusiasm in the House, and was met with ambivalence by an American public with scant knowledge of the magnitude of the lynching problem. White's bill died in the Judiciary Committee at the close of the 56th Congress in 1901.

Reduction

In addition to campaigning for anti-lynching legislation, George White challenged the House to punish southern states for disfranchising blacks by calling for a reduction in their congressional delegations. White's appeal in 1899 that southern delegations to Congress ought to be limited to "the benefit of the votes that are allowed to be cast in their representation" initially fell on unsympathetic ears, despite his declaration, "It is a question that this House must deal with some time, sooner or later."[78] Derived from Section 2 of the 14th Amendment, reduction

Lynching:

Execution without due process of law; the mob execution, usually by hanging and often accompanied by torture, of alleged criminals, especially African Americans, during the Jim Crow Era.

Anti-lynching advocates connected mob violence with an acquiescent judicial system in a 1913 cartoon from Puck Illustrated.

legislation required Congress to penalize states that sought to disqualify eligible voters by subtracting the number of disfranchised voters from the population count used to determine the number of seats each state was allotted in the House. At the high tide of Radical Republican rule in the House, the chamber passed a measure after the 1870 Census that required Congress to enforce that provision. Section 6 of the Apportionment Act of February 2, 1872, mandated that if any state denied or abridged the voting rights of eligible male inhabitants over the age of 21, "the number of Representatives apportioned in this act to such State shall be reduced in the proportion which the number of male citizens shall have to the whole number of male citizens twenty-one years of age in such state." [79]

The 1900 Census and the resultant reapportionment of U.S. House seats presented those few inclined to White's views a chance to resurrect the issue. In 1901, Congress took up its prescribed role of reapportioning House seats based on the states' population gains or declines recorded in the census.[80] Among several bills addressing the process, a measure introduced by Edgar Dean Crumpacker of Indiana received the most attention. The legislation sought to penalize Louisiana, Mississippi, North Carolina, and South Carolina, which had approved state constitutions disfranchising blacks. A former appellate judge and a prosecuting attorney from Valparaiso, Indiana, Crumpacker was first elected as a Republican in 1896 from a northwestern district that encompassed the industrial city of Gary. He appears to have first raised the issue of reduction in the late 1890s, as a member of the Select Committee on the Census. In that capacity he introduced H.R. 11982, requiring the director of the census to collect information on state suffrage laws relating to voter qualifications and to tabulate for each state the number of males over the voting age of 21. Armed with this information, Crumpacker hoped to enforce the reduction clause of the 14th Amendment. The committee reported the bill favorably to the House on the final day of the 55th Congress (1897–1899) when it was too late to take action.[81] This failed attempt to obtain a House vote on reduction would be the first of many.

On January 7, 1901, Representative Crumpacker delivered a lengthy floor speech emphasizing Congress's obligation to uphold the 14th Amendment. He urged his colleagues not to let their "coercive power" be "abrogated by passive nullification" of the Constitution. Opposing southern claims that the 15th Amendment superseded the 14th, Crumpacker declared both "active and operative" and complementary. "No state may disfranchise citizens on account of race, color, or previous condition of servitude, but they may disfranchise on any other account," Crumpacker said, taking note of state constitutional provisions for poll taxes and literacy tests. "But, sir, if they restrict the right of suffrage of male citizens 21 years of age by raising the age limit, by educational laws, by property qualifications, or by any other method within their constitutional authority, except for crime, the basis of representation [of those states in Congress] must be reduced accordingly." Crumpacker hoped to avoid a protracted struggle with southern Members over voting statistics. He proposed to reduce representation based on illiteracy rates for both whites and blacks, assuming illiterates would fail education tests that accompanied disfranchisement plans.[82] Representative George White praised Crumpacker as an exemplar "who has taken occasion to stand up in his place as a man, and has said a word in defense" of African Americans.[83] The House, which eventually voted to expand its membership, devoted considerable attention to Crumpacker's plan before voting—136 to 94—to table further consideration.[84]

The reduction debate flared again in early 1902, after Charles Dick of Ohio proposed to instruct the House Rules Committee to investigate the relationship between disfranchising states' congressional representation and the voting figures for congressional elections.[85] Southerners responded venomously. Thomas Spight of Mississippi, a Confederate veteran turned newspaper publisher, baldly declared that disfranchisement's "leading purpose was to eliminate the negro from the political equation." He added that the South would prefer to have no congressional representation if it could avoid a "return again to the state of affairs existing in the reconstruction period."[86] Nevertheless, in a party line vote, the Republican-dominated House Rules Committee supported the Dick proposal in March 1902. However, Representative Oscar Underwood of Alabama, who had just spearheaded his state's 1901 constitutional convention disfranchising virtually all blacks, successfully sabotaged the proposed investigation by exploiting a Republican division regarding a sugar tariff. Insurgent Republicans opposed leadership efforts to strike the elimination of a tariff differential amendment and thus retain a high tariff. By joining Midwestern and insurgent Republicans on an economic issue to thwart corrective federal legislation, Democrats replayed their strategy for subverting the Federal Elections Bill of 1890. In delivering the Democratic Caucus vote to these Republicans, Underwood secured their promise to vote down the Rules Committee investigation after it came to the floor.[87]

HISTORICAL LEGACY

Reduction's failure was but one symptom of the greater disorder afflicting southern blacks. In 1901, anticipating his imminent displacement, George White—the last African American remaining in Congress—retired, a victim of North Carolina's disfranchisement schemes. On the eve of his departure from the House, White lamented, "The mule died long ago and the land grabbers have obtained the 40 acres."[88] Audible in his tone was the frustration that underlay more than 30 years of broken promises made to African Americans. In his farewell speech, White observed, "This, Mr. Chairman, is perhaps the negroes' temporary farewell to the American Congress. But let me say, Phoenix-like he will rise up someday and come again."[89] It would be 28 years before another African American was elected to Congress.

The legacy of Black Americans in Congress during the 19th century has often been regarded as a footnote to discussions of their famous contemporaries, such as Frederick Douglass, Booker T. Washington, and Senator Charles Sumner. During the early 20th century, Jim Crow-Era scholars disparaged blacks' role in Reconstruction, citing black Representatives's lack of legislative successes.[90] Columbia University professor William Dunning introduced this interpretation: "The negro had no pride of race and no aspiration or ideals save to be like whites," he wrote in 1907. One of his contemporaries, Ohio businessman and historian James Ford Rhodes, asserted that black Representatives "left no mark on the legislation of their time; none of them, in comparison with their white associates, attained the least distinction."[91]

Former Representative John Lynch of Mississippi helped initiate the refutation of the Dunning interpretation, noting in *The Journal of Negro History* that black officeholders, "not only gave satisfaction to the people whom they served, but they reflected credit upon themselves, their race, their party and the community that was so fortunate as to have the benefit of their services." W. E. B. Du Bois, a leading intellectual and activist, also praised the black Representatives in his classic work, *Black Reconstruction*. Writing in 1935, Du Bois reviewed some of their most famous speeches. "The words of these black men were," Du Bois concluded, "perhaps, the last clear, earnest expression of democratic theory of American government in Congress."[92]

The civil rights movement of the 1950s and 1960s forced scholars to re-evaluate the significance of the black Reconstruction-Era Representatives. Additionally, unprecedented numbers of African Americans participating in politics during the 1960s and 1970s inspired renewed interest in the lives and careers of their 19th-century forebears—many of whom were the subjects of extended biographies.[93] The fuller historical picture that emerged fundamentally altered the earlier, derisive interpretations of Reconstruction-Era black Representatives. Modern scholars observe that early black officeholders were prevented from fulfilling their potential. Eric Foner describes their political careers as fraught with obstacles, noting that "the rising presence [of blacks] in office did not always translate into augmented power." Carol Swain remarks that "no matter how responsible these pioneers may have been, the times, the precariousness of their situations, and the attitude of their colleagues kept them from accomplishing much in the way of substantive representation." Their example, Swain adds, "undoubtedly helped—however modestly—to break down their white colleagues' notions of black inferiority."[94] Another scholar concludes, "Something magnificent happened between 1870 and 1901," noting that "the significance of the African-American congressmen . . . goes beyond the number of bills they pushed through Congress." Their courage and perseverance in their attempts to create a more democratic government form the core of their collective symbolism.[95]

A Generation Lost

For a long generation, lacking a single black Representative or Senator and absent direction from a line of ambivalent or hostile Presidents, the parties in Congress deferred—sometimes scuttled—meaningful civil rights protections and the consideration of equal educational and economic opportunity. Southern politicians routinely and loudly invoked the threat of federal intervention in southern race relations to stir the electorate, but the specter amounted to little more than a harmless bogeyman. In sharp contrast to the Reconstruction Era, Congress adopted a hands-off approach to the issue of race in the South during the early decades of the 20th century, with few exceptions. A handful of dogged reformers such as Edgar Crumpacker, Leonidas Carstarphen Dyer of Missouri, and George Holden Tinkham of Massachusetts brought significant measures before the House. But congressional action consisted more of punitive threats and partisan maneuvering than of positive reaffirmations of the federal government's commitment to the 14th or 15th Amendment.

Also at work were pervasive social theories that assumed the racial superiority of whites and the inferiority of blacks.[96] These ideas were subscribed to not only by unreconstructed southern spokesmen of white supremacy but also by many of the

An 11-term Representative, Leonidas Dyer of Missouri crusaded against lynching. In 1918, he introduced H.R. 11279, "a bill to protect citizens of the United States against lynching in default of protection by the States."

most progressive minds of the era—including those in Congress who theoretically supported voting rights for southern blacks. "No one questions the superiority of the white race, but that superiority is grounded in the rugged virtues of justice and humanity," Representative Crumpacker told colleagues. In a sense, his plan to punish states disfranchising black voters was as much about teaching recalcitrant southern whites a lesson in *noblesse oblige* as it was about elevating the status of southern blacks, whom he described as being "in the childhood of civilization . . . [in] want of manly virtues." He continued, "It is surely no credit to American manhood to bind and shackle a helpless race to avoid the temporary embarrassments that would attend its proper development."[97]

Congressional ambivalence toward racial legislation derived from the general disinterest of the American public and many prevalent stereotypes. By the late 19th century, popular opinion turned apathetic toward black civil rights and supportive of returning unencumbered self-governance to southerners. For many disaffected northerners, segregation and disfranchisement seemed viable—even rational—alternatives to mounting racial violence in the South. Federal inaction mirrored public complacency. In this social context, congressional inertia and a series of devastating Supreme Court rulings were "broadly reflective" of an American public that was not receptive to the concept of a multiracial society.[98] As one historian concludes, the passivity of the federal government on the issue of disfranchisement enabled and encouraged other southern states to follow the example of Louisiana, Mississippi, and the Carolinas.[99]

By the early 20th century, the Supreme Court had essentially eroded the legal basis for black equality and bolstered states' efforts to stringently separate the races.[100] Among the high court's most devastating rulings were *Plessy v. Ferguson* (1896), *Williams v. Mississippi* (1898), and *Giles v. Harris* (1903).[101] In upholding the constitutionality of an 1890 Louisiana law that required rail companies to provide "equal but separate accommodations for the white and colored races," *Plessy* sanctioned the system of segregation then crystallizing in the South.[102] In *Williams,* a black man convicted of murder by an all-white jury appealed the decision based on the 14th Amendment. The Supreme Court unanimously upheld the jury's decision, endorsing the disfranchising laws that prevented black men from serving on juries.[103] Several years later, *Giles* upheld the grandfather clause, one of the chief disfranchising methods used at southern constitutional conventions at the turn of the 20th century.

The decline of African-American civil rights coincided with one of the nation's most fervent bursts of social reform. Spanning the 1890s through World War I, the Progressive Era was a period when a broad and diverse group of social reformers moving from local to national arenas pushed for the modernization and democratization of American society.[104] Progressives sought to advance public safety and welfare through professionalization and standardization across the spectrum of American life. Their efforts included regulating food content and production, establishing laws for child labor and guidelines for industrial safety, and implementing conservation, temperance, and even experimental welfare programs. Progressives also ushered in political reforms, including direct primary elections, the popular election of U.S. Senators, and women's suffrage.

Though Progressivism would seem a democratizing force positioned against segregationists, in fact, the movement often complemented Jim Crow. The

Progressives' focus on the necessity for expertise provided an important rationale for limiting the franchise to voters who were deemed to be qualified.[105] Order, organization, and rational decision-making within a rapidly industrializing, sometimes chaotic, society lay at the heart of the Progressive impulse and often trumped democratic reform. "Whenever general anxieties rose across the nation, followers of the bureaucratic way had to turn for help to one of the several traditional techniques for achieving tighter cohesion," observes historian Robert Weibe. "One of the time-honored devices was exclusion: draw a line around good society and dismiss the remainder."[106] Moreover, Progressives' obsession with scientific method spread "social Darwinism" (sometimes referred to as "scientific racism" or eugenics), which postulated that Anglo-Saxon social success was rooted in superior biological and evolutionary traits. The resulting rationalization of white supremacist thinking via a national political, social, and scientific movement only emboldened proponents of segregation.[107]

African Americans participated as fully as possible in a society that had marginalized them. As George White once noted in a characteristically upbeat floor speech, "We are ramifying and stretching out as best we can in all departments of life, with a view to making ourselves good citizens."[108] These efforts were marked by significant milestones: the founding of advocacy groups such as the National Association for the Advancement of Colored People (NAACP) in 1909, African-American contributions to World War I, and the black intellectual and artistic flowering of the Harlem Renaissance in the 1920s. Faced with a repressive system of segregation in the South, African Americans sought new opportunities outside the region, as an ever-stronger current of southern blacks moved into northern cities. This demographic shift and the nascent political activism of northern urban blacks portended change for the future.

SEGREGATIONIST LEGISLATION AND THE RISE OF THE NAACP

When, in 1913, Democrats gained control of Congress and the White House for the first time since the mid-1890s, southern Members of the party were tempted to expand segregation into areas of federal jurisdiction.[109] In the first two Congresses of the Woodrow Wilson administration (the 63rd and 64th, 1913–1917), southern Members introduced bills to segregate the federal civil service, the military, and public transportation in Washington, DC. Others introduced bills to repeal the 15th

Founded in 1909, the National Association for the Advancement of Colored People (NAACP) became a primary advocacy group for early civil rights causes. The 1929 annual meeting in Cleveland, pictured here, included NAACP staff W.E.B. Du Bois, James Weldon Johnson, Walter White, William Pickens, Arthur Spingarn, Daisy Lampkin, and Robert Bagnall.

Amendment. Though Congress enacted none of these measures, the significance of these proposals lay in the fact that they were entertained at all. Having solidified absolute control over race issues in the South, southern Members of Congress were sufficiently emboldened to prod Congress to endorse a nationalized racial apartheid.[110]

Political power brokers in the Capitol and in the Wilson administration harbored segregationist sympathies even if they were unable to promote them by imparting the full weight of federal legislative sanction. In 1913, President Wilson acceded to the wishes of several Cabinet members, who quickly segregated various executive departments. Soon, dining facilities and restrooms throughout the federal government were racially segregated, although not uniformly. Wilson issued no formal executive order, and no laws were enacted, but segregation was tacitly encouraged and widely practiced.[111] Congress, which had the responsibility of administering the nation's capital, did much to promote the practice of segregation in Washington. From 1913 to 1921 and after 1933, southerners largely controlled the panels that appropriated funds and those that dealt with the administrative details of city government. In places where Congress could have overturned Jim Crow practices—in public parks, at Union Station, in theaters, restaurants, and innumerable other locations—it did nothing. Instead, its record in managing the District of Columbia was "profoundly segregationist."[112]

In part, the emergence of African-American public advocacy groups such as the NAACP—founded by Mary White Ovington and Oswald Garrison Villard, descendants of prominent abolitionists—counterbalanced efforts to introduce federal segregation laws.[113] Although its original organizers were largely white, the NAACP included black intellectuals such as W. E. B. Du Bois, anti-lynching reformer Ida Wells-Barnett, and women's rights leader Mary Church Terrell, establishing its headquarters in New York City under the leadership of Moorefield Storey, a former president of the American Bar Association. Du Bois soon began publishing *The Crisis,* the organization's journal, which served as an outlet for reformers and literary contributors and as a tool to inform the American public about issues critical to African Americans. The NAACP quickly experienced a growth spurt: During World War I, membership swelled 900 percent to include more than 90,000 individuals in 300 cities and towns nationwide. In the 1910s it began a methodical apprenticeship, learning to lobby Congress and to organize national public opinion campaigns.

WORLD WAR I AND THE GREAT MIGRATION

Throughout American history, wartime necessity has often opened new political and social avenues for marginalized groups. This familiar scenario played out after the United States intervened in the First World War in April 1917. By participating in the war effort, women suffrage activists made a compelling, and ultimately successful, case for voting rights: After all, how could America protect democracy abroad without extending it to half the population at home? Likewise, Black Americans furthered their claim for racial equality at home by their contributions on European battlefields and on the home front filling industrial jobs.

Congress passed the Selective Service Act on May 10, 1917, which required all able-bodied men ages 21 to 31 to register for military duty.[114] On registration day, July 5, 1917, more than 700,000 black men enrolled. By war's end, nearly 2.3 million had answered the call. In less than two years, more than four million draftees

African-American troops of the 351st Field Artillery gather on the deck of the U.S.S. Louisville *in February 1919 during their return voyage home from Europe.*

IMAGE COURTESY OF NATIONAL ARCHIVES AND RECORDS ADMINISTRATION

Great Migration:

The mass movement during the 1910s through the 1950s from the rural, segregated South to the urban North and West of African Americans in pursuit of economic, social, and political opportunities.

African-American families lined the streets of New York to celebrate the homecoming of the 369th Army infantry unit in 1919.

IMAGE COURTESY OF NATIONAL ARCHIVES AND RECORDS ADMINISTRATION

swelled the ranks of the U.S. military. Of these, 367,000 were African Americans who were drafted principally into the U.S. Army. Segregation in military service reflected the segregation in civilian life. Blacks were barred from the Marine Corps and the Army Air Corps, and in the U.S. Navy they were assigned only menial jobs. African Americans had to fight to establish a black officer training program.[115] On the battlefield, many infantry units in the all-black 92nd U.S. Army Division distinguished themselves.[116]

Arguably the most profound effect of World War I on African Americans was the acceleration of the multi-decade mass movement of black, southern rural farm laborers northward and westward in search of higher wages in industrial jobs and better social and political opportunities. This Great Migration led to the rapid growth of black urban communities in cities like New York, Chicago, St. Louis, and Los Angeles.[117] While relatively small groups of southern African Americans migrated after Reconstruction to border states such as Kansas and into the Appalachians, it was not until the imposition of Jim Crow segregation and disfranchisement in the South that large numbers of blacks left their homes and families to search elsewhere for a better life. Still, in 1910, nearly 90 percent of American blacks lived in the South, four-fifths of them in rural areas.

Emigration from the South gained more traction with the advent of several important developments, chiefly economic, beginning in the second decade of the 20th century. [118] In the South the depressed cotton market and a series of natural disasters reduced even the rare independent black landowner to sharecropping or tenant farming, trapping him in a cycle of indebtedness. Military conscription and the slackening of European immigration caused massive labor shortages in the North, just as war production created an insatiable demand for industrial goods. Labor shortages provided blacks with jobs in the steel, shipbuilding, and automotive industries as well as in ammunition and meat packing factories.

Many found the promise of economic opportunity irresistible, though this was not the only element pulling blacks northward. Contemplating departure from the

In 1917, New Yorkers silently protested the race riots in East St. Louis, Illinois.

IMAGE COURTESY OF LIBRARY OF CONGRESS

South, Representative George White said to the *Chicago Daily Tribune*, "I cannot live in North Carolina and be a man and be treated as a man." In an interview with the *New York Times*, he encouraged southern black families to migrate west, "los[ing] themselves among the people of the country."[119] Historian Steven Hahn suggests that a "pronounced self-consciousness" encompassed both social and political motivations for emigrating: "searches for new circumstances in life and labor, new sites of family and community building, new opportunities to escape economic dependence. . . ." Hahn explains that the movement not only created new political vistas for migrating blacks but "also served as a large and powerful political transmission belt that moved and redeployed the experiences, expectations, institutions, and networks" forged in the black community during slavery and in Reconstruction, which would fundamentally shape emerging centers of African-American culture and thought in the North.[120]

Whether their motivation was economic, political, individual, or communal, immense numbers of African Americans streamed northward. By one estimate, roughly a half-million blacks migrated to northern cities between 1915 and 1920, and between 750,000 and one million left the South in the 1920s. Chicago's black population soared 600 percent between 1910 and 1930. In the same 20-year period, Detroit's African-American community grew 2,000 percent—from 6,000 individuals to about 120,000.

This massive demographic shift dramatically altered African-American history culturally, politically, and socially, producing during the 1920s a period of black artistic expression in literature, music, and thought known as the Harlem Renaissance. Among those who participated in this cultural moment in northern Manhattan, which raised black consciousness nationally, were poet Langston Hughes, writer Zora Neale Hurston, and scholar and intellectual W. E. B. Du Bois. A new sense of African-American culture emerged, stoked by such leaders as Marcus Garvey, an advocate for black separatism and repatriation to Africa. Garvey emigrated from Jamaica to New York City in 1916 and, within a few years, founded

A civil rights pioneer, James Weldon Johnson was the NAACP's executive secretary and the chief congressional anti-lynching lobbyist.

the Universal Negro Improvement Association (UNIA), enlisting thousands of members.[121] Interestingly, UNIA found much support in the recently transplanted community of southern blacks, who helped establish many UNIA chapters in the South by sharing the organization's literature with their relatives back home.[122] Skyrocketing black populations in urban wards created new opportunities for political activism. Slowly, African Americans were elected to important political offices; for example, Oscar De Priest, a native Alabamian and future Member of Congress, became a member of the Chicago city council in 1915.

ANTI-LYNCHING LEGISLATION RENEWED

The passage of anti-lynching legislation became one of the NAACP's central goals. Slow to join the cause of pursuing legislation to remedy lynching because of the leadership's concerns about the constitutionality of such an undertaking, the NAACP eventually embraced the movement, using it to educate the often ambivalent American public so as to jar it into substantive action.

Statistics supported the NAACP's increased urgency in the anti-lynching campaign. Between 1901 and 1929, more than 1,200 blacks were lynched in the South. Forty-one percent of these lynchings occurred in two exceptionally violent states: Georgia (250) and Mississippi (245).[123] The NAACP report, *Thirty Years of Lynching in the United States, 1889–1919,* created momentum for congressional action. The anti-lynching effort provided the NAACP valuable experience waging a mass public relations campaign and mastering the art of congressional relations.[124] In the 1920s, through the organizational leadership and diverse talents of its secretary, James Weldon Johnson, the NAACP became a significant vehicle for marshaling public opinion. Johnson's biographer describes him as "truly the 'Renaissance man' of the Harlem Renaissance"—a poet, composer, writer, and activist.[125] Acting as the group's chief congressional lobbyist, he pushed for the reduction scheme during the larger congressional debate over reapportionment and decisively shaped the NAACP's campaign against lynching. Of his anti-lynching lobbying experience, Johnson recalled, "I tramped the corridors of the Capitol and the two office buildings so constantly that toward the end, I could, I think, have been able to find my way about blindfolded."[126]

Pushed vigorously by Johnson and NAACP assistant executive secretary Walter White (a civil rights activist from Atlanta), anti-lynching reform awaited only a legislative entrepreneur in Congress and, regrettably, a triggering event. Activists found Representative Leonidas C. Dyer to be a willing ally. Dyer, a Spanish-American War veteran and a former aide to Missouri Governor Herbert S. Hadley, represented a thin sliver of the southern and eastern sections of St. Louis. Heavily industrialized, part of the district hugged the Mississippi River and included growing African-American neighborhoods.[127] Since his election to the House in 1911, Dyer had demonstrated a disposition toward advocating for the black community.[128]

Dyer had a front-row seat to some of the nation's most virulent wartime race violence. In the summer of 1917, just across the Mississippi River from his district, a riot in East St. Louis, Illinois, drew national attention and widespread condemnation. A hub for southern blacks migrating northward, East St. Louis had seen its black population triple in the first decade of the 20th century. Its racial tensions, stoked by competition for jobs and prejudice, struck a chord among many white northerners apprehensive about black migration. On July 1, 1917, white assailants drove through a black neighborhood, firing indiscriminately. Two plainclothes police officers sent to investigate the disturbance arrived in a vehicle similar to the one driven by the shooters. Fearful residents mistakenly opened fire on the policemen, both of whom were killed. White residents' attempt to retaliate on July 2 flared into a merciless episode of mob sadism. The death toll climbed to 47 persons, including 38 African-American men, women, and children. Much of the black population fled the city.[129] On the House Floor, Dyer decried the event as one of "the most dastardly and most criminal outrages ever perpetrated in this country." Large numbers of refugees flowed across the river and into his district, compelling Dyer to tackle the problem of lynching and mob violence.

The rash of wartime mob violence nationwide provided new impetus for legislative action.[130] After months of consultation with legal experts and the NAACP, Representative Dyer introduced H.R. 11279 on April 18, 1918, "to protect citizens of the United States against lynching in default of protection by the States." Dyer's bill, which provided the blueprint for all subsequent NAACP-backed anti-lynching measures, sought to charge lynch mobs with capital murder charges and to try lynching cases in federal court. It levied on each county where a lynching occurred, a fine of between $5,000 and $10,000 that would be paid to the victim's immediate family or, if none existed, to the U.S. government to facilitate prosecution of the case. The Dyer Bill also mandated jail time and imposed a fine of up to $5,000 on state and local law enforcement officials who refused to make a reasonable effort to prevent a lynching or surrendered a prisoner in their custody to a lynch mob. Finally, the bill sought to establish guidelines for fair courtroom proceedings by excluding lynch mob participants and supporters from juries.[131]

Dyer's rationale was elegantly simple: Lynching—and states' refusal to prosecute the perpetrators—violated victims' 14th Amendment rights. Anticipating that Members would object to the bill because it involved federal control over social policy, he cited the slate of child labor laws the chamber had enacted and Congress's December 1917 passage of the 18th Amendment, which forbade the production, transportation, or sale of alcohol within the United States: "If Congress has felt its duty to do these things, why should it not also assume jurisdiction and enact laws to protect the lives of citizens of the United States against lynch law and mob violence? Are the rights of property, or what a citizen shall drink, or the ages and conditions under which children shall work, any more important to the Nation than life itself?"[132] In the Democrat-controlled 65th Congress (1917–1919), however, the measure remained stuck in the Judiciary Committee.

But advocates' hope was renewed when Republicans gained majorities in the House and Senate at the start of the 66th Congress in 1919. In early 1921, James Weldon Johnson paid his first visit to Representative Dyer's office, recognizing that the St. Louis Representative was a valuable contact.[133] Throughout this process, the NAACP played a significant role in keeping the issue alive in Congress, and at several junctures, Johnson bolstered Dyer, urging him not to accept compromises to attain passage of legislation and encouraging him to resist pressure from the Republican Conference to abandon legislation many of his colleagues felt was unpopular.[134]

Under the NAACP's intense lobbying pressure, the House began to move toward consideration of a bill derived from Dyer's earlier efforts—first adopting a rule for consideration and then, in early January 1922 commencing consideration on

Racial violence in Tulsa, Oklahoma, in 1921, left the African-American community in smoldering ruins. Competition for jobs and housing, deep-seated racial mistrust, and informal segregation practices, were at the heart of tensions in many urban areas.

IMAGE COURTESY OF LIBRARY OF CONGRESS

In 1917, 75 sixth-graders shared a single room and teacher in segregated Muskogee, Oklahoma.

IMAGE COURTESY OF LIBRARY OF CONGRESS

Hatton W. Sumners of Texas opposed anti-lynching laws during his 17 terms in the House of Representatives, arguing that the individual states could handle the problem of mob violence against African Americans.

A mix of black and white British members of the NAACP protested the lack of anti-lynching laws in the United States in hopes of bringing more international attention to the epidemic.

the legislation.[135] Southern opponents attempted to impede debate several times, refusing to come to the House Chamber so as to prevent a quorum. On such occasions Speaker Frederick H. Gillett of Massachusetts ordered the chamber doors locked and dispatched the Sergeant at Arms to search for errant Members.[136] The debate came to a head on January 25 and 26, 1922, when the House considered a bill that contained many of the essentials of Dyer's original measure. Though the provision seeking to ensure an impartial jury had been removed, the bill sought to levy a $10,000 fine on counties where lynchings occurred—as well as on counties through which victims were transported.

Southern Democrats rebuffed the measure, mustering familiar practical and constitutional defenses. Hatton W. Sumners of Texas, a Dallas attorney who later served 16 years as chairman of the House Judiciary Committee, led the defense. In two lengthy debates, Sumners compared the bill to an act of legislative "mob" violence and suggested Congress let southern states resolve the lynching issue on their own. "I say to you that you cannot pass this bill unless you pass it under the influence of the same spirit which this bill denounces, *viz.*, the mob spirit," Sumners said to laughter and applause on the House Floor. "You say that the folks down in the South are not doing this thing fast enough, and the folks in the South say the officers are not doing this thing fast enough, and you each get ropes and they go after the criminal and you go after the Constitution."[137]

African Americans packed the House Gallery, intensely monitoring the debate, and on several occasions they cheered loudly, in violation of gallery rules. Some traded derogatory barbs with southern House Members below on the floor, whose speeches repeatedly referred to NAACP activists as "race agitators."[138] The glare of publicity pushed cautious House leaders to move swiftly for a vote. In the end, the Dyer Bill passed the Republican-controlled chamber on January 26, 1922, by a vote of 231 to 119, with four Members voting "present" and 74 others not voting.[139] Among the 119 who voted "no" were four future Speakers of the House, each a southern Democrat who eventually presided over the chamber after Democrats assumed control of the House in 1931: John Nance Garner of Texas, Joseph Byrns of Tennessee, William Bankhead of Alabama, and Sam Rayburn of Texas.[140]

In the Senate, a combination of ambivalent Republican backing and spirited southern opposition doomed the Dyer Bill to legislative limbo. It withered in the Judiciary Committee under the unsympathetic oversight of Chairman William Borah of Idaho, who doubted its constitutionality. Nevertheless, Borah pledged not to block consideration of the measure if a majority of his colleagues assented. The measure passed out of the committee 8 to 6 in the summer of 1922—with Borah dissenting.[141] The NAACP proceeded to engage in a formidable public campaign, increasing direct pressure on Majority Leader Henry Cabot Lodge of Massachusetts (who faced re-election that fall). Lodge, who had authored the Federal Elections Bill in 1890, had greatly moderated his previously progressive stance on federal oversight of black civil rights. He reluctantly brought the measure to the Senate Floor in September, but his choice of a manager to shepherd the bill through debate— Samuel Shortridge, California's junior Senator and a relative novice—suggested he had little enthusiasm for the endeavor. Byron (Pat) Harrison of Mississippi swiftly upstaged Shortridge by gaining control of the debate. Further consideration was forestalled until after the November 1922 elections, relieving Senators of electoral pressure.[142]

When the bill came up for consideration in late November after the elections, southern Members again halted Shortridge with parliamentary maneuvers. As he had with the reduction issue two decades earlier, Alabama's Oscar Underwood, now Senate Minority Leader, played a key role in killing the Dyer measure. Underwood threatened Lodge and the Republicans with a filibuster that would shut down end-of-session business in the Senate. Fearful they would be unable to secure a ship subsidy bill desired by the Harding administration, the members of the Senate Republican Conference voted to abandon the Dyer Bill. Though Representative Dyer reintroduced the measure in each new Congress in the 1920s, it failed to gain significant political traction. However, the public awareness campaign relentlessly pushed by the NAACP likely contributed to a general decline in lynching after the 1920s. It would be 15 years before Congress would seriously consider the subject again. In the words of historian Robert Zangrando, anti-lynching legislation was "displaced by the indifference of its friends and the strategy of its enemies."[143]

REDUCTION REDUX

Although the subject of reduction arose occasionally in Congress, "increasingly it was becoming a posture rather than a policy."[144] Republican party leaders seemed content to raise the issue because it permitted them to lay claim to the moral high ground, but upon meeting stiff opposition, they readily let it die a quiet death in the interest of political expediency. Moreover, fortified by widespread social ambivalence and sensing the weakness of their opponents, southern Representatives became bolder and coordinated their efforts to repulse the reduction movement.[145]

Reduction eventually became absorbed in the larger reapportionment struggle in the House after the 1920 Census, which pitted rural and urban factions against one another for much of the next decade.[146] At several junctures during this nearly decade-long debate, Representative George Holden Tinkham of Massachusetts spoke on behalf of disfranchised blacks. A Republican who rose through the Boston common council, the board of aldermen, and the Massachusetts state senate, Tinkham was frank and fiercely independent. In 1914, he won election to a U.S. House seat—the first of his 14 terms in Congress—representing a wide multi-ethnic swath of Boston. He became one of the institution's more colorful characters.[147] A biographer described him as "the conscience of the House" in the 1920s, based on his repeated efforts to rally colleagues to the cause of investigating disfranchisement of southern blacks in violation of the 14th and 15th Amendments.[148]

On May 6, 1921, Tinkham interrupted consideration of an Army appropriations bill by introducing a resolution instructing the House Committee on the Census to investigate disfranchisement efforts by the states and report back to the full House to provide information for a debate about reapportioning to expand the chamber's membership. As usual, he did not mince words, describing southern disfranchisement schemes as "the most colossal electoral fraud the world has ever known." He added, "On this question moral cowardice and political expediency dominate the Republican leadership of the House."[149] Clearly annoyed that his planned appropriations debate had been hijacked, House Majority Leader Frank W. Mondell of Wyoming dismissed Tinkham's address as an expression of "fancy" and a "stump speech," echoing southern complaints that the reduction proposal was

George Holden Tinkham of Massachusetts became known as "the conscience of the House" for his efforts to protect voting rights for blacks. He also was one of Congress's most colorful characters. Newspapers reported that he was the first American to fire a shot against the Central Powers in World War I, when, on a congressional visit to the Allied front in 1917, an Italian army commander persuaded him to pull the firing lanyard on an artillery piece trained on Austrian forces. An avid big-game hunter, Tinkham also named his trophies for political opponents.

IMAGE COURTESY OF LIBRARY OF CONGRESS

Sixteen-term House Member John E. Rankin of Mississippi defended southern white supremacy. Later in Rankin's congressional career, Representative Adam Clayton Powell, Jr., of New York, regularly needled Rankin by sitting as near to him as possible in the House Chamber.

IMAGE COURTESY OF OFFICE OF THE CLERK, U.S. HOUSE OF REPRESENTATIVES

Left to right: U.S. Senator James Vardaman of Mississippi, U.S. Representative James Heflin of Alabama, and U.S. Senator Ollie James of Kentucky built their congressional careers on promoting segregation and white supremacy.

IMAGE COURTESY OF LIBRARY OF CONGRESS

merely an electoral enticement for northern black voters.[150] When Speaker Gillett rejected Tinkham's argument that his measure was constitutionally privileged, the full House overwhelmingly backed the ruling, 286 to 47.[151]

Later that fall during floor debate about a bill sponsored by Census Committee Chairman Isaac Siegel of New York to expand Membership of the House from 435 to 483, Tinkham again injected into the dialogue the issue of upholding the 14th Amendment, noting that the word "shall" in Section 2 compelled Congress "unconditionally" to enforce reduction. "Franchise equality is fundamental and profound," Tinkham declared, adding "national elections can no longer be half constitutional and half unconstitutional."[152] Tinkham registered unconcealed contempt for House leaders who declined to investigate southern voting fraud. "For this refusal by the leaders of the majority party I do not possess a command of language strong enough to use in denunciation and reprobation," he said. "The real anarchists in the United States, the real leaders of lawlessness, are the Members of this House of Representatives who refuse obedience to the Constitution which they have sworn to obey."[153] Representative Wells Goodykoontz of West Virginia, former president of the West Virginia Bar Association, was the sole Member to join Tinkham in calling for enforcement of the 14th Amendment. He provided statistical evidence based on November 1920 voting returns in his district (85,587 votes were cast) versus the total votes recorded for the entire congressional delegations in South Carolina (67,737) and Mississippi (70,657).[154]

The man who emerged as one of the white supremacist South's most ardent congressional defenders, John Elliott Rankin of Mississippi, offered the rejoinder to Tinkham. In 1921, Rankin was a freshman Member of the House, embarking on a 32-year career representing the northeastern corner of Mississippi. A World War I veteran, he served 20 years as chairman of the Committee on World War Veterans Legislation (later Veterans' Affairs). When he died in 1960, the press called him "one of the most turbulent political figures in modern congressional history."[155] Had reduction been adopted, Mississippi's delegation would have been halved, from 8 to 4. Rankin countered Tinkham by arguing that the 15th Amendment—in prohibiting disfranchisement because of race or color—had "by implication" superseded and voided the part of the 14th Amendment that called for reduction.[156] Conjuring up the specter of Reconstruction, Rankin continued, "the time has passed when a man or a party can successfully make political capital by holding out to the Negro the hope or promise of social and political equality."[157] The House brushed aside Tinkham's amendment on an unrecorded voice vote.[158]

Roiled and divided by major issues like immigration, tax policy, a soldier's bonus, and international questions such as U.S. participation in the League of Nations, Congress postponed work on the reapportionment issue from 1921 to 1927.[159] Tinkham made at least two more attempts to add reduction amendments before passage of a comprehensive reapportionment bill in 1929, but he was unsuccessful.[160] As one scholar notes, it is not surprising that congressional leaders failed to vigorously protect black voting rights, given pervasive notions among national political leaders and strategists that extending the franchise might be more harmful than the alternative.[161]

POWER OF THE SOUTHERN BLOC IN CONGRESS

The reduction and anti-lynching failures occurred during the heyday of southern demagogues in Congress. Innumerable racist slanders were uttered on the House and Senate floors with virtual impunity from 1890 through the 1920s. Among the practitioners of white supremacist bile was James Kimble Vardaman of Mississippi, a powerful orator who served as governor from 1904 to 1908 before winning election in 1912 to a single term in the U.S. Senate. Known by his followers as the "White Chief," Vardaman ran state and federal campaigns that unabashedly supported white supremacy and constantly sought to take money from schools for blacks. "To educate a negro is to spoil a good field hand," Vardaman once declared.[162] Others of this ilk included Ben Tillman of South Carolina, a 23-year veteran of the Senate and the architect of disfranchisement in South Carolina; the Populist-turned-race baiter Tom Watson of Georgia, who served a term in the House from 1891 to 1893 and a partial term in the U.S. Senate 30 years later; and James Thomas Heflin, a Representative and Senator of Alabama, who said the right to vote was "an inherent right with the white man and a privilege with the Negro."[163]

For such men, white supremacy was a closely held belief. For others, it was a mechanism to engage voters. The southern political system promoted—and even rewarded—a certain level of recklessness, sensationalism, and demagoguery. Race became the most potent topic available for striking powerful chords with southern voters, who by 1900 were essentially white and often disengaged from politics. "Deprived of the normal party channels of rising to power and getting support in elections, politicians were practically forced to blare recklessly in an effort to become known to an amorphous public," notes historian J. Morgan Kousser.[164] Race, as political scientist V. O. Key observed in his landmark study of southern politics in the 1940s, became the keystone of the one-party, solid Democratic South that emerged around 1900 and lasted until the civil rights movement of the 1950s. "Southern sectionalism and the special character of southern political institutions have to be attributed in the main to the Negro," Key explained. He added, "the predominant consideration in the architecture of southern political institutions has been to assure locally a subordination of the Negro population and, externally, to block threatened interferences from the outside with these local arrangements."[165]

Southern Members of Congress who opposed race reforms in the 1910s and 1920s soon became influential enough to thwart such "interferences." Accruing seniority, many ascended to powerful positions on Capitol Hill during the 1930s. Benefiting from the longevity conferred by their party, which held a virtual lock on elective office in the South, many southern House Members served long terms in secure districts, earning important leadership posts. For instance, when Democrats gained control of the House in 1931, southerners wielded the chairman's gavel on 29 of 47 committees—including virtually all the most influential panels: Ways and Means (James W. Collier of Mississippi), Rules (Edward W. Pou of North Carolina), Rivers and Harbors (John J. Mansfield of Texas), Naval Affairs (Carl Vinson of Georgia), Military Affairs (Percy Quin of Mississippi), Judiciary (Hatton Sumners of Texas), Interstate and Foreign Commerce (Sam Rayburn of Texas), Banking and Currency (Henry B. Steagall of Alabama), Appropriations (Joseph W. Byrns of Tennessee), and Agriculture (John Marvin Jones of Texas). Of the 10 most attractive committees, southerners chaired nine (J. Charles Linthicum of Maryland, a border state, chaired the Foreign Affairs Committee).[166] Southerners also held two of the top three positions in House leadership: John Nance Garner of Texas served as Speaker, and John McDuffie of Alabama was the Majority Whip.

The Ku Klux Klan's resurgence in the early 1900s ushered in a reign of violence, buttressed by public shows of power like this demonstration, just outside the U.S. Capitol in 1926.

IMAGE COURTESY OF LIBRARY OF CONGRESS

In the Senate, which went Democratic with the election of Franklin D. Roosevelt to the presidency in 1932, southern influence, although less pronounced, was nonetheless significant. Southerners chaired 13 of the chamber's 33 committees in 1933, including some of the most influential panels: Agriculture and Forestry (Ellison D. Smith of South Carolina), Appropriations (Carter Glass of Virginia), Banking and Currency (Duncan U. Fletcher of Florida), Commerce (Hubert D. Stephens of Mississippi), Finance (Pat Harrison of Mississippi), Military Affairs (Morris Sheppard of Texas), and Naval Affairs (Park Trammell of Florida). In addition, Walter F. George of Georgia wielded the chairman's gavel on the Privileges and Elections Committee, through which any voting rights bill would have to pass. Setting the chamber's agenda was Senate Majority Leader Joseph T. Robinson of Arkansas, who served in that capacity until his death in 1937.

PARTY REALIGNMENT

The political realignment of black voters set in motion at the close of Reconstruction gradually accelerated in the early 20th century, pushed by demographic shifts such as the Great Migration and by black discontent with the increasingly conservative racial policies of the Republican Party in the South. A decades-long process ensued in which blacks were effectively pushed outside or left the Republican fold because of its increasingly ambiguous racial policies. By the end of this era, the major parties' policies and a re-emergent activism among younger African Americans positioned blacks for a mass movement in the early and mid-1930s to the northern Democratic Party.[167]

Weakened to the point of irrelevancy, southern Republicans after 1900 curried favor with the political power structure to preserve their grasp on local patronage jobs dispensed by the national party. Therefore, southern white GOP officials embraced Jim Crow. Through political factions such as the "lily white" movement, which excluded blacks, and "black and tan" societies, which extended only token political roles to blacks, the party gradually ceased to serve as an outlet for the politically active cadre of southern African Americans.

Gradually, African-American leaders at the national level began to abandon their loyalty to the GOP. While the party's political strategy of creating a competitive wing in the postwar South was not incompatible with the promotion of black civil rights, by the 1890s party leaders were in agreement that this practical political end could not be achieved without attracting southern whites to the ticket. "Equalitarian ideals," explains a leading historian, "had to be sacrificed to the exigencies of practical politics."[168]

However, mutually exclusive opportunities presented themselves to the national Republican Party as late as the 1920s. On the one hand, GOP officials sensed an opportunity to present the party as a moderate alternative to the segregationist policies endorsed by the outgoing Woodrow Wilson administration—to make inroads into the growing urban centers of African-American voters. On the other hand, in campaign efforts against northern Democrats such as Al Smith of New York, Republicans perceived the chance to cultivate southern white voters by adopting racially conservative positions. "The dilemma," writes historian Lewis L. Gould, "was that the politics that spoke to one group alienated the other."[169] The party chose a middle course. GOP Presidents in the 1920s hosted black leaders to discuss touchstone issues such as anti-lynching legislation, though they did little more for fear of alienating southern whites. The party's relative lack of enthusiasm for changing segregation practices in the civil service, enforcing the reduction clause of the 14th Amendment, or endorsing fully the enactment of anti-lynching legislation convinced many African Americans that the political priorities of the party of Lincoln were no longer compatible with those of the black community. At its 1926 national convention, the NAACP pointedly resolved, "Our political salvation and our social survival lie in our absolute independence of party allegiance in politics and the casting of our vote for our friends and against our enemies whoever they may be and whatever party labels they carry."[170]

The Republicans' presidential nominee in 1928 cast more doubt in black voters' minds.[171] Herbert Hoover's handling of the relief efforts after the devastating 1927 Mississippi River floods disappointed the African-American community. Tone deaf to issues that resonated with blacks, Hoover catered to the lily-white delegations at the Republican National Convention. The platform contained no substantive concessions to black interests besides a perfunctory sentence about the necessity for anti-lynching legislation. Furthermore, during the campaign Hoover devised a southern strategy against Democratic nominee Al Smith, who was perceived negatively in the South because he was Catholic and was believed to represent ethnic and black interests. By courting the racially conservative white vote with tacit support for the segregationist status quo, Hoover fractured the solid South and captured the electoral votes of five southern states: Virginia, North Carolina, Tennessee, Florida, and Texas.[172]

The 1928 presidential campaign marked a significant step toward the eventual black exodus from Republican ranks. Though a majority of African Americans cast their vote for Hoover, black defection from the party was greater than in any prior election. Manufacturers of public opinion within the black community, including the *Chicago Defender* and the *Baltimore Afro-American*, supported Al Smith.[173] Meanwhile, the party of Lincoln seemed unresponsive to the changing electorate and lacked a strategy for adjusting to new political realities. "As Negroes moved to the North and to the cities, they became part of the new urban constituency," explains historian Richard Sherman. "Just as America had ceased to be predominantly Anglo-Saxon, so had black-white relations ceased to be primarily a problem for the South. . . . In short, Republicans failed to develop a program which could attract major elements of the new, urban America," a constituency that formed the core of the Roosevelt New Deal coalition that propelled Democrats into power in the 1930s.[174]

Conclusion

W. E. B. Du Bois insightfully observed that the dominant theme of 20th-century America would be the "color line." As historian Manning Marable points out, that line, dating back to Reconstruction, was remarkably resilient, outlasting the southern experiment in multiracialism, economic depressions, foreign wars, and massive migrations of Black Americans from the South to the North. Congress's management (or avoidance) of the issue of race relations in this era strongly confirms Marable's assessment of the durability of racial prejudice and the pervasive nature of segregation in America. Throughout the first half of the 20th century, Congress lagged behind the executive and the judicial branches—and sometimes behind popular will—in terms of racial issues.[175]

Change would arise from a "Second Reconstruction"—a civil rights movement derived from the people, not imposed on them—one shaped by everyday African Americans operating largely outside of political channels who would slowly convince society of the need for change. By then blacks would have allies and advocates within the federal government, such as Oscar De Priest, who was elected to the U.S. House from his Chicago-based district in 1928. In ending African Americans' long exile from Congress, De Priest's election would infuse millions with hope—and validate the power of organized black politics in northern cities.

NOTES

1 "The Negro in Politics," 12 December 1887, *Washington Post*: 5.

2 Michael K. Fauntroy, *Republicans and the Black Vote* (Boulder, CO: Lynne Rienner Publishers, 2007): 41.

3 C. Vann Woodward, *The Strange Career of Jim Crow* (New York: Oxford University Press, 2002): 82.

4 Woodward, *The Strange Career of Jim Crow*: 69.

5 A rich historical literature details this process. Aside from *The Strange Career of Jim Crow*, see Woodward's seminal work, *The Origins of the New South, 1877–1913* (Baton Rouge: Louisiana State University, 1951) and Edward Ayers, *The Promise of the New South: Life After Reconstruction* (New York: Oxford University Press, 1992). For African-American political activism in the South from slavery into the Jim Crow and Great Migration eras, see Steven Hahn's *A Nation Under Our Feet: Black Political Struggles from Slavery to the Great Migration* (Cambridge, MA: Belknap Press, 2003).

6 Woodward, *The Strange Career of Jim Crow*: 108.

7 All the black Jim Crow-Era Representatives were born in 1849 or later, except John Langston, who was born in 1829, and lived most of his life in privilege in Ohio. He achieved an education and a level of experience that was comparable, if not superior, to that of his late-19th-century colleagues.

8 Several historians discuss the impact of skin color on the stratification of free and enslaved black communities in different regions of the South from the colonial to the postbellum periods. Winthrop D. Jordan discusses the colonial period in "American Chiaroscuro: The Status and Definition of Mulattoes in the British Colonies," in Edward Countryman, ed., *How Did American Slavery Begin?* (Boston: Bedford/St. Martin's, 1999). Both Eugene D. Genovese and Paul D. Escott discuss stratification within slave communities in the antebellum period: Genovese, *Roll, Jordan, Roll: The World the Slaves Made* (New York: Pantheon Books, 1974) and Escott, *Slavery Remembered: A Record of Twentieth-Century Slave Narratives* (Chapel Hill: University of North Carolina Press, 1979). For the racial tensions within the free black communities in the antebellum period, see Ira Berlin, *Slaves Without Masters: The Free Negro in the Antebellum South* (New York: The New Press, 1974). Joel Williamson provides a thorough history of racial miscegenation in the United States in *New People: Miscegenation and Mulattoes in the United States* (New York: The Free Press, 1980). Willard Gatewood examines the effects of skin color on the postbellum elite communities in *Aristocrats of Color: The Black Elite, 1880–1920* (Fayetteville: University of Arkansas Press, 2000).

9 Senator Hiram Revels of Mississippi graduated from Knox College in Galesburg, Illinois, in 1857, and Representative Richard Cain of South Carolina attended Ohio's Wilberforce University in the early 1860s.

10 "John Mercer Langston," in Jessie Carney Smith, ed., *Notable Black American Men* (Farmington Hills, MI: Gale Research, Inc., 1999): 693–698. Former Representatives Josiah Walls of Florida and James O'Hara of North Carolina were admitted to the bar in a similar fashion, although O'Hara received some formal training at Howard University.

11 Benjamin R. Justesen, *George Henry White: An Even Chance in the Race of Life* (Baton Rouge: Louisiana State University Press, 2001): 39, 135–144.

12 During the 1890s, GOP corruption at the state and national levels challenged the notion of patronage. Black Members of Congress vehemently supported the Republican defense of these favors. Representative Robert Smalls of South Carolina was in the minority voting against passage of the Pendleton Act in the 47th Congress (1881–1883), which made hiring procedures for the civil service more competitive. See *Congressional Record*, House, 47th Cong., 2nd sess. (4 January 1883): 837. While in office, black Representatives regularly doled out patronage positions. For example, throughout his career, Henry Cheatham gave friends and constituents in North Carolina and Washington, DC, federal positions, bestowing more than 80 appointments in the postal, internal revenue, and judicial services.

13 Thomas Adams Upchurch, *Legislating Racism: The Billion Dollar Congress and the Birth of Jim Crow* (Lexington: The University Press of Kentucky, 2004): 9–12, 74–84; Charles W. Calhoun, *Conceiving a New Republic: The Republican Party and the Southern Question, 1869–1900* (Lawrence: University Press of Kansas, 2006): 7–32.

14 *Congressional Record*, House, 56th Congress, 2nd sess. (7 January 1901): 74.

15 Michael Perman, *Struggle for Mastery: Disfranchisement in the South, 1888–1908* (Chapel Hill: University of North Carolina Press, 2001): 229.

16 *Congressional Record*, House, 51st Cong., 2nd sess. (14 February 1891): 2694.

17 Upchurch, *Legislating Racism*: 12; Samuel P. Hays, *The Response to Industrialism, 1885–1914* (Chicago: University of Chicago Press, 1957; reprint, 1995): 7–24.

18 Frederick Jackson Turner, "The Significance of the Frontier in American History," in Martin Ridge, ed., *Frederick Jackson Turner: Wisconsin Historian of the Frontier* (Madison: State Historical Society of Wisconsin, 1986): 26–47.

19 Robert H. Wiebe, *The Search for Order, 1877–1920* (New York: Hill and Wang, 1967): 11–12.

20 Robert D. Marcus, *Grand Old Party: Political Structure in the Gilded Age: 1880–1896* (New York: Oxford University Press, 1971): 10–11, 19.

21 Marcus, *Grand Old Party*: 20, 90–91, 93.

22 J. Morgan Kousser, *The Shaping of Southern Politics: Suffrage Restriction and Establishment of the One-Party South, 1880–1910* (New Haven: Yale University Press, 1974): 238–240; see especially the chart on page 239.

23 Kousser, *The Shaping of Southern Politics*: 46–53; quotation on pages 39–40. See also Woodward, *The Strange Career of Jim Crow*: 83–86.

24 For population statistics and election results, see Stanley B. Parsons et al., *United States Congressional Districts, 1843–1883* (New York: Greenwood Press, 1986): 213; Stanley B. Parsons et al., *United States Congressional Districts, 1883–1913* (New York: Greenwood Press, 1990): 143, 279, 281; Michael J. Dubin et al., *U.S. Congressional Elections, 1788–1997* (Jefferson, NC: McFarland & Company, Inc., Publishers, 1998): 254, 262, 269, 276, 284, 292, 301, 310.

25 *Congressional Record*, House, 53rd Cong., 1st sess. (5 October 1893): 2159.

26 Dubin et al., *U.S. Congressional Elections, 1788–1997*: 319.

27 The Confederacy included South Carolina, Mississippi, Florida, Alabama, Georgia, Louisiana, Texas, Virginia, Arkansas, North Carolina, and Tennessee.

28 Michael Perman, *Road to Redemption: Southern Politics 1869–1879* (Chapel Hill: University of North Carolina Press, 1984): 193–220; Kousser, *The Shaping of Southern Politics*: 139–181.

29 See Stephen Kantrowitz, *Ben Tillman and the Reconstruction of White Supremacy* (Chapel Hill: University of North Carolina Press, 2000).

30 Perman, *Struggle for Mastery*: 96.

31 Ibid.

32 Ibid., 93.

33 George Brown Tindall, *South Carolina Negroes, 1877–1900* (Columbia: University of South Carolina Press, 2003; reprint of 1952 edition): 78.

34 Perman, *Struggle for Mastery*: 96.

35 "South Carolina's Plan," 4 November 1895, *New York Times*: 7.

36 Tindall, *South Carolina Negroes*: 88.

37 Perman, *Struggle for Mastery*: 225–226.

38 Woodward, *The Strange Career of Jim Crow*: 85; Perman, *Struggle for Mastery*: 313.

39 John Hope Franklin and Alfred A. Moss, *From Slavery to Freedom: A History of African Americans*, 8th edition (New York: Alfred A, Knopf, 2000): 288. Additionally, as southern states legally disfranchised hundreds of thousands of Black Americans, violence wracked southern cities. On November 10, 1898, in the coastal town of Wilmington, North Carolina, local whites violently evicted elected city officials including the white mayor and sheriff—who were part of a "fusion" Populist government that had the support of a thriving and politically active African-American community. Former U.S. Representative Alfred M. Waddell of North Carolina (1871–1879), a newspaper editor and an ex-Confederate cavalry colonel, led a mob of whites who ransacked black neighborhoods in the city and the offices of the local black newspaper. Eleven African Americans were killed, and the black community's leaders were sent into exile. For more on this topic, see the extensive report of the Wilmington Race Riot Commission, published in 2006: http://www.ah.dcr.state.nc.us/1898-wrrc/default.htm (accessed 1 December 2007); contemporary newspaper

accounts include "Negro Rule Ended," 11 November 1898, *Washington Post*: 1. For more on Waddell, see "Waddell, Alfred Moore," *Biographical Directory of the United States Congress, 1774–Present*, available at http://bioguide.congress.gov/scripts/biodisplay.pl?index=W000002.

40 For more on "packing" and "cracking" as gerrymandering strategies, see Bernard Grofman, *Political Gerrymandering and the Courts* (New York: Algora Publishing, 1990): especially pages 178–179.

41 See, for example, the borders between the South Carolina's 1st and 7th districts from 1893 to 1895 in Parsons et al., *United States Congressional Districts, 1883–1913*: 275.

42 Eric Anderson, *Race and Politics in North Carolina, 1872–1901* (Baton Rouge: Louisiana State University Press, 1981): 3–4, 141; Parsons et al., *United States Congressional Districts, 1843–1883*: 201; Parsons et al., *United States Congressional Districts, 1883–1913*: 255–257.

43 Kousser, *The Shaping of Southern Politics*: 11, 13–14, 261.

44 For more on this phenomenon see, Helen G. Edmonds, *The Negro and Fusion Politics in North Carolina* (New York: Russell and Russell, 1951; reprint 1972).

45 Thomas Holt explains the origins of the tensions between mulatto and dark skinned candidates. See *Black Over White: Negro Political Leadership in South Carolina During Reconstruction* (Urbana: University of Illinois Press, 1977): 59–64.

46 Quoted in William C. Hine, "Miller, Thomas Ezekiel," *American National Biography* 15 (New York: Oxford University Press, 1999): 518–520 (hereinafter referred to as *ANB*).

47 John F. Marszalek, *A Black Congressman in the Age of Jim Crow: South Carolina's George Washington Murray* (Gainesville: University Press of Florida, 2006): 37.

48 Quoted in Tindall, *South Carolina Negroes, 1877–1900*: 58.

49 Marszalek, *A Black Congressman in the Age of Jim Crow*: 109.

50 Anderson, *Race and Politics*: 208–209.

51 Ibid., 213.

52 Justesen, *George Henry White*: 199.

53 Jeffrey A. Jenkins, "Partisanship and Contested Election Cases in the House of Representatives, 1789–1902," *Studies in American Political Development* 18 (Fall 2004): 113.

54 Chester H. Rowell, *A Historical and Legal Digest of All the Contested Election Cases* (Washington, DC: Government Printing Office, 1901). Though Rowell is one of the most comprehensive sources on the activities of the Committee on Elections for this era, his data are incomplete. At least six contested elections cases involving black men are missing from his volume.

55 William J. Gaboury, "George Washington Murray and the Fight for Political Democracy in South Carolina," *Journal of Negro History* 62 (July 1977): 266. The demands placed a considerable burden on members of the Committee on Elections, which was charged with investigating disputed results and reporting its findings back to the full House. In the 54th Congress (1895–1897), facing 38 contested election cases (28 of which originated in the South), the Committee on Elections split into three separate panels named Elections #1, Elections #2, and Elections #3. The three committees remained until the Legislative Reorganization Act of 1946 combined them under the jurisdiction of the Committee on House Administration.

56 For a discussion of surrogate representation using modern examples, see Jane Mansbridge, "Should Blacks Represent Blacks and Women Represent Women? A Contingent 'Yes,'" *Journal of Politics* 61 (1999): 628–657.

57 *Congressional Record*, House, 55th Cong., 2nd sess. (22 April 1898): 4194.

58 Charles Stewart III, "Committee Hierarchies in the Modernizing House, 1875–1947," *American Journal of Political Science* 36 (1992): 845–846. Cheatham was ranked fifth out of six minority members of the Agriculture Committee in the 52nd Congress (1891–1893); White was ranked last out of 11 majority members on the Agriculture Committee in the 55th Congress (1897–1899).

59 For a thorough discussion of U.S. monetary policy in the late 19th century, see Irwin Unger, *The Greenback Era: A Social and Political History of American Finance, 1865–1880* (Princeton, NJ: Princeton University Press, 1964); Alan Weinstein, *Prelude to Populism: Origins of the Silver Issue, 1867–1878* (New Haven, CT: Yale University Press, 1970); Milton Friedman and Anna J. Schwartz, *A Monetary History of the United States, 1867–1960* (Princeton, NJ: Princeton University Press, 1963).

60 *Congressional Record*, House, 52nd Cong., 1st sess. (13 July 1892): 6133. The rest of the Republicans voting in favor of the bill were from silver-mining states.

61 *Congressional Record*, House, 53rd Cong., 1st sess. (24 August 1893): 859.

62 Woodward, *The Strange Career of Jim Crow*: 72–74.

63 Recent historical literature suggests that racism at home cooled enthusiasm for imperialism abroad. One historian argues that segregationists often opposed imperialists because they were unwilling to incorporate foreign, dark-skinned citizens. See Eric T. Love, *Race Over Empire: Racism and U.S. Imperialism, 1865–1900* (Chapel Hill: University of North Carolina Press, 2004).

64 *Congressional Record*, House, 55th Cong., 3rd sess. (26 January 1899): 1126.

65 Quoted in Upchurch, *Legislating Racism*: 86.

66 Charles W. Calhoun, *Benjamin Harrison* (New York: Henry Holt and Company, 2005): 33, 55.

67 Upchurch, *Legislating Racism*: 94.

68 Ibid., 95.

69 *Congressional Record*, House, 51st Cong., 1st sess. (26 June 1890): 6544.

70 *Congressional Record*, House, 51st Cong., 1st sess. (28 June 1890): 6728.

71 Calhoun, *Conceiving a New Republic*: 242–243.

72 *Congressional Record*, House, 51st Cong., 2nd sess. (16 January 1891): 1480–1481.

73 *Congressional Record*, House, 51st Cong., 2nd sess. (12 January 1891): 1216.

74 See W. Fitzhugh Brundage, ed., *Under Sentence of Death: Lynching in the South* (Chapel Hill: University of North Carolina Press, 1997); see also Brundage's *Lynching in the New South: Georgia and Virginia, 1880–1930* (Urbana: University of Illinois Press, 1993). For a classic study of lynching, see NAACP secretary Walter White's, *Rope and Faggot: A Biography of Judge Lynch* (Notre Dame, IN: University of Notre Dame Press, 2001; reprint of 1929 Knopf edition).

75 Susan Carter et al., eds., *Historical Statistics of the United States: Government and International Relations* 5 (New York: Oxford University Press, 2006): 252–255. While this figure represents the most recent scholarship available, it almost certainly underrepresents the actual number of white-on-black lynchings in the South. Figures exist for 10 of the original Confederate states (Alabama, Arkansas, Florida, Georgia, Louisiana, Mississippi, North Carolina, South Carolina, Tennessee, and Virginia). Figures for Texas are not included in this analysis. Statistics for Kentucky, a border state, are included in this figure. See also Stewart Tolnay and E. M. Beck, *A Festival of Violence: An Analysis of Southern Lynchings, 1882–1930* (Urbana: University of Illinois Press, 1995).

76 *Congressional Record*, House, 56th Cong., 1st sess. (20 January 1900): 1021.

77 *Congressional Record*, House, 56th Cong., 1st sess. (23 February 1900): 2151–2154; quotations on pages 2153, 2151.

78 *Congressional Record*, House, 55th Cong., 3rd sess. (26 January 1899): 1125. See also Justesen, *George Henry White*: 263.

79 House of Representatives, 56th Cong., 2nd sess. (20 December 1900), report no. 2130: 15. This document, which contained a section entitled "History of Apportionment," accompanied H.R. 12740 and was generated by the Select Committee on the Twelfth Census. Later efforts to enforce that provision, following the wave of state constitutional conventions that drafted statutes to eliminate black voters, were pursued on several occasions but were feeble, halting and, ultimately, ineffective. The enforcement section was struck and never reinserted into subsequent decennial apportionment bills.

80 Charles W. Eagles, *Democracy Delayed: Congressional Reapportionment and Urban–Rural Conflict in the 1920s* (Athens: The University Georgia Press, 1990): especially pages 21–31.

81 House of Representatives, 55th Cong., 3rd sess. (3 March 1899), report no. 2354: 1–2.

82 *Congressional Record*, House, 56th Cong., 2nd sess. (7 January 1901): 67–75; Perman, *Struggle for Mastery*: 228–229. States with additional poll taxes and property exclusions would potentially lose even more seats.

83 *Congressional Record*, House, 56th Cong., 2nd sess. (8 January 1901): 737.

84 Ibid., 748.

85 Perman, *Struggle for Mastery*: 238–239.

86 *Congressional Record*, House, 58th Cong., 2nd sess. (27 January 1904): 1276. Quotation in Perman, *Struggle for Mastery*: 240.

87 "A Bomb in Caucus: Republican Proposition to Southern Democrats," 18 April 1902, *Washington Post*: 1; Perman, *Struggle for Mastery*: 239–240. Subsequent reduction legislation also failed. In 1903, Crumpacker assumed the chairmanship of the House Committee on the Census, affording him a prime perch from which to push for enforcement of the 14th Amendment. During the 59th Congress (1905–1907), Crumpacker, working with former Speaker of the House Joseph Keifer of Ohio, introduced a measure to reduce southern representation by 37 House seats. The bill never made it to the floor for a vote. See *Congressional Record*, House, 59th Cong., 1st sess. (16 March 1906): 3885–3894; "Crusade Against South as Result of Campaign for 'Disfranchisement,'" 27 February 1906, *Atlanta Constitution*: 1; "Gen. Keifer's New Reconstruction," 3 March 1906, *Washington Post*: 6; "Disfranchisement and Reapportionment," 4 March 1906, *Atlanta Constitution*: C4. In May 1908, Crumpacker managed to attach a reduction rider to a campaign contribution reform bill. The amended measure passed the House, despite condemnations from southern Members, but the campaign bill and its rider died quietly in the Senate Committee on Privileges and Elections at the end of the 60th Congress (1907–1909). See *Congressional Record*, House, 60th Cong., 1st sess. (22 May 1908): 6763–6768; "Minority Is Hard Hit: House Republicans pass the Crumpacker Bill," 23 May 1908, *Washington Post*: 4. For Williams's quotation, see "House Upholds Stroke at South by Crumpacker," 23 May 1908, *Atlanta Constitution*: 1. For southern reaction, see "The Crumpacker Menace," 24 May 1908, *Atlanta Constitution*: A4; and "Fooling With Dynamite," 27 May 1908, *Atlanta Constitution*: 6.

88 *Congressional Record*, House, 55th Cong., 3rd sess. (26 January 1899): 1124.

89 *Congressional Record*, House, 56th Cong., 2nd sess. (29 January 1901): 1638.

90 Howard N. Rabinowitz provides a detailed essay chronicling the history of Reconstruction-Era scholarship; see "Introduction: The Changing Image of Black Reconstructionists," in Howard Rabinowitz, ed., *Southern Black Leaders of the Reconstruction Era* (Urbana: University of Illinois Press, 1982): xi–xxiv.

91 William Archibald Dunning, *Reconstruction Political and Economic* (New York: Harper & Brothers Publishers, 1907): 213; James Ford Rhodes, *History of the United States From the Compromise of 1850*, Volume 7 (New York: MacMillian Company, 1906): 169.

92 John R. Lynch, "Some Historical Errors of James Ford Rhodes," *The Journal of Negro History* 2 (October 1917): 357; W. E. B. Du Bois, *Black Reconstruction in America* (New York: Harcourt, Brace, 1935, under the title *Black Reconstruction*; reprint, New York: Free Press, 1998): 629 (citations are to the Free Press edition).

93 Most biographies appeared in the 1970s. See, for example, Okun Edet Uya, *From Slavery to Political Service: Robert Smalls, 1839–1915* (New York: Oxford University Press, 1971); Peggy Lamson, *The Glorious Failure: Black Congressman Robert Brown Elliott and the Reconstruction in South Carolina* (New York: Norton, 1973); Peter D. Klingman, *Josiah Walls: Florida's Black Congressman of Reconstruction* (Gainesville: University of Florida Press, 1976); and Loren Schweninger, *James T. Rapier and Reconstruction* (Chicago: The University of Chicago Press, 1978). Recent scholars, too, have shown a renewed interest in the lives of 19th-century black Representatives. See, for example, Justesen, *George Henry White* (2001) and Marszalek, *A Black Congressman in the Age of Jim Crow* (2006).

94 Eric Foner, *Freedom's Lawmakers: A Directory of Black Officeholders During Reconstruction* (New York: Oxford University Press, 1993): 538; Carol Swain, *Black Faces, Black Interests: The Representation of African Americans in Congress* (Cambridge: Harvard University Press, 1993): 29.

95 Stephen Middleton, ed., *Black Congressmen During Reconstruction: A Documentary Sourcebook* (Westport, CT: Praeger, 2002): xx.

96 See Richard Hofstadter, *Social Darwinism in American Thought* (Philadelphia: University of Pennsylvania Press, 1944 under the title *Social Darwinism in American Thought, 1860–1915*; reprint, Boston: Beacon Press, 1992).

97 *Congressional Record*, House, 56th Cong., 2nd sess. (7 January 1901): 74. For Crumpacker's motivations, see Perman, *Struggle for Mastery*: 229.

98 Michael J. Klarman, "Court, Congress, and Civil Rights," in *Congress and the Constitution*, Neal Devins and Keith E. Whittington, eds. (Durham, NC: Duke University Press, 2005): 175.

99 Richard B. Sherman, *The Republican Party and Black America from McKinley to Hoover, 1896–1933* (Charlottesville: University Press of Virginia, 1973): 19.

100 Gloria J. Browne-Marshall, *Race, Law, and American Society, 1607 to Present* (New York: Routledge, 2007): 115–136, especially pages 118–122.

101 Plessy v. Ferguson 163 U.S. 537 (1896); Williams v. Mississippi 170 U.S. 213 (1898); Giles v. Harris 189 U.S. 475 (1903).

102 For more on Plessy v. Ferguson, see Charles A. Lofgren, *The Plessy Case: A Legal Historical Interpretation* (New York: Oxford University Press, 1987).

103 The cases are discussed in detail in Kermit L. Hall, ed., *The Oxford Companion to The Supreme Court of the United States* (New York: Oxford University Press, 1992).

104 The rich literature on the Progressive movement includes Arthur S. Link and Richard L. McCormick, *Progressivism* (Arlington Heights, IL: Harlan Davidson, Inc., 1983); Wiebe, *The Search for Order, 1877–1920*; and Hays, *The Response to Industrialism, 1885–1914*. For a survey of the era, see John Milton Cooper, *Pivotal Decades: The United States, 1900–1920* (New York: W. W. Norton, 1990).

105 Kousser, *The Shaping of Southern Politics*: 260–261. In the South, Progressivism provided an intellectual lynchpin for efforts to eradicate party competition and to exclude blacks from political participation. Kousser writes, "Suffrage restriction was entirely consonant with the Progressive urge to rationalize the economic and political system, to substitute public for private agreements, to enact reforms which disarmed radical critics while actually strengthening the status quo. . . . How much more rationalized was the South after 1900! Virtually every elected officeholder was a white Democrat. . . . Where the Redeemers had had to count out opponents during and after elections, Progressives stopped them from running at all by disfranchising their potential followers."

106 Wiebe, *The Search for Order, 1877–1920*: 156.

107 For more on social Darwinism, see Stephen Jay Gould, *The Mismeasure of Man*, revised and expanded edition (New York: Norton, 1996); Allan Chase, *The Legacy of Malthus: The Social Costs of the New Scientific Racism* (Urbana: University of Illinois Press, 1980); Hofstadter, *Social Darwinism in American Thought*.

108 *Congressional Record*, House, 55th Cong., 2nd sess. (26 January 1899): 1125.

109 For an exhaustive study on segregation in the federal government, see Desmond King, *Separate and Unequal: Black Americans and the US Federal Government* (New York: Oxford, 1995): especially pages 9, 20–27.

110 See, for example, H.R. 5968 (63rd Congress, 1913–1915), H.R. 7540 (64th Congress, 1915–1917), H.R. 3573 (65th Congress, 1917–1919); King, *Separate and Unequal*: 218, appendix A1.3.

111 From 1914 and lasting until 1940, persons seeking civil service jobs were required to submit a photograph with their application—a *de facto* method of discrimination based on race and color. Successful African-American job seekers were assigned to a disproportionate number of menial positions (custodial, clerical, and laborer jobs) and very few supervisory positions. See King, *Separate and Unequal*: 4, 29, 48. As a result, the percentage of African-American civil servants declined from 6 to 4.9 percent of the federal workforce during the Wilson administration, though that figure was somewhat misleading because the actual total increased due to the growth of the federal government during the war production effort. Kendrick A. Clements, *The Presidency of Woodrow Wilson* (Lawrence: University Press of Kansas, 1992): 45–46, 60–61. See also Joel Williamson *The Crucible of Race: Black-White Relations in the American South Since Emancipation* (New York: Oxford University Press, 1984). For percentages of African Americans in the federal workforce, see King, *Separate and Unequal*: 49. Even after Wilson left office, however, discrimination in the federal government remained pervasive. King, *Separate and Unequal*: 16, 20, 222, 229 (appendices A2.2 and A3.2).

112 King, *Separate and Unequal*: 26–27.

113 For a history of the NAACP, see Gilbert Jonas, *Freedom's Sword: The NAACP and the Struggle Against Racism in America, 1909–1969* (New York: Routledge, 2005).

114 See Adam P. Plant, "Selective Service Act of 1917," in Brian K. Landsberg, ed., *Major Acts of Congress*, Volume 3 (New York: Macmillan Reference/Thompson Gale, 2004): 178–181; see also Robert W. Mullen, *Blacks in America's War: The Shift in Attitudes From the Revolutionary War to Vietnam* (New York: Monad Press, 1973).

115 Franklin and Moss, *From Slavery to Freedom*: 361–362.

116 Ibid., 366–374. Among these, the 15th New York Regiment of the 369th U.S. Infantry stood out. It was the first Allied unit to reach the German border on the Rhine River, and never yielded a trench or lost a member to capture. The French awarded the entire regiment the *Croix de Guerre*.

117 For more on black migrations in the post-Reconstruction period and the 20th century, see Nicholas Lemann's *The Promised Land: The Great Black Migration and How It Changed America* (New York: Knopf, 1991); Nell Irvin Painter, *Exodusters: Black Migrants to Kansas After Reconstruction* (Lawrence: University Press of Kansas, 1986); Douglas Flamming, *Bound for Freedom: Black Los Angeles in Jim Crow America* (Berkeley: University of California Press, 2005). For a concise essay on the historical literature on this topic, see Joe William Trotter, "Great Migration: An Interpretation," in *Africana* 3, Kwame Appiah and Henry Louis Gates, Jr., eds. (New York: Oxford University Press, 2005): 53–60.

118 See the chart on regional black population shifts at the end of this essay. Migration was a long and vexing question in the South and among African-American communities generally. In 1822, the American Colonization Society (ACS) acquired a small tract of land in the British colony of Sierra Leone in sub-Saharan Africa and named it "Liberia"—a settlement of people "made free." Approximately 15,000 free blacks from the United States migrated to Liberia over the next 20 years. Though the ACS initially received support from several prominent politicians, vocal objectors and an economic depression in Liberia killed the project by the 1830s. After Reconstruction, the issue of African migration was rekindled; however, many leading blacks, among them John Langston, opposed foreign emigration. "Abuse us as you will, gentlemen," Langston told Democrats. "There is no way to get rid of us. This is our native country." *Congressional Record*, House, 51st Cong., 2nd sess. (16 January 1891): 1480–1482; see also William Cohen, *At Freedom's Edge: Black Mobility and the Southern White Quest for Racial Control, 1861–1915* (Baton Rouge: Louisiana State University Press, 1991).

119 "Sees No Hope in South," 26 August 1900, *Chicago Daily Tribune*: 7; "Southern Negro's Complaint," 26 August 1900, *New York Times*: 8. White lived in Washington and Philadelphia for the rest of his life. He was among eight black Congressmen in the 19th century who left the South after their service in Washington.

120 See Hahn's discussion in *A Nation Under Our Feet*: 465–476; quotations on pages 465, 466.

121 Edmund David Cronon, *Black Moses: The Story of Marcus Garvey and the Universal Negro Improvement Association* (Madison: University of Wisconsin Press, 1955): especially pages 204–207, 212–220.

122 Hahn, *A Nation Under Our Feet*: 470–473.

123 Carter et al., *Historical Statistics of the United States: Government and International Relations* 5: 252–255.

124 William B. Hixson, Jr., "Moorefield Storey and the Defense of the Dyer Anti-Lynching Bill," *New England Quarterly* 42 (March 1969): 65–81; Robert L. Zangrando, *The NACCP Crusade Against Lynching, 1909–1950* (Philadelphia: Temple University Press, 1980): 18–19, 80–83, 214.

125 The standard biography on Johnson is Robert Fleming, *James Weldon Johnson* (New York: Twayne Publishers, 1987).

126 For more on Johnson and his role in lobbying for the Dyer Bill, see his memoir, *Along This Way* (New York: DaCapo Press, 2000; reprint of 1933 Viking Press edition): especially pages, 361–373; quotation on page 363.

127 *Congressional Directory*, 65th Congress; *Biographical Directory of the United States Congress, 1774–Present*, available at http://bioguide.congress.gov.

128 Zangrando, *The NAACP Crusade Against Lynching, 1909–1950*: 42–43.

129 Ibid., 36–37.

130 *Congressional Record*, House, 65th Cong., 1st sess. (9 July 1917): 4879; *Congressional Record*, House, 65th Cong., 1st sess. (6 July 1918): 8827. See also Zangrando, *The NAACP Crusade Against Lynching*: 43. The East St. Louis tragedy epitomized wartime racial violence in cities— spurred in large measure by the growing influx of southern blacks and immigrant whites and increased competition for industrial employment and housing. Over the next two years, riots occurred in Houston, Texas; Chester, Pennsylvania; Washington, DC; Knoxville, Tennessee; Omaha, Nebraska; and Chicago, Illinois. The summer of 1919, known widely as the "Red

Summer," was particularly violent—with 26 race riots reported nationwide resulting in hundreds of deaths. For a representative account of a particularly violent episode in 1919, see William M. Tuttle, Jr., *Race Riot: Chicago in the Red Summer of 1919* (New York: Atheneum, 1980).

131 *Congressional Record*, House, 65th Cong., 2nd sess. (7 May 1918): 6177.

132 *Congressional Record*, House, 65th Cong., 2nd sess. (7 May 1918): 6177–6178.

133 Zangrando, *The NAACP Crusade Against Lynching, 1909–1950*: 54–55, 61–62; Johnson, *Along This Way*: 362–364.

134 Zangrando, *The NAACP Crusade Against Lynching, 1909–1950*: 61–62.

135 For the entire debate, see the *Congressional Record*, House, 67th Cong., 2nd sess. (26 January 1922): 1773–1796.

136 Zangrando, *The NAACP Crusade Against Lynching, 1909–1950*: 63. Members were rounded up for a quorum on three dates: December 19 and December 20, 1921, and January 25, 1922. *Congressional Record*, House, 67th Cong., 2nd sess. (25 January 1922): 1697–1698; *Congressional Record*, House, 67th Cong., 2nd sess. (19 December 1921): 541–562.

137 *Congressional Record*, House, 67th Cong., 2nd sess. (4 January 1922): 797, 799; *Congressional Record*, House, 67th Cong., 2nd sess. (26 January 1922): 1775. For Sumners's complete speech on January 26, see pages 1774–1786. Sumners's defense rested principally on the suppositions that such an intrusion of federal power on states' rights was unconstitutional, that it placed state officers under federal control and, moreover, that proposed fines levied against local municipalities and individuals were excessively punitive. During the climax of the debate, Sumners taunted Dyer directly by using the analogy of the accused in a jailhouse besieged by the mob at the front door: "Today the Constitution of the United States stands at the door, guarding the governmental integrity of the States, the plan and the philosophy of our system of government, and the gentleman from Missouri, rope in hand, is appealing to you to help him lynch the Constitution." *Congressional Record*, House, 67th Cong., 2nd sess. (26 January 1922): 1774.

138 Johnson, *Along This Way*: 366; *Congressional Record*, House, 67th Cong., 2nd sess. (26 January 1922): 1784.

139 *Congressional Record*, House, 67th Cong., 2nd sess. (26 January 1922): 1795–1796.

140 Bankhead was the only one of these Members to deliver a lengthy floor speech. In his conclusion, he declared, "If it is a monstrously evil thing, as it is, to lynch a citizen, I answer that it is equally as felonious and culpable for a lawmaker knowingly to assassinate the Constitution." *Congressional Record*, House, 67th Cong., 2nd sess. (26 January 1922): 1792.

141 Zangrando, *The NAACP Crusade Against Lynching, 1909–1950*: 66.

142 Ibid., 66–67; *Congressional Record*, House, 67th Cong., 2nd sess. (21 September 1922): 13075–13079, 13082–13086.

143 Zangrando, *The NAACP Crusade Against Lynching, 1909–1950*: 69.

144 Perman, *Struggle for Mastery*: 240.

145 With the exception of requiring a minimum of one Representative per state and no more than one Representative per 30,000 people, the Founders were vague as to how large future Congresses should be. This problem vexed Congress throughout history. For 120 years Congress used several methods to calculate the distribution of House seats. Sometimes in combination and sometimes by ignoring the inconvenient calculations of one system and embracing those of another, the House successfully reapportioned itself through the first 12 censuses—usually within a timely fashion and in a manner that expanded, or at least preserved, the representation of most states. Problems arose in the late 19th century when, according to one formula, which distributed some House seats based on fractions, smaller rural states began to lose representation to larger states as membership was increased. See Eagles, *Democracy Delayed*: 29; Office of the Clerk, "Congressional Apportionment," available at http://clerk.house.gov/art_history/house_history/congApp.html.

146 In the 1920s, for the first (and only) time in its history, the House failed to reapportion itself based on the most recent census figures. For nine years the House haltingly debated the method for reapportioning itself, and the membership remained at the level set after the 1910 Census: 435 seats. In addition to disputing the proper statistical procedure for determining apportionment, Members contended with a number of thorny issues: Would the House become less efficient as it grew larger? How could the chamber physically hold the continually expanded memberships (required to ensure that no states lost representation)? Should African Americans and aliens be

counted in the population counts, even though most could not vote? For the single best study of the fight over congressional reapportionment and the decision to cap the House Membership at 435 Representatives, see Eagles, *Democracy Delayed*.

147 "Former Rep. Tinkham Dies, 86; Fired First U.S. Shot at Austria," 29 August 1956, *Washington Post*: 16; "George Tinkham, Legislator, Dead," 29 August 1956, *New York Times*: 28.

148 Richard H. Gentile, "Tinkham, George Holden," *ANB* 21: 696.

149 *Congressional Record*, House, 67th Cong., 1st sess. (6 May 1921): 1124–1126; the entire debate is on pages 1124–1131. For a brief account, see Sherman, *The Republican Party and Black America from McKinley to Hoover, 1896–1933*: 170–171.

150 *Congressional Record*, House, 67th Cong., 1st sess. (6 May 1921): 1127.

151 *Congressional Record*, House, 67th Cong., 1st sess. (6 May 1921): 1130–1131; Sherman, *The Republican Party and Black America from McKinley to Hoover, 1896–1933*: 171.

152 *Congressional Record*, House, 67th Cong., 1st sess. (14 October 1921): 6311–6312. See Eagles, *Democracy Delayed*: 47; Sherman, *The Republican Party and Black America from McKinley to Hoover, 1896–1933*: 171.

153 *Congressional Record*, House, 67th Cong., 1st sess. (14 October 1921): 6312.

154 Ibid.; Eagles, *Democracy Delayed*: 47. For more information on Goodykoontz, see the *Biographical Directory of the United States Congress, 1774–Present*, available at http://bioguide.congress.gov/scripts/biodisplay.pl?index=G000308. For a specific case study of election fraud and the call for reduction in Florida, see Paul Ortiz, *Emancipation Betrayed* (Berkeley: University of California Press, 2005): especially, 224–228.

155 For more on Rankin, see Walter Goodman, *The Committee: The Extraordinary Career of the House Committee on Un-American Activities* (New York: Farrar, Straus and Giroux, 1968). Also useful are his obituaries: "John Rankin Dies; Ex-Legislator, 78," 27 November 1960, *New York Times*: 86; "Rep. John Rankin, 78; Lost House Seat in '52," 28 November 1960, *Washington Post*: B3.

156 *Congressional Record*, House, 67th Cong., 1st sess. (14 October 1921): 6315–6316; Eagles, *Democracy Delayed*: 47–48.

157 *Congressional Record*, House, 67th Cong., 1st sess. (14 October 1921): 6316.

158 In late 1922, Representative Tinkham wrote President Warren G. Harding an open letter urging him to support such an investigation. He ventured as far as to warn President Harding that "the very tenure of the office you hold and the representation of the lower House of Congress is tainted with unconstitutionality." See "Negro Right to Vote Is Urged on Harding," 4 December 1922, *New York Times*: 2.

159 Eagles, *Democracy Delayed*: 51–53.

160 In early December 1927, Tinkham reintroduced an (ultimately unsuccessful) amendment to create a special House panel to investigate disfranchisement by linking it to the larger issue of equitable distribution of House seats between urban and rural constituencies. See "Will Urge Congress to Investigate South," 5 December 1927, *New York Times*: 3. In 1929, amid the deal-cutting for a key combined census and apportionment measure that permanently set the House Membership at 435, Tinkham secured enough votes to pass two amendments to a comprehensive reapportionment bill that had passed the Senate; however, Speaker Nicholas Longworth of Ohio intervened in conjunction with Majority Leader John Q. Tilson of Connecticut to kill the Tinkham provisions. House leaders feared an open debate on the issue would undo the delicate coalition of support for the overall reapportionment package. See *Congressional Record,* House, 71st Cong., 1st sess. (3 June 1929): 2348. For more on his efforts during debate on the general bill, see pages 2238–2243, 2271–2275, 2361–2364, and 2448–2449. See also Sherman, *The Republican Party and Black America from McKinley to Hoover, 1896–1933*: 221–222; Eagles, *Democracy Delayed*: 79–80.

161 Sherman, *The Republican Party and Black America from McKinley to Hoover, 1896–1933*: 222–223.

162 For more on Vardaman, see William F. Holmes, *The White Chief: James K. Vardaman* (Baton Rouge: Louisiana State University Press, 1970) and *James Kimble Vardaman: Southern Commoner* (Jackson, MS: Hederman Brothers, 1981). See also "Vardaman, James Kimble," *Biographical Directory of the United States Congress, 1774–Present*, available at http://bioguide.congress.gov/scripts/biodisplay.pl?index=V000070.

163 Kousser, *The Shaping of Southern Politics*: 170.

164 Ibid., 232–236, quotations on page 237.

165 V. O. Key, *Southern Politics in State and Nation* (Knoxville: University of Tennessee Press, 1984; reprint of 1949 Knopf edition): 665.

166 For House Members' perceptions of committee rankings based on desirability, see Stewart, "Committee Hierarchies in the Modernizing House, 1875–1947."

167 Fauntroy, *Republicans and the Black Vote*: 41, 42–55. See also Nancy Weiss's treatment in *Farewell to the Party of Lincoln: Black Politics in the Age of FDR* (Princeton, NJ: Princeton University Press, 1983): 209–235.

168 Sherman, *The Republican Party and Black America from McKinley to Hoover, 1896–1933*: 256. A significant break between the black elite and the Republican Party occurred in the aftermath of the August 1906 Brownsville affair. A garrison of African-American soldiers stationed near Brownsville, Texas, were accused (on the basis of scant evidence) of several shootings in the town. Three companies of black troops (167 enlisted men) were discharged without honor by recommendation of the U.S. Army command. President Theodore Roosevelt swiftly approved the findings. When Republican Senator Joseph B. Foraker of Ohio (a would-be contender for the 1908 party's presidential nomination) rose to defend the accused and criticized the White House, Roosevelt bristled and refused to reconsider the case. Aside from the injustice to the dishonorably discharged troops, the most lasting legacy was the alienation of a number of young black leaders, including Mary Church Terrell and Archibald Grimke.

169 Lewis L. Gould, *Grand Old Party: A History of the Republicans* (New York: Random House, 2003): 224–225.

170 *Annual Report of the NAACP* (1926): 32; cited in Sherman, *The Republican Party and Black America from McKinley to Hoover, 1896–1933*: 224.

171 For more on Hoover and African Americans, see Sherman, *The Republican Party and Black America from McKinley to Hoover, 1896–1933*: 224–259.

172 For an insightful analysis of Hoover's southern strategy, see Donald J. Lisio, *Hoover, Blacks & Lily-Whites: A Study of Southern Strategies* (Chapel Hill: University of North Carolina Press, 1985).

173 Sherman, *The Republican Party and Black America from McKinley to Hoover, 1896–1933*: 232.

174 Ibid., 258.

175 Manning Marable, *Race, Reform, and Rebellion* (Jackson: University of Mississippi Press, 1984): 10; Klarman, "Court, Congress, and Civil Rights," especially pages 177–180.

"This, Mr. Chairman,
is perhaps the negroes'
temporary farewell to the
American Congress," said
George White of North
Carolina in his final House
Floor speech. "But let me say,
Phoenix-like he will rise up
someday and come again."

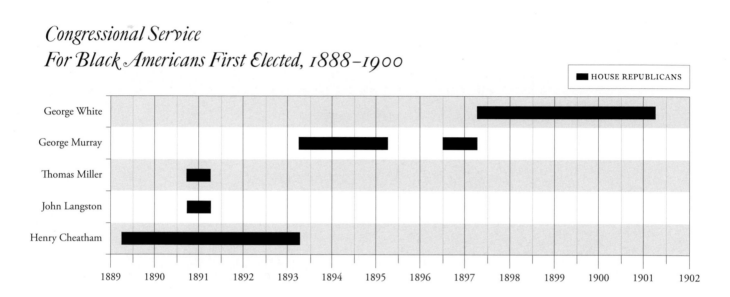

Congressional Service
For Black Americans First Elected, 1888–1900

■ HOUSE REPUBLICANS

George White

George Murray

Thomas Miller

John Langston

Henry Cheatham

1889 1890 1891 1892 1893 1894 1895 1896 1897 1898 1899 1900 1901 1902

Source: *Biographical Directory of the United States Congress, 1774–2005* (Washington, DC: Government Printing Office, 2005); also available at http://bioguide.congress.gov.

Party Divisions in the House of Representatives

50th–70th Congresses (1887–1929)

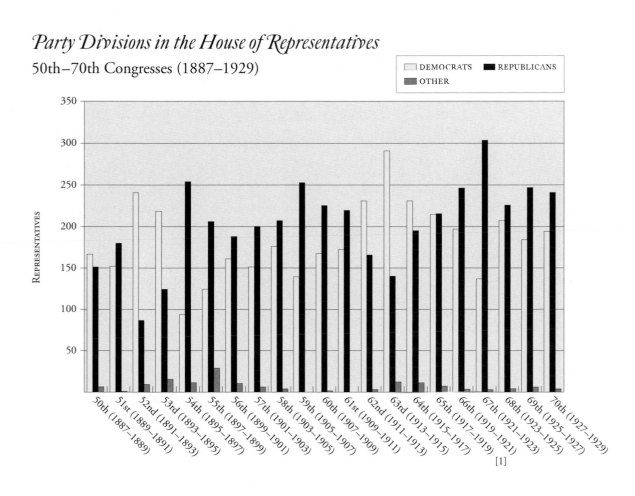

[1] The portion of the chart indicating party divisions in the 65th Congress (1917–1919) reflects the Election Day results: 215 Republicans; 214 Democrats; 3 Progressives; 1 Independent Republican; 1 Prohibitionist; 1 Socialist. Democrats, with the help of third-party Members, organized the House and elected James Beauchamp (Champ) Clark of Missouri as Speaker.

Source: Office of the Clerk, U.S. House of Representatives.

Party Divisions in the Senate
50th–70th Congresses (1887–1929)

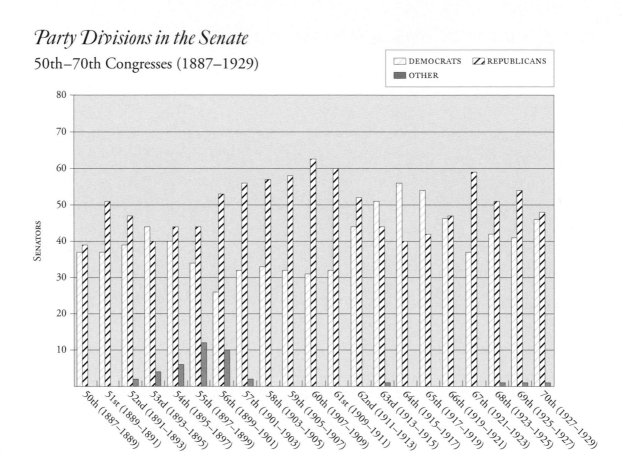

Source: U.S. Senate Historical Office.

Black Population Gains
in Selected Northern States, 1900–1950

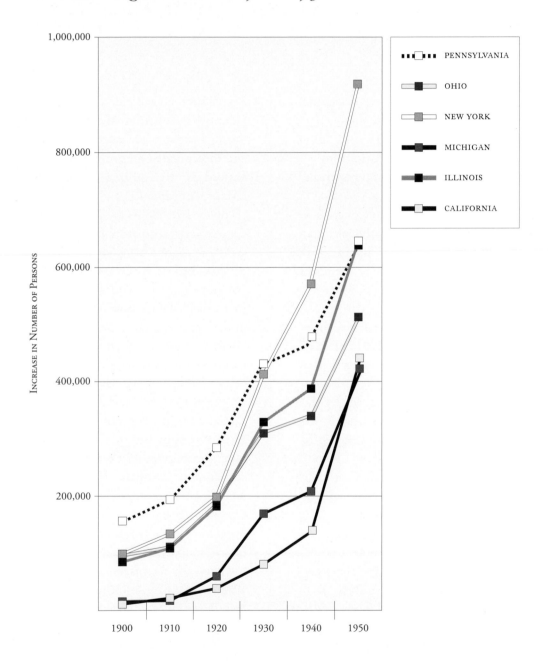

Source: U.S. Census Bureau.

Henry Plummer Cheatham
1857–1935

UNITED STATES REPRESENTATIVE ★ 1889–1893
REPUBLICAN FROM NORTH CAROLINA

A lifelong proponent of education and of the recognition of African-American achievements in the post-emancipation years, Henry Cheatham won back the "Black Second" district in eastern North Carolina, recapturing the seat formerly held by Representatives John Hyman and James O'Hara. "Politically, I am a Republican," he told the *Washington Post* in 1889. "I was elected to Congress by the Republican party and upon Republican principles and there is no question about my not cheerfully supporting the party."[1] However, Cheatham's political loyalty was tempered by his increasing frustration with the party's ambivalence toward Black Americans.

Henry Plummer Cheatham was born into slavery in Henderson, North Carolina, on December 27, 1857. His mother was a plantation-house slave, and his father was rumored to be a prominent local white man. Cheatham was emancipated at the end of the Civil War at age eight, and because of his relative youth, his formal education was more extensive than most of his future black congressional colleagues'. Cheatham attended Henderson Public School, a makeshift school for free black children. With financial help from a white friend, Robert A. Jenkins, Cheatham attended North Carolina's first college for African Americans, Shaw University Normal School in Raleigh, earning his A.B. degree in 1882. In 1887, the school awarded him an honorary master's degree.[2] While studying at Shaw, he met his first wife, fellow student Louise Cherry, who later became a music teacher. The Cheathams had three children: Charles, Mamie, and Henry Plummer, Jr. After Louise Cherry Cheatham died in 1899, Henry Cheatham married Laura Joyner, with whom he had three more children: Susie, Richard, and James.

Initially an educator, Cheatham soon found himself more interested in politics. In 1883, he was named principal of North Carolina's Plymouth Normal School.

A year later, he was elected register of deeds for Vance County. Cheatham made valuable political connections during his two terms as register. In 1887, he founded and incorporated an orphanage for black children in Oxford, North Carolina, and in 1888, he made his first bid for Congress.

By the late 1880s, the Democratic-controlled North Carolina state legislature had tightened suffrage laws, greatly restricting black voters. Jim Crow statutes had disfranchised nearly 60 percent of the voting base in the "Black Second," a predominantly African-American district that snaked along coastal sections of the northeastern part of the state.[3] A split in the African-American vote enabled "Black Second" Democrat Furnifold Simmons, to defeat incumbent Representative James O'Hara and another black candidate, Israel Abbott, in 1886.

The initial stages of the 1888 campaign pointed to a similar outcome. Simmons's chances for re-election were further strengthened by continued infighting among local Republicans. At a tumultuous Republican district convention, Cheatham topped 10 other candidates, including former Representatives John Hyman and James O'Hara.[4] Though he was eventually nominated without opposition, eight delegates abstained, indicating a tepid base of support. Black candidate George Allen Mebane used his early popularity at the district convention to run against Cheatham in the general election, claiming he had the backing of the Republican executive committee.[5] Cheatham declined Mebane's invitation to debate, refusing to recognize any other party candidate for the seat, and each candidate spent the summer of 1888 blaming the other for sustained Republican divisions. The rivalry continued unabated until October, when Mebane suddenly withdrew and asked his supporters to back Cheatham. Though Republicans praised him for acting for the sake

IMAGE COURTESY OF MOORLAND–SPINGARN RESEARCH CENTER, HOWARD UNIVERSITY

of party unity, Democrats spread rumors that Cheatham supporters had bought off Mebane.[6] Simmons remained strategically neutral on racial issues, though as a Senator he would emerge as an extremist in the white supremacy movement. He also retained a relatively large African-American following until a few weeks before the election, but his partisans were not as cautious.[7] Unable to depend on the divided vote that aided Simmons in 1886, district Democrats used white North Carolinians' racial fears against Cheatham.[8] The black candidate fought back, warning black voters that Democrats wanted to return them to slavery.[9] Cheatham defeated Simmons by a narrow 51 percent (a margin of roughly 600 votes).[10] Across the state, Republicans had their best showing since 1872, claiming three of the state's nine congressional seats.[11]

Cheatham arrived in Washington nearly a year early to familiarize himself with the legislative process. When the House organized itself in December 1889, he was the only black Member in the 51st Congress (1889–1891).[12] Reactions to his arrival were curious, but favorable. Friendly newspapers emphasized his strong educational background, which earned him an assignment on the Committee on Education.[13] Cheatham also served on the Committee on Expenditures on Public Buildings in the 51st Congress. The North Carolina Representative was a behind-the-scenes legislator, focusing on his committee work and giving few speeches on the House Floor.[14]

Cheatham proved loyal to some of the principal Republican monetary policies of the early 1890s. He favored the McKinley Tariff, which raised duties an average of 45 percent to protect local manufacturers from foreign competitors.[15] He noted that "the leading incentive of the great tariff system of America has always been to stimulate and protect home industries, and this has become the spirit of the age."[16] However, his only speech in the first session opposed a protective tax on compound lard made from pig fat and cottonseed oil. Cheatham explained that destitute farmers in his district began producing the hybrid lard after a fully animal-based product became too expensive due to an epidemic that had wiped out North Carolina's hog

population. "Our people are … anxiously waiting to see if their friends in the North will take away from them the last blessing they have in the form of cheap food," he pleaded with his colleagues, "a blessing, let me say, which materially affects the colored people's condition at the South."[17]

Cheatham's black constituents faced unraveling economic and political conditions. During his first term, the teetering economy in eastern North Carolina plunged into depression. The prices of two staple crops, cotton and corn, dropped dramatically, squeezing small farmers.[18] Poor economic prospects led to a decline in the black voter base in Cheatham's district. By 1890, many emigrated from the economically depressed Carolinas in search of better opportunities in Arkansas, Texas, and Mississippi. In an attempt to stem the flight, Cheatham returned to his district in the first month of the 51st Congress and appealed to his constituents.[19] But disfranchisement laws—including rigid requirements for proving birthplace and heritage, which necessitated documentation many freedmen did not possess—further discouraged local blacks.[20] African Americans urged Cheatham and his Republican colleagues from North Carolina, Representatives John Bower and Hamilton Ewart, to withdraw from the House Republican Conference to protest the party's perceived indifference to their plight. Black Republican voters insisted Republican leaders should be reminded of their dependence on black voters in the South. A loyal adherent to his party, Cheatham refused their demand.[21]

The Democratic Party's loss to an African-American candidate two years before in the "Black Second" district convinced local leaders to embrace white supremacy campaigns by 1890. The cautious, neutral approach taken by Democrat Furnifold Simmons during his term in Congress was rapidly displaced by more extremist positions and the application of tremendous pressure on white Republican residents of the eastern black belt to vote against their African-American neighbors.[22] But the Democrats, too, were divided by local economic depression. Wealthier party leaders, primarily lawyers and editors, argued with farmers about how to resolve the business crisis.[23] The Democrats eventually nominated James M. Mewboorne, a business agent for the powerful North Carolina Farmers' Alliance, which had connections to the national Populist Party.[24] Seeking to attract whites to his camp, Cheatham vowed to aid depressed farmers. He maintained his ties to black voters by railing against steel magnate Andrew Carnegie for hiring foreign laborers instead of blacks in his northern mills.[25] Cheatham won re-election by roughly 1,000 votes, or 52 percent.[26] He was the only Republican in the North Carolina delegation and the only black Member of the 52nd Congress (1891–1893). Despite an overwhelmingly Democratic Congress, Cheatham won a plum assignment to the Committee on Agriculture.[27]

Cheatham's and his wife Louise's poor health caused the Representative to be absent from most of the 52nd Congress. When present, Cheatham focused on advocating legislation publicly by emphasizing black citizens' contributions to American society since emancipation. On May 25, 1892, Cheatham asked the House to appropriate $100,000 for an exhibit of African-American arts, crafts, tools, and industrial and agricultural products at the World's Columbian Exhibition in Chicago in October 1893. However, Cheatham's request was rejected after the debate degenerated into an argument on the Republican-backed Federal Elections Bill to reinforce the 15th Amendment. Democrats hijacked the debate, ominously warning that the "Force Bill" would only make life harder for southern blacks in the face of virulent white opposition.[28] Cheatham openly lamented the direction of the debate, solemnly noting, "I regret exceedingly that this question has assumed a hot political phase. . . . It seems to me that whenever the colored people of this country ask for anything, something unfortunate intervenes to hinder their getting what they asked."[29]

Cheatham also sought to boost the failing economy in his district by introducing measures to protect individual farmers and arguing for federal regulation on the sales of options and futures to protect rural communities, a

stance supported even by his opponents.[30] The strong partisan flair he showed in his first term faded in the face of so much opposition—from within the GOP and from outside—to his legislative initiatives. "I am exceedingly anxious that the Democratic and Republican parties shall get together when you come to the Negro and that all will be willing to join in the effort to do something for him," he admitted in a floor speech.[31] Cheatham broke with the Republican Party over the coinage of silver, joining the entire North Carolina delegation in voting for the unsuccessful measure.[32]

By 1892, the Democratic state legislature had carved up the "Black Second" district, virtually destroying its traditional voting base. The old district's three southeastern counties—including Craven County, whose population was 65 percent black—were cut off.[33] State election laws also limited the ability of North Carolina blacks to vote. The uneasy alliance between North Carolina Populists and Republicans dissolved. The third party nominated its own candidate for Congress, Edward Alston Thorne, who had strong connections to the Farmers' Alliance.[34] Democrats were optimistic, declaring that the "cloud of blackness which has hovered over this section for so long" had lifted.[35] The Democrats selected Frederick A. Woodard, who had lost to former Representative James O'Hara in 1884. Cheatham easily gained the support of the district's Republican convention. The Populist Party, however, siphoned off some of the Republican base in the general election, luring African-American voters by offering a few black men patronage positions and nominations.[36] Cheatham lost his seat to Woodard by more than 2,000 votes (38 percent to Woodard's 45 percent). Thorne placed third, with 17 percent of the vote.[37]

Cheatham did not relinquish his political career in Washington quietly. He won the Republican nomination for his old seat in 1894 but lost in the general election. Two years later, he lost the GOP nomination to his brother-in-law, George White, an outspoken political rival. Cheatham returned to Washington in 1897 when President William McKinley, a Republican and a former colleague in the House, appointed him recorder of deeds for the District of Columbia. The U.S. Senate confirmed Cheatham for the post and he served four years. Cheatham remained active in African-American politics in the nation's capital, attending conferences with other prominent black men, including Frederick Douglass and Representative White, with whom he mended relations in the late 1890s. In 1907, Cheatham became the superintendent of the Oxford, North Carolina, orphanage he had founded two decades earlier. For the next 28 years, he expanded its facilities and surrounding farmland. At the time of his death in Oxford, on November 29, 1935, the orphanage housed 200 children.

FOR FURTHER READING

Anderson, Eric. *Race and Politics in North Carolina, 1872–1901* (Baton Rouge: Louisiana State University Press, 1981).

"Cheatham, Henry Plummer," *Biographical Directory of the United States Congress, 1774–Present*, http://bioguide. congress.gov/scripts/biodisplay.pl?index=C000340.

Logan, Frenise A. *The Negro in North Carolina, 1876–1894* (Chapel Hill: The University of North Carolina Press, 1964).

Reid, George W. "Four in Black: North Carolina's Black Congressmen, 1874–1901," *The Journal of Negro History* 64 (Summer 1979): 229–243.

MANUSCRIPT COLLECTION

The New York Public Library (New York, NY) Manuscripts, Archives and Rare Books Division, Schomburg Center for Research in Black Culture. *Papers:* In the Henry Plummer Cheatham Papers, 1912–1941, two file folders. Persons represented include Henry Plummer Cheatham's father, Representative Henry Plummer Cheatham.

NOTES

1 "Cheatham No Kicker," 29 July 1889, *Washington Post*: 2.

2 Cheatham also received legal training under white Republican Robert E. Hancock, Jr., but he never practiced law. See Stephen Middleton ed., *Black Congressmen During Reconstruction: A Documentary Sourcebook* (Westport, CT: Praeger, 2002): 59.

3 Stanley B. Parsons et al., *United States Congressional Districts, 1883–1913* (New York: Greenwood Press, 1990): 97–99.

4 Eric Anderson, *Race and Politics in North Carolina, 1872–1901* (Baton Rouge: Louisiana State University Press, 1981): 147–149.

5 Frenise A. Logan, *The Negro in North Carolina, 1876–1894* (Chapel Hill: University of North Carolina Press, 1964): 37; Maurine Christopher, *Black Americans in Congress* (New York: Thomas Y. Crowell Company, 1976): 156.

6 Christopher, *Black Americans in Congress*: 157.

7 Anderson, *Race and Politics*: 159.

8 Ibid., 154–155.

9 Leonard Schlup, "Cheatham, Henry Plummer," *American National Biography* 4 (New York: Oxford University Press, 1999): 765–766 (hereinafter referred to as *ANB*).

10 Michael J. Dubin et al., *United States Congressional Elections, 1788–1997* (Jefferson, NC: McFarland and Company, 1998): 282.

11 Anderson, *Race and Politics*: 161.

12 Black Members Thomas Miller of South Carolina and John Langston of Virginia were seated at the end of the first session.

13 "Why We Are 'Suckers,'" 8 April 1889, *Chicago Daily Tribune*: 1; "The Solitary Colored Member," 6 December 1888, *Washington Post*: 2.

14 Anderson, *Race and Politics*: 170.

15 Steven W. Stathis, *Landmark Legislation, 1774–2002: Major U.S. Acts and Treaties* (Washington, DC: Congressional Quarterly Press, 2003): 134.

16 *Congressional Record*, House, 51st Cong., 1st sess. (23 August 1890): A625.

17 Ibid., A624.

18 Anderson, *Race and Politics*: 171–172.

19 "Cheatham's Constituents," 11 January 1890, *Washington Post*: 1.

20 Anderson, *Race and Politics*: 167.

21 "Tanner's Vacant Chair," 4 October 1889, *New York Times*: 5.

22 Anderson, *Race and Politics*: 165.

23 Ibid., 172.

24 For an indication of the political power behind the Farmers' Alliance, see "North Carolina Republicans," 31 July 1890, *Atlanta Constitution*: 1. Mewboorne's name is occasionally spelled "Mewborne."

25 Schlup, "Cheatham, Henry Plummer," *ANB*; Anderson, *Race and Politics*: 178.

26 Dubin et al., *U.S. Congressional Elections, 1788–1997*: 291.

27 Mildred L. Amer, "Black Members of the United States Congress: 1870–2007," 27 September 2007, Report RL30378, Congressional Research Service, Library of Congress, Washington, DC. The Agriculture Committee assignment was one of the most attractive committee posts during this period. Political scientist Charles Stewart III ranks it as the eighth-most-desired assignment, using data collected from 1877 to 1947. See Stewart, "Committee Hierarchies in the Modernizing House, 1875–1947," *American Journal of Political Science* 36 (1992): 845. It is unclear why Cheatham received such an important committee assignment, especially as the Democrats held the majority in the 52nd Congress; however, Stewart notes that in some late-19th-century Congresses, the Minority Leader was given jurisdiction over minority committee assignments (Ibid., 842).

28 Christopher, *Black Americans in Congress*: 157.

29 *Congressional Record*, House, 52nd Cong., 1st sess. (25 May 1892): 4683.

30 Anderson, *Race and Politics*: 188.

31 *Congressional Record*, House, 52nd Cong., 1st sess. (25 May 1892): 4683.

32 *Congressional Record*, House, 52nd Cong., 1st sess. (13 July 1892): 6133. The rest of the Republicans who voted for the bill were from silver-mining states.

33 See Anderson, *Race and Politics*: 141, 186. For maps of congressional districts over time, see Parsons et al., *United States Congressional Districts, 1883–1913*: 255–257.

34 Anderson, *Race and Politics*: 194.

35 Quoted from the Tarboro (NC) *Southern* in Anderson, *Race and Politics*: 186.

36 Anderson, *Race and Politics*: 199.

37 Dubin et al., *United States Congressional Elections, 1788–1997*: 299.

John Mercer Langston
1829–1897

UNITED STATES REPRESENTATIVE ★ 1890–1891
REPUBLICAN FROM VIRGINIA

One of the most prominent African Americans in the United States before and during the Civil War, John Mercer Langston was as famous as his political nemesis, Frederick Douglass.[1] One of the first African Americans to hold elective office in the United States (he became Brownhelm, Ohio, township clerk in 1855), Langston topped off his long political career by becoming the first black man to represent Virginia in the U.S. House of Representatives.

John Mercer Langston was born free in Louisa, Virginia, on December 14, 1829.[2] His father, Ralph Quarles, was a plantation owner and had been a captain in the Revolutionary War. Langston's mother, Lucy, was a free Native American-black woman who had been Ralph Quarles's slave. Quarles emancipated Lucy and their daughter, Maria, in 1806. Lucy Langston left Quarles shortly after she was freed and had three children outside their relationship: William, Harriet, and Mary Langston. The couple later reunited, though state law forbade them to marry, and had three more children: Gideon, Charles Henry, and John Mercer. When John Langston's parents died in 1834, his father's estate was divided among his three sons and held in trust. Four-year-old John Langston moved in with a family friend, William Gooch, and his family in Chillicothe, Ohio. When Langston was 10 years old, Gooch made plans to move to Missouri, then a slave state. John's half brother, William, sued to relinquish Gooch's custody over his brother, fearing the move would jeopardize John's freedom and his substantial inheritance. The court prevented Gooch from taking the child to Missouri, and Langston became the ward of Richard Long, an abolitionist who had purchased William Gooch's Ohio farm.[3] In 1840, John Langston's brother Gideon brought John to live with him in Cincinnati. One of the city's leading black figures, Gideon ensured that his brother received a good education. In Cincinnati, John Langston heard some of the strongest antislavery rhetoric in the pre–Civil War North, and experienced the violent race riots of 1841 and the restrictive "Black Laws" imposed as a consequence.[4] In 1843, William Langston took custody of John and returned with him to Chillicothe.

John's older brothers and their colleagues, who were among the first black graduates of Oberlin College in Ohio, inspired him to attend their alma mater. Langston received a B.A. in 1849 and an M.A. in theology in 1852. Langston wanted to become a lawyer, a profession only three black men in the nation had officially achieved nationwide in the early 1850s. After two law schools denied him admission, he studied under local abolitionists in Elyria, Ohio. In September 1854, a committee on the district court confirmed his knowledge of the law, deeming him "nearer white than black," and admitted him to the Ohio bar. He commenced his practice in Brownhelm, Ohio.[5] In 1854, he married Caroline Wall, also a former student at Oberlin, who was active in the abolitionist movement and the Liberty Party.[6] The couple raised five children: Arthur, Ralph, Chinque, Nettie, and Frank.[7]

Langston's political involvement started with the Ohio conventions. A series of public meetings held statewide by prominent African Americans, the conventions called for the enfranchisement of black men and promoted their political participation. In 1852, Langston officially allied himself with the Free Democrats, who condemned the Fugitive Slave Law, allowed black delegates at their conventions, and elected Frederick Douglass as the national party secretary.[8] Langston's political career soared throughout the 1850s and 1860s. On April 22, 1855, he became one of the first African Americans elected to public office in the United States when Brownhelm Township voted him clerk on the Liberty Party ticket.[9] In 1856, he

left Brownhelm for Oberlin and served on the town's board of education. During the Civil War, Langston recruited black soldiers in the Midwest. He never served in the Union Army, but hired a substitute to take his place—a practice common among wealthy white men.[10] Following the war, he served on the Oberlin city council. In 1867, Langston served as Inspector General of the Freedmen's Bureau, touring the postwar South and encouraging freedmen to seek educational opportunities. He regularly spoke out against segregated facilities, including churches.[11]

For the first two decades of the postwar era, Langston held prominent political and educational appointments. In 1868, he returned to Washington, DC, where he established the law department at Howard University, a new college founded to educate African Americans. In the early 1870s, Senator Charles Sumner of Massachusetts sought Langston's aid in drafting his Civil Rights Bill. In 1871, Langston received an appointment from President Ulysses S. Grant (for whom he had campaigned in 1868) to the District of Columbia Board of Health. Langston served as Howard University's dean from 1868 to 1875 and from 1874 to 1875 as vice president and acting president of Howard; however, he resigned from the university when the board of trustees failed to offer him a full term as president.

In 1877, President Rutherford B. Hayes appointed Langston resident minister to Haiti and chargé d'affaires in Santo Domingo. Following his departure in 1885, Langston petitioned the Court of Claims for over $7,000 withheld from him after the Democratically controlled House appropriated less than his fixed diplomatic salary. The U.S. Supreme Court ruled in his favor in 1886. From 1885 to 1887, Langston served as president of the Virginia Normal and Collegiate Institute in Petersburg. He left after the college's board of governors fell into Democratic hands.

Settling in south-central Virginia, Langston was viewed as a celebrity by his black neighbors. In 1888, a citizen's committee asked Langston to run for a seat in the U.S. House, representing the "Black Belt of Virginia," a region whose population was 65 percent black.[12] Although

Langston had been assured that his nomination and election were nearly guaranteed, he began an aggressive campaign for the Republican ticket.[13] Langston lobbied both white and black delegates to the district convention at a lavish party hosted by several prominent black women in Petersburg.[14]

His efforts were thwarted by strong opposition from white Republicans led by scalawag Confederate General William Mahone, a central figure in Virginia Republican politics.[15] Using his formidable power over district Republicans—both black and white—Mahone orchestrated a separate district convention, excluding Langston's supporters, to nominate white candidate Judge R. W. Arnold. Though his appeal for support from the National Republican Executive Committee was unsuccessful, Langston obtained the backing of a biracial committee of district Republicans, entered the race as an Independent Republican, and methodically canvassed the district.[16]

The election brought out stark racial divisions. Democratic candidate Edward Venable refused to share a debate platform with Langston throughout the campaign.[17] Moreover, because Langston's candidacy threatened to divide the Republican vote, several prominent African Americans campaigned against him.[18] Frederick Douglass, chief among Langston's detractors, wrote a letter denouncing his candidacy, and the Mahone faction spread copies throughout the district.[19] On Election Day, Langston dispatched supporters to monitor every precinct for irregularities. His lieutenants instructed voters to say Langston's name after voting, as evidence of their support. Separate lines for blacks and whites at the polls meant black voters had to wait as long as three hours to vote. Ballot boxes were allegedly emptied of Langston's votes; Langston's supporters were not permitted to witness the count.[20] As predicted, the Republican vote split; initial results indicated that Langston lost by 641 votes to Venable. Arnold was a distant third.[21]

Langston contested the result in the House. At first, he had trouble hiring a lawyer; most attorneys in the district were white, and even sympathetic Republicans feared social and political ostracism.[22] Langston finally hired a biracial team of lawyers (the white lawyers charged an exorbitant fee). The case took several twists. One of Langston's witnesses was cross-examined for six days, an incident Langston interpreted as a stalling tactic.[23] Langston meanwhile tried to mend political fences in his district and even agreed to work on Mahone's gubernatorial campaign.[24] The Republican majority on the Committee on Elections ruled in Langston's favor on June 16, 1890, but the whole House delayed hearing his case for three months.[25] Democrats repeatedly blocked the case from coming to a vote on the floor, primarily by vacating the chamber to prevent a quorum, leaving only a few Members to address their interests.[26]

On September 23, 1890, Langston's case finally came to a vote before a crowded gallery occupied primarily by African Americans.[27] All but nine of the 152 Democratic Members retired to the hallway to avoid a quorum. But Republican discipline prevailed; the majority doggedly mustered enough Members, primarily from their own ranks.[28] Over Democratic protests that a quorum was not present, the House declared Langston the winner in a lopsided vote of 151 to 1.[29] The vote gave Langston Venable's seat for the remaining seven months of the Congress. Most Democratic Members boycotted Langston's swearing in a few minutes later, but a few offered him cordial congratulations upon re-entering the chamber.[30]

Langston's experience in higher learning earned him a position on the Committee on Education.[31] He immediately assisted the Republican majority by voting in favor of the controversial McKinley Tariff, a protective measure designed to drive up the price of cheap goods manufactured abroad. A Democratic newspaper commented that Langston's position on tariffs represented "a wall about the country so high and so great that the British lion would never have been able to get over it without the aid of dynamite or a scaling ladder."[32]

Only one week after arriving in Congress, Langston had to return home to campaign for re-election. Despite their previous "truce," William Mahone, now the governor,

refused to support Langston as his district's Republican candidate. Antagonized by Langston's Independent run for office in 1888, Mahone accused him of purposely dividing the electorate by race.[33] Langston responded that Mahone was blinded by racism and "almost a Democrat."[34] The district convention backed Langston, whose strong support was primarily from the black population. Republican newspaper accounts indicate that President Benjamin Harrison, congressional Republicans, and the GOP national leadership supported Langston's re-election.[35] However, many white Republicans in the district followed Mahone's lead and abandoned Langston, in some measure because of his unpopular vote on the McKinley Tariff.[36] Langston lost the election to Democratic candidate James Epes by about 3,000 votes in the state's first Democratic sweep since before secession.[37] Democratic newspapers blamed black voters' apathy for their party's solid victory in the state, but the contest mirrored a national trend: From nearly a 20-Member deficit, Democrats in the U.S. House captured a 100-Member majority.[38] Langston believed the election was tainted by fraud—as evidenced by long lines for black Republicans at the polls, missing ballots in black strongholds, and undue pressure by Mahone supporters.[39] But he feared contesting the election in the strongly Democratic Congress would be expensive.[40]

Returning in December 1890 as a lame duck to his first full session in Congress, Langston made his first speech on January 16, 1891. He emphasized blacks' U.S. citizenship, condemning calls for foreign emigration and what he deemed the Democratic Party's attempt to thwart black freedom. "Abuse us as you will, gentlemen," Langston told Democrats, "we will increase and multiply until, instead of finding every day five hundred black babies turning their bright eyes to greet the rays of the sun, the number shall be five thousand and still go on increasing. There is no way to get rid of us. This is our native country." Frequent, loud applause from the Republican side of the chamber interrupted Langston's speech. Newspapers admitted that Langston's speech rambled, but deemed him one of the most eloquent speakers on the House Floor.[41] One day after his speech, Langston asked the U.S. Attorney General to send the House all documentation of suits on alleged violations of voting rights.[42] The Judiciary Committee agreed to Langston's resolution, and it was adopted in the whole House. However, the Attorney General's office never complied, and the disfranchisement of southern freedmen continued.

Not all of Langston's legislative efforts were successful. Langston submitted bills to establish a national industrial university to teach blacks useful labor skills and to observe as national holidays the birthdays of former Presidents Abraham Lincoln and Ulysses S. Grant, but the bills died in committee.[43] Langston was unable to secure the appointments of several black candidates to the U.S. Military Academy at West Point and the U.S. Naval Academy at Annapolis.[44] On February 27, 1891, Langston returned to the House Floor to debate a civil appropriations bill. He used his experience as a diplomat in the Caribbean to advocate protection for American shipping interests.[45]

Langston returned to Petersburg, Virginia, at the end of the 51st Congress. In 1892, Republicans in his Virginia district asked him to run again, but he refused, noting that a white candidate would likely have more success. He continued to be active in politics, often speaking publicly about the achievements of his race.[46] Promised a federal judicial appointment as well as several Treasury Department patronage positions, Langston began campaigning for President Benjamin Harrison's re-election in 1892; however, when the administration withdrew the promised positions, he backed rival Republican James G. Blaine's quest for the nomination. Langston spent the remainder of his life traveling between Petersburg and Washington and working on his autobiography, *From the Virginia Plantation to the National Capitol*, which was published in 1894. Langston died at home in Washington, DC, on November 15, 1897.

FOR FURTHER READING

Cheek, William and Aimee Lee Cheek. *John Mercer Langston and the Fight for Black Freedom, 1829–1865* (Urbana: University of Illinois Press, 1989).

"Langston, John Mercer," *Biographical Directory of the United States Congress, 1774–Present*, http://bioguide. congress.gov/scripts/biodisplay.pl?index=L000074.

Langston, John Mercer. From the Virginia Plantation to the National Capitol, ed. William Loren Katz (New York: Arno Press, 1999; reprint of an 1894 edition by the American Publishing Co. [Hartford, CT]).

MANUSCRIPT COLLECTIONS

Fisk University (Nashville, TN) Special Collections, John Hope and Aurelia E. Franklin Library. *Papers:* 1853–1898, approximately three feet (900 items). The papers of John Mercer Langston consist of correspondence, speeches, drafts of writings, receipts, estate papers, banking papers, handbills, passports, minutes, a scrapbook, and newspaper clippings. Subjects covered in the papers include slavery in the United States, the abolition movement, Reconstruction, American relations with Haiti and the Dominican Republic, Howard University, the War Department, and the Bureau of Refugees, Freedmen and Abandoned Lands.

Howard University (Washington, DC) Moorland–Spingarn Research Center. *Papers:* 1870–1891, two linear feet. The scrapbooks of John Mercer Langston contain newspaper clippings, broadsides, programs, and invitations relating to race relations and politics in the United States. Includes information about the Virginia Normal and Collegiate Institute (now Virginia State University) in Petersburg, Virginia, and the John G. Whittier Historical Association in Memphis, Tennessee. A finding aid is available in the repository.

Library of Congress (Washington, DC) Manuscript Division. *Microfilm:* 1853–1898, one reel. The papers of John Mercer Langston consist of correspondence, speeches, drafts of writings, receipts, estate papers, banking papers, handbills, passports, minutes, a scrapbook, and newspaper clippings. Subjects covered in the papers include slavery in the United States, the abolition movement, Reconstruction, American relations with Haiti and the Dominican Republic, Howard University, the War Department, and the Bureau of Refugees, Freedmen and Abandoned Lands. The original papers are at Fisk University.

NOTES

1   For a comparison of the two men's fame, see, for example, "Mahone Makes a Dicker," 16 September 1889, *New York Times*: 1.

2   Though Stephen Middleton notes that Langston's status at birth—slave or free—is controversial, most sources indicate that his mother was freed long before his birth and that he was born free. Some ambiguity stems from whether Lucy Langston was subject to strict Virginia Black Codes and not considered legally free. See Stephen Middleton ed., *Black Congressmen During Reconstruction: A Documentary Sourcebook* (Westport, CT: Praeger, 2002): 125.

3   "John Mercer Langston," in Jessie Carney Smith, ed., *Notable Black American Men* (Farmington Hills, MI: Gale Research, Inc., 1999): 693–698 (hereinafter referred to as *NBAM*).

4   "John Mercer Langston," *NBAM*. Black Laws included, "bonding, return of all fugitive slaves, repudiation of the doctrines and activities of abolitionists, and…the total disarmament and arrest of black lawbreakers."

5   Ibid.

6   Maurine Christopher, *Black Americans in Congress* (New York: Thomas Y. Crowell Company, 1976): 140.

7   Eric Foner, *Freedom's Lawmakers: A Directory of Black Officeholders During Reconstruction*, revised edition (New York: Oxford University Press, 1996): 128.

8   "John Mercer Langston," *NBAM*.

9   Most standard secondary sources cite Langston's election as clerk of Brownhelm Township as the first time a black man was elected to public office in the United States. See, for example, Foner, *Freedom's Lawmakers*: 128; William Cheek and Aimee Lee Cheek, *John Mercer Langston and the Fight for Black Freedom, 1829–1865* (Urbana: University of Illinois Press, 1989): 260. However, this honor likely went to Alexander Twilight, who was elected to the Vermont state house of representatives and presented his credentials on October 13, 1836. See *Journal of the House of Representatives of the State of Vermont*, 1836 (Middlebury, VT: American Office, 1836): 7; Joanne Pope Melish, *Disowning Slavery: Gradual Emancipation and "Race" in New England, 1780–1860* (Ithaca: Cornell University Press, 1998): 40. Some sources list the date of Langston's election as April 2, 1885, whereas others list it as April 22. There is also disagreement about his party affiliation: Some sources list him as an Independent Democrat, while others list him as a member of the Free Soil or Liberty parties.

10   Christopher, *Black Americans in Congress*: 141.

11   Frank R. Levstik, "Langston, John Mercer," *Dictionary of American Negro Biography* (New York: Norton, 1982): 382–384.

12   William Cheek and Aimee Lee Cheek, "Langston, John Mercer," *American National Biography 13* (New York: Oxford, 1999): 164–166; Stanley B. Parsons et al., *United States Congressional Districts, 1883–1913* (New York: Greenwood Press, 1990): 157–158; John Mercer Langston, *From the Virginia Plantation to the National Capitol*, ed. William Loren Katz (New York: Arno Press, 1999; reprint of the American Publishing Co. [Hartford, CT], 1894 edition): 451.

13   Langston, *From the Virginia Plantation to the National Capitol*: 439.

14   Ibid., 442.

15   Mahone's influence is illustrated in several sources. See, for example, "Revolt Against Mahone," 20 September 1888, *New York Times*: 1; "Mahone's Lost Power," 21 September 1888, *New York Times*: 1.

16   Langston, *From the Virginia Plantation to the National Capitol*: 454–455, 458; "Campaign Features," 11 August 1888, *Washington Post*: 2. Langston credited local black women with his electoral success; though unable to vote, they were adept at organizing local meetings.

17   Christopher, *Black Americans in Congress*: 145; Langston, *From the Virginia Plantation to the National Capitol*: 462.

18   See, for example, J. W. Cromwell, "Letters from the People," 23 August 1888, *Washington Post*: 7.

19   Christopher, *Black Americans in Congress*: 145; Langston, *From the Virginia Plantation to the National Capitol*: 466–467.

20   Christopher, *Black Americans in Congress*: 145; Langston, *From the Virginia Plantation to the National Capitol*: 477–481.

21   Michael J. Dubin et al., *U.S. Congressional Elections, 1788–1997* (Jefferson, NC: McFarland & Company, Inc., Publishers, 1998): 284.

22   Langston, *From the Virginia Plantation to the National Capitol*: 487–489.

23   Ibid., 492.

24   Ibid., 495; "Virginia Political Notes," 4 August 1889, *Washington Post*: 12.

25 Considerable coverage of the contested election is included in the *Congressional Record*. See *Congressional Record*, House, 51st Cong., 1st sess. (9 September 1890): 9917–9923; *Congressional Record*, House, 51st Cong., 1st sess. (17 September 1890): 10152–10169; *Congressional Record*, House, 51st Cong., 1st sess. (19 September 1890): 10241–10244.

26 The "disappearing quorum" was a dilatory parliamentary tactic frequently employed by members of the minority party who refused to answer roll calls, and thus prevented the House from conducting business by not allowing it to achieve a working quorum. Republican Thomas Brackett Reed of Maine had resorted to the tactic when he was Minority Leader in the 1880s. Yet, as Speaker, with his party firmly in the majority, Reed refused to allow Democrats to stall legislation in this manner. On January 29, 1890, he ordered that the Democrats lingering in the hallways outside the chamber and those in the chamber refusing to vote be considered present. Reed also threatened to leave unsigned legislation requiring his signature before presidential approval until the House considered majority legislation; this would hold up several bills important to southern lawmakers. The Speaker's iron fist soon earned him the epithet "Czar Reed." See Charles W. Calhoun, "Reed, Thomas B.," in Donald C. Bacon et al., eds., *The Encyclopedia of the United States Congress* Volume 3 (New York: Simon and Schuster, 1995): 1687–1690. For newspaper coverage documenting Democratic stall tactics in Langston v. Venable, see, for example, "Wanted—A Quorum in the House," 22 September 1890, *Chicago Daily Tribune*: 2; "Reed Is Wild," 20 September 1890, *Boston Daily Globe*: 1; "Speaker Reed Annoyed," 20 September 1890, *New York Times*: 1.

27 E. W. B., "Republicans Steal," 24 September 1890, *Atlanta Constitution*: 1.

28 For contemporary accounts of Republican efforts to achieve a quorum, see "Langston Gets His Seat," 24 September 1894, *Chicago Daily Tribune*: 71; E. W. B., "Republicans Steal."

29 The lone vote against Langston came from Republican Representative Joseph Cheadle of Indiana. Cheadle remained a devoted Mahone supporter, insisting that the divided Republican vote in the Virginia district was the sole reason for Democratic victory and that seating Langston was an abuse of power. The Indiana Representative would defect to the Democratic and Populist parties in 1896. See "Cheered by Democrats," 18 September 1890, *Chicago Daily Tribune*: 7; "Pleading for Right," 18 September 1890, *Atlanta Constitution*: 9; "Cheadle, Joseph Bonaparte," *Biographical Directory of the United States Congress, 1774–Present*, available at http://bioguide.congress.gov/scripts/biodisplay.pl?index=C000339. Though Langston recalled that two other Republicans remained in the chamber to maintained the

quorum, but refused to vote, 14 members (four Republicans) were officially recorded as present and not voting. See Langston, *From the Virginia Plantation to the National Capitol*: 499; a full account of Langston's seating can be found in the *Congressional Record*, House, 51st Cong., 1st sess. (23 September 1890): 10338–10339.

30 Langston, *From the Virginia Plantation to the National Capitol*: 500–501; Thomas Miller of South Carolina was seated one day after Langston. Langston recalled being offered a seat next to Henry Cheatham of North Carolina, the only other black Member in the House.

31 "Pleading for His Race," 1 March 1888, *Atlanta Constitution*: 1.

32 "The Influence of Mahone," 10 October 1890, *New York Times*: 5.

33 "Mahone May Oppose Langston," 27 September 1890, *New York Times*: 5; "Mahone and Langston," 31 October 1890, *Washington Post*: 1.

34 "Langston's Next Fight," 15 November 1890, *Washington Post*: 2.

35 "Langston Is Confident," 8 October 1890, *Washington Post*: 1.

36 "Negroes His Only Support," 30 October 1890, *Washington Post*: 1; "The Issues in Virginia," 29 October 1890, *New York Times*: 5.

37 Dubin et al., *U.S. Congressional Elections, 1788–1997*: 292; "Solid in Virginia: The Apathy of the Negroes a Feature in the Contest," 6 November 1890, *New York Times*: 2.

38 See Office of the Clerk, "Political Divisions of the House of Representatives (1789 to Present)," available at http://clerk.house.gov/art_history/house_history/partyDiv.html.

39 "Langston's Next Fight."

40 "Langston Will Not Contest," 10 March 1891, *Washington Post*: 5.

41 Christopher, *Black Americans in Congress*: 147.

42 *Congressional Record*, House, 51st Cong., 2nd sess. (17 January 1891): 1524.

43 In 1885, President George Washington's birth date (February 22) became a federal holiday. Since the 1971 passage of the Uniform Monday Holidays Act, Washington's Birthday has been celebrated on the third Monday in February and is known as "President's Day" in recognition of all Presidents.

44 Langston, *From the Virginia Plantation to the National Capitol*: 517.

45 *Congressional Record*, House, 51st Cong., 2nd sess. (27 February 1891): 3490–3493.

46 See, for example, "Langston Upholds His Race," 8 January 1894, *Washington Post*: 5; "Emancipation at Alexandria," 23 September 1895, *Washington Post*: 7.

Langston emphasized blacks'
U.S. citizenship, condemning
calls for foreign emigration
and what he deemed the
Democratic Party's attempt
to thwart black freedom.
"Abuse us as you will,
gentlemen," Langston told
Democrats. "...There is no
way to get rid of us. This is
our native country."

Thomas Ezekiel Miller
1849–1938

UNITED STATES REPRESENTATIVE ★ 1890–1891
REPUBLICAN FROM SOUTH CAROLINA

A seasoned local and state politician, Thomas Miller brought his extensive experience fighting for freedmen's rights in post–Civil War South Carolina to his abbreviated term in the 51st Congress (1889–1891). With little time to legislate, Miller asserted himself as a staunch supporter of the Federal Elections Bill, chiding congressional colleagues about the deterioration of civil rights in the South. "I shall not be muffled here," Miller declared on the House Floor. "I am in part the representative . . . of those whose rights are denied; of those who are slandered by the press . . . and I deem it my supreme duty to raise my voice, though feebly, in their defense."[1] Though Miller was proud of his African-American heritage, his fair complexion often left him straddling the black and white communities and was used by opponents to cut short his tenure in the House of Representatives.

Thomas Ezekiel Miller was born on June 17, 1849, in Ferrebeeville, South Carolina. He was raised by Richard and Mary Ferrebee Miller, both former slaves, but his fair skin color caused much speculation about his biological origins.[2] Ferrebeeville was named after his mother's likely master, whose last name she inherited. The Millers, who were freed sometime around 1850, adopted him. Later in life, Miller's apparent mixed-race heritage availed him political opportunities, but also forced him to navigate a complicated racial middle ground in the postwar South. Thomas Miller struggled his entire life to find acceptance in the black and white communities. African-American political rivals dismissed him as a white imposter attempting to take advantage of the post–Civil War black electorate. Yet, Miller, who embraced the black heritage nurtured by his adoptive parents, was also ostracized by white colleagues.[3]

In 1851, the Millers moved to Charleston, where

Thomas attended illegal schools for free black children and sold *Mercury* newspapers at hotels. During the Civil War, Miller delivered newspapers on a Charleston railroad line running to Savannah, Georgia. He was conscripted into the military when the Confederate Army seized the railroads. Captured by Union forces in January 1865, he spent two weeks in prison before his release. When the Civil War ended, Miller went to Hudson, New York, where once again he sold newspapers on a railroad line. He finished his education at the Hudson School, just north of New York City, before earning a scholarship to Lincoln University, a school for African-American students, in Chester County, Pennsylvania. After graduating in 1872, Miller returned to South Carolina, where he won his first elective office as school commissioner of coastal Beaufort County. He subsequently moved to Columbia and studied law at the newly integrated University of South Carolina. He continued his studies under the tutelage of state solicitor P. L. Wiggins and state supreme court justice Franklin L. Moses, Sr., a future governor of South Carolina. Admitted to the bar in December 1875, Miller set up his practice in Beaufort, South Carolina. In 1874, he married Anna Hume, with whom he had nine children.[4]

Shortly after moving to Beaufort, Thomas Miller was elected to the state general assembly, where he served until 1880 before securing a term in the state senate. Miller was deeply involved in attempts to revive the flagging South Carolina Republican Party after Reconstruction ended in 1877. He was a member of the Republican state executive committee from 1878 to 1880 and the state party chairman in 1884. The party nominated him for lieutenant governor in 1880, but Democratic threats of violence frightened Republicans from officially putting forward a statewide ticket.[5] Miller also was a customs

inspector and served on the state militia throughout the 1880s before returning to the state house of representatives in 1886 for one year.

In 1888, Miller entered the race for a seat in the U.S. House of Representatives that was formerly occupied by black Representative and Civil War hero Robert Smalls. The "shoestring district" was thus named because its narrow borders twisted from Sumter County in the center of the state to Georgetown and parts of Charleston on the coast.[6] Covering the black belt of South Carolina, including the center of the state's pre–Civil War rice and cotton plantations, the gerrymandered district boasted a population that was 82 percent black. Miller greatly admired Robert Smalls, calling him "the greatest politician of any one of us."[7] District Republicans expected Smalls to run in 1888 to avenge his loss to Democrat William Elliott in 1886, an election Smalls unsuccessfully contested. But Miller supporters convinced Smalls to defer.[8] Facing the incumbent, Miller received financial backing from Randall D. George, one of the wealthiest black men in the state, who made his money distributing rosins and turpentine in the region.[9] Representative Elliott was initially declared the winner by slightly more than 1,000 votes in a light turnout, with 54 percent to Miller's 45 percent.[10]

Miller contested the election, charging that many registered black voters were prohibited from casting their ballots. He vehemently opposed the "eight box ballot law," a state statute that required multiple ballot boxes at each polling station to confuse black voters.[11] Though the Republican-dominated Committee on Elections in the 51st Congress ruled in Miller's favor, his case did not come up on the House Floor until September 23, 1890, immediately after a vote seating Virginia's first black Representative, John Langston. Inspired by their success seating Langston (complicated by Democrats, who deserted the House Chamber in an effort to prevent a quorum), House Republicans decided to take up Miller's claim. Representative Charles O'Ferrall of Virginia, who was charged with looking after the Democratic Party's interests during the Langston vote, protested that the case

was unexpected and reiterated previous complaints that a quorum was not present. Daniel Kerr of Iowa asked for 20 minutes to debate the nomination, but Republican Speaker Thomas Brackett Reed of Maine stonewalled all protest and accused the Democrats of conspiring to delay Miller's consideration. Shouts from the packed Republican side of the floor reinforced the Speaker. Members were recorded crying, "Vote! Vote!"[12] A vote was taken over O'Ferrall's vehement protests. The House seated Miller by a vote of 157 to 1. He was sworn in the following day and given a position on the Committee on Labor.[13]

After only a week, Miller returned to South Carolina to run for re-election to the 52nd Congress (1891–1893). In November 1890, in a campaign once again funded by Randall George, Miller won an apparent victory in a three-way contest that included white Republican candidate Ellery M. Brayton and former Representative Elliott, the recently unseated Democrat. Elliott insisted the vote count was fraudulent and contested the results.[14] On November 9, the South Carolina supreme court ruled that Elliott was the winner because Miller's ballots were illegal: They had a "distinctly yellow tinge" and said "for Representative" instead of "Representative."[15]

Miller contested the court's decision before the House of Representatives, which would have the final say in the case, and returned to the final session of the 51st Congress with the election still unresolved. He had no time to submit substantive legislation and spoke only twice during the three-month session. On January 12, 1891, Miller spoke in favor of Massachusetts Representative Henry Cabot Lodge's bill authorizing the federal government to oversee federal elections and protect voters from violence and intimidation, ignoring threats that his support of the bill would endanger his ability to win the pending election. Miller urged the Senate to follow the House's example in passing the Lodge proposal, emphasizing southern blacks' desire for basic equality rather than simple political patronage: for fair pay, property, and safety. "Ah, gentlemen," he lamented, "what we need in this land is not so many [political] offices. Offices are only emblems of what we need and what we ought to have. We need protection at home in our rights, the chiefest of which is the right to live."[16] On February 14, 1891, Miller rebutted controversial allegations leveled by Senator Alfred H. Colquitt of Georgia. In his address, Colquitt blamed southern freedmen for slowing regional economic development. Miller replied that white southerners encouraged economic stagnation by exploiting black farmers and denying blacks full citizenship.[17]

When the House convened for the 52nd Congress on December 7, 1891, Miller, now a private citizen, pleaded with his former colleagues to overturn the state supreme court decision and declare him the winner of the 1890 contest against Elliott. However, the makeup of the new Congress was drastically different: Democrats now outnumbered Republicans nearly two to one.[18] Their firm majority meant the Committee on Elections could stall consideration of Miller's contest. The panel did not take up the case until one month before the end of the Congress—February 1893—giving the seat to Elliott. Shortly before the committee reached its decision, future black Representative George Murray defeated Miller for the Republican nomination for the 53rd Congress (1893–1895). Miller's light skin became a decisive campaign issue, as Murray, who was dark-skinned, lambasted him for being only "one sixty-fourth black."[19]

Miller returned to the state assembly for a single term in 1894. For the next 40 years, he remained active in politics, making a steady living as an attorney for local Beaufort merchant D. H. Wall. He also was one of several prominent South Carolina black politicians who served as delegates to the 1895 state constitutional convention. Despite their best efforts, however, the convention disfranchised many South Carolina blacks by passing laws requiring voters to take a literacy test or to prove they owned more than $300 in property. When Chaflin College in Orangeburg—a black school originally staffed by northern whites that opened in 1869—lost its federal funding, Miller helped establish the State Negro College (now South Carolina State University).[20] The college hired only black teachers. Miller later successfully lobbied the state to hire only black teachers in black public schools. In March 1896, he became president of the State Negro College, but was forced to resign in 1911 when Governor Coleman L. Blease, whom Miller had opposed during his gubernatorial campaign, took office. Miller later retired to Charleston, where he remained active in civic affairs. He supported American entry into World War I, helping to recruit more than 30,000 black soldiers. He served on a black subcommittee of the all-white state committee on civic preparedness during the war. In 1923 he moved to Philadelphia, but returned to Charleston in 1934. The last of the nineteenth-century generation of African-American Representatives, Miller died on April 8, 1938.

FOR FURTHER READING

"Miller, Thomas Ezekiel," *Biographical Directory of the United States Congress, 1774–Present,* http://bioguide. congress.gov/scripts/biodisplay.pl?index=M000757.

Tindall, George Brown. *South Carolina Negroes, 1877–1900,* 2nd ed. (Columbia: University of South Carolina Press, 2003; reprint of the 1952 edition).

NOTES

1   *Congressional Record,* House, 51st Cong., 2nd sess. (14 February 1891): 2695.

2   Miller's origins remain unclear. In some sources, his biological parents were rumored to be an unwed white couple. Other historians claim Miller was the son of the light-skinned mulatto daughter of Judge Thomas Heyward, Jr., a signer of the Declaration of Independence, and a wealthy white father. The father's family disapproved of the couple's relationship and forced their son to give up the child for adoption. William C. Hine, "Miller, Thomas Ezekiel," *American National Biography* 15 (New York: Oxford University Press, 1999): 518–520 (hereinafter referred to as *ANB*). See also Maurine Christopher, *Black Americans in Congress* (New York: Thomas Y. Crowell Company, 1976): 113; Stephen Middleton, ed., *Black Congressmen During Reconstruction: A Documentary Sourcebook* (Westport, CT: Praeger, 2002): 227–228; Thomas Holt, "Miller, Thomas Ezekiel," *Dictionary of American Negro Biography* (New York: Norton, 1982): 439–440 (hereinafter referred to as *DANB*); Eric Foner, *Freedom's Lawmakers: A Directory of Black Officeholders During Reconstruction,* revised edition (New York: Oxford University Press, 1996): 149. Middleton and Foner provide the most thorough accounts of Miller's parentage.

3   George Brown Tindall, *South Carolina Negroes, 1877–1900,* 2nd ed. (Columbia: University of South Carolina Press, 2003; reprint of the 1952 edition): 48–49.

4   Hine, "Miller, Thomas Ezekiel," *ANB.* The names of Miller's children are not known.

5   Christopher, *Black Americans in Congress*: 114; Holt, "Miller, Thomas Ezekiel," *DANB.*

6   Stanley B. Parsons et al., *United States Congressional Districts, 1883–1913* (New York: Greenwood Press, 1990): 143.

7   Quoted in Christopher, *Black Americans in Congress*: 113.

8   Ibid., 114.

9   Tindall, *South Carolina Negroes*: 128.

10   Michael J. Dubin et al., *U.S. Congressional Elections, 1788–1997* (Jefferson, NC: McFarland & Company, Inc., Publishers, 1998): 284.

11   Christopher, *Black Americans in Congress*: 114; Middleton, *Black Congressmen During Reconstruction*: 228.

12   For a full account of Miller's case, see *Congressional Record,* House, 51st Cong., 1st sess. (23 September 1890): 10339.

13   Several newspaper articles indicate Miller was in South Carolina campaigning for the 1890 election when the House voted to seat him; however, it is unlikely that he was in South Carolina on September 23 and seated in Washington, DC, a day later. See, for example, "Republicans Steal," 24 September 1890, *Atlanta Constitution*: 1; "Langston Gets His Seat," 24 September 1890, *Chicago Daily Tribune*: 7.

14   Christopher, *Black Americans in Congress*: 114; Hine, "Miller, Thomas Ezekiel," *ANB*; Holt, "Miller, Thomas Ezekiel," *DANB*; Middleton, *Black Congressmen During Reconstruction*: 229. However, Michael Dubin indicates that Elliott won by more than 400 votes—45 to 39 percent in a small turnout. Brayton won 16 percent of the vote. See Dubin et al., *U.S. Congressional Elections, 1788–1997*: 292.

15   Quoted in Hine, "Miller, Thomas Ezekiel," *ANB*; "Elliott Re-Elected to Congress," 10 November 1890, *New York Times*: 1; see also "Will They Heed the Lesson?" 17 November 1890, *Washington Post*: 4.

16   *Congressional Record,* House, 51st Cong., 2nd sess. (12 January 1891): 1216.

17   *Congressional Record,* House, 51st Cong., 2nd sess. (14 February 1891): 2694.

18   See Office of the Clerk, "Political Divisions of the House of Representatives (1789 to Present)," available at http://clerk.house.gov/art_history/house_history/partyDiv.html.

19   Quoted in Foner, *Freedom's Lawmakers*, 150; Tindall, *South Carolina Negroes*: 49.

20   According to William C. Hine, the institution was originally named the Colored Normal, Industrial, Agricultural, and Mechanical College of South Carolina. See Hine, "Miller, Thomas Ezekiel," *ANB.*

Miller emphasized southern blacks' desire for basic equality rather than simple political patronage: "Ah, gentlemen," he lamented, "what we need in this land is not so many [political] offices. . . . We need protection at home in our rights, the chiefest of which is the right to live."

George Washington Murray
1853–1926

UNITED STATES REPRESENTATIVE ★ 1893–1895; 1896–1897
REPUBLICAN FROM SOUTH CAROLINA

A former slave, Representative George Murray was the only black Member in the 53rd and 54th Congresses (1893–1897). Murray was highly regarded by his peers because of his position. An 1893 newspaper called him "the most intellectual negro in the [Sumter] county."[1] However, Murray's detractors doubted his eloquence, accusing him of hiring a ghostwriter for his floor speeches. Employing his formidable oratorical skills, Murray fought the disfranchisement laws that beset the South in the early 1890s. He was a political pragmatist who worked for his constituents while placating the hostile political base necessary for his election campaigns.[2] Unable to defeat the overwhelming tide of white supremacy, either nationally or at home, Murray left the House, marking the end of black representation in South Carolina for nearly 100 years.[3]

George Washington Murray was born on September 22, 1853, near Rembert, in Sumter County, South Carolina. His parents, whose names are not known, were slaves and died before the end of the Civil War; however, Murray had at least two brothers, Prince and Frank. Murray never received a formal primary education, but in 1874 he entered the University of South Carolina in Columbia after it was opened to black students by the Republican state government.[4] After federal withdrawal from the South following the end of Reconstruction in 1877, Murray and the other black students were forced out of the university. He eventually graduated from the nearby State Normal Institution. Murray married Ella Reynolds in 1877, and they had two children, Edward and Pearl. Murray also had an illegitimate son, William, who was born sometime in the 1890s.[5]

Working as a farmer, a teacher, and a lecturer in Sumter County, Murray obtained eight patents for various farming tools.[6] His farming success garnered him local recognition, and his selection as the Sumter County delegate to the 1880 Republican Party state convention sparked his interest in politics. Murray's support of Republican President Benjamin Harrison during the 1888 campaign won him a patronage appointment as customs inspector at the port of Charleston in February 1890. That same year he sought the nomination for the South Carolina "shoestring district," which included sections of Charleston and Georgetown on the coast and twisted narrowly to the northeast to include central portions of the state.[7] Two black Representatives had been elected in the district: Civil War hero Robert Smalls and incumbent Thomas Miller. Miller defeated Murray for the Republican nomination but eventually lost the seat to Democrat William Elliott.

In 1892, Murray ran again for the congressional seat. Conducting a campaign that emphasized his African roots (his opponent, Thomas Miller, was light-skinned), Murray defeated Miller and white candidate E. W. Brayton to capture the Republican nomination.[8] Though the "shoestring district" had been modified slightly by reapportionment, nearly 75 percent of the population was black.[9] During the general election, especially in areas outside Charleston, precinct workers rejected votes for Murray for insignificant reasons, for example, the candidate's ballots were one-eighth or three-sixteenths of an inch too short, the ballot boxes were not opened at the appointed time, or the precinct managers failed to record the name of the precinct before sending the election returns to Columbia.[10] However, Murray's chances were strengthened by divisions within the district's Democratic Party. Governor Benjamin Tillman, who led a statewide white supremacy political machine, found himself at odds with the district's Democratic candidate, E. M. Moise. Moise disagreed with the governor in rejecting Populist economic issues such as the coinage of silver, which emerged as a national issue during the 1892 election. The

IMAGE, D.W. CULP, ED. *TWENTIETH CENTURY NEGRO LITERATURE*
(NAPERVILLE, IL: J.L. NICHOLS & CO., 1902)

primarily agricultural residents of the "shoestring district," who had been hit hard by economic depression, supported free silver coinage as a form of debt relief. The complicated political atmosphere made for a close election. Though Moise was originally declared the winner, canvassers for the state board of election (Democratic supporters of Governor Tillman) exacted revenge on their party's maverick by confirming that Murray was victorious by 40 votes.[11] He received an assignment to the Committee on Education, but most of Murray's work in Congress was outside the jurisdiction of this committee.

Murray's position as the only black Member during his two terms in Congress defined his career. One of the first things he did after arriving in Washington was to visit newly inaugurated Democratic President Grover Cleveland. In a personal meeting with the President, Murray told Cleveland that southern blacks were concerned about their welfare under a Democratic President but that the new administration had a fresh opportunity to welcome African Americans into the Democratic Party. Murray asked Cleveland to consider appointing more blacks to political offices through patronage, but neither the President nor his congressional allies prioritized building political capital among black Americans.[12]

When a financial panic gripped the country in early 1893, President Cleveland blamed much of the economic instability on the 1890 Sherman Silver Purchase Act. He sought to repeal the law, which required the federal government to trade 4.5 million ounces of silver bullion each month in exchange for legal tender. Cleveland called a special session of Congress to deal with the crisis. During this session, Murray and other supporters joined the 12 Populists and Silverites in defending the Silver Purchase Act. Speaking on the House Floor on August 24, 1893, Murray argued that most of his constituents earned little and were disadvantaged by the diminishing supply of gold. Believing continued silver coinage would help to stabilize the economy in his district, Murray noted that his constituents traced their overwhelming poverty to "the circulating medium [gold], which like a viper with its

victim in its coils, has been drawing its cords tighter and tighter around their prosperity, until it is dead. I am of the opinion that the only sure and permanent remedy is a lengthening of the cords, an enlargement of the volume of money."[13] Although Murray spoke at 10 p.m.—the last time slot of the legislative day—a large crowd gathered in the gallery to hear his maiden speech.[14] Proponents of silver coinage were unable to secure the necessary votes and, despite an 80-day filibuster by Senate Silverites, President Cleveland secured the congressional repeal of the Sherman Silver Purchase Act on November 1, 1893.

In 1893, when Representative Henry Tucker of Virginia authored a bill to remove impartial election supervisors and federal marshals from southern polling places, Murray fearlessly sought to block the legislation.[15] On several occasions, he interrupted Tucker's allies on the House Floor, citing personal experiences of discrimination.[16] On October 2, 1893, Murray interrupted freshman Representative (and future Speaker) Beauchamp (Champ) Clark of Missouri, who was insisting that state officials adequately monitored polling places. Murray noted that these officials were often prejudiced appointees of white supremacist Democratic state governments. He also refuted Clark's claim that federal Republican officials coerced black voters into voting as one bloc. Three days later, Murray made a long speech against Representative Tucker's legislation. He ended by repeating his plea to President Cleveland: "While I can not persuade myself that there can be found here and in the Senate enough cruel and wicked men to make this law effective, still if I am disappointed in that . . . I hope that the broad-souled and philanthropic man occupying the Executive chair is too brave and humane to join in this cowardly onslaught to strike down the walls impaling the last vestige of liberty to a helpless class of people."[17] A long thunderous bout of applause from the Republican side of the chamber followed Murray's speech, which earned him the epithet the "Black Eagle of Sumter."[18] Though Murray was absent on October 10 when the Tucker legislation came to a vote, he called upon black voters to study the roll call vote and defeat any Member who voted in its favor in the next election.[19] The bill passed both chambers and was signed into law by President Cleveland in February 1894.[20]

In 1894, Murray faced an uphill battle for re-election to the 54th Congress. The South Carolina legislature dissolved the "shoestring district," cutting off much of Charleston and Murray's black voting base.[21] Democratic infighting ceased when former Representative William Elliott won the Democratic nomination. Elliott emerged with 60 percent of the vote in the general election, but several precincts reported instances of fraud.[22] Murray appealed to the state board of election canvassers, but they rejected his claim.

As a result, Murray spent the third session of the 53rd Congress (1893–1895) preparing to contest Elliott's election before the House. He submitted a massive amount of testimony indicating election fraud; the paperwork was reported to be nearly a foot thick.[23] Murray's evidence revealed that ballot boxes in three of four heavily Republican counties in his new district were never opened, that black voters were issued fraudulent registration certificates or paperwork was withheld entirely, and that precincts in black regions failed to open. Witnesses also reported that William Elliott himself stood in front of ballot boxes taunting black men and preventing them from submitting their votes. The worst fraud occurred in the small portion of southern Charleston that remained in Murray's district. A precinct compromising 2,000 more registered black voters than white declared 2,811 votes for Elliott and 397 for Murray.[24] After reviewing the testimony, the House Committee on Elections—composed of a strong Republican majority—concluded that the final victory belonged to Murray by 434 votes. The whole House first took up the case late in the first session of the 54th Congress on June 3, 1896. Democrats spent several hours trying to prove that South Carolina registration laws had been explained to black voters and that Murray was not favored by all African-American voters and thus could not claim the district's majority based on his race.[25] The next

day, the House voted to seat Murray, 153 to 33. With only seven days remaining in the first session, Murray was again assigned to the Committee on Education and was also appointed to the Committee on Expenditures in the Treasury Department.

Political trouble at home prevented Murray from attending the final two sessions of the 54th Congress. In 1895, Tillman Democrats in the state legislature passed a referendum to revise the 1868 state constitution. Murray tried to organize black voters to elect sympathetic delegates to the constitutional convention, but only six black delegates were sent, including former Representatives Robert Smalls and Thomas Miller. The results were disastrous for black South Carolina voters. The primarily white, Democratic convention created new requirements for proving residency, instituted poll taxes, established property requirements, and created literacy tests—all aimed at disfranchising black voters.[26] Murray and fellow Republicans asked Governor Tillman to call a special session of the state legislature in March 1896. The governor ignored the appeal. In July 1896, Murray and others authored the address "To the People of the United States," requesting national support for federal intervention in the South Carolina elections. Murray spent most of 1896 raising money to pay legal fees for challenges to the new registration laws in federal courts, vowing that fighting "lawfully, not unlawfully . . . we shall create such conditions that the United States is bound to take a hand."[27] Murray's optimistic prediction fell short. Legal action brought a poll tax case before the Supreme Court in 1895 in *Mills v. Green*, but the court ruled that the tax did not violate the 14th Amendment. The same ruling on a similar case brought before the high court—*Williams v. Mississippi* in 1898—nearly halted the legal battle against disfranchisement laws and virtually sealed off national elected office for African Americans in the South.[28] Indeed, the new provisions for voting registration dimmed Murray's chances for re-election in 1896; Elliott easily defeated him, with 67 percent of the vote.[29]

Returning to Congress as a lame duck in February 1897, Murray announced he would object to South Carolina's nine electoral votes in the presidential election—which went to Democratic candidate William Jennings Bryan—if Congress did not investigate the state's new election laws. He submitted a petition signed by hundreds of South Carolina Republicans, alleging that more than 100,000 eligible black men had been refused the vote in the 1896 election. Influential Republicans attempted to dissuade Murray, fearful that disrupting the electoral vote count would impede Republican William McKinley's apparent victory. Murray dropped his objection but not his call for a federal investigation. He submitted a resolution requesting an investigation. However, Congress adjourned in March, ignoring his request.[30]

After leaving Congress, Murray returned to his South Carolina farm. He invested in more land, which he sold to black tenant farmers. In 1905, Murray was convicted in a circuit court for forgery related to a contract dispute between two of his tenants.[31] Murray fled to Chicago to avoid the sentence of three years' hard labor, insisting he had received an unfair sentence because of his race.[32] Ella Murray was unwilling to leave South Carolina, and the two divorced. Murray married Cornelia Martin in 1908 and gained a stepdaughter, Gaynell. The Murrays adopted a 10-year-old boy, Donald, in the 1920s and parented numerous foster children.[33]

Murray became active in the Republican Party in Chicago. His distrust of local Democrats eventually led him to request that the House investigate the powerful Cook County Democratic political machine. He also tried a number of unsuccessful business ventures.[34] Late in his life, Murray lectured across the country. He compiled many of his speeches into two books on race relations: *Race Ideals: Effects, Cause and Remedy for Afro-American Race Troubles* (1914) and *Light in Dark Places* (1925).[35] Both books posited that discrimination would persist until Americans appreciated the worth and dignity of African Americans. Following Murray's death on April 21, 1926, his longtime Chicago neighbor, former Mississippi Representative John Roy Lynch delivered his eulogy.

FOR FURTHER READING

Gaboury, William J. "George Washington Murray and the Fight for Political Democracy in South Carolina," *Journal of Negro History* 62 (July 1977): 258–269.

Marszalek, John F. *A Black Congressman in the Age of Jim Crow: South Carolina's George Washington Murray* (Gainesville: University of Florida Press, 2006).

"Murray, George Washington," *Biographical Directory of the United States Congress, 1774–Present*, http://bioguide. congress.gov/scripts/biodisplay.pl?index=M001106.

Murray, George Washington. *Light in Dark Places* (Chicago: Light in Dark Places Pub. Co., 1925).

_____. *Race Ideals: Effects, Cause and Remedy for Afro-American Race Troubles* (Princeton, IN: Smith & Sons Publishing, 1914).

MANUSCRIPT COLLECTIONS

University of Illinois Press (Champaign, IL) *Papers:* In the Booker T. Washington Papers, 1889–1895, one volume. Correspondents include George Washington Murray. For more information, visit http://www.historycooperative.org/btw/Vol.3/html/451.html.

University of South Carolina (Columbia, SC) South Caroliniana Library. *Papers:* In the J. Mitchell Reames Papers, 1907–1990, 12.5 linear feet. Correspondents include George Washington Murray.

NOTES

1   Quoted from the Baltimore-based newspaper *Afro-American* (20 April 1893) in William J. Gaboury, "George Washington Murray and the Fight for Political Democracy in South Carolina," *Journal of Negro History* 62 (July 1977): 259; John F. Marszalek, *A Black Congressman in the Age of Jim Crow: South Carolina's George Washington Murray* (Gainesville: University Press of Florida, 2006): 67.

2   Maurine Christopher, *Black Americans in Congress* (New York: Thomas Y. Crowell Company, 1976): 118–119.

3   Representative James Clyburn, who took his seat in the 103rd Congress in 1993, was the next African-American Representative from South Carolina. Clyburn is related to Murray; see "Clyburn, James Enos," *Biographical Directory of the United States Congress, 1774–Present*, available at http://bioguide.congress.gov/scripts/biodisplay.pl?index=C000537.

4   Previous editions of *Black Americans in Congress* indicate Murray attended public schools, but most other sources indicate he was self-taught prior to entering college. See Bruce A. Ragsdale and Joel D. Treese, *Black Americans in Congress, 1870–1989* (Washington, DC: Government Printing Office, 1990): 97; Stephen Middleton, ed., *Black Congressmen During Reconstruction: A Documentary Sourcebook* (Westport, CT: Praeger, 2002): 245.

5   Marszalek, *A Black Congressman in the Age of Jim Crow*: 9, 157–158.

6   Middleton, *Black Congressmen During Reconstruction*: 245.

7   Stanley B. Parsons et al., *United States Congressional Districts, 1883–1913* (New York: Greenwood Press, 1990): 143.

8   The *New York Times* once reported that "judging by [Murray's] face, there is not a drop of white blood running in his veins." See, "The Debate in the House," 25 August 1893, *New York Times*: 8.

9   Parsons et al., *United States Congressional Districts, 1883–1913*: 278–279; Marszalek, *A Black Congressman in the Age of Jim Crow*: 37.

10 Gaboury, "George Washington Murray and the Fight for Political Democracy in South Carolina": 260.

11 Thomas Holt, "Murray, George Washington," *Dictionary of American Negro Biography* (New York: Norton, 1982): 465; Marszalek, *A Black Congressman in the Age of Jim Crow*: 47–50.

12 Marszalek, *A Black Congressman in the Age of Jim Crow*: 51. For anecdotal information about Murray's life as the only black Representative in the 53rd Congress, see pages 52–53, 63–65.

13 *Congressional Record*, House, 53rd Cong., 1st sess. (24 August 1893): 858.

14 Gaboury, "George Washington Murray and the Fight for Political Democracy in South Carolina," 260–261; Marszalek, *A Black Congressman in the Age of Jim Crow*: 57–58.

15 For more information on Tucker's bill, see *Congressional Record*, House, 53rd Cong., 1st sess. (10 October 1893): 107.

16 Marszalek, *A Black Congressman in the Age of Jim Crow*: 60–63.

17 *Congressional Record*, House, 53rd Cong., 1st sess. (5 October 1893): 2161.

18 Gaboury, "George Washington Murray and the Fight for Political Democracy in South Carolina": 259.

19 Murray frequently sought leaves of absence in both terms of Congress, often citing personal illness or sick family members; see *Congressional Record*, Index, 53rd Cong.; *Congressional Record*, Index, 54th Cong.

20 Christopher, *Black Americans in Congress*: 120. Christopher notes that the legislation passed both Houses. However, Representative Tucker's original bill, H.R. 2331, passed the House but was tabled in the Senate (see *Congressional Record*, Index, 53rd Cong., 1st sess.). A substitute bill passed the Senate.

21 Parsons et al., *United States Congressional Districts, 1883–1913*: 278–279; Marszalek, *A Black Congressman in the Age of Jim Crow*: 68, 75–81.

22 Michael J. Dubin et al., *U.S. Congressional Elections, 1788–1997* (Jefferson, NC: McFarland & Company, Inc., Publishers, 1998): 310.

23 Gaboury, "George Washington Murray and the Fight for Political Democracy in South Carolina": 266; Christopher, *Black Americans in Congress*: 121; Marszalek, *A Black Congressman in the Age of Jim Crow*: 79.

24 Christopher, *Black Americans in Congress*: 121.

25 *Congressional Record*, House, 54th Cong., 1st sess. (3 June 1896): 6072–6077, A445–452; Marszalek, *A Black Congressman in the Age of Jim Crow*: 101. Marszalek asserts the debate took place on June 5.

26 For details on the 1895 South Carolina constitutional convention, see J. Morgan Kousser, *The Shaping of Southern Politics: Suffrage Restriction and Establishment of the One-Party South, 1880–1910* (New Haven: Yale University Press, 1974): 145–152.

27 Quoted in Stephen Kantrowitz, *Ben Tillman and the Reconstruction of White Supremacy* (Chapel Hill: University of North Carolina Press, 2000): 208.

28 Gaboury, "George Washington Murray and the Fight for Political Democracy in South Carolina": 263–267.

29 Dubin et al., *U.S. Congressional Elections, 1788–1997*: 327.

30 Gaboury, "George Washington Murray and the Fight for Political Democracy in South Carolina": 266; Marszalek, *A Black Congressman in the Age of Jim Crow*: 107–108.

31 Marszalek, *A Black Congressman in the Age of Jim Crow*: 132–136, provides a detailed description of the trial.

32 Ibid., 142–143. Marszalek argues that the Murray trial exemplified the practice of "legal whitecapping, a way to rid the community of a troublesome black."

33 Ibid., 145–146, 157–158.

34 Christopher, *Black Americans in Congress*: 122; Marszalek, *A Black Congressman in the Age of Jim Crow*: 144–145.

35 Marszalek, *A Black Congressman in the Age of Jim Crow*: 146–151.

Believing continued silver coinage would help to stabilize the economy in his district, Murray noted that his constituents traced their overwhelming poverty to "the circulating medium [GOLD], which like a viper with its victim in its coils, has been drawing its cords tighter and tighter around their prosperity, until it is dead."

George Henry White
1852–1918

UNITED STATES REPRESENTATIVE ★ 1897–1901
REPUBLICAN FROM NORTH CAROLINA

George H. White's bold legislative proposals combating disfranchisement and mob violence in the South distinguished him from his more reserved contemporaries. The lone African-American Representative at the dawn of the 20th century, White spoke candidly on the House Floor, confronting Booker T. Washington's call to work within the segregated system. The onslaught of white supremacy in his home state assured White that to campaign for a third term would be fruitless, and he departed the chamber on March 3, 1901. It would be 28 years before another black Representative set foot in the Capitol. "This, Mr. Chairman, is perhaps the negroes' temporary farewell to the American Congress," White declared in his final months as a Representative, "but let me say, Phoenix-like he will rise up someday and come again."[1]

George Henry White was born in Rosindale, North Carolina, on December 18, 1852. His father, Wiley F. White, was a free, working-class farmer. His mother, Mary, was a slave.[2] White boasted Native-American and Irish ancestry as well as his African heritage and was notably light-skinned.[3] George White had one sister, Flora. At the end of the Civil War, the young teenager helped out on the family farm and assisted in the family's funeral home business while intermittently attending public schools in Columbus County, North Carolina. In 1873, he entered Howard University in Washington, DC, graduating in 1877.[4] White joined the North Carolina bar in 1879, and served as the principal at several black public schools. He married Fannie B. Randolph in 1879 and, six years after her death in 1880, he married Cora Lena Cherry. White had four children: a daughter, Della, with his first wife, and two daughters and a son—Mary Adelyne, Beatrice Odessa, and George Henry White, Jr.—with his second wife.[5]

White's political career began with his election to the North Carolina house of representatives in 1880. That same year, he served as a delegate to the Republican National Convention. White initially focused on legislation pertaining to education, securing funding and authorization to open four black normal schools and provide training for black teachers. After establishing a second residence in Tarboro, North Carolina, he was elected solicitor and prosecuting attorney in 1886 in the "Black Second" district, a boot-shaped entity with a large black majority, winding from the Virginia border to the southern coast.[6] White considered seeking national office at this point but decided to garner recognition among district voters through a favorable record as a solicitor.

In 1888 and 1890, White reluctantly deferred candidacy for the district's congressional seat to his brother-in-law Representative Henry Cheatham, whose calculated, conciliatory demeanor contrasted with White's forthright, demanding, and unyielding personality.[7] Cheatham lost his 1892 re-election campaign, and though the two men had an uneasy relationship, they were not outright political enemies until White made a serious bid for the "Black Second" congressional seat in 1894.[8] Cheatham planned to capitalize on the redistricting that added a large number of black voters in north-central Vance and Craven counties to the existing district. Amicability between the brothers-in-law disintegrated until 1898, when Cheatham relented, supporting White for a second term.[9]

In addition to the fractious family rivalry, the Populist Party—a national third party made up primarily of disenchanted and economically depressed farmers—continued to challenge Republican political hegemony in the "Black Second." The volatile political situation divided delegates at the hotly contested 1894 Republican district convention. After 13 ballots, both White and Cheatham emerged claiming the nomination.[10] After both candidates

canvassed the district for several months, the two men brought their still-undecided case to Washington, DC, before the Republican National Committee (RNC).[11] After hearing each man's arguments, a seven-member RNC committee agreed to support Cheatham.[12] But Cheatham failed to capture the interest of the Populists; in a three-way general election, the former black Representative lost handily to incumbent Democratic Representative Frederick A. Woodard and a third Populist candidate who siphoned off a large fraction of the white Republican vote.

Cheatham's second consecutive loss sank his political career, leaving George White the district's favored African-American son. In 1896, White handily defeated Cheatham for the nomination. Possessing the full support of the Republican Party, White appealed to the Populists to avoid suffering Cheatham's fate in a three-way election. White distanced himself from the national Republican adherence to the gold standard, embracing the Populist platform calling for the free coinage of silver.[13] His chances for election improved greatly when Republican and Populist district leaders agreed on a "fusion" plan in the fall of 1896. White also benefited when a friendly 1894 state legislature reversed many of the Democratic election laws that impeded African-American voters—each of the three parties provided a judge and registrar at every polling place to ensure a fair election.[14] Turnout among black voters in North Carolina rose to record levels of more than 85 percent.[15] White defeated Representative Woodard with 52 percent of the vote. Woodard, who took 41 percent of the vote, was most hampered by rebel Populist candidate D. S. Moss, who siphoned off 7 percent of the vote.[16]

The only African American in the 55th Congress (1897–1899), George White was part of a large Republican majority that was swept into office on the coattails of presidential victor William McKinley.[17] He received a seat on the Agriculture Committee, an assignment that recognized the large number of farmers among his constituents.

The first order of business in the 55th Congress, the protectionist Dingley Tariff, allowed George White to support a major plank in the Republican platform. He voted in favor of the high tariff to protect eastern North Carolina's economically depressed timber industry. White missed the vote to go to war against Spain on April 19, 1898, while traveling from North Carolina. The following morning, he announced on the House Floor that he supported the invasion of Cuba, and he later declared his unqualified support for the colonial acquisition of Cuba and the Philippines.[18] White also missed the vote to annex the Hawaiian Islands, probably intentionally. Critical of the apparent mistreatment of the native Hawaiians, White remained loyal to Republican foreign-policy objectives out of a desire to avoid conflict with his colleagues who overwhelmingly supported annexation.[19] White later offered an amendment to legislation creating the Hawaiian territorial government, aimed at ensuring the voting rights of Hawaiian residents.[20] White once used the subject of U.S. imperialism to open a discussion about race issues in his native South.[21]

White's focus in Congress was not late-19th century foreign policy debates but defending the civil rights of his black constituents. For instance, White offered a resolution providing relief for the widow and surviving children of a black postmaster murdered in Lake City, South Carolina. The man and his infant daughter were killed by a white mob. Though the resolution was read aloud on the House Floor, White never spoke at length about the tragedy because Representative Charles Bartlett of Georgia objected to his request to elaborate.[22] White also sought to commission an all-black artillery unit in the U.S. Army. At the end of the session, White called on President McKinley to discuss honoring black soldiers fighting in the Spanish–American War. Finally, White unsuccessfully sought $15,000 in federal funding for an exhibit on black achievement at the 1900 Paris Exposition.

Returning home to campaign for re-election, George White was the primary target of white supremacist politicians, who feared a renewal of the Republican–Populist political fusion. The Raleigh *News and Observer* was particularly scathing, alleging White was the mastermind behind the "Negro domination" of local politics and businesses and citing as proof his refusal to give his seat to a white Republican.[23] White armed himself with endorsements. Republican colleague George Southwick of New York published a glowing endorsement in the African-American newspaper the *Colored American*.[24] District Republicans expressed solidarity with White by renominating him without opposition in May 1898.[25] Patronage became a pivotal issue in the election. White defended his frequent appointment of black men to patronage positions at the Republican state convention in July 1898, noting, "I am not the only negro who holds office. There are others. . . . The Democrats talk about the color line and the Negro holding office. I invite the issue."[26]

Though White received thunderous applause, those few sentences elicited vicious replies from North Carolina Democratic newspapers, declaring White had started an all-out race war. White's speech also inspired the White Government Union, led by former Representative Furnifold Simmons, to organize unity among white voters. Moreover, White's strong language at the convention infuriated white Populists, who broke from standing fusion agreements and nominated their own candidate, James B. Lloyd.[27] The final week of campaigning descended into chaos. After Lloyd refused to run on a platform of white supremacy, William Fountain added his name to the ballot as an Independent Populist. Fountain sought to swing the Populist Party against George White.[28] South Carolina Senator (and former governor) Ben Tillman and his famous Red Shirts rode into North Carolina to intimidate black voters—though White refuted a newspaper account that he was trapped aboard a train by Red Shirts on a campaign stop in Kinston.[29] Black voter turnout was low, but the confusion of a four-way race divided the vote in White's favor.[30] The post-election ramifications in North Carolina were tremendous. White supremacists in Wilmington, the biggest metropolis in the largely rural state, incited race riots in the city as an excuse to seize power from a fusion city government. Eleven black men

were killed, and 25 were injured.[31]

The bloody Wilmington riots troubled White as he returned to Washington for the final session of the 55th Congress, and he vented his frustration in his first substantive floor speech, on January 26, 1899. During a debate to extend the standing army after victory against Spain, White abruptly changed the subject to disfranchisement, arguing in favor of the bold proposal that states with discriminatory laws should have decreased representation in the U.S. House, proportionate to the number of eligible voters they prevented from going to the polls. "If we are unworthy of suffrage, if it is necessary to maintain white supremacy," White chastised his colleagues, "then you ought to have the benefit only of those who are allowed to vote, and the poor men, whether they be black or white, who are disfranchised ought not go into representation of the district of the state." Republicans greeted his speech with long applause.[32]

The 56th Congress (1899–1901) convened with a Republican majority, and White was given a second assignment on the District of Columbia Committee, which administered the capital city's government. But White's second term was focused on his pursuit of anti-lynching legislation, despite President McKinley's lack of support. On January 20, 1900, White introduced an unprecedented bill to make lynching a federal crime, subjecting those who participated in mob violence to potential capital punishment—a sentence equivalent to that for treason.[33] White's anti-lynching bill subsequently died in the Judiciary Committee.

White announced his intention not to run for renomination to the 57th Congress (1901–1903) in a speech on June 30, 1900, and declared his plans to leave his home. Several factors contributed to his decision. In 1899, the North Carolina state legislature followed the lead of neighboring states and passed new registration laws further restricting black voters. White also lost popularity within his own party. White Republicans resented his seemingly radical disfranchisement legislation and anti-lynching proposals, claiming he had belligerently "drawn the color line in this district."[34] Without strong Republican support, White had little chance of defeating his formidable Democratic opponent Claude Kitchin, scion of one of the most politically powerful families in the state.[35] In addition, White was discouraged because noticeably fewer black delegates attended the Republican National Convention in Philadelphia in mid-June. Compounding his disappointment, the convention rejected the addition of anti-lynching and franchise protection planks to the national party platform.[36] White noticed the strain on his family, particularly his sickly wife, Cora, for whom he believed another campaign would be fatal. "I cannot live in North Carolina and be a man and be treated as a man," he lamented to the Chicago *Daily Tribune*.[37] He told the *New York Times*, the "restrictive measure against the negro is not really political. The political part of it is a mere subterfuge and is a means for the general degradation of the negro." He encouraged southern black families to migrate west and remain farmers, not settling in colonies, but "los[ing] themselves among the people of the country. . . . Then their children will be better educated."[38] On January 29, 1901, White gave his famous valedictory address to the 56th Congress, predicting the return of African Americans to Congress. His speech, which filled more than four pages in the *Congressional Record*, pleaded for respect and equality for American blacks. "The only apology that I have to make for the earnestness with which I have spoken," White concluded, "is that I am pleading for the life, the liberty, the future happiness, and the manhood suffrage of one-eighth of the entire population of the United States."[39]

George White began a second successful career, as a lawyer and an entrepreneur. He opened a law practice in Washington, DC, in 1901. At the same time, he organized a town for black citizens to show that "self-sufficient blacks could not only survive but flourish, if . . . left alone in a neutral, healthy environment." Dubbed Whitesboro, the town was built on 1,700 acres of land in Cape May, New Jersey, and by 1906, its population had swelled to more than 800 people.[40] In 1905, White left Washington to found another law practice in Philadelphia. He also opened the People's Savings Bank, to help potential black home and business owners. Though he never again sought political office, White actively supported the National Association for the Advancement of Colored People, founded in 1909, and was a benefactor of the Frederick Douglass Hospital in Philadelphia. A year after his bank failed, George White died in Philadelphia on December 28, 1918.

FOR FURTHER READING

Anderson, Eric. *Race and Politics in North Carolina, 1872–1901* (Baton Rouge: Louisiana State University Press, 1981).

Justesen, Benjamin R. *George Henry White: An Even Chance in the Race of Life* (Baton Rouge: Louisiana State University Press, 2001).

Reid, George W. "Four in Black: North Carolina's Black Congressmen, 1874–1901," *Journal of Negro History* 64 (Summer 1979): 229–243.

"White, George Henry," *Biographical Directory of the United States Congress, 1774–Present*, http://bioguide.congress.gov/scripts/biodisplay.pl?index=W000372.

NOTES

1   *Congressional Record*, House, 56th Cong., 2nd sess. (29 January 1901): 1638.

2   Benjamin R. Justesen, *George Henry White: An Even Chance in the Race of Life* (Baton Rouge: Louisiana State University Press, 2001): 2–3. Mary's surname is not known.

3   Eric Anderson, "White, George Henry," *American National Biography* 23 (New York: Oxford University Press, 1999): 205–206 (hereinafter referred to as *ANB*).

4   Justesen, *George Henry White*: 35–36.

5   George W. Reid, "Four in Black: North Carolina's Black Congressmen, 1874–1901," *Journal of Negro History* 64 (Summer 1979): 235. Beatrice Odessa White (commonly referred to by her middle name) died in infancy in 1892; see Justesen, *George Henry*

White: 166.

6 Stanley B. Parsons et al., *United States Congressional Districts, 1883–1913* (New York: Greenwood Press, 1990): 97–99.

7 Justesen, *George Henry White:* 151–152.

8 Ibid., 179.

9 Parsons et al., *United States Congressional Districts, 1883–1913*: 100–102; Justesen, *George Henry White*: 257–258.

10 Justesen, *George Henry White:* 185. Justesen discusses the proceedings of the 1894 Republican district convention at length; see 190–195.

11 Ibid., 187.

12 Ibid., 188–189. Some sources note that White withdrew from the race voluntarily to avoid fracturing the Republican Party, though other sources indicate that his supporters abandoned him for Cheatham before his withdrawal; see, for example, Maurine Christopher, *Black Americans in Congress* (New York: Thomas Y. Crowell Company, 1976): 161.

13 Justesen, *George Henry White*: 206.

14 Ibid., 210; see also H. Leon Prather, Sr., *We Have Taken a City: Wilmington Racial Massacre and Coup of 1898* (Rutherford, NJ: Associated University Presses, 1984): 34–35.

15 Justesen, *George Henry White*: 211.

16 Michael J. Dubin et al., *U.S. Congressional Elections, 1788–1997* (Jefferson, NC: McFarland & Company, Inc., Publishers, 1998): 318. Dubin spells Woodard's name "Woodward."

17 Justesen, *George Henry White*: 213; There were two George Whites in the 55th Congress. Republican George Elon White of Illinois also was re-elected to his second (and final) term; see "White, George Elon," online *Biographical Directory of the United States Congress, 1774–Present,* available at http://bioguide.congress.gov/scripts/biodisplay.pl?index=W000371.

18 *Congressional Record*, House, 55th Cong., 2nd sess. (14 April 1898): 4086; *Congressional Record*, House, 55th Cong., 3rd sess. (26 January 1899): 1124.

19 Justesen, *George Henry White*: 235.

20 *Congressional Record*, House, 56th Cong., 1st sess. (5 April 1900): 3814.

21 *Congressional Record*, House, 56th Cong., 1st sess. (23 February 1900): 2151.

22 *Congressional Record*, House, 55th Cong., 2nd sess. (3 March 1898): 2427.

23 Anderson, "White, George Henry," *ANB*.

24 A synopsis of Southwick's endorsement is found in Justesen, *George Henry White*: 233–234.

25 Ibid., 232.

26 Quoted in Christopher, *Black Americans in Congress*: 163; and Justesen, *George Henry White*: 238. Both sources quote White slightly differently. Various forms of this speech were printed in newspapers throughout North Carolina. For a discussion of the different accounts, see Justesen, *George Henry White*: 238–241.

27 Justesen, *George Henry White*: 241.

28 Ibid., 246.

29 Christopher, *Black Americans in Congress*: 163. Justesen notes that most accounts of intimidation by Red Shirts were exaggerated or falsified; see Justesen, *George Henry White*: 245.

30 Helen G. Edmonds, *The Negro and Fusion Politics in North Carolina* (New York: Russell and Russell, 1973; reprint of the 1951 edition): 163–164.

31 Edmonds, *The Negro and Fusion Politics in North Carolina*: 163–164; John Hope Franklin and Alfred A. Moss, *From Slavery to Freedom: A History of African Americans,* 8th ed. (New York: Alfred A. Knopf, 2000): 288. For more on this topic, see the extensive report of the Wilmington Race Riot Commission, published in 2006: http://www.ah.dcr.state.nc.us/1898-wrrc/default.htm (accessed 1 December 2007).

32 *Congressional Record*, House, 55th Cong., 3rd sess. (26 January 1899): 1125; Justesen, *George Henry White*: 263.

33 Edmonds, *The Negro and Fusion Politics in North Carolina*: 86.

34 Quoted in Justesen, *George Henry White*: 290; the quote is attributed to white district leader Hiram L. Grant.

35 Claude Kitchin's father, William Hodges (Buck) Kitchin, served the district in the 46th Congress (1879–1880). Claude's brother, William Walton Kitchin, was finishing up his second term representing a central North Carolina district. Claude and William Walton Kitchin's nephew (and William Hodges Kitchin's grandson), Alvin Paul Kitchin, served in Congress from 1957 to 1962. For more on these individuals, see the online *Biographical Directory of the United States Congress,* available at http://bioguide.congress.gov. Claude himself later became the Democratic Leader in the House, serving as Majority Leader in the 64th and 65th Congress (1915–1919); see "Majority & Minority Leaders," Office of the Clerk, available at http://clerk.house.gov/art_history/house_history/leaders.html.

36 Justesen, *George Henry White*: 292–293.

37 "Sees No Hope In South," 26 August 1900, *Chicago Daily Tribune*: 7.

38 "Southern Negro's Plaint," 26 August 1900, *New York Times*: 8.

39 *Congressional Record*, House, 56th Cong., 2nd sess. (29 January 1901): 1638.

40 Justesen, *George Henry White*: 356.

Keeping the Faith:

AFRICAN AMERICANS RETURN TO CONGRESS, 1929–1970

With his election to the U.S. House of Representatives from a Chicago district in 1928, Oscar De Priest of Illinois became the first African American to serve in Congress since George White of North Carolina left office in 1901 and the first elected from a northern state. But while De Priest's victory symbolized renewed hope for African Americans struggling to regain a foothold in national politics, it was only the beginning of an arduous journey. The election of just a dozen more African Americans to Congress over the next 30 years was stark evidence of modern America's pervasive segregation practices.

The new generation of black lawmakers embarked on a long, methodical institutional apprenticeship on Capitol Hill. Until the mid-1940s, only one black Representative served at any given time; no more than two served simultaneously until 1955. Arriving in Washington, black Members confronted a segregated institution in a segregated capital city. Institutional racism, at turns sharply overt and cleverly subtle, provided a pivotal point for these African-American Members—influencing their agendas, legislative styles, and standing within Congress. Pioneers such as Adam Clayton Powell, Jr., of New York, Charles C. Diggs, Jr., of Michigan, and Augustus (Gus) Hawkins of

Adam Clayton Powell, Jr., of New York, a charismatic and determined civil rights proponent in the U.S. House, served as a symbol of black political activism for millions of African Americans.

California participated in the civil rights debates in Congress and helped shape fundamental laws such as the Civil Rights Act of 1964. For the first time, African Americans made substantive, not merely symbolic, gains within the institution. William L. Dawson of Illinois and Representative Powell became the first blacks to chair standing congressional committees. Eight of these trailblazers would eventually lead one or more standing House committees.

Demographic shifts continued to transform the black political base during these decades, fundamentally recasting the background and experiences of black Members of Congress. None of the black Members from this period represented a southern district or state—a testament to the near-complete disfranchisement of southern blacks and a massive, decades-long migration of millions of African Americans employed in agricultural work in the South to urban areas in the North in search of industrial jobs. While their representation of northern cities alone would have distinguished this group of black Members from their Reconstruction-Era predecessors, they were also overwhelmingly Democratic, sharply contrasting with the uniformly Republican 19th-century African Americans in Congress. New Deal reforms providing a modicum of economic relief—and, more compellingly, the promise of fuller participation in American life—drew Black Americans away from the party of Lincoln and into a durable Democratic coalition built by President Franklin D. Roosevelt. With the exception of De Priest and Senator Edward Brooke of Massachusetts, all the black Members of Congress from this era were Democrats.

An atomistic individualism characterized the careers of African-American congressional pioneers in the early decades of this era. The burden of advocating black interests fell on the shoulders of a few Representatives: De Priest and Arthur Mitchell of Illinois in the 1930s and Powell and Dawson in the 1940s, joined by Diggs and Robert Nix of Pennsylvania in the 1950s. Seven of the 13 individuals to serve in this era were not elected until the 1960s, just as the civil rights movement led by Reverend Martin Luther King, Jr., crested and compelled the federal government to enact legislative reforms. Yet this cohort formed a political vanguard that, in many respects, mirrored the experiences and trends reconfiguring black participation in modern American politics. Brooke—the first black U.S. Senator since Blanche Bruce of Mississippi during Reconstruction—entered the upper chamber in 1967; two years later, Representative Shirley Chisholm of New York became the first black woman to serve in Congress.

Like their Reconstruction-Era predecessors, these African-American Members endured racist slurs and prejudicial slights that complicated their development as legislators. Too few to effect change as a voting bloc within Congress, they acted either as public advocates commanding the spotlight on behalf of racial equality or as patient insiders who sought to deliver economic and political benefits to black constituents by accruing influence within the existing power structure. Yet the symbolism of this handful of black congressional careers initiated between the onset of the Great Depression and the social ferment of the late 1960s far exceeded the sum of its parts. Arguably for the first time, Black Americans who sent Representatives to Capitol Hill were substantively rewarded with legislative efforts made expressly on their behalf. "Keep the faith, baby," Representative Powell famously intoned, "spread it gently and walk together, children."[1] His oft-repeated words captured the essence of African Americans' growing collective political activism.

Elected in 1964, John Conyers of Michigan was featured on the front cover of Jet *magazine in an article titled, "Nation Gets Sixth Negro Congressman."*

COLLECTION OF U.S. HOUSE OF REPRESENTATIVES

PRE-CONGRESSIONAL EXPERIENCE

Numerous parallels can be drawn between the black Congressmen of the Reconstruction Era and the 13 African Americans who were elected to Congress between 1929 and 1970. Many were born in the South, some into well-to-do circumstances. All were well educated, especially compared to the general population, and they drew from a growing reserve of political experience. Like most of their white congressional colleagues, 20th-century black Members of Congress tended to be selected from the elite of their communities. Each had bridged the gulf that separated blacks from the opportunities enjoyed by better-educated, more-affluent whites. A leading political scientist notes that "in terms of education, income, and occupation, these black representatives resemble their white counterparts more than they do their African-American constituents."[2]

Six of the blacks elected to Congress from 1929 to 1970 were born into racially segregated circumstances in the South.[3] Some participated in the Great Migration to northern and western urban areas with their parents (or, later, as young adults), attracted by better economic, social, and cultural opportunities.[4] Born in Florence, Alabama, Oscar De Priest was 7 when his family joined the 1878–1879 exodus of some 60,000 black families from the Lower Mississippi Valley to Kansas; he eventually moved to Chicago as a young man. His successor, Arthur Mitchell, was born in Lafayette, Alabama, and taught school in the South before attending northern colleges to earn his law degree, eventually settling in Chicago in the 1920s—a decade when nearly 750,000 blacks moved to the North. William Dawson, who succeeded Mitchell, was born in Albany, Georgia, and attended school in the South before moving to Chicago prior to World War I. It was not until mid-century that the first black Members of Congress were elected to represent the cities where they were born and raised. These included Charles Diggs of Detroit (1954), John Conyers, Jr., of Detroit (1964), Louis Stokes of Cleveland (1968), William L. Clay, Sr., of St. Louis (1968), Shirley Chisholm of Brooklyn (1968), and George W. Collins of Chicago (1970).

Service in the U.S. Army played a formative role in the lives of a majority of these Members of Congress.[5] For those born in the North, the military was a brusque introduction to blatantly segregationist practices. Both Diggs and Stokes, who were stationed in the Deep South, recalled instances of discrimination when African-American soldiers were refused food service, while white GIs and German prisoners of war dined together. "That was the shock of recognition to me, that an enemy was more welcome than a black," Diggs observed.[6] That experience sparked Diggs's future political commitment to securing equal rights for African Americans. Shortly after taking office in 1943, William Dawson, who had graduated from the country's first black officers' candidate school in 1917, declared, "I know what segregation in the army means. . . . It is a damnable thing anywhere and I resent it."[7] As a Member of Congress during World War II, Dawson was a vocal proponent of integrating U.S. forces and, in 1944, when Secretary of War Henry L. Stimson suggested that black soldiers were unfit for combat duty, Dawson demanded his removal.[8] Edward Brooke, who served during World War II in Europe in the segregated 366th Combat Infantry Regiment and later in the 224th Engineering Battalion, recalled, "The prejudice Negro soldiers faced in the army was underscored by the friendliness of the Italians, who were colorblind with regard to race. . . . It was maddening to be given lectures on the evils of Nazi

Jim Crow reigned in North Carolina in the 1950s, where water fountains on the Halifax County courthouse lawn bore the signs of segregation.

IMAGE COURTESY OF LIBRARY OF CONGRESS

Nearly one million blacks served in World War II, most in the segregated U.S. Army. This 1942 picture of a military policeman astride his motorcycle on a base in Columbus, Georgia, underscored the reality that Jim Crow practices prevalent in civilian life were also a part of military service.

IMAGE COURTESY OF NATIONAL ARCHIVES AND RECORDS ADMINISTRATION

racial theories and then be told that we should not associate with white soldiers
or white civilians."[9] After being drafted in 1953, five years after the services were
integrated by presidential order, William Clay, Sr., was stationed at Fort McClellan
in Alabama—an army post that was still largely segregated, in Clay's words,
"with all the insobriety of the last Confederate general and the insolence of the
last Confederate infantryman." Clay organized a boycott against the segregated
barbershop, a whites-only Post Exchange restaurant, and a segregated swimming
pool. Later, Representative Diggs launched an investigation into base practices at
Fort McClellan.[10]

Like their Reconstruction predecessors, 20th-century black political pioneers
in Congress were exceedingly well educated—eclipsing the educational level
of the average American and far surpassing the educational level of their fellow
Black Americans.[11] All graduated from high school. Only one, De Priest, did not
receive at least a partial college education; seven studied law at elite historically
black institutions and Ivy League schools. As organs of political protest and racial
advancement, African-American churches played a central role in the larger civil
rights movement of the 1950s and 1960s, but religious studies and service in the
pulpit were not a prerequisite for black Members of Congress. Among these black
Members, only Adam Clayton Powell, who succeeded his father as pastor of New
York's Abyssinian Baptist Church, was trained in the ministry.

Political opportunities were more often secular. The majority of the African
Americans elected to Congress during this period had experience in elective
office. Five served on city councils in major urban areas as a result of the growing
population and influence of blacks in northern cities: De Priest, Dawson, and
Collins served in Chicago, Powell served in New York City, and Clay served in
St. Louis. Diggs, Hawkins, and Chisholm served in state legislatures. Edward
Brooke served two terms as Massachusetts attorney general, becoming one of the
highest-ranking African-American law enforcement officials in history.[12] Only
Stokes, Nix, and Conyers won election to the House without having held an
elective office, but all three had extensive local political experience.[13]

Reflecting inroads made by the modern women's rights movement, gender diversity became a reality for Black Americans in Congress during this era.[14] In 1968, Shirley Chisholm won a newly redistricted seat in Brooklyn, becoming the first African-American woman elected to Congress. She ran against James Farmer, a famous civil rights activist nominated as the Liberal-Republican candidate partly because he argued that the Democrats had for too long "thought they had [the black vote] in their pockets." Chisholm and Farmer staked out similar economic and social positions, and their campaigns were nearly identical, but Farmer argued that women had been "in the driver's seat" in black communities for an extensive period and that the district needed "a man's voice in Washington."[15] Chisholm prevailed, becoming an overnight symbol of crumbling barriers for blacks in national political office. Within five years, Yvonne Brathwaite Burke of California, Barbara Jordan of Texas, and Cardiss Collins of Illinois joined her in the House. "The black man must step forward," Chisholm was fond of saying, "but that doesn't mean that black women have to step back."[16]

LEGISLATIVE AND ELECTORAL CHARACTERISTICS

Committee Assignments

As in the Reconstruction Era, African-American Members through the mid-20th century were assigned largely to middling committee positions.[17] Among black Members' committee assignments were Invalid Pensions (3), Interior and Insular Affairs (3), Veterans' Affairs (3), Indian Affairs (2), Post Office and Post Roads (2), Expenditures in the Executive Departments (2), and District of Columbia (2). No black Members served on the Agriculture Committee (despite House leaders' initial attempt to assign Shirley Chisholm to the panel), largely because they represented northern industrialized districts. As in the 19th century, the Education and Labor Committee—which had oversight of federal laws affecting schools, workplaces, and unions—was the most common assignment, with four black Members in this era.

There were a few exceptions to this pattern, however. William Dawson served on the Irrigation and Reclamation Committee in the 78th and 79th Congresses (1943–1947). That panel, which had wide-ranging jurisdiction over public lands and water projects, ranked in the top third of "attractive" committees. In 1965, John Conyers won a seat as a freshman on the influential Judiciary Committee, which was then under the leadership of liberal Democrat Emanuel Celler of New York. At the time, the assignment was an elite one, as Judiciary ranked behind only Ways and Means and Appropriations in terms of the number of Members who sought assignment there.[18] Members also considered the Foreign Affairs Committee to be among the upper tier of House committee assignments because of its relative visibility. Charles Diggs won a seat on this panel in 1959, becoming its first African-American Member. Diggs's appointment to the committee signified African Americans' increasing interest in Cold War policies, particularly as they affected the rise of postcolonial independent states in Africa. By 1969, he chaired the Subcommittee on Africa and served as one of the principal organizers of the congressional anti-apartheid movement. Since Senators' committee responsibilities tend to be broader than those of their House counterparts, the increased workload opened avenues onto important panels for Edward Brooke, who won assignments to the Senate Appropriations Committee, the Armed Services Committee, and the Joint Defense Production Committee.[19]

Cold War:

A state of ideological, economic, political, military, and cultural warfare between the United States and the Soviet Union (USSR) from 1947 until 1991. Developing from divergent American and Soviet foreign policies concerning the restoration of Europe after World War II, the conflict spread from Europe to the rest of the world. Although there were no direct military conflicts, the Soviet and American superpowers tried to alter the international balance of power in their favor by competing globally for allies, strategic locations, natural resources, and influence in Asia, Africa, and Latin America. The Cold War ended with the collapse and disintegration of the USSR in 1991.

As commemorated on this fan, the 85th Congress (1957–1959) was the first Congress since Reconstruction with four black lawmakers serving simultaneously.

COLLECTION OF U.S. HOUSE OF REPRESENTATIVES

Unlike Adam Clayton Powell, Jr., William Dawson of Illinois preferred to stay out of the limelight and work within institutional pathways to effect civil rights change.

COLLECTION OF U.S. HOUSE OF REPRESENTATIVES

Longevity and Seniority

The turnover rate for incumbent black Members of Congress in the 20th century remained low. The creation of majority-black districts, particularly in the late 1960s and the 1970s, provided electoral safety for black House Members. Of all the African Americans who were elected to the House and the Senate from 1928 through 2007, only four were defeated in a general election: De Priest (1934), Brooke (1978), Delegate Melvin Evans of the Virgin Islands (1980), and Senator Carol Moseley-Braun of Illinois (1998). All the other African-American Members who lost their seats (12) were defeated in the Democratic primaries (usually by other African Americans). These trends reflected the growing power of incumbency among the general congressional membership.[20]

During this period, black Members of Congress tended to be slightly older upon their first election than the rest of the congressional population.[21] The average age of African-American Members at their first election was 46.4 years; their white colleagues, who began their careers at marginally earlier ages, enjoyed a statistical, if not a determinative, advantage in accruing seniority at a younger age. Roughly one-third of black Members during this era were elected in their 30s, as was the general House population that was elected between 1930 and 1960. Moreover, four African-American Members elected in their thirties—Powell, Diggs, Conyers, and Clay—all had unusually long careers and eventually held a variety of leadership posts. At 31 years of age, Diggs was the youngest black Member elected during this period. Nix was the oldest; elected to the House for the first time at age 59, he claimed to be eight years younger than he actually was.

The trend toward increasing electoral safety led to longevity on Capitol Hill. Of the 13 African Americans elected to Congress between 1928 and 1970, 10 served at least 10 years; eight served more than 20 years.[22] Longevity allowed Members to gain the seniority on committees they needed to advance into the leadership or request more-desirable committee assignments. Consequently, a number of milestones were established during this era. Representative Dawson became the first African American to chair a standing congressional committee when he earned the gavel on the House Expenditures in the Executive Departments Committee (later named the Government Operations Committee) in 1949. With the exception of the period from 1953 to 1955, when Republicans controlled the chamber, Dawson chaired the panel until his death in 1970. Representative Powell served as chairman of the Education and Labor Committee from 1961 to 1967, overseeing much of the education reform legislation passed during the Great Society. Additionally, Dawson, Powell, Diggs, and Nix chaired 10 subcommittees on six separate standing committees during this era.[23]

Incumbency conferred a substantial amount of power. It discouraged opposition from within the party because in many instances the incumbent Member controlled or influenced much of the local political machinery. It also strengthened the intangible bonds between voter and Member. In some measure the electoral longevity of this set of African-American Members can be attributed to the power of the entrenched political machines that brought them to office. But Representatives' familiarity, established through their longevity, also fostered loyalty among their constituents. Viewed by their primarily African-American communities as advocates for black interests, most of these Members cultivated unusually cohesive bases of support.[24] These relationships endured even when incumbents such as Adam Clayton Powell and Charles Diggs faced ethics charges or legal problems.[25]

PARTY REALIGNMENT AND THE NEW DEAL

The political realignment of black voters that began in the late 1920s proliferated during this era. This process involved a "push and pull"; the racial policies of Republicans alienated many black voters, while those of the northern wing of the Democratic Party attracted them.[26] In 1932, incumbent President Herbert Hoover received between two-thirds and three-quarters of the black vote in northern urban wards, despite his attempts to ingratiate himself with southern segregationists and his failure to implement economic policies to help blacks laid low by the Great Depression.[27] But most blacks cast their votes less because of Republican loyalty than because they were loath to support a candidate whose party had zealously suppressed their political rights in the South. Blacks mistrusted Franklin D. Roosevelt because of his party label, his evasiveness about racial issues in the campaign, and his choice of a running mate, House Speaker John Nance Garner of Texas.[28] As late as the mid-1930s, John R. Lynch, a former Republican Representative who represented Mississippi during Reconstruction and in the years immediately afterward, summed up the sentiments of older black voters and upper-middle-class professionals: "The colored voters cannot help but feel that in voting the Democratic ticket in national elections they will be voting to give their indorsement [sic] and their approval to every wrong of which they are victims, every right of which they are deprived, and every injustice of which they suffer."[29]

The Illinois First Congressional District provides a window into the process of black political realignment in northern cities. Prior to becoming solidly Democratic in 1934, the South Chicago district elected Republican Oscar De Priest in 1928, 1930, and 1932. Chicago's Republican machine was firmly established and headed by William Hale (Big Bill) Thompson, who served as mayor from 1915 through 1923 and again from 1927 through 1931. Southern blacks, who swelled the city's population during that period (giving it the second-largest urban black population nationally by 1930), encountered a Republican machine that courted the black vote and extended patronage jobs. The party offered these migrants an outlet for political participation that was unimaginable in the Jim Crow South. African Americans voted in droves for machine politicians like Thompson, who regularly corralled at least 60 percent of the vote in the majority-black Second and Third Wards. Mayor Thompson and the machine promoted black politicians such as De Priest who, in 1915, became the city's first African-American alderman (the equivalent of a city councilman). Black voters remained exceedingly loyal to the Republican ticket, both nationally and locally.[30]

Indeed, the most common political experience of African-American Members of this era came through their involvement in politics at the ward and precinct levels. The Chicago political machines run by Thompson and, later, Democrats such as Edward J. Kelly and Richard J. Daley, sent nearly one-third of the black Members of this era to Capitol Hill. Political machines awakened to and courted the growing African-American urban population long before the national parties realized its potential. At the beginning of this era, the relationship between black politicians and their sponsors was strong—and many black Members of Congress placed party loyalty above all else. But by the late 1960s, as black politicians began to assemble their own power

Realignment:

A new or unique merging of disparate political parties, philosophies, or organizations.

Great Depression:

The economic crisis and period of minimal business activity in the United States and other industrialized nations that began in 1929 and continued through the 1930s. During the 1920s in the United States, speculation on the stock market led to changes in federal monetary policy. The subsequent decline in personal consumption and investments triggered the stock market crash of 1929, which, along with World War I debts and reparations, precipitated the Great Depression.

Oscar De Priest's successful election campaign to represent a lakeshore district in Chicago initiated the trend of black representation in northern cities, where the Great Migration sharply increased African-American populations.

COLLECTION OF U.S. HOUSE OF REPRESENTATIVES

Born in Alabama, Representative Oscar De Priest became the first African American elected from the North and the first to be elected in the 20th century.

IMAGE COURTESY OF SCURLOCK STUDIO RECORDS, ARCHIVES CENTER, NATIONAL MUSEUM OF AMERICAN HISTORY, SMITHSONIAN INSTITUTION

New Deal:

A period of political, economic, and social activity spanning President Franklin D. Roosevelt's first two terms in office (1933–1941). Working with Congress, the Roosevelt administration provided an unprecedented level of emergency intervention in response to the Great Depression that was designed to revive the economy and to provide basic welfare to citizens.

bases, carving out a measure of independence, they often challenged the machine when party interests conflicted with racial issues that were important to the black community. Unlike earlier black Members, who relied on the established political machines to launch their careers, these Members, most of whom were native to the cities they represented, managed to forge political bases separate from the dominant party structure through long-established familial and community relations and civic engagement—and they routinely clashed with the entrenched political powers.[31]

Discontent with the Hoover administration's halting efforts to revive the Depression-Era economy also loosened African-American ties to the party. Nationally, the staggering financial collapse hit blacks harder than most other groups. Thousands had already lost agrarian jobs in the mid-1920s due to the declining cotton market.[32] Others had lost industrial jobs in the first stages of economic contraction, so blacks nationally were already in the grips of an economic depression before the stock market collapsed in October 1929. By the early 1930s, 38 percent of blacks were unemployed (compared to 17 percent of whites).[33] A Roosevelt administration study found that blacks constituted 20 percent of all Americans on the welfare rolls, even though they accounted for just 10 percent of the total population. In Chicago, one-fourth of welfare recipients were black, although blacks made up just 6 percent of the city's total population.[34]

Political opportunity (both for personal advancement and for the improvement of the black community) in the early 1930s also convinced some African-American politicians to change their party allegiance.[35] Arthur Mitchell and William Dawson epitomized a younger cadre of African Americans who were "ambitious and impatient with the entrenched black Republican leadership, [seeking] a chance for personal advancement in the concurrent rise of the national Democratic party. . . ."[36] Paid to speak on behalf of Hoover's 1928 presidential campaign, Mitchell encountered the De Priest campaign at a Chicago engagement and shortly thereafter joined the Second Ward Regular Republican Organization; he hoped to make an intraparty challenge to the incumbent. But after evaluating De Priest's control of the machine, he switched parties to campaign for Roosevelt in 1932 and two years later successfully unseated De Priest, even though the incumbent retained the majority of the black vote. Mitchell became the first African American elected to Congress as a Democrat—running largely on a platform that tapped into urban black support for the economic relief provided by New Deal programs. "I was elected partly on the achievement of your administration . . . ," Mitchell wrote President Roosevelt shortly after starting his term in office, "and partly on the promise that I would stand [in] back of your administration."[37]

Even more telling was the defection of De Priest's protégé, William Dawson, who, with the Representative's backing, in 1932 won election as a Republican Second Ward alderman to the Chicago city council. After defeating De Priest in the 1938 GOP primary, failing to unseat Mitchell in the general election, and then losing his seat on the city council when De Priest allies blocked his renomination, Dawson seized the opportunity extended by his one time opponents. Allying with Democratic mayoral incumbent Ed Kelly, Dawson changed parties and became Democratic committeeman in the Second Ward, clearing a path to succeed Mitchell upon his retirement from the House in 1942. Dawson's case epitomized the willingness of Democratic bosses like Kelly to recruit African Americans by using patronage positions.[38]

Additionally, black voters nationwide realigned their party affiliation because of the growing perception that the interests of the black community were intertwined with local Democratic organizations. Local patronage positions and nationally administered emergency relief programs in Depression-Era Chicago and other cities proved alluring.[39] While New Deal programs failed to extend as much economic relief to Black Americans as to whites, the tangible assistance they provided conferred a sense that the system was at least addressing a few issues that were important to African Americans. For those who had been marginalized or ignored for so long, even the largely symbolic efforts of the Roosevelt administration inspired hope and renewed interest in the political process.[40] As younger black voters displaced their parents and grandparents, their electoral experiences and loyalties evolved largely alongside and within the Democratic machines that came to dominate northern city wards. By 1936, only 28 percent of blacks nationally voted for Republican nominee Alf Landon—less than half the number who had voted for Hoover just four years before.[41] Over time, the party affiliations of blacks in Congress became equally one-sided. Including Oscar De Priest, just five black Republicans were elected to Congress between 1929 and 2007 (about 5 percent of the African Americans to serve in that time span).[42]

At the urging of First Lady Eleanor Roosevelt (center), Mary McLeod Bethune (left), a leading African-American educator, was appointed to head the Division of Negro Affairs of the National Youth Administration.

The Limits of New Deal Reform

President Franklin Roosevelt remained aloof and ambivalent about black civil rights largely because his economic policies may have been compromised had he raised racial issues, angering southern congressional leaders. During Roosevelt's first term, the administration's emphasis was squarely on mitigating the economic travails of the Depression. This required a close working relationship with Congresses dominated by racially conservative southern Democrats, including several Speakers and most of the chairmen of key committees. "Economic reconstruction took precedence over all other concerns," observes historian Harvard Sitkoff. "Congress held the power of the purse, and the South held power in Congress."[43] There were no plausible scenarios in which the President could have confronted white supremacy head-on during the Depression.

However, other institutional and structural reforms implemented by the administration eclipsed the President's impassivity toward black civil rights activists.[44] Absent Roosevelt's hands-on involvement, progressive New Dealers advanced the cause of African Americans, transforming many blacks' perceptions about the Democratic Party.[45] First Lady Eleanor Roosevelt prodded her husband to be more responsive and cultivated connections with black leaders, such as educator and women's rights activist Mary McLeod Bethune. One historian describes the First Lady as an "unofficial ombudsman for the Negro."[46] Harold Ickes, a key Roosevelt appointee and Secretary of the Interior Department, was another prominent advocate for blacks. A former president of the Chicago National Association for the Advancement of Colored People (NAACP) and a one-time Republican, Ickes banned segregation from his department; other heads of executive agencies followed his example. As director of the Public Works Administration, Ickes also stipulated that the agency's federal contractors must hire a percentage of blacks equal to or higher than the percentage of blacks recorded in the 1930 occupational census.[47]

Nevertheless, another failed attempt to push for anti-lynching legislation made it apparent that the extent of reform was limited. In this instance—unlike in the early 1920s when there were no blacks serving in Congress—an African-American

Members of the NAACP New York City Youth Council picketed on behalf of anti-lynching legislation in front of the Strand Theater in New York City's Times Square. In 1937, an anti-lynching bill passed the U.S. House, but died in the Senate.

World War II brought women of all races out of the home and into the workplace. With millions of men serving overseas in the military, women filled many factory jobs. Above, two women worked together at the North American Aviation Company Plant.

IMAGE COURTESY OF FRANKLIN D. ROOSEVELT PRESIDENTIAL LIBRARY AND MUSEUM, HYDE PARK, NY

Lt. Harriet Ida Pickens and Ens. Frances Willis, the first two African-American Navy "WAVES," or "Women Accepted for Voluntary Emergency Service," posed for a picture during World War II. Thousands of women in this and other military auxiliary units filled a range of jobs from nurses and clerical workers to parachute riggers, machinists, and even ferry pilots.

IMAGE COURTESY OF NATIONAL ARCHIVES AND RECORDS ADMINISTRATION

Member of Congress, Arthur Mitchell, refused to endorse legislation supported by the NAACP. Moreover, Mitchell introduced his own anti-lynching bill in the 74th Congress (1935–1937), which critics assailed as a diluted measure that provided far more lenient sentences and contained many legal ambiguities. Given the choice, southerners favored Mitchell's bill, although they amended it considerably in the Judiciary Committee, further weakening its provisions. Meanwhile, Mitchell waged a public relations blitz, including a national radio broadcast, on behalf of his bill. Only when reformers convincingly tabled Mitchell's proposal early in the 75th Congress (1937–1939) did he enlist in the campaign to support the NAACP measure—smarting from the realization that Judiciary Committee Chairman Hatton Sumners of Texas had misled and used him. The NAACP measure passed the House in April 1937 by a vote of 277 to 120 but was never enacted into law. Instead, southerners in the Senate effectively buried it in early 1938 by blocking efforts to bring it to an up-or-down vote on the floor.[48] The rivalry between Mitchell and the NAACP forecast future problems while revealing that African-American Members and outside advocacy groups sometimes worked at cross-purposes, confounding civil rights supporters in Congress and providing opponents a wedge for blocking legislation.

THE SECOND WORLD WAR

World War II marked a watershed moment in African-American history. It brought economic opportunities and opened new avenues for participation in American society. On the eve of the war, roughly 75 percent of American blacks lived in the South, two-thirds of them in rural areas. For the year 1939, 87 percent of black families were estimated to live below the federal poverty level (compared to less than half of white families), and blacks' per capita income was 39 percent that of whites. The war effort produced immense change by renewing the Great Migration, which had stalled during the Great Depression. Between 1940 and 1960, more than 4.5 million African Americans emigrated from the South to the urban North and the West. During the war years alone, approximately 700,000 black civilians left the South for destinations such as Los Angeles to take industrial jobs created by the demands of full-scale mobilization and to seek opportunities for political participation that did not exist in the South—where less than 5 percent of blacks were allowed to vote.[49]

Roughly one million blacks served in the U.S. armed forces during World War II, with approximately half serving overseas. The war effort offered more opportunities than ever for African Americans to defend their country, though discrimination and segregation circumscribed their ability to contribute. While thousands of African Americans served in combat—among them the army's 92nd and 93rd all-black divisions, as well as the famed 99th Pursuit Squadron (known as the Tuskegee Airmen)—the most common assignments for black servicemen were rear-guard mopping-up actions and menial supply and requisition roles. A lack of education among blacks generally and the prejudice of local draft boards and the military leadership accounted for much of the army's reluctance to assign African Americans to combat roles.[50] In 1942, Representative Mitchell repeatedly called attention to British military reverses in Singapore, noting that the colonial power failed "due in part to its own discriminations" against the native people, which undermined morale. "America might suffer a like fate," Mitchell warned, "if we insist upon destroying the morale of one-tenth of its fighting strength."[51] The American call to arms, Mitchell noted bitterly while reflecting on segregation in the army and the navy, "is for white people only, except where Negroes are needed to do the most menial service. Is this democracy? How long will this American practice be kept up? . . . While we are adjusting affairs the world over, we must not fail to adjust affairs in our own country and in our own hearts."[52]

Wartime experiences also mobilized black political activism. Enrollment in the NAACP, which soared from 50,000 on the eve of U.S. intervention in the war to 450,000 in 1946, constituted one measure of renewed political activity. The organization's "Double V" campaign, with its slogan "Democracy Abroad—At Home," called for victory over fascism abroad and victory over racism at home. In *A Rising Wind* (1945), influential NAACP Secretary Walter White suggested that although African Americans were maltreated and maligned even during the war effort, they were too resilient to wallow in "defeatist disillusionment." Instead, White predicted, as the United States demobilized its wartime effort against the Axis Powers, homeward-bound African-American servicemen would enlist in the effort to conquer Jim Crow, "convinced that whatever betterment of their lot is achieved must come largely from their own efforts. They will return determined to use those efforts to the utmost."[53] In this way African Americans' wartime experiences helped foster the modern civil rights movement.

Equally significant, the war against fascism and totalitarian regimes reminded millions of Americans of democracy's shortcomings on the segregated home front. A number of southern states still used the poll tax—a fee as high as $2, earmarked for school improvements, that voters had to pay before casting their ballots. The cost was prohibitive for poor voters, who were overwhelmingly black.[54] In a brief speech on the House Floor during a 1943 debate on a bill to outlaw the poll tax, freshman Representative William Dawson recalled his meager public education as a boy in Georgia, which was supplemented by private schooling, his family "slaved" to pay for. "You know that any method used to try to keep a citizen from exercising [the right to vote] is against the true spirit of the Constitution of the United States," he told colleagues. "In the cause of the 13,000,000 patriotic and loyal Negro citizens I beseech the passage of this bill." Several hours later, the House approved the measure by a sound 265 to 110 vote. However, the bill never cleared the Senate. In 1945, 1947, and 1949, the House again passed anti-poll tax bills. Over time, the measure became less controversial because fewer states employed the poll tax. Still, southern Senators blocked the legislation from being enacted.[55]

Fair Employment Practices Committee

A critical moment in the development of black political activism came in 1941 when civil rights proponents, led by A. Philip Randolph, threatened to march on Washington, DC, to protest discrimination against blacks in the war industry. President Roosevelt consented to act only grudgingly, when his efforts to cajole and dissuade black leaders from vigorously protesting his inaction had been completely exhausted. On June 25, 1941, Roosevelt issued Executive Order 8802, which declared "full participation in the national defense program by all citizens of the United States, regardless of race, creed, color, or national origin," based on "the firm belief that the democratic way of life within the Nation can be defended successfully only with the help and support of all groups within its borders." The order required that the federal government, unions, and defense industries "provide

Fair Employment Practices Committee (FEPC):

Created in June 1941, this federal office was charged with enforcing Executive Order 8802, which outlawed racial discrimination in wartime industry by conducting investigations, gathering evidence, and reporting abuses. At its peak, the FEPC had 13 regional offices around the nation and was the first agency in U.S. history to appoint blacks to policy-making positions. The FEPC was disbanded in 1946.

In February 1950, Adam Clayton Powell, Jr., (second from right) worked towards gaining permanent status for the Fair Employment Practices Committee (FEPC). While Powell and others successfully shepherded a FEPC bill through the House, the measure was blocked in the Senate.

IMAGE COURTESY OF LIBRARY OF CONGRESS

Mary Norton of New Jersey, who chaired the House Committee on Labor from 1937 to 1947, sympathized with the goals of the Fair Employment Practices Committee. Women in Congress often served as important allies of early African-American Members.

OIL ON CANVAS (DETAIL), ELAINE HARTLEY, 1935, COLLECTION OF U.S. HOUSE OF REPRESENTATIVES

On September 24, 1957, President Dwight D. Eisenhower addressed the nation concerning the integration of Central High School in Little Rock, Arkansas. The President dispatched the 101st Army Airborne Division and U.S. Marshals to protect the students and to maintain order in Little Rock.

IMAGE COURTESY OF NATIONAL PARK SERVICE, PROVIDED BY DWIGHT DAVID EISENHOWER PRESIDENTIAL LIBRARY

for the full and equitable participation of all workers."[56] The President intended to mollify black protest in the face of probable U.S. intervention in World War II, but in issuing his executive order, he inspired black activists, who viewed it, and widely portrayed it, as a milestone victory in bending the federal government to their cause.

Roosevelt's order also created the Fair Employment Practices Committee (FEPC) in the federal Office of Personnel Management to investigate complaints about hiring practices. Thousands availed themselves of the FEPC mechanism, though it drew harsh criticism from opponents of the administration's New Deal programs and racial conservatives. In May 1944, congressional opponents of the FEPC, led by Representative Malcolm C. Tarver of Georgia, introduced a measure to repeal the $500,000 annual appropriation for the committee, presenting arguments on several fronts. Tarver suggested that the FEPC was an executive fiat "and does not have the approval or legislative sanction of Congress."[57] Segregationist and avowed New Deal foe John Elliott Rankin of Mississippi declared that the FEPC was "the beginning of a communistic dictatorship, the likes of which America never dreamed."[58]

Only one African American—William Dawson of Chicago—served in Congress and could defend the record of the committee. Noting that he spoke for "more than a million Negro Americans fighting today with our armed forces and more than 13,000,000 here at home," Dawson argued that the FEPC finally ensured blacks a fair part in the war production effort. "So when I hear some Members stand here and refer to it as a dictatorial committee, bent on making people do something that they do not wish to do, I know that they are not stating the facts to you. They are merely making statements in order to carry out their own purposes."[59] Later that afternoon, the House voted 139 to 95 to agree to the amendment to pull funding for the FEPC. But the Labor Committee, chaired by sympathetic Representative Mary Norton of New Jersey, held hearings on permanently establishing the FEPC—a move that was backed by First Lady Eleanor Roosevelt—and funding was temporarily restored.[60] Opponents of the FEPC prevailed in 1946, when they garnered enough support in both chambers to let the FEPC lapse. Twice, proponents of creating a permanent commission—prodded by liberals like Adam Clayton Powell and California Representative Helen Gahagan Douglas, who represented a large black constituency in Los Angeles—brought an FEPC bill before the House. A version of the bill passed the House in February 1950, but southern opponents had fatally weakened its enforcement powers. The measure, which provided only for investigatory and proposal functions, died later that year when it was filibustered in the Senate.

POSTWAR FOREIGN POLICY AND AFRICAN-AMERICAN CIVIL RIGHTS

The Cold War, the great power rivalry that evolved between the United States and the Soviet Union in the aftermath of World War II, riveted international attention on U.S. segregation practices.[61] Discrimination against millions of African Americans at home prompted criticism from allies and provided Kremlin propagandists with ample public relations opportunities. Members of the U.S. policymaking elite, who tended to cast the Soviet–American rivalry in terms of good versus evil, were keenly aware of the gap between their rhetoric about defending the "Free World" from communist "aggression" and democratic shortcomings at home, such as the Little Rock crisis of September 1957, when the Dwight D. Eisenhower administration was compelled to dispatch federal troops and marshals to integrate the city's Central High School. Surveying the episode, widely respected foreign policy commentator Walter Lippmann noted, "the work of the American propagandist is not at present a happy one." Segregation "mocks us and haunts us whenever we become eloquent and indignant in the United Nations. . . . The caste system in this country, particularly when as in Little Rock it is maintained by troops, is an enormous, indeed an almost insuperable, obstacle to our leadership in the cause of freedom and human equality."[62]

U.S. officials viewed domestic civil rights through an ideological lens shaped by the Cold War that at times produced contrarian impulses.[63] In some measure, American officials' increasing receptiveness to calls for civil rights at home in the 1950s and 1960s must be examined within the context of their desire to promote a positive image of America abroad, particularly in the contest for support in developing, decolonized countries in Africa, Asia, and Latin America—principal proxy arenas for the Cold War.[64] As historian Thomas Borstelmann observes, U.S. officials often sought "to try to manage and control the efforts of racial reformers at home and abroad. . . . They hoped effectively to contain racial polarization and build the largest possible multiracial, anti-Communist coalition under American leadership."[65] Conversely, opponents of civil rights—often to great effect—labeled progressive reforms as communist-inspired. Moreover, investigatory panels such as the communist-hunting House Un-American Activities Committee (backed by arch segregationists such as Representative John E. Rankin) called prominent African Americans to testify during this era, questioning their ties to the American Communist Party and, by inference and innuendo, calling their patriotism into question.[66]

African Americans' participation in the international dialogue about civil rights and postcolonial self-determination is noteworthy. NAACP Secretary Walter White remarked that World War II gave African Americans "a sense of kinship with other colored—and also oppressed—peoples of the world," a belief "that the struggle of the Negro in the United States is part and parcel of the struggle against imperialism and exploitation in India, China, Burma, Africa, the Philippines, Malaya, the West Indies, and South America."[67] The Cold War certainly magnified these issues. As bellwethers of this international cognizance, Representatives Powell and Diggs made significant strides inserting themselves into the foreign policy debate, suggesting a growing black influence in shaping public perceptions about racism that transcended U.S. borders.[68]

Powell emerged as a foreign policy innovator. Representing a polyglot district, the Harlem Representative catered to the many nationalist impulses of his constituency, pushing for more liberal immigration policies, which were important to the large West Indian immigrant community in his district. He often met with visiting African heads of state and, as a freshman Member of the House, introduced legislation that allowed for the naturalization of Filipinos and South Asian Indians.[69] A critic of the containment policy adopted by the Eisenhower administration, and particularly of the emphasis of Secretary of State John Foster Dulles on the need for allies to conform to liberal democratic ideals, he was stingingly critical of racial discrimination in the U.S. foreign policy apparatus. Noting in 1953 that the U.S. was "the most hated nation in the world today," Powell called for immediate civil

The historic 1954 Supreme Court case, Brown v. the Board of Education of Topeka (KS), desegregated the nation's public schools. In September 1957, nine African-American students enrolled at the whites-only Central High School in Little Rock, Arkansas. Students were escorted to school by 101st Airborne Division soldiers. More than 40 years later, Congress recognized the bravery of the "Little Rock Nine" by awarding them the Congressional Gold Medal.

IMAGE COURTESY OF LIBRARY OF CONGRESS

Decolonization:

A process that took place from 1945 to 1993 characterized by the dissolution of European colonial institutions in Africa and Asia and the emergence of postcolonial indigenous governments.

In this 1966 photo, Education and Labor Committee Chairman Adam Clayton Powell, Jr., (left) walked down a hallway of the Rayburn House Office Building accompanied by his administrative assistant, Chuck Stone.

IMAGE COURTESY OF LIBRARY OF CONGRESS

Shortly after becoming the first Black American to serve in the U.S. Senate in nearly a century, Edward Brooke of Massachusetts met with President Lyndon B. Johnson in the Oval Office in January 1967.

PHOTOGRAPH BY YOICHI R. OKAMOTO, COURTESY OF THE LBJ LIBRARY

rights reforms, warning that otherwise "communism must win the global cold war by default."[70]

In April 1955, Powell attended the Bandung, Indonesia, Afro-Asian Conference, a gathering of developing nations which opposed the "neocolonialism" of the superpowers and included representatives from India, Pakistan, Indonesia, Egypt, Ceylon, and Burma. U.S. officials refused to send an official representative to the conference, so Powell went as a private citizen even though the government asked him not to attend. His mere presence, he later told President Eisenhower, was "living proof to the fact that there is no truth in the Communist charge that the Negro is oppressed in America."[71] Powell, however, also powerfully endorsed the notion that smaller nations could remain unaligned and neutral in the larger Cold War struggle and questioned Washington's embrace of the containment strategy and its missionary zeal for promoting free market trade. His efforts prodded the administration to install several African Americans as United Nations delegates and alternates in 1956.[72]

Diggs and Powell also became the first black Members of Congress to visit Africa. Diggs was part of an official U.S. delegation led by Vice President Richard M. Nixon in 1957 that participated in Ghana's celebration of independence from British rule and the inauguration of Kwame Nkrumah as prime minister. Powell, who had a longtime connection with Nkrumah—an attendee of his Abyssinian Baptist Church in the 1930s as a merchant seaman and as a foreign student—joined Diggs in an unofficial capacity in Ghana's capital, Accra.[73] Diggs recalled that he and Powell "stood out there with tears coming down our cheeks" as the Union Jack (the British flag) was lowered and the new Ghanaian flag was raised in its place.[74] Diggs later attended the All-African Peoples Conference in Accra, organized by Nkrumah, as a show of Third World solidarity. Diggs returned from that visit convinced that the United States was "in danger of losing the present advantage it holds in Africa to the Soviet Union." He added, "our Nation needs to be educated on the tremendous significance of the development of Africa."[75] Believing he "could make a contribution" to improve relations between Washington and postcolonial African governments, Diggs requested and was awarded a spot on the Foreign Affairs Committee in January 1959.

American intervention in the Vietnamese civil war—between the communist regime in Hanoi and the U.S.-backed government in Saigon—was another key foreign policy issue for black Members of Congress. Representative Gus Hawkins opposed the war, based partly on impressions he formed while visiting South Vietnam in 1970 that the government routinely violated prisoners' human rights. Others, such as Representative Robert Nix, supported the foreign policies of the two Democratic presidents—John F. Kennedy and Lyndon B. Johnson—who broadened the U.S. military commitment and mission in Southeast Asia. As a Senate candidate in 1966, Edward Brooke was initially skeptical about the war. After an official visit to Vietnam, he asserted that the military policy of the Johnson administration was prudent because there was no prospect of meaningful negotiations with the North Vietnamese. Brooke tacked back toward a dissenting position when, in 1970, he opposed the Nixon administration's policy of attacking communist sanctuaries in Cambodia. He eventually voted for the Cooper–Church Amendment of 1970, which prohibited the deployment of U.S. forces outside Vietnam.

THE CIVIL RIGHTS MOVEMENT AND THE SECOND RECONSTRUCTION, 1945–1968

The broad period from the end of World War II until the late 1960s, often referred to as the "Second Reconstruction," consisted of a grass-roots civil rights movement coupled with gradual but progressive actions by the Presidents, the federal courts, and Congress to provide full political rights for African Americans and to begin to redress longstanding economic and social inequities. While African-American Members of Congress from this era played prominent roles in advocating for reform, it was largely the efforts of everyday Americans who protested segregation that prodded a reluctant Congress to pass landmark civil rights legislation in the 1960s.[76]

During the 1940s and 1950s, executive action, rather than legislative initiatives, set the pace for measured movement toward desegregation. President Harry S. Truman "expanded on Roosevelt's limited and tentative steps toward racial moderation and reconciliation."[77] Responding to civil rights advocates, Truman established the President's Committee on Civil Rights. Significantly, the committee's October 1947 report, *To Secure These Rights*, provided civil rights proponents in Congress a legislative blueprint for much of the next two decades. Among its recommendations were the creation of a permanent FEPC, the establishment of a permanent Civil Rights Commission, the creation of a civil rights division in the U.S. Department of Justice, and the enforcement of federal anti-lynching laws and desegregation in interstate transportation. In 1948, President Truman signed Executive Order 9981, desegregating the military. Truman's civil rights policies contributed to the unraveling of the solid Democratic South. Alienated by the administration's race policies, a faction of conservative southerners split to form the Dixiecrats, a racially conservative party that nominated South Carolina Governor (and future U.S. Senator) Strom Thurmond as its presidential candidate in 1948.[78] President Dwight D. Eisenhower, though more cautious, also followed his predecessor's pattern—desegregating Washington, DC, overseeing the integration of blacks to the military, and promoting minority rights in federal contracts.[79]

A Herblock cartoon from March 1949 depicts a glum-looking President Harry S. Truman and "John Q. Public" inspecting worm-ridden apples representing Truman's Fair Deal policies such as civil rights and rent controls. The alliance of conservative southern Democrats and Republicans in Congress who successfully blocked many of Truman's initiatives is portrayed by the worm labeled "Coalition."

IMAGE COURTESY OF LIBRARY OF CONGRESS

Democratic governors met in February 1948 to protest President Harry S. Truman's civil rights reforms and the desegregation of the military. In this picture Senator J. Howard McGrath (seated) of Rhode Island, chairman of the Democratic National Committee, rejected the demands to dismantle President Truman's civil rights program presented by governors (from left to right) Ben T. Laney of Arkansas, R. Gregg Cherry of North Carolina, William P. Lane, Jr., of Maryland, J. Strom Thurmond of South Carolina, and B. H. Jester of Texas.

IMAGE COURTESY OF LIBRARY OF CONGRESS

The federal courts also carved out a judicial beachhead for civil rights activists. In *Smith v. Allwright* (321 U.S. 649, 1944), the U.S. Supreme Court, by an 8 to 1 vote, outlawed the white primary, which by excluding blacks from participating in the Democratic Party primary in southern states had effectively disfranchised them since the early 1900s. A decade later, the high court under Chief Justice Earl Warren handed down a unanimous decision in *Brown v. Board of Education* (347 U.S. 483, 1954), a case that tested the segregation of school facilities in Topeka, Kansas. *Brown* sparked a revolution in civil rights with its plainspoken ruling that separate was inherently unequal. "In the field of public education, separate but equal has no place," the Justices declared. Then, in the early 1960s, the Supreme Court rendered a string of decisions known as the "reapportionment cases" that fundamentally changed the voting landscape for African Americans by requiring that representation in the federal and state legislatures be based substantially on population. *Baker v. Carr* (369 U.S. 186, 1962) upheld the justiciability of lawsuits that challenged districts apportioned to enforce voting discrimination against minorities. *Gray v. Sanders* (372 U.S. 368, 1963) invalidated Georgia's county unit voting system, giving rise to the concept "one man, one vote." Two decisions in 1964, *Wesberry v. Sanders* (376 U.S. 1) and *Reynolds v. Sims* (377 U.S. 533), proved seminal. The court nullified Georgia's unequal congressional districts in *Wesberry* while validating the 14th Amendment's provision for equal representation for equal numbers of people in each district. In *Reynolds*, the Supreme Court solidified the "one man, one vote" concept in an 8 to 1 decision that expressly linked the 14th Amendment's equal protection clause to the guarantee that each citizen had equal weight in the election of state legislators.

However, Congress lagged behind the presidency, the judiciary, and, often, public sentiment during much of the postwar civil rights movement.[80] Southern conservatives still held the levers of power. Southerners continued to exert nearly untrammeled influence as committee chairmen (coinciding with the apex of congressional committee influence in the House and the Senate), in an era when Democrats controlled the House almost exclusively. In the 84th Congress (1955–1957), for instance, when Democrats regained the majority after a brief period of Republican control and embarked on 40 consecutive years of rule, 12 of the 19 House committees, including some of the most influential panels—Education and Labor, Interstate and Foreign Commerce, Rules, and Ways and Means—were chaired by southerners, who were largely unsympathetic to black civil rights.[81] The powerful coalition of southern Democrats and northern Republicans that had arisen during the late 1930s as a conservative bloc against the economic and social programs of the New Deal continued for various reasons to impede a broad array of social legislation.

Several factors prevented the few African Americans in Congress from playing prominent legislative roles in institutional efforts to pass the major acts of 1957, 1964, and 1965. Black Members were too scarce to alter institutional processes or form a consequential voting bloc. Until the fall 1964 elections, there were only five African Americans in Congress: Dawson, Powell, Diggs, Nix, and Hawkins. John Conyers joined the House in 1965 and Brooke entered the Senate in 1967. These new Members had a limited amount of influence, although Hawkins scored a major success as a freshman when he helped shape the Equal Employment Opportunity Commission as a member of Powell's Education and Labor Committee, and Brooke helped secure the housing anti-discrimination provision of the Civil Rights Act of

Sworn in to the United States Senate on January 3, 1967, Edward Brooke of Massachusetts (second from right) became the first black Senator since 1881. Vice President Hubert Humphrey administered the oath of office, while Senators Mike Mansfield of Montana, Everett Dirksen of Illinois, and Edward M. (Ted) Kennedy of Massachusetts observed.

1968 during his first term in the Senate. Yet while they were determined, energetic, and impassioned, there were too few African Americans in Congress to drive a policy agenda. Moreover, black Members themselves disagreed as to the best method to achieve civil rights advances, and individual legislative styles, conflicting loyalties (party versus activist agendas), and personality differences circumscribed their ability to craft a black issues agenda. Consequently, their uncoordinated and sporadic actions mitigated their potential effect. At key moments, some were excluded from the process or were inexplicably absent. Their symbolic leader, Powell, was too polarizing a figure for House leaders to accord him a highly visible role in the process. This perhaps explains why the Harlem Representative, despite his public passion for racial justice and his ability to deliver legislation through the Education and Labor Committee, was sometimes unusually detached from the legislative process.[82]

With few well-placed allies, civil rights initiatives faced an imposing gauntlet in a congressional committee system stacked with southern racial conservatives. Under the leadership of Chairman Emanuel Celler for most of this period, the House Judiciary Committee offered reformers a largely friendly and liberal forum. On the House Floor, a group of progressive liberals and moderate Republicans, including Celler, Clifford Case of New Jersey, Jacob Javits of New York, Hugh D. Scott of Pennsylvania, Frances Bolton of Ohio, and Helen Gahagan Douglas, emerged as civil rights advocates. Case (1954), Javits (1956), and Scott (1958) were elected to the Senate and would influence that chamber's civil rights agenda. But no matter how much support the rank-and-file membership provided, any measure that passed out of Judiciary was sent to the House Rules Committee, which directed legislation onto the floor and structured bills for debate. Chaired by arch segregationist Howard Smith of Virginia, this hugely influential panel became the killing ground for a long parade of civil rights proposals. Measures were watered down or were never considered. Smith often shuttered committee operations, retreating to his farm in Virginia's horse country to stall deliberations. When he explained one of his absences by noting that he needed to inspect a burned-down barn, Leo Allen of Illinois, the ranking Republican on the Rules Committee, remarked, "I knew the Judge was opposed to the civil rights bill. But I didn't think he would commit arson to beat it."[83]

The Senate's anti-majoritarian structure magnified the power of southern racial conservatives. In contrast to the rules of the House, which strictly limited Members' ability to speak on the floor, the Senate's long-standing tradition of allowing Members to speak without interruption played into the hands of obstructionists. The filibuster, a Senate practice that allowed a Senator or a group of Senators to prevent a vote on a bill, became the chief weapon of civil rights opponents. In this era, too, Senate rules were modified, raising the bar needed to achieve cloture, i.e., to end debate and move to a vote on legislation. From 1949 to 1959, cloture required the approval of two-thirds of the chamber's entire membership, rather than two-thirds of the Members who were present. Influential southern Senators held key positions in the upper chamber and, not surprisingly, were among the most skilled parliamentarians. Richard Russell of Georgia, a master of procedure, framed the opposition's defense on constitutional concerns about federal interference in states' issues, making him a more palatable figure than many of the Senate's earlier racial conservatives such as Mississippi's James K. Vardaman or Theodore Bilbo.[84] Russell attracted northern and western Republicans to his cause based on their opposition to the expansion of federal powers that would be necessary to enforce civil rights in

Howard Smith of Virginia, chairman of the House Rules Committee, routinely used his influential position to thwart civil rights legislation. Smith often shuttered committee operations by retreating to his rural farm to avoid deliberations on pending reform bills.

OIL ON CANVAS (DETAIL), VICTOR L'ALLIER, CA. 1974, COLLECTION OF U.S. HOUSE OF REPRESENTATIVES

Cloture:

A parliamentary procedure in the U.S. Senate requiring the approval of a super-majority of Senators to end debate on a pending proposal and bring legislation to final consideration and a vote.

As an NAACP activist in Montgomery, Alabama, Rosa Parks famously refused to give up her seat to a white rider on a public bus in 1955. Her act of civil disobedience galvanized the U.S. civil rights movement. Congress later honored Parks with a Congressional Gold Medal and by making her the first woman to lie in honor in the Capitol Rotunda after her death. Above, Parks rides on a desegregated bus.

IMAGE COURTESY OF LIBRARY OF CONGRESS

In September 1963, the African-American community in Birmingham, Alabama, mourned the deaths of four young girls killed by a bomb at the 16th Street Baptist Church. The city experienced such a dramatic rise in violence that it earned the nickname "Bombingham."

IMAGE COURTESY OF LIBRARY OF CONGRESS

the South. Mississippi's James Eastland, another procedural tactician, who presided over the Judiciary Committee beginning in March 1956, bragged that he had special pockets tailored into his suits where he stuffed bothersome civil rights bills. Between 1953 and 1965 more than 122 civil rights measures were referred to the Senate Judiciary Committee, but only one was reported back to the full Senate.[85]

Despite such official intransigence, the nonviolent civil rights movement—contrasting sharply with the vicious southern backlash against it—transformed public opinion. Driven increasingly by external events in the mid-1950s—the *Brown v. Board of Education* decision and the rise of Martin Luther King, Jr.'s Southern Christian Leadership Conference (SCLC)—support for the passage of major civil rights legislation grew in Congress. In Montgomery, Alabama, local activists led by King (then a 27-year-old Baptist preacher), had launched a boycott against the city's segregated bus system. The protest began after the arrest of Rosa Parks, a seamstress and a member of the NAACP who defied local ordinances in December 1955 by refusing to yield her seat on the bus to a white man and move to the rear of the vehicle.[86] The year-long—and, ultimately, successful—boycott forged the SCLC, brought national attention to the struggle, and launched King to the forefront of a grass-roots, nonviolent humanitarian protest movement that, within a decade, profoundly changed American life.

Racial violence in the South, which amounted to domestic terrorism against blacks, continued into the middle of the 20th century and powerfully shaped public opinion. Though more sporadic than before, beatings, cross burnings, lynchings, and myriad other forms of white-on-black intimidation went largely unpunished. Nearly 200 African Americans are thought to have been lynched between 1929 and 1964, but that figure likely underrepresents the actual number.[87] In August 1955, a particularly gruesome killing galvanized activists and shocked a largely complacent nation. Emmett Till, a 14-year-old from Chicago who was visiting family in Mississippi, was shot in the head, and his lifeless body was dumped off a bridge, for the alleged "crime" of whistling at a white woman. Determined to expose the brutality of the act, his mother allowed the national press to photograph the boy's remains, and thousands of mourners streamed past the open casket.

Charles Diggs's visible role in the wake of the Till lynching "catapulted" him into the "national spotlight."[88] At considerable personal risk, Diggs accompanied Till's mother to the September 1955 trial at which the two accused murderers were acquitted in kangaroo court proceedings. Diggs's presence in Mississippi demonstrated solidarity with (and hope for) many local African Americans. A black reporter covering the trial recalled that Diggs "made a difference down there . . . people lined up to see him. They had never seen a black member of Congress. Blacks came by the truckloads. Never before had a member of Congress put his life on the line protecting the constitutional rights of blacks."[89] Diggs, who earlier had pushed for a U.S. Justice Department probe of the defrauding of black Mississippi voters, proposed to unseat the Members of the Mississippi delegation to the U.S. House on the grounds that they were elected by only a fraction of the state's voters.[90] Diggs's performance contrasted sharply with that of William Dawson, who represented the Chicago district where Till's mother lived. In an open 1956 letter to Dawson, the NAACP questioned his failure to comment publicly on the Till lynching. Expressing further disappointment with Dawson's support for reform legislation as a member of the Democratic committee writing the civil rights plank for the national party, the

NAACP denounced him for "silence, compromise, and meaningless moderation" on civil rights matters.[91]

Adam Clayton Powell, dubbed "Mr. Civil Rights," garnered national headlines during the 1940s and 1950s for his "Powell Amendment," a rider prohibiting federal funds for institutions that promoted or endorsed segregation. Powell attached his amendment to a variety of legislative measures, beginning with a school lunch program bill that passed the House on June 4, 1946. "From then on I was to use this important weapon with success," Powell recalled, "to bring about opportunities for the good of man and to stop those efforts that would harm democracy's progress forward." Beginning in 1955, Powell vowed to attach his rider to all education bills, starting with appropriations for school construction.[92] His actions riled southern racial conservatives and stirred unease among otherwise liberal allies concerned that the amendment jeopardized social legislation.

Southern defiance, on display on Capitol Hill, crystallized in a bold proclamation conceived by Senators Russell, Strom Thurmond of South Carolina, and Harry Flood Byrd, Sr., of Virginia. Titled the "Declaration of Constitutional Principles" and known colloquially as the Southern Manifesto, it attacked the Supreme Court's *Brown* decision, accusing the Justices of abusing judicial power and trespassing upon states' rights. Signed on March 12, 1956, by 82 Representatives and 19 Senators (roughly one-fifth of Congress), it urged southerners to exhaust all "lawful means" in the effort to resist the "chaos and confusion" that would result from school desegregation.

Civil Rights Act of 1957

In 1956, partly at the initiative of outside advocacy groups such as the NAACP, proposals by Eisenhower's Justice Department under the leadership of Attorney General Herbert Brownell, and the growing presidential ambitions of Senate Majority

In August 1955, a Chicago teenager, Emmett Till, was brutally murdered in Mississippi while visiting family. Till was lynched for the alleged "crime" of allegedly whistling at a white woman. The episode riveted national attention on violence against blacks in the South. Across the nation, groups like the Metropolitan Community Church of Chicago, pictured here, signed petitions to President Dwight D. Eisenhower condemning the violence.

IMAGE COURTESY OF LIBRARY OF CONGRESS

On October 11, 1956, Adam Clayton Powell, Jr., announced to reporters his decision to support incumbent Republican President Dwight D. Eisenhower. Known as a political maverick, Powell had backed Democratic candidate Adlai Stevenson in 1952, but broke with Stevenson in 1956 because of his ambivalent position on civil rights. Powell noted Eisenhower's "great contribution in the civil rights field."

IMAGE COURTESY OF NATIONAL PARK SERVICE, PROVIDED BY DWIGHT DAVID EISENHOWER PRESIDENTIAL LIBRARY

African-American demonstrators occupied a lunch counter after being refused service in Nashville, Tennessee, in 1960. Sit-ins like this one took a toll on segregated businesses across the South. Many establishments relented and ended segregation practices because of the ensuing loss of business.

IMAGE COURTESY OF LIBRARY OF CONGRESS

House Speaker Sam Rayburn of Texas spearheaded the successful effort in 1961 to expand the membership of the House Rules Committee. Rayburn's actions undercut the power of southern conservatives, including Rules Committee Chairman Howard Smith of Virginia.

OIL ON CANVAS, DOUGLAS CHANDOR, 1941, COLLECTION OF U.S. HOUSE OF REPRESENTATIVES

Leader Lyndon B. Johnson, a civil rights bill began to move through Congress. Southern opponents such as Senators Russell and Eastland, realizing that some kind of legislation was imminent, slowed and weakened reform through the amendment process. The House passed the measure by a wide margin, 279 to 97, though southern opponents managed to excise voting protections from the original language. Adam Clayton Powell and Charles Diggs argued passionately on the House Floor for a strong bill. Powell particularly aimed at southern amendments that preserved trials by local juries because all-white juries (since blacks were excluded from the voting process, they were also barred from jury duty) ensured easy acquittals for white defendants accused of crimes against blacks. "This is an hour for great moral stamina," Powell told colleagues. "America stands on trial today before the world and communism must succeed if democracy fails. . . . Speak no more concerning the bombed and burned and gutted churches behind the Iron Curtain when here in America behind our 'color curtain' we have bombed and burned churches and the confessed perpetrators of these crimes go free because of trial by jury."[93] In the Senate, Paul H. Douglas of Illinois and Minority Leader William F. Knowland of California circumvented Eastland's Judiciary Committee and got the bill onto the floor for debate. Lyndon Johnson played a crucial role, too, discouraging an organized southern filibuster while forging a compromise that allayed southern concern about the bill's jury and trial provisions.[94] On August 29 the Senate approved the Civil Rights Act of 1957 (P.L. 85-315) by a vote of 60 to 15.

The resulting law, signed by President Eisenhower in early September 1957, was the first major civil rights measure passed since 1875. The act established the U.S. Commission on Civil Rights (CCR) for two years and created a civil rights division in the Justice Department, but its powers to enforce voting laws and punish the disfranchisement of black voters were feeble, as the commission noted in 1959. A year later, the Civil Rights Act of 1960 (P.L. 86-449)—again significantly weakened by southern opponents—extended the life of the CCR and stipulated that voting and registration records in federal elections must be preserved. However, southerners managed to strike a far-reaching provision to send registrars into southern states to oversee voter enrollment.

Though southern Members were heartened by these successes, consequential internal congressional reforms promised to end obstructionism. In 1961, Speaker Sam Rayburn of Texas challenged Chairman Howard Smith directly by proposing to expand the Rules Committee by adding three more Members to the roster, a move that was intended to break Smith's stranglehold over social legislation. Rayburn recruited a group of roughly two dozen northern Republicans who supported the reform and declared their intention to "repudiate" a GOP alliance with southern Democrats "to attempt to narrow the base of our party, to dull its conscience, to transform it into a negative weapon of obstruction."[95] The forces of reform prevailed by a margin of 217 to 212. The support of moderate Republicans presaged the development of a coalition that would undercut the power of southern racial conservatives and pass sweeping civil rights laws.

Civil Rights Act of 1964

Pressure for change, as it did throughout the Second Reconstruction, came from outside the institution. By 1963, the need for a major civil rights bill weighed heavily on Congress and the John F. Kennedy administration. Protests at lunch counters in Greensboro, North Carolina, in 1960 were followed in 1961 by attempts to desegregate interstate buses by the Freedom Riders, who were arrested in Jackson, Mississippi. In April 1963, Martin Luther King, Jr., led a large protest in Birmingham, Alabama, that was greeted with brutality. Birmingham Police Commissioner Eugene (Bull) Connor unleashed police dogs, and high-powered hoses on protesters. The images coming out of the Deep South horrified Americans from all walks of life. In August 1963, King and other civil rights leaders organized the largest-ever march on Washington, DC. Addressing hundreds of thousands of supporters from the steps of the Lincoln Memorial, the world-renowned leader of a movement that rivaled that of his model, Mahatma Gandhi, delivered his famous "I Have a Dream" speech.

A reluctant Kennedy administration began coordinating with congressional allies to pass a significant reform bill. Freshman Representative Gus Hawkins observed in May 1963 that the federal government had a special responsibility to ensure that federal dollars did not underwrite segregation practices in schools, facilities for vocational education, libraries, and other municipal entities, saying, "those who dip their hands in the public treasury should not object if a little democracy sticks to their fingers." Otherwise "do we not harm our own fiscal integrity, and allow room in our conduct for other abuses of public funds?"[96] After Kennedy's assassination in November 1963, his successor, Lyndon B. Johnson, invoked the slain President's memory to prod reluctant legislators to produce a civil rights measure.

In the House, a bipartisan bill supported by Judiciary Chairman Celler and Republican William McCulloch of Ohio worked its way to passage. McCulloch and Celler forged a coalition of moderate Republicans and northern Democrats while deflecting southern amendments determined to cripple the bill. Standing in the well of the House defending his controversial amendment and the larger civil rights bill, Representative Powell described the legislation as "a great moral issue . . . what we are doing [today] is a part of an act of God."[97] On February 10, 1964, the House, voting 290 to 130, approved the Civil Rights Act of 1964; 138 Republicans helped pass the bill. In scope and effect, the act was among the most far-reaching pieces of legislation in U.S. history. It contained sections prohibiting discrimination in public accommodations (Title II); state and municipal facilities, including schools (Titles III and IV); and—incorporating the Powell Amendment—in any program receiving federal aid (Title V). The act also prohibited discrimination in hiring and employment, creating the Equal Employment Opportunity Commission (EEOC) to investigate workplace discrimination (Title VII).[98]

Having passed the House, the act faced its biggest hurdle in the Senate. President Johnson and Senate Majority Leader Mike Mansfield of Montana tapped Hubert Humphrey of Minnesota to build Senate support for the measure and fend off the efforts of a determined southern minority to stall it. One historian notes that Humphrey's assignment amounted to an "audition for the role of Johnson's running mate in the fall presidential election."[99] Humphrey, joined by Republican Thomas Kuchel of California, performed brilliantly, lining up the support of influential Minority Leader Everett Dirksen of Illinois. By allaying Dirksen's unease about the enforcement powers of the EEOC, civil rights proponents then co-opted the support of a large group of midwestern Republicans who followed Dirksen's lead.[100] On June 10, 1964, for the first time in its history, the Senate invoked cloture on a civil rights bill (by a vote of 71 to 29), thus cutting off debate and ending a 75-day filibuster—the longest in the chamber's history. On June 19, 1964, 46 Democrats

In 1963, Birmingham, Alabama, became the focal point of the civil rights movement. Throughout the spring and summer, protesters challenged segregation practices. Images such as this one, showing Birmingham firefighters turning powerful hoses on nonviolent protesters, convinced many average Americans of the need to end Jim Crow in the South.

IMAGE COURTESY OF AP/ WIDE WORLD PHOTOS

As the finale to the massive August 28, 1963, March on Washington, Martin Luther King, Jr. gave his famous "I Have a Dream" speech on the steps of the Lincoln Memorial. This photograph showed the view from over the shoulder of the Abraham Lincoln statue while marchers gathered along the length of the Reflecting Pool.

IMAGE COURTESY OF LIBRARY OF CONGRESS

On July 2, 1964, President Lyndon B. Johnson signed the Civil Rights Act of 1964 into law. Those gathered behind President Johnson at the bill signing included civil rights leader Martin Luther King, Jr., and future District of Columbia Delegate Walter Fauntroy. The Civil Rights Act of 1964 was a landmark piece of legislation, prohibiting segregation in public accommodations, facilities, and schools, and outlawing discrimination in federally funded projects.

As chairman of the House Judiciary Committee, Emanuel Celler of New York was a prime mover behind the passage of the Civil Rights Act of 1964.

and 27 Republicans joined forces to approve the Civil Rights Act of 1964, 73 to 27. President Johnson signed the bill (P.L. 88-352) into law on July 2, 1964.

Voting Rights Act of 1965

Passage of the Civil Rights Act of 1964 dealt the deathblow to southern congressional opposition. Momentum for tougher voting rights legislation—expanding on the provisions of Section I of the 1964 act—built rapidly because of President Johnson's continued determination and unfolding civil rights protests. On March 7, 1965, marchers led by future U.S. Representative John R. Lewis of Georgia were savagely beaten at the foot of the Edmund Pettus Bridge in Selma, Alabama. Many of the protestors were kneeling in prayer when state troopers clubbed and gassed them on what would later be known as "Bloody Sunday." Television cameras captured the onslaught and beamed images into the homes of millions of Americans. As with the brutality in Birmingham, public reaction was swift and, if possible, even more powerful. "The images were stunning—scene after scene of policemen on foot and horseback beating defenseless American citizens," Lewis wrote years later. "This was a face-off in the most vivid terms between a dignified, composed, completely nonviolent multitude of silent protestors and the truly malevolent force of a heavily armed, hateful battalion of troopers. The sight of them rolling over us like human tanks was something that had never been seen before."[101]

After President Johnson addressed a Joint Session of Congress to speak about the events in Selma, legislative action was swift. A bill moved through both chambers that suspended the use of literacy tests for a five-year period and provided for sending federal poll watchers and voting registrars to states with persistent patterns of voting discrimination. It required Justice Department pre-clearance of any change to election statutes. Finally, the bill made obstructing an individual's right to vote a federal crime. On May 26, 1965, the Senate passed the Voting Rights Act by a vote of 77 to 19. Among the African-American Members who spoke on behalf of the bill on the House Floor was freshman John Conyers, Jr. Joined by Representatives Diggs, Hawkins, and Powell, Conyers had visited

Selma in February 1965 as part of a 15-Member congressional delegation that investigated voting discrimination.[102] The experience convinced him that there was "no alternative but to have the federal Government take a much more positive and specific role in guaranteeing the right to register and vote in all elections . . . surely this Government cannot relax if even one single American is arbitrarily denied that most basic right of all in a democracy—the right to vote."[103] The House passed the act by a vote of 333 to 85 on July 9, 1965. An amended conference report passed both chambers by wide margins and President Johnson signed the Voting Rights Act of 1965 (P.L. 89-110) into law on August 6, 1965.[104]

The measure dramatically increased voter registration in the short term. By 1969, 60 percent of all southern blacks were registered. Predictably, the bill's impact was most dramatic in the Deep South. In Mississippi, for instance, where less than 7 percent of African Americans qualified to vote in 1964, 59 percent were on voter rolls by 1968.[105] By 1975, approximately 1.5 million African Americans had registered to vote in the South.[106]

Coupled with the "one man, one vote" standard, which set off a round of court-ordered redistricting, the Voting Rights Act of 1965 reshaped the electoral landscape for African Americans. In southern states, particularly in cities such as Atlanta, Houston, and Memphis, the creation of districts with a majority of African-American constituents propelled greater numbers of African Americans into Congress by the early 1970s. In northern urban areas, too, the growing influence of black voters reshaped Congress. Blacks constituted a growing percentage of the population of major U.S. cities (20 percent in 1970 versus 12 percent in 1950), partly because in the 1960s whites left the cities in droves for the suburbs.[107] In 1968, Louis Stokes (Cleveland), Bill Clay (St. Louis), and Shirley Chisholm (Brooklyn) were elected to Congress from redrawn majority-black districts in which white incumbents chose not to run.[108] By 1971, the number of African-American Members in the House was more than double the number who had served in 1965.

Baton-wielding Alabama state troopers waded into a crowd of peaceful civil rights demonstrators led by the Student Nonviolent Coordinating Committee Chairman John Lewis (on ground left center, in light coat) on March 7, 1965, in Selma, Alabama. Known later as "Bloody Sunday," images of the violent event shocked millions of Americans from all walks of life and built momentum for the Voting Rights Act of 1965.

IMAGE COURTESY OF LIBRARY OF CONGRESS

Black Panthers (or Black Panther Party for Self-Defense):

An organization formed in 1966 by Huey Newton and Bobby Seale to monitor police activity and brutality against residents in Oakland, California. In contrast to the southern civil rights movement's advocacy of nonviolent resistance, the Black Panthers promoted local self-help, community activism, and armed defense against the use of excessive force by police. The Black Panthers also called for the restructuring of American society to ensure social, political, and economic equality for all races.

Civil Rights Act of 1968

The era's final major piece of civil rights legislation reflected the changing emphasis of the civil rights movement itself: Having secured a measure of political rights, black leaders now emphasized the importance of equal economic and educational opportunity. Congressional action in this area was measured; the national mood and major events had begun to turn against reform. The ambitious agenda of federal programs known as the Great Society had begun to wane. Initiated by President Johnson in the mid-1960s, these programs were in many ways conceived of as an extension of New Deal reforms. Great Society legislation marked the zenith of federal activism—addressing civil rights, urban development, the environment, health care, education, housing, consumer protection, and poverty. With Democratic majorities in both houses of Congress, the administration won the enactment of a number of far-reaching programs, among them several that exist today, such as Medicare, which provides health coverage for the elderly, and Medicaid, which provides the poor with access to hospitalization, optional medical insurance, and other health care benefits.[109]

But the cost of the deepening U.S. military commitment in Vietnam rapidly bled dry Great Society programs that, in part, addressed concerns about economic equality raised by black leaders. Moreover, middle-class whites in northern and western states who had empathized with the nonviolent protests of southern blacks were far more skeptical of the civil rights militants who were bent on bringing the movement to their doorsteps, typified by Stokely Carmichael, the Black Panthers, and the Black Power movement. Major urban rioting, particularly the devastating 1965 riot in Watts, Los Angeles (in Representative Gus Hawkins's district) turned mainstream white opinion even further from the cause. Widespread rioting in April 1968 after the assassination of Martin Luther King, Jr.—federal troops were deployed even in Washington, DC—reinforced white alienation. Nevertheless, in early March 1968, the Senate approved the Civil Rights Act of 1968 by a 71 to 20 vote. The measure outlawed discrimination in the sale and rental of roughly 80 percent of U.S. housing (the proportion handled by agents and brokers) by 1970 and meted out federal punishment to persons engaged in interstate activities to foment or participate in riots. The bill also extended constitutional rights to Native Americans. Days after King's murder in Memphis, Tennessee, the House followed the Senate's lead by a vote of 250 to 172.

CRAFTING AN INSTITUTIONAL IDENTITY

Confronting Racism

Across the decades, African-American Members' encounters with institutional racism and segregation on Capitol Hill, though gradually declining in intensity, provided a common and uniting experience. In the years leading up to the Depression and World War II, Washington had the feel of a slow, sleepy, southern town in contrast to the bustle and cultural multiplicities of northern metropolitan cities like New York, Boston, and Chicago. Washington also embraced southern segregationist practices. Southbound travelers embarking on journeys at the Union Station terminal boarded segregated train cars. Formal as well as informal racial codes also existed in the city's restaurants, department stores, movie theaters, and boarding houses well into the 1950s. Washington's legion of federal civil servants were separated according to race; until the eve of World War II, applicants for federal jobs were required to submit a personal photograph, providing a *de facto* method of racial discrimination. Even after the Eisenhower administration officially desegregated the capital city, blacks and whites remained separate, living in distinct neighborhoods, attending separate churches, and enrolling in separate schools.[110]

Congress itself practiced latent and blatant institutional racism, ranging from the denial of prominent committee assignments and any real voice in the leadership to segregated barbershops and dining facilities and the open disparagement of black Members by their colleagues. For instance, in 1929 southern Members objected to being sworn in on the House Floor with Representative De Priest, occupying an office next to his, or serving on a committee with him.[111] Capitol Hill associations and social clubs with congressional ties were uneasy welcoming black Members or their families. The Congressional Club—an organization chartered in the early 1900s initially for spouses and daughters of Representatives and Senators, Supreme Court Justices, and Cabinet members—considered a bylaw that would deny membership to De Priest's wife, Jessie, but rejected it due to the scrutiny of the national press.[112]

Despite the segregation prevalent on Capitol Hill during this era, growing numbers of African Americans were employed there. In 1949, Alice Dunnigan of the Associated Negro Press—one of the first black journalists credentialed to work in both the Senate and the House press galleries—wrote a four-part series titled "A Visit to the Nation's Capitol" that appeared in the Tuskegee Institute's *Service* magazine. Dunnigan interviewed dozens of African Americans, some of whom had been employed on Capitol Hill for three decades or more in a variety of capacities: barber, messenger, library assistant, doorkeeper, guard, head waiter, chef, filing clerk, driver, carpenter, secretary, guard, and committee clerk. According to Dunnigan, one-third of the 1,500 persons employed by the Office of the Architect of the Capitol in 1949 were African Americans. Among the individuals Dunnigan interviewed were Jesse Nichols, a document clerk and librarian who was one of the first blacks to hold a clerical position in the Senate.[113] Dunnigan also chronicled the story of Christine Ray Davis, the first African-American chief clerk of a

In 1929, Jessie De Priest, the wife of Representative Oscar De Priest of Illinois, received an invitation to a tea hosted by First Lady Lou Hoover. The invitation roiled southern Members of Congress and their wives. The Mississippi state legislature passed a resolution imploring the Herbert Hoover administration to give "careful and thoughtful consideration to the necessity of the preservation of the racial integrity of the white race." Mrs. De Priest attended a specially scheduled tea with Lou Hoover, but the episode underscored pervasive segregation practices in the U.S.

IMAGE COURTESY OF SCURLOCK STUDIO RECORDS, ARCHIVES CENTER, NATIONAL MUSEUM OF AMERICAN HISTORY, SMITHSONIAN INSTITUTION

Representative William L. Dawson of Illinois chaired the Committee on Expenditures in the Executive Departments, later Government Operations, beginning in the 81st Congress (1949–1951). Dawson was the first African American to chair a House standing committee.

IMAGE COURTESY OF NATIONAL ARCHIVES AND RECORDS ADMINISTRATION

congressional committee—a position she assumed in 1949 when William Dawson became chairman of the House Committee on Expenditures in the Executive Department. As chief clerk, Davis was the highest-paid black woman in the federal government and, Dunnigan noted, the first African-American congressional aide with unrestricted access to the House Floor.[114]

Speaking Out Against Segregation

Black Members of Congress facing segregation were left with two alternatives that were less than ideal: meet institutional segregation frontally to publicize the folly of racist practices, or minimize its significance by gaining positions of influence, thereby ameliorating segregation from within the institution. Individuals' personalities often governed that choice, though just as often, purposeful legislative calculations factored into black Members' response to racism in the House and the Senate. There was little middle ground. Those who confronted racism openly suffered the wrath of white supremacists, and those perceived as less than zealous in the pursuit of civil rights were scorned by black activists.

Oscar De Priest chose to combat segregation in Congress directly by addressing the issue on the House Floor and by using the power of the press.[115] His arrival on Capitol Hill was met with outright contempt. One well-publicized episode involved an invitation to his wife, Jessie, to a traditional White House tea hosted by First Lady Lou Henry Hoover. Southern legislators howled in indignation, and the Mississippi legislature passed a resolution calling on President Herbert Hoover to give "careful and thoughtful consideration to the necessity of racial preservation of the racial integrity of the white race," because "such an exhibition of social equality at the White House tends to destroy such racial integrity."[116] The First Lady divided the party into sessions, carefully selecting invitees to Jessie De Priest's group and providing the wives of southern Members an alternative time to attend. Undeterred, Jessie De Priest attended the event while her husband dismissed critics as "cowards."

De Priest became an advocate for desegregation because of the environment he encountered, not because of his political background. During a tough re-election bid in 1934, his anti-segregationist rhetoric increased as Election Day approached. Initially inclined to win over his House colleagues by his example as a Member, he later declared, "but if securing their respect means sacrificing my race, that respect I do not seek any longer." De Priest continued, "I am sorry I have to devote my time trying to watch the needs of the American Negro. I wish I could devote my time, like you gentlemen devote your time, trying to watch the interests of all the American people instead of just 12,000,000 of them."[117] In 1934, the Illinois Representative waged a public campaign to stop segregation in the House Restaurant. "If we allow segregation and the denial of constitutional rights under the Dome of the Capitol, where in God's name will we get them?" De Priest demanded. Though De Priest shamed the House into creating a special investigatory committee, the majority of its members were Democrats who acceded to the wishes of southern racial conservatives by refusing to recommend reforms.[118] De Priest also protested efforts to segregate other House facilities, such as the barbershop, and pressured Speaker Henry T. Rainey of Illinois to permit a black minister to offer an opening session prayer in the House.[119]

Despite his raw personal courage, De Priest failed to achieve any lasting reform—a setback that made him look ineffective in the eyes of his Chicago-area constituents and left him vulnerable to political attack. His lack of legislative influence also diminished his national status as a hero among African Americans. Some even implied that he lacked familiarity with the larger black community and the resolve to pursue and achieve substantive legislative victories. Even after De Priest had begun advocating federal pensions for former slaves, the African-American *Atlanta Daily World* complained he was "conspicuous by his silence on important questions. As a legislator, as a statesman, as a student of those things affecting the Negro's welfare, he has been a grand and glorious flop."[120]

The role of agitator and public advocate for civil rights suited Adam Clayton Powell. Charismatic, flashy, and photogenic, Powell developed a national following based as much on his style as on his legislative substance. In an era in which the press proved exceedingly forgiving of politicians' personal eccentricities, Powell stood out: driving a blue Jaguar, dressing impeccably, smoking cigars, and enjoying the company of beautiful women. He was as much at home on the French Riviera as he was in Harlem. "For years his life was so flamboyant that it verged on caricature, yet he got away with it, not only politically but somehow esthetically," noted one observer. While others advocated Black Power, Powell "stood for Black Pleasure."[121]

Substantively, Powell served as a prototype of the new, activist African-American politician. His loyal Harlem constituency provided a solid base of support that allowed him to pursue issues affecting the black community nationwide. Some anticipated his arrival on Capitol Hill, others dreaded it. But no one doubted it would be eventful. Speaker Sam Rayburn, who often counseled new Members on the folkways of the institution, called Powell into his office and lectured him from behind his desk. "Adam, everybody down here expects you to come with a bomb in both hands. Now don't do that, Adam. . . . Just see how things operate here. Take your time. Freshmen members of Congress are not supposed to be heard and not even to be seen too much. There are a lot of good men around here. Listen to what they have to say, drink it all in, get reelected a few more times, and then start moving. But for God's sake, Adam, don't throw those bombs." Powell replied, "Mr. Speaker, I've got a bomb in each hand, and I'm going to throw them right away." Rayburn burst into jovial laughter, and according to Powell, the exchange marked the beginning of a long friendship.[122]

On multiple fronts, Powell waged a direct, combative campaign against segregation on Capitol Hill. He helped to desegregate the House Press Gallery and to make available more opportunities for black reporters. He repeatedly challenged House Restaurant policy by bringing black staffers and guests to the segregated dining room. He also publicly confronted some of the most ardent segregationists in the House. His long-standing feud with Representative John E. Rankin often spilled out onto the House Floor. At one point Powell said he planned "to baptize Rankin or drown him." Rankin, who called Powell's election to the House a "disgrace," refused to sit near him on the floor, but Powell stalked Rankin and sat as close to him as possible (forcing him one day to move five times).[123] Powell used his personal charisma calculatingly, providing the black community with an unflinching, activist political hero. "I've always got my mouth open, sometimes my foot is in it, but it is always open," Powell said. "It serves a purpose; it digs at the white man's conscience."[124] But it also incurred substantive legislative costs. Whereas Powell's flamboyance and public refusals to brook racist policies won him many supporters, they also limited his effectiveness as a legislator; a growing contingent of politicians found it impossible to work with such a militant Member.

In 1967, cartoonist Gib Crockett depicted the growing controversy in Congress over Adam Clayton Powell, Jr. In January 1967, the House of Representatives removed Powell from his position as Chairman of the Committee on Education and Labor and refused to seat the New York Representative in the 90th Congress (1967–1969). The House approved a measure to deny Powell his seat for five weeks while a nine-member bipartisan special committee examined ethics charges against him. After the special committee recommended several punishments for Powell, including censure, the House voted 307 to 116 to exclude him from the 90th Congress.

IMAGE COURTESY OF LIBRARY OF CONGRESS

Serving 14 terms in the House of Representatives, Augustus (Gus) Hawkins of California chaired four committees: the Committee on House Administration, Committee on Education and Labor, Joint Committee on Printing, and Joint Committee on Library.

COLLECTION OF U.S. HOUSE
OF REPRESENTATIVES

Taking note of the experiences of Members such as De Priest and Powell, other black Members of Congress purposefully pursued an institutionalist strategy. But by seeking to advance within the institutional power structure or to remain loyal to the party and/or the local political machine that propelled them into office, they often attracted the enmity of fellow blacks and civil rights advocates who believed they were subordinating the interests of the black community for their own aggrandizement. Representative Arthur Mitchell, the first black Democrat elected to Congress, chose to work within the power structure of the Democrat-controlled House. During his four terms in Congress, the Chicago Representative worked closely with many white colleagues, adopting the philosophy of patient cooperation and accommodation that was advocated by his mentor, Booker T. Washington, whom Mitchell hoped to honor by establishing a national shrine.[125] Mitchell watched the futile battle of his predecessor, De Priest, against segregationist practices in the Capitol and calculated another course. In a pointed remark aimed at De Priest, Mitchell informed constituents shortly after his first election, "I think the people are tired of bombast, ballyhoo, and noise, where we should have constructive thought, honest action and real statesmanship."[126] But Mitchell's reluctance to push issues important to the African-American community soon disappointed black civil rights activists. Particularly galling to the black press and the NAACP were his apparent lack of interest in an assignment on the District of Columbia Committee—with oversight of the capital and its large black population—and his refusal to address the poor treatment of black journalists covering Capitol Hill.[127] Yet, over time and after taking stock of the depth of segregationist sentiment in the House, Mitchell became more committed to civil rights reform, particularly legislation to curb discrimination in the federal civil service.

Other black Representatives drew similar criticism. The NAACP excoriated William Dawson, Mitchell's successor, arguing that he did not adequately support reforms. Dawson's loyalty to the Daley political machine in Chicago created constant tension with his black House colleagues because he rarely took a public stance regarding race relations. But Dawson's association with Daley accorded him tangible power in the House. For these reasons, his career often is juxtaposed with that of Powell's in analyses of the legislative styles and strategies of black Members of Congress.[128] Unlike Dawson, Powell forswore machine politics, promising to "never be a machine man."[129] The Harlem Representative typically backed Democratic legislation and leaders, but his primary allegiance resided with his constituents and the advancement of African-American rights, not with the party.[130]

Powell's style was the exception rather than the rule. Ideological approaches and legislative strategies disposed most black Members of Congress from this era to a less confrontational style. Robert Nix rebuffed activist critics who demanded he become more vocal on race issues, suggesting that his role as an insider who rose to chair a full committee produced more tangible results for blacks. "I've seen people come into this Congress feeling it was incumbent upon them to give everybody hell, talking about the wrongs and fancied wrongs that happen every day," Nix observed. "They didn't correct a damn thing. . . . The legislation they sought to present to the House later on received little interest from any source."[131] Los Angeles Representative Gus Hawkins, who eventually chaired two full House committees, was highly successful at exerting insider influence but rarely sought the limelight. Reacting to criticism that he should do more to publicize the cause of racial equality, Hawkins

said, "I've always felt, why yell if you can get the same result by being mild? . . .
The loudmouths are well known, but they're not very effective."[132] Hawkins never
deviated from his conviction that the best way to help African Americans and other
minorities was to focus on economic issues rather than on race.[133]

Senator Brooke, who opposed the glorification of black militants, also
conformed easily to the Senate traditions that rewarded moderation and
collegiality.[134] By the late 1960s, many African-American politicians found
themselves in an uncomfortable middle ground between an entrenched and
unrepentant white power structure and younger, assertive black activists who
promoted the Black Power movement, which appealed to racial pride and called
for the creation of distinctive cultural and political organizations.[135] Adopting the
approach that blacks "must win allies, not conquer adversaries," Brooke drew harsh
criticism from more-radical black politicians, who advocated confrontational action
as an answer to racial discrimination.[136] Brooke blamed the press for focusing too
much attention on radical activists, arguing that "the emphasis should be placed
on the great, great majority of people in the Negro community who merely want
improved conditions, who want government to respond responsibly to their needs
and who at the same time recognize the need to help themselves."[137]

Of this group of contemporaries, Charles Diggs emerged as a unique figure,
able to blend Powell's activism with the institutional effectiveness of other well-
placed cohorts. Like Powell, Representative Diggs often sought out the limelight
to publicize civil rights issues, for instance, when he visited Selma, Alabama, and
interviewed local blacks in the spring of 1965. But he possessed a measure of
pragmatism Powell sometimes lacked. In addition to crafting a foreign policy agenda
for future generations of black Members, Diggs was instrumental as chairman of the
District of Columbia Committee in establishing home rule for the nation's capital
and in addressing the needs of its majority-black population. Diggs also displayed
organizational prowess by creating in 1969 the Democratic Select Committee
(DSC), a group of black Members who championed legislation important to African
Americans nationally and a precursor to the Congressional Black Caucus.

To a considerable degree, African-American Members' approaches to racial issues
on Capitol Hill were shaped by their legislative styles. Some, like Powell, preferred
the "show horse" legislative style, using the press to publicize an issue or a legislative
agenda to rally attention and build public support. Others, such as Dawson and
Hawkins, exemplified the low-key "work horse" style, focusing on committee
work, policy minutiae, and/or parliamentary procedure to cultivate their legislative
agendas.[138] These styles were self-reinforcing and usually reflected Members' status
within the organization. For instance, an insider often adopted the work horse style,
whereas the show horse style offered a remedy for those outside the institutional
circles of power and influence, who lacked the ability to introduce legislative
initiatives through normal channels.

CONCLUSION

Many of the changes that occurred during the long generation from 1929
until 1970—brought about by social movements, legal advances, and institutional
evolution—profoundly altered the landscape on Capitol Hill for the post–civil
rights generation of African-American Members. Compared with their 20th-
century predecessors, black Members who came to Capitol Hill in the 1970s would

*A 13-term Representative, Charles Diggs of
Michigan was the first black Representative
to serve on the Committee on Foreign
Affairs and was a leading critic of
apartheid in South Africa.*

COLLECTION OF U.S. HOUSE
OF REPRESENTATIVES

*First elected in 1968, Louis Stokes
of Ohio chaired two committees during
his 15 terms in Congress, the Permanent
Select Committee on Intelligence
and the Committee on Standards
of Official Conduct. Stokes also led
the Select Committee on Assassinations
and was chairman of a key
Appropriations subcommittee.*

COLLECTION OF U.S. HOUSE
OF REPRESENTATIVES

This 1965 picture of civil rights leaders includes, from left to right, future U.S. Representative Andrew Young, then-Representative William Fitts Ryan of New York, James Farmer, and future U.S. Representative John Lewis. Farmer lost a 1968 House race to Shirley Chisholm in a newly created, majority-black district in Brooklyn, New York.

Image courtesy of Library of Congress

encounter an institution that was more accessible and more favorable to their legislative interests. Court-ordered redistricting in the wake of the Supreme Court's enunciation of the "one man, one vote" principle, coupled with the Voting Rights Act of 1965, dramatically expanded the rolls of black voters and led to the creation of majority-black districts, paving the way for an increase in the number of blacks in Congress. Until 1968, men had represented the black community almost exclusively, but in the decade after Shirley Chisholm's election, black women (including some from the South and the West) won election to Congress, portending significant changes in the gender ratio of African Americans in Congress. In 1970, George Collins became the first African American in the 20th century elected to a district that was not majority-black (it would subsequently become majority-black after redistricting). During the next decade this trend accelerated, as districts where blacks did not constitute a majority elected more black Members to the House, including Parren Mitchell of Maryland, Ronald Dellums of California, and Andrew Young of Georgia.[139] Long-simmering interest in institutional reform also benefited these newcomers as reformers sought to deprive entrenched committee chairmen of their power and distribute it more evenly among the rank and file. The assignment of a number of incoming black Members to top-tier committees derived from this decentralization of power.

Perhaps the most consequential legacy of Black Americans in Congress from the pioneer era was the drive for organizing black power and interests. By the late 1960s, although African Americans were slowly making inroads in terms of committee assignments, they had relatively little power to command public and institutional attention and sustain a legislative agenda. No African American in either of the major parties held a top elected leadership position in either chamber during this 41-year era.[140] Furthermore, the limitations to black Members' ability to drive legislation were painfully apparent. Representatives Powell and Diggs became adept at garnering publicity, but as Diggs admitted, their efforts amounted to little more than "individualistic policies."[141] The multitude of expectations held by their constituents and black voters outside their districts, doubtlessly magnified black Members' frustration and sense of isolation.[142] Within this context, Diggs's efforts to create a unified caucus acquired new importance and urgency in the subsequent decade. Diggs's DSC, which evolved into the Congressional Black Caucus in the early 1970s, provided a forum for black Members to address "black interests" and shape institutional priorities. After decades in a largely unsympathetic and sometimes-hostile political wilderness on Capitol Hill, African Americans stood on the verge of achieving unprecedented influence.

NOTES

1   Thomas A. Johnson, "A Man of Many Roles," 5 April 1972, *New York Times*: 1.

2   Carol Swain, "Changing Patterns of African-American Representation in Congress," in *The Atomistic Congress: An Interpretation of Congressional Change*, Allen D. Hertzke and Ronald M. Peters, Jr., eds., (Armonk, NY: M. E. Sharpe, 1992): 107–140; quotation on page 118.

3   Aside from De Priest, Mitchell, and Dawson, the group included Robert Nix, Augustus Hawkins, and Edward Brooke.

4   See the discussion about the Great Migration in the preceding contextual essay, "The Negroes' Temporary Farewell." For more on black migrations in the post-Reconstruction period and the 20th century, see Nicholas Lemann, *The Promised Land: The Great Black Migration and How It Changed America* (New York: Knopf, 1991); Nell Irvin Painter, *Exodusters: Black Migrants to Kansas After Reconstruction* (Lawrence: University Press of Kansas, 1986); James R. Grossman, *Land of Hope: Chicago, Black Southerners, and the Great Migration* (Chicago: University of Chicago Press, 1989) and Joe William Trotter, Jr., ed., *The Great Migration in Historical Perspective: New Dimensions of Race, Class, and Gender* (Bloomington: Indiana University Press, 1991).

5   One served in World War I, four served in World War II, one saw combat in Korea, and another was drafted into service in the 1950s. Four were officers (Dawson, Brooke, Diggs, and Conyers); the rest were enlisted men. For an overview of the black experience in the military, see Bernard Nalty, *Strength for the Fight: A History of Black Americans in the Military* (New York: Free Press, 1986). For another assessment, see Robert W. Mullen, *Blacks in America's Wars: The Shift in Attitudes from the Revolutionary War to Vietnam* (New York: Monad Press, 1973).

6   "Former Congressman Diggs Enters Prison," 24 July 1980, Associated Press.

7   Harry McAlpin, "Dawson Takes Seat in House, Tells Plans," 16 January 1943, *Chicago Defender*: 9; see also Denton J. Brooks, Jr., "Fame Brings Dawson Chance to Help Race," 3 April 1943, *Chicago Defender*: 13.

8   Denton J. Brooks, Jr., "Dawson Demands Stimson's Removal," 4 March 1944, *Chicago Defender*: 1.

9   Edward Brooke, *Bridging the Divide: My Life* (New Brunswick, NJ: Rutgers University Press, 2007): 33.

10 William L. Clay, *Bill Clay: A Political Voice at the Grass Roots* (St. Louis: Missouri Historical Society, 2004): 16.

11 To put these accomplishments into perspective, by 1970 just 4.6 percent of black men and 5.1 percent of black women earned college degrees compared to 16.1 percent of white men and 9.5 percent of white women. An astounding 66.4 percent of all black males (66.7 percent of black women) in 1970 did not earn a high school diploma. These percentages were even lower in 1930 for both races and sexes and slowly increased each decade through 1970. Thus, the educational achievements of the black Representatives elected early in the period are all the more remarkable. See "College Graduation Rate, by Sex, Nativity, and Race: 1940–1997" and "High School Non-Completion Rate, by Sex, Nativity, and Race: 1940–1997," in *Historical Statistics of the United States, Volume 2: Work and Welfare*, Susan Carter et al., eds. (New York: Cambridge University Press, 2006): 469–470.

12 Former U.S. Representative Robert Elliott, a South Carolina Republican, was elected state attorney general in the 1876 election that swept Democrats back into power. He was forced from office in May 1877 under pressure from the administration of Governor Wade Hampton. For more on this episode, see Peggy Lamson, *The Glorious Failure: Black Congressman Robert Brown Elliott and the Reconstruction in South Carolina* (New York: W. W. Norton & Company, Inc., 1973): 250–270.

13 Stokes's brother and political mentor, Carl, served in the Ohio legislature and became the first African-American mayor of a major city (Cleveland) in 1967. It was Carl who convinced Louis to run for a newly drawn majority-black district in Cleveland. Nix was appointed as a deputy attorney general in Pennsylvania and also served as a Democratic committeeman in Philadelphia for 26 years, eight as chairman. Conyers worked as a legislative aide to U.S. Representative John Dingell, Jr., of Michigan, served as counsel to labor union locals, and received gubernatorial and presidential appointments before winning election to the House. As of December 31, 2007, Conyers, first elected in 1965, was the second-longest-serving current House Member: Dingell, who succeeded his father in 1955, was the longest-serving current House Member.

14   For the impact of the women's rights movement on Representatives, see Office of History and Preservation, U.S. House of Representatives, *Women in Congress, 1917–2006* (Washington, DC: Government Printing Office, 2007): 324–343.

15   John Kifner, "G.O.P. Names James Farmer for Brooklyn Race for Congress," 20 May 1968, *New York Times*: 34; John Kifner, "Farmer and Woman in Lively Bedford-Stuyvesant Race," 26 October 1968, *New York Times*: 22. See also Shirley Washington, *Outstanding Women in Congress* (Washington, DC: U.S. Capitol Historical Society, 1995): 17. Farmer echoed the findings contained in a controversial report produced by sociologist Daniel Patrick Moynihan (later a U.S. Senator from New York) titled *The Negro Family: The Case for National Action* (1965). The Moynihan Report, as it was later called, argued that the deteriorating black family structure seriously impeded the advancement of the race. More pointedly, the report suggested that a matriarchal structure in the black community undercut black men's roles as authority figures.

16   Susan Brownmiller, "This Is Fighting Shirley Chisholm," 13 April 1969, *New York Times*: SM32; see also Fred L. Zimmerman, "Negroes in Congress: Black House Members Will Add to Their Ranks in the Next Few Years," 22 October 1968, *Wall Street Journal*: 1.

17   Charles Stewart III, "Committee Hierarchies in the Modernizing House, 1875–1947," *American Journal of Political Science 36* (November 1992): 835–856.

18   Stewart, "Committee Hierarchies in the Modernizing House, 1875–1947."

19   Early women Senate pioneers, including Hattie Caraway of Arkansas and Margaret Chase Smith of Maine, also benefited from this circumstance.

20   Black Members from the post-1929 era who lost primaries include Adam Clayton Powell, Jr., of New York, Robert Nix of Pennsylvania, Katie Hall of Indiana, Charles A. Hayes of Illinois, Bennett Stewart of Illinois, Alton Waldon of New York, Lucien Blackwell of Pennsylvania, Craig Washington of Texas, Gus Savage of Illinois, Barbara-Rose Collins of Michigan, Cynthia McKinney of Georgia (twice), and Earl Hilliard of Alabama. For a standard work on the power of incumbency and the low turnover rates in the 20th century, see John R. Hibbing, *Congressional Careers: Contours of Life in the U.S. House of Representatives* (Chapel Hill: University of North Carolina Press, 1991).

21   See Allan G. Bogue, Jerome M. Clubb, Carroll R. McKibben, and Santa A. Traugott, "Members of the House of Representatives and the Processes of Modernization, 1789–1960," *Journal of American History 63* (September 1976): 275–302, especially 291–293. The average age of a freshman House Member from 1930 through 1950 was 45; from 1950 through 1960 it was 43.

22   For a graphic of the service dates for the black Members of this era, see the chart at the end of this essay. For more information on Member longevity averages, see, for instance, Mildred Amer, "Average Years of Service for Members of the Senate and House of Representatives, First through 109th Congresses," 9 November 2005, Report RL32648, Congressional Research Service, Library of Congress, Washington, DC

23   See Appendix F, Black-American Chairs of Subcommittees of Standing Committees in the U.S. House and Senate, 1885–2007. Dawson and Powell also became the first African Americans to chair full subcommittees of permanent standing committees: the Executive and Legislative Reorganization Subcommittee of Government Operations and the Mines and Mining Subcommittee of the Interior and Insular Affairs Committee, respectively. Others elected during this period who later served as full committee chairmen were Charles Diggs, Jr. (District of Columbia), Robert Nix (Post Office and Civil Service), Louis Stokes (Select Committee on Presidential Assassinations, Standards of Official Conduct, Permanent Select Committee on Intelligence), Augustus Hawkins (Joint Committee on Printing, Joint Committee on the Library, House Administration, Education and Labor), William L. Clay (Post Office and Civil Service), and John Conyers, Jr., (Government Operations, Judiciary). For a complete listing of African Americans who chaired standing congressional committees, see Appendix E, Black Americans Who Have Chaired Congressional Committees, 1877–2007.

24   For personal relations between Members and their constituents, see Richard F. Fenno, *Going Home: Black Representatives and Their Constituents* (Chicago, IL: University of Chicago Press, 2003): especially 259–261. See also Carol Swain, *Black Faces, Black Interests: The Representation of African Americans in Congress* (Cambridge, MA: Harvard University Press, 1993): 217–222. For an analysis of redistricting and black representation generally, see Kenny J. Whitby, *The Color of Representation: Congressional Behavior and Black Interests* (Ann Arbor: University of Michigan Press, 1997).

25   Diggs's Detroit area constituents returned him to Congress in November 1978 with 79 percent of the vote, despite his having been convicted of mail fraud and falsifying payroll forms weeks earlier. Similarly, in 1967, when the House voted to exclude Adam Clayton Powell, Jr., due to his legal and attendance issues, his Harlem constituents returned him to his vacant seat in a special election, with 86 percent of the vote.

26   See, for example, Nancy Weiss's treatment in *Farewell to the Party of Lincoln: Black Politics in the Age of FDR* (Princeton, NJ: Princeton University Press, 1983). For "push and pull," see Michael Fauntroy, *Republicans and the Black Vote* (Boulder, CO: Lynne Rienner, 2007): 41, 42–55.

27   Ample literature exists on the movement of black voters from the Republican Party to the Democratic Party: Weiss, *Farewell to the Party of Lincoln*; Donald J. Lisio, *Hoover, Blacks & Lily-Whites: A Study of Southern Strategies* (Chapel Hill: University of North Carolina Press, 1985); Richard Sherman, *The Republican Party and Black America from McKinley to Hoover, 1896–1933* (Charlottesville: University of Virginia Press, 1973): 134–144.

28   Lisio, *Hoover, Blacks & Lily-Whites: A Study of Southern Strategies*: 260–266; Sherman, *The Republican Party and Black America from McKinley to Hoover, 1896–1933*: 134–144.

29   See Harold F. Gosnell, *Negro Politicians: The Rise of Negro Politics in Chicago* (New York: AMS Press, 1969; reprint of 1935 University of Chicago Press edition): 24–25.

30   For more on the background of the city's Republican politics during this period, see Rita Werner Gordon, "The Change in the Political Alignment of Chicago's Negroes During the New Deal," *Journal of American History* 56 (1969): 586–588.

31   See, for example, Clay, *Bill Clay: A Political Voice at the Grass Roots*: 1–6.

32   For an analysis of how the agricultural collapse in the South contributed to black political activism, see Doug McAdam, *Political Process and the Development of Black Insurgency, 1930–1970* (Chicago: University of Chicago Press, 1982): especially 65–116.

33   John Hope Franklin and Alfred A. Moss, Jr., *From Slavery to Freedom: A History of African Americans,* 8th ed. (New York: Knopf, 2000): 421.

34   See Franklin and Moss, *From Slavery to Freedom: A History of African Americans*: 421–422; David M. Kennedy, *Freedom From Fear: The American People in Depression and War, 1929–1945* (New York: Oxford University Press, 1999): 87, 164; see also Lester Chandler, *America's Great Depression* (New York: Harper and Row, 1970): 40. The national and local GOP's inability to alleviate blacks' economic distress played a role in blacks' movement away from the party, although in 1932, black Chicagoans remained loyal to the party because the new Democratic mayoral administration stripped so many blacks of patronage jobs conferred by the old Thompson machine. See Gordon, "The Change in the Political Alignment of Chicago's Negroes During the New Deal": 591–592.

35   Weiss, *Farewell to the Party of Lincoln*: 78–95. See also William J. Grimshaw, *Bitter Fruit: Black Politics and the Chicago Machine, 1931–1991* (Chicago: The University of Chicago Press, 1992): 47–68.

36   Weiss, *Farewell to the Party of Lincoln*: 78.

37   Ibid., 88.

38   Ibid., 89–95.

39   Ibid., 212. Another scholar points to two "stages" of Chicago's black political realignment: the first consisting of registration at the polls in 1936 election (the response to New Deal emergency relief measures) and the latter occurring in 1944, when the national party under FDR embraced a larger civil rights reform agenda. See Grimshaw, *Bitter Fruit*: 52–53; see also Gordon, "The Change in the Political Alignment of Chicago's Negroes During the New Deal": 603.

40   Weiss, *Farewell to the Party of Lincoln*: 227.

41   Even in the South, African Americans were drawn toward supporting the national Democratic Party of Roosevelt and, later, Truman. "Now, if anybody thinks we ought to leave this Democratic ship and jump back into the Southern Republican skeleton and help put some meat on its bones, they have got some more thought coming," wrote a black newspaper editorialist in 1947. "Brethren, we had too hard a time getting on this ship and we are going to stay, sink or swim." Quoted in V. O. Key, *Southern Politics in State and Union* (Knoxville: University Press of Tennessee, 1984): 291; originally published by C. Blythe Andres, 29 November 1947, *Florida Sentinel* (Tampa). Between 1940 and 1960, Republican presidential candidates received between 23 and 40 percent of the black vote. Barry Goldwater's 1964 campaign transformed the decisive

Democratic advantage into a monopoly. In appealing to southern racial conservatives, Goldwater garnered just 6 percent of the African-American vote. Fauntroy, *Republicans and the Black Vote:* 56. Since then, no GOP presidential nominee has won more than 15 percent of the black vote.

42 The other black Republicans were Edward Brooke, Melvin Evans, Gary Franks, and J. C. Watts.

43 Harvard Sitkoff, *A New Deal for Blacks: The Emergence of Civil Rights as a National Issue: The Depression Decade* (New York: Oxford University Press, 1981): 44–46; quotation on page 51.

44 For a recent study suggesting that judiciary policies pursued by the Roosevelt administration had an important effect on future Supreme Court civil rights rulings, see Kevin McMahon, *Reconsidering Roosevelt on Race: How the Presidency Paved the Road to Brown* (Chicago: The University of Chicago Press, 2004): especially 177–202, 218–222. McMahon, a political scientist, maintains that Roosevelt's conclusion that southern segregation "was incompatible with his vision of a thoroughly liberal Democratic Party and with his institutional design for an executive-dominated national government served as a mainspring for the Supreme Court's later commitment to federal civil rights protection." McMahon concedes that Roosevelt's policy toward the judiciary derived from the needs of "intraparty management and his own institutional desires" rather than "a personal commitment to the African American cause." See pages 4, 7–8.

45 For an overview, see Fauntroy, *Republicans and the Black Vote*: 45–47.

46 On Eleanor Roosevelt generally, see Sitkoff, *A New Deal for Blacks*: 58–62; quotation on page 60. For a recent, comprehensive treatment of Eleanor Roosevelt, see Allida Black, *Casting Her Own Shadow: Eleanor Roosevelt and the Shaping of Postwar Liberalism* (New York: Columbia University Press, 1996).

47 Sitkoff, *A New Deal for Blacks*: 66–69.

48 For Mitchell's motivations, see Dennis S. Nordin, *The New Deal's Black Congressman: A Life of Arthur Wergs Mitchell* (Columbia: University of Missouri Press, 1997): 210–221. For the larger anti-lynching campaign in 1936 and 1937, see Robert L. Zangrando, *The NAACP Crusade Against Lynching: 1909–1950* (Philadelphia: Temple University Press, 1980): 139–165. For the legislative actions on lynching by a southern woman in the U.S. Senate in the 1930s, see "Dixie Bibb Graves," in Office of History and Preservation, *Women in Congress, 1917–2006*: 169–171.

49 For a comparative perspective on changing African-American demographics from the 1930s to the 1980s, see Gerald D. Jaynes and Robin M. Williams, Jr., *A Common Destiny: Blacks and American Society* (Washington, DC: National Academy Press, 1989): 35–42, 271–287. Statistics cited in this paragraph are drawn from pages 35, 271. A contemporaneous and hugely influential account of the plight of wartime blacks in the American South is Gunnar Myrdal's *An American Dilemma: The Negro Problem and Modern Democracy* (New York: Harper Publishers, 1944). For a concise summary of African-American participation in the war and its impact on civil rights, see Kennedy, *Freedom From Fear*: 761–776. For a standard account of the home front during the war, see John Morton Blum, *V Was for Victory: Politics and American Culture During World War II* (New York: Harcourt, Brace, Jovanovich, 1976). For more on desegregation of the military, see Richard M. Dalfiume, *Desegregation of the U.S. Armed Forces* (Columbia: University of Missouri Press, 1969).

50 See Kennedy, *Freedom From Fear*: 771–774; Franklin and Moss, *From Slavery to Freedom: A History of African Americans*: 481–491.

51 *Congressional Record*, Appendix, 77th Cong., 2nd sess. (18 February 1942): A607. See also *Congressional Record*, Appendix, 77th Cong., 2nd sess. (16 July 1942): A2790–2791.

52 *Congressional Record*, Appendix, 77th Cong., 2nd sess. (22 January 1942): A210; *Congressional Record*, Appendix, 77th Cong., 2nd sess. (28 January 1942): A290.

53 Walter White, *A Rising Wind* (Garden City, NY: Doubleday, Doran and Company, 1945): 144.

54 This was true for many southerners but especially for African Americans, the majority of whom held low-paying agricultural jobs in a tenant farmer system in the South. According to wage and salary data compiled by the U.S. Department of Commerce, the average agricultural worker in the United States earned $487 in 1940—a little more than $9 per week. See "Wage and Salary Accruals Per Full-Time Equivalent Employee, By Industry: 1929–1948," Table Ba4397–4418, Carter et al., *Historical Statistics of the United States, Volume 2*: 282.

55 *Congressional Record*, House, 78th Cong., 1st sess. (25 May 1943): 4853, 4889. In 1945, when the House again debated a measure to ban the poll tax, Dawson blasted Mississippi Representative

John E. Rankin, who claimed the tax was necessary to support public schools. "Why is it then that so many of these people cannot meet the minimum educational requirement?" Dawson rebutted, calling attention to the literacy tests used to disfranchise many southern blacks. See Venice T. Sprags, "Anti-Poll Tax Bill Faces Bilbo Filibuster Threat," 23 June 1945, *Chicago Defender*: 2.

56 "Executive Order 8802: Establishing the Committee on Fair Employment Practices," 25 June 1941, published as part of the American Presidency Project, University of California, Santa Barbara, http://www.presidency.ucsb.edu (accessed 1 February 2008). For a discussion of FDR's political position, see Sitkoff, *A New Deal for Blacks*: 320–323. See also Kennedy, *Freedom From Fear*: 768. Kennedy observes that while the FEPC was hardly a "second Emancipation Proclamation," it provided the seed for civil rights reform. "Coming at a moment that was kindled with opportunities for economic betterment and social mobility, Executive Order 8802 fanned the rising flame of black militancy and initiated a chain of events that would eventually end segregation once and for all and open a new era for African Americans."

57 *Congressional Record*, House, 78th Cong., 2nd sess. (26 May 1944): 5053.

58 Ibid., 5054.

59 Ibid. The full debate is on pages 5050–5068, quotation on page 5059.

60 *Congressional Record*, Appendix, 78th Cong., 2nd sess. (15 June 1944): A3033–3035. In June 1944, Representative Dawson testified before Norton's committee about the "psychological attitude" of "great bitterness" felt by African Americans who had been excluded from wartime work. The FEPC promised to alleviate the despair of discrimination. "Sooner or later, here in this country, we have got to face the question and settle it right for all times in the minds of the people. And there is no better way to begin to face the problem than to assure to every people that they will have the opportunity to work, along with all the other peoples in this nation of ours."

61 For a recent and important study of the topic, see Thomas Borstelmann, *The Cold War and the Color Line: American Race Relations in the Global Arena* (Cambridge, MA: Harvard University Press, 2001).

62 Walter Lippmann, "Today and Tomorrow: The Grace of Humility," 24 September 1957, *Washington Post*: A15.

63 President Kennedy worried about Soviet propaganda arising from a horrific, May 1963 Associated Press picture of Birmingham, Alabama, officials unleashing police dogs on young civil rights protestors. "What a disaster that picture is," Kennedy moaned. "That picture is not only in America but all around the world." See Nick Bryant, *The Bystander: John F. Kennedy and the Struggle for Black Equality* (New York: Basic Books, 2006): 388, 472.

64 See Mary L. Dudziak, *Cold War Civil Rights: Race and the Image of American Democracy* (Princeton, NJ: Princeton University Press, 2002).

65 Borstelmann, *The Cold War and the Color Line*: 2–8, quotation on page 2.

66 The best single source on HUAC is Walter Goodman, *The Committee: The Extraordinary Career of the House Committee on Un-American Activities* (New York: Farrar, Strauss & Giroux, 1968). For the debate surrounding the establishment of a permanent HUAC and a synopsis, see Raymond Smock, ed., *Landmark Documents on the U.S. Congress* (Washington, DC: Congressional Quarterly Inc., 1999): 367–374; *Congressional Record*, House, 79th Cong., 1st sess. (3 January 1945): 10–15. Rankin resuscitated HUAC from the brink of elimination. Established as a select committee in 1938, the panel initially investigated domestic fascist groups. Under the control of Chairman Martin Dies, Jr., of Texas, however, it rapidly became a soapbox from which New Deal programs were denounced and real and imagined communist subversives were routed out. Many Representatives resented the committee's costs and its tendency to conduct witch hunts. Most believed it would lapse after Dies's retirement in early 1945. But Rankin, a committee member and a devout segregationist and anti-communist, outmaneuvered House leaders and introduced a resolution to confer HUAC full, standing status at the opening of the 79th Congress (1945–1947). Faced with a roll call vote, many Members were reluctant to oppose a measure voters might perceive as strengthening America against the communist threat. Rankin's amendment carried 208 to 186, with 40 Members not voting. At the height of the Cold War rivalry between the United States and the Soviet Union, HUAC's influence soared and contributed to a climate of domestic fear stoked by its sensational and often unsubstantiated investigations.

67 White, *A Rising Wind*: 144.

68 See, for example, Penny M. Von Eschen, *Race Against Empire: Black Americans and Anticolonialism, 1937–1957* (Ithaca, NY: Cornell University Press, 1997); Brenda Gayle Plummer, *Rising Wind: Black Americans and U.S. Foreign Affairs, 1935–1960* (Chapel Hill: University of North Carolina Press, 1996).

69 Plummer, *Rising Wind*: 249.

70 Ibid.

71 Borstelmann, *The Cold War and the Color Line*: 96.

72 Plummer, *Rising Wind*: 248–253; quotation on page 251.

73 Ibid., 292.

74 Carolyn P. DuBose, *The Untold Story of Charles Diggs: The Public Figure, the Private Man* (Arlington, VA: Barton Publishing House, Inc., 1998): 62–65.

75 "Diggs Urges Better U.S. Attitude Toward Africa," 23 December 1958, *Chicago Defender*: 7.

76 The literature on the civil rights movement is vast, accessible, and well documented. Standard treatments include Taylor Branch's three-volume history, which uses Martin Luther King, Jr., as a lens through which to view the movement: *Parting the Waters: America in the King Years, 1954–63* (New York: Simon and Schuster, 1988); *Pillar of Fire: America in the King Years, 1963–65* (New York: Simon and Schuster, 1998); *At Canaan's Edge: America in the King Years, 1965–68* (New York: Simon and Schuster, 2006). See also David J. Garrow, *Bearing the Cross: Martin Luther King, Jr., and the Southern Christian Leadership Conference* (New York: William Morrow, 1986); William H. Chafe, *Civilities and Civil Rights: Greensboro, North Carolina, and the Black Struggle for Freedom* (New York: Oxford University Press, 1980), an account of one of the protest movement's seminal moments. For an overview of the movement and its impact on late-20th-century black America see Manning Marable, *Race, Reform, and Rebellion: The Second Reconstruction and Beyond in Black America, 1945–2006,* 3rd edition (Jackson: University Press of Mississippi, 2007).

For the evolution of civil rights legislation in Congress, see Robert Mann, *When Freedom Would Triumph: The Civil Rights Struggle in Congress, 1954–1968* (Baton Rouge: Louisiana State University Press, 2007)—an abridged version of Mann's *The Walls of Jericho: Lyndon Johnson, Hubert Humphrey, Richard Russell and the Struggle for Civil Rights* (New York: Harcourt Brace, 1996); Hugh Davis Graham, *The Civil Rights Era: Origins and Development of National Policy, 1960–1972* (New York: Oxford, 1990): especially pages 125–176; and James L. Sundquist, *Politics and Policy: The Eisenhower, Kennedy, and Johnson Years* (Washington, DC: The Brookings Institution, 1968): 221–286. A useful overview of Congress and civil rights is Timothy N. Thurber, "Second Reconstruction," in *The American Congress: The Building of Democracy*, ed. by Julian E. Zelizer (Boston: Houghton-Mifflin Company, 2004): 529–547. Another useful secondary work, which touches on aspects of the voting rights reform legislative effort, is Steven F. Lawson's *Black Ballots: Voting Rights in the South, 1944–1969* (New York: Columbia University Press, 1976).

77 Fauntroy, *Republicans and the Black Vote*: 47–49. For Truman and civil rights, see Alonzo Hamby, *Man of the People: A Life of Harry S. Truman* (New York: Oxford University Press, 1995); and Donald R. McCoy, *The Presidency of Harry S. Truman* (Lawrence: University Press of Kansas, 1984): 106–109, 167–171.

78 For more on the Dixiecrats, see Kari Frederickson, *The Dixiecrat Revolt and the End of the Solid South, 1932–1968* (Chapel Hill: University of North Carolina Press, 2001): see especially pages 67–117.

79 For a widely held critical analysis of Eisenhower and his position on civil rights, see Chester Pach, Jr., and Elmo Richardson, *The Presidency of Dwight D. Eisenhower,* revised edition (Lawrence: University Press of Kansas, 1991): 137–157.

80 See Michael J. Klarman, "Court, Congress, and Civil Rights," in *Congress and the Constitution*, Neal Devins and Keith E. Whittington, eds. (Durham, NC: Duke University Press, 2005): 173–197.

81 The congressional committees system was consolidated after passage of the 1946 Legislative Reorganization Act.

82 In part, Powell's frequent absences fit the maverick image he cultivated. Nevertheless, his failure to cast a vote for the final conference report for the Civil Rights Act of 1964 while on an extended European trip under the auspices of Congress raised eyebrows. Though not crucial to the final tally, Powell's vote would have held deep symbolic importance. Moreover, the bill incorporated his long-time amendment banning federal funds to institutions that practiced segregation. It exposed

the New York Representative to greater press scrutiny. Political pundit Drew Pearson noted that Powell failed to register his vote for a piece of legislation "considered the Magna Carta of Negro freedom," in order to satiate his "traveling propensities." See Drew Pearson, "Powell Absent for Rights Vote," 4 September 1964, *Los Angeles Times*: A6. Powell was present and voted for the original version of the bill, which passed the House on 10 February 1964. See *Congressional Record*, House, 88th Cong., 2nd sess. (10 February 1964): 2804.

83 Thurber, "The Second Reconstruction": 529–547. For a full-length biography of Chairman Smith, see Bruce J. Dierenfeild, *Keeper of the Rules: Congressman Howard W. Smith of Virginia* (Charlottesville: University Press of Virginia, 1987): Allen quotation on page 158. This quotation is often attributed to Speaker Sam Rayburn; see Thurber, "The Second Reconstruction": 531.

84 For more on Russell's position on race, see Mann, *When Freedom Would Triumph*: 22–24.

85 Thurber, "The Second Reconstruction": 531. For a perceptive summary of Eastland's career, see David Broder, "Eastland: End of an Era," 26 March 1978, *Washington Post*: C7.

86 For more on the Congressional Gold Medals awarded to Parks and other civil rights pioneers, such as Martin Luther King, Jr., and Coretta Scott King, as well as the Little Rock Nine, visit the "Congressional Gold Medal Recipients" page on the Web site of the Clerk of the U.S. House of Representatives available at http://clerk.house.gov/art_history/house_history/goldMedal.html.

87 "Reported Victims of Lynching, by Race: 1882–1964," *Historical Statistics of the United States, Volume 5: Governance and International Relations*, Carter et al., eds.(New York: Cambridge University Press, 2006): 251.

88 DuBose, *The Untold Story of Charles Diggs*: 46–60, quotation on page 46. For press coverage, see Mattie Smith Colin, "Till's Mom, Diggs Both Disappointed," 1 October 1955, *Chicago Defender*: 1.

89 DuBose, *The Untold Story of Charles Diggs*: 50.

90 Drew Pearson, "5 House Members," 12 January 1956, *Washington Post*: 31; Ethel L. Payne, "U.S. Probes Mississippi Vote Bias," 27 August 1955, *Chicago Defender*: 1.

91 "NAACP Criticizes Rep. Dawson," 1 September 1956, *Washington Post*: 38. For more on the Till lynching, see Stephen J. Whitfield, *A Death in the Delta: The Story of Emmett Till* (Baltimore: Johns Hopkins University Press, 1991).

92 Adam Clayton Powell, Jr., *Adam by Adam: The Autobiography of Adam Clayton Powell, Jr.* (New York: Dial Press, 1971): 81, 120–121.

93 *Congressional Record*, House, 85th Cong., 1st sess. (14 June 1957): 9192–9193; for Diggs's comments, see *Congressional Record*, House, 85th Cong., 1st sess. (10 June 1957): 8704–8705.

94 It was during the debate that Senator Strom Thurmond of South Carolina held the floor for more than 24 hours in a personal filibuster against the bill. Mann, *When Freedom Would Triumph*: 40–60. For more on the act, as well as its legal and social legacy, see Gilbert Paul Carrasco, "Civil Rights Act of 1957," in *Major Acts of Congress*, Volume 1, Brian K. Landsberg, ed. (New York: Thompson-Gale, 2004): 104–109. For more on Johnson's role in brokering the 1957 act, consult Robert A. Caro, *Master of the Senate* (New York: Knopf, 2002).

95 Julian E. Zelizer, *On Capitol Hill: The Struggle to Reform Congress and Its Consequences, 1948–2000* (New York: Cambridge University Press): 56–60.

96 *Congressional Record*, House, 88th Cong., 1st sess. (9 May 1963): 8256.

97 *Congressional Record*, House, 88th Cong., 2nd sess. (7 February 1964): 2465.

98 For a concise overview of the bill and its legal and social significance, see Melanie B. Abbott, "Civil Rights Act of 1964," in *Major Acts of Congress*, Volume 1: 109–115.

99 Mann, *When Freedom Would Triumph*: 175.

100 Ibid., 187–199.

101 John Lewis with Michael D'Orso, *Walking With the Wind: A Memoir of the Movement* (New York: Simon and Schuster, 1998): 331; for the full account, see pages 323–332.

102 John D. Morris, "Johnson Pledges Alabama Action," 5 February 1965, *New York Times*: 17.

103 *Congressional Record*, House, 89th Cong., 1st sess. (9 February 1965): 2434–2435. Like other African-American colleagues, Conyers stressed the foreign policy implications of voting fraud: "We are weak before our enemies if our goals abroad are so shamelessly ignored and subverted here at home." See *Congressional Record*, House, 89th Cong., 1st sess. (8 July 1965): 16000.

104 For an overview and analysis of the legal and social effects of the act, see William D. Araiza, "Voting Rights Act of 1965," in *Major Acts of Congress*, Volume 3: 271–278.

105 Thurber, "The Second Reconstruction": 543.

106 Not only were more blacks registered to vote, but also more ran for and won state and local political office. In 1965, in the 11 original Confederate states, there were just 72 black elected officials. A decade later, 1,587 held office. From 1966 to 1967, the number of blacks serving in state legislatures essentially doubled to 152. The effect was most dramatic in states that were once the strongholds of segregation: in Georgia, African Americans went from 0 to 11 seats in the state legislature in one election cycle. See *Congressional Record*, House, 94th Cong., 1st sess. (2 June 1975): 16241; John Allan Long, "Negroes Widen Political Power," 4 November 1967, *Christian Science Monitor*: 9.

107 For a recent analysis of this phenomenon, see Kevin M. Kruse, *White Flight: Atlanta and the Making of Modern Conservatism* (Princeton, NJ: Princeton University Press, 2005).

108 See, for example, Fred L. Zimmerman, "Negroes in Congress: Black House Members Will Add to Their Ranks in the Next Few Years," 22 October 1968, *Wall Street Journal*: 1.

109 For more on the origins and history of the Great Society, see James T. Patterson, *Grand Expectations: The United States, 1945–1970* (New York: Oxford University Press, 1996): 524–592; Robert Dallek, *Flawed Giant: Lyndon Johnson and His Times, 1961–1973* (New York: Oxford University Press, 1998).

110 For more about discrimination in the federal civil service, see Desmond King's standard work *Separate and Unequal: Black Americans and the US Federal Government* (New York: Oxford, 1995). For Eisenhower and his position on civil rights, see Pach and Richardson, *The Presidency of Dwight D. Eisenhower*: 137–157.

111 Weiss, *Farewell to the Party of Lincoln*: 81, footnote 9.

112 "Social Elite Aim Dart at Mrs. De Priest," 26 January 1929, *Chicago Defender*: 1; "Congressional Club Fails to Bar Mrs. De Priest," 16 February 1929, *Chicago Defender*: 4.

113 For more on Nichols, see his interview with the Senate Historical Office: http://www.senate.gov/artandhistory/history/oral_history/Jesse_R_Nichols.htm (accessed 4 February 2008).

114 Dunnigan's articles appeared in four parts under the title "A Visit to the Nation's Capitol" in *Service*, the magazine of the Tuskegee Institute; see November 1949: 9–12, 30–31; December 1949: 11–16; January 1950: 17, 20–21; and February 1950: 11–12, 21–22.

115 Modern political scientists generally characterize De Priest as having provided only "modest descriptive representation." While De Priest's substantive legislative achievements were modest, it should be noted that the unsympathetic and rigidly segregationist institution in which he worked, and his service as a Member in the minority party for most of his career, severely diminished his ability to effect reform. For a standard treatment of De Priest, see Carol Swain, "Changing Patterns of African-American Representation in Congress": 119.

116 "Pass De Priest Resolution," 26 June 1929, *New York Times*: 9; "Mrs. De Priest Visit Stirs Mississippian," 26 June 1929, *Washington Post*: 2.

117 *Congressional Record*, House, 73rd Congress, 2nd sess. (21 March 1934): 5049.

118 For a detailed account, see Elliott M. Rudwick, "Oscar De Priest and the Jim Crow Restaurant in the U.S. House of Representatives," *Journal of Negro Education* 35 (Winter 1966): 77–82.

119 "De Priest Adds Racial Demand: Opening Prayer in House by Colored Minister Requested," 28 January 1934, *Washington Post*: 7.

120 "Oscar De Priest," 30 March 1932, *Atlanta Daily World*: 6. Interestingly, after De Priest's effort to change Jim Crow practices in the House Restaurant in 1934, much of the African-American press rallied to his support. *The Atlanta Daily World* noted that De Priest "has shown himself to be no compromiser. He has measured head and shoulder to the stature of the statesman." See "Let Us Help Oscar De Priest," 4 April 1934, *Atlanta Daily World*: 6; E. N. Davis, "Race Losing Out Under NRA, AAA De Priest States Asking Negro Economic Progress," 20 May 1934, *Atlanta Daily World*: 1.

121 Joyce Haber, "A Question of Style: You Have It or You Don't," 22 January 1967, *Los Angeles Times*: C8; see also Richard L. Lyons, "Adam Clayton Powell, Apostle for Blacks," 6 April 1972, *Washington Post*: B5.

122 Powell, *Adam by Adam*: 72–73.

123 Ibid.

124 Swain, "Changing Patterns of African-American Representation in Congress": quotation on page 123.

125 "Plans Booker Washington Honor," 8 September 1937, *New York Times*: 13; *Congressional Record*, House, 77th Cong., 2nd sess. (14 October 1942): 8189.

126 "De Priest's Record Is Object of Attack by New Congressman," 19 November 1934, *Atlanta Daily World*: 2.

127 Nordin, *The New Deal's Black Congressman:* 89–90, 201–207.

128 For instance, see James Q. Wilson, "Two Negro Politicians: An Interpretation," *Midwest Journal of Political Science* 5 (1960): 349–369; Carol Swain, "Changing Patterns of African-American Representation in Congress": 123–125.

129 "Powell Declares 'Negro First' Aim," 9 April 1944, *New York Times*: 25.

130 Robert Singh, *The Congressional Black Caucus: Racial Politics in the U.S. Congress* (Thousand Oaks, CA: Sage Publications, 1998): 46–47.

131 Jessie Carney Smith, ed., *Notable Black American Men* (Detroit, MI: Gale Research, 1998): 878.

132 William J. Eaton, "Hawkins Retiring—But Not Quitting," 23 December 1990, *Los Angeles Times*: 3A.

133 Eaton, "Hawkins Retiring—But Not Quitting."

134 John Henry Cutler, *Ed Brooke: Biography of a Senator* (Indianapolis, IN: Bobbs-Merrill, 1972): 247.

135 See, for example, Ray Rogers, "Negro Politicians Caught Between Warring Factions," 7 December 1967, *Washington Post*: H3.

136 John H. Henton, "A Dapper Mr. Brooke Goes to Washington," 2 January 1967, *New York Times*: 22.

137 Cutler, *Ed Brooke: Biography of a Senator*: 247.

138 For more on the differences between the "work horse" and "show horse" styles, see Donald R. Matthews, "The Folkways of the United States Senate: Conformity to Group Norms and Legislative Effectiveness," *American Political Science Review* 53 (December 1959): 1064–1089. The same patterns have been observed in the House. See, for example, Charles L. Clapp, *The Congressman: His Work as He Sees It* (Garden City, NY: Doubleday, 1964): 22–23; and James L. Payne, "Show Horses and Work Horses in the United States House of Representatives," *Polity* 12 (Spring 1980): 428–456.

139 Swain, *Black Faces, Black Interests*: 117; David E. Rosenbaum, "3 White Districts Choose Negroes for House Seats," 5 November 1970, *New York Times*: 28.

140 Shirley Chisholm, elected in 1968, would serve as secretary of the Democratic Caucus in the 1970s.

141 For more on Diggs's motivations, see Singh, *The Congressional Black Caucus*: 54–55, 73; see also DuBose, *The Untold Story of Charles Diggs*: 79–80.

142 The more individual blacks in Congress embraced such a representational strategy, the more demands were put on their finite time and resources. After decades of neglect by white officials and an indifferent if not hostile system, an avalanche of long-deferred requests, many from people residing far outside their districts, sometimes overwhelmed black officeholders. Bill Clay recalled that black constituents often demanded "the impossible from black leaders," placing exorbitant expectations on them: "personally returning all phone calls . . . attending all PTA and block unit meetings; securing jobs; cosigning personal loans; fixing traffic tickets; providing free legal service; acting as a marriage counselor, child psychologist, and medical adviser." Calls and requests from African Americans nationwide who identified with Representative Shirley Chisholm because of her gender and her race, "deluged" her congressional staff. See, for example, Clay, *Bill Clay: A Political Voice at the Grass Roots*: 7; Charlayne Hunter, "Shirley Chisholm: Willing to Speak Out," 22 May 1970, *New York Times*: 31.

AFRICAN AMERICANS RETURN TO CONGRESS, 1929–1970 ★ 273

Congressional Service
For Black Americans First Elected 1929–1970

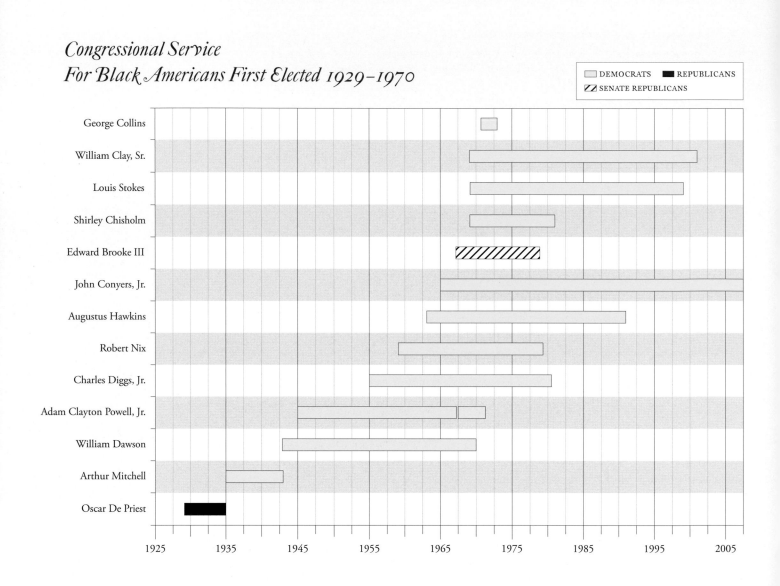

Legend:
- DEMOCRATS
- REPUBLICANS
- SENATE REPUBLICANS

Source: *Biographical Directory of the United States Congress, 1774–2005* (Washington, DC: Government Printing Office, 2005); also available at http://bioguide.congress.gov.

Party Divisions in the House of Representatives

71st–91st Congresses (1929–1971)*

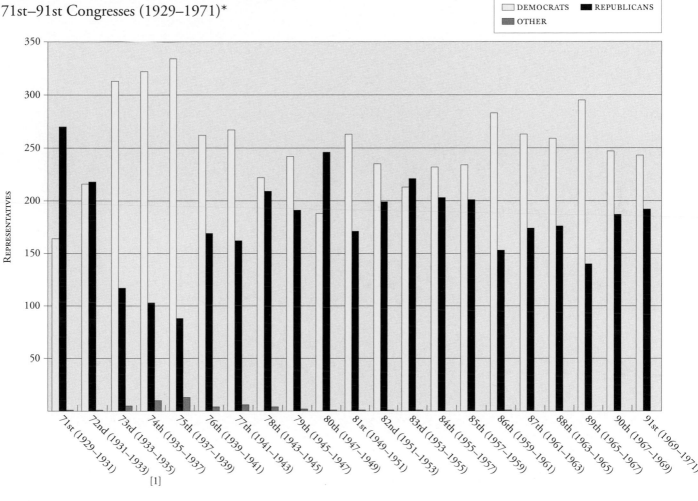

[1] Republicans won a majority of House seats on election day, but before the first day of 72nd Congress on December 7, 1931, 19 Representatives-elect died. In 14 instances, party control of the seat changed with the special election, enabling a Democratic majority to organize the House.

Source: Office of the Clerk, U.S. House of Representatives.

*Does not include Delegates or Resident Commissioners.

Party Divisions in the Senate
71st–91st Congresses (1929–1971)

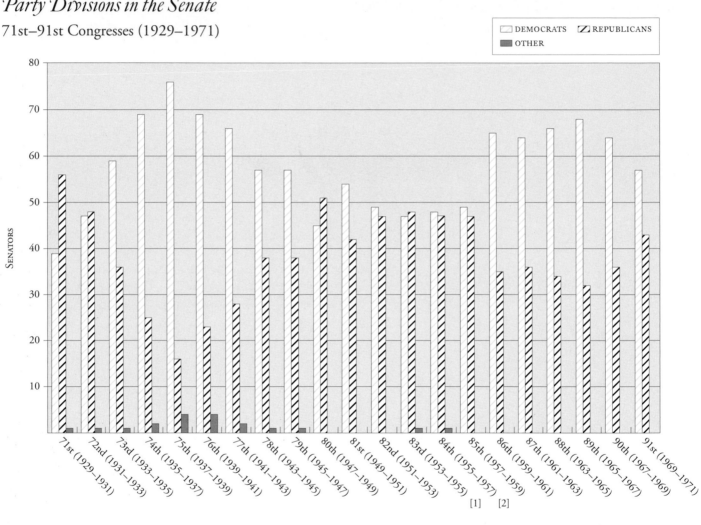

[1] The election of 1952 produced a closely divided United States Senate, with 48 Republicans, 47 Democrats, and one Independent. The Republican Party organized the Senate in January of 1953, making committee assignments, choosing Senate officers, and assigning committee chairs. During the 83rd Congress, nine senators died and one resigned, shifting the party division in the Senate with each new replacement.

[2] Strom Thurmond (SC) was an Independent Democrat during this Congress until his resignation on April 4, 1956. In November of that year he was elected as a Democrat to fill the vacancy created by his resignation.

Source: U.S. Senate Historical Office.

Black Americans First Elected to Congress by Decade, 1920–2007

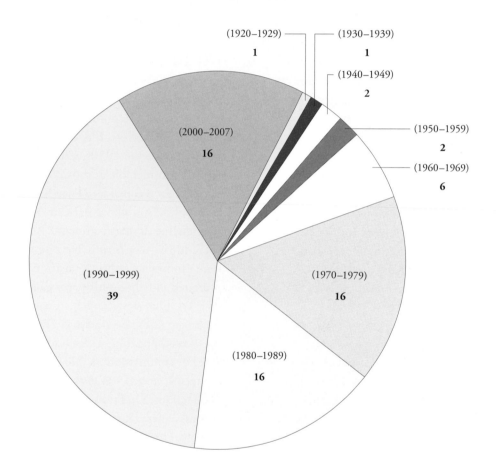

(1920–1929)
1

(1930–1939)
1

(1940–1949)
2

(2000–2007)
16

(1950–1959)
2

(1960–1969)
6

(1990–1999)
39

(1970–1979)
16

(1980–1989)
16

Source: Appendix B: Black-American Representatives and Senators By Congress, 1870–2007.

Oscar Stanton De Priest
1871–1951

UNITED STATES REPRESENTATIVE ★ 1929–1935
REPUBLICAN FROM ILLINOIS

Oscar De Priest was the first African American elected to Congress in the 20th century, ending a 28-year absence of black Representatives. De Priest's victory—he was the first black Member from the North—marked a new era of black political organization in urban areas, as evidenced by the South Side district of Chicago, whose continuous African-American representation began with De Priest's election in 1928. Although he made scant legislative headway during his three terms in Congress, De Priest became a national symbol of hope for African Americans, and he helped lay the groundwork for future black Members of the House and Senate.[1]

Oscar Stanton De Priest was born to former slaves Alexander and Mary (Karsner) De Priest in Florence, Alabama, on March 9, 1871. His father later worked as a teamster and a farmer, while his mother found part-time employment as a laundress.[2] In 1878, the De Priest family, along with thousands of other black residents of the Mississippi Valley, moved to Kansas. The migrants from Mississippi, Louisiana, and Alabama sought to escape poor economic and social conditions after Democrats and former Confederates regained control of southern state governments at the end of Reconstruction. These families, one historian wrote, were "pushed by fears of damnation and pulled by belief" in a better life in Kansas.[3] De Priest graduated from elementary school in Salina and enrolled in a business course at the Salina Normal School, where he studied bookkeeping. In 1889 he settled in Chicago before the great wave of African-American migration to northern cities during and after World War I. In Chicago, De Priest worked as an apprentice plasterer, house painter, and decorator, and he eventually established his own business and a real estate management firm. He married Jessie Williams on February 23, 1898, and the couple had one child, Oscar Stanton, Jr.[4]

De Priest's foray into politics was facilitated by Chicago's budding machine organization. Divided into wards and precincts, Chicago evolved into a city governed by a system of political appointments, patronage positions, and favors. Unable to consolidate control of the city before the 1930s, Chicago mayors nonetheless wielded considerable authority.[5] De Priest recognized the potential for a career as a local leader in a city with few black politicians whose African-American population was experiencing dramatic growth.[6] At first comfortable with a behind-the-scenes role, De Priest eventually assumed a more prominent political position as a loyal Republican interested in helping his party gain influence in Chicago. By 1904, De Priest's ability to bargain for and deliver the black vote in the Second and Third Wards gained him his first elected position: a seat on Chicago's Cook County board of commissioners. He retained this position for two terms, from 1904 through 1908.[7] Caught between rival factions, De Priest failed to secure a third term as commissioner. During a seven-year break from politics, he turned his attention to real estate, and became an affluent businessman.[8]

To revive his political career, De Priest curried favor with powerful Republican officials such as Chicago Mayor William Hale (Big Bill) Thompson and longtime U.S. Representative Martin Madden. He became Chicago's first black alderman, enabling him to sit on the influential city council from 1915 to 1917.[9] De Priest's service on the council ended abruptly; he resigned from office at the urging of local Republican leaders after being indicted for accepting money from a gambling establishment. "I shall devote myself unreservedly to proving my innocence and restoring my good name in this community," proclaimed De Priest, announcing his decision not to seek another term in office.[10] With Clarence Darrow—who later became

IMAGE COURTESY OF LIBRARY OF CONGRESS

one of the most famous trial lawyers in the country—as his defense counsel, De Priest was acquitted of the charges, but his political future remained uncertain because of several outstanding indictments.[11] After failing to gain the Republican nomination in 1918, De Priest unsuccessfully attempted to regain his council seat by running as an Independent.[12] However, he recovered enough power by 1924 to be elected Third Ward committeeman.[13]

The turning point in De Priest's career occurred when Martin Madden, the influential Chicago Representative and chair of the House Appropriations Committee, died suddenly after he had secured the Republican nomination for a likely 13th term in Congress. The Republican machine, led by Mayor Thompson, selected De Priest to replace Madden as the nominee in the lakeshore congressional district encompassing Chicago's Loop business section—a cluster of ethnic white neighborhoods—and a predominantly black area that included the famous Bronzeville section of the South Side.[14] Some black leaders in Chicago balked at the choice, contending that the credentials of other African-American politicians were better than De Priest's.[15] In the November election De Priest squared off against Democrat Harry Baker and three Independents, including William Harrison, an African-American assistant attorney general.[16] De Priest narrowly defeated his opponents with only a plurality, securing 48 percent of the vote; Harrison siphoned off some of the black votes in the district.[17] In his two subsequent congressional elections, De Priest won by more sizable margins, earning 58 and 55 percent of the vote, respectively.[18] As the first African American elected to Congress for nearly three decades, De Priest initiated a trend of black representation in urban northern cities repopulated by the Great Migration.

As De Priest prepared to take his seat in the 71st Congress (1929–1931) on April 15, 1929, he faced a potential obstacle. After his election in November, the local press speculated that the House might attempt to exclude De Priest because of an investigation involving outstanding "charges of sponsoring and protecting vice and gambling in the colored section of Chicago's South Side."[19] Although he had been cleared of the charges a few days before the start of the new Congress, Ruth McCormick, another newly elected Republican from Illinois, enlisted the assistance of Speaker Nicholas Longworth of Ohio to thwart potential challenges by southern Democrats to De Priest's seat.[20] Allegedly at the request of his wife, Alice, a personal friend of Representative-elect McCormick's, the Speaker dispensed with the traditional procedure for swearing in Members by state delegation and administered the oath of office simultaneously to prevent Members sworn in before De Priest from disputing the legality of his joining the 71st Congress.[21] De Priest's first day in Congress attracted the interest of the press and of many African Americans, some of whom watched the proceedings from the segregated visitors' gallery.[22]

The election of the new black Representative challenged the segregation pervasive in the nation's capital in the early 20th century. One of the most publicized incidents involving De Priest's arrival in Washington, DC, was the First Lady's White House tea for congressional wives. First Lady Lou Hoover's invitation to Mrs. Jessie De Priest provoked a wave of condemnation across the South. Several southern state legislatures, including Mississippi's, passed resolutions imploring the Herbert Hoover administration to give "careful and thoughtful consideration to the necessity of the preservation of the racial integrity of the white race."[23] The First Lady divided the reception into four separate sessions in an attempt to avoid a boycott by the wives of southern Members; Mrs. De Priest attended the smallest of the four gatherings with a few women who had been "screened" by the administration.[24] De Priest called the southern legislators cowards. "I've been elected to congress the same as any other member," he exclaimed. "I'm going to have the rights of every other congressman—no more and no less—if it's in the congressional barber shop or at a White House tea."[25] Nevertheless, he sought to make the most of the publicity resulting from the White House tea. Less than two weeks later, De Priest sponsored a noteworthy fundraiser in the nation's capital for the National Association for the Advancement of Colored People. The Illinois Representative invited all his Republican colleagues in the House except the two he believed had slighted him because of his race.[26]

Discriminatory practices existed in the Capitol as well. Many southern Democrats, in particular, resented De Priest's presence on the Hill and found ways to express their displeasure—such as refusing to accept offices near the newly elected black Representative.[27] Representative Fiorello LaGuardia of New York rebuked his colleagues, asserting, "It is manifestly unfair to embarrass a new member and I believe it is our duty to assist new members rather than humiliate them."[28] In January 1934, Representative Lindsay C. Warren, a Democrat from North Carolina and chairman of the House Committee on Accounts, ordered De Priest's secretary, Morris W. Lewis, and Lewis's son expelled from the House's whites only public restaurant. (There was a separate public facility for black customers next to the kitchen in the basement of the House.) The incident made headlines when De Priest introduced a resolution calling for an official investigation.[29] On the House Floor he refuted Warren's claim that African Americans had always been banned from the restaurant, recalling that he and other black patrons had frequented the Capitol establishment. De Priest implored his colleagues to support his resolution, remarking, "If we allow segregation and the denial of constitutional rights under the Dome of the Capitol, where in God's name will we get them?" He later said, "If we allow this challenge to go without correcting it, it will set an example where people will say Congress itself approves of segregation."[30] With his resolution referred to the hostile Rules Committee, which controls the flow of legislation in the House (then chaired by southern Democrat and future Speaker William Bankhead), De Priest kept his measure alive by using a parliamentary procedure: The Illinois Representative collected 145 Member signatures on a discharge petition to bring his legislation to the floor for a vote. The House ultimately voted in favor of De Priest's call for an investigatory committee, but the panel created to study the House Restaurant's policy of segregation split along party lines (three Democrats, two Republicans), refusing to recommend any revisions.[31] During his tenure, De Priest also lobbied for equality in the daily protocol of the House Chamber. In 1934, he requested that an African-American preacher be allowed to offer the opening prayer.[32]

The only African American in Congress during his three terms, De Priest discovered that in many respects he represented not only his Chicago district, but the entire black population of the United States. His entry into the national spotlight established a pattern for future black Representatives, who typically found their legislative records scrutinized in terms of their effectiveness in advancing African-American rights. Mindful of such expectations and eager to use his position to promote racial equality, De Priest proposed a reduction in the number of seats for states that disfranchised blacks, legislation originally introduced more than 30 years earlier by George White of North Carolina. In 1932, he introduced a bill to provide monthly pensions for former slaves older than 75 "to give recognition and do justice to those who are now living who were emancipated by the Emancipation Proclamation issued by Abraham Lincoln in 1863."[33] A response to the acute economic problems of the Great Depression, rather than the chronic problem of economic disparity between races, this proposal echoed social welfare plans advanced by Dr. Francis Townshend and Father Coughlin.[34] De Priest introduced a joint resolution in 1933 authorizing federal courts to change the location of a trial if a defendant's right to impartiality was compromised by consideration of race, color, or creed. This move was prompted by the infamous Scottsboro, Alabama, case in which nine African-American boys were sentenced to death by an all-white jury for the alleged rape of two white women, despite a lack of credible evidence.[35] Outlining several high-profile cases involving unfair treatment of African Americans in the judicial system, De Priest said in a speech, "I am making these remarks because I want you to know that the American Negro is not satisfied with the treatment he receives in America, and I know of no forum where I can better present the matter than the floor of Congress."[36] De Priest also backed a measure to hold states and counties responsible for the prevention of lynching. The unsuccessful legislation he introduced in 1934 would have fined and imprisoned local authorities if prisoners in their jurisdiction were lynched. In 1931 De Priest introduced a bill to make Abraham Lincoln's birthday a legal holiday—a symbolic gesture for African Americans.[37]

Although most of his legislative efforts to promote civil rights were unsuccessful, De Priest had a few victories. His most notable triumph occurred in March 1933, when he succeeded in adding an antidiscrimination rider to a $300 million unemployment relief and reforestation measure.[38] The final version of the bill, which launched the Civilian Conservation Corps (CCC), incorporated De Priest's amendment outlawing "discrimination because of race, color, creed, or criminal records" in the selection of workers for the program. Nevertheless, discrimination in the CCC remained rampant. By 1934 only 6 percent of CCC enrollees were African Americans, and the figures were disproportionately low even in majority-black states, such as Mississippi. That figure increased to almost 10 percent by the end of the decade, and while roughly a quarter million African Americans served in the CCC, only one in 10 was based in an integrated camp.[39] While in the House, De Priest nominated several African-American men from his district to the military academies—a practice replicated by his black successors from the Chicago area.[40] De Priest exclaimed proudly, "I've done more for the Negroes than any congressman since the time of Washington."[41]

De Priest did not inherit the favorable committee assignments of his predecessor, Representative Madden. During his three terms in the House he served on the Indian Affairs, Invalid Pensions, and Enrolled Bills committees. De Priest also was a member of the Post Office and Post Roads Committee during the 73rd Congress (1933–1935). Though the Post Office and Post Roads assignment ranked just outside the top

third of desirable House committees (14th overall), it was significant for a black Member. The year De Priest first won election to the House, the U.S. Post Office Department employed 45 percent of the federal government's African-American workers.[42]

In many respects, De Priest adhered to the general policy of the national Republican Party of the era. Like other Republicans, De Priest generally opposed federal programs for economic relief in the Depression, preferring to focus on such efforts at the state and community levels. Foreshadowing its importance in Congress in the coming years, De Priest denounced communism and warned of its spread in urban areas experiencing the acute effects of the Great Depression. Fearful that communists would spread propaganda among disgruntled African Americans, he lobbied unsuccessfully for a special House committee to investigate the leftist party.[43]

De Priest's refusal to support Roosevelt's remedial economic measures alienated many voters in his inner-city district. Ultimately, his loyalty to the Republican Party and his inability to provide economic relief for his constituents cost him his seat in the House. In the November 1934 general election, De Priest faced a formidable challenge from Arthur Mitchell, a former Republican lieutenant in Chicago's political machine who switched to the Democratic Party and became an ardent supporter of Roosevelt and the New Deal. In a campaign that received national attention because both candidates were African American, Mitchell attacked De Priest's refusal to vote for emergency federal aid to the poor and criticized his ineffective protest of segregation in the House Restaurant.[44] De Priest earned just 47 percent of the vote in a losing cause, paving the way for Mitchell to become the first black Democrat elected to Congress.[45] The De Priest–Mitchell contest reflected a larger political trend occurring in Chicago and many other northern cities: African Americans were changing their allegiance from the Republican Party to the Democratic Party because of dissatisfaction with the GOP response to the plight of Black Americans during the Depression and because of New

Deal relief policies. Two years later De Priest failed to regain his congressional seat. In 1943, De Priest again was elected Third Ward alderman and served once more on the Chicago city council. Defeated for re-election in 1947, De Priest remained active in his real estate business until he died in Chicago on May 12, 1951, of complications after he was hit by a bus.[46]

FOR FURTHER READING

Day, S. Davis. "Herbert Hoover and Racial Politics: The De Priest Incident," *Journal of Negro History* 65 (Winter 1980): 6–17.

"De Priest, Oscar Stanton," *Biographical Directory of the U.S. Congress, 1774–Present*, http://bioguide.congress.gov/scripts/biodisplay.pl?index=D000263.

Rudwick, Elliott M. "Oscar De Priest and the Jim Crow Restaurant in the U.S. House of Representatives," *Journal of Negro Education* 35 (Winter 1966): 77–82.

MANUSCRIPT COLLECTION

Chicago Historical Society (Chicago, IL). *Papers:* 1871–1951, approximately 60 items. The Oscar De Priest papers contain condolence letters and materials relating to the death of Oscar De Priest's son. Also included are an application to place the De Priest home on the National Register of Historic Places (1974), De Priest family genealogical information, and various news clippings about Representative De Priest. *Photographs:* In the Oscar De Priest Photograph Collection, ca. 1900–1949, 10 photographic prints and one photomechanical print, including portraits and group portraits of Oscar De Priest and his family. *Prints:* In the Visual Material Relating to Oscar Stanton De Priest, ca. 1910–1949, 17 photographic prints, three drawings, and one photomechanical print, including photoprints primarily relating to the political career of Oscar De Priest and three original editorial cartoons relating to African-American Representative William Dawson.

NOTES

1 Carol M. Swain, *Black Faces, Black Interests: The Representation of African Americans in Congress* (Cambridge, MA: Harvard University Press, 1993): 29.

2 Harold F. Gosnell, *Negro Politicians: The Rise of Negro Politics in Chicago* (Chicago: University of Chicago Press, 1967): 164.

3 Nell Irvin Painter, *Exodusters: Black Migration to Kansas After Reconstruction* (Lawrence: University of Kansas Press, 1986): 140–159, 184–201; quote on page 184.

4 Robert L. Johns, "Oscar S. De Priest," in Jessie Carney Smith, ed., *Notable Black American Men* (Farmington Hills, MI: Gale Research, Inc., 1999): 295 (hereinafter referred to as *NBAM*); Maurine Christopher, *Black Americans in Congress* (New York: Thomas Y. Crowell, 1976): 168–169.

5 For more about the Chicago political machine, see David Fremon's *Chicago Politics, Ward by Ward* (Bloomington: Indiana University Press, 1988) or William F. Gosnell's *Machine Politics, Chicago Model* (New York: AMS Press, 1969; reprint of 1937 edition).

6 In 1920 approximately 110,000 African Americans resided in Chicago. See James R. Grossman, *The Encyclopedia of Chicago* (Chicago: University of Chicago Press, 2004): 357.

7 William L. Clay, *Just Permanent Interests: Black Americans in Congress, 1870–1991* (New York: Amistad Press, 1992): 62.

8 Clay, *Just Permanent Interests*: 62–63; Gosnell, *Negro Politicians*: 168–169.

9 Clay, *Just Permanent Interests*: 63–64; Parke Brown, "De Priest Put on Ballot for Madden Place," 2 May 1928, *Chicago Daily Tribune*: 1.

10 "De Priest Quits Election Race at G.O.P. Order," 27 January 1917, *Chicago Daily Tribune*: 12.

11 Kristie Miller, "De Priest, Oscar Stanton," *American National Biography* 6 (New York: Oxford University Press, 1999): 461–463 (hereinafter referred to as *ANB*); Gosnell, *Negro Politicians*: 172–174; "Jury Acquits De Priest," 9 June 1917, *Chicago Daily Tribune*: 1.

12 "De Priest Files His Petition as an Independent," 9 March 1918, *Chicago Daily Tribune*: 4.

13 Miller, "De Priest, Oscar Stanton," *ANB*; "Negro for Madden's Seat," 2 May 1928, *New York Times*: 27.

14 "Seat in the House Won by Chicago Negro," 8 November 1928, *Washington Post*: 3; Fremon, *Chicago Politics, Ward by Ward*: 29.

15 Parke Brown, "De Priest Put on Ballot for Madden Place," 2 May 1928, *Chicago Daily Tribune*: 1; "Rivals Divided; Machine Backs Oscar De Priest," 13 May 1928, *Chicago Daily Tribune*: 24.

16 "Rivals Divided; Machine Backs Oscar De Priest."

17 "Election Statistics, 1920 to Present," available at http://clerk.house.gov/member_info/electionInfo/index.html; "Chicago Negro Elected," 8 November 1928, *Los Angeles Times*: 2.

18 "Election Statistics, 1920 to Present," available at http://clerk.house.gov/member_info/electionInfo/index.html.

19 "De Priest Wins Congress by Slim Margin," 8 November 1928, *Chicago Daily Tribune*: 14.

20 "Drops De Priest Charges," 11 April 1929, *New York Times*: 38.

21 *Congressional Record*, House, 71st Cong. 1st sess. (15 April 1929): 25; Gosnell, *Negro Politicians*: 183–184; Clay, *Just Permanent Interests*: 65–66.

22 Carlisle Bargeron, "Crowds Watch Congress Open Extra Session," 16 April 1929, *Washington Post*: 1.

23 "Pass De Priest Resolution," 26 June 1929, *New York Times*: 9; "Mrs. De Priest Visit Stirs Mississippian," 26 June 1929, *Washington Post*: 2.

24 Davis S. Day, "Herbert Hoover and Racial Politics: The De Priest Incident," *Journal of Negro History* 65 (Winter 1980): 9.

25 "De Priest Calls Legislators of Dixie Cowards," 2 July 1929, *Chicago Daily Tribune*: 1.

26 Day, "Herbert Hoover and Racial Politics: The De Priest Incident": 11–12; "Two Congressmen at De Priest Party," 22 June 1929, *Washington Post*: 1.

27 Shirley Washington, *Outstanding African Americans of Congress* (Washington, DC: U.S. Capitol Historical Society, 1998): 25.

28 "Acts for Negro in the House," 9 April 1929, *New York Times*: 64.

29 "De Priest Heads House Into Race Question Clash," 25 January 1934, *Chicago Daily Tribune*: 4; *Congressional Record*, House, 73rd Cong., 2nd sess. (21 March 1934): 5047.

30 *Congressional Record*, House, 73rd Cong., 2nd sess. (21 March 1934): 5047–5048.

31 "Bar on Negroes in Restaurant in House Is Upheld," 10 June 1934, *Chicago Daily Tribune*: 3; Elliott M. Rudwick, "Oscar De Priest and the Jim Crow Restaurant in the U.S. House of Representatives," *Journal of Negro Education* 35 (Winter 1966): 77–82.

32 "De Priest Adds Racial Demand," 28 January 1934, *Washington Post*: 7.

33 *Congressional Record*, House, 72nd Cong., 2nd sess. (19 March 1932): 6508. In the 51st Congress (1889–1891), Representative William J. Connell of Nebraska introduced an ex-slave pension bill. According to a 2007 Congressional Research Service report, during the late 19th century, several bills were put forth to provide financial compensation for older freedmen; none of the bills passed. Garrine P. Laney, "Proposals for Reparations for African Americans: A Brief Overview," 22 January 2007, Report RS20740, Congressional Research Service, Washington, DC.

34 For more on economic recovery plans that competed with the New Deal during the 1930s, see Alan Brinkley, *Voices of Protest: Huey Long, Father Coughlin, and the Great Depression* (New York: Knopf, 1982). For more on Townshend and his plan for elderly pensions, see the Social Security Administration Web site at http://www.ssa.gov/history/towns5.html (accessed 10 December 2007).

35 For more on the national dimensions of the Scottsboro case, see Dan T. Carter, *Scottsboro: A Tragedy of the American South* (Baton Rouge: Louisiana State University Press, 1969).

36 *Congressional Record*, House, 73rd Cong., 1st sess. (3 May 1933): 2823; Washington, *Outstanding African Americans of Congress*: 27; Miller, "De Priest, Oscar Stanton," *ANB*.

37 "Holiday on Lincoln's Birthday Is Asked in Bill by De Priest," 12 December 1931, *New York Times*: 6; Clay, *Just Permanent Interests*: 69.

38 Washington, *Outstanding African Americans of Congress*: 27.

39 "Forestry Bill Is Voted Amid Hubbub," 30 March 1933, *Washington Post*: 1; "House Passes Bill for Forestry Jobs," 30 March 1933, *New York Times*: 1. For figures on African Americans and the CCC, see Harvard Sitkoff, *A New Deal for Blacks: The Emergence of Civil Rights as a National Issue: The Depression Decade* (New York: Oxford, 1981): 51, 74–75.

40 "Negro Congressman Names Two of Race for Naval Academy, One for West Point," 7 May 1929, *New York Times*: 1.

41 "De Priest Seeks Negro Party to Advance Race," 22 July 1929, *Chicago Daily Tribune*: 6.

42 For committee desirability, see Charles Stewart III, "Committee Hierarchies in the Modernizing House, 1875–1947," *American Journal of Political Science* 36 (November 1992): 835–856. For statistics on African-American employment in the federal government in the 1920s, see Desmond King, *Separate and Unequal: Black Americans and the US Federal Government* (New York: Oxford, 1995): 228–229.

43 "De Priest Warns of Reds' Menace," 23 February 1931, *Washington Post*: 3; Johns, "Oscar S. De Priest," *NBAM*: 295.

44 "Negro Opposes De Priest," 29 October 1934, *New York Times*: 2.

45 "Election Information, 1920 to Present," available at http://clerk.house.gov/member_info/electionInfo/index.html.

46 "Oscar De Priest Dies; 1st Negro in City Council," 13 May 1951, *Chicago Daily Tribune*: 40; "O.S. De Priest Dies; Ex-Congressman," 13 May 1951, *New York Times*: 88; "Oscar De Priest, 79, South Side Political Figure, Hit by Bus," 17 January 1951, *Chicago Daily Tribune*: 1.

Arthur Wergs Mitchell
1883–1968

UNITED STATES REPRESENTATIVE ★ 1935–1943
DEMOCRAT FROM ILLINOIS

The first African American elected to Congress as a Democrat, Arthur Mitchell served four terms in the U.S. House, illustrating a shift among black voters, who traditionally backed Republican candidates. Throughout his congressional career, Mitchell faithfully supported President Franklin D. Roosevelt and the New Deal legislation that attracted many black voters during the Great Depression. As the only black Representative between 1935 and 1943, Mitchell was expected by African Americans in his Chicago district and across the country to use his political power to represent his race. Despite the pressure he faced to combat discrimination and promote civil rights, the Illinois Representative remarked upon taking office, "I don't plan to spend my time fighting out the question of whether a Negro may eat his lunch at the Capitol or whether he may be shaved in the House barber shop," an approach he adhered to during his tenure in Congress.[1]

The son of former slaves Taylor Mitchell and Ammar Patterson, Arthur Wergs Mitchell was born on a farm near Lafayette, Alabama, on December 22, 1883.[2] He attended public schools and entered Tuskegee Institute in 1897, working his way through college as a farm laborer and an assistant for Booker T. Washington. He taught in rural schools in Georgia and Alabama and attempted to put Washington's theories on farm management and land ownership into practice by founding the Armstrong Agricultural School in West Butler, Alabama. He served as president of the institution for 10 years. Before being admitted to the bar in Washington, DC, in 1927, Mitchell attended both Columbia and Harvard.[3] He practiced law in the nation's capital, and when he moved to Chicago in 1929, he continued his career as an attorney while also becoming involved in the real estate business.[4] Mitchell married Eula Mae King, who died in 1910, and then Annie Harris, who died in 1947. One year after the death

of his second wife, he married Clara Smith Mann. He had one son, Arthur Wergs Mitchell, Jr., with his first wife.[5]

Mitchell entered politics as a Republican, but like many Black Americans, shifted his allegiance to the Democratic Party in the early days of the New Deal. In the 1934 Democratic primary for the majority African-American congressional district encompassing Chicago's South Side, Mitchell squared off against Harry Baker. Mitchell lost to Baker (by fewer than 1,000 votes), but Baker died before the general election, and party leaders in the district selected Mitchell to take his place.[6] The congressional campaign between Mitchell and Oscar De Priest garnered national attention because both the challenger and the incumbent were African American (De Priest faced white Democratic opponents in three previous general elections).[7] Mitchell turned the contest against the venerable Republican Representative into a referendum on President Franklin D. Roosevelt's public-relief policies. Capitalizing on growing support for the New Deal, Mitchell orchestrated an aggressive campaign that forced De Priest to defend the Republican Party, whose influence was waning locally, in part due to Chicago's Democratic Mayor, Edward J. Kelly, who actively courted African-American voters.[8] On November 7, 1934, Mitchell narrowly beat De Priest, becoming the first African-American Democrat elected to Congress.[9] In his three successive elections, Mitchell continued to win by a slim margin—defeating De Priest again in 1936, future Representative William Dawson two years later, and former Illinois State Senator William E. King in 1940—with an average of 53 percent of the vote.[10] Shortly after taking his seat in the 74th Congress on January 3, 1935, Mitchell reiterated one of his campaign promises: "What I am interested in is to help this grand President of ours feed the hungry and clothe

the naked and provide work for the idle of every race and creed."[11] Mitchell was assigned to the Committee on the Post Office and Post Roads, and retained this position throughout his eight years in the House.

During his congressional career, Mitchell remained a loyal supporter of President Roosevelt and the New Deal.[12] In 1936 the Illinois Representative gave a seconding speech for Roosevelt's renomination at the Democratic Convention and served as western director of minority affairs for the President's re-election campaign. As one of Roosevelt's consistent backers, Mitchell maintained that the New Deal addressed many of the problems faced by "America's largest and most neglected minority group," the black populace.[13] Citing programs such as the Work Projects Administration (WPA; later renamed the Works Progress Administration) and the Public Works Administration (PWA), Mitchell praised the President's economic answer to the Depression, noting that the New Deal had produced the best conditions for Black Americans since they became free citizens.[14] The WPA constructed thousands of massive public works projects including buildings, roads, bridges, and airports, and oversaw such diverse activities as the Federal Art Project and the Federal Writers' Project. Led by Harry Hopkins, the agency went to great lengths to treat blacks equally—after 1936, blacks made up 15 to 20 percent of its workforce—and through wages and public works initiatives brought millions of federal dollars to devastated black communities. Likewise, under the direction of Harold Ickes, the PWA hired many African Americans and helped construct public buildings worth millions of dollars in economically depressed black locales.[15] Mitchell also defended Roosevelt's controversial plan to reorganize the federal judiciary in 1937, noting that blacks had been victimized over the years by unfavorable Supreme Court rulings, and charged that the Court had often used the 14th Amendment to protect large corporations and property holders instead of using it as it was intended: to defend the citizenship rights of blacks.

While in Congress, Mitchell worked to provide

opportunities for Black Americans. Like his predecessor, De Priest, he nominated a number of black candidates for the United States military academies.[16] Mitchell also used his position to draw attention to racial discrimination. He challenged several labor unions for agreeing to contracts that excluded blacks and supported legislation that would outlaw the poll tax. During the Second World War, Mitchell criticized the treatment of black soldiers, remarking that the discrimination endured by African-American troops undermined the U.S. objective "to extend and protect the doctrine of genuine democracy."[17] Mitchell also repeatedly offered bills that would outlaw racial discrimination in the civil service. Calling the requirement of submitting a photograph for civil service job applications "racial discrimination," Mitchell proposed that fingerprints be used instead.[18]

As the only African American in Congress, Mitchell found himself scrutinized by black leaders and organizations across the country. Criticized for what some perceived as an overly cautious stance toward civil rights, Mitchell was accused of squandering an opportunity to make a significant legislative impact on behalf of his race. A major point of contention was an anti-lynching bill submitted by Mitchell that was considered too lenient by the National Association for the Advancement of Colored People and other civil rights groups.[19] When the House ultimately rejected his measure in favor of one with stricter penalties for offenders, Mitchell remarked, "The authorship of this bill means absolutely nothing as compared with the importance of its passage."[20] Although Mitchell resented claims he could do more to help African Americans, he did not want to be identified solely by his race. "I am not going into Congress as a Negro with a chip on my shoulder thinking I am of an inferior race and that every man's hand is against me," he commented shortly after his election to the House. "I am going in as an American citizen, entitled to my rights, no more, no less, and I shall insist on them. I'm going as the representative of all the people of my district."[21] During his four terms in Congress, Mitchell worked closely with many of his white colleagues, adopting a philosophy rooted in cooperation and patience—much like his mentor Booker T. Washington, whom Mitchell hoped to honor by establishing a national shrine.[22]

Ironically, Mitchell's greatest contribution to desegregation arguably transpired outside the halls of Congress. In April 1937, Mitchell traveled from Chicago to Hot Springs, Arkansas, on the Chicago, Rock Island and Pacific Railroad. When the train crossed into Arkansas, a conductor forced Mitchell out of the Pullman car, for which he had two first-class tickets. The Representative rode the rest of the journey in a car designated for black passengers that he described as "filthy and foul smelling."[23] Following in the footsteps of James E. O'Hara, a black Reconstruction-Era Representative, Mitchell challenged transport segregation. He sued the railroad and filed a complaint with the Interstate Commerce Commission (ICC), contending that interstate trains should be exempt from the Arkansas law requiring "separate but equal" train accommodations. After the ICC and a federal district court dismissed his complaint, Mitchell made history by joining a select number of sitting Members of Congress to argue a case before the Supreme Court. In April 1941 the high court unanimously held in *Mitchell v. United States et al.* that black passengers had the right to the same accommodations and treatment whites did. Mitchell hailed the decision as a "step in the destruction of Mr. Jim Crow himself," but the ICC did not prohibit segregation on interstate trains or buses or in the public waiting rooms of railroad or bus stations until 1955.[24]

Under circumstances his biographer describes as "ambiguous," Mitchell declined to run for re-nomination to the 78th Congress in 1942.[25] Officials in Mayor Kelly's Chicago political organization were angry that Mitchell had defied machine orders in pursuing his lawsuit against a Chicago-based rail company and let Mitchell know they planned to withdraw their support. Democratic officials chose his rival, William Dawson, partially because they believed he would be a better candidate against a potentially tough field of African Americans on the Republican side. Publicly, Mitchell gracefully accepted

his political downfall, claiming (somewhat truthfully) that he was ready for a new phase in his public-service career and that he preferred to improve race relations by working through groups active in the South. After retiring from the House in January 1943, he moved to Petersburg, Virginia, where he had bought a large tract of land, and devoted himself to farming, lecturing, and the activities of organizations such as the Southern Regional Council. He died in Petersburg on May 9, 1968.

FOR FURTHER READING

"Mitchell, Arthur Wergs," *Biographical Directory of the U.S. Congress, 1774–Present*, http://bioguide.congress.gov/scripts/biodisplay.pl?index=M000805.

Nordin, Dennis. *The New Deal's Black Congressman: A Life of Arthur Wergs Mitchell* (Columbia: University of Missouri Press, 1997).

MANUSCRIPT COLLECTION

Chicago Historical Society (Chicago, IL). *Papers:* 1898–1968, 30 linear feet. The collection contains correspondence, speeches, news clippings, and other papers of Arthur Mitchell. The papers contain many letters about racial issues, from all over the country. Additional topics include Mitchell's election campaigns against Oscar De Priest and others, service in the House and on the Post Office and Post Roads Committee, anti-lynching legislation, Mitchell's U.S. Supreme Court case concerning discrimination on a railroad, and activities as director of the Western Division of Colored Voters of the Democratic National Campaign Committee during the 1936 presidential election. *Photographs:* ca. 1930–1965 (one box), relate to Mitchell's life and career.

NOTES

1 "Arthur Mitchell, an Ex-Lawmaker," 10 May 1968, *New York Times*: 47.

2 Dennis S. Nordin, *The New Deal's Black Congressman: A Life of Arthur Wergs Mitchell* (Columbia: University of Missouri Press, 1997): 1.

3 "Arthur Mitchell, an Ex-Lawmaker"; Nordin, *The New Deal's Black Congressman*: 21, 33.

4 "Arthur W. Mitchell, 85, Dies: 1st Negro Democrat in the House," 11 May 1968, *Washington Post*: B3; Nordin, *The New Deal's Black Congressman*: 39.

5 Nordin, *The New Deal's Black Congressman*: 9–10, 14, 122–123, 283, 290–291.

6 "Democrats Pick Flynn as County Clerk Candidate," 4 August 1934, *Chicago Daily Tribune*: 9.

7 S. J. Duncan-Clark, "Voters Confused in the Lake States," 4 November 1934, *New York Times*: E6; "Negro Opposes De Priest," 29 October 1934, *New York Times*: 2.

8 Nordin, *The New Deal's Black Congressman*: 62–63; Janice L. Reiff et al., eds., *Encyclopedia of Chicago*; see http://www.encyclopedia.chicagohistory.org/pages/371.html (accessed 25 October 2007).

9 Arthur Evans, "Later Returns Cut Democrat Gain in Illinois," 8 November 1934, *Chicago Daily Tribune*: 2; "Election Statistics, 1920 to Present," available at http://clerk.house.gov/member_info/electionInfo/index.html.

10 "Election Statistics, 1920 to Present," available at http://clerk.house.gov/member_info/electionInfo/index.html; Harold Smith, "G.O.P. Candidates See Victory," 20 October 1940, *Chicago Daily Tribune*: S1.

11 "Arthur W. Mitchell, 85, Dies; 1st Negro Democrat in the House."

12 Harold Smith, "Each New Deal Roll Call Gets Mitchell's 'Aye!,'" 7 February 1940, *Chicago Daily Tribune*: 2.

13 *Congressional Record*, House, 76th Cong., 2nd sess. (18 March 1940): 3019.

14 Ibid., 3019–3026.

15 Harvard Sitkoff, *A New Deal for Blacks: The Emergence of Civil Rights as a National Issue: The Depression Decade* (New York: Oxford University Press, 1981): 68, 70–71.

16 For an example, see "Negro Youth Qualifies, Enters Naval Academy," 16 June 1936, *New York Times*: 31.

17 *Congressional Record*, Appendix, 77th Cong., 2nd sess. (16 July 1942): A2790.

18 "Mitchell Protests Race 'Job Barrier,'" 25 January 1936, *Washington Post*: 2; Carol M. Swain, *Black Faces, Black Interests: The Representation of African Americans in Congress* (Cambridge, MA: Harvard University Press, 1993): 30–31.

19 Maurine Christopher, *Black Americans in Congress* (New York: Thomas Y. Crowell Company, 1976): 177.

20 *Congressional Record*, House, 75th Cong., 1st sess. (1937): 3385; Christopher, *Black Americans in Congress*: 179.

21 "Arthur Mitchell, an Ex-Lawmaker."

22 "Plans Booker Washington Honor," 8 September 1937, *New York Times*: 13; *Congressional Record*, House, 77th Cong., 2nd sess. (14 October 1942): 8189.

23 "Court Backs Rights of Negro on Trains," 29 April 1941, *New York Times*: 1; "Mitchell Fights Jim Crow Rule in High Court," 14 March 1941, *Washington Post*: 25; Nordin, *The New Deal's Black Congressman*: 249–250.

24 "Court Backs Rights of Negro on Trains."

25 Nordin, *The New Deal's Black Congressman*: 247–248.

"I AM NOT GOING INTO
CONGRESS AS A NEGRO WITH A
CHIP ON MY SHOULDER THINKING
I AM OF AN INFERIOR RACE
AND THAT EVERY MAN'S HAND
IS AGAINST ME," MITCHELL
COMMENTED SHORTLY AFTER
HIS ELECTION TO THE HOUSE.
"I AM GOING IN AS AN AMERICAN
CITIZEN, ENTITLED TO MY RIGHTS,
NO MORE, NO LESS, AND I SHALL
INSIST ON THEM. I'M GOING AS
THE REPRESENTATIVE OF ALL THE
PEOPLE OF MY DISTRICT."

William Levi Dawson
1886–1970

UNITED STATES REPRESENTATIVE ★ 1943–1970
DEMOCRAT FROM ILLINOIS

The third African American elected to Congress in the 20th century and the first black Member to chair a standing committee, William L. Dawson served in the House of Representatives for nearly three decades. A product of the influential Chicago Democratic machine, Dawson remained loyal to the organization and the political party that propelled his long congressional career. Committed to the cause of civil rights, Dawson recognized the importance of "forceful but behind-the-scenes action through regular political channels."[1] His reserved demeanor and his reluctance to alienate the political establishment led many African-American leaders of the era to question his commitment to civil rights reform and undermined his role as a national leader in the movement for racial equality. Dawson, who described himself as a "congressman first and a Negro second," avoided highlighting his race, preferring instead to build a base of power using the established seniority system of the House of Representatives.[2]

William Levi Dawson was born in Albany, Georgia, on April 26, 1886, to Levi Dawson, a barber, and Rebecca Kendrick. William had six siblings. He credited his father and sister with keeping his family together after his mother died when he was a child.[3] Upon graduating from Albany Normal School in 1905, Dawson worked his way through Fisk University in Nashville, Tennessee, as a porter and a waiter. He graduated in 1909 with a bachelor's degree, and three years later he moved to Chicago. After attending Kent College of Law and Northwestern University—both in Chicago—Dawson enlisted in the U.S. Army during World War I.[4] In 1917 he became a first lieutenant with the 365th Infantry of the American Expeditionary Force. After returning to Chicago, he resumed his studies at Northwestern and was admitted to the Illinois bar in 1920. Dawson married Nellie Brown on December 20,

1922, and the couple had two children, William Dawson, Jr., and Barbara.[5]

Dawson represented the GOP when he entered the Chicago political scene. In 1928, he waged an unsuccessful bid in the Republican primary against incumbent Martin Madden for the urban congressional district that encompassed much of the black population residing on Chicago's South Side. Undeterred by the loss, Dawson continued to pursue a career in politics. He became an ally of Chicago's first African-American alderman, Oscar De Priest, who won a special election to fill the vacancy left by Representative Madden's death in 1928.[6] In 1933, with De Priest's critical backing, Dawson won election to the Chicago city council. Two years later, backed by Chicago's Democratic Mayor, Edward J. Kelly, Dawson won re-election to a four-year term; he served a total of six years as an alderman.[7] In his second attempt to win a House seat in 1938—an off-year election in which Republicans ran well nationally—Dawson earned the Republican nomination by defeating De Priest but lost to Democratic incumbent Arthur W. Mitchell in the general election, 53.4 to 46.6 percent.[8] Dawson's support from the Democratic mayor and his decision to challenge De Priest reflected the pull of the Democratic Party on Chicago blacks, the lure of patronage rewards within the Democratic machine, and a general impatience with the old guard of black leaders tied to the GOP.[9] Having challenged his mentor, Dawson effectively severed his ties to leading black Republicans, who passed him over for the party nomination for another term on the city council. Running as an Independent, he failed to secure re-election.[10]

Dawson's political career revived in 1939 with his acceptance of Mayor Kelly's offer of the post of Democratic committeeman for Chicago's Second Ward. In line with the growing shift of many African Americans from the

OIL ON CANVAS (DETAIL), ROBERT B. WILLIAMS, 1968,
COLLECTION OF U.S. HOUSE OF REPRESENTATIVES

Republican to the Democratic Party, Dawson cited "the influence and liberalism of Franklin D. Roosevelt" as his primary motivation for changing parties. As a committeeman, Dawson efficiently organized his political base, using his precinct workers to help transform other predominantly black wards into Democratic voting blocs. In time, Dawson's followers controlled as many as five wards that generally offered overwhelming majorities to local, state, and national Democratic candidates. When Arthur Mitchell chose not to seek a fifth term in the House in 1942, Dawson opted to run for Congress a third time—as a Democrat. With the solid backing of the Democratic machine, Dawson earned the party nomination by defeating Earl Dickerson, a Chicago alderman.[11] Dawson went on to beat Republican William E. King, a former Illinois state senator and his longtime political nemesis, in the general election—earning 53 percent of the vote—to begin a congressional career that lasted nearly three decades.[12] An experienced public servant with solid community support, Dawson benefited from his close ties to the Chicago political machine, which actively courted aspiring African-American politicians.[13] Shortly after beginning his first term in the House, Dawson remarked that he hoped to play a role in the "enhancing of the American Dream."[14] Throughout his tenure in Congress he remained focused on bettering the lives of the African Americans in his district.

During his first two terms in office, Dawson was on the Coinage, Weights, and Measures; Invalid Pensions; and Irrigation and Reclamation committees. He also served on the Expenditures in the Executive Departments Committee (renamed Government Operations in 1952) from the 78th through the 80th Congress (1943–1949) before ascending to committee chair in 1949. The first African American to chair a standing committee, Dawson held the post until 1970, with the exception of a single term in the 83rd Congress (1953–1955), when Republicans controlled the House.[15] Dawson downplayed the fanfare associated with his historic chairmanship, which included a dinner in his honor hosted by leading national and Illinois Democratic leaders. "I'm not interested in that particular phase," he commented. "I just want to do a good job."[16] Dawson also served on the Insular Affairs Committee (later named Interior and Insular Affairs) from 1943 to 1946 and from 1951 to 1952 and on the District of Columbia Committee from 1955 to 1970.

In some respects Dawson was an atypical politician and machine leader. He disliked personal publicity, was wary of the media, and lived unpretentiously. Also, he personally attended to many of the details of his office. When in his district, Dawson spent part of each day at his headquarters listening to his constituents' complaints, requests, and opinions. He kept a firm grip on his share of power in Chicago, dispensing patronage and favors through his political machine and its ancillary organizations.[17] A prominent figure in the upper echelons of the Chicago Democratic machine, Dawson played a key role in Richard J. Daley's election as mayor of the Windy City in 1955.[18] In 1960, John F. Kennedy's narrow victory in the key state of Illinois was largely dependent on the voters in Dawson's wards, leading to widespread speculation among the press that the President-elect would express his gratitude by inviting Dawson to become Postmaster General. When the offer came, the 74-year-old Dawson declined, saying he would be more useful to the new administration as a senior Representative in the House.[19]

During his first term in the House, Dawson was the only African American serving in Congress. Two years later, a second black Representative, Adam Clayton Powell, Jr., of New York, joined Dawson. Dawson and Powell drew intense media attention and scrutiny because of their race and their strikingly different legislative styles.[20] Powell, who epitomized the more militant wing of the civil rights movement, publicized racial inequality, including segregation in certain areas of the Capitol, at every conceivable opportunity. Dawson, on the other hand, eschewed issues that focused exclusively on race. Unlike Powell, he rarely challenged racial discrimination publicly, choosing instead to work behind the scenes to pass legislation to assist his district and the Democratic

Party. Dawson's workman-like approach and unswerving loyalty to the party eventually brought him a position of national prominence: vice chair of the Democratic National Committee (DNC).[21] Throughout his 27 years in Congress, Dawson consistently supported the interests of the Democratic Party. Even when most other African-American leaders, including Martin Luther King, Jr., denounced Lyndon B. Johnson's foreign policy in Southeast Asia, Dawson remained an enthusiastic backer of the Democratic President. In 1965, Dawson used Johnson's phrase "nervous Nellies" to describe critics of the Vietnam War, comparing those who underestimated the communist threat in Southeast Asia to those who underestimated Hitler's potential power before the outbreak of the Second World War.[22]

His philosophy of working within the establishment and his perceived passivity to discriminatory practices drew criticism from some civil rights groups, who believed Dawson squandered the opportunity to use his authority as a committee chair and a leader of the DNC to promote meaningful change for African Americans. The National Association for the Advancement of Colored People condemned his "silence, compromise and meaningless moderation" on issues concerning African Americans, including his refusal to back the Powell Amendment, aimed initially at prohibiting federal funding for segregated schools. Although Dawson opposed the measure because he feared the rider would undermine all aid to education, his caution disappointed many of his own staff members.[23] Powell intimated that Dawson cared more about his position in Mayor Daley's Chicago political machine than the success of the civil rights movement—a sentiment shared by other prominent black leaders.[24]

Dawson reacted angrily when detractors charged he failed to adequately represent his race. "How is it," he wondered, "that after fighting all my life for the rights of my people, I suddenly awaken in the September of life to find myself vilified and abused, and those who know me well and what I have stood for are accusing me of being against civil rights."[25] Reacting to criticism that his

infrequent speeches in Congress were a sign of ineffective leadership, Dawson defended his approach to politics while maligning some of his outspoken black colleagues, noting, "I use speeches only as the artisan does his stone, to build something. I don't talk just to show off."[26]

Dawson occasionally chose a public forum to draw attention to racial injustice. The Daley machine, which had propelled him to office, had been largely unattuned to the needs of Chicago-area blacks—preferring to recruit pliant black elites who eschewed activism. With the 1960s civil rights movement, the machine's practice of "racial containment"—segregation in public housing, school districts, and jobs in the city's police and fire departments—intensified.[27] A significant personal exception to Dawson's legislative approach was his introduction of a major civil rights bill on the House Floor in 1963. Dawson's bill was not novel or radical; it echoed many of the proposals then being considered in Congress and eventually rolled into the 1964 Civil Rights Act: voting rights, ending discrimination in public accommodations, the creation of a Commission on Equal Employment Opportunity, and the prohibition of discrimination in federally funded programs. "There is a crisis in America that is now a national danger," he pronounced, carefully enunciating his petition on behalf of the "citizens of the First Congressional District of Illinois. . . . Unless something is done about it, and it must be done soon, this crisis will become a national calamity."[28]

During his tenure in the House, Dawson sought better appointments for blacks in the federal civil service and judiciary, supported southern voter registration drives, and blocked congressional efforts to undermine the integration of public schools in Washington, DC. He also opposed poll taxes and legislation he thought placed an excessive tax burden on low-income citizens. A dedicated supporter of equal employment opportunities, Dawson remarked, "The right to work is the right to live" and "every American citizen is entitled to a job in this country."[29] In 1951, Dawson played an integral role in ensuring that the Universal Military Training Act furthered the desegregation of the armed forces initiated in 1948; he helped defeat the Winstead Amendment, which would have permitted military personnel to choose whether they wanted to serve in white or black units. Dawson made a rare speech on the House Floor during the debate to urge his colleagues to end racial discrimination in the military, mentioning that an injury he sustained during World War I would not have become a lifelong affliction had he been allowed access to a white hospital. Commenting proudly that he "led Americans in battle," Dawson proclaimed, "If there is one place in America where there should not be segregation, that place is in the armed services, among those who fight for this country."[30]

Despite his longevity and influence, Dawson never assumed a leadership role among African Americans in Congress. His disinclination to place race before the party clashed with the confrontational spirit adopted by many black leaders during the 1960s. When black Members drafted political statements to publicize issues of importance to minorities and promote a sense of unity among African-American Representatives, Dawson's name was often absent—an indication of the growing rift between Dawson and his black colleagues.[31] By the end of his career, the Illinois Representative found himself on the defensive for failing to disassociate himself from the Daley machine, which by the late 1960s was widely perceived as insufficiently committed to the cause of civil rights.[32]

Dawson rarely faced any significant opposition in his re-election bids from the predominantly black district. Regardless of the mounting criticism against him, he typically earned between 70 and 80 percent of the vote.[33] Even when poor health prevented him from playing an active role in Congress and on the campaign trail during his final few terms in the House, Dawson continued to enjoy comfortable victories against his opponents. However, by the mid-1960s Dawson's organization exhibited signs of decay. Burdened by age and ill health, he skillfully receded into the background while continuing to groom the African-American ward leaders of Chicago's South Side whom he helped place in power. On November 9, 1970, only six days after his handpicked successor, Ralph Metcalfe, won election to his seat, Dawson died of pneumonia in Chicago.[34] "Politics with me is a full-time business," Dawson once remarked. "It is not a hobby to be worked on in leisure hours, but it's a job—a full-time job that pays off only if a man is willing to apply the energy, start from scratch and profit by his experience."[35]

FOR FURTHER READING

"Dawson, William Levi," *Biographical Directory of the U.S. Congress, 1774–Present*, http://bioguide.congress.gov/scripts/biodisplay.pl?index=D000158.

Wilson, James Q. "Two Negro Politicians: An Interpretation," *Midwest Journal of Political Science* 4 (November 1960): 346–369.

MANUSCRIPT COLLECTIONS

Chicago Historical Society (Chicago, IL). *Papers:* 1943–1970, approximately 150 items. Correspondence, speeches, newspaper clippings, press releases, testimonials, and other papers relating to the career of William L. Dawson, a Chicago, Ill., lawyer, alderman, and U.S. Representative (Democrat). Includes material on the elections of 1944, 1948, 1952, and 1964 and letters from Presidents Harry S. Truman, John F. Kennedy, and Lyndon B. Johnson.

Fisk University (Nashville, TN), Special Collections, Library and Media Center. *Papers:* 1938–1970, 20.8 feet. The papers of William Levi Dawson contain correspondence (1930s to 1960s) with major U.S. political figures; speeches by Dawson before the House of Representatives, the Democratic National Convention, church groups, and other organizations; biographical data; scrapbooks of clippings; certificates, plaques, and awards; printed matter; and photos. A finding aid is available in the repository.

Howard University (Washington, DC), Manuscript Division, Moorland–Spingarn Research Center. *Papers:* ca. 1942–1972, approximately five linear feet. The congressional papers of William Levi Dawson consist of correspondence, writings about Dawson, speeches, legislation, voting records, and subject files. Also included are photographs, sound recordings, and memorabilia. A finding aid is available in the repository.

NOTES

1   For observations about Dawson's legislative style, see William L. Clay, *Just Permanent Interests: Black Americans in Congress, 1870–1991* (New York: Amistad, 1992): 366; Robert Nelson, "Political Goals Emerge: Chicago Negroes Rallied to Ballot," 30 October 1963, *Christian Science Monitor*: 3.

2   Ellen Hoffman, "Rep. William L. Dawson Dies," 10 November 1970, *Washington Post*: B6.

3   "People in the News," 2 January 1949, *Washington Post*: M2.

4   Thaddeus Russell, "William Levi Dawson," *American National Biography* 6 (New York: Oxford University Press, 1999): 258–259 (hereinafter referred to as *ANB*); Maurine Christopher, *Black Americans in Congress* (New York: Thomas Y. Crowell Company, 1971): 185.

5   Hoffman, "Rep. William L. Dawson Dies"; Christopher, *Black Americans in Congress*: 185.

6   Robert L. Johns, "William L. Dawson," in Jesse Carney Smith, ed., *Notable Black American Men* (Detroit, MI: Gale Research Inc., 1998): 270 (hereinafter referred to as *NBAM*).

7   Nancy Weiss, *Farewell to the Party of Lincoln: Black Politics in the Age of FDR* (Princeton, NJ: Princeton University Press, 1983): 87, 89–90.

8   "Election Statistics, 1920 to Present," available at http://clerk.house.gov/member_info/electionInfo/index.html.

9   See, for example, Weiss, *Farewell to the Party of Lincoln*: 78–95; and William J. Grimshaw, *Bitter Fruit: Black Politics and the Chicago Machine, 1931–1991* (Chicago: The University of Chicago Press, 1992): 47–68.

10 Grimshaw, *Bitter Fruit: Black Politics and the Chicago Machine, 1931–1991*: 75–77.

11 Harold Smith, "Congress Fight in 1st District Holds Spotlight," 22 February 1942, *Chicago Daily Tribune*: S5.

12 Harold Smith, "Feud Heightens King's Chances in the 1st District," 8 March 1942, *Chicago Daily Tribune*: S2; "Election Information, 1920 to Present," available at http://clerk.house.gov/member_info/electionInfo/index.html.

13 See Weiss, *Farewell to the Party of Lincoln*: 89–91.

14 "William L. Dawson," *Current Biography, 1945* (New York: H.W. Wilson and Company, 1945): 144.

15 "Negro in Congress Hailed," 22 January 1949, *New York Times*: 6.

16 "People in the News"; "Negro in Congress Hailed," 22 January 1949, *New York Times*: 6.

17   James Q. Wilson, "Two Negro Politicians: An Interpretation," *Midwest Journal of Political Science* 4 (November 1960): 358–360.

18   George Tagge, "Dawson Praises Daley and Defends the Machine," 11 February 1955, *Chicago Daily Tribune*: 1; George Tagge, "Kennelly Men Blast Dawson; Fight Promised," 12 January 1955, *Chicago Daily Tribune*: 16.

19   Arthur Schlesinger, Jr., *A Thousand Days: John F. Kennedy in the White House* (New York: Fawcett Press, 1965): 140. According to historian and administration chronicler Arthur Schlesinger, Jr., President-elect Kennedy initially had no intention of offering the post to Dawson. In large part, Kennedy did not want to offend powerful southern chairmen in Congress like Senator Olin D. Johnston of South Carolina, who headed the Post Office and Civil Service Committee and who complained that the proposed offer to Dawson was an attempt by political opponents to make him take a picture with the black nominee that could be used against him in his next primary campaign. In what Schlesinger described as a "comedy of complication," Kennedy made the offer to end the speculation. As scripted by the White House, Dawson declined.

20   For a detailed comparison of Representatives Dawson and Powell, see Wilson, "Two Negro Politicians: An Interpretation": 346–369.

21   Alden Whitman, "Power in Chicago," 10 November 1970, *New York Times*: 50; Percy Wood, "Congressman Dawson! Chicago Democrat with a Clout," 6 February 1955, *Chicago Daily Tribune*: 5; Drew Pearson, "Democrats Pick Negro for Job," 3 December 1949, *Washington Post*: B15.

22   Christopher, *Black Americans in Congress*: 190–191.

23   "NAACP Criticizes Rep. Dawson," 1 September 1956, *Washington Post*: 38; Hoffman, "Rep. William L. Dawson Dies"; Robert Singh, *Congressional Black Caucus: Racial Politics in the U.S. Congress* (Thousand Oaks, CA: Sage Publications, Inc.): 46–47; Carol M. Swain, *Black Faces, Black Interests: The Representation of African Americans in Congress* (Cambridge, MA: Harvard University Press, 1993): 34–35.

24   Hoffman, "Rep. William L. Dawson Dies"; Russell, "William Levi Dawson," *ANB*; Adam Fairclough, *Better Day Coming: Blacks and Equality, 1890–2000* (New York: Viking, 2001): 301.

25   Johns, "William L. Dawson," *NBAM*: 271.

26   "Dawson Lauded for Leadership," 18 March 1956, *New York Times*: 85.

27   One scholar of Chicago politics noted, "As the racial demands escalated, the machine increasingly took on the retrograde character of a southern white supremacist Democratic party." See Grimshaw, *Bitter Fruit: Black Politics and the Chicago Machine 1931–1991*: 117–118.

28   *Congressional Record*, House, 88th Cong., 1st sess. (29 October 1963): 20425. In light of Dawson's loyalty to the machine, the speech was likely sanctioned by Mayor Daley to help defuse rising unrest in urban black communities about continued political and social discrimination, and economic disparities.

29   *Congressional Record*, House, 79th Cong., 1st sess. (12 July 1945): 7485.

30   *Congressional Record*, House, 82nd Cong., 1st sess. (12 April 1951): 3765; John G. Norris, "Republican Efforts to Restrict Clauses Mostly Beaten Off; Conferees Act Next," 14 April 1951, *Washington Post*: 1; "Dawson Lauded for Leadership": 85.

31   Christopher, *Black Americans in Congress*: 192; Johns, "William L. Dawson," *NBAM*: 271.

32   Francis Ward, "Dawson Dies; Pioneer Black Congressman," 10 November 1970, *Los Angeles Times*: A19; Russell, "William Levi Dawson," *ANB*.

33   "Election Information, 1920 to Present," available at http://clerk. house.gov/member_info/electionInfo/index.html; Hoffman, "Rep. William L. Dawson Dies."

34   Hoffman, "Rep. William L. Dawson Dies."

35   Johns, "William L. Dawson," *NBAM*: 271.

"POLITICS WITH ME IS A FULL-TIME BUSINESS," DAWSON ONCE REMARKED. "IT IS NOT A HOBBY TO BE WORKED ON IN LEISURE HOURS, BUT IT'S A JOB—A FULL-TIME JOB THAT PAYS OFF ONLY IF A MAN IS WILLING TO APPLY THE ENERGY, START FROM SCRATCH AND PROFIT BY HIS EXPERIENCE."

Adam Clayton Powell, Jr.
1908–1972

UNITED STATES REPRESENTATIVE ★ 1945–1967; 1967–1971
DEMOCRAT FROM NEW YORK

An unapologetic activist, Adam Clayton Powell, Jr., left his mark on Congress during his 12 terms in the House of Representatives. Viewed by his Harlem constituents as a dedicated crusader for civil rights, Powell earned the loyalty and respect of many African Americans with his confrontational approach to racial discrimination. Never one to shun the spotlight, the outspoken New York minister and politician—regarded as an irritant by many of his congressional colleagues—relished his position as a spokesperson for the advancement of African-American rights. Although Powell fought tirelessly on behalf of minorities, his legal problems and unpredictable behavior eventually undermined his influential but controversial political career. "Keep the faith, baby; spread it gently and walk together, children," was a legendary slogan of the charismatic and flamboyant Representative.[1]

Adam Clayton Powell, Jr., was born in New Haven, Connecticut, on November 29, 1908. At the age of six months he moved to New York City with his older sister Blanche and his parents, Mattie Fletcher Schaffer and Adam Clayton Powell, Sr., a Baptist preacher. The family relocated to New York when Adam Clayton Powell, Sr., was assigned to serve as a minister at the century-old Abyssinian Baptist Church in midtown Manhattan. Under his leadership, the congregation grew into one of the largest in the United States. Adam Clayton Powell, Sr., oversaw the move of the church and his family during the black migration to Harlem in the 1920s.[2]

After graduating from Townsend Harris High School in New York (also attended by Powell's future African-American House colleague Robert N. C. Nix of Pennsylvania), Powell enrolled in the City College of New York. In 1926 he transferred to Colgate University in Hamilton, New York. As an undergraduate, he often circumvented the socially accepted racial barriers of the

period because his light skin allowed him to pass as a white student.[3] A year after graduating from Colgate in 1930, Powell earned an M.A. in religious education from Columbia University. Though his choice to enter the ministry pleased his father, his decision to marry Isabel Washington—a recently separated Catholic actress—in 1933 did not. Powell later adopted Washington's son Preston from her previous marriage.[4] After divorcing his first wife, the future Representative married two more times: Hazel Scott in 1945 and Yvette Flores in 1960. Both marriages ended in divorce, too, and Powell had one son with each wife; both sons were Powell's namesake.[5]

Powell used his position as assistant minister and business manager of the Abyssinian Church to press for change in the predominantly African-American community. In 1930, he organized picket lines and mass meetings to demand reforms at Harlem Hospital, which had dismissed five doctors because they were black. Beginning in 1932, he administered a church-sponsored relief program that provided food, clothing, and temporary jobs for thousands of Harlem's homeless and unemployed. During the Great Depression, Powell established himself as a charismatic and commanding civil rights leader, directing mass meetings, rent strikes, and public campaigns that forced employers including restaurants, utilities, Harlem Hospital, and the 1939 World's Fair in New York City to hire or promote black workers. Powell's early social activism earned him the steadfast support of Harlem residents and helped lay the foundation for his future political career.[6]

In 1937, Powell succeeded his father as pastor of the Abyssinian Baptist Church. A popular community leader, he decided to enter the local political scene. After earning the endorsement of New York City Mayor Fiorello LaGuardia, the 33-year-old Powell easily won a seat on the

New York City council in 1941.[7] During World War II, Powell maintained his attacks on racial discrimination in the military and on the domestic front. Airing his views on racism through speaking engagements and columns in *The People's Voice*, a weekly newspaper he published and edited from 1941 to 1945, the feisty politician attracted national attention. Powell gained additional political experience during the war years by serving on the New York State Office of Price Administration. The creation in 1942 of a new U.S. congressional district that encompassed much of Harlem, along with name recognition and political skill, positioned Powell for a strong bid for a vacant House seat in 1944.[8]

Running on a platform that focused on the advancement of African-American rights through the promotion of fair employment practices and a ban on poll taxes and lynching, Powell received support from two of New York City's most influential organizations, the Abyssinian Church and the local Democratic machine, Tammany Hall. Asked to expand upon his political goals, Powell promised to "represent the Negro people first and after that all the other American people." However, he later said he would represent the people of his Harlem district "irrespective of race, creed, or political affiliation."[9] Despite Powell's overwhelming popularity among Harlem's black voters (approximately 90 percent of the district), his aggressive political style alienated some local leaders, causing a scramble by the Republican Party to locate a viable opponent in the upcoming election. Sara Speaks, a Harlem lawyer endorsed by the Republican Party, and Powell took advantage of state election laws allowing candidates to run in multiple party primaries. But Speaks proved no match for Powell, who won both the Democratic primary (82 to 18 percent) and the GOP primary (57 to 43 percent). Powell also received the American Labor Party designation, allowing him to run unopposed in the general election and subsequently to earn a spot in the 79th Congress (1945–1947).[10] He was the first African-American Member to represent New York. Powell's demand for racial equality and his

uncompromising demeanor resonated with his Harlem constituents, whose support essentially guaranteed Powell a House seat for the majority of his career. Like many of his future African-American House colleagues, Powell parlayed his strong record of civil rights at the local level into a congressional career.

When Congress convened on January 3, 1945, William Dawson of Illinois, the only other black Member, escorted Powell into the House Chamber for his first day in office. Powell and Dawson remained the only African-American Representatives from 1945 to 1955.[11] During his first term in Congress, Powell served on the Indian Affairs, Invalid Pensions, and Labor committees. In 1947, the Education Committee and the Labor Committee were merged, and Powell remained on the new panel for 11 terms, three of them as chairman. Powell was also a member of the Committee on Interior and Insular Affairs from 1955 until 1961.

Aware that Powell was an atypical freshman Representative because of his race and his independent nature, Speaker Sam Rayburn of Texas encouraged him to wait before making any waves in Congress, and Powell's reserved demeanor during his first month on the Hill surprised many reporters. Powell later said Democratic leaders had convinced him his "maiden speech in the House should be constructive and on as high a plane as possible."[12] After his initial reticence, Powell quickly recaptured the flair that made him such a dynamic public figure. During his first term, he introduced legislation to extend the civil rights of District of Columbia residents, to outlaw lynching and the poll tax, and to end discrimination in the armed forces, housing, employment, and transportation. He attached an anti-discrimination clause to so many pieces of legislation, the rider became known as the Powell Amendment. Initially considered a symbolic maneuver, his rider was included in the 1964 Civil Rights Act.[13] His commitment to prohibit federal funding to groups advocating unequal treatment of Black Americans earned him the epithet "Mr. Civil Rights" and infuriated some of his congressional colleagues.[14]

During a July 1955 meeting of the Education and Labor Committee, avowed segregationist and West Virginia Democrat Cleveland Bailey punched Powell in the jaw out of anger from what he perceived as Powell's continued efforts to undermine the committee's legislative efforts with his rider. The encounter, which drew national attention, apparently ended with a conciliatory handshake. Asked to comment on the skirmish, Powell said, "Cleve Bailey and I smoke cigars together, and are old friends." He added, "We always will be."[15]

Soon after his arrival in Washington, Powell challenged the informal regulations forbidding black Representatives from using Capitol facilities reserved for Members. Following the lead of Oscar De Priest, Powell often took black constituents to the whites-only House Restaurant and ordered his staff to eat there. Always looking for ways to advance racial equality, Powell also successfully campaigned to desegregate the press galleries.[16] Powell's aggressive stance on discrimination within Congress led to numerous confrontations with John E. Rankin, a Democrat from Mississippi and one of the chamber's most notorious segregationists. Even before Powell's election to Congress, Rankin disparaged attempts to integrate the Capitol. "That gang of communistic Jews and Negroes . . . tried to storm the House Restaurant and went around here arm in arm with each other" was Rankin's inflammatory response to a 1943 protest and characteristic of his stance on civil rights.[17] When Rankin made known his intention to avoid sitting near an African-American Member, Powell responded to the slight by sitting close to the southern politician whenever possible.[18] Also, Powell retorted, "I am happy that Rankin will not sit by me because that makes it mutual. The only people with whom he is qualified to sit are Hitler and Mussolini."[19] The two men did not confine their mutual dislike to seating arrangements. Powell spoke on the House Floor to condemn Rankin's racial attack on Jewish journalist Walter Winchell. "Last week democracy was shamed by the uncalled for and unfounded condemnation of one of America's great minorities." Powell continued, "I am not a member of that great minority,

but I will always oppose anyone who tries to besmirch any group because of race, creed or color. Let us give leadership to this nation in terms of racial and religious tolerance and stop petty bickering in this body."[20] Powell also denounced the racial slurs uttered in the House by Rankin and other southern Democrats, demanding an inquiry by the House Parliamentarian into the use of "disparaging terms" on the floor.[21]

In 1945, Powell looked to expose the prejudicial practices of the long-standing Daughters of the American Revolution (DAR) after the organization refused to allow his second wife, Hazel Scott, a jazz pianist, to perform in Constitution Hall. Hopeful that First Lady Bess Truman's reaction would be similar to First Lady Eleanor Roosevelt's when the DAR barred African-American Marian Anderson from singing in the concert hall, Powell became enraged when Mrs. Truman refused to intercede. His characterization of Bess Truman as the "last lady" of the land, in response to her decision to attend a previously scheduled DAR tea, instigated a lingering feud between President Harry S. Truman and the New York Democrat that resulted in Powell's exile from the White House during Truman's years in office.[22] The disagreement also fueled a heated debate on the House Floor in which Representative Rankin alleged that Powell's criticism of the situation had a communist origin.[23]

Powell spent considerable time drawing attention to the plight of poor Africans and Asians. In 1955, he attended the Bandung Conference in Indonesia, despite efforts by U.S. officials to dissuade him. Privately, State Department officials expressed concern that Powell's presence at Bandung was "bad" and might be construed as a sign of tacit U.S. approval for a discussion among nations that, for the most part, wished to remain neutral in the Cold War conflict between the Americans and the Soviets.[24] While observing the meeting of newly independent African and Asian nations, Powell was confronted by communist reporters who asked about the appalling conditions faced by African Americans. Acknowledging the existence of discrimination in the United States, Powell pointed to himself as an example of improved circumstances for minorities. Upon his return, he urged President Dwight D. Eisenhower and other American policymakers to stand firm against colonialism and to pay greater attention to the emerging Third World.[25] To keep the issue in the public eye, Powell made speeches on the House Floor that celebrated the anniversaries of the independence of nations such as Ghana, Indonesia, and Sierra Leone.[26]

During much of his tenure in Congress, Powell occupied the public spotlight. Known as a political maverick, he received national attention when he broke ranks with the Democratic Party to endorse President Eisenhower's re-election bid in 1956. Powell threw his support behind the Eisenhower administration because he was dissatisfied with the Democratic nominee for President, Adlai Stevenson, and his choice for Vice President, Alabama Senator John Sparkman.[27] Southern Democrats sought to retaliate against Powell, calling for Democratic leaders to strip him of his seniority. The National Association for the Advancement of Colored People rose to Powell's defense, persuading Speaker Sam Rayburn and liberal Emanuel Celler—dean of the New York delegation and chairman of the Judiciary Committee—not to take punitive action. Nevertheless, Powell's House enemies prevailed in an effort to fire two of Powell's patronage appointees. Of greater consequence, Education and Labor Committee Chairman Graham Barden of North Carolina, a fervent segregationist, denied Powell one of the five subcommittee chairmanships, even though Powell was the third-ranking Democrat on the full committee.[28]

In the late 1950s, Powell began to make headlines outside the political realm. He was indicted for income tax evasion by a federal grand jury in 1958, and the federal government continued to investigate his finances, even though the well publicized 1960 trial ended with a hung jury.[29] The immediate political fallout from the indictment and trial proved negligible. Tammany Hall withdrew its support for Powell in the 1958 Democratic primary—a decision machine leaders claimed stemmed from the New

York Representative's support for Eisenhower, not his legal problems—and backed black candidate Earl Brown, a Harlem city councilman. Powell easily captured the nomination for his Harlem district, even with Tammany's defection.[30]

The New York Representative was also criticized for taking numerous trips abroad at public expense, payroll discrepancies, and a high level of absenteeism for House votes. Asked to justify his erratic attendance record on the Hill, Powell replied, "You don't have to be there if you know which calls to make, which buttons to push, which favors to call in."[31] For most of his career, Powell remained relatively unscathed by the public attention he incurred from such lapses. Instead of retreating from the limelight, he used the publicity to his advantage. By refusing to alter his defiant behavior, Powell earned the respect of many African Americans who viewed his actions as bold and rebellious. "Arrogant, but with style," a characterization Powell relished, aptly described the politician who captivated his constituents throughout his career.[32]

When Representative Barden retired after the 86th Congress (1959–1961), Powell, next in seniority, assumed the chairmanship of the Committee on Education and Labor, a position he held for three terms until January 1967. Powell's service as chairman marked the most productive period of his congressional career. The committee approved more than 50 measures authorizing federal programs for increases in the minimum wage, education and training for the deaf, school lunches, vocational training, student loans, and standards for wages and work hours as well as aid for elementary and secondary schools and public libraries. "We have been a more productive committee in the last year and a half than the New Deal," a committee member noted in 1965. "You talk about Roosevelt's one hundred days—what the hell, look at what we've done. It's been under Powell's chairmanship and you've got to give him credit for that."[33] The legislation introduced by Powell's committee helped shape much of the social policy of the John F. Kennedy and Lyndon B. Johnson administrations. A personal supporter of President Kennedy and, especially, President Johnson (Powell once claimed Johnson was "the only man who could bridge the bleeding gap between the North and the South"), Powell benefited from the agendas of both Presidents.[34]

By the mid-1960s, however, Powell was being criticized not only by longtime enemies but also by committee members dismayed by his irregular management of the committee budget. Those who often interacted with Powell as a committee chairman noted his "erratic" work style, his "quixotic unpredictability," and his frequent absences.[35] His highly publicized jet-setting lifestyle elicited such judgments and raised serious concerns about his effectiveness as a committee leader. Powell's refusal to pay a 1963 slander judgment to New Yorker Esther James, who Powell alleged served as a "bag woman," transporting money from gamblers to corrupt police officers, further irked his colleagues. The public case, which lasted several years, led to Powell's self-imposed exile from his district. To avoid arrest, Powell made brief weekend appearances in Harlem since state law prohibited serving civil contempt warrants on Sundays.[36] Powell's biographer Charles V. Hamilton observed that the Harlem Representative miscalculated the toll of such actions on his House career. Powell often viewed his attainment of important positions within an indifferent, often unfriendly, institution as proof of the potential of the powerless multitudes. And while clearly his achievements provided a beacon of hope to millions of Black Americans, his personal foibles left him vulnerable and oddly impassive to obvious consequences. "If the political system could for so long oppress and permit the subjugation of a whole people," Hamilton wrote, "then why would [Powell] expect, as a spokesman for that people, to be accorded any better treatment?"[37]

Weary of Powell's legal problems and his unpredictable antics, the House Democratic Caucus stripped the New York Representative of his committee chairmanship on January 9, 1967. The full House refused to seat him until the Judiciary Committee completed an investigation. The following month, the committee recommended that Powell be censured, fined, and deprived of seniority, but on March 1, 1967, the House rejected these proposals

and voted—307 to 116—to exclude him from the 90th Congress (1967–1969). Unimpressed by the House's mandate to ban their Representative, Harlem's voters sent Congress a resounding message during the special election to fill Powell's seat on April 11, 1967. Powell received 86 percent of the vote but refused to take his seat and spent most of the term on the island of Bimini in the Bahamas. After he was re-elected to a 12th term in November 1968, the House voted to deny Powell his seniority and to fine him for misusing payroll and travel finances.

The Supreme Court helped vindicate Powell with its June 1969 ruling that the House acted unconstitutionally by excluding him from the 90th Congress. "From now on, America will know the Supreme Court is the place where you can get justice," Powell declared.[38] Despite the legal absolution, Powell never regained his former influence or authority in Congress. Still confident he would earn another term in the House, Powell entered the Democratic primary in 1970. Although Powell said, "My people would elect me . . . even if I had to be propped up in my casket," some of his constituents had grown tired of his legal troubles, negative publicity, and infrequent attendance in Congress.[39] His strongest opponent in the primary, Harlem-based New York State Assemblyman Charles Rangel, highlighted Powell's absenteeism, using campaign literature marking the major votes he had missed.[40] Even in the face of a formidable primary challenge, Powell adhered to his characteristic laidback campaigning, making few public appearances. Benefiting from redistricting that diluted Powell's base of power in Harlem by adding to the district a slice of the mostly white Upper West Side, Rangel edged out the controversial Representative in the primary by approximately 200 votes to become the Democratic candidate and the eventual Representative for his district.[41] Consistent with his determined nature, Powell contested the election results, but although the recount reduced the margin of victory from 203 to 150 votes, Rangel still prevailed.[42]

Diagnosed with cancer in 1969, Powell declined rapidly after he left Congress. He retired as minister of the

Abyssinian Baptist Church in 1971 and spent his waning days in Bimini. He died on April 4, 1972, in Miami, Florida.[43] Once asked to describe his political career, Powell said, "As a member of Congress, I have done nothing more than any other member and, by the grace of God, I intend to do not one bit less."[44]

FOR FURTHER READING

Hamilton, Charles V. *Adam Clayton Powell, Jr.: The Political Biography of an American Dilemma* (New York: Atheneum, 1991).

"Powell, Adam Clayton, Jr.," *Biographical Directory of the U.S. Congress, 1774–Present*, http://bioguide.congress.gov/scripts/biodisplay.pl?index=P000477.

Powell, Adam Clayton, Jr. *Adam by Adam: The Autobiography of Adam Clayton Powell, Jr.* (New York: Dial Press, 1971).

_____. *Marching Blacks: An Interpretive History of the Rise of the Black Common Man* (New York: Dial Press, 1945).

MANUSCRIPT COLLECTIONS

National Archives and Records Administration (Washington, DC), Center for Legislative Archives. *Papers*: In the Committee on Education and Labor Records, 80th through the 89th Congresses, amount unknown. Adam Clayton Powell, Jr., served on the committee from the 80th Congress forward; he served as chairman from the 87th through the 89th Congresses. *Papers:* In the Committee on Interior and Insular Affairs Records, 84th through 86th Congresses, amount unknown. Powell also is represented in oral histories and papers in the following presidential libraries: Dwight D. Eisenhower, Gerald R. Ford, Lyndon B. Johnson, John F. Kennedy, Richard M. Nixon, and Harry S. Truman.

The New York Public Library (New York, NY), Schomburg Center for Research in Black Culture Library. *Photographs*: ca. 1935–1969, 109 prints. Portraits of Adam Clayton Powell, Jr., mainly from his congressional years through his exile to Bimini and his return to the United States. The collection includes views of Powell preaching at the Abyssinian Baptist Church, speaking to students at the University of California at Los Angeles, at the Lincoln Memorial, holding press conferences, with wife Hazel Scott

Powell and their son Adam III, campaigning, surrounded by crowds, attending political functions, blowing out birthday candles, participating in an awards ceremony, and posing with attorneys.

NOTES

1   Thomas A. Johnson, "A Man of Many Roles," 5 April 1972, *New York Times*: 1. "Keep the faith, baby" was one of Powell's more memorable responses to questions regarding the move by the House to exclude him from Congress. He later used the phrase as the title for a book of his sermons.

2   Peter Wallenstein, "Powell, Adam Clayton, Jr.," *American National Biography* 17 (New York: Oxford University Press, 1999): 771–773 (hereinafter referred to as *ANB).*

3   Charles V. Hamilton, *Adam Clayton Powell, Jr.: The Political Biography of an American Dilemma* (New York: Atheneum, 1991): 47–50.

4   Simon Glickman, "Adam Clayton Powell, Jr.," *Contemporary Black Biography* 3 (Detroit: Gale Research Inc., 1992) (hereinafter referred to as *CBB).*

5   Wallenstein, "Powell, Adam Clayton, Jr.," *ANB*; Shirley Washington, *Outstanding African Americans of Congress* (Washington, DC: U.S. Capitol Historical Society, 1998): 71; Ilene Jones-Cornwell, "Adam Clayton Powell, Jr.," in Jessie Carney Smith, ed., *Notable Black American Men* (Farmington Hills, MI: Gale Research, Inc., 1999): 954–957 (hereinafter referred to as *NBAM).*

6   Johnson, "A Man of Many Roles"; Wallenstein, "Powell, Adam Clayton, Jr.," *ANB*; Bruce A. Ragsdale and Joel D. Treese, *Black Americans in Congress, 1870–1989* (Washington, DC: Government Printing Office, 1990): 196.

7   Richard L. Lyons, "Adam Clayton Powell, Apostle for Blacks," 6 April 1972, *Washington Post*: B5.

8   Washington, *Outstanding African Americans in Congress*: 68; Hamilton, *Adam Clayton Powell, Jr*: 144.

9   "Powell Declares 'Negro First' Aim," 9 April 1944, *New York Times*: 25; "Powell Revises Pledge," 30 April 1944, *New York Times*: 40.

10 "Election Statistics, 1920 to Present," available at http://clerk.house.gov/member_info/electionInfo/index.html; Hamilton, *Adam Clayton Powell, Jr.*: 149–156; Glickman, "Adam Clayton Powell, Jr.," *CBB*; Johnson, "A Man of Many Roles."

11 Jones-Cornwell, "Adam Clayton Powell, Jr.," *NBAM*: 956; Wil Haygood, *King of the Cats: The Life and Times of Adam Clayton Powell, Jr.* (New York: Amistad, 2006): 113.

12 Haygood, *King of the Cats*: 115.

13 Washington, *Outstanding African Americans of Congress*: 70.

14 Wallenstein, "Powell, Adam Clayton, Jr.," *ANB*.

15 William J. Brady, "Bailey Punches Powell in Row Over Segregation," 21 July 1955, *Washington Post*: 1; John D. Morris, "Powell Is Punched by House Colleague," 21 July 1955, *New York Times*: 1; Hamilton, *Adam Clayton Powell, Jr.*: 235.

16 Wallenstein, "Powell, Adam Clayton, Jr.," *ANB*.

17 *Congressional Record*, House, 78th Cong., 1st sess. (1 July 1943): A3371.

18 Adam Clayton Powell, Jr., *Adam by Adam: The Autobiography of Adam Clayton Powell, Jr.* (New York: Dial Press, 1971): 73; Washington, *Outstanding African Americans of Congress*: 69–70; Alfred Friendly, "Jefferson and Rankin," 14 April 1947, *Washington Post*: 7.

19 Hamilton, *Adam Clayton Powell, Jr.*: 178.

20 *Congressional Record*, House, 79th Cong., 1st sess. (13 February 1945): 1045; Wil Haygood, "Power and Love; When Adam Clayton Powell Jr. Met Hazel Scott, Sparks Flew," 17 January 1993, *Washington Post Magazine*: W14.

21 Hamilton, *Adam Clayton Powell, Jr.*: 186–187.

22 Ibid., 165; "Powell Demand for D.A.R. Snub Draws Refusal," 13 October 1945, *Los Angeles Times*: 2; Glickman, "Adam Clayton Powell, Jr.," *CBB*.

23 "Congress Debates D.A.R. Hall Row," 17 October 1945, *New York Times*: 19; "Rankin Calls DAR Attacks 'Communist,'" 18 October 1945, *Washington Post*: 4; Haygood, "Power and Love."

24 For more on Powell and the Bandung Conference, see Brenda Gayle Plummer, *Rising Wind: Black Americans and U.S. Foreign Affairs, 1935–1960* (Chapel Hill: University of North Carolina Press, 1996): 248–253. For the "bad" quote in a telephone conversation between Secretary of State John Foster Dulles and a CIA official, see U.S. Department of State, Office of the Historian, *Foreign Relations of the United States, 1955–1957, Volume 21: Asian Security, Cambodia, and Laos* (Washington, DC: Government Printing Office, 1989): 77.

25 Washington, *Outstanding African Americans of Congress*: 71; Haygood, *King of the Cats*: 200–204.

26 Throughout his career, Powell made many of these speeches. For an example see, *Congressional Record*, House, 91st Cong., 1st sess. (29 July 1969): 21212.

27 Glickman, "Adam Clayton Powell, Jr.," *CBB*.

28 Hamilton, *Adam Clayton Powell, Jr.*: 276–279.

29 "Powell Gives Innocent Plea in Tax Case," 17 May 1958, *Washington Post*: A2; "Tax-Charge Deadlock Dismisses Powell Jury," 23 April 1960, *Washington Post*: A3.

30 For more on Powell's rift with Tammany Hall, see Hamilton, *Adam Clayton Powell, Jr.*: 299–312. "Powell Gives Innocent Plea in Tax Case"; Leo Egan, "Powell, Lindsay Win in Primaries by Wide Margins," 13 August 1958, *New York Times*: 1; "Powell Victory Is an Old Story," 13 August 1958, *New York Times*: 18.

31 Johnson, "A Man of Many Roles."

32 Wallenstein, "Powell, Adam Clayton, Jr.," *ANB*.

33 Richard F. Fenno, Jr., *Congressmen in Committees* (Boston: Little, Brown, and Company, 1973): 128.

34 "'Think Big, Black,' Powell Urges," 29 March 1965, *Washington Post*: D3. For more on Powell's relationship with President Johnson, see Hamilton, *Adam Clayton Powell, Jr.*: 369–374.

35 Fenno, *Congressmen in Committees*: 130–131.

36 Hamilton, *Adam Clayton Powell, Jr.*: 434–437; John J. Goldman, "Adam Clayton Powell, 63, Dies; Politician, Preacher and Playboy," 5 April 1972, *Los Angeles Times*: A1.

37 Hamilton, *Adam Clayton Powell, Jr.*: 485.

38 Johnson, "A Man of Many Roles."

39 Glickman, "Adam Clayton Powell, Jr.," *CBB*.

40 David Shipler, "Powell, in Race, Has Faith in Himself," 16 June 1970, *New York Times*: 50; Thomas Ronan, "Rangel, Calling Powell a Failure, Says He Will Seek Congressional Post," 21 February 1970, *New York Times*: 24.

41 Michael J. Dubin et al., *United States Congressional Elections, 1788–1997* (Jefferson, NC: McFarland Publishing Company, Inc., 1998): 672; Hamilton, *Adam Clayton Powell, Jr.*: 473–478.

42 "Powell Defeat Confirmed by Recount," 28 June 1970, *New York Times*: 29; "Powell Loser in Recount of Primary Vote," 28 June 1970, *Chicago Tribune*: A3.

43 Jones-Cornwell, "Adam Clayton Powell, Jr.," *NBAM*; Hamilton, *Adam Clayton Powell, Jr.*: 478.

44 Johnson, "A Man of Many Roles."

"As a member of Congress,

I have done nothing more

than any other member

and, by the grace of God,

I intend to do

not one bit less,"

Powell once remarked.

Charles Coles Diggs, Jr.
1922–1998

UNITED STATES REPRESENTATIVE ★ 1955–1980
DEMOCRAT FROM MICHIGAN

Elected to the House of Representatives in 1954 at age 31, Charles C. Diggs, Jr., was the first African American to represent Michigan in Congress. Despite his reserved demeanor, Diggs served as an ardent supporter of civil rights and an impassioned advocate of increased American aid to Africa. As a principal architect of home rule for the District of Columbia and the driving force behind the formation of the Congressional Black Caucus (CBC), Diggs crafted a national legacy during his 25 years in the House. John Conyers, Jr., of Detroit, Diggs's House colleague of many years said, "Congressman Diggs paved the way for an entire generation of black political leaders, not just in his home state, but through the nation."[1]

Charles Coles Diggs, Jr., the only child of Charles Diggs, Sr., and Mamie Ethel Jones Diggs, was born in Detroit, Michigan, on December 2, 1922. Prominent in Detroit, the Diggs family owned a local mortuary, a funeral insurance company, and an ambulance service. In the 1920s, the city that would become the hub of the U.S. automobile industry underwent a massive transformation as southern blacks streamed northward in search of wage labor. Between 1920 and 1930, Detroit's black population tripled—growing at a faster rate than any other major northern city.[2] Charles Diggs, Sr., personified rising black influence in Detroit, becoming the first African-American Democrat elected to the Michigan state senate.[3] After graduating from Detroit's Miller High School in 1940, Charles Diggs, Jr., enrolled at the University of Michigan at Ann Arbor. After two years, Diggs transferred to Fisk University in Nashville, Tennessee. While still an undergraduate in Tennessee, he entered the United States Army Air Forces as a private on February 19, 1943. During World War II, Diggs was a member of a segregated unit that trained at an airstrip in Alabama. Commissioned a second lieutenant in 1944,

Diggs was discharged from the military on June 1, 1945. Diggs resumed his academic career, enrolling in Detroit's Wayne College of Mortuary Science. After graduating in June 1946, the newly licensed mortician joined his father's funeral business, serving as chairman of the House of Diggs, Inc. Diggs also delivered commentary on current affairs (interspersed with gospel music) as part of a weekly radio show sponsored by his business. Married four times, Charles Diggs, Jr., had six children.[4]

Although it was not his original intent, Diggs ultimately followed in his father's political footsteps. Elected to the Michigan state senate in 1936, Charles Diggs, Sr., was caught up in a legislative bribery scandal in 1944, bringing his public service to a grinding halt.[5] Upon his release from prison in 1950, Diggs, Sr., sought to reclaim his position in the legislature. He won his election bid, but in an unprecedented move, the Republican-controlled Michigan senate refused to seat him and another member-elect because of their criminal records.[6] Outraged by the events that prevented his father from resuming his political career, Charles Diggs, Jr., interrupted his studies at the Detroit School of Law to enter the special election for his father's seat. Diggs won the election and served in the Michigan senate for three years before setting his sights on the United States Congress.[7] Using the campaign slogan "Make Democracy Live," he defeated incumbent Representative George D. O'Brien by a two-to-one margin in the August 1954 Democratic primary in the overwhelmingly Democratic, majority-black Detroit district.[8] Building on the momentum from the primary, Diggs easily bested Republican Landon Knight—the son of John S. Knight, editor and publisher of the *Detroit Free Press*—in the general election, capturing 66 percent of the vote to become Michigan's first African-American Representative.[9] After winning a seat in the 84th Congress (1955–1957),

Diggs remarked, "This is a great victory for the voters of the Democratic Party, and it also settles deeper issues—the racial issue. This is proof that the voters of the Thirteenth District have reached maturity."[10] Diggs rarely faced serious opposition in subsequent elections, typically winning by more than 70 percent in an impoverished urban district that saw a rapid decline in population and a substantial rise in black residents during his House tenure.[11]

Diggs began his congressional career on January 3, 1955, as a member of the Committee on Interior and Insular Affairs and the Veterans' Affairs Committee. But Diggs's committee service did not follow the upward trajectory to which many Members aspired.[12] Rather than seeking out high-profile posts on top-tier panels as he accrued seniority, Diggs chose assignments that allowed him to positively influence African-American lives, and international human rights issues. In 1959, Diggs joined the Foreign Affairs Committee (later International Relations Committee), remaining there until he left Congress in 1980. Diggs became a member of the Committee on the District of Columbia (with jurisdiction over the nation's capital, which had undergone a shift from a majority-white population to majority-black after schools were desegregated in the 1950s) in 1963 and was on the panel for the remainder of his congressional tenure.

In the 84th Congress, Diggs joined black Representatives Adam Clayton Powell, Jr., of New York and William L. Dawson of Illinois. For a young Representative learning the institutional ropes, Powell and Dawson could not have provided two more different role models.[13] Flamboyant and flashy, Powell was a leading civil rights figure who grabbed headlines while constantly challenging the status quo. Dawson, reserved and businesslike and ever the party and machine man, used his chairmanship on the Government Operations Committee to exert influence from the inside. Diggs drew upon both these legislative styles throughout his career.

While a freshman Member of the House, Diggs demonstrated his commitment to ending racial discrimination. In September 1955, the Michigan Representative

garnered attention from the national media when he attended the trial of two white Mississippians accused of murdering Emmett Till, a 14-year-old African-American boy, for allegedly whistling at a white woman.[14] When Diggs discovered that the county where the trial was being held had no registered black voters, he suggested that Mississippi's representation in Congress should be reduced—echoing Members from earlier decades who called for the enforcement of Section Two of the 14th Amendment, requiring reduced congressional representation for states that discriminated against qualified voters.[15] Two months later, Diggs proposed that President Dwight D. Eisenhower convene a special session of Congress to consider civil rights issues. He also was an outspoken advocate of the Civil Rights Act of 1957.[16]

Representative Diggs frequently participated in events to attract publicity for the civil rights movement. In February 1965, he interviewed residents of Selma, Alabama, in an attempt to expose discrimination in federally funded programs in the South. Diggs also marched with 12,000 people in Charleston, South Carolina, in May 1969 to support black hospital workers who were seeking the right to organize and bargain collectively.[17] A leader in the fight to desegregate public schools, Diggs, as well as Powell, believed schools that refused to abide by the 1954 Supreme Court decision *Brown v. Board of Education* should lose federal funding.[18] During a speech aimed at promoting civil rights in Jackson, Mississippi, Diggs confidently proclaimed, "integration is as inevitable as the rising sun—even in Mississippi."[19]

Nearly a decade after he joined the Committee on the District of Columbia, Diggs ascended to the chairman's post when the former head, South Carolina segregationist John L. McMillan, failed to win renomination to his House seat. "I don't plan to be the unofficial mayor of Washington," Diggs said about his new position. "The city already has a mayor and City Council. I don't intend to become involved with the day-to-day operations of the city government."[20] Instead, Diggs sought to increase the autonomy of the District of Columbia by continuing to fight for home rule for the nation's capital. In 1973 he succeeded in bringing a bill to the House Floor authorizing partial self-government for Washington, DC. Before the legislation was voted on, he reminded his colleagues, "When we talk about self-determination for the District of Columbia we are not only talking about a matter of local interest, but because of the unique role of this capital community, it is of concern to each one of the Members of the 435 districts across this country."[21] Under the direction of Chairman Diggs, the House overwhelmingly passed the measure; on December 24, 1973, President Richard M. Nixon signed the District of Columbia Self-Government and Governmental Reorganization Act, enabling residents of the nation's capital to elect their mayor and city council for the first time since 1874. During his tenure as chairman of the Committee on the District of Columbia, Diggs also helped establish the University of the District of Columbia and led the movement to make Frederick Douglass's historic house in Anacostia a national monument.[22]

Throughout his career in Congress, Diggs looked for ways to forge connections with other black Members. Dissatisfied with the typically informal bonds between African-American Representatives, Diggs organized the Democratic Select Committee (DSC) in 1969 to promote the exchange of ideas between black Members. Black Representatives newly elected to the 91st Congress (1969–1971), such as Shirley Chisholm of New York, William Clay, Sr., of Missouri, and Louis Stokes of Ohio, embraced the idea of a network for African Americans in the House but pressed for a more formal organization with political clout. This transformation occurred in 1971 when the DSC was reorganized into the Congressional Black Caucus (CBC). The first chair of the CBC (1971–1973), Diggs called the new caucus "the first departure from the individualistic policies that characterized black congressmen in the past."[23] Also, Diggs's involvement in the Michigan redistricting after the 1960 Census helped increase black representation in the House; the subsequent reapportionment created another majority-black district in Detroit. With the congressional election of John Conyers, Jr., in 1964, Michigan became the first state since Reconstruction with two African-American Representatives.[24]

In addition to promoting a civil rights agenda on the domestic front, Diggs focused on legislation shaping U.S. policy toward Africa. Eventually dubbed "Mr. Africa" because of his dedication to and knowledge of African affairs, Diggs accompanied Vice President Nixon on a tour of Africa two years after taking office, and in 1958 he attended the All-African Peoples Conference in Ghana. In February 1969, he headed a fact-finding mission to civil war-torn Nigeria to investigate relief programs for civilians and to explore a possible cease-fire. After being named chair of the Foreign Affairs Subcommittee on Africa in 1969, Diggs continued to pursue his goal of making Africa a higher priority in American international relations. In his new leadership role, which he held for a decade, he emphasized the importance of increased American aid to the newly independent African countries.[25]

Diggs led the early charge by African-American Members to denounce the apartheid regime in South Africa. He conducted a series of hearings to investigate how some American businesses and government programs helped the economy of South Africa, despite the official U.S. opposition to the country's racist policies. In 1971 he oversaw a bipartisan delegation to South Africa to observe firsthand its business practices and apartheid system.[26] The Michigan Representative directed a study of the Civil Aeronautics Board's decision to provide South African Airways with landing rights in the United States.[27] His aggressive stance and outspoken criticism of apartheid led the South African government to bar him from the country during a trip in 1975.

Diggs also demonstrated his commitment to influencing U.S.–African relations during the political controversy involving Southern Rhodesia (now Zimbabwe). In response to the United Nations's 1968 trade embargo against Southern Rhodesia, in southeast Africa, Senator Harry Byrd of Virginia drafted an amendment that would except strategic materials. Since the bulk of U.S. trade with Southern Rhodesia involved chrome, the Byrd Amendment effectively stated that the United States would not abide by the embargo. Diggs led an unsuccessful charge against the amendment in the House.[28] In December 1971, he resigned from the U.S. delegation to the United Nations—a position he held for only a few months—to protest what he perceived as the continued "stifling hypocrisy" of U.S. government policy toward Africa.[29] At Diggs's urging, the CBC later filed suit against the American government for continuing to import Rhodesian chrome. Diggs and the CBC argued that the government had no basis for categorizing chrome as strategic since American companies used chrome for consumer supplies.[30]

In the early 1970s Diggs emerged as the leading House critic of continued Portuguese colonialism in Angola and Mozambique. During his brief stint as a U.N. delegate, he urged the United States to stop opposing U.N. resolutions condemning Portugal's policy. In 1975, after a new regime took power in Portugal, Angola and Mozambique were given their independence, but a civil war erupted in Angola between communist forces backed by Cuba and the Soviet Union and noncommunists (UNITA) supported by South Africa. After press reports revealed the CIA was covertly assisting UNITA, Diggs used his position as chairman of the Africa Subcommittee to help win House support to cut off funding for the operation. The Senate's adoption of the Clark Amendment, a rider attached in early 1976 to legislation concerning foreign aid, officially banned covert aid to Angola.[31]

Diggs's political fortunes declined when he became the focus of a federal investigation. In March 1978, a grand jury indicted Diggs on multiple charges, including taking kickbacks from his congressional staff.[32] After a nine-day trial, he was convicted on October 7, 1978, in a Washington, DC, district court of committing mail fraud and falsifying payroll forms.[33] Throughout the trial and

the appeals process, he asserted his innocence, claiming he was a victim of "selective prosecution" because of his race.[34] Despite the controversy surrounding his candidacy, voters from Diggs's Michigan district demonstrated their resounding support by re-electing him in November with 79 percent of the vote.[35] After his re-election, Diggs, voluntarily relinquished his committee and subcommittee chairmanships because of his conviction but voiced his determination to vote on the floor.[36] The CBC did not discourage him, not wishing to deprive Diggs's constituents of their guaranteed representation.[37] Diggs's decision to serve out his term until his appeals were exhausted aroused the indignation of many in the House, especially freshman Representative and future Speaker Newt Gingrich of Georgia, who spearheaded an unsuccessful effort to expel Diggs from Congress.[38] Ultimately, based mainly on a report by the Committee on Standards of Official Conduct, the House unanimously censured Diggs on July 31, 1979. After the Supreme Court refused to review his conviction, Diggs resigned from the 96th Congress (1979–1981) on June 3, 1980. One month later, he entered a minimum-security prison in Alabama; he served seven months of a three-year federal sentence.[39] In a 1981 interview, Diggs stated, "I considered myself a political prisoner during my incarceration. I was a victim of political and racist forces. I will go to my grave continuing to profess my innocence."[40]

After his release from prison, Diggs opened a funeral home in suburban Maryland and resumed his education, earning a bachelor's degree in political science from Howard University in 1983.[41] Diggs launched a brief and unsuccessful political comeback in 1990, losing a bid for a seat in Maryland's house of delegates.[42] On August 24, 1998, Charles Diggs, Jr., died of complications from a stroke in Washington, DC.

FOR FURTHER READING

"Diggs, Charles Coles, Jr.," *Biographical Directory of the U.S. Congress, 1774–Present*, http://bioguide.congress.gov/scripts/biodisplay.pl?index=D000344.

DuBose, Carolyn P. *The Untold Story of Charles Diggs: The Public Figure, the Private Man* (Arlington, VA: Barton Publishing, Inc., 1998).

MANUSCRIPT COLLECTIONS

Howard University (Washington, DC), Manuscript Division, Moorland–Spingarn Research Center. *Papers:* 1920–1998, approximately 1,000 linear feet. The Charles Diggs Collection includes personal, business, and congressional papers, as well as correspondence, photographs, motion picture film, videotape, sound recordings, and memorabilia. The collection is unprocessed, and prior arrangements are required for access. *Oral History:* In the Ralph J. Bunche Oral History Collection, 1970, 34 pages, including an interview of Charles Diggs conducted by Robert Wright on January 28, 1970. Diggs discusses his visit to South Africa, the plight of black Africans, and the relationship of the U.S. civil rights movement to their situation. Also discussed are the causes of the 1967 Detroit riot, the Black Panther Party, home rule for Washington, DC, and the Inner City Business Improvement Forum, a Detroit group that provides services for black entrepreneurs.

Lyndon B. Johnson Library (Austin, TX). *Oral History:* 1969, 13 pages. An interview with Diggs conducted on March 13, 1969. Diggs discusses civil rights, the 1967 Detroit riots, Vietnam bombing policy, and the reorganization of the District of Columbia. A transcript of the interview is available at: http://webstorage4.mcpa.virginia.edu/lbj/oralhistory/diggs_charles_1969_0313.pdf.

NOTES

1 Francesca C. Simon, "Diggs Dies of a Stroke at the Hospital; Ex-Lawmaker Lauded as Home-Rule Author," 26 August 1998, *Washington Times*: C4.

2 For more on Detroit and the Great Migration, see Elizabeth Anne Martin, *Detroit and the Great Migration, 1916–1929* (Ann Arbor, MI: The Bentley Historical Library, 1993): statistics from page 3.

3 "Four-Story Plunge Is Fatal to Michigan Negro Leader," 26 April 1967, *New York Times*: 34; Egan Paul, "Minorities Make a Mark," 26 March 1999, *Lansing State Journal*: 12TAB; Niraj Warikoo, "Advocate of Civil Rights in Congress," 26 August 1998, *Detroit Free Press*: 1C; Carolyn P. DuBose, *The Untold Story of Charles Diggs: The Public Figure, the Private Man* (Arlington, VA: Barton Publishing, Inc., 1998): 184. Sources conflict as to whether Charles Diggs, Sr., was the first African American or the first African-American Democrat to hold this position.

4 Maurine Christopher, *Black Americans in Congress* (New York: Thomas Y. Crowell Company, 1976): 212; Thura Mack, "Charles C. Diggs, Jr.," in Jessie Carney Smith, ed., *Notable Black American Men* (Farmington Hills, MI: Gale Research, Inc., 1999): 304 (hereinafter referred to as *NBAM*); Irvin Molotsky, "Charles Diggs, 75, Congressman Censured Over Kickbacks," *New York Times*, 26 August 1998: 18D.

5 Paul, "Minorities Make a Mark"; Christopher, *Black Americans in Congress*: 209.

6 "Two Senators Elect Ousted in Michigan," 15 January 1951, *Christian Science Monitor*: 3; "Sets Elections to Fill Seats of 2 in Senate," 13 January 1951, *Chicago Daily Tribune*: 10.

7 Christopher, *Black Americans in Congress*: 209–210; Mack, "Charles C. Diggs, Jr.," *NBAM*: 301–302; "Diggs, Charles C(ole), Jr.," *Current Biography, 1957* (New York: H. W. Wilson Company, 1957): 144.

8 "Diggs, Charles C(ole), Jr.," *Current Biography, 1957*: 145.

9 Michael J. Dubin et al., *U.S. Congressional Elections, 1788–1997* (Jefferson, NC: McFarland & Company, Inc., Publishers, 1998): 599; "Michigan's First Negro Congressman Elected," 4 November 1954, *Los Angeles Times*: 6.

10 Christopher, *Black Americans in Congress*: 210.

11 *Almanac of American Politics, 1974* (Washington, DC: National Journal Inc., 1973): 497–499; *Almanac of American Politics, 1978* (Washington, DC: National Journal Inc., 1977): 425–426.

12 For a perspective on the relative strength of Diggs's early and latter committee assignments, see Bruce A. Ray, "Committee Attractiveness in the U.S. House, 1963–1981," *American Journal of Political Science* 26 (August 1982): 610.

13 For more on Powell's and Dawson's divergent styles, see James Q. Wilson, "Two Negro Politicians: An Interpretation," *Midwest Journal of Political Science* 5 (1960): 349–369.

14 "Boy's Mother 'Not Surprised,'" 24 September 1955, *New York Times*: 38.

15 Mack, "Charles C. Diggs, Jr.," *NBAM*: 302. See the second contextual essay in this book, "'The Negroes' Temporary Farewell,'" covering the period from 1887 to 1929.

16 Arthur Kranish, "House Ends Debate on Rights Bill," 11 June 1957, *Washington Post*: A15; *Congressional Record*, House, 85th Cong., 1st sess. (10 June 1957): 8704–8705.

17 "Charles Diggs," in Harry A. Ploski, ed., *The Negro Almanac* (New York: Bellwether Company, 1971): 322.

18 For more on the *Brown* decision, see James T. Patterson, *Brown v. Board of Education: A Civil Rights Milestone and Its Troubled Legacy* (New York: Oxford University Press, 2001); Michael J. Klarman, *Brown v. Board of Education and the Civil Rights Movement*; an abridged edition of *From Jim Crow to Civil Rights: The Supreme Court and the Struggle for Racial Equality* (New York: Oxford University Press, 2007).

19 Christopher, *Black Americans in Congress*: 211–212.

20 Stephen Green, "Diggs Wants New Look at Home Rule," 26 September 1972, *Washington Post*: A1.

21 *Congressional Record*, House, 93rd Cong., 1st sess. (17 December 1973): 42036.

22 Richard Pearson, "Charles Diggs Dies at 75; Former Congressman From Mich.," 26 August 1998, *Washington Post*: B06; DuBose, *The Untold Story of Charles Diggs*: 188–190.

23 Robert Singh, *The Congressional Black Caucus: Racial Politics in the U.S. Congress* (Thousand Oaks, CA: Sage Publications, Inc.): 54–55, 73; DuBose, *The Untold Story of Charles Diggs*: 79–80. See also Molotsky, "Charles Diggs, 75, Congressman Censured Over Kickbacks."

24 John Flesher, "Ex-Congressman Seeks One-Time Return to Politics," 16 April 1990, Associated Press; Pearson, "Charles Diggs Dies at 75."

25 Molotsky, "Charles Diggs, 75, Congressman Censured Over Kickbacks."

26 "Black Legislator to Continue His Tour of South Africa," 14 August 1971, *New York Times*: 28; Paul Dold, "Congressman Jolts Along on African Visit," 14 August 1971, *Christian Science Monitor*: 1; DuBose, *The Untold Story of Charles Diggs*: 122–127.

27 Christopher, *Black Americans in Congress*: 212–213.

28 Mack, "Charles C. Diggs, Jr.," *NBAM*: 302–303; "Rep. Diggs Resigns as a U.N. Delegate," 18 December 1971, *New York Times*: 1.

29 "Rep. Diggs Resigns as a U.N. Delegate"; "Diggs Hits U.S. Stand, Quits Post on U.N. Unit," 18 December 1971, *Washington Post*: A18; William Fulton, "Rep. Diggs Quits U.S. Delegation to U.N.," 18 December 1971, *Chicago Tribune*: A8.

30 "Black Caucus Sues Against Rhodesia Ore"; Mack, "Charles C. Diggs, Jr.," *NBAM*: 302–303.

31 Robert David Johnson, *Congress and the Cold War* (Cambridge: Cambridge University Press, 2006): 223.

32 Jo Thomas, "Rep. Diggs of Michigan Indicted on 35 Counts in Kickback Case," 24 March 1978, *New York Times*: 11; DuBose, *The Untold Story of Charles Diggs*: 198–200.

33 Lawrence Meyer, "Congressman Convicted of Illegally Diverting Funds," 8 October 1978, *Washington Post*: A1; "Rep. Diggs' Fraud Trial Goes to Jury," 7 October 1978, *Los Angeles Times*: A9.

34 Pearson, "Charles Diggs Dies at 75; Former Congressman From Mich."

35 Dubin et al., *United States Congressional Elections, 1788–1997*: 710.

36 "House Sidesteps Diggs Ouster; Probe Planned," 2 March 1979, *Chicago Tribune*: 6.

37 Mary Russell, "Caucus Won't Tell Diggs to Refrain From Voting," 1 March 1979, *Washington Post*: A9.

38 Damon Chappie, "On Traficant, Talk of Expulsion," 11 March 2002, *Roll Call*; "The Diggs Dilemma," 3 August 1979, *New York Times*: A22.

39 "Former Rep. Diggs Begins Prison Term," 25 July 1980, *Washington Post*: A11; Molotsky, "Charles Diggs, 75, Congressman Censured Over Kickbacks."

40 Warikoo, "Advocate of Civil Rights in Congress."

41 DuBose, *The Untold Story of Charles Diggs*: 218; James M. Manheim, "Charles C. Diggs," *Contemporary Black Biography 21* (Detriot: Gale Research Inc., 1999).

42 "Ex-Rep. Diggs Back in Politics," 8 March 1990, *New York Times*: B9; Warikoo, "Advocate of Civil Rights in Congress."

"WHEN WE TALK ABOUT
SELF-DETERMINATION FOR THE
DISTRICT OF COLUMBIA," DIGGS
ONCE SAID, "WE ARE NOT ONLY
TALKING ABOUT A MATTER OF
LOCAL INTEREST, BUT BECAUSE
OF THE UNIQUE ROLE OF THIS
CAPITAL COMMUNITY, IT IS OF
CONCERN TO EACH ONE OF THE
MEMBERS OF THE 435 DISTRICTS
ACROSS THIS COUNTRY."

Robert Nelson Cornelius Nix, Sr.
1898–1987

UNITED STATES REPRESENTATIVE ★ 1958–1979
DEMOCRAT FROM PENNSYLVANIA

After gaining experience in Philadelphia politics, Robert N. C. Nix earned a seat in the U.S. House of Representatives in a special election in 1958. Nix served in Congress for more than two decades. As the first African American to represent the state of Pennsylvania and only the third black Member to chair a standing committee in the House, he dedicated himself "to ending the oppression of black people."[1] However, critics claimed Nix fell short of this goal, placing party politics before the national black agenda. Loyal to the local Democratic machine that helped begin his career on the Hill, Nix was disinclined to demand radical change for minorities, an approach that conflicted with many of his African-American colleagues' more militant politics during the 1960s and 1970s.

Robert Nelson Cornelius (N. C.) Nix, Sr. was born on August 9, 1898, in Orangeburg, South Carolina.[2] The third of four children of Nelson Nix—a former slave and future dean of South Carolina State College—and Sylvia Nix, Robert Nix later moved to New York City to live with relatives.[3] Nix graduated from Townsend Harris High School in New York City (also attended by Nix's future African-American House colleague Adam Clayton Powell, Jr. of New York), before enrolling in Lincoln University in Oxford, Pennsylvania.[4] After earning a B.A. in 1921, Nix continued his education at the University of Pennsylvania Law School, from which he graduated three years later. In 1925, Nix began practicing law in Philadelphia. He first became active in politics when he was elected a Democratic committeeman from the 44th Ward in 1932. He retained this position for 26 years, serving as chairman for the final eight.[5] From 1934 to 1938, Nix worked for the Commonwealth of Pennsylvania as a special deputy attorney general in the revenue department and as a special assistant deputy attorney general. Nix and his wife, the former Ethel Lanier, had one son, Robert N. C. Nix, Jr.

When five-term Democratic Representative Earl Chudoff resigned in 1958 to become a Philadelphia judge, Nix entered the special election to fill the vacant congressional seat encompassing sections of Philadelphia on both sides of the Schuylkill River.[6] With solid backing from the local Democratic machine, Nix won the unexpired term, defeating Republican Cecil B. Moore, an African-American attorney, with 64 percent of the vote.[7] House colleagues applauded as Nix was sworn in as a Member of the 85th Congress (1957–1959) on May 20, 1958, joining black Representatives William Dawson of Illinois; Adam Clayton Powell; and Charles Diggs, Jr., of Michigan.[8] That same year, Nix was chosen unanimously as chairman of Philadelphia's 32nd Ward, a position he held until his death in 1987.[9]

During his first two terms in the House, Nix served on the Merchant Marine and Fisheries and Veterans' Affairs committees. In the 87th Congress (1961–1963) Nix relinquished his initial assignments for a spot on Foreign Affairs (later named International Relations); he remained on this committee for the rest of his tenure in the House and chaired the Foreign Economic Policy and Asian and Pacific Affairs subcommittees.[10] After 14 years as a member of the Committee on the Post Office and Civil Service, Nix became the chairman.

A landmark study of House committees during the 1960s described the Post Office and Civil Service Committee as a "low-energy, low-influence, low-prestige" assignment. Though considered a valuable assignment by Members who sought to improve their chances of re-election by concentrating on constituency-service goals—particularly those related to the many postal carriers—the committee was also characterized by turnover.[11] Nix may have decided to remain on the committee partially because it allowed him to influence the working conditions of

the numerous African Americans employed by the U.S. Postal Service. First named head of the committee for the 95th Congress (1977–1979), Nix faced opposition instead of congratulations. A group of young Representatives contended that Nix's "record of inactivity" and age (68) disqualified him from the leadership position. The Congressional Black Caucus (CBC)—an organization of African-American Members formed in 1971 to promote legislation that concerned blacks—thwarted the move to block his appointment, promising Nix would be a competent and committed chair.[12] During his two years as chairman, Nix led a movement to "require congressional approval of major policy changes" by the U.S. Postal System in an effort to improve service.[13] He also backed a controversial bill put forth by President James Earl (Jimmy) Carter to restructure the civil service system.[14] Portrayed as a plan to improve the efficiency of the federal government, the proposed reform was criticized by many veterans' groups and federal unions that feared the legislation would undermine the rights of civil service workers.[15]

A politician who rarely sought publicity, Nix usually followed the Democratic Party line by supporting the liberal legislation of the John F. Kennedy and Lyndon B. Johnson administrations. Although some of his Democratic colleagues criticized America's involvement in the Vietnam War, Nix, a senior member of the Foreign Affairs Committee, consistently backed executive foreign policy initiatives.[16] As chairman of the Subcommittee on Foreign Economic Policy, Nix led an investigation of the use of funds by defense contractors to pay foreign consultants, agents, governmental officials, and political parties. He later introduced an amendment to the Foreign Military Sales Act requiring the Defense Department to provide Congress with information on the identities of and fees received by agents who negotiated arms sales for American firms.

Throughout his tenure on the Hill, Nix remained connected to the political machine that helped him earn a spot in Congress. Accordingly, he promoted legislation that reflected the concerns of his urban constituents, sponsoring bills to preserve the Philadelphia Navy Yard and

to establish a "senior service corps" to employ workers older than 60. He also dedicated considerable effort to lowering unemployment, arguing, "This is the richest and most technically advanced country in the world. Every citizen should enjoy the opportunity to make a living consistent with his abilities and skills."[17] In line with the practices of the machine organization, Nix held regular Saturday hours in his district office to listen to his constituents' concerns.[18]

As one of the few black Members in the House and the Representative of many African Americans living in Philadelphia, Nix backed a national civil rights agenda. In 1959, early in his congressional career, Nix introduced a measure to end racial discrimination in the armed forces. "To treat a man who wears that uniform with [contempt] merely because of the color of his skin is an insult to America and to everything for which our country stands," Nix said on the House Floor.[19] He supported passage of the landmark civil rights bills of the 1960s, with a focus on protecting of voting rights for Black Americans. In 1963, seeking to enforce the second section of the 14th Amendment, Nix authored a bill to decrease a state's representation when voters' rights were violated—echoing previous measures introduced unsuccessfully in the House for six decades.[20] During the House debate on the Voting Rights Act of 1965, Nix countered critics who maintained that African Americans from his native state of South Carolina had ample opportunity to register to vote. He highlighted the many levels of intimidation and the barriers that hindered significant black representation in the southern state.[21] Disturbed by rumors that the March on Washington to secure equal rights for minorities, scheduled for August 1963, might result in rioting and violence, Nix made an impassioned speech to his House colleagues expressing his hope that the marchers' campaign would be peaceful. "The promised land is here," he proclaimed, "now, awaiting only the complete and immediate removal, by our fellow Americans, of the racial fence which has surrounded it and kept Negroes out for 300 years."[22] The Pennsylvania Representative also sought to prevent the House from denying Representative Powell, his seat in the 90th Congress (1967–1969). Declaring "justice will prevail," Nix argued that Powell "did not receive the fair and impartial trial guaranteed to every American citizen." He added, "The Congress of the United States is honor bound to admit its error, and to correct its wrong."[23]

Despite his work to pursue equal rights for African Americans, many black leaders, including some fellow House Members, denounced Nix for failing to use his political position to secure significant gains for minorities. A reserved man who preferred to avoid controversy, Nix increasingly found himself in the minority among other black Members, whose approach to race relations was more militant. By 1974, Nix was the second-most-senior black Representative, behind Charles Diggs. However, Nix never emerged as a leader of the CBC, the symbolic power source of African-American legislators, but deferred to less senior Members of the House.

Another source of concern for the Philadelphia Representative was his high rate of absenteeism. Dubbed the "phantom" legislator by some of his congressional opponents, Nix appeared rarely at high-profile events, and his unwillingness to make himself available to the press magnified his image as an ambivalent Representative. This experience was not wholly without precedent for a machine politician like Nix who spent his final years in Congress contending with the decline of the local political network that brought him to power.[24] Throughout his career Nix also dealt with age-related concerns. After Nix's death in 1987, his son Robert, a former chief justice of the Pennsylvania supreme court, released a statement that his father was seven years older than the age he indicated upon entering the special election in 1958; aware that his age could impede his congressional career, Nix misled his constituents and colleagues in the House.[25]

Redistricting necessitated by Philadelphia's declining population modified the House district Nix represented, which came to encompass portions of northern and western Philadelphia that included poor areas populated mainly by African Americans in addition to some middle-class black areas and affluent white neighborhoods.[26] Although the constituency remained overwhelmingly Democratic, Nix did not possess a safe seat, facing frequent primary challenges from younger African Americans who criticized his close relationship with the Philadelphia Democratic machine. By the mid-1970s, with the local political establishment waning, Nix was politically vulnerable. In 1976, the Representative barely survived a primary challenge from a young African-American minister, William H. Gray III, capturing only 48 percent of the vote.[27] Two years later, Nix and Gray squared off in a Democratic primary rematch. The incumbent emphasized his congressional experience, contending that his chairmanship of a House standing committee was "the best weapon for helping this district."[28] Nix performed poorly at the polls, with only 40 percent of the vote versus Gray's 58 percent.[29]

After leaving the House in January 1979, Nix remained active in politics as the leader of Philadelphia's 32nd Ward until his death in Philadelphia on June 22, 1987. Representative Gray praised his predecessor, observing, "Because of him, I feel as if I'm standing on the shoulders of the congressmen who opened the doors so the next generation of black elected officials, like Bill Gray, can do the things they are doing now."[30]

FOR FURTHER READING

"Nix, Robert Nelson Cornelius, Sr.," *Biographical Directory of the U.S. Congress, 1774–Present,* http://bioguide.congress.gov/scripts/biodisplay.pl?index=N000113.

NOTES

1   Gordon K. Lee, "Robert N.C. Nix, Sr.," in Jessie Carney Smith, ed., *Notable Black American Men* (Farmington Hills, MI: Gale Research, Inc., 1999): 878 (hereinafter referred to as *NBAM*).

2   Tyree Johnson, "Ex-Rep. Nix, 'Pathfinder,' Dead at 88," 23 June 1987, *Philadelphia Daily News*: 4.

3   Lee, "Robert N.C. Nix, Sr.," *NBAM*: 876.

4   For more on the early education of Adam Clayton Powell, Jr., see Wil Haygood, *King of the Cats: The Life and Times of Adam Clayton Powell, Jr.* (New York: Amistad, 2006): 3–4.

5   *Congressional Directory*, 86th Cong., 1st sess. (Washington, D.C: Government Printing Office, 1959): 135–136.

6   Kenneth C. Martis, *The Historical Atlas of Political Parties in the United States Congress: 1789–1989*, (New York: Macmillan Publishing Company, 1989): 211.

7   "Election Statistics, 1920 to Present," available at http://clerk.house.gov/member_info/electionInfo/index.html; William G. Weart, "Party Men Fight in Pennsylvania," 30 March 1958, *New York Times*: 52; William G. Weart, "Stassen Swamped in Pennsylvania Bid," 21 May 1958, *New York Times*: 1, 24.

8   "4th Negro in Congress Sworn in," 5 June 1958, *Washington Post*: A2; Maurine Christopher, *Black Americans in Congress* (New York: Thomas Y. Crowell Company, 1976): 216.

9   "Congressman Robert N.C. Nix Sr. Dies," 22 June 1987, PR Newswire; Johnson, "Ex-Rep. Nix, 'Pathfinder,' Dead at 88"; Lee, "Robert N.C. Nix, Sr.," *NBAM*.

10 Nix also served brief tenures on the Select Committee on Standards of Official Conduct in 1966 (89th Congress), and the Select Committee on Crime from 1969 to 1971 (91st Congress).

11 Richard F. Fenno, Jr., *Congressmen in Committees* (Boston: Little, Brown, and Company, 1973): 252–255.

12 "Robert N.C. Nix Sr., 88, Dies; Ex-Congressman from Pa.," 23 June 1987, *Washington Post*: B4; William L. Clay, *Just Permanent Interests: Black Americans in Congress, 1870–1991* (New York: Amistad, 1992): 90–91.

13 *Congressional Record*, House, 95th Cong., 1st sess. (8 September 1977): 28335–28336.

14 Kathy Sawyer, "Nix Loss Not Seen Affecting Civil Service Reform," 18 May 1978, *Washington Post*: A2; Clay, *Just Permanent Interests*: 91–92.

15 Sawyer, "Nix Loss Not Seen Affecting Civil Service Reform"; Mike Causey, "2 Hangups in Reform Plan," 24 April 1978, *Washington Post*: A1.

16 "Robert N.C. Nix Sr., 88, Dies; Ex-Congressman from Pa."

17 Christopher, *Black Americans in Congress*: 216.

18 Johnson, "Ex-Rep. Nix, 'Pathfinder,' Dead at 88."

19 *Congressional Record*, House, 86th Cong., 1st sess. (27 August 1959): 17230.

20 *Congressional Record*, House, 88th Cong., 1st sess. (12 June 1963): 10741.

21 *Congressional Record*, House, 89th Cong., 1st sess. (12 May 1965): 10293.

22 *Congressional Record*, House, 88th Cong., 1st sess. (22 August 1963): 15618.

23 *Congressional Record*, House, 90th Cong., 1st sess. (13 July 1967): 18727, 18732.

24 Johnson, "Ex-Rep. Nix, 'Pathfinder,' Dead at 88."

25 Ibid.

26 David S. Broder, "The Ambassador, the Congressman and the Problem," 2 May 1978, *Washington Post*: A1; *Almanac of American Politics, 1974* (Washington, DC: National Journal Inc., 1973): 856–857.

27 *Almanac of American Politics, 1978* (Washington, DC: National Journal Inc., 1977): 723.

28 Broder, "The Ambassador, the Congressman and the Problem."

29 *Almanac of American Politics, 1980* (Washington, DC: National Journal Inc., 1979): 748.

30 Johnson, "Ex-Rep. Nix, 'Pathfinder,' Dead at 88."

"THE PROMISED LAND IS
HERE," NIX PROCLAIMED,
"NOW, AWAITING ONLY THE
COMPLETE AND IMMEDIATE
REMOVAL, BY OUR FELLOW
AMERICANS, OF THE RACIAL
FENCE WHICH HAS SURROUNDED
IT AND KEPT NEGROES OUT
FOR 300 YEARS."

Augustus Freeman (Gus) Hawkins
1907–2007

UNITED STATES REPRESENTATIVE ★ 1963–1991
DEMOCRAT FROM CALIFORNIA

Augustus F. Hawkins's political career spanned 56 years of public service in the California assembly and the U.S. House of Representatives. As the first black politician west of the Mississippi River elected to the House, Hawkins guided countless pieces of legislation aimed at improving the lives of minorities and the urban poor. More reserved than many other African-American Representatives of the period, Hawkins worked behind the scenes to accomplish his legislative goals. Known by his colleagues on the Congressional Black Caucus (CBC) as the "Silent Warrior," the longtime Representative earned the respect of black leaders because of his determination to tackle social issues like unemployment and his commitment to securing equal educational opportunities for impoverished Americans.[1] "The leadership belongs not to the loudest, not to those who beat the drums or blow the trumpets," Hawkins said, "but to those who day in and day out, in all seasons, work for the practical realization of a better world—those who have the stamina to persist and remain dedicated."[2]

Augustus Freeman (Gus) Hawkins was born in Shreveport, Louisiana, on August 31, 1907. The youngest of five children, he moved to Los Angeles, California, with his parents, Nyanza and Hattie (Freeman) Hawkins, and siblings in 1918. Nyanza Hawkins, a pharmacist and formerly an African explorer, left his native England for the United States.[3] Resembling his paternal English grandfather, Gus was often mistaken for a Caucasian throughout his lifetime. After graduating from Los Angeles's Jefferson High School in 1926, he earned a bachelor's degree in economics from the University of California at Los Angeles in 1931.[4] Although he planned to study civil engineering in graduate school, Hawkins's lack of financial support, exacerbated by the Great Depression, forced him to alter his career path. He

opened a real estate company with his brother Edward and took classes at the University of California's Institute of Government. Newly interested in politics, Hawkins supported the 1932 presidential bid of Franklin D. Roosevelt and the 1934 gubernatorial campaign of Upton Sinclair, a famous muckraker and author of *The Jungle*.[5] Hawkins quickly converted his political awareness into a career by defeating 16-year veteran Republican Frederick Roberts to earn a spot in the California assembly, the lower chamber of the state legislature. During the campaign, Hawkins criticized Roberts for remaining in office too long; ironically, the future Representative became known for the longevity of his public service. While serving in the state assembly, Hawkins married Pegga Adeline Smith on August 28, 1945. After she died in 1966, he married Elsie Taylor on June 30, 1977.[6]

As a member of the California assembly from 1935 to 1963, Hawkins compiled a substantial legislative record that centered on the interests of his predominantly African-American and Hispanic Los Angeles district. In addition to chairing the joint legislative organization committees, he introduced a fair housing act, a fair employment practices act, legislation for low-cost housing and disability insurance, and provisions for workmen's compensation for domestics. In 1958, Hawkins lost a bid to become assembly speaker—widely considered the second-most-powerful elected office in the state behind the governor—to Ralph M. Brown of Modesto, but Brown named Hawkins chairman of the powerful rules committee.[7] After two years in that post, Hawkins set his sights on the U.S. Congress. "I felt that as a Congressman I could do a more effective job than in the [state] Assembly," Hawkins remarked. In 1962, Hawkins entered the Democratic primary to represent a newly created majority-black congressional district encompassing

central Los Angeles.[8] His campaign received a boost when President John F. Kennedy endorsed him. With an established civil rights record, Hawkins easily defeated his three opponents—Everette Porter, an attorney, Ted Bruinsma, a business consultant, and Merle Boyce, a physician—with more than 50 percent of the vote.[9] His momentum continued as he won the general election by a landslide, capturing 85 percent of the vote against an African-American attorney, Republican Herman Smith, to earn a spot in the 88th Congress (1963–1965).[10] After the election, Hawkins remarked, "It's like shifting gears—from the oldest man in the Assembly in years of service to a freshman in Congress."[11] Even though the California state legislature reapportioned the Los Angeles district four times after Hawkins's initial election, the district remained predominantly African American and Hispanic and consistently supported Hawkins, who won by more than 80 percent throughout his career.[12]

As a Representative, Hawkins championed many of the same causes he promoted in the California assembly. During his first term in Congress, he sat on the Education and Labor Committee, which was chaired by the flamboyant and controversial Adam Clayton Powell, Jr., of New York. Eventually rising to chairman, a position he held from the second session of the 98th Congress (1983–1985) until his retirement at the end of the 101st Congress (1989–1991), Hawkins wielded considerable authority over issues relating to education and employment. He also served on the House Administration Committee from the 91st through the 98th Congresses (1969–1985), acting as chairman for the final two terms. Hawkins chaired the Joint Committee on the Library during the 97th Congress (1981–1983) and the Joint Committee on Printing during the 98th Congress. He left all three panels when he assumed the chairmanship of the Education and Labor Committee.[13] The California Representative served on the Joint Economic Committee from the 97th Congress to the 101st Congress.

Only one term after he took office, Hawkins was thrust into the political spotlight by the 1965 Watts riots,

which leveled an impoverished section of Los Angeles in his district. Hawkins challenged his fellow lawmakers to help his constituents, saying, "The trouble is that nothing has ever been done to solve the long-range underlying problems."[14] He described the rioting as an expression of desperation, partially due to the absence of long-promised federal antipoverty funds, but did not condone the violence.[15] Throughout his career, Hawkins also eschewed the militant approach of some of his congressional colleagues, arguing, "We need clearer thinking and fewer exhibitionists in the civil rights movement."[16]

From the beginning of his career on the Hill, Hawkins worked to improve the quality of life for minorities. In 1964 he toured the South with three white Representatives to champion African-American voter registration and to observe discrimination. Praising the volunteers who risked their lives to fight oppression, Hawkins recalled, "Being congressmen didn't exempt us from the constant terror felt by anyone challenging established racial practices."[17] Among Hawkins's most notable accomplishments in his early years in the House was the establishment of the Equal Employment Opportunity Commission—a federal agency to prevent discrimination in the workplace—in Title VII of the Civil Rights Act of 1964. Hawkins believed targeting discrimination in the workforce was essential to the advancement of civil rights. Although pleased with the passage of the legislation, he called the civil rights bill "only a beginning." He added, "It is incomplete and inadequate; but it represents a step forward."[18] Hawkins also succeeded in obtaining an honorable discharge for 167 black soldiers who were dismissed from the 25th Infantry Regiment of the U.S. Army after being falsely accused of a public disturbance in Brownsville, Texas, in 1906.[19]

Hawkins's modest role in the CBC strongly suggested his divergence from the tactics of black leaders. Selected vice chairman of the organization during its first term of existence (1971–1973), Hawkins never occupied another leadership position in the CBC.[20] In 1980, he remarked that the CBC "could do a better job," since "now it's 85 percent social and 15 percent business."[21] Hawkins's nonconfrontational manner did not conform with the radical and militant civil rights movement that swept through much of the country during the 1960s. While other African-American Representatives of the period, such as Adam Clayton Powell, Jr., and William L. Clay, Sr., of Missouri, routinely voiced their outrage about racial discrimination on the public stage, Hawkins focused on producing change through legislation. But despite his dedication to the civil rights movement and his legislative efforts to promote racial equality, Hawkins's political pragmatism conflicted with the militant tactics of the other black Members. Explaining his position, Hawkins said, "Racializing an issue defeats my purpose—which is to get people on my side."[22] Unlike some African Americans who worked on civil rights legislation only with other black politicians, Hawkins formed alliances with labor groups and white ethnic groups to increase the likelihood of advancing his agenda.[23]

Hawkins enthusiastically backed much of President Lyndon B. Johnson's Great Society legislation, but he found fault with the administration's foreign policy in Southeast Asia. Though he did not believe the Vietnam War undermined domestic efforts to end poverty, he noted that the United States made a mistake in "believing we can impose our way of life on other people."[24] Hawkins's criticism of the war escalated throughout the 1960s and continued into President Richard M. Nixon's administration. Serving on a select committee to provide specialized information to the House about U.S. involvement in Vietnam, Hawkins and 11 congressional colleagues set off on a fact-finding mission to Southeast Asia in June 1970.[25] During the trip, Hawkins and Democratic Representative William Anderson of Tennessee—the only Representatives to tour a South Vietnamese prison for civilians on Con Son Island— reported witnessing prisoners, including women and children, locked in "tiger cages" and suffering from extreme malnutrition.[26] They drafted a House Resolution urging Congress to "condemn the cruel and inhumane treatment" of prisoners in South Vietnam. The two Representatives

also pressured President Nixon to send an independent task force to investigate the prison and "prevent further degradation and death."[27] Hawkins's 1970 tour of Vietnam convinced him that America should withdraw its troops from Southeast Asia.[28]

Hawkins was determined to use his position as a Member of Congress to curb unemployment in the United States. In 1975, an economic downturn caused unemployment to soar to 8.5 percent—the highest rate in a generation. The joblessness rate for nonwhites—nearly 14 percent—was especially devastating to inner-city African Americans.[29] From 1974 to 1975, Hawkins worked with Senator (and former Vice President) Hubert Humphrey of Minnesota to draft legislation aimed at reducing unemployment levels to three percent over a period of 18 months. Introduced in 1976, the bill took two years until passage. On the House Floor, he rebuked his colleagues for allowing the measure to lose momentum and urged immediate action, saying both chambers of Congress had "a serious responsibility for coming to grips with the formulation of a national economic policy."[30] The Full Employment and Balanced Growth Act of 1978, also known as the Humphrey–Hawkins Act, set a target of reducing the unemployment rate to 4 percent by 1983, but the final version of the bill, which only vaguely resembled the ambitious first draft, contained few substantive guidelines for reaching the target level.[31] At the October 1978 White House signing ceremony, President James Earl (Jimmy) Carter observed that the legislation was a tribute to Senator Humphrey, who had died earlier that year. Hawkins, who received a standing ovation for his role in the bill, recalled, "the legislation was clearly symbolic"— a judgment shared by many experts.[32]

Hawkins dedicated much of his career to enacting legislation concerning education, job training, and equality in the workplace. In 1974, he authored the Juvenile Justice and Delinquency Prevention Act. Four years later, he served as floor manager for a measure to increase the effectiveness of the Comprehensive Employment and Training Act; his efforts led to the creation of 660,000 new jobs.[33] That same year, Hawkins sponsored the Pregnancy Disability Act to increase the rights of working women. In an impassioned plea to his colleagues, he said, "We have the opportunity to ensure that genuine equality in the American labor force is more than an illusion and that pregnancy will no longer be the basis of unfavorable treatment of working women."[34] With the passage of the bill in 1978, discrimination against pregnant employees became illegal.

In 1984 Hawkins became chairman of the Education and Labor Committee a month after the sudden death of the former chair, Representative Carl Perkins.[35] As chairman, Hawkins continued his aggressive pursuit of increased educational opportunities for the underprivileged. During the 1980s he focused on legislation to increase spending for adult literacy and childhood education. In 1988 he helped secure the passage of the School Improvement Act (also known as the Hawkins–Stafford Act), a bill that altered the Elementary and Secondary Education Act (1965)—landmark legislation that authorized federal aid to U.S. schools—by stipulating that only schools demonstrating improved academic achievement would receive federal aid.[36] By the time Hawkins took over the Education and Labor Committee, his liberal politics contrasted with those of a conservative President. He sparred repeatedly with President Ronald W. Reagan regarding marked increases in military spending, while his New Deal-style proposals were periodically opposed by Republicans and by many younger Democrats.

During his final terms in office, Hawkins suffered a series of major legislative setbacks. Unable to muster enough support for an extensive overhaul of the welfare system, he also failed to push through a federal childcare program and a substantial increase in the minimum wage.[37] The final blow was President George H. W. Bush's veto of a civil rights bill sponsored by Hawkins. Passed by both the House and Senate, the Civil Rights Act of 1990 sought to increase job protection for minorities and women.[38] Even with a presidential veto looming, Hawkins uncharacteristically declined to compromise, declaring, "We have had enough input from all parties on the bill."[39] Hawkins portrayed the President's decision as a "national retreat from civil rights," and when the Senate failed to overturn the veto, Hawkins's legislation did not become law.[40]

In the face of increased opposition, Hawkins continued to support federally funded education and employment programs. He refused to shift his ideology, despite the fact that many in the Democratic Party considered his beliefs outdated. His frustration with the tenor of the institution and his age led him to retire at the end of the 101st Congress in 1991.[41] For many years he lived on Capitol Hill. Months after his 100th birthday, Hawkins died on November 10, 2007, in Bethesda, Maryland. "He passed on a new tradition," noted former House colleague Yvonne Burke of California, "that African Americans can be elected, get high position in committees and set the tone and become leaders."[42]

FOR FURTHER READING

"Hawkins, Augustus Freeman (Gus)," *Biographical Directory of the U.S. Congress, 1774–Present,* http://bioguide.congress.gov/scripts/biodisplay. pl?index=H000367.

MANUSCRIPT COLLECTIONS

Howard University (Washington, DC), Manuscript Division, Moorland–Spingarn Research Center. *Oral History*: In the Ralph J. Bunche Oral History Collection, 1969, 26 pages. An interview with Representative Augustus (Gus) Hawkins conducted by Robert Wright on February 28, 1969. Representative Hawkins discusses the history of Title VII (equal employment) of the 1964 Civil Rights Act, antipoverty programs and their relationship to the 1965 Watts Riots, and the operations of congressional committees.

University of California, Los Angeles (Los Angeles, CA), Department of Special Collections, Library. *Papers:* 1935–1990, 137 linear feet. The Augustus Hawkins Collection contains the series Legislative Files, Subject Files, Correspondence Files, District Office Files, Education and Labor Committee Files, California State Assembly Files, and Miscellaneous Material. The papers cover subjects such as civil rights, employment, equal opportunity, education, job training, and childcare. The two series with perhaps the greatest research value are the legislative files, since they document Hawkins's attempts to enact legislation and his committee service; and the subject files, which provide background information, including Hawkins's handwritten notes, for many of his legislative efforts. A finding aid is available in the repository and online.

NOTES

1   William L. Clay, *Just Permanent Interests: Black Americans in Congress, 1870–1991* (New York: Amistad Press, Inc, 1992): 94.

2   *Congressional Record*, House, 101st Cong., 2nd sess. (27 October, 1990): E3656.

3   "Hawkins, Augustus," *Current Biography, 1983* (New York: H. W. Wilson Company, 1983): 176.

4   Shirley Washington, *Outstanding African Americans of Congress* (Washington, DC: United States Capitol Historical Society, 1998): 39.

5   For the most recent work on Roosevelt's 1932 election, see Donald A. Ritchie, *Electing FDR: The New Deal Campaign of 1932* (Lawrence: University Press of Kansas, 2007). See also Greg Mitchell, *The Campaign of the Century: Upton Sinclair's Race for Governor of California and the Birth of Media Politics* (New York: Random House, 1992).

6   Maurine Christopher, *Black Americans in Congress* (New York: Thomas Y. Crowell Company, 1976): 221–223; Washington, *Outstanding African Americans of Congress*, 39–40; "Hawkins, Augustus," *Current Biography, 1983*: 176–179.

7   "Still Seeks Assembly Post, Hawkins Says," 14 November 1958, *Los Angeles Times*: 6; "Both Parties Fill Posts in Legislature," 5 January 1961, *Los Angeles Times*: 13.

8   Gladwin Hill, "16 Men Battling in California for Eight New Seats in House," 20 October 1962, *New York Times*: 10; Richard Bergholz, "Democrats Facing Primary Problems," 31 May 1962, *Los Angeles Times*: A1.

9   Richard Bergholz, "District Changes Listed for Voters," 8 April 1962, *Los Angeles Times*: A2.

10   "Election Statistics, 1920 to Present," available at http://clerk. house.gov/member_info/electionInfo/index.html; Hill, "16 Men Battling in California for Eight New Seats in House."

11   "Negro, Congress-Bound, Loath to Leave State," 8 November 1962, *Los Angeles Times*: 16.

12   William J. Eaton, "Hawkins Retiring—But Not Quitting," 23 December 1990, *Los Angeles Times*: 3A.

13   Hawkins also served as acting chairman of the Joint Committee on Printing during the 96th Congress (1979–1981). See Garrison Nelson et al., *Committees in the U.S. Congress, 1947–1992: Committee Histories and Member Assignments* Volume 2 (Washington, DC: Congressional Quarterly, Inc., 1994): 395.

14   Peter Bart, "Officials Divided in Placing Blame," 15 August 1965, *New York Times*: 81.

15   Augustus Hawkins, Oral History Interview, 29 February 1969, Manuscript Division, Moorland–Spingarn Research Center, Howard University, Washington, DC: 10–11.

16 "Augustus F. Hawkins," *Politics in America, 1989* (Washington, DC: Congressional Quarterly Inc., 1988): 181.

17 Drew Pearson, "Negro Congressman Tours South," 5 August 1964, *Los Angeles Times*: A6.

18 *Congressional Record*, House, 88th Cong., 2nd sess. (10 February 1964): 2733.

19 Paul Houston, "Black Ex-Soldier," 2 December 1972, *Los Angeles Times*: 1; John Dreyfuss, "Waiting Pays Off," 19 April 1973, *Los Angeles Times*: A3. For a useful overview of the Brownsville affair, see Ann J. Lane, *The Brownsville Affair: National Crisis and Black Reaction* (Port Washington, NY: Kennikat Press, 1971). For an additional perspective on Theodore Roosevelt's role in the Brownsville affair, see Edmund Morris, *Theodore Rex* (New York: Random House, 2001): 452–455, 464–467.

20 Robert Singh, *The Congressional Black Caucus: Racial Politics in the U.S. Congress* (Thousand Oaks, CA: Sage Publications, 1998): 65.

21 Jacqueline Trescott, "Caucus Critiques," 27 September 1980, *Washington Post*: D1.

22 *Politics in America, 1990* (Washington, DC: Congressional Quarterly Inc., 1989): 181.

23 Augustus Hawkins, Oral History Interview: 20; "Hawkins, Augustus," *Current Biography, 1983*: 177.

24 Augustus Hawkins, Oral History Interview: 18.

25 Ibid., 20; "Hawkins, Augustus," *Current Biography, 1983*: 177; Richard L. Lyons, "House Names Panel of 12 for War Zone Inspection Trip," 16 June 1970, *Washington Post*: A12.

26 Gloria Emerson, "Americans Find Brutality in South Vietnamese Jail," 7 July 1970, *New York Times*: 3; George C. Wilson, "S. Viet Prison Found 'Shocking'," 7 July 1970, *Washington Post*: A1.

27 Felix Belair, Jr., "House Panel Urges U.S. to Investigate 'Tiger Cage' Cells," 14 July 1970, *New York Times*: 1.

28 "Hawkins, Augustus," *Current Biography, 1983*: 177.

29 See "Table Ba583–596, Unemployment Rate, By Age, Sex, Race, and Hispanic Origins: 1947–2000," *Historical Statistics of the United States, Volume 2: Work and Welfare*, Susan B. Carter et al., eds (New York: Cambridge University Press, 2006): 95.

30 *Congressional Record*, House, 95th Cong., 2nd sess. (18 August, 1978): 27021.

31 "Coalition Set Up to Back Full Employment Bill," 23 November 1977, *New York Times*: 68; Washington, *Outstanding African Americans of Congress*: 41–42.

32 Jacqueline Trescott, "The Long Haul of Rep. Gus Hawkins; At 83, the Steady Champion of Civil Rights Is Retiring From a Battle That Won't End," 24 October 1990, *Washington Post*: D1; Edward Walsh, "Humphrey–Hawkins Measure Is Signed by the President," 28 October 1978, *Washington Post*: A9; "President Signs Symbolic Humphrey–Hawkins Bill," 28 October 1978, *Los Angeles Times*: 17.

33 Washington, *Outstanding African Americans of Congress*: 42–43.

34 *Congressional Record*, House, 95th Cong., 2nd sess. (18 July 1978): 21435.

35 "Reps. Hawkins and Annunzio in Line for Perkins' Panel Posts," 5 August 1984, *Washington Post*: A2; "Reps. Hawkins, Annunzio Receive New Assignments," 7 September 1984, *Los Angeles Times*: B24.

36 Washington, *Outstanding African Americans of Congress*: 42; Irvin Molotsky, "A 5-Year Extension of Education Law Adopted by House," 20 April 1988, *New York Times*: A1. The Elementary and Secondary Education Act of 1965 is briefly mentioned on page 25 of Congressman Hawkins's 1969 oral history.

37 Eaton, "Hawkins Retiring—But Not Quitting"; *Politics in America, 1990*: 181–183.

38 Steven A. Holmes, "President Vetoes Bill on Job Rights; Showdown Is Set," 23 October 1990, *New York Times*: A1.

39 Steven A. Holmes, "No Compromise, Say Civil Rights Bill's Sponsors," 24 July 1990, *New York Times*: A14.

40 Trescott, "The Long Haul of Rep. Gus Hawkins"; Helen Dewar, "Senate Upholds Civil Rights Bill Veto, Dooming Measure for 1990," 25 October 1990, *Washington Post*: A15.

41 Trescott, "The Long Haul of Rep. Gus Hawkins." See also Eaton, "Hawkins Retiring—But Not Quitting."

42 Quoted in Claudia Luther and Valerie J. Nelson, "Augustus F. Hawkins: 1907–2007; A Pioneer for Black Lawmakers in L.A.," 13 November 2007, *Los Angeles Times*. See also Adam Bernstein, "Augustus Hawkins; Calif. Congressman," 14 November 2007, *Washington Post*: B7; Brandace Simmons, "Trailblazing Ex-Rep. Hawkins Dies at 100," 14 November 2007, *Roll Call*; "Rep. John Lewis Mourns Death of Rep. Augustus Hawkins and Celebrates His Accomplishments," 13 November 2007, States News Service.

"The leadership belongs
not to the loudest,
not to those who beat the
drums or blow the trumpets,"
Hawkins said, "but to those
who day in and day out,
in all seasons, work for the
practical realization of a
better world—those who
have the stamina to persist
and remain dedicated."

Edward William Brooke III
1919–

UNITED STATES SENATOR ★ 1967–1979
REPUBLICAN FROM MASSACHUSETTS

Edward W. Brooke's election to the U.S. Senate in 1966 ended an 85-year absence of African-American Senators.[1] Brooke was the first popularly elected Senator and the first black politician from Massachusetts to serve in Congress. While he professed loyalty to the Republican Party, he was an independent thinker who acted according to his conscience. Throughout his political career, Brooke demonstrated resiliency and defined himself as a representative of his entire constituency rather than as an African-American Senator seeking solely to advance black interests.

Edward William Brooke III, was born in Washington, DC, on October 26, 1919. Named for his grandfather, father, and deceased sister Edwina, he lived with his father, Edward Brooke, Jr., a graduate of Howard University Law School and a longtime lawyer with the Veterans Administration; his mother, Helen Seldon; and his older sister, Helene.[2] After graduating from Dunbar High School in Washington, DC, in 1936, Ed Brooke enrolled in Howard University. Originally intending to pursue a career in medicine, he decided to major in sociology, earning a bachelor of science degree in 1941. Shortly after the Japanese bombed Pearl Harbor on December 7, 1941, Brooke entered the U.S. Army as a second lieutenant. Before serving overseas in World War II, Brooke was stationed with the segregated 366th Infantry Regiment at Fort Devens in Ayer, Massachusetts. Like many black Members of the era, Brooke felt keenly the irony of fighting for democracy abroad while facing racial discrimination in the armed forces. The Massachusetts base implemented a whites-only policy for all clubs, as well as the swimming pool, the tennis courts, and the general store. "In every regard, we were treated as second-class soldiers, if not worse, and we were angry," Brooke recalled. "I felt a personal frustration and bitterness I had

not known before in my life."[3] While stateside, Brooke defended black enlisted men in military court. Despite a lack of legal training, he earned a reputation as a competent public defender and a "soldier's lawyer."[4] His experience on the Massachusetts military base inspired him to earn an LL.B. in 1948 and an LL.M. in 1949 from Boston University.[5]

Brooke spent 195 days with his unit in Italy. His fluent Italian and his light skin enabled him to cross enemy lines to communicate with Italian partisans. By the war's end, Brooke had earned the rank of captain, a Bronze Star, and a Distinguished Service Award. During his tour in Europe, he also met Italian-born Remigia Ferrari-Scacco. After a two-year long-distance relationship, they married on June 7, 1947, in Roxbury, Massachusetts.[6] The couple had two daughters: Edwina and Remi. Brooke divorced in 1978 and married Anne Fleming in 1979. Brooke and his second wife had a son, Edward W. Brooke IV.

Brooke declined offers to join established law firms, choosing instead to start his own practice in the predominantly African-American community of Roxbury. At the urging of friends from his former army unit, Brooke interrupted his law career to run for the Massachusetts house of representatives in 1950. Lacking party affiliation, Brooke took advantage of a state law allowing candidates to cross-file. Despite his nonexistent political experience, he received the endorsement of the Republican Party for the house seat representing Roxbury. Unsuccessful in the general election, Brooke entered the race two years later, winning the Republican nomination but losing to his Democratic opponent.[7]

Brooke resumed his law career after his failed attempts at election to the Massachusetts legislature. During his hiatus from politics, he established himself as a successful lawyer and built community ties that would prove significant

in future bids for elected office.[8] In 1960, he re-entered the political fray, running for Massachusetts secretary of state. Although Brooke lost once again, he surprised many people by capturing more than one million votes in an election in which John F. Kennedy of Massachusetts was the Democratic Party's presidential nominee.[9] During this period, Brooke attained valuable name recognition and a reputation as an honest and determined public servant. In recognition of his strong performance in the campaign, Republican Governor John Volpe of Massachusetts appointed Brooke chairman of the Boston Finance Commission, whose purpose was to uncover corruption in the city's municipal agencies. During his two-year tenure, Brooke transformed the commission into a respectable and effective organization, and his position helped make him one of the most popular political figures in the state.[10]

In 1962, Brooke achieved his goal to win an elected position. After earning the Republican nomination for Massachusetts attorney general, he easily defeated the Democratic challenger. As the only member of his party to win statewide election in 1962 and the first African American to serve as a state attorney general, Brooke garnered national attention.[11] Brooke continued his efforts to thwart corruption in the state government. He also recommended a series of measures to protect consumers' rights and fought to end housing discrimination. Civil rights leaders criticized Brooke's refusal to support a 1964 boycott by African-American students to protest segregation in the Boston school system. "I am not a civil rights leader, and I don't profess to be," Brooke once declared, explaining the divergence between legal interpretation and his personal views on racial equality.[12] His moderate response to the proposed protest won him invaluable backing from many voters in the predominantly white state.[13]

In 1966 Brooke authored *The Challenge of Change: Crisis in Our Two-Party System*, outlining many of his political principles, including his beliefs about civil rights. The "issue [civil rights] is pressing on the nation, and cries out for a solution," Brooke wrote, arguing that in addition to legislation, African Americans needed access to a quality education to compete with whites.[14] While he promoted change, Brooke steadily maintained that militancy undermined the civil rights movement.

After two terms as attorney general (1962–1966), Brooke announced his candidacy in 1965 for the U.S. Senate seat left vacant by the retirement of Leverett Saltonstall. During the campaign against Democrat Endicott Peabody, formerly the governor of Massachusetts (he was unopposed in the Republican primary), Brooke vowed to work for "the establishment of peace, the preservation of freedom for all who desire it, and a better life for people at home and abroad."[15] Labeling himself a "creative Republican," Brooke successfully courted voters from both parties by emphasizing his moderate viewpoints.[16] His criticism of militant civil rights activists resonated with many voters in Massachusetts. Despite the enthusiastic backing of popular Massachusetts Senator Edward (Ted) Kennedy, Peabody could not best Brooke on Election Day. On November 8, 1966, Brooke earned a seat in the 90th Congress (1967–1969), winning 62 percent of the vote.[17] His victory met with considerable fanfare, both in Massachusetts and the nation; Brooke was the first African American elected to the Senate since the Reconstruction Era. Asked to comment on his victory, Brooke praised the people of Massachusetts for their ability to "judge you on your merit and your worth alone." He promised to use his position to "unite men who have not been united before," reiterating his pledge to represent his constituents equally regardless of race.[18]

On the opening day of the 90th Congress, Senator Kennedy, the senior Senator of Massachusetts, escorted the newly elected Brooke down the aisle of the Senate Chamber by long-standing tradition. The Senators greeted Brooke with a standing ovation. "I felt like a member of the club," Brooke said. "They didn't overdo it. They didn't underdo it."[19] Unlike many of his African-American colleagues in the House, Brooke experienced little institutional racism in the Senate. "In all my years in the Senate, I never encountered an overt act of hostility," the Massachusetts Senator asserted.[20] Brooke later recalled using the Senate gym and the adjoining facilities without incident. Early in his first term, Brooke went to the Senators' swimming pool in the Russell Senate Office Building. Southern Democrats and staunch segregationists John Stennis of Mississippi, John McClellan of Arkansas, and Strom Thurmond of South Carolina, greeted Brooke and invited him to join them in the pool. "There was no hesitation or ill will that I could see," Brooke recollected of this positive reception by his Senate colleagues. "Yet these were men who consistently voted against legislation that would have provided equal opportunity to others of my race. I felt that if a senator truly believed in racial separatism I could live with that, but it was increasingly evident that some members of the Senate played on bigotry purely for political gain."[21]

Initially assigned to the Aeronautical and Space Sciences, Banking and Currency, and Government Operations committees, Brooke also served on the Armed Services and the Joint Committee on Bicentennial Arrangements committees for one Congress.[22] During the 92nd to the 95th Congresses (1971–1979), Brooke was on the Appropriations, Special Aging, and Banking, Housing, and Urban Affairs committees. Brooke also sat on the Select Equal Education Opportunity Committee, the Joint Committee on Defense Production, and the Select Standards and Conduct Committee. His ability to secure assignments on prominent committees such as Banking and Currency and Armed Services while a junior Member was due in large measure to the "Johnson rule," instituted by Lyndon B. Johnson of Texas during his tenure as Senate Democratic Minority Leader in the early 1950s; senior Democrats believed giving junior Members at least one important committee assignment benefited the entire caucus. Johnson made sure the junior Members knew that it was *he* who conferred the plum assignments and considered the practice a means to ensure their fealty. He continued this system as Majority Leader, and senior Senate Republican leaders, such as Everett Dirksen of Illinois (who was Minority Leader when Brooke was first

elected), adopted it as well.[23]

President Lyndon B. Johnson appointed Brooke to the President's Commission on Civil Disorders shortly after he was elected to the Senate. Governor Otto Kerner of Illinois led the group, also known as the Kerner Commission. Charged with outlining the causes of the urban riots of 1967, the Kerner Commission also proposed solutions for the epidemic of racial unrest in American cities. The commission reported that American society was sharply divided along racial lines. The 11-member commission, including Brooke, suggested the government fund a series of programs to increase educational, housing, and employment opportunities for minorities living in urban areas. Although President Johnson was dedicated to bettering the circumstances of minorities, his preoccupation with the Vietnam War and his decision not to seek re-election rendered the commission's recommendations ineffective.[24]

Working with Democratic Senator Walter Mondale of Minnesota, Brooke succeeded in attaching an anti-discrimination amendment to the groundbreaking Civil Rights Act of 1968. Title VIII of the legislation included provisions to combat racial discrimination in housing. "Fair housing does not promise an end to the ghetto," Brooke cautioned. "It promises only to demonstrate that the ghetto is not an immutable institution in America."[25] The African-American Senator cited his difficulties finding a home after he returned from service in World War II to illustrate the prejudice in the American housing market.[26] Brooke proposed that to combat the "unconscionable bitterness between white and Black Americans, it is encumbent [*sic*] upon our Government to act, and to act now."[27] In 1975, Brooke vehemently defended the need to extend the 1965 Voting Rights Act. When a proposed Senate amendment threatened to dilute the historic voting rights legislation, Brooke joined the debate. "I just cannot believe that here in 1975 on the floor of the Senate we are ready to say to the American people, black or white, red or brown, 'You just cannot even be assured the basic right to vote in this country.'"[28] Brooke's eloquent and impassioned plea to his colleagues helped extend the landmark measure seven years.[29]

Shortly after the assassination of Martin Luther King, Jr., Brooke urged his congressional colleagues to recognize the renowned civil rights leader by declaring January 15 (King's birthday) a national holiday. Arguing that it "would be fitting to pay our respects to this noble figure by enduring public commemoration of his life and philosophy," the Massachusetts Senator earned the support of many African Americans.[30] Brooke also made headlines when he traveled to Jackson State College in Mississippi in May 1970 to help ease tensions resulting from the fatal shootings of two black students by the police. Despite his support of the civil rights movement and his desire to promote equal rights for African Americans, Brooke often found himself at odds with other African-American leaders. The marked increase of black Members in the House of Representatives led to the formation of the Congressional Black Caucus (CBC) in 1971. Although the CBC was billed as a nonpartisan organization to promote economic and social issues affecting Black Americans, the Republican Brooke did not join the group.[31] When the CBC announced it would boycott President Richard M. Nixon's 1971 State of the Union address to protest his refusal to meet with the caucus, the Senator was not asked to participate because the black Representatives expected Brooke to place party interests ahead of race. Brooke repudiated the CBC's boycott by publicly declaring, "It is my duty as a United States Senator to be present, to listen and to consider his recommendations."[32]

Although Brooke supported the Republican Party, his stances were often contrary to the official party line. He typically adopted a liberal agenda with regard to social issues. During his two terms in the Senate, Brooke backed affirmative action, minority business development, and public housing legislation. He also favored extending minimum wage standards to unprotected jobs held by unskilled workers, providing tax incentives to companies with management training programs, and increasing operating subsidies for commuter rail services and mass transit systems.[33] At times Brooke even broke party ranks to work with Democrats in the Senate and the House. For example, Brooke and House Majority Leader Thomas (Tip) O'Neill of Massachusetts recommended a swift increase in Social Security benefits in 1972.[34]

Initially a supporter of President Nixon, Brooke grew increasingly critical of the Republican executive. "Deeply concerned about the lack of commitment to equal opportunities for all people," Brooke denounced the White House for neglecting the black community and failing to enforce school integration.[35] He also made waves with the Republican Party and Nixon when he opposed three of the President's Supreme Court nominees: Clement F. Haynsworth, Jr., G. Harrold Carswell, and William H. Rehnquist. In May 1973 he introduced a resolution authorizing the attorney general to appoint a special prosecutor to serve in all criminal investigations arising from the Watergate scandal. Six months later Brooke became the first Senator to publicly call for President Nixon's resignation. "There is no question that the President has lost his effectiveness as the leader of this country, primarily because he has lost the confidence of the people of the country," Brooke remarked. "I think, therefore, that in the interests of this nation that he loves that he should step down, tender his resignation."[36] Brooke was also one of the few Republicans to disagree publicly with President Gerald R. Ford's pardon of Nixon, deeming it a "serious mistake."[37]

Concerned primarily with issues that would affect the residents of his state, Brooke also demonstrated interest in foreign affairs, especially the Vietnam War. During his run for the Senate in 1966, Brooke called for increased negotiations with the North Vietnamese rather than an escalation of the fighting.[38] Determined to become an expert, he participated in a fact-finding mission in Southeast Asia in 1967. The Massachusetts Senator reported on his three-week trip during his first formal speech on the Senate Floor. Interpreted as a reversal of his position on Vietnam, his speech made national headlines. Brooke commented that his trip had convinced him "that the enemy is not disposed to participate in any meaningful negotiations," which led him to believe that Johnson's "patient" approach to Vietnam did in fact have merit.[39] Brooke was praised by those who found his willingness to publicly change his position courageous, and criticized by many civil rights activists who believed the Vietnam War siphoned valuable funding away from vital domestic programs.[40] Years later, Brooke maintained that his speech had been misinterpreted by the press because his continued support of a reduction of American involvement in the region was overlooked.[41] As a moderate Republican, Brooke grew impatient with the Nixon administration's aggressive Southeast Asian policies, which escalated the conflict with few signs of success. In 1970, he and 15 members of his party voted for the Cooper–Church Amendment, which originated in response to Nixon's decision to invade Cambodia and prohibited the use of American troops outside Vietnam. Brooke further challenged the President's war effort by voting for legislation that established a time limit for the withdrawal of American troops from Vietnam.[42]

In November 1972, Brooke easily defeated Democrat John J. Droney, the Middlesex County district attorney, earning 64 percent of the vote to win a second term in the Senate.[43] After his re-election, Brooke continued his active role in domestic politics. In November 1975 he and seven colleagues on the Banking Committee rejected President Ford's nomination of former Georgia Representative Benjamin B. Blackburn to the Federal Home Loan Bank Board because of Blackburn's opposition to the 1968 Fair Housing Act. During the James Earl (Jimmy) Carter administration, Brooke reaffirmed his support of appropriations for low-income rental housing programs, construction of public housing, and the purchase and refurbishment of existing units. He successfully fought a 1977 amendment to a Health, Education and Welfare (HEW) bill that would have prevented the department from enforcing quotas to meet affirmative action goals, but he failed to block an anti-busing clause from a HEW funding measure.

Brooke's solid support base in Massachusetts began to wane as a result of his acrimonious and public divorce in 1978 in addition to allegations of financial misconduct.[44] In the Republican primary, Brooke faced a challenge from conservative television talk show host Avi Nelson. Although he managed to rebuff Nelson's bid, Brooke entered the general election campaign in a weakened position.[45] In November 1978, Democrat Paul Tsongas, a Massachusetts Representative representing a House district including the historic mill towns of Lowell and Lawrence, defeated Brooke 55 to 45 percent.[46]

After leaving office, the former Senator resumed the practice of law in Washington, DC. In 1984 he became chairman of the Boston Bank of Commerce, and one year later he was named to the board of directors of Grumman. Upon being diagnosed with breast cancer in 2002, Brooke returned to the public spotlight to increase awareness of breast cancer in men. Asked to comment about his public advocacy, Brooke responded, "You never know in life what you're going to be called upon to do."[47] In 2004 President George W. Bush awarded Brooke the Presidential Medal of Freedom, the nation's highest civilian honor.[48] In 2007, Brooke, who currently resides in Miami, published his autobiography, *Bridging the Divide: My Life*.[49]

FOR FURTHER READING

"Brooke, Edward William III," *Biographical Directory of the U.S. Congress, 1774–Present*, http://bioguide.congress.gov/scripts/biodisplay.pl?index=B000871.

Brooke, Edward W. *Bridging the Divide: My Life* (New Brunswick: Rutgers University Press, 2007).

_____. *The Challenge of Change: Crisis in Our Two-Party System* (Boston: Little Brown, 1966).

Cutler, John Henry. *Ed Brooke: Biography of a Senator* (New York: Bobbs-Merrill Company, 1972).

MANUSCRIPT COLLECTIONS

Broadcast Pioneers Library (College Park, MD), University of Maryland Hornbake Library. *Audiotapes:* In the Westinghouse Broadcasting Company Collection, ca. 1945–1981, 18 audiotapes.

Gerald R. Ford Library (Ann Arbor, MI). *Papers:* ca. 1974–1977. Correspondence between President Ford and Senator Edward Brooke, as well as briefing papers of Senator Brooke. Finding aids are available in the repository and online.

Library of Congress (Washington, DC), Manuscript Division. *Papers:* ca. 1956–1988, 273.6 linear feet. The papers of Edward Brooke document his tenure as attorney general of Massachusetts and also include his senatorial papers. Included are correspondence, reports, notes, subject files, draft and printed legislation, briefing books, press releases, and photographs. Other topics covered include the bicentennial of the American Revolution, civil energy policy, fishing rights, foreign policy, military base closures, military policy, the financial crisis of New York City, nominations of Clement H. Haynsworth and G. Harrold Carswell to the U.S. Supreme Court, the Vietnam War, and the Watergate scandal. The papers document Edward Brooke's participation in Republican Party politics as well as his private legal practice in Washington, DC, relating primarily to cases involving the National Association for the Advancement of Colored People. Access restrictions apply. A finding aid is available in the library and online. *Film reels, film rolls, videocassettes, and videoreels*: ca. 1963–1978; 12 film reels, 26 film rolls, three videocassettes, nine videoreels comprising government and commercially produced works and unedited footage. Most of the materials relate to Brooke's political career. Access restrictions apply.

Library of Congress (Washington, DC), American Folklife Center, Archive of Folk Culture. *Oral History*: In the National Visionary Leadership Project Interviews and Conference Collection, 1997–2003, amount unknown. Interviewees include Senator Edward Brooke.

NOTES

1 The two previous black Senators, Hiram Revels and Blanche K. Bruce (both of Mississippi), were elected by state legislatures. John H. Fenton, "Brooke, A Negro, Wins Senate Seat," 9 November 1966, *New York Times*: 1.

2 Linda M. Carter, "Edward W. Brooke," in Jessie Carney Smith, ed., *Notable Black American Men* (Detroit, MI: Gale Research, Inc., 1999): 121 (hereinafter referred to as *NBAM*); John Henry Cutler, *Ed Brooke: Biography of a Senator* (New York: Bobbs-Merrill Company, 1972): 16.

3 Edward W. Brooke, *Bridging the Divide: My Life* (New Brunswick: Rutgers University Press, 2007): 22.

4 Brooke, *Bridging the Divide*: 22.

5 Carter, "Edward W. Brooke," *NBAM*.

6 Ibid; Shirley Washington, *Outstanding African Americans of Congress* (Washington, DC: U.S. Capitol Historical Society, 1998): 12.

7 Brooke, *Bridging the Divide*: 54–60; Carter, "Edward W. Brooke," *NBAM*.

8 "Edward Brooke," *Contemporary Black Biography* Volume 8 (Detroit: Gale Research Inc., 1994) (hereinafter referred to as *CBB*).

9 Washington, *Outstanding African Americans of Congress*: 12; Carter, "Edward W. Brooke," *NBAM*: 122.

10 Carter, "Edward W. Brooke," *NBAM*: 122. For more information on Brooke's tenure on the Boston Finance Commission, see Brooke, *Bridging the Divide*: 71–79.

11 "Edward Brooke," *CBB*; Brooke, *Bridging the Divide*: 96; Layhmond Robinson, "Negroes Widen Political Role; Georgians Elect State Senator," 8 November 1962, *New York Times*: 42; "Big Political Gains Scored by Negroes," 8 November 1962, *Washington Post*: C16.

12 Quoted in Maurine Christopher, *Black Americans in Congress* (New York: Thomas Y. Crowell Company, 1976): 231.

13 American Bar Association, Black History Month 2002, "Edward W. Brooke III," http://www.abanet.org/publiced/bh_brooke.html (accessed 22 September 2004); "Edward Brooke," *CBB*. For more information on the boycott, see Brooke, *Bridging the Divide*: 106–107.

14 Edward R. Brooke, *The Challenge of Change: Crisis in Our Two-Party System* (Boston: Little, Brown, 1966): 159.

15 David S. Broder, "Negro Announces for Senate Race," 31 December 1965, *New York Times*: 6.

16 Christopher, *Black Americans in Congress*: 231.

17 John H. Henton, "A Dapper Mr. Brooke Goes to Washington," 2 January 1967, *New York Times*: 22.

18   Edgar J. Mills, "Brooke Seizes Spotlight," 10 November 1966, *Christian Science Monitor*: 1.

19   "Edward Brooke," *CBB*; Henton, "A Dapper Mr. Brooke Goes to Washington."

20   Brooke, *Bridging the Divide*: 150.

21   Ibid., 149.

22   As a member of the Joint Committee on Bicentennial Arrangements, Brooke played an instrumental role in the publication of the first edition of *Black Americans in Congress*.

23   Robert Caro, *Master of the Senate* (New York: Knopf, 2002): especially 562–565. See also Donald A. Ritchie, "Oral History Interview with Howard E. Shuman," 19 August 1987, U.S. Senate Historical Office, Washington, DC: 206–207: http://www.senate.gov/artandhistory/history/resources/pdf/Shuman_interview_4.pdf (accessed 12 December 2007).

24   Brooke, *Bridging the Divide*: 172–174; Christopher, *Black Americans in Congress*: 232–233.

25   Brooke, *Bridging the Divide*: 176.

26   Washington, *Outstanding African Americans of Congress*: 14; Christopher, *Black Americans in Congress*: 232–233; "History of Fair Housing," U.S. Department of Housing and Urban Development, http://www.hud.gov/offices/fheo/aboutfheo/history.cfm (accessed 12 October 2004).

27   *Congressional Record*, Senate, 90th Cong., 2nd sess. (6 February 1968): 2281.

28   *Congressional Record*, Senate, 94th Cong., 1st sess. (23 July 1975): 24226.

29   Brooke, *Bridging the Divide*: 217–219; Bill Boyarsky, "Voting Rights Bill Survives Ford's Letter," 24 July 1975, *Los Angeles Times*: B1.

30   *Congressional Record*, Senate, 90th Cong., 2nd sess. (8 April 1968): 9227; Cutler, *Ed Brooke: Biography of a Senator*: 290–291.

31   Sources are ambiguous as to whether the CBC formally extended an offer of membership to Brooke.

32   William L. Clay, Sr., *Just Permanent Interests: Black Americans in Congress, 1870–1991* (New York: Amistad Press, Inc., 1992): 142–143; William Raspberry, "Sen. Brooke and Black Americans," 13 February 1971, *Washington Post*: A15; Robert Singh, *The Congressional Black Caucus: Racial Politics in the U.S. Congress* (Thousand Oaks, CA: Sage Publications, 1998): 55–56.

33   Carter, "Edward W. Brooke," *NBAM*.

34   Marjorie Hunter, "Brooke Joins Democrats in Urging Speedy Rise in Social Security Benefits," 5 May 1972, *New York Times*: 10.

35   "Brooke Says Nixon Shuns Black Needs," 12 March 1970, *New York Times*: 25.

36   Richard L. Madden, "Brooke Appeals to Nixon to Resign for Nation's Sake," 5 November 1973, *New York Times*: 1; Brooke, *Bridging the Divide*: 208–209.

37   Harold M. Schmeck, Jr., "Reaction to Pardon of Nixon Is Divided, But Not Entirely Along Party Lines," 9 September 1974, *New York Times*: 25.

38   "Brooke Calls Vietnam a Prime Issue," 29 August 1966, *Washington Post*: A2.

39   John Herbers, "Brooke Shifts War View and Supports President," 24 March 1967, *New York Times*: 1.

40   Herbers, "Brooke Shifts War View and Supports President."

41   Brooke, *Bridging the Divide*: 162–164.

42   Richard L. Strout, "'Vote Serves to Warn the President…,'" 2 July 1970, *Christian Science Monitor*: 1; Brooke, *Bridging the Divide*: 165–167.

43   "Election Statistics, 1920 to Present," available at http://clerk.house.gov/member_info/electionInfo/index.html; Brooke, *Bridging the Divide*: 212.

44   George B. Merry, "A Cloud Crosses Brooke Path," 30 May 1978, *Christian Science Monitor*: 3; "Brooke Admits to False Statement, Under Oath, About a $49,000 Loan," 27 May 1978, *New York Times*: 47. See also Brooke's autobiography, in which he discusses his divorce and financial statements, *Bridging the Divide*: 243–249.

45   [No title], 19 September 1978, Associated Press.

46   "Election Statistics, 1920 to Present," available at http://clerk.house.gov/member_info/electionInfo/index.html.

47   David Perera, "Into the Spotlight; Bout With Breast Cancer Turns Ex-Sen. Brooke Into Spokesman," 19 June 2003, *Roll Call*. See Brooke's autobiography for more information on his bout with cancer and his public service concerning breast cancer awareness for men, *Bridging the Divide*: 297–302.

48   Rebecca Dana, "Lucky 13: President Honors Nation's Best; Grosvenor, Podhoretz Among Medal of Freedom Recipients," 24 June 2004, *Washington Post*: C01.

49   Donna Gehrke-White, "A Vote for Miami: Former Sen. Edward Brooke Promotes His New Memoir From His New Home," 19 March 2007, *Miami Herald*; Lynette Clemetson, "A Senator's Ambitious Path Through Race and Politics," 21 February 2007, *New York Times*: E2.

Shirley A. Chisholm
1924–2005

UNITED STATES REPRESENTATIVE ★ 1969–1983
DEMOCRAT FROM NEW YORK

The first African-American Congresswoman, Shirley Anita Chisholm represented a newly reapportioned U.S. House district centered in Brooklyn, New York. Elected in 1968 because of her roots in the Bedford-Stuyvesant neighborhood, Chisholm was catapulted into the national limelight by virtue of her race, gender, and outspoken personality. In 1972, in a largely symbolic undertaking, she campaigned for the Democratic presidential nomination. But "Fighting Shirley" Chisholm's frontal assault on many congressional traditions and her reputation as a crusader limited her influence as a legislator. "I am the people's politician," she once told the *New York Times*. "If the day should ever come when the people can't save me, I'll know I'm finished. That's when I'll go back to being a professional educator."[1]

Shirley Anita St. Hill was born on November 20, 1924, in Brooklyn, New York. She was the oldest of four daughters of Charles St. Hill, a factory laborer from Guyana, and Ruby Seale St. Hill, a seamstress from Barbados. For part of her childhood, Shirley St. Hill lived in Barbados on her maternal grandparents' farm, receiving a British education while her parents worked during the Great Depression to settle the family in Bedford-Stuyvesant. The most apparent manifestation of her West Indies roots was the slight, clipped British accent she retained throughout her life. She attended public schools in Brooklyn and graduated with high marks. Accepted to Vassar and Oberlin colleges, Shirley St. Hill attended Brooklyn College on scholarship and graduated *cum laude* with a B.A. in sociology in 1946. From 1946 to 1953, Chisholm worked as a nursery school teacher and then as the director of two daycare centers. She married Conrad Q. Chisholm, a private investigator, in 1949. Three years later, Shirley Chisholm earned an M.A. in early childhood education from Columbia University. She served as an educational consultant for New York City's Division of Day Care from 1959 to 1964. In 1964, Chisholm was elected to the New York state legislature; she was the second African-American woman to serve in Albany.

A court-ordered redistricting that carved a new Brooklyn congressional district out of Chisholm's Bedford-Stuyvesant neighborhood convinced her to run for Congress. The influential Democratic political machine, headed by Stanley Steingut, declared its intention to send an African American from the new district to the House.

The endorsement of the machine usually resulted in a primary victory, which was tantamount to election in the heavily Democratic area. In the primary, Chisholm faced three African-American challengers: civil court judge Thomas R. Jones, a former district leader and New York assemblyman; Dolly Robinson, a former district co-leader; and William C. Thompson, a well-financed state senator. Chisholm roamed the new district in a sound truck that pulled up outside housing projects while she announced: "Ladies and Gentlemen . . . this is fighting Shirley Chisholm coming through." Chisholm capitalized on her personal campaign style. "I have a way of talking that does something to people," she noted. "I have a theory about campaigning. You have to let them feel you."[2] In the primary in mid-June 1968, Chisholm defeated Thompson, her nearest competitor, by about 800 votes in an election characterized by light voter turnout.

In the general election, Chisholm faced Republican-Liberal James Farmer, one of the principal figures of the civil rights movement, a cofounder of the Congress for Racial Equality, and an organizer of the Freedom Riders in the early 1960s. The two candidates held similar positions on housing, employment, and education issues, and both opposed the Vietnam War. Farmer charged that the Democratic Party "took [blacks] for granted and

thought they had us in their pockets. . . . We must be in a position to use our power as a swing vote."[3] But the election turned on the issue of gender. Farmer hammered away, arguing that "women have been in the driver's seat" in black communities for too long and that the district needed "a man's voice in Washington," not that of a "little schoolteacher."[4] Chisholm, whose campaign motto was "unbought and unbossed," met that charge head-on, using Farmer's rhetoric to highlight discrimination against women and explain her unique qualifications. "There were Negro men in office here before I came in five years ago, but they didn't deliver," Chisholm countered. "People came and asked me to do something . . . I'm here because of the vacuum." Chisholm portrayed Farmer as an outsider (he lived in Manhattan) and used her fluent Spanish to appeal to the growing Hispanic population in the Bedford-Stuyvesant neighborhood. (Puerto Rican immigrants accounted for about 20 percent of the district vote.) The deciding factor, however, was the district's overwhelming liberal tilt: More than 80 percent of the voters were registered Democrats. Chisholm won the general election by a resounding 67 percent of the vote.[5]

Chisholm's freshman class included two African Americans of future prominence: Louis Stokes of Ohio and William L. (Bill) Clay, Sr., of Missouri—and boosted the number of African Americans in the House from six to nine, the largest total up to that time.[6] Chisholm was the only new woman to enter Congress in 1969.

Chisholm's welcome in the House was not warm, due to her immediate outspokenness. "I have no intention of just sitting quietly and observing," she said. "I intend . . . to focus attention on the nation's problems." She did just that, lashing out against the Vietnam War in her first floor speech on March 26, 1969. Chisholm vowed to vote against any defense appropriation bill "until the time comes when our values and priorities have been turned right-side up again."[7] She was assigned to the Committee on Agriculture, a decision she appealed directly to House Speaker John McCormack of Massachusetts

(bypassing Ways and Means Committee Chairman Wilbur Mills of Arkansas, who oversaw Democratic committee appointments). McCormack told her to be a "good soldier," at which point Chisholm brought her complaint to the House Floor. She was reassigned to the Veterans' Affairs Committee which, though not one of her top choices, was more relevant to her district's makeup. "There are a lot more veterans in my district than trees," she quipped.[8] From 1971 to 1977 she served on the Committee on Education and Labor, having won a place on that panel with the help of Hale Boggs of Louisiana, whom she had endorsed as Majority Leader.[9] She also served on the Committee on Organization Study and Review (known as the Hansen Committee), whose recommended reforms for the selection of committee chairmen were adopted by the Democratic Caucus in 1971. From 1977 to 1981, Chisholm served as Secretary of the Democratic Caucus. She eventually left her Education Committee assignment to accept a seat on the Rules Committee in 1977, becoming the first black woman—and the second woman ever—to serve on that powerful panel. Chisholm also was a founding member of the Congressional Black Caucus (CBC) in 1971 and the Congressional Women's Caucus in 1977.

Chisholm continued to work for the causes she had espoused as a community activist. She sponsored increases in federal funding to extend the hours of daycare facilities and a guaranteed minimum annual income for families. She was a fierce defender of federal assistance for education, serving as a primary backer of a national school lunch bill and leading her colleagues in overriding President Gerald R. Ford's veto on this measure. However, Chisholm did not view herself as a "lawmaker, an innovator in the field of legislation"; in her efforts to address the needs of the "have-nots," she often chose to work outside the established system. At times she criticized the Democratic leadership in Congress as much as she did the Republicans in the White House. She was an explorer and a trailblazer rather than a legislative artisan.[10]

True to this approach, Chisholm declared her candidacy

for the 1972 Democratic nomination for President, charging that none of the other candidates represented the interests of blacks and the inner-city poor. She campaigned across the country and succeeded in getting her name on 12 primary ballots, becoming as well known outside her Brooklyn neighborhood as she was in it. At the Democratic National Convention she received 152 delegate votes, or 10 percent of the total, a respectable showing given her modest funding. A 1974 Gallup Poll listed her as one of the top 10 most-admired women in America—ahead of Jacqueline Kennedy Onassis and Coretta Scott King and tied with Indian Prime Minister Indira Gandhi for sixth place.[11] But while the presidential bid enhanced Chisholm's national profile, it also stirred controversy among her House colleagues. Chisholm's candidacy split the CBC. Many black male colleagues felt she had not consulted them or that she had betrayed the group's interests by trying to create a coalition of women, Hispanics, white liberals, and welfare recipients.[12] Pervasive gender discrimination, Chisholm noted, cut across racial lines: "Black male politicians are no different from white male politicians. This 'woman thing' is so deep. I've found it out in this campaign if I never knew it before."[13] Her presidential campaign also strained relations with other women Members of Congress, particularly Bella Abzug of New York, who endorsed George McGovern instead of Chisholm.

By 1976, Chisholm faced a stiff challenge from within her own party primary by a longtime political rival, New York City Councilman Samuel D. Wright. Born and raised in Bedford-Stuyvesant, Wright was a formidable opponent who had represented Brooklyn in the New York assembly for a number of years before winning a seat on the city council. He criticized Chisholm for her absenteeism in the House, brought on by the rigors of her presidential campaign, and for a lack of connection with the district. Chisholm countered by playing on her national credentials and her role as a reformer of Capitol Hill culture. "I think my role is to break new ground in Congress," Chisholm noted. She insisted that her strength was in bringing

legislative factions together. "I can talk with legislators from the South, the West, all over. They view me as a national figure and that makes me more acceptable."[14] Two weeks later Chisholm turned back Wright and Hispanic political activist Luz Vega in the Democratic primary, winning 54 percent of the vote to Wright's 36 percent and Vega's 10 percent.[15] She won the general election handily with 83 percent of the vote.[16]

From the late 1970s onward, Brooklyn Democrats speculated that Chisholm was losing interest in her House seat. Her name was widely floated as a possible candidate for several jobs related to education, including president of the City College of New York and chancellor of the New York City public school system.[17] In 1982, Chisholm declined to seek re-election. "Shirley Chisholm would like to have a little life of her own," she told the *Christian Science Monitor*, citing personal reasons for her decision to leave the House; she wanted to spend more time with her second husband, Arthur Hardwick, Jr., a New York state legislator she had married about six months after divorcing Conrad Chisholm in 1977.[18]

Other reasons, too, factored into Chisholm's decision to leave the House. She had grown disillusioned over the conservative turn the country had taken with the election of President Ronald W. Reagan in 1980. Also, there were tensions with people on her side of the political fence, particularly African-American politicians who, she insisted, misunderstood her efforts to build alliances. While her rhetoric about racial inequality could be passionate at times, Chisholm's actions toward the white establishment in Congress were often conciliatory. Chisholm maintained that many members of the black community did not understand the need for negotiation with white politicians. "We still have to engage in compromise, the highest of all arts," Chisholm noted. "Blacks can't do things on their own, nor can whites. When you have black racists and white racists it is very difficult to build bridges between communities."[19]

After leaving Congress in January 1983, Chisholm

helped cofound the National Political Congress of Black Women and campaigned for Jesse Jackson's presidential bids in 1984 and 1988. She also taught at Mt. Holyoke College in 1983. Though nominated as U.S. Ambassador to Jamaica by President William J. Clinton, Chisholm declined due to ill health. She settled in Palm Coast, Florida, where she wrote and lectured, and died on January 1, 2005, in Ormond Beach, Florida.

FOR FURTHER READING

Brownmiller, Susan. *Shirley Chisholm* (New York: Doubleday, 1970).

"Chisholm, Shirley Anita," *Biographical Directory of the United States Congress, 1774–Present*, http://bioguide. congress.gov/scripts/biodisplay.pl?index=C000371.

Chisholm, Shirley. *The Good Fight* (Boston: Houghton Mifflin, 1973).

——. *Unbought and Unbossed* (Boston: Houghton Mifflin, 1970).

MANUSCRIPT COLLECTIONS

Howard University (Washington, DC), Manuscript Division, Moorland–Spingarn Research Center. *Oral History*: In the Ralph J. Bunche Oral History Collection, 1973, 30 pages. An interview with Shirley Chisholm conducted by Edward Thompson III on May 2, 1973. Congresswoman Chisholm comments on initial political involvement, failures of the National Black Political Convention and its leaders, Delegate Fauntroy's promise to deliver her candidacy delegate votes from the District of Columbia, support she received from the general public, retiring from politics, how her involvement with the women's liberation movement was misconstrued, and corruption permeating the American political system.

Rutgers University Library (New Brunswick, NJ), Center for American Women and Politics, Eagleton Institute of Politics. *Papers:* 1963–1994, approximately 3.7 cubic feet. The papers of Shirley Chisholm consist of speeches, 1971–1989, on a wide variety of topics; congressional files, 1965–1981, composed primarily of complimentary letters received and presidential campaign materials; general files, 1966–1986, consisting chiefly of biographical materials, including information on Chisholm's record in Congress; newspaper clippings, 1969–1990, in the form of editorials written by Chisholm, as well as coverage of her speeches, writings, and retirement; constituent newsletters, 1969–1982, complemented by selected press releases; photographs (including photocopies and other reproductions), 1969–1990, many of which depict Chisholm with other political figures; publications, 1969–1992, with additional coverage of Chisholm's political career and her retirement; and campaign miscellany, 1969 and 1972, including buttons from her presidential campaign and political posters.

NOTES

1 Susan Brownmiller, "This Is Fighting Shirley Chisholm," 13 April 1969, *New York Times*: SM32.

2 Brownmiller, "This Is Fighting Shirley Chisholm."

3 John Kifner, "G.O.P. Names James Farmer for Brooklyn Race for Congress," 20 May 1968, *New York Times*: 34; John Kifner, "Farmer and Woman in Lively Bedford-Stuyvesant Race," 26 October 1968, *New York Times*: 22.

4 Shirley Washington, *Outstanding Women in Congress* (Washington, DC: U.S. Capitol Historical Society, 1995): 17.

5 "Election Statistics, 1920 to Present," available at http://clerk.house.gov/member_info/electionInfo/index.html.

6 In November 1970, George W. Collins of Illinois won a special election to the remainder of the 91st Congress (1969–1971), bringing the House total to 10 black Members.

7 *Current Biography, 1969* (New York: H. W. Wilson and Company, 1969): 94; Hope Chamberlin, *A Minority of Members: Women in Congress* (New York: Praeger, 1973): 325.

8 Karen Foerstel, *Biographical Dictionary of Congressional Women* (Westport, CT: Greenwood Press, 1999): 56.

9 Jane Perlez, "Rep. Chisholm's Angry Farewell," 12 October 1982, *New York Times*: A24.

10 Marcy Kaptur, *Women of Congress: A Twentieth-Century Odyssey* (Washington, DC: Congressional Quarterly Press, 1996): 150–151; see also Shirley Chisholm, *Unbought and Unbossed* (Boston: Houghton Mifflin, 1970): 70, 112.

11 "The Gallup Poll: Meir, Betty Ford Are Most Admired," 2 January 1975, *Washington Post*: B3.

12 Kaptur, *Women of Congress*: 150; William L. Clay, Sr., *Just Permanent Interests: Black Americans in Congress, 1870–1991* (New York: Amistad Press, 1993): 222.

13 Karen Foerstel and Herbert Foerstel, *Climbing the Hill: Gender Conflict in Congress* (Westport, CT: Praeger, 1996): 30.

14 Charlayne Hunter, "Chisholm-Wright Feud in Brooklyn Is Eroding Blacks' Political Power," 20 March 1976, *New York Times*: 24; Ronald Smothers, "Rep. Chisholm Battling Wright in Showdown Race in Brooklyn," 30 August 1976, *New York Times*: 26; Ronald Smothers, "Wright, Mrs. Chisholm Trade Charges in Face-to-Face Debate in Brooklyn," 3 September 1976, *New York Times*: A14.

15 "Voting in Primaries for U.S. House and State Legislature," 16 September 1976, *New York Times*: 34.

16 "Election Statistics, 1920 to Present," available at http://clerk.house.gov/member_info/electionInfo/index.html.

17 Marcia Chambers, "School Post Weighed for Mrs. Chisholm," 18 February 1978, *New York Times*: B13; Samuel Weiss, "Rep. Chisholm Is a Candidate for College Job," 19 February 1981, *New York Times*: B12.

18 Julia Malone, "Advice From Retiring Insiders on Shaping Better Congress," 3 November 1982, *Christian Science Monitor*: 1.

19 Malone, "Advice From Retiring Insiders on Shaping Better Congress."

William Lacy (Bill) Clay, Sr.
1931–

UNITED STATES REPRESENTATIVE ★ 1969–2001
DEMOCRAT FROM MISSOURI

The first African-American Representative from Missouri, Bill Clay, Sr., served in the House for more than three decades—longer than any other former black Member of the House. During his extensive tenure, he used his experience as a civil rights activist and labor union representative in St. Louis to promote legislation to help minorities and U.S. workers. Clay zealously represented his impoverished inner-city constituents, who he believed needed a strong voice in Congress. Never one to avoid confrontation, the fiery dean of the Missouri delegation observed, "I didn't get so tied to the job that it stopped me from speaking out. People used to say to me, 'How can you do that? You won't get re-elected.' I would say, 'I didn't come here to stay forever.'"[1]

William Lacy (Bill) Clay was born in St. Louis on April 30, 1931, to Irving Clay, a welder, and Luella (Hyatt) Clay. His political epiphany occurred in 1949, after police arrested him, hauled him to a district police station, and tried to coerce him to confess involvement in a brutal crime with which he had no connection. His aunt, a housekeeper for a member of the St. Louis board of police commissioners, telephoned her employer, and detectives were swiftly dispatched to end the interrogation. That episode, Clay recalled decades later, "convinced me that survival and political influence are inseparable in American society."[2] In 1953, he graduated from St. Louis University with a B.S. in history and political science. Drafted into the U.S. Army, Clay served from 1953 to 1955. While on duty in Alabama, he responded to the racial discrimination he and other African Americans faced by organizing demonstrations; once, Clay led a boycott of the base barbershop to protest its policy of serving black soldiers only one day a week. His experiences in the armed forces contributed to his future career as a social activist and politician.[3] Clay returned to St. Louis and

briefly worked as a real estate broker and a manager with a life insurance company. He won his first elective office in 1959 as an alderman from a predominantly African-American St. Louis ward and served in this position through 1964. As a local politician, Clay continued to promote civil rights by participating in a series of protests. In 1963 he was arrested and jailed for nearly four months for his role in a demonstration against the hiring practices of a St. Louis bank. "I think things were accomplished that far outweighed the 112 days I spent in jail," Clay remarked, alluding to a subsequent change in bank policy that increased the number of African Americans in professional positions.[4] Clay continued to gain experience in local politics as a St. Louis committeeman from 1964 to 1967.[5] His early political career coincided with his activity as a union official. Clay worked as a business representative for the city employees' union from 1961 to 1964 and as an education coordinator with a local steamfitter's union in 1966 and 1967.[6] Clay married Carol Ann Johnson, and the couple had three children: William Lacy, Jr.; Vicki; and Michele.[7]

A 1964 Supreme Court decision mandating the equal population of congressional districts paved the way for Clay's entry to the House. Three years later, the Missouri legislature passed a bill that reapportioned the state's districts in compliance with the high court's ruling. One of the new constituencies incorporated the north side of St. Louis and some of its outlying suburbs.[8] When the 22-year incumbent Frank Karsten of Missouri chose not to seek re-election in the newly redrawn majority-black district, Clay entered the 1968 Democratic primary for the open congressional seat.[9] He defeated five candidates for the nomination, earning 41 percent of the vote. His closest opponent, Milton Carpenter, a white state auditor and state treasurer and formerly a city comptroller, collected 30

IMAGE COURTESY OF OFFICE OF THE CLERK, U.S. HOUSE OF REPRESENTATIVES

percent.[10] Clay faced Curtis Crawford, formerly a St. Louis assistant circuit attorney, in the general election. Against the backdrop of a turbulent period of racial unrest highlighted by the assassination of Martin Luther King, Jr., the 1968 campaign received national attention because the Missouri House election uncharacteristically featured two black candidates.[11] Clay emphasized his support for employment opportunities for African Americans and the promotion of civil rights. He also pledged to represent the needs of his predominantly urban district, saying, "The conditions of poverty found in the First District and other areas of the country must be immediately addressed by our federal government to bring faith and hope to our people, before we can talk of quelling unrest and civil disorder."[12] Clay ultimately defeated his opponent in the heavily Democratic district with 64 percent of the vote, becoming the first African American to represent Missouri in Congress.[13]

As a new Member of the 91st Congress (1969–1971), Clay joined two other African-American freshmen: Representatives Shirley Chisholm of New York and Louis Stokes of Ohio.[14] The three vowed to focus on issues affecting their urban constituents, who they believed had been neglected by the government. Shortly into his first term, Representative Clay, who embraced his radical reputation, predicted, "This country is on the verge of a revolution and it is not going to be a revolution of blacks, but of dissatisfied American people, black and white."[15] Assigned in 1969 to the Committee on Education and Labor, Clay served on this panel throughout his career. He eventually chaired the Subcommittee on Labor–Management Relations and was in line to lead the full committee before the Republicans took control of the House in 1995. He also served on the Committee on House Administration from the 99th to the 103rd Congress (1985–1995), chairing the Subcommittee on Libraries and Memorials. Clay reaped the benefits of the House seniority system, rising through the ranks of the Post Office and Civil Service Committee (chairing two subcommittees) to head the full panel during the 102nd and 103rd Congresses (1991–1995) after nine

terms of service. "From the day you are sworn into Congress, you dream of the day that you will rise to chair a full committee—and today that time has come," Clay declared in 1990.[16] His tenure as chairman ended in 1995 when the committee was abolished after the Republicans took control of the House. Clay also was a member of the Joint Committee on the Library during the 101st Congress (1989–1991).

Clay was one of the 13 founding members of the Congressional Black Caucus (CBC). Officially formed in 1971, the CBC sought to provide a formal network for African-American Members to focus on legislative issues directly affecting black citizens. Clay successfully lobbied to make the CBC nonpartisan—hoping to coax Senator Edward Brooke of Massachusetts, the lone black Republican of the 92nd Congress (1971–1973), to join the nascent organization; however, Senator Brooke did not become a member.[17] Soon after its creation, the CBC made headlines because of its public dispute with President Richard M. Nixon. Unhappy with the Nixon administration's policies toward African Americans, the CBC boycotted the January 1971 State of the Union address. Clay drafted the letter outlining the reasons for the CBC's boycott: "We now refuse to be part of your audience," the letter stated in response to the President's persistent refusals to meet with the black Members of Congress.[18] When Nixon ultimately met with the CBC in March 1971, each member addressed a major point of concern for the black community. Clay spoke about the need for student grants to help impoverished African-American students who could not repay educational loans.[19]

The CBC was also involved with civil rights abroad, most notably advocating U.S. sanctions against the apartheid government of South Africa. Some black Representatives, including Clay, demonstrated at the South African Embassy. "South Africa is the most oppressive government in the world," Clay stated before being arrested for civil disobedience.[20] Reflecting on the significance of the CBC, Clay called it "the single most effective political entity we have had in articulating, representing, protecting and advancing the interests of black people in this nation over the past twenty years."[21]

During his congressional career, Clay oversaw the passage of notable legislation. For nearly two decades, he worked to revise the Hatch Act of 1939, which restricted the political activities of federal workers. Clay's measure, which became law in 1993, amended the Hatch Act, permitting government employees to publicly endorse candidates and to organize political fundraisers, among other rights that were previously prohibited.[22] "It's exhilarating to see your efforts finally rewarded," Clay remarked after President William J. (Bill) Clinton signed the measure at a White House ceremony.[23] Clay also spent several years promoting the Family and Medical Leave Act, which passed earlier the same year, mandating that companies with more than 50 workers offer up to 12 weeks of unpaid leave for employees to care for a newborn or attend to a family medical emergency.[24] Clay called the Family and Medical Leave Act "landmark legislation, in the same category as legislation against child labor, on minimum wage, and occupational safety, and health."[25] Although Clinton signed Clay's amendment to the Hatch Act and the Family and Medical Leave Act, which previously had been vetoed by President George H. W. Bush, Clay and Clinton did not always agree. Clay criticized the controversial North American Free Trade Agreement (NAFTA), calling it "badly designed" and "fatally flawed." Concerned that NAFTA would undermine workers' well-being, Clay attempted to convince his colleagues of the pitfalls of the bill. "Approval of this measure will increase the downward pressures on the wages of workers in the United States; nullify any movement toward greater labor-management cooperation; discourage efforts to improve the education and skills of low-wage workers; and exacerbate the inequitable distribution of income."[26] However, with the backing of President Clinton, NAFTA passed the House on November 17, 1993, by a vote of 234 to 200.

From his seat on the Education and Labor Committee, Representative Clay guided many initiatives through the House. In 1996, he served as the floor manager for a bill to raise the federal minimum wage. Shortly after the measure passed the House, Clay commented, "The American people came to know how unfair it was to relegate people at the bottom of the economic scale to a wage that is unlivable."[27] Clay also sponsored revisions to a pension law that was incorporated in the Tax Reform Act of 1986. With his background in labor relations, he supported the mandatory notification of plant closings and the protection of unions' negotiating rights. Clay successfully sponsored legislation in the House to ban the permanent replacement of striking workers, but he was frustrated with the Clinton administration for what he perceived as a lackluster attempt to break a filibuster that caused his bill to languish in the Senate.[28] An advocate of improving the education of inner-city students, Clay worked to reduce class sizes, to increase the number of college grants for disadvantaged students, and to boost federal funding for historically black colleges. "If America is to be prosperous and stay competitive, we must continue to improve educational opportunities for students of all ages," Clay commented in response to a growing backlash in the Republican-controlled House against President Clinton's agenda targeting public schools.[29]

Extremely popular among his St. Louis constituents, Clay made clear his intention to defend the rights of people he believed lacked an adequate voice in the government, even in the face of a shifting political environment.[30] "I don't represent all people," Clay declared. "I represent those who are in need of representation. I have no intention of representing those powerful interests who walk over the powerless people."[31] Clay's passionate approach to politics, which was manifested in a "show-horse," or publicity-driven legislative style, resonated with many of his voters. Much like Adam Clayton Powell, Jr., of New York, Clay viewed his position in Congress as an opportunity to publicize issues that concerned African Americans in his district and throughout the nation. "Rule number one is, take what you can, give up what you must," Clay mused when discussing political tactics. "Rule number two is, take it whenever, however, and from whomever. Rule number three is, if you are not ready to abide by the first two rules, you are not qualified for a career in politics."[32]

Clay's consistent support from black voters and organized labor enabled him to retain his seat—despite a series of alleged ethical violations ranging from tax evasion to the misuse of congressional funds. Throughout his career, the Missouri Representative argued that he was the victim of an unfounded government "witch hunt" because of his race and his outspoken stance on civil rights.[33] "Not many elected officials, black or white, have suffered harassment, humiliation, or intimidation to the degree and extent that I have," Clay angrily remarked.[34] He further contended that African-American leaders faced more scrutiny than their white counterparts.[35] In the early 1990s, Clay withstood a significant political setback in the wake of a scandal involving the House "bank," an informal, institutional facility some Members used to deposit their congressional pay. The revelation of the bank's longstanding practice of allowing Representatives to write checks with insufficient funds caused a public outcry. Clay vehemently denied "abusing the system" when records revealed he was responsible for a number of overdrafts. "No rules were broken, and no public money was lost," he said.[36] Clay's constituents remained loyal; both in the 1992 primary and in the general election, where he earned 68 percent of the vote.[37] Moreover, despite several reapportionments that

resulted in a growing number of conservative white voters in the outlying suburbs of his district—a consequence of St. Louis's declining population—Clay handily retained his congressional seat. His stiffest opposition for the overwhelmingly Democratic district often emerged in the primaries. Active in local politics throughout his congressional career, Clay faced a series of challenges from African-American and white candidates alike in tumultuous St. Louis politics, but despite this steady opposition, Clay typically won the primaries with ease.[38]

In May 1999, Clay announced his decision to retire at the conclusion of the 106th Congress (1999–2001). "I will continue to speak loudly, boisterously, about the inequities in our society," Clay promised of his remaining time in the office.[39] Clay's colleagues offered many tributes honoring his "brilliant career," ranging from his legislation on behalf of American workers to his commitment to increasing funding for education, especially for minorities. The longtime Representative also received praise for his 1992 book, *Just Permanent Interests: Black Americans in Congress, 1870–1991*.[40] In 2000 Clay's son, William Lacy Clay, Jr., was elected to represent his father's former St. Louis district, making the Clays the second African-American father and son ever to serve in Congress (Harold E. Ford and Harold Ford, Jr., were the first). In 2004, Clay published a political memoir, *A Political Voice at the Grass Roots*.

FOR FURTHER READING

"Clay, William Lacy Sr.," *Biographical Directory of the U.S. Congress, 1774–Present*, http://bioguide.congress.gov/scripts/biodisplay.pl?index=C000488.

Clay, William L. *Just Permanent Interests: Black Americans in Congress, 1870–1991* (New York: Amistad Press, Inc., 1992).

_____. *A Political Voice at the Grass Roots* (St. Louis: Missouri Historical Society Press, 2004).

MANUSCRIPT COLLECTIONS

Harris-Stowe State University (St. Louis, MO), Henry Givens Administrative Building. *Papers*: 1968–2000, amount unknown. The papers of William Lacy (Bill) Clay, Sr., contain documents, papers, correspondence, and artifacts generated throughout his congressional career. The papers are restricted until processing is completed.

Howard University (Washington, DC), Manuscript Division, Moorland–Spingarn Research Center. *Oral History*: In the Ralph J. Bunche Oral History Collection, 1968, 18 pages. An interview with William L. Clay conducted by Robert Wright on November 25, 1968. In the interview, Representative Clay reviews the early civil rights activities in Missouri that led to his jail sentence. He also discusses his congressional campaigns and elections, the role of a black Representative, and his efforts to desegregate labor unions.

NOTES

1   Deirdre Shesgreen, "I Didn't Come Here to Stay Forever," 16 May 1999, *St. Louis Dispatch*: A7.

2   Bill Clay, *A Political Voice at the Grass Roots* (St. Louis: Missouri Historical Society Press, 2004): 13–14.

3   Clay, *A Political Voice at the Grass Roots*: 16; John LoDico, "William Lacy Clay," *Contemporary Black Biography*, Volume 8 (Detroit: Gale Research Inc., 1994) (hereinafter referred to as *CBB*); Maurine Christopher, *Black Americans in Congress* (New York: Thomas Y. Crowell Company, 1971): 250.

4   Christopher, *Black Americans in Congress*: 250–251.

5   *Politics in America, 1982* (Washington, DC: Congressional Quarterly Inc., 1981): 679.

6   "William L. Clay, Sr.," Associated Press Candidate Biographies, 1998.

7   "William L. Clay, Sr.," Associated Press Candidate Biographies, 1998; Clay, *A Political Voice at the Grass Roots*: 16, 175.

8   "Redistricting Bill Passed in Missouri," 29 June 1967, *New York Times*: 23; Clay, *A Political Voice at the Grass Roots*: 155.

9   *Congressional Record*, House, 99th Cong., 1st sess. (13 November 1985): E5135; John Herbers, "Congress to Get Three More Negroes," 3 October 1968, *New York Times*: 43; LoDico, "William Lacy Clay," *CBB*.

10 Clay, *A Political Voice at the Grassroots*: 156, 165. One of Clay's five opponents withdrew from the contest shortly before the election, but his name remained on the ballot.

11 "Long Calls Missouri Defeat 'Victory for Snooper,'" 8 August 1968, *New York Times*: 26; "Long Calls Defeat Wiretappers' Victory," 8 August 1968, *Chicago Tribune*: 2.

12 William L. Clay, Sr., *Just Permanent Interests: Black Americans in Congress, 1870–1991* (New York: Amistad Press, Inc., 1992): 115–116.

13 "Election Statistics, 1920 to Present," available at http://clerk.house.gov/member_info/electionInfo/index.html.

14 The winner of a special election for the remainder of the 91st Congress and an election for a full term in the 92nd Congress, George W. Collins of Illinois was sworn in to office on November 3, 1970, as the fourth African-American freshman Member in the 91st Congress. Collins therefore began his congressional service after Clay, Chisholm, and Stokes began theirs.

15 Robert C. Maynard, "New Negroes in Congress Focus on City Problems," 10 August 1969, *Washington Post*: 2.

16 Robert L. Koenig, "Clay Voted Chairman of House Committee," 6 December 1990, *St. Louis Post-Dispatch* (Missouri): 19A.

17 Robert Singh, *The Congressional Black Caucus: Racial Politics in the U.S. Congress* (Thousand Oaks, CA: Sage Publications, 1998): 55–56. Sources are ambiguous as to whether the CBC formally extended an offer of membership to Brooke.

18 "Black Congressmen to Boycott Nixon," 22 January 1971, *Washington Post*: A2; Clay, *Just Permanent Interests*: 139–143.

19 Clay, *Just Permanent Interests*: 145–147.

20 "Congressmen, Bishop, Nobel Prize Winner Arrested," 6 December 1984, United Press International.

21 Singh, *The Congressional Black Caucus*: 210.

22 Robert L. Koenig, "House Passes Clay's Changes to Hatch Act," 4 March 1993, *St. Louis Post-Dispatch*: 10A.

23 Robert L. Koenig, "Clinton Signs Family Leave, Praises Clay; President Proclaims End to Washington Gridlock," 6 February 1993, *St. Louis Post-Dispatch*: 1A.

24 Steven W. Stathis, *Landmark Legislation, 1774–2002: Major U.S. Acts and Treaties* (Washington, DC: Congressional Quarterly Press, 2003): 347.

25 Robert L. Koenig, "Clay Beams as Clinton Signs Hatch Act," 7 October 1993, *St. Louis Post-Dispatch*: 1A.

26 *Congressional Record*, House, 103rd Cong., 1st sess. (17 November 1993): 29782; "Area Lawmakers React to NAFTA," 15 September 1993, *St. Louis Post-Dispatch*: 8A.

27 Bill Lembrecht, "Minimum-Wage Victory Lifts Democrats; Party Leaders Hope This Is an Issue They Can Ride Right Up to November," 26 May 1996, *St. Louis Post-Dispatch*: 1B.

28 Robert L. Koenig, "Clinton Shares in Loss of Strike Bill," 14 July 1994, *St. Louis Post-Dispatch*: 5B.

29 William Clay, "Saving Schools Will Require Bipartisanship," 7 December 1998, *Roll Call*.

30 Tim Poor, "Still Liberal and Proud of It," 7 October 1996, *St. Louis Post-Dispatch*: 5C.

31 Nathaniel Sheppard, Jr., "Race Is Key Issue in Primary for House Seat in St. Louis," 3 August 1982, *New York Times*: A12.

32 Clay, *Just Permanent Interests*: xiv.

33 "Rep. Clay Urges Speed on Inquiry," 9 May 1975, *Washington Post*: A4; Clay, *Just Permanent Interests* 322–331.

34 Clay, *Just Permanent Interests*: 322.

35 Ibid., 335–337.

36 Fred W. Lindecke and Robert L. Koenig, "Check List Puts Clay Near Top; 'I Categorically Deny Abusing the System,' the Congressman Says," 15 March 1992, *St. Louis Post-Dispatch*: 1A.

37 *Almanac of American Politics, 1994* (Washington, DC: National Journal Inc., 1993): 734–735; "Election Statistics, 1920 to Present," available at http://clerk.house.gov/member_info/electionInfo/index.html.

38 See, for example, Representative Clay's detailed description of the 1974 Democratic primary, in which he faced African-American businessman Clifford Gates; Clay, *A Political Voice at the Grass Roots*: 208–221. See also *Almanac of American Politics, 1992* (Washington, DC: National Journal Inc., 1991): 706–707; *Politics in America, 2000* (Washington, DC: Congressional Quarterly Inc., 1999): 775–776; Sheppard, "Race Is Key Issue in Primary for House Seat in St. Louis."

39 Ed Schafer, "Era Ends: Clay Announces Retirement," 25 May 1999, Associated Press.

40 "Tribute to the Honorable William L. Clay, Sr.," *Congressional Record*, House, 106th Cong., 2nd sess. (27 October 2000): H11422–11430.

"RULE NUMBER ONE IS, TAKE WHAT YOU CAN, GIVE UP WHAT YOU MUST," CLAY MUSED WHEN DISCUSSING POLITICAL TACTICS. "RULE NUMBER TWO IS, TAKE IT WHENEVER, HOWEVER, AND FROM WHOMEVER. RULE NUMBER THREE IS, IF YOU ARE NOT READY TO ABIDE BY THE FIRST TWO RULES, YOU ARE NOT QUALIFIED FOR A CAREER IN POLITICS."

Louis Stokes
1925–

UNITED STATES REPRESENTATIVE ★ 1969–1999
DEMOCRAT FROM OHIO

Louis Stokes rose from the local housing projects to serve 30 years in the U.S. House, becoming a potent symbol for his Cleveland-based majority-black district. Reluctant to enter the political arena, Stokes was persuaded to run for office by his prominent brother and by community members he had served for decades as a civil rights lawyer. His accomplishments were substantive and of historic proportions. The first black to represent Ohio, Stokes chaired several congressional committees (including the Permanent Select Intelligence Committee) and was the first African American to win a seat on the powerful House Appropriations Committee. He used his success to try to increase opportunities for millions of African Americans, saying, "I'm going to keep on denouncing the inequities of this system, but I'm going to work within it. To go outside the system would be to deny myself—to deny my own existence. I've beaten the system. I've proved it can be done—so have a lot of others." Stokes continued, "But the problem is that a black man has to be extra special to win in this system. Why should you have to be a super black to get someplace? That's what's wrong in the society. The ordinary black man doesn't have the same chance as the ordinary white man does."[1]

Louis Stokes was born on February 23, 1925, in Cleveland, Ohio, to Charles and Louise Cinthy (Stone) Stokes.[2] His father worked in a laundromat and died when Louis was young. Stokes and his younger brother, Carl, were raised by their widowed mother, whose salary as a domestic was supplemented by welfare payments. The boys' maternal grandmother played a prominent role, tending to the children while their mother cleaned homes in wealthy white suburbs far from downtown Cleveland. Years later, Louise Stokes recalled that she had tried to instill in her children "the idea that work with your hands is the hard way of doing things. I told them over and over

to learn to use their heads."[3] Louis Stokes supplemented the family income by shining shoes around the Cleveland projects and clerking at an Army/Navy store. He attended Cleveland's public schools and served as a personnel specialist in the U.S. Army from 1943 to 1946. Much of his tour of duty was spent in the segregated South, driving home for Stokes the basic inequities facing blacks—even those who wore their country's uniform.[4] He returned home with an honorable discharge, taking jobs in the Veterans Administration and Treasury Department offices in Cleveland while attending college at night with the help of the GI Bill. He attended the Cleveland College of Western Reserve University from 1946 to 1948. Stokes eventually earned a J.D. from the Cleveland Marshall School of Law in 1953 and, with his brother, opened the law firm Stokes and Stokes. On August 21, 1960, Louis Stokes married Jeanette (Jay) Francis, and they raised four children: Shelly, Louis C., Angela, and Lorene.

Initially, Louis Stokes harbored few, if any, ambitions for elective office. He devoted himself to his law practice, where he became involved in a number of civil rights-related cases—often working pro bono on behalf of poor clients and activists. He was an active participant in civic affairs, joining the Cleveland chapter of the National Association for the Advancement of Colored People (NAACP), the board of the Cleveland and Cuyahoga bar associations, and the Ohio State Bar Association's criminal justice committee, where he served as chairman.[5] He eventually served as vice president of the NAACP's Cleveland chapter and chaired its legal redress committee for five years. His brother, Carl, pursued a high-profile career in elective office, serving two terms in the Ohio legislature, and in 1967, he won election as mayor of Cleveland, becoming the first black to lead a major U.S. city. "For a long time, I had very little interest in politics,"

Louis Stokes recalled. "Carl was the politician in the family and I left politics to him."[6]

Meanwhile, Louis Stokes enjoyed a growing reputation as a prominent Cleveland attorney. Working on behalf of the Cleveland NAACP, Stokes helped challenge the Ohio legislature's redistricting in 1965 that followed the Supreme Court's "one man, one vote" decision. The state legislature had fragmented the congressional districts that overlay Cleveland, diluting black voting strength. Stokes joined forces with Charles Lucas, a black Republican, to challenge that action. They lost their case in U.S. District Court, but based on Stokes's written appeal, the U.S. Supreme Court agreed with the brief in 1967. From that decision followed the creation of Ohio's first majority-black district.[7] Later that year, in December 1967, Stokes made an oral argument before the U.S. Supreme Court in *Terry v. Ohio*, a precedent-setting case that defined the legality of police search and seizure procedures.[8]

At his brother Carl's behest Louis Stokes made his first run for elective office in 1968. He sought to win the seat in the newly created congressional district that encompassed much of the east side of Cleveland—including Garfield Heights and Newburgh Heights—where African Americans accounted for 65 percent of the population. Stokes was hardly a typical newcomer to the political campaign. First, his brother, Mayor Stokes, put the services of his political network at Louis's disposal. "I ran my brother Louis," Carl Stokes recalled, "and put behind him all the machinery that just elected me mayor."[9] With Carl's help, Louis cofounded the Twenty-First Congressional District Caucus—a political organization that would serve as his base throughout his long congressional career. It provided the supporters, volunteers, and organizational structure that sustained Stokes in the absence of support of the local Democratic machine; it was a loyal cadre that would do everything, from stuffing envelopes and knocking on doors to holding an annual picnic that became a highlight of the community's annual calendar. The caucus fulfilled Stokes's twin representational goals: to develop black political power in Cleveland and to inspire black pride among his constituents.[10] Finally, Louis

Stokes's credentials within the black community were sterling. He won two vital endorsements: the support of the *Call & Post*, the influential local black newspaper, and the backing of the vast majority of the local church ministers in the new district.

Stokes perceived the election as a barometer of the way newly enfranchised and empowered blacks would organize their political clout—less an expression of black pride than an experiment in creating a power base outside the Democratic Party, which in many urban areas represented a competing rather than a supportive entity. As Stokes put it, "Carl's race represented a cause symbolizing the hopes of the Negro race. Mine isn't."[11] The 20 candidates who entered the May 1968 primary, many of them African Americans, bore out that analysis. However, Stokes's organization proved far superior to his competition's. He successfully portrayed himself as a unity candidate who could best serve the diverse factions within Cleveland's black community. He won the primary with 41 percent of the vote—double the total of his closest competitor, black city councilman Leo A. Jackson. None of Stokes's primary opponents ever challenged him again. "We took all the starch out of them, when we beat them so badly in the first primary," he observed.[12] Stokes faced minimal opposition in his 14 subsequent primaries. Once, white leaders in the local Democratic machine recruited one of the incumbent's former staffers to run against him in 1976. Stokes won by a landslide.[13]

In the 1968 general election, Stokes faced Republican Charles Lucas, an African American and a one-time ally in the fight to create a majority-black district. During several debates in the campaign between Lucas and Stokes, "law and order" emerged as a central theme. Stokes unrelentingly tied Lucas to Republican presidential candidate Richard M. Nixon (as well as to conservative segregationists like Independent George Wallace of Alabama and Republican Strom Thurmond of South Carolina), arguing they would not promote legislation that advanced black interests.[14] Stokes prevailed with 75 percent of the vote.[15] He won his subsequent 14 general elections by lopsided margins in the heavily Democratic district—taking as much as 88 percent of the vote.[16] Gradually, reapportionment changed the makeup of the state, eliminating five of Ohio's 24 House seats. Stokes's district expanded to include traditionally white communities like cultural hubs Shaker Heights and Cleveland Heights. Reapportionment in the early 1990s brought in working-class white neighborhoods including Euclid in east Cleveland. While the proportion of blacks in the district fell to 59 percent, Stokes was largely unaffected.[17]

As a freshman Representative, Stokes received assignments on the Education and Labor Committee and the Internal Security Committee (formerly the House Un-American Activities Committee). He enthusiastically accepted the former assignment, believing Education and Labor would be a prime platform from which he could push the agenda for his urban district: job training, economic opportunity, and educational interests. But Stokes was less pleased with the Internal Security panel, which had lapsed into an increasingly irrelevant entity since its heyday investigating communists in the 1940s and 1950s. (House leaders disbanded it entirely in the mid-1970s.)

During his second term in the House, Stokes earned a seat on the powerful Appropriations Committee, with oversight of all federal spending bills. This exclusive assignment required him to relinquish his other committee assignments. During more than two decades on the committee, Stokes steered hundreds of millions of federal dollars into projects in his home state. He eventually became an Appropriations subcommittee chair, or "cardinal," for Veterans, HUD, and Independent Agencies—controlling more than $90 billion annually in federal money.[18] Stokes was the second African-American "cardinal" ever (the first, Julian Dixon of California, chaired the DC Subcommittee). Years later, Stokes said of the Appropriations Committee, "It's the only committee to be on. All the rest is window dressing."[19] In addition to chairing an Appropriations subcommittee, Stokes is one of fewer than two dozen African Americans ever to chair a House committee and one of just a handful

to wield the gavel on multiple panels: the Permanent Select Committee on Intelligence (100th Congress), the Committee on Standards of Official Conduct (97th–98th Congresses, 102nd Congress), and the Select Committee on Assassinations (95th Congress).

The growing ranks of black Members sought to create a power base, realizing—in the words of Representative William (Bill) Clay, Sr. of Missouri they "had to parlay massive voting potential into concrete economic results."[20] As freshman House Members, Stokes and Clay quickly developed an enduring friendship and became strong supporters of the formation of the Congressional Black Caucus (CBC), to promote economic, educational, and social issues that were important to African Americans. This strategy dovetailed with Stokes's perception of his role as an advocate for the "black community" in his district.[21] Stokes served as chairman of the CBC for two consecutive terms beginning in 1972, after Chairman Charles Diggs, Jr., of Michigan resigned from the post.[22] A centrist, Stokes was widely credited with shepherding the group away from the polarizing politics of various black factions toward a more stable and organized policy agenda.[23]

Using his position as CBC chairman and his increasing influence on the Appropriations Committee, Representative Stokes pushed a legislative agenda that mirrored the needs of his majority-black district. He earned a reputation as a congenial but determined activist for minority issues, consistently scoring as one of the most liberal Members of the House in the Americans for Democratic Action and the American Federation of Labor and Congress of Industrial Organizations vote tallies. He advocated more funding for education (particularly for minority colleges), affirmative action programs to employ more blacks, housing and urban development projects, and initiatives to improve access to health care for working-class Americans. In the 1980s, Stokes vocalized black concerns that the Ronald W. Reagan administration was intent on rolling back minority gains made in the 1960s and 1970s. He described conservative efforts to scale back school desegregation efforts and affirmative action programs—as well as massive spending on military programs—as a "full scale attack" on the priorities of the black community.[24] He also was an early advocate of federal government intervention in the fight against HIV/AIDS.

From his seat on the Permanent Select Committee on Intelligence, Stokes was a particularly forceful critic of the Reagan administration's foreign policy. He gained national prominence as a member of the House Select Committee to Investigate Covert Arms Transactions with Iran when he grilled Lieutenant Colonel Oliver North in 1987 about his role in funding anticommunist Nicaraguan Contras through weapons sales to Tehran. At one juncture he reminded North, "I wore [the uniform] as proudly as you do, even when our government required black and white soldiers in the same Army to live, sleep, eat and travel separate and apart, while fighting and dying for our country."[25]

House leaders repeatedly sought to capitalize on Stokes's image as a stable, trustworthy, and competent adjudicator—turning to him to lead high-profile committees and handle controversial national issues, as well as the occasional ethics scandals in the House. When Representative Henry Gonzalez of Texas abruptly resigned as chairman of the Select Committee on Assassinations after a dispute with staff and Members, Speaker Thomas P. (Tip) O'Neill of Massachusetts tapped Stokes to lead the panel, which was investigating the circumstances surrounding the deaths of President John F. Kennedy and Dr. Martin Luther King, Jr. In 1978, Stokes's committee filed 27 volumes of hearings and a final report that recommended administrative and legislative reforms. While the panel found that the King and the Kennedy murders may have involved multiple assassins (James Earl Ray and Lee Harvey Oswald have traditionally been described as lone killers), it concluded there was no evidence to support assertions of a broad conspiracy involving domestic groups or foreign governments—an assessment that has been upheld for the past three decades.[26] The committee did suggest that Oswald may

have had an accomplice on Dealey Plaza, where Kennedy was killed in November 1963.[27]

Stokes's chairmanship of the Select Committee on Assassinations led to his appointment by Speaker O'Neill in 1981 as chairman of the House Committee on Standards of Official Conduct (often called the Ethics Committee). Stokes steered the panel through a turbulent period that included investigations of Members implicated in the Federal Bureau of Investigation's ABSCAM sting and a sex scandal that involved two House Members and current and former House Pages. In the latter case, Stokes's panel recommended reforms that overhauled the Page program. Stokes left the post in 1985 but returned to lead the panel in early 1991. In 1992, after Stokes was linked to the House "Bank" scandal (he wrote 551 overdrafts against an informal account maintained by the House Sergeant at Arms), his status as an ethics overseer was somewhat diminished—but constituents still re-elected him by a wide margin.[28]

During the 1990s, Stokes's seniority made him an influential voice on the Appropriations Committee. In 1993, at the start of the 103rd Congress, he assumed the chairman's gavel of the Subcommittee on VA, HUD, and Independent Agencies, which controlled one of the largest chunks of discretionary spending in the federal budget. Stokes prodded federal agencies to hire and serve more minorities.[29] Republicans praised him for his nonpartisan leadership of the subcommittee, but when the GOP won control of the House in the 1994 elections, and Stokes became the Ranking Member of the panel, he often found himself fighting Republican efforts to trim federal spending that involved cutting welfare programs, including public housing. In one committee meeting, Stokes noted that he and his brother, Carl, had grown up in public housing, and that without such assistance "[we] would be either in jail or dead, we'd be some kind of statistic." Appropriations Committee Chairman Robert L. Livingston of Louisiana responded, "We can play this compassion game all day but it won't cut it."[30]

In January 1998, Stokes announced his retirement

from the House, noting that he wanted to leave "without ever losing an election."[31] He conceded that politics had lost some of its appeal since his brother Carl's death from cancer two years earlier. "We used to talk every day. We could run things by one another," he recalled. "We could think and strategize on political issues. I guess without him here, it really has taken away a lot of what I enjoy about politics. It's not the same."[32] Moreover, a new generation of rising black politicians in Cleveland was displacing those of Stokes's generation.[33] Among his proudest accomplishments as a Representative, Stokes cited his ability to bring Appropriations Committee money to his district to address needs in housing and urban development and the opportunities that allowed him to set "historic precedents" as an African American in the House.[34] "When I started this journey, I realized that I was the first black American ever to hold this position in this state," Stokes told a newspaper reporter. "I had to write the book . . . I was going to set a standard of excellence that would give any successor something to shoot for."[35] As his replacement, Stokes supported Stephanie Tubbs Jones, an African-American judge and a former prosecutor who prevailed in the Democratic primary and easily won election to the House in 1998. After his congressional career, Louis Stokes resumed his work as a lawyer and resides in Silver Spring, Maryland.

FOR FURTHER READING

Fenno, Richard F. *Going Home: Black Representatives and Their Constituents* (Chicago: University of Chicago Press, 2003).

"Stokes, Louis," *Biographical Directory of the U.S. Congress, 1774–Present*, http://bioguide.congress.gov/scripts/biodisplay.pl?index=S000948.

MANUSCRIPT COLLECTIONS

Howard University (Washington, DC), Manuscript Division, Moorland–Spingarn Research Center. *Oral History:* In the Ralph J. Bunche Oral History Collection, 1973, 17 pages. An interview with Louis Stokes (March 14, 1973) in which he discusses his reasons for entering politics. Other subjects include the Congressional Black Caucus, including its origin and goals and divisions within the group, Stokes's relationship with President Richard M. Nixon's administration, the Black National Political Convention in Indiana (1972), and black support of Democratic and Republican presidential candidates.

Western Reserve Historical Society (Cleveland, OH). *Papers:* The Carl Stokes Papers, 1957–1972, 104.51 linear feet. The papers include material relating to Carl Stokes's brother, Louis.

NOTES

1   Richard F. Fenno, *Going Home: Black Representatives and Their Constituents* (Chicago: The University of Chicago Press, 2003): 22.

2   "Louise Stokes, Mother of Congressman and Mayor," 13 February 1978, *New York Times*: D8.

3   David Hess, "She Urged Sons 'To Be Somebody,'" 16 December 1968, *Christian Science Monitor*: 6.

4   Tom Brazaitis, "Stokes Era Comes to End," 18 January 1998, *Cleveland Plain Dealer*: 1A.

5   *Congressional Directory, 91st Congress* (Washington, DC: Government Printing Office, 1969): 141.

6   Fenno, *Going Home*: 14.

7   Ibid., 15.

8   Kermit L. Hall, *The Oxford Companion to the Supreme Court of the United States* (New York: Oxford University Press, 1992): 865–866.

9   Fenno, *Going Home*: 16.

10 Ibid., 37.

11 Roldo Bartimole, "Negroes' Election in Nonwhite Areas Isn't Automatic, Cleveland Race Shows," 6 May 1968, *Wall Street Journal*: 12.

12 Fenno, *Going Home*: 28.

13 Ibid., 42–43, 49.

14 William L. Clay, *Just Permanent Interests: Black Americans in Congress, 1870–1991* (New York: Amistad Press, 1992): 113–114.

15 "Election Statistics, 1920 to Present," available at http://clerk.house.gov/member_info/electionInfo/index.html.

16 Ibid.

17 *Politics in America, 1994* (Washington, DC: Congressional Quarterly Inc., 1993): 1204.

18 An allusion to the "College of Cardinals," who elect and advise the Pope of the Roman Catholic Church, the cardinal title is meant to convey the power and authority vested in the handful of Appropriations Committee Members who shape federal expenditures. At the time, Stokes was one of 13 Appropriations subcommittee chairs.

19 Fenno, *Going Home*: 188.

20 Clay, *Just Permanent Interests*: 111, 173–174. Clay also observed that he, Chisholm, and Stokes "considered ourselves, along with other black representatives, to have a mandate to speak forcefully and loudly in behalf of equitable treatment of minorities by government."

21 Fenno, *Going Home*: 62.

22 Paul Delaney, "Rep. Stokes Heads the Black Caucus," 9 February 1972, *New York Times*: 23.

23 Marguerite Ross Barnett, "The Congressional Black Caucus," *Proceedings of the Academy of Political Science* 32 (Volume 1975, Number 1): 39–40.

24 Jeffrey M. Elliot, *Black Voices in American Politics* (New York: Harcourt Brace Jovanovich 1986): 40–41.

25 *Politics in America, 1990* (Washington, DC: Congressional Quarterly Inc., 1989): 1206.

26 See, for example, Gerald Posner's *Case Closed: Lee Harvey Oswald and the Assassination of JFK* (New York: Anchor Books, 2003); Vincent Bugliosi's *Reclaiming History: The Assassination of President John F. Kennedy* (New York: W. W. Norton & Co., 2007); and Taylor Branch, *At Canaan's Edge: America in the King Years, 1965–68* (New York: Simon and Chuster, 2006).

27 George Lardner, Jr., "JFK-King Panel Finds Conspiracy Likely in Slayings," 31 December 1978, *Washington Post*: A1.

28 See, for example, *Politics in America, 1994*: 1203; Fenno, *Going Home*: 181.

29 *Politics in America, 1996* (Washington, DC: Congressional Quarterly Inc., 1995): 1043; see also *Politics in America, 1994*: 1203–1205.

30 *Politics in America, 1998* (Washington, DC: Congressional Quarterly Inc., 1997): 1140–1142; quote on 1140.

31 "Louis Stokes, Ohio Democrat, Plans to Retire from Congress," 18 January 1998, *New York Times*: 23; Tom Brazaitis and Sabrina Eaton, "Rep. Stokes to Retire; Congressman Won't Seek Re-Election; Clevelander Rose From Poverty to Heights of Power," 17 January 1998, *Cleveland Plain Dealer*: 1A.

32 Brazaitis, "Stokes Era Comes to End."

33 *Politics in America, 1994*: 1204.

34 Fenno, *Going Home*: 188–189.

35 Brazaitis, "Stokes Era Comes to End."

"I'M GOING TO KEEP ON
DENOUNCING THE INEQUITIES OF
THIS SYSTEM, BUT I'M GOING TO
WORK WITHIN IT," STOKES SAID.
"TO GO OUTSIDE THE SYSTEM
WOULD BE TO DENY MYSELF—TO
DENY MY OWN EXISTENCE.
I'VE BEATEN THE SYSTEM. I'VE
PROVED IT CAN BE DONE—SO
HAVE A LOT OF OTHERS."

George Washington Collins
1925–1972

UNITED STATES REPRESENTATIVE ★ 1970–1972
DEMOCRAT FROM ILLINOIS

A diligent but reserved public servant, George Collins served only two years in Congress. He entered the political scene at the local level in Chicago, and converted his loyal service to Mayor Richard Daley's Democratic machine to a seat in the U.S. House of Representatives. Unaffected by the redistricting many experts predicted would lead to his political demise, Collins won a second term in the House. His untimely death in a plane crash ended a promising House career but launched a long term of service by his widow, Cardiss.

George Washington Collins was born in Chicago, Illinois, on March 5, 1925. The son of Wash and Leanna Collins, George grew up during the Great Depression in the impoverished Cabrini-Green neighborhood, an area in the North Side of Chicago that was later known for its failed public housing experiment.[1] After graduating from Waller High School in Chicago, Collins entered the U.S. Army as a private in 1943. He served with the Engineers Corps in the South Pacific during World War II before being discharged as a sergeant in 1946. Upon returning to civilian life, Collins continued his education, earning a business law degree in 1957 from Northwestern University. On August 5, 1958, he married Cardiss Robertson. The couple had one son, Kevin.[2]

Collins gained his first political experience in the local Democratic organization headed by Mayor Daley. Appointed precinct captain in 1954 for Chicago's 24th Ward on the West Side—a section of the city known for its loyalty to the Democratic Party and the local machine—he went on to serve as deputy sheriff of Cook County from 1958 to 1961. Collins ascended further in local government as secretary to veteran alderman Benjamin Lewis of the 24th Ward and as an administrative assistant to the Chicago Board of Health.[3] After Lewis's brutal murder in 1963—he was handcuffed and shot in his ward office—Collins succeeded his former supervisor as 24th Ward alderman, a position he held until his election to Congress in 1970.[4]

When Representative Daniel J. Ronan of Illinois died during his third term in Congress in August 1969, Collins decided to run for the vacant seat. As a faithful member of the Cook County Democratic organization, Collins received the solid backing of Mayor Daley in the special election for Ronan's unexpired term for the 91st Congress (1969–1971) and for the election for a full term in the 92nd Congress (1971–1973). The March 1970 Democratic primary for the congressional district encompassing Chicago's predominantly black West Side and two working-class white suburbs, Cicero and Berwyn (once labeled the "Selma of the North" by Martin Luther King, Jr.), received national media attention because both candidates were African American.[5] During the campaign, Collins emphasized his political experience and his ability to bring improvements to the district because of his connections with city hall. He easily defeated his opponent Brenetta Howell, an outspoken community activist, social worker, and mother, with 86 percent of the vote.[6] Due in great part to the citywide influence of the Daley machine, Collins bested Alex Zabrosky—a white engineer and steel executive who resided in Berwyn—in the general election, 56 to 44 percent.[7] With this victory, Collins became the first African-American Member of the 20th century to represent a minority-black district. (Two black Members from districts without a black majority—Ron Dellums of California and Parren Mitchell of Maryland—joined Collins in the House in the 92nd Congress.[8]) Collins's 1970 election also marked the first time two African Americans represented Chicago simultaneously in Congress.[9]

Sworn in on November 3, 1970, Collins was assigned to the Public Works and Government Operations committees.

Vowing to serve his constituents "in any way," he made frequent trips to Chicago to ensure that he kept in touch with voters.[10] To advance the interests and concerns of his urban district, the Illinois Representative promoted a wide range of legislation aimed at improving the lives of the poor in American cities. Although Collins supported President Richard M. Nixon's proposals to provide a minimum federal payment to low-income families with children and to share federal tax revenues with states and localities, he judged funding levels to be inadequate. Collins sought to increase spending for the Elementary and Secondary Education Act and advocated the passage of federal highway legislation that addressed the needs of mass transit programs and of urban residents uprooted from their neighborhoods by road construction. He introduced a bill requiring the Treasury Department to provide free tax preparation to low- and moderate-income taxpayers and backed a measure to offer fiscal relief to states burdened by high welfare costs.[11] Collins participated in efforts to reform the Federal Housing Administration after hearings conducted by the Government Operations Subcommittee on Legal and Monetary Affairs revealed that low-income homeowners had been defrauded by speculators, real estate brokers, and home repair companies.

As a veteran of World War II, Collins cared deeply about the welfare of American soldiers, and he devoted particular attention to ending racial discrimination in the armed services. In 1971, Collins and nine other members of the Congressional Black Caucus (CBC)—the newly-formed organization created to promote economic, educational, and social issues affecting African Americans—toured American military bases to investigate widespread allegations of racial discrimination. He and his CBC colleagues conducted a series of hearings to investigate the complaints.[12] Known as a Member who preferred to work quietly behind the scenes, Collins made only occasional speeches on the floor during his tenure in the House. When Vice President Spiro Agnew accused African-American Representatives of exaggerating the desperate circumstances of many blacks living in the United States, several members of the CBC, including Collins, reproached him. "Mr. Agnew, take off those rose-colored glasses," Collins retorted. "When the black leadership talk about social, economic, and financial conditions of the black and the poor, it is very real."[13]

Despite a comfortable margin of victory in his initial election to office, Collins's bid for a second term in Congress was met with uncertainty. As a result of a court-ordered redistricting plan for the state of Illinois, Collins found himself facing another product of the Chicago Democratic machine, Frank Annunzio—an Illinois Representative first elected in the 89th Congress (1965–1967)—in a newly drawn district extending east to west from the heart of downtown Chicago to the western portion of the city.[14] Unconcerned with the restructuring that would potentially pit two Daley followers against one another, Annunzio confided to friends on Capitol Hill that the situation "will be taken care of by the organization."[15] Allegedly offered a position in the city administration in return for not opposing Annunzio, Collins defied the mayor, declaring his intention to enter the upcoming election. In a different political climate, Daley might not have tolerated such insubordination. But relations between the Chicago Democratic machine and the city's African-American political leadership had deteriorated in the aftermath of a split between the mayor and South Side Representative Ralph Metcalfe, William Dawson's successor. Metcalfe had accused Daley of devoting insufficient attention to the death of an unarmed black teenager shot by a Chicago policeman. Given his difficulties with Metcalfe, Daley could not afford to alienate the city's other African-American Representative, so he accommodated Collins's wishes to stand for another term.[16] In an attempt to avoid a direct contest between the two politicians, Daley successfully encouraged Annunzio to run for an open congressional seat in a more affluent Chicago district vacated by Representative Roman Pucinski, who unsuccessfully challenged Republican Senator Charles Percy.[17] With a formidable foe eliminated, Collins handily defeated Rhea Mojica

Hammer, an associate producer of a Spanish-language television program, in the March primary.[18] In the heavily Democratic district, Collins trounced his Republican opponent, real estate broker Thomas Lento, in the general election, garnering 83 percent of the vote.[19]

On December 8, 1972, a month after his re-election to a second term, Collins died in an airplane crash that killed 45 of the 61 passengers and the crew onboard a flight from Washington, DC, to Chicago, where Collins had planned to organize a Christmas party for children in his district.[20] Then-CBC chairman Louis Stokes of Ohio eulogized his congressional colleague: "The legacy which George Collins leaves is an abiding devotion to the people. . . .Those of us who served with him saw his strength and balance. The legacy he left all of us is that we should renew our devotion to mankind."[21] Shortly after Collins's death, his widow, Cardiss, entered and won the special election to fill his vacant congressional seat. The only African-American widow to succeed her husband in Congress, Cardiss Collins served 24 years in the House.

FOR FURTHER READING

"Collins, George Washington," *Biographical Directory of the U.S. Congress, 1774–Present*, http://bioguide.congress.gov/scripts/biodisplay.pl?index=C000637.

NOTES

1   James S. Stephens, "Collins Lauded at Rites," 22 December 1972, *Chicago Daily Defender*: 29. This article lists Collins's parents as Wash and Leanna. Wash is presumably short for Washington, which is George Collins's middle name. See also Maurine Christopher, *Black Americans in Congress* (New York: Thomas Y. Crowell Publishers, 1976): 266.

2   Christopher, *Black Americans in Congress*: 266; "Crash Takes Life of Congressman," 9 December 1972, *New York Times*: 70.

3   Grayson Mitchell, "Rep. George Collins (D.-Ill.) Killed in Chicago Jet Crash," 10 December 1972, *Washington Post*: B4; "Crash Takes Life of Congressman."

4   "Ben Lewis' Aid Named as 24th Ward Leader," 4 July 1963, *Chicago Tribune*: 7; "Aid of Lewis Named to Fill His Ward Job," 9 July 1963, *Chicago Tribune*: 14.

5   David E. Rosenbaum, "3 White Districts Choose Negroes for House Seats," 5 November 1970, *New York Times*: 28; Guy Halverson, "Few New Blacks Expected to Land Seats in Congress," 30 October 1970, *Christian Science Monitor*: 1; "Crash Takes Life of Congressman."

6   Francis Ward, "Chicago Congress Race Tests Black Militancy," 1 February 1970, *Los Angeles Times*: L4; Michael Kilian, "Most Exciting Contest to Be in 6th District," 22 February 1970, *Chicago Tribune*: W3; Michael Kilian, "Congressional Race Contested in the 6th," 15 March 1970, *Chicago Tribune*: W8; Michael Kilian, "Daley Choices Win Key Tests," 18 March 1970, *Chicago Tribune*: 1.

7   "Election Statistics, 1920 to Present," available at http://clerk.house.gov/member_info/electionInfo/index.html; *Almanac of American Politics, 1972* (Washington, DC: National Journal Inc., 1971): 205–206; Becky Beaupre, "Alex J. Zabrosky, Steel Company Exec.," 4 February 2001, *Chicago Sun Times*, http://findarticles.com/p/articles/mi_qn4155/is_20010204/ai_n13896147 (accessed 12 September 2007).

8   Rosenbaum, "3 White Districts Choose Negroes for House Seats"; Carol M. Swain, *Black Faces, Black Interests: The Representation of African Americans in Congress* (Cambridge, MA: Harvard University Press, 1993): 117; "Crash Takes Life of Congressman"; Philip Warden, "2 Democrats Battle Over New District," 11 November 1971, *Chicago Tribune*: 12.

9   The other African-American Representative representing Chicago, William Dawson, died just six days after Collins's election. Representative Ralph Metcalfe succeeded Dawson in the House, thereby keeping two African Americans representing Chicago.

10   Christopher, *Black Americans in Congress*: 266.

11   *Congressional Record*, House, 92nd Cong., 1st sess. (17 November 1971): 41864.

12   Thomas A. Johnson, "10 in Black Caucus Visit Bases in Study of Charges of Bias," 16 November 1971, *New York Times*: 62; Mitchell, "Rep. George Collins (D.-Ill.) Killed in Chicago Jet Crash."

13   *Congressional Record*, House, 92nd Cong., 1st sess. (21 July 1971): 26518.

14   John Elmer, "House Remap May Give G.O.P. 3 Seats," 23 September 1971, *Chicago Tribune*: 2; Warden, "2 Democrats Battle Over New District."

15   R. W. Apple, Jr., "Blacks May Lose in Redistricting," 25 October 1971, *New York Times*: 15.

16   R. W. Apple, Jr., "Black Leader's Rebellion Is Hurting Daley Machine," 10 May 1972, *New York Times*: 36.

17   Joel Weisman, "Daley Seen Re-Slating Negro," 10 December 1971, *Washington Post*: A3; Christopher, *Black Americans in Congress*: 267.

18   Stephen Crews, "2 Democrats Face Spunky Challengers in 5th, 7th District," 19 March 1972, *Chicago Tribune*: SCL6; Stephen Crews, "Mikva, Young Easy Winners in 10th Dist.; Hanrahan in 3d," 22 March 1972, *Chicago Tribune*: 3; Stephen Crews, "Novice Shakes Slate," 16 March 1972, *Chicago Tribune*: S1.

19   "Election Statistics, 1920 to Present," available at http://clerk. house.gov/member_info/electionInfo/index.html; Michael J. Dubin et al., *United States Congressional Elections, 1788–1997* (Jefferson, NC: McFarland and Company, Inc., 1998): 678; "Split Ballots Threat to Coattail Theory," 15 October 1972, *Chicago Tribune*: W3.

20   "Rep. George Collins (D.-Ill.) Killed in Chicago Jet Crash"; John Kifner, "Toll in Chicago Crash Rises to 45 as 2 More Bodies Are Found," 10 December 1972, *New York Times*: 77; Christopher, *Black Americans in Congress*: 267–268.

21   Stephens, "Collins Lauded at Rites."

"Mr. Agnew, take off those
rose-colored glasses,"
Collins remarked when
Vice President Spiro Agnew
accused African-American
Representatives of exaggerating
the desperate circumstances
of many black people
living in the United States.
"When the black leadership
talk about social, economic,
and financial conditions of
the black and the poor,
it is very real."

Permanent Interests:

THE EXPANSION, ORGANIZATION, AND RISING INFLUENCE OF AFRICAN AMERICANS IN CONGRESS, 1971–2007

The modern era of African Americans' nearly 140-year history in Congress began in 1971. Black Members enjoyed a tremendous surge in numbers, at least in the House, reflecting a larger historical process, as minority groups and women exercised their new freedom to participate in American society. Fully 71 percent of all African Americans who have served in Congress entered the House or Senate after 1970 (84 Representatives and two Senators).[1] These startling gains derived from the legacy of the Voting Rights Act of 1965 and its subsequent extensions, as well as from Supreme Court decisions requiring legislative redistricting so that black voters could be represented more equitably.

Greater numbers of African-American Members provided renewed momentum for convening a formal group and, in 1971, 13 individuals created the Congressional Black Caucus (CBC).[2] The CBC became a focal point for addressing issues important to blacks nationally by acting as an advocacy group for African Americans within the institution and forming a potent bloc for pushing legislative items. A growing influence, more focused and forceful than in previous generations, accompanied the organizational trend. The electoral longevity of African-American Members (boosted by districts that were drawn with black majorities), coupled with the CBC's lobbying of House leaders and progressive

On January 4, 2005, the Congressional Black Caucus (CBC) swore in its first male Senator, Barack Obama of Illinois. Representatives Eddie Bernice Johnson of Texas and Donald Payne of New Jersey take the CBC oath in the foreground. Since 1971, the CBC has played a major role in advocating African-American issues and advancing black Members within the institution of Congress.

IMAGE COURTESY OF AP/WIDE WORLD PHOTOS

institutional reforms in the 1970s, placed many black Members in key committee and party leadership positions. Over time, black advancement within the institution changed Members' legislative strategies. "Many of the [early] Black Caucus members came out of the heat of the civil rights struggle," William (Bill) Gray III of Pennsylvania observed. "We have a group of new members whose strategies were shaped in the post-civil rights movement—who use leverage within the system. We see ourselves not as civil rights leaders, but as legislators . . . the pioneers had made it possible for us to be technicians."[3]

The post-1970 generation of black Americans in Congress marked a watershed in American history—a transition from a period of prolonged protest to full political participation. Similar to other minority groups on Capitol Hill entering a stage of institutional maturity, African Americans faced new and sometimes unanticipated challenges resulting from their numerical, organizational, and leadership successes. Redistricting that dramatically boosted the numbers of African-American Members in the early 1990s evoked opposition that sought to roll back or dilute black voting strength. Moreover, by the end of the decade, redistricting had largely run its course in areas where black votes could be concentrated with a goal of electing more African Americans to Congress. The net result was that the number of African Americans in Congress leveled off by the early 1990s and hovered in the high 30s and low 40s for eight election cycles from 1992 through 2006. Although organizational trends provided African-American Members a forum to discuss their legislative agendas and strategies, black Members disagreed about many issues, partially because each Member represented the interests of a unique constituency. Finally, while African-American Members enjoyed unprecedented leadership strength for most of this era, greater power often placed black leaders in a quandary when the imperatives of promoting the leadership or party agenda conflicted with perceived "black interests."

BACKGROUND AND PRECONGRESSIONAL EXPERIENCE

Like earlier generations of black legislators on Capitol Hill, the 86 African Americans who entered Congress in the period from 1971 through 2007 generally ranked far above the norm in terms of education, professional attainment, and civic achievements. Successful careers in state government propelled the large numbers of African Americans elected to Congress in the 1990s.[4] Like all the previous generations of black Members, these individuals were typical of their peers among the general membership of the House and Senate—composed largely of business, law, public service, and other professional elites. They were exceedingly well educated, as was the general congressional membership, and their level of education ranked far above the statistical averages for the general U.S. population.[5] They also largely experienced trends that were prevalent among the general congressional population, including a decline in prior military experience and a higher median age at first election.[6]

Civil Rights Activism

A defining precongressional experience for many in this generation was their shared background in local and national civil rights protests. Many of the Members from this era, especially those first elected in the 1970s and 1980s, came of age during the civil rights movement. Some were prominent figures. John R. Lewis of Georgia (elected in 1986) cofounded and led the Student Nonviolent Coordinating Committee (SNCC), which became a pillar of the movement—staging sit-ins in segregated stores, participating in the Freedom Rides of 1961, and helping to organize the 1963 March on Washington for Jobs and Freedom. Andrew Young of Georgia (elected in 1972) was a principal aide to Martin Luther King, Jr., serving as executive director and executive vice president of the Southern Christian Leadership Conference (SCLC). King also tapped a young Washington minister, Walter Fauntroy, as director of the city's SCLC bureau. As the SCLC's congressional lobbyist, Fauntroy (elected the District of Columbia's Delegate in 1971) honed his skills as a coalition-builder.

Early in their political careers, some future black Members of Congress also grappled with internal divisions in the civil rights movement between those who embraced King's nonviolent protests and those who preferred a more aggressive and militant stance (such as Stokely Carmichael, who succeeded Lewis as head of SNCC).[7] Out of this schism came the Black Power movement and the more

In 1963, civil rights leaders, from left to right, John Lewis (future Georgia Representative), Whitney Young, Jr., A. Philip Randolph, Martin Luther King, Jr., James Farmer, and Roy Wilkins met at the Hotel Commodore in New York City for a strategy session.

IMAGE COURTESY OF LIBRARY OF CONGRESS

Ronald Dellums of California, who ran as a peace candidate and Vietnam War opponent, won a seat on the Armed Services Committee in 1973. The first African American to serve on the committee, Dellums's goal was to rein in the military's budget.

IMAGE COURTESY OF OFFICE OF THE CLERK, U.S. HOUSE OF REPRESENTATIVES

Harold Washington of Illinois used his seat in the House as a springboard for his successful effort to become the first black mayor of Chicago.

COLLECTION OF U.S. HOUSE OF REPRESENTATIVES

radical black nationalist factions of the latter 1960s, such as the Black Panthers. "Black Power" had different meanings within the movement. For Carmichael's cohorts, Black Power expressed frustration and rage with intransigent racism and advocated black separatism and the use of violence, if necessary, to achieve a measure of independence for African Americans. Adam Clayton Powell, Jr., of New York, who served in the House in 1966 when Carmichael first employed the term, briefly allied himself with the "new black militants" and defined Black Power as "a new philosophy for the tough, proud young Negroes who categorically refuse to compromise any longer for their rights."[8] John Lewis, who resigned from SNCC in July 1966 because of its militancy and confrontational rhetoric, recalled that SNCC had used a similar phrase during the Selma protests but that "it had more to do with self-reliance than with black supremacy." Lewis added that as articulated by Carmichael, Black Power "tended to create a schism, both within the movement itself and between the races. It drove people apart rather than brought them together."[9]

Ronald Dellums of California, who represented an Oakland–Berkeley House district, found himself at the center of a virtual war between Black Panthers and the Oakland police force in the late 1960s. "The Black Panther Party for Self Defense" had been formed in 1966 by Huey Newton and Bobby Seale to counter what both men believed to be a long history of police abuses against African-American citizens of Oakland. As a member of the Berkeley city council, Dellums once convinced Seale to disperse an angry, agitated crowd of Panther supporters at a council meeting, probably avoiding bloodshed. Dellums noted that juggling the complex and competing agendas of radical factions developed his political acumen by forcing him "to employ all the skills at my command to build legislative majorities." A former member of the Chicago Black Panthers, Bobby Rush, who quit the group in the early 1970s because of its violent tactics, served a decade as a Chicago city councilman before winning election to the U.S. House in 1992.

Prior Elective Office

This generation's elective experience differed significantly from that of previous generations. The vast majority of African Americans who entered Congress after 1970 held prior elective office (68 of the 86, or 79 percent), with a substantial increase in the numbers with service in state legislatures. Half (43) of the African Americans elected to Congress from 1971 through 2007 served as state legislators, 19 in the lower chamber, six in the upper chamber, and 18 in both chambers of their respective statehouses. Of these, several performed leadership functions in their respective chambers, including Barbara Jordan (president *pro tempore* of the Texas senate), Harold E. Ford, Sr., (majority whip of the Tennessee house of representatives), and Carol Moseley-Braun (assistant majority leader of the Illinois house of representatives).[11] This development, perhaps more than any other precongressional characteristic, brought black Members of Congress into near-total congruence with the experiential background of the general population of House and Senate membership.

Voting rights reforms and redistricting drove diversity trends in the state legislatures in the decades after Congress enacted civil rights legislation. For instance, between 1970 and 1992, the number of African Americans serving in state legislatures increased 274 percent (from 168 to 463). The growth occurred fastest in the South—where the largest number of blacks lived and where voting rights legislation and court decisions provided greater access to the ballot. From 32 seats in 1970, blacks held 226 in 1992—a gain of 894 percent.[12] These trends have continued, albeit more slowly, in the last 15 years. According to 2003 figures from the National Conference of State Legislators, 595 African Americans held seats in the upper or lower house in state legislatures, accounting for 8.1 percent of all (7,382) state legislators nationwide.[13]

At the state and the national levels, these gains have been particularly striking among women. Over time, African-American women have accounted for an increasing percentage of the sum total of black legislators in state capitals and in Washington, DC. For instance, in 1970 there were only 15 black women state legislators—accounting for less than 10 percent of all African-American state legislators. By 1992, the number of black women state legislators had increased to 131, or roughly 28 percent of all black state legislators. As with other women in Congress, legislative experience at the state level provided a vehicle for election to the U.S. Congress. In 1971, there was only one African-American woman in Congress—Shirley Chisholm of New York—among a total of 14 blacks in Congress. By late 2007, African-American women accounted for nearly one-third of all the sitting black Members of Congress.[14]

State legislatures were just one avenue to attain higher office. Traditional experience in local and municipal elective office also typified this post-1971 cohort of black Members of Congress. Fifteen served on city councils, and five were elected county council members or commissioners. Four persons served as mayors, nine served as local or municipal judges, and several others held other elected positions, such as school board member, recorder of deeds, and justice of the peace. Three individuals held high-ranking state or territorial positions: Mervyn Dymally, lieutenant governor of California; Melvin Evans, governor of the Virgin Islands; and G. K. Butterfield, North Carolina supreme court justice. Finally, several individuals held prominent federal positions prior to winning their first congressional election, including Eleanor Holmes Norton, commissioner of the Equal Employment Opportunity Commission in the 1970s and Diane Watson, U.S. Ambassador to the Federated States of Micronesia from 1999 through 2000.

CREATION AND EVOLUTION OF THE CONGRESSIONAL BLACK CAUCUS

As the number of African Americans serving in Congress grew, a long-desired movement to form a more unified organization among black legislators coalesced. When Charles C. Diggs, Jr., of Michigan entered the House of Representatives in 1955, he joined black Members William Dawson of Illinois and Adam Clayton Powell—the largest delegation of African Americans on Capitol Hill since Reconstruction. "In Congress, there was little, if any communication between Dawson and Powell," Diggs noted. "Their styles were different. In terms of exercise between them, there was not any."[15] Diggs keenly felt the isolation endured by black Members due to their small numbers in Congress and, in some cases, an inability to connect on a personal level. Frustrated that black Representatives lacked a forum to discuss common concerns and issues, Diggs proposed the organization of the Democratic Select Committee (DSC) at the opening of the 91st Congress (1969–1971), maintaining that the DSC would fill a significant void by fostering the exchange of information among the nine African Americans serving in Congress, as well as between black Representatives and House leadership. "The sooner we get organized for group action, the more effective we can become,"

Barbara Jordan became the first black female state senator in the United States when she was elected to the Texas senate in 1966. This 1968 photograph shows Jordan at a White House meeting with President Lyndon B. Johnson (not pictured) and other legislators. When Jordan was elected to the U.S. House in 1972, Johnson persuaded congressional leaders to assign Jordan to the influential Judiciary Committee.

PHOTOGRAPH BY YOICHI R. OKAMOTO, COURTESY OF LBJ LIBRARY

More women joined the first black Congresswoman, Shirley Chisholm of New York, on Capitol Hill during this period. Pictured from left to right are: Cardiss Collins of Illinois, Yvonne Brathwaite Burke of California, and Chisholm. In the 110th Congress (2007–2009), women account for one-third of the total number of African-American Members.

IMAGE COURTESY OF MOORLAND–SPINGARN RESEARCH CENTER, HOWARD UNIVERSITY

John Conyers, Jr., of Michigan, Charles Diggs, Jr., of Michigan, Bill Clay, Sr., of Missouri, Louis Stokes of Ohio, Charles Rangel of New York, Parren Mitchell of Maryland, George Collins of Illinois, and Walter Fauntroy of the District of Columbia gathered as a show of unity among black Members of Congress of the 92nd Congress (1971–1973).

IMAGE COURTESY OF U.S. HOUSE OF
REPRESENTATIVES PHOTOGRAPHY OFFICE

Caucus:

A meeting of party members in each chamber (House Republicans, Senate Democrats, and Senate Republicans refer to their respective gatherings as "Conferences"). These meetings are used primarily to select candidates for office and to consider other important business for furthering party interests. The term also describes an organization of House and Senate Members that is devoted to a special interest or legislative area.

Diggs remarked.[16] The informal group held sporadic meetings that were mainly social gatherings and had no independent staff or budget.

Newly elected Members and beneficiaries of court-ordered redistricting, William (Bill) Clay, Sr., of Missouri, Louis Stokes of Ohio, and Shirley Chisholm embraced the concept of a group for black legislators to "seize the moment, to fight for justice, to raise issues too long ignored and too little debated"—all of which quickly translated into a more influential association for African-American Members.[17] Representative Clay and Stokes formed a fast and enduring friendship. Their close personal relationship boosted momentum to craft a permanent organization. Stokes drew upon his efforts to forge an independent political organization within his own district. "The thrust of our elections was that many black people around America who had formerly been unrepresented, now felt that the nine black members of the House owed them the obligation of also affording them representation in the House," Stokes explained. He added that "in addition to representing our individual districts, we had to assume the onerous burden of acting as congressman-at-large for unrepresented people around America."[18]

With the opening of the 92nd Congress (1971–1973), the number of black Representatives rose to 13—the greatest number of African Americans ever to serve simultaneously in Congress. The DSC met on February 2, 1971, and accepted a recommendation put forth by Clay to create a nonpartisan, formal network for African-American Members.[19] Charles Rangel of New York, who narrowly defeated longtime Representative Powell in 1970, thought of a new name for the group: the Congressional Black Caucus.[20] The CBC elected Diggs as its first chairman. "Black people have no permanent friends, no permanent enemies … just permanent interests," Clay declared—a theme that set the tone for the CBC during its formative years and evolved into its motto.[21] Unlike many Members of Congress, Clay surmised, the participants in the new caucus did not owe their elections to traditional liberal or labor bases of support. "We were truly uninhibited, really free to decide our own issues, formulate our own policies, and advance our own programs," Clay recalled. "Our mission was clear. We had to parlay massive voting potential into concrete economic results."[22]

In the midst of its transition to a more formal organization, the CBC waged its first public battle during the early months of 1971.[23] Upset with President Richard M. Nixon's refusal to meet with the group, African-American Members made national headlines when they boycotted the January 1971 State of the Union address. "We now refuse to be part of your audience," Clay wrote on behalf of the caucus, explaining that it perceived the President's persistent refusal to grant them a White House meeting as symptomatic of the administration's abandonment of African-American interests.[24] The group won a public relations victory when Nixon agreed to a March 1971 meeting. "Our people are no longer asking for equality as a rhetorical promise," Diggs declared. "They are demanding from the national Administration, and from elected officials without regard to party affiliation, the only kind of equality that ultimately has any real meaning—equality of results."[25] Press coverage provided instant national recognition for the CBC.[26] The CBC thereafter skillfully used such tactics to wield clout and build a reputation as a congressional irritant.[27]

After an August 1974 meeting with President Gerald R. Ford, the CBC posed for a picture. Standing from left to right are: Ronald Dellums of California, Robert Nix, Sr., of Pennsylvania, John Conyers of Michigan, Shirley Chisholm of New York, Andrew Young, Jr., of Georgia, Assistant to the President Stan Scott, Ralph Metcalfe of Illinois, Walter Fauntroy of the District of Columbia, Barbara Jordan of Texas, Louis Stokes of Ohio, Charles Diggs, Jr., of Michigan. Seated left to right are: Gus Hawkins of California, Cardiss Collins of Illinois, Charles Rangel of New York, Yvonne Brathwaite Burke of California, Bill Clay, Sr., of Missouri, and Parren Mitchell of Maryland.

IMAGE COURTESY OF MOORLAND–SPINGARN RESEARCH CENTER, HOWARD UNIVERSITY

A rapid transformation took place in the organization's early years as it began a maturation process. Heavy expectations were placed upon the group, initially leading the CBC to adopt a collective approach to representation to present a unified voice for black America.[28] The CBC collected and disseminated information on African-American preferences regarding policy, assisted individual black Americans with a range of requests by providing casework services, and spoke on behalf of special interest groups within the black community.[29]

Countervailing currents pushed and pulled at the CBC membership, who represented diverse constituencies and practiced individual legislative styles. Representative Diggs, a strong backer of the collective leadership model, attempted to organize a national black political convention in 1972. Ultimately, the caucus declined to sponsor the event for fear it would lead to future obligations in which the CBC would not have direct oversight.[30] Shirley Chisholm's 1972 presidential campaign also proved disuniting. The only woman among the CBC's founders, Chisholm claimed that her gender, in addition to her willingness to form coalitions with liberal whites, Hispanics, and women, irritated her CBC colleagues. Indeed, some felt she betrayed the unified mission of the caucus by reaching out to other groups and undermined the effectiveness of the organization by placing gender

The first African-American woman to campaign for the presidency, Shirley Chisholm of New York ran with the slogan of "Unbought and Unbossed." This 1972 campaign poster featured her famous mantra.

COLLECTION OF U.S. HOUSE OF REPRESENTATIVES

above race. Only Ronald Dellums and Parren Mitchell of Maryland publicly endorsed Chisholm for President.[31]

Given the burdens and tensions that arose from collective representation, the organization shifted its emphasis. CBC members began classifying themselves as "just" legislators—moving away from the national spotlight and back to responding to the needs of their constituencies.[32] That shift in priorities occurred largely under Stokes's leadership after he succeeded Diggs in 1972 as CBC chairman.[33] During his two terms leading the CBC, Stokes downplayed the role of the caucus as a champion of African-American issues. "We had to analyze what our resources were, what we should be doing, and how best to do it," he explained. "And our conclusion was this: if we were to be effective, if we were going to make the meaningful contribution to minority citizens in this country, then it must be as legislators. This is the area in which we possess expertise—and it is within the halls of Congress that we must make this expertise felt."[34]

According to political scientist Marguerite Ross Barnett, after spending its early years reacting to events, the CBC entered another stage of maturation in 1975 when it sought to foster a proactive, anticipatory method for crafting a legislative agenda. Key elements of the earlier organizational strategies informed this approach. By balancing collective leadership with individual representation, the CBC fully embraced the challenge of the dual role African-American legislators faced—speaking for the concerns of black America while simultaneously representing unique constituencies. Political scientist Carol Swain maintains that the group followed this blended leadership approach into the 1990s.[35]

During this period the CBC also confronted questions about its identity and core values. In 1975, Fortney (Pete) Stark, a white Member representing a congressional district in Oakland, California, with a substantial African-American population, asked to join the all-black caucus. After intense deliberation, the group rejected Stark's application. "The caucus symbolizes black political development in this country," CBC Chairman Charles Rangel explained. "We feel that maintaining this symbolism is critical at this juncture in our development."[36] The CBC retained its unwritten rule to limit membership to African Americans but briefly allowed whites to join as nonvoting associates. In 1988, 41 white Representatives joined the CBC when the caucus instituted its new policy.[37]

INSTITUTIONAL ADVANCEMENT

Member Characteristics: Electoral Longevity

Incumbency success rates for Members of Congress have risen throughout the 20th century for the entire congressional population. African Americans, of course, have been elected in their greatest numbers in an era in which incumbency rates have remained consistently at 95 percent (the rate in 1970) or greater—indeed in the late 1980s and the 1990s it reached 98 percent.[38] While the longevity of all Members of Congress increased, African-Americans' longevity has exceeded the norm. From the World War II Era forward, black Members have served longer than the general membership.[39]

The average length of service for former African-American Members elected between 1964 and 2004 reached 10.1 years—higher than the 8.65-year average for the entire congressional population during that time span.[40] Of the black Members who entered Congress after 1970, Charles Rangel has had the longest span of service: nearly 37 years at the end of 2007. In the history of African Americans in Congress, Rangel ranked second only to John Conyers of Michigan (also a current Member of the 110th Congress, 2007–2009), a Member for nearly 43 years by late 2007. During this era, Bill Clay, Sr., and Louis Stokes also accumulated more than three decades of service, with 32 and 30 years, respectively, at their retirements. By the 110th Congress, active African-American Members held an even more consequential service advantage: While the average length of service for the entire congressional population was at a near all-time high of 10.1 years, black Members averaged 12 years.[41]

Member Characteristics: Seniority and Leadership Posts

Longevity meant that many black Members of Congress in this era benefited from the long-standing tradition of parceling out desirable committee assignments and leadership positions to those who had accrued the most years of continuous service. The trend that awarded perquisites based on committee seniority solidified in the second decade of the 20th century in the House and remained dominant through the 1970s (and still figures prominently in the way assignments are distributed).[42] "When I first came to Congress, I was opposed to the seniority system," District of Columbia Delegate Walter Fauntroy remarked. However, he later said, "The longer I am here, the better I like it."[43] Indeed, seniority boosted the influence of black Representatives and that of the CBC in the latter part of the century. "We don't really think that racism in this country has so diminished that given the opportunity to vote on individuals based on their experience and ability that we could overcome that without the assistance of the seniority system," Representative Rangel acknowledged.[44]

Between 1971 and 1975, African-American Members eclipsed long-standing barriers on the three elite House committees: Appropriations, which originates all federal spending bills; Ways and Means, with power over taxation and revenue measures; and Rules, which reviews and structures bills passed by various committees in preparation for debate and vote by the full House. In 1971, Louis Stokes won a seat on the Appropriations Committee, becoming the first of 12 African Americans to serve on the panel in this era (the first black woman, Yvonne Brathwaite Burke of California, joined the committee in 1975). Stokes eventually served as one of the Appropriations "cardinals."[45] As chairman of the Subcommittee on Veterans Affairs, Housing and Urban Development, and Independent Agencies in the 103rd Congress (1993–1995), Stokes oversaw a huge percentage of the discretionary spending in the annual federal budget. The first African American to lead an Appropriations subcommittee was Representative Julian Dixon of California, who chaired the District of Columbia Subcommittee beginning in the 97th Congress (1981–1983).

During this period, black House Members capitalized upon decentralizing reforms to solidify and extend gains in terms of committee assignments and leadership positions. In 1974, control of committee assignments of Democratic Members was transferred from the Ways and Means Committee (then chaired by Wilbur Mills of Arkansas) to the Democratic Steering and Policy Committee, chaired by the Speaker of the House. The CBC used the opportunity to pressure House leaders, including Speaker Carl Albert of Oklahoma, to place African Americans on prominent committees. Under Representative Rangel's leadership, the group struck a deal with Speaker Albert stipulating that at least one African-

Representative Charles Rangel of New York, featured in this 2007 image, has the second longest career in congressional history among African Americans.

IMAGE COURTESY OF U.S. HOUSE OF REPRESENTATIVES PHOTOGRAPHY OFFICE

Seniority:

Priority or precedence in office or service; superiority in standing to another of equal rank by reason of earlier entrance into the service or an earlier date of appointment.

Representatives Yvonne Brathwaite Burke of California, Harold Ford, Sr., of Tennessee, Walter Fauntroy of the District of Columbia, and Louis Stokes of Ohio were members of the House Select Committee on Assassinations. The committee, chaired by Stokes, investigated the assassinations of Dr. Martin Luther King, Jr., and President John F. Kennedy. In this image of a committee hearing, Burke (upper left), Fauntroy (second from upper left), and Stokes (fifth from upper left) listen to witness testimony.

In the 103rd Congress (1993–1995), a large turnover among the House Membership allowed Lucien Blackwell of Pennsylvania to make the largest jump in seniority of any returning Member. Blackwell traded his assignment on Merchant Marine and Fisheries for a coveted position on the Budget Committee.

American Member would serve on each of the major standing committees.[46] The ability of the CBC to attain more-attractive committee assignments was one of a handful of "clear achievements of black representatives organizing as a Caucus."[47] As a result of the new agreement between the CBC and the House leadership, each of the highest-ranking House committees included at least one African-American Member on its roster during the 94th Congress (1975–1977).[48]

Throughout its history, the CBC continued to rally to the support of individual black Members seeking to make institutional inroads that would better position them to secure some of their legislative goals. One example was the case of Ronald Dellums, a vocal critic of the Vietnam War, who faced resistance when he announced his interest in serving on the Armed Services Committee, chaired by longtime southern Democrat F. Edward Hébert of Louisiana. The CBC, led by Stokes and Clay, drafted a letter to the Democratic leadership on behalf of Dellums. When Speaker Albert informed Stokes that the CBC could have a black Member on Armed Services, but not Dellums, Stokes angrily replied that "white people don't tell black people who their leaders are."[49] With the backing of the CBC, Dellums became the first black to serve on the Armed Services Committee.

Rising rank within the committee system had a reinforcing effect on the CBC. By the 99th Congress (1985–1987), CBC membership had grown to 20—only seven more than the original number in 1971.[50] But despite this modest numerical gain, African Americans chaired an unparalleled five standing committees, two select committees, and 16 subcommittees in the 99th Congress.[51] "We don't have to go hat in hand begging anybody," Representative Clay observed. "In fact, it's just the reverse. Now a lot of people have to come hat in hand [to us] asking us for favors."[52]

Of the 18 African Americans who have held House committee chairmanships in congressional history, 16 attained those positions in the post-1970 era. Five have held at least two chairmanships, and Augustus (Gus) Hawkins of California held chairmanships on four committees: Education and Labor; House Administration; Joint Committee on Printing; and Joint Committee on the Library.[53] Additionally, of the 46 African-American Members who have chaired subcommittees in Congress, 41 attained those posts for the first time in the post-1970 period.[54] Such presence within the echelons of the leadership constituted a significant base of institutional support. In summary, these developments indicated that African Americans were now represented throughout the committee structure of the House—ranging from constituency-oriented panels to power committees—and provided powerful evidence of their assimilation into the institution.[55]

During the era from 1971 through 2007, black Members made history by attaining posts in the leadership ranks of both major parties in the House. John Conyers made the first effort to attain a leadership post by challenging then-Majority Leader Carl Albert for the speakership in 1971. Conyers lost the Democratic Caucus vote 220 to 20 in what was widely described as a symbolic undertaking.[56] But African-American Members made inroads in other leadership routes during this era. Barbara Jordan of Texas, Ralph Metcalfe of Illinois, and Harold E. Ford, Sr., of Tennessee, for instance, were early appointees to the Democratic Steering and Policy Committee, which set the parameters of the party's legislative agenda in addition to parceling out committee assignments. In 1983, Speaker Thomas P. (Tip) O'Neill of Massachusetts chose Representative Rangel as a Deputy Majority Whip, making the

New York Representative one of the most powerful Democrats in the House. John Lewis later served as Chief Deputy Democratic Whip.[57]

Just four African Americans have held elected positions within the Democratic Caucus and Republican Conference. Shirley Chisholm held the position of Democratic Caucus Secretary in the 95th and 96th Congresses (1977–1981). Bill Gray made the most dramatic climb up the leadership ladder: After winning the position of Democratic Caucus chairman in December 1988, he made history six months later when his colleagues elected him Democratic (Majority) Whip. As the first African American to hold the post, Gray was the third-ranking Democrat in the House. Others followed his lead. In 1999, J. C. Watts of Oklahoma became the highest-ranking African American in the history of the Republican Party when his GOP colleagues elected him Chairman of the Republican Conference; he held the position until his retirement from the House in 2003.[58] James Clyburn of South Carolina served as Chairman of the Democratic Caucus for part of the 109th Congress, relinquishing that post to Rahm Emanuel of Illinois in November 2006, and becoming the second African American to hold the position of Majority Whip.[59]

LEGISLATIVE INTERESTS

The legislative agendas of African-American Members in the post-1970 era reflected the diversity of their committee assignments and the range of interests within the general membership of Congress. Most sought to advance a broad progressive legislative agenda supported by advocacy groups such as the National Urban League and the National Association for the Advancement of Colored People (NAACP)—extending voting rights protections, improving educational and economic opportunities, fostering urban renewal, and providing access to better health care. With greater frequency, some departed from traditional "black interests" and pursued legislative agendas that reflected the unique needs of their constituencies or their personal positions on issues.[60]

Voting Rights

Extensions of civil rights era voting protections were a touchstone for African-American Members of Congress. Efforts to retain and expand upon the provisions of the Voting Rights Act of 1965—which Barbara Jordan once referred to as the "frontispiece" of the civil rights movement—provided continuity between Members of the civil rights generation and their successors in the post-1970 generation of Black Americans in Congress. Two extensions were of particular importance: the Voting Rights Acts of 1975 and 1982.

The Voting Rights Act of 1975 (P.L. 94–73) strengthened the provisions of the Voting Rights Act of 1965 (as well as its 1970 extension).[61] The House passed the act on June 4, 1975, by a vote of 341 to 70. After Senate passage, and House acceptance of some Senate amendments, President Gerald R. Ford signed the measure into law on August 6, 1975, the 10th anniversary of the original landmark bill. As with earlier acts, jurisdictions covered by the 1975 extension had to submit to the U.S. Attorney General any changes in local and state election law for "preclearance"—a determination of whether the modification had discriminatory intent. The 1975 act also increased jurisdictions covered by the act to include locations in the North and West. Moreover, it applied not just to African Americans, but also "language minorities," including Spanish speakers, Native Americans, and Asian Americans.

In 1994, J.C. Watts of Oklahoma received the Republican nomination for his district and won election as one of only five black Republicans to serve in Congress in the 20th century. "I knew what I was doing would not be popular," Watts recalled. "It created some strain, even in relationships I had built over the years. But I knew in my heart that this was the right road, the honest road for me to take and remain true to my own principles."

COLLECTION OF U.S. HOUSE OF REPRESENTATIVES

Whip:

An assistant House or Senate Floor leader who helps round up party members for quorum calls and important votes. Coined in the British Parliament, this term is derived from "whipper-in," a person who kept the dogs from straying during a fox hunt.

As a Member of the U.S. House, Mickey Leland of Texas successfully lobbied Congress to create the Select Committee on Hunger in 1984. Leland was killed in a 1989 airplane crash while ferrying relief supplies to Ethiopia.

It required bilingual elections in areas where there were large numbers of minorities whose English literacy was below the national average.[62]

African-American Members played a prominent part in this debate. "The voting rights act may have overcome blatant discriminatory practices," noted Barbara Jordan, testifying before the House Judiciary Subcommittee on Civil Rights and Constitutional Rights. But she added, "it has yet to overcome subtle discriminatory practices." Charles Rangel agreed that the protections were needed. "Malevolent local government must not be exposed to any temptation to take back the political rights and powers that have so recently come to southern blacks," Rangel said.[63] Andrew Young pointed to vastly improved registration numbers in the seven southern states covered by the original 1965 act (29 percent registered in 1964 had expanded to 56 percent in 1972) as well as in the number of elected black officials in the South (72 in 1965 compared with 1,587 in 1975). "The remarkable effect of this act is that it has a preventative effect," Young observed. "There are some reports that the threat of suing examiners has a deterrent effect—that local registrars began to register black voters so that federal examiners would be kept out."[64]

The 1982 Voting Rights Act (P.L. 97–205) extension provided another victory for the civil rights movement and also paved the way for the expansion of Black American representation in Congress in the 1990s.[65] During floor debate prior to overwhelming passage by the House, a number of black Members of Congress spoke on behalf of the bill. Representative Bill Clay, Sr., cast the debate in broad terms: "Are we willing to continue our forward momentum in America's bold and noble attempt to achieve a free and just democratic society? Or, will we embrace the politics of reversal and retreat; the super rich against the wretchedly poor, the tremendously strong against the miserably weak?"[66] The bill extended the act's major provisions for 25 years. It also established a procedure by which jurisdictions that maintained a clean voting rights record for at least a decade could petition a panel of judges to be removed from the preclearance list. The bilingual election materials requirements established in the 1975 act were also enacted for another decade. Mickey Leland, who succeeded Representative Jordan in her Houston-centered district, addressed the House in Spanish to make a point about the need for extending those provisions. "Many of you cannot understand me," Leland said in Spanish, "and if you cannot understand me . . . nor can you understand 17 percent of all the adult workers in the Southwest. . . . And even though you cannot understand me when I speak Spanish maybe you can begin to understand the hypocrisy of our political system which excludes the participation of Hispanic-Americans only for having a different culture and speaking a different language."[67]

Most significant, the Voting Rights Act of 1982 established that certain voting rights violations could be proven to be the result of voting modifications, even if intent could not be established. That section of the bill overturned a 1980 Supreme Court decision in *Mobile v. Bolden* (446 U.S. 55) that found a violation could be proven only if the intent to discriminate could be substantiated. This legislative instrument provided the basis for a round of creating majority-black districts following the 1990 Census, particularly in southern states.

Economic Opportunity

Another primary area of legislative concern for numerous African-American Members of this generation was the desire to promote economic opportunities for blacks as a means to further the political civil rights advances won in the 1960s. Economic disparities among racial groups remained a problem throughout this time period. One of Congress's strongest supporters of urban economic aid, Representative Floyd Flake of New York noted, "We in America have created a Third World within our borders, if we conglomerate all of the rural and all of the urban communities in this Nation who are not able to provide the basic necessities for people who are part of those communities."[68] For instance, from 1980 to 1990 the unemployment rate for blacks was more than double that of whites. Throughout that decade, the median income for African Americans constituted just 60 percent of the median income for whites.[69] Many of the Members profiled in this generation supported an array of programs to advance African-American economic equality, including job training programs, urban renewal projects, affirmative action programs, and "empowerment zones" (urban and rural areas designated to receive federal grants and loans for job training and tax incentives for minority-owned businesses). At times these positions were championed by the CBC; at others, individual Members acted as policy entrepreneurs.

The CBC consistently made the economic advancement of African Americans a top priority in its legislative agenda. For example, the caucus strongly backed the extension of the Office of Economic Opportunity programs under the Economic Opportunity Act of 1964 (P.L. 88–452).[70] From 1974 to 1975, Gus Hawkins and Senator Hubert Humphrey of Minnesota drafted a measure to drastically cut unemployment in the United States, which reached 8 percent among the general population and more than 13 percent for nonwhites by the mid-1970s.[71] Concerned about the disproportionate joblessness rate for African Americans, each member of the CBC cosponsored the Humphrey–Hawkins Full Employment and Balanced Growth Act of 1978 (P.L. 95–523).[72] Among its provisions, the act declared the federal government's intention to promote full employment, real income gains, price stability, and a balanced budget. Signed into law on October 28, 1978, the final version of the bill failed to include the more ambitious full employment goals drafted by Humphrey and Hawkins, leading some analysts to describe the legislation as "an empty symbol."[73] But the CBC's ability to persuade President James Earl (Jimmy) Carter to publicly support a bill linked so closely to the caucus resulted in

Affirmative Action:

First used in the United States during the 1960s and 1970s, a policy to promote opportunities for minorities and women by favoring them in hiring and promotion in government and private jobs, college admissions, and the awarding of government contracts as a means to compensate for their historic exclusion or underrepresentation.

The Humphrey–Hawkins Full Employment Act of 1978 attempted to resolve persistent unemployment in the United States. The CBC placed its support behind the bill. Civil rights activist Jesse Jackson, Sr., (center) marched to draw attention to the legislation.

IMAGE COURTESY OF LIBRARY OF CONGRESS

In 1950, Parren Mitchell of Maryland successfully sued the University of Maryland at College Park for admission. He became the school's first African-American graduate student. Mitchell eventually became a professor of sociology and taught at Morgan State College in Baltimore. In 1970, he was elected to the first of eight consecutive terms in the House, representing a Baltimore district.

During President Ronald Reagan's eight years in office, he met once with the CBC. Pictured at the White House on February 3, 1981, the CBC sought Reagan's assistance on domestic issues.

a noteworthy victory.[74] "We would never have struggled so hard to get this act passed if we did not consider it significant," declared Representative Parren Mitchell.

Mitchell, the brother of longtime NAACP lobbyist Clarence Mitchell, Jr., used a networking strategy to help push legislation aimed at business development in African-American communities through the House. Primarily interested in promoting economic opportunities in inner cities, Mitchell assembled a "brain trust" of national advisers (mostly businessmen, lawyers, bankers, and economists) to make recommendations on policy and legislation.[75] The CBC embraced this approach, often calling upon subject experts for assistance in crafting legislation. Mitchell also employed his encyclopedic knowledge of House procedures—another facet of effective representation that many CBC Members refined during the period to promote the organization's legislative agenda. Called the "Little General" for his ability to organize and coordinate support for key legislation, the Maryland Representative attached an amendment to a $4 billion public works program that required state and local governments applying for federal contracts to reserve 10 percent of the money for minority-owned companies.[76] Signed into law in 1977, the measure constituted not only a personal triumph for Mitchell but also a significant early legislative victory for the CBC. That success lent credibility to the group's coalition-building efforts and burnished its reputation for using House procedures to achieve its legislative goals.

During the 1970s the CBC sporadically presented budget proposals that emphasized increased spending for domestic programs. However, in 1981 the group answered President Ronald W. Reagan's call for alternatives to his fiscal plan, which emphasized defense spending, by drafting their own detailed budget.[77] The CBC plan received national attention but little backing in the House. As an annual offering of the period, the CBC alternative included a consistent call to increase federal funding for domestic programs, to slash defense spending, and to raise taxes for the wealthiest Americans. "Even in defeat we have a responsibility to fight the

fight," Dellums remarked about the persistent failure of an alternative annual budget to attract meaningful support in the House. "We have to articulate the alternative."[78]

District of Columbia

Another issue of ongoing importance to black Members of Congress was the matter of representation and "home rule" (self-government) for the city of Washington, DC. Since its creation after the Residence Act of 1790, the capital had been administered by a patchwork of governing mechanisms: an appointed mayor and elected city council (both a board of aldermen and common council); briefly, a territorial government in 1871, when the city was designated the "District of Columbia"; a presidentially appointed commission; and congressional committees. After 1960, because of its new majority-black urban population, congressional debates about representation and the administration of the District resonated within the larger African-American community.

Representative Charles Diggs, an ardent advocate for Washingtonians, became chairman of a District of Columbia subcommittee in 1967. Six years later, he chaired the full committee, symbolically marking the end to the exclusive history of white congressional control over the capital. In 1970, with Diggs's leadership, the House passed the District of Columbia Act, which reinstituted the post of Delegate to represent the city in the House.[79] In March 1971, District residents elected Walter Fauntroy, a minister and civil rights activist, as the city's first congressional Delegate in a century.

Fauntroy tirelessly advocated "home rule" in the District of Columbia. The CBC, seeking to increase the independence of the predominantly African-American population, joined him. Fauntroy oversaw a lobbying campaign aimed at building support from white Members who represented southern districts with a substantial black constituency. The effort prevailed. In December 1973, Congress passed a compromise measure—the District of Columbia Self-Government and Governmental Reorganization Act—that gave the District limited self-rule, permitting citizens to elect a mayor and a city council.[80]

Based partially on the success of the "Fauntroy strategy," the CBC later created the Action-Alert Communications Network (AACN) to mobilize support from nonblack legislators on a range of policy issues affecting black Americans.[81] Encompassing the National Black Leadership Roundtable and the Black Leadership Forum, the AACN tapped into a network of national black organizations suited for grass-roots campaigns capable of applying pressure on white leaders with large African-American populations. "We are organizing ourselves to impact the political process, to reach out on a very careful basis in coalition with those whose interests coincide with ours," Fauntroy remarked.[82]

Other African-American Members played key roles in later decades. Julian Dixon, a District native who represented a Los Angeles-area district, became chairman of the House Appropriations Committee's Subcommittee on the District of Columbia. During the 1980s and 1990s, Dixon was one of the city's primary congressional allies during an era of budget woes. In 1991, after Fauntroy's retirement from the House, Eleanor Holmes Norton won election as Delegate. An advocate for full congressional voting rights for the District, Norton has served as the District's Delegate since then.

Walter Fauntroy, the former Southern Christian Leadership Conference's congressional lobbyist, became the District of Columbia's first Delegate in nearly 100 years.

IMAGE COURTESY OF OFFICE OF THE CLERK, U.S. HOUSE OF REPRESENTATIVES

Delegate:

A Member of Congress who represents a U.S. territory. Able to serve and vote in committees, Delegates cannot participate in the final vote on a bill.

Conflicting Interests

Some Members promoted policy positions that put them at odds with the majority of their CBC colleagues—either because they were required to balance the unique demands of their constituencies or because of their individual ideological beliefs. For instance, Mike Espy of Mississippi was elected from a farming district in the 1980s with considerable cross-over support from white voters, making him the first black Representative from that state in more than a century. His legislative agenda reflected the conservative ideological contours of his rural constituency. Consequently, Espy belonged to a group of centrist Democrats; he opposed gun control measures and supported the death penalty—positions that were largely contradictory to those of black Representatives from urban areas.

Welfare policy proved to be a contentious subject during the latter decades of the 20th century. The CBC often found itself in conflict with the Reagan administration during the 1980s. Reagan met only once with the CBC—a marked reversal from the Carter administration, which, while it did not always back the organization's initiatives, regularly consulted with African-American Members.[83] At the heart of this struggle lay the CBC's fundamental disagreement with President Reagan's core agenda: vastly increasing the defense budget to outpace the Soviets in a climactic Cold War arms race while scaling back social programs established in the 1960s.

Not all African-American Members were consonant on welfare. As chairman of the Ways and Means Subcommittee on Public Assistance in the 1980s, Harold E. Ford, Sr., proposed a welfare overhaul plan that linked benefits to work. Dubbed the "Family Support Program," it required parents of children six and older to participate. In many respects Ford's plan foreshadowed welfare reforms enacted in the mid-1990s.[84] Representative Floyd Flake, a minister representing a constituency in Queens, also staked out an independent position on welfare reform. Flake's bipartisanship with the new Republican majority in Congress in the mid-1990s caused friction with black colleagues. Republican House Speaker Newt Gingrich of Georgia convinced Flake to cosponsor the Community Renewal Act in 1997, which offered tax breaks and school vouchers (credits given to parents for partial or full reimbursement for their children to attend private school) to poor, urban neighborhoods.[85] Flake's support of school vouchers, partially on the grounds that such schools had better graduation rates and that vouchers might force public schools to craft better curricula and focused budgets, drew the most criticism from his fellow Democrats.[86] "We get caught up in group-thought ideology, and we think that we all have to think alike, speak alike, say the same things, do the same things," Flake observed after abruptly resigning from the House to return to the ministry. "I've never seen a leader who allows himself to be kept in the box. I am beyond race and party now."[87]

After many decades of near-exclusive Democratic Party affiliation among African Americans, three black Republican Members were elected to the House: Delegate Melvin Evans of the Virgin Islands (1979–1981), Representative Gary Franks of Connecticut (1991–1997), and Representative J. C. Watts (1995–2003). During his brief tenure in the House, Delegate Evans made history by becoming the first Republican member of the CBC. Franks, the first Republican African-American Representative elected to the House since Oscar De Priest, joined the CBC in the 102nd Congress (1991–1993). His contentious relationship with the organization revealed a new dynamic of conflicting partisan affiliations in the CBC. From

Floyd Flake, a proponent of urban economic development in the 1990s, served on the influential House Budget Committee.

IMAGE COURTESY OF OFFICE OF THE CLERK, U.S. HOUSE OF REPRESENTATIVES

its inception, the overwhelmingly Democratic organization billed itself as being nonpartisan, but the CBC denied Franks access to strategy sessions, and some individual members complained his presence undermined their mission. Franks eventually opted to skip CBC meetings, though he refused to resign.[88] Watts chose not to join the group.

Commemorative Legislation

African-American Members of Congress often used their influence to pass legislation commemorating great leaders and seminal events in the civil rights movement and to call attention to unrecognized black contributions to American history. Such efforts included the designation of February as Black History Month and, in the 1990s, the awarding of Congressional Gold Medals to distinguished African-American citizens. Some African-American Members also called for Congress to apologize for the institution of slavery and to study remedies, including reparations, for the harm done to blacks by slavery and subsequent racial discrimination.[89]

One landmark commemorative achievement was the designation of the Reverend Martin Luther King, Jr.'s birthday as a national holiday. That effort began only days after King's death in 1968 when Representative Conyers introduced legislation to designate a federal holiday in his honor; Conyers sponsored similar measures in each successive Congress for the next 15 years.[90] Senator Edward Brooke of Massachusetts offered a compromise measure in the Senate to mark King's birthday as a "day of commemoration" when it became clear that Conyers and the CBC could not rally enough support for their bill in the House.[91] His alternative measure failed to make headway in the Senate. By the mid-1970s, the CBC had elevated the King holiday to a major legislative priority. The caucus directed a successful campaign to build congressional support and to increase public knowledge of the bill.[92] In 1979, the legislation had enough support to pass the House; however, the CBC withdrew the bill when an attached amendment called for a Sunday observance of the holiday instead of the originally proposed observance of King's birthday on January 15, a compromise measure for Members concerned about the high cost of shutting down the federal government.[93]

Freshman Representative Katie Hall of Indiana, chairwoman of the Post Office and Civil Service's Subcommittee on Census and Population—the panel with jurisdiction over the bill—provided the necessary spark in the 98th Congress (1983–1985) when the CBC tapped her to introduce the legislation and to serve as the floor manager. Hall courted detractors by moving the proposed public holiday from a fixed date—King's January 15 birthday—to the third Monday of January to prevent government offices from opening twice in one week, thereby saving money.[94] The House passed her version of the King holiday bill by a vote of 338 to 90; the Senate followed suit, 78 to 22. President Reagan, who initially opposed the legislation, signed the bill into law on November 2, 1983.[95] Some viewed the episode as a symbolic victory, but it constituted an important triumph for the CBC, which marshaled public support and exerted decisive institutional pressure to overcome an unsupportive President and also organized opposition in the Senate.

African-American Members also undertook numerous other efforts to recognize civil rights icons and distinguished public figures. In 1977, singer Marian Anderson became the first Black American to be awarded a Congressional Gold Medal—the highest honor the nation can bestow on outstanding citizens.[96] Representative Julia

Congress enacted legislation in 1983 to commemorate the birth date of Martin Luther King, Jr., as a national holiday— marking a major legislative triumph for the CBC. This hand bill, noting the anniversary of King's 1968 assassination, sought to rally public support for the creation of the holiday.

IMAGE COURTESY OF LIBRARY OF CONGRESS

Carson of Indiana played a central role securing legislation to recognize Rosa Parks, whose act of civil disobedience (refusing to give up her seat on a segregated bus in Montgomery, Alabama, in 1955) galvanized the modern civil rights movement. Additionally, Congress conferred an unprecedented honor on Parks by passing a resolution to have her body lie in honor in the Capitol Rotunda from October 30 to 31, 2005—a right normally reserved for Presidents, military leaders, and other statesmen. Parks was the first woman ever accorded this honor.[97]

In the 21st century, African-American Members of Congress pressed successfully for greater recognition of blacks' contributions to congressional history in the art of the Capitol. Portraits of pioneering Representatives Joseph Rainey of South Carolina and Shirley Chisholm, as well as Senator Blanche K. Bruce of Mississippi, were commissioned. Congress also created a task force to document the work of enslaved African Americans who labored to build the Capitol itself.

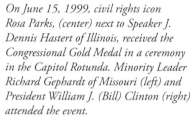

On June 15, 1999, civil rights icon Rosa Parks, (center) next to Speaker J. Dennis Hastert of Illinois, received the Congressional Gold Medal in a ceremony in the Capitol Rotunda. Minority Leader Richard Gephardt of Missouri (left) and President William J. (Bill) Clinton (right) attended the event.

IMAGE COURTESY OF U.S. HOUSE OF REPRESENTATIVES PHOTOGRAPHY OFFICE

Foreign Policy: Africa and Apartheid

Since the 1950s, black Members of Congress perceived the Cold War through a complex frame of reference. Even the most outspoken Members, such as Adam Clayton Powell, broadly endorsed the Cold War containment strategy and the necessity to combat communist international aggression. But African Americans were keenly aware of the gap between American rhetoric about the necessity to defend democratic freedoms abroad and the practice of racial segregation at home. Further, they questioned Washington's generous support for authoritarian regimes abroad, particularly in sub-Saharan African nations emerging from the yoke of decades of European imperialism. In the post-1970 period, leading African-American Members of Congress questioned the massive budgetary outlays that funded America's decades-long struggle against the Kremlin.[98] Representatives Dellums and Mitchell warned that excessive spending on Cold War initiatives was especially detrimental to minority groups, postponing or eliminating long-delayed domestic social programs and urban renewal projects. Dellums opposed the military buildup under the Reagan administration in the 1980s and sharply criticized nuclear weapons programs such as the MX missile—a land-launched weapon that could deliver multiple, independently targeted nuclear warheads when it re-entered the earth's atmosphere.

No single foreign policy issue united African Americans in Congress more than their efforts to overturn the South African government's system of apartheid, the strict segregation of the races that began in 1948 and was imposed by whites descended from colonial immigrants. Even before the formation of the CBC in 1971, Charles Diggs used his position as chairman of the Foreign Affairs Subcommittee on Africa to call attention to racial discrimination in South Africa. Other black Members followed suit, and ending apartheid became a central policy concern. During the next 15 years the CBC oversaw a torrent of activism to enact economic sanctions against South Africa.

According to political scientist Alvin Tillery, Representative Powell kindled Diggs's interest in African foreign policy.[99] Diggs, who became the first black Member to travel to Africa (1957) and the first to serve on the Foreign Affairs Committee (1959), was known as "Mr. Africa" because of his knowledge of Sub-Saharan issues. When the Detroit-area Representative was appointed chairman of the Foreign Affairs Subcommittee on Africa in 1969, he effectively used his position to draw attention to the continent. "I think if I had any one priority, it is to try to put Africa in proper perspective, to try to get the attention of policy makers in the government, the attention of the American investors in Africa and the attention of the American public, in general, and to arouse the substantive interest of black Americans," Diggs remarked.[100]

Diggs held a series of hearings on South Africa and led many fact-finding missions during his tenure on the Foreign Affairs Committee to highlight what he described as "an appalling amount of racial injustice in South Africa—a blatant, ever-present, and all-pervasive discrimination based on race, color, and creed."[101] From 1969 to 1971, he led an unsuccessful charge against the renewal of a special U.S. sugar quota for South Africa. "I have been in over 37 African countries, and the first question that is always asked at a press conference is when we are going to implement our pronouncements in the United Nations, and stop being inconsistent, by providing this kind of subsidy to South Africa, which is one of the most racist countries in the world."[102] Diggs cosponsored legislation calling for an end to the subsidy.[103] He also kept apartheid in the congressional spotlight with his criticism of the labor conditions of American companies in South Africa. He faulted the National Aeronautics and Space Administration and major U.S. carmakers for the discriminatory practices in their South African facilities. In 1971 he introduced a measure to implement fair employment practices for U.S. firms eligible for government contracts. Diggs also urged an end to new American investment in South Africa to protest apartheid.[104]

With the establishment of the CBC in 1971, Diggs cultivated the group's international agenda. "Diggs being the great leader that he was reckoned that getting us involved in foreign policy would make a big splash on the Hill," Representative Clay recalled.[105] The CBC adopted this strategy to lend credibility to the fledgling caucus, and from its inception, the CBC took an active stance in the anti-apartheid movement.[106] In February 1971, Ronald Dellums introduced the first legislation for U.S. economic sanctions against South Africa, on behalf of the CBC.[107] Though the measure had little chance of passing the House, Dellums recollected, "Nonetheless,

A leader behind the congressional movement to end apartheid in South Africa, Charles Diggs, Jr., of Michigan was an authority on African-related issues. Representative Diggs and a House Page posed for this image in his office in the 1970s.

IMAGE COURTESY OF U.S. HOUSE OF REPRESENTATIVES PHOTOGRAPHY OFFICE we had raised the issue before the elected representatives of the American people, and our resolution provided an organizing device for those on the outside to use to begin to build pressure on Congress for legislative action."[108] The anti-apartheid bill emerged from a petition drafted by employees from a major U.S. camera and film company, who demanded that the corporation cease operations in South Africa. Responsible for producing photographs for the mandatory identity passbooks carried by blacks in South Africa—a major symbol of the racial oppression prevalent in the country—the corporation eventually bowed to public pressure and withdrew its business.[109]

In 1975, the CBC helped establish the Black Forum on Foreign Policy, a legislative support group interested in better representation of black interests abroad. The Black Forum's early mission epitomized a "detached study group" rather than a formal lobbying assembly.[110] At a 1976 CBC conference, caucus members recognized the need for a more influential vehicle to shape American foreign policy in Africa and the Caribbean. The new lobbying group, renamed TransAfrica, began operations in Washington, DC, in 1978. TransAfrica employed a grass-roots strategy that mobilized local black leaders who were interested in foreign policy. The group

President Jimmy Carter hosted members of the CBC at this 1978 White House meeting.

also adopted an aggressive posture on South Africa, refusing to accept donations from U.S. corporations with business ties to South Africa and calling for tough economic sanctions against the African nation.[111]

TransAfrica received a boost when Representative Andrew Young, one of the primary architects of the Black Forum on Foreign Policy, resigned from Congress in 1977 to accept President James Earl (Jimmy) Carter's appointment as U.S. Ambassador to the United Nations. Young became a conduit for black lobbyists to the Oval Office. But while TransAfrica advocated a boycott by American businesses in South Africa, Young and the Carter administration maintained that promoting U.S. economic involvement in South Africa would have a liberalizing effect on the white-controlled regime.[112] At the time, the internal resistance movement against apartheid had been sparked by the Soweto uprising of June 1976. When students gathered for a mass protest to oppose a new government regulation that instructors teach school in Afrikaans, the government brutally dispersed protestors; in the ensuing riots, hundreds were killed, including many children. The event shocked international observers and initiated a long period of internal turmoil in South Africa.

In 1981, the Reagan administration implemented a policy of "constructive engagement," or maintaining diplomatic and economic relations with South Africa while advocating domestic reforms. Fearful that Reagan's 1984 re-election would be interpreted as a mandate for the status quo of racial discrimination in South Africa, TransAfrica's executive director Randall Robinson changed the tenor of the movement.[113] On November 21, just weeks after the President's landslide victory, Robinson, DC Delegate Walter Fauntroy, and Mary Frances Berry from the U.S. Commission on Civil Rights staged a sit-in at the South African Embassy in Washington, DC.[114] The resulting arrests of the high-profile protesters garnered national attention and sparked a new "direct action" approach by TransAfrica and the CBC. Fauntroy described the demonstration as an act of "moral witness" and indicated that a "national campaign" against apartheid would follow; a few days after the incident, Robinson, Fauntroy, and Berry formed the Free South Africa Movement (FSAM) to publicize racial inequality in South Africa and pressure the Reagan administration to toughen its stance toward the apartheid regime.[115] The FSAM orchestrated a series of demonstrations outside the South African Embassy that tapped into the long domestic civil rights tradition of nonviolent protest. Representative Charles Hayes of Illinois, Clay, and Dellums were among the first Representatives who were arrested. "I knew immediately why Fauntroy was calling," Dellums remarked, recalling the coordinated effort by the FSAM to draw attention to South Africa. "'Hello, Walter' I said. 'It's a good day to go to jail. Where do you want me to be and what time?' He laughed. 'How did you know?' 'I just knew that it would one day be my turn, so when you called it was pretty easy to figure out why.'"[116] The movement drew black and white Americans from all walks of life: national and local leaders, celebrities, teachers and students, and even Members of Congress who had been ambivalent about the issue. "It was very interesting to see colleagues from both sides of the aisle and of all races, who had previously paid little attention to our efforts, scramble to get arrested in front of the South African embassy and introduce sanctions when the [effects of the] movement hit home in their districts," Dellums later observed.[117] The protests, which eventually spread beyond the South African Embassy in Washington, DC, to other American cities, kept apartheid in the public eye.[118]

More than any other congressional cohort, African-American Members consistently drew attention to apartheid. Between the 92nd and 99th Congresses (1971–1987), black Representatives introduced more than 100 pieces of legislation concerning South Africa, encompassing issues such as diplomatic relations, economic sanctions, and trade restrictions.[119] Representative Bill Gray, chairman of the House Committee on the Budget, compared the situation in South Africa to the history of segregation in the United States. "It took us 200, 300 years to eradicate apartheid here by law," Gray observed. "People forget that only 20 years ago, when I came here to Washington, DC, as a boy, I couldn't go into the downtown hotels. . . . We are only 20 years away from our own story, and that plays a part in our double standard" toward South Africa.[120] In 1985, Gray introduced a bill endorsed by the House leadership banning new loans and implementing limited economic sanctions in South Africa to "stop the future financing of apartheid."[121] The House approved

Serving a total of nearly 13 years in the House, William (Bill) Gray III, of Pennsylvania became the first African American to serve as Majority Whip. House Democrats elected him in 1989.

the Anti-Apartheid Act of 1985 by a vote of 295 to 127, but soundly defeated a stronger disinvestment substitute put forth by Representative Dellums and backed by the CBC. The next month the Senate overwhelmingly passed a weaker version of the House anti-apartheid bill by a vote of 80 to 12.[122] Wary of the mounting public pressure for action against South Africa, the President avoided a direct confrontation with Congress and a potential veto override by signing an executive order in September that included some of the congressionally approved sanctions. Gray described the action as "an ill-disguised and ill-advised attempt to circumvent an overwhelmingly bipartisan consensus in Congress."[123]

The push for a comprehensive sanctions bill against South Africa reached a crescendo in the second session of the 99th Congress. Gray's anti-apartheid bill made it to the House Floor again for a vote, where it was expected to pass. For a second time, Dellums offered a substitute. In an unexpected move, the House approved Dellums's measure by a voice vote. The bill called for a trade embargo and total disinvestment; it was the first legislation that mandated a withdrawal of American companies to pass either chamber. Elated and stunned, Dellums proclaimed, "We haven't simply altered the debate on apartheid, we've changed the environment. Whatever the dynamics of that moment, its effect can't be changed."[124] A Senate bill sponsored by Richard Lugar of Indiana, which passed 84 to 14, resembled Gray's more modest anti-apartheid legislation. In the interest of securing passage of a sanctions bill, CBC members, including Dellums, supported Lugar's measure, which passed the House in September 1986 by a 308 to 77 vote.[125] President Reagan vetoed the anti-apartheid legislation, but on October 2, 1986, the Comprehensive Anti-Apartheid Act (CAAA) of 1986 became law when the Senate overrode the veto, following the House.[126] The historic legislation marked the first congressional override of a presidential veto on a major foreign policy issue since the enactment of the War Powers Resolution in 1973.[127] Mickey Leland observed, "This is probably the greatest victory we've ever experienced. The American people have spoken and will be heard around the world."[128]

After the passage of the CAAA, black Members continued their fight to abolish apartheid. In 1986, for instance, Gray led a delegation of Representatives to tour South Africa and observe the effects of the sanctions.[129] Leading the anti-apartheid movement on the Hill, Dellums persisted in introducing legislation for comprehensive economic sanctions.[130] When President George H. W. Bush considered rescinding sanctions against South Africa, Dellums and the CBC remained firm in their conviction that "sanctions should be lifted only when the oppressed people of South Africa say they should be lifted."[131] With the release of Nelson Mandela in 1990 and the establishment of majority rule in South Africa in 1994, the CBC achieved its longtime goal of contributing to the abolishment of apartheid.[132]

CRAFTING AN IDENTITY ON CAPITOL HILL

As African-American Members entered Congress during this era, they encountered an institution that, like American society generally, was becoming more accessible and offered more opportunities for minority participation. Though there were exceptions, the culture of overt racism of earlier decades—discrimination in the House Restaurant and barbershop, insulting floor tirades by pro-segregationist Members, and many other, unspoken slights—had largely vanished. Black Members now embarked on the mature phase of their institutional advancement by accruing service, winning better committee assignments, and gaining the attention and trust of House and Senate leadership. However, their ascent in Congress was accompanied by new challenges and questions about their identity and legislative strategies on Capitol Hill.

Like their predecessors in the previous century, African-American Members of Congress who served after 1970 generally perceived themselves as surrogate representatives for the larger black community. In the CBC's 1971 meeting with President Nixon, Representative Diggs said, "Our concerns and obligations as members of Congress do not stop at the boundaries of our districts, our concerns are national and international in scope. We are petitioned daily by citizens living hundreds of miles from our districts who look on us as Congressmen-at-large for black people and poor people in the United States."[133] Cardiss Collins, one of the few women members of the caucus in its early years, agreed: "Our main goal is to have greater influence. It's that simple. When we represent black people in our districts, we are representing all black people because their needs are very similar."[134]

Never a monolithic group, the black Members of Congress became, if anything, more fragmented in the modern era because of their changing stature and growing numbers within the institution. While most black Members understood and accepted their role as surrogate representatives, there was no consensus on how to pursue the legislation that was important to their broad constituency. "We all have basically the same goals," Mickey Leland observed. "The question is how to attain those goals."[135]

Some, such as Barbara Jordan, chose an insider route that often took precedence over racial or gender issues. "I sought the power points," she once said. "I knew if I were going to get anything done, [the congressional and party leaders] would be the ones to help me get it done." Jordan was careful not to align herself too closely with the agenda of any special interest group, including the CBC and the Women's Caucus, both of which she nevertheless joined. "I am neither a black politician nor a woman politician," Jordan said in 1975. "Just a politician, a professional politician." Her choice of seating in the House Chamber was revealing. Jordan chose to sit in the center aisle (away from the section customarily occupied by the CBC) because she could hear better, be seen by the presiding officer, and save a seat for colleagues who wanted to stop and chat. Her seating preference as well as her loyalty to the Texas delegation agitated fellow CBC members, but both were consistent with Jordan's strategy for seeking congressional influence.[136] Similarly, Julian Dixon accrued influence in the institution by working quietly with various factions. Syndicated political columnist David Broder observed, "Dixon is a fascinating example of the emerging alternative style of black leadership: a person who makes his way not by the militance of his advocacy of civil rights or other racially linked issues, but on the basis of personal and intellectual qualities that cross racial and ideological divisions and make an effective bridge-builder."[137]

In many respects, Representatives Jordan and Dixon introduced a new legislative style that emerged among black Members during this generation: In de-emphasizing race, they served to foster a consensus-crafting approach among various factions. One political observer described this shift among black House Members in the 1980s, suggesting they bore "striking similarities" to their "independent" contemporary colleagues in both major parties. "First, they worked painstakingly to

Following the unexpected death of George W. Collins of Illinois, his widow, Cardiss Collins, won the special election for his seat. Congresswoman Collins served nearly 24 years in Congress.

COLLECTION OF U.S. HOUSE OF REPRESENTATIVES

In 1976, Barbara Jordan of Texas, a captivating public speaker, became the first woman and the first African American to deliver a keynote address at a Democratic National Convention.

IMAGE COURTESY OF LIBRARY OF CONGRESS

In this 1971 photograph, freshman House Members and outspoken peace advocates Ronald Dellums of California (center) and Bella Abzug of New York (in hat, at Dellums's left), speak to reporters about their proposal to conduct an unofficial inquiry into alleged U.S. war crimes in Vietnam. Two years later, at the insistence of House leaders who overrode Chairman F. Edward Hébert of Louisiana, Dellums earned a seat on the House Armed Services Committee, which had jurisdiction over every facet of the defense establishment.

IMAGE COURTESY OF MOORLAND–
SPINGARN RESEARCH CENTER,
HOWARD UNIVERSITY

build their own organizations to win election," political commentator Richard Cohen wrote. "Once in the House, they have become issue activists and coalition builders eager for influence, not necessarily inclined to await the delayed rewards of the seniority system."[138] Political scientists also noted a gradual shift in the style of African-American representation during this era. During the 1960s and 1970s, legislative reformers and civil rights advocates emphasized the need for "descriptive" representation, i.e., electing more blacks to Congress with the goal of providing better representation for the African-American community. But by the latter part of the 20th century, many black Members of Congress had a new focus: "substantive" representation, which involved a connection between constituents and their Representatives that was based on legislative agenda and achievements rather than solely on the color of their skin.[139]

Even those who were elected to Congress because they dissented from the prevailing political establishment underwent a process of institutional integration that conferred upon them legislative success and leadership positions. Several Members adapted their activism to prevailing institutional norms. Elected to Congress from the epicenter of the anti–Vietnam War movement, Ronald Dellums was a prime example. Soon after being elected to the House, he introduced legislation to investigate alleged U.S. war crimes in Southeast Asia, as well as a measure to impose penalties on the apartheid regime in South Africa. Dellums declared, "I am not going to back away from being called a radical. If being an advocate of peace, justice, and humanity toward all human beings is radical, then I'm glad to be called a radical."[140] He worked his way onto the Armed Services Committee largely to try to curb vast Pentagon expenditures. Dellums was literally denied a seat at the table when he first joined that panel: He was forced to share a single chair with Patricia Schroeder of Colorado (then the only woman on the committee) by Chairman F. Edward Hébert of Louisiana as a sign of contempt.[141] But Dellums's activism was tempered by the need to craft legislation through compromise. Contrary to opponents' expectations, Dellums forged a reputation as an effective coalition builder to achieve his legislative goals; for instance, he allied with fiscal conservatives to halt production of the controversial B-2 bomber in the early 1980s. In 1993, partially reflecting the degree to which the Bay Area Representative had mastered institutional politics, Dellums became the senior Democrat and assumed the chair of the Armed Services Committee. "If you are around the House long enough, you learn its rules and customs and come to understand that no point of principle is served by remaining a permanent outsider," Dellums reflected in retirement. "My constituency, like any other, had sent me to Washington to legislate. I owed them nothing less than my best."[142]

Other Members of this generation followed a similar trajectory. For instance, Delegate Walter Fauntroy drew upon his experience in the civil rights movement and as a community activist in Washington, DC, to develop effective coalitions in the House on issues ranging from apartheid to home rule in the District of Columbia; he eventually chaired more than a half-dozen House subcommittees.[143] As supporters, and in some cases, participants, in the civil rights movement, many of the founding members of the CBC initially believed that working outside the system—following Powell's militant example during his House career—would best serve African Americans. But gradually it became apparent that working with House leaders, particularly with high-ranking Democratic Members, could produce measurable and substantive results. Mickey Leland, a self-described "revolutionary," explained that many of his black colleagues could now bargain for legislative goals from a position of strength. "We understand that in order to get our point across we don't have to jump up and down on the table or shoot off fireworks to get the attention of the leadership," Leland remarked. "We go in and negotiate."[144]

Over time, black Members forged alliances with congressional groups with similar policy goals. "The technique now is coalitions," Julian Dixon remarked in the 1980s. "I don't think we want to stand alone on the issues. The numbers tell us we won't be successful."[145] Representative Schroeder, a cofounder of the Women's Caucus, acknowledged the necessity for cooperative efforts among minorities in Congress during the 1980s: "It seemed that the three chairpersons of the women's, black and Hispanic caucuses have been sewn together around issues of equal concern, such as hunger, the feminization of poverty, the extension of the Voting Rights Act and the reauthorization of the civil rights commission."[146]

African-American politicians' electoral success in the latter half of the 20th century presented new challenges. New black Members, including more women and southern blacks, altered the gender and the geographic composition of the CBC. In 1997, Maxine Waters of California became the first woman elected to head the CBC since Cardiss Collins held the position in the 96th Congress (1979–1981), indicating the growing influence of women in the caucus; in the subsequent decade, Eddie Bernice Johnson of Texas (107th Congress, 2001–2003) and Carolyn Cheeks Kilpatrick of Michigan (110th Congress) also chaired the CBC.[147] The influx of new Members from rural and suburban districts modified the substance of the caucus, which historically had fielded Representatives from northern cities.[148] New committee assignments and issues that were significant to southern and rural districts, such as support for the space industry and tobacco farmers, were included in black Members' more diversified approach to the political landscape.[149]

Consequently, the CBC had difficulty sustaining the collective voice envisioned by its founders in 1971. Although most black Members still represented majority-black districts, the swelling membership of the caucus and the conflicting opinions of its individual members resulted in internal divisions.[150] Still, the group managed to focus on the common goals of opposing racism and backing equal opportunity. "Like coalition building in any context, holding the Black Caucus together required fluidity and flexibility, the constant search for common ground, and no rigid tests of membership," Representative Dellums later noted, "otherwise the fate of other caucuses and coalitions that had arisen during the same period would have befallen the CBC as well."[151]

In 1992, with the election of the second Democratic President during the CBC's history, William J. (Bill) Clinton, political commentators believed the group would be able to advance a broad legislative agenda. Yet, much as with President Carter, the CBC was often at odds with the Clinton administration, particularly because of its willingness to compromise with conservatives on Capitol Hill.[152] Many black Members dissented from key administration policies, such as portions of the 1993 Clinton budget, the North American Free Trade Agreement, relations with Haiti, and the controversial nomination (and then withdrawal) of civil rights scholar Lani Guinier for Assistant U.S. Attorney General for Civil Rights. However, the CBC's clout ensured that the President seriously considered the group's point of view and often consulted the caucus regarding policy affecting African Americans.[153]

Representative Carolyn Cheeks Kilpatrick of Michigan presented the Tuskegee Airmen of World War II with the Congressional Gold Medal in 2007. In the 110th Congress, Congresswoman Kilpatrick chairs the CBC.

IMAGE COURTESY OF U.S. HOUSE OF REPRESENTATIVES PHOTOGRAPHY OFFICE

In June 1993, the CBC met with President William J. (Bill) Clinton. Though the CBC agreed with Clinton on many issues, the group sometimes was critical of the Democratic President because of his willingness to compromise with conservative lawmakers on efforts to reduce the federal budget deficit by curtailing entitlement programs.

IMAGE COURTESY OF WILLIAM J. CLINTON PRESIDENTIAL LIBRARY

A reserved but influential advocate for civil rights, Gus Hawkins of California once said, "The leadership belongs not to the loudest, not to those who beat the drums or blow the trumpets, but to those who day in and day out, in all seasons, work for the practical realization of a better world—those who have the stamina to persist and remain dedicated."

After the Republicans won control of Congress in 1995—and a majority in the House for the first time in 40 years—the CBC's legislative momentum and hard-fought institutional gains dissipated. The institutional structure of the House, which favors the majority, relegated Democratic black Representatives to a secondary role, much like the status of their white Democratic colleagues. Nevertheless, many members of the caucus promised to continue their mission, regardless of the party change. "The Congressional Black Caucus has got to yell louder and scream or be steamrollered," asserted Cynthia McKinney of Georgia, epitomizing the pitched partisanship during the latter half of the decade.[154] Political scientist Robert C. Smith, writing shortly after the GOP takeover, voiced widely shared frustration with black Members' inability to advance a legislative agenda. Despite numerical gains, the attainment of leadership positions, and prominent civil rights efforts, "blacks in Congress are frequently an isolated, invisible, inconsequential minority unable to enact (or often even to get serious debate and deliberation on) proposals it deems minimally necessary to meliorate the problems of joblessness, crime and dispossession that plague its core constituency."[155]

Still, the change in party control—largely the result of southern white Democrats in the House being replaced by an insurgent Republican Party in the South—had ancillary benefits for black Members. In the minority Democratic Party, black Members now represented a larger percentage of the Democratic Caucus.[156] Given the relative electoral safety of their districts, this increase portended significant consequences for boosting blacks into a greater share of leadership roles in the party as they collectively accounted for greater percentages of the more experienced cadre of Democrats.[157]

Conflicting Imperatives: Black Interests Versus Party Agenda

While the institutional headway made by African-American Members during the 1970s and 1980s strengthened the collective authority of the CBC, it posed new challenges to the cohesiveness of the organization. Its success advancing black Representatives into the upper echelons of the institutional establishment raised expectations for the group and for individual Members to produce immediate, tangible results for Black Americans. Moreover, some black Members began to experience conflicting pressures between their allegiance to the CBC, their responsibilities as committee and party leaders, and their debt to the Democratic leaders who had placed them in positions of power. The development of conflicts between individual aspirations and collective goals was a sign of African-American institutional maturation, and other minority groups in Congress experienced such conflicts as well. A similar process unfolded among women Members of Congress, often creating tension between the institutional apprenticeship generation of the 1940s and 1950s, who had attained leadership positions, and the feminist activists who followed them.[158]

This theme recurs throughout the service of this generation of Black Americans in Congress. The career of Representative Bill Gray provides an illustrative example. As chairman of the House Budget Committee for the 99th and 100th Congresses (1985–1989), Gray asserted his independence: "I am not here to do the bidding of somebody just because they happen to be black. If I agree with you, I agree with you. I set my policy."[159] Once he rose to the chairmanship of the Budget Committee, Gray encouraged the CBC to continue submitting an alternative budget, although he did not publicly support it. His decision to vote "present" when the CBC measure came to the House Floor disrupted the public solidarity of the organization and angered some of his black colleagues, who thought Gray was placing personal interests ahead of caucus goals.[160] Similarly, Julian Dixon, who chaired the CBC in the 98th Congress, refused to bring the Caucus's alternative budget to the House Floor for a vote. House leaders had asked Dixon, also a subcommittee chairman of the Appropriations Committee, to pledge his support for the House Budget Committee's budget proposal to attract rank-and-file Democrats' votes for the measure. Knowing he could extract some concessions for his support, the CBC chairman agreed. "Our purpose, hopefully, is not to go down to defeat with honor," Dixon explained. "Our purpose is to have some success."[161]

Investigations, Corruption, and Race

Concerns about public corruption became commonplace in the post-Watergate Era as the number of Americans who trusted their government decreased. That distrust was magnified by a growing adversarial relationship between the press and public officials. Throughout this period, a number of African-American officeholders, including a significant number of black Members of Congress, observed that federal investigations into political corruption unfairly targeted black politicians.[162] This perception may have been partially due to an increase in the total number of corruption probes conducted by the federal government, which soared more than 2,300 percent between 1970 (63) and 1991 (1,452).[163] Additionally, the number of black officials who held public positions increased from 1,469 in 1970 to 6,681 in 1987. Nevertheless, African-American officials seemed disproportionately targeted. One study found that of the 465 political corruption probes initiated by the Justice Department between 1983 and 1988, 14 percent investigated black officeholders— even though they represented just 3 percent of all U.S. officeholders.[164] Black Members of Congress often believed they were the targets of such investigations, asserting that they were singled out for scrutiny on racial grounds and were held to higher standards than their white counterparts. Some interpreted such scrutiny as a coordinated effort to silence black officeholders by "diluting [their] influence and credibility."[165] Representative Bill Clay, Sr., maintained that the legal problems encountered by Adam Clayton Powell, Jr., and Harold Ford, Sr., were examples of a "pattern" of investigatory practices and "harassment."[166]

From 1981 to 1993, roughly half the members of the CBC were the subjects of federal investigations or indictments, though few were convicted.[167] Bill Clay, Sr., claimed that federal investigations and political corruption probes into the careers and personal lives of black officeholders were often part of a long-standing "conspiracy to silence dissent." According to Clay, business and "elite" interests—using government, judicial, and law enforcement mechanisms as well as a pliant press—sought to ruin the reputations of those who spoke out about racial, economic, or social inequality.[168] Some political observers did not fully agree with that viewpoint. "There is no question there is real racism in our country," said African-American journalist Juan Williams in 1987, but he added, "Unfortunately, it is not the case that racism explains all charges of corruption." Some prominent black officials, such as then-Virginia Governor L. Douglas Wilder and Representative John Lewis, publicly disputed the conspiracy viewpoint. An official from a black political organization succinctly described the relationship between blacks' new role in the political process and the increased scrutiny by public officials: "White folks are in a fishbowl; they get to swim. Black folks are in a test tube; they have to go straight up or down."[169]

Elected to the House at age 29, Harold Ford, Sr., of Tennessee later became one of the youngest Members ever to chair a subcommittee on Ways and Means. He left his position as chairman amid legal problems, but regained his seniority and chairmanship after his acquittal.

Former union leader Charles Hayes of Illinois won his first-ever campaign for elective office when he prevailed in a 1983 special election to succeed Harold Washington, who had been elected as Chicago's first black mayor.

COLLECTION OF U.S. HOUSE
OF REPRESENTATIVES

Apportionment:

The allocation of congressional seats in the House of Representatives in proportion to states' populations as tabulated by the U.S. Census Bureau every 10 years. Although the House determines the total number of Representatives, states determine the size and boundaries of their congressional districts based on population changes revealed in each census.

Within Congress, African-American Members were appointed to chair the House Standards of Official Conduct (Ethics) Committee more often than any other congressional panel.[170] In the 1980s and 1990s, respected insiders such as Representatives Stokes and Dixon led the Ethics Committee, once during a highly sensitive investigation into alleged standards violations by Speaker Jim Wright of Texas. The scandal with the strongest effect on black Members during this era occurred in 1992 when the press publicized General Accounting Office and House internal investigations revealing that dozens of lawmakers (some 220 former and current Members) had overdrawn their accounts at the informal House "Bank" run by the House Sergeant at Arms. Nine African-American Members revealed that they had written checks without sufficient funds, and five were on the list of the "worst offenders" that was released by the House Ethics Committee.[171] The occurrence of the scandal in an election year, with the economy in recession, magnified voters' discontent with incumbents. However, only one black incumbent, Charles Hayes, lost his primary re-election campaign in the Chicago district he had represented for a decade; his name appeared on a list that was leaked days before the contest.[172] As in the preceding generation, African Americans who faced such investigations or congressional disciplinary actions enjoyed unusually strong loyalty from their constituencies.

REDISTRICTING AND "DERACIALIZATION": OPPORTUNITIES AND LIMITS

The return of African Americans to Congress in the third generation (1929–1970) and the phases of rapid expansion (1971–1977, 1991–1995) in the fourth generation are attributable to unique historical forces, the intervention of the courts, and legislative remedies. These developments include the Great Migration, which concentrated blacks in northern cities; the passage and implementation of the landmark 1965 Voting Rights Act (and its extensions); and court decisions in subsequent decades that supported the creation of majority or minority congressional districts.

Title 2 of the Voting Rights Act Amendment of 1982 was critical to the development of racial redistricting after the 1990 Census. That provision marked a significant shift from an emphasis on "process-oriented" remedies, which focused on providing minority voters equal access and opportunity (such as the Civil Rights Act of 1964 and the Voting Rights Act of 1965) to an emphasis on end results achieved by prohibiting electoral arrangements that had the intent or the effect of diluting minority votes. In addition, the growing number of African-American state legislators on key committees with oversight of election and redistricting issues (by one account, 17 percent of all black state legislators in 1992 served on such committees) significantly boosted black electoral prospects in the early 1990s.[173]

Redistricting imposed by the courts and the decennial reapportionment mandated by the Constitution were carried out by state legislatures and accounted for major changes in 1992, in combination with an anti-incumbent mood and the election of a Democratic President for the first time in 12 years. That year, more blacks were elected to Congress than in any previous decade (16 Representatives and one Senator), and 13 of the 16 newly elected black House Members were from districts that had been redrawn for black majorities. The other new black Representatives succeeded retiring or defeated black incumbents.[174] "I think the Congressional Black

Caucus has moved to a whole other level," Ronald Dellums observed. "We can win. We've gone beyond just being 'the conscience of the House.'"[175]

At the opening of the 103rd Congress African-American representation reached a then-historic high of 40, including the first black woman Senator, Carol Moseley-Braun. Moseley-Braun's election was significant for other reasons, too: She became just the fourth African American ever to serve in the upper chamber and the first to be elected as a Democrat. She won decisively in majority-black districts in Chicago but also drew broad-based support from voters from across the state, including a core black constituency, women, and liberal whites.[176] Her campaign strategy was essentially one of "deracialization," a term coined by political scientists to describe an African-American candidate running in a majority-white jurisdiction (often against a white opponent) and energetically seeking white voter support. Black candidates who employed this method avoided strong racial appeals. This strategy was not new; in the 1980s, House Members John Lewis and Mike Espy both won election in districts that, while majority black, required them to develop significant coalitions of both white and African-American voters.[177]

Nevertheless, African Americans seeking election to the Senate faced an obstinate, seemingly insuperable barrier. Lingering racial prejudices, difficulty in securing funding, and the diminished strength of black voting blocs in statewide elections cumulatively discouraged many qualified blacks from seeking a Senate seat. The major parties nominated only nine African Americans as Senate candidates in the 20th century, and these included Brooke and Moseley-Braun.[178] Reflecting on his career as the longest-serving African American in the chamber's history, Senator Brooke noted that when he came to Washington in 1967, Margaret Chase Smith of Maine, a former House Member, was the lone woman. But by 2007, 16 women served in the Senate—many of whom had served in the House. No such transition has yet occurred for black Members. To date, no African-American Representatives have been elected to the Senate, though several have attempted to make this transition, including Alan Wheat, Denise Majette, and Harold Ford, Jr. The lack of black representation in the Senate "deeply saddened" Brooke and, he added, remained "a blight on the American electorate that should be removed."[179] In 2004, Barack Obama—a theretofore little-known Illinois state senator—won election to a seat held by retiring incumbent Peter Fitzgerald, who had defeated Senator Moseley-Braun in her 1998 re-election bid. Employing a campaign strategy (running against African-American GOP nominee Alan Keyes) that echoed Moseley-Braun's efforts, the charismatic and energetic Senator Obama rapidly evolved into a serious contender for the 2008 Democratic presidential nomination. However, halfway through his first Congress he remained the only African-American Senator, as were his four African-American predecessors.

While race-based redistricting of the early 1990s dramatically boosted the number of black Americans in the House, it also produced a tide of lawsuits by voters whose former districts were bifurcated and dissected by state legislatures. In 1993, the U.S. Supreme Court rendered a judgment in *Shaw v. Reno* (509 U.S. 630) that reinstated a suit by five North Carolinians who charged that one of the state's new congressional districts (a district represented by Representatives Mel Watt that wound along the I-85 corridor and took in several urban areas) violated their 14th Amendment rights to equal protection under the law by diluting their votes. In a 5 to 4 decision, the court questioned the constitutionality of drawing congressional

The first black woman to serve in the U.S. Senate, Carol Moseley-Braun of Illinois won her 1992 campaign with a coalition of African Americans, women, and liberal white voters. In this image taken after she left the Senate, she is seen testifying during Senate confirmation hearings on her concurrent appointment in 1999 as U.S. Ambassador to both New Zealand and Samoa.

IMAGE COURTESY OF U.S. SENATE HISTORICAL OFFICE

Senator Edward Brooke of Massachusetts (left) confers with Senator Robert Taft, Jr., of Ohio in this undated photograph. Brooke was the first popularly elected African-American Senator and one of just two to serve in the 20th century. Brooke later noted that the lack of black Senators was "a blight on the American electorate that should be removed."

IMAGE COURTESY OF U.S. SENATE HISTORICAL OFFICE

districts with "bizarre" shapes. While the decision did not overturn a lower-court ruling that rejected the suit, it was returned to the lower courts with what seemed to be a new standard for scrutiny.[180]

Within a few years, *Shaw v. Reno* spawned redistricting challenges in a number of states, with the potential to affect the boundaries of roughly a dozen U.S. congressional districts represented by African Americans. On June 29, 1995, the Supreme Court struck down Georgia's congressional district map in the case of *Miller v. Johnson* (515 U.S. 900), a case brought by plaintiffs in a district represented by Representative Cynthia McKinney that stretched from Atlanta to the Georgia coast—some 260 miles away.[181] The judgment called into question the creation of any district in which race was the "predominant factor." Writing for the majority, Justice Anthony M. Kennedy explained, "just as the state may not, absent extraordinary justification, segregate citizens on the basis of race in its public parks, buses, golf courses, beaches, and schools," the government also "may not separate its citizens into different voting districts on the basis of race." The decision reconfigured McKinney's district, as well as that of another African-American Member from Georgia, Sanford Bishop. Over the course of the next several years, lawsuits challenged the boundaries of African American-held seats in Florida, Texas, Virginia, and South Carolina.[182]

Virtually all of the black Members whose districts were reconfigured midway through the decade emerged unscathed, and in many cases, reapportionment after the 2000 Census reinforced their positions. Cleo Fields of Louisiana, who spent much of his second term in Congress fighting redistricting challenges in court, was the only casualty. In 1996 a federal district court that relied on the *Shaw v. Reno* and *Miller v. Johnson* rationale struck down the Louisiana legislature's redrawing of Cleo Fields's Z-shaped district, which included jurisdictions in the state's northern, eastern, and southern quadrants. Fields's district was reconfigured so that it no longer had a majority-black population; of even greater significance, his hometown was outside the boundaries of the new district. Consequently, Fields declined to run against the longtime incumbent who represented the new district.

The long-term impact of these decisions was ambiguous, with opinion closely divided over the issue. Racially gerrymandered districts remained a politically contentious electoral device on both sides of the political spectrum.[183] Liberals believed the districts offered "descriptive" rather than "substantive" representation, and those from the civil rights generation suggested that lumping blacks into specially designated districts ran counter to the movement's goal of fostering commonality among blacks and whites. In the mid-1990s, John Lewis expressed the concern that majority-black districts could "ensnare blacks in separate enclaves, the exact opposite of what the civil rights movement intended."[184] Conservatives have argued that the creation of the districts endorsed a kind of "racial apartheid" and, more pointedly, that those elected from such districts—which were created to express the interests of a particular racial group—would as a matter of practical politics place their primary allegiance with that group rather than the entire constituency.

Despite major gains in the 1990s, African Americans were still considerably underrepresented in Congress and the state legislatures. According to figures from the 2000 Census, African Americans constituted roughly 12.5 percent of the U.S. population, but accounted for 8.1 percent of the total number of state legislators nationally in 2003 and just 8 percent of the membership in the 110th Congress.[185]

CONCLUSION

The post-1970 generation of Black Americans in Congress exemplified the maturation of African-American influence on Capitol Hill in nearly every quantifiable measure. By the beginning of the 21st century, the number of black Members of Congress had increased dramatically, expanding their hold on leadership positions, practicing legislative entrepreneurship, developing important coalition- and consensus-building specialties, and winning key legislative triumphs. Despite the attendant growing pains, these were remarkable achievements in an institution that was often resistant to change.

The inception and growth of the CBC during this era marked a principal institutional development in the story of Black Americans in Congress. The caucus acquired stature rapidly, transforming itself from a congressional irritant to a potent bloc for advocating issues and promoting African Americans to positions of power within Congress. Examining the historic power of the CBC to shape legislation, political scientist Milton D. Morris observes, "There is no clear evidence of influence beyond routine advocacy and/or a contact point for the interested black public, but as a vehicle for articulating positions held by African American members of Congress it almost certainly strengthens their voice on selected issues."[186] The marked increase in the number of Black Americans in Congress during the 1990s renewed hope and expectations that the CBC would play a more influential role in Congress.

A new era began in the 110th Congress when the Democrats regained control of the House for the first time in 12 years. The change in party control amplified the power of the all-Democratic CBC. Once again, seniority positioned the longest-serving African Americans for influential roles throughout the committee system and the House leadership. When the 110th Congress convened in January 2007, African Americans held the chairmanships of five full House committees and 17 subcommittees. In all, 22 of the 43 African Americans in Congress—51 percent—held committee leadership positions.[187] Leadership positioning for African

Americans crystallized as a significant institutional strength—an ironic development in light of the immense power wielded just decades earlier by entrenched southern conservative committee chairs who used it to thwart civil rights legislation.

The debate about minority districts during the 1990s touched on a broader dialogue about representation in a democratic government. Whether descriptive or substantive representation best advanced the interests of African Americans was not resolved. Some believed majority–minority districts to be necessary for the democratization of the political process: Most important, they provide historically underrepresented African-American voters representation in Congress, and instead of promoting the notion that only blacks can or should represent black voters, they foster political commonality. As political scientist David T. Canon explains, "factions within the African-American community produce candidates with different ideological backgrounds and different visions of the representation of racial interests. One significant effect of this ideological diversity among black candidates is to give a centrist coalition of moderate white and black voters the power to elect the black candidate of their choice in many districts."[188] In essence, descriptive representation and substantive representation were not mutually exclusive.

Such coalition-building may well be the key to creating an even larger and more influential role for future Black Members of Congress. Undoubtedly, new challenges lie ahead, but even a brief survey of African-American history on Capitol Hill since 1870 reveals a pattern: Through distinct stages—symbolic, apprentice, and mature—black Americans have persisted, overcoming obstacles to achieve a position of unprecedented influence in Congress. In legislating for an uncertain future, current black Members and their successors will be able to draw strength from their predecessors' historic accomplishments and experiences.

NOTES

1   On December 31, 2007, the figure stood at 86 of the 121 who had served in all of congressional history.

2   According to Robert Singh, "The central function of caucuses is to bring together legislators with shared interests, backgrounds, and policy goals." Robert Singh, *The Congressional Black Caucus: Racial Politics in the U.S. Congress*, (Thousand Oaks, California: Sage, 1998): 58. As internal congressional organizations, caucuses like the CBC formed in great part to pursue a collective agenda with a "strength in numbers" strategy.

3   Quoted in Singh, *The Congressional Black Caucus*: 51.

4   For a discussion of this phenomenon among women Members, see Office of History and Preservation, U.S. House of Representatives, *Women in Congress, 1917–2006* (Washington, DC: Government Printing Office, 2006): 326–327, 545.

5   Ninety-one percent (78 individuals) held an undergraduate degree; three others took coursework at the college level. Additionally, 66 percent (57 individuals) earned a graduate degree—11 of these held multiple graduate degrees. Nearly 40 percent of all the individuals (34) from this era held law degrees. African-American Members also held 20 master's degrees, four MBA degrees, and three MSW degrees. Three individuals were Ph.Ds, and two were MDs. While in line with the educational backgrounds of the general congressional membership, African-American Members of Congress far outstripped the education rates for the general U.S. population. As recently as 1997, just 16.3 percent of all black males and 16.5 percent of all black females graduated from college (compared with 30.1 percent of white men and 26.6 percent of white women, respectively). See Matthew Sobek, "Table Bc798–805, College Graduation Rate, by Sex, Nativity, and Race, 1940–1997," and "Table Bc806 – 813, High School Noncompletion Rate, by Sex, Nativity, and Race: 1940–1997," in *Historical Statistics of the United States, Volume 2: Work and Welfare*, Susan B. Carter et al., eds. (New York: Cambridge University Press, 2006): 469–470.

6   Reflecting a trend among the general congressional population, relatively few African-American Members from this era were service veterans. Among black Members of Congress elected from 1971 through 2007, slightly more than 17 percent served in the U.S. military. Most of these served in the U.S. Army. Four were World War II veterans, and one was a Korean War veteran. With the end of the compulsory draft in 1971, fewer Americans served in the military; unlike earlier generations, for whom military service was a common formative experience, this generation had fewer members that were linked by the commonalities of life in uniform. After 1970, the average age of African-American Members upon their first election to Congress was 46.4 years. Men (61 individuals) won their first elections at an average age of 45 years; women (25 individuals) averaged 50 years of age at the time of first election. This consequential statistical difference, in theory, benefited men who had more time to accrue seniority necessary to attain leadership positions and high-ranking or prestigious committee assignments. The youngest Members elected during this era were a father–son duo: Harold E. Ford, Jr., who succeeded his father in a Memphis, Tennessee, district in the 1996 elections, was 26 years of age (Ford, Sr., was 29 at the time of his first election in 1974). The younger Ford has the distinction of being the second-youngest African American ever elected to Congress: John Roy Lynch of Mississippi first won election to Congress in 1872 at the age of 25. The oldest African American elected during this time period was George Crockett of Michigan, who was 71 when he succeeded Charles Diggs, Jr., in 1980.

7   For a comprehensive treatment of the civil rights movement—its origins, triumphs, principal leaders, and internal divisions—see the three-volume history by Taylor Branch: *Parting the Waters: America in the King Years, 1954–63* (New York: Simon and Schuster, 1988); *Pillar of Fire: America in the King Years, 1963–65* (New York: Simon and Schuster, 1998); and *At Canaan's Edge: America in the King Years, 1965–68* (New York: Simon and Schuster, 2006).

8   Charles V. Hamilton, *Adam Clayton Powell, Jr.: The Political Biography of an American Dilemma* (New York: Atheneum, 1991): 28.

9   John Lewis with Michael D'Orso, *Walking With the Wind: A Memoir of the Movement* (New York: Simon and Schuster, 1998): 371.

10 Ronald V. Dellums and H. Lee Halterman, *Lying Down With the Lions: A Public Life From the Streets of Oakland to the Halls of Power* (Boston: Beacon Press, 2000): 44–45.

11   At least three other African-American Members held leadership positions in their respective state legislatures: Mervyn Dymally (chairman of the California senate's Democratic caucus), Elijah Cummings (speaker *pro tempore* of the Maryland house of delegates), and Gwen Moore (president *pro tempore* of the Wisconsin senate). President *Pro Tempore* is a Senator who serves as presiding officer of the chamber when the Vice President is absent. (The president *pro tempore* position is also used in state senates, in the absence of the Lieutenant Governor.) Latin for "the time being" or "temporarily," the president *pro tempore* not only presides over the U.S. Senate but is also empowered to swear in Senators and sign legislation. After World War II, the Senate began electing the senior member of the majority party to this position. This person may hold the office until retirement or until the party loses its majority status. Since 1947, the position is third in line for the presidency, behind the Vice President and the Speaker of the House. The House Member appointed to preside over chamber activities when the Speaker of the House is absent is called the Speaker *pro tempore*. In accordance with House Rules, the Speaker *pro tempore* typically serves for only one legislative day at a time.

12   Milton D. Morris, "African American Legislators," in the *Encyclopedia of American Legislative Systems*, Volume 1, Joel Silbey ed. (New York: Charles Scribner's Sons, 1994): 375–376. For an even wider perspective, see Andrew Young's remarks in the *Congressional Record*, citing Voter Education Project figures for the number of blacks holding elective office in 11 Deep South states in 1965 (72) versus 1975 (1,587). See *Congressional Record*, House 94th Cong., 1st sess. (2 June 1975): 16241–16242.

13   The largest recent gains for African-American state legislators have been made in state senates. For more on black state legislators, their effect on their institutions and public policy, their representational patterns, and their peers' perceptions about them, see Kerry L. Haynie, *African American Legislators in the American States* (New York: Columbia University Press, 2001). The figures from 2003, the most recent year for which racial breakdowns are available, are reported in "Numbers of African-American Legislators, 2003," National Conference of State Legislators: http://www.ncsl.org/programs/legismgt/about/afrAmer.htm (accessed 19 November 2007).

14   Minority women comprise a larger percentage of their ethnic group in Congress than does the general population of Congresswomen relative to the entire Membership—16.6 percent (90 of 540). Groups of other minority women are much smaller, but of roughly equal proportions to black women: Asian-American women in the 110th Congress accounted for a third of current Asian Americans in Congress (2 of 6), and Hispanic-American women accounted for about 29 percent of all current Hispanic Americans in Congress (7 of 24). Caucasian women accounted for about 14 percent of all Caucasians in Congress (67 of 467). For statistics on women in state legislatures through the mid-1990s, see Morris, "African American Legislators": 376.

15   Carolyn P. DuBose, *The Untold Story of Charles Diggs: The Public Figure, the Private Man* (Arlington, Virginia: Barton Publishing House, Inc., 1998): 33.

16   Singh, *The Congressional Black Caucus*: 54–55; Norman C. Miller, "Negroes in the House Join Forces for Black Interests," 31 March 1970, *Wall Street Journal*: 1.

17   William L. Clay, *Just Permanent Interests: Black Americans in Congress, 1870–1991* (New York: Amistad Press Inc., 1992): 116–117; For more on Clay, Stokes, and Chisholm, see Robert C. Maynard, "New Negroes in Congress Focus on City Problems," 10 August 1969, *Washington Post*: 2.

18   Richard Fenno, *Going Home: Black Representatives and Their Constituents* (Chicago: University of Chicago Press): 62.

19   Singh, *The Congressional Black Caucus*: 55–56. According to Singh, Clay's strategy for crafting a nonpartisan organization included an unsuccessful attempt to coax the lone black Republican of the 92nd Congress, Senator Edward Brooke of Massachusetts, to join the CBC. Sources are ambiguous about whether the CBC formally extended an offer of membership to Brooke. See also Clay, *Just Permanent Interests, Black Americans in Congress, 1870–1991*: 116–117.

20   Clay, *Just Permanent Interests: Black Americans in Congress, 1870–1991*: 121. For a brief history of the CBC and additional information on the organization, see http://www.avoiceonline.org. See also the Congressional Black Caucus Foundation, Inc.: http://www.cbcfinc.org/About/ CBC/index.html. There were 13 founding members of the CBC: Shirley Chisholm, Bill Clay, Sr., George Collins, John Conyers, Ronald Dellums, Charles Diggs, Walter Fauntroy, Augustus Hawkins, Ralph Metcalfe, Parren Mitchell, Robert Nix, Charles Rangel, and Louis Stokes.

21 Clay, *Just Permanent Interests, Black Americans in Congress, 1870–1991*: ix, 165.

22 Ibid., 173–174. Clay also observed that he, Chisholm, and Stokes "considered ourselves, along with other black representatives, to have a mandate to speak forcefully and loudly in behalf of equitable treatment of minorities by government." Ibid., 111.

23 At the time of the boycott, the group was still referred to as the DSC, but by the time it met with Nixon, the organization had been re-established as the more formal CBC. To avoid confusion, in this account the group is referred to as the CBC for the entire episode.

24 "Black Congressmen to Boycott Nixon," 22 January 1971, *Washington Post*: A2; Clay, *Just Permanent Interests: Black Americans in Congress, 1870–1991:* 139–143. "Benign neglect" of African Americans, postulated by senior Nixon advisor (and later New York Senator) Daniel Patrick Moynihan, became a subject of public debate when an internal White House memo he drafted on race legislation was leaked to the press in March 1970. Black Americans, Moynihan wrote, had made "extraordinary progress" in the previous decade, adding that a cooling-off period would serve the advancement of civil rights, which were "too much talked about" and "too much taken over to hysterics, paranoids and boodlers on all sides." Moynihan concluded, "the time may have come when the issue of race could benefit from a period of 'benign neglect.'" See Peter Kihss, "'Benign Neglect' on Race Is Proposed by Moynihan," 1 March 1970, *New York Times*: 1; "Is 'Benign Neglect' the Real Nixon Approach?" 8 March 1970, *New York Times*: E1. For a modern assessment of President Nixon's policy of "benign neglect" that stresses the administration's "schizophrenic" but nevertheless "surprisingly progressive record" on minority and civil rights see Melvin Small, *The Presidency of Richard Nixon* (Lawrence, University Press of Kansas, 1999): 161–177, 162 ("schizophrenic"), 183 ("surprisingly progressive").

25 *Congressional Record*, House, 92nd Cong., 1st sess. (30 March 1971): 8710–8714; "Key Proposals of Black Caucus," 26 March 1971, *Washington Post*: A6; Paul Delaney, "Blacks in House Get Nixon Pledge," 26 March 1971, *New York Times*: 1. For a more detailed version of the meeting between President Nixon and the CBC, see Clay, *Just Permanent Interests: Black Americans in Congress, 1870–1991:* 145–148, and DuBose, *The Untold Story of Charles Diggs*: 96–103.

26 Marguerite Ross Barnett, "The Congressional Black Caucus," *Proceedings of the Academy of Political Science* 32 (1975): 36.

27 Barnett, "The Congressional Black Caucus": 36–39. Barnett concluded that the group's greatest virtue "was the brilliance of political innovation inherent in the decision of black representatives to work together to represent the interests of the black community." During the 1970s, the CBC struggled to pass meaningful legislation as it worked on building a reputation as an effectual House organization. Representing only a fraction of the total House membership, it faced formidable challenges: small enrollment, initial lack of seniority among individual Members, and, apart from the black community, a lack of popular support.

28 Ibid., 36–38.

29 Ibid., 36. See also Carol M. Swain, *Black Faces, Black Interests: The Representation of African Americans in Congress* (Cambridge, Massachusetts: Harvard University Press, 1993): 38.

30 Barnett, "The Congressional Black Caucus": 37–38; Singh, *The Congressional Black Caucus*: 76.

31 Singh, *The Congressional Black Caucus*: 77.

32 Barnett, "The Congressional Black Caucus": 39.

33 Paul Delaney, "Rep. Stokes Heads the Black Caucus," 9 February 1972, *New York Times*: 23.

34 Quoted in Barnett, "The Congressional Black Caucus": 39. Under Stokes's direction, however, the CBC continued to pursue unified efforts. In 1972, the CBC issued a "Black Declaration of Independence" that included a "Black Bill of Rights" intended to "create a society which is truly founded upon the principles of freedom, justice and full equality." The CBC's demands, meant to influence the Democratic Party platform and presidential nominee selection process, encompassed issues ranging from national health insurance to increased foreign aid to Africa. See also Austin Scott, "Black Caucus Warns Democrats," 2 June 1972, *Washington Post*: A6; Paul Delaney, "House Caucus Lists 'Black Bill of Rights,'" 2 June 1972, *New York Times*: 22.

35 Barnett, "The Congressional Black Caucus": 48; Singh, *The Congressional Black Caucus*: 38. The internal structure of the CBC remained quite consistent throughout this period and it developed a considerable administrative staff. Established in 1976, the Congressional Black Caucus Foundation (CBCF), a nonpartisan, nonprofit organization, complemented the CBC

by conducting research and technical assistance and promoting the political participation of African Americans. The CBCF grew more important when, in 1981, the House Administration Committee wrote new regulations stipulating that Legislative Service Organizations (LSOs), including the CBC, using House office space, supplies, and equipment could no longer receive funding from outside sources such as corporations or nonprofit foundations. However, LSOs could continue to use tax-exempt foundations for research and other caucus activities. The CBC responded to the rule change by transferring most of its responsibilities to the CBCF. In 1995, when the Republican majority abolished LSOs across the board, forcing all caucuses to operate without House resources, the CBC's administrative functions were entirely subsumed by the CBCF. See Singh, *The Congressional Caucus*: 63, 68; Dorothy Collin, "Time of Growth for Black Caucus," 19 September 1982, *Chicago Tribune*: A3; Lynn Norment, "Our Team on Capitol Hill," *Ebony* 39 (August 1984): 44; David C. Ruffin and Frank Dexter Brown, "Clout on Capitol Hill," *Black Enterprise* 15 (October 1984): 100. See also the CBCF Web site, at http://www.cbcfinc.org/.

36 "Congress Caucus for Blacks Only," 22 June 1975, *Chicago Tribune*: 30; Paul Houston, "Black Caucus Won't Let White Congressman Join," 19 June 1975, *Los Angeles Times*: B18. The issue of white membership in the CBC would surface again in 2007. See Josephine Hearn, "Black Caucus: Whites Not Allowed," 24 January 2007, *Roll Call*.

37 Swain, *Black Faces, Black Interests*: 38. This development roughly paralleled the decision by the Women's Caucus to admit dues-paying male members on a nonvoting basis in 1982. See Office of History and Preservation, *Women in Congress, 1917–2006*: 548.

38 Morris P. Fiorina, "Legislative Incumbency and Insulation," in *The Encyclopedia of American Legislative Systems*, Volume 1, Silbey, ed.: 516–518.

39 Roughly one-third (32 of the 97 African Americans to enter the House since 1943) have served more than 14 years—compared with roughly 29 percent of all House Members, and nearly 18 percent (17 of 97) have served 20 or more years—compared with about 15 percent of the general membership. General House Member statistics are drawn from David C. Huckabee, "Length of Congressional Service: First Through 107th Congresses," 9 August 2002, Report RS21285, Congressional Research Service (hereinafter referred to as CRS), Library of Congress, Washington, DC.

40 See, for instance, Mildred Amer, "Average Years of Service for Members of the Senate and House of Representatives, First through 109th Congresses," 9 November 2005, Report RL32648, CRS.

41 See the chart on Members' terms of service from 1965 through 2007, at the end of this essay. See also Mildred Amer, "Membership of the 110th Congress: A Profile," 12 September 2007, Report RS22555, CRS. The Congress with the longest average length of service was the 102nd (1991–1993), which was 10.4 years.

42 On the general topic of centralization of power in the House that gave rise to the hierarchical committee system, see Peter Swenson, "The Influence of Recruitment on the Structure of Power in the U.S. House, 1870–1940," *Legislative Studies Quarterly* VII (February 1982): 7–36. For an analysis of committee seniority, see Michael Aboam and Joseph Cooper, "The Rise of Seniority in the House of Representatives," *Polity* 1 (Fall 1968): 52–84. For an analysis of factors that mitigate seniority as the determining factor in committee hierarchy as well as a discussion of when the seniority system solidified in the House, see Nelson Polsby, Miriam Gallaher, and Barry S. Rundquist, "The Growth of the Seniority System in the U.S. House of Representatives," *American Political Science Review* 63 (September 1969): 787–807.

43 Eric Pianin, "Black Caucus Members Face Dilemma of Hill Loyalties," 23 September 1987, *Washington Post*: A1.

44 Milton Coleman, "Black Caucus Comes of Age," 7 January 1985, *Washington Post*: A1.

45 "Cardinals" alludes to the College of Cardinals of the Catholic Church who set church policy. In this usage, the term conveys the authority of the Appropriations Committee subcommittee chairs—each of whom has control over allocations for a portion of the federal budget.

46 Swain, *Black Faces, Black Interests*: 38.

47 Barnett, "The Congressional Black Caucus": 46.

48 Richard D. Lyons, "Ways and Means in Liberal Shift," 12 December 1974, *New York Times*: 38. The elite committee Members included Louis Stokes on Appropriations, Charles Rangel and Harold Ford, Sr., on Ways and Means, and Andrew Young on Rules. During this era, African Americans also registered major gains on second-tier committees where none had previously served, including Banking and Currency (Parren Mitchell, 1971), Budget (Mitchell, 1974),

Energy and Commerce (Cardiss Collins and Mickey Leland, 1981), and Public Works (George Collins and Charles Rangel, 1971). The most common committee assignment for African-American Members during this era was the Small Business Committee, created in 1974. Including the first, Parren Mitchell, a total of 31 black Members have served on the committee through 2007. Since 1971, a total of 21 black Members have served on the Transportation and Infrastructure Committee (and its previous iterations, Public Works and Public Works and Transportation), another 21 African Americans have served on the Oversight and Government Reform Committee (and its previous iterations, Government Reform, Government Reform and Oversight, and Government Operations), and 20 have served on the Education and Labor Committee (and its predecessor, Education and the Workforce).

49 Quoted in Singh, *The Congressional Black Caucus*: 79. According to Dellums's recollections in *Lying Down With the Lions*, the CBC helped him get a spot on Armed Services in 1973.

50 At the opening of the 99th Congress there were 20 African Americans in Congress. Alton Waldon, Jr., of New York became the 21st black Member to serve in the 99th Congress after he won a special election on June 10, 1986.

51 Nadine Cohadas, "Black House Members Striving for Influence," *Congressional Quarterly Weekly Report* 43 (13 April 1985): 675; Singh, *The Congressional Black Caucus*: 92; Coleman, "Black Caucus Comes of Age."

52 Cohadas, "Black House Members Striving for Influence": 675.

53 See Appendix E, Black Americans Who Have Chaired Congressional Committees. In the modern era, no African Americans have held full or select committee chairmanships in the Senate. Only Blanche Bruce of Mississippi has led Senate panels: the Select Committee to Investigate the Freedmen's Savings and Trust Company in the 46th Congress and the Select Committee on the Mississippi River in the 44th Congress.

54 See Appendix F, Black-American Chairs of Subcommittees of Standing Committees in the U.S. House and Senate, 1885–2007. James O'Hara, Adam Clayton Powell, William Dawson, Robert Nix and Charles Diggs, held subcommittee chairmanships before 1970. Nix and Diggs also held subcommittee chairman posts after 1970.

55 See, for example, Carol Swain, "Changing Patterns of African-American Representation in Congress," in *The Atomistic Congress: An Interpretation of Congressional Change*, Allen D. Hertzke and Ronald M. Peters, Jr. (Armonk, NY: M.E. Sharpe, Inc., 1992): 132.

56 Swain, "Changing Patterns of African-American Representation in Congress": 129.

57 Black Members also held minor leadership positions during this era. For example, Shirley Chisholm served as Secretary of the Democratic Caucus, Cardiss Collins was the first black woman to serve as an At-Large Democratic Whip, and Parren Mitchell also served as an At-Large Democratic Whip.

58 For an analysis of J. C. Watts's House career with an emphasis on his challenging task of building bridges between the Republican Party and black voters, see Jake Tapper, "Fade to White: The Only African American Republican in Congress Is Headed Home. Can the Party of Lincoln—and Trent Lott—Afford the Loss of J. C. Watts?" 5 January 2003, *Washington Post Magazine*: W06.

59 For analyses of Clyburn's leadership and his ascendancy within the context of the rising influence of southern blacks in Congress, see Richard E. Cohen, "A Different Kind of Whip," 20 January 2007, *National Journal*: 42–44; David Rogers, "Clyburn Leads Southern Blacks' Ascent to Top Posts in Congress," 3 January 2007, *Wall Street Journal*: A5; and Jennifer Yachnin, "No 'Sharp Elbows' for Whip Clyburn," 11 December 2006, *Roll Call*.

60 Swain, "Changing Patterns of African-American Representation in Congress": 132–133.

61 For a detailed legislative history, see "Congress Clears Voting Rights Act Extension," *Congressional Quarterly Almanac, 94th Congress, 1st Session, 1975*, Volume 1 (Washington, DC: Congressional Quarterly, 1976): 521–532. For a listing of major civil rights bills, see Appendix J, Constitutional Amendments and Major Civil Rights Acts of Congress Referenced in the Text.

62 Representative Barbara Jordan was instrumental in sponsoring a bill to expand the definition of literacy tests to include election registration materials printed only in English in areas with large non-English-speaking populations—in the case of her Houston district, Hispanics. "I am persuaded that the only means available to language minority citizens, and specifically Mexican-Americans in Texas, to gain equal access to the franchise is through application of the remedies of the Voting Rights Act." See "Congress Clears Voting Rights Act Extension": 525.

63   Ibid.

64   Ibid., 527. See also Young's floor remarks and statistics in the *Congressional Record*, House, 94th Cong., 1st sess. (2 June 1975): 16241–16242.

65   For a legislative history of the bill, see "Voting Rights Act Extended, Strengthened," *Congressional Quarterly Almanac, 97th Cong., 2nd sess., 1982* (Washington, DC: Congressional Quarterly Inc., 1983): 373–377.

66   *Congressional Record*, House, 97th Cong., 1st sess. (5 October 1981): 23204.

67   Ibid., 23187–23188. For comments by Cardiss Collins and Shirley Chisholm, see pages 23199–23201, 23202–23203.

68   *Congressional Record*, House, 103rd Cong., 1st sess. (28 July 1993): H5431.

69   U.S. Department of Commerce figures (1991) cited in Haynie, *African American Legislators in the American States*: 20–21.

70   Barnett, "The Congressional Black Caucus": 40; Austin Scott, "Blacks Assail Nixon's Budget," 1 February 1973, *Washington Post*: A1; Paul Houston, "Black Caucus Assails Nixon Budget Cuts," 1 February 1973, *Los Angeles Times*: 11.

71   For U.S. unemployment rates in the post–World War II period, see "Table Ba583-596, Unemployment Rate, by Age, Sex, Race, and Hispanic Origin: 1947–2000," in Carter et al., eds., *Historical Statistics of the United States, Volume 2: Work and Welfare*: 95.

72   Clay, *Just Permanent Interests: Black Americans in Congress, 1870–1991*: 95.

73   Robert C. Smith, *We Have No Leaders: African Americans in the Post-Civil Rights Era* (Albany: State University of New York Press, 1996): 187–210, quotation on page 206.

74   Barbara Reynolds, "Carter Endorses Andy Young, Jobs Bill," 1 October 1978, *Chicago Tribune*: 12; Paul Houston, "Black Congressmen, Carter Clash Over Employment Bill," 27 October 1978, *Los Angeles Times*: B1; Singh, *The Congressional Black Caucus*: 86–90.

75   Barnett, "The Congressional Black Caucus": 43; Singh, *The Congressional Black Caucus*: 84.

76   Shirley Washington, *Outstanding African Americans of Congress* (Washington, DC: U.S. Capitol Historical Society, 1998): 64; Thomas Goldwasser, "Liberal's Liberal Mitchell Is Fiscal Conservative," 15 September 1980, *Washington Post*: A1; Sandra Sugawara, "Retiring Mitchell Still Has Passion for Justice," 1 December 1985, *Washington Post*: 37.

77   Singh, *The Congressional Black Caucus*: 97.

78   Tom Kenworthy, "Congressional Black Caucus Facing New Circumstances After 20 Years," 17 September 1989, *Washington Post*: A22.

79   For a historical overview of nonvoting Delegates, including Resident Commissioners, see Earl S. Pomeroy, *The Territories of the United States, 1861–1980* (Seattle: University of Washington Press, 1969); Betsy Palmer, "Territorial Delegates to the U.S. Congress: Current Issues and Historical Background," 6 July 2006, Report RL32340, CRS; R. Eric Petersen, "Resident Commissioner from Puerto Rico," 31 March 2005, Report RL 31856, CRS; Michael Fauntroy, "District of Columbia Delegates to Congress," 4 April 2001, Report RS 20875, CRS. See also "At the Starting Gate for the Delegate Race," 25 September 1970, *Washington Post*: A24. While the position of Delegate was previously reserved for territories that were likely to become states, the District of Columbia Act of 1970 launched a new trend, creating Delegates for areas without statehood on the legislative horizon: District of Columbia, 1970; U.S. Virgin Islands and Guam, 1972; and American Samoa, 1978. Currently, a Resident Commissioner represents Puerto Rico.

80   "After 8 Years, House Will Weigh District of Columbia Home Rule," 8 October 1973, *New York Times*: 22; "Home Rule Bill for Washington Signed," 25 December, 1973, *Los Angeles Times*: 4;

81   For more information on the AACN, see Charles E. Jones, "Testing a Legislative Strategy: The Congressional Black Caucus's Action-Alert Communications Network," *Legislative Studies Quarterly* 4 (November 1987).

82   Singh, *The Congressional Black Caucus*: 156. For more on the establishment of the AACN, see Thomas A. Johnson, "Black Conferees Establish Network to Influence White Congressman," 28 May 1979, *New York Times*: A7; William Raspberry, "A Black Voter Network," 19 October 1981, *Washington Post*: A1.

83   Singh, *The Congressional Black Caucus*: 93.

84 "Top House Democrats Back 'Workfare,'" 20 March 1987, Associated Press. The plan called for developing "a system requiring education, training, or work for many recipients. States would have to provide a minimum level of cash assistance, and child support collections would be strengthened." Ford figured the program "would cost the federal government roughly $600 to $850 million in fiscal 1988 and about $2.5 billion when phased in fully."

85 "Floyd H. Flake," *Contemporary Black Biography*, Volume 18 (Detroit, MI: Gale Research Inc., 1998) (hereinafter referred to as *CBB*); Jonathan P. Hicks, "Rep. Flake Breaks with Party to Back School Vouchers," 12 March 1997, *New York Times*: B3.

86 "Floyd H. Flake," *CBB*. Terry M. Neal, "Ex-Lawmaker Refuses to be Boxed In; The Rev. Flake Left Congress to Pursue Urban Renewal Beyond Party Lines," 10 January 1998, *Washington Post*: A1.

87 Neal, "Ex-Lawmaker Refuses to be Boxed In."

88 Singh, *The Congressional Black Caucus*: 101; Jill Zuckman, "Black Republican Says Party Lags on Ending Preferences," 6 August 1995, *Boston Globe*: 19; Tapper, "Fade to White."

89 Such proposals had been considered by Congress since the Reconstruction Era. See Garrine P. Laney, "Proposals for Reparations for African Americans: A Brief Overview," 22 January 2007, Report RS20740, CRS.

90 Douglas Reid Weimer, "Dr. Martin Luther King, Jr.: Commemorative Works and Other Honors Authorized by Congress," 17 December 2007, Report RL 33704, CRS.

91 Edward W. Brooke, *Bridging the Divide: My Life* (New Brunswick: Rutgers University Press, 2007): 178–179.

92 Singh, *The Congressional Black Caucus*: 95.

93 Mary Russell, "King Holiday Frustrated," 6 December 1979, *Washington Post*: A6.

94 Larry Margasak, "Courting Conservatives to Back King Holiday," 14 August 1983, Associated Press.

95 For a detailed account of the legislative history of the Rev. Martin Luther King, Jr., holiday, see *Congressional Quarterly Almanac 1983* (Washington DC: Congressional Quarterly Press, 1983): 600–602. The federal holiday honoring King was first observed in 1986.

96 Other black recipients followed, including sports legends, military heroes, and social activists such as boxer Joe Louis (1982), Olympic track and field gold medalist Jesse Owens (1987), General Colin Powell (1991), educator Dr. Dorothy Height (2003), and the Tuskegee Airmen (2006). The award also celebrated the contributions of civil rights leaders and icons Roy Wilkins (1984), the Little Rock Nine (1998), Rosa Parks (1999), and the Rev. Martin Luther King, Jr., and his wife, Coretta Scott King (2004). See "Congressional Gold Medal Recipients," available at http://clerk. house.gov/art_history/house_history/goldMedal.html; see also Stephen W. Stathis, "Congressional Gold Medals, 1776–2007," 30 January 2008, Report RL30076, CRS.

97 See "Individuals Who Have Lain in State or in Honor," available at http://clerk.house.gov/art_ history/house_history/lieinstate.html.

98 The Center for Defense Information, a Washington, DC-based nonprofit, estimated that the total cost of the Cold War U.S. military budgets (excluding intelligence and foreign aid) exceeded $13 trillion (in 1996 dollars) from 1948 until the collapse of the Soviet Union in 1991. See http:// www.cdi.org/issues/milspend.html (accessed 15 February 2008).

99 Alvin B. Tillery, Jr., "Foreign Policy Activism and Power in the House of Representatives: Black Members of Congress and South Africa," *Studies in American Political Development* 20 (Spring 2006): 95–96.

100 DuBose, *The Untold Story of Charles Diggs*: 76.

101 Paul Dold, "U.S. Firms in South Africa: New Pressure," 20 August 1971, *Christian Science Monitor*: 1.

102 *Congressional Record*, House, 92nd Cong., 1st sess. (10 June 1971): 19110.

103 Spencer Rich, "South Africa Sugar Quota Draws Fire," 16 April 1969, *Washington Post*: A2. Diggs was not alone in the early battle to bring the issue of racial segregation in South Africa to the House Floor; Louis Stokes of Ohio introduced a measure to terminate the sugar quota during the 91st Congress (1969–1971), and William (Bill) Clay, Sr., of Missouri cosponsored a similar bill. When the House voted to extend the South Africa sugar quota in 1971, the CBC voiced its disapproval, characterizing the decision as "complicity with apartheid." See David E. Rosenbaum, "Sugar Vote Voted by House, 229–128," 11 June 1971, *New York Times*: 44.

104 Jesse W. Lewis, "Diggs Presses Anti-Apartheid Bill," 31 March 1972, *Washington Post*: A2; DuBose, *The Untold Story of Charles Diggs*: 129–133; Paul Dold, "U.S. Firms in South Africa: New Pressure"; *Congressional Record*, House, 92nd Cong., 2nd sess. (29 March 1972): 10931.

105 Tillery, "Foreign Policy Activism and Power in the House of Representatives: Black Members of Congress and South Africa": 93.

106 For more on the CBC's role in the anti-apartheid movement, see http://www.avoiceonline.org/aam/history.html (accessed 8 February 2008).

107 *Congressional Record*, House, 92nd Cong., 2nd sess. (16 February 1972): 4247. In his memoirs, Dellums provides a detailed account of how he and Representative John Conyers met with Polaroid employees to discuss their petition and subsequently drafted a bill to terminate business interests in South Africa and other African countries with discriminatory policies. See Dellums and Halterman, *Lying Down With the Lions*: 122–124. According to the *Congressional Record*, Dellums and Conyers first introduced a sanctions bill in December 1971. The bill was re-introduced in February on behalf of the CBC. See *Congressional Record*, House, 92nd Cong., 1st sess. (15 December 1971): 47236.

108 Dellums and Halterman, *Lying Down With the Lions*: 123; "Polaroid Cuts Off Goods to S. Africa," 22 November 1977, *Los Angeles Times*: A1.

109 "Polaroid Cuts Off Goods to S. Africa."

110 Robert K. Massie, *Loosing the Bonds: The United States and Africa in the Apartheid Years* (New York: Nan A. Talese/Doubleday, 1997): 405; Paula Stern, "Ethnic Groups: Shaping the Course of American Foreign Policy," 10 January 1976, *Washington Post*: A15.

111 Harold J. Logan, "A Black Political Group Set Up as Africa Lobby," 21 May 1978, *Washington Post*: A18; "New Lobby of Blacks Will Seek to Influence U.S. Policy in Africa," 22 April 1978, *Washington Post*: A9; Tillery, "Foreign Policy Activism and Power in the House of Representatives: Black Members of Congress and South Africa": 100.

112 David L. Hostetter, *Movement Matters: American Antiapartheid Activism and the Rise of Multicultural Politics* (New York: Routledge, 2006): 78–79. On a 1977 trip to South Africa, Young was quoted as saying, "I'm not advocating [a boycott] because to do so would be to interfere in your internal affairs. I'm a sophisticated diplomat and I wouldn't want to do that." Massie, *Loosing the Bonds*: 413. Young's short tenure as U.S. Ambassador to the United Nations ended with his resignation in 1979.

113 Massie, *Loosing the Bonds*: 558–560.

114 Eleanor Holmes Norton, then a Georgetown law professor, and Fauntroy's eventual successor as DC Delegate, accompanied Fauntroy, Berry, and Robinson to the South African Embassy, but left before the group's arrest to notify the press of the protest. Dorothy Gilliam, "DC Sit-In Led the Way," 9 September 1985," *Washington Post*: A1; "Capital's House Delegate Held in Embassy Sit-In," 22 November 1984, *New York Times:* B10.

115 Massie, *Loosing the Bonds*: 558–560; Kenneth Bredemeier and Michael Marriott, "Fauntroy Arrested in Embassy," 22 November 1984, *Washington Post*: 1; Courtland Milloy, "Blacks Form 'Free S. Africa Movement,'" 24 November 1984, *Washington Post*: C1; "Capital's House Delegate Held in Embassy Sit-In."

116 Dellums and Halterman, *Lying Down With the Lions:* 128.

117 Quoted in Tillery, "Foreign Policy Activism": 100.

118 Karlyn Barker and Michael Marriott, "Protest Spreads to Other U.S. Cities," 4 December 1984, *Washington Post*: A1; "New Tactics on South Africa," 10 May 1986, *New York Times*: 8.

119 According to the *Congressional Record* more than 100 bills and resolutions were introduced during this period. In some cases, Members introduced similar legislation on several occasions, thereby increasing this number. For example, Charles Diggs introduced a Joint Resolution entitled "A Joint Resolution to Protect United States Domestic and Foreign Policy interests by Making Fair Employment Practices in the South African Enterprises of United States Firms a Criteria for Eligibility for Government Contracts" seven times during the 93rd and 94th Congresses. In his article "Foreign Policy Activism and Power in the House of Representatives: Black Members of Congress and South Africa, 1968–1986," political scientist Alvin Tillery writes that African-American Representatives introduced 12 bills on South Africa in the 91st Congress and 26 bills in the 92nd Congress. According to the *Congressional Record*, three bills on South Africa were introduced in the House during the 91st Congress, followed by eight in the House during the

92nd Congress. In addition, two bills were introduced in the Senate during the two Congresses. Of the 11 bills on South Africa in the House, five were sponsored by black Members. Many of the measures consisted of resolutions condemning the regime or requests urging the U.S. government to change its policy toward South Africa. Whereas the majority of legislation sponsored by CBC members never made it to the floor for a vote, a few resolutions passed the House. In the 95th Congress (1977–1979), for example, a concurrent resolution introduced by Cardiss Collins of Illinois "expressing concern about the recent acts of repression by the Government of the Republic of South Africa" passed the House. George Crockett of Michigan successfully sponsored the "Mandela Freedom Resolution" in 1984, calling for the release of the imprisoned South African leader; an identical resolution passed the Senate. Despite a low rate of success, the steady flow of legislation on South Africa that was put forth by African-American Representatives kept the issue of apartheid in the congressional spotlight. With a new sense of vigor spurred by the embassy demonstrations and increased violence in South Africa, black Members of Congress intensified their legislative effort to fight apartheid. According to Representative Clay, the CBC sponsored 24 bills concerning U.S. policy toward South Africa between 1985 and 1986. See Clay, *Just Permanent Interests: Black Americans in Congress, 1870–1991*: 281; Omang, "Rep. Crockett and the Volley From the Right."

120 Juan Williams, "Antiapartheid Actions Await Turn of Events; Rep. Gray Says U.S. Moves Depend Upon South Africa," 28 September 1985, *Washington Post*: A7.

121 Jonathan Fuerbringer, "House Votes Sanctions Against South Africa," 6 June 1985, *New York Times*: A1.

122 Bob Secter, "S. Africa Sanctions Passed by the Senate," 12 July 1985, *Los Angeles Times*: A1.

123 George da Lama and Dorothy Collin, "Reagan Slaps S. Africa's Wrist," 10 September 1985, *Chicago Tribune*: 1.

124 James R. Dickenson, "Dellums: Exoneration Is His," 20 June 1986, *Washington Post*: A17; Edward Walsh, "House Would Require U.S. Disinvestment From South Africa," 19 June 1986, *Washington Post*: A1. Dellums provides a detailed account of the floor action concerning the anti-apartheid legislation in his memoirs, *Lying Down With the Lions*: 132–138.

125 Typical protocol dictated that a conference report would be drafted as a compromise between the House and Senate bills. However, leaders from both chambers decided to adopt the Senate bill to avoid the possibility of a pocket veto by President Reagan. See Massie, *Loosing the Bonds*: 617–618; Dellums and Halterman, *Lying Down With the Lions*: 136–138.

126 The Senate voted 78 to 21 and the House voted 313 to 83 to override the presidential veto. "Senate Overrides Reagan's Veto Sanctions 78 to 21," 2 October 1986, *Los Angeles Times*: A1; Edward Walsh, "House Easily Overrides Veto of South African Sanctions," 30 September 1986, *Washington Post*: A1.

127 "Hill Overrides Veto of South Africa Sanctions," *1986 Congressional Quarterly Almanac* (Congressional Quarterly Inc.: Washington, DC, 1987): 359.

128 Desson Howe, "Cheers for Sanctions Vote," 4 October 1986, *Washington Post*: G1.

129 Allister Sparks, "6 Congressmen Begin Tour of S. Africa," 8 January 1986, *Washington Post*: A1.

130 E. A. Wayne, "Congress Considers Boosting Sanctions Against South Africa," 5 November 1987, *Christian Science Monitor*: 3; Dellums wrote about his continued attempts to pass stricter sanctions against South Africa in his memoirs. See Dellums, *Lying Down With the Lions*: 138–148.

131 Dellums, *Lying Down With the Lions*: 143. President Bush eventually lifted the majority of U.S. sanctions due to what he perceived as a "profound transformation" in the attempt to promote racial equality in South Africa. See Ann Devroy and Helen Dewar, "Citing S. Africa's 'Transformation,' Bush Ends Most Sanctions," 11 July 1991, *Washington Post*: A23.

132 Scholars have yet to systematically examine the effect of the anti-apartheid campaign on the CBC's institutional powers: Did it gain legislative savvy and increased influence on other issues? Did it make any new congressional allies? Or did it achieve an expanded national prominence?

133 *Congressional Record*, House, 92nd Cong., 1st sess. (30 March 1971): 8710.

134 "A Time of Testing for Black Caucus as Its Members Rise to Power in House," 27 April 1985, *National Journal*: 911.

135 Cohadas, "Black House Members Striving for Influence": 680.

136 See Fenno, *Going Home*: 106–109.

137 David Broder, "Ethics Committee Head Passes Colorblind Test," 17 April 1989, *St. Louis Post-Dispatch*: 3B.

138 Richard Cohen, "New Breed for Black Caucus," 26 September 1987, *National Journal*: 2432.

139 For a discussion of the topic, see Swain, *Black Faces, Black Interests*: 5–6, 207–225. For a countervailing viewpoint, see Kenny J. Whitby, *The Color of Representation: Congressional Behavior and Black Interests* (Ann Arbor: University of Michigan Press, 1997): especially 135–144.

140 Ray Mosley, "Violence Disavowed by Rep. Dellums," 14 February 1971, *Washington Post*: 113.

141 Dellums and Halterman, *Lying Down With the Lions*: 149–150.

142 Ibid., 175.

143 See Appendix F, Black-American Chairs of Subcommittees of Standing Committees in the U.S. House and Senate, 1885–2007.

144 Coleman, "Black Caucus Comes of Age."

145 Cohadas, "Black House Members Striving for Influence": 681.

146 Ruffin and Brown, "Clout on Capitol Hill": 102.

147 See Appendix I, Congressional Black Caucus Chairmen and Chairwomen, 1971–2007; Juliet Eilperin, "Black Caucus Taps Rep. Maxine Waters as New Chair; First Woman Since 1979," 21 November 1996, *Roll Call*: 18.

148 For more on changing southern representation in the late 20th-century Congresses, see Nelson Polsby, *How Congress Evolves: Social Bases of Institutional Change* (New York: Oxford University Press, 2004).

149 Jeremy Derfner, 27 March–10 April 2000, *The American Prospect*: 16. In his autobiography, Dellums discusses the growing diversity of the CBC during the 1990s and also reflects upon an incident in which he mistakenly assumed the CBC would back one of his proposals based on past experience. Dellums and Halterman, *Lying Down With the Lions*: 117–121.

150 For example, while the CBC as a group publicly denounced the controversial North American Free Trade Agreement (NAFTA) in 1993, nine members of the caucus voted in favor of the measure. Eight House Members from the CBC voted in favor of NAFTA in addition to the lone black Senator, Carol Moseley-Braun. See Singh, *The Congressional Black Caucus*: 183.

151 Dellums and Halterman, *Lying Down With the Lions*: 120.

152 For more on the CBC's relationship with President Clinton, see Singh, *The Congressional Black Caucus*: 178–192. Clinton's nearly 1,000-page memoirs contain no substantive policy discussion or debate involving the CBC. See Bill Clinton, *My Life* (New York: Alfred A. Knopf, 2004).

153 Ronald A. Taylor, "Congressional Black Caucus Displays Growing Clout," 13 September 1993, *Washington Times*: A10; Adam Clymer, "Black Caucus Threatens Revolt on Clinton Budget," 10 June 1993, *New York Times*: A22; "The Black Caucus," 16 July 1993, *Christian Science Monitor*: 18. See also, for example, Brent Staples, "Wanted: A Million Black Republicans," 21 June 1993, *New York Times*: A18; Max Boot, "Black Caucus Feels Left Out of Clinton Plans," 30 June 1993, *Christian Science Monitor*: 1; Michael Wines, "Democrats Expect Tight Budget Vote," 26 July 1993, *New York Times*: A12.

154 John E. Yang, "Black Caucus Adjusts to New Political Scene," 23 September 1995, *Washington Post*: A15.

155 Smith, *We Have No Leaders: African Americans in the Post-Civil Rights Era*: 211–225, quotation on page 222.

156 For instance, in the 103rd Congress (1993–1995), after the landmark 1992 elections brought a record number of 40 blacks to the House, African Americans constituted 15 percent of the House Democrats. In the following Congress, the 41 black Representatives accounted for 20 percent of the Democratic Caucus. These totals reflect the largest number of blacks serving at any one time during a Congress, not the total that served during the Congress. See Mildred Amer, "Black Members of the United States Congress, 1870–2007," 27 September 2007, Report RL30378, CRS.

157 For an early example of such analysis, see Alan Gerber, "African Americans' Congressional Careers and the Democratic House Delegation," *The Journal of Politics* 58 (August 1996): 831–845.

158 See for example, Office of History and Preservation, *Women in Congress, 1917–2006*: 3–5, 340–341, 546–547. Some outside critics of this transformation implied that the process amounted to a cooptation that marginalized the interests of the black community. Political scientist Robert C. Smith concluded in the mid-1990s that, "The institutional norms and folkways of the House encourage exaggerated courtesy, compromise, deference, and above all loyalty to the institution. And the black members of Congress are probably more loyal to the House and their roles in it than they are to blacks." See Smith, *We Have No Leaders: African Americans in the Post-Civil Rights Era*: 225.

159 Eric Pianin, "Black Caucus Members Face Dilemma of Hill Loyalties," 23 September 1987, *Washington Post*: A1.

160 Pianin, "Black Caucus Members Face Dilemma of Hill Loyalties"; Kenworthy, "Congressional Black Caucus Facing New Circumstances After 20 Years."

161 Richard Simon and Nick Anderson, "Respected Lawmaker Julian Dixon Dies," 9 December 2000, *Los Angeles Times*: B1.

162 See, for example, the chapter titled, "A Conspiracy to Silence Dissent," in Clay, *Just Permanent Interests: Black Americans in Congress 1870–1991*: 312–338. For more on the subject, see George D. Musgrove, "The Harassment of Black Elected Officials: Race, Party Realignment, and State Power in the Post-Civil Rights United States," Ph.D Dissertation, New York University, 2005.

163 Richard Sutch, "Table Ec1356–1370, Federal Prosecutions of Public Corruption: 1970–1996," in Carter et al., eds., *Historical Statistics of the United States, Volume 5: Governance and International Relations*: 331.

164 Gwen Ifill, "Black Officials: Probes and Prejudice—Is There a Double Standard for Bringing Indictments? The Jury's Still Out," 28 February 1988, *Washington Post*: A9.

165 Clay, *Just Permanent Interests: Black Americans in Congress, 1870–1991*: 314–337. For a countervailing viewpoint, see Ifill, "Black Officials: Probes and Prejudice."

166 Clay, *Just Permanent Interests: Black Americans in Congress, 1870–1991*: 82–83, 332–334. Of the accusations made against Powell, writes Clay, they "could have been leveled against every chairman of every full committee in the House of Representatives. He did no more, and no less, than any other in terms of exercising traditional legal privileges that accompanied the powerful position of committee chairman. His private life, including intimate relations with numerous and glamorous women, was routine activity for many members of Congress, committee chairmen or not."

167 "Were Black Office-Holders More Routinely Investigated During the '80s?" 19 December 1993, *Atlanta Daily World*: 5.

168 Clay, *Just Permanent Interests: Black Americans in Congress, 1870–1991*: 312–316, 335–337.

169 For the Juan Williams quote, see Charles J. Abbott, "Panel Says Smear Tactics Used to Discredit Black Politicians," 10 October 1987, *New Pittsburgh Courier*: 1. For "fishbowl" and "test tube," see Ifill, "Black Officials: Probes and Prejudice."

170 Indeed, from 1981 forward, when Democrats controlled the House Chamber (e.g., eight Congresses) African Americans have led the Standards of Official Conduct Committee for all but one Congress. The black chairs were Louis Stokes (1981–1985; 1991–1993), Julian Dixon (1985–1991), and Stephanie Tubbs Jones (2007 to present).

171 "The 22 Worst Offenders," 17 April 1992, *Los Angeles Times*: A18; "List of Members of the House of Representatives Who Acknowledge Having Written Checks on Insufficient Funds at the House Bank," 13 April 1992, Associated Press.

172 "House Check-Kiter List Official: 2 Names Missing from Panel's Record of Worst Abusers," 2 April 1992, *Chicago Tribune*: 6.

173 Morris, "African American Legislators": 379, 381; David T. Canon, *Race, Redistricting, and Representation: The Unintended Consequences of Black Majority Districts* (Chicago: The University of Chicago Press, 1999): 1.

174 See, for instance, Carol Swain, "Black Members: Twentieth Century," in the *Encyclopedia of the United States Congress*, Volume 1, Donald Bacon et al. (New York: Simon and Schuster, 1995): 173–176.

175 Kenneth J. Cooper, "For Enlarged Congressional Black Caucus, a New Kind of Impact," 19 September 1993, *Washington Post*: A4. "The conscience of the House" was the self-described role of the CBC shortly after its establishment in 1971.

176 Roger K. Oden, "The Election of Carol Moseley-Braun in the U.S. Senate Race in Illinois," in *Race, Politics, and Governance in the United States*, Huey L. Perry, ed. (Gainesville: University Press of Florida, 1996): 47–61, quotation on page 57.

177 Huey L. Perry, "Introduction: An Analysis of Major Themes in the Concept of Deracialization," in *Race, Politics, and Governance in the United States*, Perry, ed.: 1–11, especially 4–5.

178 John Mercurio, "The Senate Color Barrier: Just Nine African-Americans Nominated in 20th Century," 8 November 1999, *Roll Call*: 13. The article relied on statistics compiled in a report on elected black officials by the Joint Center for Political and Economic Studies. For more on this phenomenon and possible explanations, see Linda F. Williams, "White/Black Perceptions of Electability of Black Political Candidates," *The National Political Science Review* 2 (1990): 45–64; and Gerber, "African Americans' Congressional Careers and the Democratic House Delegation": 833.

179 Brooke, *Bridging the Divide: My Life*: 305.

180 For a brief overview of Shaw v. Reno, see Kermit Hall, ed., *The Oxford Companion to the Supreme Court of the United States*, 2nd ed. (New York: Oxford University Press, 2005): 913.

181 Linda Greenhouse, "The Supreme Court: Congressional Districts—Justices, in 5–4 Vote, Reject Districts Drawn with Race the 'Predominant Factor'; New Voting Rules," 30 June 1995, *New York Times*: A1. For a brief overview of Miller v. Johnson, see Hall, *The Oxford Companion to the Supreme Court of the United States*: 637.

182 For concise annual summaries of redistricting cases, see *Congressional Quarterly Almanac, 1995* (Washington, DC: Congressional Quarterly Press, 1996): 12-3–5, 6-39–40; *Congressional Quarterly Almanac, 1996* (Washington, DC: Congressional Quarterly Press, 1997): 5-48–50.

183 The clustering of black votes has electoral repercussions for the major parties, irrespective of their stated ideological preferences. For instance, particularly in the South during the 1980s and 1990s, Democrats lost seats in districts coterminous with black majority districts, when redistricting had shifted sizeable minority populations from their old districts into the new borders of black majority districts. "Thus," explains political scientist David T. Canon, "Republicans tend to oppose the districts on principle, but quietly support them for political reasons, while many white Democrats support the districts in principle but privately hope they will be abolished." See Canon, *Race, Redistricting, and Representation*: 5; Bernard Grofman, ed., *Race And Redistricting in the 1990s* (NY: Agathon Press, 1998).

184 Sean Wilentz, "The Last Integrationist: John Lewis's American Odyssey," 1 July 1996, *The New Republic*: 19–26; Canon, *Race, Redistricting, and Representation*: 5.

185 Some analysts believe the numbers may already have peaked. Political scientist Carol Swain has observed problems arising from the concentration of the black population in majority-black districts, particularly as the voting-age populations in these districts decline. That factor and the natural population level of African Americans create a ceiling that prevents greater gains. See, for instance, Swain, "Black Members: Twentieth Century": 175–176; see also Swain, *Black Faces, Black Interests*: 207–225. For the 2003 figures (the most recent available) on state legislator demographics, see the National Conference of State Legislators Web site at http://www.ncsl.org/programs/legismgt/about/afrAmer.htm (accessed 11 December 2007).

186 Morris, "African American Legislators": 383.

187 This figure includes Juanita Millender-McDonald, who led the House Administration Committee from January 2007 until her death in April 2007. The percentage of African Americans in Congress holding committee leadership positions far exceeded that of women in committee leadership. For instance, women chaired six full committees and 28 subcommittees in the House and Senate combined at the start of the 110th Congress. With 90 women combined in both chambers, this constituted 38 percent in committee leadership posts. Smaller minority groups in the 110th Congress compared favorably to black Members in this regard. Of the 27 Hispanic Americans in the House and Senate, 15 held full and subcommittee gavels (55.5 percent). An equal percentage of Asian-Pacific Islander Americans (five of the nine) combined held committee leadership positions in both chambers.

188 Canon, *Race, Redistricting, and Representation*: 3, 261–264; see also Perry, "Introduction: An Analysis of Major Themes in the Concept of Deracialization": 1–11.

Congressional Service for Former Black Members
First Elected, 1971–2005

	HOUSE DEMOCRATS	■ HOUSE REPUBLICANS
■ HOUSE INDEPENDENTS		SENATE DEMOCRATS

Source: *Biographical Directory of the United States Congress, 1774–2005* (Washington, DC: Government Printing Office, 2005); also available at http://bioguide.congress.gov.

Party Divisions in the Senate
92nd–110th Congresses (1971–2009)*

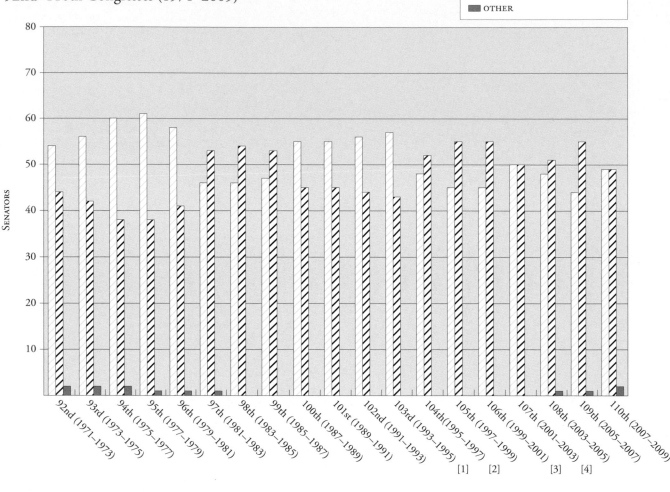

*110th Congress through December 31, 2007.

[1] Party division changed to 56 Democrats and 44 Republicans after the June 5, 1993, election of Kay B. Hutchison (R-TX).

[2] Party ratio changed to 53 Republicans and 47 Democrats after Richard Shelby of Alabama switched from the Democratic to Republican Party on November 9, 1994. It changed again, to 54 Republicans and 46 Democrats, when Ben Nighthorse Campbell of Colorado switched from the Democratic to Republican Party on March 3, 1995. When Robert Packwood (R-OR) resigned on October 1, 1995, the Senate divided between 53 Republicans and 46 Democrats with one vacancy. Ron Wyden (D) returned the ratio to 53 Republicans and 47 Democrats when he was elected to fill the vacant Oregon seat.

[3] As the 106th Congress began, the division was 55 Republican seats and 45 Democratic seats, but this changed to 54-45 on July 13, 1999, when Senator Bob Smith of New Hampshire switched from the Republican Party to Independent status. On November 1, 1999, Smith announced his return to the Republican Party, making the division once more 55 Republicans and 45 Democrats. Following the death of Senator Paul Coverdell (R-GA) on July 18, 2000, the balance shifted again, to 54 Republicans and 46 Democrats, when the governor appointed Zell Miller, a Democrat, to fill the vacancy.

[4] From January 3 to January 20, 2001, with the Senate divided evenly between the two parties, the Democrats held the majority due to the deciding vote of outgoing Democratic Vice President Al Gore. Senator Thomas A. Daschle served as majority leader at that time. Beginning on January 20, 2001, Republican Vice President Richard Cheney held the deciding vote, giving the majority to the Republicans. Senator Trent Lott resumed his position as Majority Leader on that date. On May 24, 2001, Senator James Jeffords of Vermont announced his switch from Republican to Independent status, effective June 6, 2001. Jeffords announced that he would caucus with the Democrats, giving the Democrats a one-seat advantage, changing control of the Senate from the Republicans back to the Democrats. Senator Thomas A. Daschle again became Majority Leader on June 6, 2001. Senator Paul D. Wellstone (D-MN) died on October 25, 2002, and Independent Dean Barkley was appointed to fill the vacancy. The November 5, 2002 election brought to office elected Senator James Talent (R-MO), replacing appointed Senator Jean Carnahan (D-MO), shifting balance once again to the Republicans, but no reorganization was completed at that time since the Senate was out of session.

Source: U.S. Senate Historical Office.

Party Divisions in the House of Representatives
92nd–110th Congresses (1971–2009) [1]

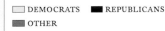

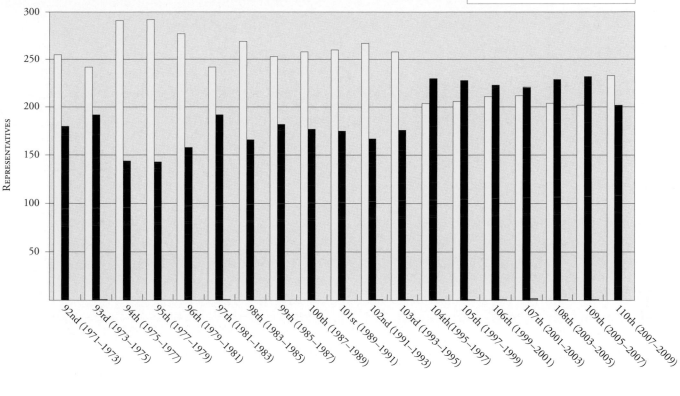

Length of Service of Current Black Members of Congress

(42 Individuals as of December 31, 2007) [2]

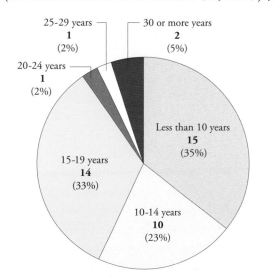

Black Americans as a Percentage of Congress, 110th Congress (2007–2009)

as of December 31, 2007 [3]

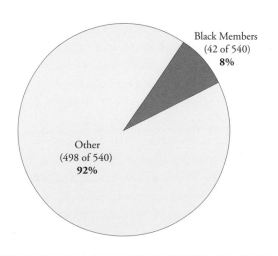

[1] Does not include Delegates or Resident Commissioners; 110th Congress through December 31, 2007.

[2] Including Delegates.

[3] Including Delegates and Resident Commissioners.

Source: Office of the Clerk, U.S. House of Representatives.

Ronald V. Dellums
1935–

UNITED STATES REPRESENTATIVE ★ 1971–1998
DEMOCRAT FROM CALIFORNIA

Born and raised in the northern California district
that founded the free speech movement and
the Black Panthers in the 1960s, Ronald Dellums
embraced the activist spirit of the region, taking his
seat in Congress in 1971 as an outspoken critic of the
Vietnam War. Throughout his nearly three decade career
in the House, Dellums remained true to his antiwar
principles, consistently working to reduce the military
budget. Initially a politician who believed more could be
accomplished outside the establishment, the California
Representative chaired two standing committees and
became adept at building congressional coalitions to
achieve his legislative agenda. "It was never about personal
battles," Dellums recalled upon his retirement from the
House. "It has always been about ideas. Individuals come
and go, but ideas must ultimately transcend, and ideas
must ultimately prevail."[1]

Ronald V. Dellums was born on November 24, 1935, in
Oakland, California, to Verney Dellums, a Pullman porter
and a longshoreman, and Willa Dellums, a beautician and
government clerk. His uncle, C. L. Dellums—a leader in
the Brotherhood of Sleeping Car Porters union—served
as a role model and as a political influence. Ron Dellums
attended McClymonds High School before graduating
from Oakland Technical High School in 1953. After a
short stint at San Francisco City College, he enlisted in
the Marine Corps in 1954. While in the service, Dellums
married and had two children: Michael and Pam. He and
his wife Athurine later divorced. In 1956, at the end of his
two-year enlistment in the Marines, he enrolled at Oakland
City College, where he earned an associate's degree in
1958. He continued his education at San Francisco State
College, graduating with a B.A. in 1960. Two years later
he was awarded a master's degree in social work from
the University of California at Berkeley.[2] In 1962 he

married Leola Roscoe Higgs, an attorney; the couple had
a daughter, Piper, and two sons, Erik and Brandy. They
divorced in 1999, and Dellums married Cynthia Lewis
in 2000.[3]

After earning his master's degree, Dellums worked in a
series of social work jobs that promoted his involvement
with community affairs and local politics in the Bay Area.
He began his career as a psychiatric social worker for the
California department of mental hygiene from 1962 to
1964. Between 1964 and 1968, Dellums directed several
area programs, including the Bayview Community Center
in San Francisco, Hunter's Point Youth Opportunity
Council, and the San Francisco Economic Opportunity
Council. He later found employment at San Francisco
State College and the University of California at Berkeley
as a lecturer and was employed as a senior consultant for
manpower programs at Social Dynamics, Inc., from 1968
through 1970.[4] At the urging of friends and members of
the community, Dellums made his first foray into politics
when he sought and won a seat on the Berkeley city
council in 1967. Asked to describe his approach to politics,
he responded, "I'd listen and try to understand what people
had to say, but then I'd act on my own beliefs. That's the
only way anyone should run for office."[5]

From his seat on the council, Dellums, who had
become a spokesperson for minorities and the disadvantaged, mounted a campaign in 1970 for the congressional
seat encompassing the liberal bastion of Berkeley and
nearby Oakland, one of the most populated and
impoverished cities in California. In the primary, Dellums
squared off against the six-term incumbent Jeffery
Cohelan. Running on an antiwar platform, he criticized
Cohelan's late opposition to America's involvement in
Vietnam.[6] As a young (34-year-old), African-American
candidate, Dellums connected with the anti-establishment

current that was prevalent in Berkeley and Oakland. He also made a concerted effort to appeal to voters of various races in the diverse district. "[I] entered the campaign for Congress with a fervent belief that beyond ethnicity, it would be possible to bring women, labor, seniors, youths, and the poor into a coalition of the 'powerless,'" he later recollected.[7] Dellums's grass-roots campaigning ultimately helped him upset Cohelan. After garnering 55 percent of the vote, Dellums remarked that the race "brought up the new versus the old generation issue, war versus peace, open versus closed politics."[8] The November general election attracted national attention despite the fact that Dellums was virtually assured of winning the heavily Democratic district. Vice President Spiro Agnew campaigned against the vocal critic of the Richard M. Nixon administration's policy in Vietnam, labeling Dellums an "out-and-out radical" and an "enthusiastic backer of the Black Panthers."[9] The Vice President's visit to the district did little to slow Dellums's momentum and, in fact, seemed to generate more publicity for his campaign. "One person I forgot to thank," Dellums quipped in his victory speech, "my public relations agent, Spiro T. Agnew."[10] Dellums defeated Republican candidate John Healy, a 25-year-old accountant, and third-party candidate Sarah Scahill with 57 percent of the vote to become one of the first African Americans to represent a majority-white congressional district.[11]

With his election to the 92nd Congress (1971–1973), Dellums quickly made headlines in his district and around the country. Unlike many freshman Members of Congress, who chose to learn the ropes quietly, Dellums adopted an active and vocal approach, introducing more than 200 pieces of legislation.[12] Groomed in the radical tradition of his district, he displayed little patience for congressional customs and the inner workings of the institution. After the House refused to conduct an investigation on possible American war crimes in Vietnam, he spearheaded a plan to hold his own ad hoc hearings—an unusual and controversial move that provoked scorn from some longtime politicians but drew considerable media

attention.[13] "I am not going to back away from being called a radical," Dellums remarked defiantly during his first term. "If being an advocate of peace, justice, and humanity toward all human beings is radical, then I'm glad to be called a radical."[14] He also convened informal hearings on racism in the military, an issue of personal importance because of the discrimination he encountered in the Marines.[15]

Dellums continued to make waves in the House, introducing a measure for comprehensive economic sanctions in South Africa during the 92nd Congress. The first legislator to propose such severe restrictions against the apartheid regime, Dellums, alongside the Congressional Black Caucus (CBC), waged a long, intense battle to highlight the discriminatory practices of South Africa.[16] "We are serious in our determination that positive action be taken soon to terminate U.S. business relationships with apartheid and repression in Africa," Dellums affirmed on behalf of the CBC in 1972. As one of the 13 Members who founded the organization in 1971 and served as its chairman for the 101st Congress (1989–1991), Dellums discovered an outlet for his activism with the CBC.[17] During the next 15 years, the California Representative led the charge against apartheid by sponsoring numerous bills to end U.S. support for the South African government and participating in a series of peaceful demonstrations— which, on one occasion, led to his arrest at the South African Embassy in Washington, DC.[18] In 1986, Dellums achieved one of his most significant legislative triumphs. As the floor manager of a bill calling for a U.S. trade embargo against South Africa and divestment by American companies of their holdings in the African nation, Dellums edged out a similar bill put forth by another black Member, William (Bill) Gray III of Pennsylvania, that included more modest sanctions. In an unusual turn of events, the opposition chose not to request a recorded roll call vote after a voice vote passed Dellums's measure. Dellums expressed shock at how easily the bill had passed as well as profound satisfaction: "This is the highest point of my political life, the most significant and personally rewarding," Dellums rejoiced. "It's been a long journey to this moment."[19] Although the Senate ultimately passed a less stringent measure than the House, the two chambers united to override a veto by President Ronald W. Reagan easily. The Comprehensive Anti-Apartheid Act became law on October 2, 1986.[20]

One of Dellums's long-standing goals as a Representative was to slash the military budget. To pursue this objective effectively he sought a seat on the powerful Armed Services Committee for the 93rd Congress (1973–1975). While this decision may have seemed out of character for an antiwar politician, the Representative explained that if he could become well versed in military affairs, he would be better able to argue the merits of his views on military oversight.[21] The CBC drafted a letter to the Democratic leadership on Dellums's behalf, but the chair of Armed Services, F. Edward Hébert of Louisiana, and the Committee on Committees opposed the appointment of an outspoken war critic. Refusing to yield, the CBC, led by Louis Stokes of Ohio and William (Bill) Clay, Sr., of Missouri, won the backing of Speaker Carl Albert of Oklahoma to place Dellums on the panel. He became the first African American to serve on the committee.[22] Retaliating for Dellums's addition and that of a woman (Patricia Schroeder of Colorado) to his committee roster, Hébert set aside one seat for the two newcomers at the first Armed Services meeting in 1973. "Let's not give these guys the luxury of knowing they can get under our skin," Dellums urged Schroeder. "Let's sit here and share this chair as if it's the most normal thing in the world."[23]

Despite this inauspicious start, Dellums rose through the ranks of Armed Services, serving on the panel for the rest of his House career. In 1983 he became chairman of the influential Subcommittee on Military Installations and Facilities. A decade later he made history as the first African-American chairman of Armed Services.[24] Initially some Members warned that Dellums's record of opposition to defense appropriations would stymie the committee. But Dellums surprised his critics with his impartial

leadership that allowed a continued ban on gays in the military, a pay increase for the armed services, and a boost in anti-missile funding—all despite his objections.[25] He retained the chairmanship for one term but became the Ranking Member in 1995 when the Republicans took control of the House for the first time in 40 years.

Throughout his tenure on Armed Services, Dellums sought to build coalitions—even on the other side of the aisle—to accomplish his legislative goals. On several occasions, he worked with Republican John Kasich of Ohio to stop production of the B-2 bomber.[26] Dellums also consistently challenged another Cold War weapon, the MX missile—a land-based intercontinental ballistic missile that could deploy as many as 10 re-entry rockets, each topped by a 300-kiloton nuclear warhead. Beginning in 1977, he offered amendments to block its funding, and in 1980, after receiving a symbolic and short-lived nomination for President (he withdrew from contention moments later), Dellums used the forum to make a fervent speech about the need to cease MX manufacturing and "to reject war and inflation-combating policies that caused a rise in unemployment."[27] In 1982 he proposed an alternative military budget—mirroring the CBC's substitute budget—that slashed spending by more than $50 billion. Though the resolution received little support outside the CBC, Dellums considered it one of his most meaningful legislative endeavors. "We will be back next year and the year after that and the year after that until we right the wrongs in this madness," he asserted.[28] Dellums remained steady in his opposition to most U.S. military operations, including the American invasion of Grenada in 1983 and the Persian Gulf War in 1991, but he did support some peacekeeping efforts in Africa and the Caribbean.[29] His unswerving commitment to reduce military funding became a hallmark of his House tenure.

Assigned to the District of Columbia Committee during his first term in office, Dellums eventually chaired the panel from the 96th to the 102nd Congresses (1979–1993). Under his direction, the committee examined a range of issues affecting the nation's capital and other urban areas, such as transportation, schools, housing, and public safety.[30] Envisioning himself as "an advocate, not an overseer, of District affairs," Dellums worked to achieve one of his major priorities, which he first introduced in 1971: statehood for Washington, DC.[31] "There should be no colonies in a democracy, and the District of Columbia continues to be a colony," Dellums said after the committee voted in favor of a statehood measure in 1987.[32] As as Representative, he also served on the Foreign Affairs, Post Office and Civil Service, and Select Intelligence committees.

Dellums rarely faced serious re-election challenges, averaging more than 60 percent of the vote throughout most of his House career. Although Dellums reportedly had more than 800 overdrafts from the House "Bank," his popularity among his constituents, especially in the urban areas of Oakland and Berkeley, allowed him to escape the fate of several Members who lost their congressional seats after they were linked to the House "Bank" scandal in the 102nd Congress (1991–1993). The reapportionment that took effect in 1992 created a safer district for the incumbent; with the elimination of the outlying suburbs, Dellums captured more than 70 percent of the vote in his three remaining contests.[33]

In February 1998, the 14-term Representative shocked his colleagues when he resigned from the House, citing personal reasons.[34] In his farewell speech, Dellums reflected on his long and successful career in the House: "To get up every day and put on your uniform and put on your tie and march on the floor of Congress knowing that, in your hands, in that card, in your very being, you have life and death in your hands, it is an incredible thing."[35] After Congress, Dellums worked as a lobbyist, starting his own firm in Washington, DC. In 2006, he returned to the political spotlight when he was elected mayor of Oakland at age 70. "You just asked an old guy to come out of the comfort zone and play one more game," Dellums observed.[36]

FOR FURTHER READING

"Dellums, Ronald V.," *Biographical Directory of the U.S. Congress, 1774–Present,* http://bioguide.congress.gov/scripts/biodisplay.pl?index=D000222.

Dellums, Ronald V., and H. Lee Halterman. *Lying Down with the Lions: A Public Life from the Streets of Oakland to the Halls of Power* (Boston: Beacon Press, 2000).

James, Victor V., Jr. "Cultural Pluralism and the Quest for Black Citizenship: The 1970 Ronald V. Dellums Congressional Primary Campaign." Ph.D. dissertation, University of California at Berkeley, 1975.

MANUSCRIPT COLLECTION

African American Museum and Library at Oakland (Oakland, CA). *Papers:* ca. 1971–1998, approximately 235 cubic feet. The papers of Ronald V. Dellums are closed until processing is completed.

NOTES

1 *Congressional Record*, House, 105th Cong., 2nd sess. (5 February 1998): H363.

2 Ronald V. Dellums and H. Lee Halterman, *Lying Down With the Lions: A Public Life From the Streets of Oakland to the Halls of Power* (Boston: Beacon Press, 2000): 9–12, 17–19, 25; Helen R. Houston, "Ronald V. Dellums," in Jessie Carney Smith, ed., *Notable Black American Men* (Detroit, MI: Gale Research, Inc., 1999): 289 (hereinafter referred to as *NBAM*); "Dellums, Ronald V.," *Current Biography, 1972* (New York: H. W. Wilson and Company, 1972): 104.

3 Sources conflict regarding Dellums's divorce and remarriage dates. See Houston, "Ronald V. Dellums," *NBAM*: 289; Guy Ashley, "City Holds Breath for Dellums," 27 September 2005, *Contra Costa Times* (Walnut Creek, CA): F4.

4 "Dellums, Ronald V.," *Current Biography, 1993* (New York: H.W. Wilson and Company, 1993): 152.

5 Dellums and Halterman, *Lying Down With the Lions*: 41.

6 Daryl Lembke, "Cohelan Faces Strong Challenge in the Primary," 27 May 1970, *Los Angeles Times*: 30.

7 Carol M. Swain, *Black Faces, Black Interests: The Representation of African Americans in Congress* (Cambridge: Harvard University Press, 1993): 134.

8 "Black Defeats Veteran White Congressman," 4 June 1970, *Chicago Tribune*: E11; Daryl Lembke, "Cohelan Upset in Congress Race by Negro," 4 June 1970, *Los Angeles Times*: 3.

9 Daryl Lembke, "Welcomes Attack by Agnew, Dellums Says," 10 October 1970, *Los Angeles Times*: 9; Bill Boyarsky, "Veysey Takes Lead in Tunney's Old District," 4 November 1970, *Los Angeles Times*: A33; William Chapman, "Agnew Says Democrats Embrace Radicalism," 9 October 1970, *Washington Post*: A12.

10 "Nixon Backer, Agnew Target Win Contests," 5 November 1970, *Los Angeles Times*: A3.

11 "Election Statistics, 1920 to Present," available at http://clerk.house.gov/member_info/electionInfo/index.html; Swain, *Black Faces, Black Interests*: 133–140.

12 Swain, *Black Faces, Black Interests*: 139.

13 Dellums led the movement for informal hearings on alleged war crimes in Vietnam. He was joined by three other Democrats: Bella Abzug of New York, John Conyers, Jr., of Michigan, and Parren Mitchell of Maryland. See "4 in the House Plan Hearings on War," 7 April 1971, *New York Times*: 10; Lois Romano, "Ron Dellums, Waging Peace: The Longtime Anti-War Activist, From Grandstander to Seasoned Player," 20 February 1991, *Washington Post*: C1; William Chapman, "4 Congressmen to Hold Inquiry on War Crimes," 7 April 1971, *Washington Post*: A8.

14 Ray Mosley, "Violence Disavowed by Rep. Dellums," 14 February 1971, *Washington Post*: 113.

15 In his memoirs, Dellums describes how an overt act of racism disqualified him for consideration as an officer in the Marines. See Dellums and Halterman, *Lying Down With the Lions*: 22–23.

16 Ronald V. Dellums Interview: Conversations With History; Institute of International Studies, UC Berkeley: http://globetrotter.berkeley.edu/people/Dellums/dellums-con0.html (accessed 10 February 2000); Dellums and Halterman, *Lying Down With the Lions*: 121–123; *Congressional Record*, House, 92nd Cong., 2nd sess. (16 February 1972): 4247. In his memoirs, Dellums cites February 1972 for the introduction of the measure, matching the *Congressional Record*. However, there is an earlier listing for proposed sanctions against South Africa by Dellums and Congressman John Conyers, Jr. See *Congressional Record*, House, 92nd Cong., 1st sess. (15 December 1971): 47236.

17 Robert Singh, *The Congressional Black Caucus: Racial Politics in the U.S. Congress* (Thousand Oaks, CA: Sage, 1998): 65.

18 For example, see "Dellums Arrested in Ongoing South African Protest," 29 November 1984, Associated Press; "Apartheid Protest Greets President Reagan at Capitol," 7 February 1985, *Washington Post*: A19. For a detailed account of his arrest, see Dellums and Halterman, *Lying Down With the Lions*: 127–129.

19 James R. Dickerson, "Dellums: Exoneration Is His," 20 June 1986, *Washington Post*: A17; Edward Walsh, "House Would Require U.S. Disinvestment From South Africa," 19 June 1986, *Washington Post*: A1.

20 Helen Dewar, "Congress Votes Sanctions on South Africa," 13 September 1986, *Washington Post*: A1; Edward Walsh, "House Easily Overrides Veto of South Africa Sanctions," 30 September 1986, *Washington Post*: A1; "Senate Overrides Reagan's Veto of Sanctions 78 to 21," 2 October 1986, *Los Angeles Times*: A1. Dellums provides a detailed account of the legislative effort in *Lying Down With the Lions*: 97–98.

21 Dellums and Halterman, *Lying Down With the Lions*: 97–98.

22 Ibid., 99–103; Romano, "Ron Dellums, Waging Peace."

23 Dellums and Halterman, *Lying Down With the Lions*: 149–150. Historian Julian Zelizer referred to this incident and also detailed the downfall of Hébert as chairman of Armed Services in the post-Watergate reform era. See *On Capitol Hill: The Struggle to Reform Congress and Its Consequences, 1948–2000* (Cambridge: Cambridge University Press, 2004): 135, 167–169.

24 "Dellums Approved to Head House Armed Services Committee," 27 January 1993, Associated Press.

25 Gilbert A. Lewthwaite, "Dellums' Lonely Fight in Armed Services," 19 March 1994, *Baltimore Sun*: 2A.

26   Eric Schmitt, "House Panel Votes to Cut Off Bomber," 1 August 1990, *New York Times*: B6; Romano, "Ron Dellums, Waging Peace"; Dellums and Halterman, *Lying Down With the Lions*: 118.

27   Herbert Denton Washington, "Dellums Uses His Brief Candidacy to Try to 'Energize' the Gathering," 14 August 1980, *Washington Post*: A15; Dellums and Halterman, *Lying Down With the Lions*: 87.

28   Dellums and Halterman, *Lying Down With the Lions*: 171; Dickenson, "Dellums: Exoneration Is His."

29   Lewthwaite, "Dellums' Lonely Fight in Armed Services"; *Politics in America, 1998* (Washington, DC: Congressional Quarterly Inc., 1997): 113.

30   Dellums and Halterman, *Lying Down with the Lions*: 95–96.

31   Donald P. Baker, "Dellums to Be 'Advocate' for DC," 27 January 1979, *Washington Post*: B1; "Fauntroy Attacks Plan on Statehood," 15 July 1971, *Washington Post*: E2.

32   "House Committee OKs Bill to Make District of Columbia a State," 4 June 1987, Associated Press.

33   "Election Statistics, 1920 to Present," available at http://clerk.house.gov/member_info/electionInfo/index.html; *Politics in America, 1998*: 113–114; Clifford Krauss, "Committee Names All Who Overdrew at the House Bank," 17 April 1992, *New York Times*: A1.

34   "House Welcomes New Member, Bids Farewell to 27-Year Veteran," 5 February 1998, Associated Press. Dellums provided more insight on his decision to retire from the House in his memoirs. "While for thirty years I had been willing to accept the call to service, it was now time for me to recapture my life. I had never had any intention of being 'carried out' of the Congress. I had always imagined returning to private life." See *Lying Down With the Lions*: 195.

35   *Congressional Record*, House, 105th Cong., 2nd sess. (5 February 1998): H363.

36   Guy Ashley, "Dellums Announces Run for Mayor," 8 October 2005, *Contra Costa Times*; Heather MacDonald, "Dellums Promises Oakland Revival; City's 48th Mayor Focuses on Street Violence During Fiery Inaugural Speech at Famous Paramount Theatre," 9 January 2007, *Contra Costa Times*: F4.

"I AM NOT GOING TO BACK AWAY
FROM BEING CALLED A RADICAL,"
DELLUMS REMARKED DEFIANTLY
DURING HIS FIRST TERM.
"IF BEING AN ADVOCATE OF
PEACE, JUSTICE, AND HUMANITY
TOWARD ALL HUMAN BEINGS IS
RADICAL, THEN I'M GLAD TO BE
CALLED A RADICAL."

Ralph Harold Metcalfe
1910–1978

UNITED STATES REPRESENTATIVE ★ 1971–1978
DEMOCRAT FROM ILLINOIS

Ralph Metcalfe achieved worldwide fame as an Olympic athlete years before he became involved in politics on Chicago's South Side. Like William Dawson, his predecessor from the predominantly black, urban Illinois district, Metcalfe rose through the ranks of the Chicago Democratic political machine before winning a seat in Congress. However, Metcalfe differentiated himself from other machine loyalists of the period by elevating race above local party interests. Metcalfe's willingness to risk his political career to follow his conscience won him loyal support among the majority of his constituents and his black colleagues in the House. "I know the political reality of what I am doing, but I am prepared to let the chips fall where they may," Metcalfe remarked. "I'm willing to pay whatever political consequences I have to, but frankly, I don't think there will be any. . . . In the caucus we have decided to put the interests of black people first—above all else, and that means even going against our party or our political leaders if black interests don't coincide with their positions."[1]

Ralph Harold Metcalfe was born in Atlanta, Georgia, on May 29, 1910, to Marie Attaway, a seamstress, and Clarence Metcalfe, a stockyard worker.[2] As a child, he moved with his family to the South Side of Chicago. After graduating from Chicago's Tilden Technical School in 1930, Metcalfe attended Marquette University where he received a bachelor of philosophy degree in 1936. He completed his education by earning an M.A. in physical education from the University of Southern California in 1939. During high school Metcalfe began a long and successful career as a track athlete. "I was told by my coach that as a black person I'd have to put daylight between me and my nearest competitor," Metcalfe recalled. "I forced myself to train harder so I could put that daylight behind me."[3] Metcalfe became a household name in the United

States when he medaled in the 1932 and 1936 Olympics. During the infamous Berlin Games of 1936, Metcalfe and Jesse Owens led the American 400-meter relay team to a world record, much to the dismay of German onlookers, especially Adolf Hitler, who expected the German athletes to prove their superiority by sweeping all the track and field events.[4] Years later, Owens credited Metcalfe with helping his black teammates overcome the many distractions they faced. "He said we were not there to get involved in the political situation. We were there for one purpose—to represent our country."[5]

Following his retirement from competitive sports in 1936, Metcalfe taught political science and coached track at Xavier University in New Orleans until 1946. He also served in the U.S. Army Transportation Corps from 1942 to 1945, where he rose to the rank of first lieutenant and earned the Legion of Merit for his physical education training program. After World War II, Metcalfe returned to Chicago in 1945 to become director of the civil rights department of the Chicago Commission on Human Relations, a position he held until 1949. He then headed the Illinois State Athletic Commission from 1949 to 1952. In 1947, Metcalfe married Madalynne Fay Young. The couple had one child, Ralph Metcalfe, Jr.[6]

In 1952, Metcalfe began his political career by winning election as Chicago's Third Ward Democratic committeeman. Quickly earning the respect and trust of Richard J. Daley, Chicago's mayor and leader of the city's powerful political machine, Metcalfe secured more prominent positions in the local government. After becoming an alderman in 1955, he was later selected by Daley to serve as president *pro tempore* of the Chicago city council.[7] When the powerful but aging Representative William L. Dawson, a longtime member of the Democratic machine, decided to retire from the

House, he chose Metcalfe to replace him in Congress. In the Democratic primary, Metcalfe faced A. A. (Sammy) Rayner, an alderman and an undertaker, who blamed the predominantly white power structure of Chicago for the problems facing many African Americans in the urban district. Running on a platform of "law and order," Metcalfe defended his ties to Daley's machine, reassuring voters that the political organization "is structured in a businesslike manner to get things done and, therefore, it is an asset."[8] With the backing of Daley and Dawson, Metcalfe defeated Rayner and went on to win election to the House easily, with 91 percent of the vote against Republican Jayne Jennings, a schoolteacher, a few days before Dawson's death in November 1970.[9] Metcalfe entered the House on January 3, 1971, and was assigned to the Committee on Merchant Marine and Fisheries and the Interstate and Foreign Commerce Committee; he served on both committees throughout his tenure in the House.

Metcalfe's appointment to the influential Interstate and Foreign Commerce Committee marked the first time an African-American Member served on the panel in the 20th century.[10] The Illinois Representative also served on the Post Office and Civil Service Committee during the 95th Congress (1977–1979).

Metcalfe's legislative focus in the House, like his predecessor's, was assisting the residents on Chicago's South Side. Using his experience as chairman of the Chicago city council's housing committee, Metcalfe introduced legislation to increase the availability of home improvement loans and federal housing programs to benefit the many impoverished people living in his district. He also advocated funding for security measures to protect residents in public projects and fought to eliminate "redlining," the practice of withholding funds for home loans and insurance from low-income neighborhoods. Defending the need for such measures, Metcalfe asserted, "It is essential that individuals living in our cities, or individuals of low or moderate income residing in rural areas, be provided with the means and incentive to remain in their communities."[11] As a strong

proponent of gun control, the Illinois Representative introduced legislation to prohibit the manufacture and sale of handguns, stating, "The people in the First Congressional District of Illinois know the terror of uncontrolled handguns. They know that the only solution to this epidemic of violent handgun crime is an absolute ban on the manufacture, sale, and distribution of these weapons throughout the United States."[12]

Throughout his House career, Metcalfe also advanced issues that extended beyond his congressional district. He drafted provisions to the Railroad Revitalization and Regulatory Reform Act to combat discrimination in the industry present more than a decade after the passage of the landmark Civil Rights Act of 1964.[13] Concerned about the quality of health care for minorities, the Illinois Representative criticized the Richard M. Nixon administration for failing to support legislation aimed at improving health services for those most in need and exhorted his House colleagues to "design a health care package which adequately meets the needs and aspirations of poor and minority groups."[14] Drawing on his own athletic experience, Metcalfe cosponsored the Amateur Sports Act of 1978, which provided federal funding for American Olympic athletes and increased opportunities for minorities, women, and disabled Americans to participate in amateur sports.[15]

Although his legislative agenda focused heavily on domestic issues, Metcalfe had an interest in U.S. foreign policy. As chairman of the Merchant Marine and Fisheries Subcommittee on the Panama Canal, he advocated more opportunities for education, housing, and jobs in the Canal Zone and worked to secure the passage of legislation that eventually ceded American control of the Panama Canal.[16] Like other African-American Members of the era, Metcalfe called for increased U.S. involvement in African affairs, especially in South Africa. In 1975 he introduced a measure to cease American support for South Africa to protest its government-sanctioned policy of racial discrimination. Metcalfe praised the recommendations of the Organization of African Unity

(OAU) for the South African region, which included ending apartheid in South Africa and instituting majority rule in Rhodesia. "In order to insure [sic] that the tremendous potential for violent conflict in southern Africa, a potential born of people's desire to throw off the yoke of oppression and racism, is not realized, it is imperative that the United States follow the lead of the OAU and reassess its own policies in Southern Africa."[17]

Metcalfe received national attention when he publicly broke ranks in 1972 with Chicago Mayor Richard Daley, his friend and political ally, and the Democratic machine. Outraged by what he perceived as Daley's lenient stance on police brutality in the black community—specifically with regard to a violent raid of the local Black Panthers and two incidents that involved the harassment of black dentists—Metcalfe declared, "the Mayor doesn't understand what happens to black men on the streets of Chicago, and probably never will."[18] Metcalfe used his position on the Interstate and Foreign Commerce Committee to conduct public hearings for victims and witnesses of police brutality and organized a citizens' group to lobby the city government for reforms.[19] "I've always spoken out for my people—for what I believe but in the past I've tried to remedy situations on a case-by-case basis, trying to work within the party or official government circles," Metcalfe said. "In the brutality field, however, I can't just stand by while each and every case is investigated. I want the system changed."[20] When Metcalfe backed William Singer, Daley's opponent in the 1975 Chicago mayoral primary, the powerful political boss retaliated by depriving the Illinois Representative of his Third Ward patronage positions and orchestrating a challenge in the 1976 Democratic primary for Chicago's South Side congressional seat.[21] In a fight against what he termed a "political dictatorship" in Chicago, Metcalfe asserted, "There is only one issue. The right of black people to choose their own public officials and not have them picked from downtown."[22] With the outspoken support of the Congressional Black Caucus (CBC)—an organization Metcalfe helped found in 1971—he handily defeated Daley aide Erwin A. France with more than 70 percent of the vote in the bitterly contested primary. "This is a people's victory," the Chicago Representative declared.[23] After reapportionment in 1972, the metropolitan district continued to boast a predominantly black population, even with the significant change in boundaries that included a largely white neighborhood surrounding the University of Chicago. As with the two previous general elections for the Chicago congressional district, Metcalfe faced little Republican opposition, and he easily earned a seat in the 95th Congress.[24]

With the death of Mayor Daley in December of 1976, tensions eased between Metcalfe and the Chicago machine.[25] However, Metcalfe called attention to racial discrimination in Chicago and also continued to try to improve police service for his constituents residing in impoverished neighborhoods. "If we want to strengthen and rebuild Chicago, then we must help the people who are sticking it out in the inner city to survive."[26] During the 95th Congress, Metcalfe demonstrated his determination to recognize the accomplishments of African Americans, sponsoring several resolutions to declare February as Black History Month.

Metcalfe's congressional career ended when he died suddenly of an apparent heart attack on October 10, 1978, only a month before his almost certain re-election to a fifth term. Representative Louis Stokes of Ohio praised Metcalfe's dedication to his district and the CBC. "Ralph was a man who had the ability to inspire people," Stokes recalled. "The type of individual who, as you came to know him, you would have to admire."[27]

FOR FURTHER READING

"Metcalfe, Ralph Harold" *Biographical Directory of the U.S. Congress, 1774–Present,* http://bioguide.congress.gov/scripts/biodisplay.pl?index=M000675.

MANUSCRIPT COLLECTION

The Metcalfe Collection (Chicago, IL). *Papers:* ca. 1932–1977, amount unknown. The collection documents Ralph Metcalfe's athletic pursuits, including his Olympic track victories; his public service, including his tenure with the U.S. House of Representatives; and his involvement with the civil rights movement. The collection has not yet been processed.

NOTES

1   "Ralph Harold Metcalfe," 14 October 1978, *Washington Post*: A16.

2   David L. Porter, "Metcalfe, Ralph Harold," *American National Biography* 15 (New York: Oxford University Press, 1999): 386 (hereinafter referred to as *ANB*). *ANB* lists Metcalfe's mother's first name as Marie, whereas other sources indicate her first name was Mayme.

3   "Rep. Ralph Metcalfe," 11 October 1978, *Chicago Tribune*: D2.

4   Jean R. Hailey, "Rep. Ralph H. Metcalfe Dies," 11 October 1978, *Washington Post*: C8; Darius L. Thieme, "Ralph H. Metcalfe," in Jessie Carney Smith, ed., *Notable Black American Men* (Farmington Hills, MI: Gale Research, Inc., 1999): 803–804 (hereinafter referred to as *NBAM*); Porter, "Metcalfe, Ralph Harold," *ANB*. For more information on the 1936 Olympics, see Alan Gould, "Metcalfe Runs Second to Ohio Negro in Sprint Finals," 4 August 1936, *Washington Post*: X15 and Shirley Povich, "What Price Olympic Glory?—America's Sports Public Demands," 16 August 1936, *Washington Post*: B5.

5   Dorothy Collin, "Jesse Owens Recalls a Beloved Teammate," 11 October 1978, *Chicago Tribune*: 1.

6   Thieme, "Ralph H. Metcalfe," *NBAM*.

7   Hailey, "Rep. Ralph H. Metcalfe Dies."

8   Michael Kilian, "Daley Choices Win Key Tests," 18 March 1970, *Chicago Tribune*: 1; Norman C. Miller, "A Primary in Chicago Between Two Blacks Is Big Test for Daley," 24 February 1970, *Wall Street Journal*: 1.

9   "Election Statistics, 1920 to Present," available at http://clerk.house.gov/member_info/electionInfo/index.html; Maurine Christopher, *Black Americans in Congress* (New York: Thomas Y. Crowell Company, 1976): 264.

10   Charles Stewart III, "Committee Hierarchies in the Modernizing House, 1875–1947," *American Journal of Political Science* 36 (1992): 845–846.

11   *Congressional Record,* House, 93rd Cong., 2nd sess. (30 April 1974): 12437–12438; *Congressional Record,* House, 93rd Cong., 2nd sess. (20 May 1974): 15592.

12   *Congressional Record,* House, 94th Cong., 1st sess. (26 February 1975): 4491; Christopher, *Black Americans in Congress*: 265.

13   *Congressional Record,* House, 94th Cong., 1st sess. (17 December 1975): 41339; *Congressional Record,* House, 94th Cong., 2nd sess. (28 January 1976): 1357; Porter, "Metcalfe, Ralph Harold," *ANB*.

14   *Congressional Record,* House, 93rd Cong., 1st sess. (31 January 1973): 2845–2846; C. Gerald Fraser, "Wider Health Care Urged for Blacks," 12 December 1971, *New York Times*: 77.

15 *Congressional Record*, House, 95th Cong., 2nd sess. (26 September 1978): 31671.

16 *Congressional Record*, House, 95th Cong., 2nd sess. (18 April 1978): 10453–10454; Porter, "Metcalfe, Ralph Harold," *ANB*; "Ralph Metcalfe," *Contemporary Black Biography*, Volume 26 (Detroit, MI: Gale Group, 2000).

17 *Congressional Record*, House, 94th Cong., 1st sess. (8 May 1975): 13646.

18 R. W. Apple, Jr., "Black Leader's Rebellion Is Hurting Daley Machine," 10 May 1972, *New York Times*: 36; Nathaniel Sheppard, Jr., "19 Seeking House Seat Vacated by Chicago Mayor," 8 July 1983, *New York Times*: A7.

19 *Congressional Record*, House, 93rd Cong., 1st sess. (6 December 1973): 39929–39930; Christopher, *Black Americans in Congress*: 264.

20 "Police Acts Create New Daley Critic," 7 May 1972, *Washington Post*: A14.

21 As was the case with other machine politicians, Metcalfe retained his local leadership positions in Chicago until his death. See Hailey, "Rep. Ralph H. Metcalfe Dies"; Barbara Reynolds, "Track Star Metcalfe Running Hard," 7 March 1976, *Chicago Tribune*: 28.

22 Vernon Jarrett, "Ralph Metcalfe Comes Out Fighting," 23 January 1976, *Chicago Tribune*: A4; Barbara Reynolds, "Metcalfe Seeks New Term, Rips 'Dictator,'" 12 November 1975, *Chicago Tribune*: 3.

23 Barbara Reynolds, "Metcalfe Victory Seen as Freedom From Daley," 17 March 1976, *Chicago Tribune*: 3; Reynolds, "Track Star Metcalfe Running Hard"; Vernon Jarrett, "France Has Bitter Taste of Politics," 9 April 1976, *Chicago Tribune*: A4; "5 Congressmen Here to Aid Rep. Metcalfe," 15 February 1976, *Chicago Tribune*: 20.

24 "Election Statistics, 1920 to Present," available at http://clerk.house.gov/member_info/electionInfo/index.html.

25 "Ralph Metcalfe Is Dead at 68," 11 October 1978, *Los Angeles Times*: E11.

26 The *Chicago Tribune* printed an article based on a speech by Metcalfe that outlined his goals for improvements in law enforcement in Chicago. See "Police Protection Is Everyone's Right," 11 June 1977, *Chicago Tribune*: S10.

27 *Congressional Record*, House, 95th Cong., 2nd sess. (11 October 1978): 35723.

Parren James Mitchell
1922–2007

UNITED STATES REPRESENTATIVE ★ 1971–1987
DEMOCRAT FROM MARYLAND

A lifelong activist who carried on his family's tradition of public service, Parren Mitchell won election to the U.S. House in 1970, becoming the first African-American Representative from Maryland. As a Member of Congress, he earned a reputation as a dedicated and successful legislator who focused on improving the economic welfare of minorities residing in his Baltimore district and other urban centers. Mitchell's passion and determination to extend the gains made in the civil rights movement—mainly through increased opportunities for minority-owned businesses—guided his eight terms in the House. After Mitchell's death in May 2007, Representative Elijah Cummings of Maryland described him as "a true servant leader, never concerning himself about fame or fortune but, rather, devoting himself entirely to uplifting the people he represented."[1]

Parren James Mitchell was born in Baltimore, Maryland, on April 29, 1922, to Clarence Mitchell, Sr., a waiter, and Elsie Davis Mitchell. His older brother, Clarence Mitchell, Jr., became an influential and longtime lobbyist for the National Association for the Advancement of Colored People (NAACP), serving as director of the Washington bureau from 1950 to 1978.[2] In their youth, Clarence and Parren participated in demonstrations protesting segregation in Baltimore. This early activism fostered Parren Mitchell's interest in promoting civil rights, which shaped much of his future legislative career. Mitchell's political family tree also extended to his sister-in-law, Juanita Jackson Mitchell, who led the Maryland office of the NAACP, and a nephew who served in the Maryland state senate.[3] After graduating from Douglass High School in Baltimore in 1940, Parren Mitchell joined the U.S. Army in 1942, serving as a commissioned officer and a company commander with the all-black 92nd Infantry Division. Mitchell earned a Purple Heart

during his World War II service in Italy.[4] Following his discharge from the armed services in 1946, Mitchell used funding from the 1944 GI Bill of Rights to enroll in Morgan State College in Baltimore. After graduating with an A.B. from Morgan State in 1950, he sued the University of Maryland for admission to the main campus in College Park. Mitchell became the school's first African-American graduate student, earning an M.A. in sociology in 1952.[5] After becoming an instructor of sociology at his undergraduate alma mater, Morgan State, from 1953 to 1954, Mitchell supervised probation work for the Supreme Bench of Baltimore City from 1954 to 1957. He was appointed the executive secretary of the Maryland Commission on Interracial Problems and Relations in 1963 and oversaw the implementation of the state's new public accommodations law.[6] Mitchell also led the Baltimore Community Action Agency, an antipoverty program, from 1965 to 1968, before returning to Morgan State as a professor of sociology and the assistant director of its Urban Affairs Institute. In 1969 Mitchell became president of Baltimore Neighborhoods, Inc., a nonprofit fair housing organization.[7] Mitchell never married and had no children.

Persuaded by local community groups to run for elective office, Mitchell believed he could best help the inner-city residents of Baltimore from Congress. Consequently, he entered the 1968 Democratic primary for the Maryland House seat that encompassed much of western Baltimore and its bordering suburbs. During the campaign, Mitchell accused the 16-year incumbent and chairman of the Committee on House Administration, Samuel Friedel, of losing touch with his constituents, saying, "He doesn't understand the dimensions of the urban crisis, the mood of the people."[8] Mitchell ultimately lost his first election by 5,000 votes.[9] Two years later,

he again challenged Friedel in the Democratic primary. Mitchell countered his opponent's political experience by accentuating his family's civil rights activism and deep roots in Baltimore. In a grass-roots campaign that focused on his antiwar stance and record of community outreach, Mitchell won by a razor-thin margin of 38 votes.[10] He went on to defeat his Republican opponent, lawyer Peter Parker, in the overwhelmingly Democratic district, becoming the first African American to represent the state of Maryland in Congress. Mitchell also became one of the first black Members to win election in a minority-black congressional district.[11] After his Maryland district was redrawn in 1971, Mitchell rarely encountered any serious opposition in his bids for re-election. Once predominantly Jewish and African American, the district now encompassed much of Baltimore's minority population; most of the white suburbs were eliminated. With this shift, the district became even safer for Democrats.[12]

After being sworn in as a member of the 92nd Congress (1971–1973) on January 3, 1971, Mitchell reflected, "I was part of that breed that came in with some clear-cut objectives. I was part of that movement in the country that was deeply dissatisfied with the way the political process was working, and deeply dissatisfied with involvement in Vietnam."[13] Early in his first term, Mitchell used his seat in the House to speak out against the war. The Maryland Representative joined nine of his congressional colleagues on a national tour in 1971 criticizing American foreign policy in Southeast Asia.[14] He and 22 Members of Congress also sought to publicize the antiwar movement by drafting a lawsuit demanding an end to the American bombing and mining of North Vietnamese ports.[15] Mitchell and a handful of Representatives sought to force President Richard M. Nixon to end a bombing campaign in Cambodia, declaring the action unconstitutional since Congress had not authorized it.[16] Frustrated because the allotment of money to subsidize the war in Vietnam drained funding for social programs, Mitchell balked at a Nixon administration proposal to provide North Vietnam financial aid "to contribute to healing the wounds of war

and to postwar reconstruction of the Democratic Republic of Vietnam and throughout Indochina."[17]

Mitchell served on the Banking and Currency Committee (later Banking, Finance, and Urban Affairs) for the duration of his House tenure and on the House Budget panel from the 93rd to the 95th Congresses (1973–1979). He also was a member of the Small Business Committee for the 94th Congress (1975–1977) and from the 96th to the 99th Congresses (1979–1987), serving as chairman from 1981 to 1987.[18] As a Representative, Mitchell also sat on two joint committees: Defense Production and Economic. Mitchell's legislative focus took shape while he was a member of the Small Business Committee. Throughout his congressional career, he directed a series of measures promoting minority-owned businesses and small firms. In 1976 the Maryland Representative attached an amendment to a $4 billion public works program that required state and local governments applying for federal contracts to reserve 10 percent of this money for minority-owned companies. He later described this effort as "my proudest congressional accomplishment."[19] Mitchell achieved another major legislative triumph in 1982 when he guided a bill through the House to set aside funding for small businesses whose owners were economically disadvantaged.[20] Despite criticism that his affirmative action proposals constituted a quota system, Mitchell and other proponents maintained that such legislation was necessary to balance the economic scales.[21] To provide small businesses with more opportunities to procure contracts from the Defense Department, he fought to remove constraints on the number of companies that were permitted to bid for spare parts contracts. Mitchell strongly supported the Small Business Administration (SBA) and opposed efforts to increase interest rates on loans to small businesses and efforts to reduce SBA disaster loans. He also resisted the establishment of a subminimum wage for workers aged 18 and younger.

As one of the 13 founding members of the Congressional Black Caucus (CBC), Mitchell played a significant role in crafting the identity of the fledgling organization. Dubbed the "Little General" for his ability to assemble and organize caucus members with little notice, Mitchell chaired the CBC during the 95th Congress (1977–1979).[22] Representative Cardiss Collins of Illinois noted that Mitchell's efficient and selfless leadership helped lend credibility to the organization. "Parren works hard to make sure each person gets his share of spotlight. He's forging the caucus forward because now we are acting rather than reacting," she said.[23]

Throughout his career in Congress, Mitchell consistently opposed increased funding for the military.[24] In 1977, for instance, he proposed transferring $15 million from the military budget for programs to increase employment opportunities in the U.S. "I have no great fear of the Soviet Union or China," Mitchell remarked. "If this democracy should ever fail it will come from within because of the enormous disparity between the rich and the poor."[25] Under his direction, the CBC took a more public stance to curb defense spending. He lashed out against the James Earl (Jimmy) Carter administration's proposed 1979 fiscal year budget, which allotted a 3 percent hike for military spending. Calling the boost "unconscionable," Mitchell added, "I certainly feel duped in so far as the military budget is concerned."[26] In 1980 Mitchell sponsored a CBC-backed amendment as an alternative to the House Budget Committee's legislation to balance the budget. Mitchell's unsuccessful proposal would have increased funding for domestic programs for education, job training, and income assistance. According to the Maryland Representative, the measure put forth by the Budget Committee plunged "an economic dagger into the bodies of the poor, the nearly poor and the elderly."[27] The following year, the CBC launched its own comprehensive substitute budget—an initiative put forth annually by the caucus—emphasizing the need for increased funding for domestic programs.

Mitchell's legislative agenda stretched beyond national borders; he was an outspoken supporter of strong economic sanctions against South Africa's apartheid government. When the House passed a watered-down version of a bill to limit trade between the United States and South Africa, he angrily remarked, "You can't compromise with total evil. You can't take a mid-point on immorality."[28] Mitchell also urged U.S. participation in the African Development Fund, an international financial institution that focused on providing money for basic infrastructure projects in Africa. "A brief cost-analysis will show that the benefits received by the United States far exceeds [sic] the cost of participating in the African Development Fund, mainly because African countries serve the commercial interests of the United States," Mitchell informed his House colleagues.[29]

Mitchell was known as an outspoken and passionate legislator. One of the first to call for President Nixon's resignation after the Watergate scandal, he routinely criticized the White House during his eight terms in the House for what he perceived as a willingness to neglect the needs of poor Americans. Mitchell's characterization in the press as an "unhappy warrior" with "seething anger" stemmed from his frustration with Black Americans' lack of economic advancement. "I know I get emotional. But it's been more than 20 years from 1954 (the year of the landmark Supreme Court decision on school desegregation). How many people have been jailed, lost, and now you see those gains unraveling."[30]

During the 1980s, Mitchell often sparred with the Ronald W. Reagan administration. Against the backdrop of the Cold War, the Maryland Representative accused President Reagan of excessive defense spending without regard for vital social programs. In particular, he criticized budget initiatives he believed neglected the welfare of America's neediest citizens. At a time when he thought Democrats should stand firm in their commitment to help the poor, Mitchell claimed his party was "trying to out-Republican the Republicans."[31] As a conservative mood swept the electorate in the early 1980s, Mitchell also disputed the growing backlash against the term "liberal": "I'm a liberal, not a post-liberal or a neo-liberal or a reformed liberal, and I plan to stay that way."[32] Mitchell took great pride in his determination to stay in close contact with his constituents—he commuted to the Capitol every day from Baltimore to ensure his accessibility to voters. "I know it sounds hokey, but I enjoy all this work," Mitchell admitted. "When you're asked to take this job, you're asked to perform a public service. And that's what I think I do."[33]

Mitchell's announcement in September 1985 that he would not seek re-election to a ninth term came as a surprise to many. "I'm concerned about what you might call the heart of Congress," he said, adding, "Those who are poor are generally treated with contempt. The concerns of minorities are no longer the concerns of this Congress. . . . It's a step backward."[34] Mitchell denied speculation that his retirement resulted from an ideological rift with the Democratic Party, saying he was leaving because "16 years is a long time to be here."[35] In 1986, he accepted an invitation from Maryland Attorney General Stephen H. Sachs to join his gubernatorial ticket as a candidate for state lieutenant governor; Mitchell's political aspirations ended when he and Sachs failed to win the Democratic nomination.[36] After his retirement from Congress, Mitchell continued to promote economic opportunities for minorities, founding the Minority Business Legal Defense and Education Fund, a private organization that offered legal assistance for the minority business community.[37]

Mitchell died on May 28, 2007, in Baltimore, Maryland, of complications from pneumonia. "If you believe in fighting racism, you make a commitment for the rest of your life," Mitchell said after he retired from the House. "There's no getting off that train. You can't say, 'I've put five years in fighting racism and now I am finished.' No, you are not finished. Our job is to fight it every day, to continue to shove it down and when it rises up to shove it down even harder."[38]

FOR FURTHER READING

"Mitchell, James Parren," *Biographical Directory of the U.S. Congress, 1774–Present,* http://bioguide.congress.gov/scripts/biodisplay.pl?index=M000826.

MANUSCRIPT COLLECTIONS

Howard University (Washington, DC), Moorland–Spingarn Research Center. *Oral History:* 1973, 20 pages. An oral history interview with Parren J. Mitchell conducted by Edward Thompson III on February 22, 1973. In the interview, Parren Mitchell discusses the Congressional Black Caucus, including its accomplishments and relationship to Democratic National Committee. Mitchell also comments on the 1972 National Black Political Convention, describes the purpose and function of the Committee on Banking and Currency and its importance to blacks, and discusses the usurpation of congressional power by President Nixon and the economic policies of his administration. Mitchell also recalls his congressional campaign.

John F. Kennedy Library and Museum (Boston, MA), Oral History Collection. *Oral History:* 1988, 110 pages. An interview with Parren Mitchell by Anthony Shriver in 1988. The interview concerned John F. Kennedy's telephone call to Coretta Scott King during the 1960 presidential campaign.

Morgan State University (Baltimore, MD). *Papers:* Memorabilia.

NOTES

1 Joe Holley, "Parren Mitchell; Politician, Civil Rights Activist; Activist Was Maryland's 1st Black Congressman," 30 May 2007, *Washington Post*: B05; Kelly Brewington, "Fighter, Pioneer, Activist, Mentor; Hundreds Attend Service to Honor, Laud Parren Mitchell," 6 June 2007, *Baltimore Sun*: 1A. Representative Cummings has represented Mitchell's former Maryland congressional district since 1996.

2 For more information on Clarence Mitchell, Jr., see Denton L. Watson, *Lion in the Lobby: Clarence Mitchell, Jr.'s Struggle for the Passage of Civil Rights Laws* (New York: William Morrow & Company, 1990).

3 Sandra Sugawara, "Retiring Mitchell Still Has Passion for Justice," 1 December 1985, *Washington Post*: 37; Jacqueline Trescott, "'One of God's Angry Men,'" 23 September 1977, *Washington Post*: C1; Richard M. Cohen, "Mitchell Victory Seen in Black, Liberal Turnout," 17 August 1970, *Washington Post*: B1.

4 Shirley Washington, *Outstanding African Americans of Congress* (Washington, DC: U.S. Capitol Historical Society, 1998): 61–62; Delphine Ava Gross, "Parren J. Mitchell," in Jessie Carney Smith, ed., *Notable Black American Men* (Farmington Hills, MI: Gale Research Inc., 1999): 825 (hereinafter referred to as *NBAM*).

5 Washington, *Outstanding African Americans of Congress*: 62; Jacqueline Trescott, "Mitchells of Maryland: Standing Up and Speaking Out," 1 February 1976, *Washington Post*: 93; Gross, "Parren J. Mitchell," *NBAM*; "Negro Admitted to Baltimore Unit of Maryland U.," 31 August 1950, *Washington Post*: 1; "Accept Negro Student," 31 August 1950, *New York Times*: 31.

6 William Chapman, "Negro Appointed Secretary of Maryland Commission," 11 April 1963, *Washington Post*: B1; "Civil Rights Workshop Set in Mount Pleasant," 25 September 1964, *Washington Post*: C6. Most contemporary newspaper articles refer to the commission as the Maryland Commission on Interracial Problems and Relations; however, variations of the name appear in other sources. Mitchell was most likely appointed to the commission by the governor of Maryland, J. Millard Tawes.

7 "Parren James Mitchell," *Who's Who Among African Americans, 2002* (New York: Gale Research, 2002); "Parren J. Mitchell," Associated Press Candidate Biographies, 1986; Gross, "Parren J. Mitchell," *NBAM*. For more information on the history of Baltimore Neighborhoods, Inc., see http://www.bni-maryland.org/about/index.htm (accessed 3 December 2007).

8 According to a contemporary newspaper article, Mitchell did not reside in the district when he ran for the open congressional seat in Maryland. For more information on Mitchell's first campaign for elective office, see Richard Homan, "Negro Poses Solid Threat to Friedel," 25 August 1968, *Washington Post*: C1; Washington, *Outstanding African Americans of Congress*: 63; Friedel became

chairman of the Committee on House Administration on July 30, 1968, when the previous chairman, Omar Burleson of Texas, moved to the House Committee on Ways and Means. See Garrison Nelson, *Committees in the U.S. Congress 1947–1992*, Volume 2 (Washington, DC: Congressional Quarterly Press, 1994): 545.

9 Cohen, "Mitchell Victory Seen in Black, Liberal Turnout"; Washington, *Outstanding African Americans of Congress*: 63.

10 Richard M. Cohen, "Mandel to Aid Parren Mitchell as Race Issue Surfaces in Drive," 7 October 1970, *Washington Post*: C2; "Maryland's Friedel Concedes," 6 October 1970, *New York Times*: 36; Cohen, "Mitchell Victory Seen in Black, Liberal Turnout."

11 "Election Statistics, 1920 to Present," available at http://clerk.house.gov/member_info/electionInfo/index.html; David E. Rosenbaum, "3 White Districts Choose Negroes for House Seats," 5 November 1970, *New York Times*: 28.

12 Cohen, "Mandel to Aid Parren Mitchell as Race Issue Surfaces in Drive"; Cohen, "Mitchell Victory Seen in Black, Liberal Turnout"; *Politics in America, 1982* (Washington, DC: Congressional Quarterly Inc., 1981): 535.

13 Sugawara, "Retiring Mitchell Still Has Passion for Justice."

14 "10 in House Open an Antiwar Tour," 8 May 1971, *New York Times*: 13.

15 Washington, *Outstanding African Americans of Congress*: 61–62; Bart Barnes, "Rallies on War Stir Capitol," 12 May 1972, *Washington Post*: A1.

16 Trescott, "'One of God's Angry Men'"; Paul Hodge, "Anti-Bombing Suit Loses Second Test," 25 July 1973, *Washington Post*: A6.

17 Herbert H. Denton, "U.S. Aid to North Vietnam Opposed in Lawmakers' Mail," 22 March 1973, *Washington Post*: B1.

18 Mitchell stepped down from the Small Business Committee on May 15, 1975, to serve on the Budget Committee. He returned to the Small Business Committee at the beginning of the 96th Congress (1979–1981). See Nelson, *Committees in the U.S. Congress 1947–1992*, Volume 2: 624.

19 Washington, *Outstanding African Americans of Congress*: 64; Thomas Goldwasser, "Liberal's Liberal Mitchell Is Fiscal Conservative," 15 September 1980, *Washington Post*: A1.

20 Sugawara, "Retiring Rep. Mitchell Still Has Passion for Justice"; Martin Weil and Gwen Hill, "Rep. Mitchell to Retire," 1 October 1985, *Washington Post*: D1.

21 Washington, *Outstanding African Americans of Congress*: 64.

22 Trescott, "'One of God's Angry Men.'"

23 Ibid.

24 Ibid.; Sugawara, "Retiring Mitchell Still Has Passion for Justice."

25 Jean Campbell, "A Move to Transfer $15 Billion From Defense," 23 April 1977, *Los Angeles Times*: B4.

26   John K. Colley, "US Budget Critics Rally in Congress," 29 January 1979, *Christian Science Monitor*: 9; John Dillin, "Carter Arms Budget Draws Flak From Liberals," 1 February 1978, *Christian Science Monitor*: 5.

27   Robert Parry, "House Liberals Fail to Rewrite 1981 Budget," 1 May 1980, Associated Press; Robert Parry, "House Rejects Republican Plan on Revenue Sharing," 30 April 1980, Associated Press.

28   Mary Russell, "Ex-Im Bank Curb for S. Africa Voted," 3 June 1978, *Washington Post*: A6; "Black Caucus Asks New Ban on S. Africa," 29 October 1977, *Washington Post*: A7.

29   *Congressional Record*, House, 94th Cong., 1st sess. (9 December 1975): 39381; William L. Clay, *Just Permanent Interests: Black Americans in Congress, 1870–1991* (New York: Amistad Press, Inc., 1992): 382.

30   Trescott, "'One of God's Angry Men'"; Sugawara, "Retiring Mitchell Still Has Passion for Justice."

31   Sandra Sugawara and Michel McQueen, "Rep. Mitchell: Time for Something New," 2 October 1985, *Washington Post*: B1.

32   Thomas Korosec, "Blacks in Congress: Frustration and Bitterness," 28 March 1982, *Chicago Tribune*: A1.

33   Goldwasser, "Liberal's Liberal Mitchell Is Fiscal Conservative."

34   Sugawara, "Retiring Mitchell Still Has Passion for Justice."

35   Sugawara and McQueen. "Rep. Mitchell: Time for Something New."

36   Tom Kenworthy, "Mitchell Teams With Sachs in Md. Race," 3 June 1986, *Washington Post*: B1; Tom Kenworthy and Michael McQueen, "Shaefer, Mikulski Win," 10 September 1986, *Washington Post*: A1.

37   Washington, *Outstanding African Americans of Congress*: 65–66.

38   "Parren J. Mitchell, 85; Maryland Congressman Championed Civil Rights," 30 May 2007, *Los Angeles Times*: B6.

When the House passed a watered-down version of a bill to limit trade between the United States and South Africa, Mitchell angrily remarked, "You can't compromise with total evil. You can't take a mid-point on immorality."

Walter Edward Fauntroy
1933–

DELEGATE ★ 1971–1991
DEMOCRAT FROM THE DISTRICT OF COLUMBIA

Walter Fauntroy's leadership in the civil rights movement paved the way for his two-decade career as the District of Columbia's Delegate in the House of Representatives. While he was concerned with many issues during his tenure, Fauntroy dedicated much of his career to attaining home rule (a municipal government elected by the people) for Washington, DC, and to ending apartheid in South Africa. "When you carry a big stick you can walk quietly," Fauntroy once remarked, revealing his political strategy, which embraced compromise and coalition-building to accomplish his legislative goals.[1]

Walter Edward Fauntroy was born in Washington, DC, on February 6, 1933, the fourth of seven children of Ethel (Vine) and William Fauntroy, a U.S. Patent Office clerk. Fauntroy graduated from Dunbar High School in Washington, DC, in 1952 and earned a B.A. from Virginia Union University in 1955. On August 3, 1957, Fauntroy married Dorothy Simms. The couple had a son, Marvin, and later adopted a baby girl, Melissa Alice. After receiving a bachelor of divinity degree from Yale University Divinity School in 1958, Fauntroy became pastor of Washington's New Bethel Baptist Church.[2]

Through his ministry and his devotion to improving conditions for African Americans, Fauntroy, like many other black clerics of the era, became actively involved in the civil rights movement. Impressed by the DC minister's organizational skills and commitment to the movement, civil rights leader Martin Luther King, Jr., appointed Fauntroy director of the Washington bureau of the Southern Christian Leadership Conference (SCLC).[3] After honing his political skills as the SCLC's lobbyist in Congress, Fauntroy urged President Lyndon B. Johnson and Congress to pass civil rights legislation. President Johnson subsequently appointed Fauntroy vice chairman of the 1966 White House Conference "To Fulfill These

Rights," which focused on recommendations for improving the lives of African Americans after the passage of the landmark 1964 Civil Rights Act.[4] Fauntroy also served as the District of Columbia coordinator for the March on Washington for Jobs and Freedom on August 28, 1963. In preparation for the Washington march, Fauntroy and other leading civil rights activists, such as future Representative Andrew Young of Georgia, assisted King with his famous "I Have a Dream" speech. When Fauntroy learned that King would have only eight minutes to speak, he indignantly told his mentor, "They can't limit you—the spokesman of the movement—to that."[5] Fauntroy also helped organize the 1965 march from Selma, to Montgomery, Alabama, and was national coordinator of the 1968 Poor People's Campaign, an extended vision of King's plan to draw attention to poverty and force government action to combat it.[6]

Fauntroy centered many of his civil rights, antipoverty, and neighborhood revitalization activities on the nation's capital as the founder and director of the Shaw Urban Renewal Project, an economic initiative to restore the historic African-American neighborhood of Washington, DC, where Fauntroy grew up.[7] He served as vice chair of the District of Columbia Council from 1967 until he resigned in 1969 to spend time with the Model Inner City Community Organization, a neighborhood planning agency he founded with other Washington ministers. The following year, Fauntroy's political fortunes advanced when Congress passed the District of Columbia Delegate Act. The legislation reinstituted a nonvoting Delegate to represent the nation's capital in the House of Representatives, a position last held by Norton Chipman from 1871 to 1875.[8] In the crowded January 1971 Democratic primary, Fauntroy ran on a platform of instituting home rule for the District, eliminating job

discrimination for African Americans, and providing federally funded daycare.[9] With the help of campaign appearances by Coretta Scott King, the widow of the famous civil rights leader, and strong support from local black churches, Fauntroy orchestrated a surprising upset over six opponents, garnering 44 percent of the vote.[10] Overwhelmingly elected in the March general election with a 59 percent majority, Fauntroy routed his closest opponent, Republican John Nevius, a white lawyer with a strong civil rights record, to become the first African American to represent the District of Columbia.[11] "It was an exhilarating experience in learning the ways of politics, in being Americans for the first time," Fauntroy exclaimed after his victory.[12] Fauntroy won by comfortable margins in his subsequent re-election bids in the predominantly African-American and Democratic city.[13]

Sworn in to the House of Representatives on April 19, 1971, Delegate Fauntroy immediately began work on accomplishing his major campaign promise: achieving home rule for the District of Columbia. Although as a Delegate Fauntroy was unable to vote on the House Floor, he could serve on and vote in committees and introduce legislation. Fauntroy used his seat on the District of Columbia Committee—a position he retained throughout his tenure in the House—to build support among his colleagues and in the capital for a measure that would provide self-government for the residents of the District, who had lacked the ability to choose their own municipal government since a failed experiment during the Reconstruction Era.[14] "The election of a congressman is but the first step toward full self-government for the District," Fauntroy commented. "The immediate next step is that of organizing the people for political action to make their congressman effective."[15] Only a few months after becoming a Delegate, Fauntroy introduced a home rule bill to expand the independence of the District by removing some of Congress's oversight authority and allowing DC residents to select their own local officials.[16] He also ran as a "favorite-son" candidate in the 1972 DC Democratic presidential primary in a symbolic move to draw attention to home rule and issues affecting Black Americans. After winning the election, he threw his support (the 15 votes of the Washington, DC, delegation) behind the eventual Democratic nominee, George McGovern, who endorsed much of Fauntroy's DC agenda. "We must learn to use our power and stop relying on simple benevolence," Fauntroy declared.[17]

In 1972, the defeat of District of Columbia Committee Chairman John L. McMillan of South Carolina, a longtime opponent of home rule, removed a critical obstacle from the pursuit of self-government for the nation's capital. Fauntroy, Charles Diggs, Jr., of Michigan, the new chairman of the District of Columbia Committee, and the Congressional Black Caucus (CBC) helped pass the District of Columbia Self-Government and Governmental Reorganization Act in December 1973. The bill gave the District limited self-rule, permitting citizens to elect a mayor and a city council.[18] Although pleased with this progress, Fauntroy continued his efforts to attain greater independence for the District from the federal government. In 1978 he helped guide a proposed constitutional amendment through the House to give the District full representation in both bodies of Congress—one of his most significant accomplishments. The vote "reaffirmed my great faith in the American people," asserted an elated Fauntroy.[19] Despite his intense lobbying efforts, which included nationwide speaking tours, the DC Voting Rights Amendment failed to achieve ratification, with only 16 of the necessary 38 states approving the measure by 1985. Some critics blamed the DC Delegate for neglecting to muster enough support for the amendment and for causing a public backlash against the legislation after a controversial meeting with Palestine Liberation Organization leader Yasser Arafat.[20] "The District is too urban, too liberal, too Democratic and too black," Fauntroy remarked bitterly after the defeat of the proposed amendment.[21] Undaunted by the earlier failure, Fauntroy and Senator Edward M. (Ted) Kennedy of Massachusetts each introduced (unsuccessful) legislation in 1987 that would have granted the District of Columbia statehood and full representation without amending the Constitution.[22]

As chairman of several subcommittees on the District of Columbia Committee, Fauntroy vowed to improve conditions for his many poor constituents, focusing on affordable housing and antidrug legislation. He introduced a measure to convert vacant land on the former Bolling-Anacostia military complex into affordable housing and hospitals.[23] Fauntroy criticized urban renewal efforts in the nation's capital that adversely affected its many impoverished black residents. In 1978 he compiled a housing and community proposal to address common neighborhood problems such as housing shortages, abandoned buildings, resident displacement, and inadequate community services.[24] He also cosponsored antidrug bills as a member of the House Select Committee on Narcotics and a resolution to create an organization to battle regional drug trafficking.[25]

During his tenure in the House, Fauntroy served on the Banking and Currency Committee (later named the Banking, Currency, and Housing Committee and subsequently the Banking, Finance, and Urban Affairs Committee) from the 93rd to the 101st Congresses (1973–1991) and chaired three of its subcommittees, including the influential Domestic Monetary Policy Subcommittee.[26] He also served on the Select Assassinations Committee during the 94th and 95th Congresses (1975–1979).

Despite his nonvoting status in the House, Fauntroy played an active role in the CBC, seeking to use his position to highlight issues concerning African Americans, both in the District and nationwide. As chairman of the CBC during the 97th Congress (1981–1983), he criticized the economic and social policies of President Ronald W. Reagan, insisting that they undermined progress made during the civil rights movement.[27] In 1977, Fauntroy sought to increase the CBC's effectiveness by founding the National Black Leadership Roundtable (NBLR), a group of national organizations encompassing black civil rights, business, and labor leaders, to promote the public policy

agenda of the caucus. Under Fauntroy's direction, the NBLR successfully promoted the election of more African Americans to federal office.[28]

Fauntroy's legislative interests extended beyond domestic affairs, and he used his position in the House to effect change internationally. The DC Delegate made headlines on November 21, 1984, along with Mary Frances Berry, a member of the U.S. Commission on Civil Rights, and Randall Robinson, director of the foreign policy advocacy organization TransAfrica. The group was arrested for refusing to vacate the premises of the South African Embassy in Washington, DC, while protesting the imprisonment of several South African labor and civil rights leaders. Their arrest, the first of many until the passage of comprehensive economic sanctions by the United States against South Africa in 1986, sparked a national wave of civil disobedience. "We knew we had to humble ourselves and go to jail," explained Fauntroy after his highly publicized arrest.[29] The three subsequently launched the Free South Africa Movement (FSAM) to publicize racial inequality in South Africa and to pressure the Reagan administration into stiffening its foreign policy toward the apartheid regime.[30] Fauntroy drew upon his experience as a civil rights leader to help orchestrate a relentless campaign of peaceful demonstrations outside the South African Embassy that included many high-profile figures, such as Members of Congress, civil rights leaders, and celebrities.[31] In January 1986, he joined five congressional colleagues on a tour of South Africa to assess the effects of limited economic sanctions imposed by the United States during the first session of the 99th Congress (1985–1987).[32] Fauntroy continued his work with the FSAM and the CBC to pressure Congress to pass stronger sanctions against South Africa. On October 2, 1986, the Comprehensive Anti-Apartheid Act became law after the House and Senate mustered enough votes to override a veto by President Reagan.[33]

Fauntroy also spent considerable time during his congressional career highlighting human rights violations in Haiti and promoting economic development for the impoverished country.[34] Believing he should use his position to focus on international affairs as well as domestic affairs, Fauntroy responded to critics who argued he spent too much time away from the nation's capital. "When I sought the office of delegate, I ran on the theme that once elected I would build a network of friends for the District, and my traveling is for the purpose of strengthening that network."[35]

Fauntroy opted to leave his safe congressional seat to run for mayor of Washington, DC, in 1990. While the longtime Delegate indicated his decision to run surfaced from a desire to heal a polarized and beleaguered city, some speculated he had become frustrated with his limited authority as a Delegate. Fauntroy joined a crowded field in the Democratic primary to replace Mayor Marion Barry, who had been arrested, imprisoned, and later entered a rehabilitation facility to be treated for drug addiction. During the campaign, Fauntroy had difficulty convincing his political base that he understood the problems facing the District—a criticism that stemmed from his global approach to politics as a Delegate. "The people do not know me," Fauntroy admitted. "They don't know what I do on the Hill."[36] After winning less than 10 percent of the vote in the Democratic primary, Fauntroy noted, "I am disappointed, of course, that I did not win and that I will not have the opportunity to personally implement solutions to some of the most serious problems facing any city in this nation."[37] In 1995, Fauntroy was sentenced to two years of probation for filing a false financial report in 1988 when he served in Congress.[38] Fauntroy currently serves as pastor of the New Bethel Baptist Church in Washington, DC—a position he held while in Congress —and has been involved in a series of community projects.

FOR FURTHER READING

"Fauntroy, Walter Edward," *Biographical Directory of the U.S. Congress, 1774–Present*, http://bioguide.congress.gov/scripts/biodisplay.pl?index=F000046.

MANUSCRIPT COLLECTION

The George Washington University, Special Collections, Gelman Library (Washington, DC). *Papers:* ca. 1963–1991, 681 boxes. The papers of Walter Fauntroy include materials generated during his 39 years of community service. The collection includes 623 boxes that have not been processed, and portions may be restricted. A finding aid for the papers is available in the repository.

NOTES

1   Martha M. Hamilton, "Outspoken Fauntroy Manner Changes in His Second Term," 15 July 1973, *Washington Post*: B1.

2   "Walter E. Fauntroy," *Contemporary Black Biography* (Detroit, MI: Gale Research Inc., 1996); Marcia Slacum Greene, "Fauntroys Welcome New Baby," 2 June 1990, *Washington Post*: B3; Shirley Washington, *Outstanding African Americans of Congress* (Washington, DC: U.S. Capitol Historical Society, 1998): 29. For more information on Delegate Walter Fauntroy, see http://www.walterfauntroy.com/home.html (accessed 4 December 2007).

3   For more on King's early years in the civil rights movement, see Taylor Branch, *Parting the Waters: America in the King Years, 1954–1963* (New York: Simon and Schuster, 1988).

4   Cortez Rainey, "Walter E. Fauntroy," in Jesse Carney Smith, ed., *Notable Black American Men* (Detroit, MI: Gale Research Inc., 1998): 397 (hereinafter referred to as *NBAM*); Washington, *Outstanding African Americans of Congress*: 30; Robert E. Baker, "Civil Rights Talks Begin Here Today," 1 June 1966, *Washington Post*: A1.

5   Stephen B. Oates, *Let the Trumpet Sound: The Life of Martin Luther King, Jr.* (New York: Harper & Row, 1982): 256.

6   "Fauntroy, Walter," *Current Biography, 1979* (New York: H. W. Wilson and Company, 1979): 124–127.

7   Willard Clopton Jr., "$18 Million Grant Goes to Shaw Area," 24 October 1966, *Washington Post*: A1.

8   Michael Fauntroy, "District of Columbia Delegates to Congress," 4 April 2001, Report RS208785, Congressional Research Service, Library of Congress, Washington, DC; "At the Starting Gate for the Delegate Race," 25 September 1970, *Washington Post*: A24. The position of House Delegate was previously reserved for territories that were likely to become states. The District of Columbia Act launched a new trend of creating Delegates for areas without statehood on the legislative horizon: the District of Columbia (1970), the U.S. Virgin Islands and Guam (1972), and American Samoa (1978).

9   "Fauntroy Plans Plank on Job Bias," 17 October 1970, *Washington Post*: E2; Washington, *Outstanding African Americans of Congress*: 30.

10   "Delegate Hopefuls Push Hard as Campaigning Nears End," 9 January 1971, *Washington Post*: B1; R. W. Apple, Jr., "Dr. King Aide Wins Capital Primary," 14 January 1971, *New York Times*: 24.

11   Washington, *Outstanding African Americans of Congress*: 30; R. W. Apple, Jr., "Black Minister Wins Election as House Delegate for Capital," 24 March 1971, *New York Times*: 24.

12   "Fauntroy Exhilarated Over Victory," 24 March 1971, *Washington Post*: A10.

13   "Election Statistics, 1920 to Present," available at http://clerk.house.gov/member_info/electionInfo/index.html.

14   The mayor and the city council of the District of Columbia were appointed by the President before the passage of the District of Columbia Self-Government and Governmental Reorganization Act. See, for example, Washington, *Outstanding African Americans of Congress*: 30.

15   Joseph D. Whitaker, "Fauntroy, Negro Congressmen Urge Nixon to Back Home Rule," 26 March 1971, *Washington Post*: A6.

16   "Fauntroy Introduces Home Rule Bill," 30 June 1971, *Washington Post*: A7.

17   R. W. Apple, Jr., "Black in the Capital to Enter Primary," 8 December 1971, *New York Times*: 26; Richard E. Prince, "Fauntroy May Scrap 'Favorite-Son Strategy,'" 25 May 1972, *Washington Post*: B1; *Current Biography, 1979*: 126.

18   "After 8 Years, House Will Weigh District of Columbia Home Rule," 8 October 1973, *New York Times*: 22; "Home Rule Bill for Washington Signed," 25 December 1973, *Los Angeles Times*: 4.

19   "House Approves Full Vote Rights on Hill for DC," 3 March 1978, *Washington Post*: A1.

20   Jacqueline Trescott, "Walter Fauntroy—His Days of Trial," 7 November 1979, *Los Angeles Times*: C8; Rainey "Walter E. Fauntroy," *NBAM*: 398.

21   Barbara Gamarekians, "A Legislator With Statehood on His Mind," 30 November 1986, *New York Times*: 77.

22   Eric Pianin, "Fauntroy Renews Bid for DC Statehood," 8 January 1987, *Washington Post*: D7.

23   David R. Boldt, "Fauntroy Challenges Nixon to Build Housing at Bolling," 5 January 1971, *Washington Post*: B4; *Current Biography, 1979*: 126.

24   Patricia Camp, "Fauntroy Heckled on DC Housing Plan," 12 May 1978, *Washington Post*: B2.

25   Sandra Sugawara, "Lawmakers Propose Metropolitan Drug Authority," 7 June 1985, *Washington Post*: C7.

26   Gamarekians, "A Legislator With Statehood on His Mind."

27 "Congressional Black Caucus Picks Fauntroy as Chairman," 13 December 1980, *Washington Post*: A28; Rainey "Walter E. Fauntroy," *NBAM*: 399.

28 Gamarekians, "A Legislator With Statehood on His Mind"; William L. Clay, *Just Permanent Interests: Black Americans in Congress, 1870–1991* (New York: Amistad Press, Inc., 1992): 269–272. According to the National Black Leadership Roundtable Web site, Fauntroy currently serves as the chairman of the organization, see http://www.nblr.us/index.html (accessed 4 December 2007).

29 Eleanor Holmes Norton, then a Georgetown University law professor, and Fauntroy's eventual successor as DC Delegate, accompanied Fauntroy, Berry, and Robinson to the South African Embassy but left prior to the group's arrest to notify the press of their protest. Dorothy Gilliam, "DC Sit-In Led the Way," 9 September 1985, *Washington Post*: A1; "Capital's House Delegate Held in Embassy Sit-In," 22 November 1984, *New York Times*: B1.

30 Kenneth Bredemeier and Michael Marriott, "Fauntroy Arrested in Embassy," 22 November 1984, *Washington Post*: 1; Courtland Milloy, "Blacks Form 'Free S. Africa Movement,'" 24 November 1984, *Washington Post*: C1; "Capital's House Delegate Held in Embassy Sit-In." For more information on the formation of the Free South Africa Movement, see Robert Kinloch Massie, *Loosing*

the Bonds (New York: Nan A. Talese/Doubleday, 1997): 558–560.

31 Ed Bruske, "Fauntroy: District's Man in Congress," 1 September 1986, *Washington Post*: B1; Massie, *Loosing the Bonds*: 559–560.

32 Allister Sparks, "Six Congressmen Begin Tour of S. Africa," 8 January 1986, *Washington Post*: A1; Eric Pianin, "DC Statehood Fauntroy's Big Loss," 12 November 1987, *Washington Post*: C1.

33 Helen Dewar, "Congress Votes Sanctions on South Africa," 13 September 1986, *Washington Post*: A1; Edward Walsh, "House Easily Overrides Veto of South Africa Sanctions," 30 September 1986, *Washington Post*: A1; "Senate Overrides Reagan's Veto of Sanctions 78 to 21," 2 October 1986, *Los Angeles Times*: A1.

34 "Fauntroy Faults Haiti," 13 April 1985, *Washington Post*: B6; "Fauntroy Explores Financial Aid for Haiti Development," 7 April 1985, *Washington Post*: C2.

35 Bruske, "Fauntroy: District's Man in Congress."

36 R. H. Melton, "Fauntroy's Giant Leap of Faith," 5 March 1990, *Washington Post*: E1; R. H. Melton, "Underdog Reprising a Familiar Role," 28 August 2000, *Washington Post*: A1.

37 Mary Ann French and Keith Harriston, "Fauntroy Sanguine in the Face of Resounding Defeat," 12 September 1990, *Washington Post*: A21.

38 "Former Delegate to Congress Is Sentenced," 10 August 1995, *New York Times*: 16A.

"THE ELECTION OF A
CONGRESSMAN IS BUT THE FIRST
STEP TOWARD FULL
SELF-GOVERNMENT FOR
THE DISTRICT," FAUNTROY
COMMENTED. "THE IMMEDIATE
NEXT STEP IS THAT OF
ORGANIZING THE PEOPLE FOR
POLITICAL ACTION TO MAKE
THEIR CONGRESSMAN EFFECTIVE."

Yvonne Brathwaite Burke
1932–

UNITED STATES REPRESENTATIVE ★ 1973–1979
DEMOCRAT FROM CALIFORNIA

Yvonne Brathwaite Burke was a rising star in California and national politics years before she won a seat in the U.S. House. In 1966, she became the first African-American woman elected to the California assembly. At the 1972 Democratic National Convention she served as vice chair of the platform committee, gaining national television exposure. That same year she became the first black woman from California (and one of only three black women ever) elected to the House. Her meteoric career continued with a prime appointment to the Appropriations Committee and her election as the first woman chair of the Congressional Black Caucus (CBC). But Burke's most notable distinction in the eyes of much of the public occurred in 1973, when she became the first Congresswoman to give birth and be granted maternity leave while serving in Congress.

Perle Yvonne Watson was born on October 5, 1932, in Los Angeles, California, the only child of James Watson, a custodian at the MGM film studios, and Lola (Moore) Watson, a real estate agent in East Los Angeles. Yvonne (she rejected the name Perle) grew up in modest circumstances and at first was enrolled in a public school.[1] At age four she was transferred to a model school for exceptional children. Watson became the vice president of her class at Manual Arts High School in Los Angeles. She enrolled at the University of California at Berkeley in 1949 but transferred to the University of California at Los Angeles, where she earned a B.A. in political science in 1953. She became only the second black woman to be admitted to the University of California School of Law, earning her J.D. and passing the California bar in 1956. After graduating, she found that no law firms would hire an African-American woman and, consequently, entered into her own private practice, specializing in civil, probate, and real estate law. In addition to her private practice,

she served as the state's deputy corporation commissioner and as a hearing officer for the Los Angeles Police Commission. In 1957, Yvonne Watson wed mathematician Louis Brathwaite. The marriage ended in divorce in 1964. Yvonne Brathwaite organized a legal defense team for Watts rioters in 1965 and was named by Governor Edmond Brown to the McCone Commission, which investigated the conditions that led to the riot. A year later she won election to the California assembly. She eventually chaired the assembly's committee on urban development and won re-election in 1968 and 1970.[2]

Brathwaite ultimately grew impatient with the pace of social legislation in the California assembly and, when court-mandated reapportionment created a new congressional district, decided to enter the race for the seat. The district encompassed much of southwest Los Angeles, was nearly 75 percent registered Democrats, and had a large African-American constituency. In the Democratic primary, Brathwaite faced Billy Mills, a popular African-American Los Angeles city councilman. She amassed 54 percent of the vote to defeat Mills and three other challengers. Just days after the primary, on June 14, 1972, Yvonne Brathwaite married businessman William Burke, who had been an aide to Mills. Less than a month later, Yvonne Brathwaite Burke garnered national media attention as the vice chair of the Democratic National Convention in Miami Beach that nominated George McGovern. She spent much of the convention controlling the gavel during the long and sometimes-raucous platform deliberations, eventually helping to pass revised rules that gave minorities and young voters a greater voice in shaping party policy.[3]

The convention exposure only added to Burke's luster, though it was hardly a factor in the general election that November in the heavily Democratic district. Burke faced 31-year-old Gregg Tria, a recent law school graduate, who

ran on an anti-busing and anti-abortion platform. Burke defeated Tria easily, winning 73 percent of the vote. In Burke's subsequent re-election bids in 1974 and 1976, she won 80 percent of the vote against Republicans Tom Neddy and Edward Skinner, respectively.[4]

In Burke's first term during the 93rd Congress (1973–1975), she received assignments on two committees: Public Works and Interior and Insular Affairs. She gave up both of those panels in December 1974 to accept a seat on the powerful Appropriations Committee, where she served for the duration of her House career. Burke's appointment to the panel occurred at a time when African Americans began to serve simultaneously on the most influential House committees: Appropriations (Burke and Louis Stokes of Ohio), Ways and Means (Charles Rangel of New York and Harold E. Ford of Tennessee), and Rules (Andrew Young of Georgia).[5] In the 94th Congress (1975–1977), Burke was appointed chair of the Select Committee on the House Beauty Shop, an honorific position that rotated among the women Members.

Burke made national headlines again as a freshman Member when she revealed in the spring of 1973 that she was expecting a child. When Autumn Roxanne Burke was born on November 23, 1973, Yvonne Burke became the first Member to give birth while serving in Congress, "a dubious honor," she observed.[6] The House subsequently granted Burke maternity leave, another first in congressional history.[7] The Burkes also had a daughter, Christine, from William Burke's previous marriage.

Representative Burke recognized that the civil rights struggle had shifted to a phase in which less overt discrimination must be confronted. "The kinds of things we faced in my generation were easy to understand," she explained. "Your parents said, 'They don't let you sit down here, they don't let you go to that place.' Everybody knew. But now it is so complex, so frustrating to young people when they are led to believe that everything is fine, yet at the same time it is not fine."[8] Minority interests were always at the forefront of Burke's legislative agenda. During her first term in office she fought the Richard

M. Nixon administration's efforts to unravel some of the programs established under Lyndon B. Johnson's Great Society, particularly the Office of Economic Opportunity (OEO), which Nixon stripped of many of its programs. One of Burke's earliest House Floor speeches defended the OEO.[9]

Burke also fought for equal opportunities for minority-owned businesses in the construction of the Trans-Alaskan Pipeline by adding two amendments to the bill that provided the framework for the nearly 800-mile-long project. One amendment required that affirmative action programs be created to award some pipeline contracts to minority businesses. A later version of that amendment would require that any project funded with federal dollars must provide affirmative action incentives, reminiscent of the legislative technique used by Adam Clayton Powell, Jr., of New York, which involved the attachment of antidiscrimination riders to legislation involving federal funding. "The construction of the Alaskan Pipeline will create substantial employment opportunities, and it therefore seems desirable and appropriate to extend the existing programs for non-discrimination and equal employment opportunity" to that project, Burke told colleagues on the House Floor.[10] Burke's second amendment to the bill, the Buy America Act, required that the materials to construct the pipeline be manufactured in the United States "to the maximum extent feasible."[11] Despite voicing strong concerns about potential environmental problems, Burke continued to back the Alaska pipeline project, believing it would help the impending energy crisis in the United States.[12]

In the House, Burke earned a reputation as a legislator who avoided confrontation and controversy yet worked determinedly behind the scenes to effect changes she believed were important. "I don't believe in grand-standing but in the poverty areas, if there is something we need, then I'll go after it," she explained.[13] Using her experience as a former state legislator in the California assembly, Burke chose her positions carefully and usually refrained from partisan rhetoric in debates. She also seemed to take to heart the advice of former President Johnson, who had counseled her as a freshman Member, "Don't talk so much on the House Floor."[14]

With quiet determination, Representative Burke supported most major feminist issues and joined the Congressional Women's Caucus when it was founded in 1977, serving as the group's first treasurer.[15] She was part of a successful effort to extend the time limit for ratification of the Equal Rights Amendment by an additional three years.[16] That same year, the California Representative introduced the Displaced Homemakers Act, which authorized the creation of job training centers for women entering the labor market, particularly middle-aged, self-supporting women who were re-entering the job market after an absence of many years. The purpose of the bill, which also provided health and financial counseling, was "to help displaced homemakers make it through a readjustment period so that they may have the opportunity to become productive, self-sufficient members of society," Burke explained.[17] In 1977, she vigorously criticized the Hyde Amendment, which prohibited the use of federal Medicaid funds for abortions. "The basic premise which we cannot overlook is that if the Government will not pay for an indigent woman's abortion, she cannot afford to go elsewhere," Burke wrote in a *New York Times* op-ed piece.[18] In 1978, Burke introduced a bill to prohibit pregnancy-related discrimination in the workplace, particularly employer policies that kept women out of their jobs for long periods before and after childbirth.[19]

Despite her prominent committee assignments and her role as chair of the CBC, which she assumed in 1976, Representative Burke never seemed completely at home on Capitol Hill. Publicly, she expressed her desire to have a more direct and administrative effect on policy than the demands of her job allowed her. However, associates believed that by 1977 the distance from her husband and her 4-year-old daughter in Los Angeles and the 3,000-mile biweekly commute had left her exhausted and unhappy.[20]

In 1978, Burke declined to run for re-election to the 96th Congress (1979–1981), in order to campaign for the office of California attorney general, the chief law enforcement position for the state (and a position no woman had ever held in any state government). She won the Democratic nomination but lost to Republican State Senator George Deukmejian in the general election. In June 1979, California Governor Jerry Brown appointed Burke to the Los Angeles County board of supervisors, making her the first black person ever to sit on the panel. In 1980, she lost her bid to a new four-year term and returned to private law practice. In 1984, Burke was the vice chair of the Los Angeles Olympics Organizing Committee. Burke became the first African American to win outright election as an L.A. County supervisor in 1992, defeating future Representative Diane Watson by a narrow margin.[21] A year later, she became the first woman and the first member of a racial minority group to chair the board. Burke has been re-elected three times, chairing the board of supervisors in 2002–2003 and, most recently, in 2007–2008. She resides in her native Los Angeles.[22]

FOR FURTHER READING

"Burke, Yvonne Brathwaite," *Biographical Directory of the United States Congress, 1774–Present*, http://bioguide. congress.gov/scripts/biodisplay.pl?index=B001102.

Gray, Pamela Lee. "Yvonne Brathwaite Burke: The Congressional Career of California's First Black Congresswoman, 1972–1978." Ph.D. diss., University of Southern California, 1987.

MANUSCRIPT COLLECTIONS

University of California (Berkley, CA), The Bancroft Library. *Oral History:* 1982, 46 pages. The title of the interview is "New Arenas of Black Influence." The interview includes a discussion of Representative Burke's political offices, including her drive for social legislation, her entry into Democratic Party politics, and her tenure in the California assembly during Governor Ronald W. Reagan's administration, as well as a discussion about minorities and women.

University of Southern California (Los Angeles, CA), Regional Cultural History Collection, Department of Special Collections, Doheny Memorial Library. *Papers:* 1966–1980, 452 feet. Correspondence, photographs, sound recordings, and memorabilia relating to Representative Burke's years in the California assembly, U.S. Congress, and Los Angeles County board of supervisors. Also included are materials relating to her campaign for attorney general of California. Some restrictions pertain to the collection. A finding aid is available in the repository.

NOTES

1   Leroy F. Aarons, "Legislator With a Subtle Touch," 22 October 1972, *Washington Post*: K1.

2   "Yvonne Brathwaite Burke," *Notable Black American Women*, Book 1 (Detroit, MI: Gale Research: 1992).

3   Leroy F. Aarons, "That Woman in the Chair Aims for Hill," 14 July 1972, *Washington Post*: A8.

4   "Election Statistics, 1920 to Present," available at http://clerk. house.gov/member_info/electionInfo/index.html.

5   "Committee Sizes Shift in the House," 13 December 1974, *Washington Post*: A2.

6   "Rep. Burke: 'A Dubious Honor,'" 5 July 1973, *Washington Post*: C7; "7-lb. 9-oz. Girl for Rep. Burke," 24 November 1973, *New York Times*: 19.

7   "Congressional First," 24 November 1973, *Washington Post*: D3.

8   Yvonne Burke, "'The World I Want for My Child,'" 27 March 1974, *Christian Science Monitor*: 20. This is an op-ed piece based on excerpts of an *Ebony* article from March 1974 that Burke had authored.

9   *Congressional Record*, House, 93rd Cong., 1st sess. (31 January 1973): 2835–2836.

10 *Congressional Record*, House, 93rd Cong., 1st sess. (2 August 1973): 27655.

11 Ibid., 27710; "Trade Proposals Causing Concern," 3 September 1973, *New York Times*: 23.

12 *Congressional Record*, House, 93rd Cong., 1st sess. (2 August 1973): 27653–27655.

13 "2 Black Women Head for House," 7 October 1972, *New York Times*: 18.

14 Dorothy Gilliam, "He'd Have Said, Go 'Head,'" 25 January 1973, *Washington Post*: C1.

15 Irwin Gertzog, *Congressional Women: Their Recruitment, Integration, and Behavior* (Westport, CT: Praeger, 1995): 186.

16 *Congressional Record*, House, 95th Cong., 2nd sess. (15 August 1978): 26226–26232.

17 *Congressional Record*, House, 94th Cong., 2nd sess. (25 May 1976): 15449–15450; *Congressional Record*, House, 94th Cong., 1st sess. (21 October 1975): 33482–33483.

18 Yvonne Brathwaite Burke, "Again, 'Back-Alley and Self-Induced Abortions,'" 22 August 1977, *New York Times*: 23.

19 *Congressional Record*, House, 95th Cong., 2nd sess. (18 July 1978): 21442.

20 Lacey Fosburgh, "Women's Status a Key Factor in Race by Rep. Burke," 13 May 1978, *New York Times*: 10.

21 "Ex-Lawmaker Seems Victor in Los Angeles," 22 November 1992, *New York Times*: 29.

22 "Biography of the Honorable Yvonne B. Burke," at http://burke. lacounty.gov/bio.htm (accessed 1 March 2008).

In the House, Burke earned
a reputation as a legislator
who avoided confrontation
and controversy yet worked
determinedly. . . . "I don't
believe in grand-standing but
in the poverty areas, if there
is something we need, then
I'll go after it," she explained.

Barbara Jordan
1936–1996

UNITED STATES REPRESENTATIVE ★ 1973–1979
DEMOCRAT FROM TEXAS

Barbara Jordan emerged as an eloquent and powerful interpreter of the Watergate impeachment investigation at a time when many Americans despaired about the Constitution and the country. As one of the first African Americans elected from the Deep South since 1898 and the first black Congresswoman ever from that region, Jordan lent added weight to her message by her very presence on the House Judiciary Committee.

Barbara Charline Jordan was born in Houston, Texas, on February 21, 1936, one of three daughters of Benjamin M. Jordan and Arlyne Patten Jordan. Benjamin Jordan, a graduate of Tuskegee Institute, worked in a local warehouse before becoming pastor of Good Hope Missionary Baptist Church, which his family had long attended. Arlyne Jordan was an accomplished public speaker. Barbara Jordan was educated in the Houston public schools and graduated from Phyllis Wheatley High School in 1952. She earned a B.A. from Texas Southern University in 1956 and a law degree from Boston University in 1959. That same year she was admitted to the Massachusetts and Texas bars, and she began to practice law in Houston in 1960. To supplement her income (she worked temporarily out of her parents' home), Jordan was employed as an administrative assistant to a county judge.[1]

Barbara Jordan's political turning point occurred when she worked on the John F. Kennedy presidential campaign in 1960. She eventually helped manage a highly organized get-out-the-vote program that served Houston's 40 African-American precincts. In 1962 and 1964, Jordan ran for the Texas house of representatives but lost both times, so in 1966 she ran for the Texas senate when court-enforced redistricting created a constituency that consisted largely of minority voters. Jordan won, defeating a white liberal and becoming the first African-

American state senator in the U.S. since 1883 as well as the first black woman ever elected to that body.[2] The other 30 (male, white) senators received her coolly, but Jordan won them over as an effective legislator who pushed through bills establishing the state's first minimum wage law, antidiscrimination clauses in business contracts, and the Texas Fair Employment Practices Commission. On March 28, 1972, Jordan's peers elected her president *pro tempore* of the Texas legislature, making her the first black woman in America to preside over a legislative body. In seconding the nomination, one of Jordan's male colleagues on the other side of the chamber stood, spread his arms open, and said, "What can I say? Black is beautiful."[3] One of Jordan's responsibilities as president *pro tempore* was to serve as acting governor when the governor and lieutenant governor were out of the state. When Jordan filled that largely ceremonial role on June 10, 1972, she became the first black chief executive in the nation.

In 1971, Jordan entered the race for the Texas congressional seat encompassing downtown Houston. The district had been redrawn after the 1970 Census and was composed of a predominantly African-American and Hispanic-American population. In the 1972 Democratic primary, Jordan faced Curtis Graves, another black state legislator, who attacked her for being too close to the white establishment. Jordan blunted Graves's charges with her legislative credentials. "I'm not going to Washington and turn things upside down in a day," she told supporters at a rally. "I'll only be one of 435. But the 434 will know I am there."[4] Jordan took the primary with 80 percent of the vote. In the general election, against Republican Paul Merritt, she won 81 percent of the vote. Along with Andrew Young of Georgia, Jordan became the first African American in the 20th century elected to Congress from the Deep South. In the next two campaign cycles, Jordan

overwhelmed her opposition, capturing 85 percent of the total vote in both general elections.[5]

Representative Jordan's political philosophy from her days in the state legislature led her to focus on local issues. Civil rights and women's rights activists sometimes criticized her when she chose to favor her community interests rather than theirs. She followed this pattern in the House. "I sought the power points," she once said. "I knew if I were going to get anything done, [the congressional and party leaders] would be the ones to help me get it done."[6] Jordan was reluctant to commit herself fully to any one interest group or caucus, such as the Congressional Black Caucus (CBC), of which she was a member. House women met informally too, but Jordan's attendance at those meetings was irregular, and she was noncommittal on most issues that were brought before the group. She was especially careful not to attach herself too closely to an agenda she had little control over that might impinge on her ability to navigate and compromise within the institutional power structure. "I am neither a black politician nor a woman politician," Jordan said in 1975. "Just a politician, a professional politician."[7]

In both her Texas legislative career and in the U.S. House, Jordan made the conscious decision to pursue power within the established system. One of her first moves in Congress was to establish relations with Members of the Texas delegation, which had strong institutional connections. Her attention to influence inside the House was demonstrated by where she sat in the House Chamber's large, theater-style seating arrangement. CBC members traditionally sat to the far left of the chamber, but Jordan chose to sit near the center aisle because she could hear better, be seen by the presiding officer, and save an open seat for colleagues who wanted to stop and chat. Her seating preference as well as her loyalty to the Texas delegation agitated fellow CBC members, but both were consistent with Jordan's model of seeking congressional influence.[8]

Jordan also believed that an important committee assignment, one where she would be unique because of her gender and race, would magnify her influence. Thus, she disregarded suggestions that she accept a seat on the Education and Labor Committee, and used her connection with Texan Lyndon Johnson—she had been his guest at the White House during her time as a state legislator—to secure a plum committee assignment on the Judiciary Committee. Securing former President Johnson's intercession with Wilbur Mills of Arkansas, the chairman of the Committee on Committees, she landed a seat on the Judiciary Committee, where she served for her three terms in the House. In the 94th and 95th Congresses (1975–1979), she was also assigned to the Committee on Government Operations.

It was as a freshman Member of the Judiciary Committee, however, that Jordan earned national recognition. In the summer of 1974, as the committee considered articles of impeachment against President Richard M. Nixon for crimes associated with the Watergate scandal, Jordan delivered opening remarks that shook the committee room and the large television audience tuned in to the proceedings. "My faith in the Constitution is whole, it is complete, it is total," Jordan said. "I am not going to sit here and be an idle spectator to the diminution, the subversion, the destruction of the Constitution." She then explained the reasoning behind her support of each of the five articles of impeachment against President Nixon. In conclusion, Jordan said that if her fellow committee members did not find the evidence compelling enough, "then perhaps the eighteenth-century Constitution should be abandoned to a twentieth-century paper shredder."[9] Reaction to Jordan's statement was overwhelming. Jordan recalled that people swarmed around her car after the hearings to congratulate her. Impressed by her articulate reasoning and her knowledge of the law, many people sent the Texas Representative letters of praise. One person even posted a message on a series of billboards in Houston: "Thank you, Barbara Jordan, for explaining the Constitution to us."[10] The Watergate impeachment hearings helped create Jordan's reputation as a respected national politician.

From her first days in Congress, Jordan encouraged colleagues to extend the federal protection of civil rights to more Americans. She introduced civil rights amendments to legislation authorizing law enforcement assistance grants and joined seven other Members on the Judiciary Committee in opposing Gerald R. Ford's nomination as Vice President, citing a mediocre civil rights record. In 1975, when Congress voted to extend the Voting Rights Act of 1965, Jordan sponsored legislation that broadened the provisions of the act to include Hispanic Americans, Native Americans, and Asian Americans. Although she voted for busing to enforce racial desegregation in public schools, she was one of the few African-American Members of Congress to question the utility of the policy.[11]

Jordan's talent as a speaker continued to contribute to her national profile. In 1976, she became the first woman and the first African-American keynote speaker at a Democratic National Convention. Appearing after a subdued speech by Ohio Senator John Glenn, Jordan energized the convention with her oratory. "We are a people in search of a national community," she told the delegates, "attempting to fulfill our national purpose, to create and sustain a society in which all of us are equal. . . . We cannot improve on the system of government, handed down to us by the founders of the Republic, but we can find new ways to implement that system and to realize our destiny."[12] Amid the historical perspective of the national bicentennial, and in the aftermath of the Vietnam War and Watergate, Jordan's message, like her commanding voice, resonated with Americans. She campaigned widely for Democratic presidential candidate James Earl (Jimmy) Carter, who defeated President Ford in the general election. Though Carter later interviewed Jordan for a Cabinet position, he did not offer her the position of U.S. Attorney General, the one post she said she would accept.

In 1978, downplaying reports about her poor health, Jordan declined to run for what would have been certain re-election to a fourth term, citing her "internal compass," which she said was pointing her "away from demands that are all consuming."[13] She also said she wanted to work more directly on behalf of her fellow Texans. Jordan was appointed the Lyndon Johnson Chair in National Policy at the LBJ School of Public Affairs at the University of Texas in Austin, where she taught until the early 1990s. She continued to lecture widely on national affairs. In 1988 and 1992, she delivered speeches at the Democratic National Convention. Her 1992 keynote address was delivered from a wheelchair while she was in the midst of a lengthy battle with multiple sclerosis. In 1994, President William J. (Bill) Clinton appointed her to lead the Commission on Immigration Reform, a bipartisan group that delivered its findings in September of that year. Jordan received nearly two dozen honorary degrees and, in 1990, was named to the National Women's Hall of Fame in Seneca, New York. She never married and carefully guarded her private life. Jordan died in Austin, Texas, on January 17, 1996, from pneumonia that was a complication of leukemia.

FOR FURTHER READING

Bryant, Ira Babington. *Barbara Charline Jordan: From the Ghetto to the Capital* (Houston: D. Armstrong, 1977).

Fenno, Richard F. *Going Home: Black Representatives and Their Constituents* (Chicago, IL: University of Chicago Press, 2003).

"Jordan, Barbara Charline," *Biographical Directory of the United States Congress, 1774–Present*, http://bioguide. congress.gov/scripts/biodisplay.pl?index=J000266.

Jordan, Barbara, and Shelby Hearon. *Barbara Jordan: A Self-Portrait* (Garden City, NY: Doubleday, 1979).

Rogers, Mary Beth. *Barbara Jordan: American Hero* (New York: Bantam Books, 1998).

MANUSCRIPT COLLECTIONS

Lyndon B. Johnson Library (Austin, TX). *Oral History:* March 28, 1984. 16 pages. Description in library.

Texas Southern University (Houston, TX). *Papers:* 1966–1996, 462 linear feet. The papers are divided into three major groups: State senate papers, U.S. House of Representatives papers, and personal papers. A finding aid is available in the repository and online.

NOTES

1   For information on Jordan's early life, see Barbara Jordan and Shelby Hearon, *Barbara Jordan: A Self-Portrait* (Garden City, NY: Doubleday, 1979) and Mary Beth Rogers, *Barbara Jordan: American Hero* (New York: Bantam Books, 1998).

2   *Current Biography, 1993* (New York: H. W. Wilson and Company, 1993): 291; Rogers, *Barbara Jordan.*

3   Richard Fenno, *Going Home: Black Representatives and Their Constituents* (Chicago: University of Chicago Press): 106–109.

4   Fenno, *Going Home*: 89–92.

5   "Election Statistics, 1920 to Present," available at http://clerk. house.gov/member_info/electionInfo/index.html.

6   Susan Tolchin, *Women in Congress* (Washington, DC: Government Printing Office, 1976): 96–97.

7   Fenno, *Going Home*: 106–109.

8   Ibid.

9   Quotations from Barbara Jordan and Shelby Hearon, "Barbara Jordan: A Self-Portrait," 7 January 1979, *Washington Post*: A1.

10   Jordan and Hearon, "Barbara Jordan: A Self-Portrait."

11   *Current Biography, 1993*: 291. See also Tolchin, *Women in Congress*: 96–97.

12   *Current Biography, 1993*: 292.

13   Ibid.

"I am neither a
black politician nor
a woman politician,"
Jordan said in 1975.
"Just a politician,
a professional politician."

Andrew Jackson Young, Jr.
1932–

UNITED STATES REPRESENTATIVE ★ 1973–1977
DEMOCRAT FROM GEORGIA

A senior aide to Martin Luther King, Jr., in the Southern Christian Leadership Conference (SCLC) during the 1960s, Andrew Young had a meditative temperament that shaped his views as a proponent of nonviolent resistance. By the time he was sworn in to Congress in 1973, Young was committed to bringing King's vision of civil rights to the nation and the world.[1] His experiences in the grass-roots politics of the civil rights movement and his diplomatic perspective allowed Young to take principled but pragmatic stands for his constituents.

Andrew Jackson Young, Jr., was born in New Orleans, Louisiana, to Andrew and Daisy Fuller Young. His father was a dentist and his mother was a schoolteacher. Andrew and his younger brother Walt "grew up as the only black children in a middle-class, predominantly Irish and Italian neighborhood" in New Orleans.[2] After graduating from Gilbert Academy in 1947, he attended Dillard University for one year and then transferred to Howard University in Washington, DC. Young earned a bachelor of science degree in biology in 1951. After graduating from Howard, Young considered a career in dentistry, but decided to pursue a career in the ministry instead. He attended the Hartford Theological Seminary in Hartford, Connecticut, earning a bachelor of divinity degree from Hartford in 1955, and was ordained a minister in the United Church of Christ. While at seminary, Young met his future wife, Jean Childs, a teacher, in 1952; after a brief courtship, they married on June 7, 1954. They had four children: Andrea, Lisa, Paula, and Andrew III. Two years after his wife died of cancer in 1994, Young married Carolyn Watson, an elementary school teacher.[3] After graduating from the seminary, Young served as a pastor, teacher, and civil rights activist in Marion, Alabama, and in Thomasville, and Beachton, Georgia, until he was invited to work in the Youth Work Division of the National Council of Churches in New York City, where he served as assistant director from 1957 to 1961. In 1961, Young returned to the South to participate in a voter education program sponsored by the United Church of Christ. He moved from New York to Atlanta and joined the SCLC.

Young organized a citizenship training program at the SCLC and collaborated with its members. By mid-1962, he began to work closely with Reverend King's staff, including civil rights leader Ralph Abernathy. Arrested for training students to register voters, King and Abernathy relied on Young to handle various duties while incarcerated in Albany, Georgia, for seven weeks. Young also served as a mediator between the SCLC and the Albany police. He subsequently volunteered to mediate between the SCLC and white southerners.[4] His effectiveness multiplied his responsibilities: in 1964, King named Young executive director of the SCLC. In his leadership role, Young provided logistical and legal support for prominent demonstrations and legislation such as the Civil Rights Act of 1964 and the Voting Rights Act of 1965.

When civil rights activist Julian Bond declined to run in the Democratic primary for the congressional district encompassing metropolitan Atlanta, Georgia, and its northern suburbs, Young resigned from the SCLC in 1970 to enter the race. Young suggested his campaign was motivated by the belief that he could initiate change from inside the political power structure, rather than from outside: "There just comes a time when *any* social movement has to come in off the street and enter politics."[5] He also benefited from a reapportionment that increased the number of black voters in the Atlanta district to almost 40 percent.[6] Young advocated what he called the New South Coalition, which he defined as "black votes, liberal votes, [and] white labor votes," acknowledging, "The problem is to involve those new white voters without

stirring up the dyed-in-the-wool racists in the process."[7] The New South Coalition was a base of electoral support that Young and other Atlanta politicians such as Mayor Sam Massell and future Mayor Maynard Jackson relied upon. In the Democratic primary, Young defeated Wyman C. Lowe, a white lawyer, in a runoff election, with 60 percent of the vote.[8] However, in the general election Young lost to two-term incumbent Republican Fletcher Thompson, who garnered 57 percent of the vote.[9] Young believed that "if a little more than half of the 35,000 registered . . . who did not vote had gone to the polls, he would have defeated the Republican incumbent."[10] After losing the general election, he chaired Atlanta's Community Relations Commission. This position allowed Young to acclimate himself with the political environment of the Fifth District and provided him greater exposure to local constituents.[11]

In 1972 Young orchestrated a second campaign for the House when the incumbent, Thompson, ran for the U.S. Senate. After defeating three primary opponents with 60 percent of the vote, he ran in the general election against Republican Rodney Cook, a veteran politician who served four terms in the Georgia house and also on the Atlanta board of aldermen.[12] Young opposed highway building and commercial development along the Chattahoochee River, both issues that resonated with Atlanta residents. He also described a four-point plan for improving public education that advocated federal and state grants instead of property taxes for funding, greater community involvement, a curriculum that was relevant to its urban constituents, and racial integration at all levels of the system.[13] Young ran a savvy campaign that incorporated aggressive voter registration and a media blitz. He also benefited from redistricting that added blacks while reducing the number of conservative white communities.[14] As a result, he achieved victory in the majority-white district, winning an estimated 95 percent of the black vote and 23 percent of the white vote.[15]

Young was the first black Representative from Georgia since Jefferson Long's election a century earlier. Young

and Barbara Jordan of Texas, also entering Congress for the first time, served as the first black Members from the Deep South since Reconstruction. "I consider this victory a little more than just being the first Black man to go to Congress from this deep South state," Young noted. "I see this as a city-wide mandate of people of both races working together to achieve the kind of representation that this area so badly needs."[16] During the 93rd Congress (1973–1975), he sought to improve public education and the social infrastructure of his district by serving on the Committee on Banking and Currency and its Subcommittee on Housing, Transportation, and Finance.[17]

During his first term, Young developed a record as a liberal advocate who supported governmental solutions to complications arising from social disfranchisement and promoted economic opportunities to benefit society.[18] One of his early initiatives was the Urban Mass Transportation Assistance Act, a program to facilitate the building of mass transit systems such as MARTA in Atlanta. Although a public transportation system would help all Atlanta businesses, the Georgia Representative argued that blacks would benefit directly from the $1 billion in federal support. He also insisted that residents should have a voice in such mass transit development.[19] Young ensured that he visited his district on weekends because he understood the importance of being visible to his constituents, especially newly enfranchised black voters. "[W]e're terribly cynical about people we don't see," Young once remarked. "We don't read too much about our men in the paper, so it's their physical presence and accessibility that counts."[20]

Young also joined the Congressional Black Caucus (CBC), and established a liberal voting record on domestic issues. He rejected cuts in domestic spending for the poor while supporting an increase in wages for workers in the public sector.[21] Young criticized the Richard M. Nixon administration's cuts in rural spending by linking the rural poverty with forced migration to urban centers and the problems that ensued. He also argued that both black and white middle-class families could suffer because of Nixon's economic policies, such as the federal moratorium on financing new housing.[22] Throughout his congressional career, both on his own and through the CBC, Young challenged the President to preserve legislation that benefited black constituents. He denounced the Nixon administration for an anti-busing bill and for failing to support mass transit, suggesting that some of these policies could hurt white middle-class constituents as much as black constituents.[23] In a CBC forum called the "True State of the Union," Young declared, "the overall goal [for Congress] must be to return the economy to a system which generates growth and production instead of death and destruction," and to "provide the aggressive leadership in rebuilding an economy of peace and justice."[24]

Young was able to work successfully with Republicans across the aisle by approaching them one-on-one to discuss political issues. Using negotiating skills he developed in the SCLC—dubbed "the Atlanta style"—he reached compromises with political allies and opponents.[25] Although Young clearly staked out his position as a Democratic liberal, he exhibited a shrewd political pragmatism that surprised his allies. It was noted that the Atlanta Representative, "avoids[s] the appearance of doctrinaire politics, while fulfilling the promise implicit in his progression from black civil rights leader to U.S. Congressman—the promise of effective representation for black as well as white citizens."[26] In October 1973, Young was the only CBC member who voted for Republican Minority Leader Gerald Ford of Michigan as Richard Nixon's Vice President, despite their political disagreements. Young explained, "I decided that here was a guy I wanted to give a chance. He was certainly better than a Reagan or any of the other alternatives at the time. Besides, Atlanta was going to need to work very closely with the next administration."[27]

Young developed a keen interest in U.S. foreign policy, especially concerning Africa, Asia, and Latin America. One of his earliest bills called for barring U.S. government contracts to companies that practiced racial discrimination in South Africa.[28] Young also made congressional visits to South Africa in 1972 and to Zambia, Kenya, and Nigeria in 1975.[29] He opposed the Byrd Amendment and testified before the Senate against the nomination of Nathaniel Davis for Assistant Secretary of State for African Affairs, due to his ambassadorship to Chile during a CIA-sponsored coup d'état against its president in 1973.[30]

In July 1973, Young and some southern Republicans successfully lobbied for a foreign aid bill provision that authorized the President to cancel aid that Portugal would use for military action in its African colonies. The House passed the amendment.[31] Young commented "[s]ome of the people I disagree with the most are some of the people I have come to respect the most . . . I can usually swing Democratic support, but unless you can get Republican support, nothing happens around here. I'm not going to ask them . . . to do anything that's going to hurt them politically and they know better than to ask me."[32]

Young won re-election to a second term with 72 percent of the vote in 1974.[33] In the 94th Congress (1975–1977), he became the first black Representative appointed to the House Rules Committee.[34] Young was also elected treasurer of the CBC and a member of its executive committee. In the summer of 1975 he worked to pass an extension of the Voting Rights Act of 1965. During deliberations on the House Floor, Young delivered a prepared statement that outlined the successes of the Voting Rights Act: increasing the number of black elected officials in the South, boosting black voter turnout, initiating monitoring by federal examiners and observers, and helping "language minorities," such as Latinos. He believed the Voting Rights Act was necessary to ensure minority participation in voting and argued that the act allowed politicians to appeal to a cross-section of society instead of only to a privileged few. "There was a time, when, in order to be elected from our part of the country, you had to present yourself at your worst," Young observed. "The man who was the chairman of my campaign . . . had to run as a segregationist when he wanted to run statewide." Following these deliberations, the House voted 341 to 70 to extend coverage of the Voting Rights Act.[35]

For the remainder of the Congress, Young continued to seek ways to improve the lives of his rural and urban constituents. He sponsored bills that outlined comprehensive health care plans and testified on behalf of bills that preserved food stamp programs and economic development in his district and in Africa. Young sponsored the Food Stamp Act of 1976, an act that proposed an overhaul of the program.[36]

During the early 1970s, Young became acquainted with James Earl (Jimmy) Carter, who was the governor of Georgia. Carter's sincerity and the men's mutual interest in promoting human rights formed the basis for a strong relationship. The Georgia Representative supported Carter's bid for the presidency in 1976 with a seconding speech at the Democratic National Convention in New York City and organized voter registration drives in urban areas for the successful Carter campaign.[37] In 1976, Young won re-election to a third term in the House with 80 percent of the vote.[38] On January 25, 1977, after accepting President Carter's offer to serve as U.S. Ambassador to the United Nations, Young resigned from Congress.

As the U.S. Ambassador to the United Nations, Young became the initial point of contact for the Carter administration's foreign policy in Africa and Asia. By using the network of contacts that had been developing since the 1950s, he played an active role in articulating Carter's position on human rights and liberal capitalism in Rhodesia, South Africa, and Angola.[39] Young resigned the ambassadorship in 1979 in the wake of severe criticism following his meeting with Zehdi Labib Terzi, the U.N. observer for the Palestine Liberation Organization. From 1982 to 1990, he served as mayor of Atlanta. He spent a great deal of time traveling nationally and internationally to build Atlanta's reputation as a financial competitor on the world stage. Young also succeeded in bringing the Olympic Games to the city in 1996. In 1990, he launched a gubernatorial bid, but lost to Lieutenant Governor Zell Miller, who garnered 65 percent of the vote in a runoff election.[40] He eventually formed a consulting firm dedicated to fostering economic development in Africa and the Caribbean.[41] In 2003, Young considered a run for the U.S. Senate, but declined because winning "would mean I would spend the next seven years in Washington, and Washington is not always the center of action."[42] Young remains involved with a number of consulting firms and nonprofit organizations in the Atlanta area.

FOR FURTHER READING

DeRoche, Andrew J. *Andrew Young: Civil Rights Ambassador* (Wilmington, DE: Scholarly Resources, 2003).

Gardner, Carl. *Andrew Young: A Biography* (New York: Drake, 1978).

Young, Andrew. *An Easy Burden: The Civil Rights Movement and the Transformation of America* (New York: HarperCollins, 1996).

"Young, Andrew Jackson, Jr.," *Biographical Directory of the U.S. Congress, 1774–Present,* http://bioguide.congress.gov/scripts/biodisplay.pl?index=Y000028.

MANUSCRIPT COLLECTION

The Auburn Avenue Research Library on African-American Culture and History (Atlanta, GA). *Papers:* Dates and amount unknown.

NOTES

1   Andrew J. DeRoche, *Andrew Young: Civil Rights Ambassador* (Wilmington, DE: Scholarly Resources, 2003): xi.

2   *Current Biography, 1977* (New York: H. W. Wilson Company, 1977): 449.

3   "Jean C. Young, 61, an Educator and Wife of Ex-Envoy to U.N.," 17 September 1994, *New York Times*: 12; Nadine Brozan, "Chronicle," 21 May 1996, *New York Times*: B5.

4   DeRoche, *Andrew Young*: 15–19.

5   Hamilton Bims, "A Southern Activist Goes to the House," *Ebony* 28 (February 1973): 84.

6   Because of the large number of black voters and liberal white voters, black political leaders in Atlanta believed a black candidate could win the seat. For a detailed discussion about antagonism between rural and urban southerners, see V.O. Key, *Southern Politics in State and Nation* (Knoxville: University of Tennessee Press, 1984): 378–382.

7   Bims, "A Southern Activist Goes to the House": 84. Young observed, "In 1970, when I ran and lost, we sent white volunteers into certain white areas. It didn't work. Many of the whites were as resentful of those kids as they would have been of black people banging on their doors. In 1972, we did it a little differently: more low-key, I suppose, and apparently, we succeeded."

8   Bruce Galphin, "Former King Aide Wins Runoff in Ga.," 24 September 1970, *Washington Post*: A2; Earl Caldwell, "Negro's Aides Optimistic on House Race in White-Dominated District in Atlanta." 9 August 1970, *New York Times*: 26.

9   *Almanac of American Politics, 1974* (Boston: Gambit Press, 1973): 232.

10   Kenneth Reich, "Black Vote Disappoints Ga. Candidate," 19 November 1970, *Washington Post*: H4. Young cited two reasons why black turnout wasn't larger. The first reason was the "'extreme mobility' of poor black people . . . All of the public housing projects have a high transient rate. . . . People register there, move away, and don't come back to vote." The second reason was "a lack of transportation in the black community" and the fact that "many blacks hold down two jobs," hampering their ability to get to the polls.

11   DeRoche, *Andrew Young*: 42–43.

12   William L. Chaze, "Atlanta Black Wooing Votes," 1 October 1972, *Washington Post*: F20; *Current Biography, 1977*: 450.

13   "At the Hungry Club, Young Talks of Education Plans for the 70's," 12 May 1972, *Atlanta Daily World*: 1.

14   Chaze, "Atlanta Black Wooing Votes." Voter registration drives in black areas also added roughly 5,000 new voters to the rolls.

15   *Almanac of American Politics, 1974*: 232; Bims, "A Southern Activist Goes to the House": 90; "The South's Black Congressman Reflects on His Stunning Victory," 18 November 1972, *New York Amsterdam News*: B9.

16   "'Will Work Hard to Deserve Victory,' for the People, Young Says," 10 November 1972, *Atlanta Daily World*: 1.

17   *Almanac of American Politics, 1974*: 232. Young sat on the following Banking and Currency subcommittees: Consumer Affairs; International Finance; International Trade; and Urban Mass Transportation.

18   De Roche, *Andrew Young*: 44; *Current Biography, 1977*: 450.

19 Carl Gardner, *Andrew Young: A Biography* (New York: Drake, 1978): 181; *Congressional Record*, House, 93rd Cong., 1st sess., (3 October 1973): 32796; "Grants Revealed for 5th District," 19 January 1973, *Atlanta Daily World*: 1.

20 *Current Biography, 1977*: 450; Bims, "A Southern Activist Goes to the House": 84.

21 "Young Urges Pay Hike for Maids, Youths," 17 June 1973, *Atlanta Daily World*. Young argued that domestic work "is a profession that has never been given the respect of a profession. If you do not believe it, just stay home one day and try to clean house from top to bottom, wash and iron all the clothing, take care of the dishes and the children, and then you will realize what a significant accomplishment it is when someone can do this systematically and routinely, and what a contribution this makes to one's home." Subsequently, the House "voted to include domestic workers and youth in a bill to increase the federal minimum wage and extend its coverage to 6 million additional workers."

22 Gardner, *Andrew Young*: 181. Young "pointed out that the moratorium hurt more white people than black through its effect on the building trades and the savings and loan association."

23 Ibid., 181–182.

24 *Congressional Record*, House, 93rd Cong., 1st sess. (22 February 1973): 5077.

25 *Congressional Record*, House, 93rd Cong., 2nd sess. (11 April 1974): 10793.

26 Ibid.

27 *Current Biography, 1977*: 451.

28 "Young Seeks Biased Firms Funds Halt," 16 February 1973, *Atlanta Daily World*: 8.

29 DeRoche, *Andrew Young*: 53, 59.

30 Murray Marcer, "Role in Chile Haunts Pick for State Job," 20 February 1975, *Washington Post*: A2.; DeRoche, *Andrew Young*: 44–45, 54–55. The Byrd Amendment of 1971, sponsored by Harry Byrd of Virginia, allowed the United States to import chrome from Rhodesia. After Prime Minister Ian Smith declared Southern Rhodesia's independence from Great Britain in 1965, the United Nations imposed sanctions. The Lyndon B. Johnson administration supported the U.N. sanctions. After the passage of the amendment, the United States joined Portugal and South Africa in accepting Rhodesian chrome. According to DeRoche, Young and the CBC were ahead of their time, calling attention to an issue that was not addressed by the House until 1974.

31 Gardner, *Andrew Young*: 182.

32 *Congressional Record*, House, 93rd Cong., 2nd sess. (11 April 1974): 10794; Gardner, *Andrew Young*: 182; *Congressional Quarterly Almanac, 1973* (Washington, DC: Congressional Quarterly Inc., 1974): 826.

33 *Current Biography, 1977*: 451.

34 DeRoche, *Andrew Young*: 54; John S. Lewis, Jr., "3 Blacks Named to Powerful Congressional Committees," 21 December 1974, *New Pittsburgh Courier*: 1.

35 *Congressional Record*, House, 94th Cong., 1st sess. (3 June 1975): 16774; John W. Lewis, Jr., "Black Congressmen Wage Fight For Extension of Voting Rights Act,"14 June 1975, *New Pittsburgh Courier*: 1.

36 "Young Introduces Bill for Health Care of All People," 2 May 1975, *Atlanta Daily World*: 5; "Young Defends U.S. Food Stamp Program," 17 October 1975, *Atlanta Daily World*: 5; "Young Reports MARTA Grant, Africa Development Fund," 19 December 1975, *Atlanta Daily World*: 2; "Young Introduces Bill Revising Food Program," 1 April 1976, *Atlanta Daily World*: 2.

37 *Current Biography, 1977*: 451.

38 Ibid., 450.

39 For a detailed articulation of Young's humanitarian and political pragmatism toward Africa, see Andrew Young, "The Promise of U.S. Africa Policy," 17 May 1976, *Washington Post*: A21.

40 Jim Barber, "Young Loses Democratic Gubernatorial Primary," 7 August 1990, United Press International.

41 DeRoche, *Andrew Young*: 151–159; "Ex-UN Envoy Andrew Young Replaces Leon Sullivan as Summit Chair," 20 August 2001, *Jet*: 16; Sheila M. Poole, "Catching Up With Atlanta's Mr. International," 30 October 2002, *Atlanta Journal-Constitution*: 2.

42 Dick Pettys, "Young Rejects Bid for Senate, Send State Democrats Scrambling," 4 October 2003, *Chattanooga Times Free Press*: B1.

"BLACKS DON'T SAY,
'GO UP THERE AND DO A GOOD
JOB.' THEY SAY, 'DON'T FORGET
ABOUT US, HEAR?' WE'VE BEEN
BETRAYED AND USED SO MUCH
IN THE PAST THAT WE MUST BE
CONSTANTLY ASSURED THAT
OUR POLITICIANS ARE WITH US,"
YOUNG ONCE REMARKED.

Cardiss Collins
1931–

UNITED STATES REPRESENTATIVE ★ 1973–1997
DEMOCRAT FROM ILLINOIS

Elected to 12 consecutive terms in the U.S. House of Representatives, Cardiss Collins ranks as one of the longest-serving minority women in the history of Congress. Succeeding her late husband, Representative George Collins, after his death in 1972, Cardiss Collins continued his legacy as a loyal politician in the Chicago Democratic organization directed by Mayor Richard Daley. One of only a handful of women to serve in Congress for more than 20 years, and the only black woman in the chamber for six years, Representative Collins evolved into a dedicated legislator who focused on the economic and social needs of her urban district.

Cardiss Hortense Robertson was born on September 24, 1931, in St. Louis, Missouri, to Finley, a laborer, and Rosia Mae Robertson, a nurse. Upon graduating from the Detroit High School of Commerce in Michigan, she began work in a factory tying mattress springs while living with her maternal grandmother in Chicago. She later found employment as a stenographer at a carnival equipment company. Attending night classes at Northwestern University, she earned a business certificate in 1966 and a diploma in professional accounting one year later.[1] After graduation, Cardiss Robertson remained in Chicago, where she worked for the Illinois department of labor as a secretary and later with the Illinois department of revenue as an auditor until her election to Congress.

Robertson gained her first political experience serving as a committeewoman for Chicago's Democratic ward organization. In 1958 she married George Washington Collins and participated in his various campaigns for alderman, committeeman, and U.S. Representative, while raising their son, Kevin.[2] On November 3, 1970, George Collins won both a special and a general election to fill a U.S. House seat representing Chicago that was vacant following the death of Illinois

Representative Daniel J. Ronan. In his two terms in Congress, Collins served on the House Government Operations and Public Works committees. As a World War II veteran, the Democratic Representative worked to improve conditions for African Americans serving in the military. Known as a diligent, but quiet, Member who rarely spoke on the House Floor, Collins had close political ties to Richard Daley.[3]

In December 1972, shortly after George Collins won election to another term in Congress, he died in an airplane crash near Chicago's Midway Airport. His widow later recalled, "I never gave politics a thought for myself. When people started proposing my candidacy right after the crash, I was in too much of a daze to think seriously about running."[4] Collins overcame her initial reluctance, however, and announced her candidacy for the special election to fill the vacant congressional seat that encompassed the predominantly African-American west side of Chicago.[5] Created in the apportionment of 1947, the inner-city district was one of five congressional seats located in Chicago, each a product of the local political machine.[6] With the solid backing of Mayor Daley's Cook County Democratic organization, Collins handily defeated her opponents Otis Collins, a former state representative, and Milton Gardner, a Columbia University law student, in the Democratic primary, winning 84 percent of the vote.[7] On June 5, 1973, she became the first African-American woman to represent the state of Illinois in Congress by defeating Republican contender Lar Daly and Independent Angel Moreno, with a convincing 92 percent of the vote.[8]

Although she was anxious to continue the work begun by her husband in Congress, Collins had much to learn. Her lack of political experience, exacerbated by her entrance midterm, led to unfamiliarity with

congressional procedures. During her early tenure, Collins often relied upon her colleagues in the House to teach her more about the basic rules of Congress. Collins also had to overcome her reserved demeanor. A few years after taking office, she noted, "Once people learned I had something to say, I gained confidence."[9]

During her first term in Congress, Collins served on the Committee on Government Operations (later Government Reform and Oversight). As a member of the panel throughout her tenure in Congress, Collins chaired two Government Operations subcommittees: Manpower and Housing and Government Activities and Transportation. As chair of the latter subcommittee from 1983 to 1991, Collins worked to improve safety in air travel and fought for stricter controls on the transportation of toxic materials. She eventually rose to the position of Ranking Democrat of the full committee during the 104th Congress (1995–1997). Collins also served on the Committee on International Relations (later Foreign Affairs) from 1975 to 1980, the District of Columbia Committee during the 95th Congress (1977–1979), and the influential Committee on Energy and Commerce (later Commerce) from the 97th through the 104th Congresses (1981–1997), chairing the Commerce, Consumer Protection, and Competitiveness Subcommittee in the 102nd and the 103rd Congresses (1991-1995). Additionally, Collins was the first African American and woman selected as a Democratic Whip At-Large.

Four years after taking office in 1973, Collins commented that her primary objective as a Representative was to "provide better living and working conditions for people [on Chicago's west side] and other low and moderate income people throughout the country." Known for her commitment to the issues directly affecting her constituents, Collins spent eight days each month in her district to ensure that she stayed abreast of their concerns.[10] The close attention Collins paid to her district reaped benefits at the polls. For more than two decades, Collins won by comfortable margins in the strongly Democratic district, typically defeating her Republican opponents by

more than 80 percent.[11] Collins did, however, experience some difficult primary races during the mid-1980s (against Danny Davis, who later succeeded her)—a consequence of the decline in power of the Cook County Democratic organization that accelerated with the death of Richard Daley in 1976.[12] She proved resilient without the influential machine that helped launch her congressional career; devoid of its strict control, Collins was able to develop as a politician and to pursue her own legislative interests.

During the 96th Congress (1979–1981), Collins became the chairwoman of the Congressional Black Caucus (CBC), augmenting both her influence and her standing in the House. As only the second woman to hold the leadership position in the CBC and as the fourth black woman ever to serve in the U.S. House of Representatives, Collins found herself in the spotlight. The high visibility of her position encouraged her to become more outspoken. At one fundraiser, Collins voiced the growing disillusionment of the CBC, declaring, "We will no longer wait for political power to be shared with us, we will take it."[13] Members of the CBC praised Collins, citing her ability to lead with fairness and to create an atmosphere that encouraged unity through debates rather than arguments.[14] As chairwoman, Collins voiced disapproval with President James Earl (Jimmy) Carter's record on civil rights. She criticized the President for failing to gather enough congressional support to pass legislation making Martin Luther King, Jr.'s, birthday a federal holiday. Collins also disparaged the House for its failure to pass the bill, alleging that "racism had a part in it."[15]

Throughout her 24 years in Congress, Collins dedicated herself to the advancement of African Americans and other minorities. According to Collins, some federal agencies, such as the National Endowment for the Humanities, the Federal Trade Commission, and the U.S. Justice Department, were not upholding the provisions of the Civil Rights Act requiring agencies that received federal funding to provide information on their affirmative action programs. Her 1985 findings as chair of the

House Subcommittee on Government Activities and Transportation led her to ask Congress to curb funding to specific agencies, arguing, "Laws that have been debated and passed by the courts cannot arbitrarily be negated by individuals." In the 1980s, she continued her defense of affirmative action by drawing attention to the hiring practices of U.S. airlines, which rarely placed African Americans in professional positions.[16] Representative Collins's push for equality in the aviation industry helped pave the way for an amendment to the Airport and Airway Safety, Capacity, and Expansion Act of 1987, requiring that 10 percent of all concession stands in airports be run by minority- and women-owned businesses.

Collins also worked to prevent federal tax write-offs for advertising firms that discriminated against minority-owned media companies. Hoping to "provide black and other minority station owners with a mechanism for redress," Collins argued that financial penalties for offending agencies would help combat discrimination and level the playing field for all media organizations. She also crusaded against gender and racial inequality in broadcast licensing. On several occasions, Collins introduced legislation to preserve Federal Communications Commission policies designed to increase the number of women and minorities owning media companies.[17]

In an effort to promote equal opportunities for women in sports at colleges and universities, Collins introduced the Equality in Athletic Disclosure Act on February 17, 1993. This amendment to the Higher Education Act of 1965 directed colleges and universities to publicize the rate of participation in athletic programs by gender. In recognition of her commitment to gender equity in athletics, Collins was inducted into the Women's Sports Hall of Fame in 1994.[18] Collins also cosponsored the Universal Health Care Act and the Health Security Act in 1993 and urged the National Institutes of Health to focus on the health issues that concern minorities, since "little use has been made of studies on minority prone diseases despite the significant disproportionate array of health conditions."[19] A longtime advocate of increasing breast cancer awareness, Collins drafted legislation to help elderly and disabled women receive Medicare coverage for mammograms and introduced a law designating October as National Breast Cancer Awareness Month.

Collins declined to run for re-election to the 105th Congress (1997–1999). Although she vowed to remain active in Democratic politics, she decided to end her career in elective office, telling reporters, "I'm going to be 65 next year, and that's the time many people retire."[20] After completing her last term, Collins returned to Chicago, Illinois. She later moved to Alexandria, Virginia.

FOR FURTHER READING

"Collins, Cardiss," *Biographical Directory of the United States Congress, 1774–Present,* http://bioguide.congress.gov/scripts/biodisplay.pl?index=C000634.

NOTES

1   Marie Garrett, "Cardiss Collins," in Jessie Carney Smith, ed., *Notable Black American Women* (Detroit, MI: Gale Research, 2003): 204 (hereinafter referred to as *NBAW*).

2   Garrett, "Cardiss Collins," *NBAW.*

3   "Rep. George Collins (D-Ill.) Killed in Chicago Jet Crash," 10 December 1972, *Washington Post*: B4.

4   Garrett, "Cardiss Collins," *NBAW*: 205.

5   Joel Weisman, "Congressman's Widow Elected in His Place," 6 June 1973, *Washington Post*: A7.

6   Leo M. Snowiss, "Congressional Recruitment and Representation," *American Political Science Review* 60 (1966): 628–629.

7   "House Race Won By Widow," 18 April 1973, *Washington Post*: A22.

8   "Widow Wins a Bid for Husband Seat," 18 April 1973, *New York Times*: 42; Andrew H. Malcolm, "Illinois Elects Its First Black Woman to Congress, on 92% of Vote," 7 June 1973, *New York Times*: 11; "Election Statistics, 1920 to Present," available at http://clerk.house.gov/member_info/election.html.

9   Jacqueline Trescott, "The Coming Out of Cardiss Collins," 21 September 1979, *Washington Post*: C1.

10   Garrett, "Cardiss Collins," *NBAW.*

11   "Election Statistics, 1920 to Present," available at http://clerk.house.gov/member_info/election.html.

12   Roger Biles, *Richard J. Daley: Politics, Race and the Governing of Chicago* (DeKalb: Northern Illinois University Press, 1995): 221–222, 232; *Politics in America, 1994* (Washington, D.C: Congressional Quarterly Press, 1993): 474–475.

13   Jacqueline Trescott and Elisabeth Bumiller, "The Raucous Caucus," 24 September 1979, *Washington Post*: B1.

14   Trescott, "The Coming Out of Cardiss Collins."

15   *Politics in America, 1990* (Washington, DC: Congressional Quarterly Inc., 1989): 345.

16   "Cardiss Collins," *Contemporary Black Biography*, Volume 10 (Farmington Hills, MI: Gale Group, 2002) (hereinafter referred to as *CBB*). See also *Congressional Record,* House, 99th Cong., 1st sess. (26 February 1985): E633.

17   *Congressional Record*, House, 102nd Cong., 1st sess. (3 January 1991): E32.

18   Karen Foerstel, *Biographical Dictionary of Congressional Women* (Westport, CT: Greenwood Press, 1999): 63; "Colleges Told to Publish Sports Costs," 3 December 1995, *New York Times*: 37.

19   "Cardiss Collins," *CBB.*

20   "A Chicago Democrat is Quitting Congress," 9 November 1995, *New York Times*: B14.

… Collins commented that her primary objective as a Representative was to "provide better living and working conditions for people [on Chicago's west side] and other low and moderate income people throughout the country."

Harold Eugene Ford, Sr.
1945–

UNITED STATES REPRESENTATIVE ★ 1975–1997
DEMOCRAT FROM TENNESSEE

The first African American to represent Tennessee in the U.S. Congress, Harold E. Ford transformed his family's entrepreneurial success into a political dynasty that shaped state and national politics. Ford's membership on the influential House Ways and Means Committee enabled him to build support among his constituents by directing ample federal funding to his district. Elected at age 29, Ford was one of the youngest Members ever to chair a subcommittee on Ways and Means. During his more-than-two-decade career in the House, Ford strongly advocated government assistance for the poor and set out to reform welfare in the United States. "Harold Ford has been a staunch defender of justice and equality," acknowledged William (Bill) Clay, Sr., of Missouri upon his colleague's retirement at the end of the 104th Congress (1995–1997). "He has shown a special dedication to representing the needs of the underprivileged and has left his signature on our Nation's welfare and employment programs."[1]

The eighth of 15 children, Harold Eugene Ford was born on May 20, 1945, in Memphis, Tennessee. Ford's father, Newton, worked as an undertaker; his mother, Vera, was a housewife. Ford earned a bachelor of science degree from Tennessee State University in 1967 and an associate of arts degree in mortuary science from John Gupton College in Nashville, Tennessee, in 1969. On February 10, 1969, he married Dorothy Bowles. The couple had three children—Harold, Newton Jake, and Sir Isaac—before divorcing in 1999.[2] Ford later earned a master's degree in business administration from Howard University in 1982. After entering the family mortuary business, he ran for a seat in the Tennessee state house of representatives. "This fellow came in looking for a campaign contribution for his race for the state legislature," Ford later recalled. "When he stepped out the door, I decided to run." Ford lobbied support from "the silent majority—through

churches, civic clubs, PTAs" and other groups of affluent blacks in Memphis. His well-organized campaign also tapped into his father's mortuary business—an invaluable community network that laid the groundwork for his victorious bid for the state legislature in 1972. Ford made his mark early in the Tennessee house of representatives. Named majority whip in his first term, he also chaired a legislative committee that investigated utility rates and practices. During his political career, Ford used his family's deep roots in the community to assemble a formidable machine in Memphis politics. Raised with respect for public service—his great-grandfather held a county office, and his father (unsuccessfully) campaigned for a seat in the Tennessee house—Ford also benefited from changes in the political landscape. With a spike in the number of African-American voters in the Memphis area, Ford and his family were able to solidify a power base that included representation at the federal, state, and local levels.[3]

At the urging of local black politicians, Ford ran for a seat in the U.S. House in 1974 after two terms as a state legislator.[4] He easily defeated his three opponents—Mary A. Guthrie, a Catholic nun; Joan Best, a schoolteacher; and Lee Whitman, a lawyer—in the Democratic primary, with 63 percent of the vote.[5] Ford faced Dan Kuykendall, a four-term incumbent Republican Member, in the general election. The southwestern Tennessee congressional district boasted a diverse constituency; although redistricting increased the number of African-American voters, Ford faced an uphill battle in the majority-white district. To strengthen his standing with black voters and the liberal whites in the district, Ford ran on a bipartisan platform that emphasized economic development for the community. "Inflation knows no color . . . that's what the people will vote on," Ford remarked.[6] His campaign enlisted an army of paid workers and volunteers that

included blacks and whites and received financial support from black churches and luminaries such as Isaac Hayes, an African-American singer. An energetic campaigner, Ford "organized the headquarters and phone banks . . . put together caravans that . . . would wind slowly through residential neighborhoods carrying campaign workers who would put up yard signs and hand out candy to kids."[7] With the Watergate scandal as a backdrop to the early part of the campaign, Ford called for the immediate impeachment of President Richard M. Nixon. Kuykendall, who had faced little previous opposition, had difficulty separating himself from the embattled President.[8] After contesting the initial results, Ford narrowly won the general election by 744 votes, becoming the first black Representative to represent Tennessee.[9] He joined an influx of freshman Members of the House elected to the 94th Congress (1975–1977). Dubbed the "Watergate Babies," the 75 new Democratic Representatives capitalized on an anti-Republican sentiment in the wake of the scandal.[10]

In his subsequent re-election campaigns, Ford typically won by comfortable margins. He locked in the black vote and a larger number of white voters in his district to win 61 percent of the vote in 1976.[11] Before the 1976 election, redistricting eliminated 12,000 white suburban voters, increasing the black constituency to more than 45 percent. During the 1980s, Ford increased his margins of victory, typically garnering more than 70 percent of the vote. In his latter terms on the Hill, he failed to secure as many dominant victories, partially because of a series of legal problems; however, his constituents remained loyal, consistently electing him with more than 50 percent of the vote.[12]

During his first term, Ford was assigned to the Committee on Banking, Currency, and Housing, the Committee on Veterans' Affairs, the Select Committee on Aging, and the Select Committee on Assassinations. In September 1975, the Tennessee Representative became the second African American selected to serve on the prestigious House Ways and Means Committee, which set federal tax and revenue policy.[13] In 1987, Speaker of

the House Jim Wright of Texas appointed Ford to the powerful Democratic Steering and Policy Committee, which makes committee assignments for Democratic Members of the House.

Ford focused on helping lower-income constituents with government-sponsored aid such as job training and maintaining a social safety net through programs such as welfare. He also sought opportunities for economic development to assist both rich and poor constituents through his representation and grass-roots efforts. During the 95th Congress (1977–1979), Ford attempted to cultivate public support for President James Earl (Jimmy) Carter's comprehensive urban policy plan—an initiative to rebuild American cities that had suffered economic setbacks. Ford informed his constituents that they were "in a position to impact directly upon the 5–10 pieces of legislation which are required to implement these proposals . . . Only through such actions can we as black people ever make the 'system' work as it should."[14] As a member of the Ways and Means Committee's Subcommittee on Health, Ford tried to assist senior citizens who needed health care in his district. He cosponsored the extension of the Older Americans Health Services Act, which was due to expire in 1978. To draw constituent support for the measure, Ford scheduled hearings in his district. "The response . . . has been overwhelming with 'aging' enthusiasts in my district who are anxious to have their voices heard," Ford said.[15]

In the 97th Congress (1981–1983), Ford became chairman of the Ways and Means Subcommittee on Public Assistance and Unemployment Compensation. In his new leadership role, he attacked President Ronald W. Reagan's efforts to curtail government-sponsored programs aimed at assisting the poor. He fought against administration initiatives to reduce Medicare funding and to force the poor to pay for food stamps. The Tennessee Representative also attempted to block a measure by the Ways and Means Committee to cut more than $1.7 billion from Medicare.[16]

Ford used his Ways and Means subcommittee chairmanship to secure federal government aid for unemployed workers who had exhausted state benefits.

Through his efforts, a supplemental benefits program was added to existing tax legislation.[17] During the 99th Congress (1985–1987), Ford led an unsuccessful battle to extend the life of the supplemental benefits.[18] Ford proposed a welfare overhaul plan that linked benefits to work. Called the Family Support Program, it was an alternative to Aid to Families With Dependent Children. The work component, called the National Education, Training, and Work program (NETWork), would require the participation of parents whose children were age six or older and would outline "specific education, employment, and counseling services" for the states. Although the initial cost was high, Ford pointed out, "We will save revenue for the federal government three to four years down the road."[19]

Ford's ambition to reform welfare hit a major roadblock when the veteran lawmaker was indicted in 1987 on 19 federal counts that included charges of obstruction against the Internal Revenue Service, mail and bank fraud, and embezzlement.[20] The Congressional Black Caucus (CBC) publicly backed Ford, pledging to raise $250,000 to help pay his legal bills. Like Ford, the CBC questioned the legitimacy of the investigation, arguing that it was racially or politically motivated.[21] Ford fought to remain effective on Capitol Hill despite having to resign his subcommittee chairmanship.[22] He supported a bill to raise the ceiling on the number of immigrants admitted to the United States, and introduced legislation that would provide college scholarships and job training for the poor. In tune with his legislative focus on local issues, Ford helped attain a multimillion-dollar development project for downtown Memphis. During his congressional tenure he also obtained federal funding for public housing improvements and upgrades for Memphis International Airport, as well as increased opportunities for minority businesses in his Tennessee district.[23]

After a mistrial was declared in April 1990, a federal judge ruled that Ford's second trial would take place in Memphis, but that jurors would be selected from several outlying counties due to the publicity from the first proceeding. House leaders filed an *amicus curiae* brief on Ford's behalf arguing that the Representative's right to a fair trial had been violated by the decision to bus jurors in from rural western Tennessee.[24] Ford's defense team and the CBC made an unsuccessful request for a review by the Justice Department.[25] In April 1993, the predominantly white jury acquitted Ford of all charges.[26]

After his acquittal, Ford's seniority privileges were restored, and he reclaimed his position as chair of the Ways and Means Subcommittee on Human Resources following a six-year absence.[27] "I don't think I can walk in on Day One and be fully alert . . . In ample time, four to six weeks, I think I should be back in the swing of things," Ford admitted upon his return. The Tennessee Representative continued his dedication to welfare reform. He agreed with President William J. (Bill) Clinton's proposal to change welfare, but opposed a finite limitation on benefits. "I don't think welfare reform worked . . . I'm not going to wait to see [Clinton's] package. We're going to hit the road running." Ford proposed a more gradual approach to getting people off of welfare that included standardizing and increasing benefits rather than abruptly ending services.[28] He also put forward a more ambitious welfare-to-work plan that would pay workers a minimum of $9 to $9.50 an hour. In return for receiving double the minimum wage, workers would relinquish welfare benefits such as food stamps and housing subsidies. "What I'm looking at, on a national level, is replacing welfare with a jobs program," Ford noted.[29] Ultimately, the 1995 welfare reform bill signed into law by President Clinton failed to include Ford's comprehensive initiatives.

For several years, speculation swirled around Ford's possible retirement from the House. "I didn't want history to show I was on my way down," Ford revealed when asked if he had thought of stepping down after his legal vindication in 1993.[30] Three years later, Ford announced his decision to leave Congress. "I'm going to leave while I'm on top," he remarked. "I've been there (in Congress) a long time. I've seen how members of Congress stayed beyond the level of capacity where they can really be effective."[31] Ford's son, Harold, Jr., won his father's House seat for the 105th Congress (1997–1999), making Harold Ford the first African-American Representative whose son succeeded him in Congress. After his career in the House, Ford managed a political consulting firm in Tennessee.

FOR FURTHER READING

"Ford, Harold Eugene," *Biographical Directory of the U.S. Congress, 1774–Present,* http://bioguide.congress.gov/scripts/biodisplay.pl?index=F000261.

NOTES

1   *Congressional Record*, House, 104th Cong., 2nd sess. (30 September 1996): E1889.

2   "Ford, Harold Eugene," *The Complete Marquis Who's Who Biographies*, 11 February 2003; James W. Brosnan, "Harold, Dorothy Ford Avoid Divorce Trial With Agreement," 31 March 1999, *Commercial Appeal* (Memphis, TN): B2.

3   Dorothy Gilliam, "Harold Ford," 23 February 1975, *Washington Post*: H1; Charles Bernsen, "Political Machine of Ford Clan Took a Century to Build," *Commercial Appeal*, 1 July 1990: A1; Charles Bernsen, "Ford Team Scored Big in 1974," 2 July 1990, *Commercial Appeal*: A1; *Almanac of American Politics, 1996* (Washington, DC: National Journal Inc., 1995): 1253.

4   Bernsen, "Ford Team Scored Big in 1974."

5   *Almanac of American Politics, 1976* (Washington, DC: National Journal Inc., 1975): 809–810; Bill Terry, "Nun, Mortician Vie in Tenn. Hill Race," 1 August 1974, *New York Times*: A12.

6   Terry, "Nun, Mortician Vie in Tenn. Hill Race." A contemporary noted that Ford "was liberated from the notion that he had to be in an all black area in order to win an election"; see Gilliam, "Harold Ford."

7   Bernsen, "Ford Team Scored Big in 1974."

8   Terry, "Nun, Mortician Vie in Tenn. Hill Race"; Haynes Johnson, "Nixon's the One Hurting the GOP," 27 October 1974, *Washington Post*: C1.

9   Bernsen, "Ford Team Scored Big in 1974;" *Politics in America, 1982* (Washington, DC: Congressional Quarterly Inc., 1981): 1140–1141; "Election Statistics, 1920 to Present," available at

http://clerk.house.gov/member_info/electionInfo/index.html; Mildred L. Amer, "Black Members of the United States Congress: 1870–2007," 27 September 2007, Report RL30378, Congressional Research Service, Library of Congress, Washington, DC; Gilliam, "Harold Ford."

10   "'Freshmen Have Never Been Treated So Well,'" 15 January 1975, *Washington Post*: B1. While entertaining Memphis constituents, Ford "couldn't get tickets for them for the swearing-in ceremony itself, so he borrowed a large committee room and restaged the oath-taking for their benefit." Ford's congressional style resembles one of the archetypes outlined by Richard Fenno, Jr., *Home Style: House Members in Their Districts,* (New York: Longman, 2003): 114–124.

11   Henry Mitchell, "A Symbolic Gathering," 6 January 1977, *Washington Post*: D9; *Politics in America, 1982*: 1141.

12   "Election Statistics, 1920 to Present," available at http://clerk.house.gov/member_info/electionInfo/index.html. For example, Ford won 82 percent of the vote in 1988. Two years later he garnered 58 percent in the general election.

13   Charles Rangel of New York was the first black member of the panel when he joined the committee at the beginning of the 94th Congress.

14   Harold Ford, "Carter's Urban Policy: A Workable Mish-Mash?" 20 April 1978, *Atlanta Daily World:* 4.

15   *Congressional Record*, House, 95th Cong., 1st sess. (4 November 1977): 37420.

16   Ford "tried to persuade the committee to restore $71 million in Medicare cuts, but failed. In the past, he has backed legislation to expand Medicare payments to cover dentistry, chiropractic treatment, eyeglasses, and hearing aids." Quoted in *Politics in America, 1982*: 1140. See also *Congressional Quarterly Almanac, 97th Congress, 1st Session, 1981: Volume 38* (Washington, DC: Congressional Quarterly Press, 1982): 479.

17   *Congressional Directory, 98th Congress* (Washington, DC: Government Printing Office, 1983): 356; *Politics in America, 1990* (Washington, DC: Congressional Quarterly Press, 1989): 1416.

18   *Politics in America, 1990*: 1416.

19   "Top House Democrats Back 'Workfare,'" 20 March 1987, Associated Press. The plan would incorporate "a system requiring education, training, or work for many recipients. States would have to provide a minimum level of cash assistance, and child support collections would be strengthened." Ford figured the program "would cost the federal government roughly $600 to $850 million in fiscal 1988 and about $2.5 billion when phased in fully."

20 Howard Kurtz, "Tennessee Rep. Ford Indicted on Tax, Bank Fraud Charges," 25 April 1987, *Washington Post*: A1. The most controversial aspects of the case stemmed from the establishment of a "sham corporation" that processed a $350,000 loan from the financiers to Ford's funeral home business. The indictment alleged that instead of using the money for those purposes, Ford used the loan for personal reasons. C. H. Butcher, a bank financier, pleaded guilty to conspiracy and bankruptcy fraud charges and agreed to cooperate with prosecutors. Another member of the Butcher family was serving a 20-year prison term for defrauding depositors.

21 Woody Baird, "Congressman Says His Indictment Racially Motivated," 28 April 1987, Associated Press; Kenneth B. Noble, "Blacks in Congress Join to Help Indicted Colleague," 28 May 1987, *New York Times*: A20. With legal costs then estimated at $750,000, Ford raised $500,000 from two sources, the CBC and 200 black ministers from Memphis, in a successful grass-roots effort. For more on Ford's legal problems, see William L. Clay, *Just Permanent Interests: Black Americans in Congress, 1870–1991* (New York: Amistad Press, Inc., 1992): 332–334.

22 "Ford's Defense," 24 July 1987, *New York Times*: 14. "All contributions to his political committee, the Harold Ford Committee for Better Government, in the first six months of the year have been used for his defense . . . taking in just over $75,000 and spending just over $75,000 on attorney fees." According to the *1987 Congressional Quarterly Almanac*, a Democratic Caucus rule required Members indicted for "serious felonies" to resign their chairmanships until they were acquitted. *Congressional Quarterly Almanac, 100th Congress, 1st Session, 1987: Volume 43* (Washington, DC: Congressional Quarterly Press, 1988): 479.

23 James W. Brosnan, "Tennessee Congressmen Line Up Solidly Against Immigration Bill, But Still Lose," 5 October 1990, *Commercial Appeal*: A5; "Ford Offers Two Measures to Aid Poor," 19 October 1990, *Commercial Appeal*: A13. "Sundquist, Ford Will Try to Revive Peabody Place Bill," 29 October 1990, *Commercial Appeal*: B1; James W. Brosnan, "No Apologies, Ford Is Proud of Liberal Legacy," 21 April 1996, *Commercial Appeal*: 5B.

24 Susan B. Glasser, "Hill Leadership Intervenes in Rep. Ford's Fraud Case," 2 May 1991, *Roll Call*.

25 Susan Glasser, "Six Years After Indictment, Rep. Ford's Second Trial on Fraud Charges Begins," 4 February 1993, *Roll Call*; Chris Conley and James W. Brosnan, "Justice to Join Ford, Seek New Jury; U.S. Atty. Bryant Resigns; Prosecutors Leave Case," 20 February 1993, *Commercial Appeal*: A1; Chris Conley, "Ford Case Returns to Court Amid Questions Over Jury, Prosecutors," 21 February 1993, *Commercial Appeal*: A1; "Turner Cited 'Tactics,' Coverage in Decision on Jury in Ford Trial," 23 February 1993: A8; Chris Conley, "Appeals Court Affirms Ford Jury," 27 February 1993, *Commercial Appeal*: A8; Susan Glasser, "GOP Asks Probe of Justice Dept. Over Ford Trial," 1 March 1993, *Roll Call*; "Clinton Says No Improprieties Intruded on Rep. Ford's Case," 7 March 1993, Reuters.

26 *Almanac of American Politics, 1994* (Washington, DC: National Journal Inc., 1993): 1196–1197; Alan Fram, "Exonerated Congressman Wants Government to Pay His Legal Costs," 14 April 1993, Associated Press; Susan Glasser, "Acquitted, Rep. Ford Moves to Settle Some Scores, Wants the US to Pay His Legal Bills," 15 April 1993, *Roll Call*.

27 Previously named the Subcommittee on Public Assistance and Unemployment Compensation, it had been renamed the Subcommittee on Human Resources by the time Ford resumed his chairmanship.

28 Leslie Phillips, "For Congressman, Reputation Retrieval," 21 April 1993, *USA Today*: 8A; Kenneth J. Cooper, "Rep. Ford Finds New Faces, Old Issues; Long-Absent Subcommittee Chairman Retakes Helm and Tackles Welfare Overhaul," 22 April 1993, *Washington Post*: A21.

29 William M. Welch, "Ford 'Ready' to Redo Welfare," 27 January 1994, *USA Today*: 5A.

30 Brosnan, "No Apologies, Ford Is Proud of Liberal Legacy."

31 James W. Brosnan, "Harold Ford Will Announce Today Decision to Retire From Congress," 11 April 1996, *Commercial Appeal*: 1A.

Julian Carey Dixon
1934–2000

UNITED STATES REPRESENTATIVE ★ 1979–2000
DEMOCRAT FROM CALIFORNIA

For more than two decades, Representative Julian Dixon operated as a congressional insider who succeeded in several key committee assignments because of his low-key, evenhanded style. "I don't mean to be critical of anyone else's style, but I think it's better to have an impact on the issue than to give a speech that gets picked up in the national press," Dixon said.[1] A native of Washington, DC, who represented a Los Angeles district, Dixon became the first African American to head an Appropriations subcommittee in 1980 when he took over the chairmanship of the Subcommittee on the District of Columbia. Additionally, he chaired the Committee on Standards of Official Conduct, which investigated allegations that Speaker Jim Wright of Texas had violated House rules (the investigation eventually precipitated Wright's resignation in 1989). He also held a high-ranking position on the sensitive Permanent Select Committee on Intelligence, solidifying his status as one of the House's important behind-the-scenes institutionalists.

Julian Carey Dixon was born in Washington, DC, on August 8, 1934. His father was a longtime postal worker. Dixon attended Monroe Elementary School in northwest Washington, DC, before moving to the Culver City section of Los Angeles with his mother at age 11.[2] He graduated from Dorsey High School in 1953. From 1957 to 1960, Dixon served in the U.S. Army, attaining the rank of sergeant. In 1962, he graduated with a bachelor of science degree from Los Angeles State College; five years later he earned a law degree from Southwestern University in Los Angeles. Dixon married Felicia Bragg, and the couple had a son, Cary Gordon, before divorcing. Dixon later married Betty Lee.[3]

Dixon's political career began when he became a legislative aide to California State Senator Mervyn Dymally. In 1972, he won election to the California

assembly, filling the seat of Yvonne Burke, who embarked on a successful campaign for a Los Angeles-based seat in the U.S. House. Dixon registered as an immediate force in Sacramento, chairing the assembly's Democratic caucus—he was the first freshman legislator to hold that post—and attaining positions on the influential ways and means and criminal justice committees. His signal piece of legislation was a criminal and juvenile justice measure that brought $55 million in state funding to California counties. Dixon built a network of important allies in addition to Dymally and Governor Jerry Brown, including Speaker Leo T. McCarthy, Assemblyman Henry Waxman, and Assembly Majority Leader Howard Berman. (The latter two eventually served alongside Dixon in the U.S. House of Representatives.[4])

When three-term U.S. Representative Yvonne Burke announced she was retiring from the House to run for the post of California attorney general in 1978, Dixon entered the race for the vacant House seat. The district encompassed much of West Los Angeles, including Culver City, Inglewood, and Palms, a neighborhood adjacent to Beverly Hills. With registered Democrats composing 76 percent of the constituency, the district contained a cross section of wealthy, middle-class, and working-class voters and a plurality-black population (estimated at 38 percent of the district); the constituency also included a large white population and a growing Hispanic segment.[5] Dixon was one of three major contenders in a field of eight that vied for the Democratic nomination, including two other prominent African Americans: California State Senator Nate Holden and Los Angeles City Councilman David S. Cunningham. The primary reflected an ongoing conflict among three political factions competing for control of the black vote in Los Angeles. Dixon was supported by Lieutenant Governor Dymally, Holden

was backed by Los Angeles County Supervisor Kenneth Hahn, and Los Angeles Mayor Tom Bradley endorsed Cunningham.[6] During the primary, Dixon relied on his connections to state legislators such as Berman and Waxman, using their help to launch a complex direct-mail campaign that challenged Holden's credentials as a state legislator.[7] Berman's brother, Michael, served as Dixon's campaign manager. In September, Dixon handily won the primary, with 48 percent of the vote; Holden was runner-up, with 34 percent.[8] That win assured Dixon a House seat. Without an opponent in the general election, he did not maintain a campaign headquarters and did little campaigning, emphasizing health care and moderately priced housing for seniors, as well as energy issues, during his relatively few appearances.[9] Redistricting after the 1980 and 1990 censuses changed the geography of the district, eliminating some precincts, but did not dilute the district's heavily Democratic composition; African Americans still accounted for roughly 40 percent of the population after 1980, and that percentage remained steady through 2000. In his subsequent 11 re-election bids, Dixon won by lopsided margins, capturing between 73 and 87 percent of the vote.[10]

When Dixon claimed his seat in the House in January 1979, he won a coveted assignment on the Appropriations Committee—a rare coup for a freshman Member. Dixon later claimed that he had convinced party leaders to give him the seat "using three hats": First, his predecessor, Yvonne Burke, had served on the panel for the previous two Congresses; second, he had experience in the appropriations process in the California assembly; finally, he suggested the panel needed more minority representation.[11] Dixon remained on the Appropriations Committee for the rest of his long House career. In 1980 he became the first African American to win a subcommittee chairmanship on the Appropriations panel, taking over as head of the District of Columbia Subcommittee. In the 98th Congress (1983–1985), Dixon received an additional assignment on the Committee on Standards of Official Conduct (widely known as the

Ethics Committee). In 1993, House leaders tapped Dixon for a seat on the influential Permanent Select Committee on Intelligence, where he remained through the 106th Congress (1999–2001), by which time he had become the Ranking Democrat on the panel.

Dixon quickly earned a reputation as an institutional player who worked effectively behind the scenes and shunned the limelight. "I do not work the press," he said. "I never had a press aide, as such. I realize that there are sexy issues one can get a lot of public attention working on. I have not avoided those issues but I have not pursued them."[12] Dixon's quiet, but effective, approach brought him several difficult assignments, demonstrating the level of trust House leadership placed in him. He was eventually tapped as chairman of the rules committee for the 1984 Democratic National Convention—another first for an African American. At the start of the 99th Congress (1985–1987), House leaders chose Representative Dixon to head a sensitive post as chairman of the Ethics Committee. Political columnist David Broder, called Dixon's selection as Ethics Committee chairman a "sign of the maturation of American politics," adding, "Dixon is a fascinating example of the emerging alternative style of black leadership: a person who makes his way not by the militance of his advocacy of civil rights or other racially linked issues, but on the basis of personal and intellectual qualities that cross racial and ideological divisions and make an effective bridge-builder."[13] It was during the following Congress that Dixon presided over an investigation into a book deal that critics suggested had earned Speaker Jim Wright outside income in violation of House rules. Numerous other complaints were filed against Wright after the investigation began. Under Dixon's leadership, the Ethics Committee released a 456-page report by an outside counsel indicating that the Speaker had violated House rules on numerous counts. When the committee signaled its willingness to investigate the allegations in the report, Wright stepped down in June 1989.[14] Dixon was lauded as a fair-minded, effective leader who imparted a bipartisan ethos to the committee's deliberations and conclusions.

Dixon also chaired the Congressional Black Caucus (CBC) in the 98th Congress. His role as a conciliator sometimes caused friction among the members of the caucus. In 1983, several CBC members criticized Dixon for refusing to bring the caucus's alternative budget to the House Floor for a vote. Submitted annually, the CBC budget was a symbolic effort to highlight the legislative needs and programs that were important to the African-American community. Speaker Thomas P. (Tip) O'Neill of Massachusetts had asked Dixon to pledge support for the House Budget Committee measure in an effort to secure rank-and-file Democrats' votes. Knowing he could extract some concessions for his support, the CBC chairman agreed. "Our purpose, hopefully, is not to go down to defeat with honor," Dixon explained. "Our purpose is to have some success."[15]

Dixon's other principal focus was the District of Columbia Subcommittee of the Appropriations Committee. He took over the post from Representative Charlie Wilson of Texas in early 1980, having said, "because of my background in dealing with urban problems in the state legislature, and my fondness for the District by way of birth, I would take it if it became available."[16] While some Members would have considered the post an insular burden because it afforded little opportunity to address issues in individual districts, Dixon believed his subcommittee chairmanship dovetailed nicely with the interests of his urban and working-class constituents: "My people aren't parochial," he explained. "They have expanded horizons."[17]

From that post, Dixon balanced competing tensions and political impulses in the House between those seeking to grant the federal city greater autonomy on the path to complete home rule and those who sought to exercise a greater oversight role of the capital, particularly through the power of the purse. Throughout the 1980s and early 1990s, Dixon sought to bring the District of Columbia's budget under control while appropriating federal dollars for important programs. Some political observers noted that he had as much impact on the city as its congressional

delegates during that period. The editors of the *Almanac of American Politics* summed up Dixon's approach to the District and its various leaders, such as longtime Mayor Marion S. Barry, as "sympathetic but not sycophantic."[18] Eventually, Dixon grew disillusioned with the actions of city officials as the city fell deeper into debt and Barry was beset by legal problems because of his use of illicit drugs. "I have personally come to the conclusion that the District government has not acted in good faith with the Congress," Dixon said at an Appropriations Committee hearing in 1995. "I wanted to think the best. Now I believe the worst."[19] Even then, he fought efforts by the Republican-led House to cut the city's federal payment.

Dixon also pursued legislative items pertaining to issues that were important to the African-American community. He authored a resolution, passed by the House, to award the Presidential Medal of Freedom to Dr. Benjamin Mays, the longtime president of Morehouse College in Atlanta and a mentor to Dr. Martin Luther King, Jr. He also sponsored a resolution designating September 1983 Sickle Cell Anemia Awareness Month. Among Dixon's legislative interests that related directly to his district were initiatives to establish a mass transit system in Los Angeles (for which he secured more than $3.8 billion in federal funding from 1983 to 2000), as well as programs to promote low-and moderate-income housing and better access to health care. He also helped secure federal relief funding for Los Angeles after the 1992 race riots and the 1994 Northridge earthquake. In a 1997 omnibus measure, he managed to win a $400 million loan for the development of the Alameda Corridor, which connected the ports of Los Angeles and Long Beach with national rail lines.[20] Dixon also worked to create a loan guarantee program for small businesses and contractors that were hurt economically by military base closings in southern California.[21] Although he campaigned only minimally in his district, Dixon remained close to his constituency and was widely regarded as a facilitator between the political and ethnic factions of the area. At several points, Dixon was mentioned as a possible candidate for a seat on the powerful Los Angeles

County board of supervisors (where his predecessor served after she left the House), but he chose to remain in the U.S. House.

From his seat on the Subcommittee on Foreign Operations of the Appropriations Committee, Representative Dixon influenced U.S. assistance to foreign countries. During his tenure on the subcommittee, he drafted legislation that required the United States to oppose loans by the International Monetary Fund to any country that employed apartheid. As further evidence of his resolve to draw attention to apartheid, in December 1984, Dixon, along with two other leaders, was arrested outside the South African Embassy in Washington, DC, in a peaceful demonstration against the minority-white apartheid government.[22] Dixon also was instrumental in securing increased aid for development for sub-Saharan Africa, disaster assistance for Jamaica, and scholarships for disadvantaged South African students.

Just a month after being re-elected to a 12th consecutive term, Representative Dixon died of a heart attack on December 8, 2000, in Los Angeles. A close friend and fellow House Member from Los Angeles, Representative Howard Berman of California, described Dixon as "unique for the political class because he had his ego under control. . . . His interest was in accomplishing things and in loyalty to the institution."[23] Recalling his service on the Appropriations Subcommittee on the District of Columbia, the *Washington Post* eulogized Dixon for his "unfailing respect for city residents," calling him a Washington native "who never forgot his roots . . . one of the best friends the District ever had."[24]

FOR FURTHER READING

"Dixon, Julian Carey," *Biographical Directory of the U.S. Congress, 1774–Present*, http://bioguide.congress.gov/scripts/biodisplay.pl?index=D000373.

MANUSCRIPT COLLECTION

California State University, Los Angeles (Los Angeles, CA). Special Collections, University Library. *Papers:* Details are not yet available.

NOTES

1 Betty Cuniberti, "Rep. Dixon Named One of Unsung Heroes on the Hill," 12 September 1985, *Los Angeles Times*: Section 5, page 1.

2 Donald P. Baker, "Californian Heads Hill Unit on DC Funds," 5 March 1980, *Washington Post*: A1; Courtland Milloy, "Mr. Dixon," 2 August 1984, *Washington Post*: A1.

3 Baker, "Californian Heads Hill Unit on DC Funds"; Vernon Jarrett, "Can Black Voters Renew Their Faith?" 25 April 1980, *Chicago Tribune*: D4; David Stout, "Julian C. Dixon Is Dead at 66; Longtime Member of Congress," 9 December 2000, *New York Times*: C15. Some sources spell Julian Dixon's second wife's name "Bettye."

4 Doug Shuit, "Power Factions Clash in Congress Race," 26 April 1978, *Los Angeles Times*: E1; Donald P. Baker, "Dixon Hopes to Change Attitudes; New District Appropriations Boss Sees No Quick Shift," 6 March 1980, *Washington Post*: B2.

5 *Almanac of American Politics, 1980* (New York: E. P. Dutton, 1979): 107.

6 Shuit, "Power Factions Clash in Congress Race."

7 Dixon and his opponents called on both black and white politicians in an effort to court African-American voters.

8 *Almanac of American Politics, 1980*: 108.

9 Jean Merl, "Two Candidates Have It All to Themselves," 29 October 1978, *Los Angeles Times*: WS1; Doug Shuit, "Bitter Campaign by Mail Rages in 28th District," 4 June 1978, *Los Angeles Times*: D1.

10 "Election Statistics, 1920 to Present," available at http://clerk.house.gov/member_info/electionInfo/index.html.

11 Baker, "Dixon Hopes to Change Attitudes; New District Appropriations Boss Sees No Quick Shift."

12 Cuniberti, "Rep. Dixon Named an Unsung Hero: Only Californian to Make Editor's 'Underrated' List."

13 David Broder, "Bridge-Builder in Congress," 12 April 1989, *Washington Post*: A23.

14 *Politics in America, 1998* (Washington, DC: Congressional Quarterly Inc., 1997): 180; Tom Kenworthy, "House Ethics Panel to Release Unabridged Report on Wright," 8 April 1989, *Washington Post*: A2.

15 Richard Simon and Nick Anderson, "Respected Lawmaker Julian Dixon Dies," 9 December 2000, *Los Angeles Times*: B1.

16 Baker, "Californian Heads Hill Unit on DC Funds."

17 Baker, "Dixon Hopes to Change Attitudes; New District Appropriations Boss Sees No Quick Shift."

18 *Almanac of American Politics, 1988* (Washington, DC: National Journal Inc., 1987): 142; see also *Politics in America, 1990* (Washington, DC: Congressional Quarterly Inc., 1989): 179.

19 Stout, "Julian C. Dixon Is Dead at 66; Longtime Member of Congress."

20 *Politics in America, 1998*: 178.

21 Simon and Anderson, "Respected Lawmaker Julian Dixon Dies."

22 Lexie Verdon, "Political Precedent Worries Some Members," 6 May 1983, *Washington Post*: A1; "Arrests in 3 Cities," 19 December 1984, *New York Times*: A28.

23 Simon and Anderson, "Respected Lawmaker Julian Dixon Dies"; Stout, "Julian C. Dixon Is Dead at 66; Longtime Member of Congress."

24 Editorial, "Julian C. Dixon," 10 December 2000, *Washington Post*: B6.

Melvin Herbert Evans
1917–1984

DELEGATE ★ 1979–1981
REPUBLICAN FROM THE VIRGIN ISLANDS

Melvin Evans achieved distinction as the first popularly elected governor of the Virgin Islands— a multi-island territory in the eastern Caribbean. As the first black Delegate to represent the American territory in the U.S. Congress, Evans used his political experience to promote health care, education, and other areas of concern to his constituents during his brief tenure in the House of Representatives. "A man of conviction and high integrity, Congressman Evans would not be swayed from his principles," asserted Representative Donald Clausen of California. "A spokesman for the common man, he assured that the interests of his constituents were never overlooked."[1]

Melvin Herbert (Mel) Evans was born in Christiansted, St. Croix, on August 7, 1917, soon after the United States purchased the Virgin Islands from Denmark. After graduating from high school on St. Thomas, Evans received a bachelor of science degree in 1940 from Howard University and an M.D. from the Howard University College of Medicine in 1944. In 1945, Evans married Mary Phyllis Anderson, a nurse he met in a New York hospital; the couple had four sons: William, Melvin, Jr., Robert, and Cornelius.[2] During the next 15 years he served in a variety of medical and public health posts at hospitals and institutions in the United States and the Virgin Islands. From 1959 to 1967 Evans served as the Commissioner of Health for the Virgin Islands; he also was the chairman of the Governor's Commission on Human Resources from 1962 to 1966. In 1967 he furthered his academic credentials by earning a master's degree in public health from the University of California at Berkeley. He returned to private practice for two years before President Richard M. Nixon appointed him governor of the Virgin Islands. In August 1968 Congress passed the Virgin Islands Elective Governor Act, providing for the election of a governor by the territory's residents. Evans was elected as a Republican to the governor's office in 1970 and served until 1975. After his unsuccessful bid for re-election in 1974, he was Republican National Committeeman from the Virgin Islands and chairman of the board of trustees of the College of the Virgin Islands.[3]

In 1972, Congress authorized nonvoting Delegates for the Virgin Islands and Guam in the House of Representatives.[4] When the first Delegate of the Virgin Islands, Democrat Ron de Lugo, announced his decision to leave the House at the end of the 95th Congress (1977–1979) to run for governor of the American territory, Evans entered the 1978 general election to fill his open seat. In a tight race, Evans narrowly defeated Democrat Janet Watlington, a congressional aide to de Lugo, with 52 percent of the vote, to become the Virgin Islands's first black Delegate.[5] Sworn in to the 96th Congress (1979–1981) on January 3, 1979, Evans served on the Armed Services, Interior and Insular Affairs, and Merchant Marine and Fisheries committees.

During his congressional career, Evans paid close attention to the needs of his unique constituency, focusing on a legislative agenda to improve education and health care in the Virgin Islands. He secured federal funds to provide the territory's public education system with additional programs and services for its expanding school-age population. A longtime professional in the medical field, Evans introduced legislation to alleviate the critical shortage of doctors at local health facilities by permitting foreign physicians to practice in the Virgin Islands. "I firmly believe that the 120,000 people of the U.S. Virgin Islands, in addition to the 1.5 million tourists who annually visit our islands, must be provided adequate medical assistance to which they are entitled," he told his colleagues on the House Floor.[6] He also urged

the House to authorize funding to build two hospitals to accommodate the growing population of the territory.[7]

Determined to improve the quality of life on the Virgin Islands, Evans used his position in Congress to bring awareness to a variety of local issues and concerns. He attempted to make farm credit loans available to local fishing and agricultural industries and succeeded in having the Virgin Islands classified as a 'state,' making the territory eligible to receive full law enforcement funding.[8] Following the devastation wrought by Hurricane David and Tropical Storm Frederic in 1979, Evans urged Congress to approve flood control measures for the islands. In 1980 he organized congressional hearings in St. Croix and St. Thomas to investigate chronic delays in mail delivery between the United States and the Virgin Islands.[9] Evans also successfully sponsored a bill allowing federal recognition for National Guard officers from the Virgin Islands.

As one of only 17 blacks serving in the 96th Congress, Evans advocated increased rights for blacks. Shortly after joining the House, he remarked, "No one who has not been disenfranchised does not understand what it means to be disenfranchised." He added, "I'm from an area, you know, that got its first delegate to Congress only six years ago."[10] Despite his Republican affiliation, the entirely Democratic Congressional Black Caucus (CBC) welcomed Evans, contending that partisanship should not play a role in advancing the rights of minorities.[11] The Virgin Islands Delegate and the first-ever Republican caucus

member expressed great satisfaction at joining the CBC but warned, "Not only do I speak with a Republican point of view but I represent it in the caucus."[12] During his one term, Evans supported efforts to designate a national holiday for Martin Luther King, Jr., and after the death of A. Philip Randolph in May 1979, he eulogized the civil rights leader on the House Floor.[13] He strongly opposed a proposed constitutional amendment to eliminate court-ordered busing in public schools: "When people protest how strongly they favor civil rights and how vehemently they oppose segregation and then seek to remove one of the only, if not the only remedies, however imperfect without offering a viable alternative, it causes serious concern."[14] Evans's dedication to civil rights also extended to international politics. He joined many of his House colleagues in expressing outrage against the South African government's practice of racial segregation.[15]

Evans lost his 1980 re-election bid against Ron de Lugo, who had returned to seek his old seat after failing to win his bid for governor of the territory. Evans garnered 47 percent of the vote in a close contest.[16] Many Members of the House paid tribute to the retiring Evans, commending his commitment to the Virgin Islands, even though he served in the House for only two years.[17] In 1981, President Ronald W. Reagan nominated Evans as United States Ambassador to Trinidad and Tobago. Evans served in that office until his death of a heart attack in Christiansted on November 27, 1984.[18]

FOR FURTHER READING

"Evans, Melvin Herbert," *Biographical Directory of the U.S. Congress, 1774–Present*, http://bioguide.congress.gov/scripts/biodisplay.pl?index=E000254.

NOTES

1 *Congressional Record*, House, 96th Cong., 2nd sess. (9 December 1980): 32938.

2 "Dr. Melvin H. Evans Is Dead; Served as Envoy to Trinidad," 28 November 1984, *New York Times*: D27; Roderick Nordell, "Island Governor's Wife and Life," 19 January 1971, *Christian Science Monitor*: 10; "Deaths Elsewhere," 28 November 1984, *Washington Post*: B7.

3 "Dr. Melvin H. Evans Is Dead; Served as Envoy to Trinidad"; "Deaths Elsewhere"; "Washington News," 6 November 1981, United Press International.

4 Betsy Palmer, "Territorial Delegates to the U.S. Congress: Current Issues and Historical Background," 6 July 2006, Report RL32340, Congressional Research Service, Library of Congress, Washington, DC. House Delegates from the Virgin Islands, Guam, American Samoa, and the District of Columbia can vote in committee and introduce legislation but cannot vote on the House Floor or offer a motion to reconsider a vote.

5 "Governor of Virgin Islands Wins a Full Term on 'No-Party' State," 12 November 1978, *New York Times*: 52; "Election Statistics, 1920 to Present," available at http://clerk.house.gov/member_info/electionInfo/index.html.

6 *Congressional Record*, House, 96th Cong., 1st sess. (8 June 1979): 14073.

7 "Two Hospitals in Virgin Islands Are Warned of Cutoffs in Funds," 20 May 1979, *New York Times*: 46.

8 *Congressional Record*, House, 96th Cong., 1st sess. (19 July 1979): 19527.

9 Ellen Hume, "Rep. Wilson Presides at Hearings in Virgin Islands," 12 April 1980, *Los Angeles Times*: A3.

10 Donnie Radcliffe, "Honoring Newcomers to the Black Caucus," 6 February 1979, *Washington Post*: A1.

11 Luix Overbea, "Jobs—Still Black Caucus Priority," 24 November 1978, *Christian Science Monitor*: 5.

12 Radcliffe, "Honoring Newcomers to the Black Caucus."

13 *Congressional Record*, House, 96th Cong., 1st sess. (5 December 1979): 34759; *Congressional Record*, House, 96th Cong., 1st sess. (21 May 1979): 12001.

14 *Congressional Record*, House, 96th Cong., 1st sess. (24 July 1979): 20379.

15 *Congressional Record*, House, 96th Cong., 2nd sess. (24 March 1980): 6225.

16 "Election Statistics, 1920 to Present," available at http://clerk.house.gov/member_info/electionInfo/index.html.

17 *Congressional Record*, House, 96th Cong., 2nd sess. (9 December 1980): 32937–32941.

18 "Dr. Melvin H. Evans Is Dead; Served as Envoy to Trinidad."

William Herbert Gray III
1941–

UNITED STATES REPRESENTATIVE ★ 1979–1991
DEMOCRAT FROM PENNSYLVANIA

A third-generation pastor of a large Philadelphia-area Baptist church and community activist, William Gray defeated a longtime incumbent to take his first elected office in the United States House of Representatives. Though new to elective office, Gray proved adept at Capitol Hill politics, rising meteorically in power during his 12 years in Congress primarily because he was skilled at lobbying for top posts. "If preachers, lawyers, business entrepreneurs, and teachers can engage in politics, why not a Baptist minister?" Gray asked. "Congress needs a strong moral force within its chambers. What better person than a man of moral integrity to serve his district?"[1] Gray was the first black Member of Congress to chair the powerful and partisan Budget Committee and the first black Representative to become the third-ranking Democrat in the House. Yet, at the height of his political career, he abruptly resigned to take a position to assist historically black colleges and to return to the pulpit.

William Herbert (Bill) Gray III was born in Baton Rouge, Louisiana, on August 20, 1941. The second child of Dr. William H. Gray, Jr., and Hazel Yates Gray, he had an older sister, Marion. William Gray spent the first nine years of his life in St. Augustine, and Tallahassee, Florida, where his father served as president of Florida Normal and Industrial College (now Florida Memorial College) and Florida Agricultural and Mechanical College (now Florida A&M University). His mother was a high school teacher and once served as dean of Southern University in Baton Rouge, Louisiana. When William Gray III's grandfather and namesake died in 1949, the Grays moved to North Philadelphia, where William Gray, Jr., took over his father's pastoral position at Bright Hope Baptist Church, which William Gray, Sr., had held since 1925. William Gray III graduated from Simon Gratz High School in Philadelphia in 1959 and earned a B.A. from Franklin and Marshall

College in Lancaster, Pennsylvania, in 1963. Gray majored in sociology, but one of his professors encouraged him to become involved in politics. During his senior year in college, Gray interned for Philadelphia Representative Robert N. C. Nix.[2]

After college, Gray followed his father and grandfather into the ministry. He received a master's degree in divinity from Drew Theological Seminary in Madison, New Jersey, in 1966 and a master's degree in theology from Princeton Theological Seminary in 1970. He became a community activist in 1970 while living in Montclair, New Jersey, after he won a housing discrimination suit against a landlord who denied him an apartment because of his race. The New Jersey superior court awarded him financial damages, setting a legal precedent and earning Gray national attention.[3] Gray founded the nonprofit Union Housing Corporation in Montclair to build affordable homes for low- and moderate-income tenants. In 1971, he married Andrea Dash, a marketing consultant. They raised three sons: William IV, Justin, and Andrew.

After his father died in 1972, Gray assumed the pastor's position at Philadelphia's Bright Hope Baptist Church.[4] The congregation swelled to more than 4,000 members, and Gray continued his community activism. In 1975, he cofounded the Philadelphia Mortgage Plan, an organization that helped people in low income communities to obtain mortgages.[5] Concern about community housing issues and the high unemployment rate in his West Philadelphia neighborhood drew Gray back into politics in 1976. Never having held elected office, Gray took interest in the northwest Philadelphia congressional district that was represented by his former boss, Representative Nix, a longtime Representative and a Philadelphia political powerbroker. Gray had become disillusioned with what he perceived as Nix's

OIL ON CANVAS, SIMMIE KNOX, 1996,
COLLECTION OF U.S. HOUSE OF REPRESENTATIVES

unresponsiveness to his constituents, nearly one-third of whom lived below the poverty line. Since the registered voters in northwest Philadelphia were overwhelmingly Democratic, winning the Democratic primary was tantamount to victory in the general election.[6] Gray narrowly lost the 1976 primary election by about 300 votes.[7] Gray returned in 1978, dubbing Nix "the phantom" due to the infrequency of the aging Representative's visits to his district. Gray also called attention to the district's ailing economy, which had the highest unemployment rate in the state.[8] Encouragement from former Representative Andrew Young of Georgia, who was serving as U.S. Ambassador to the United Nations, gave Gray the confidence to enter elective politics. "Bill, if you can pastor Bright Hope Baptist Church, Congress will not be difficult," Gray recalls Young telling him. "It is essentially pastoring, ministering to the folks in your district."[9] Bright Hope Baptist members played an integral part in Gray's campaign, hosting events and helping him plan strategy.[10] He defeated the incumbent in the 1978 primary, with 58 percent to Nix's 41 percent.[11]

Unconcerned about the general election in his overwhelmingly Democratic district, Gray spent the time between the primary and the November elections lobbying for choice committee posts. His friendship with Young provided Gray with important connections in Washington.[12] After winning the general election by a wide margin (82 percent) over Republican Roland Atkins, Gray received several plum committee assignments in the 96th Congress (1979–1981) as a result of his earlier lobbying efforts. In addition to a seat on the Committee on the District of Columbia, the only post he would hold for his entire career, Gray occupied seats on the prestigious Budget and Foreign Affairs panels. The Democratic leadership as well as the leaders of the Congressional Black Caucus (CBC) took note of his political acumen and pegged him as a rising star. CBC Chairman Parren Mitchell of Maryland called Gray's skills "top flight."[13] The caucus elected Gray as its secretary and in his second term he served as vice chairman. Also, Gray's fellow freshman

Democrats elected him as their representative to the Steering and Policy Committee, which sets committee assignments for Democratic Members and writes party policy. Gray later served on the House Administration Committee (102nd Congress, 1991–1993) and the Joint Committee on Deficit Reduction (100th Congress, 1987–1989).

Gray typically won re-election with little opposition, garnering margins of at least 90 percent.[14] Careful not to suffer the same fate as Nix, he kept in close contact with the district and remained attentive to the needs of the black community. Throughout his congressional career, Gray continued to preach two Sundays per month at Bright Hope Church. "I was elected to Congress," he once told the *Washington Post*, "I was called to preach. One I do because people allow me to do it. The other I *have* to do."[15] In May 1985, Gray's dedication to his constituents was tested. His district was the scene of disaster after members of MOVE, a radical, black Muslim cult, clashed with police. The violence led to 11 deaths, and several city blocks in a West Philadelphia neighborhood were burned. Gray escaped the political fallout for the massacre; Philadelphia Mayor Wilson Goode bore the brunt of the criticism. Gray responded to his constituents' needs by touring the scene of the destruction and obtaining federal aid for the victims from the Department of Housing and Urban Development (HUD).[16]

Gray's work on the Foreign Affairs Committee focused on Africa. Though he left the committee after his freshman term, throughout his career, Gray requested aid for Africa on a scale that was later compared to the Marshall Plan, which provided billions of dollars to war-torn Europe after World War II.[17] In his freshman term, Gray sponsored a bill that created the African Development Foundation, which delivered U.S. aid to African villages.[18] In 1983, he sponsored a series of allotments guaranteeing minority-owned businesses, private agencies, and historically black universities greater participation programs in Africa that were administered by the U.S. Agency for International Development. Gray also was one of the first politicians in the early 1980s to predict an impending famine in Ethiopia. In 1984 he led the House in providing emergency food rations to the starving nation. Three years later, he made a rare break from his own party, supporting a Republican-sponsored bill to condemn Ethiopia's communist leaders for human rights violations and for exacerbating the famine.[19] Also, Gray was a chief opponent of South Africa's apartheid system.

Gray received his initial position on the Budget Committee with the blessing of outgoing panel member Representative Parren Mitchell, who was eager to find a CBC member to replace him on the committee in 1979.[20] Serving his first term on the Budget Committee, Gray grew increasingly frustrated with the committee Democrats' seemingly weak defense against cuts in social spending. He was one of a few Members who regularly voted against his party's budgets. Gray left the Budget Committee in 1981 for a spot on the Appropriations panel, where he would remain for the rest of his career, and returned to the Budget Committee in 1983 at the beginning of the 98th Congress (1983–1985). With seats on the Budget and Appropriations panels, Gray occupied a position of power and was much more receptive to compromise. He began working to persuade Democrats to accept more moderate proposals, and he arbitrated differences between House and Senate versions of the federal budget.[21] Gray's political expertise and integrity earned him a solid reputation. In 1984, conservative Democrat Charles Stenholm of Texas noted, "Bill's shown flexibility and a mastery of the budget process. He's very articulate and he's always been fair."[22]

House rules allowed Members to serve on the Budget Committee for a maximum of six successive years. In 1984, sitting chairman Representative Jim Jones of Oklahoma faced the end of his allotted term. He and outgoing Representative Leon Panetta of California, who also aspired to the chairmanship, sought a change in the rule so that they could continue serving, but last-minute opposition from Speaker Thomas (Tip) O'Neill of Massachusetts thwarted their plan. Having quietly secured

support in case the rule had not changed, Gray was the only member of the panel who had enough votes for the chairmanship upon Jones's departure, despite a last-minute bid by Democratic Texas Representative Martin Frost.[23] Nearly two thousand of Gray's proud constituents organized by Bright Hope congregants flooded the Capitol to watch his swearing-in as the first black chairman of the Budget Committee.[24] Gray downplayed the symbolism. "There is no title here called 'Black America Budget Chairman'," Gray declared. "It's called House Budget Committee Chairman. I happen to be black and there is no conflict in that. . . . it's been proven over the years that blacks can provide leadership in Congress."[25]

A natural politician who was comfortable on the House Floor, Chairman Gray tactfully managed the often-explosive, partisan Budget Committee. Gray's congressional colleague Washington Democrat Mike Lowry speculated about the origins of Gray's ability to broker compromises: "It's maybe his professional training as a minister. He's a great judge of knowing how far he can push his members. He never gets mad."[26] Gray often was successful in unifying an increasingly diverse Democratic Party—and some Republicans—around a budget that incorporated his commitment to social spending. He also quelled initial Democratic concerns about the message a liberal northeastern African American in his powerful position would send to more-moderate voters by forging a strong coalition that spanned the party's broad fiscal spectrum. Surprisingly, Gray found strong allies in the "boll weevils," southern Democrats who tended to support the Ronald W. Reagan administration's cuts in social spending; two boll weevils, Representatives Marvin Leath and Stenholm, both from Texas, were among Gray's biggest supporters.[27]

Despite his reputation for compromise, Gray did not back down from creating a budget that was consistent with his liberal Democratic ideals. He guided four successive Democratic budget resolutions through the House— often over vehement protests from many committee Republicans. One observer remarked, "Gray treated the budget process as a political puzzle, not an economic problem; he saw the budget for what it is: a political statement rather than a blueprint for fiscal governance."[28] However, the increasing federal deficit became a sticking point. Gray battled Republican attempts to reduce deficit spending. His focus was preserving funding for social programs, and he believed efforts to reduce the deficit should not override compassionate spending.[29] "A balanced budget is good for the country, the affluent and poor alike," Gray noted. "I seek [a budget] that doesn't sacrifice programs for the poor and minorities, one that is fair and equitable."[30] The Budget Committee under Gray virtually ignored the Gramm–Rudman–Hollings Act of 1985 (revised in 1987), which demanded automatic budget cuts across the board if the President and Congress were unable to cap the deficit at a specific annual level.[31] As a result, Gray oversaw the first trillion-dollar budget in U.S. history for fiscal year 1988. The Democratic Party's show of unity regarding the Gray budgets was impressive, especially in view of the party's growing fiscal diversity. Few of the Democratic rank and file voted against Gray's budgets. A record low of 15 Democrats refused to support their party's budget resolution in Gray's first year as chairman. His first three budget resolutions combined totaled 53 "nay" votes from Democrats; previously, this figure was more typical for a single year.[32]

Capitalizing on his favorable reputation in Democratic circles, Gray sought to move up in the party leadership. In 1987, Gray began lobbying to succeed Representative Richard Gephardt of Missouri as Chairman of the House Democratic Caucus in order to head party efforts to develop a consensus and dole out committee assignments. Though his work on the Budget Committee reflected Gray's ability to unite Democrats, it was his efforts as chairman of the committee drafting the party platform for the 1988 Democratic Convention that truly shone. Gray's committee brought together the broad coalition of Democrats under a platform of "that which uniquely binds us together as Democrats."[33] The House Democratic Caucus overwhelmingly elected Gray to Gephardt's former position in December 1988. Again, Gray downplayed the milestone he had achieved as the first African-American chairman of the House Democratic Caucus, noting that his new position called for building coalitions, not representing one arm of the Democratic Party. "I hope we can tie our ropes together so we can be one party and show the nation what we stand for as Democrats," Gray declared.[34] Just six months later, Gray took one more step up the leadership ladder when he succeeded Representative Tony Coelho of California as Majority Whip. In this position Gray was responsible for determining and coalescing votes from the Democratic Members for issues of party interest. With his ascent to Majority Whip, the third-ranking leadership position in the House, Gray became the highest-ranking African American in congressional history.

At the peak of his political power, Gray abruptly announced his resignation from Congress on June 20, 1991, effective the following September 11. He outlined his plan to head the United Negro College Fund (later known as the College Fund/UNCF)—which allocates federal money to augment the facilities, programs, and faculty at historically black colleges and universities— saying his new duties were "just as important as being a member of the leadership in Congress." Gray's departure sent shockwaves through the political community.[35] Gray served as President and CEO of the College Fund/UNCF until March 2004.[36] In 1994, President William J. (Bill) Clinton asked Gray to serve as his special adviser on Haiti, which was then embroiled in civil war. Gray's efforts to restore democracy to the island nation won him a Medal of Honor from Haitian President Jean-Bertrand Aristide.

FOR FURTHER READING

"Gray, William Herbert, III," *Biographical Directory of the United States Congress, 1774–Present*, http://bioguide.congress.gov/scripts/biodisplay.pl?index=G000402.

MANUSCRIPT COLLECTION

The New York Public Library, Schomburg Center for Research in Black Culture (New York, NY). *Papers:* 1979–1991, 90 feet. The congressional papers of William Herbert Gray III have not yet been processed.

NOTES

1   Luix Overbea, "Pennsylvania's Gray—Budgeteer, Congressman, and Minister," 21 October 1985, *Christian Science Monitor*: 11.

2   "William H. Gray III," in Jessie Carney Smith, ed., *Notable Black American Men* (Farmington Hills, MI: Gale Research Inc., 1999): 478–481 (hereinafter referred to as *NBAM*).

3   "William H. Gray III," *NBAM*; Ronald Sullivan, "Negro, Denied Apartment, Wins $50 Court Award for 'Trauma,'" 6 May 1970, *New York Times*: 1.

4   Gray served as pastor of Bright Hope Baptist Church until 2007. The position of head pastor was filled by a member of the Gray family for more than 80 years; see Philadelphia Baptist Association, "Our Churches" at http://www.philadelphiabaptist.org/PBAChurches.htm (accessed 27 February 2006).

5   "William H. Gray III," *NBAM*.

6   *Politics in America, 1988* (Washington, DC: Congressional Quarterly Inc., 1987): 1284; Brooks Jackson, "Many Blacks Show Little Urge to Vote," 3 October 1980, *Wall Street Journal*: 1.

7   "William H. Gray III," *NBAM*.

8   "Gray, William H., 3d," *Current Biography, 1988* (New York: H. W. Wilson Company, 1988): 198.

9   Carla Hall, "Bill Gray, Baron of the Budget," 24 May 1985, *Washington Post*: B1.

10 Hall, "Bill Gray, Baron of the Budget."

11 *Politics in America, 1988*: 1285.

12 Hall, "Bill Gray, Baron of the Budget."

13 Mary Russell, "Minister Proves Skillful Politician," 21 January 1979, *Washington Post*: A3.

14 The only exception was in 1982, when Republican activist Milton Street ran as an Independent because he missed the filing date. However, Street's misconduct, which included assault charges and unpaid taxes, boosted support for Gray, and he won easily, with 76 percent of the vote. See "Election Statistics, 1920 to Present," available at http://clerk.house.gov/member_info/election.html.

15 Hall, "Bill Gray, Baron of the Budget" (author's emphasis).

16 "Gray, William H., 3d," *Current Biography, 1988*: 200; Hall, "Bill Gray, Baron of the Budget."

17 "Gray, William H., 3d," *Current Biography, 1988*: 200.

18 Though Gray's bills (H.R. 5509 and H.R. 6288) did not pass, his measure was folded into a successful omnibus international development bill (H.R. 6942), which Gray cosponsored. See *Congressional Record*, 96th Cong., 2nd sess.

19 "William H. Gray III," *Contemporary Black Biography* Volume 3 (Detroit, MI: Gale Research Inc., 1992) (hereinafter referred to as *CBB*).

20 Shirley Washington, *Outstanding African Americans of Congress* (Washington, DC: United States Capitol Historical Society, 1998): 34.

21 "Gray, William H., 3d," *Current Biography, 1988*: 198.

22 Dan Balz, "Minister May Head Budget Panel; Rep. Gray Has Quietly 'Done All the Right Things'," 6 December 1984, *Washington Post*: A4.

23 Washington, *Outstanding African Americans of Congress*: 35; *Politics in America, 1988*: 1284.

24 Washington, *Outstanding African Americans of Congress*: 36.

25 Hall, "Bill Gray, Baron of the Budget."

26 Ibid.

27 Washington, *Outstanding African Americans of Congress*: 36.

28 *Politics in America, 1990* (Washington, DC: Congressional Quarterly Inc., 1989): 1273.

29 "William H. Gray III," *NBAM*; Washington, *Outstanding African Americans of Congress*: 36.

30 Overbea, "Pennsylvania's Gray—Budgeteer, Congressman, and Minister."

31 See James A. Thurber, "Balanced Budget and Emergency Deficit Control Act," in Donald C. Bacon et al., *The Encyclopedia of the United States Congress*, Volume 1 (New York: Simon and Schuster, 1995): 129–130.

32 *Politics in America, 1988*: 1283.

33 "Gray, William H., 3d," *Current Biography, 1988*: 200. See also Herbert S. Parmet, "Election of 1988," in Arthur M. Schlesinger, Jr., ed., *History of American Presidential Elections, 1789–2001*, Volume XI (Philadelphia: Chelsea House Publishers, 2002): 4229–4239.

34 Elaine S. Povich, "Black Democrat Gets No. 4 Post in House," 6 December 1988, *Chicago Tribune*: 4.

35 "Gray Tells Colleagues His Reasons for Resigning," 20 June 1991, *Seattle Post-Intelligencer*: A3; quoted in "William H. Gray III," *NBAM*. A 1989 Justice Department probe into Gray's office staff as well as his personal and congressional finances fueled rumors that fiscal misconduct spurred his resignation. Accusations against Gray weakened when a top aide for U.S. Attorney General Dick Thornburgh was charged with leaking information on the investigation. Thornburgh repeatedly denied that Gray was the specific target of an investigation, and charges against Gray were never filed. See Paul M. Rodriguez and Jerry Seper, "Gray Quit After Start of Probe in FBI," 21 June 1991, *Washington Times*: A1; Washington, *Outstanding African Americans of Congress*: 37; "William H. Gray III," *CBB*; "Outgoing House Whip Says Financial Probe Just a Rumor," 22 June 1991, Associated Press.

36 See Michael Anft, "A Politician and Fund Raiser Returns to the Ministry," 30 October 2003, *The Chronicle of Higher Philanthropy*, at http://www.philanthropy.com/free/articles/v16/i02/02006201.htm (accessed 18 April 2008).

"THERE IS NO TITLE HERE CALLED 'BLACK AMERICA BUDGET CHAIRMAN'," GRAY DECLARED. "IT'S CALLED HOUSE BUDGET COMMITTEE CHAIRMAN. I HAPPEN TO BE BLACK AND THERE IS NO CONFLICT IN THAT. . . . IT'S BEEN PROVEN OVER THE YEARS THAT BLACKS CAN PROVIDE LEADERSHIP IN CONGRESS."

George Thomas (Mickey) Leland
1944–1989

UNITED STATES REPRESENTATIVE ★ 1979–1989
DEMOCRAT FROM TEXAS

Inspired by an extended stay on the continent as a young legislator, Representative Leland poured his energy into focusing attention on a disastrous East African famine and raising funds for relief efforts. Leland worked tirelessly as chairman of the House Select Committee on Hunger, which he had lobbied Congress to create. Responding to critics who felt he should focus on domestic poverty first, Leland retorted, "I am as much of a citizen of this world as I am of this country. To hell with those people who are critical of what I am able to do to help save people's lives. I don't mean to sound hokey, but I grew up on the Christian ethic which says we are supposed to help the least of our brothers."[1] This statement encapsulated Leland's career and life goals. He became a martyr for the cause of eradicating world hunger, perishing in a plane crash on a humanitarian mission to transport supplies to an Ethiopian refugee camp.

George Thomas (Mickey) Leland was born in Lubbock, Texas, on November 27, 1944, to Alice Rains.[2] It was Leland's maternal grandfather who nicknamed him "Mickey." Shortly after Leland's birth, his parents separated. Alice Rains moved with her two sons, Mickey and Gaston, to a poor section of Houston, where she worked as a short-order cook. Rains put herself through school and became a teacher. Mickey Leland graduated from Phyllis Wheatley High School in Houston in 1963 and attended Houston's Texas Southern University. Earning his degree in pharmacy in 1970, Leland worked as an instructor of clinical pharmacy at Texas Southern before taking a job as a pharmacist. He also served with several university organizations, setting up free clinics and other aid for the Houston-area poor.

Influenced by diverse doctrines—the writings of black activists and the emphasis of his Roman Catholic faith on helping the disadvantaged—Leland was active in the civil rights movement as a student in the late 1960s, often participating in unruly protests, and describing himself as a "Marxist" and a "revolutionary."[3] His arrest while demonstrating against police brutality in Houston proved to be a pivotal moment in his life, persuading Leland to work within the political system rather than against it. Leland was first elected to the Texas state house of representatives in 1972 and served his polyglot Houston neighborhood from 1973 to 1979. He quickly earned a reputation as a militant, firebrand politician in the state legislature, appearing on the first day in a tie-dyed dashiki shirt, an Afro haircut, and platform shoes.[4] While in the state legislature, Leland made his first trip to Africa. The young politician developed a deep affection for the continent, staying in Tanzania for three months rather than his scheduled three weeks.[5] "Nobody knew where I was," Leland recalled, "My mother thought I was dead. But the fact is that I got totally absorbed in Africa."[6] Leland stepped onto the national political scene by serving as a delegate to the Democratic National Convention in 1972. He also served as a delegate to the Texas state constitutional convention in 1974, where he helped rewrite Texas's 97-year-old Jim Crow-Era constitution, focusing on reforming the judicial and executive branches of the state government.[7]

In 1978, three-term Houston Representative Barbara Jordan announced her retirement from Congress. The first Member to serve the newly created district, Jordan represented central city neighborhoods where the population was almost three-quarters minority, dominated by lower- and middle-class African and Mexican Americans.[8] Leland entered the May 6 Democratic primary, garnering 48 percent of the vote against seven other candidates. Falling short of the necessary 50 percent to win the nomination, Leland faced the primary runner-

IMAGE COURTESY OF OFFICE OF THE CLERK, U.S. HOUSE OF REPRESENTATIVES

up, African-American candidate Anthony Hall, in a runoff primary on June 3. Hall had won 24 percent of the May 6 votes. Hall and Leland had remarkably parallel backgrounds: they were both age 33, grew up in similar Houston neighborhoods, and served simultaneously in the state legislature. Though Jordan refused to endorse any one candidate, Leland's ability to garner support from both the district's black and Hispanic constituents sealed his victory over Hall, with 57 percent of the vote.[9] Without official opposition in the general election, Leland won 97 percent of the vote for the 96th Congress (1979–1981). He was re-elected five times, typically winning majorities of 90 percent or more.[10]

Upon his arrival in Washington, Leland won a seat on the powerful Interstate and Foreign Commerce Committee (later Energy and Commerce)—often sought after by Members because of its regulatory powers across a broad swath of industry. He was also assigned to the Post Office and Civil Service Committee, where he chaired the Subcommittee on Postal Operations and Services. In addition, Leland served on the Committee on the District of Columbia and became an active member of the Congressional Black Caucus (CBC). Leland later chaired the CBC in the 99th Congress (1985–1987). While attending an annual CBC weekend party in 1982, Leland met 24-year-old Georgetown University Law student Alison Walton. The two married in 1983, and Alison Leland worked as an investment banker. In 1986, the couple celebrated the birth of their first son, Jarrett.[11]

Leland proved an active advocate for all minorities, focusing particularly on the needs of his black and Hispanic constituents. To best serve the large Mexican-American population in his district, Leland learned Spanish. He once shocked his colleagues by arguing in Spanish on the House Floor in favor of maintaining the bilingual clauses in the Voting Rights Act.[12] His bilingualism allowed him to develop a controversial working relationship with Cuban leader Fidel Castro. Leland disagreed emphatically with Castro's philosophy but admired his political influence among poorer nations.

Leland continued to look abroad, focusing on international cooperation and exchange. One of his first acts in Congress was to fund a six-week trip to Israel to allow underprivileged black teenagers from the Houston area to learn about Jewish culture and to create a cross-cultural dialogue between the youths in the two countries.[13] Leland also led the demand for increased hiring quotas for women and minorities at telecommunications companies, taking on television executives and advocating more minority hires for on and off screen positions. In 1984 Leland supported the presidential candidacy of his longtime friend Vice President Walter Mondale over that of black civil rights activist Jesse Jackson, angering several of his African-American colleagues. However, Leland returned as Jackson's lead fundraiser for the 1988 presidential campaign.[14]

Leland's greatest passion developed from his three-month stay in East Africa. He spent most of his congressional career attempting to redirect American foreign policy away from the military imperatives of the Cold War confrontation between superpowers toward examining the inequalities between rich and poor nations. When famine struck East Africa in the mid-1980s, Leland was an outspoken advocate for alleviating hunger on the continent. Throughout his first two terms, he lobbied for the creation of a congressional committee to focus on world poverty and hunger. While sympathetic to his cause, many Members provided less support than Leland requested, as they believed it would only add to the institution's mounting bureaucracy.[15] While critics claimed Leland should focus on domestic hunger before turning his attention abroad, he also involved himself in domestic poverty and hunger issues, proposing tax exemptions for American companies that donated to food banks. In 1987, he spent a night on a Washington, DC, steam grate to emphasize the plight of the homeless.[16] Leland regularly raised aid for Houston-area food banks, which provided him with greater leverage for creating a committee on hunger.[17] Leland often invoked two images from his frequent trips to Ethiopian refugee camps: a throng of starving people rubbing their stomachs and pleading for food and an Ethiopian girl who died in his arms as he turned to ask her caretakers about her condition. "Every day I see her face," Leland said.[18]

After gathering 258 cosponsors and the support of 60 national organizations, Leland realized his goal in 1984 of creating a congressional committee to examine global hunger and poverty.[19] Leland's Hunger Committee resolution passed on February 22 by a vote of 309 to 78.[20] He was appointed the first chairman of the Temporary Select Committee on Hunger in the 98th Congress (1983–1985). Modeled after a similar panel (the Committee on Children, Youth and Families), the Hunger Committee studied the effects of domestic and international hunger and poverty. In 1984, partially aided by publicity from American and British musicians, Leland's committee pushed through Congress an aid package for famine relief of nearly $800 million.[21] Though successful in raising awareness about hunger, Leland complained of his congressional colleagues' lack of interest.

Leland traveled frequently to Africa, often guiding Members and their staffs to refugee camps so they could witness firsthand how aid money was being used in Africa. On August 7, 1989, he took advantage of the congressional summer recess to check on the progress of a refugee camp near the Sudanese–Ethiopian border. Shortly after his plane took off from Addis Ababa, it crashed over a mountainous region in Ethiopia while navigating a storm. All 15 people aboard were killed, including Leland

and three congressional aides. Out of mutual respect for Leland, the United States and Ethiopia temporarily repaired their strained diplomatic relations, and Ethiopian military leader Mengistu Haile Mariam allowed American military spy planes to search for Leland's downed aircraft.[22] The U.S. military discovered the wreckage after seven days of searching, and a congressional delegation accompanied Leland's remains to Texas for burial.

Representative Leland was widely eulogized. Visitors poured into his Capitol Hill office to offer their condolences. Staff in the neighboring office occupied by Representative George Crockett of Michigan helped field the overwhelming number of phone calls.[23] Communities touched by Leland were quick to honor him: The CBC renamed its humanitarian award for him in 1989, Houston International Airport named its largest terminal for him, and the National Association for the Advancement of Colored People sponsored a project to plant trees in Africa in his name.[24] The tragedy of Leland's death was compounded when Alison Leland gave birth in January 1990 to premature twin sons, Cameron George and Austin Mickey, five months after her husband's death. Democratic leaders in the House led a fundraiser to collect donations for Leland's three children. Alison Leland declined an offer to run for her husband's vacant House seat. With her support, Houston-area legislator Craig Washington succeeded Leland in the December 9 special election. Without Leland's forceful support and leadership, the Select Committee on Hunger was eventually eliminated in the 103rd Congress (1993–1995).

FOR FURTHER READING

"Leland, George Thomas (Mickey)," *Biographical Directory of the United States Congress, 1774–Present*, http://bioguide.congress.gov/scripts/biodisplay.pl?index=L000237.

MANUSCRIPT COLLECTION

Texas Southern University (Houston, TX). The Leland Archives, The Mickey Leland Center on World Hunger and Peace. *Papers:* 1970–1989, 653 boxes. The collection documents Mickey Leland's public service career as a Texas state representative and as a U.S. Representative from Texas. Materials include correspondence, news clippings, artifacts, photographs, audio and videotapes, speeches, news releases, committee testimony, and casework. Topics include health care rights for the poor, prison reform, police harassment and brutality, racial discrimination, affirmative action, budget discrimination in higher education, labor legislation, political election organization, infant mortality, minority rights in business, health education, parks and recreation for the indigent, apartheid and racial discrimination issues worldwide, Third World development, emergency shelters for the homeless, nutrients for the malnourished, and food security for victims of hunger. A finding aid database is available in the repository.

NOTES

1   Lisa Belkin, "Representative Mickey Leland, 44, Dies in Crash," 14 August 1989, *New York Times*: D9.

2   Leland's father is unknown.

3   Stephen Chapman, "Mickey Leland: Good Intentions, Serious Errors," 17 August 1989, *Chicago Tribune*: 29C.

4   *Politics in America, 1984* (Washington, DC: Congressional Quarterly Inc., 1983): 1495.

5   Shirley Washington, *Outstanding African Americans of Congress* (Washington, DC: United States Capitol Historical Society, 1998): 56.

6   Belkin, "Representative Mickey Leland, 44, Dies in Crash."

7   Molly Ivins, "Constitution Time Again in Texas," 20 January 1974, *Washington Post*: C3.

8   *Almanac of American Politics, 1986* (Washington, DC: National Journal Inc., 1985): 1327.

9   *Politics in America, 1982* (Washington, DC: Congressional Quarterly Inc., 1981): 1191.

10 "Election Statistics, 1920 to Present," available at http://clerk.house.gov/member_info/election.html.

11 Washington, *Outstanding African Americans of Congress*: 57.

12 *Congressional Record*, House, 97th Cong., 1st sess. (5 October 1981): 23187.

13 "Mickey Leland," *Contemporary Black Biography*, Volume 2 (Detroit: Gale Research Inc., 1992).

14 Jacqueline Trescott, "Leland and the War on Hunger," 27 September 1985, *Washington Post*: B1.

15 Washington, *Outstanding African Americans of Congress*: 57.

16 Chapman, "Mickey Leland: Good Intentions, Serious Errors."

17 Lori Rodriguez, "Leland's Legacy In Need of Boost," 28 March 1992, *Houston Chronicle*: A25; "Select Committee on Hunger," in Garrison Nelson, *Committees in the U.S. Congress, 1947 to 1992*, Volume 2 (Washington, DC: Congressional Quarterly Press, 1994): 1035; *Congressional Record*, House, 98th Cong., 2nd sess. (22 February 1984): 2967–2968.

18 Belkin, "Representative Mickey Leland, 44, Dies in Crash."

19 *Congressional Record*, House, 98th Cong., 2nd sess. (22 February 1984): 2967; "Select Committee on Hunger," in Nelson, *Committees in the U.S. Congress, 1947 to 1992*, Volume 2: 1035.

20 *Congressional Record*, House, 98th Cong., 2nd sess. (22 February 1984): 2986–2987.

21 Washington, *Outstanding African Americans of Congress*: 57.

22 *Politics in America, 1986* (Washington, DC: Congressional Quarterly Inc., 1985): 1524.

23 Richard L. Berke, "Friends and Relatives Mourn Texas Lawmaker," 14 August 1989, *New York Times*: A10.

24 "NAACP Launches African Tree-Planting: To Honor Congressman Mickey Leland," 6 July 1991, *Michigan Citizen*: 2.

"I AM NOW AN ACTIVIST

ON BEHALF OF HUMANITY

EVERYWHERE, WHETHER IT IS

ETHIOPIA... SOUTH AFRICA

... ANY PART OF THE WORLD

WHERE PEOPLE ARE DESPERATE

AND HUNGRY FOR FREEDOMS

AND RIGHTS THEY [DESERVE]

AS HUMAN BEINGS. THAT IS

MY COMMUNITY, THAT IS

MY BATTLEGROUND," LELAND

TOLD THE *WASHINGTON POST*

IN 1985.

Bennett McVey Stewart
1912–1988

UNITED STATES REPRESENTATIVE ★ 1979–1981
DEMOCRAT FROM ILLINOIS

Elected to succeed Representative Ralph Metcalfe after his sudden death shortly before the general election in 1978, Bennett McVey Stewart continued the tradition of African-American representation of Chicago's South Side that began with the election of Oscar De Priest in 1928. A product of the once-powerful Chicago machine, Stewart never gained a solid footing in his district during his one term in the U.S. House. His re-election defeat in 1980 symbolized the waning influence of the local political organization and marked the end of a historic era of machine dominance in Chicago.

Bennett McVey Stewart was born in Huntsville, Alabama, on August 6, 1912, to Bennett Stewart and Cathleen Jones. He attended public schools in Huntsville and graduated from high school in Birmingham, Alabama. In 1936, Stewart received a B.A. from Miles College, in Birmingham, Alabama. While attending college, Stewart met his future wife, Pattye Crittenden. The couple married in 1938 and had three children: Bennett, Jr., Ronald, and Miriam.[1] From 1936 to 1938 he served as assistant principal of Irondale High School in Birmingham. Stewart returned to Miles College as an associate professor of sociology from 1938 until 1940, when he joined an insurance company as an executive. In 1950 he became Illinois state director for the company, a position he held for 18 years. Stewart's subsequent position—as an inspector with Chicago's building department of urban renewal advising property owners on financing renovations—sparked his involvement with politics. Following a path similar to those of other influential African-American politicians in Chicago, Stewart won election to the Chicago city council as an alderman from the 21st Ward in 1971. A year later he was elected Democratic committeeman for the same ward; he held both offices until 1978.

When Representative Ralph Metcalfe died unexpectedly in October 1978, Stewart became a central figure in the power struggle that emerged to fill the vacant House seat. Desperate to regain control of the political scene in Chicago after the death of Mayor Richard J. Daley and the much-publicized falling-out between Metcalfe and the machine organization, the ward committeemen from the Chicago district named Stewart the Democratic candidate for the general election. Recognized as a party loyalist, Stewart resembled previous machine-backed candidates for Congress who had a clear allegiance to the Democratic city organization. Stewart's candidacy was controversial among many constituents in the predominantly black urban district who had recently grown accustomed to a new style of representation that placed race above local party concerns.[2] Although speculation surfaced that Metcalfe's son would seek the Democratic nomination, or that black leaders would stage a write-in campaign to re-elect Metcalfe posthumously in order to force a special election, Stewart ultimately prevailed as the Democratic nominee.[3] Stewart was originally slated to run against political novice and shoe salesman Jackie Brown, but Republican leaders, sensing the untested Stewart's vulnerability, hoped to make a late substitution on the ballot. A. A. (Sammy) Rayner, a former alderman and perennial candidate for the congressional seat, filed suit when the Illinois state board of elections rejected a petition to replace Brown.[4] Rayner eventually won his case, but Stewart proved victorious in the November election, defeating his Republican opponent with 58 percent of the vote.[5] Despite Rayner's claim of voting fraud, Stewart earned a spot in the 96th Congress (1979–1981) on January 3, 1979, and received a premier assignment on the Committee on Appropriations.[6]

During his short tenure in the House, Stewart focused on the needs of his urban constituents. He vigorously supported federal loan guarantees for the financially

IMAGE COURTESY OF MOORLAND–SPINGARN RESEARCH CENTER, HOWARD UNIVERSITY

troubled Chrysler Corporation, which employed more than 1,500 workers in his Chicago district.[7] As a member of the Appropriations Committee, Stewart backed federal emergency relief to provide low-income constituents with heating assistance. Declaring that the appropriation was "a small price to pay to help alleviate the burdens imposed on the poor," Stewart praised his House colleagues for passing the measure, which helped many of his constituents.[8] The Illinois Representative also worked to extend the length of public service employment programs, citing the necessity for a longer transition period for residents of cities like Chicago, which had a higher rate of unemployment than the national average.[9] In 1980, Stewart requested a General Accounting Office (GAO) analysis of the Chicago Housing Authority (CHA). Prompted by a charge of financial misconduct, the GAO revealed that inefficient management had driven the CHA to the verge of bankruptcy.[10]

Although not as outspoken on racial issues as some black Members of the 96th Congress, at times Stewart drew attention to matters concerning African Americans. In 1979, he criticized a proposed constitutional amendment to prohibit public school busing. Recalling the humiliating segregation practices he had grown up with in Birmingham, he branded the proposal an "attempt to undermine the Fourteenth Amendment" and an effort to re-establish segregation in the United States.[11] Stewart carried on the efforts of Ralph Metcalfe when he introduced a resolution designating February as Black History Month. "We must not continue to permit the history and heritage of black people to be ignored," Stewart exclaimed. "If we educate our Nation's youth, black and white, about the heritage of our whole society we may be able to eliminate racial tensions that have existed in the past."[12] A vocal supporter of the establishment of Martin Luther King, Jr., Day as a federal holiday, he remarked that recognizing the civil rights leader in this manner would be an important step in promoting equality among the races in the United States. In 1983 Congress passed a law designating the third Monday in January as a public holiday honoring King.[13]

Having secured the endorsement of the Democratic committeemen from the South Side for a second term in Congress, Stewart nonetheless faced mounting dissension in his party. Some local politicians harbored residual anger regarding the strong-arm tactics of party leaders who chose Stewart to replace Metcalfe after his sudden death.[14] In an atypical open Chicago Democratic primary (for much of the century, the local organization selected a loyal nominee to run for Congress, who in turn rarely had any real opposition), Stewart faced three well-known opponents: Harold Washington, an Illinois state senator; John Stroger, a Cook County commissioner; and Ralph Metcalfe, Jr., the son of the late Representative.[15] The results of the crowded and competitive primary indicated the growing rift between machine-backed candidates and politicians who wanted to disassociate themselves from city hall: Stewart placed a distant third behind Metcalfe, and the victorious Democratic nominee, Washington, who earned nearly 50 percent of the vote.[16]

After leaving Congress, Stewart served as interim director of the Chicago Department of Inter-Governmental Affairs from 1981 to 1983 and was one of Chicago Mayor Jane Byrne's administrative assistants.[17] Stewart remained a resident of Chicago until his death on April 26, 1988.

FOR FURTHER READING

"Stewart, Bennett McVey," *Biographical Directory of the U.S. Congress, 1774–Present*, http://bioguide.congress.gov/scripts/biodisplay.pl?index=S000902.

NOTES

1   "Bennett Stewart, 76; Former Congressman," 28 April 1988, *Chicago Tribune*: 10C; Leo J. Daugherty III, "Stewart, Bennett McVey," *American National Biography* 20 (New York: Oxford University Press, 1999): 744–745 (hereinafter referred to as *ANB*).

2   William J. Grimshaw, *Bitter Fruit: Black Politics and the Political Machine, 1931–1991* (Chicago: University of Chicago Press, 1995): 153–154.

3   F. Richard Ciccone and David Axelrod, "Dems Name Ald. Stewart to Replace Metcalfe on Ballot," 17 October 1978, *Chicago Tribune*: 3; "Ralph Metcalfe's 'Replacement,'" 18 October 1978, *Chicago Tribune*: B2; Jay Branegan and David Axelrod, "Rayner Sues State in Bid for Metcalfe Job," 25 October 1978, *Chicago Tribune*: 3.

4   Branegan and Axelrod, "Rayner Sues State in Bid for Metcalfe Job"; David K. Fremon, *Chicago Politics, Ward by Ward* (Bloomington: Indiana University Press, 1988): 53–54.

5   Jay Branegan, "Rayner on Ballot, Court Rules," 28 October 1978, *Chicago Tribune*: S3; "Election Information, 1920 to Present," available at http://clerk.house.gov/member_info/electionInfo/index.html; Fremon, *Chicago Politics: Ward by Ward*: 53.

6   "Rayner Charges Vote Fraud," 23 December 1978, *Chicago Tribune*: B11; Bruce A. Ray, "Committee Attractiveness in the U.S. House, 1963–1981," *American Journal of Political Science* 26 (August 1982): 610.

7   *Congressional Record*, House, 96th Cong., 1st sess. (13 December 1979): 35758–35759.

8   "Fuel Aid for Poor Gets House OK," 26 October 1979, *Chicago Tribune*: 2; *Congressional Record*, House, 96th Cong., 1st sess. (30 October 1979): 30149–30150.

9   *Congressional Record*, House, 96th Cong., 1st sess. (27 September 1979): 26580.

10 "Bennett Stewart, 76; Former Congressman"; "And Now the CHA," 9 May 1980, *Chicago Tribune*: D2; "CHA Board to Conduct Own Audit," 14 May 1980, *Chicago Tribune*: A2.

11 *Congressional Record*, House, 96th Cong., 1st sess. (24 July 1979): 20404.

12 *Congressional Record*, House, 96th Cong., 2nd sess. (21 February 1980): 3506. The legislation, referred to the House Committee on Post Office and Civil Service, never made it to the floor for a vote. Metcalfe introduced several measures during his tenure to "recognize the heritage of black citizens in the United States."

13 *Congressional Record*, House, 96th Cong., 1st sess. (13 November 1979): 32142.

14 David Axelrod, "A Tossup at Polls in the 1st District," 26 February 1980, *Chicago Tribune*: A1; David Axelrod, "Dems Endorse Stewart for Re-election in 1st District," 4 December 1979, *Chicago Tribune*: B9; William L. Clay, *Just Permanent Interests: Black Americans in Congress, 1870–1991* (New York: Amistad Press, Inc., 1992): 262–263.

15 Axelrod, "A Tossup at Polls in the 1st District."

16 Aldo Beckman, "Campaign '80: The Illinois Primary," 20 March 1980, *Chicago Tribune*: B6. Washington, a former machine politician who severed ties with the local organization, served a little more than a term in the House before he was elected as the first African-American mayor of Chicago.

17 Daugherty, "Stewart, Bennett McVey," *ANB*: 745.

George William Crockett, Jr.
1909–1997

UNITED STATES REPRESENTATIVE ★ 1980–1991
DEMOCRAT FROM MICHIGAN

George Crockett won a seat in the U.S. House of Representatives in 1980 after a lengthy career as a lawyer and a judge. At age 71, he was the oldest African-American Member ever elected to Congress. The Michigan Representative came to the House with a reputation as a tireless civil rights advocate and a staunch defender of civil liberties. An earlier prison sentence for contempt of court that resulted from the zealous representation of his clients in a contentious federal trial shaped much of his outlook on American justice and politics: "If there's one thing you learn in a place like this, it is patience. Time is always passing, and your time is bound to come."[1]

Born in Jacksonville, Florida, on August 10, 1909, Crockett was the son of George Crockett, Sr., a carpenter, and Minnie Jenkins Crockett. He attended public schools in his native city and graduated with an A.B. from Morehouse College in Atlanta in 1931. Crockett went north to study law at the University of Michigan, where he earned a J.D. in 1934. That same year he married Dr. Ethelene Jones, the first black woman to practice obstetrics and gynecology in Michigan and the first woman president of the American Lung Association.[2] The couple had three children: Elizabeth Ann Hicks, George William Crockett III, and Ethelene Crockett Jones. After his wife died in 1978, Crockett remarried two years later, to Harriette Clark Chambliss, a pediatrician with two sons.[3]

Crockett worked in Jacksonville, Florida, and Fairmont, West Virginia, as a lawyer in private practice. His involvement with labor law took him to Washington in 1939 as the first African-American attorney with the U.S. Department of Labor.[4] In 1943 President Roosevelt appointed Crockett a hearing examiner with the newly formed Fair Employment Practices Committee. A year later, he moved to Detroit to direct a Fair Employment Practices office with the United Auto Workers. During this time he remained active in the defense of labor unions and civil rights organizers, representing clients before the House Un-American Activities Committee (HUAC) and the U.S. Supreme Court. Crockett gained notoriety in 1949 for his participation in a highly publicized federal trial in which 11 communist leaders were convicted of subversion against the U.S. government under the Smith Act, a law which made teaching about the overthrow of the government a criminal offense. Upon the conclusion of the nine-month proceedings, the judge sentenced Crockett and the other defense attorneys to jail for alleged attempts to delay and confuse the proceedings. The Supreme Court eventually upheld the penalty.[5] Recalling his four-month prison term, the Michigan lawyer said, "I think I have always been a champion of the underdog in our society and, if anything, that segregated prison life probably pushed me a little farther along the road."[6] Crockett also argued before the Supreme Court on behalf of Eugene Dennis, the top defendant in the 1949 trial, for an earlier sentence for contempt of Congress and was one of the defense lawyers in the influential case *Dennis v. United States*, which upheld the convictions of the communist leaders and the constitutionality of the controversial Smith Act.[7]

During his career before Congress, Crockett established a solid civil rights record. He helped found Michigan's first integrated law firm and organized the Mississippi Project to provide free legal services for civil rights workers imprisoned in Mississippi.[8] As a judge of the Recorder's Court in Detroit from 1966 to 1978 and the presiding official of the court for the latter four years, Crockett often dispensed lenient sentences for defendants arrested in civil rights protests.[9] Of the belief that African-American judges should be the "conscience of the judiciary," Crockett garnered national attention in 1969 when he released more than 100 members of a black separatist group after

a violent encounter with the Detroit police.[10] Crockett defended his actions by asking, "Can any of you imagine the Detroit police invading an all-white church and rounding up everyone in sight to be bused to a wholesale lockup in a police garage?"[11] After retiring from the Recorder's Court, he served as a visiting judge on the Michigan Court of Appeals and as corporation counsel for the City of Detroit.[12]

As a celebrated leader in Detroit's black community, Crockett entered the race for the House seat left vacant by the resignation of Charles Diggs, Jr., in 1980. The overwhelmingly Democratic congressional district, entirely within the city limits of Detroit, encompassed the downtown commercial center. During his campaign Crockett promised to fight unemployment, improve health care and provide housing opportunities for the residents of Detroit.[13] His integrity and civil rights record, along with the backing of Detroit Mayor Coleman Young and former Representative Diggs, helped Crockett secure the Democratic nomination with a 42 percent plurality in the crowded August primary.[14] He went on to defeat his Republican opponent, Theodore Wallace, easily with 92 percent of the vote in the 1980 special election to fill the vacancy for the remainder of the 96th Congress (1979–1981). He also trounced Republican M. Michael Hurd in the general election for the full term in the 97th Congress (1981–1983), again earning 92 percent of the vote.[15] Crockett retained his House seat for another four terms, rarely facing any formidable challenge in the majority-black, inner-city district, except in his final primary run against future Representative Barbara-Rose Collins, when he collected only 51 percent of the vote.[16]

Sworn in to office on November 12, 1980, Crockett briefly served on the Small Business Committee before switching to the Judiciary Committee—a spot he retained from 1982 through the 101st Congress (1989–1991). He also served on the Select Committee on Aging from the 97th Congress until his retirement at the end of the 101st Congress and on the Committee on Foreign Affairs for his entire congressional career. During the 100th and

101st Congresses (1987–1991), Crockett chaired the Foreign Affairs Subcommittee on Western Hemisphere Affairs, which oversaw United States policy in Latin America and the Caribbean. His appointment earned the disdain of some conservative groups that categorized Crockett as a security risk. "I've never collaborated with the Communist Party as such," Crockett responded. "Admittedly, some of the positions I've taken, dictated by the U.S. Constitution, have coincided with desires and positions of the Communist Party, like supporting freedom of speech."[17] In his position as chairman of the Western Hemisphere subcommittee, the Detroit Representative strongly denounced President Ronald W. Reagan's policy in the region, speaking out against the administration's support of the contras in Nicaragua.[18] He also participated in lawsuits against the President—for authorizing military aid to El Salvador and the American invasion of Grenada.[19] Greatly interested in U.S. foreign policy, Crockett served as a member of the United States delegation to the 42nd General Assembly of the United Nations in 1987 and 1988. He also traveled with a U.S. congressional delegation to the Inter-Parliamentary Conference in Havana, Cuba, in 1981 and to the Seventh U.N. Congress on Prevention of Crime meeting in Milan, Italy, in 1984.[20]

During his congressional tenure, Crockett rarely introduced any measures on the House Floor. The Michigan Representative explained, "We have enough legislation now to take care of just about every situation that arises, if we will just enforce it and apply it."[21] He did, on occasion, make exceptions to this practice. In 1984, for instance, Crockett authored a resolution calling for the release of Nelson Mandela, the imprisoned South African leader; the Mandela Freedom Resolution went on to pass the House.[22] Throughout his tenure in Congress, he remained a consistent critic of the apartheid regime and was arrested in 1984 for participating in a demonstration outside the South African Embassy.[23]

Only a few months after President George H. W. Bush proposed a more stringent antidrug policy in September 1989, Crockett made headlines as the first Member of

Congress to call for the decriminalization of drugs. The former judge, known for taking controversial positions, noted, "Our courts are burdened down with these drug cases and there is nothing we can do about it." He went on to point out that federal money slotted for drug enforcement could be invested in programs to help his urban constituents and other impoverished Americans.[24]

In March 1990, at the age of 80, Crockett announced his intention to retire from the House: "After 68 years of working, I'm hoping to enjoy a little time off." The Michigan Representative denied that his decision had been influenced by the prospect of another difficult primary race against Barbara-Rose Collins. "I've just gotten older and wiser," he said.[25] In his retirement Crockett continued his record of activism, joining the Detroit branch of the National Association for the Advancement of Colored People in its fight in 1996 to prevent the closing of the Detroit Recorder's Court, the court where Crockett began his career as a judge.[26] On September 7, 1997, Crockett died of complications from cancer and a stroke.[27]

FOR FURTHER READING

"Crockett, George William, Jr.," *Biographical Directory of the U.S. Congress, 1774–Present,* http://bioguide.congress.gov/scripts/biodisplay.pl?index=C000919.

MANUSCRIPT COLLECTIONS

Howard University (Washington, DC). Moorland–Spingarn Research Center. Papers: 1980–1990, approximately 155 linear feet. The papers of George Crockett consist of speeches, photographs, correspondence, and other material documenting his legislative activities, particularly his service on the Select Committee on Aging, the Committee on Foreign Affairs, and the Judiciary Committee. An inventory is available in the repository.

Wayne State University (Detroit, MI). Walter P. Reuther Library Archives of Labor and Urban Affairs. *Oral History:* 1968, 42 leaves. Oral history interview with George W. Crockett, Jr.

NOTES

1   Iver Peterson, "Judge Caps Career in Race for House," 10 August 1980, *New York Times*: 25.

2   George Crockett, Jr., *Contemporary Black Biography*, Volume 10 (Detroit, MI: Gale Research Inc., 1995); "People," 13 August 1981, *Washington Post*: DC4.

3   Kathleen E. Bethel, "George W. Crockett Jr.," in Jessie Carney Smith, ed., *Notable Black American Men* (Farmington Hills, MI: Gale Research, Inc., 1999): 236 (hereinafter referred to as *NBAM*); Martin Weil, "Former Rep. George Crockett Jr., 88, Dies," 9 September 1997, *Washington Post*: B06.

4   Weil, "Former Rep. George Crockett Jr., 88, Dies."

5   "11 Top Reds Found Guilty and Medina Jails Counsel," 15 October 1949, *Washington Post*: 1; Lewis Wood, "Top Court Upholds Contempt Jailing," 11 March 1952, *New York Times*: 11.

6   Weil, "Former Rep. George Crockett Jr., 88, Dies."

7   "Justices to Review Dennis' Conviction," 8 November 1949, *New York Times*: 14; Willard Edwards, "Court Upholds Prison Terms for 11 Top Reds," 5 June 1951, *Chicago Daily Tribune*: 6. For more on the Supreme Court case, Dennis v. United States, see Kermit L. Hall, *The Oxford Companion to the Supreme Court of the United States* (New York: Oxford University Press, 1995): 225–226.

8   Bethel, "George W. Crockett Jr.," *NBAM*; Bill McGraw, "Activist Crockett Fighting for Life; Retired Congressman Comatose After Stroke," 5 September 1997, *Detroit Free Press*: 1A; Robert Mcg. Thomas, Jr., "George W. Crockett Dies at 88; Was a Civil Rights Crusader," 15 September 1997, *New York Times*: B7.

9   Weil, "Former Rep. George Crockett Jr., 88, Dies."

10 William K. Stevens, "Black Judges Becoming a Force in U.S. Justice," 19 February 1974, *New York Times*: 1.

11 Jerry M. Flints, "Judge in Detroit Answers Critics," 4 April 1969, *New York Times*: 18.

12 Bethel, "George W. Crockett Jr.," *NBAM*.

13 Peterson, "Judge Caps Career in Race for House."

14 John Hyde, "13 Democrats Vie for Diggs' Old Seat in Detroit Primary," 4 August 1980, *Washington Post*: A1; *Politics in America, 1982* (Washington, DC: Congressional Quarterly Inc., 1981): 610.

15 "Election Statistics, 1920 to Present," available at http://clerk. house.gov/member_info/electionInfo/index.html; Michael J. Dubin et al., *United States Congressional Elections, 1788–1997* (Jefferson, NC: McFarland & Company, Inc., 1998): 714, 720.

16 *Almanac of American Politics, 1990* (Washington, DC: National Journal Inc., 1989): 620.

17 Joanne Omang, "Rep. Crockett and the Volley From the Right," 10 February 1987, *Washington Post*: A19.

18 John Flesher, "Outspoken Liberal to Retire," 28 March 1990, Associated Press.

19 Omang, "Rep. Crockett and the Volley From the Right"; Martin Tolchin, "45 in House Sue to Bar Bush From Acting Alone," 21 November 1990, *New York Times*: A11; Bethel, "George W. Crockett Jr.," *NBAM*.

20 Bethel, "George W. Crockett Jr.," *NBAM*.

21 Omang, "Rep. Crockett and the Volley From the Right"; "George W. Crockett, Jr., 88, Detroit Judge, Rights Activist," 15 September 1997, *Chicago Tribune*: 6N; Thomas, "George Crockett Dies at 88; Was a Civil Rights Crusader."

22 Bethel, "George W. Crockett Jr.," *NBAM*.

23 Ed Bruske, "Apartheid Foes Freed Without Arraignment," 2 December 1984, *Washington Post*: B1.

24 "Michigan's Crockett First Congressman on Record for Decriminalization," 17 December 1989, Associated Press; Thomas, "George Crockett Dies at 88; Was a Civil Rights Crusader"; Bernard Weinraub, "President Offers Strategy for U.S. on Drug Control," 6 September 1989, *New York Times*: A1.

25 "Michigan Rep. Crockett to Retire," 29 March 1990, *Washington Post*: A4.

26 "Civil Rights Veterans Coleman Young, and George Crockett, Jr. Join Detroit NAACP Campaign to Save Recorder's Court," 7 October 1996, PR Newswire.

27 McGraw, "Activist Crockett Fighting for Life; Retired Congressman Comatose After Stroke"; Weil, "Former Rep. George Crockett Jr., 88, Dies."

"IF THERE'S ONE THING YOU LEARN IN A PLACE LIKE THIS, IT IS PATIENCE," CROCKETT WROTE WHILE SERVING A PRISON SENTENCE FOR CONTEMPT OF COURT AS A RESULT OF HIS ZEALOUS REPRESENTATION OF HIS CLIENTS' CIVIL RIGHTS IN A CONTENTIOUS FEDERAL TRIAL. "TIME IS ALWAYS PASSING, AND YOUR TIME IS BOUND TO COME."

Mervyn Malcolm Dymally
1926–

UNITED STATES REPRESENTATIVE ★ 1981–1993
DEMOCRAT FROM CALIFORNIA

A Caribbean immigrant, a longtime member of the California legislature, and the first black elected to statewide office in California, Mervyn Dymally represented a southern Los Angeles County district in the U.S. House of Representatives for 12 years. Representative Dymally eventually served as a subcommittee chairman on the Foreign Affairs Committee, where he was an outspoken advocate for international human rights and economic development, particularly in Africa and the Caribbean. "I have an obligation as a Third World person. I make no excuses," Dymally explained. "I do have a very keen interest in the Third World. We do not live in just 50 states. We contribute significant sums of taxpayer money in the Third World."[1]

Mervyn Malcolm Dymally was born on May 12, 1926, in Cedros, Trinidad, in the British West Indies, to Hamid A. and Andreid S. (Richardson) Dymally. He attended Cedros Government School and graduated from St. Benedict and Naparima Secondary School in Trinidad in 1944. Dymally worked as a janitor and a labor organizer early in his career. He also worked as a reporter, covering labor issues for *The Vanguard*, a weekly newspaper published by the Oil Workers' Trade Union. Inspired by the story of Booker T. Washington, Dymally arrived in the U.S. to study journalism at Lincoln University in Jefferson City, Missouri.[2] After a semester, he transferred to Chapman University in southern California. Dymally earned a B.A. in education from California State University in Los Angeles in 1954. After college, he taught students with exceptional needs for six years in Los Angeles. He earned an M.A. in government from California State University in Sacramento in 1969 and a Ph.D. in human behavior from the United States International University (now Alliant International University) in San Diego in 1978. He married the former Alice M. Gueno, an educator

from New Orleans, and they raised two children, Mark and Lynn.

While a teacher, Dymally volunteered as a campaign worker and joined the California Young Democrats, where he served as state treasurer. In 1960, he worked for the Democratic National Convention in Los Angeles, where John F. Kennedy was chosen as the party's presidential nominee. He later served as field coordinator for the Kennedy presidential campaign.

Dymally's political career began in 1962 when he won election to the California state assembly to succeed assemblyman Augustus (Gus) Hawkins (who had won a U.S. House seat) in a district representing southern Los Angeles County, becoming the first foreign-born black elected to the California legislature. Four years later, Dymally became the first black ever elected to the California senate. He chaired the senate Democratic caucus, three full committees on social welfare, military and veterans affairs, and elections and reapportionment, and the joint committee on legal equality for women, from which he authored the legislation that eventually resulted in the state's ratification of the Equal Rights Amendment. He also was chairman of the California state black caucus. "I see politics as becoming the cutting edge in the entire civil rights movement," Dymally told the *Christian Science Monitor* in a retrospective article on the Watts Riots of 1965.[3] In 1974, Dymally was elected lieutenant governor of California—becoming the first black elected to statewide office. His campaign focused on the state's energy and environmental problems as well as on equal rights for women. "I'm not shying away from race questions, but neither am I running a campaign on black issues," he noted during the contest.[4] He served in that capacity until 1979, heading the State Commission for Economic Development and the Commission of the

Californias. In his 1978 re-election bid, Dymally won just 43 percent of the vote, losing to Republican candidate Mike Curb.

In 1980, Dymally entered the Democratic primary for a U.S. congressional district that encompassed suburbs in southern Los Angeles County: Gardena, Compton, Torrance, and Hawthorne. Representative Charles H. Wilson had represented the Democratic-leaning district for nearly two decades, with no serious opposition until the late 1970s. Wilson entered the primary while under investigation for "financial misconduct" stemming from his acceptance of a gift from businessman Tongsun Park, the center of the Koreagate scandal, which involved suspected influence buying in Congress by Korean business interests. (A week after the primary of June 3, 1980, the House censured Wilson.[5]) Joining the field of contenders was former U.S. Representative Mark W. Hannaford of California. Dymally had a core group of support among African-American voters, who accounted for about 36 percent of the district's population. He also had backing from the political machine run by California Assemblyman Howard Berman and U.S. Representative Henry A. Waxman—two of his allies from his days in the state legislature.[6] With a large financial advantage over the other candidates, Dymally relied on a targeted mass mailing campaign. In the Democratic primary, he received 51 percent of the vote while Hannaford and Wilson received just 25 and 16 percent, respectively. In the general election, Dymally won handily over Republican candidate Don Grimshaw, capturing 64 percent of the vote.[7]

One of the most ethnically and culturally diverse localities in California, the district remained heavily Democratic (more than 70 percent by the end of the 1980s), though its borders changed due to reapportionment during Dymally's 12 years in office. By 1992, it included large portions of Watts, Carson, and Wilmington in addition to Compton and Lynwood. Also, the district was one of the poorest in the state, with seven housing projects.[8] In his subsequent five re-election campaigns Dymally prevailed easily, with 70 percent or more of the vote.[9]

When Dymally took his seat in the House in January 1981, he won assignments on the Foreign Affairs, District of Columbia, and Science and Technology committees. In the 99th Congress (1983–1985), Dymally left his post on Science and Technology for a seat on the Post Office and Civil Service Committee. He served on that panel, Foreign Affairs, and the District of Columbia until he retired in 1993. For a single term in the 99th Congress (1985–1987), Dymally also served on the Education and Labor Committee. In the 100th Congress (1987–1989), he chaired the Congressional Black Caucus (CBC).

As chairman of the Foreign Affairs Subcommittee on International Operations, Dymally became a leading spokesperson on human rights and economic development, particularly in Africa, the Middle East, and the Caribbean. He was an outspoken critic of apartheid in South Africa and advocated imposing sanctions against the minority-white government. Dymally also emphasized the necessity of economic development. As a member of the Subcommittee on Africa, Dymally made numerous trips to Africa and pushed the committee to focus on a wider spectrum of issues from "human relations to trade." He observed, "Most African countries are moving toward democracy; human rights belongs to a subcommittee on human rights; and there is an absence of trade between Africa and African Americans, in particular, and America, in general. We've been building up a network and trying to convince Africans about the importance of trade. It is proper to want to get Africans out of jail. But, I want to get them out of poverty, too."[10]

Dymally's interest in human rights extended to other parts of the globe as well. Having emigrated from the Caribbean, Representative Dymally was sensitive to political, economic, and immigrant concerns affecting countries in the Caribbean Basin. He was an advocate for Haitian immigrants in the United States, explaining, "The Haitian system is very oppressive . . . The taking of a life is like pouring a cup of coffee. Poor people have no rights at all."[11] He was critical of the Soviet Union (for refusing to allow Russian Jews to emigrate to Israel), of Israel (for continuing its trade with South Africa and suppressing Palestinian protest efforts in the West Bank and Gaza Strip), and of Iran's fundamentalist Islamic government (for engaging in bellicose rhetoric aimed at Israel). Dymally was also a steadfast supporter of Palestinian self-determination, advocating the creation of a Palestinian state on the West Bank. Dymally weighed in on many internal political practices in developing countries from Zaire to Micronesia and, in the 1980s, was critical of U.S. aid to authoritarian regimes in Latin America, and particularly the Nicaraguan contras.

As a member of the District of Columbia and the Post Office and Civil Service committees, and as chairman of the CBC, Dymally consistently spoke about the minority issues that were important to his urban constituency. He chaired the District of Columbia's Subcommittee on Judiciary and Education and supported statehood for the majority-black city and increased funding for education programs for minorities. Representative Dymally was also an advocate for blue-collar Capitol Hill workers and staff, many of whom were African American. He backed an increase in federal contracts for minority businesses, including those that leased federal lands for oil and gas development. He served briefly as chairman of the Post Office and Civil Service Committee's Subcommittee on Census and Population, advocating an upward adjustment of the 1990 Census figures to compensate for projected undercounts in urban districts with large African-American and Hispanic populations. This issue was significant because federal aid was allocated partially on the basis of the census.

Dymally's reputation in Congress—and his portrayal by the media—was sometimes that of a brash and blunt insider. "Merv builds a lot of good will," said his friend Representative Julian Dixon, who represented a neighboring Los Angeles district, "but he certainly

has his controversial side." Dixon added that Dymally's legacy was his role as "a mentor, responsible, in part, for a lot of elected people in the black community."[12] He received some criticism in his district for being aloof and seemingly more interested in affairs overseas than in South Los Angeles. Dymally argued that the Reagan administration's emphasis on slashing entitlement programs in the 1980s, had been exceedingly difficult for urban districts and the Members who represented them. "It's a very serious dilemma. How do you get help for your constituents?" Dymally asked. "You have to measure the worth of a congressman in the context of the administration's cuts in services."[13] Of his more controversial legislative positions Dymally said, "I do not seek to be popular. I seek to be right."[14]

In February 1992, Dymally announced that he would retire from the U.S. House at the end of the 102nd Congress in January 1993. "I did not get elected to stay in office forever," Dymally remarked. "I have no regrets. The people have supported me. They have permitted me to be independent and even wrong sometimes."[15] Though he endorsed his daughter, Lynn, to succeed him, Compton Mayor Walter R. Tucker III won the Democratic primary and easily prevailed in the general election for Dymally's vacant seat.

In his retirement, Dymally worked as a foreign affairs consultant for Caribbean, African, and Asian interests. In 2002, he was elected to the California state assembly to represent a district that encompassed South Los Angeles and the cities of Compton, Paramount, and Long Beach. He topped his closest opponent, Paramount Mayor Diane J. Martinez, by a 2 to 1 margin in a race that ran counter to electoral trends favoring Hispanic over black candidates in California's urban areas.[16] Dymally's peers elected him chairman of the assembly's Democratic study group, which develops and promotes progressive legislation.

FOR FURTHER READING

"Dymally, Mervyn Malcolm," *Biographical Directory of the U.S. Congress, 1774–Present*, http://bioguide.congress.gov/scripts/biodisplay.pl?index=D000592.

MANUSCRIPT COLLECTIONS

California State University (Los Angeles, CA). Special Collections, University Library. Papers: ca. 1962–1993, approximately 440 linear feet. The papers of Mervyn Malcolm Dymally document his service in the U.S. House of Representatives, the California state assembly, California state senate, and his tenure as lieutenant governor of California.

University of California (Los Angeles, CA). Oral History Program. *Oral History:* 1996–1997, three volumes. Oral history interviews with Mervyn Dymally conducted by Elston L. Carr between 1996 and 1997. In the interviews, Representative Dymally discusses his family background and education, his decision to move to California, the lack of opportunities for blacks to become politically active, and his joining the American Federation of Teachers. Dymally also discusses gaining support in the 1962 campaign for the 53rd Assembly District, the impact of the Watts Riots, running for the 29th senate district seat in 1966, legislation to teach black history in public schools (Early Childhood Education Act and the California Fair Plan), prison reform, and 1965 reapportionment. The interview continues with events leading to Dymally's decision to run for lieutenant governor in 1974, endorse Jerry Brown for President in 1976, and run for a seat in the U.S. House of Representatives after his loss for a second term as lieutenant governor in 1978, as well as issues he focused on during his tenure in the U.S. House and the reasons for his decision to leave Congress in 1992 after 12 years of service.

NOTES

1 Jeffrey L. Rabin, "Outspoken Dymally Favored to Win Re-Election to Congress," 6 October 1988, *Los Angeles Times*: Metro 8.

2 A. S. Young, "An Interview With Dymally," 29 January 1992, *Los Angeles Sentinel*: 7.

3 Curtis J. Sitomer, "Watts . . . Six Years Later: Optimism Vies With Despair," 3 February 1972, *Christian Science Monitor*: 1.

4 Albert R. Hunt, "The New Black Pragmatism," 23 May 1974, *Wall Street Journal*: 14.

5 For more on the House reprimand of Wilson, see the Committee on Standards of Official Conduct historical database, available at http://www.house.gov/ethics/Historical_Chart_Final_Version.htm (accessed 4 December 2007).

6 *Politics in America, 1982* (Washington, DC: Congressional Quarterly Inc., 1981): 156.

7 "Election Statistics, 1920 to Present," available at http://clerk.house.gov/member_info/electionInfo/index.html.

8 *Politics in America, 1990* (Washington, DC: Congressional Quarterly Press, 1989): 189; Tina Griego, "Stormy Race for 37th District Seat Steals the Thunder," 31 May 1992, *Los Angeles Times*: J1.

9 "Election Statistics, 1920 to Present," available at http://clerk.house.gov/member_info/electionInfo/index.html; *Politics in America, 1990*: 189.

10 A. S. Young, "Dymally Interview, II," 12 February 1992, *Los Angeles Sentinel*: 7.

11 Young, "Dymally Interview, II."

12 Tina Griego, "Dymally to Retire; Blazed Path for Blacks in Politics," 11 February 1992, *Los Angeles Times*: B1.

13 Rabin, "Outspoken Dymally Favored to Win Re-Election to Congress."

14 Ibid.

15 Griego, "Dymally to Retire; Blazed Path for Blacks in Politics."

16 "Mervyn Dymally Wins Calif. Assembly Seat in Political Comeback," 25 March 2002, *Jet*: 7.

"I HAVE AN OBLIGATION AS A

THIRD WORLD PERSON.

I MAKE NO EXCUSES," DYMALLY

EXPLAINED. "I DO HAVE A VERY

KEEN INTEREST IN THE THIRD

WORLD. WE DO NOT LIVE IN

JUST 50 STATES."

Gus Savage
1925–

UNITED STATES REPRESENTATIVE ★ 1981–1993
DEMOCRAT FROM ILLINOIS

Gus Savage ascended to Congress as an outsider to elective politics. A veteran civil rights activist and pioneer African-American journalist, he used his strong community ties to earn a seat in the U.S. House from South Chicago. During his 12 years in Congress, Savage's flamboyant personality and militant approach to highlighting racial inequalities in his district and around the nation made headlines and often provoked controversy.[1] "I value my independence," Savage avowed. "And I view struggle as desirable. I don't crave acceptance. I march to my own tune. If the machine doesn't like it, that's tough. If my colleagues don't like it, that's also tough."[2]

Born in Detroit, Michigan, on October 30, 1925, Gus Savage moved to the South Side of Chicago with his family at age five.[3] He attended public schools in Chicago, graduating from Wendell Phillips High School in 1943. Savage served in a segregated unit of the U.S. Army from 1943 to 1946; the racial discrimination he witnessed contributed to his future radicalism.[4] After he completed a tour of duty in World War II, Savage attended Roosevelt University in Chicago, where he earned a B.A. in philosophy in 1951. Enrolled in Chicago-Kent College of Law during 1952 and 1953, he changed his career to journalism in 1954 and later edited and published *Citizen Newspapers*, a chain of independent weekly newspapers based in Chicago.[5] Savage married Eunice King on August 4, 1946. The couple had two children: Thomas James and Emma Mae. Savage's wife died of lung cancer in 1981, and he never remarried.[6]

A lifelong civil rights advocate, Savage fought against discrimination in housing, employment, and labor unions. In the 1960s he chaired Chicago's South End Voters Conference and the Protest at the Polls. Savage also served as the campaign manager for the Midwest League of Negro Voters.[7] Savage organized and participated in a series of protests, including one against the National Tea Co. (an advertiser in his newspapers) to draw attention to the company's poor record on minority hiring practices.[8] He also played an important role in publicizing the brutal murder of Emmett Till by printing a photograph of the body of the 14-year-old African-American boy from Chicago who was killed in Mississippi for allegedly whistling at a white woman. The shocking photographs of the boy's dead body, first published by Savage in *The American Negro: A Magazine of Protest*, as well as *Jet* and the *Chicago Defender*, caused a public outcry.[9]

Savage entered political life in 1948 as a Progressive Party organizer for former Vice President Henry A. Wallace's presidential campaign against the incumbent, Harry S. Truman.[10] The future Representative became involved in local politics as an outspoken critic of Mayor Richard J. Daley and the Chicago machine. Beginning in the 1960s, Savage used his newspapers to express his discontent with the white power structure that dominated the city during much of the 20th century. Not satisfied with watching from the sidelines, he made five unsuccessful bids for elective office at the local and the national levels before eventually earning a seat in Congress.[11] Savage entered two Democratic primaries for one of Chicago's U.S. House seats; in 1968 he lost to five-term incumbent William T. Murphy, and in 1970 he lost to the machine-backed candidate, Morgan Murphy, Jr.[12]

When Representative Morgan Murphy announced his retirement in December 1979, Savage joined the race to succeed him. Created in 1971, the predominantly African-American working-class congressional district formed a U-shape that encompassed much of Chicago's far South Side, several suburban neighborhoods, and the industrial section surrounding Lake Calumet.[13] In the Democratic primary, Savage faced the machine candidate,

Reginald Brown, who was the principal of the Chicago Vocational School, in addition to Leon Davis and Robert Unger.[14] Throughout the campaign, Savage emphasized his reputation as an independent politician and an alternative to the Chicago machine. After winning the primary by earning 45 percent of the vote, Savage commented, "All those years, you see, the machine was getting weaker, and I was getting stronger."[15] In the general election, Savage trounced his Republican opponent, Marsha Harris, a 25-year-old registered nurse, garnering 88 percent of the vote to become the district's first African-American Representative.[16] "For 32 years, some battles I've won and some I've lost," Savage remarked after the election. "But those who know me know my objective in life has never been personal; so my satisfaction now is not personal." He joined two other black politicians from Chicago in the 97th Congress (1981–1983)—Cardiss Collins and Harold Washington; it was the first time three African Americans represented Chicago simultaneously and an indication of the growing influence of Chicago's black community.[17]

Savage became a Member of Congress on January 3, 1981. He later observed that he viewed his election to the House as "a vehicle to effect change."[18] During his six terms he served on the Post Office and Civil Service, Public Works and Transportation, and Small Business committees. Savage chaired the Public Works and Transportation Subcommittee on Economic Development during the 101st and 102nd Congresses (1989–1993).

Savage's primary concerns as a Representative focused on advancing the rights of African Americans and improving conditions in his Chicago district. In 1986 he sponsored an amendment to the National Defense Authorization Act for Fiscal Year 1987. A major legislative triumph, the amendment imposed the largest federal contract set-aside program in history on all military procurements, providing a possible $25 billion for minority-owned and -controlled businesses and institutions and historically black colleges. "I would only remind our colleagues that our great Nation, America, was founded on an impossible dream, and America was built by doing the improbable," Savage had

proclaimed, attempting to persuade the House to back his measure. "Do not limit your goal to the attainable; set your goal at what is right."[19] In 1988 he sponsored legislation to build a new federal office building in his district and urged the use of minority contractors for the expensive project.[20] Savage also sponsored measures to reduce home mortgages in poor communities and fought to curb toxic pollution in his Chicago district.[21]

Savage used his position in the House to highlight issues he believed harmed African Americans. The Chicago Representative joined his Congressional Black Caucus (CBC) colleagues in blasting President Ronald W. Reagan's economic agenda during the 1980s: "Reagan is a reverse Robin Hood, robbing the poor and giving to the rich," Savage quipped, referring to a 1981 administration proposal that included tax cuts for wealthy Americans and decreased federal spending for programs to assist the poor.[22] He also found fault with much of the President's foreign policy, including the U.S. invasion of Grenada.[23] The Illinois Representative favored military cuts for programs such as the Strategic Defense Initiative—a space-based missile defense system touted by the Reagan administration—and called for a reduction of the armed forces. "I don't want to take young men into the Army to train them to kill," he said. "I'd rather we send them to college to train them to heal."[24] A proponent of increased American attention on Africa, Savage toured the continent on several occasions, including congressional visits to Zimbabwe, South Africa, Zaire, Somalia, Angola, and Kenya.[25]

One of the more outspoken Members of the House, Savage often lashed out against Congress's record on civil rights, accusing the government of applying many "Band-Aids and salves" but failing to succeed in the "liberation of black people."[26] He also provoked anger from some for implying that the U.S. was excessively concerned with Israeli interests because of a strong Jewish lobbying presence. One of only three Members of the House who voted against a resolution requesting the United States to withhold funds from the United Nations if Israel was barred from participating in General Assembly proceedings, Savage declared, "the powerful Zionist lobby in this country must understand that it can no longer dictate to every member of Congress."[27] Savage also found his actions scrutinized on several occasions, including a confrontation with the District of Columbia police involving a traffic violation committed by his son, an investigation by the Federal Election Commission of incomplete financial reports for his campaign, and his congressional attendance and voting records.[28] In 1989, the House Ethics Committee, chaired by Savage's fellow CBC member Julian Dixon of California, investigated allegations of sexual misconduct involving a Peace Corps volunteer while he was on an official congressional visit to Zaire. The subsequent public report condemned the Representative's behavior but did not recommend punishment, citing Savage's effort to apologize to the volunteer.[29] Covered widely by the media, the incident soured an already-volatile relationship between Savage and the press. Questioned by reporters, Savage said the "white racist" press had attacked him unfairly, asserting, "Black leadership is under attack in this county, and I'm the No. 1 target."[30] Savage granted few interviews as a Representative, preferring to disseminate information about his House record through his weekly newsletter.

Unable to capitalize on his status as an incumbent, Savage had many competitive primary races during his career and never received more than 52 percent of the vote.[31] In three successive primaries he was opposed by Mel Reynolds, a former Rhodes Scholar and a South Side professor. However, Savage had the advantage of running against multiple contenders until his final primary election on March 17, 1992, in which he faced only Reynolds.[32] Redistricting, in addition to the intense rivalry between the two candidates, complicated Savage's bid for a seventh term in the House. The district's redrawn boundaries encompassed more suburban neighborhoods, which ultimately aided Reynolds by depriving Savage of some of his most loyal urban voting base.[33] Savage lost by an unexpectedly wide margin of 63 to 37 percent.[34] In his concession speech, he stated, "I have tried to serve as best as I know how."[35] Savage resides in Washington, DC.

FOR FURTHER READING

"Savage, Gus," *Biographical Directory of the U.S. Congress, 1774–Present,* http://bioguide.congress.gov/scripts/biodisplay.pl?index=S000081.

MANUSCRIPT COLLECTION

The HistoryMakers (Chicago, IL). *Oral History:* 2001, six Betacam SP videocassettes and one half-document box containing accompanying materials. Interview with Gus Savage conducted by Julieanna Richardson on April 26, 2001, in Washington, DC.

NOTES

1   Richard Wolf, "Congressman Again in Eye of the Storm," 10 March 1992, *USA Today*: 2A.

2   Jeffrey M. Elliot, ed., *Black Voices in American Politics* (New York: Harcourt Brace Jovanovich, 1986): 8.

3   Frank James, "Behind the 'Scenes': Who Is Gus Savage and Why Does a Ruckus Follow Him Wherever He Goes?" 31 July 1989, *Chicago Tribune*: 1C; Elliot, *Black Voices in American Politics*: 3.

4   James, "Behind the 'Scenes': Who Is Gus Savage and Why Does a Ruckus Follow Him Wherever He Goes?"

5   "Gus Savage," 1992 Associated Press Candidate Biographies.

6   "Rep. Savage's Wife Dies of Lung Cancer," 24 February 1981, *Chicago Tribune*: A7.

7   Gary Rivlin, *Fire on the Prairie: Chicago's Harold Washington and the Politics of Race* (New York: Henry Holt and Company, 1992): 51.

8   James, "Behind the 'Scenes': Who Is Gus Savage and Why Does a Ruckus Follow Him Wherever He Goes?" For a brief summary of Savage's involvement in the civil rights movement see, Elliot, *Black Voices in American Politics*: 4–5.

9   John Bachtell, "From the Emmett Till Case to the Election of Harold Washington; Arlene Brigham; Foot Soldier for Equality," 13 August–19 August 2005, *People's Weekly World*: 10; Michael McQueen, "Rep. Savage's Controversial Style, Values Face Critical Test in Tough Democratic Race," 15 March 1990, *Wall Street Journal*: A16; Sheila Dewan, "How Photos Became Icon of Civil Rights Movement," 28 August 2005, *New York Times*: 12.

10 James, "Behind the 'Scenes': Who Is Gus Savage and Why Does a Ruckus Follow Him Wherever He Goes?"

11 George de Lama, "Gus Savage Wins; City Puts Three Blacks in House," 5 November 1980, *Chicago Tribune*: C1.

12 "William Murphy, Congressman From Illinois for 12 Years," 1 February 1978, *Washington Post*: C4; Michael Killian, "Savage Courts Whites in 3d District Primary," 1 March 1979, *Chicago Tribune*: SCL5.

13   Michael Arndt, "Rep. Savage Draws Crowd of Opponents for Primary," 26 February 1986, *Chicago Tribune*: 1C; "Gus Savage," *Politics in America, 1990* (Washington, DC: Congressional Quarterly Inc., 1989): 420.

14   David Axelrod, "Contests Heat up on S. Side for Two Seats in U.S. House," 17 January 1980, *Chicago Tribune*: W_A3.

15   Jeff Lyon, "Savage to Fight on the Inside for a Change," 24 March 1980, *Chicago Tribune*: 5.

16   "Election Information, 1920 to Present," available at http://clerk. house.gov/member_info/electionInfo/index.html; De Lama, "Gus Savage Wins; City Puts Three Blacks in House"; "Our Choices for Congress," 23 October 1980, *Chicago Tribune*: B2.

17   De Lama, "Gus Savage Wins; City Puts Three Blacks in House."

18   Elliot, *Black Voices in American Politics*: 8.

19   *Congressional Record*, House, 99th Cong., 2nd sess. (14 August 1986): 21718.

20   John Gorman, "Loop to Get Third Federal Office Building in '91," 30 December 1988, *Chicago Tribune*: 1C; "Rep. Savage Urges Minority Contracting," 26 April 1988, *Chicago Tribune*: 4C.

21   Elliot, *Black Voices in American Politics*: 4, 11.

22   Robert Shepard, 19 February 1981, United Press International.

23   Howard Kurtz, "Black Legislators Seek Withdrawal of American Forces From Grenada," 29 October 1983, *Washington Post*: A7.

24   Tom Brune and Michael Briggs, "Past Troubles Shape Savage, Reynolds Race," 3 March 1992, *Chicago Sun-Times*: 8.

25   "Congressional Delegation Heading to Africa," 4 August 1981, Associated Press.

26   Juan Williams, "Lawmaker Tells Muslims Congress Isn't Liberator," 24 February 1985, *Washington Post*: A5.

27   Mike Robinson, "Savage Condemns 'Zionist Lobby,'" 12 May 1982, Associated Press.

28   Robert Davis, "Rep. Savage Familiar With Controversy," 20 July 1989, *Chicago Tribune*: 11C. In a published interview with Jeffrey Elliot, Savage responded to criticism concerning his sporadic voting record: "I'm one of the hardest-working, most able, and loyal servants of the people in Washington. I believe that members should be judged more by *how* they vote than merely by the number of times they vote." See Elliot, *Black Voices in American Politics*: 10.

29   See House Report No. 101-397, 101st Cong., 2nd sess. (1990); and the historical summary on the Committee on Standards of Official Conduct Web page: http://www.house.gov/ethics/ Historical_Chart_Final_Version.htm (accessed 11 March 2008). See also Holmes, "Panel Is Critical of Representative." According to one newspaper account, Representative Savage denied ever writing a letter of apology. See Susan F. Rasky, "Congressman in Sex Case Bitterly Attacks Critics," 2 February 1990, *New York Times*: A15.

30   David Dahl, "Savage Lashes Out at Media," 27 June 1991, *St. Petersburg Times* (Florida): 10A; for more detail on Savage's rocky relationship with the press, see Elliot, *Black Voices in American Politics*: 14–16.

31   *Politics in America, 1992* (Washington, DC: Congressional Quarterly Inc., 1991): 360–361.

32   Steve Neal, "Reynolds Is Upbeat About His Third Race," 3 January 1992, *Chicago Sun-Times*: 25.

33   Neal, "Reynolds Is Upbeat About His Third Race"; Craig Winneker, "Reynolds Whips Savage on 3rd Try, 63-37%; Shooting May Have Helped," 19 March 1992, *Roll Call*; Carol M. Swain, *Black Faces, Black Interests: The Representation of African Americans in Congress* (Cambridge, MA: Harvard University Press, 1995): 66–67.

34   Winneker, "Reynolds Whips Savage on 3rd Try, 63-37%."

35   Ibid; Robert A. Davis and Tom Cruze, "Savage Loses to Reynolds; Hayes, Rush Tight; Rosty, Lipinski Win," 18 March 1992, *Chicago Sun-Times*: 6.

Harold Washington
1922–1987

UNITED STATES REPRESENTATIVE ★ 1981–1983
DEMOCRAT FROM ILLINOIS

Born and raised in a political family, Harold Washington converted his early access to prominent lawmakers and the local government structure into a memorable career as a Chicago politician. Like his early mentor Representative Ralph Metcalfe, Washington ascended the ranks of the powerful Chicago political machine, only to break with the organization later because he resented the lack of independence and power he experienced as a black politician.[1] Washington abandoned an outwardly safe congressional seat after winning a second term in the U.S. House in order to run for mayor of Chicago, and he made history when he became the first African American to hold the influential elective position. "The reason my face and my name are known all over is because of the history of the Chicago political machine and the movement that brought it down," Washington remarked. "I just happened to be there at the right time to capitalize on it."[2]

Harold Washington was born on April 15, 1922, in Chicago, Illinois. His mother, Bertha Price, left his father, Roy Lee Washington, a minister, lawyer, and Democratic politician, and her four children when Harold was a toddler.[3] After his parents divorced in 1928, Washington lived with his father, who married Arlene Jackson, an area schoolteacher, in 1935.[4] Roy Washington's connections with the influential black Democrats in Chicago, forged while he was a precinct captain in the predominantly black South Side, provided his son with many political contacts. Accompanying his father to political rallies and meetings, Washington learned about Chicago politics by observing future Representative Arthur Mitchell, William Dawson, and Ralph Metcalfe.[5] Harold Washington attended Forrestville School and DuSable High School in Chicago before dropping out to work in a meat-packing factory. Interested in athletics, he competed as an amateur boxer

and a hurdler.[6] In 1941, Washington married Dorothy Finch. The couple had no children and divorced in 1951.[7] Drafted into the military in 1942, Washington served with the U.S. Air Force Engineers in the Pacific until 1946. After World War II, he attended Roosevelt University in Chicago, one of the few integrated universities in the nation. During his senior year he was class president—the first elective position of his career. After earning a B.A. in political science in 1949, he went on to receive a J.D. from Northwestern University's School of Law in 1952, joining his father in a private law practice in Chicago once he passed the bar in 1953.[8]

When Roy Washington died in 1953, Harold Washington succeeded him as a precinct captain in the Third Ward regular Democratic organization in 1954. He also continued practicing law, joining the city corporation counsel's office as an assistant prosecutor from 1954 to 1958. Beginning in 1960, he served for four years as an arbitrator for the Illinois Industrial Commission.[9] Washington bolstered his political experience and credentials by serving in the Illinois state house of representatives from 1965 to 1976 and in the Illinois state senate from 1976 to 1980.[10] As a state legislator, Washington revealed an independent streak that foreshadowed his eventual rift with the Chicago machine. Although he often followed the "idiot card"—the derogatory name for the voting instructions assembled for machine candidates, Washington defied organization leaders on occasion, backing liberal agendas such as the Equal Rights Amendment (ERA), a fair housing code, and the establishment of a statewide holiday honoring civil rights leader Martin Luther King, Jr.[11] Despite some legal problems—Washington spent a month in jail on a 1971 conviction for failure to file income tax returns—he managed to maintain political viability.[12]

In 1977, Washington entered the special primary held to replace Chicago Mayor Richard J. Daley after his sudden death. Aggravated by the Democratic organization, which he believed stifled independent black politicians, Washington decided to challenge the machine-backed candidate, Michael Bilandic, for the Democratic mayoral nomination. Unable to raise sufficient funds, he focused much of his attention on Chicago's South Side. During the campaign, he likened the city's black population to a "sleeping giant," predicting that if "the potential black vote ever woke up, we'd control the city."[13] Washington finished a distant third, with only 11 percent of the vote, in a field of four contenders.[14] Unapologetic after his failed mayoral bid, Washington went on the offensive, promising voters that his split with the machine would be permanent. "I'm going to do that which maybe I should have done 10 or 12 years ago," Washington exclaimed. "I'm going to stay outside that damned Democratic Party and give it hell."[15]

True to his word, Washington jumped at the chance to challenge freshman Representative Bennett Stewart, the machine incumbent in the 1980 Democratic primary for Chicago's South Side seat in the House. Well known in the majority-black district, which included middle-class and poor neighborhoods running southward along Lake Michigan as well as the downtown commercial Loop, Washington emphasized his independence from City Hall during his campaign.[16] Garnering nearly 50 percent of the vote in the primary, Washington defeated Stewart, who placed third in a field of four candidates including Ralph Metcalfe, Jr. (the son of the late Representative).[17] In the November general election, Washington trounced his Republican opponent, George Williams, securing 95 percent of the vote and earning a seat in the 97th Congress (1981–1983).[18] Sworn in on January 3, 1981, Washington received assignments on three favorable committees: Education and Labor, Judiciary, and Government Operations.

The sixth in a succession of African-American Representatives from his inner-city district, beginning with Oscar De Priest's election in 1928, Washington differed from his predecessors in that he lacked the backing of the Chicago political machine.[19] At the Capitol, Washington continued his anti-machine posture. Of the 30 freshman Members who held positions in their respective state legislatures, the Chicago native was the only one who refused to resign his seat in the statehouse.[20] Furious with Chicago Mayor Jane Byrne, who inherited the Daley machine and intended to replace him with a party regular from her personal staff, Washington protested for several weeks before ultimately relinquishing his position. Conceding "I must go about my business in Congress," Washington nonetheless took the opportunity to criticize the machine organization, declaring, "I was elected to Congress because the people are sick and tired of downtown bosses who want to handpick individuals to control our political lives."[21]

Elected to office at the same time as President Ronald W. Reagan, Washington spent much of his short tenure on Capitol Hill attacking the President's proposed spending cuts for social programs and his supply-side economic plan. Fearful that reduced funding for initiatives such as college financial aid would hinder many of his urban constituents who relied upon federal assistance, the South Side Representative deemed such cuts "unfairly targeted," and predicted that diminished accessibility to a college education would have a detrimental effect on the economy.[22] Washington repeatedly condemned the administration's budget and tax proposals, convinced they would help rich Americans at the expense of the poor, such as those residing in his district, and he urged his colleagues to reject proposals "to balance the budget on the backs of the poor."[23] During the 1981 budget reconciliation process, rather than agree to a proposal by the Education and Labor Committee to cut $11.7 billion from student aid, employment training, and child nutrition programs, Washington voted "present." Washington also disagreed with much of the President's foreign policy, especially the increased production of nuclear weapons, the emphasis on defense spending, and U.S. military intervention in Central America.[24]

Washington's most enduring influence as a Representative was his commitment to civil rights. Unlike many freshman Members, who lacked extensive legislative experience, Washington had a long career in local and state government, which paved the way for his prominent role in the effort to extend the provisions of the 1965 Federal Voting Rights Act. The Congressional Black Caucus (CBC), which Washington labeled "the one forum by which black leaders can speak to the nation," chose the Illinois Representative as its floor manager for the significant legislation.[25] As the CBC's representative and a member of the Judiciary Committee, Washington helped negotiate an extension of sections of the 1965 Voting Rights Act that disallowed jurisdictions with a history of voting rights abuses from using "bail-out" provisions to avoid inclusion under the measure.[26] During his time in the House, Washington denounced proposals to weaken the enforcement of affirmative action and reiterated one of his positions as an Illinois state legislator: endorsement of the Equal Rights Amendment (ERA).[27] After the defeat of the ERA, he expressed regret and blamed the Reagan administration for its failed ratification. "To me, the ERA is a nondebatable issue," Washington noted. "Black people have suffered from discrimination, degradation, and inequality in all areas of life. So, on this issue of peoples' rights, it is easy to identify with the inequities women are facing."[28]

Concerned that Mayor Byrne and other local machine leaders would launch a significant challenge to his re-election bid, Washington spent considerable time campaigning in Chicago during his first term.[29] But despite his apprehension, he ran unopposed in the Democratic primary and easily won a second term in the House, garnering 97 percent of the vote in the general election.[30]

Shortly after his victory in November 1982, Washington announced his candidacy for mayor of Chicago. Approached by several African-American groups interested in fielding a strong black candidate to oppose Byrne, Washington, who was content with his position in Congress, agreed to run only after a campaign to register

voters added more than 100,000 blacks to Chicago's rolls.[31] Throughout his campaign in the Democratic primary against the incumbent mayor and Richard M. Daley, the son of the late former mayor, Washington used a grass-roots approach, emphasizing his anti-machine record, especially when courting African-American voters. "It's our turn," Washington said repeatedly. "We're not going to apologize for it and we're not going to waste a lot of time explaining it. It's our turn—that's all."[32] Drastically outspent by both his opponents, Washington nonetheless stunned the nation by emerging victorious in the competitive Democratic primary, which boasted its largest turnout in 25 years—bolstered by thousands of newly registered black voters.[33] In the general election, Washington narrowly defeated former Illinois state legislator Republican Bernard Epton to become Chicago's first African-American mayor. Aware of the magnitude of his victory, Washington commented shortly after his election that "the whole Nation was watching and Chicago sent a profound message out of the crucible of our city's most trying election."[34] On April 30, 1983, a little more than two weeks after the election, he resigned his House seat.[35]

Washington struggled to reform the Chicago political scene, but he eventually experienced some success in weakening the power of the machine. Seven months after winning election to a second term, Washington died suddenly of a heart attack on November 25, 1987.[36] "Losing our mayor is like losing a black folk hero," noted a Chicago constituent. Even the *Chicago Tribune*, which had at times criticized Mayor Washington, observed that few people "have made quite so powerful an impact" on the city. The newspaper also noted that though he experienced discrimination, "Harold Washington did not neglect white Chicago the way his predecessors neglected black Chicago, and let that be a permanent part of his legacy and a lasting tribute to him."[37] During a salute to his former colleague on the House Floor, Mervyn Dymally of California recognized Washington's political legacy: "He was purposeful and constantly focused, for his battle did not begin and end with the roll call, but extended into a crusade to heal the cancerous lesions of race hatred and generations of divisive political warfare."[38]

FOR FURTHER READING

Levinsohn, Florence Hamlish. *Harold Washington: A Political Biography* (Chicago: Chicago Review Press, 1983).

Rivlin, Gary. *Fire on the Prairie: Chicago's Harold Washington and the Politics of Race* (New York: Henry Holt, 1992).

Travis, Dempsey. *Harold: The People's Mayor: An Authorized Biography of Mayor Harold Washington* (Chicago: Urban Research Press, 1989).

"Washington, Harold," *Biographical Directory of the U.S. Congress, 1774–Present,* http://bioguide.congress.gov/scripts/biodisplay.pl?index=W000180.

MANUSCRIPT COLLECTION

Chicago Public Library, Harold Washington Archives & Collections, Special Collections & Preservation Division Reading Room (Chicago, IL). *Papers*: 1981–1983, 54 linear feet. The congressional records of Harold Washington document his promotion and sponsorship of legislation, his committee work, and his involvement with the Congressional Black Caucus. The papers contain correspondence and other contacts with his constituents, including casework, fundraising, and the organization of task forces for such issues as housing and health. A finding aid is available in the repository.

NOTES

1 Paul Taylor, "Washington: A Thoughtful Legislator," 24 February 1983, *Washington Post*: A7.

2 Quoted in a December 1987 *Ebony* article that was entered into the *Congressional Record* as part of a tribute to Harold Washington after his death in 1987. See *Congressional Record*, House, 100th Cong., 1st sess. (2 December 1987): 33747.

3 Florence Hamlish Levinsohn, *Harold Washington: A Political Biography* (Chicago: Chicago Review Press, 1983): 23.

4 Jessie Carney Smith, ed., "Harold Washington," *Notable Black American Men* (Detroit, MI: Gale Research Inc., 1998).

5 Shirley Washington, *Outstanding African Americans of Congress* (Washington, DC: U.S. Capitol Historical Society, 1998): 73; Taylor, "Washington: A Thoughtful Legislator"; Levinsohn, *Harold Washington: A Political Biography*: 20–21.

6 Washington, *Outstanding African Americans of Congress*: 73.

7 "Harold Washington," *Contemporary Black Biography* (Detroit, MI: Gale Research Inc., 1994). Several sources refer to his wife as Dorothy Finch; however, one source, *Notable Black American Men* (1999), mentions Harold Washington's meeting and later marrying Nancy Dorothy Finch, who lived in the same building as the Washington family after 1935.

8 Thaddeus Russell, "Washington, Harold" *American National Biography* 22 (New York: Oxford University Press, 1999): 768–769 (hereinafter referred to as *ANB*).

9 Washington, *Outstanding African Americans of Congress*: 74.

10 William E. Schmidt, "Leader Who Personified Black Rise to Urban Power," 26 November 1987, *New York Times*: 19D.

11 Gary Rivlin, *Fire on the Prairie: Chicago's Harold Washington and the Politics of Race* (New York: Henry Holt, 1992): 55–56; Levinsohn, *Harold Washington: A Political Biography*: 101.

12 Neil Mahler and David Axelrod, "Blacks Favor Mayor Bid by Washington," 20 January 1977, *Chicago Tribune*: 10.

13 Roger Biles, *Richard J. Daley: Politics, Race, and the Governing of Chicago* (DeKalb: Northern Illinois University Press, 1995): 234.

14 Rivlin, *Fire on the Prairie*: 56–57; Taylor, "Washington: A Thoughtful Legislator."

15 Vernon Jarrett, "For Washington, the Party's Over," 11 May 1977, *Chicago Tribune*: A4.

16 William L. Clay, *Just Permanent Interests: Black Americans in Congress, 1870–1991* (New York: Amistad Press, 1992): 262; Levinsohn, *Harold Washington: A Political Biography*: 135–136.

17 Aldo Beckman, "Campaign '80: The Illinois Primary," 20 March 1980, *Chicago Tribune*: B6; "Election 80—New Faces in the House," 23 November 1980, *Washington Post*: A15.

18 "Election Statistics, 1920 to Present," available at http://clerk.house.gov/member_info/electionInfo/index.html.

19 Even though Ralph Metcalfe ultimately severed ties with Mayor Daley's organization, his initial election owed much to machine support.

20 T. R. Reid, "New House Member Won't Yield State Senate Seat to Byrne Machine," 18 January 1981, *Washington Post*: A7; Sam Smith, "Washington Won't Resign His Seat in State Senate," 18 January 1981, *Chicago Tribune*: 16.

21 Robert Benjamin, "Rep. Washington Resigns His Seat in Illinois Senate," 21 January 1981, *Chicago Tribune*: D1.

22 *Congressional Record*, House, 97th Cong., 1st sess. (11 March 1981): 4075.

23 *Congressional Record*, House, 97th Cong., 1st sess. (24 February 1981): 2945.

24 Russell, "Washington, Harold," *ANB*.

25 "The Power Seekers: Chicago's Mayoral Races," 13 February 1983, *Chicago Tribune*: A1; Washington, *Outstanding African Americans of Congress*: 76.

26 Levinsohn, *Harold Washington: A Political Biography*: 171; Schmidt, "Leader Who Personified Black Rise to Urban Power"; Russell, "Washington, Harold," *ANB*; Taylor, "Washington: A Thoughtful Legislator."

27 John C. White, "Rep. Washington Criticizes Plans to Relax Affirmative Action Rules," 27 August 1981, *Chicago Tribune*: A13.

28 *Congressional Record*, House, 97th Cong., 2nd sess. (14 July 1982): 16116.

29 William J. Grimshaw, *Bitter Fruit: Black Politics and the Chicago Machine, 1931–1991* (Chicago: University of Chicago Press, 1992): 169.

30 "Election Statistics, 1920 to Present," available at http://clerk.house.gov/member_info/electionInfo/index.html.

31 Kevin Klose, "Chicago Mayoral Primary; Rep. Washington Leads Byrne," 23 February 1983, *Washington Post*: A1; David Axelrod, "Washington Key Black in Mayor Race," 26 July 1982, *Chicago Tribune*: A1; "The Power Seekers: Chicago's Mayoral Race," 13 February 1983, *Chicago Tribune*: A1.

32 Taylor, "Washington: A Thoughtful Legislator."

33 Frederick C. Klein, "Chicago Is Likely to Get First Black Mayor After Rep. Washington's Primary Victory," 24 February 1983, *Wall Street Journal*: 19; Kevin Klose, "Black Turnout, Split White Vote Aided Rep. Washington," 24 February 1983, *Washington Post*: A1.

34 Quoted in a tribute to Washington's victory delivered by fellow Chicago Representative Gus Savage. See *Congressional Record*, House, 98th Cong., 1st sess. (13 April 1983): 8369.

35 Ibid.

36 Bob Secter and Wendy Leopold, "Washington, 1st Black Mayor of Chicago Dies," 26 November 1987, *Los Angeles Times*: 1.

37 "Harold Washington and Chicago," 26 November 1987, *Chicago Tribune*: 30; Jerry Thornton and Cheryl Devall, "It's 'Like Losing a Black Folk Hero,'" 26 November 1987, *Chicago Tribune*: 6.

38 *Congressional Record*, House, 110th Cong., 1st sess. (2 December 1987): 33746.

Katie Beatrice Hall
1938–

UNITED STATES REPRESENTATIVE ★ 1982–1985
DEMOCRAT FROM INDIANA

Unable to exercise her constitutional right to vote before the civil rights era and subject to segregation laws, Katie Hall felt trapped in her tiny southern hometown until she heard speeches by African-American Representatives Adam Clayton Powell, Jr., of New York and William Dawson of Illinois that led her to believe she could attain a quality education and a better life outside Mississippi.[1] Hall eventually sought public office and became the first African American from Indiana to serve in the House of Representatives. Among her chief accomplishments was piloting a bill through Congress to make Martin Luther King, Jr.'s birthday a national holiday.

On April 3, 1938, Katie Beatrice Green was born to Jeff and Bessie Mae Hooper Green, in Mound Bayou, Mississippi. One of 12 children, Katie attended the public schools in Mound Bayou and received a bachelor of science degree from Mississippi Valley State University in 1960. During her junior year of college, in 1957, she married John H. Hall. The couple had three children: Jacqueline, Junifer, and Michelle. In 1968, Katie Hall received an M.S. degree from Indiana University in Bloomington. She subsequently taught social studies in Gary, Indiana, an industrial city on the south shore of Lake Michigan. Hall's early political involvement included campaigning for black lawyer Richard Hatcher, a Gary mayoral candidate. This experience encouraged her to enter electoral politics herself. Hall ran an unsuccessful campaign for the Indiana state house of representatives in 1972 but won a seat in 1974. Two years later, Hall was elected to the state senate, where she served from 1976 until 1982. She also served as the chairwoman of the Lake County Democratic Committee from 1978 to 1980 and chaired the 1980 Indiana Democratic convention.

In September of 1982, Indiana Democratic Representative Adam Benjamin, Jr., died suddenly of a heart attack. Katie Hall attended a public forum a week after the Representative's death to discuss a possible successor and was surprised to hear her name mentioned, although her aspiration to national office was not new. "I had always thought about running for Congress," she admitted, but refrained because "I saw Adam as a very highly respected Congressman who did the job very well. I saw him as a person who was undefeatable."[2] Patricia Benjamin, the Representative's widow, also expressed interest in succeeding her husband. Under Indiana law, the chairman of the district's Democratic committee selected the nominee to fill the vacancy for the remainder of the 97th Congress (1981–1983).[3] Then-chairman Richard Hatcher, whom Hall considered her political mentor, remembered Hall's support for his mayoral campaigns.[4] He selected his protégé to run for the vacant seat that represented the northwest corner of the state, anchored by Gary. At the same time, the committee nominated Hall—with Hatcher casting the deciding vote—for a full term in the 98th Congress (1983–1985) to represent a newly reapportioned district.[5] The district's boundaries remained relatively unchanged after the reapportionment, and white northern Indiana Democrats expressed concern over Hall's electability because of her race. Although downtown Gary was primarily black, the racial composition of the entire district was 70 percent white.[6] A legal battle ensued when Patricia Benjamin's supporters claimed that, as chairman of the old district, Hatcher did not have the right to select a candidate for the new district.[7] The courts refused to overturn Hatcher's decision. Hall's nomination as the Democratic nominee for both the vacancy and the full term was tantamount to election in the working-class, Democratic district and she defeated her Republican opponent, Thomas Krieger, with 63 percent to win election to the remainder of the 97th Congress.[8] She simultaneously

IMAGE COURTESY OF NATIONAL ARCHIVES AND RECORDS ADMINISTRATION

won election with 56 percent of the vote for the 98th Congress.[9] Upon her election, Hall became the first black woman from Indiana to serve in the U.S. Congress.

When she arrived in Washington to be sworn in on November 2, 1982, Representative Hall received seats on the Committee on Post Office and Civil Service and the Committee on Public Works and Transportation, assignments that were typical for freshman Members. Representative Hall voted with the Democratic majority against much of the Ronald W. Reagan administration's legislative agenda, focusing on education, labor, and women's issues. In addition, Representative Hall became involved in the fight to alleviate famine in Africa when she witnessed widespread suffering during a congressional trip to northern Ethiopia. Hall also supported a variety of measures designed to reduce her urban, industrial district's high rate of unemployment and to mitigate the attendant social problems of crime, family debt and bankruptcy, and alcohol and drug abuse. As a member of the House Steel Caucus, Hall endorsed the Fair Trade in Steel Act, which was intended to revitalize Gary's ailing steel industry.

Katie Hall made her most lasting legislative contribution as chairwoman of the Post Office and Civil Service Subcommittee on Census and Population. Devoted to commemorating the memory of Dr. Martin Luther King, Jr., in July 1983 Hall introduced a bill to make King's birthday a federal holiday. Since King's assassination in 1968, similar measures had been introduced annually, but all had failed. As a nod to her negotiating abilities, Hall was assigned as the floor manager for the measure. The primary argument against the bill, advanced by fiscal conservatives, was the large cost of the holiday to the federal government, estimated at $18 million in holiday overtime pay and lost work time.[10] Hall courted detractors by moving the holiday from a fixed date—King's January 15 birthday—to the third Monday in January to prevent government offices from having to open twice in one week and thereby saving money. Under Hall's leadership, the House Subcommittee on Census and Population passed the measure in a five to one vote, sending it to the House

Floor. In opening the debate on the House Floor, Hall reminded her colleagues, "The legislation before us will act as a national commitment to Dr. King's vision and determination for an ideal America, which he spoke of the night before his death, where equality will always prevail."[11] Hall's persistence paid off. On August 2, 1983, more than 15 years after King's assassination, the bill passed the House by a vote of 338 to 90. On November 2, 1983, President Ronald Reagan signed the measure into law.[12] Impressed by Hall's success, veteran lawmaker William (Bill) Gray III of Pennsylvania observed, "Sometimes when you get to the goal line it's good to go to someone fresh and new to take it over. She brought a freshness of approach, a spirit of reconciliation to what had sometimes been a bitter battle."[13]

In her 1984 bid for renomination and re-election to the 99th Congress (1985–1987), Katie Hall faced a formidable challenge. Despite her many widespread supporters, including Speaker Thomas P. (Tip) O'Neill of Massachusetts, two strong Democrats challenged Hall in her district primary: former Adam Benjamin aide Peter Visclosky and county prosecutor Jack Crawford. Hall maintained that intraparty opposition was based partially on her race and gender. During one debate Hall declared, "If I wasn't black and female, there wouldn't be a contest."[14] Reverend Jesse Jackson, whose name appeared on the primary ballot for the Democratic presidential nominee, also rallied to her aid.[15] In the May primary, Hall lost the Democratic nomination to Visclosky by a margin of 2,367 votes and immediately cited racial injustice.[16] However, the most detrimental development was that aside from Hatcher, prominent African-American officials in Gary had failed to support her, resulting in only a 50 percent voter turnout in the predominantly black city.[17] Hall also questioned returns in areas where polls indicated she ran stronger than the final count.[18] She filed a petition and won a suit for a recount of the primary results; however, the recount only confirmed her losing margin.

After Congress, Hall continued to be active in Indiana Democratic politics. In 1986 and in 1990, she tried unsuccessfully to recapture the Democratic nomination in her old House district. Hall returned to Gary and served as the vice chair of the city's housing board. Hall became the Gary city clerk in 1985. She resigned in January 2003 after pleading guilty to charges of federal mail fraud.[19]

FOR FURTHER READING

Catlin, Robert A. "Organizational Effectiveness and Black Political Participation: The Case of Katie Hall," *Phylon* 46 (September 1985): 179–192.

"Hall, Katie Beatrice," *Biographical Directory of the United States Congress, 1774–Present,* http://bioguide.congress. gov/scripts/biodisplay.pl?index=H000058.

NOTES

1 Steven V. Roberts, "Mississippi Gets a Representative From Indiana," 26 November 1982, *New York Times*: B8.

2 Jan Carroll, "Katie Hall Could Be First Black Representative From Indiana," 21 September 1982, Associated Press.

3 "Black Woman Nominated to Succeed Benjamin," 13 September 1982, Associated Press.

4 Carroll, "Katie Hall Could Be First Black Representative From Indiana."

5 James R. Dickerson, "Indiana Democrats Feud Over Benjamin's Seat," 19 September 1982, *Washington Post*: A10.

6 "Black Woman Nominated to Succeed Benjamin"; for statistics on the white majority, see *Almanac of American Politics, 1984* (Washington, DC: National Journal Inc., 1983): 387; Julia Malone, "Folks Back Home Speak Their Piece to Representatives," 8 September 1982, *Christian Science Monitor*: 1.

7 Dickerson, "Indiana Democrats Feud Over Benjamin's Seat."

8 "Gary Indiana Newspaper Rejects Candidate's Newspaper Ad," 27 October 1982, United Press International; Roberts, "Mississippi Gets a Representative From Indiana."

9 "Election Information, 1920 to Present," available at http://clerk. house.gov/member_info/electionInfo/index.html.

10 Larry Margasak, "Courting Conservatives to Back King Holiday," 14 August 1983, Associated Press.

11 *Congressional Record*, House, 98th Cong., 1st sess. (2 August 1983): 22208.

12 A three-year grace period also was part of the compromise; see Sandra Evans Teeley, "King Holiday Bill Approved by House Panel," 1 July 1983, *Washington Post*: A10. The Martin Luther King, Jr., holiday was first observed on January 20, 1986. See Steven V. Stathis, *Landmark Legislation, 1774–2002* (Washington, DC: Congressional Quarterly Press, 2003). See also the House bill history in the final *House Calendar* for the 98th Congress. For the Reagan bill signing, see David Hoffman, "King Is Saluted as President Signs Holiday Into Law," 3 November 1983, *Washington Post*: A1.

13 Margasak, "Courting Conservatives to Back King Holiday."

14 E. R. Shipp, "Rep. Katie Hall Facing Tough Fight in Indiana," 7 May 1984, *New York Times*: B8.

15 David S. Broder and Kevin Klose, "Two States' House Primaries Will Involve Interracial Battles," 5 May 1984, *Washington Post*: A7.

16 "Mrs. Hall Loses Bid for Renomination in Indiana; Racism Charged," 10 May 1984, *Washington Post*: B19.

17 "Racism, Low Voter Turnout Blamed for Black Congresswoman's Defeat," 9 May 1984, Associated Press.

18 "Black Congresswoman Seeks Recount After Loss in Democratic Primary," 22 May 1984, Associated Press.

19 Barbara Sherlock, "Gary Official Resigns After Pleading Guilty; City Clerk Accepts Mail Fraud Charges," 29 January 2003, *Chicago Tribune*: N2.

Major Robert Odell Owens
1936–

UNITED STATES REPRESENTATIVE ★ 1983–2007
DEMOCRAT FROM NEW YORK

Trained as a librarian, civil rights activist Major Owens was a community reformer who went on to serve in the New York state senate and then won the seat of legendary Brooklyn Representative Shirley Chisholm—the first African-American woman elected to Congress—when she retired from the U.S. House. Owens became a significant advocate for education during his 12 terms in the House.[1] "Education is the kingpin issue," he explained. "Proper nurturing of and attention to the educational process will achieve a positive domino reaction which will benefit employment and economic development. . . . The greater the education, the lesser the victimization by drugs, alcoholism, and swindles. . . . We have to believe that all power and progress really begins with education."[2]

Major Robert Odell Owens was born in Collierville, Tennessee, on June 28, 1936, to Ezekiel and Edna (Davis) Owens. Owens's father, a day laborer in a furniture factory who espoused President Franklin D. Roosevelt's New Deal philosophy, shaped Owens's political views at an early age. "I can't remember a time when I wasn't aware of the fact that a much bigger world than my own personal universe was out there," Owens once remarked. "We were very poor and always had to struggle to make ends meet. Still, I was also aware that we were not alone—that millions of people, in this country and abroad, faced similar kinds of problems. I also realized that what happened in the larger world affected my family and its personal welfare."[3] He also recalled that his mother, "the scholar of the family," influenced his approach to academics. His parents' optimism about their children's future left Owens with the attitude that "there was no reason why I couldn't go out and scale life's summits."[4] Early on, he aspired to be a novelist. He attended public schools in Memphis, Tennessee, graduating from Hamilton High School. In 1956, Owens earned a B.A. with high honors from Morehouse College in Atlanta, Georgia. A year later, he completed an M.A. in library science at Atlanta University (now Clark Atlanta). In 1956, he married Ethel Werfel. They raised three children—Christopher, Geoffrey, and Millard—before divorcing in 1985. Geoffrey, an actor, landed a regular part on *The Cosby Show*; Chris became a community activist and ran unsuccessfully for city council in 1989. Major Owens later married Marie Cuprill, the staff director of an Education and Labor subcommittee in the U.S. House.[5] She brought two children, Carlos and Cecilia, to the marriage.

Once out of school, Owens took a job as a librarian at the Brooklyn Public Library in 1958, where he worked until 1966. He became active in the Democratic Party during that time and was involved in community organizations and the broader civil rights movement. In 1961, Owens joined the Brooklyn chapter of the Congress of Racial Equality (CORE), later chairing the organization. He also was vice president of the metropolitan New York council of housing. Additionally, Owens taught as an adjunct professor of library science and was director of the Community Media Program at Columbia University. From 1966 to 1968, he served as the executive director of the Brownsville community council. One observer described him as "the most canny and capable of the community corporation directors."[6] That post brought widespread recognition in the borough and its president designated September 10, 1971, "Major R. Owens Day." Based on his work on antipoverty programs in the Brownsville neighborhood, New York Mayor John Lindsay appointed Owens the commissioner of the community development agency, giving him responsibility for the city's antipoverty programs.[7] Owens left the post in late 1973 near the end of Lindsay's term as mayor, charging that there was corruption within the antipoverty and school

programs in Brownsville and further asserting that newly elected African-American New York City Councilman Samuel Wright had awarded school board contracts as "political payoffs."[8] That episode sparked a feud between Wright and Owens that persisted into the 1980s. In 1972, Owens served on the International Commission on Ways of Implementing Social Policy to Ensure Maximum Public Participation and Social Justice for Minorities at The Hague in the Netherlands. Owens also participated in the 1979 White House Conference on Libraries.

Owens first ran for elective office in 1974, winning a seat in the New York state senate, where he chaired the senate democratic operations committee. Eventually, Owens served on the finance committee and the social services committee, and was ranking member of the chamber's daycare task force. He also tended to back local and statewide candidates from outside the Brooklyn Democratic machine—a role he would take on in a U.S. congressional race in the early 1980s.

After Representative Shirley Chisholm announced her retirement in 1982, Owens became a candidate for her Brooklyn-based seat, which encompassed the neighborhoods of Bedford-Stuyvesant, Brownsville, and Crown Heights. The district was roughly 80 percent black, overwhelmingly Democratic, and was afflicted by a high poverty rate and urban blight. Also, voter turnout was traditionally low. In the Democratic primary, Owens faced former New York State Senator Vander L. Beatty. Considered the leading reformer among local politicians, Owens had grass-roots support and the endorsement of the *New York Times*. Beatty, a wealthy African American, was backed by many top Democratic leaders, including Representative Chisholm; the Brooklyn political machine led by Borough President Howard Golden; and a patronage network Beatty had cultivated from Albany. Owens exploited Beatty's connection to corrupt local officials, stressing his own honesty and independence from the local political machine. Winning the endorsements of the *Amsterdam News* (a well-respected newspaper in the black community) and the *Village Voice*, he prevailed in the

primary by 2,400 votes and he survived a court challenge from Beatty and his backers, who questioned the results. Six months later, Beatty was indicted on charges of election fraud.[9] In the general election, Owens cruised to victory, defeating Republican David Katan with 91 percent of the vote.

Like his predecessor, Representative Chisholm, Owens monitored potential primary challengers, especially since he came from outside the political establishment, but he lacked significant opposition for most of his congressional career. Although he did face a serious primary challenge in 2000, Owens never stumbled in any of his general election campaigns, despite redistricting that reconfigured his district after the 1990 Census. He won each of his 10 subsequent elections with at least 89 percent of the vote.[10]

When Representative Owens took his seat in the House, he received assignments on the Education and Labor Committee (later Education and the Workforce) and the Government Operations Committee (later Government Reform). He remained on both panels throughout his House career. In 1987, Owens became chair of the Education and Labor Subcommittee on Select Education and Civil Rights—a position he held until the Republicans won control of the chamber in the 1994 elections and abolished the subcommittee. By the 109th Congress (2005–2007), Representative Owens was the third-ranking Democrat on the Education and the Workforce and the Government Reform committees. In addition, he served as the Ranking Minority Member on the Education and the Workforce Subcommittee on Workforce Protections. Owens also was a member of the Congressional Black Caucus (CBC) and the Progressive Caucus, which comprised the House's most liberal Members.[11]

As a junior Member in the House, surveying the effects of the depressed economy in the early 1980s, Owens explained that he planned to "push the prerogatives of a congressman to the limit" to publicize the needs of inner-city Americans. "My principal focus is on jobs and employment. From my perspective the Democratic-controlled House has been extremely negligent in this area. It has shown little, if any, urgency about the plight of the unemployed."[12] As a Representative, Owens focused on a cause near to his heart: advocating more federal money for education and libraries, which dovetailed with the needs of his urban district. From his post as chairman of the Subcommittee on Select Education and Civil Rights, Owens focused on restoring federal funding for library services, institutions of higher learning, and programs to alleviate the high school dropout crisis in the black community. In 1985, he wrote portions of a higher education bill that provided a fund of $100 million to improve the programs and the infrastructure of historically black colleges. He called the measure "the payment of a long overdue debt" in response to critics who charged it was "unwarranted special treatment."[13] Owens also served as chairman of the Congressional Black Caucus Higher Education Brain Trust. When the Cold War ended in the early 1990s, Owens advocated that money being shifted from military to domestic programs should be appropriated for American inner cities. "We need our fair share of this peace divided, in particular to rehabilitate crumbling and dilapidated inner-city schools, and to guarantee a first-rate education for urban youths," he said.[14] Owens criticized budgets under Republican Presidents Ronald W. Reagan and George H. W. Bush, asserting that they neglected the pressing need of minorities. On the House Floor in 1990, he belted out some lines from a rap song he wrote: "At the big white DC mansion/There's a meeting of the mob/And the question on the table/Is which beggars they will rob."[15]

From his subcommittee post, Representative Owens was a primary backer and a floor manager of the Americans with Disabilities Act of 1990, a landmark law Owens said set forth "clear, strong, consistent, enforceable standards addressing discrimination against individuals with disabilities."[16] Among the provisions were the first guidelines prohibiting discrimination against persons with disabilities in businesses and public spaces and the establishment of standards for accessibility to public buildings. The measure also contained provisions to promote development programs for preschool children and to introduce new technologies to assist students with disabilities, which Owens had championed earlier.[17] "A civilized and moral government which is also seeking to enhance its own self-interest must strive to maximize the opportunities for the educational development, equal access and productive employment of all its citizens," Owens noted. "Greater than all the physical barriers are the barriers of entrenched attitudes and the silent insistence that people with disabilities should be grateful for minimal governmental protection and assistance."[18]

Representative Owens was the lead sponsor of the Domestic Volunteer Service Act, providing for major reforms to the long-established Volunteers in Service to America (VISTA) program, which assigns volunteers to community-based aid agencies to combat urban and rural poverty. Additionally, he was a key backer of the Child Abuse Prevention Challenge Grants Reauthorization Act of 1989, which renewed a measure first passed in 1974. The bill provided states federal funding to assess, investigate, and prosecute cases of child abuse; conduct research; and compile data. The bill also defined child abuse and neglect. In the early 1990s, Owens helped reauthorize legislation that encouraged states to offer people with disabilities jobs through rehabilitation centers and homes where they could live independently. From his seat on the Education and the Workforce Committee in the late 1990s, Owens supported hikes in the federal minimum wage, opposed efforts to eliminate cash compensation for overtime work, advocated the continued need for the Occupational Safety and Health Administration (OSHA), and defended organized labor.[19] Since many of his constituents were of Caribbean descent, Owens also sponsored two pieces of legislation that were important to immigrants: a bill that prevented the Immigration and Naturalization Service from deporting the parents of American-born children under age 18 and a measure that extended citizenship to immigrant children under age 12 who were in the U.S. without their parents.[20]

Over time, the makeup of Owens's Brooklyn-based district changed. In the early 1990s, following reapportionment after the 1990 Census, blacks still made up a sizable majority of the district; 19 percent was white, and 12 percent was Hispanic. That round of reapportionment expanded the western borders of the district to take in the wealthy Park Slope neighborhood and middle-class Kensington.[21] During the 1980s and 1990s, large numbers of Haitians began moving into the district, making it the second-largest community of Haitians in the country, second to Miami. Roughly two-thirds of the district's black population (then 55 percent) were from nations in the Caribbean Basin. Immigrant groups complained that Owens was "totally out of touch with the Haitian community," willing to support the return to power of ousted President Jean-Bertrand Aristide, but less active regarding issues such as housing and political asylum. Owens dismissed such charges as "total distortion," ascribing them to members of the Haitian community who did not approve of his support for Aristide.[22] In 2000, Owens received a stiff primary challenge from New York City Councilwoman Una Clarke, a Jamaican-born politician with roots among the growing number of Caribbean immigrants in Owens's district. A one-time political ally of Owens's, Clarke capitalized on simmering immigrant discontent and ran against the Representative, charging he had not done enough to bring federal economic aid to the district and that he was unresponsive to immigration issues. Owens relied on support from First Lady and New York Senate candidate Hillary Rodham Clinton and other prominent Democrats. The race revealed frictions between the growing community of Caribbean blacks and African Americans. Owens eventually turned back Councilwoman Clarke's primary challenge by a 54 to 46 percent margin.

Reapportionment following the 2000 Census did not significantly reconfigure the district and increased its proportion of blacks to 59 percent. Owens cruised to re-election in 2002, but when he announced in early 2003 that he would seek re-election in 2004 and then retire in 2007, two young female New York City council members jumped into the primary. Yvette Clarke, daughter of Owens's 2000 primary opponent, drew 29 percent of the vote, while Tracy Boyland won 22 percent of the vote. Representative Owens won the primary with 45 percent of the vote and election to his final term with 94 percent of the vote. Among those who announced their candidacy for his open seat in 2006 was Owens's son Chris. Yvette Clarke eventually won the Democratic primary and the general election to succeed Representative Owens. In retirement, Owens suggested he would pursue his interest in literature. "It's something that I have always wanted to do," Owens said. "I even began writing a novel when I was younger. And that's one of the things I want very much to get back to."[23] In late 2006, Representative Owens was named a distinguished visiting scholar at the John W. Kluge Center at the Library of Congress. He is currently at work on a case study of the CBC and its impact on national politics.[24]

FOR FURTHER READING

"Owens, Major Robert Odell," *Biographical Directory of the U.S. Congress, 1774–Present*, http://bioguide.congress.gov/scripts/biodisplay.pl?index=O000159.

MANUSCRIPT COLLECTION

University at Albany, SUNY (Albany, NY). M. E. Grenander Department of Special Collections and Archives. *Papers:* ca. 1983–2006, 106 cubic feet. The collection includes the office files and personal papers of Representative Major Owens from his 24 years in the U.S. House of Representatives.

NOTES

1   Quoted in "Major R. Owens: The Predicament of Power," in Jeffrey M. Elliot, *Black Voices in American Politics* (New York: Harcourt Brace Jovanovich, 1986): 68.

2   Quoted in "Major Owens," *Contemporary Black Biography*, Volume 6 (Detroit, MI: Gale Research Inc., 1994) (hereinafter referred to as *CBB*).

3   "Biography of Congressman Major R. Owens," undated (c. 1990) official news release from the Office of Representative Owens, files of the Office of History and Preservation, U.S. House of Representatives.

4   Elliot, *Black Voices in American Politics*: 56–57.

5   *Politics in America, 1994* (Washington, DC: Congressional Quarterly Inc. 1993): 1052.

6   Charles R. Morris, *The Cost of Good Intentions: New York City and the Liberal Experiment, 1960–1975* (New York: W.W. Norton and Company, 1980): 65.

7   Peter Kihss, "Brooklyn Negro Leader Named Head of a City Poverty Agency," 13 March 1968, *New York Times*: 38.

8   Peter Kihss, "Community Aide Charges Corruption in Brownsville," 29 November 1973, *New York Times*: 48.

9   Beatty was found guilty of forgery and conspiracy in December 1983. See Joseph P. Fried, "Beatty Is Guilty of a Conspiracy in Vote Forgery," 23 December 1983, *New York Times*: A1; *Almanac of American Politics, 1984* (Washington, DC: National Journal Inc., 1983): 811–812; Ronald Smothers, "2 Ex-State Senators Vie for Rep. Chisholm's Job," 16 September 1982, *New York Times*: B8; "Primary Day Choices," 23 September 1982, *New York Times*: A26; *Almanac of American Politics, 1988* (Washington, DC: National Journal Inc., 1987): 1036.

10   "Election Statistics, 1920 to Present," available at http://clerk.house.gov/member_info/election.html; for the 2000 primary, see Jonathan P. Hicks, "Bitter Primary Contest Hits Ethnic Nerve Among Blacks," 31 August 2000, *New York Times*: A1.

11   "Official Biography of Major Owens," at http://www.house.gov/owens/biography.htm (accessed 17 May 2006); Mildred L. Amer, "Black Members of the United States Congress, 1870–2007," 27 September 2007, RL30378, Congressional Research Service, Library of Congress, Washington, DC.

12   Quoted in Elliot, *Black Voices in American Politics*: 68–69.

13   *Politics in America, 1988* (Washington, DC: Congressional Quarterly Inc., 1987): 1036.

14   "Major Owens," *CBB*.

15   "Colorful Characters," 22 May 1994, *New York Times*: CY13.

16   Stephen W. Stathis, *Landmark Legislation, 1774–2002* (Washington, DC: CQ Press, 2003): 336.

17   *Politics in America, 1994*: 1052.

18   *Congressional Record*, House, 101st Cong., 1st sess. (2 August 1989): E2814.

19   *Politics in America, 2006* (Washington, DC: Congressional Quarterly Inc., 2005): 717–718; "Official Biography of Major Owens."

20   *Politics in America, 2006*: 718.

21   *Politics in America, 1994*: 1053.

22   Garry Pierre-Pierre, "Haitians Seek New Influence in Local Politics," 7 August 1994, *New York Times*: CY7.

23   Jonathan P. Hicks, "Congressman From Brooklyn Will Seek One Final Term," 23 November 2003, *New York Times*: 33.

24   "U.S. Congressman Major Owens Named Distinguished Visiting Scholar at John W. Kluge Center," 26 December 2006, Library of Congress press release, at http://www.loc.gov/today/pr/2006/06-237.html (accessed 20 September 2007).

Alan Dupree Wheat
1951–

UNITED STATES REPRESENTATIVE ★ 1983–1995
DEMOCRAT FROM MISSOURI

Alan Wheat's rare appointment as a freshman Member to the prestigious House Committee on Rules shaped his congressional career. "Rules gave me the opportunity to immediately start making an impact on the House of Representatives," the Missouri Representative once remarked. "Perhaps not so much as a sponsor of legislation but being able to have an impact on legislation as it came through the committee."[1] During his six terms in Congress, Wheat used his position on the influential panel to skillfully represent a broad constituency in his majority-white Missouri district. Known for his ability to forge alliances between African-American and white groups, Wheat wielded considerable political clout by working within the institution to push through legislation important to his district and the Democratic Party.

Alan Dupree Wheat was born in San Antonio, Texas, on October 16, 1951, to James Wheat, an officer and civil engineer in the U.S. Air Force, and Emogene (Jean) Wheat, a teacher. Wheat grew up on military bases and attended schools in Wichita, Kansas, and Seville, Spain, before graduating from Airline High School in Bosier City, Louisiana, in 1968. After earning a B.A. in economics from Grinnell College, in Iowa, Wheat joined the Department of Housing and Urban Development as an economist in 1972. He worked in the same capacity for the Mid-America Regional Council in Kansas City from 1973 to 1975. Wheat then served as an aide to Jackson County, Missouri, executive Mike White in 1975 and 1976 and won election to the Missouri general assembly in 1976 at age 25. Wheat served three terms in the Missouri state legislature, where he chaired the urban affairs committee. On August 11, 1990, Wheat married Yolanda Townsend, a lawyer; the couple had two children: Christopher and Nicholas. Wheat also had another daughter, Alynda, from a previous relationship.[2]

When longtime Missouri Representative Richard W. Bolling announced his retirement in August 1981, Wheat joined seven other candidates in the Democratic primary to represent the majority-white, predominantly Democratic district encompassing much of Kansas City, including the downtown area, and Independence, Missouri, hometown of President Harry S. Truman. The only African-American candidate in the crowded field, Wheat narrowly earned the Democratic nomination, with 31 percent of the vote. He went on to win the general election against Republican Missouri State Representative John Sharp, with 58 percent of the vote, by appealing to middle- and working-class voters with his criticism of President Ronald W. Reagan's economic policies and his promise to continue the legislative agenda of Representative Bolling.[3] Wheat became the first African-American Member to represent Kansas City and the second black Representative in Congress from Missouri.[4]

Elected to the 98th Congress (1983–1985) in November 1982 at age 31, Wheat received a spot on the House Rules Committee (previously chaired by his predecessor, Dick Bolling), which controls the flow of legislation on the House Floor. He used his committee assignment to secure federal funding for a series of projects affecting his district, ranging from flood control initiatives to highway and transit spending and the building of a new Kansas City courthouse. He also played a significant role in the passage of legislation to prohibit the foreign servicing of American planes—which saved the jobs of hundreds of Kansas City-based airline employees—as well as the passage of legislation to expand the Harry S. Truman National Historic Site.[5] Wheat's seat on the Rules Committee was instrumental in allowing him to push contentious legislation through the House. In 1989, he helped institute a ban on smoking on most domestic flights

by attaching the bill to a routine procedural measure so as to avoid undue attention from tobacco lobbyists and other opponents.[6] From the 99th to the 103rd Congresses (1985–1995), Wheat served on the District of Columbia Committee, chairing the Government Operations and Metropolitan Affairs Subcommittee during his final four terms in office. Wheat was also a member of the House Select Committee on Children, Youth, and Families and a member of the Select Committee on Hunger.

Wheat's legislative approach in Congress appealed to a broad voting base. "My job is to do what's best for my country and district," he noted. "What I do legislatively has ramifications for both."[7] By focusing attention on issues affecting his Missouri district and the domestic front, he effectively balanced the interests of African-American and white voters. In 1994, Wheat responded to constituent concerns about neighborhood violence with his enthusiastic backing of the Violent Crime Control and Law Enforcement Act.[8] His consistent votes along party lines resonated with the constituents in his Democratic district. However, Wheat eschewed the political labels (mainly liberal) his opponents used to categorize his outspoken support for issues such as free speech and gun control and his opposition to the death penalty. "The only label I'd accept is Democrat," he asserted. "That's because I believe Roosevelt, Truman, Kennedy and Johnson did a pretty damned good job."[9]

Throughout his tenure in the House, Wheat advocated a strong stance on civil rights. In his position on the Rules Committee he played an integral part in the passage of the Civil Rights Bill of 1990, a comprehensive measure to combat employment discrimination—Wheat called it "the single most important civil rights legislation since the 1964 Civil Rights Act"—ensuring that the version that reached the House Floor retained much of its original language.[10] In the 102nd Congress (1991–1993) he joined fellow Missouri Representative William (Bill) Clay, Sr., in co-sponsoring legislation to provide financial assistance to historically black colleges and universities; the measure became part of the Higher Education Act of 1992.[11] As

vice chair of the Congressional Black Caucus (CBC) during the 100th and 101st Congresses (1987–1991), Wheat instituted a policy that allowed whites to join the organization as associate members, reflecting his ability to address the interests of both black and white constituents. Although he was a vocal supporter of the CBC, Wheat emphasized his political independence: "I apply the same standard to the activities of the Black Caucus as to the activities of other groups. If I agree, I participate. If not, I don't."[12] Additionally, Wheat served as president of the Congressional Black Caucus Foundation, an independent, nonprofit organization geared toward public policy analysis.

Also concerned with civil rights abroad, Wheat denounced South Africa's apartheid regime. The Missouri Representative was a member of a congressional delegation that visited the African nation in 1990. After meeting with South African President Frederik de Klerk, and touring the country, Wheat remarked, "It is true that a start has been made, but it is only a start down the long road that must be trod toward freedom in South Africa."[13] He urged his colleagues to maintain economic sanctions against South Africa until the country instituted full demographic reforms.[14] Wheat's interest in foreign affairs extended beyond Africa. He opposed the U.S. invasion of Grenada in 1983 and President Reagan's decision to furnish military aid to the contras in Nicaragua. In 1991, Wheat joined the Democratic majority in condemning the Persian Gulf War resolution.[15]

Wheat's commitment to the constituents of his district paid off at the polls, where he enjoyed comfortable margins of victory. During his re-election bids he reminded voters of his valuable position on the Rules Committee and employed clever campaign advertisements with wheat stalks—a play on his name and a symbol of midwestern agriculture.[16] Wheat suffered a temporary political setback in 1992 when his name appeared on a list of dozens of Members who overdrew their accounts at the informal House "Bank" managed by the Sergeant at Arms. Records revealed that Wheat had many overdrawn checks.

However, Wheat was elected to a sixth term in the House, with 59 percent of the vote (the lowest percentage since his first run for Congress), avoiding the fate of some other Representatives whose careers were ended by the controversy.[17]

When Republican Senator John Danforth announced his decision to retire at the conclusion of the 103rd Congress (1993–1995), Wheat entered the race to fill the vacant Senate seat. "I want my career to be meaningful," he stated. "I don't want to look back after 30 or 40 years' service and have nothing to say except that I grew in seniority and inherited a committee chairmanship."[18] Wheat narrowly earned the Democratic nomination, with 41 percent of the vote, against Jackson County executive Marsha Murphy, becoming the first African American in Missouri to be nominated for statewide office. In the general election he faced an uphill battle against former Missouri Governor John Ashcroft. The competitive primary had depleted Wheat's campaign funds, and a rising anti-incumbent sentiment put Wheat on the defensive. In an election year in which the GOP gained control of the House and the Senate for the first time since the Eisenhower Era, Ashcroft soundly defeated Wheat, who garnered only 36 percent of the vote.[19]

After his congressional service, Wheat served as vice president of SmithKline Beecham pharmaceutical company and as vice president of public policy and government relations of the global relief organization CARE. In 1996 he resumed his political career, accepting a position as deputy campaign manager for the Clinton-Gore presidential re-election campaign. Two years later in 1998, he founded Wheat Government Relations, a political consulting firm in Virginia.[20]

FOR FURTHER READING

"Wheat, Alan Dupree," *Biographical Directory of the U.S. Congress, 1774–Present*, http://bioguide.congress.gov/scripts/biodisplay.pl?index=W000326.

MANUSCRIPT COLLECTION

University of Missouri-Kansas City, Western Historical Manuscript Collection (Kansas City, MO). *Papers:* ca. 1982–1994, 257 cubic feet. The papers of Alan Dupree Wheat consist of his congressional files, including press releases, newsletters, correspondence, individual voting records, office files, calendars, speeches, photographs, and videotapes.

NOTES

1   Andrew C. Miller, "Wheat's Influence Felt Behind the Scenes," 25 September 1994, *Kansas City Star*: A23.

2   Jon Sawyer, "Wheat Answers Critics, Touts Record in Senate Race," 15 July 1994, *St. Louis Post-Dispatch*: 1C; "Alan Wheat," *Who's Who Among African Americans* (New York: Gale Research, 2002); "Alan Wheat," *Contemporary Black Biography* Volume 14 (Detroit, MI: Gale Research Inc., 1997) (hereinafter referred to as *CBB*). The *CBB* entry lists Wheat's father as James Weldon.

3   Carol M. Swain, *Black Faces, Black Interests: The Representation of African Americans in Congress* (Cambridge, MA: Harvard University Press, 1993): 120–121; "Alan Wheat," *CBB*; "Election Statistics, 1920 to Present," available at http://clerk.house.gov/member_info/electionInfo/index.html; *Politics in America, 1994* (Washington, DC: Congressional Quarterly Inc., 1993): 881–882.

4   Mark Schlinkmann, "Broad Support Gives Wheat 5th District Win," 3 November 1982, *Kansas City Times*.

5   Miller, "Wheat's Influence Felt Behind the Scenes;" Swain, *Black Faces, Black Interests*: 125; Katherine Tate, *Black Faces in the Mirror: African Americans and Their Representatives in the U.S. Congress* (Princeton: Princeton University Press, 2003): 101.

6   Miller, "Wheat's Influence Felt Behind the Scenes."

7   Swain, *Black Faces, Black Interests*: 127.

8   "Alan Wheat," *CBB*.

9   Sawyer, "Wheat Answers Critics, Touts Record in Senate Race."

10 Robert Shepard, "House Debates Civil Rights Bill," 2 August 1990, United Press International; William L. Clay, *Just Permanent Interests: Black Americans in Congress, 1870–1991* (New York: Amistad Press, Inc., 1992): 392; Richard L. Berke, "House Approves Civil Rights Bill; Veto Is Weighed," 4 August 1990, *New York Times*: 1. The 1990 civil rights legislation also passed the Senate but was vetoed by President George H. W. Bush.

11 *Politics in America, 1994*: 881.

12 Swain, *Black Faces, Black Interests*: 127.

13 *Congressional Record*, House, 101st Cong., 2nd sess. (6 February 1990): 1283.

14 *Politics in America, 1994*: 881.

15 Sawyer, "Wheat Answers Critics, Touts Record in Senate Race;" Swain, *Black Faces, Black Interests*: 126.

16 Swain, *Black Faces, Black Interests*: 122, 124.

17 Miller, "Wheat's Influence Felt Behind the Scenes"; Robert L. Koenig, "303 Lawmakers Wrote Bad Checks," 17 April 1992, *St. Louis Post-Dispatch*: 1A; *Politics in America, 1994*: 882–883.

18 Miller, "Wheat Answers Critics, Touts Record in Senate Race."

19 "Alan Wheat," *CBB*; "Former Governor Wins Missouri G.O.P. Primary for Governor," 3 August 1994, *New York Times*: A22; Richard L. Berke, "Blow for Clinton: Democratic Mainstays Ousted in Big Upsets Around the Nation," 9 November 1994, *New York Times*: A1; "Election Statistics, 1920 to Present," available at http://clerk.house.gov/member_info/electionInfo/index.html.

20 "Alan Wheat," *CBB*; "The Honorable Alan Wheat: Wheat Government Relations, Inc.," at http://www.wheatgr.com/alanwheat.html (accessed 21 March 2007); Philip Dine, "Wheat May Be Compromise for Labor Department Post," 19 December 1996, *St. Louis Post-Dispatch*: 13C.

ALTHOUGH HE WAS A VOCAL
SUPPORTER OF THE CBC, WHEAT
EMPHASIZED HIS POLITICAL
INDEPENDENCE:
"I APPLY THE SAME STANDARD TO
THE ACTIVITIES OF THE BLACK
CAUCUS AS TO THE ACTIVITIES
OF OTHER GROUPS. IF I AGREE,
I PARTICIPATE. IF NOT, I DON'T."

Charles Arthur Hayes
1918–1997

UNITED STATES REPRESENTATIVE ★ 1983–1993
DEMOCRAT FROM ILLINOIS

Elected in his first bid for public office, Charles Arthur Hayes succeeded Representative Harold Washington when he resigned from the 98th Congress (1983–1985) to become mayor of Chicago. During his five terms in the House, Hayes gradually sought to separate himself from the shadow of his popular predecessor when representing his South Side Chicago constituents, by combining his major interests and strengths: labor and civil rights. "Charlie Hayes was a giant in the history of the struggle for civil rights and political rights for Americans of African descent," Senator Carol Moseley-Braun of Illinois said after Hayes died in 1997. "He was a trailblazer in the trade-union movement and to the end maintained his passionate commitment to working men and women."[1]

Born in Cairo, Illinois, on February 17, 1918, Charles Arthur Hayes graduated from Cairo's Sumner High School in 1935. After high school, Hayes worked in Cairo as a machine operator. His long career of union activism began when he helped organize Local 1424 of the United Brotherhood of Carpenters and Joiners of America. Hayes served as president of this organization from 1940 to 1942. In 1943, he joined the grievance committee of the United Packinghouse Workers of America (UPWA) and became a UPWA field representative in 1949. He served as district director for the UPWA's District One from 1954 to 1968. From 1979 until his retirement in September 1983, Hayes served as the international vice president of the United Food and Commercial Workers Union.[2] As a trade unionist, he promoted increased benefits and improved conditions for workers, fought to eliminate segregation and discrimination in hiring and promotion in industry, and provided African-American and women workers with opportunities to serve as leaders in the labor movement. Twice widowed and once divorced, Hayes had four children.[3]

Although he had no direct experience as a politician, Hayes was not a stranger to Congress. In 1959, the future Representative testified before the House Un-American Activities Committee. Questioned about his alleged ties to the Communist Party as a trade union leader, he denounced communism but declined to answer questions about any personal connections with the party.[4] As a veteran meatpacking union lobbyist, Hayes gained valuable experience about the inner workings of Congress.[5] Interested in politics at the local level as well, he actively supported the anti-establishment candidate Harold Washington in his bids for mayor of Chicago—his unsuccessful run in 1977 and his victorious campaign in 1983. Like Washington, Hayes opposed the powerful Chicago political machine, preferring a more independent style of governing that focused on the welfare of the city's many impoverished black residents.[6] The friendship of the two Chicago leaders figured prominently in Hayes's unlikely path to Congress.

Following Washington's resignation from the House on April 30, 1983, upon his election as Chicago's first African-American mayor, Hayes joined 13 other candidates in the special Democratic primary to fill the vacant congressional seat. Well known in certain areas of the community because of his extensive labor activities, Hayes nonetheless faced an array of challengers with more name recognition, including Ralph Metcalfe, Jr., the son of a former Representative; civil rights leader Al Raby; and Lu Palmer, a newspaper columnist and community activist. During the campaign, the 65-year-old Hayes promised to help the many poor people living in the congressional district encompassing Chicago's predominantly black South Side. In particular, he ran on a platform advocating federal assistance for public housing and employment programs.[7] With the enthusiastic backing of organized labor and the newly elected Mayor

IMAGE COURTESY OF OFFICE OF THE CLERK, U.S. HOUSE OF REPRESENTATIVES

Washington, Hayes emerged victorious with 45 percent of the vote in the crowded and competitive primary on July 26, 1983.[8] Although Washington's active campaigning on Hayes's behalf contributed to his win, Hayes assured his supporters that "I'm not going to be a mouthpiece for him." He continued, "If I can just do what he did when he was there [Congress], just do my own thing as a representative, I'll be all right."[9] One month later, Hayes easily defeated his Republican opponent, community newspaper columnist Diane Preacely, in the special election with 94 percent of the vote.[10]

Hayes began his second career when he took his seat in Congress on September 12, 1983, to complete the remainder of Washington's term. During his tenure in the House he served on the Education and Labor, Small Business, and Post Office and Civil Service committees. As a member of the Education and Labor Committee, Hayes authored one of his most significant pieces of legislation: the Dropout Prevention and Reentry Act. Concerned about the high dropout rate among students in Chicago, which far exceeded the national average, Hayes successfully proposed that the federal government allocate $500 million to state and local government officials to alleviate the problem. In 1986, the Illinois Representative remarked, "The greatest security our Nation can have is to have our children properly educated."[11] Echoing many of his African-American colleagues in the House, Hayes questioned the Ronald W. Reagan administration's commitment to education. He criticized President Reagan's proposed budget cuts of the mid-1980s, labeling the federal spending reduction "a callous disregard for the dreams and aspirations of millions of poor and disadvantaged children and young adults."[12]

During his congressional career, Hayes attempted to follow through on his campaign promise to help the unemployed in his district and nationwide. He sponsored bills to reduce high unemployment rates, to provide disadvantaged youth with job training, and to create public works programs to rebuild the infrastructures of cities like Chicago. Alarmed by the rising unemployment in his district that was precipitated by the economic recession of the early 1980s, Hayes urged lawmakers to support legislation to assist workers laid off in the massive plant closings in Chicago.[13] He frequently expressed a determination to strengthen the 1978 Humphrey–Hawkins Full Employment and Balanced Growth Act, which was crafted to promote employment opportunities in accordance with a growth in productivity.[14] Hayes sponsored the Income and Jobs Action Act of 1985 to reinforce the principles outlined in the 1978 measure and to "focus attention and find solutions to the problem of unemployment and stop acting as though the problem does not exist."[15] Drawing on his experience as a labor leader, Hayes consistently supported legislation to protect American workers through higher wages, restrictions on imports, and more-comprehensive benefits for children and health care.[16]

Hayes boasted a strong record of civil rights activism spanning four decades. He joined Martin Luther King, Jr., in the 1955 Montgomery, Alabama, bus boycott, and worked closely with the Southern Christian Leadership Conference and Operation PUSH (People United to Save Humanity).[17] Once elected to the House, he viewed the Congressional Black Caucus (CBC) as an important tool for advancing the rights of African Americans. Hayes once remarked, "to say that a person can just go (to Congress) and change it all—it doesn't work that way." He believed that working cooperatively with the CBC would help him to achieve one of his primary legislative goals: the endorsement of racial equality in Chicago and in the nation.[18] A consistent opponent of South Africa's white-minority government, Hayes introduced legislation to impose economic and diplomatic sanctions against the African nation as a means of ending apartheid.[19] In November 1984, he protested at the South African Embassy in Washington, DC. As one of several Members arrested during the staged protests, Hayes defended the demonstrations, remarking "these acts should force the South African Government to stop oppressing, jailing, and killing its black citizens who are only seeking justice."[20]

Throughout his time in the House, Hayes faced little opposition in his re-election bids, typically winning more than 90 percent of the vote.[21] In the 1992 Democratic primary, however, several factors contributed to an unusually difficult campaign for the five-term incumbent. Partially because of a decline in population during the 1980s in Hayes's impoverished urban district, the boundaries were redrawn, changing the composition of the constituency. Although the district still included the predominantly African-American South Side, it also picked up several white neighborhoods and suburban areas of southwest Chicago.[22] Hayes had a formidable challenger in the primary—Bobby Rush, a Chicago alderman and a former member of the Black Panther Party. During the campaign, Rush accused Hayes of making many promises to his constituents but failing to secure enough substantial legislative victories.[23] Despite the potential obstacles to his re-election, Hayes seemed to be on his way to securing another term in Congress until his name was linked to a breaking Capitol Hill scandal just days before the March 18 primary. A Government Accounting Office study indicated that many Members consistently overdrew their accounts in the House "Bank," an informal service provided by the House Sergeant at Arms. The ensuing investigation by the House Ethics Committee revealed that Hayes wrote 716 checks exceeding his account balance in a 39-month period.[24] He had the dubious distinction of being identified as one of the roughly two dozen "abusers" (the Members with the worst records of bouncing checks).[25] "I believe the whole thing is a personal matter," Hayes commented after his overdrafts became public. "It did not cost the taxpayers a dime and is a side issue when our nation is in a serious crisis."[26] Reluctant to accept blame or apologize to his constituents, Hayes lost to Rush 42 to 39 percent.[27] In 1993, the Justice Department cleared Hayes of any criminal wrongdoing for bouncing checks while he was a Member of the House.[28]

Hayes remained active in labor and community affairs after his congressional career.[29] Stricken with cancer, he died in Chicago on April 8, 1997.[30] In 1999, the Charles A. Hayes Family Investment Center, a nonprofit technology center for disadvantaged Chicago residents that was named for the former Representative, opened in a historic building previously used by the UPWA.[31]

FOR FURTHER READING

"Hayes, Charles Arthur," *Biographical Directory of the U.S. Congress, 1774–Present*, http://bioguide.congress.gov/scripts/biodisplay.pl?index=H000388.

NOTES

1 Steve Neal, "Former Lawmaker Charles Hayes Dies," 10 April 1997, *Chicago Sun-Times*: 4.

2 "Former S. Side Congressman Charles Hayes Dies at 79," 9 April 1997, *Chicago Tribune*: 2C; "Charles Arthur Hayes," 1992 Associated Press Candidate Biographies.

3 "Charles Hayes, 79, Former Chicago Lawmaker," 13 April 1997, *New York Times*: 38; *Congressional Directory*, 99th Congress (Washington, DC: Government Printing Office, 1985): 52.

4 Mitchell Locin and Robert Davis, "Lifetime of Union Work Leads Hayes to Threshold of Congress," 28 July 1983, *Chicago Tribune*: A9.

5 "Former S. Side Congressman Charles Hayes Dies at 79."

6 Locin and Davis, "Lifetime of Union Work Leads Hayes to Threshold of Congress."

7 "Chicago Mayor's Candidate Wins Primary for House Seat," 28 July 1983, *New York Times*: A17.

8 David Axelrod and Mitchell Locin, "Hayes Wins 1st District House Race," 27 July 1983, *Chicago Tribune*: 1; Kevin Klose, "For Chicago Mayor, a Change in Fortune," 28 July 1983, *Washington Post*: A8.

9 Locin and Davis, "Lifetime of Union Work Leads Hayes to Threshold of Congress."

10 Michael J. Dubin et al., *United States Congressional Elections, 1788–1997: The Official Results* (Jefferson, NC: McFarland & Company, Inc., 1998): 735; "Labor Leader Wins Easily in Chicago Special Election," 24 August 1983, *Washington Post*: A3. Dubin et al. spell Hayes's opponent's surname, "Pracely," whereas the contemporary *Washington Post* uses the spelling "Preacely."

11 *Congressional Record*, House, 99th Cong., 2nd sess. (7 August 1986): 19646.

12 *Congressional Record*, House, 99th Cong., 1st sess. (26 February 1985): 3534.

13 *Congressional Record*, House, 99th Cong., 1st sess. (12 November 1985): 31409.

14 Stephen W. Stathis, *Landmark Legislation, 1774–2002: Major U.S. Acts and Treaties* (Washington, DC: Congressional Quarterly Press, 2003): 302.

15 *Congressional Record*, House, 100th Cong., 1st sess. (9 April 1987): 8654; *Politics in America, 1990* (Washington, DC: Congressional Quarterly Inc., 1989): 417.

16 *Congressional Record*, House, 100th Cong., 1st sess. (9 April 1987): 8655; *Politics in America, 1990*: 417.

17 "Funeral Held for Former Rep. Hayes," 14 April 1997, United Press International; "Chicago Mayor's Candidate Wins Primary for House Seat," 28 July 1983, *New York Times*: A17.

18 Andrew Herrmann, "Rush, Hayes Put Records on the Line in 1st District," 21 February 1992, *Chicago Sun-Times*: 8.

19 *Congressional Record*, House, 99th Cong., 1st sess. (28 February 1985): 4165.

20 "Congressman and Rights Leader Arrested at South African Embassy," 27 November 1984, *New York Times*: A20; "Rep. Hayes, SCLC Head Are Arrested in Protest," 27 November 1984, *Wall Street Journal*: 64; "2 Congressmen Held After Embassy Protest," 1 December 1984, *New York Times*: 10.

21 "Election Statistics, 1920 to Present," available at http://clerk.house.gov/member_info/electionInfo/index.html.

22 Robert Davis, "Well-known Name Plays Role in 1st District Race," 21 September 1992, *Chicago Tribune*: 1; *Politics in America, 1994* (Washington, DC: Congressional Quarterly Inc., 1993): 455–456.

23 "Hayes Targets Jobless Voters With $5 Billion Public Works Bill," 28 January 1992, *Chicago Tribune*: C2.

24 Amy Keller, "Members Misbehaving: Congress' Top Scandals," 14 June 2005, *Roll Call*.

25 Steve Johnson and Teresa Wiltz, "Rep. Hayes Bounced 716 Checks, List Shows," 15 March 1992, *Chicago Tribune*: 1C.

26 Larry Margasak, "Rep. Hayes Listed Among Top Abusers of House Bank," 15 March 1992, *Chicago Sun-Times*: 3.

27 Adam Clymer, "The Rumble of Discontent Rattles Illinois Incumbents," 19 March 1992, *New York Times*: A20.

28 "Hayes Cleared in Check-Writing Scandal," 19 May 1993, *Chicago Tribune*: 14.

29 "Charles Hayes, Former Congressman," 10 April 1997, *Milwaukee Journal Sentinel*: 7.

30 "Charles Hayes, 79, Former Chicago Lawmaker"; "Former S. Side Congressman Charles Hayes Dies at 79."

31 "Governor Unveils Computer Lab for Disabled at Charles A. Hayes Center," 28 April 2004, *Chicago Defender*: 3.

Concerned about the high dropout rate among students in Chicago, which far exceeded the national average, Hayes successfully proposed that the federal government allocate $500 million to state and local government officials to alleviate the problem. In 1986, the Illinois Representative remarked, "The greatest security our Nation can have is to have our children properly educated."

Alton R. Waldon, Jr.
1936–

UNITED STATES REPRESENTATIVE ★ 1986–1987
DEMOCRAT FROM NEW YORK

Upon being sworn in to the U.S. House of Representatives after a heated special election, Alton Waldon, Jr., noted of the U.S. Capitol: "This is a nice place to work for a man whose father had a strong back and not much else. I'm a bit of a romantic, a bit of a dreamer. This is a place that is the repository of the history of America."[1] Declaring, "I want to devote myself to being a 24-hour-a-day, seven-day-a-week, Congressman," Walton devoted his short term to protesting apartheid in South Africa.[2] Though he served in the House for less than six months, Waldon made his mark as the first black Representative elected from New York's Queens borough.

Alton Ronald Walton, Jr., was born on December 21, 1936, in Lakeland, Florida. His parents, Rupert Juanita Wallace and Alton R. Waldon, Sr., moved to New York City when their son was six years old, and he grew up in the Bedford-Stuyvesant section of Brooklyn. Alton Waldon, Sr., worked as a longshoreman. Waldon, Jr., joined the U.S. Army in 1953 and served until he was discharged in 1959 as a Specialist, 4th Class. He married Barbara DeCosta, a graphic designer, in 1961. They had three children: Alton III, Dana, and Ian. Waldon spent his first few years out of the military pursuing a professional singing career before he joined the New York City housing authority's police force in 1962. The housing authority police, which provided security for residents of the city's public housing, was at the time separate from the New York City Police Department. Before leaving the force in 1975, Waldon advanced from the rank of patrolman to captain. He also became chief administrator and commander of the police academy for the New York City housing department. Waldon received a B.S. in criminal justice from John Jay College in New York City in 1968, and earned a J.D. from New York University Law School in 1973. During his time in law school, Waldon won

the prestigious Thurgood Marshall Fellowship, awarded every three years to promising minority law students by the New York state trial lawyers association. In 1975, Waldon was appointed deputy commissioner of the New York state division of human rights. In 1981 and 1982, he served as assistant counsel for the New York state office of mental retardation and developmental disabilities. In 1982, Waldon won election to represent his Queens neighborhood in the New York state assembly, where he served until 1986.

In April 1986, Representative Joseph Addabbo, after a long battle, succumbed to cancer. Addabbo had risen to chair the House Defense Appropriations Subcommittee during his 25-year congressional tenure. During that span, his southeastern Queens district grew by about 25 percent, transforming from a primarily white lower- to middle-class neighborhood to a community that was nearly 65 percent black.[3] In May 1986, Queens Democrats nominated Waldon to run for Addabbo's seat in the June 10 special election. If elected in the crowded five-way race, Waldon would be the first black man to represent the overwhelmingly Democratic district in Congress. Three Democrats joined the canvass under third party banners. Floyd Flake, a popular pastor of the Allen African Methodist Episcopal (AME) Church in Jamaica, ran as a Unity Party candidate. New York City health department official Kevin McCabe entered the race as the Good Government Party candidate. State senator Andrew Jenkins, who was runner-up to Waldon for the Democratic nomination, ran on the Liberal Party ticket. Lone Republican-Conservative Richard Dietl also joined the race.

Though he did not have the backing of the Democratic Party, Flake was considered Waldon's strongest opponent. Flake's position in the religious community gained him the

support of nearly all of the black ministers in the district. Churches were instrumental in influencing voters, and also provided transportation to the polls.[4] Flake gained the endorsement of the *New York Times* just five days before the election, though the newspaper also portrayed Waldon favorably.[5] At the close of polls on Election Day, Flake led by 197 votes (out of more than 40,000 cast), but absentee ballots had yet to be counted. Flake's name did not appear on the absentee ballots because a filing technicality had temporarily eliminated him from the race; by the time his candidacy was reinstated right before the election, it was too late to change the absentee ballots.[6] The final count put Waldon ahead of Flake by a mere 278 votes. Flake attempted to discard the absentee ballots in court, but a three-judge federal appeals panel ruled in Waldon's favor on July 25.[7] Waldon was in Washington, DC, visiting Representative Charles Rangel of New York when he received the news of his election. He was sworn in five days later on July 29, 1986. "How sweet it is," he declared. "I'm the son of a man who could not read and write. Only in America could this happen, to have someone to come from abject poverty . . . and sit in this august body."[8]

During his brief term, Waldon received assignments to the Committee on Education and Labor and the Committee on Small Business, but his focus was primarily on U.S. relations with South Africa. Waldon entered Congress at the height of the battle for strict sanctions against South Africa's white-minority government to condemn its apartheid system. Waldon and other black Members led the fight to override President Ronald W.

Reagan's veto of a bill calling for sanctions against South Africa. "America is the cradle of freedom," Waldon declared on the House Floor. "But unless we move with determination and dispatch, the babe of hope will be stillborn in Pretoria."[9] He also opposed aid to Angolan rebels, who received support from South Africa's white-minority government and called on President Reagan to participate in a summit with the leaders of the nations bordering South Africa.[10] Waldon also submitted legislation combating drug abuse, focusing on reducing the use of crack cocaine. Recalling his father's inability to read and write, he called for a national task force to focus on illiteracy, describing the inability to read as a "corrosive force that is silently eroding the social infrastructure of our Nation."[11]

Just two months after he took his seat, Waldon found himself battling Flake for re-election. Though Waldon had the benefit of incumbency as well as support from New York Governor Mario Cuomo, Flake returned with his strong base as well as support from New York City Mayor Edward Koch. Waldon lost the nomination to Flake by about 3,000 votes.[12]

Waldon left Congress in January 1987 and received an appointment to the New York state investigation commission, where he served until 1990. The following year, he won a seat in the New York state senate, serving in that body for a decade. In 2000, Waldon accepted a judicial appointment to the New York court of claims in New York City.

FOR FURTHER READING

"Waldon, Alton R., Jr.," *Biographical Directory of the United States Congress, 1774–Present*, http://bioguide. congress.gov/scripts/biodisplay.pl?index=W000038.

NOTES

1   Esther B. Fein, "Warmth and Work Greet Waldon," 31 July 1986, *New York Times*: B3.

2   "Man in the News; After Court Victory, A Congressman-Elect: Alton Ronald Waldon, Jr.," 26 July 1986, *New York Times*: A31.

3   "Good—and Better—in Queens," 5 June 1986, *New York Times*: A26.

4   Dan Jacobson, "Queens Elects First Black Congressman," 11 June 1986, United Press International.

5   "Good—and Better—in Queens."

6   "Election Laws on Trial in Queens," 20 June 1986, *New York Times*: A30.

7   "Man in the News; After Court Victory, A Congressman-Elect: Alton Ronald Waldon, Jr."

8   *Congressional Record*, House, 99th Cong., 2nd sess. (29 July 1986): 17956.

9   *Congressional Record*, House, 99th Cong., 2nd sess. (29 September 1986): 27094.

10 *Congressional Record*, House, 99th Cong., 2nd sess. (26 September 1986): 26410.

11 *Congressional Record*, House, 99th Cong., 2nd sess. (8 October 1986): 29605.

12 Esther B. Fein, "Flake Defeats Waldon; Abzug Leading Teicher," 10 September 1986, *New York Times*: B5.

Alphonso Michael (Mike) Espy
1953–

UNITED STATES REPRESENTATIVE ★ 1987–1993
DEMOCRAT FROM MISSISSIPPI

As the only black student at a newly integrated high school, Mike Espy learned firsthand how to navigate the strict racial division between blacks and whites in his home state of Mississippi. This ability won him a seat in the U.S. House of Representatives—the first held by a black Mississippian in more than 100 years—in his first bid for elective office in 1986. "Service, service, service" was the way Espy described his legislative strategy; he focused on economic development and procuring aid for farmers in his impoverished rural district.[1] His centrist approach to politics won over constituents of both races and eventually earned him a top position in the Cabinet of his friend President William J. (Bill) Clinton.

Alphonso Michael (Mike) Espy was born in Yazoo City, Mississippi, on November 30, 1953. He and his twin, Althea Michelle, were the youngest of Henry and Willie Jean (Huddelston) Espy's seven children. Though Yazoo City was located in an impoverished section of the Mississippi River Delta, the Espy family was affluent. Educated (along with his wife) at Alabama's Tuskegee Institute, Henry Espy served as a county agent for the U.S. Department of Agriculture in the 1930s.[2] He later joined his father-in-law's family-owned funeral home business. Mike Espy's maternal grandfather, T. J. Huddleston, Sr., founded a chain of nursing homes and built the first black hospital in Mississippi in 1921. Huddleston, who died in the 1950s, was a local celebrity and one of the wealthiest black men in the South.[3] The prosperous family business initially sheltered the Espy children from segregated public schools. Mike Espy attended a local parochial school through his first two years of high school. After the school closed, in 1969, he transferred to Yazoo City High School. Espy was the only black student, and he carried a stick to fend off racist attacks from fellow students.[4] "Relative to the civil rights experiences of snarling dogs and whips and

things it was pretty tame," Espy recalled of his schooldays. "But I'd always have a fight. The teacher would leave the room, and then you're among 35 in the classroom and they'd make racial jeers."[5] A year later, in 1970, Yazoo City High School was fully integrated, and Espy was elected president of the black student body in his senior year. (The white students had their own president.) Espy went on to earn a B.A. in political science from Howard University in Washington, DC, in 1975. He earned a J.D. from Santa Clara University Law School, near San Jose, California, in 1978, and then returned to Mississippi to practice law. He married Sheila Bell and the couple had two children, Jamilia and Michael, before divorcing.

Espy began his political career working in several state government positions. He served as the first black assistant secretary of state, managing the Mississippi central legal services division from 1978 to 1980. For the next four years, Espy served as assistant secretary of state for the public lands division, in charge of enforcing a state law that set aside one of every 36 square miles for educational purposes. From 1984 to 1985, Espy was assistant state attorney general for the consumer protection division. Espy also drew national attention within the Democratic Party when he served on the rules committee for the 1984 national convention.

Following the 1980 Census—nearly 100 years after the last black Representative to serve Mississippi (John Roy Lynch) departed the House in 1883—a statewide redistricting effort created a majority-black congressional district that stretched along the Mississippi River on the western side of the state and encompassed the cities of Vicksburg and Greenville. In 1984, black state legislator Robert Clark came close to unseating white freshman Republican incumbent Webb Franklin in a racially charged campaign. In 1986, the U.S. Justice Department

supervised the redrawing of district lines to include more black voters in response to the 1965 Voting Rights Act, which called for higher black percentages in single districts.[6] The new Mississippi district, with its slight black majority, was the most impoverished in the country; 42 percent of its residents lived below the national poverty line and five counties had an unemployment rate of at least 20 percent.[7] Studying the 1984 election, Espy believed he could improve on Clark's campaign.[8] Narrowly avoiding a runoff election, Espy won a 50 percent plurality in the Democratic primary against runner-up Paul B. Johnson, a grandson of a former Mississippi governor, and Hiram Eastland, a cousin of the late segregationist U.S. Senator James Eastland.

In the general election, Espy faced the incumbent, Franklin. Both candidates realized that voter turnout would be key since the district's population was evenly divided between blacks and whites—particularly in a state where race was still a significant dividing line.[9] For example, Mississippi was the only state that still categorized drivers' licenses by skin color, and blacks and whites coexisted in generally peaceful, but separate worlds. Social, civic, and educational institutions practiced an almost *de facto* segregation—black churches held services down the street from white churches; black lawyers served black clients and vice versa; and black children dominated the public schools down the road from the private schools that were mostly white.[10] Combating black voters' traditionally low turnout, Espy went door-to-door, calling on supporters to volunteer transportation and other services on Election Day. "I need you; I can't do it by myself," he implored. "Please sir, please ma'am, turn out, serve as a poll watcher or a driver or a food-fixer. The answer is in your hands."[11] A lifelong Baptist campaigning in a religious area, Espy adopted the slogan, "Stand by Me, Pray for Me, Vote for Me."[12] Espy stepped across the deep racial divide to court white voters, too. Describing the balancing act required by his strategy, Espy said, "You must excite your black voters and not incite your white voters."[13] He promised to combat the agricultural depression that plagued his white constituents (widely known as "planters" in local circles), touting a letter from House Speaker Jim Wright of Texas ensuring him a seat on the powerful Agriculture Committee.[14] The strategy paid off. Espy won 12 percent of the white turnout, while many other white voters stayed home in a show of *de facto* support.[15] Espy took 52 percent of the total returns to Franklin's 48 percent, winning his first elective office and becoming the only black Representative in the 100th Congress (1987–1989) to represent a rural district.[16] Asked by a *Washington Post* reporter how he felt after his victory, Espy responded, "peaceful," belying the frenzy of national attention.[17] Espy's ability as a black candidate to attract white voters was unprecedented in a Mississippi federal election.[18] Espy's election, declared a state newspaper, "did more than shatter the age-old color barrier. . . . It is further evidence that Mississippi is ready for a change."[19]

House leaders rewarded Espy with favorable committee assignments for a freshman Representative, enabling him to look after the interests of his rural district.[20] He took his promised seat on the Agriculture Committee as well as an assignment on the equally prestigious Budget Committee. He also served on the Select Committee on Hunger. Espy was re-elected three times. His 1988 campaign was difficult, but he won with 65 percent of the vote. Espy's opponent, Republican attorney Jack Coleman, accused him of supporting the "radical left" and insinuated that Espy had defaced his home with racial epithets in order to elicit sympathy from voters.[21] In Espy's next two election campaigns in 1990 and 1992, he defeated Republican Dorothy Bedford with 84 and 76 percent of the vote, respectively.[22]

Espy attributed his electoral success to his focus on constituent service.[23] As a freshman, he sponsored the Lower Mississippi River Valley Delta Development Act, enlisting the aid of fellow Mississippi Democrat and powerful Appropriations Committee Chairman Jamie Whitten, who helped secure $3 million to fund the project.[24] The bill established a nine-member panel to study the region's widespread poverty and created a plan for economic development along the banks of the Mississippi River. The governors of participating states (Mississippi, Louisiana, Arkansas, Tennessee, Kentucky, Missouri, and Illinois) selected the commission's members. Espy also helped create the Lower Mississippi Delta Congressional Caucus, later serving as its chairman. The group persuaded Congress to pass the 1990 Housing and Community Development Act, which funneled money to underserved areas. In addition, Espy became a spokesman for the Mississippi Delta's fastest-growing enterprise: catfish farming. He sought huge federal grants for the thousand-acre pools to breed the fish and sponsored a resolution declaring June 25 National Catfish Day. He even persuaded the U.S. Army to serve soldiers catfish at least once a week.[25]

Reflecting the nearly even racial and political divisions among his constituents, Espy embraced the political center to a greater degree than did many of his African-American colleagues in Congress.[26] Espy's voting record received high ratings from liberal groups. As an active member of the liberal Congressional Black Caucus, he generally disagreed with President Ronald W. Reagan's focus on the Cold War military buildup and he supported abortion rights. Yet Espy also embraced some conservative positions on social issues: For instance, he was in favor of school prayer and advocated the death penalty for those who committed drug-related crimes. A longtime member of the National Rifle Association—a conservative organization whose primary interest was to protect Second Amendment rights to gun ownership—Espy made headlines as the first federal lawmaker to appear in one of the organization's advertisements.[27] He also favored U.S. funding for the Nicaraguan contras, who were fighting communist insurgents.[28]

Espy developed a close working relationship with fellow moderate, then-Arkansas Governor Bill Clinton. Both politicians served on the Democratic Leadership Council, a centrist coalition that was shunned by most black lawmakers. In an effort to support self-reliance over welfare handouts, the coalition often sided with Republican-sponsored economic enterprises. The council also promoted "microenterprises," through which welfare recipients would receive loans from local banks to start their own small businesses. Espy endorsed the idea, noting that similar programs had been successful in developing countries such as Bangladesh and the Dominican Republic.[29]

As one of the first Democratic lawmakers to endorse Clinton's 1992 candidacy for President, Espy benefited from his election to the presidency. Having won a fourth term in Congress, Espy sought a promotion to chair an Agriculture subcommittee or a seat on the prestigious Appropriations Committee. Receiving neither, Espy reportedly sent the President-elect a memo with the top 10 reasons he should head the U.S. Department of Agriculture (USDA).[30] Clinton offered him the post, and Espy resigned from Congress on January 22, 1993, to begin his new position.

Most occupants of the USDA's top post had been Midwesterners, and Espy was the first African American and the first Mississippian to receive the appointment. As the fourth-largest federal department, the USDA oversaw services ranging from the administration of food stamp programs to farm subsidies. The agency also had a reputation as a top-heavy bureaucracy. Espy directed several noteworthy achievements at the USDA, including improved meat inspections after an outbreak of illness caused by the bacterium E. coli in fast-food hamburgers. He also trimmed the agency's bureaucracy and provided relief for farming areas following devastating Mississippi River floods in 1993. However, his career in the Clinton Cabinet ended prematurely when he resigned on December 31, 1994, after being charged with ethics violations. Although he was indicted on federal bribery and fraud charges, Espy was acquitted.[31] He returned to Jackson, Mississippi, to practice law.[32]

FOR FURTHER READING

"Espy, Alphonso Michael (Mike)," *Biographical Directory of the United States Congress, 1774–Present*, http://bioguide. congress.gov/scripts/biodisplay.pl?index=E000218.

MANUSCRIPT COLLECTION

Mississippi State University Libraries, Congressional and Political Research Center (Mississippi State, MS). *Papers:* ca. 1987–1994, 100 cubic feet. The collection includes papers, publications, photographs, and memorabilia documenting Mike Espy's tenure on the following House committees: Agriculture, Budget, and the Select Committee on Hunger. The collection is closed pending processing.

NOTES .

1   Robin Toner, "Real-Life Politics in Deep South," 30 March 1989, *New York Times*: B7.

2   "Mike Espy," *Contemporary Black Biography* Volume 6 (Detroit, MI: Gale Research Inc., 1994) (hereinafter referred to as *CBB*).

3   Carla Hall, "Espy's Mississippi Milestone," 19 December 1986, *Washington Post*: C1.

4   "Espy, Mike," *Current Biography, 1993* (New York: H. W. Wilson Company, 1993): 184.

5   Quoted in Hall, "Espy's Mississippi Milestone."

6   Kenneth Martis, *The Historical Atlas of Political Parties in the United States Congress: 1789–1989* (New York: Macmillan, 1989): 235–239; *Almanac of American Politics, 1988* (Washington, DC: National Journal Inc., 1987): 655.

7   *Current Biography, 1993*: 185; James R. Dickerson, "House Rivals Tread Fine Line in Race-Conscious Mississippi," 29 October 1986, *Washington Post*: A1.

8   *Current Biography, 1993*: 185.

9   Dickerson, "House Rivals Tread Fine Line in Race-Conscious Mississippi."

10   See Hall, "Espy's Mississippi Milestone" for a summary of racial divisions in Espy's Mississippi district.

11   Dickerson, "House Rivals Tread Fine Line in Race-Conscious Mississippi."

12   *Current Biography, 1993*: 185.

13   Quoted in "Mike Espy," *CBB*.

14   Dickerson, "House Rivals Tread Fine Line in Race-Conscious Mississippi"; Marshall Ingwerson, "In Deepest of Deep South, Black Lawmaker Wins Many Whites," 21 October 1988, *Christian Science Monitor*: NL7.

15   Ingwerson, "In Deepest of Deep South, Black Lawmaker Wins Many Whites."

16   Robin Toner, "Real-Life Politics in Deep South."

17   Hall, "Espy's Mississippi Milestone."

18   Marshall Ingwerson, "Espy's Mississippi Victory," 22 December 1986, *Christian Science Monitor*: 1.

19   Quoted in Hall, "Espy's Mississippi Milestone."

20   Bruce A. Ragsdale and Joel D. Treese, *Black Americans in Congress, 1870–1989* (Washington, DC: Government Printing Office, 1990): 50.

21   *Current Biography, 1993*: 185.

22   "Election Statistics, 1920 to Present," available at http://clerk. house.gov/member_info/election.html.

23   Toner, "Real-Life Politics in Deep South."

24   Helen Dewar, "For Impoverished Mississippi River Delta, Change Is in the Air," 17 April 1988, *Washington Post*: A3.

25   *Current Biography, 1993*: 186.

26   Toner, "Real-Life Politics in Deep South."

27   Ibid.

28   "Mike Espy," *CBB*.

29   Ibid.

30   *Current Biography, 1993*: 185.

31   "The Dizzying Fall of Mike Espy," 5 October 1994, *Chicago Tribune*: 20. Espy was indicted on felony bribery and fraud charges when it was discovered that various food companies had paid his way to sporting events and awarded his girlfriend a scholarship. Also, Espy drove a car leased with government funds on non–work-related visits to Mississippi. He was acquitted in 1998. See, for example, Bill Miller, "Espy Acquitted in Gifts Case," 3 December 1998, *Washington Post*: A1.

32   Lori Michelle Muha, "Mike Espy," in Jessie Carney Smith, ed., *Notable Black American Men* (Farmington Hills, MI: Gale Research, Inc., 1999): 380.

Espy's ability as a black candidate to attract white voters was unprecedented in a Mississippi federal election. Espy's election, declared a state newspaper, "did more than shatter the age-old color barrier.... It is further evidence that Mississippi is ready for a change."

Floyd Harold Flake
1945–

UNITED STATES REPRESENTATIVE ★ 1987–1997
DEMOCRAT FROM NEW YORK

Although Floyd Flake arrived in Congress without having held public office, he was bolstered by his experience managing one of the largest churches in New York City: the Allen African Methodist Episcopal (AME) Church. As a provider of a broad range of social services, the church was the economic focal point of the Queens neighborhood of Jamaica. Flake was part of a new generation of black Representatives who sought to work within the congressional hierarchy and who viewed race as less important in their role as Representatives. A Democrat, Flake often found himself teamed with Republicans to fund urban renewal efforts. But Flake's calling ultimately remained his church, and halfway through his sixth term in Congress he left to return to New York. "I realize I could never be a Beltway politician," Flake noted. "[Back home] there are real people with real everyday problems that need to be addressed."[1]

Floyd Harold Flake was born in Los Angeles, California, on January 30, 1945, one of 13 children of Robert Flake, Sr., a janitor, and Rosie Lee Johnson-Flake, a homemaker. Both his parents had only an elementary school education.[2] The Flakes moved to Houston, Texas, where Floyd Flake attended public schools and joined the AME church at the age of ten. Flake was the first in his family to attend college. He graduated from Ohio's historically black college, Wilberforce University, with a B.A. in psychology in 1967, and subsequently did graduate work at Payne Theological Seminary at Wilberforce before earning his master's degree in divinity at the United Theological Seminary in Dayton, Ohio, in 1995.[3] Flake later studied business administration at Northeastern University in Boston. Between his studies, he was employed as a social worker in Dayton, Ohio, a salesman for a large tobacco company, and a marketing analyst for an international technology and document management company. Flake

eventually drew on his background in religious studies and education, working as the director of the Martin Luther King, Jr. Afro-American Center and the chaplain at Boston University. Flake married Margaret Elaine McCollins, also an ordained minister, and they raised four children: Aliya, Nailah, Robert Rasheed, and Harold Hasan.

In 1976, Flake and his wife took over the Allen AME Church in Jamaica, a primarily black neighborhood and one of the poorest sections of the mostly middle-class Queens Borough in New York. Named for Richard Allen of the Free African Society, Flake's church was the oldest AME church in Queens, dating back to the 1860s.[4] Under Flake's leadership, Allen AME became the second-largest black church in New York City, swelling from 1,000 to more than 5,000 members in a little more than a decade.[5] As a provider of community outreach services such as a health clinic, a primary school, and affordable housing, Allen AME became the economic focal point of the Jamaica neighborhood.[6] Other local black pastors spoke highly of Flake's ministry. "He is a master builder," noted a local Pentecostal reverend. A regional Baptist leader called him "a role model for the clergy."[7]

Flake did not consider running for public office until Joseph Addabbo, a longtime Representative from southeastern Queens, died in April 1986, opening a House seat. Democratic leaders sought a black man to replace Addabbo, whose constituency had changed dramatically during his 25-year career—from a large, middle-class Irish and Italian majority to one that was 65 percent black. Excluding Flake's impoverished neighborhood in Jamaica, the district constituted one of the largest black middle-class communities in the nation.[8] Flake lost the party's nomination for the seat to Alton Waldon, Jr., a black community lawyer and a former police officer. In a crowded special election, Flake ran on the Unity Party

platform. Several other Democrats also joined the race on third-party tickets, providing Waldon with competition in the overwhelmingly Democratic district. Flake was Waldon's chief opponent; he enjoyed the endorsement of the *New York Times* as well as the powerful support of local clergy.[9] Flake won the initial canvass in June by a mere 197 votes, but Waldon took the lead by 276 votes after the absentee ballots were counted. Flake's name was not the absentee ballots, due to a filing error that occurred shortly before the election. Although Flake attempted to nullify the absentee ballots in federal court, he was unsuccessful.[10] "It was mindboggling," Flake noted of his loss to Waldon. "One day you go to bed having won an election. A week later you discover you've lost because of absentee ballots."[11] Flake returned three months later to face Waldon for the Democratic nomination for the 100th Congress (1987–1989). In addition to his Jamaica base, Flake also enjoyed an endorsement from New York City Mayor Edward Koch, who delivered him some of the heavily Jewish and Italian neighborhoods that remained in the district. Flake defeated the incumbent in the primary by 3,000 votes.[12] Tantamount to a win in the Democratic district, Flake's nomination propelled him into the general election, where he won with 68 percent of the vote.

Flake won re-election five times, typically garnering between 60 and 70 percent of the vote in somewhat-crowded general elections.[13] In 1992, a well-publicized legal controversy catapulted Flake into a primary battle. Black Democrat Simeon Golar, a local judge, challenged his nomination.[14] Golar claimed that Flake focused more on his church and its surrounding neighborhood than on his congressional duties and neighborhoods outside Jamaica.[15] The Democratic establishment in Queens chose to support Golar in the primary.[16] Flake retaliated by providing a slate of candidates for local elections who were loyal to him and running against the party's handpicked candidates. Election officials threw several of Flake's candidates off the ballot for failure to observe filing rules.[17] Despite the Democrats' anger at his defiance, Flake remained on the primary ballot and emerged victorious.

Flake's background in business and urban redevelopment won him appointments to the Banking and Small Business committees. Following the loss of several incumbents on the Banking Committee in the 1992 elections, Flake rose to chair the panel's Subcommittee on General Oversight.[18] Flake effectively used his committee assignments to help steer federal money toward urban renewal projects in his district. In 1995, a New York publication cited him as one of the most effective downstate New York Representatives regarding the procurement of federal funds.[19] Flake's willingness to work with Republicans and their traditional corporate constituents often helped him to meet his goals. In 1993, taking advantage of his new chairmanship on a Banking subcommittee, Flake introduced a comprehensive community development plan that outwardly opposed a plan advanced by Democratic President William J. (Bill) Clinton. Along with the Ranking Member on the Banking Committee, Representative Jim Leach of Iowa, Flake crafted legislation that redirected one-third of the funding for the Clinton proposal from local community development banks to large lending institutions.[20] According to Flake, this move provided incentives for big banks to lend to poor communities—first, by underwriting local lenders in order to help small businesses get off the ground and second, by encouraging larger lenders to take on the businesses as they matured. Parts of Flake's legislation were later incorporated into the Community Development Banking and Financial Institutions Act, which was signed into law in 1994.[21]

Flake's support for portions of the GOP's Contract With America was controversial. House Democrats almost unanimously opposed the 1994 list of campaign promises for reform legislation, but the contract helped vault Republicans into power in the House in 1995. Flake's support was not without reservation; he informed new GOP Speaker and Contract With America champion Newt Gingrich of Georgia that the legislative agenda ignored urban America. Gingrich later took note of Flake's work at Allen AME and brought him on in

1997 to cosponsor another Republican reform bill, the Community Renewal Act, which offered tax breaks and school vouchers to poor urban neighborhoods.[22] Flake's support of school vouchers—tax credits given to parents so their children could attend private schools—drew the most criticism from within his party. Citing the successful Allen AME Christian School, Flake argued that private schools used fewer tax dollars per student annually and graduated more students than did public schools. He also believed that vouchers would motivate public schools to better manage their finances and curricula.[23] Most Democrats viewed the program as an across-the-board abandonment of the public school system. Foes included the Congressional Black Caucus (CBC) and a powerful lobby composed of many New York City teachers and administrators. Many of these teachers were members of Allen AME. House Minority Leader Richard Gephardt of Missouri noted, "I've been to Floyd Flake's school, and I've seen how truly remarkable it is. But if we're going to rip the rug from underneath public schools, we've made a grave error."[24]

Yet Flake voted with the Democrats more often than not. Though wary of dependence on government assistance, the passage of a 1996 welfare reform bill caused Flake to rail against the slashes in programs, which he noted would cost New Yorkers $750 million in lost federal benefits. Flake noted the role of the federal safety net in keeping the poor in major cities afloat.[25] He also was an active member of the CBC and supported its broad mission. "With those 39 votes, we were able to do a very effective job of lobbying the President and Congress because those votes made a big difference," Flake noted after an increase in the caucus membership following the 1992 elections. But he cautioned against the CBC's leftward lean in the face of the increasingly conservative Congress. The caucus should "become more bipartisan," Flake concluded, as well as "work with [President Bill Clinton with the] understanding that he, as the leader of the nation, cannot afford to make policies that were effective for us in the 1970s."[26]

Allen AME remained a significant part of Flake's life, and in July 1997 he announced that he was resigning from Congress to concentrate on his pastoral duties. "My calling in life is as a minister," Flake told reporters, "so I had to come to a real reconciliation . . . and it is impossible to continue the sojourn where I am traveling back and forth to DC."[27] Flake served out the remainder of the session, officially leaving on November 15. Candidates who hoped to succeed Flake immediately sought his endorsement, recognizing the local political power of Allen AME's thousands of congregants.[28] Flake backed the eventual winner, former state assemblyman Gregory Meeks.

Flake continued to be politically active following his departure from Congress, writing op-ed pieces for the *New York Post* and working for various conservative think tanks to promote school vouchers. "The best thing that's happened to me is getting out of Congress," Flake declared in a 1997 interview, "Because I'm going to be a real hell-raiser from now on!"[29] In addition to fulfilling his duties as head pastor at Allen AME, Flake also was appointed president of Wilberforce University in October 2002, after serving six months as interim president.

FOR FURTHER READING

"Flake, Floyd Harold," *Biographical Directory of the United States Congress, 1774–Present*, http://bioguide.congress.gov/scripts/biodisplay.pl?index=F000184.

NOTES

1   Robert M. Garsson, "Rep. Flake, a New York Liberal—a Bank Defender," 2 August 1993, *The American Banker*: 15.

2   James Traub, "Floyd Flake's Middle America," 19 October 1997, *New York Times*: 245.

3   Whether Flake received his graduate degree at the Payne Theological Seminary of Wilberforce, Ohio, or at United Theological Seminary in Dayton, Ohio, is unclear. According to Flake's Allen AME biography, he received his degree from United and did some graduate work at Payne. See "Professional Profile: Rev. Dr. Floyd H. Flake," *The Greater Allen A.M.E. Cathedral of New York*, http://www.allencathedral.org (accessed 5 April 2006).

4   Josh Barbanel, "Congressman Flake's Indictment: Good Works or Greed?" 6 August 1990, *New York Times*: B1.

5   The congregation of Allen A.M.E. has grown significantly since the 1980s. In a 2004 interview, Flake claimed more than 18,000 members. See Public Broadcasting System (PBS), "Interview: Floyd Flake," 24 September 2004, *Religion and Ethics Newsweekly*, at http://www.pbs.org/wnet/religionandethics/week804/interview.html (accessed 5 April 2006).

6   Barbanel, "Congressman Flake's Indictment: Good Works or Greed?"

7   Ibid.

8   "Good—and Better—in Queens," 5 June 1986, *New York Times*: A26; Traub, "Floyd Flake's Middle America."

9   Dan Jacobson, "Queens Elects First Black Congressman," 11 June 1986, United Press International; "Good—and Better—in Queens."

10 "Election Laws on Trial in Queens," 20 June 1986, *New York Times*: A30; "Man in the News; After Court Victory, A Congressman-Elect: Alton Ronald Waldon Jr.," 26 July 1986, *New York Times*: 31.

11 Ken Fireman, "The Crazy Case of Floyd Flake," 12 September 1988, *Newsday* (New York): 22.

12 Esther B. Fein, "Flake Defeats Waldon; Abzug Leading Teicher," 10 September 1986, *New York Times*: B5.

13 "Election Statistics, 1920 to Present," available at http://clerk.house.gov/member_info/election.html.

14 In 1990, Floyd and Elaine Flake were charged with income tax evasion and embezzlement of federal funds appropriated to build the church's senior citizen housing complex in 1981. The Flakes maintained their innocence, and their supporters claimed the charges were politically and racially motivated. Following a well publicized, three-week trial in March 1991, a judge dismissed the charges against the Flakes, declaring the prosecution's evidence insufficient. See "Floyd H. Flake," Associated Press Candidate Biographies, 1996; "Floyd H. Flake," *Contemporary Black Biography* (Detroit, MI: Gale Research, Inc., 2002) (hereinafter referred to as *CBB*); Susan B. Glasser, "Rep. Flake Is Indicted in Church Fraud Plot," 6 August 1990, *Roll Call*; Joseph P. Fried, "Flake Pleads Not Guilty to All Charges," 21 August 1990, *New York Times*: B1; Murray Kempton, "The Quiet Trial of U.S. Rep. Flake," 13 March 1991, *Newsday* (New York): 11; Barbanel, "Congressman Flake's Indictment: Good Works or Greed?"; M. A. Farber, "U.S. Dismisses Charges Faced by Rep. Flake," 4 April 1991, *New York Times*: A1.

15 Joseph P. Fried, "Rep. Flake Is Fighting Hard Race in Queens," 24 August 1992, *New York Times*: B3.

16 *Politics in America, 1996* (Washington, DC: Congressional Quarterly Inc., 1995): 897.

17 "Rev. Flake Loses Bid for District Leader in Queens," 26 August 1992, *New York Voice* (Volume 34, Number 20): 1.

18 Though Flake also sought more powerful assignments on the Budget and Appropriations committees, the Democratic leadership passed him over. This snub was attributed to his reputation as an independent lawmaker. See *Politics in America, 1990* (Washington, DC: Congressional Quarterly Inc., 1989): 1014; Jack Sirica, "Dems Bypass Flake," 8 December 1992, *Newsday*: 106.

19 Traub, "Floyd Flake's Middle America."

20 *Politics in America, 1996*: 895.

21 See 103rd Cong., 1st sess., H.R. 2707 and H.R. 3474.

22 "Floyd H. Flake," *CBB*; Jonathan P. Hicks, "Rep. Flake Breaks With Party to Back School Vouchers," 12 March 1997, *New York Times*: B3.

23 "Floyd H. Flake," *CBB*.

24 Terry M. Neal, "Ex-Lawmaker Refuses to Be Boxed In; The Rev. Flake Left Congress to Pursue Urban Renewal Beyond Party Lines," 10 January 1998, *Washington Post*: A1.

25 Ralph Roach, "A Conversation With Cong. Floyd Flake," 10 August 1996, *New York Amsterdam News*: 11.

26 Ed Laiscell, "Congressman Floyd Flake Prepares to Leave Congress," 17 September 1997, *Washington Informer*: 18.

27 Laiscell, "Congressman Floyd Flake Prepares to Leave Congress."

28 Jonathan P. Hicks, "Flake to Leave Congress to Devote Time to Church," 1 August 1997, *New York Times*: B3.

29 Ronald Powers, "Flake Leaves Congress to Work at His Church," 15 November 1997, *Telegraph Herald* (Dubuque, IA): B10.

"MY CALLING IN LIFE IS AS
A MINISTER," FLAKE TOLD
REPORTERS [EXPLAINING HIS
DECISION TO RETIRE IN 1997],
"SO I HAD TO COME TO A REAL
RECONCILIATION . . . AND IT IS
IMPOSSIBLE TO CONTINUE THE
SOJOURN WHERE I AM TRAVELING
BACK AND FORTH
[FROM QUEENS] TO DC"

Kweisi Mfume
1948–

UNITED STATES REPRESENTATIVE ★ 1987–1996
DEMOCRAT FROM MARYLAND

An epiphany in his mid-20s called Frizzell Gray away from the streets of Baltimore and into politics under a new name: Kweisi Mfume, which means "conquering son of kings" in a West African dialect. "Frizzell Gray had lived and died. From his spirit was born a new person," Mfume later wrote.[1] An admirer of civil rights leader Dr. Martin Luther King, Jr., Mfume followed in his footsteps, becoming a well-known voice on Baltimore-area radio, the chairman of the Congressional Black Caucus (CBC), and the leader of one of the country's oldest advocacy groups for African Americans, the National Association for the Advancement of Colored People (NAACP).

Kweisi Mfume, formerly named Frizzell Gray, was born on October 24, 1948, in Turners Station, Maryland, a small town 10 miles south of Baltimore. His mother, Mary Elizabeth Gray, was employed in odd jobs that included positions as a maid and a worker in an airplane components factory. His stepfather, Clifton Gray, a truck driver, left the family in 1959.[2] In 1960, Mary Gray and her children moved to West Baltimore, where they struggled financially. Education was segregated, and Gray recalled being confused about having to pass three schools on the way to his own.[3] The Grays drew inspiration from Martin Luther King, Jr., and President John F. Kennedy. In 1962, Gray heard President Kennedy speak in Baltimore. A year later, the Grays wanted to attend King's civil rights March on Washington but could not afford the trip.[4]

Two events changed Gray's life when he was a young man. In 1965, his mother died in his arms after battling cancer. Though the Gray children were parceled out among relatives, Gray felt responsible for the well-being of his sisters: Darlene, LaWana, and Michele. At 16, he left high school and worked as many as three jobs simultaneously, finding employment as a grocery clerk, a bread factory employee, and a shoe shiner. Eventually succumbing to stress and frustration, Gray quit his jobs. He hung out on street corners, participated in illegal gambling, joined a gang, and fathered five sons (Ronald, Donald, Kevin, Keith, and Michael) with four different women. In the summer of 1972, Gray saw a vision of his mother's face, convincing him to leave his life on the streets.[5] Earning a high school equivalency degree, Gray changed his name to symbolize his transformation. He adopted the name Kweisi Mfume at the suggestion of an aunt who had traveled through Ghana. An earlier encounter with future Baltimore-area Representative Parren Mitchell, who challenged Mfume to help solve the problems of poverty and violence, profoundly affected the troubled young man.[6] "I can't explain it, but a feeling just came over me that I shouldn't be [on the streets] and I had to change. I was headed nowhere," he later told reporters.[7] Mfume continued to provide for his sons. He married Linda Shields in July 1972, but they later divorced.

A renewed Mfume began classes at the Community College of Baltimore and served as an announcer for WEBB Radio Baltimore, which was owned by legendary singer James Brown. Mfume volunteered for Parren Mitchell's 1968 campaign. Though Mitchell lost the primary election (he was elected to Congress in 1970 and would serve 16 years in the House), the experience sparked Mfume's interest in politics. He soon went from introducing popular records on the radio to hosting his own ad hoc political talk show.[8] From 1974 to 1976, Mfume was the dee-jay for "Ebony Reflections," a radio show that discussed African-American political concerns between musical selections and aired recordings of Malcolm X and King.[9] Uncomfortable with the show's political content, Brown eventually dismissed Mfume.[10] After transferring to Morgan State University, Mfume helped start a college radio station. By the time Mfume

earned his bachelor of science degree in urban planning in 1976, he was the program director for the station.[11]

In 1978, Mfume ran for a seat on the Baltimore city council. Adopting the slogan "Beat the Bosses," he conducted a massive, but disorganized, door-to-door campaign.[12] Mfume won the seat by a mere three votes.[13] Shortly after Mfume's razor-thin victory, a mentor encouraged him to change his attire from more-eclectic, African-inspired clothing to suits and ties. Mfume followed the advice; however, he remained outspoken and often instigated famously heated battles with Democratic Mayor William Donald Schaefer. Yet he soon tempered his confrontational style. "I realized I had to find a way to put together a majority of the votes on the council, and that meant developing a consensus," Mfume said.[14] In his eight years as a city councilman, Mfume rose to chair the city's health subcommittee and led Baltimore's divestment from companies doing business in South Africa. He also earned a master's degree in liberal arts from Johns Hopkins University in 1984.

In 1985, Representative Parren Mitchell announced his retirement after more than a decade and a half in the House. Rooted in inner-city Baltimore, Mitchell's district was overwhelmingly black (73 percent) and Democratic presidential candidates regularly received 80 percent of the vote throughout the 1980s.[15] Mfume entered a crowded 1986 Democratic primary to succeed Mitchell as a dark horse among well-recognized names. Front-runner Clarence Mitchell III (Parren Mitchell's nephew), a 24-year state senate veteran, entered the race. Wendell H. Phillips, a civil rights activist and pastor of a large Baltimore church, proved to be Mitchell's closest rival. Phillips had the full support of former Mayor Schaefer, who was running for governor. As Phillips and Mitchell attacked one another, Mfume emerged as a viable compromise and unexpectedly won the nomination with 47 percent of the vote.[16] In the general election, Mfume faced Republican Saint George I. B. Crosse III. Crosse attacked Mfume by drawing attention to his former life on the street. In front of a

media entourage, Crosse held up a cup and challenged Mfume to take a drug test.[17] Mfume deflected the attacks by pointing to his changed life and easily won the election, with 87 percent of the vote. Though redistricting in 1993 added some rural communities west of the city to his constituency, the district remained predominantly black (71 percent) due to African-American migration to the suburbs.[18] Mfume won all of his subsequent elections by margins greater than 80 percent, and he ran unopposed in 1988.[19]

Mfume's background led him to focus on urban economic renewal, and his committee assignments reflected this emphasis. Mfume received assignments on the Banking, Finance, and Urban Affairs Committee and the Small Business Committee. He also received an assignment on the Select Committee on Hunger. In 1990, he convinced the Subcommittee on Housing of the Banking, Finance, and Urban Affairs Committee to include an amendment that would prorate rents in public housing on the basis of real income—less alimony and child support payments—rather than net income.[20] Mfume presided over a debate that preceded the passage of the civil rights bill by the House in 1991; the measure facilitated the collection of damages by victims of job discrimination based on race, sex, disability, or national origin.[21] In 1993, Mfume teamed with Connecticut Republican Christopher Shays on a bill to create enterprise zones and provide tax breaks for minority businesses.[22] "People are being discriminated against by mortgage lenders based on the color of their skin," Mfume told the *New York Times*. "Banks have a long way to go for meeting the legitimate needs of neighborhoods."[23] Mfume's experience on the streets motivated him to craft legislation to help inner-city youth and he proposed the Youth Employment Services Act, which sought to connect local businesses and governments with teenage workers.[24] Mfume also received national attention in the 101st Congress (1989–1991) when he attempted to restrict the sale of beepers to young people, claiming the devices made drug transactions easier.[25] In the 102nd Congress (1991–1993), Mfume earned an additional assignment on the Joint Economic Committee. He continued to advocate urban renewal projects as chairman of the Small Business Committee in the 103rd Congress (1993–1995). To revitalize urban areas, Mfume unveiled a seven-point plan that included the expansion of the enterprise zones program and the development of nationally sponsored service projects for urban youth.

Mfume was an active member of the CBC from the beginning of his congressional career. As a freshman in the 100th Congress (1987–1989), he served as CBC treasurer. The following Congress, he was vice chairman. In the 103rd Congress, he sought the caucus chairmanship. Mfume's promise of bold leadership helped him prevail against Representative Craig Washington of Texas, and he won the chairmanship by a vote of 27 to 9.[26]

As CBC chairman, Mfume quickly established that the caucus would not automatically support the policies of Democratic President William J. (Bill) Clinton. In April 1993, Mfume led the CBC and a handful of other Democrats in a threat to join Republicans in blocking Clinton's request for a line-item veto (the ability to strike certain provisions of an appropriations bill without vetoing it). Explaining his stance as a "pure position of principle," Mfume argued that granting the President's request would give him too much power. "Even the most naïve student of constitutional history knows that no legislator since the beginning of this nation has come to the point that we are at today, to cede unto the executive branch, those powers," he declared. Mfume and other liberals were also uneasy about the power that could be given to a future conservative executive.[27] Realizing they were hemorrhaging votes, Democratic leaders quickly pulled the measure from the floor. After several weeks of cajoling black Members to get on board with the line-item veto, the leadership managed to pass the measure; Mfume voted against it.[28] Under Mfume's leadership the CBC also challenged the Clinton administration's budget-cutting priorities as it scaled back welfare and other entitlement programs.[29] The CBC also weighed in on foreign affairs. The caucus's pressure on the Clinton administration affected the President's policies toward former Haitian President Jean-Bertrand Aristide. The CBC wanted to help reinstate the exiled leader and change American policy toward Haitian refugees, many of whom were sent back to Haiti when they arrived in the United States.[30] In April 1994, Mfume was one of six Members of Congress—five of them CBC members—who were arrested after a sit-in at the White House to protest the Clinton administration's Haitian policy.[31] Mfume and the caucus pushed the Clinton administration to turn its attention to Africa's problems: war, famine, and slow development.[32] Additionally Mfume and the CBC denounced the North American Free Trade Agreement, a Clinton proposal to relax trade restrictions with neighboring countries.

Mfume stepped down as CBC chairman after one term in December 1994, per caucus tradition, though he remained active in a supporting role. In December 1994, Mfume unsuccessfully campaigned for chairman of the Democratic Caucus—an organization that set congressional party policy—for the 104th Congress (1995–1997) against Representative Vic Fazio of California.[33] The "Republican Revolution" in the 1994 election, which ushered in the first GOP majority in 40 years, also discouraged Mfume and reduced the political power of the liberal CBC.[34] In December 1995, he announced his retirement from his safe congressional seat to head the NAACP, whose headquarters are in Baltimore. Mfume faced the daunting task of revitalizing an organization that was beset by financial difficulties, internal bickering, and scandal.[35] By February 1997, Mfume had nearly erased the organization's $3 million debt and had rekindled interest in the association.[36] Mfume left the NAACP after nine years of service to spend time with his sons. (He adopted a sixth son, four-year-old Christopher, in 2004.[37]) Reflecting on his political career, Mfume mused, "I could just stand on the side and be a spectator.

But politics is not a spectator sport. And in Washington, it's a contact sport. I don't play to tie, I try to play to win. But you can only win if you are in the game."[38] Mfume attempted a return to elective political office in 2005, when he announced his candidacy to succeed retiring U.S. Senator Paul Sarbanes in the 2006 election. In a crowded Democratic primary, Mfume lost by a narrow four-point margin to Maryland Representative Ben Cardin, taking 40 percent of the vote.[39]

FOR FURTHER READING

"Mfume, Kweisi," *Biographical Directory of the United States Congress, 1774–Present*, http://bioguide.congress.gov/scripts/biodisplay.pl?index=M000687.

Mfume, Kweisi with Ron Stodghill II. *No Free Ride: From the Mean Streets to the Mainstream.* (New York: One World, 1996).

NOTES

1   Kweisi Mfume with Ron Stodghill II, *No Free Ride: From the Mean Streets to the Mainstream* (New York: One World Books, 1996): 187.

2   Family friend Rufus Tate later revealed that he was Mfume's biological father. Damien Bayard Ingram, "Kweisi Mfume," in Jessie Carney Smith, ed., *Notable Black American Men* (Detroit, MI: Gale Research Inc., 1999): 809 (hereinafter referred to as *NBAM*).

3   "Kweisi Mfume," *Contemporary Heroes and Heroines*, Volume 3 (Detroit, MI: Gale Group, 1998) (hereinafter referred to as *CHH*).

4   Mfume, *No Free Ride*: 109.

5   "Kweisi Mfume," *CHH*; Ingram, "Kweisi Mfume," *NBAM*; Mfume, *No Free Ride*: 176–177. See also "Kweisi Mfume," *Contemporary Black Biography*, Volume 6 (Detroit, MI: Gale Research Inc., 1994) (hereinafter referred to as *CBB*).

6   Mfume, *No Free Ride*: 165–166.

7   Kent Jenkins, Jr., "Mfume on the Move," 8 December 1992, *Washington Post*: D1.

8   "Kweisi Mfume," *CBB*.

9   Ingram, "Kweisi Mfume," *NBAM*.

10   Mfume, *No Free Ride*: 210.

11   Jenkins, "Mfume on the Move."

12   "Kweisi Mfume," *CBB*; "Mfume, Kweisi," *Current Biography, 1996* (New York: H. W. Wilson Company, 1996): 368.

13   Jenkins, "Mfume on the Move."

14 Quoted from *Washington Post* profile on the Representative in "Mfume, Kweisi," *Current Biography, 1996*: 368.

15 *Politics in America, 1990* (Washington, DC: Congressional Quarterly Inc., 1989): 671.

16 Mfume, *No Free Ride*: 268.

17 Sandra Sugawara, "Maryland Democrats Talk of Sweeping 8 Races for U.S. House," 1 November 1986, *Washington Post*: D11.

18 *Politics in America, 1994* (Washington, DC: Congressional Quarterly Inc., 1993): 703.

19 "Election Statistics, 1920 to Present," available at http://clerk.house.gov/member_info/electionInfo/index.html.

20 "Mfume, Kweisi," *Current Biography, 1996*: 369.

21 Adam Clymer, "17 Short of Goal," 6 June 1991, *New York Times*: A1.

22 "Mfume, Kweisi," *Current Biography, 1996*: 369.

23 "Blacks' Woes in Borrowing," 8 May 1992, *New York Times*: D13.

24 *Politics in America, 1990*: 670.

25 Paul W. Valentine, "Law Urged to Curb Sale of Beepers to Youths," 14 March 1989, *Washington Post*: A6.

26 "Mfume, Kweisi," *Current Biography, 1996*: 369; *Politics in America, 1994*: 702.

27 *Politics in America, 1994*: 702; Clifford Krauss, "A Line-Item Veto Is Passed, But It Has Key Restrictions," 30 April 1993, *New York Times*: A14.

28 *Politics in America, 1994*: 702.

29 Neil A. Lewis, "Says He Had Not Read Her Academic Writings," 4 June 1993, *New York Times*: A1.

30 "Mfume, Kweisi," *Current Biography, 1996*: 369.

31 Steven Greenhouse, "U.S. Says Later That It Will Pressure His Foes; Six Lawmakers Arrested During Protest," 22 April 1994, *New York Times*: A1.

32 Steven A. Holmes, "Administration Seeks Ways to Ease Africa's Wars and Debt Burden," 18 May 1993, *New York Times*: A9.

33 Adam Clymer, "Congress Returns to Select Leaders for the New Term," 28 November 1994, *New York Times*: A1.

34 "Kweisi Mfume," *CHH*.

35 Rob Howe et al., "The Bootstrap Method; Having Salvaged Himself, Kweisi Mfume Strives to Revive the NAACP," 26 February 1996, *Time*: 55.

36 "Kweisi Mfume," *CHH*.

37 Christopher's mother was an employee of the NAACP with whom Mfume reportedly had a relationship. See Matthew Moss and Cheryl W. Thompson, "Mfume Accused of Favoritism at NAACP," 28 April 2005, *Washington Post*: A1.

38 Quoted in "Kweisi Mfume," *CHH*.

39 Maryland State Board of Elections, "Official 2006 Gubernatorial Primary Election Results for U.S. Senator," at http://www.elections.state.md.us/elections/2006/results/primary/office_US_Senator.html (accessed 15 November 2007).

Craig Anthony Washington
1941–

UNITED STATES REPRESENTATIVE ★ 1989–1995
DEMOCRAT FROM TEXAS

Elected to fill the House seat of the late Mickey Leland, Craig Washington proved to be a staunch supporter of civil rights and the rights of criminal defendants. However, his career in a downtown Houston district that boasted African-American representation since its creation in 1973 ended abruptly when constituents eventually rejected his maverick and often-erratic voting record. Washington frequently voted with the minority in lopsided roll call votes and he took pride in his independence. "I did this my way," he said, conceding his loss in the 1994 Democratic primary to future Representative Sheila Jackson Lee. "There are a lot of easier ways to be a congressman or run for Congress. I wanted people to hear the truth."[1]

Craig Anthony Washington was born to Roy and Azalea Washington on October 12, 1941, in Longview, Texas. He received a bachelor of science degree in 1966 from Prairie View A&M University, a historically black college located 40 miles northwest of Houston. In 1969, he received a J.D. from Texas Southern University. Washington was on the law school faculty from 1969 to 1970, before opening his own criminal defense practice in Houston.[2] In 1973, Washington was elected a Texas state representative in a freshman class that included future U.S. Representative Mickey Leland. In 1983, Washington moved to the Texas state senate, where he proved to be a commanding orator and legislative strategist. Washington soon became one of the foremost faces in the Texas civil rights movement. He worked to increase the participation of minorities and women in state government, supported Texas divestment from South Africa, and coordinated his state's fight against the spread of HIV/AIDS. Washington married twice and raised five children.[3]

On August 7, 1989, popular Houston Representative Mickey Leland died in a plane crash in Ethiopia while en route to a United Nations' refugee camp. Leland's district had been served by an African American since its creation. (Representative Barbara Jordan preceded Leland, deciding not to run for re-election in 1978.) A longtime Leland ally, Washington entered the primary election to succeed him after Leland's widow, Alison, declined to run.[4] Under the campaign slogan, "Pass the Torch," emphasizing the Leland family's support of his candidacy, Washington was the top vote-getter in the nonpartisan primary. In a December 9 special election, Washington easily defeated Houston City Councilman Anthony Hall (who had lost to Leland in 1978) with 56 percent of the vote.[5] Washington invoked Leland's memory in his victory speech: "I claim this victory not for myself," he told reporters, "but for our brother who died on the side of a hill in Ethiopia."[6] Taking his oath of office on January 23, 1990, on the opening day of the second session for the 101st Congress (1989–1991), Washington said, "I could never replace Mickey Leland. I'm merely his successor."[7] Washington filled Leland's vacant seat on the Select Committee on Hunger, which the former Representative had created. Continuing his predecessor's focus on world hunger, Washington admitted, "I may not be a champion on the issue of hunger. But I will be a drum major."[8] Washington's legal background won him appointments to the Judiciary Committee and the Committee on Education and Labor. After easily winning two re-election campaigns in his liberal district—running unopposed in 1990 and capturing 65 percent of the vote in 1992—Washington traded his seat on the Education and Labor Committee for a place on the highly desirable Energy and Commerce Committee in the 103rd Congress (1993–1995).[9]

Whereas Leland had made his name as an advocate for hunger, Washington earned a reputation as an independent politician. Compiling a solid liberal record, Washington frequently voted with the handful of Members

in the minority of a one-sided vote. He was one of five Representatives (all African-American) who opposed sending U.S. troops into Kuwait in 1991 to drive out Iraqi forces under President Saddam Hussein.[10] Instead, Washington proposed a resolution calling for an up-or-down vote on the use of force against Iraq. "Either you are for war or you are against war," Washington declared on the House Floor. "Let it be said by history that the Congress of the United States saw its duty and we did it."[11] He also cast some perplexing votes against proposed projects that would have benefited his state and district. Washington was one of two Texans to vote against continuing funding for the superconducting super collider in 1993. The project, which would enable scientists to study small particles of matter, was sited for East Texas and would have brought the state millions of federal dollars. Washington was also the only Texan to vote against building a space station whose construction and maintenance would have employed constituents of his Houston district, which was home to the National Aeronautics and Space Administration's (NASA) Lyndon B. Johnson Space Center. Washington justified both votes by asserting that federal dollars would be better spent on more-basic needs, such as education, health care, and social services.[12] Yet at other times he voted in favor of his district's interests. Washington was one of seven Texans to vote against the North American Free Trade Agreement (NAFTA), despite its support by Houston-area businesses, arguing that the measure would ship 3,000 jobs from his district to Mexico.[13]

Washington's experience as a defense lawyer and a civil rights activist influenced his work on the Judiciary Committee. He was one of the more vocal opponents of the 1991 Civil Rights Bill, which was backed by President George H. W. Bush. Bush had vetoed a 1990 bill seeking to reverse a series of Supreme Court decisions that narrowed the scope of laws against employment discrimination based on race, sex, or ethnicity. The 1990 bill required employers to meet controversial racial quotas, whereas the 1991 compromise focused less on racial quotas

than on greater gender equity in the job market.[14] From his seat on the Judiciary Committee, Washington argued for the return of racial quotas, calling the compromise measure a "hollow shell of a civil rights bill."[15] "Where did the quotas go?" he asked on the House Floor. "They swam upstream like red herrings often do."[16] Washington was the only Democrat to vote against the 1991 compromise bill.

Washington was also a strict defender of Members' rights and privacy within Congress. In 1992, he came out strongly against a federal subpoena for House "Bank" records, despite a public outcry following the revelation that Members had overdrawn their accounts. Also, Washington was one of two Members who voted against restricting franking privileges from within Members' districts. "I don't have a right to tell other members of Congress where they should mail," he declared. "If the people don't like [the mailing practices] they will respond in kind at election time."[17] The former criminal defense lawyer also upheld the rights of those accused of crimes. Washington argued against the 1994 Omnibus Crime Bill, which he deemed overly punitive, calling for a greater focus on crime prevention. Washington was particularly concerned about trying juveniles as adults. As a member of the Judiciary Subcommittee on Crime and Criminal Justice, Washington quipped, "Certifying 13-year-olds as adults is an oxymoron." Though the final bill classified young teenagers participating in violent criminal activity as adults, it attempted to balance prevention programs with harsher punishments for particularly violent crimes.[18]

In January 1991, Washington filed for bankruptcy, admitting he owed $250,000 in federal taxes and $65,000 in local taxes. Yet in spite of personal financial trouble, he ran for chairman of the Congressional Black Caucus (CBC) in 1992. The 103rd Congress (1993–1995) was pivotal for the CBC, whose membership skyrocketed by 50 percent following the 1992 elections. Washington proposed assigning a caucus member to every House subcommittee and cited his independent voting record as proof of his commitment to bold leadership. However, he lost the bid to Maryland Democrat Kweisi Mfume.

Washington faced further difficulty when *Congressional Quarterly* reported that he was absent from nearly 25 percent of the votes during the 102nd Congress (1991–1993), giving him the worst attendance record in the Texas delegation and the second-worst record of any Representative.[19] Washington expressed exasperation with the lengthy voting process, claiming he skipped votes that had no bearing on his Houston districts so he could meet with constituents and focus on projects closer to home.[20] Washington began logging his missed votes and recording his alternative activities. "When it comes to a choice between form and substance, I choose substance," he declared.[21]

In 1994, Washington's district was redrawn. The new boundaries included a few wealthier Houston suburbs but retained a predominantly minority constituency that was 51 percent black and 15 percent Hispanic.[22] Washington's financial troubles, poor attendance, and maverick voting record inspired a strong challenge from Houston City Councilwoman Sheila Jackson Lee, a Democrat who ran under a slogan "Representation You Can Be Proud Of," an allusion to Washington's controversial positions. Houston-area businessmen rallied around Jackson Lee, upset that Washington had voted against NASA projects and against NAFTA. Six of Washington's congressional colleagues flew to Houston to show their support for his re-election. Charlie Rose of North Carolina noted re-electing Washington would add to his power in Congress by increasing his seniority. "Texas is not powerful in Washington because it changes its congresspeople every two or three terms," Rose advised.[23] Nevertheless, Washington lost the nomination to Jackson Lee, who handily defeated the incumbent with 63 percent of the vote. Easily winning the general election, Jackson Lee continued the district's trend of African-American representation.

Following his departure from Congress, Washington resumed practicing law and bought a farm outside Houston. He expressed no interest in returning to politics. "I loved it when I did it, but there's not a snowball's chance in hell that I'd ever run again," he remarked in 2001. "It'd be like putting my hand back in the meat grinder."[24]

FOR FURTHER READING

"Washington, Craig Anthony," *Biographical Directory of the United States Congress, 1774–Present*, http://bioguide.congress.gov/scripts/biodisplay.pl?index=W000177.

NOTES

1 Todd Ackerman, "Election '94: Craig Washington Goes Down to Defeat Fighting," 9 March 1994, *Houston Chronicle*: A21.

2 While a defense attorney, Washington faced possible jail time for failing to appear for two of his clients' court dates. He claimed he was not aware of the court dates; however, he was sentenced for contempt of court. Washington settled the matter without serving the prescribed jail time. See Karen Timmons, "Facing Jail, Washington Becomes Congressman," 24 January 1990, United Press International*; Politics in America, 1994* (Washington, DC: Congressional Quarterly Inc., 1993): 1502.

3 Based on a c.v. provided by the Honorable Craig Washington's law firm, the names of his children are: Craig Anthony, II; Chival Antoinette; Alexander Haller; Cydney Alexandra; and Christopher Alfred. For additional information, see *Who's Who Among African-Americans*, 15th Ed. (Gale Group, 2002).

4 Craig Winneker, "Washington Wins Last Special of '89," 14 December 1989, *Roll Call*.

5 "Craig Anthony Washington," Associated Press Candidate Biographies, 1992.

6 Ibid.

7 Quoted in "Craig Anthony Washington," Associated Press Candidate Biographies, 1994.

8 Ibid.

9 "Election Statistics, 1920 to Present," available at http://clerk.house.gov/member_info/election.html; Garrison Nelson, *Committees in the U.S. Congress, 1947 to 1992*, Volume 2 (Washington, DC: Congressional Quarterly Press, 1994): 916.

10 Six Members, several of them African-American, also voted "present." Twenty-four Members were recorded as absent. See "Final Vote Results for Roll Call 10," Office of the Clerk, available at http://clerk.house.gov/evs/1991/roll010.xml.

11 *Congressional Record*, House, 102nd Cong., 1st sess. (10 January 1991): H115.

12 Alan Bernstein, "U.S. Representative, District 18," 25 October 1992, *Houston Chronicle*: 3.

13 Alan Bernstein, "U.S. Representative, District 18," 27 February 1994, *Houston Chronicle*: 4.

14 *Congress and the Nation, 1989–1992,* Volume 8 (Washington, DC: Congressional Quarterly Press, 1993): 780–785.

15 Quoted in *Politics in America, 1994*: 1500.

16 *Congressional Record*, House, 102nd Cong., 1st sess. (7 November 1991): H9538.

17 Alan Bernstein, "Washington, Blum Spar Over Free Stamps," 26 June 1992, *Houston Chronicle*: A22.

18 "Jesse Jackson Says Crime Bill Is 'Fascist'," 23 February 1994, *The Record*: 8; *Congressional Quarterly Almanac, 1994* (Washington, DC: Congressional Quarterly Inc., 1995): 278–279; 287–294.

19 Jim Simmon, "The New Year Rings With . . . Politics," 4 January 1994, *Houston Chronicle*: A11; Washington's 74 percent voting record tied that of Representative Joseph McDade of Pennsylvania and was second only to that of Representative Harold Ford, Sr. of Tennessee, who had a 69 percent attendance record; see *Congressional Quarterly Almanac, 1993* (Washington, DC: Congressional Quarterly Inc., 1994): 34C–35C. The *Washington Post* vote database lists Washington as having the most absences in the 103rd Congress. See "The U.S. Congress Votes Database," 103rd Congress, House: http://projects.washingtonpost.com/congress/103/house/ (accessed 26 July 2006).

20 Bernstein, "U.S. Representative, District 18" (1994).

21 *Politics in America, 1994*: 1501.

22 Ibid.

23 Jennifer Leinhart, "Rep. Washington Gets 'Fly-In' Help From Capitol Hill Peers," 6 March 1994, *Houston Chronicle*: A31.

24 Brian D. Sweany, "Craig Washington," *Texas Monthly* (September 2001): 51.

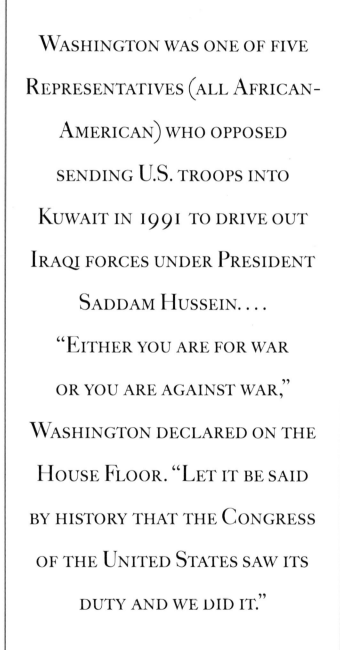

Washington was one of five Representatives (all African-American) who opposed sending U.S. troops into Kuwait in 1991 to drive out Iraqi forces under President Saddam Hussein.... "Either you are for war or you are against war," Washington declared on the House Floor. "Let it be said by history that the Congress of the United States saw its duty and we did it."

Barbara-Rose Collins
1939–

UNITED STATES REPRESENTATIVE ★ 1991–1997
DEMOCRAT FROM MICHIGAN

A longtime community activist and single mother, Barbara-Rose Collins was elected to Congress in 1990 on a platform to bring federal dollars and social aid to her economically depressed neighborhood in downtown Detroit. In the House, Collins focused on her lifelong advocacy for minority rights and on providing economic aid to and preserving the family in black communities.

The eldest child of Lamar Nathaniel and Lou Versa Jones Richardson, Barbara Rose Richardson was born in Detroit, Michigan, on April 13, 1939. Her father supported the family of four children as an auto manufacturer and later as an independent contractor in home improvement. Barbara Richardson graduated from Cass Technical High School in 1957 and attended Detroit's Wayne State University majoring in political science and anthropology. Richardson left college to marry her classmate, Virgil Gary Collins, who later worked as a pharmaceutical salesman to support their two children, Cynthia and Christopher.[1] In 1960, the couple divorced, and, as a single mother, Barbara Collins was forced to work multiple jobs. She received public financial assistance until the physics department at Wayne State University hired her as a business manager, a position she held for nine years. Collins subsequently became an assistant in the office of equal opportunity and neighborhood relations at Wayne State. In the late 1960s, Collins heard a speech by black activist Stokely Carmichael at Detroit's Shrine of the Black Madonna Church. Inspired by Carmichael's appeal to African Americans to improve their own neighborhoods, Collins purchased a house within a block of her childhood home and joined the Shrine Church, whose sociopolitical agenda focused on uplifting black neighborhoods. In 1971, Collins was elected to Detroit's region one school board, earning widespread recognition for her work on school safety and academic achievement. Encouraged by the

Shrine Church pastor, Collins campaigned for a seat in the state legislature in 1974, hyphenating her name, Barbara-Rose, to distinguish herself from the other candidates.[2] Victorious, she embarked on a six-year career in the statehouse. Collins chaired the constitutional revision and women's rights committee, which produced *Women in the Legislative Process*, the first published report to document the status of women in the Michigan state legislature.[3]

Bolstered by her work in Detroit's most downtrodden neighborhoods, Collins considered running for the U.S. House of Representatives in 1980 against embattled downtown Representative Charles Diggs, Jr.; however, Collins's mentor Detroit Mayor Coleman Young advised her to run for Detroit city council instead, and she did successfully.[4] Eight years later in the Democratic primary, she challenged incumbent U.S. Representative George W. Crockett, who had succeeded Diggs. In a hard-fought campaign, Collins held the respected, but aging, Crockett to a narrow victory with less than 49 percent of the vote. Crockett chose not to run for re-election in 1990, leaving the seat wide open for Barbara-Rose Collins. Collins's 1990 campaign focused on bringing federal money to Detroit, an economically depressed city whose population was moving to the suburbs. Her district's rapidly rising crime rate (one of the highest in the nation) also affected the candidate.[5] In 1989, Collins's son was convicted of armed robbery, and she concluded that he went astray because he lacked a strong male role model. "I could teach a girl how to be a woman, but I could not teach a boy how to be a man," she later told the *Detroit Free Press*.[6] Drawing from this experience, Collins tried to strengthen black families, rallying under the banner "Save the Black Male." In a crowded field of eight candidates, Collins won her primary with 34 percent of the vote, a victory that amounted to election to Congress in the overwhelmingly Democratic

district. Collins sailed through the general election with 80 percent of the vote and was re-elected twice with even higher percentages.[7]

One of three black women in her freshman class, Collins sought the influence and counsel of longtime Michigan Representative John Dingell, Jr., who helped her gain a seat on the Public Works and Transportation Committee (later Transportation and Infrastructure).[8] She also received assignments to the Committee on Science, Space, and Technology and the Select Committee on Children, Youth, and Families. She later traded these two panels for Government Operations (later named Government Reform and Oversight) and the Post Office and Civil Service Committee, where she chaired the Subcommittee on Postal Operations and Services in the 103rd Congress (1993–1995). A member of the Congressional Black Caucus and the Congressional Women's Caucus, Representative Collins was appointed a Majority Whip At-Large from 1993 until 1994.

Collins's career was focused on her campaign promises of economic and social aid for the urban black poor. In October 1992 Collins began encouraging agricultural growers to donate excess food that would otherwise go to waste to urban food banks and shelters.[9] Collins generally supported President William J. (Bill) Clinton's economic and job stimulus initiatives; however, she vocally opposed adopting the North American Free Trade Agreement, arguing that opening American borders to cheaper Mexican products would take domestic manufacturing jobs away from urban minority workers.[10] Though she favored the bill's final version, she voted against the President's April 1994 omnibus crime bill, objecting to its extension of the death penalty to several more federal crimes and opposing a section that mandated life in prison for people convicted of three felonies. Collins argued that these provisions would affect minorities disproportionately, declaring, "I think justice is dispensed differently for people of color, be they black or Hispanic."[11] Collins's family advocacy was apparent in her enthusiastic support of the October 1995 Million Man March, a mass rally of African-American men in Washington, DC, to demonstrate commitment to family. Collins planned to provide water for the marchers, "The idea is electrifying. . . . Black men will be reaffirming their responsibility for black women and for the black family," she said.[12] Collins also advocated considering housework, childcare, volunteer work, and time devoted to a family business as components of the gross national product. "If you raise the status of women," she declared, "we would be more conscious of the family unit."[13]

With her focus on domestic issues, Representative Collins generally opposed increasing foreign aid. "Our cities are hurting," she observed. "We must learn how to take care of America first."[14] However, in April 1994 Collins and five other Democratic House Members were arrested after staging a sit-in at the White House to protest American policy toward Haiti. In the wake of the island nation's military coup, the protestors called for greater acceptance of Haitian refugees and demanded a stronger embargo against Haiti.[15] "What's being done to Haitians is inhumane and immoral," Collins said. "The fact of the matter is we welcome Hungarians with open arms, we welcome Vietnamese with open arms, we welcome Cubans with open arms, but when it comes to black Haitians, we tell them, 'Stand back we don't want you,' the result being that hundreds are drowned at sea, children and women eaten by sharks."[16] All six Members were fined and released.

While Collins was popular among her constituents, she drew negative publicity when the Justice Department and the House Ethics Committee investigated her office in 1996 for the alleged misuse of campaign and scholarship funds.[17] Though Collins was initially unopposed in the 1994 primary, six opponents entered the race following the controversy. Challenger Carolyn Cheeks Kilpatrick defeated the incumbent in the primary by a 21-point margin and went on to win the general election. Barbara-Rose Collins remained active in local politics. In 2001, she won a seat on the Detroit city council. Collins was re-elected to the council for a second term in 2005.

FOR FURTHER READING

"Collins, Barbara-Rose," *Biographical Directory of the United States Congress, 1774–Present*, http://bioguide. congress.gov/scripts/biodisplay.pl?index=C000633.

NOTES

1 The couple's third child died in infancy.

2 DeWitt S. Dykes, Jr., "Barbara-Rose Collins," *Notable Black American Women,* Volume 2, Jessie Carney Smith, ed. (Detroit, MI: Gale Research Inc., 1996): 135 (hereinafter referred to as *NBAW*). The couple's third child died in its infancy.

3 Dykes, "Barbara-Rose Collins," *NBAW*.

4 Ibid.

5 *Almanac of American Politics, 1996* (Washington, DC: National Journal Inc., 1995): 710.

6 Dykes, "Barbara-Rose Collins," *NBAW*.

7 "Election Statistics, 1920 to Present," available at http://clerk. house.gov/member_info/electionInfo/index.html.

8 Dykes, "Barbara-Rose Collins," *NBAW*.

9 *Congressional Record*, House, 102nd Cong., 2nd sess. (5 October 1992): 3074.

10 *Congressional Record*, House, 103rd Cong., 1st sess. (21 October 1993): 8336; *Congressional Record*, House, 103rd Cong., 1st sess. (26 October 1993): 8436.

11 *Politics in America, 1996*: 685.

12 Francis X. Clines, "Organizers Defend Role of Farrakhan in March by Blacks," 13 October 1995, *New York Times*: A1.

13 Maria Odum, "If the G.N.P. Counted Housework, Would Women Count for More?" 5 April 1992, *New York Times*: E5.

14 Adam Clymer, "House Votes Billions in Aid to Ex-Soviet Republics," 7 August 1992, *New York Times*: A1.

15 Peter H. Spiegel, "Members Arrested in Haiti Protest," 25 April 1994, *Roll Call*.

16 Kenneth R. Bazinet, "Congressmen Arrested Outside White House," 21 April 1994, United Press International.

17 In January 1997, the House Standards of Official Conduct Committee found Representative Collins guilty of violating 11 House rules and federal laws; however, the panel did not recommend disciplinary action because Collins had already left office. A historical chart of all formal House ethics actions is available at http://www.house.gov/ethics/Historical_Chart_ Final_ Version.htm. See also Robyn Meredith, "Ethical Issues Pose Test to a Detroit Lawmaker," 2 August 1996, *New York Times*: A10; Sarah Pekkanen, "Ethics Committee Issues Scathing Report on Collins," 8 January 1997, *The Hill*.

Gary A. Franks
1953–

UNITED STATES REPRESENTATIVE ★ 1991–1997
REPUBLICAN FROM CONNECTICUT

As the first black Republican Representative to serve in the U.S. House in nearly six decades, the GOP promoted Gary Franks as its newest African-American spokesperson when he won his seat in Congress in 1990.[1] Franks was a zealous champion of conservative causes, including welfare reform, opposition to affirmative action, and support for Supreme Court nominee Clarence Thomas. "The whole Republican philosophy is self-help," Franks avowed. "I believe in less government. I believe that we don't have to tax and spend constantly to maintain our society."[2] Ultimately, Franks's difficulty connecting with his primarily middle-class white constituency, as well as his contentious fights with the Congressional Black Caucus (CBC), and at times, with the leadership within his own party, contributed to his political defeat.

Gary Alvin Franks was born in Waterbury, Connecticut, on February 9, 1953. He was the youngest of six children of Janery Petteway Franks and Richard Franks, a mill worker who left school in the sixth grade. Education was valued in the Franks home; all the children attended college, and three earned doctoral degrees.[3] Gary Franks was an all-state basketball player at Sacred Heart High School in Waterbury. In 1975 he earned a B.A. from Yale University. After working as an industrial relations agent for three companies in Connecticut, Franks started his own real estate firm in Waterbury. Inspired by his friend, Representative John Rowland of Connecticut, Franks entered politics to bring "new blood" to the Waterbury Republicans.[4] Franks ran unsuccessfully for state comptroller in 1986. That same year, he was elected to the Waterbury board of aldermen, where he served until 1990. Franks married Donna Williams in 1990, gaining a stepdaughter, Azia. The couple's daughter, Jessica, was born in 1991, and their son, Gary, Jr., arrived in 1994.

In 1990, Rowland, whose district encompassed a mix of working-class and wealthy towns in western and central Connecticut, including Gary Franks's hometown of Waterbury, vacated his House seat to run for governor of Connecticut. Franks sought the Republican nomination based on his conservative politics, winning the GOP endorsement by beating out five candidates at the district's Republican convention in July 1990.[5] In the general election, Franks faced former Democratic Representative and television anchor Toby Moffett. Formerly representing a neighboring district, Moffett was elected to Congress in 1974, serving four terms before losing bids for the U.S. Senate in 1982 and the Connecticut governor's post in 1986.[6] The campaign drew national attention. Though a Republican had held the district since Rowland upset the Democratic incumbent in 1984, the seat was considered vulnerable. Registered Democrats outnumbered Republicans almost three to two. The district contained only a small black population (under 10 percent), and Franks's campaign did not emphasize his race.[7] The campaign came down to a referendum on economic policy, as the northeastern economy spiraled toward recession. Franks ran on a conservative platform, promising no new taxes, supporting a cut in the capital gains tax, and advocating a constitutional amendment outlawing the desecration of the American flag. He also attacked the American welfare system for creating a "spiral of government dependency."[8] Moffett tried to tie Franks's platform to former President Ronald W. Reagan's economic policies, claiming that the former administration had left the economy flat in its wake.[9] The tight race drew high-powered endorsements and campaign appearances. President George H. W. Bush, First Lady Barbara Bush, and Vice President Dan Quayle visited the district on Franks's behalf. Actor Robert Redford and former Speaker Thomas P. (Tip) O'Neill campaigned for Moffett. Franks

won the election with 52 percent of the vote.[10] He was the first African-American Representative to be elected from Connecticut. Franks's unique position immediately attracted a barrage of media attention, making him one of the most recognizable Members of his freshman class.[11] He won assignments on the Armed Services and Small Business committees, as well as on the Select Committee on Aging.

The CBC—a traditionally liberal organization that was then composed entirely of Democrats—accepted Franks as a member upon his election. Franks spoke regularly at caucus meetings during his first term, and he often disagreed with the other members of the CBC. For example, Franks voted against the 1990 Civil Rights Bill, which the CBC almost universally supported. Although he had experienced discrimination, Franks said he did not approve of a system requiring employers to hire a certain percentage of minorities; he argued that enforced quotas would encourage employers to move jobs from his Connecticut district to states that were more racially homogeneous to avoid the requirements.[12] Furthermore, Franks said, "I question whether some Democrats truly want a civil rights bill or if they want a political issue."[13] President George H. W. Bush rejected the bill, primarily because of the quotas provision, and the House failed to override his veto.[14]

Franks also attracted national attention as the only member of the CBC to support the nomination of federal Judge Clarence Thomas—an African American who was slated to replace Thurgood Marshall, the first black Supreme Court Justice, when he retired. The CBC rejected Thomas's conservative record, particularly his opposition to affirmative action. By contrast, Franks defended him, calling the CBC's failure to endorse Thomas "politics at its worst." Franks noted that Thomas's "approach to issues may be different from liberals, but his determination and concern for fairness and justice would be the same."[15] Black conservatives rallied behind Thomas, and the Senate confirmed him on October 15, 1991, by a vote of 52 to 48 that was split nearly along party lines.[16]

In 1992, Franks faced the first of a series of tough re-election campaigns. Though a looming national figure, two strong candidates opposed Franks: Democratic probate judge James Lawlor and Independent Lynn Taborsak, a former Democratic state representative.[17] Both opponents attacked what they called Franks's weak stance on federal plans to cancel the construction of Seawolf submarines in Groton, Connecticut. The project was important to the state's economy and, as Connecticut's sole member on the Armed Services Committee, Franks received mail from constituents about the rumored closing of the military base in Groton. Concerned voters claimed he was often unavailable for comment on the subject.[18] Franks dismissed the attacks as a liberal smear campaign spawned by fear that he would lure African-American voters to the Republican Party. He ultimately benefited from a split Democratic vote, winning with a 44 percent plurality.[19]

Franks relinquished his seat on the Armed Services Committee for an assignment to the Committee on Energy and Commerce (later Commerce), a highly desirable panel that usually requires Members to give up all other committee assignments. He also returned as a member of the CBC, which added 14 Representatives after the 1992 elections, bringing the organization's membership to 40 and establishing it as a significant voting bloc. Courting a sympathetic Democratic President, William J. (Bill) Clinton, liberals in the caucus began to assert their authority. Previously a link between the CBC and Republican President George H. W. Bush, Franks lost power within the caucus. Several members objected to Franks's attendance at the caucus's strategy sessions, insisting that he was a mole for the Republicans, and the CBC unofficially ejected Franks from these meetings.[20]

An exasperated Franks publicly announced his intention to resign from the CBC on Friday, June 14, 1993, but recanted the following Monday, citing an influx of phone calls and mail from constituents imploring him not to resign.[21] Though he continued to criticize some of the caucus's policies, Franks declared, "As long as I am a Member of Congress and black, I will continue to belong to the CBC."[22] However, Franks was soon barred from the first half-hour of CBC meetings—traditionally reserved for lunch—marking the first official barrier to his membership. Faced with growing negative publicity, CBC chairman Kweisi Mfume of Maryland eventually smoothed over the rift, announcing in August 1993 that Franks would be allowed full participation in all caucus activities and promising that, during his tenure as chairman, the caucus would embrace "diversity and plurality."[23] Yet Franks remained at odds with the majority of the caucus and eventually stopped attending meetings.

In the 1994 election, Connecticut State Senator James Maloney overcame a close primary to win the Democratic nomination, and using a strategy employed by Franks's previous opponents, he accused the incumbent of being out of touch with his constituents. Television ads became a focal point in the campaign. In the weeks leading up the election, Maloney unleashed a series of ads attacking Franks's positions. Franks responded with television spots focusing on his support for business and welfare reform. Franks's strategy proved effective; he won a narrow victory, with 52 percent of the vote.[24] Franks took his place in the first Congress in 40 years to have a Republican majority.

Franks played a significant role in crafting the GOP welfare reform package, which was launched in the fall of 1995. The plan set strict penalties for welfare recipients who refused to look for work after having collected benefits for two years, and made welfare difficult for immigrants to access. Also, mothers who could not determine their children's paternity would have more difficulty receiving benefits.[25] Franks spoke candidly about his own relatives' experience in the system, praising the Republican plan as one that encouraged the achievement of economic independence. "Our welfare system continues to play the role of fish-delivery man for able-bodied people. Instead, we should help—and insist—that able-bodied people catch their own fish," Franks said, explaining his party's position.[26] In 1995, Franks was appointed to attend the conference to resolve the differences between the House and Senate versions of the reformed welfare system. Franks fought to save his own proposals, which would cap the amount of money per child that was given to families on welfare and provide a debit card for food stamps.[27]

Franks opposed affirmative action more zealously than many of his GOP colleagues, who had championed the issue in their campaign to recapture the congressional majority. The 1995 Supreme Court ruling in *Adarand Constructors, Inc. v. Peña* held that affirmative action policies had to withstand "strict scrutiny," meaning that they must show clear evidence of righting a past discriminatory practice. The contemporary policy in the federal government provided special set-asides and preferences for minorities and women. Franks argued that the extra entitlements were a form of discrimination. "I do not want my children to feel that they are inferior to white children," he declared. "I do not want someone to put their thumb on the scale in order for them to succeed."[28] Congressional Republicans supported Franks's efforts; however, many GOP House Members objected to the speediness with which Franks proposed to implement the changes.[29] "I question the sincerity of a number of Republicans on the issue," Franks said to reporters. "They love to get the political mileage out of it, but when it comes time to vote, they don't want to do it."[30] Franks questioned the veracity of Speaker Newt Gingrich of Georgia, claiming Gingrich had promised his support for the amendment. Franks later apologized to Gingrich, noting that he would follow the Speaker's lead on the issue.[31]

Maloney returned for a rematch against Franks in a 1996 campaign that was largely a referendum on the implementation of the GOP's Contract With America. With more support from the national and local Democratic Party, Maloney defeated Franks 52 to 46 percent.[32] Though the long coattails from President Clinton's decisive re-election victory factored into Franks's defeat, he also attributed his loss to a lack of support from the Republican Party—noting that the GOP estimated he was well ahead in the polls just months before the election and had refused to pay for what seemed like a safe district—and to the united front between labor and liberals. He also observed that several prominent black liberals had made appearances in his district "to spread lies, and half-truths about my record."[33]

Franks refused to step out of the political spotlight. As he hinted in his 1996 autobiography, Franks made a bid against incumbent Democratic Senator Christopher Dodd in 1998. The campaign was considered a long shot against the entrenched Dodd, an 18-year veteran of the Senate whose father, Thomas, had preceded him in the chamber.[34] Franks pulled in support from Republicans, including former Vice President Dan Quayle, who stumped for him.[35] Describing himself as a "real conservative and a real Republican," Franks campaigned on the national issues he had championed in Congress.[36] He supported the creation of a modified flat income tax and the elimination of capital gains and inheritance taxes. Franks also endorsed a strong national defense, the preservation of Medicare and Social Security, and the death penalty. However, Dodd ran away with the race, with 65 percent to Franks's 32 percent.[37] After Franks lost the election, he returned to his real estate business in Waterbury.

FOR FURTHER READING

Franks, Gary. *Searching for the Promised Land: An African American's Optimistic Odyssey* (New York: Reagan Books, 1996).

"Franks, Gary A.," *Biographical Directory of the United States Congress, 1774–Present*, http://bioguide.congress.gov/scripts/biodisplay.pl?index=F000348.

NOTES

1 Republican Senator Edward Brooke of Massachusetts also served 12 years in the Senate, departing in 1979. Delegate Melvin Evans of the Virgin Islands served from 1979 to 1981.

2 Peter Viles, "Connecticut Alderman Tries to Break 55-Year House Lockout," 27 August 1990, Associated Press.

3 Nick Ravo, "A Black Congressional Hope in Connecticut," 9 August 1990, *New York Times*: B1.

4 Gary Franks, *Searching for the Promised Land: An African American's Optimistic Odyssey* (New York: Regan Books, 1996): 38–39.

5 Franks, *Searching for the Promised Land*: 38–39.

6 Ibid.

7 Nick Ravo, "Ghost of Reagan in Connecticut Race," 22 October 1990, *New York Times*: B4.

8 Ravo, "A Black Congressional Hope in Connecticut."

9 Ravo, "Ghost of Reagan in Connecticut Race"; Viles, "Connecticut Alderman Tries to Break 55-Year House Lockout"; Jacqueline Trescott, "Rep. Gary Franks, Unexpected Republican," 31 July 1991, *Washington Post*: B1.

10 "Election Statistics, 1920 to Present," available at http://clerk.house.gov/member_info/election.html.

11 *Politics in America, 1994* (Washington, DC: Congressional Quarterly Inc., 1993): 299.

12 Bill Whalen, "The Reluctant Republican Star," 8 March 1991, *Washington Times*: E1.

13 Trescott, "Rep. Gary Franks, Unexpected Republican."

14 *Congressional Quarterly Almanac, 1990* (Washington, DC: Congressional Quarterly Inc., 1991): 473.

15 Bob Dart, "Fight Over Seating Thomas Splits Blacks," 19 July 1991, *Atlanta Journal and Constitution*: A2.

16 Senate Roll Call Vote 220, 102nd Cong., 1st sess.. See "U.S. Congress Votes Database," *Washington Post*: http://projects. washingtonpost.com/congress/102/senate/1/votes/220/ (accessed 7 February 2008).

17 Lindsey Gruson, "Franks Gets a Lift From an Opponent," 24 October 1992, *New York Times*: 28.

18 Miranda Spivack, "A Rising Star in the Nation's Capital Loses Luster For Some Back Home," 10 February 1992, *Hartford Courant*: A1.

19 "Election Statistics, 1920 to Present,"available at http://clerk.house.gov/members/electionInfo/elections.html.

20 "Black Republican Allowed to Vote in CBC Group," 23 August 1993, *National Report*: 5; Mary Jacoby, "GOP's Franks to Quit Black Caucus," 14 June 1993, *Roll Call*.

21 Mary Jacoby, "Whoops! Franks Does About-Face, Will Stay in CBC," 17 June 1993, *Roll Call*.

22 Jacoby, "Whoops! Franks Does About-Face, Will Stay in CBC."

23 "Black Republican Allowed to Vote in CBC Group"; Franks, *Searching for the Promised Land*: 124.

24 "Election Statistics, 1920 to Present," available at http://clerk.house.gov/member_info/election.html.

25 *Congressional Quarterly Almanac, 1995* (Washington, DC: Congressional Quarterly Inc., 1996): 7-40.

26 Michael Remez, "Franks Speaks for GOP in Welfare Debate," 5 May 1994, *Hartford Courant*: F1.

27 David Daley, "Franks Appointed to Welfare Conference Committee," 29 September 1995, States News Service.

28 Jill Zuckman, "Black Republican Says Party Lags on Ending Preferences," 6 August 1995, *Boston Globe*: 19.

29 David Lightman, "Franks to Lead Battle in Congress," 13 July 1995, *Harford Courant*: A3.

30 Zuckman, "Black Republican Says Party Lags on Ending Preferences."

31 David Lightman, "Franks Apologizes to Gingrich," 7 September 1995, *Washington Post*: A6.

32 "Election Statistics, 1920 to Present," available at http://clerk.house.gov/members/electionInfo/elections.html.

33 Mike McIntire, "Franks Blames GOP, Liberals, Labor, and Rat Ads for His Loss," 7 November 1996, *Hartford Courant*: A17; Nancy E. Roman, "Black Democrat Rips Franks for Votes 'Suicidal' To His Race," 21 November 1996, *Washington Times*: A4. Representative William Lacy (Bill) Clay, Sr., of Missouri lambasted the outgoing Representative in a six-page letter circulated on Capitol Hill, branding Franks "a pariah, who gleefully assists in suicidal conduct to destroy his own race."

34 Melissa B. Robinson, "Former Rep. to Run for Senate," 19 January 1998, Associated Press.

35 Robinson, "Former Rep. to Run for Senate."

36 "Gary Alvin Franks," Associated Press Candidate Biographies, 1998.

37 "Election Statistics, 1920 to Present," available at http://clerk.house.gov/member_info/election.html.

Lucien Edward Blackwell
1931–2003

UNITED STATES REPRESENTATIVE ★ 1991–1995
DEMOCRAT FROM PENNSYLVANIA

A long-time resident of West Philadelphia, Lucien Blackwell appealed to his primarily African-American, blue-collar constituents because of his image as a "common man." The popular former city councilman successfully navigated Philadelphia's Democratic Party machinery, emerging as one of the city's most recognized politicians. Making his congressional debut in a special election to succeed powerful Representative William (Bill) Gray III, the former union president focused on helping working-class Americans who were suffering from the recession of the early 1990s. "The American worker is marching down the street asking for unemployment compensation because he has lost his job," Blackwell said to his colleagues. "I ask every Congressman who does not vote for unemployment compensation tonight, give up your wages, give up your employment, give up what you've earned here, and then tell me it is all right to live off nothing."[1] However, Blackwell's congressional career, marking a transitional phase in Philadelphia politics, proved to be short as the 73-year-old machine politician contended with a new generation of black leaders.

Lucien Edward Blackwell was born on August 1, 1931, to Thomas and Mary Blackwell in Whiset, Pennsylvania. He had at least one sibling, a sister named Audrey.[2] As a young child, Lucien Blackwell moved to a West Philadelphia neighborhood known as "the Bottom," where his father opened a grocery store. He lived in that neighborhood all his life. Lucien Blackwell dropped out of West Philadelphia High School in 1947 to take a job as a dockworker on the Philadelphia waterfront. He briefly pursued a boxing career, winning a novice Diamond Belt Championship in 1949 before being drafted into the United States Army in 1953 to fight in the Korean War. During his military service, he was awarded a unit commendation, two bronze stars, and a good conduct medal.[3] After returning to civilian life, he joined the International Longshoreman's Union, serving as president of its Philadelphia branch from 1973 to 1991. Blackwell married and divorced at a young age. He met his second wife, Jannie, while she was teaching at a school attended by his sons, Lucien, Jr., and Thomas W. Blackwell IV.[4] The couple married in 1972 and had four daughters: Patricia, Barbara, Brenda, and Audrey.

Blackwell's union work introduced him to politics. Living in a predominantly black, liberal neighborhood, he was a self-described Democrat "from the tip of my head to the bottom of my feet."[5] Blackwell first served in the Pennsylvania house of representatives from 1973 to 1975, but he made his mark as a Philadelphia city councilman, holding the office from 1975 to 1991. Blackwell earned the nickname "Lucien the Solution" for his attention to the needs of his constituents in West and South Philadelphia. He ran unsuccessfully for Philadelphia mayor as the Consumer Party candidate in 1979 against controversial incumbent Frank Rizzo, who was under investigation for fostering police brutality in Blackwell's Ward. Both Rizzo and Blackwell lost to Democrat William J. Green. In 1986, Blackwell lost a bid for the Democratic city committee chairmanship to future Representative Robert A. Brady. He nevertheless held key chairmanships of two Philadelphia political groups: the Black Elected Officials and the United Black Ward Leaders. In 1991, Blackwell made his second mayoral run, finishing second to eventual winner Edward Rendell in a hotly contested Democratic primary. Blackwell's first taste of national politics came through his work on Jesse Jackson's presidential campaigns in 1984 and 1988.

In June 1991, Representative Bill Gray, the House Majority Whip and third-ranking Democrat, retired abruptly from his seat encompassing West Philadelphia,

which boasted a black majority (82 percent) and a long Democratic voting record. Believing that the special election would take place on November 5—the same day Philadelphia voters would select a new mayor and a United States Senator—Blackwell declared his intention to run for the vacant seat and quickly became the front-runner. However, Gray postponed his resignation until September, citing the need to train the new House Majority Whip, Representative David Bonior of Michigan. According to Pennsylvania state law, special elections could take place no sooner than 60 days after a former Member resigned. Gray's late departure pushed the special election back to early 1992, leaving Blackwell's rivals a chance to organize their campaigns. Blackwell supporters accused Gray of thwarting their candidate's chances, as the two had previously been political rivals.[6] A federal court denied Blackwell's request to return the election date to November 5; however, he subsequently appealed to the Pennsylvania state court, which ruled in his favor on October 1. During a whirlwind campaign the following month, Democratic ward leaders overwhelmingly supported Blackwell, as many district residents voted a straight Democratic ticket. Blackwell's closest rivals included the young, charismatic state senator Chaka Fattah, a Democrat who was running as a Consumer Party candidate; and the former head of the Pennsylvania welfare department, John F. White, Jr., who was running as an Independent. Drawing upon the strength of the Democratic machine and his rapport as councilman with the city's working class, Blackwell prevailed with 39 percent of the vote. Fattah and White each won 28 percent.[7] Blackwell took his seat in the 102nd Congress (1991–1993) on November 13, 1991.

Just five months later, Blackwell faced C. Delores Tucker in the Democratic primary for the 103rd Congress (1993–1995). Having been considered by the Democratic machine the previous November, Tucker—a black woman who was formerly the secretary of the Commonwealth of Pennsylvania—proved a formidable opponent. Redistricting had cut the black majority in the district to 62 percent, forcing both candidates to broaden their appeal

to a bloc of wealthier white voters in the northwestern section of the city. Well funded by national women's groups and civil rights leaders, Tucker accused Blackwell of being a "puppet" of the Philadelphia party bosses. Blackwell emphasized his party and union support. Although Tucker won favor in the district's new neighborhoods, Blackwell defeated her with 54 percent of the vote. He went on to defeat Republican Larry Hollin with a sound 77 percent in the general election.[8]

In the House, Blackwell received appointments to the Public Works Committee and the Merchant Marine and Fisheries Committee. Blackwell also served as a member of the Congressional Black Caucus (CBC). In the 103rd Congress, overwhelming turnover allowed him to make the largest jump in seniority of any returning Member.[9] Blackwell traded his assignment on Merchant Marine and Fisheries for a coveted position on the Budget Committee, formerly chaired by his predecessor, Representative Bill Gray, in the 99th and 100th Congresses (1985–1989). Yet Blackwell retained his "common man" appeal. He claimed he was not seeking powerful committee or leadership posts, saying, "I come here not in a braggadocio way."[10] Instead, his focus throughout his congressional career was improving the quality of life of his Philadelphia neighbors. He was known for bringing federal dollars to the district.[11]

Blackwell's constituent-centered agenda—and the focus of the 102nd and 103rd Congresses as well as that of President William J. (Bill) Clinton—included lifting the national economy out of a recession. He agreed with Democratic colleagues who opposed an amendment to the Constitution requiring a balanced federal budget. Blackwell feared most politicians "believe that a balanced budget amendment is a magic wand. One quick wave over the document that represents the heart and soul of this nation, and the budget will be balanced, the economy restored, and the recession shattered by this almighty amendment."[12] He asserted that reducing the deficit was necessary to improve the economy and recommended that Congress take steps toward this goal by providing new jobs, creating fair trade, changing tax laws, enacting national health insurance legislation, and improving life in American cities. Blackwell also joined fellow Democrats in supporting the Clinton administration's economic initiatives, proposed in February 1993, which called for reduced federal spending and tax increases for the wealthy.[13]

Drawing on his union experience, Blackwell acted as an advocate for unemployed laborers. He introduced a bill in the 102nd Congress to protect the credit ratings of employees who had lost their jobs because their employers relocated overseas. Blackwell backed the Clinton reform package guaranteeing all Americans basic health coverage, and he supported family medical leave to care for family members who were unwell. He also sponsored a bill to protect job applicants from discrimination based on genetic factors, such as vulnerability to certain diseases. Blackwell favored extending the amount of time benefits were paid under the Emergency Unemployment Compensation Act, citing his concern for the high rate of unemployed workers in his district.[14]

In the May 1994 Democratic primary, Blackwell faced his former opponent Chaka Fattah. Blackwell appeared strong enough to defend his seat, receiving an endorsement from Mayor Rendell as well as the nominal endorsement of the local Democratic Party. However, individual Democrats were divided between Blackwell and Fattah. One ward leader observed, "Lu's in the fight of his life and Chaka's right on his heels."[15] Though immensely popular among his black, working-class neighbors, voters from the wealthier northwestern section of the district abandoned the incumbent because of his inability to connect with the district's white voters. Among a younger generation of black politicians, the youthful community activist Fattah proved better able to bridge the gaps between the city's races.[16] The challenger defeated Blackwell with 58 to 42 percent of the vote. In his concession speech Blackwell said, "What I have to do now is take a look at Lucien Blackwell and see what God has in store for him. And I'll show you that God isn't through with me yet."[17]

In May 1995, Blackwell joined the Washington-based lobbying firm Whitten & Diamond, which boasted the City of Philadelphia as one of its largest clients. Blackwell used his congressional connections, particularly through the CBC, to work on defense conversion as well as welfare reform.[18] He also acted as a consultant for a Philadelphia debt collection company. In 1996, Blackwell successfully fought the disintegration of the Philadelphia branch of the International Longshoreman's Association, led by his son Thomas W. Blackwell. He also served as a delegate to the Democratic National Convention that same year. In 1997, Blackwell considered running in a special election to replace Philadelphia Representative Thomas Foglietta, who was appointed U.S. Ambassador to Italy. Blackwell was inspired by the fact that Foglietta's district contained some areas that he had lost in the 1992 redistricting. However, Blackwell later bowed out of the race, claiming he had "just decided it was time to go."[19] On January, 24, 2003, after returning home from a morning walk, Blackwell suddenly died of a heart attack. The City of Philadelphia hosted a funeral that drew nearly 3,000 mourners.[20]

FOR FURTHER READING

"Blackwell, Lucien Edward," *Biographical Directory of the United States Congress, 1774–Present*, http://bioguide. congress.gov/scripts/biodisplay.pl?index=B000517.

NOTES

1   *Congressional Record*, House, 102nd Cong., 1st sess. (2 June 1992): H4414.

2   Blackwell paid tribute to his sister, Audrey Blackwell Farthing, in the *Congressional Record*. There is no mention of other siblings. See *Congressional Record*, Extension of Remarks, 103rd Cong., 1st sess. (15 June 1993): E1508.

3   *Congressional Directory*, 103rd Cong., 1st sess. (Washington, DC: Government Printing Office, 1993): 250–251.

4   The only information available about Blackwell's first wife is that she was the mother of Lucien, Jr., and Thomas W. Blackwell IV.

5   "Former ILA Local 1332 President, U.S. Congressman and Philadelphia City Councilman Lucien Blackwell Passes," *ILA Newsletter*, Spring 2003, at http://ilaunion.org/news/nlp_spr03_page16.htm (accessed 13 September 2004).

6   *Politics in America, 1994* (Washington, DC: Congressional Quarterly Inc., 1993): 1293.

7   Michael J. Dubin et al., *U.S. Congressional Elections, 1788–1997* (Jefferson, NC: McFarland & Company, Inc., Publishers, 1998): 774.

8   "Election Statistics, 1920 to Present," available at http://clerk. house.gov/member_info/electionInfo/index.html.

9   Peter H. Spiegel, "Seniority Lineup in the 103rd," 18 January 1993, *Roll Call*.

10 *Politics in America, 1994*: 1292.

11 James J. Kilpatrick, "Excise Pork From Federal Budget," 25 April 1992, *Chicago Sun-Times*: 19.

12 *Congressional Record*, House, 102nd Cong., 1st sess. (10 June 1992): H4511.

13 *Congressional Quarterly Almanac, 1995* (Washington, DC: Congressional Quarterly Inc., 1996): 7D–12D; Jennifer Babson, "Blackwell Summoned to White House for Clinton Talk," 13 February 1993, State News Service.

14 *Congressional Record*, House, 103rd Cong., 1st sess. (24 February 1993): H832.

15 Nicole Weisensee, "Blackwell, Fattah Too Close to Call?" 29 April 1994, *Philadelphia Daily News*: 13.

16 Ronald A. Taylor, "Power of Incumbency Wanes for Blacks Too," 14 May 1994, *Washington Times*: A1; Richard Fenno, *Going Home: Black Representatives and Their Constituents* (Chicago: University of Chicago Press): 114–115, 124–125.

17 "Lucien Blackwell," Associated Press Candidate Biographies, 1994.

18 Dave Davies, "Lucien Blackwell's Back on Taxpayers' Payroll," 5 May 1995, *Philadelphia Daily News*: 5.

19 "Blackwell Ends Run, Decides It's 'Time to Go'," 2 February 1998, *Roll Call*.

20 Dave Davies, "Farewell, Mr. Blackwell," 25 January 2003, *Philadelphia Daily News*: 3.

In Congress,

Blackwell retained his

"common man" appeal.

He claimed he was not

seeking powerful committee

or leadership posts, saying,

"I come here [to the House]

not in a braggadocio way."

Eva M. Clayton
1934–

UNITED STATES REPRESENTATIVE ★ 1992–2003
DEMOCRAT FROM NORTH CAROLINA

The first African-American woman to represent North Carolina in Congress, Eva Clayton became the state's first black Representative since 1901. From her post on the House Agriculture Committee, Clayton advanced the interests of her rural district in the northeastern part of her state and called attention to the economic inequalities that affected African Americans nationally.

Eva McPherson was born in Savannah, Georgia, on September 16, 1934. She grew up in Savannah and received a bachelor of science degree in biology from Johnson C. Smith University in Charlotte, North Carolina, in 1955. In 1962, she earned an M.S. in biology and general science from North Carolina Central University in Durham. She originally planned to become a doctor and travel to Africa to do missionary work. Shortly after receiving her undergraduate degree, Eva McPherson married Theaoseus Clayton, who became a prominent lawyer. They raised four children: Theaoseus Jr., Martin, Reuben, and Joanne.

The civil rights movement mobilized Eva Clayton to become active in civic and political affairs. At one point, she even picketed her husband's law office to protest Theaoseus's and his white law partner's ownership of a building that contained a segregated restaurant.[1] As early as 1968, Eva Clayton was recruited by civil rights activist Vernon Jordan to seek election to Congress in a north-central North Carolina district. Though Clayton won 31 percent of the vote in the Democratic primary, incumbent Lawrence Fountain prevailed. However, Clayton's campaign had the intended effect of spiking black voter registration.[2] "In 1968, the timing wasn't there," she later admitted.[3] After the birth of her fourth child, Clayton reluctantly withdrew from law school. "I wasn't super enough to be a supermom," Clayton recalled years later. "I left to be a mom. My husband was supportive, but I

felt enormously guilty. I think I would do it differently now. I think I would know how to demand more of my husband."[4] In the early 1970s, she worked for several public/private ventures, including the North Carolina Health Manpower Development Program at the University of North Carolina. In 1974 she cofounded and served as the executive director of Soul City Foundation, a housing organization that renovated dilapidated buildings for use as homeless shelters and daycare centers. Two years later, she worked on the successful gubernatorial campaign of Jim Hunt, who later appointed Clayton the assistant secretary of the North Carolina department of natural resources and community development. Clayton served in that capacity from 1977 until 1981. After leaving state government, she founded an economic development consulting firm. In 1982 she won election to the Warren County Board of Commissioners, which she chaired until 1990. Over the next decade, Clayton helped steer more than $550 million in investments into the county and also successfully passed a bond issue for the construction of new schools.

When Representative Walter Jones, Sr., announced his retirement in 1992, Clayton entered the Democratic primary to fill his seat. Recently reapportioned by the state legislature, the congressional district was one of two in North Carolina that had a black majority. Jones died in September 1992, and his son Walter, Jr., who was considered the favorite in the primary, captured 38 percent to Clayton's 31 but fell two points shy of winning the nomination outright. In the runoff, Clayton secured the support of her other primary opponents and won 55 percent to Jones's 45 percent. In the general election, Clayton ran on a platform of increased public investment and job training for rural areas in the district, which encompassed a large swath of eastern North Carolina including the towns of Goldsboro, Rocky Mount, and

Greenville. She advocated slashing the defense budget to lower the federal deficit. "We went into the projects and knocked on doors and got people out" to vote, Clayton recalled.[5] On November 3, 1992, she won the special election to fill the last two months of Walter Jones, Sr.'s unexpired term in the 102nd Congress (1991–1993) and defeated Republican Ted Tyler for a full term in the 103rd Congress (1993–1995). Mel Watt, an African American, also won election from a North Carolina district to the House on November 3, but because Clayton was elected to the 102nd Congress, she became the first African-American Representative from North Carolina since George White, who left Congress in 1901. In her subsequent four bids for re-election, she won comfortably, with 60 percent or more of the vote. She defeated Tyler three times, even in 1998, after court rulings reshaped the district once again by adding 165,000 new constituents and shrinking the African-American majority by 7 percent, effectively dividing the district between black and white constituents. In 2000, the GOP ran Duane E. Kratzer, Jr., who managed just 33 percent of the vote to Clayton's 66 percent.

Clayton claimed her seat in the 102nd Congress on November 5, 1992, but did not receive committee assignments until the 103rd Congress convened in January 1993. She won spots on the Agriculture and Small Business committees. Clayton eventually became the Ranking Democratic Member on the Agriculture Committee's Operations, Oversight, Nutrition, and Forestry Subcommittee. Her Democratic colleagues also elected her the first woman president of the freshman class. In 1995, she was appointed to the Democratic Advisory Committee to formulate party strategy. In the 105th Congress (1997–1999) she dropped her Small Business assignment for a seat on the prestigious Budget Committee. Clayton was also assigned to the Social Security Task Force.

Clayton became a staunch defender of the rural and agricultural interests of her district, which comprised 20 counties with numerous peanut and tobacco growers. Along with Missouri Republican Jo Ann Emerson, she revived the Rural Caucus and rallied more than 100 Members to pledge continued federal aid to farmers, new rural jobs, and technology initiatives. In 1993 and 2000, respectively, Clayton voted against the North American Free Trade Agreement and Permanent Normal Trade Relations with China, insisting that both would adversely affect the agricultural industry and eliminate low-wage jobs from her district. "Must eastern North Carolina lose in order for the Research Triangle to win?" she asked, alluding to the state's booming high-tech corridor to the west of her district.[6] Although Clayton advocated smaller defense budgets, she remained supportive of naval contracts for projects at the nearby Newport News shipyards, which provided jobs for her constituents. From her seat on the Agriculture Committee—in contrast with many of her Democratic colleagues—Clayton supported extending tobacco subsidies to farmers at a time when critics attacked the program. "This is not about smoking," Clayton said. "This is about discriminating against the poorest of the poor of that industry. . . . They really are attacking the small farmer."[7] She also fought successfully to preserve Section 515 of the Agriculture Department's affordable housing program, which provided federal loans for multi-unit housing projects in rural areas.[8]

Clayton's district suffered a major natural disaster in 1999 when Hurricane Floyd dumped rains on the state, submerging parts of eastern North Carolina under 14 feet of water from swollen rivers. Clayton and other Members of the state delegation secured billions in relief aid. Clayton also obtained $1.5 million in federal money to reconstruct a dike along the Tar River in Princeville, one of the nation's first towns chartered by African Americans. She also assembled a volunteer force of more than 500 people, to help flood victims throughout eastern North Carolina.

As she gained seniority and prestige in the House, Clayton created a high profile for herself as an advocate for programs to help economically disadvantaged African Americans. Throughout her career, she stressed the importance of job training. "The issue of equity in jobs and fairness of opportunities is paramount," Clayton said.

"Job opportunities combined with a fair wage are key to strengthening families and communities and increasing our quality of life."[9] With fellow North Carolinian Mel Watt, Clayton, as chair of the Congressional Black Caucus Foundation, organized a campaign to help 1 million African Americans buy homes by 2005. In 1996 she also played a key part in fighting GOP efforts to cut summer job programs for young people. Declaring that she intended "to wake up" the House, Clayton said that the programs helped more than 615,000 youths in 650 cities and towns: "This is the first opportunity many of these young people have to get a job."[10]

In November 2001, Clayton declined to seek renomination to a sixth term in the House. She had been involved in intense bargaining with state legislators to ensure that her predominantly African-American district was "protected" during reapportionment after the 2000 Census. "My heart is leading me somewhere else," Clayton said. "I don't know exactly where that is, but I do want to have another opportunity for public service before I really hang it up."[11] Clayton was succeeded by an African-American, Frank Ballance, Jr., in the fall 2002 elections. After retiring in January 2003, Clayton returned to her home in Littleton, North Carolina.

FOR FURTHER READING

"Clayton, Eva M.," *Biographical Directory of the United States Congress, 1774–Present,* http://bioguide.congress.gov/scripts/biodisplay.pl?index=C000494.

MANUSCRIPT COLLECTION

Johnson C. Smith University, James B. Duke Memorial Library (Charlotte, NC). *Papers:* Eva Clayton's papers have not yet been processed.

NOTES

1   Rob Christensen, "Clayton to Retire in 2002," 21 November 2001, *Charlotte News and Observer*: A1.

2   Christensen, "Clayton to Retire in 2002."

3   Scott Mooneyham, "Clayton Announces She Will Retire From Congress," 20 November 2001, Associated Press.

4   Marian Burros, "Rep. Mom: Even in Washington's Watershed Year, Laundry Still Needs Doing," 20 June 1993, *Chicago Tribune*: woman news section, 12.

5   "Eva M. Clayton," Associated Press Candidate Biographies, 1998.

6   *Almanac of American Politics, 2002* (Washington, DC: National Journal Inc., 2001): 1139–1140.

7   *Politics in America, 2002* (Washington, DC: Congressional Quarterly Inc., 2001): 738–739.

8   *Current Biography, 2000* (New York: H. W. Wilson and Company, 2000): 121–124.

9   "Eva M. Clayton," *Contemporary Black Biography, 1998,* Volume 20 (Detroit, MI: Gale Research Inc., 1998).

10   "Congresswomen Lead Campaign for Summer Jobs for Black Youth," 15 April 1996, *Jet*: 39.

11   John Mercurio, "Going Home: Clayton Will Retire; But North Carolina Map Expected to Alter 1st District Only Slightly," 26 November 2001, *Roll Call*.

Cleo Fields
1962–

UNITED STATES REPRESENTATIVE ★ 1993–1997
DEMOCRAT FROM LOUISIANA

From an impoverished childhood, Cleo Fields rose to win a seat in the U.S. House of Representatives at age 29, serving as the youngest Member of the 103rd Congress (1993–1995). "Chills just went down my spine," Fields remarked about his swearing-in.[1] Yet the controversy over racial gerrymandering and the peculiarity of Louisiana's election law extinguished Fields's meteoric political career in the U.S. House after just two terms.

Born in Baton Rouge, Louisiana, on November 22, 1962, Cleo was one of 10 children of Isidore Fields, a dockworker, and Alice Fields, a maid. Isidore died after falling asleep behind the wheel of his car on his way home from working a double shift.[2] Poverty became a way of life for four-year-old Cleo, as the Fields household struggled to make ends meet. "I didn't know what poor was," Cleo Fields later recalled, "I thought mommas were supposed to put three patches in a pair of pants. In junior high school, it really hit me in the face. That's when I realized what my mother was going through."[3] At one point, the family was evicted from a Baton Rouge apartment. Throughout his youth, Fields worked several jobs to aid his family, taking a shift at a fast food restaurant and working at the Baton Rouge mayor's office of youth opportunity to save money for college. After graduating from McKinley High School in Baton Rouge, Fields attended cross-town Southern University, earning his bachelors and law degrees. Politics became his passion. In his early law school years, he began circulating bumper stickers to classmates that read, "I'm waiting for Cleo Fields." Fields noted, "I didn't know what office I would run for, so I didn't want to be too specific."[4]

During his final year of law school in 1986, Fields ran a grass-roots campaign for the Louisiana state senate. Without money to launch a campaign, he depended on student volunteers and the aid of his siblings to oust a well-entrenched incumbent. His eventual victory made the 24-year-old the youngest state legislator ever elected in Louisiana. Fields's slight, youthful build and five-foot, seven-inch frame were dwarfed by the round, tortoiseshell glasses that became his trademark. He once quipped to a crowd of voters, "I know I don't look like a man, but I am one."[5] While in the state legislature, Fields focused on environmental issues and economic opportunities for minorities. He also emerged as a leader in the war against illegal drugs. Fields married his high school sweetheart, Debra Horton. The couple had two sons, Cleo Brandon, born in 1995, and Christopher, born in 1998.

In 1990, Fields ran unsuccessfully against incumbent Republican Clyde Holloway for a U.S. House seat encompassing central Louisiana that included portions of the state capital, Baton Rouge. The district's population, which was 38 percent black, had voted for Democratic candidates in three of the past four presidential elections.[6] Fields was runner-up in the former open-party primary, unique to Louisiana, in which all the candidates from all the parties competed. If no candidate received more than 50 percent of the vote, the state held a runoff election between the top-two vote getters. The well-entrenched Holloway won decisively with 56 percent of the vote to Fields's 30 percent; there was no need for a runoff.

After the 1990 Census eliminated one U.S. House seat from Louisiana, Fields participated in the redistricting efforts from his state senate seat, helping to create an oddly shaped congressional district that he would seek to represent in 1992. The district hugged Louisiana's eastern border, jutting occasionally toward the central part of the state and forming a loose "Z" shape. It encompassed a large area, stretching east and west of Baton Rouge, north up the Mississippi River to the Arkansas border and west through Shreveport, taking in a wide mix of rural and urban communities, including parts of the state's five largest

cities and Louisiana State University. The state senate designed the district so that it would have a black majority (66 percent of the population), and registered Democrats outnumbered Republicans 8 to 1.[7] It was one of two black-majority districts in the state; Representative William Jefferson represented the other, which covered greater New Orleans. Fields received 48 percent of the vote, making him the top vote-getter, but he fell just short of the 50 percent needed to win outright. His nearest competitor, fellow African-American State Senator Charles (C. D.) Jones, took 14 percent. The two faced one another in a December runoff. Fields ran an energetic door-to-door campaign. He defeated Jones handily with 74 percent of the vote, emphasizing three goals he would advocate throughout his political career: creating jobs, lowering the cost of health care, and reducing the federal deficit.[8]

Fields's congressional colleagues recognized his service in the state senate by electing him parliamentarian of his freshman class. He was assigned to the Small Business Committee as well as the Banking, Finance, and Urban Affairs Committee. In 1995, Fields earned the highest marks in the Louisiana delegation for his liberal voting record, citing his support for gun control, abortion, and social spending.[9] He preferred to support the proposals put forth by the Democratic Congress and the President William J. (Bill) Clinton administration rather than take the lead on many legislative initiatives.

Fields was soon preoccupied with defending the borders of his district against several lawsuits. In April 1994, the federal court in Louisiana re-examined *Hays v. Louisiana*—a lawsuit that was previously filed by four of Fields's constituents who claimed Louisianans' voting rights were hindered by a racial "supermajority" in all the state's congressional districts. The court ruled that Fields's Z-shaped district was invalid and forced another reapportionment.[10] The new district resembled a wedge running between the northwest border of the state toward the center and Baton Rouge. The Representative's home remained within the district and the new borders still contained a majority-black population (58 percent). Not

satisfied, the same plaintiffs filed suit again. Only after the United States Supreme Court issued a stay in August did the 1994 election proceed with Fields running in the wedge-shaped district.[11] Fields won the open primary with 48 percent of the vote; he took the November 3 runoff with 74 percent over his 1992 opponent, Charles Jones.[12] However, his district lines changed four times between December 1993 and August 1994, distracting Fields from his legislative work. "For four years, I had one foot in the House and one foot across the street in the Supreme Court," Fields later recalled. "I was under a dark cloud the whole time I was up there. I never knew if I would be there the next day."[13] Fields blamed the political enemies he made during his years in the state senate for the relentless attacks on the boundaries of his district.[14]

In the midst of the battle to alter his district, Fields announced his candidacy for governor in 1995. Though Fields maintained the election was not about race, he quickly shored up as many black votes as possible.[15] In an open-primary field that was crowded with Democrats, Fields hoped his youth as well as his race would appeal to voters. Fields won 19 percent of the vote in the open primary, finishing as the runner-up to Republican Mike Foster—whose family had a history of service in the state and who switched party affiliation just weeks before the primary election. Fields lost the runoff vote—which was mostly divided on racial lines—taking only 36 percent of the vote.[16]

The final blow to Fields's congressional career came on January 5, 1996, when a U.S. District Court ruled that his wedge-shaped district was unconstitutional. Representing himself, Fields appealed the ruling to the U.S. Supreme Court; however, the state legislature—following the lead of the newly elected Governor Foster—adopted the plan in April 1996, despite Fields's plea to the statehouse.[17] The new lines, including a larger wedge running south from the northwest border through Shreveport, retained a substantial black voting bloc in the new district, but African Americans were no longer the majority. Also, Fields no longer lived in the district he was supposed to represent;

his Baton Rouge home ended up being within the same boundaries as House veteran Republican Richard Baker's residence.[18] Fields chose not to run against the very popular and well-entrenched Baker in 1996, further admitting that running in his former district would be "self-serving," as his home was no longer located there. "I don't want to leave the impression that I am bitter [about the apportionment battle]. I want people to know how honored I am," he told reporters, "Well, I got 17 percent of the white vote [in the governor's race]. For a then-33-year-old candidate like me to get 17 percent of the cross-over vote, I think that says there's a bright future ahead, a bright future."[19] Fields also was optimistic that the 2000 Census would gain Louisiana an extra House seat, noting that the loss of a seat following the 1990 Census did not account for large numbers of minority and low-income residents. However, Louisiana did not pick up a seat after the next census.

Though Fields debated running for an open U.S. Senate seat when Senator Bennett Johnston retired, he ultimately decided not to run, citing his decisive loss for governor.[20] Upon his departure, Fields pressed to eliminate the open-primary system that had been in place in Louisiana since 1978. He also was active in the 1996 presidential campaign, serving as a senior advisor on the Clinton–Gore re-election campaign. In 1997, he took an appointment in Vice President Al Gore's office directing a federal program that awarded grants and economic incentives to impoverished communities, classified as "empowerment zones" and "enterprise communities," each receiving a different level of federal aid.[21] Several of these zones were located in Fields's former Louisiana district.

Fields returned to the state senate in a special election in December 1997, serving simultaneously with his younger brother, Wilson.[22] Fields also began hosting a weekly radio program in Baton Rouge, called "Cleo Live," which drew prominent black politicians as guests, and he opened a law practice. Fields later admitted, "The more I get into my law practice, the less appealing returning to Congress becomes. It's been one of the most productive things I've done with my life." But, he also conceded, "When I was in Congress, I thought it was the greatest job in the world."[23]

FOR FURTHER READING

"Fields, Cleo" *Biographical Directory of the United States Congress, 1774–Present*, http://bioguide.congress.gov/scripts/biodisplay.pl?index=F000110.

NOTES

1   Joan McKinney, "'There's A Bright Future Ahead': Rep. Cleo Fields Plans to Rest, Get a Job—And Return to Office," 1 December 1996, *The Advocate* (Baton Rouge, LA): 1A.

2   Gwendolyn Thompkins, "Cleo Fields Reaching for the Mountaintop After a Tough Climb," 13 September 1995, *Times-Picayune* (New Orleans, LA): A1.

3   "Cleo Fields," *Contemporary Black Biography*, Volume 13 (Detroit, MI: Gale Research Inc., 1996).

4   Thompkins, "Cleo Fields Reaching for the Mountaintop After a Tough Climb."

5   Ibid.

6   *Politics in America, 1990* (Washington, DC: Congressional Quarterly Inc., 1989): 629.

7   *Politics in America, 1994* (Washington, DC: Congressional Quarterly Inc., 1993): 650.

8   "Election Statistics, 1920 to Present," available at http://clerk.house.gov/member_info/electionInfo/index.html.

9   Bruce Alpert, "Fields' Focus Earns Praise From Liberals," 29 October 1995, *Times-Picayune* (New Orleans, LA): A1.

10 Richard L. Engstrom and Jason F. Kirksey, "Race and Representational Districting in Louisiana," in Bernard Grofman ed., *Race And Redistricting In The 1990s* (New York: Agathon Press, 1998): 229–265; *Congressional Quarterly Almanac, 1993* (Washington, DC: Congressional Quarterly Inc., 1994): 22-A–23-A; *Congressional Quarterly Almanac, 1994* (Washington, DC: Congressional Quarterly Inc., 1995): 591–592.

11 Engstrom and Kirksey, "Race and Representational Districting in Louisiana:" 256, 259.

12 Michael J. Dubin et al., *U.S. Congressional Elections, 1788–1997* (Jefferson, NC: McFarland & Company, Inc., Publishers, 1998): 779.

13 John Mercurio, "Return Engagement? Ex-Rep. Fields Plotting Political Comeback," 8 June 2000, *Roll Call*.

14 Mercurio, "Return Engagement? Ex-Rep. Fields Plotting Political Comeback."

15 Tyler Bridges, "Jefferson Joins Race, Is Pitted With Fields," 9 February 1995, *Times-Picayune* (New Orleans, LA).

16 *Congressional Quarterly Almanac, 1995* (Washington, DC: Congressional Quarterly Inc., 1996): 12-5.

17 *Congressional Quarterly Almanac, 1995*: 12-5; Jack Wardlaw and Ed Anderson, "Black District Realignment OK'd," 29 March 1996, *Times-Picayune* (New Orleans, LA).

18 *Congressional Quarterly Almanac, 1996* (Washington, DC: Congressional Quarterly Inc., 1997): 11–37.

19 McKinney, "'There's A Bright Future Ahead': Rep. Cleo Fields Plans to Rest, Get a Job—And Return to Office."

20 "Black Congressman In Louisiana Decides To Skip Senate Bid," 13 July 1996, *New York Times*: 7.

21 Joan McKinney, "Fields Set To Begin Fed Work," 28 March 1997, *The Advocate* (Baton Rouge, LA).

22 "Senator Cleo Fields—District 14," *Louisiana State Senate*, at http://senate.legis.state.la.us/FieldsC/biography.asp (accessed 7 March 2007).

23 Mercurio, "Return Engagement? Ex-Rep. Fields Plotting Political Comeback."

"For four years, I had one
foot in the House and one
foot across the street in the
Supreme Court,"
Fields later recalled.
"I was under a dark cloud
the whole time I was up there.
I never knew if I would be
there the next day."

Earl Frederick Hilliard
1942–

UNITED STATES REPRESENTATIVE ★ 1993–2003
DEMOCRAT FROM ALABAMA

Earl Hilliard's long career in the state legislature catapulted him into Congress—making him the first black Representative from Alabama since Jeremiah Haralson left office during Reconstruction. "We have not had a voice in 117 years," Hilliard declared upon his first election. "I will be able to articulate the views and opinions of a group that hasn't had representation in a very long time."[1]

Earl Frederick Hilliard was born in Birmingham, Alabama, on April 9, 1942, to Iola Frazier and William Hilliard. Hilliard grew up in a segregated society and chose to attend traditionally black colleges. While a student at Morehouse College in Atlanta, Georgia, Hilliard met Dr. Martin Luther King, Jr. The meeting had a powerful effect on him, as Hilliard vowed to become "one of King's foot soldiers in the war for racial equality."[2] After receiving a B.A. from Morehouse in 1964, Hilliard received a J.D. at Howard University Law School in Washington, DC, in 1967. In 1970, he received a M.B.A. at Atlanta University in Georgia. He married Mary Franklin in 1967, and the couple had two children: Alesia and Earl, Jr.

Hilliard began his career in elective politics when he won a campaign for a seat in the Alabama state house of representatives in 1975. In 1980, he was elected to the state senate. Hilliard's senate career focused on helping the urban poor, who constituted the bulk of his Birmingham-area constituents. He also earned a reputation as a hard-fighting, tactical legislator.[3] In 1991, Hilliard declared bankruptcy after a deal to sell a radio station he owned fell through.[4] However, he thought his experience would benefit him as a legislator. "The bankruptcy gave me a chance to pay people back in an orderly manner," he noted. "I'm able to understand what it is not to be able to pay obligations."[5]

In 1992, redistricting gave the Alabama legislature a chance to create a single black-majority U.S. congressional district in a state that had not sent an African American to Congress since Reconstruction. The west-central district stretched primarily from the Mississippi–Alabama border through Selma to Montgomery. The district went as far north as Tuscaloosa, with a small offshoot through Jefferson County to Birmingham. Montgomery and Birmingham made up the bulk of the urban population; however, the rest of the district's boundaries included the poor, rural areas of the black belt and the old cotton-growing regions. The district's three major cities—Selma, Montgomery, and Birmingham—were battlegrounds at the heart of the 1960s civil rights movement. All the candidates in the Republican and the Democratic primaries were black, but because the district was overwhelmingly Democratic, a primary victory would be tantamount to winning the general election.[6] Hilliard ran an arduous campaign to win the nomination. He faced a crowded field of six candidates in his June 2 primary, the favorite being Hank Sanders of Selma, a fellow state senator.[7] The two squared off on issues of health care and job creation. Hilliard prevailed with 31 percent of the vote versus Sanders's 24 percent, sending the two into a runoff election.[8] Hilliard narrowly defeated Sanders with 51 percent of the vote in the August runoff. The following November, Hilliard defeated Republican Kervin Jones, a black Tuscaloosa farmer, with 70 percent of the vote. In his next four re-election bids, Hilliard won at least 71 percent of the vote, running unopposed in 1998.[9] He initially took assignments on the Agriculture and Small Business committees. In 1997, he traded the Small Business post for a seat on the International Relations Committee. An active member of the Congressional Black Caucus, Hilliard was elected vice chairman of the organization for the 105th Congress (1997–1999).

Hilliard's initial focus in Congress was creating economic opportunity for his constituents. He attempted

to protect and expand the Alabama military installations used by the U.S. Army and the National Aeronautics and Space Administration, suggesting that closing American military bases in Germany and Japan so that more funding would be available for domestic military installations.[10] He also worked to protect a Tuscaloosa-area airport that was difficult to sustain because of the region's sparse population. Its only airline threatened to leave in 1995 and Hilliard feared the loss of the airport would hurt business growth in the region. "Tuscaloosa and the surrounding communities would suffer terribly without local air service, and this travel option will become increasingly important as industrial development continues in the area," he wrote to a colleague.[11] Due in large part to Hilliard's lobbying, the House and Senate Appropriations committees diverted limited funding to Tuscaloosa in the Essential Air Service legislation.[12] Hilliard also was crucial in convincing a Korean-based car manufacturer to open a plant outside Montgomery. At the plant's groundbreaking ceremony in April 2002, he was a featured speaker.[13]

Hilliard attempted to assist the rural regions of his district by submitting legislation to establish a Southern Rural Development Commission, which he modeled on the Appalachian Regional Commission. The purpose of the commission was to dispense federal money to projects enhancing economic development, improving health care, and offering job training. The new commission would cover the "black belt" or agricultural region of 10 southern states; however, the measure died in committee.[14] Hilliard also offered creative legislation to help his poor farming constituents, asking to add rabbit to the list of meats that were federally inspected. Hoping federal safety inspections would increase rabbit's popularity among consumers, Hilliard speculated that his constituents could breed the animals to produce the meat quickly and cheaply.[15]

Hilliard's frequent foreign travel as a member of the International Relations (later Foreign Affairs) Committee garnered national attention.[16] In August 1997, he made an unauthorized trip to Libya. The State Department had banned American travel to Libya with a U.S. passport as well as any business and financial transactions with the country since sanctions were imposed in 1986 and Libya was declared a terrorist state. The State Department warned that traveling to the country was "contrary to U.S. policy" and was unaware that Hilliard had made the trip until he returned to the United States.[17] On September 26, International Relations Committee Chairman Ben Gilman of New York announced that the committee would review Hilliard's actions in Libya and inquire whether he had broken any laws.[18] The Committee on Standards of Official Conduct eventually took up the case at the end of September.[19]

In cooperation with the investigation, Hilliard revealed that a Swiss company headed by a wealthy Tunisian businessman that dealt in crude oil had paid nearly $5,000 for Hilliard's trip to Tunisia and Libya from August 21 to 25.[20] Hilliard claimed he went to Libya to investigate how American money was being spent abroad. "The majority of our foreign aid is spent in the Middle Eastern region between Egypt and other north African countries," Hilliard explained. "[Libya] was a country I had not been to, and I had the opportunity to go this time and I went." He noted that his trip was an attempt to "develop channels for dialogue" with the Muslim world.[21] In a letter to his constituents, Hilliard noted that he did not use his American passport to enter the country and that he did not spend any money, which was later confirmed by the U.S. Treasury Department.[22] The Standards Committee agreed with the Treasury Department's assessment and dropped the case against Hilliard in the middle of November.[23]

On December 3, 1997, a Capitol Hill newspaper published a two-part story that Hilliard had broken several House rules related to campaign staffing and financing.[24] On June 20, 2001, the Committee on Standards of Official Conduct issued a written rebuke of Hilliard's actions. By signing an agreement admitting to the violations, he received the least severe punishment the committee could administer: a three-page letter outlining the violations, signed by the committee's Chairman and Ranking Member.[25]

In the 2002 election, Hilliard faced a previous opponent, Artur Davis. The Harvard-educated Davis, a former assistant district attorney, returned to challenge the incumbent with greater Democratic support. He accused Hilliard of doing little for the district in his decade in office. Moreover, a slight change in district lines added more voters from counties that favored Davis and eliminated two counties that primarily favored Hilliard.[26] Hilliard narrowly edged out Davis in the early June primary, 46 to 43 percent, resulting in a runoff election.[27] But Davis overcame his earlier deficit to win the runoff against Hilliard on June 25, 56 percent to 44 percent. Hilliard returned to his law firm in Birmingham after his loss.

FOR FURTHER READING

"Hilliard, Earl Frederick," *Biographical Directory of the United States Congress, 1774–Present*, http://bioguide. congress.gov/scripts/biodisplay.pl?index=H000621.

NOTES

1   "Earl F. Hilliard," January 1993, *Ebony Magazine*.

2   *Politics in America, 2002* (Washington, DC: Congressional Quarterly Inc., 2001): 19.

3   *Politics in America, 1994* (Washington, DC: Congressional Quarterly Inc., 1993): 38; "Earl Frederick Hilliard," Associated Press Candidate Biographies, 1996.

4   Joe Nabbefeld, "Hilliard Liable for Debts Totaling $528,098, Records Show," 5 September 1993, *Birmingham News* (AL).

5   "Earl Frederick Hilliard," Associated Press Candidate Biographies, 1996.

6   David Pace, "Birthplace of Voting Rights Movement Getting First Black Congressman," 28 May 1992, Associated Press.

7   *Politics in America, 2002:* 20; "House Race Briefings: Featured Tuesday Primaries: AL 07," 29 May 1992, *The Hotline*; Robert B. McNeil, "Earl Hilliard Reports Spending $189,097 to Win Democratic Nomination," 20 July 1992, States News Service.

8   Tim Curran, "Alabama Runoffs Tuesday Decide Edreich Foe, Demo Nominee to Succeed Dickinson," 25 June 1992, *Roll Call*.

9   "Election Statistics, 1920 to Present," available at http://clerk. house.gov/member_info/election.html.

10   Robert Dunnavant, "Hilliard Backs Space Station Development," 27 April 1993, *Birmingham News*.

11   Mike Zapler, "Hilliard Changes Strategy on Airline Service, Targeting Callahan," 12 October 1995, State News Service.

12   Mike Zapler, "Tuscaloosa's Airline Service Spared," 26 October 1995, State News Service.

13   Mary Orndorff, "Hilliard Says, 'I Vote For The Working People,'" 23 May 2002, *Birmingham News*.

14   Michael Brumas, "Hilliard Proposes New Agency to Help South's Rural Poor," 25 January 1994, *Birmingham News*; see H.R. 3901, 103rd Cong., 2nd sess.

15 *Politics in America, 2002*: 19.

16 "Hilliard Says All Trips Were Official Business," 25 May 1995, *Birmingham News*.

17 Michael Brumas, "Hilliard Visits Off-Limits Libya State Department Says He Wasn't Acting On Its Behalf," 17 September 1997, *Birmingham News*.

18 David Pace, "Rep. Hilliard's Libya Trip Examined," 26 September 1997, Associated Press.

19 Jock Friedly, "Hilliard Trip to Libya Sponsored by Wealthy Tunisian Businessman," 1 October 1997, *The Hill*.

20 Michael Brumas, "Hilliard Confirms Traveling to Libya," 27 September 1997, *Birmingham News*.

21 Michael Brumas, "Hilliard: Libya Trip Attempt at 'Dialogue,'" 30 September 1997, *Birmingham News*.

22 Michael Brumas, "Treasury: Hilliard Trip to Libya OK 'No Indication of a Violation,'" 1 October 1997, *Birmingham News*; Val Walton, "Hilliard: Libya Trip Broke No Law," 29 September 1997, *Birmingham News*.

23 In April 1999, Hilliard claimed partial credit when Libyan officials handed over two suspects from the bombing of a Pan-Am commercial flight over Lockerbie, Scotland, in 1988. When the suspects went on trial at the International Criminal Court at The Hague, the Netherlands, in 2000, Hilliard boasted, "I'm telling you that [the trial] never would have happened had I not interceded." See Michael Brumas, "Hilliard Says He Helped Get Libya to Hand Over Suspects," 9 April 1999, *Birmingham News*; Michael Brumas, "Hilliard: Stepping on Toes Makes Him a Target," 16 May 2000, *Birmingham News*.

24 The newspaper's initial allegations are documented in Jock Friedly, "Hilliard's Finances Indicate Possible Violations of Federal Law," 3 December 1997, *The Hill*; Jock Friedly, "Hilliard Campaign Boosted His Business," 3 December 1997, *The Hill*. Hilliard had previously come under fire after a federal campaign report revealed that he paid more than $17,000 from his campaign funds to his family members in his 1992 campaign. Hilliard justified the payouts, noting that his family members worked for his campaign. See Michael Brumas, "Hilliard Pays Family With Campaign Cash," 5 August 1993, *Birmingham News*.

25 See Committee on Standards of Official Conduct history of disciplinary actions at http://www.house.gov/ethics/Historical_Chart_Final_Version.htm; Juliet Eilperin, "House Ethics Panel Launches Probe of Rep. Hilliard's Business Dealings," 29 January 1998, *Roll Call*; Michael Brumas, "Capitol Hill Paper Hits Hilliard Dealings, He Calls It GOP Attempt 'To Discredit Me,'" 4 December 1997, *Birmingham News*; Michael Brumas, "House Probe Set Off Hilliard's Finances," 24 September 1999, *Birmingham News*; Michael Brumas, "GOP Blamed for Probe Hilliard's Attorney Cites Ethics Committee Chairman," 25 September, *Birmingham News*; Philip Shenon, "House Panel Reprimands a Democrat on Finances," 22 June 2001, *New York Times*: A1; Juliet Eilperin, "House Ethics Panel Rebukes Hilliard for Funds Misuse," 22 June 2001, *Washington Post*: A7; Mary Orndorff, "Hilliard Takes Ethics Slap in Stride," 25 June 2001, *Birmingham News*.

26 John Mercurio, "Sweet Home; Hilliard Could Be Hurt by Remap in Alabama," 31 January 2002, *Roll Call*.

27 Mary Orndorff, "Hilliard Fights for Political Life Against Davis," 6 June 2002, *Birmingham News*.

"We have not had a voice in 117 years," Hilliard declared upon his election as the first black Representative from Alabama since Jeremiah Haralson left office during Reconstruction. "I will be able to articulate the views and opinions of a group that hasn't had representation in a very long time."

Cynthia Ann McKinney
1955–

UNITED STATES REPRESENTATIVE ★ 1993–2003; 2005–2007
DEMOCRAT FROM GEORGIA

The first African-American woman from Georgia to serve in Congress, Cynthia McKinney was elected to the U.S. House of Representatives in 1992. With a résumé that included graduate work in international relations, Representative McKinney's background fit her service on the Armed Services and International Relations committees, where she addressed human rights issues. The outspoken Representative, who sometimes held polarizing views on key foreign policy issues, lost her re-election bid in 2002. Two years later, voters in her DeKalb County-centered district returned her to the House for a single term, making her one of a handful of Congresswomen who served nonconsecutive terms.

Cynthia Ann McKinney was born on March 17, 1955, in Atlanta, Georgia, to Leola Christion McKinney, a nurse, and James Edward (Billy) McKinney, a police officer, civil rights activist, and longtime legislator in the Georgia house of representatives. Joining the Atlanta police department in 1948, Billy McKinney was one of its first African-American officers. Cynthia McKinney's participation in demonstrations with her father inspired her to enter politics.[1] While protesting the conviction of Tommy Lee Hines, a mentally handicapped black man charged with raping a white woman in Alabama, McKinney and other protestors were threatened by the Ku Klux Klan. "That was probably my day of awakening," McKinney recalled. "That day, I experienced hatred for the first time. I learned that there really are people who hate me without even knowing me. . . . That was when I knew that politics was going to be something I would do."[2] McKinney graduated from St. Joseph High School and, in 1978, earned a B.A. in international relations from the University of Southern California. She later pursued graduate studies at the Fletcher School of Law and Diplomacy at Tufts University in Medford, Massachusetts. In 1984 she served as a diplomatic fellow at Spelman College in Atlanta. She then taught political science at Agnes Scott College in Decatur and at Clark Atlanta University. Cynthia McKinney married Coy Grandison, a Jamaican politician. The couple had a son, Coy, Jr., before divorcing.

In 1986, Billy McKinney registered his daughter without her knowledge as a candidate for the Georgia state house of representatives. She lost that race to the incumbent but, without even campaigning, won 20 percent of the vote based on name recognition. In 1988, McKinney won election as an at-large state representative in the Georgia legislature, defeating Herb Mabry, who would later head the state AFL-CIO.[3] The McKinneys became the first father–daughter combination to serve concurrently in the same state legislature.[4] McKinney's father expected her to be a close political ally, but he was soon confronted with his daughter's independent style. "He thought he was going to have another vote," she recalled, "but once I got there, we disagreed on everything . . . I was a chip off the old block, a maverick."[5]

During the late 1980s, McKinney and other Georgia legislators pressed the U.S. Justice Department to create additional majority-black congressional districts so that African-American voters would have more equitable representation. In 1992, the Georgia legislature created two additional majority-black districts (Georgia already had one) and McKinney chose to run in the sprawling 260-mile-long district that included much of DeKalb County east of Atlanta to Augusta and extended southward to the coastal city of Savannah, encompassing or cutting through 22 counties.[6] The district took in a diverse mix of constituents, ranging from inhabitants of inner cities to the residents of outlying communities in agricultural counties. McKinney moved into the new district, and her father managed her campaign. In the five-way Democratic

primary, McKinney used a strong grassroots network to place first, with 31 percent of the vote.[7] In a runoff against second-place finisher George DeLoach—a funeral home director and the former mayor of Waynesboro, Georgia—McKinney won with 54 percent of the vote.[8] In the heavily Democratic district, she won election to the 103rd Congress (1993–1995), with 73 percent of the vote, against her Republican opponent, Woodrow Lovett. Reflecting on an election that propelled record numbers of women and African Americans into congressional office, McKinney said shortly afterward, "Now we have people in Congress who are like the rest of America. It's wonderful to have ordinary people making decisions about the lives of ordinary Americans. It brings a level of sensitivity that has not been there."[9]

When McKinney was sworn in to the 103rd Congress in January 1993, she received assignments on the Committee on Agriculture and the Committee on Foreign Affairs (later named International Relations). Over the next several Congresses she received membership on several other panels. In the 104th Congress (1995–1997) she won a seat on the Banking and Finance Committee, where she served two terms. In the 105th Congress (1997–1999) Representative McKinney was assigned to the National Security Committee (later renamed Armed Services).

Representative McKinney quickly became known by her unconventional attire, including her trademark pair of gold tennis shoes and her Mickey Mouse watch. Shortly after she entered the House in 1993, one reporter described McKinney as possessing "uncommon poise and a decidedly unpinstriped wardrobe."[10] A member of the largest class of freshman women in congressional history, McKinney also was part of a newly elected vanguard of black Congresswomen, many from the South, who emerged from state legislatures onto the national political scene.[11] Her devotion to work and her courage to stand up against the traditions of the mostly male institution impressed colleagues. "She's not a showboat, she's a workhorse," observed Representative Patricia Schroeder of Colorado, employing a term commonly used to describe Members

who work tirelessly behind the scenes. "She stands up to the old bulls, and is very strong in everything she does," Schroeder added.[12]

McKinney's confrontational legislative style, cultivated since her days as a state legislator, was congruous with her distinctive attire. In January 1991, she delivered a blistering speech attacking the first Gulf War and President George H. W. Bush: two-thirds of the legislators in the Georgia statehouse left the chamber after McKinney derided the military action as "the most inane use of American will that I have witnessed in a very long time." She added, "America must be willing to fight injustice and prejudice at home as effectively as America is ready to take up arms to fight 'naked aggression' in the international arena."[13] In 1995, she infuriated newly installed House Republican leaders when she suggested that an independent counsel investigate Speaker Newt Gingrich of Georgia for violating the chamber's gift rules because he accepted free air time on cable television to broadcast a college course.[14] In 2000, McKinney accused then-Vice President Al Gore of having a "low Negro tolerance level" for not having more African Americans on his security detail. She later claimed the remark was part of a draft press release not intended for public distribution, though she did press the William J. (Bill) Clinton administration to investigate charges of discrimination in the Secret Service.[15]

Representative McKinney also displayed a readiness to speak out on issues ranging from human rights abuses abroad to social inequities at home. As an advocate for poor and working-class Americans, McKinney opposed federal efforts to restrict abortions—particularly a long-standing measure known as the Hyde Amendment that largely eliminated Medicaid coverage for abortions. In a debate on the House Floor, McKinney described the amendment as "nothing but a discriminatory policy against poor women, who happen to be disproportionately black."[16]

A court challenge shortly after McKinney's 1994 re-election (with 66 percent of the vote) placed her at the epicenter of a national debate over the constitutionality of minority-conscious redistricting. Five voters from the rural parts of her district (including her former opponent in the Democratic primary, George DeLoach) filed a suit claiming they had been disfranchised because the state drew "an illegally gerrymandered district to benefit black voters," as one critic noted. McKinney claimed she had made great efforts to reach out to her rural constituents but that her entreaties had been met with "resistance" or "silence."[17] A U.S. Supreme Court decision in 1995 invalidated Georgia's congressional district map as a "racial gerrymander" that violated the 14th Amendment's guarantee of equal protection under the law. A panel of federal judges from three courts remapped the district before the 1996 elections, and the black population of McKinney's district dropped from 64 percent to about 33 percent. Although McKinney was forced to run in a majority-white district, the loyal political network that figured heavily in her previous campaigns helped her prevail against Republican challenger John M. Mitnick, with 58 percent of the vote.[18] McKinney won her two subsequent re-election bids by comfortable margins of about 60 percent. Reapportionment in 2002 placed McKinney in a district that again was predominantly African American (roughly 53 percent of the population).[19]

On the International Relations Committee, where she eventually served as the Ranking Member on the International Operations and Human Rights Subcommittee, McKinney tried to curb weapons sales to countries that violated human rights—sponsoring the Arms Transfers Code of Conduct, which passed the House in 1997, to prevent the sale of weapons to dictators. In 1999, she partnered with a Republican colleague to insert a similar provision into a State Department reauthorization bill. A year later, she voted against granting full trade relations with China, citing Beijing's poor human rights record. McKinney frequently challenged American foreign policy during this period, including the 1999 bombing campaign in Kosovo, long-standing U.S. sanctions against Iraq, and much of U.S. policy in the Middle East.

Representative McKinney's actions after the September 11, 2001, terrorist attacks caused her political difficulty. First, she offered to accept a check from a wealthy Saudi prince after then-New York City Mayor Rudolph W. Giuliani rejected it because the prince said the September 11 attacks were a response to U.S. policies in the Middle East.[20] Then, in a 2002 radio interview, McKinney suggested that officials in the George W. Bush administration had prior knowledge about the attacks but remained silent because they stood to gain financially from military spending in the aftermath of the attacks. Alluding to the still-contentious recount of votes in Florida in 2000, and the Supreme Court ruling that resulted in the Republican presidency, McKinney said, "an administration of questionable legitimacy has been given unprecedented power."[21] At a time when much of the nation was supportive of the administration in the wake of the September 11 attacks, McKinney's comments were met with a torrent of criticism.[22]

In the 2002 primary McKinney faced a little-known newcomer to electoral politics, Denise Majette. An African American and a former state judge, Majette ran on a platform contrasting her moderation and centrism with McKinney's rhetoric, which Majette's campaign implied had gone too far. Majette achieved a two-to-one advantage in campaign funding, raising another issue when it became evident that national Jewish and Muslim groups were funding Majette and McKinney, respectively.[23] In the August 20, 1992, primary, Majette prevailed by a 58 to 42 percent margin and went on to win the general election.

Two years later, when Majette made an ultimately unsuccessful bid for the U.S. Senate, McKinney entered the race to reclaim her old congressional seat. Benefitting from a divided Democratic field in the party primary, she won the nomination with 54 percent of the vote. McKinney ran an understated campaign that steered clear of extensive media coverage and, as in her earlier runs for Congress, relied on a vigorous grass-roots effort. In the general election, for the 109th Congress (2005–2007), McKinney won easily, with 64 percent of the vote against

Republican candidate Catherine Davis.[24] McKinney regained her assignment on the Armed Services Committee and also received a seat on the Budget Committee.

In late March 2006, McKinney allegedly hit a Capitol Hill police officer who stopped her at the entrance to one of the House office buildings and asked for identification. McKinney claimed she was a victim of racial profiling and, according to news accounts, described the police officer who stopped her as "racist." A grand jury investigated the incident but declined to indict McKinney.[25] Noting that McKinney's base of support in her predominantly African-American district remained strong, pundits predicted her renomination. Yet in the July 18, 2006, Democratic primary, DeKalb County Commissioner Hank Johnson, Jr., an African-American lawyer whose simple campaign message was "Replace McKinney," held the incumbent to just 47 percent of the vote (Johnson received 45 percent). Short of the majority required by state law, McKinney was forced into a runoff. Johnson prevailed by a 59 to 41 percent margin, garnering 60 percent of the vote in McKinney's former stronghold in DeKalb County.[26]

After leaving the House in January 2007, McKinney remained active in national politics. In December 2007 she announced her candidacy as the Green Party nominee for the 2008 presidential election.[27]

FOR FURTHER READING

"McKinney, Cynthia Ann," *Biographical Directory of the U.S. Congress, 1774–Present*, http://bioguide.congress.gov/scripts/biodisplay.pl?index=M000523.

NOTES

1   Kim Masters, "The Woman in the Hot Seat: Rep. Cynthia McKinney Just Lost Her District and She Wants It Back," 5 July 1995, *Washington Post*: C1.

2   Masters, "The Woman in the Hot Seat."

3   Steve Harvey, "The 11th District: Charm Mixed with Savvy— McKinney Has Made Meteoric Rise in Politics," 13 August 1992, *Atlanta Journal and Constitution*: B4.

4   *Current Biography, 1996* (New York: H. W. Wilson and Company, 1996): 353.

5   *Current Biography, 1996*: 353.

6   Ibid.; Harvey, "The 11th District: Charm Mixed with Savvy— McKinney Has Made Meteoric Rise in Politics."

7   Kristine F. Anderson, "Georgia House Race May Be a First," 14 September 1992, *Christian Science Monitor*: 8.

8   Steve Harvey, "Election '92: 11th District—McKinney Captures Victory Over DeLoach," 12 August 1992, *Atlanta Journal and Constitution*: D4.

9   Anne Janette Johnson, "Cynthia Ann McKinney," *Contemporary Black Biography* Volume 11 (Detroit, MI: Gale Research Inc., 1996) (hereinafter referred to as *CBB*).

10   Maureen Dowd, "Growing Sorority in Congress Edges Into the Ol' Boys' Club," 5 March 1993, *New York Times*: A1.

11   Marcia Gelbart, "Lifelong Civil Rights Advocate Watches as Supreme Court Decides Her Fate," 8 March 1995, *The Hill*.

12 Gelbart, "Lifelong Civil Rights Advocate Watches as Supreme Court Decides Her Fate."

13 "War Debate Lights Spark in State House; Aiding the Enemy or Laying Out the Facts?" 19 January 1991, *Atlanta Journal and Constitution*: A19; Rhonda Cook and Brian O'Shea, "A Day of Anguish, Prayers; In House, Legislator Lashes Out at Bush; Others Walk Out on Her," 18 January 1991, *Atlanta Journal and Constitution*: D1; Johnson, "Cynthia Ann McKinney," *CBB*.

14 Katharine Q. Seelye, "Ethics Panel Needs Weeks on Gingrich," 24 February 1995, *New York Times*: A14.

15 "Cynthia McKinney," 6 November 2004, *National Journal*: 3363–3364; *Politics in America, 2002* (Washington, DC: Congressional Quarterly Inc., 2001): 266.

16 *Current Biography, 1996*: 353; Masters, "The Woman in the Hot Seat."

17 Masters, "The Woman in the Hot Seat"; Rhonda Cook, "Redistricting: The Ruling's Impact," 1 July 1995, *Atlanta Journal and Constitution*: 12A. For an analysis of the larger phenomenon of court challenges to racially gerrymandered congressional districts in the 1990s, see David T. Canon, *Race, Redistricting, and Representation: The Unintended Consequences of Black Majority Districts* (Chicago, IL: The University of Chicago Press, 1999).

18 *Politics in America, 2002*: 267; "Election Statistics, 1920 to Present," available at http://clerk.house.gov/member_info/electionInfo/index.html.

19 "Election Statistics, 1920 to Present," available at http://clerk.house.gov/member_info/electionInfo/index.html; *Almanac of American Politics, 2002* (Washington, DC: National Journal Inc., 2001): 444; *Politics in America, 2004* (Washington, DC: Congressional Quarterly Inc., 2003): 277.

20 Betsy Rothstein, "Rep. McKinney: An In-Your-Face Crusader," 16 January 1992, *The Hill*: 1.

21 Juliet Eilperin, "Democrat Implies Sept. 11 Administration Plot," 12 April 2002, *Washington Post*: A16; *Politics in America, 2004*: 266.

22 Betsy Rothstein, "McKinney Feels Vindicated by Democratic Criticism of Bush," 22 May 2002, *The Hill*: 22.

23 Darryl Fears, "Rhetoric Haunts McKinney in Ga.: Sept. 11 Remarks Lift Little-Known Rival's Campaign," 19 August 2002, *Washington Post*: A2; Lauren W. Whittington and Chris Cillizza, "On the Move: McKinney Challenger Levels Financial Playing Field," 12 August 2002, *Roll Call*: 8. See also Thomas B. Edsall, "Questions Raised About Donors to Georgia Lawmaker's Campaign," 13 August 2002, *Washington Post*: A2; Thomas B. Edsall, "Impact of McKinney Loss Worries Some Democrats: Tension Between Blacks, Jews a Concern," 22 August 2002, *Washington Post*: A4.

24 "Georgia 4th District: Cynthia McKinney," 6 November 2004, *National Journal*: 3363–3364.

25 Eric M. Weiss and Petula Dvorak, "Indictment Rejected for Rep. McKinney; Police Union to Study Legal Options," 17 June 2006, *Washington Post*: B4; Karen Juanita Carrillo, "Grand Jury: No Indictment Against McKinney," 22 June 2006, *New York Amsterdam News*: 4; "Grand Jury Convened to Consider Charges Against McKinney," 6 April 2006, *The Frontrunner*; Josephine Hearn and Jonathan E. Kaplan, "McKinney in Fracas With Officer," 30 March 2006, *The Hill*: 1.

26 Rachel Kapochunas, "McKinney Likely to Survive Primary Despite Police Incident," 11 July 2006, *Congressional Quarterly Today*; Jonathan Weisman, "House Incumbents McKinney, Schwarz Fall in Primaries," 9 August 2006, *Washington Post*: A5.

27 Jeffry Scott, "McKinney to Run for President?" 17 October 2007, *Atlanta Journal-Constitution*: 3B; Jeffry Scott, "McKinney Takes Her Longest Shot," 24 December 2007, *Atlanta Journal-Constitution*: 1A.

Carrie P. Meek
1926–

UNITED STATES REPRESENTATIVE ★ 1993–2003
DEMOCRAT FROM FLORIDA

Carrie P. Meek won election to the House in 1992 as one of the first African-American lawmakers to represent Florida in Congress since Reconstruction. Focusing on the economic and immigration issues of her district, Meek secured a coveted seat on the House Appropriations Committee as a freshman Representative. While able to work with Republicans on health issues, she sharply criticized welfare reform efforts during the mid-1990s.

Carrie Pittman, the daughter of Willie and Carrie Pittman, was born on April 29, 1926, in Tallahassee, Florida. Her grandmother was born and raised in Georgia as a slave. Carrie Pittman's parents began their married life as sharecroppers, though her father later became a caretaker and her mother a laundress and the owner of a boarding house. Nicknamed "Tot" by her siblings, Carrie was the youngest of 12 children, and a tomboy. The Pittman family lived near the old Florida capitol in a neighborhood called the "Bottom." Carrie Pittman starred in track and field while earning a bachelor of science degree in biology and physical education at Florida A&M University in Tallahassee in 1946. She enrolled at the University of Michigan graduate school because blacks were banned from Florida graduate schools, though the state government would pay her out-of-state tuition "if we agreed to get out of Dodge," she later recalled.[1] She graduated in 1948 with an M.S. degree in public health and physical education. Afterward, Pittman taught at Bethune Cookman, a historically black college in Daytona Beach, where she coached basketball and taught biological sciences and physical education. She later taught at Florida A&M. In 1961, as a divorcée with two young children, Carrie Pittman Meek moved to Miami-Dade Community College, where she spent the next three decades teaching and administrating, eventually serving as a special assistant

to the vice president of the college. In 1978, she won election to the Florida state house of representatives, defeating 12 candidates. She served from 1979 to 1983, chairing the education appropriations subcommittee. From 1983 to 1993, Meek served in the Florida senate. She was the first African-American woman elected to that body and the first black to serve there since Reconstruction. Earning a reputation as a particularly effective legislator, she passed a minority business enterprise law and other legislation to promote literacy and reduce the dropout rate.[2]

In 1992, when incumbent Representative Bill Lehman (a 10-term Democrat) decided to retire, Meek captured the Democratic nomination for his newly reapportioned district, which ran through the northern Miami suburbs in Dade County. She ran unopposed in the general election. Since Meek essentially clinched the seat by winning the September primary in the heavily Democratic district, she later claimed to be the first African American elected to represent Florida in Congress since Reconstruction. Democrats Corrine Brown and Alcee L. Hastings, who prevailed over opponents in the November general election in two other Florida districts, were sworn in with Meek on January 3, 1993.

Meek entered Congress at age 66 and immediately launched into an ambitious agenda that contrasted with her soft southern accent and grandmotherly demeanor. "Don't let her fool you. She is not a little old lady from the ghetto," noted a Florida political observer at the time of her election. "Carrie Meek is a player."[3] Meek lobbied intensively—and successfully—for a seat on the Appropriations Committee, an assignment that was virtually unheard of for a freshman legislator. When the Republicans took control of the House in 1994, Meek was bumped off Appropriations and reassigned to the Budget Committee and the Government Reform and

Oversight Committee. In 1996, she returned to the Appropriations Committee and eventually served on two of its subcommittees: Treasury, Postal Service, and General Government and VA, HUD, and Independent Agencies.

Meek focused on the needs of her district, which included issues arising from unemployment, immigration, and a natural disaster. Shortly after arriving on Capitol Hill, Meek sought federal aid for her district, which encompassed Homestead, Florida, and bore the brunt of the devastation caused by Hurricane Andrew in August 1992. However, Meek used her Appropriations seat principally to try to expand federal programs to create jobs and provide initiatives for African Americans to open their own businesses. Meek also authored a measure to modify Social Security laws to cover household workers. On behalf of her district's Haitian community, Meek sought to extend U.S. residence for immigrants and refugees who were excluded from two 1997 bills addressing Central American immigration. In 1999, she strove to obtain more-accurate census counts in her district by providing a measure whereby welfare recipients who were familiar with their poor, traditionally undercounted neighborhoods could work temporarily for the U.S. Census Bureau without losing their benefits.[4]

On national issues Meek developed a cooperative and congenial style that was punctuated by partisan episodes. For instance, she worked with Republicans to change the warnings on cigarette labels to reflect the fact that more African Americans than whites suffer from several smoking-related diseases. She also worked with Republican Anne Northup of Kentucky to increase funding for research on lupus and to provide federal grants for college students with poor reading skills due to learning disabilities.[5] But

in early 1995 Meek denounced Speaker Newt Gingrich on the House Floor amid the controversy surrounding a $4.5 million advance for his book. "If anything, now, how much the Speaker earns has grown much more dependent upon how hard his publishing house hawks his book," Meek said. "Which leads me to the question of exactly who does this Speaker really work for. . . . Is it the American people or his New York publishing house?" Republicans shouted Meek down and struck her remarks from the *Congressional Record*.[6] She also charged that by gutting the welfare system, Republicans were balancing the budget on the backs of America's working poor, elderly, and infirm. "The spending cuts that the House approved today fall mainly on the weakest members of our society, on the sick and on the elderly," she said in June 1997. "Tomorrow we will be voting on tax cuts that mainly favor the wealthy. . . . Today, the House voted to rob from the poor so that tomorrow the majority can help the rich."[7]

In 2002 Meek declined to seek certain re-election to a sixth term, citing her age. "I wish I could say I was tired of Congress," Meek told the *Miami Herald*. "I love it still. But at age 76, understandably, some of my abilities have diminished. I don't have the same vigor that I had at age 65. I have the fire, but I don't have the physical ability. So it's time."[8] Her youngest child, 35-year-old Kendrick Meek, who served in the Florida senate, announced his candidacy for the Democratic nomination in her district. When Kendrick Meek won the November 2002 general election, he became just the second child to directly succeed his mother in Congress.[9] His election also marked just the sixth time a Congresswoman's child was chosen to serve in Congress.

FOR FURTHER READING

"Meek, Carrie P.," *Biographical Directory of the United States Congress, 1774–Present,* http://bioguide.congress.gov/scripts/biodisplay.pl?index=M000628.

MANUSCRIPT COLLECTION

Florida A&M University, Carrie Meek–James N. Eaton Southeastern Regional Black Archives Research Center and Museum (Tallahassee, FL). *Papers:* ca. 1993–2003, 250 cubic feet. The Carrie Meek Collection documents Meek's career in the U.S. House of Representatives and includes campaign materials, legislation, constituent correspondence, press releases, programs, calendars, photographs, videotapes, and a museum collection. The collection will not open for research until processing is completed; however, part of the museum collection is open.

NOTES

1   William Booth, "The Strong Will of Carrie Meek; A Florida Sharecropper's Daughter Takes Her Stand on Capitol Hill," 16 December 1992, *Washington Post*: C1.

2   "Carrie P. Meek," Associated Press Candidate Biographies, 1992; *Politics in America, 1994* (Washington, DC: Congressional Quarterly Inc., 1993): 310–311.

3   Booth, "The Strong Will of Carrie Meek."

4   *Almanac of American Politics, 2000* (Washington, DC: National Journal Inc., 1999): 409.

5   *Politics in America, 2002* (Washington, DC: Congressional Quarterly Inc., 2001): 240.

6   Karen Foerstel, *Biographical Dictionary of Women in Congress* (Westport, CT: Greenwood Press, 1999): 184.

7   *Politics in America, 2002*: 240–241.

8   Andrea Robinson and Tyler Bridges, "Carrie Meek to Retire: She Made History From Tallahassee to Capitol Hill," 7 July 2002, *Miami Herald*: A1.

9   James Kee of West Virginia, who succeeded his mother, Maude Kee, in 1965, was the first.

Carol Moseley-Braun
1947–

UNITED STATES SENATOR ★ 1993–1999
DEMOCRAT FROM ILLINOIS

The first African-American woman Senator, Carol Moseley-Braun was also only the second black Senator since the Reconstruction Era.[1] "I cannot escape the fact that I come to the Senate as a symbol of hope and change," Moseley-Braun said shortly after being sworn in to office in 1993. "Nor would I want to, because my presence in and of itself will change the U.S. Senate."[2] During her single term in office, Senator Moseley-Braun advocated for civil rights issues and for legislation on crime, education, and families.

Carol Moseley was born in Chicago, Illinois, on August 16, 1947. Her parents, Joseph Moseley, a policeman, and her mother, Edna (Davie) Moseley, a medical technician, divorced in 1963. The oldest of the four Moseley children in a middle-class family, Carol graduated from Parker High School in Chicago and earned a B.A. in political science from the University of Illinois in 1969.[3] Possessing an early interest in politics, she worked on the campaign of Harold Washington—an Illinois state representative, a U.S. Representative, and the first African-American mayor of Chicago—and the campaign of Illinois State Senator Richard Newhouse.[4] In 1972, Carol Moseley graduated from the University of Chicago School of Law. In Chicago she met and later married Michael Braun. Moseley-Braun hyphenated her maiden and married names. The couple raised a son, Matthew, but their marriage ended in divorce in 1986. Moseley-Braun worked as a prosecutor in the office of the U.S. Attorney in Chicago from 1973 until 1977. In 1978, she won election to the Illinois state house of representatives, a position she held for a decade. After an unsuccessful bid for Illinois lieutenant governor in 1986, she was elected the Cook County, Illinois, recorder of deeds in 1988, becoming the first African American to hold an executive position in Cook County.[5]

Not satisfied with her position as recorder of deeds, and believing politicians were out of touch with the average American, Moseley-Braun contemplated running for Congress. Her resolve to seek national office strengthened after she witnessed Senators' questioning of Anita Hill during the Clarence Thomas's controversial confirmation hearing for the Supreme Court in 1991. "The Senate absolutely needed a healthy dose of democracy," she observed. "It wasn't enough to have millionaire white males over the age of 50 representing all the people in the country."[6] Officially entering the race for the Senate in November 1991, Moseley-Braun focused in her Democratic primary campaign on two-term incumbent Alan Dixon's support of Clarence Thomas's appointment and the need for diversity in the Senate. Despite organizational problems and paltry fundraising, Moseley-Braun stunned the experts, defeating her two opponents, Dixon and Alfred Hofeld, an affluent Chicago lawyer, and capturing 38 percent of the primary vote.[7] "This democracy is alive and well, and ordinary people can have a voice with no money," Moseley-Braun remarked shortly afterward.[8] In the general election, she faced Republican candidate Richard Williamson, a lawyer and a former official in the Ronald W. Reagan and George H. W. Bush administrations.[9] Focusing on a message of change and diversity encapsulated by slogans such as, "We don't need another arrogant rich guy in the Senate," Moseley-Braun ultimately defeated Williamson with 53 percent of the vote.[10] In the "Year of the Woman," Carol Moseley-Braun became a national symbol of change, reform, and equality. Soon after her election to the Senate, she commented, "my job is emphatically not to be a celebrity or a full time symbol. Symbols will not create jobs and economic growth. They do not do the hard work of solving the health care crisis. They will not save the children of our cities from drugs and guns and murder."[11]

In the Senate, Moseley-Braun became the first woman to serve on the powerful Finance Committee when a top-ranking Democrat, Tom Daschle of South Dakota, gave up his seat to create a spot for her. Also, Moseley-Braun and Senator Dianne Feinstein of California became just the second and third women ever to serve on the prestigious Senate Judiciary Committee. In addition, Moseley-Braun served on the Senate Banking, Housing, and Urban Affairs Committee and on the Small Business Committee. In 1993, the Illinois Senator made headlines when she convinced the Senate Judiciary Committee not to renew a design patent for the United Daughters of the Confederacy (UDC) because it contained the Confederate flag. The patent had been routinely renewed for nearly a century, and despite the Judiciary Committee's disapproval, the Senate was poised to pass a resolution sponsored by Senator Jesse Helms of North Carolina that included a provision to authorize the extension of the federal patent. Moseley-Braun threatened to filibuster the legislation "until this room freezes over." She also made an impassioned and eloquent plea to her colleagues about the symbolism of the Confederate flag, declaring, "It has no place in our modern times, place in this body, place in our society."[12] Swayed by Moseley-Braun's argument, the Senate rejected the UDC's application to renew its patent.[13]

Moseley-Braun sparred with Senator Helms once again while managing her first bill on the Senate Floor. As a cosponsor of a measure providing federal funding for the Martin Luther King, Jr., Holiday Commission—an organization established in 1984 to promote national recognition of the holiday—Moseley-Braun helped thwart a Helms amendment to the legislation that would have replaced government money with private donations. The Illinois Senator invoked memories of her participation in a civil rights march with King in the 1960s in an attempt to win support for the legislation.[14] The Senate eventually approved the bill. Among Moseley-Braun's other triumphs involving social legislation were her prominent roles in the passage of the Child Support Orders Act, the 1994 William J. (Bill) Clinton administration crime bill, the Multiethnic Placement Act, and the Improving America's School Act.[15]

During her term in the Senate, Moseley-Braun addressed an array of issues affecting women and African Americans. She helped create legislation to assist divorced and widowed women, arguing, "Pension laws were never written for women . . . no wonder the vast majority of the elderly poor are women."[16] She also sponsored the creation of the Sacagawea coin to recognize "women of color" and a National Park Service initiative to fund historic preservation of the Underground Railroad.[17] A consistent supporter of equal opportunity and affirmative action, Moseley-Braun also spoke out against sexual harassment. In 1995 she joined five of her women colleagues in the Senate to call for public hearings on alleged sexual misconduct by Senator Bob Packwood of Oregon.[18]

Despite the high expectations following Moseley-Braun's upset victory in 1992, her term in the Senate was marked by controversy. Moseley-Braun drew criticism for alleged campaign finance violations, which eventually led to an investigation by the Federal Election Commission.[19] In 1996, the Congressional Black Caucus and human rights organizations chastised Moseley-Braun for taking a private trip to Nigeria to attend the funeral of General Sani Abacha's son despite objections by the State Department. Previously an outspoken critic of human rights violations in the African nation, Moseley-Braun reversed her position and defended the Nigerian government.[20]

Closely scrutinized, Moseley-Braun faced a difficult challenge in her 1998 bid for re-election to the Senate against Republican Peter Fitzgerald, an Illinois state senator.[21] Capturing just 47 percent of the vote, Moseley-Braun lost to her opponent, who spent nearly $12 million of his own money.[22] President Clinton appointed Moseley-Braun the U.S. Ambassador to New Zealand; she served from 1999 until 2001. Attempting to revive her political career, Moseley-Braun entered the race for the Democratic nomination for President in 2000, but she was unsuccessful. It was the second time an African-American woman had sought the nomination (Shirley Chisholm became the first in 1972). Since 2001, Moseley-Braun has taught political science at Morris Brown College (Atlanta) and DePaul University (Chicago) and managed a business consulting company in Chicago.[23] In 2004, Moseley-Braun made another unsuccessful bid for the Democratic presidential nomination.

FOR FURTHER READING

D'Orio, Wayne. *Carol Moseley-Braun* (Philadelphia, PA: Chelsea House, 2003).

"Moseley Braun, Carol," *Biographical Directory of the United States Congress, 1774–Present,* http://bioguide. congress.gov/scripts/biodisplay.pl?index=M001025.

Moseley-Braun, Carol. *Shared Prosperity Through Partnership* (Washington, DC: Division of International Studies, Woodrow Wilson International Center for Scholars, 1996).

MANUSCRIPT COLLECTIONS

Chicago Historical Society (Chicago, IL). *Papers:* 1992–1999. Senatorial papers.

University of Oklahoma (Norman, OK), The Julian P. Kanter Commercial Archive, Department of Communication. *Video reels:* 1992, eight video reels. Includes nine commercials used during Carol Moseley-Braun's campaign for the 1992 U.S. senatorial election in Illinois, Democratic Party.

NOTES

1   Senator Moseley-Braun hyphenated her name during her U.S. Senate term but stopped using the hyphen when she left Congress.

2   *Current Biography, 1994* (New York: H. W. Wilson and Company, 1994): 378.

3   Steve Johnson, "Braun's Win Turns Around a Once-Stagnant Career," 4 November 1992, *Chicago Tribune*: 19.

4   Johnson, "Braun's Win Turns Around a Once-Stagnant Career"; Sarah Nordgren, "Carol Moseley-Braun: The Unique Candidate," 26 July 1992, Associated Press.

5   *Current Biography, 1994*: 379.

6   Ibid., 380.

7   Nordgren, "Carol Moseley-Braun: The Unique Candidate"; Frank James, "Welcome to the Club: Carol Moseley-Braun's Campaign for the Senate Was Her Own Excellent Adventure," 6 December 1992, *Chicago Tribune*: 14.

8   Lynn Sweet, "A Braun Upset; First Defeat for Dixon in 42 Years," 18 March 1992, *Chicago Sun-Times*: 1.

9   Edward Walsh, "Carol Braun's Rocky Road to History; After the Upset, It's Still a Long Way to the Senate," 28 April 1992, *Washington Post*: C1.

10 James, "Welcome to the Club"; Sharon Cohen, "Carol Moseley-Braun: From Face in the Crowd to National Spotlight," 4 November 1992, Associated Press; *Current Biography, 1994*: 381.

11 *Current Biography, 1994*: 378–379; Thomas Hardy, "Clinton Elected President: Carol Moseley-Braun Sweeps to Historic Senate Victory," 4 November 1992, *Chicago Tribune*: 1.

12 Helen Dewar, "Senate Bows to Braun on Symbol of Confederacy," 23 July 1993, *Washington Post*: A1.

13 Dewar, "Senate Bows to Braun on Symbol of Confederacy"; Steve Neal, "Moseley-Braun Record Is Inconsistent," 28 July 1993, *Chicago Sun-Times*: 31.

14 Mitchell Locin, "Moseley-Braun Tangles Anew With Helms," 25 May 1994, *Chicago Tribune*: 4.

15 *Current Biography, 1994*: 381.

16 Lynn Sweet, "Bill Seeks Fair Pension Shake for Women," 12 May 1996, *Chicago Sun-Times*: 28.

17 Alaina Sue Potrikus, "Braun Has Something to Prove in Her Bid for President," 14 January 2004, *Milwaukee Journal Sentinel*: 12A.

18 Dori Meinert and Toby Eckert, "Moseley-Braun Assailed for Backing Clinton," 27 February 1998, *State Journal-Register* (Springfield, IL): 11.

19 Darryl Fears, "On a Mission in a Political Second Act; Bush's Record Forced Her to Run, Braun Says," 13 July 2003, *Washington Post*: A6.

20 Fears, "On a Mission in a Political Second Act"; *Politics in America, 1998* (Washington, DC: Congressional Quarterly Inc., 1997): 441–442.

21 Nordgren, "Carol Moseley-Braun: The Unique Candidate"; Jennifer Loven, "Peter Fitzgerald: He's Heading for Capitol Hill But What Will He Do There?" 7 November 1998, Associated Press.

22 "Carol Moseley-Braun Says She Won't Run for Office Again," 5 November 1998, Associated Press.

23 "Ambassador Carol Moseley-Braun to Keynote SLDN National Dinner," 7 March 2005, U.S. Newswire.

Mel Reynolds
1952–

UNITED STATES REPRESENTATIVE ★ 1993–1995
DEMOCRAT FROM ILLINOIS

Persistent in the face of defeat, Mel Reynolds earned a seat in the 103rd Congress (1993–1995) after two unsuccessful bids against Illinois incumbent Gus Savage in the Democratic primary. Perceived by national party leaders as a standout with political promise, Reynolds received a seat on the influential Ways and Means Committee—a rare honor for a freshman Representative—during his term in Congress.[1]

Mel Reynolds was born on January 8, 1952, in Mound Bayou, Mississippi, to Essie Mae and Reverend J. J. Reynolds. When he was a child, his family moved to Chicago, where he attended public schools, including Mather High School.[2] Reynolds received an A.A. from Chicago City College in 1972, and two years later graduated with a B.A. from the University of Illinois at Champaign-Urbana. One of the first African Americans from Illinois to be selected as a Rhodes Scholar, Reynolds earned an LL.B. from Oxford University in 1979. He also completed a master's degree in public administration at Harvard's Kennedy School of Government in 1986. While at Harvard, Reynolds met his future wife, Marisol Concepcion. The couple married in 1990 and had three children: Corean, Marisol Elizabeth, and Mel, Jr.[3]

Reynolds initially worked as an assistant professor of political science at Roosevelt University in Chicago and hosted a local radio talk show. He also launched the organization American Scholars Against World Hunger to fight famine in Africa. Reynolds earned a reputation as a community activist, participating in an antidrug campaign on Chicago's South Side and directing the Community Economic Development and Education Foundation, which provided scholarships to local students.[4] He gained valuable political experience working on the campaigns of several unsuccessful Democratic presidential candidates, including Edward M. (Ted) Kennedy, Jesse Jackson, and Michael Dukakis.[5] In 1987, Reynolds participated in Chicago Mayor Harold Washington's victorious re-election campaign.

Without experience in elective office, Reynolds challenged the four-term Democratic incumbent Gus Savage for the congressional district encompassing portions of Chicago's predominantly African-American South Side. As a young (36-year-old), untested candidate, Reynolds impressed experts with an efficient campaign that focused on his status as an outsider to Chicago's powerful ward system and on his roots in the community. "It's more of a commitment to me than just a job," he remarked during the contest. "Obviously as a black Rhodes Scholar, I can work in any corporation in America. I've chosen to be in my community."[6] Reynolds placed a distant third in the 1988 primary, garnering only 14 percent of the vote.[7] Despite the loss, he made another run for the district seat two years later, citing unhappiness with Savage's representation of the urban district. In a race featuring three candidates, Reynolds made a strong showing, with 43 percent of the vote, partly reflecting voters' growing discontent with the incumbent Savage, who had a history of making controversial remarks as well as a volatile relationship with the press.

In 1992, Reynolds orchestrated a third campaign to unseat Savage. This time, no other opponents challenged the incumbent, ensuring that votes would not be split among several candidates. Reynolds also received a boost with the 1992 redistricting that shrank Savage's stronghold in urban black neighborhoods, replacing them with white suburbs south of Chicago. In the March primary, Reynolds easily defeated Savage, 63 to 37 percent.[8] He went on to earn 78 percent of the vote in the general election against Republican candidate Ron Blackstone and third-party opponent Louanner Peters. In his subsequent election, he

bested two challengers in the Democratic primary with 56 percent of the vote and easily defeated a write-in candidate in the general election to earn a second term in the House.[9]

During his first term in Congress, Reynolds successfully lobbied for a seat on the powerful Ways and Means Committee. With the backing of longtime committee chairman Representative Daniel Rostenkowski of Illinois, Reynolds became the first freshman in 14 years to be awarded the coveted assignment.[10] In 1993, Reynolds joined Rostenkowski in voting for the North American Free Trade Agreement (NAFTA), a measure aimed at promoting economic growth between United States, Canada, and Mexico. As the only two Democrats representing Chicago to back the controversial legislation, both Members faced widespread criticism from organized labor leaders who believed the free trade program would undermine wages and job security for American workers. However, the two Representatives reaped the gratitude of President William J. (Bill) Clinton—who had pushed for NAFTA's passage in the House and Senate—aiding their re-election bids in 1994.[11]

During his short stint in the House, Reynolds sought to improve conditions for his many impoverished constituents by backing an earned income tax credit and hosting a series of job fairs in Chicago.[12] He also worked to curb crime in his district, primarily by supporting gun control. In 1993 the Chicago Representative authored a bill to facilitate lawsuits against gun manufacturers for deaths or injuries caused by their firearms. He also proposed doubling the excise tax on guns, with a portion of the additional revenue to be allocated for urban hospitals that cared for uninsured patients with gunshot injuries.[13] "If we are truly serious about addressing the senseless slaughter taking place on our streets, we must hold people and corporations responsible for their actions, as well as provide relief to those impacted so heavily by the destructive cost of gun violence," Reynolds remarked.[14]

Although Reynolds had an auspicious beginning in the House, a series of legal problems jeopardized his career.[15]

Early in his first term, published reports emerged alleging that Reynolds owed thousands of dollars in campaign debts and educational loans.[16] The Illinois Representative explained that he had delayed paying his student loans so that he could fund his three election campaigns. "It was a question of priorities, a question of me spending my life trying to do what I believe was right," Reynolds commented.[17] In August 1994 a Cook County grand jury indicted Reynolds on counts of criminal sexual assault, child pornography, and obstruction of justice. Reynolds denied having an affair in 1992 with his accuser—a 16-year-old campaign worker.[18]

Initially, Reynolds managed to weather the controversy and retain his position in Congress, winning re-election to a second term with no significant opposition in the general election.[19] With the opening of the 104th Congress (1995–1997), Republicans gained control of the House for the first time in 40 years. As the lowest-ranking Democrat on the Ways and Means Committee, Reynolds lost his position when Republicans reduced the number of seats for the panel; he received a spot on the Economic and Educational Opportunities Committee.[20] When a Chicago jury found Reynolds guilty of multiple criminal counts, including having sex with a minor and obstruction of justice, calls for his resignation among Democrats reached a crescendo.[21] Reluctantly, Reynolds resigned from the House, effective October 1, 1995.[22]

Reynolds spent two and a half years in jail for the sexual misconduct conviction. Later indicted and convicted on federal charges of bank and campaign fraud, he remained in prison until President Clinton commuted his sentence shortly before leaving office in 2001.[23] The former Representative attempted to resurrect his political career by running against Representative Jesse Jackson, Jr., who had succeeded him in office, but his comeback stalled when he received only 6 percent of the vote in the 2004 Democratic primary.[24]

FOR FURTHER READING

"Reynolds, Mel," *Biographical Directory of the U.S. Congress, 1774–Present,* http://bioguide.congress.gov/scripts/biodisplay.pl?index=R000178.

NOTES

1   Ben Johnson, "Reynolds' 1st Year Was Big Success," 22 December 1993, *Chicago Sun-Times*: 39.

2   Tom McNamee, "Controversies Shadow His Success," 23 August 1995, *Chicago Sun-Times*: 8; Ellen Warren, "Amid Hopes, Always Doubt; Early Supporters Saw Mel Reynolds as Bright, Impressive, Determined. Now They Remember Other, More Troubling Traits," 7 May 1995, *Chicago Tribune*: 1C.

3   Lee Bey, "A Life of Ups and Downs and a Career on the Rise," 16 July 1995, *Chicago Sun-Times*: 21; Richard A. Chapman, "A Quiet Mystery Surrounds Marisol," 27 August 1995, *Chicago Sun-Times*: 20; "Ex-Chicago Congressman Mel Reynolds Returns After Clinton Commutes Prison Sentence," February 2001, *Jet*.

4   Janita Poe and Helaine Olen, "Reynolds Is Injured in the Shooting," 13 March 1992, *Chicago Tribune*: 1C; Chuck Neubauer and Michael Sneed, "Reynolds' Finances Subject of Inquiry," 14 August 1994, *Chicago Sun-Times*: 12.

5   Luix Overbea, "Jesse Jackson's Boston 'Rainbow Coalition,'" 16 January 1984, *Christian Science Monitor*: 5; "Melvin J. Reynolds," Associated Press Candidate Biographies, 1996; R. Bruce Dold, "Election '88 Illinois Primary," 11 March 1988, *Chicago Tribune*.

6   Dold, "Election '88 Illinois Primary."

7   *Almanac of American Politics*, 1990 (Washington, DC: National Journal Inc., 1989): 353–354.

8   "Savage May Face Toughest Primary Yet," 16 March 1992, United Press International; Craig Winneker, "Reynolds Whips Savage on Third Try, 63-37%; Shooting May Have Helped,"19 March 1992, *Roll Call*.

9   "Election Statistics, 1920 to Present," available at http://clerk.house.gov/member_info/electionInfo/index.html; *Almanac of American Politics, 1996* (Washington, DC: National Journal Inc., 1995): 424.

10 Johnson, "Reynolds' 1st Year Was Big Success"; *Politics in America, 1996* (Washington, DC: Congressional Quarterly Inc., 1995): 399.

11 Basil Talbott, "Reynolds Goes His Own Way," 18 November 1993, *Chicago Sun-Times*: 13; *Politics in America, 1996*: 399.

12 Robert A. Davis, "Reynolds Shoots for Term 2; Challengers Say He's an 'Outsider,'" 9 February 1994, *Chicago Sun-Times*: 5.

13 Mark N. Hornung, "Gun Bill Is Thoughtful, But Flawed," 5 February 1993, *Chicago Sun-Times*: 39; "Reynolds Set To Go After His Second Term," 6 December 1993, Chicago Tribune: 2N; *Politics in America, 1996*: 399.

14 *Congressional Record*, House, 99th Cong., 1st sess. (2 February 1993): H320.

15 Johnson, "Reynolds' 1st Year Was Big Success."

16 Glenn R. Simpson, "Reynolds Sued Eight Times in Seven Years Says Report Is a 'Total Hatchet Job,'" 29 July 1993, *Roll Call*; Tom Strong, "Reynolds Lets Debts Slide in Quest for Office," 26 July 1993, Associated Press.

17 Strong, "Reynolds Lets Debts Slide in Quest for Office."

18 "Congressman Faces Sex Charges; Rep. Mel Reynolds, A Freshman Democrat from Chicago's South Side, Was Indicted by a Grand Jury Friday," 20 August 1994, *Orlando Sentinel* (Florida): A3; Brian Jackson, "Porn Charge Shocks Reynolds," 22 August 1994, *Chicago Sun-Times*: 1.

19 "Election Statistics, 1920 to Present," available at http://clerk.house.gov/member_info/electionInfo/index.html; "Lipinski Survives a Scare in the 3rd; 11th District Takes Weller over Giglio," 9 November 1994, *Chicago Tribune*: 1.

20 *Almanac of American Politics, 1990*: 422.

21 "Accuser Says Congressman Was 'Godlike'; More Colleagues Ask Reynolds to Quit the House," 25 August 1995, *Washington Post*: A8; Michelle Groenke, "Gephardt Calls for Reynolds' Resignation," 24 August 1995, United Press International.

22 Thomas Hardy and Robert Becker, "Reynolds on Live TV: I Quit; Congressman Vents Anger at Heard, Media," 2 September 1995, *Chicago Tribune*: 1N; Dirk Johnson, "Congressman to Resign," 2 September 1995, *New York Times*: 1.

23 John Chase, "Reynolds Runs Again Despite Sex Conviction; He Wants Old Congress Seat Back," 8 October 2003, *Chicago Tribune*: 1C.

24 *Politics in America, 2006* (Washington, DC: Congressional Quarterly Inc., 2005): 399; "Reynolds Suffers Loss and Lawsuit," 17 March 2004, *Chicago Tribune*: C18.

Walter R. Tucker III
1957–

UNITED STATES REPRESENTATIVE ★ 1993–1995
DEMOCRAT FROM CALIFORNIA

Hailing from a Southern California political dynasty, the well-educated and ambitious Walter R. Tucker III began his career in elected office by taking his father's seat as the youngest mayor of Compton, California. He subsequently defeated an incumbent's daughter for a seat in the U.S. House of Representatives. Tucker arrived in Washington in 1993 with the goal of "bring[ing] positive attention to Compton," a city that had recently been wracked by destructive race riots.[1]

Born May 28, 1957, Tucker was one of four children in a prominent political family in Compton, California. His father, Walter R. Tucker II, worked as a dentist who entered politics in 1967, when he won election to the Compton school board. He was eventually elected mayor of Compton. Tucker's mother, Martha, was a real estate agent and writer. The Tucker family was often referred to as the "Kennedys of Compton" because of its political power. Tucker graduated from Compton High School in 1974. He attended Princeton University from 1974 to 1976 before returning home to finish his studies at the University of Southern California in Los Angeles in 1978. Tucker went on to earn his J.D. at Georgetown University Law School in Washington, DC, in 1981, after which he returned to Compton to practice law. Tucker served as deputy district attorney for Los Angeles County from 1984 to 1986.[2] He also earned a certificate of ordination from the School of the Word and practiced as an associate minister of the Bread of Life Christian Center in Carson. Tucker's wife, Robin, and their two children—Walter IV and Autumn—lived with the extended Tucker family in a sprawling home near Compton city hall.

Tucker entered elective politics when his father died of cancer in his third term as Compton's mayor in 1991. Tucker ran to succeed him and, on April 16, 1991, became Compton's youngest mayor. Tucker's mayoral tenure focused on economic improvement in the impoverished city. Once a bustling economic center—former President George H. W. Bush had a home in the city in the late 1940s—Compton experienced an economic downturn starting when race riots broke out in 1965. High poverty, crime, and gang violence had since plagued much of the city.[3]

In 1992, six-term U.S. Representative Mervyn Dymally announced his retirement. Dymally represented a swath of the low-income neighborhoods in southwest Los Angeles, including Compton. African Americans made up 34 percent of the district, and Hispanics made up another 40 percent of the electorate.[4] Dymally endorsed his daughter, Lynn—a member of the Compton school board—to succeed him. However, Tucker emerged as the strongest of three challengers who vigorously opposed Lynn Dymally in the Democratic primary.[5] The campaign took a unique twist nearly one month before the primary, in May 1992, when a Los Angeles jury's verdict in favor of four police officers accused of beating black motorist Rodney King sparked a series of race riots in the city. Compton suffered an estimated $100 million in damage; nearly 200 buildings were vandalized, and more than 130 separate arson fires were reported.[6] As mayor, Tucker quickly took charge in the wake of the riots. Images of Tucker touring the city with black activist Reverend Jesse Jackson were shown on national television. Tucker won the nomination with 39 percent over Dymally's 37 percent. Carson City councilwoman Vera Roble DeWitt took 11 percent, with two other candidates splitting 12 percent.[7] Tucker easily won the general election in the overwhelmingly liberal district, with 86 percent of the vote.[8]

Assigned to the Public Works and Transportation and Small Business committees, Tucker emerged as a labor-friendly Representative with a liberal voting record. He

backed tax-exempt funding to construct the Alameda Corridor, a truck and rail line that would expedite the shipment of cargo from the port of Los Angeles inland through the congested city.[9] Despite heavy lobbying, Tucker made a rare break from President William J. (Bill) Clinton's administration by voting against the North American Free Trade Agreement, fearing the loss of low-wage jobs in the Los Angeles area. Tucker focused primarily on the task of alleviating unemployment and poverty in a district with chronic unemployment problems. He was credited with securing $5.9 million in extra police funds for southern California.[10] He also submitted legislation designating the week of February 14 as a period for people to perform kind deeds without expecting anything in return.[11]

In March 1994, federal prosecutors revealed that Tucker and a member of the Compton city council were the subjects of a federal bribery investigation. "I unequivocally and categorically deny all charges that have been brought against me," Tucker stated upon his indictment. "I have complete faith in God, who is my shield and my defense. I will not allow this matter to impede on the important work that I am doing in the U.S. Congress."[12] On August 22, he officially pled "not guilty" to 10 counts in a federal district court in Los Angeles. Tucker accused the Federal Bureau of Investigation and federal prosecutors of targeting him because he was a black official. Upon his arraignment, supporters rallied on the courthouse steps, holding signs reading "Tucker Is Innocent—Witch Hunt" and "Stop Racism 1994. Leave Tucker Alone."[13]

In the June 1994 Democratic primary Tucker trounced his challenger, local businessman Lew Prulitsky with 84 percent of the vote. Libertarian Guy Wilson, a merchant seaman, was Tucker's only general election challenger for his 1994 re-election campaign. Though Wilson had not planned on running a serious campaign, Tucker's indictment after the primary boosted his prospects. Yet Wilson's fringe beliefs—he claimed his first official act, if elected, would be to introduce legislation repealing the 16th Amendment, which established a federal income tax—limited his ability to run as a serious candidate.[14] Tucker was re-elected with 77 percent of the vote.[15] However, at Tucker's ongoing trial, the prosecution presented overwhelming evidence including video and audio tapes of Tucker demanding cash in exchange for public projects.[16] Jurors deliberated for two weeks before convicting Tucker on seven counts of extortion and two counts of tax evasion on December 8, 1995. Holding his Bible outside the Los Angeles courtroom, Tucker maintained his innocence: "I believe the jury made the wrong decision. I know what happened in these circumstances. The government knows what happened. It was entrapment."[17] Tucker resigned from Congress on December 15, 1995.[18] On April 17, 1996, a district court judge sentenced him to 27 months in prison—less than the recommended 30 to 57 months, partially because the citizens of Compton wrote more than 200 letters in Tucker's support.[19] Tucker was also responsible for paying $30,000 in restitution upon his release.[20]

Shortly after his resignation, Tucker endorsed his wife, Robin, to fill his vacancy in a special election to be held on March 26, the same day as the Democratic primary for the 105th Congress (1997–1999). A long-shot candidate, Robin Tucker was among eight candidates who lost the nomination to California State Assemblywoman Juanita Millender-McDonald, who prevailed with a 27 percent plurality. Robin Tucker was sixth in the crowded field with 7 percent of the vote.[21]

Before entering prison, Walter Tucker announced his desire to start a prison ministry.[22] Upon his release in September 1998, Tucker served as the Southern California director of the prison fellowship, headed by Charles (Chuck) Colson, a former aide to President Richard M. Nixon aide and a central figure in the Watergate scandal.

FOR FURTHER READING

"Tucker, Walter R., III," *Biographical Directory of the United States Congress, 1774– Present*, http://bioguide.congress.gov/scripts/biodisplay.pl?index=T000405.

NOTES

1   "New Faces of 1992," 9 November 1992, *Roll Call*.

2   *Politics in America, 1996* (Washington, DC: Congressional Quarterly Inc., 1995): 174; Tina Griego, "Tucker Rolls With Punches," 28 June 1992, *Los Angeles Times*: B1.

3   Emily Adams and Shawn Hubler, "A Wealth of Woes," 26 March 1994, *Los Angeles Times*: B1.

4   *Almanac of American Politics, 1994* (Washington, DC: National Journal Inc., 1993): 178.

5   Tina Griego, "Elections/U.S. House of Representatives; Stormy Race for 37th District Seat Steals the Thunder," 31 May 1992, *Los Angeles Times*: J1.

6   Tina Griego, "Aftermath of the Riots," 7 May 1992, *Los Angeles Times*: B1.

7   "California House: CA 37," 3 June 1992, *Hotline*.

8   "Election Statistics, 1920 to Present," available at http://clerk.house.gov/member_info/electionInfo/index.html.

9   Joan Pryde, "Case Made on Hill for Use of Munis to Finance Project for California Ports," 9 September 1993, *The Bond Buyer*. Tucker's Bill (H.R. 3231) died in the Ways and Means Committee.

10 *Almanac of American Politics, 1996* (Washington, DC: National Journal Inc., 1995): 189.

11 Dina El Boghdady, "Rep. Tucker to Introduce Random Acts of Kindness Measure," 8 February 1994, States News Service.

12 Jim Newton and Emily Adams, "Rep. Tucker Is Indicted; Denies Bribery Charges," 12 August 1994, *Los Angeles Times*: A1.

13 Committee on Standards of Official Conduct, "Historical Summary of Conduct Cases in the House of Representatives," available at http://www.house.gov/ethics/Historical_Chart_Final_Version.htm (accessed 26 March 2007); Michael Janofsky, "California Congressman Indicted by U.S.," 12 August 1994, *New York Times*: A12; Ron Russell et al., "Rep. Tucker Indicted on New Charges," 2 June 1995, *Los Angeles Times*: B1; "2 in Congress Attend Court on Charges," 23 August 1994, *New York Times*: A13.

14 Ted Johnson, "Local Elections/37th Congressional District; Foe's Indictment Spurs Libertarian," 18 October 1994, *Los Angeles Times*: B3; *Almanac of American Politics, 1996*: 189–190.

15 "Election Statistics, 1920 to Present," available at http://clerk.house.gov/member_info/electionInfo/index.html.

16 David Rosenzweig of the *Los Angeles Times* provided extensive coverage of the trial from September 11, 1995, to December 9, 1995. See, for example, "Trial Opens in Tucker Bribery Case," 4 October 1995: B3; "Witness Ends Testimony in Tucker Trial," 18 October 1995: B1; "Tucker Demanded Funds, Witness Says," 21 October 1995: B3; "Tucker, Agent Talk of Money on Tape," 27 October 1995: B1; "Tucker Says Pay Was for Consulting," 4 November 1995: B1; "Tucker Denies He Accepted $7,500 in Return for Votes," 9 November 1995: B3. Other coverage includes Gabriel Kahn, "Prosecution Rests in Tucker Trial," 2 November 1995, *Roll Call*.

17 Kathryn Wexler et al., "Rep. Tucker Convicted of Extortion; Congressman Took Bribes While Mayor of Compton, Calif.," 9 December 1995, *Washington Post*: A1.

18 Jeff Leeds et al., "Tucker to Resign From Congress to Avoid Expulsion," 13 December 1995, *Los Angeles Times*: B1.

19 David Rosenzweig, "Tucker Gets Prison Term for Extortion," 18 April 1996, *Los Angeles Times*: B1.

20 David Rosenzweig, "Tucker Loses Bid to Cut Restitution," 10 May 2000, *Los Angeles Times*: B1.

21 Jeff Leeds, "Tucker Backs Wife as House Successor," 14 December 1995, *Los Angeles Times*: B1; Eric Moses, "Tucker's Wife Vies for Husband's Calif. Seat," 10 January 1996, *The Hill*; "Final California Election Returns/Congress," 28 March 1996, *Los Angeles Times*: A16.

22 Jeff Leeds, "Former Rep. Tucker Reports to Prison for 27-Month Sentence," 4 June 1996, *Los Angeles Times*: B1.

Victor O. Frazer
1943–

DELEGATE ★ 1995–1997
INDEPENDENT FROM THE VIRGIN ISLANDS

Victor Frazer became the second black Delegate to represent the U.S. Virgin Islands in the U.S. House of Representatives after a surprise victory in 1995. During his brief stint in Congress, Frazer promoted the interests of his constituents in the American territory, focusing on procuring federal money for hurricane relief and attracting tourism to the eastern Caribbean.

Born on May 24, 1943, in Charlotte Amalie, St. Thomas, Virgin Islands, to Albert Frazer and Amanda Blyden, Victor O. Frazer was one of 10 children.[1] After graduating from Charlotte Amalie High School in 1960, Frazer earned a B.A. from Fisk University, in Nashville, Tennessee, in 1964, and a J.D. from Howard University Law School in 1971. He worked as a lawyer for the District of Columbia Office of the Corporation Counsel (later called the Office of the Attorney General of the District of Columbia) from 1974 to 1978.[2] Employed as a banker for Manufacturers Hanover Trust Company, Frazer also worked as a lawyer for the Interstate Commerce Commission and the U.S. Patent Office.[3] He later served as general counsel for the Virgin Islands Water and Power Authority from 1987 to 1989. Frazer acquired congressional experience as an administrative assistant for California Representative Mervyn Dymally, a special assistant for Michigan Representative John Conyers, and as counsel for the House Committee on the District of Columbia. Before winning a seat in the House, he also worked in a private legal practice. A divorcé, Frazer has two daughters, Kaaren and Aileene.[4]

In 1992, Frazer made an unsuccessful run for Congress against longtime Virgin Islands Delegate Ron de Lugo; Frazer, a Democrat who ran as an Independent, lost by more than 5,000 votes.[5] When de Lugo announced his retirement in 1994, Frazer orchestrated another attempt at elective office, again running as an Independent. In a four-way race to represent the Virgin Islands in the U.S. House, he placed second to Eileen Petersen, a former judge, but qualified for the runoff election on November 22 since none of the candidates earned the necessary 50 percent of the vote to secure the nomination.[6] Frazer's campaign benefited from the endorsement of retired U.S. Ambassador Terrance Todman, overcoming meager campaign funds and the support of the Congressional Black Caucus (CBC) for his Democratic opponent, Petersen.[7] He upset Petersen in the runoff, winning 55 percent of the vote and astounding the experts; congressional publishers had to scramble to locate a photograph of Frazer for inclusion with those of the other new Members of the 104th Congress (1995–1997).[8] Elated by his success, Frazer proclaimed, "This is the people's victory."[9]

During the 104th Congress, Frazer served on the Committee on International Relations. As one of the five nonvoting Delegates in the House he was allowed to vote in committee but not on the House Floor. In the 103rd Congress (1993–1995), the rights of the Delegates and the Puerto Rican Resident Commissioner were expanded, allowing them to vote in the Committee of the Whole. However, when the Republicans took control of the House in 1995, they rescinded the privilege. "We are not less American because we live in the Virgin Islands," Frazer remarked.[10] After several weeks of deliberation, Frazer opted to caucus with the Democratic Party and became one of a handful of non-Democratic Members to join the CBC.[11]

Delegate Frazer used his one term in Congress to highlight issues of concern to the residents of the Virgin Islands. When Hurricane Marilyn struck the chain of islands in 1995—St. Thomas sustained the most damage—Frazer worked with President William J. (Bill) Clinton to

ensure that the Virgin Islands received federal funds for disaster relief.[12] In the aftermath of the hurricane, Frazer emphasized the need for additional protection against natural disasters for his constituents. He urged the federal government to require private insurance companies to provide coverage for wind damage in their standard policies for homeowners in areas affected by hurricanes, such as the Caribbean islands.[13] In 1996 he sponsored legislation directing the Federal Emergency Management Agency to study the feasibility of insurance to provide protection from windstorms for residents of the Virgin Islands.[14]

Frazer also sought to revive the lagging tourism industry of the Virgin Islands—an essential segment of its economy. He backed the Travel and Tourism Partnership Act of 1995, aimed at promoting international travel and tourism to the United States because it "would enhance the limited resources of the Virgin Islands."[15] Frazer also successfully lobbied for an increase in funds to fight the growing problem of international drug trafficking in the U.S. territory.[16] Shortly after he took office in 1995, Frazer joined the Representatives from Hawaii, the Delegates from Guam and American Samoa, and the Resident Commissioner from Puerto Rico, to protest a nuclear waste shipment originating in France and traveling through the Caribbean to Japan. The radioactive materials, which originated from Japanese nuclear plants, were shipped to France to extract plutonium and back to Japan as part of an energy program sponsored by the Japanese government.[17] Also concerned with the high poverty rate among his constituents, Frazer supported an increase in the federal minimum wage, warning that even though "the

Virgin Islands is considered an American paradise," many of its residents lived below the poverty line.[18]

In his bid for re-election to the 105th Congress (1997–1999), Frazer portrayed himself as a zealous spokesperson for the Virgin Islands in the House and argued that his status as an Independent allowed him the flexibility to cross party lines so as to better represent the American territory.[19] His opponents criticized his legislative style, especially his frequent trips abroad. During his one term in office, Frazer took more than 10 trips overseas. He defended his travel as a necessary prerequisite for his membership on the International Relations Committee, assuring voters, "I have never traveled without promoting the Virgin Islands."[20] In the campaign, Frazer's two challengers contended that the incumbent should have lobbied for exemptions from the 1996 welfare reform legislation to protect the many impoverished citizens of the Virgin Islands. "No one member of Congress is going to hold back the tide of legislation," Frazer responded. "We ought not to embrace welfare as something we welcome."[21] None of the candidates in the general election earned 50 percent of the vote. Frazer finished ahead of Virgin Islands Lieutenant Governor Kenneth Mapp, but his other challenger, Donna Christian-Green, a physician, bested him 39 to 34 percent.[22] In the November 19, 1996, runoff, Frazer lost to Christian-Green by fewer than one thousand votes.[23] Shortly after the election, Frazer demanded a recount, but he failed to prove his claim of vote tampering.[24]

After his term in Congress, Frazer worked as an attorney in Washington, DC.[25]

FOR FURTHER READING

"Frazer, Victor O.," *Biographical Directory of the U.S. Congress, 1774–Present,* http://bioguide.congress.gov/scripts/biodisplay.pl?index=F000351.

NOTES

1 *Congressional Record*, House, 104th Cong., 2nd sess. (26 March 1996): E453.

2 Timothy S. Robinson and Laura A. Kiernan, "Widespread Fixing of Tickets Found; Study Finds Widespread Ticket Fixing; Law Enforcement Insiders Beneficiaries," 30 July 1978, *Washington Post*: A1; Laura A. Kiernan, "Ticket Canceling Said Common in Counsel's Office; DC Ticket Canceling Called Standard," 20 April 1978, *Washington Post*: A1.

3 *Congressional Directory, 104th Congress* (Washington, DC: Government Printing Office, 1995): 308.

4 "Victor O. Frazer," *Who's Who Among African Americans*; *Politics in America, 1996* (Washington, DC: Congressional Quarterly Inc., 1995): 1476.

5 "Election Statistics, 1920 to Present," available at http://clerk.house.gov/member_info/electionInfo/index.html.

6 "Retired Judge Wins Democratic Race to Succeed 10-Term Congressman," 13 September 1994, Associated Press.

7 "Virgin Islands Elects First Black Delegate in 20 Years," 19 December 1994, *Jet*: 8.

8 Anthony Faiola, "They're in One Hill of a Hurry; Publishers of Congressional Guides Find Power Turnover Is No Grand Old Party," 6 January 1995, *Washington Post*: B1.

9 Lynda Lohr, "Independents Break Democrats' Grip on Delegate's Seat, Government House," 22 November 1994, Associated Press.

10 "Bill Giving Delegate to Guam and Virgin Islands Goes to Nixon," 29 March 1972, *Washington Post*: A3; Doug Richards, "Reducing Voting Privileges Diminishes Meaning of Citizenship: Delegate," 5 January 1995, Associated Press; Kay Johnson, "Incumbent Delegate Takes the Heat in Televised Debate," 30 September 1996, Associated Press; Betsy Palmer, "Territorial Delegates to the U.S. Congress: Current Issues and Historical Background," 6 July 2006, Report RL 32340, Congressional Research Service, Library of Congress, Washington, DC.

11 *Almanac of American Politics, 1996* (Washington, DC: National Journal Inc., 1995): 1483.

12 Rajiv Chandrasekaran, "Hurricane Leaves 3 Dead in U.S. Virgin Islands," 17 September 1995, *Washington Post*: A8; Mireya Navarro, "Damage Heavy as Hurricane Ravages Island of St. Thomas," 17 September 1995, *New York Times*: 1.

13 Delegate Frazer made a prepared statement before the House Committee on Transportation and Infrastructure Subcommittee on Water Resources and Environment on the Natural Disaster Protection Partnership Act of 1995. See Federal News Service, 18 October 1995.

14 *Congressional Record*, House, 104th Cong., 2nd sess. (19 September 1996): 23924.

15 *Congressional Record*, House, 104th Cong., 2nd sess. (5 June 1996): E1001.

16 "Charlotte Amalie, U.S. Virgin Islands," 19 January 1996, Associated Press.

17 "6 U.S. Lawmakers Protest Japan's Nuclear Waste Shipment," 23 February 1995, Japan Economic Newswire; "Virgin Islands Broadcast News Summary," 19 January 1995, Associated Press; Andrew Pollack, "A-Waste Ship, Briefly Barred, Reaches Japan," 26 April 1995, *New York Times*: A13.

18 *Congressional Record*, House, 104th Cong., 2nd sess. (23 April 1996): 8609.

19 "Voters to Choose Territory's Only Elected Federal Official," 19 November 1996, Associated Press.

20 Kay Johnson, "Delegates' Globetrotting Raises Eyebrows in Election Year," 21 October 1996, Associated Press.

21 Johnson, "Incumbent Delegate Takes the Heat in Televised Debate."

22 "Runoff Necessary in Virgin Islands Race," 7 November 1996, *Sun-Sentinel* (Fort Lauderdale, FL): 22A; "Voters to Choose Territory's Only Elected Federal Official."

23 "Election Statistics, 1920 to Present," available at http://clerk.house.gov/member_info/electionInfo/index.html.

24 "Briefs From the Virgin Islands," 29 November 1996, Associated Press; "Incumbent Delegate to Congress Demands Vote Recount, Charges Fraud," 3 December 1996, Associated Press.

25 "Victor O. Frazer," *Who's Who Among African Americans*.

Julius Caesar (J. C.) Watts, Jr.
1957–

UNITED STATES REPRESENTATIVE ★ 1995–2003
REPUBLICAN FROM OKLAHOMA

A college football hero, charismatic conservative, and gifted public speaker, J. C. Watts had star power when he took the oath of office as a Member of the first Republican majority in 40 years. One of two black Republicans in Congress in his freshman term, Watts cited his humble roots in a segregated Oklahoma farm town as the source of his belief in self-reliance and disdain of social welfare. "I wasn't raised to be a Republican or Democrat," Watts recalled. "My parents just taught by example. They taught me and my brothers and sisters that if you lived under their roof, you were going to work."[1] Watts quickly became one of the GOP's most visible spokesmen, quickly rising to the position of Republican Conference Chair—the fourth-highest-ranking Republican in the House. His uneasy relationship with party leaders and a desire to spend more time with his family cut short Watts's Capitol Hill career in its prime.

Julius Caesar (J. C.) Watts, Jr., was born in the farming community of Eufaula, Oklahoma, on November 18, 1957. His mother, Helen Watts, a homemaker, raised six children: Melvin, Lawrence, Mildred, Gwen, J. C., and Darlene. Watts's father, Julius Caesar (Buddy) Watts, was a police officer, a businessman, and a minister. The elder Watts also served on the Eufaula city council, and along with his brother, Wade, was active in the Democratic Party and the National Association for the Advancement of Colored People (NAACP). Wade Watts headed the Oklahoma branch of the NAACP for 16 years.[2] J. C. Watts was one of the first black children to attend a previously all-white elementary school in Eufaula. At Eufaula High School, Watts was the first African-American quarterback for the school's football team; some of Watts's teammates from the mostly segregated local community protested at first.[3] While in high school, Watts fathered two daughters with two different women. One child, Tia, was adopted by Watt's Uncle Wade.[4] Watts married his other daughter's mother, Frankie Jones, whom he first met at his seventh birthday party. The couple raised five children: LaKesha, Jerrell, Jennifer, Julia, and Trey.[5]

After graduating in 1976, Watts played football and studied journalism at the University of Oklahoma in Norman. At first, he was a seventh-string quarterback. Discouraged with his minimal playing time, he left school multiple times. In each instance, his father persuaded him to return.[6] In 1979, Watts became the starting quarterback and led the Sooners to Orange Bowl victories in 1980 and 1981. He was named the bowl's most valuable player both years, and he was inducted into the Orange Bowl Hall of Fame in 1992. Watts's athletic prowess provided him with motivational speaking opportunities while he was in college.[7]

Following Watts's graduation in 1981, the New York Jets, a National Football League (NFL) team, offered him a place on their roster, but it was not in his favorite position as quarterback. Watts turned down the NFL offer and played from 1981 to 1986 in the Canadian Football League (CFL).[8] Watts then returned to Oklahoma to become a youth minister at Sunnyvale Baptist Church, in Del City, Oklahoma. Ordained in 1993, he supplemented his ministerial income by opening his own highway construction company. His discontent with government regulation of his business led him to contemplate running for office.

Despite the Watts family's long-standing public support for the Democratic Party—Buddy Watts once quipped that "a black man voting for the Republicans makes about as much sense as a chicken voting for Colonel Sanders"—J. C. Watts subscribed to the Republican message of social and fiscal conservatism.[9] He first considered changing his party allegiance when he covered a 1980 Oklahoma senate

campaign as a journalism student and found that his views were more in line with those of the Republican candidate, Don Nickles.[10] He officially changed his party affiliation in 1989. "I switched my registration not out of convenience but out of conviction," Watts later recalled. "I knew what I was doing would not be popular. It created some strain, even in relationships I had built over the years. But I knew in my heart that this was the right road, the honest road for me to take and remain true to my own principles."[11] In 1990, Watts ran for a seat on the Oklahoma corporation commission, an organization that regulated the state's telephone, oil, and gas industries. With Oklahoma party loyalty tending to split along racial lines, officials in the state Republican Party eagerly embraced Watts.[12] He won a seat on the commission, serving as chairman from 1993 until his departure in 1995.[13]

In 1994, seven-term Representative Dave McCurdy of Oklahoma announced that he was running for the U.S. Senate and local Republican businessmen urged Watts to run for McCurdy's seat. McCurdy represented a conservative southwest Oklahoma district, with several oil reserves and three major military installations. Agriculture was also a major industry and the district included the University of Oklahoma in Norman.[14] Watts entered the primary as a "textbook conservative": He favored the death penalty, school prayer, a balanced budget amendment and welfare reform. He also opposed abortion and cuts in defense spending.[15]

Watts faced a tough August primary challenge against state representative Ed Apple, winning 49 percent to Apple's 48 percent; however, state law required a runoff primary if no candidate won more than 50 percent of the vote.[16] In preparation for the September contest, Watts brought in high-powered Republicans to campaign for him, including New York Representative Jack Kemp, a football star, and National Rifle Association spokesman and actor Charlton Heston. Watts also secured the endorsement of the House Republican leadership. Apple lambasted Watts's courting of out-of-state luminaries. Comparing his local campaign to Watts's star-power

support, he declared, "It's grassroots vs. glitz."[17] The runoff remained close, but Watts prevailed with 52 percent of the vote.

Watts continued to host high-profile Republicans for his general election campaign, including former President George H. W. Bush, Kansas Senator Bob Dole, and future Republican Speaker (then Republican Whip) Newt Gingrich of Georgia.[18] He and his Democratic opponent, local attorney David Perryman, a self-described conservative, soon found themselves in a close, heated campaign. In an attempt to appeal to the district's conservative farming voters, Perryman launched an advertisement depicting Watts with his Afro hairstyle in high school juxtaposed against images of himself as a teenager posing with his prize-winning pigs.[19] The advertisement's racial overtones attracted national attention and Perryman offered to change the photograph of Watts in the advertisement.[20] Watts's firm conservative platform and his popularity among Oklahoma Sooners fans prevailed. He defeated Perryman and Independent candidate Bill Tiffee, with 52 percent of the vote.[21]

Watts's victory established several milestones. He was the first black Representative elected from Oklahoma and the first Republican to win the district in 72 years.[22] He was sworn in to the 104th Congress (1995–1997) as part of the GOP national tide, putting the party in power in the House for the first time in 40 years. Watts increased his victories in his next three re-election campaigns, winning by as much as 65 percent in 2000.[23] He received assignments on the Banking and Financial Services Committee and National Security Committee (later renamed Armed Services). The latter panel was crucial to the oversight of the three military installations in his district. Watts left the Banking and Financial Services Committee for a spot on the Transportation and Infrastructure Committee in the 105th Congress (1997–1999). In the 106th Congress (1999–2001), he turned down a position on the prestigious Appropriations Committee when a seat opened midterm; he did not want to leave the Transportation Committee.

The GOP hoped that Watts, as one of two black Republicans in the House (Representative Gary Franks was also re-elected to a Connecticut district), would court African-American voters, who overwhelmingly voted Democratic in national elections. Watts focused on promoting the GOP through black organizations. He often attended NAACP meetings and met with representatives from historically black colleges.[24] "Most black people don't think alike. Most black people just vote alike," he argued. "Why is it that so many people in the black community [who] would agree with Republican issues, why don't they vote Republican? I think that's the question we have to ask."[25] However, Watts stressed that he represented his district, rather than strictly his race. "My father raised me to be a man, not a black man," Watts declared.[26] "I am black, but that's not all of who I am," he later added.[27] Accordingly, Watts declined an invitation to join the traditionally liberal Congressional Black Caucus (CBC). "I think the CBC and I want the same things for the black community," he mused. "The difference is how we get there."[28]

Representative Watts supported a fiscally conservative agenda, voting 95 percent of the time for legislative initiatives from the Contract With America, a 1994 Republican campaign promise to limit government spending and corruption.[29] Watts's legislative emphasis was based on his belief that public assistance programs encouraged dependency in poor minorities.[30] In 1995, Watts teamed with Representative Jim Talent of Missouri to create the Renewal Community Project, legislation that provided tax breaks and the deregulation of small businesses, school vouchers allowing parents to choose their children's schools, and funding for faith-based organizations assisting low-income communities. In 2000 Watts reintroduced the legislation as the American Community Renewal Act, adding tax cuts for low-income communities as well as opportunities for home ownership. The new legislation also eliminated the capital gains tax and provided a "wage credit" for businesses that hired qualified low-income employees. Watts's goal was to help low-income families save money. "Under the current tax system, we penalize savings and investment and productivity," he argued. "Those are three things we should be rewarding."[31] The legislation gained bipartisan support. President William J. (Bill) Clinton's administration supported the measure and Speaker Dennis Hastert dubbed the bill among the GOP's top three priorities for the second session of the 106th Congress (1999–2001).[32] The legislation was signed into law in December 2000.

Though Watts embraced his role as a conservative, he attempted to remain outside the debate on affirmative action.[33] "Affirmative action isn't the problem," Watts argued. "Lousy education for black kids is the problem. Until you fix these schools don't talk to me about equal opportunity."[34] Watts's personal experience with continued racism led him to believe the United States was not ready to abolish preferences for minorities, and Watts opposed a bill submitted by fellow black Republican Gary Franks of Connecticut and Florida Republican Charles Canady in the 104th Congress to eliminate affirmative action practices in the federal government. As the bill gained momentum in the Republican House, Watts appealed directly to Speaker Newt Gingrich to block it. "Look, in principle I don't agree with affirmative action," he told Gingrich, "but in practice, we still don't have a level playing field." An emotional Watts admitted to the Speaker that he was "thinking with my heart here, not my head." Sympathetic to Watts's position, the Speaker arranged for the bill to die in the Judiciary Committee.[35]

Representative Watts's ability to draw national attention earned him a reputation as the GOP's "Great Black Hope."[36] In 1996, the Republican Party tapped him to deliver the GOP response to President Clinton's State of the Union Address.[37] He was the youngest Representative and the first African American to be accorded this honor.[38] Watts's response was generally well received. He spoke about reducing the role of government in American lives. "Government can't ease all pain. In fact, Government sometimes rubs the wound raw and makes healing harder," he argued. "I'm afraid that when the

[Clinton] Administration and others talk about race it sounds to me like the same old, same old—a bunch of sermons and sloganizing that defends the old assumption that Government can heal the racial divide." Watts concluded that the GOP's "mission is to return power to your home, to where mothers and fathers can exercise it according to their beliefs."[39] Watts was rumored as a possible vice presidential candidate in 1996, serving as co-chairman for GOP presidential candidate Bob Dole.[40] Former Representative Kemp eventually received the vice presidential nomination.

In 1998, Watts capitalized on a GOP Conference roiled by a poor showing in the midterm elections to challenge incumbent Conference Chairman John Boehner of Ohio. Though Republicans had maintained their majority, exit polls showed high African-American voter turnout in the South, the GOP's stronghold, and only 11 percent of these Black Americans voted Republican—down from 18 percent in 1996.[41] Though he claimed he was not running as a black candidate, Watts emphasized the GOP's need for broader appeal to minorities. In a letter to House Republicans, he wrote, "It is time to let the American people know that the Republican Party is the party of all Americans. We are the party of inclusiveness. Our ideas are good for everyone."[42] Supporters emphasized Watts's strong oratorical skills, noting that the GOP lacked a charismatic spokesperson. On Watts's 41st birthday, November 18, 1998, he prevailed against Boehner, 121 to 93, in the race for chairman of the House Republican Conference, the GOP's fourth highest position in the House.[43] Watts was the first African American to join the Republican leadership and was subsequently re-elected to the position for the 107th Congress (2001–2003).

However, Watts's tenure in the leadership proved difficult. Despite his elevated post, Watts often felt alienated by GOP decision makers.[44] He also found himself at odds with powerful Republican Whip Tom DeLay of Texas. Watts disagreed with DeLay's often forceful leadership. As a result, the GOP Whip's hands-on approach to gathering votes and maintaining party unity often overstepped Watts's role as the hub for communication within the GOP Conference. In July 1999, Watts threatened to resign from his leadership position to protest DeLay's alleged encroachment on his duties, but he stopped short of doing so. When Majority Leader Dick Armey of Texas announced his retirement in 2002, Watts considered running to replace him and he quietly solicited the aid of congressional allies; however, DeLay openly nailed down enough votes to secure the position before Watts made an open bid for Majority Leader.[45]

Watts also felt ignored by Republican President George W. Bush's administration. In 2002, the Pentagon considered eliminating funding for an $11 billion weapons system that would be partially assembled in Watts's district in Elgin, Oklahoma. Watts later claimed that President Bush refused to return his phone calls after targeting the project for spending cuts. When Secretary of Defense Donald Rumsfeld announced the program's demise on May 8, Watts was only given two hours' notice from the Pentagon. An early and avid supporter of the Bush administration, Watts was furious. When the President addressed the Republican Conference on Capitol Hill the next week, Watts was conspicuously absent.[46]

In 2002, Watts declined to run for re-election to the 108th Congress (2003–2005), citing a desire to spend more time with his family, who had remained in Oklahoma during his tenure in Washington. "This business is hard on families," he admitted. "I don't want to do this for the rest of my life. There are other things I want to do and can do. You have to be careful about getting on this treadmill."[47] Prominent Representatives of both parties implored him to stay, recognizing that his unique position brought diversity to the House. "I hate to see him go," noted CBC Member James Clyburn of South Carolina, a prominent Democrat. "J. C. is someone who really has been quietly and forcefully doing a lot of good."[48] Civil rights leader Rosa Parks, who, in 1955, famously refused to give up her seat on a Montgomery, Alabama, bus, wrote to Watts. "If you can," Parks implored him, "please remain as a pioneer on the Republicans' side until others come to assist you. I am glad that I stayed in my seat."[49] Though appreciative of the support, Watts noted that "the strength in this business is not hanging on. The real strength is to let go."[50] Watts's political ally, Republican Tom Cole, won his congressional seat in the 2002 election. Though Watts left Congress, he did not abandon the political spotlight. He formed a consulting business and currently serves as a nationally recognized political analyst.

FOR FURTHER READING

Watts, J. C., with Chriss Winston, *What Color Is Conservative?: My Life in Politics* (New York: HarperCollins, 2002).

"Watts, Julius Caesar, Jr. (J. C.)," *Biographical Directory of the United States Congress, 1774–Present*, http://bioguide. congress.gov/scripts/biodisplay.pl?index=W000210.

NOTES

1   Marc Sandalow, "The Republicans' Great Black Hope," 9 February 1997, *San Francisco Chronicle*: 9.

2   "J.C. Watts," *Newsmakers 1999*, Issue 2 (Detroit, MI: Gale Research Inc., 1999).

3   "J.C. Watts," *Newsmakers 1999*.

4   "Watts, J.C., Jr.," *Current Biography, 1999* (New York: H. W. Wilson Company, 1999): 591.

5   J. C. Watts, Jr., *What Color Is Conservative?* (New York: HarperCollins, 2002): 39.

6   "J. C. Watts," *Newsmakers 1999*.

7   Ibid.

8   Watts started with the Ottawa Rough Riders before joining the Toronto Argonauts in 1985. In his rookie season, he led the Rough Riders to victory in the Grey Cup (the Canadian Football League championship). See "Watts, J. C., Jr.," *Current Biography, 1999*: 591; "J.C. Watts," *Newsmakers 1999*.

9   Quoted in Jake Tapper, "Fade to White," 5 January 2003, *Washington Post Magazine*: W6.

10   "Watts, J. C., Jr.," *Current Biography, 1999*: 591.

11   Watts, *What Color is Conservative?*: 152.

12   "J. C. Watts," *Newsmakers 1999*. Though convinced of Watts's party loyalty, Republican officials worried that African-American voters who came to the polls to vote for Watts would split their tickets and cast their ballots for other Democratic candidates. Watts called this a "sick, pathetic theory." See Tapper, "Fade to White."

13   Watts's service on the commission was clouded by accusations that he accepted large campaign contributions from the oil and gas businesses he was responsible for regulating. See Jo Thomas, "Rising Congressional Leader Experienced in Self-Defense," 16 November 1998, *New York Times*: A1.

14   *Politics in America, 2002* (Washington, DC: Congressional Quarterly Inc., 2001): 825.

15   "J.C. Watts," *Newsmakers 1999*.

16   Mick Hinton, "Watts Defeats Apple in 4th," 21 September 1994, *Daily Oklahoman* (Oklahoma City, OK).

17   Mick Hinton, "Watts Gains National Help in House Race," 11 September 1994, *Daily Oklahoman*.

18 "J.C. Watts," *Newsmakers 1999*.

19 Dan Balz et al., "'Race Card' in Oklahoma," 20 October 1994, *Washington Post*: A24.

20 "Perryman Says He'll Swap Watts' Afro Photo in Ad," 21 October 1994, *Daily Oklahoman*; Thomas, "Rising Congressional Leader Experienced in Self-Defense": A1; Patrick Rogers et al., "Calling His Play; Former Gridiron Star J.C. Watts Is Now Scoring Points for the GOP," 24 March 1997, *People Magazine*: 141; Mick Hinton, "On the Campaign Trail Watts, Perryman Stump in 4th District," 31 October 1994, *Daily Oklahoman*.

21 "Election Statistics, 1920 to Present," available at http://clerk.house.gov/member_info/election.html.

22 "Julius Caesar Watts," Associated Press Candidate Biographies, 1996.

23 "Election Statistics, 1920 to Present," available at http://clerk.house.gov/member_info/election.html.

24 Chris Casteel, "Watts Striving to Reach Out to Black Voters," 15 July 2000, *Daily Oklahoman*.

25 Janelle Carter, "Watts to Bush: Get Back On Offense," 13 September 2000, Associated Press.

26 "Watts, J.C., Jr.," *Current Biography, 1999*: 591.

27 Susan Crabtree, "A Different Kind of Speakership for Watts," 24 October 2002, *Roll Call*.

28 Quoted in "J.C. Watts, Jr.," *Contemporary Black Biography*, Volume 14 (Detroit, MI: Gale Research Inc., 1997).

29 Sandalow, "The Republicans' Great Black Hope": 9.

30 "Watts, J.C., Jr.," *Current Biography, 1999*: 591.

31 Baldauf, "Oklahoman Brings Conservative Gospel to Broader Audience."

32 Jim Myers, "Watts' Plan Gets Push; Re-election Question Yet Unanswered," 7 January 2000, *Tulsa World* (Tulsa, OK).

33 Steven A. Holmes, "2 Black G.O.P. Lawmakers in House Differ Slightly on Affirmative Action," 6 August 1995, *New York Times*: 22.

34 Quoted in Tapper, "Fade to White."

35 Ibid.

36 "J.C. Watts," *Newsmakers 1999*.

37 Watts had previously rebutted President Clinton's post-election radio address in 1994. See "Watts, J.C., Jr.," *Current Biography, 1999*: 591.

38 Watts's response, delivered before a live audience in the Library of Congress, was quickly overshadowed by the announcement of a verdict in the civil trial of former NFL player O.J. Simpson. Some major networks divided their screen between Simpson and Watts, quickly returning full coverage to Simpson's trial in California at the end of the Representative's statement. Katharine Q. Seelye, "G.O.P., After Fumbling in '96, Turns to Orator for Response," 5 February 1997, *New York Times*: A1.

39 Seelye, "G.O.P., After Fumbling in '96, Turns to Orator for Response"; "J.C. Watts," *Newsmakers 1999*.

40 Tapper, "Fade to White."

41 Edward Walsh, "For Watts, A Bid to Broaden His Party's Appeal; House GOP's Only Black Member Knows Spotlight, Aspires to Join Leadership," 17 November 1998, *Washington Post*: A11.

42 Walsh, "For Watts, A Bid to Broaden His Party's Appeal."

43 See Katharine Q. Seelye, "Mix of Old and New Is to Lead House G.O.P.," 19 November 1998, *New York Times*: A1.

44 See, for example, Robert Novak, "House GOP Leaders Unhappy With J.C.," 19 December 1999, *Daily Oklahoman*; Art Pine, "Rep. Watts Says He Will Seek Reelection," 1 February 2000, *Los Angeles Times*: A10; "J.C. Watts," *Newsmakers 1999*.

45 Tapper, "Fade to White."

46 Ibid.

47 Pine, "Rep. Watts Says He Will Seek Reelection."

48 Tapper, "Fade to White."

49 Ibid.

50 Chris Casteel, "Watts Says 'It's Time to Let Go,'" 2 July 2002, *Daily Oklahoman*.

WATTS DECLINED AN INVITATION
TO JOIN THE TRADITIONALLY
LIBERAL CONGRESSIONAL
BLACK CAUCUS (CBC).
"I THINK THE CBC AND I WANT
THE SAME THINGS FOR THE
BLACK COMMUNITY," HE MUSED.
"THE DIFFERENCE IS HOW
WE GET THERE."

Juanita Millender-McDonald
1938–2007

UNITED STATES REPRESENTATIVE ★ 1996–2007
DEMOCRAT FROM CALIFORNIA

A fast-rising star in California politics, Juanita Millender-McDonald won her seat in the U.S. House of Representatives just six years after capturing her first elective office. From her position on the House Transportation and Infrastructure Committee, Representative Millender-McDonald shaped federal transportation legislation that directly affected her district and numerous federal programs. In 2007, she made history by becoming the first African-American woman to chair a standing congressional panel, the House Administration Committee.[1]

Juanita Millender was born on September 7, 1938, in Birmingham, Alabama, one of five children raised by Shelly Millender and Everlina (Dortch) Millender. After Everlina Millender's untimely death, Shelly Millender, a minister, moved his family to California. On July 26, 1955, Juanita Millender married James McDonald, Jr. By the time she was 26, the couple had five children. A homemaker for 15 years, Juanita Millender-McDonald returned to college, earning a B.S. in business administration from the University of Redlands in Redlands, California, in 1981. Millender-McDonald earned a master's degree in educational administration from California State University in Los Angeles in 1988. After teaching math and English in a public high school, she worked as an administrator in the Los Angeles Unified School District— eventually directing its gender equality programs.[2]

Millender-McDonald first entered elective politics at the local level in Los Angeles and served as a delegate to the Democratic National Conventions in 1984, 1988, and 1992. In 1982, she worked on behalf of the unsuccessful gubernatorial campaign of longtime Los Angeles Mayor Tom Bradley. Thereafter she worked on several local campaigns before entering a 1990 election for a seat on the Carson City Council. She displayed adroitness at

building networks for political support during that race. The first time she asked for the support of then-U.S. Representative Mervyn Dymally, the Representative declined, telling Millender-McDonald, "Local politics is too divisive; I don't want to get involved." But she was persistent. Dymally said, "She came back, this time with a delegation of friends and supporters. I said, 'What do you want?' She said, 'I need your endorsement.' I said, 'You have it.'"[3] Millender-McDonald became the first African-American woman elected to the council and in 1991 served as Carson City mayor *pro tempore*. In 1992, following the reapportionment of California state assembly districts, Millender-McDonald defeated two incumbent assemblymen whose Los Angeles-area districts had been merged. The contest broke down along racial lines, and Millender-McDonald prevailed when the incumbents split the white vote; she went on to serve in the California state assembly until 1996.[4] Within her first year in the assembly, she chaired two panels: the committee on insurance and the committee on revenue and taxation. From those posts, she sponsored a major transportation bill to create the Alameda Corridor, a national transportation artery designed to improve railroad and highway access to the San Pedro Bay Ports, which constitute one of the nation's largest shipping complexes.[5]

In December 1995, Millender-McDonald announced her candidacy to fill a U.S. House seat left vacant by the resignation of convicted Representative Walter R. Tucker III. Tucker's congressional district—which encompassed suburbs south of Los Angeles, including Carson and Compton—was heavily Democratic and working-class. African Americans and Hispanic Americans composed roughly 75 percent of the population. No GOP challenger entered the March 26, 1996, special election contest. Millender-McDonald and nine others, including fellow

IMAGE COURTESY OF OFFICE OF THE CLERK, U.S. HOUSE OF REPRESENTATIVES

state assemblyman Willard H. Murray and Robin Tucker, the wife of Walter Tucker, vied for election to the remainder of the term in the 104th Congress (1995–1997). With support from former longtime speaker of the state assembly and San Francisco Mayor Willie Brown, Millender-McDonald won with 27 percent of the vote; her nearest competitor, Murray, received 20 percent. In the simultaneous Democratic primary for the full term in the 105th Congress (1997–1999), Millender-McDonald prevailed over Murray by an even narrower margin: 24 to 21 percent.[6] In the fall 1996 campaign for the 105th Congress, she defeated Republican Michael E. Voetee with 85 percent of the vote. Representative Millender-McDonald won her subsequent five re-election campaigns with majorities of at least 75 percent. In 2006, she defeated Republican Herb Peters with 82 percent of the vote.[7]

After her swearing-in on April 16, 1996, Millender-McDonald served on the Transportation and Infrastructure Committee and the Small Business Committee. She kept both assignments throughout her congressional tenure. As a freshman, she was appointed Ranking Member of the Small Business Subcommittee on Workforce, Empowerment, and Government Programs. In the 106th Congress (1999–2001), Democratic leaders named her a regional party whip, and in the 107th Congress (2001–2003), she co-chaired the Democratic Caucus for Women's Issues. Then, in the 108th Congress (2003–2005), she drew assignments on the Committee on House Administration and the Joint Committee on Printing, and she was appointed Ranking Member of the Subcommittee on Tax, Finance, and Exports. In the 109th Congress (2005–2007), Democratic Minority Leader Nancy Pelosi named Millender-McDonald Ranking Member of the Committee on House Administration.[8] After the Democrats regained control of the House in the 2006 elections, she was named chairwoman of the House Administration Committee, Millender-McDonald also held the Vice-Chair post on the Joint Committee on the Library, whose membership roster was drawn from the House Administration Committee and the Senate Rules and Administration Committee.

Many of Representative Millender-McDonald's legislative initiatives came from her seat on the Transportation and Infrastructure Committee. In 2001, Millender-McDonald authored the Terrorism Threat to Public Transportation Assessment Act—a measure to evaluate vulnerabilities in the nation's mass transit systems. She also was a lead sponsor of the Nuclear Waste Responsible Component and Protection Act, which sought to ensure environmentally sound and safe means of transporting and storing chemical waste outside of inner cities. Her place on the Transportation and Infrastructure Committee also allowed her to attend to transportation projects directly affecting her district. During her first months in the House, Millender-McDonald secured $400 million in federal loan guarantees necessary to complete her state legislative work on the Alameda Corridor, a 20-mile railroad artery that connects the national rail system to the ports of Los Angeles and Long Beach. In the 108th Congress, Millender-McDonald helped draft the six-year Transportation Equity Act—which brought in more than $87 million in federal money for highway projects in and around her district. Her addition to that bill, the "Projects of National and Regional Significance," allocated more than $6.6 billion toward major transportation projects nationally.[9]

Much of Representative Millender-McDonald's House career was dedicated to the interests she held since her days in the California assembly: the Los Angeles public school system, job training, childcare, education, women's issues, and combating drug abuse. Millender-McDonald also worked on promoting awareness of health issues like cervical cancer, AIDS, asthma, and bone marrow registration. Although she worked away from the limelight, Millender-McDonald occasionally orchestrated dramatic political moments. In 1996, she brought then-Central Intelligence Agency (CIA) director John Deutsch to a Watts town hall meeting, where Deutsch fielded questions about allegations that the CIA funneled proceeds from the sale of crack cocaine to purchase arms for the Contras in Nicaragua. Three years later, seeking to boost the stalled ambassadorial appointment to New Zealand of former U.S. Senator Carol Moseley-Braun of Illinois, Millender-McDonald staged a sit-in at the office of Senator Jesse Helms of North Carolina, who was blocking the appointment.[10]

In mid-April 2007, Millender-McDonald was granted a six-week leave of absence from her House duties to receive treatment for cancer. She passed away at her home in Compton on April 22. House Speaker Nancy Pelosi of California remembered Millender-McDonald as "a trailblazer, always advocating for the full participation of all Americans in the success and prosperity of our country."[11]

FOR FURTHER READING

"Millender-McDonald, Juanita," *Biographical Directory of the U.S. Congress, 1774–Present,* http://bioguide.congress.gov/scripts/biodisplay.pl?index=M000714.

MANUSCRIPT COLLECTION

California State University, (Dominguez Hills, CA). Archives and Special Collections. Papers: The Juanita Millender-McDonald Collection has not yet been processed.

NOTES

1   Stephanie Tubbs Jones of Ohio was simultaneously appointed chairwoman of the House Committee on Standards of Official Conduct.

2   *Politics in America, 2004* (Washington, DC: Congressional Quarterly Inc., 2003): 138.

3   Quoted in Nicole Gaouette, "Juanita Millender-McDonald, 68; Southland Congresswoman," 23 April 2007, *Los Angeles Times*: B9.

4   *Politics in America, 1998* (Washington, DC: Congressional Quarterly Inc., 1997): 194.

5   *Politics in America, 2004*: 139.

6   *Politics in America, 1998*: 193–194.

7   "Election Statistics, 1920 to Present," available at http://clerk.house.gov/member_info/electionInfo/index.html.

8   *Almanac of American Politics, 2006* (Washington, DC: National Journal Inc., 2005): 270.

9   *Politics in America, 2004*: 138; "Official Biography of Juanita Millender-McDonald," http://www.house.gov/millender-mcdonald/bio.htm (accessed 22 November 2004); James Bornemeier, "Broader Horizons; Seat in Congress Opens New Doors for Juanita Millender-McDonald," 21 April 1996, *Los Angeles Times*: A3.

10 Gaouette, "Juanita Millender-McDonald, 68; Southland Congresswoman."

11 Ibid; Kelly McCormack and Sam Youngman, "Millender-McDonald Remembered for 'Dignity,' 'Determination,'" 24 April 2007, *The Hill*: 13.

Julia May Carson
1938–2007

UNITED STATES REPRESENTATIVE ★ 1997–2007
DEMOCRAT FROM INDIANA

Overcoming poverty and racism, Julia Carson served nearly two decades in the Indiana legislature and in an Indianapolis administrative office before winning election to the U.S. House in 1996. Representative Carson, the first African American and woman to represent the Indiana state capital, focused on issues that affected working-class Americans, many with which she was personally familiar. "The only thing some people learn from oppression and hatred is revenge. Others learn compassion and empathy," said former Representative Andy Jacobs, Carson's political mentor. "From the physical pain of material poverty and the mindlessly cruel persecution of nitwit racism, Julia Carson made her choice of hard work, compassion, and a pleasing sense of humor."[1]

Julia May Porter was born in Louisville, Kentucky, on July 8, 1938. Her single mother, Velma Porter, moved to Indianapolis, Indiana, to find work as a domestic. Julia Porter grew up poor, attended the local public schools, and worked part-time, waiting tables, delivering newspapers, and harvesting crops, among other jobs. In 1955, she graduated from Crispus Attucks High School in Indianapolis. Shortly thereafter she was married, and had two children, Sam and Tonya. She divorced while they were still young. She later studied at Martin University in Indianapolis and Indiana University in Bloomington. In 1965 she was working as a secretary at a local chapter of United Auto Workers when she met newly elected Representative Andy Jacobs. Jacobs was looking for a caseworker and district aide, and he hired Carson. She worked for Jacobs for seven years until 1972, when he encouraged her to run for office in the Indiana legislature. He recalled sitting in Carson's living room for an hour, trying to convince her to run. "Come on, kid," Jacobs encouraged. "This is the time to step up."[2] From 1973 to 1977, Carson served in the state house of representatives,

serving as the assistant minority caucus chair, before winning election to the Indiana senate. She served in the upper chamber until 1990, sitting on its finance committee and eventually holding the minority whip position. Throughout her service in the state legislature, Carson was employed as the human resources director at an electric company—a job she held from 1973 to 1996. In 1991, Carson won election as a Center Township trustee. In that post, she administered welfare payments in central Indianapolis, earning a reputation for defending the poor that would last throughout her career.[3] Carson successfully erased the agency's crippling debt—a $20-million deficit—leaving $7 million in the bank prior to winning a seat in Congress. "Julia Carson," observed the county's auditor, a Republican, "wrestled that monster to the ground."[4]

Representative Jacobs retired in 1996 after 15 terms representing a district encompassing greater Indianapolis. Traditionally moderate, the district was 68 percent white and 30 percent black. With Jacobs's endorsement, Carson topped the former district party chair, Ann DeLaney, in the Democratic primary with a margin of 49 to 31 percent. Political observers maintained that Carson was at a disadvantage in the general election against Republican Virginia Blankenbaker, insisting she could not win in the conservative-leaning, majority-white district. Both candidates were more liberal than their respective party's general positions, supporting abortion rights and opposing the death penalty. Carson sought to deflect attention from racial issues, insisting, "I am not your African American candidate. I am the Democratic candidate for Congress. I don't allow my opponents to stereotype me and confine me to a certain segment of the population."[5] She prevailed, with 53 percent of the vote to Blankenbaker's 45 percent.

Carson underwent heart surgery shortly after her election and was sworn in to office from her hospital

bed on January 9, 1997. She was unable to travel to Washington, DC, until early March. Her health problems led to speculation she would not return for re-election in 1998, but Carson quickly quelled the rumors.[6] Carson won her four re-election campaigns by slightly larger margins in her competitive district. Reapportionment in 2001 added more than 100,000 constituents, many of them Republican. Nevertheless, Carson was re-elected in 2004 and 2006, both times with 54 percent of the vote.[7]

When Representative Carson claimed her seat in the 105th Congress (1997–1999), she received posts on the Banking and Financial Services Committee (later renamed Financial Services) and the Veterans' Affairs Committee. In the 108th Congress (2003–2005) she left Veterans' Affairs to accept an assignment on the Transportation and Infrastructure Committee.

Representative Carson had varied legislative interests, ranging from national issues affecting children and working Americans to local programs of particular interest to her Indianapolis constituency. From her seat on the Financial Services Committee, Carson authored legislation to reform the debt consolidation industry. Boosting the "financial literacy" of average Americans was one of her chief goals. To that end, she helped create the Indiana Mortgage and Foreclosure Hotline to counsel homeowners and potential buyers about the mortgage process. Carson noted that Indiana residents had one of the country's highest rates of homeownership in 2001, only to see a record number of foreclosures in 2004. "Homeownership," Carson declared, "is the cornerstone of a healthy thriving city."[8] Carson was a regular sponsor of children's safety, health, and nutrition legislation. In 1999, she submitted comprehensive gun safety legislation, including a provision requiring safety locks on handguns. "Kids and guns are a deadly combination," she noted in 1999. "It makes no sense that it is easier for kids to operate a handgun than it is for kids to open an aspirin lid."[9]

Representative Carson's work on the Transportation and Infrastructure Committee also allowed her to support local Indiana businesses. In 2003, Carson helped win $11 million in federal funding for transportation initiatives in Indianapolis, including highway expansion, street improvements, and augmented public transportation.[10] In 2005, she sponsored the largest Amtrak re-authorization bill in history—the National Defense Rail Act. The $40 billion bill provided for the development of new rail lines including high-speed rail corridors, and Carson supported the bill partially because Amtrak's largest repair facility was located near Indianapolis. In 2000, Carson was one of the last House Members to support the extension of permanent normal trade relations with China. Intensely lobbied by President William J. (Bill) Clinton's administration to support the bill, Carson hesitated because of China's questionable human rights record and organized labor's opposition to the measure. "I feel like I have been put in a Maytag washer and put on the spin cycle," she noted before the vote. She reluctantly voted in favor of the legislation, believing that increased foreign trade would benefit Indianapolis businesses.

One of Carson's crowning legislative achievements was the bill she authored and introduced during the 106th Congress (1999–2001) to award the Congressional Gold Medal to civil rights activist Rosa Parks. It was while reading Parks's autobiography, *Quiet Strength*, in early 1998, that Carson decided the civil rights activist—whose refusal to move to the back of a segregated bus in 1955 galvanized the modern civil rights movement—should be awarded the highest civilian honor bestowed by Congress.[11] "I had a lingering kind of adoration in my own soul for Rosa," Carson noted. "I always believed in my heart that it was Rosa who paved the way for me to go to Congress and to other places. I felt like it then became my purpose to give her some honor, to repay her."[12] The Representative introduced a resolution to honor Parks with the medal on February 4, 1999—Parks's 86th birthday. Knowing the civil rights icon was watching House proceedings on her television, Carson ignored a House rule requiring Members to address only the Speaker *pro tempore*. "Mrs. Parks, I am grateful for your steadfastness," she declared. Initially, the bill attracted only 40 cosponsors—primarily

Members of the Congressional Black Caucus (CBC). Carson began a media campaign on nationally syndicated radio and television programs, eventually netting 329 cosponsors. On April 20, the House passed the bill, 424 to 1. The Senate unanimously followed suit.[13] "This is one of the best days of my life," declared a tearful Carson. "Not for anything I have done to honor her, but the honor Rosa Parks brought to this whole nation."[14] On June 15, 1999, visitors packed the Capitol Rotunda to attend the Congressional Gold Medal ceremony. Carson was among the dignitaries who spoke at the ceremony, along with President Clinton, who presented the medal to Parks. Carson later helped her colleagues pass legislation allowing Parks to lie in honor in the Capitol Rotunda when she died in October 2005. Parks was the first woman to be given this honor.[15]

In late 2007, Carson's health once again became a concern. The Representative expressed frustration with her regular battle with asthma and diabetes. After missing an important vote due to health problems, Carson noted, "I understand how an athlete feels when they sit one out to recover from an injury. The minutes move slowly, and you want nothing more than to be in for the big game."[16] In October, Carson took a two-week leave of absence to recover from a leg infection that had forced her to traverse the Capitol in a wheelchair.[17] One month later, Carson announced that she had been diagnosed with terminal lung cancer during a follow-up examination of her leg. Carson succumbed to the disease on December 15 in her Indianapolis home. She lay in state in the statehouse in Indianapolis on December 21. "Let's remember Congresswoman Carson by doing the people's work and fighting for those who don't have a voice," said her grandson, André Carson. "When you talk about Julia Carson, you're talking about an American icon. The people's champ," he concluded.[18]

FOR FURTHER READING

"Carson, Julia May," *Biographical Directory of the U.S. Congress, 1774–Present*, http://bioguide.congress.gov/scripts/biodisplay.pl?index=C000191.

NOTES

1   "Official Biography of Julia Carson," http://www.juliacarson.house.gov/display2.cfm?id=778&type=news (accessed 14 June 2002).

2   Rob Schneider, "Carson Remembered: Congresswoman Gave Voice to Disadvantaged," 16 December 2007, *Indianapolis Star*.

3   "The Quotable Julia Carson," 15 December 2007, *Indianapolis Star*.

4   "Julia Carson," *Contemporary Black Biography*, Volume 23 (Detroit, MI: Gale Research Inc., 1999).

5   *Almanac of American Politics, 1998* (Washington, DC: National Journal Inc., 1997): 552.

6   See "The Quotable Julia Carson."

7   "Election Statistics, 1920 to Present," available at http://clerk.house.gov/member_info/election.html.

8   "Hotline May Help Homeowners," 2 March 2004, *Noblesville Ledger* (Noblesville, IN).

9   "Rep. Carson to Introduce Gun Safety Bill," 29 January 1999, Associated Press.

10 Anthony Shoettle, "Carson Steps to Plate for Local Transportation Projects," 24 March 2003, *Indianapolis Star*.

11 George Stuteville, "Carson's 1st Bill Pays Tribute to Civil Rights Pioneer," 19 April 1999, *Indianapolis Star*. See also Office of the Clerk, "Congressional Gold Medal Recipients," available at http://clerk.house.gov/art_history/house_history/goldMedal.html.

12 Rob Schneider, "She Never Forgot," 16 December 2007, *Indianapolis Star* (quotation from April 1999).

13 Carson's House bill (H.R. 573) was eventually supplanted by a Senate version (S. 531), sponsored by Senator Spencer Abraham of Michigan. The Senate bill became law.

14 "The Quotable Julia Carson."

15 "Individuals Who Have Lain in State or in Honor," Office of the Clerk, available at http://clerk.house.gov/art_history/house_history/lieinstate.html.

16 "The Quotable Julia Carson."

17 Maureen Groppe, "Carson to Miss Two More Weeks," 3 October 2007, *Indianapolis Star*.

18 Bill Ruthhart, "Farewell, Friend," 22 December 2007, *Indianapolis Star*; Ken Kusner, "Mourners Bid Adieu to 'People's Champ,'" 22 December 2007, *Fort Wayne Journal Gazette*.

Harold Ford, Jr.

1970–

UNITED STATES REPRESENTATIVE ★ 1997–2007
DEMOCRAT FROM TENNESSEE

Elected in 1996, Harold Ford, Jr., established a reputation as a moderate who took an interest in the social and economic issues that affected his constituents. Ford's mother recalled that, as a four-year-old attending his father's swearing-in as a freshman House Member, Harold, Jr., raised his hand and declared, "This is what I want to be when I grow up."[1] In contrast to an earlier generation of African Americans in Congress (including Harold Ford, Sr.) who maintained the legislative legacies of the civil rights movement, Ford, Jr., developed economic and technological solutions for a broader constituency.

The eldest son of Harold Eugene and Dorothy Bowles Ford, Harold Eugene Ford, Jr., was born on May 11, 1970, in Memphis, Tennessee. His father was a member of the Tennessee state house of representatives and was elected in 1974 to the U.S. House, where he served 22 years. His mother was a longtime employee of the U.S. Department of Agriculture.[2] The Ford family moved to Washington, DC, in the late 1970s, and Harold attended the elite St. Albans School for Boys. Ford acknowledged that his studies at the school shaped his political philosophy: "For me, and for the other kids who were not white, it was a very heterogeneous place . . . I had to get along with everybody. That helped me later on when I was in situations where you had to say, 'Hey, let's all get together and try to figure this out.'"[3] In 1992, he graduated with a B.A. in history from the University of Pennsylvania and worked on William J. (Bill) Clinton's presidential campaign. Four years later, Ford earned a J.D. from the University of Michigan School of Law. He served briefly as a staff aide for the U.S. Senate Committee on the Budget and as a special assistant at the U.S. Department of Commerce. In addition, Ford worked on his father's congressional campaigns in 1992 and 1994.

After his father announced his retirement from the House in 1996, Ford ran to succeed him in the district encompassing the bulk of Memphis, Tennessee. The predominantly African-American district (60 percent) was one of the most liberal in the state and included more blacks than any southern city outside Texas.[4] Ford's father served as his chief campaign strategist. Using the Ford name to full effect among Memphis-area constituents, Harold Ford, Jr., distributed campaign buttons and T-shirts that read "Jr." Asked what being a Representative required, Ford said a "willingness to work hard, a willingness to listen and having the courage to stand up for what you believe in and having the courage to stand up for those that you represent." Ford ran on three platforms: increased federal funding for education and job training, opposition to Medicare price hikes, and crime prevention.[5] Contending against Steve Cohen, a state senator, and Rufus Jones, a state representative, Ford won the primary with 61 percent of the vote. His opponent in the general election was Rod DeBerry, a local politician who ran against Harold Ford, Sr., for the seat in 1992 and 1994.[6] The candidates both advocated economic empowerment, but proposed different strategies for achieving it. Ford stressed educational opportunities in a city with a high dropout rate, whereas DeBerry promoted a broader package that emphasized education, job opportunities, and economic development for the Memphis area.[7] Both candidates staked their positions on familiar party policies: Ford advocated government solutions to local problems, whereas DeBerry promoted local solutions and less government involvement. In the general election, Ford prevailed with 61 percent of the vote, making him the first African American to succeed a parent in Congress. In his subsequent four re-election campaigns, Ford won with 79 percent or more. He ran unopposed in 2000.[8]

Ford clarified from the beginning that his legislative style would be distinct from his father's, which was liberal

and minority-focused. "I represent this entire district . . . I respect my dad and . . . admire him a great deal," Ford noted. "But I don't think he would respect me if I didn't have the fortitude to disagree with him if I felt he was wrong." Ford remained dedicated to directing government resources toward the poor, but he emphasized expanding educational opportunities. Ford also reached out to some of his father's political rivals, such as Willie Herenton, the mayor of Memphis, with whom he had a good relationship. Ford stressed pragmatism. Memphis City Hall, he observed, is "the principal contracting agency with the federal government. I have a responsibility to secure what funds and resources I can for my state and city."[9]

Ford's determination and leadership skills laid the groundwork for his quick rise in the Democratic Party. Shortly after he entered Congress in January 1997, Ford was chosen by his Democratic colleagues as freshman class president, providing him added influence as a spokesperson for the newly elected Members and as an intermediary with House leaders. The progression of Ford's committee assignments also reflected his resolve to play a significant role in the House. He initially received assignments on Education and the Workforce and Government Reform and Oversight. He left the latter committee in the 107th Congress (2001–2003) to accept a seat on the Financial Services Committee (his father had served on the predecessor to that committee). In the following Congress, Ford won a seat on the influential Budget Committee. Pegged as one of the Democratic Party's bright young stars, Ford received widespread media attention when he delivered the keynote address at the 2000 Democratic National Convention.

Unlike the previous generation of black lawmakers, who advocated federal solutions to counteract racial and economic discrimination, Ford proposed legislation aimed at enhancing the assets of working-class Americans through savings programs and tax incentives.[10] Although Ford supported Democratic causes such as environmental protection and affirmative action, he also backed measures that were opposed by many in his party, like private school vouchers and federal funding for faith-based charities. Additionally, Ford supported Republican initiatives such as a federal amendment banning gay marriage; the USA PATRIOT Act, which was designed to deter terrorism by strengthening law enforcement; and the authorization to use military force in Iraq.[11] Among the bills sponsored by Ford were measures that would reform campaign finance, make college affordable, and hold the gun industry accountable to local authorities for gun violence.[12]

Though his approach was moderate overall, Ford maintained a comparatively liberal voting record relative to those of the other Representatives from his state.[13] He stressed his pragmatism and his ability to work with Republican colleagues across the aisle.[14] As a member of the Congressional Black Caucus (CBC), he maintained his independence by choosing his battles. On issues such as affirmative action and tax cuts, the Tennessee Representative voted with his colleagues. However, Ford's support for a balanced budget, prayer in schools, and the establishment of private accounts to bolster Social Security contrasted with the position of many of his CBC colleagues. Ford contended that the "old labels have lost a lot of their meaning . . . ideology makes it easier to resist good ideas." [15]

Ford established himself as a centrist in the House. He joined several organizations, such as the New Democrat and Blue Dog coalitions, that included a range of social moderates and fiscal conservatives. In 2002 Ford orchestrated what he described as an "underdog campaign" against Nancy Pelosi of California for the position of Democratic Leader that was vacated by Richard Gephardt of Missouri.[16] As a late entrant, Ford publicized his candidacy through media outlets rather than using the traditional and more successful method of intense behind-the-scenes campaigning. The main issue separating the two contenders was the Iraq War Resolution that Ford had backed (the war began in March 2003).[17] The Iraq issue divided Ford from many rank-and-file Democrats who believed the party's base demanded a more aggressive opposition to the administration's stance on Iraq.[18] Ultimately, Pelosi prevailed, 177 to 29, in her historic run to become the first woman to lead a party in Congress.[19]

In May 2005, Ford, who had twice considered running for the U.S. Senate, announced his candidacy for the seat that was being vacated by Senate Majority Leader Bill Frist in 2007. "[W]ith five good terms in the House behind me . . . I believe I'm ready to meet the challenges ahead of us in a way that will make Tennesseans as proud of me as I am of Tennessee," Ford said. He also believed that serving in the Senate would enhance his ability to direct federal and fiscal resources to his state; he argued, "The U.S. Senate is where all the decisions are going to be made over the next 10 to 20 years—from Social Security to Medicare to how we create better jobs in this country, and national security issues."[20]

During his senatorial campaign, Ford ran as a centrist "who appealed to moderate Republican and independent voters . . . by focusing on . . . health care, education, and economic development."[21] Throughout the campaign, Ford emphasized that his political stance derived from his personal beliefs rather than from liberal Democratic orthodoxy. "If I was doing the textbook thing that Democrats do . . . I'd say 'Republicans want to short Social Security, they want to rob poor children of their college education, they want to deny families the education system.' Don't get me wrong, there's some truth to that. But that's not me. Just let me be myself."[22] Ford's election strategy was to maintain his name recognition and base

in western Tennessee while building support in central and eastern Tennessee.[23] Analysts predicted that Ford had a good chance of winning the seat in light of widespread voter dissatisfaction with the Bush administration and minimal opposition from Democrats in the primary.[24] However, when Bob Corker, a former mayor of Chattanooga, won the Republican nomination in August 2006, the Senate race became hotly contested due to a controversial ad campaign and national media attention.[25] Ford's election strategy yielded mixed results: Although he performed well in urban areas such as Memphis, Nashville, and Chattanooga, Corker received support in suburban counties around Nashville and the eastern part of the state.[26] Corker prevailed in a narrow election with 51 percent to Ford's 48 percent.[27]

After leaving the U.S. House in January 2007, Ford served as a visiting professor at Vanderbilt University and the Lyndon B. Johnson School of Public Affairs at the University of Texas–Austin. He also succeeded Iowa Governor Tom Vilsack as chairman of the Democratic Leadership Council (DLC), an organization that fosters a moderate approach to economic development, welfare reform, and international business.[28] Ford served as a vice chairman and senior policy advisor to a major investment company and appeared as a political commentator on network television.[29] In 2007 he became engaged to Emily Threlkeld, a business manager for a fashion designer in New York City.[30]

FOR FURTHER READING

"Ford, Harold E., Jr.," *Biographical Directory of the U.S. Congress, 1774–Present,* http://bioguide.congress.gov/scripts/biodisplay.pl?index=F000262.

MANUSCRIPT COLLECTION

University of Tennessee, Modern Political Archives, Howard H. Baker, Jr., Center for Public Policy (Knoxville, TN). *Papers*: The Harold Ford, Jr., Collection is not yet available for research.

NOTES

1   *Current Biography, 1999* (New York: H. W. Wilson & Company, 1999): 204.

2   *Almanac of American Politics, 1996* (Washington, DC: National Journal Press, 1995): 1252.

3   Jonathan Darman, "The Path to Power," 30 October 2006, *Newsweek*: 4.

4   *Politics in America, 2006* (Washington, DC: Congressional Quarterly Inc., 2005): 963.

5   Nate Hobbs, "Eager Ford Embraces His Father's Legacy," 9 June 1996, *The Commercial Appeal*: 1B.

6   Terry Keeter, "Ford Jr. Wins in Landslide Despite Record Crossover," 2 August 1996, *The Commercial Appeal*: 1A; "DeBerry, Ford Jr. Pull No Punches at Forum, Schools, Experience Emerge as Main Issues," 9 October 1996, *The Commercial Appeal*: 1B.

7   Nate Hobbs, "DeBerry's Solution Is Business; Ford's Is Education,"19 September 1996, *The Commercial Appeal*: 1B.

8   Nate Hobbs, "Ford, DeBerry Want Balanced Budget Law," 20 September 1996, *The Commercial Appeal*: 2B; "DeBerry and Ford Draw Clear Differences Down Party Lines," 29 October 1996, *The Commercial Appeal*: 1A; *Politics in America, 2002* (Washington, DC, Congressional Quarterly Press, 2001): 948; *Almanac of American Politics, 2006*: 1566; "Ford Sworn-In as Youngest Member of 105th Congress," 27 January 1997, *Jet*: 4.

9   James W. Brosnan, "He Won't Be 'Puppet,' Ford Jr. Vows, Backs Dad's Urban Agenda But Plans Education Push," 7 November 1996, *The Commercial Appeal*: 7B.

10   *Politics in America, 2006*: 962; "Official Biography of Harold Ford," at http://www.house.gov/ford/about/index.shtml (accessed 16 May 2006).

11   "Harold Ford, Jr.," *Contemporary Black Biography* 16 (Detroit, MI: Gale Research Inc., 1997); "Ford, Harold E. Jr.," *Current Biography, 1999*: 205–206; *Politics in America, 2006*: 962.

12   Ford sponsored H.R. 2051 (Public Voice Campaign Finance Reform Act of 1997) in the 105th Congress (1997–1999), H.R. 1086 (Gun Industry Responsibility Act) in the 106th Congress (1999–2001), and H.R. 1631 (Make College Affordable Act of 1999) in the 106th Congress (1999–2001).

13   Darman, "The Path to Power": 5. Darman noted that Ford was "one of only three African-American members" of the Blue Dog Coalition.

14   "Official Biography of Harold Ford."

15   *Almanac of American Politics, 2006*: 1568; Lynette Clemetson, "Losing the Old Labels," 28 January 2002, *Newsweek*: 50.

16   Carl Hulse, "The Challenger," 10 November 2002, *New York Times*: 30.

17   Rob Johnson, "Ford Impresses With Ambition, Moxie Despite Loss," 18 November 2002, *The Tennessean*: 1A. For a detailed critique, see Harold Ford, Jr., "Why I Should Be Minority Leader,"13 November 2002, *Washington Post*: A27.

18   Michael Crowley, "Ford's Theater," July/August 2006, *Atlantic Monthly*: 44; Darman, "The Path to Power": 6; *Politics in America, 2006*: 963.

19   Marc Sandalow, "Savvy, Cash Clinched Job for Pelosi; Tightly Orchestrated Campaign Followed Lucrative Fund Raising," 17 November 2002, *San Francisco Chronicle*: A3.

20   Lauren Whittington, "Ford Officially Enters Tenn. Senate Contest," 26 May 2005, *Roll Call*; "Ford Drives Home His Strategy," at http://haroldfordjr2006.blogspot.com/2005/07/ford-drives-home-his-strategy.html (accessed 1 January 2007).

21 Ashley Rowland, "Impact of Race on Ford's Defeat Debated," 12 November 2006, *Chattanooga Times*: 3.

22 Darman, "The Path to Power": 2.

23 V. O. Key, Jr., *Southern Politics in State and Nation* (Knoxville: University of Tennessee Press, 1984): 75–81. East Tennessee has been a reliable base of GOP support since the Civil War, whereas central Tennessee contains a mixture of Democrats and Republicans.

24 Crowley, "Ford's Theater": 44. For a more comprehensive analysis, see Corey Dade and Nikhil Deogun, "Republicans' Hold on the South Gets Test in Tennessee," 26 October 2006, *The Wall Street Journal*: A1.

25 Crowley, "Ford's Theater": 45–46; Karen Tumulty and Perry Bacon, Jr., "Why Harold Ford Has a Shot," 14 August 2006, *Time*: 44.

26 Beth Rucker, "After Senate Defeat, What's Harold Ford Jr.'s Next Move?" 10 November 2006, Associated Press.

27 "Election Statistics, 1920 to Present," available at http://clerk.house.gov/member_info/electionInfo/index.html.

28 "Harold Ford Jr. to Be Visiting Professor at Vanderbilt," at http://www.memphisflyer.com/memphis/Content?old=23532 (accessed 29 January 2007); "New DLC Chair: Harold Ford, Jr.": http://www.ndol.org/print.cfm?contentid=254178 (accessed 12 February 2007); "Vanderbilt Class Maps Strategies for 2008 Presidential Campaign; Former Congressman Harold Ford Jr. and John Geer to Co-Teach," 20 July 2007, *Ascribe Newswire*; "Harold Ford Jr. to Teach at University of Texas," 15 October 2007, Associated Press.

29 "Former Congressman Harold Ford Joins Merrill Lynch as Vice Chairman," 14 February 2007, Associated Press; "Harold Ford Jr. Joins Fox News as Political Contributor to Network's News Programming," 14 March 2007, *Business Wire*.

30 Amy Argetsinger and Roxanne Roberts, "Harold Ford Jr.'s Next Election: To Tie the Knot," 10 October 2007, *Washington Post*: C03.

Frank W. Ballance, Jr.

1942–

UNITED STATES REPRESENTATIVE ★ 2003–2004
DEMOCRAT FROM NORTH CAROLINA

The first African American elected to the state legislature from eastern North Carolina since the Reconstruction Era, Frank Ballance won election to the U.S. House in 2002, succeeding Representative Eva Clayton in a district that included much of coastal North Carolina. During an 18-month tenure in the House that was abbreviated by health problems and a probe into his management of a nonprofit foundation, Ballance served on the Agriculture Committee—an important assignment for his predominantly rural, farm-based constituency.

Frank Winston Ballance, Jr., was born in Windsor, North Carolina, on February 15, 1942, to Frank Winston and Alice Eason Ballance. His mother, noted one political activist in eastern North Carolina, was the "political wheel" of Bertie County, organizing drives for voter registration and advocating greater representation for the area's black voters.[1] Ballance graduated in 1959 from W. S. Etheridge High School in Windsor and four years later earned a bachelor of science degree from North Carolina Central University in Durham. In 1965, Ballance graduated with a law degree from the same institution. He was employed as a professor at South Carolina State College (now South Carolina State University) from 1965 to 1966. Ballance served in the North Carolina National Guard in 1968 and continued on as a reservist until 1971. He practiced law, establishing a firm along with Theaoseus T. Clayton (the husband of future U.S. Representative Eva Clayton) in Warrenton, North Carolina. Ballance married Bernadine Smallwood, a lawyer, and they raised three children: Garey, Angela, and Valerie.

Ballance became active in local politics in the late 1960s as a youth director of the local chapter of the National Association for the Advancement of Colored People. He eventually ran two unsuccessful campaigns: for a seat as a judge on a district court in eastern North Carolina in 1968

and, after switching to the Republican Party, for a seat on the Warren County Commission in 1974. Ballance soon returned to the Democratic Party "to my people, where my votes are."[2] In 1982, Ballance became the first black in roughly a century to be elected to the statehouse from the eastern section of the state, defeating a white lawyer to represent a newly redrawn district. A local newspaper published the story under the headline "Free at Last." Ballance recalled, "Among the black community, there was great excitement that a new day had dawned and things would be different."[3] He served from 1983 to 1987 in the North Carolina state house of representatives. He was unsuccessful in his bid for a nomination to the North Carolina senate in 1986 but was elected two years later and served in the upper chamber from 1989 to 2002. As a state senator, Ballance was a leading critic of the death penalty, especially for mentally retarded convicts. He also was responsible for a four-year education plan that raised teachers' salaries statewide, a measure to fund state community colleges with local bonds, and the establishment of a mental health fund.[4]

In November 2001, when six-term Representative Eva Clayton announced her retirement from the House, Ballance entered the race to succeed her. Ballance had managed Clayton's first successful run for the U.S. House in a special election in 1992 to fill the vacancy resulting from the death of U.S. Representative Walter B. Jones. A decade later, Clayton encouraged Ballance to run in the district, which encompassed much of northeastern North Carolina, arching southward from the Virginia border along the Albemarle and Pamlico Sounds and including areas encompassed by Ballance's state legislative district. Some of its major commercial towns included Goldsboro, Kinston, and Greenville. The district was heavily Democratic (Democrats outnumbered Republicans four

IMAGE COURTESY OF U.S. HOUSE OF REPRESENTATIVES PHOTOGRAPHY OFFICE

to one) and was majority African American (50.5 percent).[5] Among those vying for the nomination were Sam Davis, a Pasquotank County commissioner; former U.S. Attorney Janice Cole; and Christine Fitch, chairwoman of the Wilson County school board. A lawsuit over state redistricting pushed the May primary back to September. Ballance campaigned on his 18 years' experience in the state legislature. In the September 10, 2002, Democratic primary, Ballance prevailed convincingly over his three competitors, with 47 percent of the vote, capturing 17 of 23 counties in the district; the nearest runner up, Davis, tallied 26 percent.[6] In the general election, Ballance defeated Republican nominee Greg Dority, a security consultant, by a margin of 64 to 35 percent.[7]

When Representative Ballance was sworn in to the House in January 2003, he received seats on the Agriculture Committee and the Small Business Committee. Weeks after winning election to the House, the Democratic freshmen chose Ballance as class president—an honor that was conferred on Ballance's predecessor, Representative Clayton.[8] The position provided some influence because the class president traditionally served as the spokesperson for their first-term colleagues and as an intermediary with House leaders.

Representative Ballance's assignment to the Agriculture Committee was key for his rural district, which relied on its large tobacco crop as well as its sizable harvest of cotton and peanuts. Two of the district's primary industrial products were textiles and lumber. Ballance called attention to the plight of thousands of textile workers in his district who had recently lost jobs, arguing that without more aid, the state would "face a crisis of chronic unemployment with shrinking safety nets to combat this crisis."[9] He also placed a priority—as had Representative Clayton—on securing federal money for education and better access to health care for his district. In 2003, he opposed a Medicare prescription drug plan backed by the George W. Bush administration, arguing that it favored health maintenance organizations (HMOs) and drug companies over the interests of many of the

elderly and poor constituents of his district.[10] Additionally, Representative Ballance joined other members of the North Carolina delegation in October 2003, to secure federal relief funding for portions of North Carolina that were devastated by Hurricane Isabel.[11]

By the fall of 2003, Representative Ballance's congressional career became mired in controversy surrounding a nonprofit substance abuse facility that he cofounded in 1985. The John A. Hyman Memorial Youth Foundation, located in Ballance's hometown of Warrenton, North Carolina, was named after the state's first African-American Representative, who represented what was known as the "Old Black 2nd District," which wound its way through eastern North Carolina. As a state senator, Ballance had secured state funding for the nonprofit while continuing to serve as chairman of the foundation's board of directors.[12] Investigations by the Federal Bureau of Investigation and North Carolina state regulators uncovered "conflicts of interests"—including payments to Ballance's family members, political allies, and campaign staff. Additionally, the foundation had failed to file state and federal nonprofit taxes for years.[13]

A number of candidates were prepared to challenge the incumbent in the 2004 Democratic primary. Late in the filing period, Ballance formally entered the race, only to withdraw several days later. On May 7, 2004, Representative Ballance announced his retirement from the House, citing myasthenia gravis, a debilitating neuromuscular disease that weakens the muscles. In explaining his decision to leave office before the end of the 108th Congress (2003–2005), Ballance commented, "We expect that with time and medication that I'd be fine. It's just that it did not appear that I was going to have the energy and strength to run this vigorous campaign that I had to run."[14] The North Carolina Representative resigned from the House effective June 11, 2004, and retired to his hometown of Warrenton. Ballance was eventually succeeded by former North Carolina Supreme Court Justice G. K. Butterfield in a special election held on July 20 to fill the vacant seat.

In early September 2004, Ballance was indicted on federal corruption charges related to his management of the Hyman Foundation.[15] In November 2004, he pled guilty to one count of conspiracy to commit mail fraud and launder money.[16] In October 2005, he received a four-year jail sentence.[17]

FOR FURTHER READING

"Ballance, Frank W.," *Biographical Directory of the U.S. Congress, 1774–Present*, http://bioguide.congress.gov/scripts/biodisplay.pl?index=B001238.

NOTES

1　Jena Heath, "Ballance Evens Scales by Breaking Barriers," 2 February 1997, *The News & Observer*: B1.

2　Heath, "Ballance Evens Scales by Breaking Barriers."

3　Ibid.

4　*Almanac of American Politics, 2004* (Washington, DC: National Journal Inc., 2003): 1197.

5　*Almanac of American Politics, 2004*: 1197.

6　"Sept. 10 Primary Election Results," 18 November 2002, *News and Observer*: B5; *Almanac of American Politics, 2004*: 1198.

7　"Election Statistics, 1920 to Present," available at http://clerk.house.gov/member_info/electionInfo/index.html.

8　"Ballance Elected to Lead Freshmen of 108th Congress," 22 November 2002, *Greensboro News and Record*: B2.

9　*Congressional Record*, House, 108th Cong., 1st sess. (14 May 2003): H4099–4100.

10　*Congressional Record*, House, 108th Cong., 1st sess. (4 March 2003): H1504–1505.

11　*Congressional Record*, House, 108th Cong., 1st sess. (1 October 2003): H9106–9107.

12　Dane Kane, "Ballance To Keep House Post," 9 September 2003, *The News & Observer*: B4;

13　Damon Chappie and Erin P. Billings, "Ballance Vows To Stay on After Harsh Audit," 23 October 2003, *Roll Call.*

14　Dan Kane, "Ballance Drops Out of Race; Scandal, Health Figure in Decision," 8 May 2004, *The News & Observer*: A1; Jim Morrill, Mark Johnson, and Staff Writers, "Ballance Ends Campaign; U.S. Congressman's Withdrawal Brings Rush of Hopefuls on Last Day of Election Filing," 8 May 2004, *Charlotte Observer*: 1B; Lauren W. Whittington and Erin P. Billings, "Embattled Ballance Retiring," 10 May 2004, *Roll Call.*

15　Matthew Eisley, "Ballance Charged With Corruption; Indictment Alleges Abuse of State Post," 3 September 2004, *The News & Observer*: A1.

16　Matthew Eisley, "Ballance Legacy in Tatters; Guilty Plea Ahead in Corruption Case," 9 November 2004, *The News & Observer*: A1; "A Trust Betrayed," editorial, 11 November 2004, *The News & Observer*: A16; "Ambition and Crime: Rep. Frank Ballance's Actions Stole the Public's Trust," editorial, 15 November 2004, *Charlotte Observer*: 16A.

17　Dan Kane, "Ballance Gets 4 Years for Misuse of Money," 13 October 2005, *The News & Observer*: A1.

Denise L. Majette
1955–

UNITED STATES REPRESENTATIVE ★ 2003–2005
DEMOCRAT FROM GEORGIA

Upsetting a veteran incumbent in the Democratic primary for a congressional seat from Georgia, Denise Majette coasted to victory in the general election, earning a spot in the U.S. House of Representatives for the 108th Congress (2003–2005). One of five new African-American Members elected in 2002, Majette described herself as "pro-choice, anti-death penalty, for protecting rights of workers and making sure that everyone has access on a level playing field."[1]

Denise L. Majette was born on May 18, 1955, in Brooklyn, New York, the daughter of Voyd Lee and Olivia Carolyn (Foster) Majette. Until 1972 she resided in New York, where one of her role models was Shirley Chisholm, the first black Congresswoman. Majette attended Yale University, graduating with a B.A. in 1976. After college, she decided to attend law school because of her anguish over President John F. Kennedy's assassination in 1963. "I wanted to be able to use the law to effect social change and make things better for people who otherwise didn't have those opportunities," she later recalled.[2] After earning a J.D. in 1979 from Duke University Law School, Majette began her professional career as a staff attorney at the Legal Aid Society in Winston-Salem, North Carolina, and later served as a clinical adjunct law professor at Wake Forest University. In 1983, Majette moved to Stone Mountain, Georgia, with her husband Rogers J. Mitchell, Jr., and their two sons from former marriages, to accept a position as law clerk for Judge R. Keegan Federal at the superior court of DeKalb County. Over the next two decades, Majette served as a law assistant to Judge Robert Benham of the Georgia court of appeals, a special assistant attorney general for the state of Georgia, and a partner in an Atlanta law firm. In 1992, Majette became a judge of administrative law for the Atlanta office of the Georgia state board of workers' compensation. On June 8, 1993,

Georgia Governor Zell Miller appointed Majette as a judge on the state court of DeKalb County. During her nearly 10 years as a judge, Majette presided over a variety of court proceedings, including criminal trials, civil cases, and hearings.[3]

On February 5, 2002, Majette resigned from the bench, announcing her candidacy as a Democrat for a seat in the Georgia congressional district encompassing the suburban area east of Atlanta—although she lacked the high profile of the Democratic incumbent, five-term Representative Cynthia McKinney. Majette said she decided to run for public office because she felt McKinney had become disconnected from the issues affecting DeKalb County. The race garnered national attention after McKinney implied that President George W. Bush deliberately ignored pre–September 11 intelligence reports suggesting an imminent terrorist attack and that his big-business supporters profited in the wake of the attacks. Majette capitalized on the controversy that surrounded her opponent's remarks. Also, she received a strong endorsement from Zell Miller, who had been elected a U.S. Senator. Middle-class voters flocked to Majette in the August 20, 2002, primary, joined by Republicans who took advantage of Georgia state law, which allowed voters to switch parties during primaries. Majette captured 58 percent of the vote. In the general election she easily defeated her Republican opponent, Cynthia Van Auken, gaining 77 percent of the vote.[4]

Upon being sworn in to the U.S. House of Representatives in January 2003, Majette observed, "I was just looking around the room and appreciating the kind of work the Congress will have to do and how that will impact the nation and the world."[5] Majette received assignments on the Budget, Education and Workforce, and Small Business committees and chaired the

Democrats' Task Force on Jobs and the Economy. She also assumed a leadership role in her brief tenure in Congress, as an Assistant Democratic Whip and as president of the Democrats' freshman class.

During her first year in Congress, Majette sponsored legislation to designate Arabia Mountain in southeast DeKalb County as a national heritage area, a classification that would increase tourism and make the metropolitan Atlanta region eligible for millions of dollars in federal funding. Testifying before the House Resources Committee's Subcommittee on National Parks, Recreation, and Public Lands, Majette called the locale "a living history lesson" and urged the preservation of the "area's unique heritage for future generations."[6] As a member of the Small Business Committee, she criticized President Bush's proposed budget for fiscal year 2005, citing concerns for the many female- and minority-owned small businesses in her district.

Majette fought to protect a variety of federally funded programs during her term in the House. She believed the Bush administration had failed to adequately fund education initiatives, and was an outspoken critic of the President's record on domestic violence against women. "It saddens me to think that millions of women continue to be abused each year, while this administration sits idly by, taking no initiative and, in some cases, decreasing resources available to battered women," Majette said.[7] She also voted against overhauling Medicare, labeling the Republican-sponsored Medicare Prescription Drug and Modernization Act of 2003 a "sham" that failed to include "adequate prescription drug coverage that our mothers and grandmothers absolutely deserve."[8] In 2003, she joined two of her Democratic colleagues, Chris Van Hollen of Maryland and John Tierney of Massachusetts, in proposing an amendment to increase spending for Head Start. "The program doesn't just teach children to read," Majette argued. "It provides nutritional support, it makes sure that children are properly vaccinated at the appropriate time, that parents are also being supported and supportive of the efforts, that children are given the overall support they need. It's not just about teaching them their colors."[9]

On March 29, 2004, Majette surprised her House colleagues, and even some of her staff, when she announced her candidacy for the Georgia Senate seat that was being vacated by the retiring Zell Miller. Not wanting to miss the opportunity to run for an open Senate seat, Majette entered the race despite the absence of a statewide fundraising network and her lack of name recognition outside the Atlanta area.[10] Forced into a runoff because she did not gain a majority in the Democratic primary, Majette defeated millionaire businessman Cliff Oxford by using an effective grassroots campaign. The first African American to earn a nomination for the U.S. Senate from the state of Georgia, Majette lost in the general election, receiving only 40 percent of the vote against three-term Republican Representative Johnny Isakson.[11]

"It was a leap of faith for me, another step in my spiritual journey," Majette remarked after her loss.[12] She expressed no regrets. In 2005, Majette began work as a judge in DeKalb County. A year later she won the Democratic nomination for Georgia superintendent of schools, a position with oversight of the daily operations of the state's department of education.[13] But she lost by a wide margin in the general election.

FOR FURTHER READING

"Majette, Denise L.," *Biographical Directory of the United States Congress, 1774–Present,* http://bioguide.congress.gov/scripts/biodisplay.pl?index=M001145.

NOTES

1   *Politics in America, 2004* (Washington, DC: Congressional Quarterly Inc., 2003): 277.

2   Jeffrey McMurray, "Majette Says Spiritual Calling Prompted Belated Senate Run," 16 June 2004, Associated Press.

3   "Who Is Denise Majette?" at http://www.majetteforcongress.org (accessed 6 November 2002).

4   "New Member Profile: Denise Majette," 9 November 2002, *National Journal*; "Election Statistics, 1920 to Present," available at http://clerk.house.gov/member_info/electionInfo/index.html.

5   Melanie Eversley, "Enormity of Duty Awes Capitol Hill: Georgia's Freshmen Sworn in," 8 January 2003, *Atlanta Journal-Constitution*: 6A.

6   Donna Williams Lewis, "Majette Makes Appeal for Heritage Area; Designation Would Make as Much as $1 Million per Year Available," 25 September 2003, *Atlanta Journal Constitution*: 1JA; Ben Smith, "Majette Coming Into Her Own in Congress," 1 May 2003, *Atlanta Journal-Constitution*: 2JA; Mae Gentry, "2004 The Year in Review; It Only Looked Like Politics Stood Alone in Reshaping the Country," 30 December 2004, *Atlanta Journal-Constitution*: 1JB.

7   *Congressional Record*, House, 108th Cong., 2nd sess. (22 June 2004): 4746; Brian Basinger, "Majette Defies Conventional Election Theories," 24 October 2004, *Florida Times-Union* (Jacksonville, FL): A1.

8   *Congressional Record*, House, 108th Cong., 1st sess. (26 June 2003): 5956.

9   Melanie Eversley, "Majette Joins Head Start Fight; Bill Urges Federal Funding," 22 July 2003, *Atlanta Journal-Constitution*: 5A.

10   Lauren W. Whittington, "Majette Shaking Up Ga. Politics," 30 March 2004, *Roll Call*; Peter Savodnik and Michael Rochmes, "Majette Seeks Senate—Colleagues Stunned," 30 March 2004, *The Hill*: 1.

11   "Election Statistics, 1920 to Present," available at http://clerk.house.gov/member_info/electionInfo/index.html; Savodnik and Rochmes, "Majette Seeks Senate—Colleagues Stunned"; Dick Pettys, "Majette Looks for Funds, Foot Soldiers in U.S. Senate Battle," 20 October 2004, Associated Press.

12   Anna Varela, "Election 2004: Isakson's Romp Beats Expectations; 18-Point Margin Laid to Turnout, High Profile," 4 November 2004, *Atlanta Journal-Constitution*: 5C.

13   Corey Dade, "Majette Accepts Job as Part-Time Judge," 22 December 2004, *Atlanta Journal-Constitution*: 2D; "Across Metro Atlanta & the State; Georgia Votes 2006: State School Superintendent," 8 November 2006, *Atlanta Journal-Constitution*: 7D.

★ PART TWO ★

Current Black-American Members

★ INTRODUCTION TO ★

Profiles of Current Members

Nearly 140 years ago, Senator Hiram Revels of Mississippi and Representative Joseph Rainey of South Carolina became the first of 121 African Americans to serve in the U.S. Congress.* The history of African Americans in Congress contains many of the same themes that resonate in the larger chronicle of American democracy: a pioneering spirit, struggle, perseverance, gradual attainment of power, advancement through unity, and outstanding achievement.

The 42 African Americans (39 Representatives, two Delegates, and one Senator) who are serving in the 110th Congress (2007–2009) are the inheritors of that long historical legacy extending back to Revels and Rainey. One of the largest groups of black legislators to serve in the history of the institution (8 percent of the lawmakers in both chambers), these African Americans account for more than one-third of all the blacks who have ever served in Congress. All of them were sworn in to Congress after 1964, and the majority first took office in the 1990s.

The biographical profiles of these current Members, like those of their predecessors, contain information on pre-congressional careers, first House or Senate campaigns, committee and leadership positions, and legislative achievements. But because these Members are incumbents, comprehensive accounts of their congressional careers must await a later date. Current Members were given the opportunity to review their profiles before the book was published. At approximately 750 words each, these profiles are about half as long as those of most former Members. Also, these profiles are arranged alphabetically rather than chronologically. The profiles in this section are of the 38 African Americans who have served for two or more Congresses. The four freshman Members of the 110th Congress are profiled in a résumé format in Appendix A.

Among the current Members who are profiled in this section is Representative John Conyers, Jr., of Michigan, who had 43 years of congressional service as of January 2008. First sworn in to Congress in 1965, Conyers is the longest-serving African American in congressional history and one of the 15 longest-serving Members in House history. Also included in this section are profiles of Representative James Clyburn of South Carolina, one of only two African Americans ever to hold one of the top-three leadership positions in the House, and Senator Barack Obama of Illinois, currently the only African-American Senator.

As incumbent Members retire, we will expand their profiles to include a more complete account of their congressional careers. As these members leave Congress, their profiles in the online version of *Black Americans in Congress*— http://baic.house.gov—will be updated to reflect these individuals' contributions to the rich history of African Americans in Congress.

*The total reflects the number who had served in Congress up to the closing date for this volume on December 31, 2007.

★ SENATOR ★

★ REPRESENTATIVE ★

★ DELEGATE ★

Sanford D. Bishop, Jr.
1947–

UNITED STATES REPRESENTATIVE
DEMOCRAT FROM GEORGIA
1993–

IMAGE COURTESY OF THE MEMBER

Sanford Bishop served 16 years in the Georgia state legislature before winning election to the U.S. House of Representatives in 1992. As an eight-term veteran of Congress, Representative Bishop now serves on the prestigious Appropriations Committee. While focusing on military and veterans issues, as well as on agricultural legislation important to his southwest Georgia district, Bishop has championed federal fiscal responsibility.

Sanford D. Bishop, Jr., was born on February 4, 1947, in Mobile, Alabama, to Sanford D. Bishop, Sr., and Minnie S. Bishop. His father served as the first president of the Bishop State Community College; his mother was the college librarian.[1] He served as student body president at Morehouse College in Atlanta, graduating in 1968 with a bachelor of arts degree in political science. Bishop served in the U.S. Army, joining the ROTC and completing basic training at Fort Benning, Georgia. He was honorably discharged in 1971, the same year he earned his J.D. at Emory University in Atlanta. Bishop initially worked as a private practice lawyer who specialized in civil rights cases. In 1976, he won election to the Georgia state house of representatives, representing a district that covered Columbus. He served there for 14 years before winning election to the Georgia senate in 1990. In the state legislature, Bishop helped establish the Georgia Commission on Equal Opportunity and the state's office of child support receiver.[2] He is married to Vivian Creighton Bishop, and they have a daughter, Aayesha J. Reese.

Backed by the Columbus business community in 1992, Bishop was one of five challengers to run against six-term incumbent Representative Charles F. Hatcher in the Democratic primary. The district encompassed much of southwestern Georgia, including portions of Columbus, Macon, Albany, Valdosta, and Fort Benning, the state's largest military installation. Reapportionment, at the urging of the U.S. Justice Department, made the district the state's third majority-black district in 1992.[3] In the primary, asserting that he represented "a new generation of leadership,"

Bishop forced Hatcher into a runoff before defeating the incumbent with 53 percent of the vote in a head-to-head contest.[4] Bishop ran in the general election as a consensus builder. "For too long we have focused on things that divide us, black versus white, rural versus urban," he said. "But throughout the district, people have the same concerns—affordable health care, safe streets, and good jobs."[5] In the general election, he defeated Republican Jim Dudley with 64 percent of the vote.

Bishop has won election to seven additional terms, despite court-ordered redrawing of his district in the mid-1990s. In 1995, a federal court ruled that the borders of his district were the result of an unconstitutional "racial gerrymander." Subsequent redistricting placed Columbus in a neighboring congressional district, reducing the African-American portion of Bishop's constituency from 52 to 39 percent.[6] In the newly configured and competitive district, Bishop won re-election in 1996 with 54 percent of the vote. In 2000, in his narrowest re-election margin, Representative Bishop defeated GOP candidate Dylan Glenn, an African American and former Senate aide, with 53 percent of the vote. Reapportionment following the 2000 Census put a large section of Muscogee County back into his district and increased the black portion of the population to 44 percent. Since then, Bishop has won with large majorities, including in 2006, when he defeated Republican Bradley Hughes with 68 percent of the vote.[7]

When Bishop was sworn in to the 103rd Congress (1993–1995), he received assignments to three committees: Agriculture, Post Office and Civil Service, and Veterans' Affairs. In the 104th Congress (1995–1997), the Post Office and Civil Service panel was subsumed under the new Government Reform Committee, and Bishop left that assignment. In the 105th Congress (1997–1999), after he left his Veterans' Affairs post, Representative Bishop received an assignment to the Permanent Select Committee on Intelligence. In the 108th Congress (2003–2005), he relinquished all of his committee assignments to serve on the exclusive Appropriations Committee. He currently serves on three Appropriations subcommittees: Defense, Agriculture, and Military Construction and Veterans Affairs.

In the House, Representative Bishop has developed a reputation as a moderate Democrat who cosponsored constitutional amendments to balance the budget, to ban flag desecration, and to allow voluntary prayer in public schools.[8] From his seat on the Appropriations Subcommittee on Agriculture, Bishop worked with House leaders to steer through the House a major farm bill that increased funding for farm support programs, including those for peanut production, a major agriculture industry in his district. Bishop also has strongly supported the defense budget, looking out particularly for veterans' issues from his seat on the Appropriations Committee's Subcommittee for Military Construction, Veterans Affairs, and Related Agencies and its Subcommittee on Defense.[9]

FOR FURTHER READING

"Bishop, Sanford Dixon, Jr.," *Biographical Directory of the U.S. Congress, 1774–Present,* http://bioguide.congress.gov/scripts/biodisplay.pl?index=B000490.

NOTES

1 "Sanford D. Bishop, Jr.," *Contemporary Black Biography*, Volume 24 (Detroit, MI: Gale Group, 2000); *Politics in America, 2006* (Washington, DC: Congressional Quarterly Inc., 2005): 285.

2 *Almanac of American Politics, 2000* (Washington, DC: National Journal Inc., 1999): 463.

3 *Politics in America, 1994* (Washington, DC: Congressional Quarterly Inc., 1993): 396–397.

4 "Democratic Congressman Loses in Georgia," 12 August 1992, *New York Times*: A16; Bill Montgomery, "Bishop Touts 'Progressive' Image in Push to Topple Hatcher," 4 August 1992, *Atlanta Journal and Constitution*: E1.

5 Bill Montgomery, "Contrasts Mark Campaign; Political Novice Faces Veteran Lawmaker in 2nd District," 20 October 1992, *Atlanta Journal and Constitution*: E3.

6 *Politics in America, 2006*: 285.

7 "Election Statistics, 1920 to Present," available at http://clerk.house.gov/member_info/electionInfo/index.html; *Politics in America, 2006*: 285.

8 "Official Biography of Sanford Bishop, Jr.," http://bishop.house.gov/display.cfm?content_id=4 (accessed 8 February 2006); *Politics in America, 2006*: 284.

9 "Official Biography of Sanford Bishop, Jr.," http://bishop.house.gov/display.cfm?content_id=4 (accessed 11 October 2007); *Politics in America, 2008* (Washington, DC: Congressional Quarterly Inc., 2007): 277.

Corrine Brown
1946–

UNITED STATES REPRESENTATIVE
DEMOCRAT FROM FLORIDA
1993–

IMAGE COURTESY OF THE MEMBER

In 1992, Corrine Brown became one of the first African Americans elected to the U.S. House from Florida since the Reconstruction Era. During her House career, from her seats on the Transportation and Infrastructure and the Veterans' Affairs committees, Representative Brown regularly brought federal programs into her Jacksonville district and earned a reputation as a tireless advocate of civil rights.[1]

Corrine Brown was born in Jacksonville, Florida, on November 11, 1946, and grew up in the city's Northside neighborhood, graduating from Stanton High School. As a single mother, she raised a daughter, Shantrel. She earned a bachelor of science degree at Florida Agriculture and Mechanical University in 1969 and an M.A. from the same institution in 1971. In 1972, Brown graduated with an Ed.S. degree from the University of Florida. She taught at the University of Florida and Edward Waters College before settling at Florida Community College in Jacksonville, where she taught and served as a guidance counselor from 1977 to 1992. Her close friend and political mentor, Gwen Cherry, was the first African-American woman elected to the Florida house of representatives. Cherry's death in a 1979 car crash prompted Brown to enter elective politics. In 1980, she was a delegate for presidential candidate Senator Edward M. (Ted) Kennedy at the Democratic National Convention. Two years later, Brown won a seat in the Florida legislature, where she served for a decade.

In 1992, reapportionment created a new district in northeastern Florida spanning the area from Jacksonville to Orlando. Brown won the Democratic nomination and ran a general election campaign that focused on improving the district's educational system, bringing more jobs to the area, and protecting Social Security and Medicare for the elderly. She won by 18 percentage points, making her one of three Florida candidates elected that year (including Alcee Hastings and Carrie Meek) who were the first African Americans to represent the state since Reconstruction. In her subsequent seven re-election campaigns, Brown won by comfortable margins. In 2006, she was elected to her eighth term without opposition.[2]

When Representative Brown took her seat in the 103rd Congress (1993–1995), she received assignments on the Government Operations Committee, the Veterans' Affairs Committee, and the Public Works and Transportation Committee (later named Transportation and Infrastructure). In the 104th Congress (1995–1997), she resigned from Government Operations. In the 110th Congress (2007–2009), Brown serves as chairwoman of the Transportation and Infrastructure Subcommittee on Railroads, Pipelines, and Hazardous Materials. She also serves as the second-ranking Democrat for the Veterans' Affairs Subcommittee on Health.[3] Brown also has served as vice chair of the Congressional Black Caucus and is a member of the Women's Caucus.

Brown's primary focus is on improving the economy within her district, steering federal funds and projects into the north Florida region. She led the effort to construct an $86 million federal courthouse in Jacksonville, while using her influence on the Transportation and Infrastructure Committee to initiate Florida rail projects to meet the state's booming transportation needs. While supporting reduction of the federal deficit by cutting welfare programs, Brown believed the system must be made "more advantageous for welfare recipients to get off welfare" by providing jobs and job training. "We must make sure that changes in the welfare system do not inadvertently hurt children," she added.[4]

Brown also supported military defense spending, in part reflecting the large military presence in her district, most notably the Jacksonville Naval Air Station. But Brown wanted more of the money to flow into personnel training, describing the military as a place where working-class Americans could find opportunities unavailable elsewhere. From her seat on the Veterans' Affairs Committee, Brown was particularly attentive to the needs of women veterans and health issues. After the 2000 elections, Brown was one of the most vocal advocates for voting reforms. To improve the voting process, especially in minority precincts, Representative Brown supported the Help America Vote Act of 2002 to streamline balloting procedures and provide money to modernize voting systems as a first step toward reform.[5]

Brown's interests extend beyond her congressional district. In 1993, she began working behind the scenes to push the William J. (Bill) Clinton administration to restore a democratic government in Haiti by installing deposed President Jean-Bertrand Aristide. She also urged officials to process the thousands of Haitians who arrived in the United States seeking political asylum.[6] Brown also has taken up the cause of Liberians, pushing to extend temporary visa status for thousands who came to America after a civil war in the African country during the early 1990s.

FOR FURTHER READING

"Brown, Corrine," *Biographical Directory of the U.S. Congress, 1774–Present*, http://bioguide.congress.gov/scripts/biodisplay.pl?index=B000911.

NOTES

1   Bruce I. Friedland, "Jacksonville's Pragmatic Liberal U.S. Rep. Corrine Brown Passionately Pushes Her Causes and Delivers Bacon Back to City," 19 July 2000, *Florida Times-Union*: A1.

2   "Election Statistics, 1920 to Present," available at http://clerk.house.gov/member_info/electionInfo/index.html.

3   "Official Biography of Corrine Brown," http://www.house.gov/corrinebrown/biography.shtml (accessed 3 December 2007); *Politics in America, 2008* (Washington, DC: Congressional Quarterly Inc., 2007): 227–228.

4   "Candidates' Forum," 6 November 1994, *Orlando Sentinel*: G7.

5   Conference Report on H.R. 3295, Help America Vote Act of 2002, *Congressional Record*, House, 107th Cong., 2nd sess. (10 October 2002): 7836.

6   "Testimony of Congresswoman Corrine Brown," 13 June 1994, Judiciary Subcommittee on International Law, Immigration, and Refugees, Federal Document Clearing House Congressional Testimony.

G. K. Butterfield
1947–

UNITED STATES REPRESENTATIVE
DEMOCRAT FROM NORTH CAROLINA
2004–

IMAGE COURTESY OF THE MEMBER

After serving for more than 15 years as a North Carolina judge, including a term on the state supreme court, G. K. Butterfield won a 2004 special election to serve in the U.S. House of Representatives. Re-elected to the 109th Congress (2005–2007) less than four months later, Representative Butterfield secured prominent committee assignments from which he tended to the agricultural and small business interests of his district.

George Kenneth (G. K.) Butterfield was born on April 27, 1947, in Wilson, North Carolina. His father, George Kenneth Butterfield, won a seat on the Wilson city council in the 1950s—making him one of a handful of African Americans to hold political office in the state since Reconstruction. Town officials later changed the election format to deprive the senior Butterfield and all black candidates of a chance to win further elections. "I saw how the political system was manipulated to obtain an unfair result," the younger Butterfield recalled. "Having seen that injustice has made me want to be involved politically."[1] Butterfield served two years in the U.S. Army as a personnel specialist, from 1968 to 1970, before graduating from North Carolina Central University in 1971 with a bachelor's degree in sociology and political science. Three years later he earned a J.D. from North Carolina Central University and commenced private law practice. Butterfield later went on to serve as president of the North Carolina Association of Black Lawyers, filing several successful voting rights lawsuits. In November 1988, he won election to the North Carolina superior court, where he served for 12 years. In 2001, North Carolina Governor Mike Easley appointed Judge Butterfield to the North Carolina supreme court, where he served for two years. In 2002, Butterfield lost his re-election bid and was subsequently appointed special superior court judge. Butterfield is divorced, with two daughters, Valeisha and Lenai.

In 2004, when incumbent Representative Frank Ballance announced his retirement from the U.S. House, Butterfield was nominated by local Democrats to run in the special election.[2] The district, which covered large swaths of eastern North Carolina, is solidly Democratic and largely rural and poor and is one of two majority-black congressional districts in the state. Butterfield ran on a platform that promised more federal dollars to help small business development revitalize the local economy. He noted, "[W]e need to understand the role that small business plays in economic development and I think that's where the congressperson can be really valuable."[3] On July 20, 2004, Butterfield won the special election with 71 percent of the vote against Republican challenger Greg Dority, to serve out the remainder of the term in the 108th Congress (2003–2005). Both men also won simultaneous primary elections for the full term in the 109th Congress. In November 2004, three times as many voters went to the polls, and Butterfield again prevailed against Dority with a 64 percent majority.[4] Representative Butterfield faced no opposition in his 2006 re-election.

Representative Butterfield was sworn in to office on July 21, 2004. "The people of the First District are no different from your constituents," Butterfield told his colleagues afterward in a floor speech. "They want our government to work to enable all people to experience the American dream."[5] He received assignments on the Agriculture and Small Business committees. He retained the Agriculture Committee assignment in the 109th Congress, but resigned from the Small Business panel to accept a seat on the Armed Services Committee. In the 110th Congress (2007–2009), Butterfield gave up these assignments for a seat on the Energy and Commerce Committee, where he serves as vice chair of the Subcommittee on Energy and Air Quality. He also serves on the Democratic Steering and Policy Committee. Butterfield is one of eight Chief Deputy Whips, making him the first Democrat from North Carolina to serve in this position.[6]

One of Representative Butterfield's chief legislative aims has been to improve the economy of his district by reducing unemployment and bringing federal money to help small businesses in northeastern North Carolina. Representative Butterfield's assignment to the Agriculture Committee was important to the region's farm-based economy, particularly tobacco farmers. In late 2004, he backed a federal buyout program for tobacco producers that eventually passed the House. From his seat on the Armed Services panel, Butterfield has opposed a navy plan to build a test airstrip where naval aviators could conduct more than 30,000 practice flights per year. He objected to the navy's site selection process and was successful in eliminating the appropriation for the project.[7]

FOR FURTHER READING

"Butterfield, George Kenneth, Jr., (G. K.)" *Biographical Directory of the U.S. Congress, 1774–Present,* http://bioguide.congress.gov/scripts/biodisplay.pl?index=B001251.

NOTES

1 *Politics in America, 2008* (Washington, DC: Congressional Quarterly Inc., 2007): 744.

2 Lauren W. Whittington and Erin P. Billings, "Embattled Ballance Retiring," 10 May 2004, *Roll Call*; *Politics in America, 2006* (Washington, DC: Congressional Quarterly Inc., 2005): 759–760.

3 William L. Holmes, "Butterfield Wins Special Election; Will Face Dority in November," 21 July 2004, Associated Press; Jay Cohen, "Ballance Casts Shadow Over 1st District N.C. Race," 14 July 2004, Associated Press.

4 Cindy George, "Former Justice Wins 1st District; Butterfield Fills Ballance's Seat," 21 July 2004, *News and Observer*: A16; Holmes, "Butterfield Wins Special Election; Will Face Dority in November"; "Election Statistics, 1920 to Present," available at http://clerk.house.gov/member_info/electionInfo/index.html.

5 *Congressional Record*, House, 108th Cong., 2nd sess. (21 July 2004): H6497.

6 *Politics in America, 2006*: 759; *Politics in America, 2008*: 743–744; "About G. K. Butterfield," http://butterfield.house.gov/aboutgk.asp (accessed 17 October 2007).

7 *Politics in America, 2006*: 759.

Donna M. Christensen
1945–

DELEGATE
DEMOCRAT FROM THE VIRGIN ISLANDS
1997–

Delegate Donna M. Christensen won election to the U.S. House of Representatives in 1997, the first woman to represent the U.S. Virgin Islands, a multi-island territory in the eastern Caribbean. The islands became part of the United States when they were purchased from Denmark in 1917. Since 1973, the territory has had nonvoting representation in the House of Representatives.[1] During her tenure, Christensen has focused on improving the social, political, and economic dynamics of the islands, especially as they relate to federal issues.

Donna Christensen was born on September 19, 1945, to the late chief judge of the Virgin Islands District Court, Almeric Christian, and Virginia Sterling Christian. She earned a bachelor of science degree from St. Mary's College at Notre Dame in 1966 and an M.D. from George Washington University School of Medicine in 1970. In addition to running an active family practice, Christensen worked as a health administrator, rising to the position of assistant commissioner of health for the Virgin Islands.

Concurrently, she began her political career in 1980 as part of the Coalition to Appoint a Native Judge, which emphasized judicial appointments from within the community, and later on as part of the Save Fountain Valley Coalition, which called for the protection of St. Croix's north side from overdevelopment. She served as Democratic National Committeewoman from 1984 to 1994, as vice chair of the Territorial Committee of the Democratic Party of the Virgin Islands, and as a member of the Platform Committee of the Democratic National Committee. From 1984 to 1986, she served as a member of the Virgin Islands Board of Education and was appointed to the Virgin Islands Status Commission from 1988 to 1992.

Christensen lost her first bid for Delegate to Congress in 1994, failing to secure the Democratic nomination. Two years later, she not only won the party's nomination, but also went on to defeat freshman Independent incumbent Victor Frazer after a three-way general election and a runoff election. In 1997, as a Member of the 105th Congress (1997–1999), she became the first female physician to serve in the House. Christensen has since won re-election to the House with at least 62 percent of the vote.[2]

As a Member of the House, she has served on the Natural Resources Committee, which oversees the affairs of the offshore territories, where she is chairwoman of the Subcommittee on Insular Affairs and the third-ranking Democrat on the Subcommittee on National Parks, Forests, and Public Lands. She has also served on the Small Business Committee and, during the 108th Congress (2003–2005), gained a seat on the Committee on Homeland Security, primarily because of her expertise in public health.

Christensen has focused on strengthening the Virgin Islands' economy and stabilizing its fiscal condition. Expanding traditional tax incentives that are central to the economy of the Virgin Islands and introducing legislation to encourage fiscal discipline have been the hallmarks of her tenure. She also has worked to expand business, housing, health, and educational opportunities in the territory.

Delegate Christensen, a member of the Congressional Black Caucus, chairs the Health Braintrust and has been at the forefront of efforts to end health disparities, fight the HIV/AIDS threat both nationally and internationally, and extend health insurance coverage to as many Americans as possible.

Delegate Christensen is married to Christian O. Christensen of St. Croix and has two daughters from a previous marriage, Rabiah and Karida Green, and three grandchildren, Nia Hamilton, Kobe George, and Nealia Williams.[3] She has four stepchildren from her 1998 marriage to Christian O. Christensen: Lisa, Esther, Bryan and David.

FOR FURTHER READING

"Christensen, Donna Marie Christian," *Biographical Directory of the U.S. Congress, 1774–Present*, http://bioguide.congress.gov/scripts/biodisplay.pl?index=C000380.

NOTES

1 "America's Caribbean Paradise: History and Geography," http://www.house.gov/christianchristensen/vi_history.htm (accessed 29 December 2004).

2 "Election Statistics, 1920 to Present," available at http://clerk.house.gov/member_info/electionInfo/index.html; *Politics in America, 2008* (Washington, DC: Congressional Quarterly Inc., 2007): 1131; "Official Biography of Donna M. Christensen," http://www.house.gov/christian-christensen/biography.htm (accessed 3 December 2007).

3 "Official Biography of Donna M. Christensen"; *Politics in America, 2006* (Washington, DC: Congressional Quarterly Inc., 2005): 1142.

William L. Clay, Jr.
1956–

UNITED STATES REPRESENTATIVE
DEMOCRAT FROM MISSOURI
2001–

IMAGE COURTESY OF THE MEMBER

Hailing from one of Missouri's most influential political families, Lacy Clay won election to the U.S. House of Representatives in 2000, succeeding his father, William (Bill) Clay, Sr., a three-decade House veteran. In Congress, Clay has focused on liberal issues ranging from protection of voting rights to creating economic development opportunities for minorities. "Although I am not my father, I am my father's son, in that we share the same values . . . and commitment to principles, such as fairness and justice," Clay once said.[1]

William Lacy Clay, Jr., was born in St. Louis, Missouri, on July 27, 1956, one of three children raised by William and Carol Ann Clay. His father, William, Sr.—a union representative and St. Louis alderman—won election to the U.S. House in 1968, where he served 32 years and was a founding member of the Congressional Black Caucus. His uncle, Irving, held several executive positions in St. Louis city government before being elected an alderman. Lacy Clay spent his teenage years in suburban Maryland, graduating with the class of 1974 from Springbrook High School in Silver Spring. He served as an assistant doorkeeper in the U.S. House of Representatives, working his way toward a bachelor of science degree in government and politics, which he earned in 1983 at the University of Maryland, College Park. "I didn't originally want to go into politics. I wanted to do something like own a business," Clay once recalled. "But I realized after working in Washington and the U.S. Congress that that was an option for me."[2] After graduating from college, Clay returned to St. Louis to run in a special election for a vacant seat in the Missouri house of representatives. He served as a state representative until 1991, when he was elected to the Missouri senate.[3] He also has served as a Missouri Democratic National Committeeman since 1992. Clay and his wife, Ivie Lewellen Clay, have two children: Carol and William III.

In 1999, when William Clay, Sr., announced his retirement from the U.S. House, Lacy Clay was an immediate favorite to succeed his father in a district that encompassed northern St. Louis and a large area of the city's suburbs in St. Louis County. During the election, Clay invoked his paternal connection to Congress: "For 32 years, your congressman has been Congressman Clay," he told voters. "I certainly hold him up as my hero. He is the one I look to; he is the one who has taught me what I need to know in this business."[4] In the August 2000 Democratic primary, he won convincingly against a field of contenders that included a popular St. Louis County councilman. In the general election, Lacy Clay easily carried the heavily Democratic district, with 75 percent of the vote. His colleagues in the Democratic freshman class elected him president of their group.[5] "It's an honor for me to succeed my father," Clay said on election night. "I certainly am looking forward to hitting the ground running, working on behalf of working families."[6] In his subsequent three re-election campaigns in 2002, 2004, and 2006, Clay won with 70, 75, and 72 percent of the vote, respectively.[7]

When Representative Clay was sworn in to the House in January 2001, he was assigned to the Financial Services and Government Reform committees. He has served on both panels since then and currently serves as chairman of the Subcommittee on Information Policy, Census, and National Archives for the Oversight and Government Reform Committee. On the Financial Services Committee, Clay serves on two subcommittees: Financial Institutions and Consumer Credit and Domestic and International Monetary Policy, Trade, and Technology.[8]

During his congressional career, Representative Clay has focused primarily on two issues: voting rights and economic development. He has been an outspoken advocate of electoral process reform, weighing in on issues ranging from electronic voting, to expansion of voter registration, to campaign finance reform. On economic issues, Representative Clay has pushed for expanded access to credit to stimulate home ownership among low-income families. He has cosponsored measures to eliminate predatory lending practices by financial institutions.[9] Clay also has stressed constituent services. "That's what I really get pleasure out of—serving people," he said. "I make sure my employees understand that we are here because of the people and we have to serve them and we have to do a good job serving them."[10]

FOR FURTHER READING

"Clay, William Lacy, Jr.," *Biographical Directory of the U.S. Congress, 1774–Present,* http://bioguide.congress. gov/scripts/biodisplay.pl?index=C001049.

NOTES

1   *Politics in America, 2008* (Washington, DC: Congressional Quarterly Inc., 2007): 578.

2   Gregory B. Freeman, "The Clays: A Missouri Dynasty," 19 January 1992, *St. Louis Post-Dispatch Magazine*: 8.

3   *Politics in America, 2008*: 578; "Congressman William 'Lacy' Clay Biography," http://www.house.gov/clay/ biography.htm (accessed 6 September 2005).

4   D. J. Wilson, "Hand-Me-Down District," 19 July 2000, *Riverfront Times*.

5   *Politics in America, 2004* (Washington, DC: Congressional Quarterly Inc., 2003): 576.

6   Mark Schlinkmann, "Lacy Clay Wins 75 Percent of the Vote in Bid to Succeed His Father in Congress," 8 November 2000, *St. Louis Post-Dispatch*: 6.

7   "Election Statistics, 1920 to Present," available at http://clerk.house.gov/ member_info/electionInfo/index.html.

8   "Subcommittee Assignments for the 110th Congress," http:// financialservices.house.gov/ subassignments.html; "Committees," http://lacyclay.house.gov/committees. htm (both sites accessed 28 November 2007).

9   *Politics in America, 2004*: 576–577; "The Federal Home Loan Bank System," Extension of Remarks, *Congressional Record*, House, 108th Cong., 1st sess. (29 January 2003): E100; "A New Direction at St. Louis Housing Authority," Extension of Remarks, *Congressional Record*, House, 107th Cong., 1st sess. (14 June 2001): E1109; "Congressman William 'Lacy' Clay, Biography."

10 David Scott, "Observers Say Missouri's 1st District Likely to Stay in Clay's Hands," 18 June 2002, Associated Press.

Emanuel Cleaver II
1944–

UNITED STATES REPRESENTATIVE
DEMOCRAT FROM MISSOURI
2005–

IMAGE COURTESY OF THE MEMBER

As a former Kansas City mayor and city councilman, Emanuel Cleaver II entered Congress with a reserve of political experience not customary for the typical U.S. House freshman Member. During his first term, Representative Cleaver earned a seat on the exclusive Financial Services Committee and focused on the needs of his Kansas City-based district.

Emanuel Cleaver II was born in Waxahachie, Texas, on October 26, 1944. He and his family lived in a small wooden house that had been a slave cabin. His family's religious roots—his great-grandfather, grandfather, and an uncle were preachers—inspired him to a life of ministry.[1] He graduated from high school in Wichita Falls, Texas, before earning a bachelor of science degree in sociology from Prairie View A&M University in Prairie View, Texas, in 1972. Two years later, Cleaver graduated with a master's degree in divinity from the St. Paul School of Theology in Kansas City, Missouri. Cleaver served as an ordained Methodist minister for a central Kansas City congregation (he still serves as senior pastor at St. James United Methodist Church). Cleaver and his wife, Dianne, a psychologist, have four children and three grandchildren.

Cleaver, who had been active in the 1960s civil rights movement, entered elective politics in 1979, successfully campaigning for a seat on the Kansas City city council. He served there until 1991, acting as mayor *pro tempore* and chairing the council's planning and zoning committee.[2] He won election as Kansas City mayor, becoming the first African American to hold that post. Cleaver served as mayor for eight years, focusing on job growth and economic development. His success earned him the distinction of being chosen the two-term president of the National Conference of Black Mayors. After he left office in 1999, Cleaver worked as a radio talk show host.

In December 2003, when five-term Democratic Representative Karen McCarthy announced she would not run for re-election in 2004, Cleaver sought the nomination for the vacant seat. "The surest path to happiness has always come when I became consumed in a cause greater than myself," Cleaver said when announcing his candidacy. "Serving in Congress at such a time as this is that great cause."[3] The district covered portions of Kansas City and some of its eastern suburbs. A majority of constituents were middle-class and Democratic, and the party had controlled the seat since before the New Deal. Cleaver turned back a spirited challenge by Jamie Metzel, a former White House Fellow and National Security Council aide. He won the August 3, 2004, primary with 60 percent of the vote.[4] In the general election, he faced Republican candidate Jeanne Patterson, a businesswoman and political newcomer. Patterson spent nearly $3 million of her own money during the campaign, arguing that she would bring more jobs to the city. Cleaver stressed his accomplishments as mayor, including his successful efforts to bring major corporations to the city.[5] In the general election, he prevailed over Patterson by 55 to 42 percent of the vote, with the remainder going to a Libertarian candidate. African Americans accounted for just 24 percent of the district population—the smallest black population of any district represented by a black Member of Congress.[6] In 2006, Cleaver was re-elected with 64 percent of the vote.[7]

When Representative Cleaver was sworn in to the House in January 2005, he received an assignment on the Financial Services Committee. He currently serves on two of that panel's subcommittees: Investigation and Oversight and Housing and Community Opportunity. In the 110th Congress (2007–2009), Cleaver joined the new Select Committee on Energy Independence and Global Warming. He also serves as a regional whip for the Democratic Caucus and as second vice chairman for the Congressional Black Caucus.[8]

Representative Cleaver has focused on many of the issues that were highlighted in his initial campaign. He has advocated federal dollars for improved education programs and affordable health care coverage. Arguing that he is in accord with voters' sentiments in northern Missouri, Cleaver opposes the continued presence of U.S. military forces in Iraq.[9] Among the measures that Representative Cleaver introduced during his freshman term was a bill to condemn the use of "racially restrictive covenants" in housing documents that sought to prohibit the sale or lease of property to racial or ethnic minorities, in violation of the Fair Housing Act of 1968. Another bill he authored condemned the Government of Mexico for producing postage stamps with Memin Pinguin, a comic book character from the 1940s that evoked racist Jim Crow-Era cartoons of blacks.[10]

FOR FURTHER READING

"Cleaver, Emanuel, II," *Biographical Directory of the U.S. Congress, 1774–Present*, http://bioguide.congress.gov/scripts/biodisplay.pl?index=C001061.

NOTES

1 Darrell McWhorter, "A Long March to Kansas City Mayor's Office," 12 May 1991, *St. Louis Post-Dispatch Magazine*: 1C.

2 "Official Biography of Emanuel Cleaver II," http://www.house.gov/cleaver/about.html (accessed 31 October 2007).

3 Steve Kraske, "Cleaver Sees 'Great Cause'; Former KC Mayor Joins Race in 5th Congressional District," 9 February 2004, *Kansas City Star*: B2.

4 Steve Kraske, "Cleaver Survives a Fierce Challenge," 4 August 2004, *Kansas City Star*: A1; Steve Kraske, "Cleaver Denounces Campaign 'Vitriol'; Metzl Says Questions 'Need to Be Asked,'" 23 July 2004, *Kansas City Star*: B1; "Rep. Emanuel Cleaver," *Almanac of American Politics, 2006* (Washington, DC: National Journal Inc., 2005): 979–980.

5 *Politics in America, 2006* (Washington, DC: Congressional Quarterly Inc., 2005): 596.

6 *Politics in America, 2008* (Washington, DC: Congressional Quarterly Inc., 2007): 586.

7 "Election Statistics, 1920 to Present," available at available at http://clerk.house.gov/member_info/electionInfo/index.html.

8 *Politics in America, 2008*: 585.

9 David Goldstein, "Mr. Cleaver Goes to Washington—and Finds It Highly Perplexing," 29 November 2004, *Kansas City Star*: A1; *Almanac of American Politics, 2006*: 980; *Politics in America, 2006*: 596.

10 *Congressional Record*, House, 109th Cong., 1st sess. (19 May 2005): H3589; *Congressional Record*, House, 109th Cong., 1st sess. (11 July 2005): H5630–5633.

James E. Clyburn
1940–

UNITED STATES REPRESENTATIVE
DEMOCRAT FROM SOUTH CAROLINA
1993–

James E. (Jim) Clyburn's 1992 election made him the first African American from South Carolina to serve in Congress since the late 19th century. Representative Clyburn has won re-election to seven additional terms, serving as chairman of the Congressional Black Caucus (CBC) and winning a seat on the influential House Appropriations Committee. On November 16, 2006, the House Democratic Caucus unanimously elected Clyburn Majority Whip, making him the first South Carolinian and the second African American to ascend to the third-ranking position in the House.[1]

James E. Clyburn was born in Sumter, South Carolina, on July 21, 1940, the eldest of three sons of Enos L. Clyburn, a minister, and Almeta Clyburn, a beauty shop operator. At age 12, he was elected president of the Sumter youth chapter of the National Association for the Advancement of Colored People. A client of his mother's once warned him against giving voice to his early political aspirations in the segregated South. "We knew what the rules were. I mean, a 12-year-old black kid talking about being in politics and government?" Clyburn recalled of that formative moment. "She was just telling me, 'Son, be careful, you can't have those kinds of dreams—you're not the right color.'"[2] He attended Mather Academy, a private all-black high school. Clyburn graduated from South Carolina State College in 1961 with a bachelor of arts degree. During the 1950s and 1960s, he organized sit-ins at an Orangeburg, South Carolina, five and dime store and was arrested and jailed for his participation in nonviolent civil rights protests.[3] During one such protest he met his future wife, the former Emily England; they have three grown daughters: Mignon, Angela, and Jennifer. Clyburn taught history in high school before working on several federal employment programs. From 1968 to 1971, he was the executive director of the South Carolina state commission for farm workers. In 1970, Clyburn ran an unsuccessful campaign for the state house of representatives, but his candidacy caught South Carolina Governor John West's attention. He joined Governor West's staff in 1971 and, three years later, was appointed head of the state commission for human affairs (the first black gubernatorial appointee in the state in more than seven decades). Clyburn lost campaigns for South Carolina secretary of state in 1978 and 1986.[4]

In 1992, at the recommendation of the U.S. Justice Department, statewide redistricting created a majority-black district in eastern South Carolina. It was a sprawling district encompassing all or part of 16 counties as well as parts of the cities of Charleston, Columbia, and Florence. The five-term incumbent Democrat, Robert (Robin) Tallon, retired, and Clyburn captured the Democratic nomination with 56 percent of the primary vote against four opponents. In the general election, he easily defeated Republican candidate John Chase with 65 percent of the vote.[5] Clyburn is a distant relative of George Washington Murray, the last African American to represent South Carolina in the U.S. House (1893–1895, 1896–1897).[6] In his subsequent seven re-election campaigns, Clyburn won with between 64 and 73 percent of the vote. In 2006, he defeated Republican Gary McLeod with a 64 percent majority.[7]

As a new Representative, Clyburn proved to be a pragmatic, enthusiastic, and effective behind-the-scenes player, moving rapidly into the leadership ranks.[8] Elected co-president of the Democratic freshman class, he won assignments on the Public Works and Transportation Committee (later named Transportation and Infrastructure) and the Veterans' Affairs Committee. He later served as Ranking Member of the Veterans' Affairs Subcommittee on Oversight and Investigation. He accepted an additional assignment with the Small Business Committee for a term in the 104th Congress (1995–1997). In the 106th Congress (1999–2001), Representative Clyburn won a seat on the exclusive Appropriations Committee.[9] He has served on that panel since. The CBC also unanimously chose Clyburn as its chairman in that Congress, making him just the second southerner to lead the group.[10] At the start of the 108th Congress (2003–2005), Clyburn's Democratic colleagues elected him Vice Chairman of the Democratic Caucus. He served in that post until he was elected Chairman of the Democratic Caucus during the 109th Congress (2005–2007).

As a Member of the House, Representative Clyburn has focused on issues important to his agricultural and low income district and the African-American community generally. He has been a strong supporter of education, seeking increased federal funding for historically black colleges in his district. He opposed efforts to overhaul the Social Security system and to dismantle affirmative action programs and has advocated a higher minimum wage and universal health care coverage. "There is no separation between the defense of our nation and the nutrition for our children," Clyburn once said. "There is no difference between the defense of our nation and a strong, educated work force."[11]

FOR FURTHER READING

Clyburn, James with Jennifer Revels. *Uncommon Courage: The Story of Briggs v. Elliott, South Carolina's Unsung Civil Rights Battle* (Spartanburg, SC: Palmetto Conservation Foundation Press, 2004).

"Clyburn, James Enos," *Biographical Directory of the U.S. Congress, 1774–Present*, http://bioguide.congress.gov/scripts/biodisplay.pl?index=C000537.

NOTES

1 "James E. Clyburn Biography," http://clyburn.house.gov/clyburn-biography.cfm (accessed 27 November 2007).

2 Betsy Rothstein, "Rep. James Clyburn (D-S.C.); Head of Congressional Black Caucus Grew Up in a Segregated World," 17 February 1999, *The Hill*: 15.

3 Matthew C. Quinn, "Gephardt's Man in S. Carolina; Can Clyburn Turn Out the Vote in Primary?" 10 December 2003, *Atlanta Journal-Constitution*: 6A.

4 Rothstein, "Rep. James Clyburn (D-S.C.)"; *Politics in America, 2006* (Washington, DC: Congressional Quarterly Inc., 2005): 931.

5 "James Clyburn," *Gale Newsmakers* (Detroit, MI: Gale Group, 1999); *Politics in America, 2006*: 931.

6 Steve Piacente, "Jim Clyburn: The 6th District Congressman Built His Career on Lessons Learned Early in Life," 27 February 1999, *Post and Courier* (Charleston, SC): D1; *Politics in America, 2006*: 931.

7 "Election Statistics, 1920 to Present," available at http://clerk.house.gov/member_info/electionInfo/index.html.

8 Stephen Delaney Hale, "Freshman Congressman Upbeat," 28 January 1993, *Augusta Chronicle* (Georgia): SC1.

9 Steve Piacente, "Rep. Clyburn Wins Seat on Appropriations Panel," 11 December 1998, *Post and Courier* (Charleston, SC): A1.

10 Mickey Leland of Texas was the first, serving from 1985 to 1987. See Appendix I, Congressional Black Caucus Chairmen and Chairwomen, 1971–2007.

11 Piacente, "Jim Clyburn."

John Conyers, Jr.
1929–

UNITED STATES REPRESENTATIVE
DEMOCRAT FROM MICHIGAN
1965–

IMAGE COURTESY OF THE MEMBER

Representative John Conyers is the longest-serving African American in congressional history. As chairman of the Judiciary Committee, Representative Conyers heads a panel that has oversight over the Department of Justice and the federal courts as well as jurisdiction over copyright, constitutional issues, consumer protection, and civil rights.

John Conyers, Jr., was born in Detroit, Michigan, on May 16, 1929, the eldest of four sons of John and Lucille (Simpson) Conyers. His father was a United Auto Workers representative. John, Jr., attended Detroit public schools, graduating from Northwestern High School in 1947. He served in the National Guard from 1948 to 1950 before enlisting as a U.S. Army private for four years. Conyers attended officer candidate school and was commissioned as a second lieutenant. He was assigned to the Army Corps of Engineers in Korea, where he served in combat for a year. In 1954, Conyers left active duty with an honorable discharge, serving three more years in the Army Reserves. In 1957, using the GI Bill's educational benefits, Conyers earned a bachelor of arts degree from Wayne State University and, a year later, an L.L.B. from Wayne State Law School. After graduating, Conyers joined the staff of Michigan Representative John Dingell, Jr. From 1958 to 1961, he served as Dingell's legislative assistant. After passing the Michigan bar in 1959, he cofounded the law firm of Conyers, Bell & Townsend. In 1961, Michigan Governor John B. Swainson appointed him as a referee for the Michigan workmen's compensation department, and he also worked as general counsel for several labor union locals. In 1963, President John F. Kennedy appointed Conyers to the National Lawyers Committee for Civil Rights Under the Law, which promoted racial tolerance in the legal profession. In 1967, the Southern Christian Leadership Conference chose him as the recipient of the Rosa Parks Award, presented by Dr. Martin Luther King, Jr. Conyers married Monica Ann Esters in June 1990. They have two sons: John III and Carl.[1]

Conyers's first political interests developed during the mid-1950s while he was a college student, when he joined the Young Democrats and served as a precinct official for the local Democratic Party. In late 1963, he ran for a newly reapportioned U.S. House seat that had been drawn from two districts that had covered Detroit. The new district encompassed middle- and upper-middle-class sections of the city, with a predominantly African-American population, and included Conyers's childhood neighborhood. Local Democratic Party officials refused to support him in the primary, arguing that the 35-year-old was too young and lacked experience in elective office. Conyers ran anyway, supported by a large volunteer force at the precinct level. With the campaign slogan "Jobs, Justice, and Peace," he defeated the party-backed candidate, Richard H. Austin, by a slim margin of 45 votes.[2] In the heavily Democratic district, Conyers easily won the general election with 84 percent of the vote. In his subsequent 20 successful re-election campaigns for his House seat, Conyers has never been seriously challenged, winning his general elections by a minimum of 82 percent of the vote. In 2006, Conyers won re-election with 85 percent of the vote against Republican Chad Miles.[3]

Upon taking his seat in the House in January 1965, Conyers won a coveted assignment on the Judiciary Committee—becoming the first African American ever to serve on that panel. He has served there ever since. In 1995, Representative Conyers became Ranking Member and, when the Democrats regained control of the House in 2007, Conyers was named chairman. He has served on two other panels: Government Operations, from the 92nd through the 103rd Congresses (1971–1993), and Small Business (1987–1993). Conyers chaired the Government Operations Committee from 1989 until early 1995, when the Republicans won control of the House. He is one of only a handful of black Members of Congress to chair multiple standing committees.

Representative Conyers played a leading role in the passage of major legislation during his four-decade career. Among the measures he helped pass are the Help America Vote Act (2002), the Violence Against Women Act (1994), the Motor Voter Bill (1993), the Jazz Preservation Act (1987), and the Martin Luther King, Jr., Holiday Act (1983). He was one of the 13 founding Members of the Congressional Black Caucus. At the start of the 110th Congress (2007–2009), Representative Conyers began his 42nd year of House service, making him the second-longest-serving House Member (behind fellow Michigan Representative John Dingell, Jr.) and one of the 25 longest-serving Members in congressional history.[4]

FOR FURTHER READING

"Conyers, John, Jr.," *Biographical Directory of the U.S. Congress, 1774–Present*, http://bioguide.congress.gov/scripts/biodisplay.pl?index=C000714.

NOTES

1 For more biographical information, see *Politics in America, 2008* (Washington, DC: Congressional Quarterly Inc., 2007): 534–535; *Current Biography, 1970* (New York: H. W. Wilson and Company, 1970): 94–95; and the official biography of John Conyers, Jr., at http://www.house.gov/conyers/news_biography.htm (accessed 30 November 2007).

2 Michael Powell, "The Democrats' Seasoned Frontman; John Conyers, Sounding a Persistent Note on the Impeachment Inquiry," 13 October 1998, *Washington Post*: D1; *Current Biography, 1970*: 94–95.

3 "Election Statistics, 1920 to Present," available at http://clerk.house.gov/member_info/electionInfo/index.html.

4 Mildred Amer, "Members Who Have Served in the U.S. Congress 30 Years or More," 7 July 2007, Report RL30370, Congressional Research Service, Library of Congress, Washington, DC.

Elijah E. Cummings
1951–

UNITED STATES REPRESENTATIVE
DEMOCRAT FROM MARYLAND
1996–

Elijah E. Cummings, a Baltimore native, has represented his hometown in public office for three decades. A seven-term veteran of the U.S. House of Representatives, Representative Cummings has been an advocate for issues affecting his predominantly African-American district. He gained national prominence as chairman of the Congressional Black Caucus in the 108th Congress (2003–2005), and in the 110th Congress (2007–2009) he is chairman of the Transportation and Infrastructure Committee's Subcommittee on Coast Guard and Maritime Transportation.

Elijah Eugene Cummings was born on January 18, 1951, in Baltimore, Maryland. He was one of seven children of Robert and Ruth Cummings.[1] He graduated from Baltimore City College High School in 1969 and went on to Howard University, where, as a member of Phi Beta Kappa, he earned a bachelor's degree in political science in 1973. At Howard, Cummings served as the sophomore class president and as the student government president. In 1976, he graduated with a J.D. degree from the University of Maryland School of Law. He founded his own law firm in Baltimore shortly after graduation—a practice he would continue until being elected to Congress two decades later. Cummings first entered public office when he won election to the Maryland house of delegates in 1982, where he served for 14 years. He represented a predominantly African-American district in southern West Baltimore. He served as vice chairman of both the constitutional and administrative law committee and the economic matters committee. In the state legislature, Cummings chaired the legislative black caucus and eventually became the first African American in Maryland history to be named speaker *pro tempore*— the house of delegates' second-highest position.

When five-term Representative Kweisi Mfume resigned from his Baltimore, Maryland-based seat in February 1996, Cummings entered the race to succeed the incumbent. The district was a crescent shaped area extending from poor and affluent areas in the center of Baltimore through a number of poor black communities on the western side of the city. It also encompassed the middle-class towns of Catonsville and Randallstown. Since 1971, the district had been represented by an African American, beginning with Representative Parren Mitchell, Maryland's first black Member of Congress. Despite the fact that 26 other candidates entered the crowded Democratic primary, Cummings's status in the state house of delegates, his ties to the community, and key endorsements by local politicians and the *Baltimore Sun* and the *Baltimore Afro-American* newspapers quickly made him a favorite. He won the primary with 37 percent of the vote, defeating his nearest rival by 13 percentage points.[2] He easily won election against Republican Kenneth Kondner in the April 16 special election, garnering 81 percent of the vote. Cummings later said that he hoped "to be the voice of those people who put their faith and trust in me. Hopefully, I will build a record . . . that reflects that goal."[3] In his subsequent six re-election campaigns, Cummings was never seriously challenged, winning 73 percent or more of the vote in the general elections. In his 2006 re-election campaign, Cummings faced no party-endorsed competition in the general election.[4]

When Representative Cummings was sworn in to office in April 1996, he was assigned to the Government Reform and Oversight Committee (later renamed Oversight and Government Reform) and the Transportation and Infrastructure Committee. He has served on both panels during his entire congressional tenure. He also serves on the Committee on Armed Services and the Joint Economic Committee.[5]

During the 110th Congress, Representative Cummings has sponsored initiatives to improve homeland security, increase access to college, promote access to quality, affordable health care, provide seniors with affordable prescription drugs, and ensure a high quality of life for veterans. He is also committed to ensuring that every child has access to a quality education, specifically through the reauthorization and full funding of the No Child Left Behind Act.

Representative Cummings serves on numerous boards and commissions. He is spearheading an effort to strengthen the maritime curriculum at the Maritime Academy in Baltimore. He also serves on the U.S. Naval Academy Board of Visitors, the Morgan State University Board of Regents, the Maryland Zoo Board of Trustees, the Baltimore Aquarium Board of Trustees, the Baltimore Area Council of the Boy Scouts of America Board of Directors, and the Yale-Howard Nursing Partnership Center to Reduce Health Disparities by Self and Family Management Advisory Committee. He is an active member of New Psalmist Baptist Church.

FOR FURTHER READING

"Cummings, Elijah Eugene," *Biographical Directory of the U.S. Congress, 1774–Present*, http://bioguide.congress.gov/scripts/biodisplay.pl?index=C000984.

NOTES

1 "Elijah E. Cummings," *Contemporary Black Biography*, Volume 24 (Detroit, MI: Gale Group, 2000).

2 Rachel Van Dongen, "The Next Special: To Succeed Mfume, Cummings Looks Like Frontrunner," 22 February 1996, *Roll Call*; Paul W. Valentine, "32 Hopefuls Seek Mfume Post," 25 February 1996, *Washington Post*: B5; Todd Spangler, "Maryland Lawmaker, Dental Technician Nominated for Mfume Seat," 6 March 1996, Associated Press.

3 Paul W. Valentine, "Welcome to Capitol Hill; Freshman Congressman Laments Effort Spent on Partisan Bickering," 24 April 1997, *Washington Post*: M1.

4 "Election Statistics, 1920 to Present," available at http://clerk.house.gov/member_info/electionInfo/index.html.

5 *Politics in America, 2008* (Washington, DC: Congressional Quarterly Inc., 2007): 473.

Artur Davis
1967–

UNITED STATES REPRESENTATIVE
DEMOCRAT FROM ALABAMA
2003–

Hailing from a poor Montgomery, Alabama, neighborhood, Artur Davis used his academic prowess to earn two Harvard degrees and to launch a political career that brought him to the U.S. House of Representatives. Elected in 2002, Davis has built a reputation as an advocate for economic opportunities for low-income Americans and as a House Member who is attuned to the needs of his constituents.[1]

Artur Davis was born on October 9, 1967, in Montgomery, Alabama. He was raised in the poor west end of Montgomery by his mother, a schoolteacher, and his grandmother after his parents divorced when he was young. He attended the city public schools, graduating from Jefferson Davis High School. In 1990, Davis earned a B.A. *magna cum laude* from Harvard University, and three years later he graduated with a J.D. from Harvard Law School. Davis immediately began positioning himself for a career in politics. He clerked for Judge Myron Thompson—one of the first African-American judges appointed in the Middle District of Alabama. Appointed an Assistant U.S. Attorney in the same district in 1994, Davis served in that capacity until 1998, when he left to make his first run for Congress. Davis is not married.

In the 2000 election campaign, Davis challenged five-term incumbent Earl F. Hilliard in the Democratic primary for a district that represented portions of Birmingham and Tuscaloosa as well as low-income agricultural counties in west-central Alabama that were part of the "Black Belt," so called for its dark, productive soils. Hilliard prevailed with a 58 percent majority.[2] Two years later, however, Hilliard ran into political trouble over perceptions of his lack of influence in the House and criticisms by pro-Israel groups that he favored the Palestinian cause.[3] Davis again challenged Hilliard in the Democratic primary, this time with support from the mayors of Birmingham and Selma. In a three-way contest, Hilliard failed to win an outright majority. In the runoff, Davis claimed 56 percent of the vote. In the general election, running against a Libertarian candidate, Davis commanded a 92 percent majority. In his subsequent re-election campaigns, Davis won handily, garnering 75 percent in 2004 and facing no major party opposition in 2006.[4]

When Davis claimed his seat in the 108th Congress (2003–2005), he received assignments on the prestigious Budget and Financial Services committees. In the 109th Congress (2005–2007), Representative Davis was appointed a member of the Senior Whip Team for the Democratic Caucus. In the 110th Congress (2007–2009), Davis left the Budget and Financial Services committees to serve on two plum committees: Judiciary and Ways and Means. He also is a member of the Committee on House Administration and the Democratic Steering and Policy Committee.[5]

As a Representative-elect, Davis described his legislative agenda as focused on the "fundamentals": schools, medical care, and transportation infrastructure.[6] Like many freshman Members, Davis committed himself to constituent services, assembling a professional staff that ran five district offices and was eight times larger than the staff of his predecessor.[7]

As a House Member, Davis earned a reputation as being liberal on economic legislation and moderately conservative on controversial social issues.[8] Davis has voted with a minority of Democrats to ban partial birth abortion and human cloning; he also supports a constitutional amendment to ban gay marriage. On issues of economic equality for Black Americans, Davis votes with his colleagues in the Congressional Black Caucus. "I think I've always been able to overcome obstacles, overcome odds," Davis said, shortly after winning his first election to the U.S. House. "That's why I refuse to accept [that] the Black Belt has to lag behind the rest of our state."[9]

The U.S. Census Bureau listed five of the 12 counties in Davis's district as being among the 100 poorest in the country. Much of his agenda focuses on improving and expanding economic and educational opportunities for his constituents. During his freshman term, Davis successfully led an effort to restore funding for minority land grant colleges—including Tuskegee University—which had been cut in the annual budget. In the 109th Congress, he restored funding for HOPE VI, a program for renovating public housing, by convincing a large number of Republicans to cross the aisle and vote for his measure. Representative Davis worked with Representative Charles Rangel of New York to expand the child tax credit for poor families. Davis also was the lead Democratic sponsor of a bill to establish a national cord blood bank that will help provide blood transfusions to patients suffering from diseases such as sickle cell anemia and diabetes.[10]

FOR FURTHER READING

"Davis, Artur," *Biographical Directory of the U.S. Congress, 1774–Present,* http://bioguide.congress.gov/scripts/biodisplay.pl?index=D000602.

NOTES

1 Jeffrey McMurray, "Davis Vows to Be 'Executive' Advocate for Poor Constituents," 1 December 2002, Associated Press.

2 *Almanac of American Politics, 2002* (Washington, DC: National Journal Inc., 2001): 77.

3 *Politics in America, 2006* (Washington, DC: Congressional Quarterly Inc., 2005): 20.

4 "Election Statistics, 1920 to Present," available at http://clerk.house.gov/member_info/electionInfo/index.html.

5 "Biography, Congressman Artur Davis," http://www.house.gov/arturdavis/biography.shtml (accessed 31 October 2007).

6 "Can You Spot the Future Majority Leader? The Hill Queries Nine Freshmen on Their Priorities and Expectations," 13 November 2002, *The Hill*: 18.

7 "Can You Spot the Future Majority Leader?"; *Politics in America, 2008*: 20; "Official Biography of Artur Davis," http://www.house.gov/arturdavis (accessed 16 February 2006).

8 *Politics in America, 2008*: 19.

9 McMurray, "Davis Vows to be 'Executive' Advocate for Poor Constituents."

10 "Official Biography of Artur Davis"; *Politics in America, 2006*: 19.

Danny K. Davis
1941 –

UNITED STATES REPRESENTATIVE
DEMOCRAT FROM ILLINOIS
1997 –

IMAGE COURTESY OF THE MEMBER

Danny K. Davis was chosen by the people of the 7th Congressional District of Illinois as their Representative in Congress on November 5, 1996. He has been re-elected by large majorities to succeeding Congresses, most recently to the 110th Congress on November 7, 2006.

In the 110th Congress (2007–2009), Representative Davis serves on the Committee on Oversight and Government Reform and the Committee on Education and Labor. Representative Davis is also a member of the Congressional Black Caucus, the Progressive Caucus, the India Caucus, the Steel Caucus, the Arts Caucus, the Hellenic Caucus, and the Community Health Centers Caucus.

Representative Davis has distinguished himself as an articulate voice for his constituents and as an effective legislator able to move major bills to passage despite his relative lack of seniority. In the 109th Congress (2005–2007), Davis introduced the Second Chance Act, legislation to facilitate the return of ex-offenders to the community at large.

Davis has developed a unique and energetic style of communication and interaction with his constituents, setting up dozens of advisory task forces to consider significant questions of public policy. He hosts several weekly television and radio shows that feature audience call-in and distributes regular written reports to every household in his district. In addition, he maintains weekly office hours in the district, is widely sought after as a speaker at district events, and sponsors more than 40 town hall meetings each year.

Prior to his election to the Congress, he served on the Cook County board of commissioners, having been elected in November 1990 and re-elected in November 1994. Previously, he served for 11 years as a member of the Chicago city council as alderman of the 29th Ward.

Before seeking public office, Representative Davis had productive careers as an educator, a community organizer, a health planner/administrator and a civil rights advocate. He has received hundreds of awards and citations for outstanding work in the areas of health, education, human relations, politics, and advocacy. He has traveled extensively throughout the United States and has spent time in Africa, Europe, the Middle East, Asia, and in South and Central America.

Representative Davis is noted for his volunteer and political work. He has served as founder/president of the Westside Association for Community Action, and president of the National Association of Community Health Centers, and was a member of the Harold Washington Campaign Committee and Transition Team in 1983, and a co-chair of the Clinton/Gore/Braun campaigns in 1992. He has also been an officer and a member of many other civic, professional, and social organizations.

Born in Parkdale, Arkansas, on September 6, 1941, Representative Davis moved to the west side of Chicago in 1961, after having earned a bachelor of arts degree from Arkansas A.M. & N. College. He subsequently earned master's and doctoral degrees, respectively, from Chicago State University and the Union Institute in Cincinnati, Ohio.

He is married to Vera G. Davis and has two sons, Jonathan and Stacey. He is a member and deacon of the New Galilee M.B. Church. Davis is a public servant, an elected official and politician whose primary concern is truly the public interest.

FOR FURTHER READING

"Davis, Danny K.," *Biographical Directory of the U.S. Congress, 1774–Present*, http://bioguide.congress.gov/scripts/biodisplay.pl?index=D000096.

Chaka Fattah
1956–

UNITED STATES REPRESENTATIVE
DEMOCRAT FROM PENNSYLVANIA
1995–

IMAGE COURTESY OF THE MEMBER

A Philadelphia native, Chaka Fattah has represented a U.S. House district covering large sections of the northern and western parts of the city for seven terms. Fattah served 12 years in the Pennsylvania state legislature before winning his first House election in 1994. "I hope my accomplishment, my achievement, will be in legislation, not in how high a position I reached," Fattah, a member of the influential Appropriations Committee, once explained. "It wouldn't matter to me what position I had if I got two or three bills passed. Very few people actually drive the policy machine. I want to be one of those people."[1]

Chaka Fattah was born Arthur Davenport on November 21, 1956, in Philadelphia, Pennsylvania, the fourth of six sons of Russell and Frances Davenport. His father was a U.S. Army sergeant, and his mother was an editor at the *Philadelphia Tribune*, the oldest black newspaper in America, and served as vice president of the Philadelphia Council of Neighborhood Organizations. His parents divorced when he was young, and Fattah's mother remarried. She renamed her son Chaka, after an African Zulu warrior. Her social activism shaped Fattah's political development. "I grew up in a home where being involved in community life was a norm," Fattah recalled.[2] Fattah attended the Community College of Philadelphia and the University of Pennsylvania's Wharton School. In 1986, he graduated with an M.A. in government administration from the University of Pennsylvania's Fels School of State and Local Government. Fattah held several community development positions before making his first bid for elective office in 1982. He unseated a Democratic incumbent by 58 votes to win a seat in the Pennsylvania house of representatives. At age 25, he was one of the youngest people ever to serve in the state legislature. In 1988, Fattah won a seat in the Pennsylvania senate.[3] As a freshman senator, Fattah chaired the education committee. Fattah is married to Renee Chenault-Fattah, and they have four children.

Fattah made his first bid for the U.S. House of Representatives in 1991, when Representative William H. Gray III retired from a seat that covered large areas of Center City Philadelphia, West Philadelphia, Chestnut Hill, and the University of Pennsylvania. In the special election to succeed Gray, City Councilman Lucien Blackwell received the Democratic nomination, and Fattah ran under the Consumer Party banner. Blackwell won with 39 percent of the vote to Fattah's 28 percent. In 1994, Fattah again challenged Blackwell in the Democratic primary and prevailed with 58 percent of the vote. In the heavily Democratic and majority-black district, he won the general election with 86 percent of the vote. In his subsequent six re-election campaigns, Fattah has won easily—most recently with 89 percent of the vote in the 2006 election.[4]

Since entering Congress in 1995, Fattah has held seats on several committees, including Economic and Educational Opportunities (later renamed Government Reform), Government Reform and Oversight (later renamed Education and Labor), Small Business, the Standards of Official Conduct, House Administration, the Joint Committee on Printing, and Appropriations. House Speaker Nancy Pelosi has appointed Representative Chaka Fattah Chairman of the Urban Caucus. The caucus brings together House Members who represent the nation's largest metropolitan areas to formulate ideas on how to best address the challenges faced in America's urban communities.

In Congress, Representative Fattah has focused on issues of access to a quality education. His biggest legislative success came in 1998 when he won congressional backing for GEAR UP (Gaining Early Awareness and Readiness for Undergraduate Programs), a federally funded measure to prepare low-income students to enter college and excel. To date, more than $2 billion has been appropriated for the program, which is available to millions of students.[5] Representative Fattah developed the College Retention Program, which gives low-income students access to low-interest loans and work study programs. In the 109th Congress (2005–2007), Fattah introduced his Student Bill of Rights Act, requiring each state to certify with the U.S. Secretary of Education that its public school system provides students with equal access to resources and qualified teachers.[6]

Fattah also has proposed legislation drawing from his background in housing reform and urban renewal projects. He has championed a plan to allow homeowners a two-year grace period from defaulting on mortgages because of unforeseen circumstances. His Transform America Transaction Fee proposal calls for the elimination of all federal taxes on individuals and businesses—and their replacement with a revenue system based on transaction fees.[7]

FOR FURTHER READING

"Fattah, Chaka," *Biographical Directory of the U.S. Congress, 1774–Present,* http://bioguide.congress.gov/scripts/biodisplay.pl?index=F000043.

Fenno, Richard F. *Going Home: Black Representatives and Their Constituents* (Chicago: University Press of Chicago, 2002): 114–177.

NOTES

1 Richard Fenno, *Going Home: Black Representatives and Their Constituents* (Chicago: University of Chicago Press, 2002): 120.

2 Fenno, *Going Home*: 117, 119.

3 "Chaka Fattah," *Contemporary Black Biography*, Volume 11 (Detroit, MI: Gale Publishing Inc., 1996).

4 "Election Statistics, 1920 to Present," available at http://clerk.house.gov/member_info/electionInfo/index.html.

5 "About Congressman Chaka Fattah," http://www.house.gov/fattah/about/about.htm (accessed 28 November 2007).

6 *Politics in America, 2006* (Washington, DC: Congressional Quarterly Inc., 2005): 872–873; "About Congressman Chaka Fattah."

7 *Politics in America, 2006*: 872; "About Congressman Chaka Fattah."

Al Green
1947–

UNITED STATES REPRESENTATIVE
DEMOCRAT FROM TEXAS
2005–

IMAGE COURTESY OF THE MEMBER

In 2005, Judge Al Green took the congressional oath of office to serve the people of Texas's new 9th Congressional District and began his first term in the United States House of Representatives. As a Houston judge and lawyer, and the Houston National Association for the Advancement of Colored People (NAACP) branch president, he has dedicated most of his life to fighting for those in society whose voices are too often unheard, taken for granted, or simply ignored.

Born in New Orleans, Louisiana, Representative Green learned the importance of education from his parents and extended family, who instilled within him the drive and determination to succeed in spite of obstacles. After graduating from Chactawhatchee High School, he attended Florida A&M University and Tuskegee Institute of Technology. Although he did not acquire an undergraduate degree, he entered law school. In 1974, Representative Green earned his law degree from the Thurgood Marshall School of Law at Texas Southern University, where he later served as an instructor.

Upon graduating from law school, Green cofounded and co-managed the law firm of Green, Wilson, Dewberry and Fitch. In 1977, he was appointed judge of a Harris County justice court, where he served for 26 years before retiring in 2004.

Throughout his career, Green has earned the respect of his colleagues and a wide cross section of community leaders. He has been recognized for his superior legal skills, impeccable character, and innate ability to communicate skillfully with people from diverse backgrounds.

For nearly 10 years, Green served as president of the Houston branch of the NAACP. Under his leadership, the organization grew to unprecedented heights, acquiring property and increasing its membership from a few hundred to thousands.

Representative Green would become known as an unwavering defender of equality and a champion of justice for all. During his tenure, he oversaw the purchase and renovation of two buildings that would serve as the Houston NAACP's headquarters. In an effort to ensure that all Houstonians could participate in their economy, Green created the Houston Fair Share Program, which encourages corporations to join with minority firms in joint ventures and to hire minority vendors. He also cofounded the Black and Brown Coalition with Judge Armando Rodriguez to bring together Houston's African-American and Latino communities to work on issues of common interest.

During his first term as a Member of the 109th Congress (2005–2007), Representative Green acquired a seat on the Financial Services Committee. He has remained an active member of that committee in the 110th Congress (2007–2009), serving on the Subcommittee on Financial Institutions and Consumer Credit as well as the Subcommittee on Housing and Community Opportunity. In the 109th Congress, he also acquired a seat on the Science Committee (later renamed Science and Technology), serving on the Space and Aeronautics Subcommittee—a key appointment considering the proximity of the 9th District to the National Aeronautics and Space Administration Johnson Space Flight Center. In the 110th Congress, Representative Green left the Science and Technology Committee to take a spot on the Homeland Security Committee. He sits on the Subcommittee on Border, Maritime, and Global Counterterrorism and the Subcommittee on Emerging Threats, Cybersecurity, and Science and Technology.

Green's chief legislative priorities for his second term in office are creating a federal living wage; reducing chemical, biological, radiological, and nuclear threats; eliminating policies and practices that have historically victimized low- and moderate-income communities; and increasing the availability of affordable housing to ensure that every American can realize the dream of having a place to call home.

While working on current priorities, Representative Green maintains his focus on his compelling goals of eliminating poverty, expanding economic opportunities, protecting Social Security, providing affordable health care, perfecting national security, improving education, and promoting world peace.

Representative Green was elected Whip of Region VI and serves as the Housing Task Force Chair for CAPAC, the Congressional Asian Pacific American Caucus.

FOR FURTHER READING

"Green, Al," *Biographical Directory of the U.S. Congress, 1774–Present*, http://bioguide.congress.gov/scripts/biodisplay.pl?index=G000553.

Alcee Hastings
1936–

UNITED STATES REPRESENTATIVE
DEMOCRAT FROM FLORIDA
1993–

IMAGE COURTESY OF THE MEMBER

The son of domestic workers, Alcee L. Hastings became Florida's first African-American federal judge and, in 1992, one of the first handful of blacks to represent the state in the U.S. Congress in the 20th century. An eight-term veteran of the House, Representative Hastings holds high-ranking positions on both the Permanent Select Committee on Intelligence and the Rules Committee.

Alcee Lamar Hastings, son of Julius C. and Mildred L. Hastings, was born in Altamonte Springs, Florida, on September 5, 1936. His parents were domestic servants who eventually left the state to take jobs to pay for his education. Hastings, who lived with his maternal grandmother, graduated from Crooms Academy in Sanford, Florida, in 1953. He earned a bachelor of arts degree in zoology and botany from Fisk University in Nashville, Tennessee, in 1958 and later attended Howard University School of Law in Washington, DC. In 1963, Hastings graduated with a J.D. from Florida Agricultural & Mechanical University in Tallahassee. In 1964, he was admitted to the Florida bar, and he practiced as a civil rights attorney for the next 13 years. Hastings is twice-divorced, with three children: Alcee Lamar III, Chelsea, and Leigh. From 1977 to 1979, Hastings served as a circuit court judge in Broward County, Florida. In 1979, President James Earl (Jimmy) Carter appointed Hastings to a U.S. District Court seat in Miami, making him the first black federal judge in Florida history.[1]

In 1992, when court-ordered reapportionment created a U.S. congressional district that was 44-percent black, covering large portions of Broward County, including West Palm Beach and western Fort Lauderdale, Hastings entered the Democratic primary for the seat. In a close race in September 1992, Hastings placed second in a five-candidate primary behind Florida State Representative Lois Frankel, although he managed to force a runoff.[2] Hastings defeated Frankel with 58 percent of the vote in the October 1 runoff.[3] The primary victory in the heavily Democratic district virtually assured Hastings a seat in the U.S. House. In the November general election, he defeated Republican candidate Ed Fielding, a real estate salesman, with 58 percent of the vote.[4] Along with newly elected Representatives Carrie Meek and Corrine Brown, Hastings became one of the first African Americans elected to the U.S. Congress from Florida since the Reconstruction Era. In his subsequent seven re-election campaigns, Hastings has won with majorities of 73 percent or more. On four occasions—1994, 1998, 2004, and 2006—he was unopposed in the general election.[5]

When Hastings entered the House in January 1993, he received assignments on three committees: Foreign Affairs, Merchant Marine and Fisheries, and Post Office and Civil Service. He served on Foreign Affairs (later renamed International Relations) through the 107th Congress (2001–2003). When Merchant Marine and Fisheries and Post Office and Civil Service were disbanded in the 104th Congress (1995–1997), he was reassigned to the Science Committee, where he served through the 105th Congress (1997–1999). In the 106th Congress (1999–2001), Hastings earned a seat on the House Permanent Select Committee on Intelligence, where he eventually served as vice chairman of the full committee and two of its subcommittees before leaving the panel at the end of 2007. During the 107th Congress, Hastings served as vice chairman of the Democratic Caucus's Special Committee on Election Reform, a panel assigned to investigate voting discrepancies in the 2000 election. In the following Congress, he won a seat on the powerful Rules Committee, which directs legislation onto the House Floor. He currently serves as chairman of the Rules Committee's Subcommittee on Legislative and Budget Process. Hastings also serves as a Senior Democratic Whip.[6]

Widely regarded as a charismatic orator, Representative Hastings is a leading voice for liberal causes in the House. But his seats on the Rules and Permanent Select Intelligence committees also provide him a platform from which he can cultivate legislation important to his district and to minorities nationally. Hastings's legislative interests center on fostering educational and economic opportunities for his constituency, including federal funding for Head Start programs, Medicare, and job training and re-education for displaced workers. He has advocated tax incentives to spur small business development. On the Intelligence Committee, Representative Hastings has prodded U.S. intelligence agencies to recruit more minorities and women, and he successfully included a provision in the 2004 intelligence authorization bill to create a pilot program to achieve that end. Hastings also is one of the institution's experts on overseas elections and serves as chairman of the U.S. Helsinki Commission and is a member of the Organization for Security Cooperation in Europe's Parliamentary Assembly.[7]

FOR FURTHER READING

"Hastings, Alcee Lamar," *Biographical Directory of the U.S. Congress, 1774–Present*, http://bioguide.congress.gov/scripts/biodisplay.pl?index=H000324.

NOTES

1 *Politics in America, 2006* (Washington, DC: Congressional Quarterly Inc., 2005): 269–270.

2 *Politics in America, 1994* (Washington, DC: Congressional Quarterly Inc., 1993): 384–385.

3 *Politics in America, 1994*: 384.

4 "Election Statistics, 1920 to Present," available at http://clerk.house.gov/member_info/electionInfo/index.html.

5 "Election Statistics, 1920 to Present."

6 "United States Representative Alcee L. Hastings," http://www.alceehastings.house.gov/index.php?option=com_content&task=view&id=60&Itemid=68 (accessed 28 Novemer 2007); "Committee Assignments," http://www.alceehastings.house.gov/index.php?option=com_content&task=view&id=101&Itemid=50 (accessed 28 November 2007).

7 *Politics in America, 2006*: 269–270; "Official Biography of Alcee L. Hastings," http://alceehastings.house.gov/biography (accessed 28 August 2006).

Jesse Jackson, Jr.
1965–

UNITED STATES REPRESENTATIVE
DEMOCRAT FROM ILLINOIS
1995–

IMAGE COURTESY OF THE MEMBER

The son of one of the foremost civil rights activists of the 20th century, Jesse Jackson, Jr., won his first campaign for elective office when he prevailed in a special election to represent a U.S. House district that stretched across South Chicago and outlying communities. From his seat on the powerful House Appropriations Committee, Jackson has focused on improving the economy of his largely suburban district and attending to key national issues such as voting reform and health disparities.

Jesse L. Jackson, Jr., was born in Greenville, South Carolina, on March 11, 1965, the second of five children of Jesse, a civil rights activist, and Jacqueline Davis Jackson. He attended Le Mans Academy, a private military preparatory school, and graduated high school from St. Albans School in Washington, DC. Jackson graduated in 1987 with a bachelor of science degree in business management from North Carolina Agricultural and Technical State University. Two years later, he earned an M.A. in theology from the Chicago Theological Seminary. In 1993, he completed his J.D. at the University of Illinois–Chicago College of Law. After earning his law degree, Jackson served two years as national field director of the Rainbow Coalition, a political organization founded by his father. Jackson's wife, Sandi, whom he married in 1991, currently serves as an alderman for Chicago's 7th Ward. The couple have two children: Jessica Donatella and Jesse L. Jackson III.[1]

In 1995, Jackson announced his intention to run for the U. S. House seat vacated by incumbent Representative Mel Reynolds of Illinois. The district, which included much of Chicago's South Side and a swath of suburbs toward the south, was 69 percent black according to the 1990 Census. It was economically diverse, with rich and poor neighborhoods, abandoned steel mills, and tract suburban housing.[2] Jackson won the Democratic special primary on November 29, 1995, with 48 percent of the vote, against Emil Jones and Alice Palmer, Illinois state senators.[3] In the special election on December 13, 1995, Jackson defeated his Republican opponent, former Chicago Heights police officer Thomas Somer, by a nearly three-to-one margin. Jackson was sworn in the following day, as Representative Sidney Yates from a nearby North Side Chicago district—then the longest-serving Member of the House—introduced him on the floor.[4] In his six re-election bids, Jackson has never been seriously challenged, winning majorities of between 89 and 94 percent of the vote.[5]

Jackson received an assignment on the Banking and Financial Services Committee when he joined the 104th Congress (1995–1997). In the 105th Congress (1997–1999), Jackson received an additional post on the Small Business Committee. In the 106th Congress (1999–2001), he left both panels after securing an exclusive post on the Appropriations Committee, which originates all federal spending bills. During the 110th Congress (2007–2009), Representative Jackson serves as the second-ranking Democrat on the Subcommittee on State, Foreign Operations, and Related Programs and the fourth-ranking Democrat on the Subcommittee on Labor, Health and Human Services, Education, and Related Agencies. He also serves on the Subcommittee on Agriculture, Rural Development, Food and Drug Administration, and Related Agencies.

Every Congress, Representative Jackson introduces several constitutional amendments for the right to vote, the right to a high quality education, and the right to high quality health care. He also wrote the legislation that will place a statue of civil rights pioneer Rosa Parks in National Statuary Hall in the Capitol. From his seat on the Appropriations Committee, Representative Jackson was the driving force in increasing the funding for the Minority HIV/AIDS initiative from $166 million in 1998 to more than $400 million currently, and he has consistently led the fight to increase funding for historically black schools for medical and health professions. He also directed the effort to create the National Center on Minority Health and Health Disparities at the National Institutes of Health in 2001.

Representative Jackson has also been successful in obtaining humanitarian aid for sub-Saharan African countries, securing $500 million in emergency humanitarian and peacekeeping assistance for the Darfur region of Sudan in 2005 and $50 million in emergency humanitarian assistance for Liberia in 2006. For his district, Jackson has secured hundreds of millions of dollars for job training, health care, education, transportation and infrastructure projects, and has championed the construction of a third Chicago-area airport south of his district to foster economic development.

FOR FURTHER READING

"Jackson, Jesse L., Jr.," *Biographical Directory of the U.S. Congress, 1774–Present*, http://bioguide.congress.gov/scripts/biodisplay.pl?index=J000283.

NOTES

1 "Official Biography of Representative Jesse L. Jackson, Jr." http://www.house.gov/jackson/Bio.shtml (accessed 27 June 2007).

2 Don Terry, "In House Election, A Familiar Name," 24 November 1995, *New York Times*: A20; *Politics in America, 1994* (Washington, DC: Congressional Quarterly Inc., 1993): 457–458.

3 Benjamin Sheffner, "His Last Name Proves Golden for Jesse Jackson Jr., Who Wins Big in Special Primary for Reynolds Seat," 30 November 1995, *Roll Call*.

4 Dirk Johnson, "Victory His, Jesse Jackson Jr. Heads to Congress," 14 December 1995, *New York Times*: B17; "Jesse Jackson, Jr. Sworn in as House Member," 15 December 1995, *New York Times*: A38; Mitchell Locin, "GOP Won't Challenge Jackson in 2nd District," 6 September 1996, *Chicago Tribune*: 1.

5 "Election Statistics, 1920 to Present," available at http://clerk.house.gov/member_info/electionInfo/index.html.

Sheila Jackson Lee
1950–

UNITED STATES REPRESENTATIVE
DEMOCRAT FROM TEXAS
1995–

IMAGE COURTESY OF THE MEMBER

Sheila Jackson Lee won election to the U.S. House of Representatives in 1994 in a Houston district once served by Barbara Jordan. From her seats on the Judiciary, Homeland Security, and Foreign Affairs committees, Representative Jackson Lee has focused on the needs of her district. She also has called attention to such national issues as bolstering the protection of our homeland while preserving civil liberties, health care, and job training for working-class Americans.

Sheila Jackson was born in Queens, New York, on January 12, 1950. Her mother was a nurse, and her father was a comic book illustrator. Jackson graduated from Jamaica High School and attended New York University. In 1969, she transferred with the first group of female undergraduates admitted to Yale College and graduated in 1972 with a B.A. in political science. Before receiving her J.D. from the University of Virginia School of Law in 1975, Sheila Jackson married fellow Yale graduate Elwyn Cornelius Lee in 1973; they raised two children, Erica and Jason. In 1977 and 1978, she worked as a staff counsel for the U.S. House Select Committee on Assassinations, which investigated the murders of Martin Luther King, Jr., and President John F. Kennedy. She left private law practice in 1987 to serve as an associate judge in the Houston municipal courts. Three years later, she won election to the first of two terms as an at-large member of the Houston city council.

In 1994, Jackson Lee challenged incumbent Craig Washington for the Democratic nomination to the Houston-area U.S. House seat. Her platform reflected broad agreement with the William J. (Bill) Clinton administration agenda. Promoting measures that would benefit the Houston economy, Jackson Lee defeated her opponent, with 63 percent of the vote, in the primary. She won handily with a 73 percent majority in the general election. In her subsequent six re-elections, Jackson Lee won easily, capturing a high of 90 percent in 1998. Jackson Lee followed a succession of prestigious Representatives from her district, including Jordan and noted humanitarian George (Mickey) Leland. Created after the 1970 Census, Jackson Lee's district was the first in Texas in which African Americans and Hispanics constituted the majority of voters.

When Jackson Lee took her seat in the 104th Congress (1995–1997), she received assignments on the Judiciary and Science (later renamed Science and Technology) committees. Her colleagues elected her Democratic freshman class president. Jackson Lee was also appointed to the Democratic Steering and Policy Committee. In 1997, she was selected as a Congressional Black Caucus (CBC) whip and thereafter as first vice chair of the CBC. By the 107th Congress (2001–2003), Jackson Lee was the top-ranking Democrat on the Immigration and Claims Subcommittee of the Judiciary Committee. In the 108th Congress (2003–2005), Jackson Lee was assigned to the Homeland Security Committee, where in the 110th Congress (2007–2009) she chairs the Subcommittee on Transportation Security and Infrastructure Protection. In 2007, Jackson Lee coauthored and ensured the passage of the Rail and Public Transportation Security Act, which authorized more than $5 billion to overhaul security for U.S. railroads, mass transit, and buses. In the 110th Congress, she also left the Science and Technology Committee for a seat on the Foreign Affairs Committee.

In Congress, Jackson Lee battled GOP initiatives to reduce welfare. In the 105th Congress (1997–1999), she pushed for legislation to protect child support and alimony payments from creditors. As a cofounder of the Congressional Children's Caucus, she also sponsored bills to create affordable childcare for working parents and to strengthen adoption laws. Jackson Lee spearheaded efforts to reduce teenage smoking addiction and authored the "Date Rape Drug Prevention Act" to curb the availability of substances used by rapists. She also strongly defended affirmative action programs. From her seat on the Science Committee, Jackson Lee sought to restore appropriations for the National Aeronautics and Space Administration in 1999, and also supported extending provisions in a 1998 bill to grow the commercial space launch industry. She persuaded the Clinton administration to make low-income Houston neighborhoods eligible for federal grants for economic development, job training, childcare facilities, and improved transportation. Jackson Lee also coauthored and helped pass the historic Notification of Federal Employees Anti-Discrimination and Retaliation ("No Fear") Act. Described as the first civil rights act of the 21st century, the measure protects federal workers, and especially whistleblowers, from acts of discrimination and retaliation.

Jackson Lee maintained that such advocacy was part of her job representing constituents. "You have an obligation to make sure that their concerns are heard, are answered," she explained. "I need to make a difference. I don't have wealth to write a check. But maybe I can be a voice arguing consistently for change."

FOR FURTHER READING

"Jackson Lee, Sheila," *Biographical Directory of the U.S. Congress, 1774–Present*, http://bioguide.congress.gov/scripts/biodisplay.pl?index=J000032.

William J. Jefferson
1947–

UNITED STATES REPRESENTATIVE
DEMOCRAT FROM LOUISIANA
1991–

When William Jefferson won election to the U.S. House in 1990 from a New Orleans-centered district, he became the first African American to represent the state of Louisiana since Reconstruction. Jefferson, who had more than a decade of experience in the Louisiana state senate, specialized in economic matters and eventually earned a seat on the influential Ways and Means Committee.

William Jennings Jefferson was born on March 14, 1947, in Lake Providence, Louisiana. Jefferson grew up in poverty in a family of 10 children in the far northeastern part of the state. In 1969, he graduated from Southern University Agricultural and Mechanical College with a B.A. degree. Three years later, on scholarship, he earned a J.D. from Harvard Law School. In 1996, Jefferson earned a Master of Laws in taxation from Georgetown University. After law school, he served for a year as a law clerk for veteran U.S. District Court Judge Alvin B. Rubin in New Orleans. From 1973 to 1975, Jefferson then served as a legislative assistant to Senator J. Bennett Johnston of Louisiana. Jefferson is married to Dr. Andrea Green-Jefferson, and they have raised five daughters: Jamila, Jalila, Jelani, Nailah, and Akilah.[1]

Jefferson entered elective politics in the late 1970s, when he defeated a white incumbent for a Louisiana senate seat that covered the affluent Uptown section of New Orleans. He served in Baton Rouge for 12 years, working on the finance committee and chairing the special budget stabilization committee, which was created to rein in state spending and develop more accurate revenue projections. He also chaired the influential governmental affairs committee, which had oversight of reapportionment.[2] In 1982 and 1986, Jefferson was an unsuccessful candidate for mayor of New Orleans.

In 1990, when 17-year House veteran Corinne C. (Lindy) Boggs announced her retirement, Jefferson entered a crowded field to succeed her. The district covered much of New Orleans proper, the wealthy Uptown section, Algiers on the west bank of the Mississippi River, and the sprawling Kenner suburbs on the city's west side. In 1983, court-ordered redistricting made it the state's first majority-black district and, by 1990, Representative Boggs was the last white Representative in the country to represent a majority black-district. Jefferson was one of four principal contenders in the October open primary, which included Marc H. Morial, son of former mayor Dutch Morial (who served from 1978 to 1986 and the city's first African-American mayor), a state senator who had been endorsed by the governor, and a prominent city school board member. Jefferson finished first with 25 percent of the vote, with Morial trailing at 22 percent.[3] In the spirited two-man November runoff, Jefferson prevailed with 53 percent of the vote. In his subsequent seven re-election campaigns, Jefferson won handily with 73 percent of the vote or more.[4]

When Jefferson took his seat in the House in the 102nd Congress (1991–1993), he earned seats on the Education and Labor and the Merchant Marine and Fisheries committees. In the following Congress, he relinquished those assignments for a coveted spot on the Ways and Means Committee. When the Republicans took control of the chamber for the 104th Congress (1995–1997) Jefferson lost his Ways and Means post and was transferred to the National Security Committee (later renamed Armed Services), the House Oversight Committee (later renamed House Administration), and the Joint Committee on Printing. In the next Congress, Jefferson again won an assignment to the exclusive Ways and Means Committee, relinquishing his prior assignments. He remained on Ways and Means until June 2006, adding an assignment to the Budget Committee in the 109th Congress. In the 110th Congress, Jefferson was assigned to the Small Business Committee.

In Congress, Jefferson specializes in trade and tax issues. New Orleans is a major U.S. port, and trade is a primary economic engine. Jefferson has advocated trade opportunities in neglected markets such as Brazil and Africa. He served as co-chair of the Africa Trade and Investment Caucus and also chaired the Congressional Black Caucus Foundation board of directors. In the wake of Hurricane Katrina, which flooded much of New Orleans and its surrounding environs in August 2005, Jefferson pushed for reforms to the Small Business Administration (SBA) disaster loan program, which was criticized in the aftermath of the storm. The House also passed Jefferson's amendment to extend the deadline for minority-owned businesses in his district to rebuild under the SBA's redevelopment program.[5]

In 2006, Jefferson was re-elected to a ninth term against Democratic challenger Karen Carter, with 57 percent of the vote.[6]

FOR FURTHER READING

"Jefferson, William Jennings," *Biographical Directory of the U.S. Congress, 1774–Present*, http://bioguide.congress.gov/scripts/biodisplay.pl?index=J000070.

NOTES

1 "Official Biography of William J. Jefferson," http://www.house.gov/jefferson/biography.shtml (accessed 2 November 2007).

2 *Politics in America, 1994* (Washington, DC: Congressional Quarterly Inc., 1993): 644.

3 *Almanac of American Politics, 1992* (Washington, DC: National Journal Inc., 1991): 513.

4 "Election Statistics, 1920 to Present," available at http://clerk.house.gov/member_info/electionInfo/index.html.

5 *Politics in America, 2008* (Washington, DC: Congressional Quarterly Inc., 2007): 435; "Official Biography of William J. Jefferson."

6 "Election Statistics, 1920 to Present," available at http://clerk.house.gov/member_info/electionInfo/index.html.

Eddie Bernice Johnson
1935–

UNITED STATES REPRESENTATIVE
DEMOCRAT FROM TEXAS
1993–

IMAGE COURTESY OF THE MEMBER

A nurse by training, Eddie Bernice Johnson was also a political veteran decades before coming to Congress in the early 1990s. In 1972, Johnson became the first African American to hold a Dallas-area political office since the Reconstruction Era, after winning election to the state legislature. Elected to the U.S. House of Representatives in 1992, Johnson has attained a high-ranking seat on the Science and Technology Committee, and a subcommittee chairmanship on the Transportation and Infrastructure Committee, and has chaired the Congressional Black Caucus (CBC) while stressing the need for minority inroads in the fields of science and technology.

Eddie Bernice Johnson was born in Waco, Texas, on December 3, 1935, the daughter of Lee Edward Johnson and Lillie Mae (White) Johnson. She graduated from A.J. Moore High School in Waco in 1952. In 1955, she received a nursing diploma from Holy Cross Central School of Nursing in South Bend, Indiana. Eddie Bernice Johnson married Lacey Kirk Johnson a year later. Before they divorced in 1970, the couple had one son, Kirk. Johnson graduated in 1967 with a B.S. from Texas Christian University in Fort Worth. She later became the chief psychiatric nurse of the Veterans Administration hospital in Dallas. In 1976, Johnson earned an M.S. in public administration from Southern Methodist University in Dallas. Johnson has three grandchildren: Kirk, Jr., David, and James.

Eddie Bernice Johnson first became involved in elective politics at the state level. She was elected as a Democrat to the Texas state legislature in 1972, becoming the first African-American woman from the Dallas area ever to hold public office. As a member of the Texas legislature, she chaired the labor committee, becoming the first woman in Texas history to lead a major committee in the statehouse. In 1977, President James Earl (Jimmy) Carter appointed her as a regional director for the Department of Health, Education, and Welfare, a post she held until 1981. After a six-year hiatus from politics, Johnson won election to the state senate, eventually serving as chair of the redistricting committee.

Following the Texas reapportionment of 1992, Johnson ran for the newly created U.S. House seat, which encompassed much of the Dallas and Irving area. She was elected as a Democrat with 72 percent of the vote. In 1996, court-ordered redistricting changed the boundaries of the Texas district, reducing the percentage of minority voters. Nevertheless, Johnson was re-elected with 55 percent of the vote. In her subsequent five re-election campaigns, Johnson won comfortably. In 2006, she won re-election to the 110th Congress (2007–2009) with 80 percent of the vote.[1]

Johnson has served on two committees since her House career began in January 1993: Transportation and Infrastructure and Science and Technology. In the 110th Congress, Johnson was appointed to serve as chairwoman of the Transportation and Infrastructure Committee's Subcommittee on Water Resources and the Environment. She also serves as a senior deputy whip.[2]

Representative Johnson's legislative interests have had both a local and a national focus. As a former nurse, Johnson has called attention to the problems facing the country's health care system and Medicare program. In 2002, she voted against a Republican-backed prescription drug plan. She also has been a proponent of a bill that called for increased federal funding for research into osteoporosis, or bone density deficiency. From her seat on the Science and Technology Committee, Representative Johnson also has pushed for a program to encourage schoolchildren to study science and math.

Johnson used her Transportation and Infrastructure Committee and Science and Technology Committee positions to look out for the economic interests of her district. Early in her career, Johnson supported the North American Free Trade Agreement, recognizing the fact that much of Dallas's business revolves around exports to Mexico. She later voted for normalizing trade relations with China, arguing that it would bring business to the Dallas–Fort Worth area. In 1998, she received a post on the Aviation Subcommittee of the Transportation and Infrastructure Committee, an important position since her district covers part of the Dallas–Fort Worth International Airport. Johnson has helped bring federal money for transportation improvements and also has supported the production of B-2 stealth bombers, which are manufactured in her district.

During her House career, Johnson has been an active member of the CBC. As chair of the organization in the 107th Congress (2001–2003), she attempted to steer the CBC toward building coalitions with business groups in addition to its traditional reliance on labor and civil rights organizations. Representative Johnson also pushed the group to hold its first summit conferences on technology and energy.[3]

FOR FURTHER READING

"Johnson, Eddie Bernice," *Biographical Directory of the U.S. Congress, 1774–Present,* http://bioguide.congress.gov/scripts/biodisplay.pl?index=J000126.

NOTES

1 "Election Statistics, 1920 to Present," available at http://clerk.house.gov/member_info/electionInfo/index.html.

2 "About Eddie Bernice Johnson," http://www.house.gov/ebjohnson/about_ebj/index.shtml (accessed 4 December 2007).

3 *Politics in America, 2004* (Washington, DC: Congressional Quarterly Inc., 2003): 1008.

Stephanie Tubbs Jones
1949–

UNITED STATES REPRESENTATIVE
DEMOCRAT FROM OHIO
1999–

IMAGE COURTESY OF THE MEMBER

Stephanie Tubbs Jones won election to the U.S. House of Representatives in 1998, becoming the first African-American woman to represent Ohio in the U.S. Congress. In the 110th Congress (2007–2009), Jones became the first African-American woman to chair a standing House committee.[1] Representative Jones, who chairs the Standards of Official Conduct Committee and holds a seat on the influential Ways and Means Committee, has focused on the economic issues affecting her Cleveland-centered district: financial literacy, access to health care, retirement security, and education.

Stephanie Tubbs was born in Cleveland, Ohio, on September 10, 1949, the youngest of three daughters raised by Mary Tubbs, a factory worker, and Andrew Tubbs, an airline skycap. Raised in Cleveland's Glenville neighborhood, Stephanie Tubbs graduated from Collinwood High School, earning 10 academic and athletic awards. At Case Western Reserve University, Tubbs founded the African-American Students Association and, in 1971, earned a B.A. in sociology with a minor in psychology. "All my life I had wanted to help others, and I had been active in helping others," she recalled. "I was always interested in service. In my day, the college watchword was relevant. . . . With a law degree, I thought I could bring about relevant change in the world."[2] She enrolled in the Case Western University Law School and graduated in 1974 with a J.D. Tubbs then served as the assistant general counsel for the equal opportunity administrator of the northeast Ohio regional sewer district. In 1976, Tubbs married Mervyn Jones. They raised a son, Mervyn. Stephanie Tubbs Jones later worked as an assistant Cuyahoga County prosecutor and trial attorney for the Cleveland district equal employment opportunity commission. When Jones and several friends worked on a successful political campaign in 1979, the group pledged to select one among them to promote for public office. Noting a lack of minority members on the bench, they chose Jones, who eventually won election as a judge on the Cleveland municipal court. Ohio Governor Richard Celeste appointed Jones to the Cuyahoga County court of common pleas, where she served from 1983 to 1991. In 1992, she was appointed the Cuyahoga County prosecutor, making her the state's first African-American prosecutor and the only black woman prosecutor in a major U.S. city. Jones was re-elected twice.[3]

In 1998, when 30-year veteran U.S. Representative Louis Stokes retired from his Ohio district seat, Jones entered the Democratic primary to succeed him. She ran on the basis of her 17-year career in public office in the district and on her well-established political connection to constituents.[4] Capturing 51 percent of the vote among five primary candidates, she later won 80 percent in the general election. Jones faced no serious challenges in her four re-election bids, winning by 75 percent or more of the vote.[5] In 2006, Jones won with 83 percent.[6]

When she took her seat in the 106th Congress (1999–2001), Jones received assignments on the Banking and Financial Services (later renamed Financial Services) and Small Business committees. In the 107th Congress (2001–2003), in addition to serving on those two panels, she served on the Standards of Official Conduct Committee, which oversees House ethics guidelines for Members and staff. In the 108th Congress (2003–2005), Jones won a seat on the prestigious Ways and Means Committee, which has jurisdiction over tax law.[7]

Representative Jones's district encompasses some of Cleveland's most affluent suburbs and parts of poor, inner-city neighborhoods. Her seat on Financial Services helped her secure funding for business and housing development. In the 108th Congress, Jones chaired the Congressional Black Caucus Housing Task Force, investigating allegations against subprime lenders and introducing legislation against predatory lenders.[8] Her seat on Ways and Means has enabled her to focus legislative efforts on shoring up Social Security and Medicare, pension law, and long-term care.

Jones also has taken a legislative interest in children's issues, health, and education. She authored and passed the Child Abuse Prevention and Enforcement Act of 1999 to increase training funds for child-protection workers through money generated from bail bonds, fines, and forfeited assets. In the 107th through the 109th Congresses (2001–2007), Representative Jones introduced the Uterine Fibroids Research and Education Act and also authored the Campus Fire Prevention Act to provide federal funds to equip college housing with fire suppression equipment. In 2005, Jones introduced the Count Every Vote Act to improve electronic voting systems. Additionally, she authored legislation to clarify the legal status of cash balance pension plans. In the 109th Congress, she chaired the Congressional Black Caucus Retirement Security Task Force.

FOR FURTHER READING

Fenno, Richard F. *Going Home: Black Representatives and Their Constituents* (Chicago: University of Chicago Press, 2003).

"Jones, Stephanie Tubbs," *Biographical Directory of the U.S. Congress, 1774–Present*, http://bioguide.congress.gov/scripts/biodisplay.pl?index=J000284.

NOTES

1 Representative Juanita Millender-McDonald of California became Chairwoman of the House Administration Committee at the same time.

2 Richard Fenno, *Going Home: Black Representatives and Their Constituents* (Chicago: University of Chicago Press, 2003): 193.

3 "Stephanie Tubbs Jones," *Contemporary Black Biography*, Volume 24 (Detroit, MI: Gale Research Inc., 2000).

4 Fenno, *Going Home*: 196–198; 201.

5 Ibid., 203.

6 "Election Statistics, 1920 to Present," available at http://clerk.house.gov/member_info/electionInfo/index.html.

7 *Politics in America, 2008* (Washington, DC: Congressional Quarterly Inc., 2007): 800.

8 *Politics in America, 2002* (Washington, DC: Congressional Quarterly Inc., 2001): 796–797.

Carolyn Cheeks Kilpatrick
1945–

UNITED STATES REPRESENTATIVE
DEMOCRAT FROM MICHIGAN
1997–

A 30-year veteran of Michigan politics, Carolyn Cheeks Kilpatrick won election to the U.S. House of Representatives in 1996. Kilpatrick was the first African-American woman to serve on the Michigan legislature's appropriations committee. In the 110th Congress (2007–2009), Representative Kilpatrick was unanimously elected chairwoman of the Congressional Black Caucus (CBC).

Carolyn Jean Cheeks was born on June 25, 1945, in Detroit, Michigan, to Marvell Cheeks, Jr., and Willa Mae (Henry) Cheeks. Raised in the AME Church, she later joined the Shrine of the Black Madonna of the Pan African Orthodox Christian Church, a politically active and powerful congregation in Detroit. She served as coordinator of political action.[1] She graduated from the High School of Commerce in Detroit as president of her class and attended Ferris State University. She earned a bachelor of science degree in education from Western Michigan University in 1972 and a master of science degree in education from the University of Michigan. In 1968, the Representative married Bernard Kilpatrick. They raised two children, Ayanna and Kwame. Early in her career, Kilpatrick worked as a Detroit public school teacher. A protégé of longtime Detroit Mayor Coleman A. Young, she left teaching in 1978 to pursue a political career and won election to nine consecutive terms in the Michigan house of representatives. Serving 18 years in the state house, Kilpatrick became the first African-American woman member of the house appropriations committee. She chaired the corrections budget and the transportation budget during 14 years on the appropriations committee. She also was a house Democratic whip—earning a reputation as a consensus-builder.[2]

Kilpatrick sought election in 1996 to represent Michigan in the U.S. House of Representatives. Among a large field of competitors in the Democratic primary, including three-term incumbent Barbara-Rose Collins, Kilpatrick prevailed with a 19 percent margin. In the general election, Kilpatrick captured an 88 percent majority. In her subsequent five re-election bids, she has won by similarly large margins, despite reapportionment in 2001.[3]

When Representative Kilpatrick took her seat in the 105th Congress (1997–1999), she received assignments on three committees: Banking and Financial Services, House Oversight (later renamed House Administration), and the Joint Committee on the Library of Congress. In the 106th Congress (1999–2001), Kilpatrick won a seat on the prestigious House Appropriations Committee, which required her to leave her other committee assignments. She is the sole Michigan Democrat to serve on the committee. She is the fifth woman to head the full CBC. Kilpatrick also is the first African-American Member of Congress to serve on the Air Force Academy Board, which oversees programs of the U.S. Air Force Academy.[4]

Much of Kilpatrick's legislative work has centered on bringing federally funded projects into the State of Michigan. She has helped garner funding for pre-college engineering, children's television programming, and enhanced rehabilitation services at the Detroit Medical Center.[5] She also initiated a transportation bill that included $24 million for an intermodal freight terminal that links rail, marine, and road delivery lines.[6] She has initiated $100 million in the current five-year U.S. transportation bill for a commuter rail system that covers more than 50 miles in southeastern Michigan. Kilpatrick's efforts brought the National Aeronautics and Space Administration engineering and aeronautics program to Michigan for students ranging from kindergarten through 12th grade. The program is housed at Wayne State University.

Representative Kilpatrick has been an outspoken advocate for affordable health care for low- and middle-income families and for raising the minimum wage. Kilpatrick also proposed legislation to provide a $1,000 per month tax credit for medical doctors who practice in underserved areas. Representative Kilpatrick has sought to encourage corporate America and the federal government to invest more money in minority- and women-owned media outlets and advertising agencies. From her seat on the Foreign Operations Subcommittee of the Appropriations Committee, Kilpatrick brought attention to health and economic woes in sub-Saharan Africa, securing more than $25 million for flood relief in Mozambique, Madagascar, Botswana, South Africa, and Zimbabwe. Representative Kilpatrick has initiated funding for HIV/AIDS programs, education, and military assistance in America and in several African countries.

The Honorable Kwame Kilpatrick succeeded Representative Kilpatrick in the Michigan house of representatives. Kwame Kilpatrick went on to become the Democratic leader of the state house of representatives. In 2001, at 30 years of age, Kwame Kilpatrick was elected mayor of the city of Detroit.

FOR FURTHER READING

"Kilpatrick, Carolyn Cheeks," *Biographical Directory of the U.S. Congress, 1774–Present*, http://bioguide.congress.gov/scripts/biodisplay.pl?index=K000180.

NOTES

1 "Carolyn Cheeks Kilpatrick," Associated Press Candidate Biographies, 2000; "Carolyn Cheeks Kilpatrick," *Contemporary Black Biography*, Volume 16 (Detroit, MI: Gale Research Inc., 1997) (hereinafter referred to as *CBB*).

2 "Carolyn Cheeks Kilpatrick," *CBB*; Hans Johnson and Peggie Rayhawk, *The New Members of Congress Almanac: 105th U.S. Congress* (Washington, DC: Almanac Publishing Inc., 1996): 58.

3 "Election Statistics, 1920 to Present," available at http://clerk.house.gov/member_info/electionInfo/index.html.

4 *Politics in America, 2008* (Washington, DC: Congressional Quarterly Inc., 2007): 532; "Official Biography of Congresswoman Carolyn Cheeks Kilpatrick," http://www.house.gov/kilpatrick/biography.shtml (accessed 5 December 2007).

5 *Almanac of American Politics, 2002* (Washington, DC: National Journal Inc., 2001): 815.

6 *Almanac of American Politics, 2002*: 814.

Barbara Lee
1946–

UNITED STATES REPRESENTATIVE
DEMOCRAT FROM CALIFORNIA
1998–

IMAGE COURTESY OF THE MEMBER

Representative Barbara Lee was first elected to represent California's 9th Congressional District in 1998, in a special election to fill the seat of retiring Representative Ronald Dellums. After serving on the International Relations and Financial Services committees, in 2007 she joined the House Appropriations Committee, which controls the federal purse strings and is widely viewed as one of the most powerful committees in Congress. On that committee, she serves on the Labor, Health and Human Services, Education, and Related Agencies Subcommittee and the State, Foreign Operations, and Related Programs Subcommittee, and is Vice Chair of the Legislative Branch Subcommittee.

She also serves as the Co-Chair of the Congressional Progressive Caucus and is a cofounder of the Out of Iraq and Out of Poverty caucuses, a Senior Democratic Whip, and First Vice Chair of the Congressional Black Caucus (CBC), where she serves as Co-Chair of the CBC Outreach Task Force and Chair of the CBC Task Force on HIV/AIDS.

Among her many legislative victories, Representative Lee's Darfur divestment bill passed Congress in late 2007 and was subsequently signed into law. She has been a leader in the bipartisan effort in Congress to end the ongoing genocide in Darfur, Sudan. She was arrested for protesting the genocide in front of the Sudanese Embassy in Washington in June 2006 and has traveled to the Darfur region several times.

Representative Lee's accomplishments in promoting effective bipartisan legislation to stop the spread of HIV/AIDS and make treatment available for those who are infected have earned her international recognition as a leader in the global fight against HIV/AIDS. Her bills to create the Global Fund to Fight HIV/AIDS, to protect AIDS orphans, and to create a $15 billion fund to fight HIV/AIDS, tuberculosis, and malaria were all signed into law. She has also been a leader in the fight to stop the spread of HIV/AIDS in the United States, particularly in the African-American community. In 1998, she helped declare a state of emergency in Alameda County in order to secure more funds to fight the disease, and the House has passed her resolution recognizing the goals of National Black AIDS Awareness Day every year since 2005.

Representative Lee's willingness to stand on principle earned her international acclaim when she was the only Member of Congress to vote against giving President George W. Bush a blank check to wage war after the horrific September 11 attacks. In addition to being one of Congress's most vocal opponents of the war in Iraq, Representative Lee has been a leader in promoting policies that foster international peace, security, and human rights. She successfully blocked funds from being used to establish permanent military bases in Iraq during the 109th Congress (2005–2007). She sponsored legislation disavowing the doctrine of preemptive war.

Representative Lee is committed to eradicating poverty, fostering opportunity, and protecting the most vulnerable in our society. In the wake of Hurricane Katrina, she authored the poverty section of the CBC's Gulf Coast reconstruction legislation and introduced a package of bills designed to make the eradication of poverty a priority for Congress.

California's 9th Congressional District encompasses most of Alameda County, including the cities of Albany, Ashland, Berkeley, Castro Valley, Cherryville, Emeryville, Fairview, Oakland, and Piedmont.

Born in El Paso, Texas, Representative Lee graduated from Mills College in Oakland and received her M.S.W. from the University of California in Berkeley. She began her political career as an intern in the office of her predecessor, then-Representative Ronald Dellums, currently the mayor of Oakland, where she eventually became his chief of staff. Before being elected to Congress, she served in the California state assembly from 1990 to 1996 and in the California state senate from 1996 to 1998.

FOR FURTHER READING

"Lee, Barbara," *Biographical Directory of the U.S. Congress, 1774–Present,* http://bioguide.congress.gov/scripts/biodisplay.pl?index=L000551.

John Lewis
1940–

UNITED STATES REPRESENTATIVE
DEMOCRAT FROM GEORGIA
1987–

IMAGE COURTESY OF THE MEMBER

Dubbed "the Conscience of the U.S. Congress," John Lewis spent his early life as one of the principal leaders of the nonviolent civil rights movement initiated by Martin Luther King, Jr.[1] Now in his 11th term in the U.S. House, Representative Lewis holds a seat on the powerful Ways and Means Committee, from which he speaks with passion and authority about issues related to the legacy of that movement.

John Robert Lewis was born on February 21, 1940, in Troy, Alabama, to Eddie and Willie Mae Lewis. His parents originally were sharecroppers before they bought a 110-acre farm, where they raised cotton and peanuts. To help support the family of 10 children, Eddie Lewis drove a school bus and Willie Mae worked as a laundress.[2] John Lewis grew up attending segregated public schools. Shy and soft-spoken, Lewis was drawn to preaching. He eventually earned a bachelor of arts degree in 1961 from the American Baptist Theological Seminary in Nashville, Tennessee. Lewis then enrolled at Fisk University, also in Nashville, graduating with a B.A. degree in religion and philosophy in 1967.

Lewis played a central role in the American civil rights movement. He was a founder and chairman of the Student Nonviolent Coordinating Committee (SNCC), eventually becoming one of the "Big Six" civil rights leaders—the others being King, Whitney Young, A. Phillip Randolph, James Farmer, and Roy Wilkins. He participated in the Freedom Rides to desegregate commercial busing in the South. He helped to organize the March on Washington, delivering a keynote address at the August 1963 gathering.[3] Lewis also led the Bloody Sunday protest in Selma, Alabama, when baton-wielding state troopers beat and tear-gassed peaceful marchers at the Edmund Pettus Bridge on March 7, 1965. That event provided the catalyst for the Voting Rights Act of 1965. Lewis later served as associate director of the Field Foundation and directed the Voter Education Project of the South Regional Council. In 1968, Lewis married Lillian Miles; the couple has one son, John.

Lewis first ran for congressional office when Atlanta Representative Andrew Young resigned his U.S. House seat in 1977 to serve as U.S. Ambassador to the United Nations. In a crowded special primary on March 15, 1977, Lewis won 29 percent of the vote—second in a field of 12, behind Atlanta City Council Chairman Wyche Fowler. In a run-off several weeks later, Fowler prevailed with 62 percent of the vote.[4] In 1977, President James Earl (Jimmy) Carter appointed Lewis to head the federal volunteer agency ACTION. He remained there four years before winning election to the Atlanta city council.

In 1986, when Fowler retired to run for the U.S. Senate, Lewis entered the Democratic primary for the seat that covered most of Atlanta and rural areas in southwest Fulton County. Reapportionment in 1982 had turned a district that formerly was half-white into one that was nearly two-thirds black. In a runoff primary against his former SNCC colleague and then-Georgia State Senator Julian Bond, Lewis went door to door in the district in a relentless grass-roots effort that won over a coalition of poor inner-city blacks and voters in majority-white precincts. He prevailed with a 52 percent majority.[5] In the general election, Lewis defeated Republican candidate Portia A. Scott with 75 percent of the vote. In his subsequent 10 re-election campaigns, Lewis has won by similar margins, running unopposed since 2002.[6]

When Lewis entered the House in January 1987, he was assigned to two committees: Public Works and Transportation and Interior and Insular Affairs. In the 101st Congress (1989–1991), he received an additional post on the House Select Committee on Aging. He relinquished all three assignments in the 103rd Congress (1993–1995) after winning a coveted seat on the powerful Ways and Means Committee, which sets tax policy. He has remained on that panel since and currently serves as Chairman of the Subcommittee on Oversight. Lewis also served in the 108th Congress (2003–2005) on the Budget Committee. In addition, Representative Lewis has served as a Chief Deputy Whip for the Democratic Caucus since 1989. In the 110th Congress (2007–2009), Lewis serves as Senior Chief Deputy Whip.

Representative Lewis's legislative interests draw chiefly from his background as a civil rights activist; he supports legislation to protect and expand voting rights measures and to provide better access to health care for minorities. Lewis's legislation creating the National Museum of African American History and Culture in Washington, DC, a unit of the Smithsonian Institution, was signed into law by President George W. Bush in 2003.

FOR FURTHER READING

"Lewis, John R.," *Biographical Directory of the U.S. Congress, 1774–Present*, http://bioguide.congress.gov/scripts/biodisplay.pl?index=L000287.

Lewis, John. *Walking with the Wind: A Memoir of the Movement* (New York: Simon & Schuster, 1998).

MANUSCRIPT COLLECTION

Howard University, Moorland–Spingarn Research Center (Washington, DC). *Oral History*: 1967, 175 pages. Interview with John Lewis includes recollections of student sit-ins in Nashville, Tennessee, in the early 1960s. Lewis also discusses the founding of the Student Nonviolent Coordinating Committee and its activities, including Freedom Rides and demonstrations in Selma, Alabama. Lewis recalls his role in the March on Washington and his association with Martin Luther King, Jr. Restrictions; no quotation or citation without Lewis's written permission.

NOTES

1 Peter Carlson, "Nonviolent Fighter; John Lewis Retraces the Route That Led to the Future," 9 June 1998, *Washington Post*: D1.

2 "John (Robert) Lewis," *Current Biography, 1980* (New York: H. W. Wilson and Company, 1980): 222.

3 John Lewis, *Walking with the Wind: A Memoir of the Movement* (New York: Simon & Schuster, 1998); see also Lewis's official biography at http://johnlewis.house.gov/index.php?option=com_content&task=view&id=17&Itemid=31 (accessed 29 October 2007).

4 *Current Biography, 1980*: 224.

5 Joe Davidson, "Lacking Issues, Veteran Civil-Rights Allies Take to the Low Road in Georgia Race for Congress," 8 August 1986, *Wall Street Journal*: 36; Art Harris, "Georgia Rivals in Bitter Runoff," 31 August 1986, *Washington Post*: A4; *Politics in America, 1988* (Washington, DC: Congressional Quarterly Inc. 1987): 366–367; *Almanac of American Politics, 1988* (Washington, DC: National Journal Inc. 1987): 298–299.

6 "Election Statistics, 1920 to Present," available at http://clerk.house.gov/member_info/electionInfo/index.html.

Kendrick B. Meek
1966–

UNITED STATES REPRESENTATIVE
DEMOCRAT FROM FLORIDA
2003–

IMAGE COURTESY OF THE MEMBER

In 2003, Kendrick Meek's election in a Florida district formerly represented by his mother, Carrie Meek, made him one of a handful of African-American Members of Congress to succeed a parent directly. A veteran of state politics, Meek won key assignments on the Armed Services Committee and the House Select Committee on Homeland Security and served as Florida's lone Representative on the powerful Ways and Means Committee.[1]

Kendrick Brett Meek was born in Miami, Florida, on September 6, 1966, the youngest of three children raised by Carrie Pittman Meek. Carrie Meek was divorced as a young mother but went on to build a political career in the Florida state legislature and, eventually, as a Member in the U.S. House of Representatives. Kendrick Meek graduated with a bachelor of science degree in criminology from Florida A&M University in 1989. After college, Meek worked for the Florida highway patrol, eventually earning the rank of captain, and for a time guarding Democratic Lieutenant Governor Kenneth Hood (Buddy) McKay. In 1994, Meek won election to the Florida state house of representatives, where he served four years before winning election to the state senate. During that time, he also worked for one of the country's largest private security firms. Meek married the former Leslie Dixon, and they raised two children, Lauren and Kendrick, Jr.

When Carrie Meek, a five-term, 76-year-old veteran of the House, announced her retirement in July 2002, Kendrick was the immediate favorite to succeed her.[2] The district, which weaved through southeast Broward County and northeast Miami-Dade County, was majority African-American and heavily Democratic. Kendrick Meek entered the Democratic primary as the sole candidate. For much of the campaign season, Meek led a citizen initiative to reduce the size of classes in Florida's public schools, which voters eventually passed during a fall

2002 referendum.[3] He also pushed a legislative agenda that included economic development, improved social services, and criminal justice initiatives. "I'm here to represent, 'We the People,'" Meek said. "Someone has to know what's going on and stand up for the rights of regular folks."[4] In the fall general election, Meek received no major party opposition and ran in large part on the basis of his mother's nearly iconic reputation in the district.[5] His election also made him just the second son to succeed his mother directly in Congress. He was sworn in to the 108th Congress (2005–2007) in January 2003 with his mother looking on. "I am very respectful of the fact that the reason I am able to assume this high office today is because of the sacrifices and struggles and the battles for equal rights that were fought by the generations that preceded me," Meek said.[6] In his 2004 and 2006 re-election campaigns, he ran unopposed in the general election.[7]

Since his freshman term, Representative Meek has served on the Armed Services Committee. Meek also served on the Homeland Security Committee for two terms, rising to the position of Ranking Member of the Subcommittee on Management, Integration, and Oversight—which has jurisdiction over airport and seaport security; customs operations; aid to local and state governments; and immigration inspections, detention, and enforcement policies. In the 110th Congress (2007–2009), Meek was appointed to the Ways and Means Committee and retained his Armed Services Committee seat. He also earned a spot on the Democratic Steering and Policy Committee. In January 2007, Meek was appointed to the NATO Parliamentary Assembly, an interparliamentary organization of legislators representing NATO Members and associate countries. He is one of only 12 members of Congress to represent the United States on the NATO Parliamentary Assembly. Meek also serves as chairman of the board of directors of the Congressional Black Caucus Foundation.[8]

Meek noted that his mother's work on the Appropriations Committee informed his sense that policy and money were intertwined. "I believe the way we appropriate sets the priorities for America," Meek said. "That's where all our principles and all our values start, where we put our money."[9] To that end, Meek has worked to ensure that minority firms have had access to contracting opportunities for the billions of federal dollars now spent on terrorism and homeland security operations.[10] Representative Meek also has used his seat on the Armed Forces Committee to push to better equip troops fighting in Iraq and Afghanistan. His top domestic priorities include health care, particularly the fight against HIV/AIDS; strengthening diversity within the senior corps of the military; and Haitian immigration.[11]

FOR FURTHER READING

"Meek, Kendrick B.," *Biographical Directory of the U.S. Congress, 1774–Present,* http://bioguide.congress.gov/scripts/biodisplay.pl?index=M001148.

NOTES

1 *Politics in America, 2008* (Washington, DC: Congressional Quarterly Inc., 2007): 251.

2 Andrea Robinson and Tyler Bridges, "Carrie Meek to Retire," 7 July 2002, *Miami Herald*: A1; Lauren Whittington, "Family Planning: Late Retirement Doesn't Always Mean Victory for Offspring," 11 July 2002, *Roll Call*.

3 "Official Biography of U.S. Rep. Kendrick B. Meek," http://kendrickmeek.house.gov/biography.shtml (accessed 3 December 2007); see also Jason T. Smith, "Meek One Step Closer to Congress," 24 July 2002, *Miami Times*: 1A.

4 Andrea Robinson, "Kendrick Meek Set to Fulfill a Legacy," 2 January 2003, *Miami Herald*: A1.

5 Shortly after being sworn in to Congress, Meek said, "People say, 'How do you feel being in the shadow of Carrie Meek?' I say the shade is *mighty* comfortable." See Betsy Rothstein, "Some New Members Arrive in Unique Manner," 8 January 2003, *The Hill*: 11.

6 "U.S. Rep. Kendrick Meek Takes Office in Historic Capitol Ceremony," *Broward Times*, 10 January 2003.

7 "Election Statistics, 1920 to Present," available at http://clerk.house.gov/member_info/electionInfo/index.html.

8 "Biography of U.S. Rep. Kendrick B. Meek"; *Politics in America, 2008*: 251.

9 *Politics in America, 2004* (Washington, DC: Congressional Quarterly Inc., 2003): 250; see also Starla Vaughns Cherin, "State Senator Kendrick Meek Runs for United States Congress," 17 July 2002, *Westside Gazette*: 1.

10 "Spotlight on Meek at CBC Conference," 17 September 2003, *Miami Times*: 1A.

11 See, for example, *Congressional Record*, House, 108th Cong., 2nd sess. (3 March 2004): H809–810; *Congressional Record*, House, 108th Cong., 2nd sess. (24 February 2004): H531; Kendrick B. Meek, "Strength in Diversity," 19 November 2007, *Army Times*.

Gregory W. Meeks
1953–

UNITED STATES REPRESENTATIVE
DEMOCRAT FROM NEW YORK
1998–

Gregory W. Meeks, a former Queens prosecutor and New York state legislator, has represented his Queens-centered House district for six terms. An advocate for business development in the African-American community, Meeks once noted that his role "as part of a new generation of African American leadership, is to take us to the new phase of the civil rights movement, that is, the economic development of our community."[1]

Gregory Weldon Meeks was born on September 25, 1953, in East Harlem, New York. His father, James, was a taxi driver and handyman, while his mother, Mary, raised Gregory and his three younger siblings. He recalled growing up in a household that was active in community affairs. His political role model was Thurgood Marshall, a civil rights advocate and the first black U.S. Supreme Court Justice. "He was someone I really admired because he was trying to make conditions better for people like me," Meeks recalled.[2] In 1975, he earned a bachelor of arts degree from Adelphi University on Long Island. In 1978, Meeks graduated with a J.D. from Howard University School of Law in Washington, DC. Meeks settled in Far Rockaway in Queens, where he was active in community organizations that aimed to improve city services and repair streets. He served two-year stints as an assistant district attorney in Queens, an assistant special narcotics prosecutor in New York, and a member of the New York State Investigation Commission. He later went into private law practice and, from 1985 to 1992, served as a judge on the New York state workers compensation board. His career in elective politics began in 1991 when he made an unsuccessful bid for the New York city council. Subsequently, Meeks was appointed supervising judge of the New York state workers compensation system. The following year Meeks won election to the New York state assembly, representing a Queens district from 1992 to 1997. Meeks and his wife, Simone-Marie, whom he married in 1997, have three daughters: Ebony, Aja, and Nia-Aiyana.

In 1997, when Representative Floyd Flake announced his retirement from a U.S. House seat representing Queens, Meeks emerged as a leading candidate to succeed the six-term veteran. Meeks received endorsements from Flake, the *New York Times,* and other figures in the Democratic establishment.[3] As the Democratic nominee, Meeks portrayed himself as "a bridge-builder" between the party's liberal and moderate wings.[4] In the five-way February 3 special election that included a New York state senator and an assemblywoman, Meeks prevailed with 57 percent of the vote. He told the *New York Times*: "I'm one who understands that, particularly in the African-American community, the key is now economic. We have to move toward the economic redistribution of our community more than we have in the past."[5] In his subsequent five re-elections, Meeks has prevailed by comfortable majorities of 97 percent or more.[6]

When Meeks was sworn in to the 105th Congress (1997–1999) on February 5, 1998, he received a seat on the Banking and Financial Services Committee (later renamed Financial Services). In the 106th Congress (1999–2001), Meeks also was appointed to the International Relations Committee (later renamed Foreign Affairs). Representative Meeks continues to serve on both panels. He is a member of the New Democratic Coalition and the Democratic Leadership Council.

In the House, Representative Meeks's legislative priorities encompass improving educational opportunities, ensuring minority business participation, expanding trade, and defending civil rights. Meeks has promoted economic redevelopment in Queens, including acquiring federal money for commercial areas and office buildings, health clinics, libraries, and infrastructure improvements. He also has been attentive to economic policies affecting JFK International Airport, which is located in his district.[7] On major trade issues, Meeks has been a "swing" vote—approving the normalization of trade relations with China in 2000 (citing the potential for new business in his district) while opposing a 2002 law that expanded the George W. Bush administration's trade authority on the grounds that Congress should not yield power to a President who did not have its strongest confidence. As a member of the Financial Services Subcommittee on Capital Markets, Insurance, and Government Sponsored Enterprises, Meeks has sought to promote home ownership and curb predatory lending practices.

From his seat on the Foreign Affairs Committee, Meeks has called for a greater role for U.S. trade and development policies in the formulation of foreign policy. He has been a leading advocate for the advancement of Afro-Latinos, increased U.S. attention to Western Hemisphere priorities, humanitarian aid to Africa, and trade adjustment assistance to spread the benefits of trade to marginalized communities. Meeks serves on three subcommittees: Western Hemisphere, Oversight and Investigations, and Asia and the Pacific, where he is vice chairman.

FOR FURTHER READING

"Meeks, Gregory W.," *Biographical Directory of the U.S. Congress, 1774–Present*, http://bioguide.congress.gov/scripts/biodisplay.pl?index=M001137.

NOTES

1 "Gregory W. Meeks," *Contemporary Black Biography* Volume 25 (Detroit, MI: Gale Research Inc., 2000).

2 Clemente Lisi, "Rep. Gregory Meeks," 15 February 2001, *New York Post*: 62.

3 "An Endorsement for Congress in Queens," 31 January 1998, *New York Times*: A14; Sarah Kershaw, "Flake Backs Meeks for Congress," 6 January 1998, *Newsday*: A31.

4 Jonathan P. Hicks, "Master of the Political Balancing Act," 5 February 1998, *New York Time*: B5; Jonathan P. Hicks, "Queens Democrats Select Legislator for House Race," 10 January 1998, *New York Times*: B3; Jonathan P. Hicks, "Race for Congressional Seat Nears a Heated Conclusion," 1 February 1998, *New York Times*: A26.

5 Hicks, "Master of the Political Balancing Act," 5.

6 "Election Statistics, 1920 to Present," available at http://clerk.house.gov/member_info/electionInfo/index.html.

7 *Politics in America, 2008* (Washington, DC: Congressional Quarterly Inc., 2007): 693–694; "Gregory W. Meeks, Biography," http://www.house.gov/meeks/en.us.about.shtml (accessed 17 October 2007).

Gwendolynne S. (Gwen) Moore
1951–

UNITED STATES REPRESENTATIVE
DEMOCRAT FROM WISCONSIN
2005–

In 2004, Gwen Moore won election as the first African American to represent Wisconsin in Congress. A state legislator and community activist with more than two decades of experience, Moore emerged as an advocate for urban issues: affordable housing, education, and access to health care. "I am really in sync with people who struggle on a day to day basis," said Moore, a single mother who once relied on welfare to help pay bills. "You don't have to have a 'D' after your name to understand that people have to eat."[1]

Gwendolynne S. (Gwen) Moore was born in Racine, Wisconsin, on April 18, 1951, the eighth of nine siblings. Her father was a factory worker, and her mother was a public school teacher. As an expectant single mother on welfare, she went to college with the help of TRIO, a program that provided educational aid to low-income Americans. Moore earned a B.A. in political science from Marquette University in 1978. In 2000, she earned a certificate for senior executives in state and local government from Harvard University. After college, Moore worked for VISTA, helping to spearhead community projects such as the start-up of a local credit union, and eventually being awarded the prestigious VISTA Volunteer of the Decade award as a result of her accomplishments. She worked for years as a housing and urban development specialist. In 1988, she entered elective politics, winning a seat in the Wisconsin house of representatives. Four years later, Moore became the first African-American woman elected to the Wisconsin senate.[2] Moore is the mother of three children: Jessalynne, Sowande, and Ade.[3]

When 11-term incumbent Democrat Gerald D. Kleczka announced his plan to retire at the end of the 108th Congress (2003–2005), Moore entered the 2004 primary as the front-runner. The district encompassed the entire city of Milwaukee and several of its surrounding suburbs. Although heavily Democratic, it was relatively new, the result of reapportionment after the 2000 Census that merged two distinct parts of the city for the first time. Moore fended off a stiff challenge from two prominent Democrats—a state senator and a former state Democratic Party chairman. The candidates agreed largely on the central issues, but the campaign reflected geographical and racial divisions highlighted during the city's mayoral contest: The African-American population lives on the north side in largely black neighborhoods, while a significant community of Polish and Eastern European descent lives on the south side in largely white neighborhoods. Moore's base of support among African Americans, mobilized by the mayoral race, proved decisive. She won the three-way primary with 64 percent of the vote.[4] In the general election, backed by African Americans, women, and progressives, Moore easily defeated Republican challenger Gerald Boyle, an Iraq War veteran, 70 to 28 percent. On election night she told reporters, "I really want people to remain engaged around the issues that brought this coalition together. We've got to come to a conclusion with this war. We've got to preserve life, preserve resources and start focusing on a domestic agenda that's going to relieve us of a dearth of jobs, a lack of health care and a divestment in educational opportunities."[5] In her 2006 re-election bid, Representative Moore defeated Republican Perfecto Rivera with 71 percent of the vote.[6]

When Moore took her seat in the 109th Congress (2005–2007), she received assignments on the Financial Services and Small Business committees. In the 110th Congress (2007–2009), Moore won a coveted seat on the influential Budget Committee.

During Representative Moore's freshman term, provisions from the SHIELD Act, which she authored, were included in the reauthorization of the landmark Violence Against Women Act. Moore's legislation provided for measures to ensure that domestic violence abusers cannot track their victims through a federal database that centralizes information on homeless persons who receive public assistance.[7]

Moore's committee assignments largely reflect her interest in economic issues, which she believes constitute "one of the next frontiers in the fight for civil rights."[8] Representative Moore has focused on many of the same issues she emphasized as a community activist and a state legislator. Among her legislative interests have been bills preventing predatory lending in minority communities, providing affordable housing, and ensuring that federal contracts are awarded equitably to minority-owned businesses. In her first term, she also secured an amendment to help public-housing recipients build up the credit record necessary for homeownership if they made timely rent payments.[9] Her interest in the effects of economic globalization led to her being asked to serve on the worldwide Parliamentary Network of the World Bank.

FOR FURTHER READING

"Moore, Gwendolynne S. (Gwen)," *Biographical Directory of the U.S. Congress, 1774–Present*, http://bioguide.congress.gov/scripts/biodisplay.pl?index=M001160.

NOTES

1 *Politics in America, 2008* (Washington, DC: Congressional Quarterly Inc., 2007): 1110–1111, quotation on 1110.

2 "Official Biography of Congresswoman Gwen Moore," http://www.house.gov/gwenmoore/bio.shtml (accessed 11 September 2007).

3 Katherine M. Skiba, "Washington Notebook: Moore Counts on Experience of Many Former Kleczka Aides," 9 January 2005, *Milwaukee Journal Sentinel*: A13.

4 *Almanac of American Politics, 2006* (Washington, DC: National Journal Inc., 2005): 1823.

5 Larry Sandler, "Moore Rewrites History; Mainstream Appeal Makes Her State's First Black Congresswoman," 3 November 2004, *Milwaukee Journal Sentinel*: A1; see also Larry Sandler and Leonard Sykes, Jr., "A Race in Which Race Didn't Matter," 4 November 2004, *Milwaukee Journal Sentinel*: B1.

6 "Election Statistics, 1920 to Present," available at http://clerk.house.gov/member_info/electionInfo/index.html.

7 "Official Biography of Congresswoman Gwen Moore."

8 Ibid.

9 *Politics in America, 2008*: 1110.

Eleanor Holmes Norton
1937–

DELEGATE
DEMOCRAT FROM THE DISTRICT OF COLUMBIA
1991–

IMAGE COURTESY OF THE MEMBER

A civil rights and constitutional lawyer, a former chair of the Equal Employment Opportunity Commission, and a tenured professor of law, Eleanor Holmes Norton has carried her lifelong commitments to Congress as the Delegate for the District of Columbia. Since 1991, Norton has tirelessly advocated DC congressional voting rights and DC statehood while using innovative approaches to obtain federal funds and legislation to improve the city's economy and tax base. "I have been elected to Congress not to further my own interests, but to bring resources and respect to the District of Columbia," she said. "The ethics of the bar require zealous representation. That's how I understand my relationship to my folks."[1]

Eleanor Holmes was born in Washington, DC, on June 13, 1937, the oldest of three daughters of Coleman Holmes, a civil servant, and Vela Lynch Holmes, a teacher. She attended Dunbar High School in Washington, DC, and earned a B.A. at Antioch College in Ohio in 1960. Norton earned an M.A. in American studies in 1963 and a law degree in 1964, both from Yale University. While a student, she worked in the civil rights movement with the Student Nonviolent Coordinating Committee and the Mississippi Freedom Democratic Party. After graduating, she clerked for federal Judge A. Leon Higginbotham in Philadelphia. She then became assistant legal director of the American Civil Liberties Union. In 1965, Eleanor Holmes married Edward Norton. The couple raised two children, Katherine and John, before divorcing in 1993. In 1970, New York Mayor John Lindsay appointed Eleanor Holmes Norton to chair the New York City Commission on Human Rights.[2] In 1977, President James Earl (Jimmy) Carter appointed her chair of the U.S. Equal Employment Opportunity Commission, where she served until 1981; she was the first woman to chair the commission. During the 1980s, she was a full-time tenured professor at Georgetown University Law Center, where she still teaches one course annually.

In 1990, Norton defeated five challengers in the Democratic primary for an open seat as the District of Columbia's Delegate in the U.S. House. In the general election, she won 62 percent of the vote in the heavily Democratic city. She has faced little or no opposition in nine re-election bids.[3]

When Norton entered the 102nd Congress (1991–1993), she won assignments on three committees: District of Columbia, Post Office and Civil Service, and Transportation and Infrastructure. In the 103rd Congress (1993–1995), she was appointed to the Joint Committee on the Organization of Congress. In 1995, the District of Columbia Committee was absorbed by the Government Reform Committee (later renamed Oversight and Government Reform), where Norton now serves. In the 108th Congress (2003–2005), Norton won a seat on the Homeland Security Committee. In the 110th Congress (2007–2009), she chairs the Transportation Committee's Subcommittee on Economic Development, Public Buildings, and Emergency Management.

For the first time in the city's history, Norton won a vote as Delegate on the House Floor in the Committee of the Whole through a new rule she requested. In subsequent decisions, the federal courts ruled that the House could grant Delegates the right to vote in the House Floor committee by rule, as it had traditionally in other committees. This vote was withdrawn in the 104th Congress (1995–1997) when the Republicans assumed control of the House, but was returned in the 110th Congress when the Democrats resumed control. Current House rules allow Delegates full participation in the legislative process, excepting full voting rights on the House Floor. Delegates may introduce legislation, speak on the House Floor, and even chair committees. Yet Norton is the only Member of Congress whose constituents have no final congressional vote, although they pay federal income taxes and serve in the military.

Norton has been a vocal and articulate leader in the fight to secure DC statehood and voting rights and to improve the city's services and infrastructure.[4] In an effort to win statehood for the District, she authored the New Columbia Admission Act, which went to an unsuccessful vote on the House Floor. She then sponsored the No Taxation Without Representation Act for congressional votes, a bill that was also introduced in the Senate. In 2007, the House passed a bipartisan bill sponsored by Norton and Representative Tom Davis of Virginia to create House seats for largely Republican Utah and the mostly Democratic District of Columbia. (The bill is pending in the Senate.) She successfully fought congressional initiatives to nullify local laws, including repeals of the city's ban on handguns, the use of local funds to lobby or seek court relief for congressional voting rights, and needle exchange programs to combat the spread of HIV/AIDS.[5]

FOR FURTHER READING

Lester, Joan Steinau. *Eleanor Holmes Norton: Fire in My Soul* (New York: Atria Books, 2003).

Marcovitz, Hal. *Eleanor Holmes Norton* (Philadelphia, PA: Chelsea House Publishers, 2003).

"Norton, Eleanor Holmes," *Biographical Directory of the U.S. Congress, 1774–Present*, http://bioguide.congress.gov/scripts/biodisplay.pl?index=N000147

NOTES

1 Joan Steinau Lester, *Eleanor Holmes Norton: Fire in My Soul* (New York: Atria Books, 2003): 274–276.

2 "Eleanor Holmes Norton," *Contemporary Black Biography*, Volume 7 (Detroit, MI: Gale Research Inc., 1994) (hereinafter referred to as *CBB*).

3 "Election Statistics, 1920 to Present," available at http://clerk.house.gov/member_info/electionInfo/index.html.

4 "Eleanor Holmes Norton," *CBB*; Lester, *Fire in My Soul*: 286.

5 *Almanac of American Politics, 2002* (Washington, DC: National Journal Inc., 2001): 358–359.

Barack Obama
1961–

UNITED STATES SENATOR
DEMOCRAT FROM ILLINOIS
2005–

IMAGE COURTESY OF THE MEMBER

In July 2004, after delivering a stirring keynote address at the Democratic National Convention, Barack Obama burst onto the national political scene, later winning a landslide victory to become a U.S. Senator from Illinois. He is only the fifth African American in congressional history to serve in the U.S. Senate.

Barack Obama was born in Honolulu, Hawaii, on August 4, 1961, the son of Barack Obama, Sr., and Ann Dunham Obama. Barack, Sr., an economist, was born and raised in Kenya and grew up raising goats with his father, who was a domestic servant for the British.[1] He met and married Ann Dunham, who grew up in a small town in Kansas, while both were students at the University of Hawaii. When Obama, Jr., was two years old, his father left to attend Harvard. Soon thereafter his parents divorced. He lived for a while in Jakarta, Indonesia, when his mother remarried to an Indonesian oil manager. The family resettled in Hawaii, where Obama attended the Punahou Academy. From 1979 to 1981, he attended Occidental College in Los Angeles, California, before completing a bachelor of arts in political science at Columbia University in 1983. He moved to Chicago in 1985 to work for a church-based group that sought to improve living conditions in impoverished neighborhoods. He then attended Harvard Law School, serving as the first African-American president of the *Harvard Law Review.* In 1991, he graduated with his J.D. and married the former Michelle Robinson. The couple have two daughters, Malia and Sasha.[2]

Obama entered local politics through his work as a community activist in a blighted South Side Chicago neighborhood. He practiced civil rights law and lectured at the University of Chicago Law School. In 1996, he was elected to the Illinois state senate. He served in that capacity from 1997 through 2004, pushing through a state earned income tax credit and an expansion of early childhood education. In 2000, he unsuccessfully challenged four-term incumbent U.S. Representative Bobby Rush in the Democratic primary for a seat representing most of Chicago's South Side.

In 2004, after incumbent U.S. Senator Peter Fitzgerald, a Republican, announced his retirement, Obama joined a crowded field of candidates in the Democratic primary for the open seat. He garnered 53 percent of the vote, topping two favored candidates—State Comptroller Daniel Hynes and a wealthy securities trader, Blair Hull (who spent $29 million on his campaign). Obama emerged as a national figure during that campaign, delivering a rousing keynote address on the second night of the Democratic National Convention in the summer of 2004, when he dared Americans to have "the audacity of hope." He explained, "It's the hope of slaves sitting around a fire singing freedom songs. The hope of immigrants setting out for distant shores. . . . The hope of a skinny kid with a funny name who believes that America has a place for him, too." Obama won a landslide 70 percent of the vote against Republican candidate Alan Keyes.[3]

When Obama took his seat at the start of the 109th Congress (2005–2007), he received assignments on three committees: Foreign Relations, Environment and Public Works, and Veterans' Affairs. In the 110th Congress (2007–2009), Obama left the Environment and Public Works panel and earned two additional committee posts: Homeland Security and Governmental Affairs and Health, Education, Labor, and Pensions. During the 110th Congress he also served as chairman of the Foreign Relations Committee's Subcommittee on European Affairs.

During his first three years in the Senate, Obama focused on issues such as lobbying and ethics reform, veterans' benefits, energy, nuclear nonproliferation, and government transparency. From his seat on the Veterans' Affairs Committee, Obama secured disability pay for veterans and advocated greater services and assistance for returning service members who served in Iraq. As a member of the Environment and Public Works Committee, Senator Obama sought to reinvigorate a national dialogue about developing more-energy-efficient vehicles and alternative energy sources. On the Foreign Relations Committee, he worked with then-Chairman Richard Lugar of Indiana to initiate a new round of nonproliferation efforts designed to find and secure nuclear and conventional weapons around the world.

In February 2007, Senator Obama announced his intention to run as a candidate for the 2008 Democratic presidential nomination.

FOR FURTHER READING

"Obama, Barack," *Biographical Directory of the U.S. Congress, 1774–Present*, http://bioguide.congress.gov/scripts/biodisplay.pl?index=O000167.

Obama, Barack. *The Audacity of Hope: Thoughts on Reclaiming the American Dream* (New York: Crown Publishers, 2006).

_____. *Dreams From My Father: A Story of Race and Inheritance* (New York: Three Rivers Press, 1995; reprint 2004).

NOTES

1   *Dreams From My Father: A Story of Race and Inheritance* (New York: Three Rivers Press, 1995, reprint 2004): 9–27.

2   William Finnegan, "The Candidate: How the Son of a Kenyan Economist Became an Illinois Everyman," 31 May 2004, *The New Yorker*; "Official Biography of Barack Obama," http://obama.senate.gov/about/ (accessed 26 October 2007); *Politics in America, 2008* (Washington, DC: Congressional Quarterly Inc., 2007): 322–323.

3   "Election Statistics, 1920 to Present," available at http://clerk.house.gov/member_info/electionInfo/index.html.

Donald M. Payne
1934–

UNITED STATES REPRESENTATIVE
DEMOCRAT FROM NEW JERSEY
1989–

IMAGE COURTESY OF THE MEMBER

Donald M. Payne, the first African American to represent New Jersey in the U.S. Congress, has emerged as a stalwart advocate for federal funding for education as well as greater U.S. engagement in Africa. An experienced community activist and Newark elected official, Payne succeeded one of the House's most recognizable figures, longtime House Judiciary Committee Chairman Peter W. Rodino, Jr., after his 1988 retirement.

Donald Milford Payne was born on July 16, 1934, in Newark, New Jersey, the son of William Evander Payne, a dockworker, and Norma Garrett Payne. He grew up in Doodletown, an Italian-American section of Newark. Payne later recalled, "Everyone, whites and blacks, worked for low wages, although we didn't think of it as living in poverty, and there was a real sense of neighborhood, of depending on one another."[1] As a teenager, Payne joined a group called "The Leaguers," which sought to assist inner-city youth by providing social, educational, and work activities.[2] The founders, Reynold and Mary Burch, were prominent African Americans in Newark and helped Payne secure a four-year scholarship at Seton Hall University. Payne graduated in 1957 with a degree in social studies, and later pursued graduate studies at Springfield College in Massachusetts. On June 15, 1958, he married Hazel Johnson, who died in 1963. Donald Payne never remarried and has three adult children. He taught English and social studies and coached football and track in the Newark public school system before working for a major insurance company. He later served as a vice president of a computer forms manufacturing company founded by his brother.

Payne became involved in politics at age 19 as manager of his brother William's successful campaign to serve as Newark's first African-American district leader.[3] He pursued community work through the local Young Men's Christian Association (YMCA). From 1970 to 1973, Payne served as president of the YMCA of the United States; he was the first black to hold that position. In 1972, he was elected to the Essex County board of chosen freeholders. During his six years as a freeholder, he eventually chaired the board. In 1982, Payne won election to the city council of Newark.

Payne twice challenged Representative Rodino in the Democratic primary for a U.S. House seat encompassing Newark and portions of Essex County. Arguing that the New Jersey congressional delegation was not representative of the racial composition of the state, Payne failed to unseat Rodino in 1980 and 1986.[4] In 1988, however, when Rodino announced his retirement, Payne became a leading contender for the nomination to fill the vacant seat. In the June 1988 Democratic primary, he defeated Ralph T. Grant by a two to one ratio. In a district that voted overwhelmingly Democratic, Payne defeated Republican opponent Michael Webb with 77 percent of the vote in the general election.[5] In his subsequent nine re-election campaigns, he has won by similar margins.[6]

After Payne was sworn in to the House on January 3, 1989, he received assignments on the Education and Labor Committee and the Foreign Affairs Committee. He has served on the Education and Labor Committee and the Foreign Affairs Committee throughout his House career. In the 110th Congress (2007–2009), he assumed the chairman's gavel of the Foreign Affairs Committee's Subcommittee on Africa and Global Health. Payne has served on the Democratic Steering Committee, which determines individual committee assignments for Democratic House Members and shapes the party's legislative agenda. As a past chairman of the Congressional Black Caucus, he developed a reputation as being thoughtful, determined, and low-key. "I think there is a lot of dignity in being able to achieve things without having to create rapture," he once noted. Payne also is a member of the Democratic Whip organization.[7]

Representative Payne's legislative interests include both domestic and foreign initiatives. Among the successful measures he has helped shape from his seat on the Education and Labor Committee are the Goals 2000 initiative to improve the quality of education, the Student Loan Bill, the School-to-Work Opportunities Act, and the National Service Act.[8] An advocate for inner-city redevelopment, Payne is a leading critic of civil rights crimes, racial profiling, and police brutality. As a senior member of the Foreign Affairs Committee, Representative Payne emerged as a forceful advocate for U.S. sanctions against the Sudanese government—particularly during a period of genocide in the Darfur region in 2004. He also has prodded both the William J. (Bill) Clinton and George W. Bush administrations for increased foreign aid for economic development and health care improvements in Africa.

FOR FURTHER READING

"Payne, Donald Milford," *Biographical Directory of the U.S. Congress, 1774–Present*, http://bioguide.congress.gov/scripts/biodisplay.pl?index=P000149.

NOTES

1 Joseph F. Sullivan, "A Victor in Jersey's Primary: From Coach to Congress Race," 9 June 1988, *New York Times*: B1.

2 *Politics in America, 2008* (Washington, DC: Congressional Quarterly Inc., 2007): 658.

3 "Donald Payne," *Contemporary Black Biography* Volume 2 (Ann Arbor, MI: Gale Research Inc., 1992); Sullivan, "A Victor in Jersey's Primary."

4 Bill Lowry, "Rodino Facing Black Rival," 10 March 1986, *Bergen Record*: B1; Joseph F. Sullivan, "Challenge to Rodino Closely Watched," 2 June 1986, *New York Times*: B2; David Blomquist, "It's Time to Step Down, Rodino's Old Allies Say Democrats in Essex Want to Elect a Black," 14 March 1988, *Bergen Record*: A1; Joseph F. Sullivan, "Black Politicians Pressure Rodino to Retire," 9 March 1988, *New York Times*: B1; Joseph F. Sullivan, "Rodino Says He Will Retire in January," 15 March 1988, *New York Times*: B1.

5 Kathleen O'Brien, "Payne Gets Rodino Seat; First Black Congressman Elected from N.J.," 9 November 1988, *Bergen Record*: A19.

6 "Election Statistics, 1920 to Present," available at http://clerk.house.gov/member_info/electionInfo/index.html.

7 *Politics in America, 2006* (Washington, DC: Congressional Quarterly Inc., 2005): 670; "Official Biography of Congressman Donald M. Payne," http://www.house.gov/payne/biography/index.html (accessed 29 October 2007).

8 "Official Biography of Congressman Donald M. Payne."

Charles B. Rangel
1930–

UNITED STATES REPRESENTATIVE
DEMOCRAT FROM NEW YORK
1971 –

IMAGE COURTESY OF THE MEMBER

As dean of the New York State delegation, Representative Charles Rangel is one of the five most senior Members in the House of Representatives and the second-longest-serving African American in congressional history. In the 110th Congress (2007–2009), Representative Rangel became the first African American to chair the powerful Ways and Means Committee and is one of a small group of blacks who have chaired multiple congressional committees.

Charles Rangel was born on June 11, 1930, in Harlem, New York City. The second of three children, he was raised by his mother, who was born Blanche Wharton, and his maternal grandfather, Charles Wharton. From 1948 to 1952, Rangel served in the U.S. Army and was awarded the Bronze Star and the Purple Heart in the Korean War after being wounded and leading 40 U.S. soldiers from behind enemy lines.[1] After graduating from DeWitt Clinton High School, Rangel, in 1957, earned a bachelor of science degree from New York University under the GI bill. Three years later, he completed a J.D. at St. John's University Law School. In 1960 Rangel passed the New York Bar and began practicing law. In 1963, he was appointed Assistant U.S. Attorney for the Southern District of New York. He later served as counsel to the speaker of the New York assembly and on the President's Commission to Revise the Draft Laws. On July 26, 1964, Rangel married the former Alma Carter. They raised two children, Steven and Alicia. They have three grandsons.

Rangel's interest in politics was piqued by his work for the state assembly and the New York City housing and redevelopment board, and by his service as a legal adviser to many individuals in the civil rights movement. In 1966, he ran successfully for a seat in the New York assembly, representing central Harlem. During his two terms in Albany, Rangel emerged as a leading advocate for inner-city constituents while forging a bipartisan friendship with Republican Governor Nelson A. Rockefeller.[2]

In the 1970 Democratic primary, Rangel narrowly defeated renowned veteran U.S. Representative Adam Clayton Powell, Jr., for his Harlem-based seat and prevailed in the general election. Powell had represented the district—encompassing Harlem, East Harlem, the Upper West Side, Washington Heights, and Inwood—since its creation in 1944. In his subsequent 18 re-election campaigns, Rangel won by lopsided majorities of 87 percent or more.[3]

Rangel took his seat at the opening of the 92nd Congress (1971–1973). In the 94th Congress (1975–1977), he became the first African-American member of the prestigious Ways and Means Committee, which writes federal tax law, and ascended to the chairmanship in 2007. He also was assigned to the Select Committee on Narcotics Abuse and Control in 1975 and chaired that panel from the 98th through the 102nd Congresses (1981–1993). Rangel cofounded the Congressional Black Caucus, serving as the group's chairman in the 94th Congress.

Representative Rangel emerged as a forceful critic of the drug trade and illicit drug use. He also focused on opening up economic opportunities for minority groups and the poor. He authored a 1993 provision providing tax breaks to promote investments and jobs in inner-city neighborhoods called "empowerment zones." Rangel authored the Low Income Housing Tax Credit—a measure that significantly boosted affordable housing built in the United States.[4] For veterans, Rangel founded the Office of Minority Affairs in the Veterans Administration.

In 1987, Rangel contributed to the demise of the apartheid government of South Africa as the author of the "Rangel Amendment." Denying certain tax benefits to U.S. corporations, the legislation forced major U.S. companies to withdraw from the country, weakening the government and clearing the way for the emergence of democracy. In 2000, the Representative's historic African Growth and Opportunity Act became law, providing for the first time incentives for U.S. trade with sub-Saharan Africa. He also founded the Rangel State Department Fellows Program, which has significantly increased the representation of minorities in the U.S. Foreign Service.

As part of an economic stimulus bill to rejuvenate the U.S. economy after the terrorist attacks of September 11, 2001, Rangel managed to extend unemployment benefits for workers; this was particularly important to those in the travel and lodging industries in New York.[5] Rangel has brought millions of dollars into his district, helping to spur the economic revitalization of Harlem.

FOR FURTHER READING

"Rangel, Charles B.," *Biographical Directory of the U.S. Congress, 1774–Present*, http://bioguide.congress.gov/scripts/biodisplay.pl?index=R000053.

Rangel, Charles B., and Leon Wynter. *And I Haven't Had a Bad Day Since: From the Streets of Harlem to the Halls of Congress* (New York: Thomas Dunne Books, 2007).

NOTES

1 "Charles B. Rangel," *Current Biography, 1984* (New York: H. W. Wilson and Company, 1984): 338.

2 See, for example, Paul Good, "A Political Tour of Harlem," 29 October 1967, *New York Times Magazine*: SM34; *Current Biography, 1984*: 338.

3 "Election Statistics, 1920 to Present," available at http://clerk.house.gov/member_info/electionInfo/index.html.

4 "Official Biography of Congressman Charles B. Rangel," http://www.house.gov/rangel/bio.shtml (accessed 27 November 2007).

5 *Almanac of American Politics, 2000* (Washington, DC: National Journal Inc., 1999): 1138; *Politics in America, 2006* (Washington, DC: Congressional Quarterly Inc., 2005): 725–726; see also "Official Biography of Congressman Charles B. Rangel."

Bobby L. Rush
1946–

UNITED STATES REPRESENTATIVE
DEMOCRAT FROM ILLINOIS
1993–

IMAGE COURTESY OF THE MEMBER

As a founder of the Illinois chapter of the Black Panther Party, an ally in Harold Washington's effort to topple the Daley Democratic machine in Chicago, and a Member of Congress, Bobby Rush has devoted his political career to bringing a measure of power to those disfranchised from the political system. An eight-term Member of the House, Representative Rush serves on the powerful Energy and Commerce Committee. "My life's mission, my life's meaning, my life's definition," he once said, "is that I am a fighter for the people."[1]

Bobby L. Rush was born on November 23, 1946, in Albany, Georgia, the son of Cora Lee, a beautician and teacher, and Jimmy Lee Rush, a taxi driver. At age seven, he and his four siblings moved to Chicago with his divorced mother.[2] His mother was a Republican precinct leader, largely because whites dominated the local Democratic machine.[3] In 1963, he joined the U.S. Army, serving five years before receiving an honorable discharge. During the 1960s civil rights movement, Rush was a member of the Student Nonviolent Coordinating Committee (SNCC). In 1968, he left SNCC to cofound the Illinois chapter of the Black Panther Party, a militant group that fought for political and economic equality. Rush helped initiate nonviolent projects in African-American communities, including a medical clinic that screened patients for sickle-cell anemia. "We were resistant to police brutality, to the historical relationship between African Americans and recalcitrant, racist whites," Rush recalled years later. Rush left the Black Panther Party in 1974 because he opposed its growing emphasis on violence and drug use. Rush earned a B.A. degree in political science from Roosevelt University in Chicago in 1973. In 1994, he earned an M.A. in political science from the University of Illinois at Chicago, and four years later he completed an M.A. in theological studies from McCormick Theological Seminary in Chicago. Rush, an ordained minister, and his wife of 28 years, Carolyn, have six children. One of their sons was murdered in 1999.

Rush made unsuccessful bids for the Chicago city council and the Illinois state house of representatives, but in 1983, his longtime friend U.S. Representative Harold Washington was elected mayor of Chicago, marking a moment of black ascendancy in Chicago politics. At the same time, Rush was elected alderman in the city's South Side 2nd Ward. By the time Washington died in office in 1987, Rush had built a formidable political base.[4]

In 1992, Rush challenged Representative Charles Hayes, a five-term veteran, in the Democratic primary. The district encompassed much of the African-American South Side in addition to several Irish-American communities. Rush defeated Hayes in the primary by three percentage points.[5] In the general election, he won handily against his Republican opponent, with 83 percent of the vote. In his seven re-election efforts since, he has won 76 percent of the vote or more, including 87 percent in his 2006 re-election campaign.[6]

As a freshman Representative, Rush received assignments on three committees: Banking, Finance, and Urban Affairs; Government Operations; and Science, Space, and Technology. He left those assignments in the 104th Congress (1995–1997) for a seat on the prestigious Energy and Commerce Committee, where he has remained. In the 110th Congress (2007–2009), he was appointed Chairman of its Subcommittee on Commerce, Trade, and Consumer Protection. Rush's Democratic freshman class colleagues elected him class president in the 103rd Congress (1993–1995), and he has been part of the Whip organization since he entered the House.

By his own estimate, Rush has brought more than $2 billion in federal money into his district since 1993.[7] As a freshman Member, Rush introduced legislation that passed the House as the Community Development and Regulatory Act. An advocate for improved access to health care for underserved populations, Rush has passed measures such as the Urban Asthma Reduction Act of 1999. In his first year as Subcommittee Chairman, Rush passed H.R. 20, the Melanie Blocker-Stokes Postpartum Depression Research and Care Act. Rush supports gun control and opposes the death penalty, and has introduced H.R. 2666, the Blair Holt Firearm Licensing and Record of Sale Act, a measure aimed at registering every gun sold in the United States.

While backing government programs to expand economic opportunities in urban communities, Rush does not view the federal government as a panacea. "Government is not going to solve all the problems that afflict the African American community," Rush noted. "We must look within ourselves, first and foremost. Capacity building and maintenance must become the top priority, both economically and politically, especially through entrepreneurship and education."

FOR FURTHER READING

"Rush, Bobby L.," *Biographical Directory of the U. S. Congress, 1774–Present*, http://bioguide.congress.gov/scripts/biodisplay.pl?index=R000515.

NOTES

1 Sarah Pekkanen, "The Many Paradoxes of Rep. Bobby Rush," 29 March 1995, *The Hill*.

2 Don Wycliff, "Soul Survivor: Bobby Rush Narrowly Escaped a Deadly Police Raid and Later Won a Long-Shot Bid for Congress," 16 November 2003, *Chicago Tribune Magazine*: 12; Dirk Johnson, "A Politician's Life, From Militant to Mainstream," 3 June 1990, *New York Times*: 22.

3 *Politics in America, 2006* (Washington, DC: Congressional Quarterly Inc., 2005): 331; Pekkanen, "The Many Paradoxes of Rep. Bobby Rush."

4 "Bobby Rush," *Contemporary Black Biography*, Volume 26 (Detroit, MI: Gale Publishing Inc., 2000).

5 Tim Curran, "Former Black Panther Leader Gets Ready to Move to Hill After Victory Over Hayes," 19 March 1992, *Roll Call*; Tim Curran, "Black Panthers' Bobby Rush Heads for Hill," 26 March 1992, *Roll Call*.

6 *Politics in America*, 2008 (Washington, DC: Congressional Quarterly Inc., 2007): 325; "Election Statistics, 1920 to Present," available at http://clerk.house.gov/member_info/electionInfo/index.html; Mike Robinson, "Former Black Panther Wins Primary," 22 March 2000, Associated Press.

7 "Official Biography of Congressman Bobby L. Rush," http://www.house.gov/rush/bio.shtml (accessed 17 October 2007).

David Scott
1946–

UNITED STATES REPRESENTATIVE
DEMOCRAT FROM GEORGIA
2003–

A 28-year veteran of the Georgia legislature, David Scott won election to the U.S. House in 2002 as a centrist Democrat representing a newly created district in suburban Atlanta. Scott's appeal in a racially mixed district illustrated the revolution in southern politics that occurred after the 1960s civil rights movement, when large portions of his district voted for George Wallace. "I want to be viewed as a Representative who happens to be African American, but one who represents all the people," Scott said.[1]

David Albert Scott was born on June 27, 1946, in Aynor, South Carolina. His father was a preacher and a chauffeur, and his mother was a maid and a hospital worker. He attended grade school in the northeast, settling with his parents as they took jobs in Scarsdale, New York. The experience was formative. Scott noted, "I learned at a very young age how to have confidence in myself and how to get along with people who don't look like me."[2] Scott graduated with a bachelor of arts degree in English and speech from Florida A&M University in 1967. As an intern at the Labor Department in Washington, DC, he met George W. Taylor, an influential labor management expert. Taylor suggested Scott apply to the Wharton School of Business at the University of Pennsylvania, where Taylor taught. In 1969, Scott received an M.B.A. from Wharton. Scott married the former Alfredia Aaron, the youngest sister of professional baseball's longtime homerun king Hank Aaron. They raised two daughters, Dayna and Marcye.

Scott's political work began in an advisory role when, for several years, he consulted for then-Governor James Earl (Jimmy) Carter of Georgia on revenue policy. In 1972, he worked on Andrew Young's successful congressional campaign. Two years later, Scott was elected to the Georgia house of representatives, where he served through 1982. He then was elected to the Georgia senate, where he served from 1983 until 2002—eventually chairing the prestigious rules committee. He authored a law that gave breast cancer patients and their doctors ultimate control over determining hospitalization and treatment measures to combat the disease as well as a law that allowed local communities to fight landfill developments.[3]

David Scott entered the race in 2002 for a newly reapportioned U.S. House district that surrounded metro Atlanta, including large parts of Fulton, Gwinnett, and Clayton counties. The district—the result of the spectacular growth of suburban Atlanta in the 1990s—also reached into eight other surrounding counties, drawing in communities that had seen a rise in the African-American population during the 1990s. The new district was 42 percent white, 41 percent black, and 10 percent Hispanic. Largely middle class with affluent pockets, it had a strong Democratic tilt. Scott faced two formidable rivals, a former state Democratic Party chairman and a popular state senator, whom the Party backed in the primary. Scott also tapped his experience as an advertising executive—organizing a billboard campaign that reached thousands of drivers who used the major interstates that crossed the spidery district. Scott prevailed in the primary and won the general election with 60 percent of the vote. He was re-elected in 2004 with no major party opposition, and won 69 percent of the vote in his successful 2006 campaign.[4]

After Representative Scott was sworn in to the U.S. House in January 2003, he received assignments on the Financial Services Committee and the Agriculture Committee. By the start of the 109th Congress (2005–2007), he was the second-ranking member on the Agriculture Subcommittee on Livestock and Horticulture. In the 110th Congress (2007–2009), Scott joined the Foreign Affairs Committee, where he serves as Vice Chair of the Terrorism, Nonproliferation, and Trade Subcommittee. He is also a member of the NATO Parliamentary Assembly, the Congressional Black Caucus, the Blue Dog Coalition, and the New Democrats.[5]

In the House, Representative Scott has earned a reputation as a problem solver. "It's very important that our party do two things," Scott told the *Atlanta Journal-Constitution* just weeks after he took his seat. "One, we've got to command the center. Secondly, we've got to energize our base."[6] He was one of just a handful of Democrats to vote for the Medicare overhaul bill, which provided prescription drug benefits for millions of American seniors. Among Scott's legislative undertakings have been his lead sponsorship of H.R. 916, the John R. Justice Prosecutors and Defenders Incentive Act, which provides student loan assistance to attorneys who work in public service, as well as the Financial Literacy for Homeowners Act, which seeks to increase homeowners' knowledge about their mortgages. Further, Representative Scott sponsors annual health fairs and jobs fairs to help bring wellness and economic assistance to his constituents.

FOR FURTHER READING

"Scott, David," *Biographical Directory of the U.S. Congress, 1774–Present,* http://bioguide.congress.gov/scripts/biodisplay.pl?index=S001157.

NOTES

1 Jill Cox, "Crossover Appeal: David Scott Represents a New Breed of Politicos Who Cross Racial Lines to Win Elections," October 2002, *Atlanta Tribune: The Magazine* 16 (No. 5): 30.

2 *Politics in America, 2006* (Washington, DC: Congressional Quarterly Inc., 2005): 302.

3 *Politics in America, 2006*: 303; "Official Biography of U.S. Representative David Scott," http://davidscott.house.gov/biography (accessed 26 September 2005).

4 "New Member Profile: David Scott (D)," 9 November 2002, *National Journal* (Vol. 34, No. 45); Henry Farber, "Scott Got Head Start on DC Connections," 14 November 2002, *Atlanta Journal-Constitution*: 4JI; "Election Statistics, 1920 to Present," available at http://clerk.house.gov/member_info/electionInfo/index.html.

5 "Official Biography of U.S. Representative David Scott," http://davidscott.house.gov/Biography/ (accessed 26 October 2007).

6 Melanie Eversley, "New Faces in Congress—David Scott: Bridge Builder Keeps Open Door to All Viewpoints," 25 February 2003, *Atlanta Journal-Constitution*: 1B.

Robert C. Scott
1947–

UNITED STATES REPRESENTATIVE
DEMOCRAT FROM VIRGINIA
1993–

IMAGE COURTESY OF THE MEMBER

Robert Cortez Scott was born in Washington, DC, on April 30, 1947, the son of Charles Waldo Scott, a doctor, and Mae Hamlin Scott, a teacher. He was raised in Newport News, Virginia. When Virginia officials resisted court-ordered public school integration in the late 1950s, Scott's parents sent him to Groton School, a college preparatory school in Massachusetts.[1] He graduated with a B.A. in liberal arts from Harvard University in the class of 1969 and four years later earned his J.D. at Boston College Law School.[2] While in law school, Scott served in the Massachusetts National Guard and later in the U.S. Army Reserve. After law school, he resettled in Newport News and opened a private law practice. From 1975 to 1980, Scott served as president of the local chapter of the National Association for the Advancement of Colored People. In 1977, he won election to the Virginia house of delegates. He served there for five years until his election to the Virginia senate, where he served for another decade. Scott is divorced and has no children. He is a member of St. Augustine's Episcopal Church in Newport News, Virginia.

Scott's first attempt to win national office took place in 1986, when he challenged two-term Republican incumbent Herbert H. Bateman for a seat in the U.S. House. The campaign garnered wide name recognition for Scott, although he lost the general election by a margin of 56 to 44 percent.[3] Following the 1990 Census, Virginia underwent reapportionment that increased its congressional delegation from 10 to 11. In order to comply with the Voting Rights Act, the Virginia assembly created a majority-black district that ran from southeast Richmond into portions of Newport News and Norfolk at the mouth of the Chesapeake Bay in southeastern

Virginia. Scott, who had represented portions of the new district in the state legislature, ran for the seat. In the Democratic primary, he received two-thirds of the vote, defeating two African-American women—a house of delegates member and the chair of the state retirement system. In the general election, he prevailed handily over Republican candidate Daniel Jenkins, with 79 percent of the vote.[4] Scott was the first black since John Mercer Langston (1890–1891) to represent the state and (because of his Filipino ancestry on his mother's side of the family) the first American of Filipino heritage to serve as a U.S. Representative.[5] Despite court-ordered redistricting in 1997, Scott has never been seriously challenged in his seven re-election bids. In 1998, in the reapportioned district, Scott won with a 78 percent majority. In 2006, Scott won with 96 percent of the vote against write-in candidates.[6]

When Scott was sworn in to the 103rd Congress (1993–1995), he was appointed to three committees: Judiciary; Education and Labor; and Science, Space, and Technology. He served on the Science, Space, and Technology Committee for one term (1993–1995) and continues to serve on the Judiciary Committee and the Education and Labor Committee—though he took a leave of absence from the Education and Labor Committee during the 108th Congress (2003–2005) to serve on the prestigious Budget Committee. In the 110th Congress (2007–2009), he serves on the Education and Labor, Budget, and Judiciary committees and as chairman on the Judiciary Committee's Subcommittee on Crime, Terrorism, and Homeland Security.

Representative Scott earned a reputation as a forthright progressive, opposing efforts to amend the Constitution to outlaw flag desecration and promote prayer in public schools.[7] He is also a strong advocate of reforming the juvenile justice system and of reducing crime by using prevention and intervention strategies. Scott has consistently fought against discrimination in employment by organizations that use federal funds. In 1997, Scott was a leading proponent of the Individuals with Disabilities Education Act, which seeks to protect the right of children with disabilities to a free, appropriate public education. He also sponsored the Death in Custody Act, signed into law in 2000, which requires states to report the death of individuals apprehended or held by police.[8] Scott has been a proponent of business interests in his district, which include major military and shipbuilding facilities such as the army's Fort Eustis and the Hampton Roads shipyards.

FOR FURTHER READING

"Scott, Robert Cortez," *Biographical Directory of the U.S. Congress, 1774–Present*, http://bioguide.congress.gov/scripts/biodisplay.pl?index=S000185.

NOTES

1 *Politics in America, 2006* (Washington, DC: Congressional Quarterly Inc., 2005): 1058; "Official Biography of Robert C. 'Bobby' Scott," http://www.house.gov/scott/about/biography.html (accessed 30 November 2007).

2 "Robert C. Scott," *Contemporary Black Biography*, Volume 23 (Detroit, MI: Gale Group, 1999) (hereinafter referred to as *CBB*).

3 "Election Statistics, 1920 to Present," available at http://clerk.house.gov/member_info/electionInfo/index.html; *Politics in America, 2006*: 1058.

4 "Election Statistics, 1920 to Present," available at http://clerk.house.gov/member_info/electionInfo/index.html; "Robert C. Scott," *CBB*.

5 "Official Biography of Robert C. 'Bobby' Scott." More than a dozen Filipinos served as Resident Commissioner for the nearly 50 years of Philippine annexation by the United States after the Spanish–American War in 1898. None of the Resident Commissioners were American citizens.

6 "Election Statistics, 1920 to Present," available at http://clerk.house.gov/member_info/electionInfo/index.html; *Politics in America, 2008* (Washington, DC: Congressional Quarterly Inc., 2007): 1044.

7 *Politics in America, 2006*: 1057.

8 "Official Biography of Robert C. 'Bobby' Scott"; *Congressional Record*, House, 106th Cong., 2nd sess. (24 July 2000): 6737.

Bennie Thompson
1948–

UNITED STATES REPRESENTATIVE
DEMOCRAT FROM MISSISSIPPI
1993–

IMAGE COURTESY OF THE MEMBER

A veteran of Mississippi politics for nearly 40 years, Bennie Thompson is an eight-term Member of the U.S. House and chairman of the Homeland Security Committee. Having grown up in the segregated South, Thompson has watched Mississippi government evolve from an era when blacks had no political clout to the present, when African Americans hold a number of the state's elective offices. His congressional career has focused on the interests of his largely agricultural constituency and on improved access for minorities to economic opportunities and health care.

Bennie G. Thompson was born in Bolton, Mississippi, on January 28, 1948, to Will and Annie Lauris Thompson. He grew up in an all-black neighborhood and was educated in segregated schools. His father, who died when Bennie was a teenager, was an auto mechanic, and his mother was a teacher. In 1968, he graduated from Tougaloo College in Tougaloo, Mississippi, with a bachelor of arts degree in political science. In college, he was a member of the Student Nonviolent Coordinating Committee and volunteered on the congressional campaign of famed civil rights activist Fannie Lou Hamer. Though Hamer did not win election to Congress, her example and the experience of registering African Americans in southern voting drives inspired Thompson to pursue a career in politics.[1] He earned a master of science degree in educational administration from Jackson State University in Jackson, Mississippi, in 1973. Thompson later pursued doctoral work in public administration at the University of Southern Mississippi in Hattiesburg. Thompson married his college sweetheart, London Johnson, a schoolteacher, and they raised one daughter, BendaLonne.[2] He briefly worked as a public school teacher in Madison, Mississippi, but when he won election to the board of aldermen in Bolton, Mississippi, white officials challenged the election in court and forced Thompson to resign his teaching position. The courts upheld the election results, and Thompson served as a town alderman from 1969 to 1973, when he won election as the town's mayor. He served in that capacity for six years. In 1980, Thompson was elected to the Hinds County board of supervisors, where he served 13 years.

In 1993, when four-term Democratic Representative Mike Espy of Mississippi resigned his seat to become Secretary of Agriculture in the William J. (Bill) Clinton administration, Thompson entered the race for the open seat. The district encompassed west-central Mississippi, taking in urban areas such as Jackson, the state capital, and a nearly 230-mile stretch of agriculturally dependent communities along the Mississippi Delta that included some of the poorest counties in the country. On the Democratic side, his two principal contenders were Henry Espy, the brother of former Representative Mike Espy, and James Meredith, a 1960s civil rights activist and the first African American to attend the University of Mississippi. In the all-party open primary in March 1993, GOP candidate Hayes Dent won with a 34 percent plurality. Thompson was second, with 28 percent. In accordance with state election law, the top two finishers squared off in the April 13 special election. Henry Espy threw his support behind Thompson, who worked hard to turn out the African-American vote. Thompson prevailed against Dent, with a 55 percent majority.[3] In his subsequent seven re-election bids, Thompson has won by comfortable margins. In 2006, he won election to his seventh term, with 64 percent of the vote, against Republican candidate Yvonne R. Brown.[4]

Representative Thompson claimed his seat in the House on April 20, 1993, and received assignments on three committees: Agriculture, Merchant Marine and Fisheries, and Small Business. Thompson remained on the Agriculture Committee through the 108th Congress (2003–2005). In the 105th Congress (1997–1999), Thompson was assigned to the influential Budget Committee, where he remained until he won a seat on the newly created Select Committee on Homeland Security. In 2005, when Homeland Security became a standing House committee, Democrats tapped Thompson as the panel's Ranking Member. In the 110th Congress (2007–2009), Thompson became the first-ever Democratic chairman of the committee.

Representative Thompson has sought federal dollars for infrastructure improvements, access to improved health care, and better schools for his district. In 2000, Thompson was a lead author and sponsor of a measure that created the National Center for Minority Health and Health Care Disparities. From his seat on the Agriculture Committee, Thompson, with support from the Congressional Black Caucus, prodded the Agriculture Department to disburse more federal aid to minorities, who Thompson argued have been discriminated against for decades. He also has been a leading defender of affirmative action programs.[5]

FOR FURTHER READING

"Thompson, Bennie," *Biographical Directory of the U.S. Congress, 1774–Present*, http://bioguide.congress.gov/scripts/biodisplay.pl?index=T000193.

NOTES

1 Jesse Carney Smith, ed., "Bennie G. Thompson," *Contemporary Black Biography*, Volume 26 (Detroit: Gale Group, 2000).

2 "Official Biography of Congressman Bennie G. Thompson," http://benniethompson.house.gov/HoR/MS02/About+Bennie/ (accessed 31 October 2007).

3 Michael J. Dubin et al., *United States Congressional Elections, 1788–1997* (Jefferson, NC: McFarland & Company, Inc., Publishers, 1998): 785; Tim Curran, "Thompson Wins, Farr Tops Calif. Field; Democrat Takes Espy Seat, 55–45%," 15 April 1993, *Roll Call*; Thomas B. Edsall, "In Mississippi Delta, House Race Is as Complex as Black and White," 14 March 1993, *Washington Post*: A8.

4 "Election Statistics, 1920 to Present," available at http://clerk.house.gov/member_info/electionInfo/index.html.

5 *Politics in America, 2008* (Washington, DC: Congressional Quarterly Inc., 2007): 566; *Almanac of American Politics, 2000* (Washington, DC: National Journal Inc., 1999): 909–910.

Edolphus Towns
1934–

UNITED STATES REPRESENTATIVE
DEMOCRAT FROM NEW YORK
1983–

Edolphus Towns, a former social worker and community activist in Brooklyn, New York, serves as a 13-term veteran in the House, where he holds an assignment on the powerful Energy and Commerce Committee. In the 110th Congress (2007–2009), Towns was appointed chairman of the Oversight and Government Reform Committee's Subcommittee on Government Management, Organization, and Procurement. He has focused on issues such as education, health care, and better access to technology for minorities.

Edolphus (Ed) Towns was born on July 21, 1934, in Chadbourn, North Carolina, the son of Versie and Dolphus Towns. His father was a sharecropper in a region where tobacco was an important agricultural product. Edolphus attended the local public schools, graduating from West Side High School in 1952. Towns earned a bachelor of science degree from North Carolina Agricultural and Technical State University in Greensboro in 1956. Towns later earned a master's degree in social work from Adelphi University in Garden City, New York. For two years after college, he served in the U.S. Army. After being discharged in 1958, Towns taught at Medgar Evers College and Fordham University in New York City, and in the city's public schools. He also worked as a program director and administrator in two city hospitals, from 1965 to 1975. Towns married the former Gwendolyn Forbes in 1960, and they have two children, Darryl and Deidra.

Edolphus Towns entered politics through his work in various civic associations. He held his first political position beginning in 1972 when he won election as the Democratic state committeeman for the New York 40th Assembly District in Brooklyn. In 1976, he was appointed Brooklyn's first African-American deputy borough president, where he served until 1982.

In 1982, Towns entered the Democratic primary for a newly created seat representing portions of the northern and eastern sections of Brooklyn, including Williamsburg, Bushwick, and Fort Greene. In the majority-black and Hispanic district, Towns defeated two Hispanic candidates, with roughly 50 percent of the vote.[1] In the general election, Towns was heavily favored and defeated Republican James W. Smith, with 84 percent of the vote. Towns has won by large pluralities in subsequent general elections, claiming 85 percent of the vote or more in his 12 re-election bids.[2] He was challenged several times in Democratic primaries (particularly after his 1997 endorsement of Republican Rudolph Giuliani for mayor); the toughest challenges occurred in the 1998 and 2000 primaries, when he defeated lawyer Barry Ford by margins of 16 and 14 percent, respectively.[3] Redistricting following the 2000 Census brought in part of Midwood in south-central Brooklyn and bolstered Towns's base. The current district is one of the state's most diverse, comprising black, Hispanic, Caribbean, and Jewish voters, and is solidly Democratic: The Democratic Party has a 13 to 1 registration advantage.[4]

When Representative Towns took his seat in the House on January 3, 1983, he was assigned to three committees: Government Operations (later renamed Oversight and Government Reform), Public Works and Transportation, and the House Select Committee on Narcotics Abuse and Control. Towns has remained on the Oversight and Government Reform Committee for his entire House career. In the 101st Congress (1989–1991), he won a seat on the prestigious Energy and Commerce Committee, where he has remained since. At the end of the 104th Congress (1995–1997), Towns left his Public Works and Transportation assignment.

Representative Towns's legislative interests have included education, health care, financial services, and the environment. Among his legislative accomplishments, Towns counts the Student Right to Know Act, which mandates that colleges report student athlete graduation rates.[5] In the 107th Congress (2001–2003), Towns introduced a measure to place sports agents under the oversight of the Federal Trade Commission in an effort to stop unethical recruitment practices.[6] He has secured federal funding for programs for the gifted and talented and for bilingual education as well as for enhanced teacher training. Towns helped create the Telecommunications Development Fund to provide capital to small and minority-owned businesses that provide high technology. In addition, in recent Congresses he has sponsored a measure to implement technology upgrades at historically black colleges and those that serve minorities generally.[7]

Representative Towns and his son, Darryl, a New York state assemblyman, are the first African-American father–son team to serve simultaneously in New York public office.

FOR FURTHER READING

"Towns, Edolphus," *Biographical Directory of the U.S. Congress, 1774–Present*, http://bioguide.congress.gov/scripts/biodisplay.pl?index=T000326.

NOTES

1 Jane Perlez, "Towns Wins in Bid for Richmond's Seat," 24 September 1982, *Washington Post*: B7.

2 "Election Statistics, 1920 to Present," available at http://clerk.house.gov/member_info/electionInfo/index.html.

3 Jonathan P. Hicks, "Congressman Squares Off With Brooklyn Challenger," 17 August 2000, *New York Times*: B3; *Almanac of American Politics, 2000* (Washington, DC: National Journal Inc., 1999): 1124.

4 *Politics in America, 2006* (Washington, DC: Congressional Quarterly Inc., 2005): 716.

5 "Official Biography of Edolphus Towns," http://www.house.gov/towns/bio.shtml (accessed 30 November 2007).

6 *Politics in America, 2006*: 715.

7 Ibid. "Official Biography of Edolphus Towns."

Maxine Waters
1938–

UNITED STATES REPRESENTATIVE
DEMOCRAT FROM CALIFORNIA
1991–

IMAGE COURTESY OF THE MEMBER

On the "My Hero" Web site, a young woman named Michelle calls U.S. Representative Maxine Waters a "community hero," explaining, "[Waters] instills the belief that you can achieve whatever you wish as long as you really strive to do so."[1] In fact, over three decades, Representative Waters has become one of the nation's most tenacious, unapologetic advocates for women, children, the poor, economic development, communities of color, human rights, and civil rights.

Waters's passionate commitment to social and economic justice can be traced to the struggles her family faced during her youth. Maxine Carr was born in St. Louis, Missouri, on August 15, 1938, the fifth of 13 children. "I know all about welfare," she recalled. "I remember the social workers peeking in the refrigerator and under the beds."[2] Although she has compiled a long list of significant accomplishments and is considered one of the most powerful women in American politics, she still remembers starting work at age 13 in factories and segregated restaurants. It is perhaps her first-hand experience that has made her one of the nation's most effective grass-roots organizers.

Waters moved to California in 1961 and, in 1970, earned a B.A. in sociology from California State University at Los Angeles. During that time, she launched her career in public service with the Head Start program, where she eventually coordinated the Parent Involvement Program. In 1976, Waters was elected to the California state assembly, where she became the first woman in state history to be elected minority whip. She eventually became chair of the Democratic caucus. As an assemblywoman, she successfully spearheaded efforts to implement the first statewide training program in the country to prevent child abuse, the largest divestment of state pension funds from South Africa, landmark affirmative action legislation, and the prohibition of strip searches by police of individuals charged with nonviolent misdemeanors.

In 1990, Waters was elected to fill the congressional seat vacated by retiring U.S. Representative Augustus (Gus) Hawkins, the first African American to represent California in the national legislature. She captured 79 percent of the vote and has not been seriously challenged since, capturing similar percentages in eight subsequent re-election campaigns.[3]

As a Member of Congress, Waters has provided $10 billion under the Section 108 loan guarantee program for economic and infrastructure development in U.S. cities, tripled funding for debt relief in poor nations, obtained $50 million for the Youth Fair Chance Program, created the Center for Women Veterans, and established the Minority AIDS Initiative. Additionally, Waters has been a leader on global peace and international human rights issues and remains actively involved in efforts to improve the plight of oppressed individuals in conflict-torn nations like Sudan, Haiti, and Liberia.

Waters's efforts have been noticed by her congressional colleagues. In 1997, she won the chair of the Congressional Black Caucus, and later her Democratic colleagues elected her to the post of Chief Deputy Minority Whip. She serves on the influential House Committee on the Judiciary and she is the Chairwoman of the Subcommittee on Housing and Community Opportunity of the Committee on Financial Services.[4] Waters has sponsored important measures on housing and community development, including legislation to reform the Section 8 voucher program, legislation to modernize the Federal Housing Administration, and legislation to improve the HOPE VI public housing revitalization program. Additional legislation includes the Section 8 Voucher Reform Act of 2007 (SEVRA), reforms in the Expanding Homeownership Act of 2007, and the HOPE VI Improvement and Reauthorization Act of 2007.

By the 110th Congress (2007–2009), Representative Waters was a leading member of the Democratic Party. She acquired that status by amplifying her record of advocacy at the local and state levels to become "a community activist in Congress," in the words of an observer.[5] In 2005, Waters cofounded and was elected chair of the 72-member Out of Iraq Congressional Caucus. One of the largest caucuses in the House of Representatives, Out of Iraq was established to consistently pressure the George W. Bush administration, to provide a voice in Congress for individuals and organizations opposed to the Iraq War, and, ultimately, to end the war and reunite U.S. troops with their families as soon as possible. Waters's family is extremely important to her. She is married to Sidney Williams, the former U.S. Ambassador to the Commonwealth of the Bahamas. She is the mother of two adult children, Karen and Edward, and has two grandchildren.

FOR FURTHER READING

Naden, Corinne J., and Rose Blue. *Heroes Don't Just Happen: Biographies of Overcoming Bias and Building Character in Politics* (Maywood, NJ: Peoples Publishing Group, 1997).

"Waters, Maxine," *Biographical Directory of the U.S. Congress, 1774–Present,* http://bioguide.congress.gov/scripts/biodisplay.pl?index=W000187.

MANUSCRIPT COLLECTION

California State Archives (Sacramento, CA). *Papers*: Maxine Waters's California State Assembly bill files, 1979–1990, 30 cubic feet. *Papers*: In miscellaneous office files of Maxine Waters, 1978–1982, 11 cubic feet. Includes schedules and itineraries, ways and means committee records, budget conference papers, and elections and reapportionment committee working papers. Also includes judiciary committee correspondence on pending legislation. *Papers*: In subject files of Assemblywoman Waters, 1977–1986, unknown amount of material. Includes documentation on the Commission on Status of Women. Restricted access.

NOTES

1 "Community Hero: Maxine Waters," http://myhero.com/myhero/hero.asp?hero=WATERS_TAFT_04 (accessed 21 July 2006).

2 *Almanac of American Politics, 2006* (Washington, DC: National Journal Inc., 2005): 261.

3 "Election Statistics, 1920 to Present," http://clerk.house.gov/member_info/electionInfo/index.html.

4 *Politics in America, 2008* (Washington, DC: Congressional Quarterly Inc., 2007): 139–140; "About Congresswoman Waters," http://www.house.gov/waters/bio/ (accessed 5 December 2007).

5 John L. Mitchell, "Undeterred Waters Crusades for Answers," 4 March 1997, *Los Angeles Times*: A3.

Diane Edith Watson
1933–

UNITED STATES REPRESENTATIVE
DEMOCRAT FROM CALIFORNIA
2001–

IMAGE COURTESY OF THE MEMBER

Formerly an educator, a state legislator, and a U.S. ambassador, Diane Watson entered the U.S. House of Representatives as an unusually experienced freshman. From her seats on the Oversight and Government Reform Committee and the Foreign Affairs Committee, Representative Watson quickly established herself as a legislator whose interests ranged from welfare reform to foreign aid for African nations facing the HIV/AIDS crisis.

Diane Edith Watson was born on November 12, 1933, in Los Angeles, California, the daughter of William Allen Louis Watson and Dorothy Elizabeth O'Neal Watson. She graduated with an A.A. from Los Angeles City College and a B.A. from the University of California, Los Angeles (UCLA) in 1956. Watson later earned an M.S. from California State University in 1967 and a Ph.D. in education administration from Claremont College in 1986. After graduating from UCLA, Watson worked as a teacher and a school psychologist in the Los Angeles public schools. She was an associate professor at California State University from 1969 to 1971 and then worked in the California department of education and served on the Los Angeles unified school board. Watson won election as a state senator in 1978, an office she held for 20 years. She was the first African-American woman in the state senate and chaired the health and human services committee. In 1998, President William J. (Bill) Clinton nominated her as U.S. Ambassador to the Federated States of Micronesia, a post she held for two years.

In December 2000, U.S. Representative Julian Dixon, who had just been re-elected to a 12th term in Congress from his central Los Angeles–Culver City district, died. In April 2001, Watson prevailed with a 33 percent plurality in the special Democratic primary to choose Dixon's successor, while her nearest competitor received 26 percent.[1] In the June 5, 2001, special election, Watson carried the heavily Democratic Los Angeles district with 75 percent of the vote. In her three subsequent re-election bids, Watson has won her district with more than 80 percent of the vote.[2]

When Watson was sworn in to the U.S. House on June 7, 2001, she was assigned seats on the Government Reform Committee (now the Oversight and Government Reform Committee) and the International Relations Committee (now the Foreign Affairs Committee). As a former ambassador, she took a keen interest in American foreign policy, particularly as it related to issues of racism and health in the developing world. In the summer of 2001, Watson attended the United Nations Conference on Racism, Xenophobia, and Other Intolerance in Durban, South Africa. She called on the United States to host its own conference on racism and reform to the education, justice, and health care systems, to make "reparations" for the practice of American slavery.[3] In early 2002, Watson took to the House Floor to support the Local Law Enforcement Hate Crimes Prevention Act, noting that incidents of violence against Arab Americans, which had risen since the 2001 terrorist attacks, were "the tip of a proverbial iceberg."[4]

Watson also called for the United States to expand aid to sub-Saharan African nations fighting an HIV/AIDS pandemic that in some countries had infected more than a quarter of the adult population. Aside from humanitarian considerations, she argued, the crisis had repercussions for regional stability and American national security because of the strain it placed on so many developing economies. The disease, she observed, "in the very near term, if more is not done, may challenge the very notion of law-based nation states." She also linked the chaos the disease could cause with instability favorable to terrorist actions. "Let us not forget that Al Qaeda terrorist leader Osama bin Laden has exploited the misery of another state where civil society has collapsed—Afghanistan—to serve as a base for his terror network," Watson said.[5]

During the 107th and 108th Congresses (2001–2005), Representative Watson established herself as an advocate for what she describes as "commonsense" welfare reform in California. Watson supported reauthorization of the Temporary Assistance for Needy Families Program, which provides education, childcare, job training, and employment to welfare recipients by providing states with federal funds to develop and manage their own welfare programs. Representative Watson also has been an advocate for increasing funding to the Cal-Learn program to help teen mothers complete their educations and get jobs.[6] In addition, she introduced several bills, including legislation to develop a state plan for responding to medical disasters in the event of a biological or chemical weapons attack.[7] She also advocated passage of a plan that would fully fund seniors' medical prescriptions.

FOR FURTHER READING

Katsimbras, Amofia, ed. *Senator Diane E. Watson, Ph.D. 1978–1998: Legislative History* (Sacramento: California State Senate, 1999).

Watson, Diane E., "The Effects of the Desegregation Controversy on Trustee Governance in the Los Angeles Unified School District 1975–1980." (Ph.D. diss., Claremont University, 1987).

"Watson, Diane Edith," *Biographical Directory of the U.S. Congress, 1774–Present*, http://bioguide.congress.gov/scripts/biodisplay.pl?index=W000794.

Watson, Diane E., and Beverly J. Rambo. *Your Career in Health Care* (New York: Gregg Division, McGraw-Hill, 1976).

MANUSCRIPT COLLECTION

California State Archives (Sacramento, CA). *Papers*: Correspondence and chronological files of state senator Diane Watson, 1978–1980, two cubic feet. Includes Sacramento and district files, miscellaneous legislative counsel drafts; constituent problems correspondence; bill files, 1979–1982, four cubic feet; bill files, 1981–1986, 1.5 cubic feet.

NOTES

1 "Diane Watson: Member of Congress, California 32, Democrat," July 2002, *Campaigns and Elections*: 18.

2 "Election Statistics, 1920 to Present," available at http://clerk.house.gov/member_info/electionInfo/index.html.

3 *Congressional Record*, House, 107th Cong., 1st sess. (6 September 2001): 5447.

4 *Congressional Record*, House, 107th Cong., 2nd sess. (7 February 2002): 219.

5 *Congressional Record*, House, 107th Cong., 1st sess. (29 November 2001): 572; *Congressional Record*, House, 107th Cong., 1st sess. (11 December 2001): 9089.

6 "Meet Congresswoman Diane Watson," http://www.house.gov/watson/meet_congresswoman.html (accessed 2 January 2005); *Congressional Record*, House, 107th Cong., 2nd sess. (17 April 2002): 384; *Congressional Record*, House, 107th Cong., 2nd sess. (8 May 2002): 2170.

7 *Politics in America, 2002*: (Washington, DC: Congressional Quarterly Inc., 2001): 130–132.

Melvin L. Watt
1945–

UNITED STATES REPRESENTATIVE
DEMOCRAT FROM NORTH CAROLINA
1993–

Melvin Watt, an eight-term House veteran from North Carolina, is a high-ranking member of the House Judiciary Committee and the House Financial Services Committee. He chaired the Congressional Black Caucus (CBC) in the 109th Congress (2005–2007). A vocal advocate for civil liberties, Watt has sought to build ties to business interests from his seat on the Financial Services Committee.

Melvin L. (Mel) Watt was born in Charlotte, North Carolina, on August 26, 1945. He attended segregated public schools in Mecklenburg County. When Watt started college, southern universities had recently been desegregated, so he was among a relatively small number of blacks enrolled in the state university system.[1] He attended the University of North Carolina at Chapel Hill, graduating Phi Beta Kappa with a business administration degree in 1967. Three years later, Watt earned his J.D. from Yale Law School. He returned to Charlotte, where he entered the North Carolina bar. For the next 20 years, Watt worked in private practice, specializing in minority business and economic development law.[2] He eventually served as president of the Mecklenburg County Bar. He married Eulada Paysour and they raised two sons, Brian and Jason. He served a single term in the North Carolina state senate, from 1985 to 1987, but left to spend more time with his teenage sons. Much of Watt's early political work was behind the scenes. He managed the successful campaigns of a rising African-American politician, Charlotte City Councilman and Mayor Harvey Gantt.

After managing Gantt's unsuccessful effort to win a U.S. Senate seat against incumbent Jesse Helms in 1990, Watt ran for elective office himself. In 1992, redistricting created a majority-black (53 percent) congressional district in central North Carolina that stretched through parts of 10 counties and included portions of Durham, Greensboro, Winston-Salem, and Charlotte.[3] In a crowded primary field, Watt carried 47 percent of the vote, defeating his closest rival, North Carolina State Representative Mickey Michaux, by 19 percentage points.[4] Against Republican Barbara Gore Washington, Watt captured 70 percent of the vote in the general election. In his subsequent seven re-election bids, Watt has won by comfortable margins, usually by 65 percent of the vote or more. In 1998, during a controversial effort to reconfigure Watt's district, Watt experienced his narrowest margin of victory, when he turned back Republican challenger John (Scott) Keadle with 56 percent of the vote. In 2006, Watt was elected to his eighth consecutive term, with 67 percent of the vote.[5]

When Watt entered the U.S. House in January 1993 he received an appointment to the Banking, Finance, and Urban Affairs Committee (later renamed Financial Services), where he currently serves as chairman of its Subcommittee on Oversight and Investigations. He also was assigned to the Judiciary Committee. Watt has served on both panels throughout his House career, and in the 109th Congress he served as Ranking Member of the Judiciary Committee's Subcommittee on Commercial and Administrative Law. For a single term in the 103rd Congress (1993–1995), he served on the Post Office and Civil Service Committee before it was abolished in the following Congress. In addition, Watt has served on the Joint Economic Committee in the 107th and 108th Congresses (2001–2005). In the 109th Congress, Watt was unanimously elected chairman of the CBC.

In Congress, Representative Watt established a reputation as an independent liberal. As a freshman in the 103rd Congress, Watt voted with the Democratic majority nearly 90 percent of the time, although he broke with President William J. (Bill) Clinton to vote against the North American Free Trade Agreement and the administration's 1994 Crime Bill.[6] During the 1990s, Watt also criticized efforts to dismantle federal welfare programs and some tough crime measures, especially those in support of the death penalty. Watt also backed a universal health care system.[7]

Watt's extensive preparation for and detailed knowledge of legislation being considered are widely recognized by his peers.[8] On the Judiciary panel, he has vigorously defended constitutional prerogatives and civil liberties. In 2001, shortly after the September 11 terrorist attacks, he was one of a minority of House Members to oppose the USA PATRIOT Act, sweeping legislation that granted expanded powers to law enforcement agencies.[9] On the Financial Services Committee, however, Watt tended to work with Republicans across the aisle and to focus on the business interests, particularly banking, that dominated his district.[10]

FOR FURTHER READING

"Watt, Melvin L.," *Biographical Directory of the U.S. Congress, 1774–Present,* http://bioguide.congress.gov/scripts/biodisplay.pl?index=W000207.

NOTES

1 Arati Sontakay, "Giving 'Em Mel: Congressman Doesn't Shy From Hot Seat," 11 September 1995, *Business Journal of Charlotte* 10 (No. 22): 3.

2 "About Congressman Watt," http://watt.house.gov/aboutmel.asp (accessed 28 November 2007).

3 Ronald Smothers, "2 Strangely Shaped Hybrid Creatures Highlight North Carolina's Primary," 3 May 1992, *New York Times*: 29.

4 Tim Curran, "In NC, Civil Rights Lawyer Watt Wins 'I-85' Primary; Walter Jones Jr. Headed for Runoff," 7 May 1992, *Roll Call.*

5 "Election Statistics, 1920 to Present," available at http://clerk.house.gov/member_info/electionInfo/2006election.pdf.

6 Ellen J. Silberman, "Watt Spent Most of First Term Learning," 4 November 1994, States News Service; Sontakay, "Giving 'Em Mel."

7 *Almanac of American Politics, 2000* (Washington, DC: Congressional Quarterly Inc., 1999): 1029–1031.

8 Sontakay, "Giving 'Em Mel."

9 *Politics in America, 2006* (Washington, DC: Congressional Quarterly Inc., 2005): 779.

10 *Politics in America, 2006*: 779.

Albert R. Wynn
1951–

UNITED STATES REPRESENTATIVE
DEMOCRAT FROM MARYLAND
1993–

Albert Wynn won election to the U.S. House of Representatives in 1992, in an affluent, predominantly African-American district in suburban Maryland. With a decade of service in the state legislature, Wynn quickly adapted to the U.S. House, eventually earning a seat on the prestigious Energy and Commerce Committee and moving into the hierarchy of the Congressional Black Caucus (CBC).

Albert Russell Wynn was born in Philadelphia, Pennsylvania, on September 10, 1951. His family moved to North Carolina, where his father farmed and his mother taught school.[1] When his father was hired by the U.S. Department of Agriculture, the family moved to a suburb of Washington, DC, where Wynn attended the public schools in Prince George's County, Maryland. In 1973, Wynn graduated with a bachelor of science degree in political science from the University of Pittsburgh. He briefly studied public administration at Howard University in Washington, DC, before entering Georgetown University and earning a law degree in 1977. Wynn later served as director of the Prince George's County consumer protection commission. After opening his own law firm in 1982, Wynn won election to the Maryland house of delegates, where he served from 1983 to 1987. He was then elected to the Maryland state senate, serving there until 1993 and rising to the post of deputy majority whip. Wynn is married to Gaines Clore Wynn, an artist and art educator. They have two daughters, Meredith and Gabrielle, and a grandson, Kaden Nicholas.

Following the 1990 Census, the Maryland state legislature created a new congressional district that encompassed sections of Prince George's and Montgomery counties inside the Capital Beltway along the border of the District of Columbia. In the 1970s and 1980s, Prince George's County had become increasingly African American as blacks from Washington, DC, moved to the suburbs. Prince George's County was home to a large group of middle- to upper-middle-class African Americans, many of whom were federal workers, and blacks accounted for 58 percent of the heavily Democratic district. In the March 3, 1992, Democratic primary, Wynn garnered 28 percent of the vote, defeating his closest opponent, Prince George's County's State's Attorney Alex Williams, by several percentage points—in large measure because he performed better than Williams in the

Montgomery County sections of the district.[2] Wynn easily prevailed in the general election, claiming 75 percent of the vote against Republican candidate Michele Dyson, an African-American business consultant. In his subsequent seven re-election bids, Wynn has won with pluralities of 75 percent or more (he received 87 percent of the vote in 1998). Reapportionment after the 2000 Census pulled several heavily Democratic sections out of Wynn's district and added more conservative locales in the suburbs of Montgomery County. Nevertheless, in 2006, Representative Wynn won re-election, with 80 percent of the vote, against Republican challenger Michael Moshe Starkman.[3]

When Wynn took his seat in the House on January 5, 1993, he received assignments on three committees: Banking, Finance, and Urban Affairs (later named Financial Services), Foreign Affairs, and Post Office and Civil Service. In the 105th Congress (1997–1999) Representative Wynn accepted a post on the prestigious Commerce Committee (later named Energy and Commerce), requiring him to yield his prior assignments. He has served on Energy and Commerce since then, and in the 110th Congress (2007–2009) he was appointed chairman of the Subcommittee on Environment and Hazardous Materials. Since 2002, Wynn has chaired the CBC's Political Action Committee and Minority Business Task Force. He heads the CBC task forces on campaign finance reform and minority business and serves as a Senior and Regional Whip.[4]

Wynn's district is home to more federal workers (70,000) than any other district in the country. In addition, a number of small businesses in Wynn's district contract with federal agencies. Much of his legislative focus is on issues affecting that constituency; for instance, Wynn has been a leading advocate for the protection of federal salaries and pensions as well as for the creation of more federal contracts for minority businesses and small businesses. Wynn has also focused on bringing federal dollars into the district for transportation and infrastructure projects.[5]

FOR FURTHER READING

"Wynn, Albert Russell," *Biographical Directory of the U.S. Congress, 1774–Present*, http://bioguide.congress.gov/scripts/biodisplay.pl?index=W000784.

NOTES

1 *Politics in America, 2008* (Washington, DC: Congressional Quarterly Inc., 2007): 468.

2 Michele L. Norris, "Montgomery Bolstered Wynn; Lower Turnout in P.G. Hurt Williams in Democratic House Primary," 5 March 1992, *Washington Post*: C1; Michele L. Norris, "4th District Nod Goes to Wynn; Rep. Byron Loses in Upset in Maryland's 6th District," 4 March 1992, *Washington Post*: A1.

3 "Election Statistics, 1920 to Present," available at http://clerk.house.gov/member_info/electionInfo/2006election.pdf.

4 "Official Biography of Congressman Albert Russell Wynn," http://www.wynn.house.gov/index.php?option=com_content&task=view&id=14&Itemid=26 (accessed 29 October 2007).

5 "Official Biography of Congressman Albert Russell Wynn"; *Politics in America, 2006* (Washington, DC: Congressional Quarterly Inc. 2005): 476.

First-Term Black-American Members of the 110th Congress*

SOURCES

Online Biographical Directory of the United States Congress, 1774–Present: http://bioguide.congress.gov; individual Member offices.

*The closing date for this volume was December 31, 2007.

Yvette Clarke

UNITED STATES REPRESENTATIVE DEMOCRAT FROM NEW YORK

CONGRESSIONAL COMMITTEES:
Education and Labor
Homeland Security
Small Business

BORN: November 21, 1964, Brooklyn, New York

FAMILY: Single

EDUCATION: Attended Oberlin College, 1982–1986

MILITARY: N/A

POLITICAL CAREER: New York city council, 2002–2006

PROFESSIONAL CAREER: Public policy, public service

Keith Ellison

UNITED STATES REPRESENTATIVE
DEMOCRAT FROM MINNESOTA

CONGRESSIONAL COMMITTEES:
Financial Services
Judiciary

BORN: August 4, 1963, Detroit, Michigan

FAMILY: Wife: Kim; children: Jeremiah, Isaiah, Elijah, and
Amirah

EDUCATION: B.A., Wayne State University, 1986; J.D.,
University of Minnesota, 1990

MILITARY: N/A

POLITICAL CAREER: Minnesota state house of
representatives, 2003–2006

PROFESSIONAL CAREER: Lawyer and
community activist

Hank Johnson

UNITED STATES REPRESENTATIVE
DEMOCRAT FROM GEORGIA

CONGRESSIONAL COMMITTEES:
Armed Services
Judiciary
Small Business

BORN: October 2, 1954, Washington, DC

FAMILY: Wife: Mereda Davis Johnson; children: Randi
and Alex

EDUCATION: B.A., Clark Atlanta University, 1979; J.D.,
Texas Southern University, 1979

MILITARY: N/A

POLITICAL CAREER: DeKalb County (GA) board
 of commissioners, 2001–2006

PROFESSIONAL CAREER: Lawyer

*Laura Richardson**

UNITED STATES REPRESENTATIVE
DEMOCRAT FROM CALIFORNIA

CONGRESSIONAL COMMITTEES:
Transportation and Infrastructure
Science and Technology

BORN: April 14, 1962, Los Angeles, California

FAMILY: Divorced

EDUCATION: B.A., political science, University
of California at Los Angeles, 1984; M.B.A., University
of Southern California, 1996

MILITARY: N/A

POLITICAL CAREER: Long Beach, California, city
council, 2000–2006, tidelands and harbor committee
chair, state legislation and environmental committee
chair, budget oversight committee chair; California state
assembly, 2006–2007, assistant speaker *pro tempore*

PROFESSIONAL CAREER: Marketing representative,
Xerox Corporation, 1987–2001; field representative
(part-time), Representative Juanita Millender-McDonald,
1996–1998; southern California director, California
Lieutenant Governor Cruz Bustamante, 2001–2005.

*Elected on August 21, 2007, to fill the vacancy caused by the death
 of U.S. Representative Juanita Millender-McDonald

Black-American Representatives and Senators by Congress, 1870–2007

CONGRESS	HOUSE	SENATE
41st (1869–1871)	Jefferson Franklin Long (R-GA) Joseph Hayne Rainey (R-SC)	Hiram Rhodes Revels (R-MS)
42nd (1871–1873)	Robert Carlos De Large (R-SC) Robert Brown Elliott (R-SC) Joseph Hayne Rainey (R-SC) Benjamin Sterling Turner (R-AL) Josiah Thomas Walls (R-FL)	N/A
43rd (1873–1875)	Richard Harvey Cain (R-SC) Robert Brown Elliott (R-SC) John Roy Lynch (R-MS) Joseph Hayne Rainey (R-SC) Alonzo Jacob Ransier (R-SC) James Thomas Rapier (R-AL) Josiah Thomas Walls (R-FL)	N/A
44th (1875–1877)	Jeremiah Haralson (R-AL) John Adams Hyman (R-NC) John Roy Lynch (R-MS) Charles Edmund Nash (R-LA) Joseph Hayne Rainey (R-SC) Robert Smalls (R-SC) Josiah Thomas Walls (R-FL)	Blanche K. Bruce (R-MS)
45th (1877–1879)	Richard Harvey Cain (R-SC) Joseph Hayne Rainey (R-SC) Robert Smalls (R-SC)	Blanche K. Bruce (R-MS)
46th (1879–1881)	N/A	Blanche K. Bruce (R-MS)
47th (1881–1883)	John Roy Lynch (R-MS) Robert Smalls (R-SC)	N/A
48th (1883–1885)	James Edward O'Hara (R-NC) Robert Smalls (R-SC)	N/A
49th (1885–1887)	James Edward O'Hara (R-NC) Robert Smalls (R-SC)	N/A
50th (1887–1889)	N/A	N/A
51st (1889–1891)	Henry Plummer Cheatham (R-NC) John M. Langston (R-VA) Thomas Ezekiel Miller (R-SC)	N/A
52nd (1891–1893)	Henry Plummer Cheatham (R-NC)	N/A
53rd (1893–1895)	George Washington Murray (R-SC)	N/A

CONGRESS	HOUSE	SENATE
54th (1895–1897)	George Washington Murray (R-SC)	N/A
55th (1897–1899)	George Henry White (R-NC)	N/A
56th (1899–1901)	George Henry White (R-NC)	N/A
57th–70th (1901–1929)	N/A	N/A
71st (1929–1931)	Oscar Stanton De Priest (R-IL)	N/A
72nd (1931–1933)	Oscar Stanton De Priest (R-IL)	N/A
73rd (1933–1935)	Oscar Stanton De Priest (R-IL)	N/A
74th (1935–1937)	Arthur Wergs Mitchell (D-IL)	N/A
75th (1937–1939)	Arthur Wergs Mitchell (D-IL)	N/A
76th (1939–1941)	Arthur Wergs Mitchell (D-IL)	N/A
77th (1941–1943)	Arthur Wergs Mitchell (D-IL)	N/A
78th (1943–1945)	William Levi Dawson (D-IL)	N/A
79th (1945–1947)	William Levi Dawson (D-IL) Adam Clayton Powell, Jr. (D-NY)	N/A
80th (1947–1949)	William Levi Dawson (D-IL) Adam Clayton Powell, Jr. (D-NY)	N/A
81st (1949–1951)	William Levi Dawson (D-IL) Adam Clayton Powell, Jr. (D-NY)	N/A
82nd (1951–1953)	William Levi Dawson (D-IL) Adam Clayton Powell, Jr. (D-NY)	N/A
83rd (1953–1955)	William Levi Dawson (D-IL) Adam Clayton Powell, Jr. (D-NY)	N/A
84th (1955–1957)	William Levi Dawson (D-IL) Charles Coles Diggs, Jr. (D-MI) Adam Clayton Powell, Jr. (D-NY)	N/A
85th (1957–1959)	William Levi Dawson (D-IL) Charles Coles Diggs, Jr. (D-MI) Robert Nelson Cornelius Nix, Sr. (D-PA) Adam Clayton Powell, Jr. (D-NY)	N/A
86th (1959–1961)	William Levi Dawson (D-IL) Charles Coles Diggs, Jr. (D-MI) Robert Nelson Cornelius Nix, Sr. (D-PA) Adam Clayton Powell, Jr. (D-NY)	N/A
87th (1961–1963)	William Levi Dawson (D-IL) Charles Coles Diggs, Jr. (D-MI) Robert Nelson Cornelius Nix, Sr. (D-PA) Adam Clayton Powell, Jr. (D-NY)	N/A
88th (1963–1965)	William Levi Dawson (D-IL) Charles Coles Diggs, Jr. (D-MI) Augustus Freeman (Gus) Hawkins (D-CA) Robert Nelson Cornelius Nix, Sr. (D-PA) Adam Clayton Powell, Jr. (D-NY)	N/A
89th (1965–1967)	John Conyers, Jr. (D-MI) William Levi Dawson (D-IL) Charles Coles Diggs, Jr. (D-MI) Augustus Freeman (Gus) Hawkins (D-CA) Robert Nelson Cornelius Nix, Sr. (D-PA) Adam Clayton Powell, Jr. (D-NY)	N/A

CONGRESS	HOUSE	SENATE
90th (1967–1969)	John Conyers, Jr. (D-MI) William Levi Dawson (D-IL) Charles Coles Diggs, Jr. (D-MI) Augustus Freeman (Gus) Hawkins (D-CA) Robert Nelson Cornelius Nix, Sr. (D-PA) Adam Clayton Powell, Jr. (D-NY)*	Edward William Brooke III (R-MA)
91st (1969–1971)	Shirley Anita Chisholm (D-NY) William Lacy Clay, Sr. (D-MO) George Washington Collins (D-IL) John Conyers, Jr. (D-MI) William Levi Dawson (D-IL) Charles Coles Diggs, Jr. (D-MI) Augustus Freeman (Gus) Hawkins (D-CA) Robert Nelson Cornelius Nix, Sr. (D-PA) Adam Clayton Powell, Jr. (D-NY) Louis Stokes (D-OH)	Edward William Brooke III (R-MA)
92nd (1971–1973)	Shirley Anita Chisholm (D-NY) William Lacy Clay, Sr. (D-MO) George Washington Collins (D-IL) John Conyers, Jr. (D-MI) Ronald V. Dellums (D-CA) Charles Coles Diggs, Jr. (D-MI) Walter Edward Fauntroy (D-DC) Augustus Freeman (Gus) Hawkins (D-CA) Ralph Harold Metcalfe (D-IL) Parren James Mitchell (D-MD) Robert Nelson Cornelius Nix, Sr. (D-PA) Charles B. Rangel (D-NY) Louis Stokes (D-OH)	Edward William Brooke III (R-MA)
93rd (1973–1975)	Yvonne Brathwaite Burke (D-CA) Shirley Anita Chisholm (D-NY) William Lacy Clay, Sr. (D-MO) Cardiss Collins (D-IL) John Conyers, Jr. (D-MI) Ronald V. Dellums (D-CA) Charles Coles Diggs, Jr. (D-MI) Walter Edward Fauntroy (D-DC) Augustus Freeman (Gus) Hawkins (D-CA) Barbara Charline Jordan (D-TX) Ralph Harold Metcalfe (D-IL) Parren James Mitchell (D-MD) Robert Nelson Cornelius Nix, Sr. (D-PA) Charles B. Rangel (D-NY) Louis Stokes (D-OH) Andrew Jackson Young, Jr. (D-GA)	Edward William Brooke III (R-MA)

*Adam Clayton Powell, Jr., was elected to the 90th Congress, but the House refused to seat him. He was subsequently elected to that Congress in a special election to fill his own vacancy, although he chose not to occupy the seat for the duration of the term.

CONGRESS	HOUSE	SENATE
94th (1975–1977)	Yvonne Brathwaite Burke (D-CA)	Edward William Brooke III (R-MA)
	Shirley Anita Chisholm (D-NY)	
	William Lacy Clay, Sr. (D-MO)	
	Cardiss Collins (D-IL)	
	John Conyers, Jr. (D-MI)	
	Ronald V. Dellums (D-CA)	
	Charles Coles Diggs, Jr. (D-MI)	
	Walter Edward Fauntroy (D-DC)	
	Harold Eugene Ford, Sr. (D-TN)	
	Augustus Freeman (Gus) Hawkins (D-CA)	
	Barbara Charline Jordan (D-TX)	
	Ralph Harold Metcalfe (D-IL)	
	Parren James Mitchell (D-MD)	
	Robert Nelson Cornelius Nix, Sr. (D-PA)	
	Charles B. Rangel (D-NY)	
	Louis Stokes (D-OH)	
	Andrew Jackson Young, Jr. (D-GA)	
95th (1977–1979)	Yvonne Brathwaite Burke (D-CA)	Edward William Brooke III (R-MA)
	Shirley Anita Chisholm (D-NY)	
	William Lacy Clay, Sr. (D-MO)	
	Cardiss Collins (D-IL)	
	John Conyers, Jr. (D-MI)	
	Ronald V. Dellums (D-CA)	
	Charles Coles Diggs, Jr. (D-MI)	
	Walter Edward Fauntroy (D-DC)	
	Harold Eugene Ford, Sr. (D-TN)	
	Augustus Freeman (Gus) Hawkins (D-CA)	
	Barbara Charline Jordan (D-TX)	
	Ralph Harold Metcalfe (D-IL)	
	Parren James Mitchell (D-MD)	
	Robert Nelson Cornelius Nix, Sr. (D-PA)	
	Charles B. Rangel (D-NY)	
	Louis Stokes (D-OH)	
	Andrew Jackson Young, Jr. (D-GA)	
96th (1979–1981)	Shirley Anita Chisholm (D-NY)	N/A
	William Lacy Clay, Sr. (D-MO)	
	Cardiss Collins (D-IL)	
	John Conyers, Jr. (D-MI)	
	George William Crockett, Jr. (D-MI)	
	Ronald V. Dellums (D-CA)	
	Charles Coles Diggs, Jr. (D-MI)*	
	Julian Carey Dixon (D-CA)	
	Melvin Herbert (Mel) Evans (R-VI)	
	Walter Edward Fauntroy (D-DC)	

*Charles Coles Diggs, Jr. resigned on June 3, 1980, and was succeeded by George Crockett on November 4, 1980.

CONGRESS	HOUSE	SENATE
96th (1979–1981) *Continued*	Harold Eugene Ford, Sr. (D-TN) William Herbert Gray III (D-PA) Augustus Freeman (Gus) Hawkins (D-CA) George Thomas (Mickey) Leland (D-TX) Parren James Mitchell (D-MD) Charles B. Rangel (D-NY) Bennett McVey Stewart (D-IL) Louis Stokes (D-OH)	
97th (1981–1983)	Shirley Anita Chisholm (D-NY) William Lacy Clay, Sr. (D-MO) Cardiss Collins (D-IL) John Conyers, Jr. (D-MI) George William Crockett, Jr. (D-MI) Ronald V. Dellums (D-CA) Julian Carey Dixon (D-CA) Mervyn Malcolm Dymally (D-CA) Walter Edward Fauntroy (D-DC) Harold Eugene Ford, Sr. (D-TN) William Herbert Gray III (D-PA) Katie Beatrice Hall (D-IN)* Augustus Freeman (Gus) Hawkins (D-CA) George Thomas (Mickey) Leland (D-TX) Parren James Mitchell (D-MD) Charles B. Rangel (D-NY) Gus Savage (D-IL) Louis Stokes (D-OH) Harold Washington (D-IL)	N/A
98th (1983–1985)	William Lacy Clay, Sr. (D-MO) Cardiss Collins (D-IL) John Conyers, Jr. (D-MI) George William Crockett, Jr. (D-MI) Ronald V. Dellums (D-CA) Julian Carey Dixon (D-CA) Mervyn Malcolm Dymally (D-CA) Walter Edward Fauntroy (D-DC) Harold Eugene Ford, Sr. (D-TN) William Herbert Gray III (D-PA) Katie Beatrice Hall (D-IN) Augustus Freeman (Gus) Hawkins (D-CA) Charles Arthur Hayes (D-IL) George Thomas (Mickey) Leland (D-TX) Parren James Mitchell (D-MD) Major Robert Odell Owens (D-NY) Charles B. Rangel (D-NY)	N/A

*Katie Beatrice Hall was elected to the 97th Congress in a special election to succeed Adam Benjamin on November 2, 1982.

CONGRESS	HOUSE	SENATE
98th (1983–1985) *Continued*	Gus Savage (D-IL) Louis Stokes (D-OH) Edolphus Towns (D-NY) Harold Washington (D-IL) Alan Dupree Wheat (D-MO)	
99th (1985–1987)	William Lacy Clay, Sr. (D-MO) Cardiss Collins (D-IL) John Conyers, Jr. (D-MI) George William Crockett, Jr. (D-MI) Ronald V. Dellums (D-CA) Julian Carey Dixon (D-CA) Mervyn Malcolm Dymally (D-CA) Walter Edward Fauntroy (D-DC) Harold Eugene Ford, Sr. (D-TN) William Herbert Gray III (D-PA) Augustus Freeman (Gus) Hawkins (D-CA) Charles Arthur Hayes (D-IL) George Thomas (Mickey) Leland (D-TX) Parren James Mitchell (D-MD) Major Robert Odell Owens (D-NY) Charles B. Rangel (D-NY) Gus Savage (D-IL) Louis Stokes (D-OH) Edolphus Towns (D-NY) Alton R. Waldon, Jr. (D-NY) Alan Dupree Wheat (D-MO)	N/A
100th (1987–1989)	William Lacy Clay, Sr. (D-MO) Cardiss Collins (D-IL) John Conyers, Jr. (D-MI) George William Crockett, Jr. (D-MI) Ronald V. Dellums (D-CA) Julian Carey Dixon (D-CA) Mervyn Malcolm Dymally (D-CA) Michael Alphonso (Mike) Espy (D-MS) Walter Edward Fauntroy (D-DC) Floyd Harold Flake (D-NY) Harold Eugene Ford, Sr. (D-TN) William Herbert Gray III (D-PA) Augustus Freeman (Gus) Hawkins (D-CA) Charles Arthur Hayes (D-IL) George Thomas (Mickey) Leland (D-TX) John R. Lewis (D-GA) Kweisi Mfume (D-MD) Major Robert Odell Owens (D-NY) Charles B. Rangel (D-NY) Gus Savage (D-IL)	N/A

CONGRESS	HOUSE	SENATE
100th (1987–1989) *Continued*	Louis Stokes (D-OH)	
	Edolphus Towns (D-NY)	
	Alan Dupree Wheat (D-MO)	
101st (1989–1991)	William Lacy Clay, Sr. (D-MO)	N/A
	Cardiss Collins (D-IL)	
	John Conyers, Jr. (D-MI)	
	George William Crockett, Jr. (D-MI)	
	Ronald V. Dellums (D-CA)	
	Julian Carey Dixon (D-CA)	
	Mervyn Malcolm Dymally (D-CA)	
	Michael Alphonso (Mike) Espy (D-MS)	
	Walter Edward Fauntroy (D-DC)	
	Floyd Harold Flake (D-NY)	
	Harold Eugene Ford, Sr. (D-TN)	
	William Herbert Gray III (D-PA)	
	Augustus Freeman (Gus) Hawkins (D-CA)	
	Charles Arthur Hayes (D-IL)	
	George Thomas (Mickey) Leland (D-TX)	
	John R. Lewis (D-GA)	
	Kweisi Mfume (D-MD)	
	Major Robert Odell Owens (D-NY)	
	Donald Milford Payne (D-NJ)	
	Charles B. Rangel (D-NY)	
	Gus Savage (D-IL)	
	Louis Stokes (D-OH)	
	Edolphus Towns (D-NY)	
	Craig Anthony Washington (D-TX)	
	Alan Dupree Wheat (D-MO)	
102nd (1991–1993)	Lucien Edward Blackwell (D-PA)	N/A
	William Lacy Clay, Sr. (D-MO)	
	Eva M. Clayton (D-NC)	
	Barbara-Rose Collins (D-MI)	
	Cardiss Collins (D-IL)	
	John Conyers, Jr. (D-MI)	
	Ronald V. Dellums (D-CA)	
	Julian Carey Dixon (D-CA)	
	Mervyn Malcolm Dymally (D-CA)	
	Michael Alphonso (Mike) Espy (D-MS)	
	Floyd Harold Flake (D-NY)	
	Harold Eugene Ford, Sr. (D-TN)	
	Gary A. Franks (R-CT)	
	William Herbert Gray III (D-PA)*	
	Charles Arthur Hayes (D-IL)	
	William Jennings Jefferson (D-LA)	

*   William Herbert Gray III resigned on September 11, 1991, and was succeeded by Lucien Edward Blackwell on November 5, 1991.

CONGRESS	HOUSE	SENATE
102nd (1991–1993) *Continued*	John R. Lewis (D-GA) Kweisi Mfume (D-MD) Eleanor Holmes Norton (D-DC) Major Robert Odell Owens (D-NY) Donald Milford Payne (D-NJ) Charles B. Rangel (D-NY) Gus Savage (D-IL) Louis Stokes (D-OH) Edolphus Towns (D-NY) Craig Anthony Washington (D-TX) Maxine Waters (D-CA) Alan Dupree Wheat (D-MO)	
103rd (1993–1995)	Sanford Dixon Bishop, Jr. (D-GA) Lucien Edward Blackwell (D-PA) Corrine Brown (D-FL) William Lacy Clay, Sr. (D-MO) Eva M. Clayton (D-NC) James Enos Clyburn (D-SC) Barbara-Rose Collins (D-MI) Cardiss Collins (D-IL) John Conyers, Jr. (D-MI) Ronald V. Dellums (D-CA) Julian Carey Dixon (D-CA) Michael Alphonso (Mike) Espy (D-MS)* Cleo Fields (D-LA) Floyd Harold Flake (D-NY) Harold Eugene Ford, Sr. (D-TN) Gary A. Franks (R-CT) Alcee Lamar Hastings (D-FL) Earl Frederick Hilliard (D-AL) William Jennings Jefferson (D-LA) Eddie Bernice Johnson (D-TX) John R. Lewis (D-GA) Cynthia Ann McKinney (D-GA) Carrie P. Meek (D-FL) Kweisi Mfume (D-MD) Eleanor Holmes Norton (D-DC) Major Robert Odell Owens (D-NY) Donald Milford Payne (D-NJ) Charles B. Rangel (D-NY) Mel Reynolds (D-IL) Bobby L. Rush (D-IL) Robert Cortez Scott (D-VA) Louis Stokes (D-OH)	Carol Moseley-Braun (D-IL)

* Michael Alphonso (Mike) Espy resigned on January 22, 1993, and was succeeded by Bennie Thompson on April 13, 1993.

CONGRESS	HOUSE	SENATE
103rd (1993–1995) *Continued*	Bennie Thompson (D-MS)	
	Edolphus Towns (D-NY)	
	Walter R. Tucker III (D-CA)	
	Craig Anthony Washington (D-TX)	
	Maxine Waters (D-CA)	
	Melvin L. Watt (D-NC)	
	Alan Dupree Wheat (D-MO)	
	Albert Russell Wynn (D-MD)	
104th (1995–1997)	Sanford Dixon Bishop, Jr. (D-GA)	Carol Moseley-Braun (D-IL)
	Corrine Brown (D-FL)	
	William Lacy Clay, Sr. (D-MO)	
	Eva M. Clayton (D-NC)	
	James Enos Clyburn (D-SC)	
	Barbara-Rose Collins (D-MI)	
	Cardiss Collins (D-IL)	
	John Conyers, Jr. (D-MI)	
	Elijah Eugene Cummings (D-MD)	
	Ronald V. Dellums (D-CA)	
	Julian Carey Dixon (D-CA)	
	Chaka Fattah (D-PA)	
	Cleo Fields (D-LA)	
	Floyd Harold Flake (D-NY)	
	Harold Eugene Ford, Sr. (D-TN)	
	Gary A. Franks (R-CT)	
	Victor O. Frazer (I-VI)	
	Alcee Lamar Hastings (D-FL)	
	Earl Frederick Hilliard (D-AL)	
	Jesse L. Jackson, Jr. (D-IL)	
	Sheila Jackson Lee (D-TX)	
	William Jennings Jefferson (D-LA)	
	Eddie Bernice Johnson (D-TX)	
	John R. Lewis (D-GA)	
	Cynthia Ann McKinney (D-GA)	
	Carrie P. Meek (D-FL)	
	Kweisi Mfume (D-MD)*	
	Juanita Millender-McDonald (D-CA)	
	Eleanor Holmes Norton (D-DC)	
	Major Robert Odell Owens (D-NY)	
	Donald Milford Payne (D-NJ)	
	Charles B. Rangel (D-NY)	
	Mel Reynolds (D-IL)**	
	Bobby L. Rush (D-IL)	
	Robert Cortez Scott (D-VA)	

* Kweisi Mfume resigned on February 15, 1996, and was succeeded by Elijah Eugene Cummings on April 16, 1996.

** Mel Reynolds resigned on October 1, 1995, and was succeeded by Jesse L. Jackson, Jr., on December 12, 1995.

104th (1995–1997) *Continued*	Louis Stokes (D-OH)	
	Bennie Thompson (D-MS)	
	Edolphus Towns (D-NY)	
	Walter R. Tucker III (D-CA)*	
	Maxine Waters (D-CA)	
	Melvin L. Watt (D-NC)	
	Julius Caesar (J. C.) Watts, Jr. (R-OK)	
	Albert Russell Wynn (D-MD)	
105th (1997–1999)	Sanford Dixon Bishop, Jr. (D-GA)	Carol Moseley-Braun (D-IL)
	Corrine Brown (D-FL)	
	Julia May Carson (D-IN)	
	Donna Christensen (D-VI)**	
	William Lacy Clay, Sr. (D-MO)	
	Eva M. Clayton (D-NC)	
	James Enos Clyburn (D-SC)	
	John Conyers, Jr. (D-MI)	
	Elijah Eugene Cummings (D-MD)	
	Danny K. Davis (D-IL)	
	Ronald V. Dellums (D-CA)***	
	Julian Carey Dixon (D-CA)	
	Chaka Fattah (D-PA)	
	Floyd Harold Flake (D-NY)****	
	Harold Eugene Ford, Jr. (D-TN)	
	Alcee Lamar Hastings (D-FL)	
	Earl Frederick Hilliard (D-AL)	
	Sheila Jackson Lee (D-TX)	
	Jesse L. Jackson, Jr. (D-IL)	
	William Jennings Jefferson (D-LA)	
	Eddie Bernice Johnson (D-TX)	
	Carolyn Cheeks Kilpatrick (D-MI)	
	Barbara Lee (D-CA)	
	John R. Lewis (D-GA)	
	Cynthia Ann McKinney (D-GA)	
	Carrie P. Meek (D-FL)	
	Gregory W. Meeks (D-NY)	
	Juanita Millender-McDonald (D-CA)	
	Eleanor Holmes Norton (D-DC)	
	Major Robert Odell Owens (D-NY)	
	Donald Milford Payne (D-NJ)	
	Charles B. Rangel (D-NY)	
	Bobby L. Rush (D-IL)	

*Walter R. Tucker III resigned on December 15, 1995, and was succeeded by Juanita Millender-McDonald on March 26, 1996.

**Donna Christensen served under the name Donna Christian-Green in the 105th Congress.

***Ronald V. Dellums resigned on February 6, 1998, and was succeeded by Barbara Lee on April 7, 1998.

****Floyd Harold Flake resigned on November 17, 1997, and was succeeded by Gregory Meeks on February 3, 1998.

CONGRESS	HOUSE	SENATE
105th (1997–1999) *Continued*	Robert Cortez Scott (D-VA) Louis Stokes (D-OH) Bennie Thompson (D-MS) Edolphus Towns (D-NY) Maxine Waters (D-CA) Melvin L. Watt (D-NC) Julius Caesar (J. C.) Watts, Jr. (R-OK) Albert Russell Wynn (D-MD)	
106th (1999–2001)	Sanford Dixon Bishop, Jr. (D-GA) Corrine Brown (D-FL) Julia May Carson (D-IN) Donna Christensen (D-VI) William Lacy Clay, Sr. (D-MO) Eva M. Clayton (D-NC) James Enos Clyburn (D-SC) John Conyers, Jr. (D-MI) Elijah Eugene Cummings (D-MD) Danny K. Davis (D-IL) Julian Carey Dixon (D-CA) Chaka Fattah (D-PA) Harold Eugene Ford, Jr. (D-TN) Alcee Lamar Hastings (D-FL) Earl Frederick Hilliard (D-AL) Jesse L. Jackson, Jr. (D-IL) Sheila Jackson Lee (D-TX) William Jennings Jefferson (D-LA) Eddie Bernice Johnson (D-TX) Stephanie Tubbs Jones (D-OH) Carolyn Cheeks Kilpatrick (D-MI) Barbara Lee (D-CA) John R. Lewis (D-GA) Cynthia Ann McKinney (D-GA) Carrie P. Meek (D-FL) Gregory W. Meeks (D-NY) Juanita Millender-McDonald (D-CA) Eleanor Holmes Norton (D-DC) Major Robert Odell Owens (D-NY) Donald Milford Payne (D-NJ) Charles B. Rangel (D-NY) Bobby L. Rush (D-IL) Robert Cortez (Bobby) Scott (D-VA) Bennie Thompson (D-MS) Edolphus Towns (D-NY) Maxine Waters (D-CA) Melvin L. Watt (D-NC) Julius Caesar (J. C.) Watts, Jr. (R-OK) Albert Russell Wynn (D-MD)	N/A

CONGRESS	HOUSE	SENATE
107th (2001–2003)	Sanford Dixon Bishop, Jr. (D-GA)	N/A
	Corrine Brown (D-FL)	
	Julia May Carson (D-IN)	
	Donna Christensen (D-VI)	
	William Lacy Clay, Jr. (D-MO)	
	Eva M. Clayton (D-NC)	
	James Enos Clyburn (D-SC)	
	John Conyers, Jr. (D-MI)	
	Elijah Eugene Cummings (D-MD)	
	Danny K. Davis (D-IL)	
	Chaka Fattah (D-PA)	
	Harold Eugene Ford, Jr. (D-TN)	
	Alcee Lamar Hastings (D-FL)	
	Earl Frederick Hilliard (D-AL)	
	Jesse L. Jackson, Jr. (D-IL)	
	Sheila Jackson Lee (D-TX)	
	William Jennings Jefferson (D-LA)	
	Eddie Bernice Johnson (D-TX)	
	Stephanie Tubbs Jones (D-OH)	
	Carolyn Cheeks Kilpatrick (D-MI)	
	Barbara Lee (D-CA)	
	John R. Lewis (D-GA)	
	Cynthia Ann McKinney (D-GA)	
	Carrie P. Meek (D-FL)	
	Gregory W. Meeks (D-NY)	
	Juanita Millender-McDonald (D-CA)	
	Eleanor Holmes Norton (D-DC)	
	Major Robert Odell Owens (D-NY)	
	Donald Milford Payne (D-NJ)	
	Charles B. Rangel (D-NY)	
	Bobby L. Rush (D-IL)	
	Robert Cortez Scott (D-VA)	
	Bennie Thompson (D-MS)	
	Edolphus Towns (D-NY)	
	Maxine Waters (D-CA)	
	Diane Edith Watson (D-CA)*	
	Melvin L. Watt (D-NC)	
	Julius Caesar (J.C.) Watts, Jr. (R-OK)	
	Albert Russell Wynn (D-MD)	
108th (2003–2005)	Frank W. Ballance, Jr. (D-NC)**	N/A
	Sanford Dixon Bishop, Jr. (D-GA)	
	Corrine Brown (D-FL)	
	George Kenneth (G. K.) Butterfield, Jr. (D-NC)	

*Diane Edith Watson was elected by special election on June 5, 2001, to succeed Julian Dixon.

**Frank W. Ballance, Jr., resigned on June 11, 2004, and was succeeded by George Kenneth (G. K.) Butterfield, Jr., on July 20, 2004.

CONGRESS	HOUSE	SENATE
108th (2003–2005) *Continued*	Julia May Carson (D-IN) Donna Christensen (D-VI) William Lacy Clay, Jr. (D-MO) James Enos Clyburn (D-SC) John Conyers, Jr. (D-MI) Elijah Eugene Cummings (D-MD) Artur Davis (D-AL) Danny K. Davis (D-IL) Chaka Fattah (D-PA) Harold Eugene Ford, Jr. (D-TN) Alcee Lamar Hastings (D-FL) Jesse L. Jackson, Jr. (D-IL) Sheila Jackson Lee (D-TX) William Jennings Jefferson (D-LA) Eddie Bernice Johnson (D-TX) Stephanie Tubbs Jones (D-OH) Carolyn Cheeks Kilpatrick (D-MI) Barbara Lee (D-CA) John R. Lewis (D-GA) Denise L. Majette (D-GA) Kendrick B. Meek (D-FL) Gregory W. Meeks (D-NY) Juanita Millender-McDonald (D-CA) Eleanor Holmes Norton (D-DC) Major Robert Odell Owens (D-NY) Donald Milford Payne (D-NJ) Charles B. Rangel (D-NY) Bobby L. Rush (D-IL) David Scott (D-GA) Robert Cortez Scott (D-VA) Bennie Thompson (D-MS) Edolphus Towns (D-NY) Maxine Waters (D-CA) Diane Edith Watson (D-CA) Melvin L. Watt (D-NC) Albert Russell Wynn (D-MD)	
109th (2005–2007)	Sanford Dixon Bishop, Jr. (D-GA) Corrine Brown (D-FL) George Kenneth (G. K.) Butterfield, Jr. (D-NC) Julia May Carson (D-IN) Donna Christensen (D-VI) William Lacy Clay, Jr. (D-MO) Emanuel Cleaver II (D-MO) James Enos Clyburn (D-SC) John Conyers, Jr. (D-MI) Elijah Eugene Cummings (D-MD)	Barack Obama (D-IL)

CONGRESS	HOUSE	SENATE
109th (2005–2007) *Continued*	Artur Davis (D-AL) Danny K. Davis (D-IL) Chaka Fattah (D-PA) Harold Eugene Ford, Jr. (D-TN) Al Green (D-TX) Alcee Lamar Hastings (D-FL) Jesse L. Jackson, Jr. (D-IL) Sheila Jackson Lee (D-TX) William Jennings Jefferson (D-LA) Eddie Bernice Johnson (D-TX) Stephanie Tubbs Jones (D-OH) Carolyn Cheeks Kilpatrick (D-MI) Barbara Lee (D-CA) John R. Lewis (D-GA) Cynthia Ann McKinney (D-GA) Kendrick B. Meek (D-FL) Gregory W. Meeks (D-NY) Juanita Millender-McDonald (D-CA) Gwendolynne S. (Gwen) Moore (D-WI) Eleanor Holmes Norton (D-DC) Major Robert Odell Owens (D-NY) Donald Milford Payne (D-NJ) Charles B. Rangel (D-NY) Bobby L. Rush (D-IL) David Scott (D-GA) Robert Cortez Scott (D-VA) Bennie Thompson (D-MS) Edolphus Towns (D-NY) Maxine Waters (D-CA) Diane Edith Watson (D-CA) Melvin L. Watt (D-NC) Albert Russell Wynn (D-MD)	
110th (2007–2009)	Sanford Dixon Bishop, Jr. (D-GA) Corrine Brown (D-FL) George Kenneth (G. K.) Butterfield, Jr. (D-NC) Julia May Carson (D-IN)* Donna Christensen (D-VI) Yvette Diane Clarke (D-NY) William Lacy Clay, Jr. (D-MO) Emanuel Cleaver II (D-MO) James Enos Clyburn (D-SC) John Conyers, Jr. (D-MI) Elijah Eugene Cummings (D-MD)	Barack Obama (D-IL)

*Julia May Carson died on December 15, 2007. A special election to fill Representative Carson's vacant seat had not been held as of the closing date of this volume, on December 31, 2007.

110th (2007–2009)
Continued

Artur Davis (D-AL)
Danny K. Davis (D-IL)
Keith Ellison (D-MN)
Chaka Fattah (D-PA)
Al Green (D-TX)
Alcee Lamar Hastings (D-FL)
Jesse L. Jackson, Jr. (D-IL)
Sheila Jackson Lee (D-TX)
William Jennings Jefferson (D-LA)
Hank Johnson (D-GA)
Eddie Bernice Johnson (D-TX)
Stephanie Tubbs Jones (D-OH)
Carolyn Cheeks Kilpatrick (D-MI)
Barbara Lee (D-CA)
John R. Lewis (D-GA)
Kendrick B. Meek (D-FL)
Gregory W. Meeks (D-NY)
Juanita Millender-McDonald (D-CA)*
Gwendolynne S. (Gwen) Moore (D-WI)
Eleanor Holmes Norton (D-DC)
Donald Milford Payne (D-NJ)
Charles B. Rangel (D-NY)
Laura Richardson (D-CA)
Bobby L. Rush (D-IL)
David Scott (D-GA)
Robert Cortez Scott (D-VA)
Bennie Thompson (D-MS)
Edolphus Towns (D-NY)
Maxine Waters (D-CA)
Diane Edith Watson (D-CA)
Melvin L. Watt (D-NC)
Albert Russell Wynn (D-MD)

*Juanita Millender-McDonald died on April 22, 2007, and was succeeded in a special election by Laura Richardson on August 21, 2007.

Black-American Representatives and Senators by State and Territory

States are listed in descending order according to the number of African Americans that each has sent to Congress.

STATE OR TERRITORY	MEMBER'S NAME	YEAR MEMBER TOOK OFFICE
Illinois (16)	Oscar Stanton De Priest	1929
	Arthur Wergs Mitchell	1935
	William Levi Dawson	1943
	George Washington Collins	1970
	Ralph Harold Metcalfe	1971
	Cardiss Collins	1973
	Bennett McVey Stewart	1979
	Gus Savage	1981
	Harold Washington	1981
	Charles Arthur Hayes	1983
	Carol Moseley-Braun[a]	1993
	Mel Reynolds	1993
	Bobby L. Rush	1993
	Jesse L. Jackson, Jr.	1995
	Danny K. Davis	1997
	Barack Obama[a]	2005
California (11)	Augustus Freeman (Gus) Hawkins	1963
	Ronald V. Dellums	1971
	Yvonne Brathwaite Burke	1973
	Julian Carey Dixon	1979
	Mervyn Malcolm Dymally	1981
	Maxine Waters	1991
	Walter R. Tucker III	1993
	Juanita Millender-McDonald	1996
	Barbara Lee	1998
	Diane Edith Watson	2001
	Laura Richardson	2007
New York (9)	Adam Clayton Powell, Jr.	1945
	Shirley Anita Chisholm	1969
	Charles B. Rangel	1971
	Major Robert Odell Owens	1983
	Edolphus Towns	1983
	Alton R. Waldon, Jr.	1986
	Floyd Harold Flake	1987
	Gregory W. Meeks	1998
	Yvette Diane Clarke	2007

| --- | --- | --- |
South Carolina (9)	Joseph Hayne Rainey	1870
	Robert Carlos De Large	1871
	Robert Brown Elliott	1871
	Richard Harvey Cain	1873
	Alonzo Jacob Ransier	1873
	Robert Smalls	1875
	Thomas Ezekiel Miller	1890
	George Washington Murray	1893
	James Enos Clyburn	1993
Georgia (8)	Jefferson Franklin Long	1870
	Andrew Jackson Young, Jr.	1973
	John R. Lewis	1987
	Sanford Dixon Bishop, Jr.	1993
	Cynthia Ann McKinney	1993
	Denise L. Majette	2003
	David Scott	2003
	Hank Johnson	2007
North Carolina (8)	John Adams Hyman	1875
	James Edward O'Hara	1883
	Henry Plummer Cheatham	1889
	George Henry White	1897
	Eva M. Clayton	1992
	Melvin L. Watt	1993
	Frank W. Ballance, Jr.	2003
	George Kenneth (G. K.) Butterfield, Jr.	2004
Texas (6)	Barbara Charline Jordan	1973
	George Thomas (Mickey) Leland	1979
	Craig Anthony Washington	1989
	Eddie Bernice Johnson	1993
	Sheila Jackson Lee	1995
	Al Green	2005
Alabama (5)	Benjamin Sterling Turner	1871
	James Thomas Rapier	1873
	Jeremiah Haralson	1875
	Earl Frederick Hilliard	1993
	Artur Davis	2003
Florida (5)	Josiah Thomas Walls	1871
	Corrine Brown	1993
	Alcee Lamar Hastings	1993
	Carrie P. Meek	1993
	Kendrick B. Meek	2003
Michigan (5)	Barbara-Rose Collins	1991
	John Conyers, Jr.	1965
	George William Crockett, Jr.	1980
	Charles Coles Diggs, Jr.	1955
	Carolyn Cheeks Kilpatrick	1997

STATE OR TERRITORY	MEMBER'S NAME	YEAR MEMBER TOOK OFFICE
Mississippi (5)	Hiram Rhodes Revels[a]	1870
	John Roy Lynch	1873
	Blanche K. Bruce[a]	1875
	Michael Alphonso (Mike) Espy	1987
	Bennie Thompson	1993
Maryland (4)	Parren James Mitchell	1971
	Kweisi Mfume	1987
	Albert Russell Wynn	1993
	Elijah Eugene Cummings	1996
Missouri (4)	William Lacy Clay, Sr.	1969
	Alan Dupree Wheat	1983
	William Lacy Clay, Jr.	2001
	Emanuel Cleaver II	2003
Pennsylvania (4)	Robert Nelson Cornelius Nix, Sr.	1958
	William Herbert Gray III	1979
	Lucien Edward Blackwell	1991
	Chaka Fattah	1995
Louisiana (3)	Charles Edmund Nash	1875
	William Jennings Jefferson	1991
	Cleo Fields	1993
Virgin Islands (3)	Melvin Herbert (Mel) Evans[b]	1979
	Victor O. Frazer[b]	1995
	Donna Christensen[b]	1997
District of Columbia (2)	Walter Edward Fauntroy[b]	1971
	Eleanor Holmes Norton[b]	1991
Indiana (2)	Katie Beatrice Hall	1982
	Julia May Carson	1997
Ohio (2)	Louis Stokes	1969
	Stephanie Tubbs Jones	1999
Tennessee (2)	Harold Eugene Ford, Sr.	1975
	Harold Eugene Ford, Jr.	1997
Virginia (2)	John M. Langston	1890
	Robert Cortez Scott	1993
Connecticut (1)	Gary A. Franks	1991
Massachusetts (1)	Edward William Brooke[a]	1967
Minnesota (1)	Keith Ellison	2007
New Jersey (1)	Donald Milford Payne	1989
Oklahoma (1)	Julius Caesar (J. C.) Watts, Jr.	1995
Wisconsin (1)	Gwendolynne S. (Gwen) Moore	2005

a Senator

b Delegate

Note: The following states and territories have never elected an African American to Congress: Alaska, American Samoa, Arizona, Arkansas, Colorado, Delaware, Guam, Hawaii, Idaho, Iowa, Kansas, Kentucky, Maine, Montana, Nebraska, Nevada, New Hampshire, New Mexico, North Dakota, Oregon, Rhode Island, South Dakota, Utah, Vermont, Washington, West Virginia, Wyoming, and Puerto Rico.

Black Members' Committee Assignments (Standing, Joint, Select) in the U.S. House and Senate, 1870–2007

Explanatory note: This appendix lists alphabetically all the congressional committees on which African-American Members served. Several features will help readers track black membership on committees over time.

- In instances where a committee's name (rather than its primary jurisdictional duties) has changed, a "See also" note is provided which refers researchers to prior or latter committee name iterations. These name iterations are listed in chronological order.

- In instances where a committee on which a black Member served was disbanded and its jurisdiction subsumed by another committee, a "Jurisdiction reassigned" note is provided. Researchers are referred only to the committees with expanded jurisdictions on which black Members later served.

- In instances where a committee was disbanded and no jurisdictional transfer occurred, only the Congress and date ranges of the committee are provided.

- Members' terms of service on committees reflect the years they served on the committees; the Congress range is provided in a separate column. Please be aware that because this appendix accounts for Members joining or leaving committees because of deaths, resignations, and special elections, in some instances service dates are not coterminous with Congress dates.

HOUSE STANDING COMMITTEE	TERM	CONGRESS		TERM	CONGRESS

AGRICULTURE [1820–Present]
16th Congress–Present

Richard Harvey Cain	1873–1875	43rd
Robert Smalls	1875–1877	44th
	1882–1883	47th
Henry Plummer Cheatham	1891–1893	52nd
George Henry White	1897–1901	55th–56th
Michael Alphonso (Mike) Espy	1987–1993	100th–102nd
Sanford Dixon Bishop, Jr.	1993–2003	103rd–107th
Eva M. Clayton	1993–2003	103rd–107th
Earl Frederick Hilliard	1993–2003	103rd–107th
Cynthia Ann McKinney	1993–1997	103rd–104th
Bennie Thompson	1993–2005	103rd–108th
Frank W. Ballance, Jr.	2003–2005	108th
George Kenneth (G. K.) Butterfield, Jr.	2004–2007	108th–109th
David Scott	2003–	108th–110th

APPROPRIATIONS [1865–Present]
39th Congress–Present

Louis Stokes	1971–1999	92nd–105th
Yvonne Brathwaite Burke	1975–1979	94th–95th
Julian Carey Dixon	1979–2000	96th–106th
Bennett McVey Stewart	1979–1981	96th
William Herbert Gray III	1981–1991	97th–102nd
Carrie P. Meek	1993–1995	103rd
	1999–2003	105th–107th
James Enos Clyburn	1999–2007	106th–109th
Jesse L. Jackson, Jr.	1999–	106th–110th
Chaka Fattah	2001–	107th–110th
Sanford Dixon Bishop, Jr.	2003–	108th–110th
Carolyn Cheeks Kilpatrick	1999–	106th–110th
Barbara Lee	2007–	110th

ARMED SERVICES [1947–1995; 1999–Present]
80th through 103rd Congresses; 106th Congress–Present
(See also the following standing committee: National Security)

Ronald V. Dellums	1973–1995	93rd–103rd
Melvin Herbert Evans	1979–1981	96th
Gary A. Franks	1991–1993	102nd
Cynthia Ann McKinney	1999–2003	106th–107th
	2005–2007	109th
Julius Caesar (J. C.) Watts, Jr.	1999–2003	106th–107th
Kendrick B. Meek	2003–	108th–110th
George Kenneth (G. K.) Butterfield, Jr.	2005–2007	109th
Elijah Eugene Cummings	2007–	110th
Hank Johnson	2007–	110th

BANKING AND CURRENCY [1865–1975]
39th through 93rd Congresses
(See also the following standing committees: Banking, Currency, and Housing; Banking, Finance, and Urban Affairs; Banking and Financial Services; Financial Services)

Parren James Mitchell	1971–1975	92nd–93rd
Andrew Jackson Young, Jr.	1973–1975	93rd
Walter Edward Fauntroy	1973–1975	93rd

BANKING, CURRENCY, AND HOUSING [1975–1977]
94th Congress
(See also the following standing committees: Banking and Currency; Banking, Finance, and Urban Affairs; Banking and Financial Services; Financial Services)

Parren James Mitchell	1975–1977	94th
Harold Eugene Ford, Sr.	1975–1977	94th
Walter Edward Fauntroy	1975–1977	94th

BANKING AND FINANCIAL SERVICES [1995–2001]
104th through 106th Congresses
(See also the following standing committees: Banking and Currency; Banking, Currency, and Housing; Banking, Finance, and Urban Affairs; Financial Services)

Cleo Fields	1995–1997	104th
Floyd Harold Flake	1995–1997	104th–105th
Jesse L. Jackson, Jr.	1995–1999	104th–105th
Cynthia Ann McKinney	1995–1997	104th–105th
Kweisi Mfume	1995–1996	104th
Maxine Waters	1995–2001	104th–106th
Melvin L. Watt	1995–2001	104th–106th
Julius Caesar (J. C.) Watts, Jr.	1995–1997	104th
Albert Russell Wynn	1995–1997	104th
Julia May Carson	1997–2001	105th–106th
Carolyn Cheeks Kilpatrick	1997–1999	105th
Barbara Lee	1998–2001	105th–106th
Gregory W. Meeks	1998–2001	105th–106th
Stephanie Tubbs Jones	1999–2001	106th

BANKING, FINANCE, AND URBAN AFFAIRS [1977–1995]
95th through 103rd Congresses
(See also the following standing committees: Banking and Currency; Banking, Currency and Housing; Banking and Financial Services; Financial Services)

Parren James Mitchell	1977–1987	95th–99th
Walter Edward Fauntroy	1977–1991	95th–101st
Floyd Harold Flake	1987–1995	100th–103rd
Kweisi Mfume	1987–1995	100th–103rd
Maxine Waters	1991–1995	102nd–103rd
Cleo Fields	1993–1995	103rd
Bobby L. Rush	1993–1995	103rd
Melvin L. Watt	1993–1995	103rd
Albert Russell Wynn	1993–1995	103rd

BUDGET [1974–Present]
93rd Congress–Present

Parren James Mitchell	1974–1979	93rd–95th
Louis Stokes	1975–1981	94th–96th
William Herbert Gray III	1979–1981	96th
	1983–1989	98th–100th
Michael Alphonso (Mike) Espy	1987–1993	100th–102nd
Lucien Edward Blackwell	1993–1995	103rd
Carrie P. Meek	1995–1997	104th
Eva M. Clayton	1997–2003	105th–107th
Bennie Thompson	1997–2003	105th–107th
Artur Davis	2003–2007	108th–109th
Harold Eugene Ford, Jr.	2003–2007	108th–109th
John R. Lewis	2003–2005	108th
Denise L. Majette	2003–2005	108th
Robert Cortez Scott	2003–2005	108th
	2007–	110th
Cynthia Ann McKinney	2005–2007	109th
William Jennings Jefferson	2005–2007	109th
Gwendolynne S. (Gwen) Moore	2007–	110th

COINAGE, WEIGHTS, AND MEASURES [1864–1947]
38th through 79th Congresses (Jurisdiction reassigned to the following standing committees: Banking and Currency; Interstate and Foreign Commerce)

William Levi Dawson	1943–1947	78th–79th

COMMERCE [1995–2001]
104th through 106th Congresses (See also the following standing committees: Interstate and Foreign Commerce; Energy and Commerce)

Cardiss Collins	1995–1997	104th
Gary A. Franks	1995–1997	104th
Bobby L. Rush	1995–2001	104th–106th
Edolphus Towns	1995–2001	104th–106th
Albert Russell Wynn	1997–2001	105th–106th

DISTRICT OF COLUMBIA [1808–1995]
10th through 103rd Congresses (Jurisdiction reassigned to the following standing committee: Government Reform and Oversight)

George Henry White	1899–1901	56th
William Levi Dawson	1955–1970	84th–91st
Charles Coles Diggs, Jr.	1963–1980	88th–96th
Ronald V. Dellums	1971–1995	92nd–103rd
Walter Edward Fauntroy	1971–1991	92nd–101st
Charles B. Rangel	1973–1975	93rd
William Herbert Gray III	1979–1991	96th–102nd
George Thomas (Mickey) Leland	1979–1987	96th–99th
Mervyn Malcolm Dymally	1981–1993	97th–102nd
Alan Dupree Wheat	1985–1995	99th–103rd
Eleanor Holmes Norton	1991–1995	102nd–103rd
William Jennings Jefferson	1993–1995	103rd
John R. Lewis	1993–1995	103rd

ECONOMIC AND EDUCATIONAL OPPORTUNITIES [1995–1997]
104th Congress (See also the following standing committees: Education and Labor; Education; Education and the Workforce)

William Lacy Clay, Sr.	1995–1997	104th
Chaka Fattah	1995–1997	104th
Major Robert Odell Owens	1995–1997	104th
Donald Milford Payne	1995–1997	104th
Mel Reynolds	1995	104th
Robert Cortez Scott	1995–1997	104th

EDUCATION [1883–1947]
48th through 79th Congresses (See also the following standing committees: Education and Labor; Economic and Educational Opportunities; Education and the Workforce)

Henry Plummer Cheatham	1889–1893	51st–52nd
John M. Langston	1890–1891	51st
George Washington Murray	1893–1897	53rd–54th

EDUCATION AND LABOR [1867–1883; 1947–1995; 2007–Present]

40th through 47th Congresses; 80th through 103rd Congresses; 110th Congress–Present (See also the following standing committees: Education; Economic and Educational Opportunities; Education and the Workforce)

Robert Brown Elliott	1871–1875	42nd–43rd
James Thomas Rapier	1873–1875	43rd
Charles Edmund Nash	1875–1877	44th
John Roy Lynch	1882–1883	47th
Adam Clayton Powell, Jr.	1947–1967	80th–89th
	1969–1971	91st
Augustus Freeman (Gus) Hawkins	1963–1991	88th–101st
William Lacy Clay, Sr.	1969–1995	91st–103rd
George Washington Collins	1969–1971	91st
Louis Stokes	1969–1971	91st
Shirley Anita Chisholm	1971–1977	92nd–94th
Major Robert Odell Owens	1983–1995	98th–103rd
Harold Washington	1981–1983	97th–98th
Charles Arthur Hayes	1983–1993	98th–102nd
Mervyn Malcolm Dymally	1985–1987	99th
Alton R. Waldon, Jr.	1985–1987	99th
Craig Anthony Washington	1990–1993	101st–102nd
Kweisi Mfume	1989–1991	101st
Donald Milford Payne	1989–1995	101st–103rd
	2007–	110th
William Jennings Jefferson	1991–1993	102nd
Robert Cortez Scott	1993–1995	103rd
	2007–	110th
Yvette Diane Clarke	2007–	110th
Danny K. Davis	2007–	110th

EDUCATION AND THE WORKFORCE [1997–2007]

105th through 109th Congresses (See also the following standing committees: Education and Labor; Education; Economic and Educational Opportunities)

William Lacy Clay, Sr.	1997–2001	105th–106th
Chaka Fattah	1997–2001	105th–106th
Harold Eugene Ford, Jr.	1997–2003	105th–107th
Major Robert Odell Owens	1997–2007	105th–109th
Donald Milford Payne	1997–2007	105th–109th
Robert Cortez Scott	1997–2003	105th–107th
	2005–2007	109th
Danny K. Davis	2003–2007	108th–109th
Denise L. Majette	2003–2005	108th

ENERGY AND COMMERCE [1981–1995; 2001–Present]

97th through 103rd Congresses; 107th Congress–Present (See also the following standing committees: Interstate and Foreign Commerce; Commerce)

Cardiss Collins	1981–1995	97th–103rd
George Thomas (Mickey) Leland	1981–1989	97th–101st
Edolphus Towns	1989–1995	101st–103rd
	2001–	107th–110th
Gary A. Franks	1993–1995	103rd
Craig Anthony Washington	1993–1995	103rd

ENERGY AND COMMERCE *Continued*

Albert Russell Wynn	2001–	107th–110th
Bobby L. Rush	2001–	107th–110th
George Kenneth (G. K.) Butterfield, Jr.	2007–	110th

ENROLLED BILLS [1876–1947]

44th through 79th Congresses (Jurisdiction reassigned to the following standing committee: House Administration)

Oscar Stanton De Priest	1929–1935	71st–73rd

EXPENDITURES IN EXECUTIVE DEPARTMENTS [1927–1953]

70th through 82nd Congresses (See also the following standing committees: Government Reform and Oversight; Government Operations; Government Reform; Oversight and Government Reform)

William Levi Dawson	1943–1953	78th–82nd

EXPENDITURES IN THE INTERIOR DEPARTMENT [1860–1927]

36th through 69th Congresses (Jurisdiction reassigned to the following standing committee: Expenditures in Executive Departments)

John Roy Lynch	1873–1875	43rd

EXPENDITURES IN THE NAVY DEPARTMENT [1816–1927]

14th through 69th Congresses (Jurisdiction reassigned to the following standing committee: Expenditures in Executive Departments)

Josiah Thomas Walls	1873–1875	43rd

EXPENDITURES ON THE PUBLIC BUILDINGS [1816–1927]

14th through 69th Congresses (Jurisdiction reassigned to the following standing committee: Expenditures in Executive Departments)

James Edward O'Hara	1885–1887	49th
Henry Plummer Cheatham	1889–1893	51st–52nd

EXPENDITURES IN THE TREASURY DEPARTMENT [1816–1927]

14th through 69th Congresses (Jurisdiction reassigned to the following standing committee: Expenditures in Executive Departments)

George Washington Murray	1896–1897	54th

FINANCIAL SERVICES [2001–Present]

107th Congress–Present (See also the following standing committees: Banking and Currency; Banking, Currency, and Housing; Banking, Finance, and Urban Affairs; Banking and Financial Services)

Julia May Carson	2001–2007	107th–110th
William Lacy Clay, Jr.	2001–	107th–110th
Harold Eugene Ford, Jr.	2001–2007	107th–109th
Stephanie Tubbs Jones	2001–2003	107th
Barbara Lee	2001–2007	107th–109th
Gregory W. Meeks	2001–	107th–110th
Maxine Waters	2001–	107th–110th
Melvin L. Watt	2001–	107th–110th

FINANCIAL SERVICES *Continued*

Artur Davis	2003–2007	108th–109th
Emanuel Cleaver II	2005–	109th–110th
Gwendolynne S. (Gwen) Moore	2005–	109th–110th
Al Green	2005–	109th–110th
David Scott	2003–	108th–110th
Keith Ellison	2007–	110th

FOREIGN AFFAIRS [1822–1977; 1981–1995; 2007–Present]
17th through 94th Congresses; 97th through 103rd Congresses; 110th Congress–Present (See also the following standing committee: International Relations)

Charles Coles Diggs, Jr.	1959–1975	86th–93rd
Robert Nelson Cornelius Nix, Sr.	1961–1977	87th–94th
Ronald V. Dellums	1971–1973	92nd
Cardiss Collins	1975–1977	94th
George William Crockett, Jr.	1981–1991	97th–101st
Mervyn Malcolm Dymally	1981–1993	97th–102nd
Donald Milford Payne	1989–1995	101st–103rd
	2007–	110th
Alcee Lamar Hastings	1993–1995	103rd
Cynthia Ann McKinney	1993–1995	103rd
Albert Russell Wynn	1993–1995	103rd
Sheila Jackson Lee	2007–	110th
Gregory W. Meeks	2007–	110th
David Scott	2007–	110th
Diane Edith Watson	2007–	110th

FREEDMEN'S AFFAIRS [1866–1875]
39th through 43rd Congresses (Jurisdiction reassigned to the following standing committee: Judiciary)

Joseph Hayne Rainey	1870–1873	41st–42nd

GOVERNMENT OPERATIONS [1953–1995]
83rd through 103rd Congresses (See also the following standing committees: Expenditures in the Executive Departments; Government Reform and Oversight; Government Reform; Oversight and Government Reform)

William Levi Dawson	1953–1970	83rd–91st
George Washington Collins	1970–1972	91st–92nd
John Conyers, Jr.	1971–1995	92nd–103rd
Cardiss Collins	1973–1995	93rd–103rd
Barbara Charline Jordan	1975–1979	94th–95th
Harold Washington	1981–1983	97th
Major Robert Odell Owens	1983–1995	98th–103rd
Edolphus Towns	1983–1995	98th–103rd
Donald Milford Payne	1989–1995	101st–103rd
Corrine Brown	1993–1995	103rd
Barbara-Rose Collins	1993–1995	103rd
Floyd Harold Flake	1993–1995	103rd
Bobby L. Rush	1993–1995	103rd
Craig Anthony Washington	1993–1995	103rd

GOVERNMENT REFORM [2001–2007]
106th through 109th Congresses (See also the following standing committees: Expenditures in the Executive Departments; Government Reform and Oversight; Oversight and Government Reform)

Elijah Eugene Cummings	1999–2007	106th–109th
Danny K. Davis	1999–2007	106th–109th
Chaka Fattah	1999–2001	106th
Harold Eugene Ford, Jr.	1999–2001	106th
Major Robert Odell Owens	1999–2007	106th–109th
Edolphus Towns	1999–2007	106th–109th
William Lacy Clay, Jr.	2001–2007	107th–109th
Eleanor Holmes Norton	1999–2007	106th–109th
Diane Edith Watson	2001–2007	107th–109th

GOVERNMENT REFORM AND OVERSIGHT [1995–1999]
104th and 105th Congresses (See also the following standing committees: Expenditures in the Executive Departments; Government Reform; Oversight and Government Reform)

Barbara-Rose Collins	1995–1997	104th
Cardiss Collins	1995–1997	104th
Chaka Fattah	1995–1999	104th–105th
Carrie P. Meek	1995–1997	104th
Eleanor Holmes Norton	1995–1999	104th–105th
Major Robert Odell Owens	1995–1999	104th–105th
Edolphus Towns	1995–1999	104th–105th
Elijah Eugene Cummings	1996–1999	104th–105th
Danny K. Davis	1997–1999	105th
Harold Eugene Ford, Jr.	1997–1999	105th

HOUSE ADMINISTRATION [1947–1995; 1999–Present]
80th through 103rd Congresses; 106th Congress–Present (See also the following standing committee: House Oversight)

Augustus Freeman (Gus) Hawkins	1969–1985	91st–98th
William Lacy Clay, Sr.	1985–1995	99th–103rd
William Herbert Gray III	1991	102nd
Chaka Fattah	1999–2003	106th–107th
Juanita Millender-McDonald	2003–2007	108th–110th
Artur Davis	2007–	110th

HOUSE OVERSIGHT [1995–1999]
104th and 105th Congresses (See also the following standing committee: House Administration)

William Jennings Jefferson	1995–1997	104th

HOMELAND SECURITY [2005–Present]
109th Congress–Present

Donna Christensen	2005–	109th–110th
Sheila Jackson Lee	2005–	109th–110th
Eleanor Holmes Norton	2005–	109th–110th
Kendrick B. Meek	2005–2007	109th
Bennie Thompson	2005–	109th–110th
Yvette Diane Clarke	2007–	110th
Al Green	2007–	110th

INDIAN AFFAIRS [1821–1947]
17th through 79th Congresses (Jurisdiction reassigned to the following standing committee: Public Lands, which later became Interior and Insular Affairs)

Joseph Hayne Rainey	1873–1875	43rd
Oscar Stanton De Priest	1929–1935	71st–73rd
Adam Clayton Powell, Jr.	1945–1947	79th

INSULAR AFFAIRS [1899–1947]
56th through 79th Congresses (Jurisdiction reassigned to the following standing committee: Public Lands, which later became Interior and Insular Affairs)

William Levi Dawson	1943–1947	78th–79th

INTERIOR AND INSULAR AFFAIRS [1951–1993]*
82nd through 102nd Congresses (See also the following standing committees: Natural Resources; Resources)

William Levi Dawson	1951–1953	82nd
Charles Coles Diggs, Jr.	1955–1959	84th–85th
Adam Clayton Powell, Jr.	1955–1961	84th–86th
Yvonne Brathwaite Burke	1973–1975	93rd
Melvin Herbert Evans	1979–1981	96th
John R. Lewis	1987–1993	100th–102nd

INTERNAL SECURITY [1969–1975]
91st through 93rd Congresses (Jurisdiction reassigned to the following standing committee: Judiciary)

Louis Stokes	1969–1971	91st

INTERNATIONAL RELATIONS [1977–1981; 1995–2007]
95th and 96th Congresses; 104th through 109th Congresses (See also the following standing committee: Foreign Affairs)

Cardiss Collins	1977–1981	95th–96th
Charles Coles Diggs, Jr.	1977–1980	95th–96th
Robert Nelson Cornelius Nix, Sr.	1977–1979	95th
William Herbert Gray III	1979–1981	96th
George William Crockett, Jr.	1980–1981	96th
Victor O. Frazer	1995–1997	104th
Alcee Lamar Hastings	1995–2001	104th–106th
Cynthia Ann McKinney	1995–2003	104th–107th
Donald Milford Payne	1995–2007	104th–109th
Albert Russell Wynn	1995–1997	104th
Earl Frederick Hilliard	1997–2003	105th–107th
Barbara Lee	1999–2007	106th–109th
Gregory W. Meeks	1999–2007	106th–109th
Diane Edith Watson	2001–2007	107th–109th

INTERSTATE AND FOREIGN COMMERCE [1893–1981]
53rd through 96th Congresses (See also the following standing committees: Energy and Commerce; Commerce)

Ralph Harold Metcalfe	1971–1979	92nd–95th
George Thomas (Mickey) Leland	1979–1981	96th

INVALID PENSIONS [1831–1947]
21st through 79th Congresses (Jurisdiction reassigned to the following standing committees: Judiciary; Veterans' Affairs)

Benjamin Sterling Turner	1871–1873	42nd
Joseph Hayne Rainey	1875–1879	44th–45th
James Edward O'Hara	1885–1887	49th
Oscar Stanton De Priest	1929–1935	71st–73rd
William Levi Dawson	1943–1947	78th–79th
Adam Clayton Powell, Jr.	1945–1947	79th

IRRIGATION AND RECLAMATION [1925–1947]
69th through 79th Congresses (Jurisdiction reassigned to the following standing committee: Public Lands, which later became Interior and Insular Affairs)

William Levi Dawson	1943–1947	78th–79th

JUDICIARY [1813–Present]
13th Congress–Present

John Conyers, Jr.	1965–	89th–110th
Charles B. Rangel	1972–1975	92nd–93rd
Barbara Charline Jordan	1973–1979	93rd–95th
George William Crockett, Jr.	1982–1991	97th–101st
Harold Washington	1981–1983	97th–98th
Craig Anthony Washington	1990–1995	101st–103rd
Robert Cortez Scott	1993–	103rd–110th
Melvin L. Watt	1993–	103rd–110th
Sheila Jackson Lee	1995–	104th–110th
Maxine Waters	1997–	105th–110th
Artur Davis	2007–	110th
Keith Ellison	2007–	110th
Hank Johnson	2007–	110th

LABOR [1883–1947]
48th through 79th Congresses (See also the following standing committees: Education and Labor; Education and the Workforce)

Thomas Ezekiel Miller	1890–1891	51st
Adam Clayton Powell, Jr.	1945–1947	79th

MANUFACTURES [1819–1911]
16th through 61st Congresses

Robert Carlos De Large	1871–1873	42nd
Alonzo Jacob Ransier	1873–1875	43rd
John Adams Hyman	1875–1877	44th
Robert Smalls	1884–1885	48th

MERCHANT MARINE AND FISHERIES [1947–1995]
80th through 103rd Congresses (Jurisdiction reassigned to the following standing committees: National Security; Resources; Science; Transportation and Infrastructure)

Robert Nelson Cornelius Nix, Sr.	1958–1961	85th–86th
Ralph Harold Metcalfe	1972–1978	92nd–95th
Melvin Herbert Evans	1979–1981	96th
Lucien Edward Blackwell	1992–1993	102nd
William Jennings Jefferson	1991–1993	102nd

* In the 82nd Congress (1951–1953), the committee changed names from Public Lands to Interior and Insular Affairs on February 2, 1951.

MERCHANT MARINE AND FISHERIES *Continued*

Alcee Lamar Hastings	1993–1995	103rd
Bennie Thompson	1993–1995	103rd

MILITIA [1815–1835]

14th through 23rd Congresses (Jurisdiction reassigned to the following standing committee: Military Affairs, which later became Armed Services)

Josiah Thomas Walls	1871–1875	42nd–43rd
Robert Brown Elliott	1873–1874	43rd
Robert Smalls	1877–1879	45th
	1882–1883	47th
	1884–1885	48th
John Roy Lynch	1882–1883	47th

MILEAGE [1837–1927]

25th through 69th Congresses (Jurisdiction reassigned to the following standing committee: Accounts, which later became House Administration)

Josiah Thomas Walls	1875–1876	44th

MINES AND MINING [1865–1947]

39th through 79th Congresses (Jurisdiction reassigned to the following standing committee: Public Lands, which later became Interior and Insular Affairs)

John Roy Lynch	1873–1877	43rd–44th
James Edward O'Hara	1883–1885	48th

NATIONAL SECURITY [1995–1999]

104th through 105th Congresses (See also the following standing committee: Armed Services)

Ronald V. Dellums	1995–1998	104th–105th
William Jennings Jefferson	1995–1997	104th
Julius Caesar (J. C.) Watts, Jr.	1995–1999	104th–105th
Cynthia Ann McKinney	1997–1999	105th

NATURAL RESOURCES [1993–1995; 2007–Present]

103rd and 104th Congresses; 110th Congress–Present (See also the following standing committees: Interior and Insular Affairs; Resources)

Donna Christensen	2007–	110th

OVERSIGHT AND GOVERNMENT REFORM [2007–Present]

110th Congress–Present (See also the following standing committees: Expenditures in the Executive Departments; Government Operations; Government Reform and Oversight; Government Reform)

William Lacy Clay, Jr.	2007–	110th
Elijah Eugene Cummings	2007–	110th
Danny K. Davis	2007–	110th
Eleanor Holmes Norton	2007–	110th
Edolphus Towns	2007–	110th
Diane Edith Watson	2007–	110th

POST OFFICE AND CIVIL SERVICE [1947–1995]

80th through 103rd Congresses (See also the following standing committee: Post Office and Post Roads. Jurisdiction reassigned to the following standing committees: Government Reform and Oversight; House Oversight)

Robert Nelson Cornelius Nix, Sr.	1963–1979	88th–95th
William Lacy Clay, Sr.	1973–1995	93rd–103rd
Ralph Harold Metcalfe	1977–1978	95th
George Thomas (Mickey) Leland	1979–1989	96th–101st
Ronald V. Dellums	1981–1985	97th–98th
Gus Savage	1981–1983	97th
Mervyn Malcolm Dymally	1984–1993	98th–102nd
Katie Beatrice Hall	1983–1985	98th
Charles Arthur Hayes	1989–1993	101st–102nd
Barbara-Rose Collins	1991–1995	102nd–103rd
Eleanor Holmes Norton	1991–1995	102nd–103rd
Sanford Dixon Bishop, Jr.	1993–1995	103rd
Alcee Lamar Hastings	1993–1995	103rd
Melvin L. Watt	1993–1995	103rd
Albert Russell Wynn	1993–1995	103rd

POST OFFICE AND POST ROADS [1808–1947]

10th through 79th Congresses (See also the following standing committee: Post Office and Civil Service)

Oscar Stanton De Priest	1933–1935	73rd
Arthur Wergs Mitchell	1935–1943	74th–77th

PRIVATE LAND CLAIMS [1816–1911]

14th through 61st Congresses

Richard Harvey Cain	1877–1879	45th

PUBLIC WORKS [1947–1975]

80th through 93rd Congresses (See also the following standing committees: Public Works and Transportation; Transportation and Infrastructure)

George Washington Collins	1971–1972	92nd
Charles B. Rangel	1971–1973	92nd
Yvonne Brathwaite Burke	1973–1975	93rd
Cardiss Collins	1974–1975	93rd

PUBLIC WORKS AND TRANSPORTATION [1975–1995]

94th through 103rd Congresses (See also the following standing committees: Public Works; Transportation and Infrastructure)

Gus Savage	1981–1993	97th–102nd
Katie Beatrice Hall	1983–1985	98th
Edolphus Towns	1983–1997	98th–104th
John R. Lewis	1987–1993	100th–102nd
Lucien Edward Blackwell	1991–1995	102nd–103rd
Barbara-Rose Collins	1991–1995	102nd–103rd
Eleanor Holmes Norton	1991–1995	102nd–103rd
Corrine Brown	1993–1995	103rd
James Enos Clyburn	1993–1995	103rd
Walter R. Tucker III	1993–1995	103rd
Eddie Bernice Johnson	1993–1995	103rd

PUBLIC EXPENDITURES [1814–1880; 1881–1883]
13th through 46th Congresses; 47th Congress

Jeremiah Haralson	1875–1877	44th

RESOURCES [1995–2007]
105th through 109th Congresses (See also the following standing committees: Interior and Insular Affairs; Natural Resources)

Donna Christensen	1997–2007	105th–109th

RULES [1849–Present]
31st Congress–Present

Andrew Jackson Young, Jr.	1975–1977	94th
Shirley Anita Chisholm	1977–1983	95th–97th
Alan Dupree Wheat	1983–1995	98th–103rd
Alcee Lamar Hastings	2001–	107th–110th

SCIENCE [1995–2007]
104th through 109th Congresses (See also the following standing committees: Science and Astronautics; Science, Space, and Technology; Science and Technology)

Alcee Lamar Hastings	1995–2001	104th–106th
Sheila Jackson Lee	1995–2007	104th–109th
Eddie Bernice Johnson	1995–2007	104th–109th
Barbara Lee	1998–1999	105th
Al Green	2005–2007	109th

SCIENCE AND ASTRONAUTICS [1959–1975]
86th through 93rd Congresses (See also the following standing committees: Science and Technology; Science, Space, and Technology; Science)

Charles B. Rangel	1971–1973	92nd

SCIENCE AND TECHNOLOGY [1975–1987; 2007–Present]
94th through 99th Congresses; 110th Congress–Present (See also the following standing committees: Science and Astronautics; Science, Space, and Technology; Science)

Mervyn Malcolm Dymally	1981–1985	97th–98th
Eddie Bernice Johnson	2007–	110th
Laura Richardson	2007–	110th

SCIENCE, SPACE, AND TECHNOLOGY [1987–1995]
100th through 103rd Congresses (See also the following standing committees: Science and Astronautics; Science and Technology; Science)

Eddie Bernice Johnson	1993–1995	103rd
Bobby L. Rush	1993–1995	103rd
Robert Cortez Scott	1993–1995	103rd

SMALL BUSINESS [1975–Present]
94th Congress–Present

Parren James Mitchell	1975	94th
	1979–1987	96th–99th
George William Crockett, Jr.	1981–1983	97th
Gus Savage	1981–1993	97th–102nd
Charles Arthur Hayes	1983–1991	98th–101st
Alton R. Waldon, Jr.	1985–1987	99th

SMALL BUSINESS *Continued*

John Conyers, Jr.	1987–1995	100th–103rd
Kweisi Mfume	1987–1996	100th–104th
Floyd Harold Flake	1987–1997	100th–105th
Gary A. Franks	1991–1993	102nd
Eva M. Clayton	1993–1997	103rd–104th
Cleo Fields	1993–1997	103rd–104th
Earl Frederick Hilliard	1993–1997	103rd–104th
Bennie Thompson	1993–1997	103rd–104th
Walter R. Tucker III	1993–1995	103rd–104th
Maxine Waters	1993–1996	103rd–104th
James Enos Clyburn	1995–1997	104th
Chaka Fattah	1995–1997	104th
Eleanor Holmes Norton	1995–1997	104th
Juanita Millender-McDonald	1996–2007	104th–109th
Danny K. Davis	1997–2007	105th–109th
Jesse L. Jackson, Jr.	1997–1999	105th
Donna Christensen	1999–2007	106th–109th
Stephanie Tubbs Jones	1999–2003	106th–107th
Frank W. Ballance, Jr.	2003–2004	108th
George Kenneth (G. K.) Butterfield, Jr.	2004–2005	108th
Denise L. Majette	2003–2005	108th
Gwendolynne S. (Gwen) Moore	2005–	109th–110th
Yvette Diane Clarke	2007–	110th
William Jennings Jefferson	2007	110th
Hank Johnson	2007–	110th

STANDARDS OF OFFICIAL CONDUCT [1967–Present]
90th Congress–Present

Louis Stokes	1979–1985	96th–98th
	1991–1993	102nd
Julian Carey Dixon	1983–1991	98th–101st
Kweisi Mfume	1993–1995	103rd
Chaka Fattah	1997–2001	105th–106th
Stephanie Tubbs Jones	2001–	107th–110th

TRANSPORTATION AND INFRASTRUCTURE [1995–Present]
104th Congress–Present (See also the following standing committees: Public Works; Public Works and Transportation)

Corrine Brown	1995–	104th–110th
Barbara-Rose Collins	1995–1997	104th
James Enos Clyburn	1995–1999	104th–105th
Eddie Bernice Johnson	1995–	104th–110th
Eleanor Holmes Norton	1995–	104th–110th
Walter R. Tucker III	1995	104th
Juanita Millender-McDonald	1996–2007	104th–110th
Elijah Eugene Cummings	1996–	104th–110th
Julius Caesar (J. C.) Watts, Jr.	1997–2001	105th–106th
Julia May Carson	2003–2007	108th–110th
Laura Richardson	2007–	110th

VETERANS' AFFAIRS [1947–Present]
80th Congress–Present

Charles Coles Diggs, Jr.	1955–1959	84th–85th
Robert Nelson Cornelius Nix, Sr.	1958–1961	85th–86th
Shirley Anita Chisholm	1969–1973	91st–92nd
Harold Eugene Ford, Sr.	1975	94th
Maxine Waters	1991–1997	102nd–104th
Corrine Brown	1993–	103rd–110th
Sanford Dixon Bishop, Jr.	1993–1997	103rd–104th
James Enos Clyburn	1993–1999	103rd–105th
Julia May Carson	1997–2003	105th–107th

WAR CLAIMS [1873–1947]
43rd through 79th Congresses (Jurisdiction reassigned to the following standing committee: Judiciary)

Robert Smalls	1885–1887	49th

WAYS AND MEANS [1795–Present]
4th Congress–Present

Charles B. Rangel	1975–	94th–110th
Harold Eugene Ford, Sr.	1975–1997	94th–104th
William Jennings Jefferson	1993–1995	103rd
	1997–2006	105th–109th
John R. Lewis	1993–	103rd–110th
Mel Reynolds	1993–1995	103rd
Stephanie Tubbs Jones	2003–	108th–110th
Artur Davis	2007–	110th
Kendrick B. Meek	2007–	110th

REPRESENTATIVES WHO SERVED FULL OR PARTIAL TERMS WITHOUT COMMITTEE ASSIGNMENTS

Jefferson Franklin Long	1870–1871	41st Congress

SELECT AGING [1975–1993]
94th Congress through 102nd Congresses

Harold Eugene Ford, Sr.	1975–1993	94th–102nd
George William Crockett, Jr.	1981–1991	97th–101st
John R. Lewis	1989–1993	101st–102nd
Gary A. Franks	1991–1993	102nd

SELECT COMMITTEE ON ASSASSINATIONS [1976–1979]
94th and 95th Congresses

Yvonne Brathwaite Burke	1976–1979	94th–95th
Walter Edward Fauntroy	1976–1979	94th–95th
Harold Eugene Ford, Sr.	1976–1979	94th–95th
Louis Stokes	1976–1979	94th–95th

SELECT COMMITTEE ON CENTENNIAL CELEBRATION AND THE PROPOSED NATIONAL CENSUS OF 1875 [1875–1877]
44th Congress

Joseph Hayne Rainey	1875–1877	44th

SELECT COMMITTEE ON CHILDREN, YOUTH, AND FAMILIES [1983–1993]
98th through 102nd Congresses

George Thomas (Mickey) Leland	1983–1985	98th
Alan Dupree Wheat	1983–1993	98th–102nd
Floyd Harold Flake	1987–1989	100th
Barbara-Rose Collins	1991–1993	102nd

SELECT COMMITTEE ON ENERGY INDEPENDENCE AND GLOBAL WARMING [2007–Present]
110th Congress–Present

Emanuel Cleaver II	2007–	110th

SELECT COMMITTEE ON COMMITTEES II [1979–1980]
96th Congress

William Lacy Clay, Sr.	1979–1980	96th

SELECT COMMITTEE ON CRIME [1969–1973]
91st through 93rd Congresses

Robert Nelson Cornelius Nix, Sr.	1969–1971	91st
Charles B. Rangel	1971–1973	92nd–93rd

SELECT COMMITTEE ON HOMELAND SECURITY [2002–2005]
107th and 108th Congresses (Jurisdiction reassigned to the following standing committee: Homeland Security)

Donna Christensen	2003–2005	108th
Kendrick B. Meek	2003–2005	108th
Eleanor Holmes Norton	2003–2005	108th
Bennie Thompson	2003–2005	108th

SELECT COMMITTEE ON THE HOUSE BEAUTY SHOP [1967–1977]
90th through 94th Congresses (Jurisdiction reassigned to the following standing committee: House Administration)

Yvonne Brathwaite Burke	1975–1977	94th

SELECT COMMITTEE ON HUNGER [1984–1993]
98th through 102nd Congresses

George Thomas (Mickey) Leland	1984–1989	98th–101st
Floyd Harold Flake	1987–1993	100th–102nd
Kweisi Mfume	1987–1989	100th
Michael Alphonso (Mike) Espy	1989–1993	101st–102nd
Alan Dupree Wheat	1990–1993	101st–102nd

SELECT COMMITTEE ON INTELLIGENCE [1975–1976]
94th Congress (Jurisdiction reassigned to the following select committee: Permanent Select Committee on Intelligence)

Ronald V. Dellums	1975–1976	94th

PERMANENT SELECT COMMITTEE ON INTELLIGENCE [1977–Present]
95th Congress–Present

Ronald V. Dellums	1991–1993	102nd
Louis Stokes	1983–1989	98th–100rh
Julian Carey Dixon	1993–2000	103rd–106th
Alcee Lamar Hastings	1999–2007	106th–110th
Sanford Dixon Bishop, Jr.	1997–2003	105th–107th

SELECT COMMITTEE TO INVESTIGATE COVERT ARMS TRANSACTIONS WITH IRAN [1987]
100th Congress

Louis Stokes	1987	100th

SELECT COMMITTEE TO INVESTIGATE THE VOTING IRREGULARITIES OF AUGUST 2, 2007 [2007–Present]
110th Congress–Present

Artur Davis	2007–	110th–

SELECT COMMITTEE ON NARCOTICS ABUSE AND CONTROL [1976–1993]
94th through 102nd Congresses

Charles B. Rangel	1975–1993	94th–102nd
Cardiss Collins	1979–1993	96th–102nd
Walter Edward Fauntroy	1983–1991	98th–101st

SELECT COMMITTEE ON NARCOTICS ABUSE AND CONTROL *Continued*

Edolphus Towns	1983–1993	98th–102nd
Kweisi Mfume	1989–1993	101st–102nd
Craig Anthony Washington	1991–1993	102nd
Donald Milford Payne	1991–1993	102nd

SELECT SMALL BUSINESS [1947–1975]
80th through 93rd Congresses (Jurisdiction reassigned to the following standing committee: Small Business)

Parren James Mitchell	1971–1975	92nd–93rd

SELECT COMMITTEE ON STANDARDS OF OFFICIAL CONDUCT [1966]
89th Congress (Jurisdiction transferred to the following standing committee: Standards of Official Conduct)

Robert Nelson Cornelius Nix, Sr.	1966	89th

SELECT COMMITTEE ON U.S. NATIONAL SECURITY AND MILITARY/COMMERCIAL CONCERNS WITH CHINA [1998–1999]
105th and 106th Congresses

Robert Cortez Scott	1998–1999	105th–106th

JOINT COMMITTEE ON BICENTENNIAL ARRANGEMENTS [1975–1976]
94th Congress

Edward William Brooke III, Sen.	1975–1976	94th

JOINT COMMITTEE ON DEFENSE PRODUCTION [1950–1977]
81st through 95th Congresses

Edward William Brooke III, Sen.	1975–1977	94th–95th
Parren James Mitchell, Rep.	1975–1977	94th–95th

JOINT COMMITTEE ON DEFICIT REDUCTION [1987]
100th Congress

Michael Alphonso (Mike) Espy, Rep.	1987	100th
William Herbert Gray III, Rep.	1987	100th

JOINT ECONOMIC COMMITTEE [1957–Present]
85th Congress–Present

Parren James Mitchell, Rep.	1977–1987	95th–99th
Augustus Freeman (Gus) Hawkins, Rep.	1981–1991	97th–101st
Kweisi Mfume, Rep.	1991–1996	102nd–104th
Melvin L. Watt, Rep.	2001–2005	107th–108th

JOINT COMMITTEE ON THE LIBRARY [1947–Present]
80th Congress–Present

Augustus Freeman (Gus) Hawkins, Rep.	1981–1985	97th–98th
William Lacy Clay, Sr., Rep.	1989–1991	101st
Carolyn Cheeks Kilpatrick, Rep.	1997–1999	105th
Juanita Millender-McDonald, Rep.	2003–2007	108th–110th

JOINT COMMITTEE ON THE ORGANIZATION OF CONGRESS [1992–1993]
102nd and 103rd Congresses

Eleanor Holmes Norton, Del.	1992–1993	102nd–103rd

JOINT COMMITTEE ON PRINTING [1947–Present]
80th Congress–Present

Augustus Freeman (Gus) Hawkins, Rep.	1977–1985	95th–98th
William Jennings Jefferson, Rep.	1995–1997	104th
Chaka Fattah, Rep.	1999–2003	106th–107th
Juanita Millender-McDonald, Rep.	2005–2007	109th–110th

JOINT COMMITTEE ON TAXATION [1977–Present]
94th Congress–Present

Charles B. Rangel, Rep.	1995–1999	104th–105th
	2003–2005	108th

AERONAUTICAL AND SPACE SCIENCES [1958–1977]
85th through 94th Congresses

Edward William Brooke III	1967–1969	90th

APPROPRIATIONS [1867–Present]
40th Congress–Present

Edward William Brooke III	1971–1979	92nd–95th

ARMED SERVICES [1947–Present]
80th Congress–Present

Edward William Brooke III	1969–1971	91st

BANKING AND CURRENCY [1913–1971]
63rd through 90th Congresses (See also the following standing committee: Banking, Housing, and Urban Affairs)

Edward William Brooke III	1967–1971	90th–91st

BANKING, HOUSING, AND URBAN AFFAIRS [1971–Present]
92nd Congress–Present (See also the following standing committee: Banking and Currency)

Edward William Brooke III	1971–1979	92nd–95th
Carol Moseley-Braun	1993–1999	103rd–105th

DISTRICT OF COLUMBIA [1816–1977]
14th through 94th Congresses

Hiram Rhodes Revels	1870–1871	41st

EDUCATION AND LABOR [1869–1947]
41st through 79th Congresses (Jurisdiction reassigned to the following committee: Labor and Public Welfare, which later became Health, Education, Labor, and Pensions)

Hiram Rhodes Revels	1870–1871	41st
Blanche K. Bruce	1875–1881	44th–46th

ENVIRONMENT AND PUBLIC WORKS [1977–Present]
95th Congress–Present

Barack Obama	2005–	109th–110th

FINANCE [1947–Present]
80th Congress–Present

Carol Moseley-Braun	1995–1999	104th–105th

FOREIGN RELATIONS [1947–Present]
80th Congress–Present

Barack Obama	2005–	109th–110th

GOVERNMENT OPERATIONS [1953–1993]
83rd through 102nd Congresses

Edward William Brooke III	1968–1969	90th

HEALTH, EDUCATION, LABOR, AND PENSIONS [1999–Present]
106th Congress–Present

Barack Obama	2007–	110th

HOMELAND SECURITY AND GOVERNMENTAL AFFAIRS [2005–Present]
109th Congress–Present

Barack Obama	2007–	110th

IMPROVEMENT OF THE MISSISSIPPI RIVER AND ITS TRIBUTARIES [1879–1921]
46th through 66th Congresses (See also the following select committee: Levees of the Mississippi River)

Blanche K. Bruce	1879–1881	46th

VETERANS' AFFAIRS [1971–Present]
92nd Congress–Present

Barack Obama	2005–	109th–110th

SELECT EQUAL EDUCATION OPPORTUNITY [1970–1972]
91st and 92nd Congresses

Edward William Brooke III	1970–1972	91st–92nd

SELECT COMMITTEE ON LEVEES OF THE MISSISSIPPI RIVER [1877–1879]
45th Congress, 1st, 2nd, and 3rd Sessions (See also the following standing committee: Improvement of the Mississippi River and Its Tributaries)

Blanche K. Bruce	1877–1879	45th

SELECT STANDARDS AND CONDUCT [1965–1977]
88th through 94th Congresses

Edward William Brooke III	1973–1977	93rd–94th

SPECIAL COMMITTEE ON AGING [1961–Present]
87th Congress–Present

Edward William Brooke III	1971–1979	92nd–95th
Carol Moseley-Braun	1995–1999	104th–105th

SELECT COMMITTEE TO INVESTIGATE THE FREEDMEN'S SAVINGS AND TRUST COMPANY [1879–1881]
46th Congress, 1st, 2nd, and 3rd Sessions

Blanche K. Bruce	1879–1881	46th

Sources: Mildred L. Amer, "Black Members of the United States Congress: 1870–2007," 27 September 2007, Report RL30378, Congressional Research Service, Library of Congress, Washington, DC; David T. Canon et al., *Committees in the U.S. Congress, 1789 to 1946*, 4 volumes (Washington, DC: Congressional Quarterly Press, 2002); various editions of the *Congressional Directory* (Washington, DC: Government Printing Office); various editions of the *Congressional Quarterly Almanac* (Washington, DC: Congressional Quarterly Inc.); various editions of the *Congressional Record*; Robert W. Coren et al., *Guide to the Records of the United Senate at the National Archives, 1789–1989: Bicentennial Edition* (Washington, DC: Government Printing Office, 1989); Garrison Nelson, *Committees in the U.S. Congress, 1947 to 1992*, 2 volumes (Washington, DC: Congressional Quarterly Press, 1994); Charles E. Schamel et al., *Guide to the Records of the United States House of Representatives at the National Archives, 1789–1989: Bicentennial Edition* (Washington, DC: Government Printing Office, 1989); U.S. House of Representatives, Committee on the Judiciary, *A History of the Committee on the Judiciary, 1813–2006* (Washington, DC: Government Printing Office, 2006).

Black Americans Who Have Chaired Congressional Committees, 1877–2007

CONGRESS/YEAR	MEMBER'S NAME, PARTY, STATE	HOUSE COMMITTEE
110th (2007–2009)	John Conyers, Jr. (D-MI)	Judiciary
	Stephanie Tubbs Jones (D-OH)	Standards of Official Conduct
	Juanita Millender-McDonald (D-CA)*	House Administration
	Charles B. Rangel (D-NY)	Ways and Means
	Bennie Thompson (D-MS)	Homeland Security
109th (2005–2007)	N/A	N/A
108th (2003–2005)	N/A	N/A
107th (2001–2003)	N/A	N/A
106th (1999–2001)	N/A	N/A
105th (1997–1999)	N/A	N/A
104th (1995–1997)	N/A	N/A
103rd (1993–1995)	William Lacy Clay, Sr. (D-MO)	Post Office and Civil Service
	John Conyers, Jr. (D-MI)	Government Operations
	Ronald V. Dellums (D-CA)	Armed Services
102nd (1991–1993)	William Lacy Clay, Sr. (D-MO)	Post Office and Civil Service
	John Conyers, Jr. (D-MI)	Government Operations
	Ronald V. Dellums (D-CA)	District of Columbia
	Charles B. Rangel (D-NY)	Select Narcotics Abuse and Control
	Louis Stokes (D-OH)	Standards of Official Conduct
101st (1989–1991)	John Conyers, Jr. (D-MI)	Government Operations
	Ronald V. Dellums (D-CA)	District of Columbia
	Julian Carey Dixon (D-CA)	Standards of Official Conduct
	Augustus Freeman (Gus) Hawkins (D-CA)	Education and Labor
	George Thomas (Mickey) Leland (D-TX)	Select Hunger
	Charles B. Rangel (D-NY)	Select Narcotics Abuse and Control
100th (1987–1989)	Ronald V. Dellums (D-CA)	District of Columbia
	Julian Carey Dixon (D-CA)	Standards of Official Conduct
	William Herbert Gray III (D-PA)	Budget
	Augustus Freeman (Gus) Hawkins (D-CA)	Education and Labor
	George Thomas (Mickey) Leland (D-TX)	Select Hunger
	Louis Stokes (D-OH)	Intelligence (Permanent Select)
	Charles B. Rangel (D-NY)	Select Narcotics Abuse and Control
99th (1985–1987)	Ronald V. Dellums (D-CA)	District of Columbia
	Julian Carey Dixon (D-CA)	Standards of Official Conduct
	William Herbert Gray III (D-PA)	Budget

* Juanita Millender-McDonald died on April 22, 2007.

CONGRESS/YEAR	MEMBER'S NAME, PARTY, STATE	HOUSE COMMITTEE
99th (1985–1987) Continued	Augustus Freeman (Gus) Hawkins (D-CA)	Education and Labor
	George Thomas (Mickey) Leland (D-TX)	Select Hunger
	Parren James Mitchell (D-MD)	Small Business
	Charles B. Rangel (D-NY)	Select Narcotics Abuse and Control
98th (1983–1985)	Ronald V. Dellums (D-CA)	District of Columbia
	Augustus Freeman (Gus) Hawkins (D-CA)	Education and Labor
		House Administration
		Jt. Committee on Printing
	George Thomas (Mickey) Leland (D-TX)	Select Hunger
	Parren James Mitchell (D-MD)	Small Business
	Charles B. Rangel (D-NY)	Select Narcotics Abuse and Control
	Louis Stokes (D-OH)	Standards of Official Conduct
97th (1981–1983)	Ronald V. Dellums (D-CA)	District of Columbia
	Augustus Freeman (Gus) Hawkins (D-CA)	House Administration
		Jt. Committee on the Library
	Louis Stokes (D-OH)	Standards of Official Conduct
	Parren James Mitchell (D-MD)	Small Business
96th (1979–1981)	Ronald V. Dellums (D-CA)	District of Columbia
	Augustus Freeman (Gus) Hawkins (D-CA)	Jt. Committee on Printing
95th (1977–1979)	Yvonne Brathwaite Burke (D-CA)	House Beauty Shop (Select)
	Charles Coles Diggs, Jr. (D-MI)	District of Columbia
	Robert Nelson Cornelius Nix, Sr. (D-PA)	Post Office and Civil Service
	Louis Stokes (D-OH)	Select Assassinations
94th (1975–1977)	Yvonne Brathwaite Burke (D-CA)	House Beauty Shop (Select)
	Charles Coles Diggs, Jr. (D-MI)	District of Columbia
93rd (1973–1975)	Charles Coles Diggs, Jr. (D-MI)	District of Columbia
91st (1969–1971)	William Levi Dawson (D-IL)	Government Operations
90th (1967–1969)	William Levi Dawson (D-IL)	Government Operations
89th (1965–1967)	William Levi Dawson (D-IL)	Government Operations
	Adam Clayton Powell, Jr. (D-NY)	Education and Labor
88th (1963–1965)	William Levi Dawson (D-IL)	Government Operations
	Adam Clayton Powell, Jr. (D-NY)	Education and Labor
87th (1961–1963)	William Levi Dawson (D-IL)	Government Operations
	Adam Clayton Powell, Jr. (D-NY)	Education and Labor
86th (1959–1961)	William Levi Dawson (D-IL)	Government Operations
85th (1957–1959)	William Levi Dawson (D-IL)	Government Operations
84th (1955–1957)	William Levi Dawson (D-IL)	Government Operations
82nd (1951–1953)	William Levi Dawson (D-IL)	Expenditures in the Executive Departments
81st (1949–1951)	William Levi Dawson (D-IL)	Expenditures in the Executive Departments

CONGRESS/YEAR	MEMBER'S NAME, PARTY, STATE	SENATE COMMITTEE
46th (1879–1881)	Blanche K. Bruce (R-MS)	Investigate the Freedmen's Savings and Trust Company (Select)
45th (1877–1879)	Blanche K. Bruce (R-MS)	Committee on the Mississippi River (Select)

Black-American Chairs of Subcommittees of Standing Committees in the U.S. House and Senate, 1885–2007

CONGRESS	MEMBER	COMMITTEE	SUBCOMMITTEE
110th (2007–2009)	Corrine Brown (D-FL)	Transportation and Infrastructure	Railroads, Pipelines, and Hazardous Materials
	Donna Christensen (D-VI)[a]	Natural Resources	Insular Affairs
	Elijah Eugene Cummings (D-MD)	Transportation and Infrastructure	Coast Guard and Maritime Transportation
	William Lacy Clay, Jr. (D-MO)	Oversight and Government Reform	Information Policy, Census, and National Archives
	Danny K. Davis (D-IL)	Oversight and Government Reform	Federal Workforce, Postal Service, and the District of Columbia
	Alcee Lamar Hastings (D-FL)	Rules	Legislative and Budget Process
	Sheila Jackson Lee (D-TX)	Homeland Security	Transportation Security and Infrastructure Protection
	Eddie Bernice Johnson (D-TX)	Transportation and Infrastructure	Water Resources and Environment
	John R. Lewis (D-GA)	Ways and Means	Oversight
	Eleanor Holmes Norton (D-DC)[a]	Transportation and Infrastructure	Economic Development, Public Bldgs & Emergency Management
	Barack Obama (D-IL)[b]	Foreign Relations	European Affairs
	Donald Milford Payne (D-NJ)	Foreign Affairs	Africa and Global Health
	Bobby L. Rush (D-IL)	Energy and Commerce	Commerce, Trade, and Consumer Protection
	Robert Cortez Scott (D-VA)	Judiciary	Crime, Terrorism, and Homeland Security
	Edolphus Towns (D-NY)	Oversight and Government Reform	Government Management, Organization, and Procurement
	Maxine Waters (D-CA)	Financial Services	Housing and Community Opportunity
	Melvin L. Watt (D-NC)	Financial Services	Oversight and Investigations
	Albert Russell Wynn (D-MD)	Energy and Commerce	Environment and Hazardous Materials
104th–109th (1995–2007)	No black Members chaired subcommittees	N/A	N/A
103rd (1993–1995)	William Lacy Clay, Sr. (D-MO)	House Administration	Libraries and Memorials
	William Lacy Clay, Sr. (D-MO)	Post Office and Civil Service	Oversight and Investigations
	Barbara-Rose Collins (D-MI)	Post Office and Civil Service	Postal Operations and Services
	Cardiss Collins (D-IL)	Energy and Commerce	Commerce, Consumer Protection, and Competitiveness
	John Conyers, Jr. (D-MI)	Government Operations	Legislation and National Security
	Ronald V. Dellums (D-CA)	Armed Services	Military Acquisition
	Julian Carey Dixon (D-CA)	Appropriations	District of Columbia
	Floyd Harold Flake (D-NY)	Banking, Finance and Urban Affairs	General Oversight, Investigations and the Resolution of Failed Financial Institutions
	Harold Eugene Ford, Jr. (D-TN)	Ways and Means	Human Resources
	Kweisi Mfume (D-MD)	Small Business	Minority Enterprise, Finance and Urban Development
	Eleanor Holmes Norton (D-DC)[a]	District of Columbia	Judiciary and Education
	Eleanor Holmes Norton (D-DC)[a]	Post Office and Civil Service	Compensation and Employee Benefits
	Major Robert Odell Owens (D-NY)	Education and Labor	Select Education and Civil Rights
	Charles B. Rangel (D-NY)	Ways and Means	Select Revenue Measures

CONGRESS	MEMBER	COMMITTEE	SUBCOMMITTEE
103rd (1993–1995) Continued	Louis Stokes (D-OH)	Appropriations	Veterans Affairs, Housing and Urban Development, and Independent Agencies
	Edolphus Towns (D-NY)	Government Operations	Human Resources and Intergovernmental Relations
	Alan Dupree Wheat (D-MO)	District of Columbia	Government Operations and Metropolitan Affairs
102nd (1991–1993)	William Lacy Clay, Sr. (D-MO)	House Administration	Libraries and Memorials
	William Lacy Clay, Sr. (D-MO)	Post Office and Civil Service	Investigations
	Cardiss Collins (D-IL)	Energy and Commerce	Commerce, Consumer Protection, and Competitiveness
	John Conyers, Jr. (D-MI)	Government Operations	Legislation and National Security
	Ronald V. Dellums (D-CA)	Armed Services	Research and Development
	Julian Carey Dixon (D-CA)	Appropriations	District of Columbia
	Mervyn Malcolm Dymally (D-CA)	District of Columbia	Judiciary and Education
	Mervyn Malcolm Dymally (D-CA)	Foreign Affairs	Africa
	Michael Alphonso (Mike) Espy (D-MS)	Budget	Community Development and Natural Resources
	Harold Eugene Ford, Sr. (D-TN)	Ways and Means	Human Resources
	Major Robert Odell Owens (D-NY)	Education and Labor	Select Education
	Charles B. Rangel (D-NY)	Ways and Means	Select Revenue Measures
	Gus Savage (D-IL)	Public Works and Transportation	Public Buildings and Grounds
	Alan Dupree Wheat (D-MO)	District of Columbia	Government Operations and Metropolitan Affairs
101st (1989–1991)	William Lacy Clay, Sr. (D-MO)	Education and Labor	Labor-Management Relations
	William Lacy Clay, Sr. (D-MO)	House Administration	Libraries and Memorials
	Cardiss Collins (D-IL)	Government Operations	Government Activities and Transportation
	John Conyers, Jr. (D-MI)	Government Operations	Legislation and National Security
	George William Crockett, Jr. (D-MI)	Foreign Affairs	Western Hemisphere Affairs
	Ronald V. Dellums (D-CA)	Armed Services	Research and Development
	Julian Carey Dixon (D-CA)	Appropriations	District of Columbia
	Mervyn Malcolm Dymally (D-CA)	District of Columbia	Judiciary and Education
	Mervyn Malcolm Dymally (D-CA)	Foreign Affairs	International Operations
	Michael Alphonso (Mike) Espy (D-MS)	Hunger (Select)	Domestic
	Walter Edward Fauntroy (D-DC)[a]	Banking, Finance, Urban Affairs	International Development, Finance Trade and Monetary Policy
	Walter Edward Fauntroy (D-DC)[a]	District of Columbia	Fiscal Affairs and Health
	Harold Eugene Ford, Sr. (D-TN)	Ways and Means	Human Resources
	Augustus Freeman (Gus) Hawkins (D-CA)	Education and Labor	Elementary, Secondary and Vocational
	George Thomas (Mickey) Leland (D-TX)	Post Office and Civil Service	Postal Operations and Services
	Major Robert Odell Owens (D-NY)	Education and Labor	Select Education
	Charles B. Rangel (D-NY)	Ways and Means	Select Revenue Measures
	Gus Savage (D-IL)	Public Works and Transportation	Economic Development
	Alan Dupree Wheat (D-MO)	District of Columbia	Government Operations and Metropolitan Affairs
100th (1987–1989)	William Lacy Clay, Sr. (D-MO)	Education and Labor	Labor-Management Relations
	Cardiss Collins (D-IL)	Government Operations	Government Activities and Transportation
	John Conyers, Jr. (D-MI)	Judiciary	Criminal Justice
	George William Crockett, Jr. (D-MI)	Foreign Affairs	Western Hemisphere Affairs
	Ronald V. Dellums (D-CA)	Armed Services	Military Installations and Facilities
	Julian Carey Dixon (D-CA)	Appropriations	District of Columbia
	Mervyn Malcolm Dymally (D-CA)	District of Columbia	Judiciary and Education

CONGRESS	MEMBER	COMMITTEE	SUBCOMMITTEE
100th (1987–1989) *Continued*	Mervyn Malcolm Dymally (D-CA)	Post Office and Civil Service	Census and Population
	Walter Edward Fauntroy (D-DC)[a]	Banking, Finance, Urban Affairs	International Development Institutions and Finance
	Walter Edward Fauntroy (D-DC)[a]	District of Columbia	Fiscal Affairs and Health
	Augustus Freeman (Gus) Hawkins (D-CA)	Education and Labor	Elementary, Secondary, and Vocational Education
	George Thomas (Mickey) Leland (D-TX)	Post Office and Civil Service	Postal Operations and Services
	Major Robert Odell Owens (D-NY)	Education and Labor	Select Education
	Charles B. Rangel (D-NY)	Ways and Means	Select Revenue Measures
	Gus Savage (D-IL)	Public Works and Transportation	Economic Development
	Louis Stokes (D-OH)	Intelligence (Permanent Select)	Program and Budget Authorization
	Alan Dupree Wheat (D-MO)	District of Columbia	Government Operations and Metropolitan Affairs
99th (1985–1987)	William Lacy Clay, Sr. (D-MO)	Education and Labor	Labor-Management Relations
	Cardiss Collins (D-IL)	Government Operations	Government Activities and Transportation
	John Conyers, Jr. (D-MI)	Judiciary	Criminal Justice
	Ronald V. Dellums (D-CA)	Armed Services	Military Installations and Facilities
	Julian Carey Dixon (D-CA)	Appropriations	District of Columbia
	Mervyn Malcolm Dymally (D-CA)	District of Columbia	Judiciary and Education
	Mervyn Malcolm Dymally (D-CA)	Post Office and Civil Service	Postal Personnel and Modernization
	Walter Edward Fauntroy (D-DC)[a]	Banking, Finance, Urban Affairs	Domestic Monetary Policy
	Walter Edward Fauntroy (D-DC)[a]	District of Columbia	Fiscal Affairs and Health
	Harold Eugene Ford, Sr. (D-TN)	Ways and Means	Public Assistance and Unemployment Compensation
	Augustus Freeman (Gus) Hawkins (D-CA)	Education and Labor	Elementary, Secondary, and Vocational Education
	George Thomas (Mickey) Leland (D-TX)	Post Office and Civil Service	Postal Operations and Services
	Parren James Mitchell (D-MD)	Joint Economic Committee	Investment, Jobs, and Press
	Parren James Mitchell (D-MD)	Small Business	SBA and SBIC Authority, Minority Enterprise and General Small Business Problems
	Charles B. Rangel (D-NY)	Ways and Means	Select Revenue Measures
	Louis Stokes (D-OH)	Intelligence (Permanent Select)	Program and Budget Authorization
98th (1983–1985)	William Lacy Clay, Sr. (D-MO)	Education and Labor	Labor-Management Relations
	William Lacy Clay, Sr. (D-MO)	Post Office and Civil Service	Postal Operations and Services
	Cardiss Collins (D-IL)	Government Operations	Government Activities and Transportation
	John Conyers, Jr. (D-MI)	Judiciary	Criminal Justice
	Ronald V. Dellums (D-CA)	Armed Services	Military Installations and Facilities
	Julian Carey Dixon (D-CA)	Appropriations	District of Columbia
	Mervyn Malcolm Dymally (D-CA)	District of Columbia	Judiciary and Education
	Walter Edward Fauntroy (D-DC)[a]	Banking, Finance, Urban Affairs	Domestic Monetary Policy
	Walter Edward Fauntroy (D-DC)[a]	District of Columbia	Fiscal Affairs and Health
	Harold Eugene Ford, Sr. (D-TN)	Ways and Means	Public Assistance and Unemployment Compensation
	William Herbert Gray III (D-PA)	District of Columbia	Government Operations and Metropolitan Affairs
	Katie Beatrice Hall (D-IN)	Post Office and Civil Service	Census and Population
	Augustus Freeman (Gus) Hawkins (D-CA)	Education and Labor	Employment Opportunities
	George Thomas (Mickey) Leland (D-TX)	Post Office and Civil Service	Postal Personnel and Modernization
	Parren James Mitchell (D-MD)	Small Business	SBA and SBIC Authority, Minority Enterprise and General Small Business Problems
	Charles B. Rangel (D-NY)	Ways and Means	Oversight

CONGRESS	MEMBER	COMMITTEE	SUBCOMMITTEE
97th (1981–1983)	William Lacy Clay, Sr. (D-MO)	Post Office and Civil Service	Postal Operations and Services
	Cardiss Collins (D-IL)	Government Operations	Manpower and Housing
	John Conyers, Jr. (D-MI)	Judiciary	Criminal Justice
	Ronald V. Dellums (D-CA)	District of Columbia	Fiscal Affairs and Health
	Julian Carey Dixon (D-CA)	Appropriations	District of Columbia
	Mervyn Malcolm Dymally (D-CA)	District of Columbia	Judiciary and Education
	Walter Edward Fauntroy (D-DC)[a]	Banking, Finance and Urban Affairs	Domestic Monetary Policy
	Harold Eugene Ford, Sr. (D-TN)	Ways and Means	Public Assistance and Unemployment Compensation
	William Herbert Gray III (D-PA)	District of Columbia	Government Operations and Metropolitan Affairs
	Augustus Freeman (Gus) Hawkins (D-CA)	Education and Labor	Employment Opportunities
	George Thomas (Mickey) Leland (D-TX)	Post Office and Civil Service	Postal Personnel and Modernization
	Parren James Mitchell (D-MD)	Small Business	SBA and SBIC Authority, Minority Enterprise and General Small Business Problems
	Charles B. Rangel (D-NY)	Ways and Means	Oversight
96th (1979–1981)	William Lacy Clay, Sr. (D-MO)	Post Office and Civil Service	Postal Personnel and Modernization
	Cardiss Collins (D-IL)	Government Operations	Manpower and Housing
	John Conyers, Jr. (D-MI)	Judiciary	Crime
	Ronald V. Dellums (D-CA)	District of Columbia	Fiscal Affairs and Health
	Walter Edward Fauntroy (D-DC)	District of Columbia	Government Affairs and Budget
	Augustus Freeman (Gus) Hawkins (D-CA)	Education and Labor	Employment Opportunities
	Augustus Freeman (Gus) Hawkins (D-CA)	House Administration	Printing
	Parren James Mitchell (D-MD)	Banking, Finance and Urban Affairs	Domestic Monetary Policy
	Charles B. Rangel (D-NY)	Ways and Means	Health
	Louis Stokes (D-OH)	Budget	Human and Community Resources
95th (1977–1979)	William Lacy Clay, Sr. (D-MO)	Post Office and Civil Service	Civil Service
	Cardiss Collins (D-IL)	Government Operations	Manpower and Housing
	John Conyers, Jr. (D-MI)	Judiciary	Crime
	Ronald V. Dellums (D-CA)	District of Columbia	Fiscal and Government Affairs
	Charles Coles Diggs, Jr. (D-MI)	International Relations	Africa
	Walter Edward Fauntroy (D-DC)[a]	Banking, Finance and Urban Affairs	Historic Preservation and Coinage
	Walter Edward Fauntroy (D-DC)[a]	Assassinations (Select)	Assassination of Martin Luther King Jr.
	Augustus Freeman (Gus) Hawkins (D-CA)	Education and Labor	Employment Opportunities
	Augustus Freeman (Gus) Hawkins (D-CA)	House Administration	Printing
	Ralph Harold Metcalfe (D-IL)	Merchant Marine and Fisheries	Panama Canal
	Parren James Mitchell (D-MD)	Banking and Urban Affairs	Domestic Monetary Policy
	Parren James Mitchell (D-MD)	Budget	Human Resources
	Robert Nelson Cornelius Nix, Sr. (D-PA)	Post Office and Civil Service	Investigations
	Louis Stokes (D-OH)	Budget	Community and Physical Resources
94th (1975–1977)	William Lacy Clay, Sr. (D-MO)	Post Office and Civil Service	Employee Rights and Intergovernmental Programs
	John Conyers, Jr. (D-MI)	Judiciary	Crime
	Ronald V. Dellums (D-CA)	District of Columbia	Education, Labor, and Social Services
	Charles Coles Diggs, Jr. (D-MI)	Foreign Affairs	International Resources, Food, and Energy
	Walter Edward Fauntroy (D-DC)[a]	District of Columbia	Government Operations
	Augustus Freeman (Gus) Hawkins (D-CA)	Education and Labor	Equal Opportunities
	Augustus Freeman (Gus) Hawkins (D-CA)	House Administration	Electrical and Mechanical Office Equipment
	Ralph Harold Metcalfe (D-IL)	Merchant Marine and Fisheries	Panama Canal
	Robert Nelson Cornelius Nix, Sr. (D-PA)	Foreign Affairs	International Economic Policy

CONGRESS	MEMBER	COMMITTEE	SUBCOMMITTEE
93rd (1973–1975)	John Conyers, Jr. (D-MI)	Judiciary	Crime
	Ronald V. Dellums (D-CA)	District of Columbia	Education
	Charles Coles Diggs, Jr. (D-MI)	Foreign Affairs	Africa
	Walter Edward Fauntroy (D-DC)[a]	District of Columbia	Judiciary
	Augustus Freeman (Gus) Hawkins (D-CA)	Education and Labor	Equal Opportunity
	Augustus Freeman (Gus) Hawkins (D-CA)	House Administration	Electrical and Mechanical Office Equipment
	Robert Nelson Cornelius Nix, Sr. (D-PA)	Foreign Affairs	Asian and Pacific Affairs
92nd (1971–1973)	Charles Coles Diggs, Jr. (D-MI)	Foreign Affairs	Africa
	Robert Nelson Cornelius Nix, Sr. (D-PA)	Post Office and Civil Service	Postal Service
91st (1969–1971)	Charles Coles Diggs, Jr. (D-MI)	District of Columbia	Subcommittee No. 2
	Charles Coles Diggs, Jr. (D-MI)	Foreign Affairs	Africa
	Robert Nelson Cornelius Nix, Sr. (D-PA)	Foreign Affairs	Foreign Economic Policy
	Robert Nelson Cornelius Nix, Sr. (D-PA)	Post Office and Civil Service	Postal Operations
90th (1967–1969)	William Levi Dawson (D-IL)	Government Operations	Special Studies
	Charles Coles Diggs, Jr. (D-MI)	District of Columbia	Subcommittee No. 2
89th (1965–1967)	William Levi Dawson (D-IL)	Government Operations	Executive and Legislative Reorganization
	Robert Nelson Cornelius Nix, Sr. (D-PA)	Post Office and Civil Service	Census and Statistics
	Adam Clayton Powell, Jr. (D-NY)	Education and Labor	Ad Hoc Subcommittee on the Poverty War Program
88th (1963–1965)	William Levi Dawson (D-IL)	Government Operations	Executive and Legislative Reorganization
87th (1961–1963)	William Levi Dawson (D-IL)	Government Operations	Executive and Legislative Reorganization
	Adam Clayton Powell, Jr. (D-NY)	Education and Labor	Labor Management Irregularities
86th (1959–1961)	William Levi Dawson (D-IL)	Government Operations	Executive and Legislative Reorganization
	Adam Clayton Powell, Jr. (D-NY)	Interior and Insular Affairs	Mines and Mining
49th (1885–1887)	James Edward O'Hara (R-NC)	Invalid Pensions	H.R. 6485 (Relating to increase of pension in certain cases)*

a Denotes Delegate

b Denotes U.S. Senator

*There were no official subcommittees for the Invalid Pensions Committee; however, Members were often assigned leadership roles in considering specific bills or charged with organizing petitions from specific states [Minutes of the Committee on Invalid Pensions, 49th Congress, Records of the United States House of Representatives (RG 233), National Archives Building, Washington, DC]

Black Americans in Party Leadership Positions, 1977–2007[*]

CONGRESS	MEMBER'S NAME	CAUCUS/CONFERENCE	POSITION
95th (1977–1979)	Shirley Anita Chisholm (D-NY)	Democratic Caucus	Secretary
96th (1979–1981)	Shirley Anita Chisholm (D-NY)	Democratic Caucus	Secretary
97th (1981–1983)	N/A		
98th (1983–1985)	N/A		
99th (1985–1987)	N/A		
100th (1987–1989)	N/A		
101st (1989–1991)	William Herbert Gray III (D-PA)	Democratic Caucus	Chair
	William Herbert Gray III (D-PA)	Democratic Caucus	Majority Whip
102nd (1991–1993)	John R. Lewis (D-GA)	Democratic Caucus	Chief Deputy Whip
103rd (1993–1995)	John R. Lewis (D-GA)	Democratic Caucus	Chief Deputy Whip
104th (1995–1997)	John R. Lewis (D-GA)	Democratic Caucus	Chief Deputy Whip
105th (1997–1999)	John R. Lewis (D-GA)	Democratic Caucus	Chief Deputy Whip
106th (1999–2001)	John R. Lewis (D-GA)	Democratic Caucus	Chief Deputy Whip
	Maxine Waters (D-CA)	Democratic Caucus	Chief Deputy Whip
	Julius Caesar (J. C.) Watts, Jr. (R-OK)	Republican Conference	Chair
107th (2001–2003)	John R. Lewis (D-GA)	Democratic Caucus	Chief Deputy Whip
	Maxine Waters (D-CA)	Democratic Caucus	Chief Deputy Whip
	Julius Caesar (J. C.) Watts, Jr. (R-OK)	Republican Conference	Chair
108th (2003–2005)	James Enos Clyburn (D-SC)	Democratic Caucus	Vice Chair
	John R. Lewis (D-GA)	Democratic Caucus	Chief Deputy Whip
	Maxine Waters (D-CA)	Democratic Caucus	Chief Deputy Whip
109th (2005–2007)	James Enos Clyburn (D-SC)	Democratic Caucus	Vice Chair
			Chair
	John R. Lewis (D-GA)	Democratic Caucus	Chief Deputy Whip
	Maxine Waters (D-CA)	Democratic Caucus	Chief Deputy Whip
110th (2007–2009)	James Enos Clyburn (D-SC)	Democratic Caucus	Majority Whip

[*] No African-American Senator has ever been elected to a party leadership position.

Black-American Familial Connections in Congress

CHILDREN WHO HAVE SUCCEEDED THEIR PARENTS

William Lacy Clay, Jr., of Missouri (2001–Present), son of William Lacy Clay, Sr., of Missouri (1969–2001)

Harold Eugene Ford, Jr., of Tennessee (1997–2007), son of Harold Eugene Ford, Sr., of Tennessee (1975–1997)

Kendrick B. Meek of Florida, (2003–Present), son of Carrie P. Meek of Florida (1993–2003)

WIDOWS WHO HAVE SUCCEEDED THEIR LATE HUSBANDS

Cardiss Collins of Illinois (1973–1997), wife of George Washington Collins of Illinois (1970–1972)

MISCELLANEOUS FAMILIAL CONNECTIONS

Henry Plummer Cheatham of North Carolina (1889–1893), and George Henry White of North Carolina (1897–1901) were brothers-in-law.

George Washington Murray of South Carolina (1893–1895), and James Enos Clyburn of South Carolina (1993–Present) were distant relatives.

Congressional Black Caucus Chairmen and Chairwomen, 1971–2007*

MEMBER'S NAME	CONGRESS/SESSION	YEARS OF SERVICE
Charles Coles Diggs, Jr.	92nd–1st session	1971–1972
Louis Stokes	92nd–2nd session	1972–1973
Louis Stokes	93rd–1st session	1973–1974
Charles B. Rangel	93rd–2nd session	1974–1975
Charles B. Rangel	94th–1st session	1975–1976
Yvonne Brathwaite Burke	94th–2nd session	1976–1977
Parren James Mitchell	95th	1977–1979
Cardiss Collins	96th	1979–1981
Walter Edward Fauntroy	97th	1981–1983
Julian Carey Dixon	98th	1983–1985
George Thomas (Mickey) Leland	99th	1985–1987
Mervyn Malcolm Dymally	100th	1987–1989
Ronald V. Dellums	101st	1989–1991
Edolphus Towns	102nd	1991–1993
Kweisi Mfume	103rd	1993–1995
Donald Milford Payne	104th	1995–1997
Maxine Waters	105th	1997–1999
James Enos Clyburn	106th	1999–2001
Eddie Bernice Johnson	107th	2001–2003
Elijah Eugene Cummings	108th	2003–2005
Melvin L. Watt	109th	2005–2007
Carolyn Cheeks Kilpatrick	110th	2007–Present

* In the early years of the CBC, leadership was elected twice per Congress.

Constitutional Amendments and Major Civil Rights Acts of Congress Referenced in the Text

AMENDMENT/ACT	PUBLIC LAW/ U.S. CODE	MAIN PROVISIONS
THIRTEENTH AMENDMENT	13 Stat. 567; 13 Stat. 774–775	Abolished slavery and involuntary servitude, except as punishment for a crime. Approved by the 38th Congress (1863–1865) as S.J. Res. 16; ratified by the states on December 6, 1865.
CIVIL RIGHTS ACT OF 1866	14 Stat. 27–30	Guaranteed the rights of all citizens to make and enforce contracts and to purchase, sell, or lease property. Passed by the 39th Congress (1865–1867) as S.R. 61.
FOURTEENTH AMENDMENT	14 Stat. 358–359	Declared that all persons born or naturalized in the U.S. were citizens and that any state that denied or abridged the voting rights of males over the age of 21 would be subject to proportional reductions in its representation in the U.S. House of Representatives. Approved by the 39th Congress (1865–1867) as H.J. Res. 127; ratified by the states on July 9, 1868.
FIFTEENTH AMENDMENT	16 Stat. 346; 16 Stat. 40–41	Forbade any state to deprive a citizen of his vote because of race, color, or previous condition of servitude. Approved by the 40th Congress (1867–1869) as S.J. Res. 8; ratified by the states on February 3, 1870.
FIRST KU KLUX KLAN ACT (CIVIL RIGHTS ACT OF 1870)	16 Stat. 140–146	Prohibited discrimination in voter registration on the basis of race, color, or previous condition of servitude. Established penalties for interfering with a person's right to vote. Gave federal courts the power to enforce the act and to employ the use of federal marshals and the army to uphold it. Passed by the 41st Congress (1869–1871) as H.R. 1293.
SECOND KU KLUX KLAN ACT (CIVIL RIGHTS ACT OF 1871)	16 Stat. 433–440	Placed all elections in both the North and South under federal control. Allowed for the appointment of election supervisors by federal circuit judges. Authorized U.S. Marshals to employ deputies to maintain order at polling places. Passed by the 41st Congress (1869–1871) as H.R. 2634.
THIRD KU KLUX KLAN ACT (1871)	17 Stat. 13–15	Enforced the 14th Amendment by guaranteeing all citizens of the United States the rights afforded by the Constitution and provided legal protection under the law. Passed by the 42nd Congress (1871–1873) as H.R. 320.
CIVIL RIGHTS ACT OF 1875	18 Stat 335–337	Barred discrimination in public accommodations and on public conveyances on land and water. Prohibited exclusion of African Americans from jury duty. Passed by the 43rd Congress (1873–1875) as H.R. 796.
CIVIL RIGHTS ACT OF 1957	P.L. 85–315	Created the six-member Commission on Civil Rights and established the Civil Rights Division in the U.S. Department of Justice. Authorized the U.S. Attorney General to seek court injunctions against deprivation and obstruction of voting rights by state officials. Passed by the 85th Congress (1957–1959) as H.R. 6127.

AMENDMENT/ACT	PUBLIC LAW/ U.S. CODE	MAIN PROVISIONS
CIVIL RIGHTS ACT OF 1960	P.L. 86–449	Expanded the enforcement powers of the Civil Rights Act of 1957 and introduced criminal penalties for obstructing the implementation of federal court orders. Extended the Civil Rights Commission for two years. Required that voting and registration records for federal elections be preserved. Passed by the 86th Congress (1959–1961) as H.R. 8601.
CIVIL RIGHTS ACT OF 1964	P.L. 88–352	Prohibited discrimination in public accommodations, facilities, and schools. Outlawed discrimination in federally funded projects. Created the Equal Employment Opportunity Commission to monitor employment discrimination in public and private sectors. Provided additional capacities to enforce voting rights. Extended the Civil Rights Commission for four years. Passed by the 88th Congress (1963–1965) as H.R. 7152.
VOTING RIGHTS ACT OF 1965	P.L. 89–110	Suspended the use of literacy tests and voter disqualification devices for five years. Authorized the use of federal examiners to supervise voter registration in states that used tests or in which less than half the voting-eligible residents registered or voted. Directed the U.S. Attorney General to institute proceedings against use of poll taxes. Provided criminal penalties for individuals who violated the act. Passed by the 89th Congress (1965–1967) as S. 1564.
CIVIL RIGHTS ACT OF 1968 (FAIR HOUSING ACT)	P.L. 90–284	Prohibited discrimination in the sale or rental of approximately 80 percent of the housing in the U.S. Prohibited state governments and Native-American tribal governments from violating the constitutional rights of Native Americans. Passed by the 90th Congress (1967–1969) as H.R. 2516.
VOTING RIGHTS ACT AMENDMENTS OF 1970	P.L. 91–285	Extended the provisions of the Voting Rights Act of 1965 for five years. Made the act applicable to areas where less than 50 percent of the eligible voting age population was registered as of November 1968. Passed by the 91st Congress (1969–1971) as H.R. 4249.
VOTING RIGHTS ACT AMENDMENTS OF 1975	P.L. 94–73	Extended the provisions of the Voting Rights Act of 1965 for seven years. Established coverage for other minority groups including Native Americans, Hispanic Americans, and Asian Americans. Permanently banned literacy tests. Passed by the 94th Congress (1975–1977) as H.R. 6219.
VOTING RIGHTS ACT AMENDMENTS OF 1982	P.L. 97–205	Extended for 25 years the provisions of the Voting Rights Act of 1965. Allowed jurisdictions that could provide evidence of maintaining a clean voting rights record for at least 10 years, to avoid preclearance coverage (the requirement of federal approval of any change to local or state voting laws). Provided for aid and instruction to disabled or illiterate voters. Provided for bilingual election materials in jurisdictions with large minority populations. Passed by the 97th Congress (1981–1983) as H.R. 3112.
CIVIL RIGHTS RESTORATION ACT OF 1987	P.L. 100–259	Established that antidiscrimination laws are applicable to an entire organization if any part of the organization receives federal funds. Passed by the 100th Congress (1987–1989) as S. 557.

AMENDMENT/ACT	PUBLIC LAW/ U.S. CODE	MAIN PROVISIONS
FAIR HOUSING ACT AMENDMENTS OF 1988	P.L. 100–430	Strengthened the powers of enforcement granted to the Housing and Urban Development Department in the 1968 Fair Housing Act. Passed by the 100th Congress (1987–1989) as H.R. 1158.
CIVIL RIGHTS ACT OF 1991	P.L. 102–166	Reversed nine U.S. Supreme Court decisions (rendered between 1986 and 1991) that had raised the bar for workers who alleged job discrimination. Provided for plaintiffs to receive monetary damages in cases of harassment or discrimination based on sex, religion, or disability. Passed by the 102nd Congress (1991–1993) as S. 1745.
VOTING RIGHTS ACT OF 2006	P.L. 109–478	Extended the provisions of the Voting Rights Act of 1965 for 25 years. Extended the bilingual election requirements through August 5, 2032. Directed the U.S. Comptroller General to study and report to Congress on the implementation, effectiveness, and efficiency of bilingual voting materials requirements. Passed by the 109th Congress (2005–2007) as H.R. 9.

Index

A

Abbott, Israel B., 149, 161, 200
Abernathy, Ralph, 458
ABSCAM sting, 358
Abzug, Bella, 343, *392*, 421n
Action-Alert Communications Network
(AACN), 383
Adarand Constructors, Inc. v. Peña. See,
Supreme Court, United States.
Addabbo, Joseph, 552, 562
Affirmative action, *381*, 381, 432, 448,
468–69, 527, 586, 587, 624, 641,
656, 685, 703, 737, 740. *See also,*
Discrimination.
Africa, foreign policy, 147, 148, 239,
313–14, 386–87, 418–19, 461, 462,
482, 490, 496, 498–99, 501, 512,
514, 520, 532, 703, 705, 711, 712,
719, 727, 729, 743. *See also,* South
Africa, apartheid policy.
African-American citizenship, 21, 37,
56, 82n, 88, 100, 128, 133, 146,
177, 209, 213, 217, 288. *See also,*
Fourteenth Amendment.
African-American Members of
Congress, characteristics,
affluence of, 25
committee assignments, 3, 4, 5,
32–34, 46n, 162, 187n, 239–40n,
266n, 377–79, 404n. *See,* Appendix
D: Black Members' Committee
Assignments (Standing, Joint,
Select) in the U.S. House and
Senate, 1870–2007; Appendix
E: Black Americans Who
Have Chaired Congressional
Committees, 1877–2007;
Appendix F: Black-American Chairs
of Subcommittees of Standing
Committees in the U.S. House and
Senate, 1885–2007.
discrimination against, 31–32, 36–37,
41–42, 190n, 244–47, 260–61, 359
early backgrounds, 22–23, 154–55,
237
education, 23–24, 155, 237, 238,
265n, 370–71, 401n
familial connections. *See,* Appendix
H: Black-American Familial
Connections in Congress.
historical legacy, 169–70
legislative interests, 32–39, 162–69,
245–59, 379–90
legislative style, 14n, 33–34, 161,
162–64, 260–63, 270n, 272n,
273n, 294–95, 390–95, 410–11n
military service. *See,* Military Service,
African-American Members of
Congress.
political power, 32–34, 162, 185n,
242, 250–51, 272, 273, 377–79,
402n

pre-congressional careers, 22–25,
154–55, 237–39, 370–71
pre-congressional political experience,
154–55, 238, 265n, 371–73, 402n
Washington experience, 30–32,
36–37, 46n, 259–62, 390–94
women, 7, 8, 239, *373*, 373, 397,
402n, 412n. *See also,* Women
Representatives.
see also, Congressional Black Caucus
(CBC); Democratic Party;
Disfranchisement; Elections;
Enterprise Railroad Company;
Incumbency and seniority,
influence of; Republican Party;
Senate, United States; Race;
Surrogate representation.
African Development Foundation, 490
African Methodist Episcopal (AME)
Church. *See,* Allen African
Methodist Episcopal (AME) Church
(Queens, NY); Ebenezer African
Methodist Episcopal (AME) Church
(Lincolnville, SC); Emanuel African
Methodist Episcopal (AME) Church
(Charleston, SC).
African Growth and Opportunity Act,
729
Agnew, Spiro, 364, 418
AIDS. *See,* HIV/AIDS.
Alabama,
black representation, 84–87, 110–15,
122–27, 606–11, 690–91. *See,*
Appendix C: Black-American
Representatives and Senators by
State and Territory.
civil rights protests, 252, 255–56
disfranchisement, 124–35, 169
gerrymander, 124
Ku Klux Klan, 29, 112, 113
sugar tariff differential device, 169
see also, Discrimination;
Disfranchisement; Ku Klux Klan.
Alameda Corridor, 481, 632, 646, 648
Albert, Carl, 377–78, 419
Alcorn, James, 20, 58, 116, 118
Allen, Leo, 251
Allen African Methodist Episcopal
(AME) Church (Queens, NY), 552,
562, 565
Alternative budget, 382–83, 394–95,
419, 433, 481
Amateur Sports Act, 426
American Community Renewal Act,
641
Americans with Disabilities Act, 537
Ames, Adelbert, 56, 58, 100, 116, 118
Amnesty, Confederate, 20, 26, 34, 57,
60, 62, 86, 106, 108
Amnesty Act (1872), 34, 64, 68, 70,
74, 80, 84, 86
Anderson, Marian, 303, 385
Anderson, William, 327

Annunzio, Frank, 364
Antebellum Era, *23*, 23, 24, 43n, 68. *See
also,* Postbellum.
Apartheid. *See,* South Africa, apartheid
policy.
Apportionment and redistricting,
28, 99n, *168*, 168, 192–93n, 257,
372, 372–73, 374, 396–99, 412n,
602–603, 614–15
"Black Second" district of North
Carolina, 128–31, 132n, 146–49,
160–61, 200–203, 228
"packing" and "cracking" electoral
districts, 159–60, *160*
"shoestring district" of Mississippi,
102, 103
"shoestring district" of South
Carolina, 160, 161, 216, 220, 222,
223
see also, Elections; Gerrymander;
Reduction.
Arkansas, Little Rock integration, *246*,
247, 247, 271n
Armey, Richard (Dick), 642
Arms Transfers Code of Conduct, 615
Ashley, James M., 21
At-Large Representative, 28, *30*, 30,
45n, 88, 90, 96, 121n

B

Bacon, John E., 78, 80
Bailey, Cleveland, 303
Baker, Harry, 280, 286
Baker v. Carr. See, Supreme Court,
United States.
Ballance, Frank W., Jr., 599, **660–63**,
677
Bankhead, William, 178, 192n, 281
Barden, Graham, 304
Barry, Marion S., 442, 481
Bartlett, Charles, 230
Beard, Thomas P., 70, 71n
Beatty, Vander L., 536, 539n
Beaufort Southern Standard, 25, 138. *See
also,* Newspapers, African-American.
Beebe, George, 136
Benjamin, Adam, Jr., 530
Berman, Howard, 478, 480, 514
Berman, Michael, 480
Berry, Mary Frances, 389, 408n, 441,
444n
Bethune, Mary McLeod, *243*, 243
Bisbee, Horatio, 91
Bishop, Sanford D., 398, **672–73**
Black-American Members of Congress.
See, African-American Members of
Congress, characteristics.
Black-majority congressional districts.
See, Apportionment and redistricting.
Black and Brown Coalition, 697
Black Codes, 29
Black Declaration of Independence,
403n

Black Forum on Foreign Policy, 388
Black History Month, 385, 427, 504
Black Panther Party for Self Defense,
258, 258, 372, 416, 418, 427, 549,
730
Black Power Movement, 258, 261, 263,
371–72
"Black Second" district of North
Carolina. *See,* Apportionment and
redistricting.
Blackwell, Lucien Edward, 266n, *378*,
590–95, 695
"Bloody Shirt," *157*, 157
"Bloody Sunday." *See,* Alabama.
Blount, George W., 130
Blount, James, 37
Boehner, John, 642
Boggs, Hale, 342
Boggs, Corinne C. (Lindy), 7, 704–705
Bolling, Richard W., 540
"Boll Weevils," 491
Bolton, Frances, 251
Bond, Julian, 458, 715
Bonior, David, 592
Borah, William, 178
Bowen, Christopher, 72, 74–75
Brady, Robert A., 590
Bright Hope Baptist Church
(Philadelphia, PA), 488, 490, 491
Broder, David, 391, 480
Brogden, Curtis, 130, 146
Bromberg, Frederick, 86, 124
Brooke, Edward William, III, 5, 7, 236,
239, *250*, *258*, 265n, 268n, **332–39**,
348, 352n, *397*, 397, 402n, 588n
electoral defeat, 240
legislative style, 250–51, 263
legislative interests, *248*, 248, 385
military service, 237
pre-congressional experience, 238
Brooks, Preston, 20, 78
Brown, Albert, 18, 56
Brown, Corrine, 618, **674–75**, 699
Brown, John, 32, 47n, 48n
Brownell, Herbert, 253
Brown Fellowship Society, 72
Brownsville affair, 194n, 326
Brown v. Board of Education. See, Supreme
Court, United States.
Bruce, Blanche Kelso, *8*, *10*, 10, 23,
25, *26*, 30, 31, *32*, *33*, 33, 34, 45n,
102–103, 105n, **116–21**, 134, 236,
338n, 386, 405n
Bruce, Josephine Beall Wilson, 119
Buckley, Charles, 112
Budget. *See,* Alternative budget; Military
budget.
Burke, Yvonne Brathwaite, 5, 6, *11*, 239,
373, *375*, 377, *378*, **446–51**, 478, 480
Bush, George H. W., 328, 349, 390,
409n, 508, 537, 544n, 576, 584, 586,
614, 622, 630, 640

Bush, George W., 337, 398, 615, 642, 657, 662, 664, 666, 713, 715, 719, 727, 741
Butler, Benjamin, 31, *35*, 35, 36, 38, 39, 47–48n, 70
Butler, Matthew, 106, 140
Butterfield, G. K., 373, 662, **676–77**
Buttz, Charles W., 108
Byrd, Harry, 253, 313–14, 461, 464n
Byrne, Jane, 504, 526
Byrns, Joseph, 178, 181

C

Cain, Richard Harvey, 3, 25, 27–30, 32, 38–39, 41, 48n, 78, **94–99**, 185n
Caldwell, Tod R., 160
California, black representation, 324–31, 416–23, 446–51, 478–83, 512–17, 630–33, 646–49, 712–13, 740–41, 742–43, 750. *See,* Appendix C: Black-American Representatives and Senators by State and Territory.
Cal-Learn program, 743
Cambodia, 248, 337, 432
Canon, David T., 11, 400
Carmichael, Stokely, 258, 371–72, 580
Carnegie, Andrew, 156, 203
Carpenter, Milton, 346
Carpetbaggers, 26–27, *27*, 80, 84, 88, 90, 97, 100, 112, 118, 122, 148. *See also,* Scalawag.
Carrollton County courthouse riot, 149
Carson, André, 653
Carson, Julia May, 385–86, **650–53**
Carter, James Earl (Jimmy), 320, 327, 337, 381–82, 384, *388*, 388, 393, 433, 455, 462, 468, 474, 698, 706, 715, 722, 732
Case, Clifford, 251
Cassidy, Hiram, 100
Castro, Fidel, 498
Caucus, *374. See also,* Congressional Black Caucus (CBC).
Celler, Emanuel, 239, 251, 255, *256*, 304
Census, 23, 46n, 167–68, *168. See also,* Apportionment and redistricting; Reduction.
Cessna, John, 36
Chaflin College (Orangeburg, SC), 217
Chalmers, James R., 102–103
Chamberlain, Daniel, 26–27, 97, 108, 140
Chandler, William, 164–65
Cheatham, Henry Plummer, 131, 144n, 149, 152, *159*, 160–63, 166, 185n, 187n, **200–205**, 212n, 228, 230, 233n
Chicago, IL. *See,* Elections; Emigration; Illinois, black representation; Machine politics; Till, Emmett.
Child Abuse Prevention and Enforcement Act, 709
Child Abuse Prevention Challenge Grants Reauthorization Act, 537
Chinese Exclusion Act, 118
Chisholm, Shirley A., 1, *5, 6,* 7, *11,* 236, *238, 264,* 264, **340–45**, 348, 352n, 360n, *370, 373,* 373, *375,* 379, 386, 402n, 403n, 406n, 534, 536, 664
committee assignments, 2

early background, 237
elections, 239, 257
leadership positions, 273n, 405n
legislative style, 313, 360n, 374
pre-congressional political experience, 238–39
presidential bid, 375–76, *376,* 624–25
see also, New York, African-American representation.
Christensen, Donna M., 636, **678–79**
Chudoff, Earl, 318
Civilian Conservation Corps (CCC), 282. *See also,* New Deal.
Civil rights,
Jim Crow Era decline, 40–42, 157–59, 170–71
opposition to, 35–39, 157, 158, 172–73, 178, 180–82, *249,* 249, 271n
see also, Civil rights legislation; Civil Rights Movement; Cold War; Democratic Party; Discrimination; Disfranchisement; Elections; Lynching; Reconstruction; Republican Party; Segregation; Senate, United States; Supreme Court, United States.
Civil rights legislation. *See,* Civil Rights Acts; Fourteenth Amendment, Fifteenth Amendment; Great Society legislation; Ku Klux Klan Acts; Lynching; Powell Amendment; Reduction; Thirteenth Amendment; Senate, United States; Supreme Court, United States; Voting Rights Acts; Appendix J: Selected Landmark Civil Rights Acts of Congress, 1863–2007.
Civil Rights Act of 1866, 21, 35, 790
Civil Rights Act of 1875, 3, 35–39, 40–42, 47n, 790
1874 election, and, 36
African-American Members of Congress, influence, 35–36, 64–65, 81, 83, 96, 100, 102, 106, 108, 112–13, 128
education, 38–39, 91, 108
public transportation and accommodations, 36–37
social equality, 36–39, 102
Supreme Court, United States, and, 41–42
Civil Rights Act of 1957, 253–54, 271n, 312, 790
African-American Members of Congress, influence, 250–51, 312
Civil Rights Act of 1960, 254, 791
Civil Rights Act of 1964, 5, 254–56, *256,* 270n, 791
African-American Members of Congress, influence, 250–51, 255, 270, 295, 302, 326, 438, 458
Civil Rights Act of 1968, 258–59, 791
African-American Members of Congress, influence, 335
Civil Rights Act of 1991, 576, 792
Civil Rights Bill (1990), 328, 542, 586
Civil Rights Cases. See, Supreme Court, United States.
Civil Rights Movement, 249–59, 270n

1963 March on Washington, *255,* 255, 320, 371, 568
African-American Members of Congress, influence, 5, 15n, 312–13, 371–72, 438, 458, 460, 684, 714, 730
"Bloody Sunday" (Birmingham, AL), 256, *257,* 714
communism, influence of, 247–48, 269n
Freedom Ride protests, 254–55, 340, 371, 714, 715
House Judiciary committee, influence on, 251
House Rules committee, influence on, *251,* 251
Montgomery (AL) bus boycott, *252,* 252, 386, 548, 642, 652
lunch counter protests, *254,* 254–55
racial violence, influence of, 252–53, 256
racism and segregation, transforming, 259–62
southern governors' protest, *249,* 249
Vietnam War, influence of, 258
see also, African-American Members of Congress, legislative style; Black Panther Party for Self Defense; Black Power Movement; Civil rights; Civil rights legislation; Cold War; Communism; Discrimination; Disfranchisement; King, Martin Luther, Jr.; Lynching; National Association for the Advancement of Colored People (NAACP); Reconstruction; Senate, United States; Supreme Court, United States; Till, Emmett.
Civil service, employment, 190n. *See also,* Discrimination.
Civil War, 20. *See also,* Military service, African-American Members of Congress.
Clark, Beauchamp (Champ), 222
Clark Amendment, 314
Clarke, Una, 538
Clarke, William John, 155
Clarke, Yvette, 538, **748**
Clay, William (Bill), Sr., 237, 342, **346–53**, 472, 589n, 680
committee assignments, 266n
early background, 238
elections, 257
Congressional Black Caucus (CBC), and, *370, 374,* 374, *375,* 375, 377, 378, 387, 402n, 680
investigations of African-American Members of Congress, 395, 411n
legislative interests, 380, 542
legislative style, 273n, 313, 327, 357, 360n
political influence, 240, 419
South Africa, apartheid policy, 387, 389, 407n, 408–409n
Clay, William Lacy, Jr., 350, **680–81**
Clayton, Eva M., 6, **596–99**, 660, 662
Cleaver, Emanuel, II, **682–83**
Cleveland, Grover, 142, 164, 222
Clinton, William J. (Bill), 349, *386,* *393,* 393, 410n, 455, 475, 492,

543, 556, 559, 564, 565, 571, 582, 586, 587, 588, 592–93, 602, 603, 614, 624, 628, 632, 634, 635, 636, 641–42, 644n, 652–53, 654, 675, 693, 702–703, 727, 737, 742, 745
Cloture, 251, 251, 255. *See also,* Filibuster; Senate, United States.
Clyburn, James E., 7, 225n, 379, 642, 671, **684–85**
Coelho, Tony, 492
Cohelan, Jeffery, 416, 418
Cold War, *239,* 269n, 407n
civil rights movement, influence, 246–48
legislation, influence, 239, 384, 386
College Retention Program, 695
Collins, Barbara Rose, 266n, 508, 509, **580–83**, 710
Collins, Cardiss, *5, 11,* 239, 365, *373,* *375,* 391, 391, 393, 404n, 405n, 408–409n, 433, **466–71**, 520
Collins, George Washington, 237, 238, 264, 345n, 352n, **362–67**, *370,* 374, *391,* 402n, 404–405n, 466
Colored People's Convention of 1865 (Charleston, SC), 29, 72, 94
Committee assignments. *See,* African-American Members of Congress, characteristics.
Committee on Elections. *See,* Contested Elections.
Communism, 247–48, 254, 282, 546. *See also,* Cold War.
Community Development and Regulatory Act, 731
Community Renewal Act, 384, 565
Comprehensive Anti-Apartheid Act of 1986. *See,* South Africa, apartheid policy.
Comprehensive Employment and Training Act, 327–28
Confederate states, readmission to the Union, 21, 68, 70. *See also,* Amnesty, Confederate; Disfranchisement.
Congressional Black Caucus (CBC), *5,* 5, *11, 12,* 263, 264, *368,* 368, *393,* 400, 403n
Action-Alert Communications Network, 383, 406n
alternative budget, 382, 394–95, 433
apartheid policy, 386–90, 418
conflicting interests, 383–84, 391, 410n, 586–87
Congressional Black Caucus Foundation (CBCF), 403–404n
evolution of, 5, 6, 310, 313, 342, 348, 364, *370,* 373–76, 401n, 402n, 411n. *See also,* Democratic Select Committee (DSC).
leadership, 376, *393,* 393, 468, 481, 571, 707. *See,* Appendix I: Congressional Black Caucus Chairmen and Chairwomen, 1971–2007.
legislative interests, *381,* 381–82, 383, *385,* 385, 386–90, 403n, 407n, 408n, 409n, 410n, 418, 432–33, 527, 571
legislative strategy, 368, 370, 376, 377, *380,* 381, 382, 387, 388,

390–91, 392, 393, 394, 401n, 402n, 403n, 409n, 411n
membership, 376, 384, 391, 393, 402n, 404n, 586–87
organizational structure, 402n, 403–404n
political influence, 343, 377–78, 382, 393, 394, 396, 399, 403n, 405n, 419
relationship with Presidents, 336, 347, 368–70, 375, *375*, 381, *382*, 384, *388*, *393*, 393, *398*, 403n, 410n, *520*, 624
seniority, impact of, 377–79
TransAfrica lobbying group, 388, 389, 441
True State of the Union, 461
see also, African-American Members of Congress, characteristics; Black Declaration of Independence; Black Forum on Foreign Policy; Democratic Select Committee (DSC); King, Martin Luther, Jr.; Nixon, Richard M.; South Africa, apartheid policy.
Congressional Children's Caucus, 703
Congressional districts. See, Apportionment and redistricting.
Congressional Gold Medal, *247*, *252*, 271n, 385–86, *386*, *393*, 407n, 652–53. See also, Anderson, Marian; King, Martin Luther, Jr.; King, Coretta Scott; Parks, Rosa.
Congressional Record, 11–12, 47n, 162
Congressional Women's Caucus, 342, 391, 393, 404n, 449, 582, 675
see also, Equal Rights Amendment (ERA).
Congressional Women's Club, 259
Conkling, Roscoe, 31, 116, 118, 121n
Connecticut, black representation, 584–89. See, Appendix C: Black-American Representatives and Senators by State and Territory.
Connor, Eugene (Bull), 255
Constitutional conventions, former Confederate states. *See,* Disfranchisement.
Contested elections, 30, 31, 45n, 52, 53, 162, 187n
Committee on Elections, 30, 32, 45n, *162,* 187n
see also, Elections; individual 19th-century African-American Members of Congress.
Contract With America, 564, 587, 641. See also, Republican Party.
Conyers, John, Jr., *11,* 236, 237–38, 250, 265n, 266n, 310, 313, *370,* *374,* *375,* 402n, 408n, 421n, 634, **686–87**
Judiciary Committee assignment, 239
legislative interests, 256–57, 271–72n, 385, 408n
political influence, 240, 377, 671
pre-congressional experience, 239
Speaker, bid for, 378
see also, Michigan, black representation.
Cooper–Church Amendment of 1970, 248, 337
Corker, Stephen, 70, 71n

Cox, Samuel, 31–32, 65–66, 74
Crawford, Curtis, 348
"Cracking" electoral districts, 159–60, *160. See also,* Apportionment and redistricting.
Crisis (NAACP periodical), 173
Crockett, George William, Jr., 401n, 408–409n, 499, **506–11**, 580
Crosse, Saint George I. B., III, 570
Crumpacker, Edgar, 168–69, 170, 171, 189n
Cuba, 103, 163–64, *164,* 314, 498, 508, 582. See also, Imperialism.
Cummings, Elijah E., 401–402n, 430, 435n, **688–89**

D

Daley, Richard J., 241, 262, 294, 295, 296, 298n, 362, 364, 424, 426, 427, 466, 468, 502, 518, 526, 527, 529n, 730. See also, Machine politics.
Danforth, John, 543
Darfur Divestment bill, 712. See also, Sudan.
Darrow, Clarence, 278, 280
Daschle, Tom, 414n, 624
Date Rape Prevention Drug Act, 703
Daughters of the American Revolution (DAR), 303
Davis, Artur, 609, **690–91**
Davis, Christine Ray, 259–60
Davis, Danny K., 468, **692–93**
Davis, Tom, 723
Dawson, William Levi, 5, 10, *240,* 286, 289, **292–99,** 302, 312, 318, 364, 366n, 424, 426
committee assignments, 236, 239, 240, 259–60, *260,* 266n, 405n
early background, 237, 245, 265n
legislative interests, 245, 246, 252–53, 268–69n
legislative style, 2, *240,* 242, 262–63, 373
political influence, 246, 250
pre-congressional political experience, 237, 238, 242
Till, Emmett, and, 252–53
see also, Illinois, black representation; Till, Emmett.
Death In Custody Act, 735
Declaration of Constitutional Principles, 253
Decolonization, *247. See also,* Imperialism.
Delany, Martin, 41, 74, 97
Delegate, territorial, *383,* 383, 406n. See, Evans, Melvin Herbert; Fauntroy, Walter Edward; Frazer, Victor O.; Norton, Eleanor Holmes; Christensen, Donna M.
De Large, Robert Carlos, 29, *33,* 34, 41, **72–77,** 97, 106
DeLay, Tom, 642
Dellums, Ronald V., 7, *11,* 264, 362, *370,* *372,* *375,* 380, *392,* **416–23,** 712, 713
committee assignments, 378, 392, 405n
Congressional Black Caucus (CBC), and, 387–88, 393, 396–97, 402n, 405n, 410n

legislative interests, 378, 382–83, 386, 387, 389–90, 408n, 409n
legislative style, 392
pre-congressional political experience, 372
Shirley Chisholm presidential bid, and, 375–76
see also, California, black representation.
de Lugo, Ron, 484, 486, 634
Democratic Caucus, 6, 378–79, 492, 571
Democratic Party
black voter re-alignment, 5, 14n, 58, 182–83, 236, 241–44, 266–67n, 267n, 286
Civil Rights Era, 249, 268n, 320
Congressional Black Caucus (CBC), and, 373, 384–85, 403n, 634
Jim Crow Era, 4–5, 154, 157–60, 172–73, 180–82, 190n
New Deal and Depression Era, 241–43, 282
Reconstruction Era, 29–30, 35–39, 40
see also, Apportionment and redistricting; Constitutional conventions, former Confederate states; Elections; Machine politics; Reduction; Republican Party.
Democratic Select Committee (DSC), 263, 264, 313, 373–74. See also, Congressional Black Caucus (CBC).
Dennis v. United States. See, Supreme Court, United States.
De Priest, Jessie, 259, *259,* 260, 278, 280
De Priest, Oscar Stanton, *4,* 5, 10, 184, 234, 240, *241, 242,* 243, *260,* 265n, **278–85,** 292, 303, 384
Chicago political machines, and, 241, 242
discrimination on Capitol Hill, and, 259, 260–61, 262, 272n
early background, 176, 237, 238
legislative interests, 260–61
legislative style, 1–2, 42, 236, 262, 272n
Mitchell, Arthur, political rivalry, 242, 262, 286, 288
pre-congressional political experience, 238, 241
see also, Illinois, black representation; Machine politics; Surrogate representation.
Deukmejian, George, 449
Deutsch, John, 648
Dick, Charles, 169
Dickerson, Earl, 294
Dickson, Julian, 742
Dies, Martin, Jr., 269n
Diggs, Charles Coles, Jr., 5, 6, 10, *11,* 234, 250, *263,* **310–17,** 318, 321, *370,* *374, 375,* 387, 401n, 508, 580
committee assignments, 239, 240, 266n, 383, 387, 405n
Congressional Black Caucus (CBC), and, 5, 6, *11,* 357, *374,* 374–75, 376, 387, 402n, 440
Democratic Select Committee (DSC), and, 264, 373–74

early background, 237
legal difficulties, 240–41, 267n
legislative interests, 236, 247, 248, 252–53, 254, 256–57, 271n, 273n, 383, 386–87, 407n, 408n
legislative style, *263,* 264, 391
military service, 237–38, 265n
pre-congressional political experience, 238
political influence, 240
Till, Emmett, and, 252–53, *312*
see also, Congressional Black Caucus (CBC); Democratic Select Committee (DSC); Michigan, black representation.
Dingell, John, Jr., 265n, 582, 686, 687
Dingley Tariff, 230
Dirksen, Everett, 250n, 255, 335
Discrimination, 36–37, 158, 172, 180–81, 183, 241, 243, 245–46, 246–47, 249, 252, 256, 390, 403n, 426–27
African-American, Members of Congress, experiences, 29–30, 31–32, 36–37, *41,* 169–70, 237–38, 256, *257,* 259–62, 272n, 395–96. See also, individual African-American Members of Congress.
congressional, 31–32, 249, 250, 251, 253, 254–55, 259–62, 265n, 272n, 281, 303, 335, 390
federal government, and, 5, 172–73, 190n, 282
housing, 257, 258–59
military, 118, 145n, 173–74, 237–38, 244–45, 364
railroads, 37, 41–42, 148–49, 289, 426
see also, Affirmative action; Brownsville affair; Civil rights; Civil rights legislation; Civil Rights Acts; Disfranchisement; Elections; Equal Rights Amendment (ERA); Fair Employment Practices Committee (FEPC); Gerrymander; Jim Crow; Ku Klux Klan; Lynching; Racial violence; Reduction; Segregation; Race; Slavery; Senate, United States; South Africa, apartheid policy; Supreme Court, United States; Till, Emmett; Voting Rights Acts.
Disfranchisement, 4, 29, 40–41, 157–59, 166, *168,* 190n, 256–57, 271n, 379–81, 383, 412
"eight box ballot" law, 157–58, 216, 220
constitutional conventions, former Confederate states, 21, 62, 78, 88, 94, 106, 110, 128, 138, 146, 158–59, 169, 188n, 217, 223, 226n. See also, South Carolina.
grandfather clause, *157,* 157
literacy tests, 157, 159, 256, 268n, 405n
poll tax, 33, 157, *158,* 159, 245, 268n
voter registration laws, 157–59
see also, Alabama; Apportionment and redistricting; Contested Elections; Discrimination; Elections; Gerrymander; Mississippi; North

Carolina; Reduction; South Carolina; Voting Rights Acts.

Displaced Homemakers Act, 449

District of Columbia, 302, 312–13, *383*, 383, 406n, 419–20, 438, 440, 443n, 481, 487n, 515

black representation, 438–45, 722–23. *See,* Appendix C: Black-American Representatives and Senators by State and Territory.

District of Columbia Self-Government and Governmental Reorganization Act, 313, 383, 440

District of Columbia Committee, 239, 262, 263, 266n, 312–13, 515

see also, Delegate; Diggs, Charles Coles, Jr.; Dixon, Julian; Fauntroy, Walter Edward; Norton, Eleanor Holmes.

Dixon, Allen, 622

Dixon, Julian Carey, 357, 377, 383, 391, 393, 395, 396, 411n, **478–83**, 515, 521, 742

Dodd, Christopher, 588

Domestic Volunteer Service Act, 537

Douglas, Helen Gahagan, 246, 251

Douglas, Paul H., 254

Douglass, Frederick, *8*, *32*, 122, 204, 206, 208

Droney, John J., 337

Dropout Prevention and Re-entry Act, 548

Du Bois, W.E.B., 170, *172*, 173, 183

Dunnigan, Alice, 259

Durham, Milton, 35, 38

Dyer, Leonidas, *170*, 170, 176–79, 192n

Dymally, Lynn, 512, 515, 630

Dymally, Mervyn Malcolm, 373, 402n, 478, **512–17**, 527–28, 630, 634, 646

E

East St. Louis (IL) race riot. *See,* Race riots.

Eastland, James, 252, 254

Economic policy, 162–63, 241, 243, 267n, 268n, 381–83, 406–407n

Economic Opportunity Act of 1964, 381

see also, Civilian Conservation Corps (CCC); Fair Employment Practices Committee (FEPC); Freedmen's Savings and Trust Company; Great Society legislation; New Deal legislation

Ebenezer African Methodist Episcopal (AME) Church (Lincolnville, SC), 96

"Eight box ballot" law. *See,* Disfranchisement.

Eisenhower, Dwight D., *246*, 246–47, 248, 249, 253, 254, 259, 270n, 272n, 304, 312

Eldredge, Charles, 37

Elections, *1*, 28–30, 45n, 157–62, 240, 376–77, 396–99

1872 election, *26*

1874 election, 36

1876 election, 40–41, 154

1890 election, 165–66

1928 election, 183, 242

1932 election, 242

1992 election, 410n

1994 election, 384, 571, 587, 638

violence, 29–30, 186–87n

nominating conventions, *26*, 26, 45n

black political rivalries, 160–62, 262

see also, individual states; individual African-American Members of Congress; Apportionment and redistricting; Contested elections; Democratic Party; Discrimination; Disfranchisement; Federal Elections Bill of 1890; Fifteenth Amendment; Fusion; Gerrymander; Ku Klux Klan; Incumbency and seniority, influence of; Machine politics; Race riots; Reduction; Republican Party; Voting Rights Acts.

Elliott, Robert Brown, 1, *8*, 10, 22, 29, *33*, 34–35, 36, *37*, 44n, 75, 76n, **78–83**, 94, 265n

Elliott, William, 142–43, 216, 217, 218n, 220, 223

Ellison, Keith, **749**

Emancipation Proclamation, 20

Emanuel African Methodist Episcopal (AME) Church (Charleston, SC), 25, 94

Emergency Unemployment Compensation Act, 593

Emerson, Jo Ann, 598

Emigration,

"Exodusters" (American West), 113, 174–75, 191n

Liberia (Africa), 94, 97, 191n

Great Migration (American North), *173*, 173–76, 182, 183, 191n, 199, 236, 237, *241*, 241, 244

see also, Discrimination; Disfranchisement; Reduction; World War I.

Enterprise Railroad Company, 25

Epping, J. P. M., 140

Equal Employment Opportunity Commission (EEOC), 250, 255, 326

Equality in Athletic Disclosure Act, 469

Equal Rights Amendment (ERA), 449, 512, 524, 527

Espy, Alphonso Michael (Mike), 384, 397, **556–61**, 737

Essential Air Service Bill, 608

Ethiopia, 491, 496, 498–99, 501, 532, 574

Evans, Melvin Herbert, 240, 268n, 373, 384, **484–87**, 588n

Executive Order 8802. *See,* Fair Employment Practices Committee (FEPC).

Executive Order 9981, 249. *See also,* Discrimination; Segregation.

F

Fair Employment Practices Committee (FEPC), *245*, 245–46, *246*, 249, 269n

Familial connections. *See,* African-American Members of Congress, characteristics.

Family and Medical Leave Act, 349

Family Support Program, 384, 475

Farmer, James, 239, *264*, 266n, 340, 342, *371*

Fattah, Chaka, 592, 593, **694–95**

Fauntroy, Walter Edward, *5*, *11*, *256*,

370, 371, *374*, *375*, 377, *378*, *383*, 383, 389, 392, 402n, 408n, **438–45**

Federal Elections Bill of 1890, 164–66, 169, 178, 203, 214, 216–17. *See also,* Disfranchisement; Lodge, Henry Cabot.

Fields, Cleo, 398, **600–605**

Fifteenth Amendment, *1*, 18, 22, *22*, *24*, 29, 34, 35, 41, 42, *158*, 158, 164, 165, 168, 170, 172, 179, 180

Filibuster, 165, 179, 222, 246, 251, 254, 255–56, 271n, 349, 624. *See also,* Cloture; Senate, United States.

Financial Literacy for Homeowners Act, 733

Finley, Jesse J., 91

Fitzgerald, Peter, 725

Fitzhugh, Robert, 100

Flake, Floyd Harold, 381, *384*, 384, 552, 554, **562–67**

Foner, Eric, 10, 170

Foraker, Joseph B., 194n

Force Acts. *See,* Ku Klux Klan Acts.

Force Bill. *See,* Federal Elections Bill of 1890.

Ford, Gerald R., 342, *375*, 379, 455, 461

Ford, Harold, Jr., 350, 397, 401n, 472, 476, **654–59**

Ford, Harold E., Sr., *5*, 6, *11*, 350, 372, *378*, 378, 384, *395*, 395, 401n, 404–405n, 448, **472–77**, 578n, 654

Foreign Military Sales Act, 320

Fourteenth Amendment, 21, *34*, 35, 41, 42, 56, 68, 94, 128, 136, 158, 167, 168, 170, 171, 177, 179, 180, 183, 189n, 223, 250, 288, 312, 320, 397, 615

France, Erwin A., 427

Franking privileges, 18, 576

Franks, Gary A., 384–85, **584–89**, 641

Frazer, Victor O., **634–37**, 679

Freedmen's Bureau, *21*, 21, 24, 27, *28*, 72, 88, 124

Freedmen's Savings and Trust Company (Freedmen's Bank), 33–34, 65, 96, 103, 119, 130. *See also,* Select Committee on the Freedmen's Bank.

Freedom Riders. *See,* Civil Rights movement.

Friedel, Samuel, 430, 432, 435n

Frost, Martin, 491

Fusion, *160*, 160, 186–87n, 230, 231

G

Gainesville New Era, 25, 91. *See also,* Newspapers, African-American.

Garfield, James A., *26*, 36, 66, 81, 102–103, 119–20

Garner, John Nance, 178, 181, 241

Garvey, Marcus, 175

Gaining Early Access and Readiness for Undergraduate Program (GEAR UP), 695

Gandhi, Indira, 343

Gandhi, Mahatma, 255

George, Randall D., 216

Georgia,

black representation, 68–71, 458–65, 612–17, 664–67, 672–73, 714–15, 732–33. *See,* Appendix C: Black-American Representatives and Senators by State and Territory.

disfranchisement, 70, *238*, 250, 272n, 398

lynching, *166*, 176

re-admission to the Union, 56–57, 68, 70

see also, Disfranchisement; Lynching.

Georgia Educational Association, 68

Gephardt, Richard, *386*, 492, 565, 656

Gerrymander, 28, *29*, 113, 124, 128, 141–42, 159–60, 187n, 216, 397–99, 412n, 600, 602, 603, 614–15, 617n. *See also,* Apportionment and redistricting; Elections; Disfranchisement.

Ghana, 248, 304, 313. *See also,* Africa, foreign policy.

Giles v. Harris. See, Supreme Court, United States.

Gillett, Frederick H., 178, 180

Gingrich, Newt, 314, 384, 564–65, 587, 614, 620, 640, 641

Global Fund to Fight HIV/AIDS, 713

Goals 2000 initiative, 727

Golar, Simeon, 564

Goldwater, Barry, 14n, 267–68n

Gonzalez, Henry, 358

Goode, Wilson, 490

Goodykoontz, Wells, 180, 193n

Gramm–Rudman–Hollings Act, 492

Grandfather clause, *157*, 157, 171. *See,* Disfranchisement.

Grant, Ulysses S., 25–26, *34*, 39, 58, 64, 80, 102, 106, 112, 124, 130, 134, 208, 210

Graves, Curtis, 452

Gray, Frizzell. *See,* Mfume, Kweisi.

Gray, William III (Bill), 2, 7, *390*, **488–95**, 532, 590, 592, 695

Congressional Black Caucus (CBC), and, 370

first election, 321

legislative interests, 389–90, 418

legislative style, 394

political influence, 379, 389, 394–95

see also, Economic policy; Pennsylvania, black representation; South Africa, apartheid policy.

Great Depression, 236, *241*, 241–44, 259, 281, 282, 286, 288, 300, 324, 340, 362. *See also,* New Deal legislation.

Great Migration, *173*. *See also,* Emigration.

Great Society legislation, 240, 258, 327, 448

Greeley, Horace, 26, 112

Green, Al, **696–97**

Gulf War. *See,* Iraq.

Gurney, William, 106

H

Haiti, 393, 441–42, 492, 514, 538, 571, 582, 620, 675, 717, 741

Hall, Anthony (Tony), 498

Hall, Katie Beatrice, 385, **530–33**
Hamburg massacre. *See,* South Carolina.
Hamilton, Charles V., 305
Hammer, Rhea Mojica, 364–65
Hampton, Wade, 65, 142
Hannaford, Mark, 514
Haralson, Jeremiah, 26, 29, 45n, 46n, 113, **122–27**, 161
Harris, James H., 148
Harris, John T., 32, *37*, 37, 124
Harrison, Benjamin, 120, 143, 164, 209, 210, 220
Harrison, Byron (Pat), 178, 182
Hastert, Dennis, *386*, 641
Hastings, Alcee, 618, 674, **698–99**
Hatch Act, 349
Hatcher, Richard, 530, 532
Hawaii, 163–64, 230, 724
Hawkins, Augustus Freeman (Gus), *2*, 10, *11*, 250, 258, 265n, **324–31**, *370*, *375*, *394*, 402n
   committee assignments, 262–63, 266n
   legislative interests, 234, 236, 248, 255, 256–57, *381*, 381
   legislative style, 2, 263
   political influence, *262*, 262–63, 378
   pre-congressional political experience, 238
   see also, California, black representation; Humphrey–Hawkins Full Employment and Balanced Growth Act.
Hawkins–Stafford Act. *See,* School Improvement Act.
Hayes, Charles Arthur, 389, *396*, 396, **546–51**, 731
Hayes, Rutherford B., *40*, 40–41, 97, 121n, 130, 136, 208
Hayes v. Louisiana. See, Louisiana; Supreme Court, United States.
Head Start Program, 666
Health Security Act, 469
Hébert, F. Edward, 378, *392*, 392, 419
Heflin, James, *180*, 181
Higher Education Act, 542
Hilliard, Earl Frederick, 266n, **606–11**, 690–91
HIV/AIDS, 574, 648, 679, 701, 711, 712, 717, 723, 741, 743
Hoar, George Frisbie, 31–32, 35, 164–65
Hoge, Solomon L., 78
Holden, William, 128
Holloway, Clyde, 600
Hoover, Herbert, 183, 241, 242, 243, *259*, 260, 280
Hoover, Lou Henry, *259*, 260, 280
House, John, 134
House "Bank" scandal, 350, 358, 420, 542, 549, 576
House Gallery. *See,* Segregation.
House Un-American Activities Committee (HUAC). *See,* Un-American Activities Committee (HUAC).
Housing and Community Development Act, 559
Housing discrimination. *See,* Discrimination.

Houston Fair Share program, 697
Howard, Michael, 57–58 *See,* West Point, U.S. Military Academy.
Hubbs, Orlando, 148.
Humphrey, Hubert, *250*, 255, 327, 381. *See also,* Humphrey–Hawkins Full Employment and Balanced Growth Act.
Humphrey, Lotte W., 148
Humphrey–Hawkins Full Employment and Balanced Growth Act, 6, 327, *381*, 381–82, 548
Hunger, Select Committee on, *380*, 496, 499, 542, 558, 560, 570, 574, 776
Hunt, Caleb, 30
Hunter, David, 142
Hunter, Maria, 142
Hurricanes, 598, 705, 713
Hyman, John Adams, 22–23, 50, **128–33**, 146. *See also,* John A. Hyman Memorial Youth Foundation.

I

Ickes, Harold, 243
Illinois, black representation, 278–83, 286–91, 292–99, 362–67, 424–29, 466–71, 502–505, 518–23, 524–29, 546–51, 622–25, 626–29, 692–93, 702–703, 724–25, 730–31. *See,* Appendix C: Black-American Representatives and Senators by State and Territory.
Immigration, 180
   legislation, 537–38, 620, 717
   Asian, 118
   European, 174
Imperialism,
   Decolonization, African/Asian, *247*, 247, 314
   United States, 163–64, 188n, 230
Income and Jobs Action Act, 548
Incumbency and seniority, influence of, 33, 46n, 50, 162, 181–82, 196, 240–41, 266n, 274, *376*, *377*, 376–77, 404n, 413
Indiana, black representation, 530–33, 650–53. *See,* Appendix C: Black-American Representatives and Senators by State and Territory.
Industrialization, influence of, 156–57
Iran-Contra affair, 358
Iraq, 576, 579, 615, 656–57, 683, 712, 713, 717, 721, 725, 741
Isakson, Johnny, 666

J

Jackson, Jesse, *381*, 498, 532, 590, 626, 630
Jackson, Jesse, Jr., 628, **700–701**
Jackson Lee, Sheila, **702–703**
Jacobs, Andy, 650
Jacobs, H. P., 100
James, Esther, 305
James, Ollie, *180*
Javits, Jacob, 251
Jefferson, William J., 602, **704–705**
Jim Crow, *154*, 154, 241, *255*. *See also,* Discrimination.
John A. Hyman Memorial Youth Foundation, 662
John R. Justice Prosecutors and

Defenders Incentive Act, 733
Johnson, Andrew, 20–21, 43n
Johnson, Eddie Bernice, **706–707**
Johnson, James Weldon, *172*, *176*, 176, 177. *See also,* National Association for the Advancement of Colored People (NAACP).
Johnson, Hank, 616, **749**
Johnson, Lewis E., 96
Johnson, Lyndon B., *248*, 248, 253–54, 255–56, *256*, *257*, 257, *258*, 258, 271n, 295, 297, 304–305, 306, 320, 327, 335, 336–37, *373*, 438, 448, 449, 454, 455, 464n, 542
Jones, Charles, 602
Jones, Stephanie Tubbs, 359, 411n, 649n, **708–709**
Jones, Thomas R., 340
Jones, Walter, 596, 598, 660
Jordan, Barbara, 6, 10, *11*, 239, *373*, *380*, 380, *391*, **452–57**, 460, 496, 498, 574, 702
   committee assignments, 378
   Congressional Black Caucus (CBC), and, *375*, *380*, 391
   legislative interests, 379–80, 405n
   legislative style, *391*, 391
   pre-congressional political experience, 372
   see also, Texas, black representation.
Juvenile Justice and Delinquency Prevention Act, 327

K

Karsten, Frank, 346
Keifer, Joseph Warren, 125, 189n
Kelly, Edward J., 241, 242, 286, 292. *See also,* Machine Politics.
Kellogg, Stephen, *39*, 39
Kennedy, Anthony M., 398
Kennedy, Edward M. (Ted), *250*, 334, 440, 626
Kennedy, John F., 248, 254, 255, 269n, 294, 297, 298n, 304, 306, 320, 326, 334, 358, *378*, 434, 452, 512, 542, 568, 664, 686
Kerr, Daniel, 216
Kerr, Michael, 91, 134, 136
Key, V.O., 181
Keyes, Alan, 397
Kilpatrick, Carolyn Cheeks, *393*, 393, 582, **710–11**
Kilpatrick, Kwame, 711
King, Coretta Scott, 271n, 343, 407n, 440
King, Martin Luther, Jr., 236, 252, 254–55, *255*, *256*, 258, 270n, 271n, 295, 336, 348, 358, 362, *371*, 371, *378*, 407n, 438, 458, 481, 524, 532, 548, 568, 606, 686, 687, 700, 714
   holiday, 336, *385*, 385, 407n, 468, 486, 504, 624
King, Rodney, 630, 632
King, William E., 294
Kitchin, Alvin Paul, 233n
Kitchin, Claude, 232, 233n
Kitchin, William W., 233n
Kitchin, William H., 148, 233n
Kleczka, Gerald. D., 720
Knight, Landon, 310
Knowland, William F., 254

Koreagate scandal, 514
Kousser, J. Morgan, 181, 190n
Ku Klux Klan, 29, 30, 64, 68, 70, 74, 77, 78, 80, 88, 90, 97, 106, 112, 113, 128, 140, *182*
   Ku Klux Klan Acts, 3, *34*, 34–35, 41, 47n, 64, 74, 77, 80, 165
   see also, Lynching.
Kuchel, Thomas, 255
Kuwait, 576
Kuykendall, Dan, 472, 474

L

LaFollette, Robert M., 143
LaGuardia, Fiorello, 281, 300
Langston, John Mercer, *8*, 10, *152*, 152, 153, *154*, *159*, *161*, *162*, 166, 191n, **206–13**, 735
   early background, 155, 185n
   legislative interests, 166, 191n
   pre-congressional political experience, 155
   election, *156*, 162, 196
   see also, Virginia, black representation.
Langston v. United States et al. See, Supreme Court, United States.
Lanham, Samuel, 165
Lawton, Winburn J., 71
Leach, Jim, 564
Leath, Marvin, 491
Lee, Barbara, **712–13**
Lee, Samuel, 65, 81, 142, 161
Legislative style. *See,* African-American Members of Congress, characteristics; Surrogate representation.
Lehman, Bill, 618
Leland, George Thomas (Mickey), *7*, 7, *380*, **496–501**, 574
   committee assignments, 404–405n
   legislative interests, 380, 390
   legislative style, *391*, 392
   see also, Texas, black representation.
Lewis, Barbour, 38
Lewis, John R., 395, 397, 399, **714–15**
   leadership, 379
   civil rights leader, 256, *257*, *264*, 271n, 371, *371*, 372
   see also, Georgia, black representation.
Lewis, Morris W., 281
Liberal Republican Party, 26
Liberia. *See,* Emigration.
Libya, 608, 610n
Lincoln, Abraham, 20, *21*, 142, 183, 210, 236, *255*, 281, 282
Lincolnville (SC), 96
Line-item veto, 571
Lippmann, Walter, 247
Literacy tests. *See,* Disfranchisement.
Lithicum, J. Charles, 181
Little Rock (AR), school integration, *246*, *247*, 246–47, 271n
Livingston, Robert L., 358–59
Lloyd, James B., 231
Lodge, Henry Cabot, 143, 164–66, *165*, 178
Long, Jefferson Franklin, *33*, 34–35, 41, 50, 64, 80, **68–71**, 460
Longworth, Nicholas, 193n, 280
Los Angeles (CA) 1992 riots. *See,* Race riots; King, Rodney.
Louisiana,

black representation, 134–37,
600–605, 704–705
congressional districts, 398, 600, 602
see also, Menard, John Willis;
Pinchback, Pinckney B. S.;
Appendix C: Black-American
Representatives and Senators by
State and Territory.
Lower Mississippi Delta Congressional
Caucus, 559
Lower Mississippi River Valley Delta
Development Act, 558–59
Low Income Housing Tax Credit, 729
Lucas, Charles, 356
Lunch counter protests. *See,* Civil Rights
Movement.
Lugar, Richard, 390, 725
Lynch, John Roy, 10, *26, 32,* 41, 42,
46n, 50, 56, **100–105,** 224, 241
discrimination, and, 29–30, 37, 38
early background, 24
elections, 28
historical interpretation, 169
legislative interests, 37, 38, 39, 40
pre-congressional political experience,
28
Republican Party, and, 27, 40
see also, Mississippi, black
representation.
Lynching, *166,* 166, *167,* 178, 183,
188n, 192n, 252–53
anti-lynching legislation, *4,* 164,
166–67, 175–79, *178,* 182, 183,
231, *243,* 243–44, 249, 268n
see also, Ku Klux Klan; Race riots; Till,
Emmett.

M

Machine politics, 241–43, *262,* 262,
267n, 278, 280, 282, 284n, 289, 292,
294, 295, 296, 298n, 302, 312, 318,
320, 321, 340, 356, 362, 364. *See
also,* Daley, Richard J.; Kelly, Edward
J.; Steingut, Stanley; Tammany Hall;
Thompson, William Hale (Big Bill).
Mackey, Edmund W., 97, 108, 142
Macon Union League, 68
Madden, Martin, 278, 280, 282, 292
Mahan, Alfred Thayer, 163
Mahone, William, 208–209
Majette, Denise L., 397, 615, **664–67**
Majority Whip. *See,* Whip.
Maloney, James, 587
Mansfield, Mike, *250,* 255
Mariam, Mengistu Haile, 499
Martin Luther King, Jr., holiday. *See,*
King, Martin Luther, Jr.
Maryland, black representation,
430–37, 568–73, 688–89, 746–47.
See, Appendix C: Black-American
Representatives and Senators by State
and Territory.
Massachusetts, black representation,
332–39. *See,* Appendix C: Black-
American Representatives and
Senators by State and Territory.
McCary, William, 100
McCormack, John, 342
McCormick, Ruth, 280
McCulloch William, 255

McGrath, J. Howard, *249*
McKee, George, 118
McKee, John, 138, 144n, 145n
McKinley, William, 103, 120, 143,
144n, 161, 167, 203–204, 224, 230,
231
McKinley Tariff, 166, 202, 209
McKinney, Cynthia Ann, 266n, 394,
398, 398, **612–17,** 664
McLean, William, 47–48n
McMillan, John L., 312, 440
Mebane, George Allen, 200, 202
Meek, Carrie P., **618–21,** 674, 699, 716
Meek, Kendrick B., 620, **716–17**
Meeks, Gregory W., **718–19**
Menard, John Willis, *3,* 30, 71n, 134
Metcalfe, Ralph Harold, *5, 10, 11,* 296,
364, 366n, *370, 375,* 378, 402n,
424–29, 502, 504, 524
Metcalfe, Ralph Harold, Jr., 504, 526,
546
Mewboorne, James M., 203, 205n
Mfume, Kweisi, **568–73,** 576, 587
Michigan, black representation, 310–17,
506–11, 580–83, 686–87, 710–11.
See, Appendix C: Black-American
Representatives and Senators by State
and Territory.
Middleton, Steven, 10
Military budget, 419
Military service, African-American
Members of Congress, 401n
Civil War, 54, 62, 84, 88, 94, 100,
116, 134, 138, 145n
Spanish–American War, 100, 103
World War I, 265n, 292, 296
World War II, 237–38, 244–45, 247,
265n, 302, 310, 332, 335, 362,
424, 430, 466, 518, 524
Millender-McDonald, Juanita, 412n,
632, **646–49**
Miller, Thomas Ezekiel, 143, 152, 155,
156, 157, 158, *159,* 159, 160, 161,
162, 166, 205n, 212n, **214–19,** 220,
223
Miller, Zell, 414, 462, 664, 666
Miller v. Johnson. See, Supreme Court,
United States.
Million Man March, 582
Mills, Billy, 446
Mills, Roger, 38
Mills v. Green. See, Supreme Court,
United States.
Mills, Wilbur, 454
Minnesota, black representation, 749.
See, Appendix C: Black-American
Representatives and Senators by State
and Territory.
Minority Business Legal Defense and
Education Fund, 434
Minority HIV/AIDS initiative, 701
Missionary Record (South Carolina Leader),
25, 78, 94. *See also,* Newspapers,
African-American.
Mississippi, 18, *29,* 43n, 45, 56, 60n,
116, 159, 282, 384
"Mississippi Plan," 29–30, 102, 118
black representation, 54–61,
100–105, 116–21, 556–61,
736–37.

civil rights protests, 254–55
disfranchisement, 159, 168, 169,
171, 180
electoral districts, 28, 45n, 100
racial violence, 29–30, 102, 149, 176,
188n, 252, 312
Voting Rights Act of 1965, impact
of, 257
white supremacy, 23, 119, 180–82,
259, 260, 280. *See also,* Harrison,
Byron (Pat); Rankin, John Elliott;
Vardaman, James Kimble; White
supremacy.
see also, Appendix C: Black-American
Representatives and Senators by
State and Territory.
Mississippi River Improvement
Association, 119
Missouri, black representation,
346–53, 540–45, 680–81, 682–83.
See, Appendix C: Black-American
Representatives and Senators by State
and Territory.
Mitchell, Arthur Wergs, 1, 2, 10, 265n,
282, **286–91,** 292, 294, 524
early background, 237
legislative interests, 243–45, 262
legislative style, 242, 262
pre-congressional political experience,
242
see also, Illinois, black representation.
Mitchell, Parren, *5, 11,* 264, 362, *370,
374, 375, 382,* 402n, 421n, **430–37,**
490, 491, 568, 570
committee assignments, 404–405n
legislative interests, 382, 386
legislative style, 381–82
Shirley Chisholm presidential bid,
and, 375–76
see also, Maryland, black
representation.
Mitchell v. United States et al. See, Supreme
Court, United States.
Moffett, Toby, 584
Moise, E. M., 220, 222
Mondale, Walter, 335, 498
Mondell, Frank W., 179
Monroe Doctrine, 163
Moore, Gwendolynne S., 402n, **720–21**
Moore, Joseph B., 134
Moseley-Braun, Carol, 6, *12,* 240, 372,
397, *397,* 410n, 546, **622–25,** 649
Moses, Franklin, 26–27, 108, 214
Moss, D. S., 230
Moynihan Report, 266n
Mozambique, 314. *See also,* Imperialism.
Mulatto, *23. See,* Race.
Murphy, Morgan, 518
Murphy, William T., 518
Murray, George Washington, 4, 10, 143,
152, 155, *155,* 157–58, 158–59, 160,
161, 162, 163, 217, **220–27,** 685

N

Nash, Charles Edmund, *32,* 91, **134–37**
National Association for the
Advancement of Colored People
(NAACP), *4, 5,* 5, *172, 176, 178, 238,
243, 252,* 638
African-American Members of

Congress, and, 243–44, 252–53,
262, 280–81, 288, 295, 304, 354,
356, 379, 382, 430, 499, 509, 571,
638, 641, 684, 696
activism, 176–79, 183, 243–44,
252–53, 262
World War II, and, 245, 247
founded, 172–73
leadership, 243, 430, 571, 660,
696–97, 734
voter registration drives, 238
National Defense Rail Act, 652
National Negro Labor Union (NNLU),
110, 112
Native American legislation, 90, 118–19
Nevius, John, 440
New Columbia Admission Act, 723
New Deal legislation, 236, 242, 241–44,
258, 267n, 269n, 282, 285n, 286,
288, 304. *See also,* Fair Employment
Practices Committee (FEPC); Great
Society legislation.
New Jersey, black representation,
726–27. *See,* Appendix C: Black-
American Representatives and
Senators by State and Territory.
Newton, Huey, *258,* 372
New York, black representation,
300–309, 340–45, 534–39, 552–55,
562–67, 718–19, 728–29, 738–39,
748. *See,* Appendix C: Black-American
Representatives and Senators by State
and Territory.
Newspapers, African-American, 25,
44n, 67, 78, 518. *See,* individual
newspapers.
Niblack, Silas L., 90
Nichols, Jesse, 259
Nix, Robert Nelson Cornelius, Sr., *5,
10, 11,* 236, 238, 240, 248, 250, 262,
265n, 266n, 300, **318–23,** *370, 375,*
402n, 405n
Nixon, Richard M., 248, 313, 327,
336, 337, 348, 356, 364, 375, 391,
403n, 418, 426, 432, 433, 448, 454,
460–61, 474, 484, 632
Nkrumah, Kwame, 248
Nominating conventions, *26. See,*
Elections.
North, Oliver, 358
North American Free Trade Agreement
(NAFTA), 349, 571, 576, 582, 598,
628, 632, 707, 745
North Carolina, 24
black representation, 128–33,
146–51, 200–205, 228–33,
596–99, 660–63, 676–77, 744–45
"Black Second" district. *See,*
Apportionment and redistricting.
disfranchisement, 186–87n, 202
segregation, 174–75
Wilmington race riots, 186–87n
see also, Appendix C: Black-American
Representatives and Senators by
State and Territory.
North Carolina Farmers' Alliance, 203,
205n
Northup, Anne, 620
Norton, Eleanor Holmes, 373, 383,
408n, 444n, **722–23**

Norton, Mary, *246*, 246, 269n

No Taxation Without Representation Act, 723

Nuclear Waste Responsible Component and Protection Act, 648

Nye, James, 56

O

Oates, William C., 112

Obama, Barack, *369*, 397, 671, **724–25**

O'Brien, George D., 310

O'Connor, Michael, 97

O'Ferrall, Charles, 216

Office of Economic Opportunity, 448

O'Hara, James Edward, 22, *41*, 41–42, 46–47n, 130, 132n, 144n, **146–51**, 160, 161, 185n, 200, 203, 289

Ohio, black representation, 354–61, 708–709. *See,* Appendix C: Black-American Representatives and Senators by State and Territory.

Oklahoma, black representation, 638–45. *See,* Appendix C: Black-American Representatives and Senators by State and Territory.

Older Americans Health Services Act, 474

Omnibus Crime Bill (1994), 576, 582, 624

Onassis, Jacqueline Kennedy, 343

O'Neill, Thomas P. (Tip), 336, 358, 378, 481, 491, 532, 584

Ovington, Mary White, 173

Owens, Jesse, 407n, 424

Owens, Major Robert O'Dell, **534–39**

P

"Packing" electoral districts, *160*. *See,* Apportionment and redistricting.

Park, Tongsun, 514

Parker, Peter, 432

Parks, Rosa, *252*, 252, 271n, 385–86, *386*, 407n, 642–43, 652–53, 686, 701

Payne, Donald M., *369*, **726–27**

Pelosi, Nancy, 648, 649, 656–57, 695

Pennsylvania, black representation, 318–23, 488–95, 590–95, 694–95. *See,* Appendix C: Black-American Representatives and Senators by State and Territory.

People's Savings Bank, 232

Perryman, David, 640

Phelps, William, 47n

Philippines. *See,* Imperialism.

Phillips, Wendell H., 570

Pickens, Harriet Ida, *244*

Pierce, Franklin, 43n

Perce, Legrand, 100

Pinchback, Pinckney B. S., *31*, 118, 121n, 134

Planter ammunition transport ship, 138, 141, 144n, 145n

Plessy v. Ferguson. See, Supreme Court, United States.

Political machines. *See,* Machine Politics.

Poll tax, *158*. *See,* Disfranchisement.

Populism, 160, *161*, 161, 203, 220, 222, 228, 230, 231. *See also,* Fusion.

Postbellum Era, 23, *23*, 43n. *See also,* Antebellum Era.

Powell, Adam Clayton, Jr., *2*, 10, *180*, 234, *235*, 236, *245*, 248, 250, 266n, 267n, 294, 295, **300–309**, 312, 318, 322n, 326, 327, 349, 372, 373, 374, 392, 448, 530, 729

civil rights activist, 14n, 236, 251, 253, 254, 255, 257, 261, 270–71n, 372

committee assignments, 236, 240, 266n, 405n

congressional exclusion, 266n, 305, 320–21

early background, 238

Eisenhower, support for, *253*, 253, 304

ethical and legal problems, 240–41, *261*, 304, 305, 395, 411n

legislative interests, 5, 245, 246, 247–48, 253, 256–57, 303–304, 386, 387

legislative style, 1, 2, 251, 261–62, 263, 264, 270–71n

Nix, Robert opposition, 321

political influence, 240, 251

pre-congressional political experience, 238

see also, New York, black representation; Powell Amendment.

Powell Amendment, 253, 255, 295, 302–303

Pregnancy Disability Act, 328

President's Committee on Civil Rights, 249

Progressivism, 171–72, 190n

R

Race,

mulatto, 23, *23*, 24, 43n, 80, 155, 160–61, 184n, 186n, 218n

black racial tension, 23, 44n, 160–61

Race riots, 176–77, 191–92n, 258–59, 335

East St. Louis (IL) race riot, *175*, 176–77

Carrollton County (MS) courthouse riot, 149

Los Angeles (CA) 1992 riot, 481, 630. *See also,* King, Rodney.

Tulsa (OK) race riot, *177*

Washington (DC) riot, 258

Watts (CA) race riots, 258, 326, 446

Wilmington (NC) race riot, 186–87n, 231

Racism. *See,* Discrimination.

Rail and Public Transportation Security Act, 703

Railroads. *See,* Discrimination.

Railroad Revitalization and Regulatory Reform Act, 426

Rainey, Joseph Hayne, 1, *8*, 10, *19*, *25*, *26*, 31, *32*, *33*, 44n, **62–67**, 70, 80, 96, 97, 99n, 160

committee assignments, 33

discrimination, experience with, 22–23, 30, 31, 32, 36–37, 97

early background, 22–23, 25

elections, 30

legislative interests, 33, 34, 36–37, 39, 40

pre-congressional political experience, 29

see also, South Carolina, black representation.

Rainey, Susan, 22–23, 62

Randolph, A. Philip, 245

Rangel, Charles, *5*, 11, 305, *370*, 374, 374, *375*, 376–77, *377*, 377, 378, 379, 380, 402n, 404–405n, 448, 476n, 554, 691, **728–29**

Rangel Amendment, 729

Rankin, Jeannette, 1

Rankin, John Elliott, *180*, 180, 246, 247, 261, 269n, 303

Ransier, Alonzo Jacob, 25, 27, 29, 32, 39, 41, 75, 94, 97, **106–109**

Rapier, James Thomas, Jr., 25, *26*, 28, 29, 37, 38, 39, 45n, **110–15**, 124, 127n, 161

Rayburn, Samuel, 178, 181, *254*, 254, 261, 302, 304

Rayner, A. A. (Sammy), 426, 502

Reagan, Ronald W., 328, 343, 357, 358, *382*, 382, 384, 385, 386, 389, 390, 409n, 419, 433, 441, 461, 474, 486, 491, 508, 515, 520, 526, 527, 532, 537, 540, 542, 548, 554, 559, 584, 622

Realignment, *241*, 241–43. *See also,* Democratic Party; Republican Party.

Reconstruction, *20*, 20–22, 25–27, 39–42. *See also,* Civil Rights Act of 1875; Ku Klux Klan Acts; individual 19th-century African-American Members of Congress.

Redemption, 39–42, *41*, 41–42. *See also,* White supremacy.

Redistricting. *See,* Apportionment and redistricting.

Redlining, 426. *See also,* Discrimination.

Red Shirts. *See,* South Carolina.

Redistricting, *372*. *See,* Apportionment and redistricting.

Reduction, 167–69, 179–80, 189n, 193n, 281, 312, 320. *See also,* Apportionment; Fourteenth Amendment.

Reed, Thomas Brackett, 212n, 216

Renewal Community Project, 641

Republican Party,

1994 "Republican Revolution," 571

black representation, 25–28, 384–85

black voter re-alignment, 4, 14n, *42*, 42, 58, 182–83, 236, *241*, 241–44, 267n, 286

civil rights, 20–22, 26–27

corruption and patronage, 26–27, 185n

New Deal and Depression Era, 241–44

Jim Crow Era, 154, 155–57

Reconstruction Era, 20–21, 25–28

factions, 20–21, 25–28, 155–56

see also, Apportionment and redistricting; Constitutional conventions, former Confederate states; Democratic Party; Elections; Machine politics; Reduction.

Republican Sentinel, 25, 112, 113. *See also,* Newspapers, African-American.

Revels, Hiram Rhodes, 1, 10, 18, *20*, 20, 24, *25*, *26*, *29*, *32*, *33*, 33, 34,

43n, 45n, **54–61**, 118, 338n

Reynolds, Mel, 521, **626–29**

Reynolds v. Sims. See, Supreme Court, United States.

Rice, Thomas, *154*

Richardson, John S., 65, 66

Richardson, Laura, **750**

Rifle Clubs, 29

Rizzo, Frank, 590

Robertson, Edward, 136

Roberts, Frederick, 324

Robinson, Dolly, 340

Robinson, Randall, 389, 408n

Ronan, Daniel J., 361, 362

Roosevelt, Eleanor, *243*, 243, *244*, 246, 268n

Roosevelt, Franklin D., 181, 236, 241, 242, 243, 245–46, 249, 267–68n, 282, 286, 288, 294, 303, 324, 329n, 506, 534, 542

Roosevelt, Theodore, 194n, 330n

Rostenkowski, Daniel, 628

Rumsfeld, Donald, 642

Rush, Bobby L., 372, 549, 724, **730–31**

Russell, Richard, 251–52, 253, 254

Ryan, William Fitts, 265

S

Sacagawea coin, 624

Saulsbury, Willard, 56

Savage, Gus, **518–23**, 529n, 626

Scalawag, 26, *28*, 36, 72, 88, 108, 148, 208. *See also,* Carpetbaggers.

School Improvement Act, 328

School vouchers, 565, 641, 656

Schroeder, Patricia, 392, 393, 419, 614

Scott, Hugh D., 251

Scott, David, **732–33**

Scott, Robert C., **734–35**

Scott, Robert K., 26–27, 72, 74, 75, 78, 96, 106. *See also,* South Carolina.

Seal, Roderick, 102

Seale, Bobby, *258*, 372

Second Reconstruction, 249–59

Segregation,

education, 177, 255

Executive Order 9981, 249

federal government, in, 172–73, *174*, 190n, 245–46, 259–60

health clinics, *174*

House visitors' gallery, *163*

lunch counters, *254*, 254–55

military, 14, 57–58, 118, 140, *164*, 173, *174*, 237, 237–38, 244–45, 249, 295–96

water fountains, 237

see also, Civil rights; Civil Rights Acts; Civil Rights Movement; Discrimination; Disfranchisement.

Select Committee on Hunger. *See,* Hunger, Select Committee on.

Select Committee on the Freedmen's Bank, 33–34, 64, 65, 119. *See also,* Freedmen's Savings and Trust Company (Freedmen's Bank).

Selective Service Act, influence of, 173

Senate, United States, 4, 6, *12*, 25, 35, *158*, 165, *180*, *248*, 263, 390

committees, 31, 33, 34, 46n, 182, 239, 405n

confirmations, 204, *397*, 461, 586

elections, 18, 20, 43n, 45n, 397
procedures, *4*, 251–52, 409n. *See also,*
    Cloture; Filibuster.
Senators, African-American, 18, *20*,
    20, *29*, *31*, 31, *32*, *33*, *369*, 397. *See
    also,* Brooke, Edward William, III;
    Bruce, Blanche Kelso; Moseley-
    Braun, Carol; Obama, Barack;
    Revels, Hiram Rhodes.
southern influence, 180–82, 251–52.
Sener, James, 36
Seniority, *377. See also,* Incumbency and
    seniority, influence of.
Seymour, Horatio, 122
Shaw v. Reno. See, Supreme Court,
    United States.
Shays, Christopher, 570
Shelley, Charles M., 113, 124–25
Sherman, John, 81, 164
Sherman Silver Purchase Act, 163, 222
SHIELD Act, 721
"Shoestring" district of Mississippi. *See,*
    Apportionment and redistricting.
"Shoestring" district of South Carolina.
    See, Apportionment and redistricting.
Shortridge, Samuel, 178–79
Sickles, Daniel, 29
Silver coinage monetary policy, 162–63,
    165
Simmons, Furnifold, 149, 200, 202
Simpson, William, 141
Singh, Robert, 10, 401n
Slaughterhouse Cases. See, Supreme Court,
    United States.
Slavery, 14n, 43n, 96, 185n, 202, 210,
    211
    African-American Members of
        Congress, experiences, 3, 22–24,
        43n, 86, 88, 100, 116, 128, 200
    geographic distinctions, 22–24, 155
    legacy of, 385, 743
Smalls, Robert, 10, 25–26, *32*, 91, 99n,
    138–45, 151n, 185n, 220
    committee assignments, 32
    early background, 25, 144n, 145n
    elections, 30, 157–59, 161, 216
    legislative interests, 41–42
    political influence, 216
    South Carolina constitutional
        convention, 158–59, 223
    see also, South Carolina.
Smith, Al, 182, 183
Smith, Howard, *251*, 251, 254
Smith, Robert C., 394, 410–11n
Smith Act, 506
Smith v. Allwright. See, Supreme Court,
    United States.
Social Darwinism, 172. *See also,*
    Imperialism; White supremacy.
South Africa, apartheid policy, 239,
    263, 313, 314, 348, 386–90, 418–19,
    426–27, 433, 441, 444n, 461, 482,
    486, 491, 508, 514, 515, 542, 548,
    552, 554, 570, 574, 729, 740
    Anti-Apartheid Act of 1985, 389–90
    Comprehensive Anti-Apartheid Act of
        1986 (CAAA), 390, 418–19, 441
    constructive engagement policy, 389
    see also, Congressional Black Caucus
        (CBC).

South Carolina, 26–27
    black representation, 62–67, 72–77,
        78–83, 94–99, 106–109, 138–45,
        214–19, 220–27, 684–85
    disfranchisement, 157–59, 220, 224
    Hamburg massacre, 65–66
    Red Shirt militias, 29, 64, 97, 140,
        141, 231, 233n
    Scottsboro Nine, 281
    State constitutional conventions, 62,
        78, 88, 94, 106, 110, 128, 138,
        146, 158–59, 217, 223, 226n. *See
        also,* Disfranchisement,
    see also, Black Codes; White
        supremacy; Appendix C: Black-
        American Representatives and
        Senators by State and Territory.
*South Carolina Leader. See, Missionary
    Record*; Newspapers, African-
    American.
Southern Christian Leadership
    Conference (SCLC), 252, 371, *383*,
    438, 458, 461, 548
Southern conservatives, influence of,
    172–73, 178, 180–82, 249, 250,
    251–52, 253
Southern Manifesto. *See,* Declaration of
    Constitutional Principles.
Southern Rural Development
    Commission, 608
Southwick, George, 231
Spanish–American War, 103, 163,
    164, 230. See also, Military Service,
    African-American Members.
Speaks, Sara, 302
Speer, Thomas Jefferson, 68
Stark, Fortney (Pete), 376
Stanton, Edwin, 21
State constitutional conventions. *See,*
    Disfranchisement.
Steingut, Stanley, 340. *See also,* Machine
    politics.
Stenholm, Charles, 491
Stephens, Alexander, 36, 81
Stevens, Thaddeus, 20, *22*
Stevenson, Adlai, *253*, 304
Stewart, Bennett McVey, 266n,
    502–505, 526
Stewart, William, 165
Stimson, Henry L., 237
Stockdale, Thomas, 103
Stokes, Carl, 265n, 356
Stokes, Louis, *5*, 6, *11*, 238, *263*, 313,
    342, 348, **354–61**, 365, *370*, *374*, *375*,
    378, 396, 419, 427, 448, 709
    committee assignments, 266n, 377,
        378, 402n, 403n, 404n, 411n
    Congressional Black Caucus (CBC),
        and, 6, 376, 378, 402n
    early background, 237
    elections, 257, 352n
    legislative interests, 407n
    legislative style, 374, 378, 403n
    political influence, 377
    pre-congressional political experience,
        238, 265n
    see also, Ohio, black representation.
Stone, Chuck, *248*
Storey, Moorefield, 173
Storm, John, 37

Straker, Daniel Augustus, 78
Student Bill of Rights Act, 695
Student Nonviolent Coordinating
    Committee (SNCC), *257*, 371–72,
    714, 722, 730, 736. *See also,* Lewis,
    John R.
Student Right to Know Act, 739
Sub-Saharan Africa humanitarian aid,
    701, 711, 729, 743. *See also,* Africa,
    foreign policy.
Sudan, 499, 701, 712, 727, 741
Sumner, Charles, 20, 26, 31, 35, 54, 64,
    78, 81, 108, 128, 164, 169, 208
Sumners, Hatton W., *178*, 178, 181,
    192n, 244
Supreme Court, United States, 41–42,
    171, 250, 253, 264, 268n
    Adarand Constructors, Inc. v. Peña, 587
    Baker v. Carr, 250
    Brown v. Board of Education, 247, 250,
        252, 312
    Civil Rights Cases, 41
    Dennis v. United States, 506
    Giles v. Harris, 171
    Langston v. United States, 208
    Miller v. Johnson, 398
    Mills v. Green, 223
    Mitchell v. United States et al., 289
    Plessy v. Ferguson, 171
    Powell exclusion, 305
    Reynolds v. Sims, 250
    Shaw v. Reno, 397–98
    Slaughterhouse Cases, 41
    Smith v. Allwright, 250
    Terry v. Ohio, 356
    United States v. Cruikshank, 41
    United States v. Harris, 41
    United States v. Reese, 41
    Wesberry v. Sanders, 250
    Williams v. Mississippi, 171, 223
Surrogate representation, 1–2, 27–28,
    42, 45n, 162, 187n, 391. *See
    also,* African-American Members
    of Congress, characteristics;
    Congressional Black Caucus (CBC).
Swain, Carol, 10, 170, 376

T

Talent, Jim, 641
Tammany Hall, 302, 304. *See also,*
    Machine politics.
Tarver, Malcolm C., 246
Tax Reform Act of 1986, 349
Telecommunications Development
    Fund, 739
Temporary Assistance for Needy
    Families program, 743
Tennessee, black representation,
    472–77, 654–59. *See,* Appendix C:
    Black-American Representatives and
    Senators by State and Territory.
Tennessee Negro Suffrage Convention,
    110
Tenure of Office Act, 21
Terrell, Mary Church, 173, 194n
Terrorism Threat to Public
    Transportation Assessment Act, 648
Terry v. Ohio. See, Supreme Court, United
    States.
Texas, black representation, 452–57,
    496–501, 574–79, 696–97, 702–703,

706–707. *See,* Appendix C: Black-
    American Representatives and
    Senators by State and Territory.
Thirteenth Amendment, 21, 35
Thomas, Charles R., 128
Thomas, Clarence, 584, 586, 622
Thompson, Bennie, **736–37**
Thompson, Charles P., 36
Thompson, Fletcher, 460
Thompson, Henry, 142
Thompson, William C., 340
Thompson, William Hale (Big Bill),
    241, 267n, 278, 280. *See also,*
    Machine Politics.
Thorne, Edward Alston, 203
Thurman, Allen, 57
Thurmond, Strom, *249*, 249, 253, 271n,
    335, 356
Till, Emmett, 252–53, *253*, 312, 518.
    See also, Lynching.
Tillman, Benjamin, *158*, 158–59, 161,
    181, 220, 222, 223, 231. *See also,*
    White supremacy; South Carolina.
Tillman, George D., 140–41
Tilson, John Q., 193n
Tinkham, George Holden, 170, *179*,
    179–80, 193n
To Secure These Rights, 249
Towne, Laura, 141
Towns, Edolphus, **738–39**
TransAfrica lobbying group. *See,*
    Congressional Black Caucus (CBC).
Transform America Transaction Fee, 695
Transportation Equity Act, 648
Truman, Bess, 303
Truman, Harry S., *249*, 249, 303
Trumbull, Lyman, 35
Tucker, C. Delores, 592
Tucker, Henry, 222
Tucker, Walter R., III, 515, **630–33**, 646
Tulsa race riot. *See,* Race riots.
Turner, Benjamin Sterling, 31, *33*, 34,
    84–87, 112, 122, 124
Turner, Frederick Jackson, 157

U

Un-American Activities Committee
    (HUAC), 247, 269n, 506, 546
Underwood, Oscar, 169, 179
Unemployment, 327, 381
United Negro College Fund, 492
United States v. Cruikshank. See, Supreme
    Court, United States.
United States, v. Harris. See, Supreme
    Court, United States.
United States v. Reese. See, Supreme Court,
    United States.
Universal Health Care Act, 469
Universal Military Training Act, 295–96
Universal Negro Improvement
    Association, 176
Urban Asthma Reduction Act, 731
Urban Mass Transportation Assistance
    Act, 460
Urban policy plan initiative, 474
USA PATRIOT Act, 656, 745

V

Van Hollen, Chris, 666
Vardaman, James Kimble, *180*, 181. *See
    also,* White supremacy.

Vega, Luz, 343
Venable, Edward, 208
Vietnam War, 248, 258, 295, 320, 327, 335, 336–37, 340, 342, 378, *392*, 392, 416, 418, 432
Villard, Oswald Garrison, 173
Violence Against Women Act, 687, 721
Violent Crime Control and Law Enforcement Act, 542
Virginia, black representation, 206–13, 734–35. *See,* Appendix C: Black-American Representatives and Senators by State and Territory.
Virgin Islands, 406n
    black representation, 484–87, 634–37, 678–79. *See,* Appendix C: Black-American Representatives and Senators by State and Territory.
Volpe, John, 334
Volunteers in Service to America (VISTA), 537
Voter registration drives. *See,* National Association for the Advancement of Colored People (NAACP).
Voting rights. *See,* Civil Rights Acts; Civil rights movement; Disfranchisement; Elections; National Association for the Advancement of Colored People (NAACP); Voting Rights Acts.
Voting Rights Act of 1965, 256–57, *257*, 320, 335, 368, 379
    effect on congressional districts, 257, 264, 396, 558
Voting Rights Act of 1975, 335, 379, 455, 461–62
Voting Rights Act of 1982, 379, 380–81, 396

W

Waddell, Alfred, 186–87n
Waldon, Alton R., Jr., 405n, **552–55**, 562, 564
Walls, Josiah Thomas, *25*, 25, 27, 30, 31, *33*, 33, 39, 45n, **88–93**
Warren, Lindsay C., 281
Washington, Booker T., 169, 228, 262, 286, 289
Washington, Craig Anthony, 499, 571, **574–79**
Washington, Harold, *372*, 504, 520, **524–29**, 546, 622, 626, 693, 730
Watergate scandal, 336, 433, 452, 454, 455, 474, 632
Waters, Maxine, 393, **740–41**
Watson, Diane Edith, **742–43**
Watt, Melvin, L., 598, **744–45**
Watts, Julius Caesar, Jr. (J. C.), *379*, 379, 384–85, **638–45**
Watts (CA) race riots. *See,* Race riots.
Welfare policy, 242, 281, 328, 337, 358, 364, 384, 472, 474, 475, 546, 559, 565, 571, 584, 587, 620, 636, 638, 640
Wells, G. Wiley, 118
Wells-Barnett, Ida, *166*, 173
Wesberry v. Sanders. See, Supreme Court, United States.
West Point, U.S. Military Academy, 57–58, 60n, 118, 210

Wheat, Alan Dupree, 397, **540–45**
Whip, 181, 378–79, *379*, *390*, 405n, 468, 492, 582, 590, 592, 640, 642, 648, 666
White, George Henry, 1, 6, 10, 152, 154, 160, 169, 172, 174–75, 191n, 195, **228–33**, 234
    committee assignments, 187n
    early background, 155
    legislative interests, 162–64, 166–68
    legislative style, 161
    Cheatham, Henry, and, 161–62, 203, 204
    Whitesboro (NJ), 232
    see also, North Carolina, black representation.
White, Walter, *172*, 176, 188n, 245, 247
Whitehead, Thomas, 37
White League, 29–30, 102. *See also,* Ku Klux Klan.
White supremacy, 29, 44n, 158–59, 180–81, 246–47, 335. *See also,* Discrimination; Mississippi; Segregation; Social Darwinism.
Whittaker, Johnson C., 118
Whittemore, Benjamin F., 62
Wilder, L. Douglas, 395
Williams, George H., 113
Williams, Jeremiah, 113
Williams, Juan, 395
Williams v. Mississippi. See, Supreme Court, United States.
Willis, Frances, *244*
Wilmington (NC) race riot. *See,* Race riots.
Wilson, Henry, 18
Wilson, Woodrow, 172, 173, 182, 190n
Wisconsin, black representation, 720–21. *See,* Appendix C: Black-American Representatives and Senators by State and Territory.
Women Representatives, 239, *246*, 264, 265n. *See also,* African-American Members of Congress, characteristics.
Wood, Robert, 100
Woodard, Frederick A., 148, 161–62, 203, 230
Woodward, C. Vann, 10, 154, 185n
World War I, *173*, 173–74, 191n. *See also,* Military service, African-American Members of Congress.
World War II, *237*, *244*, 244–46
    employment discrimination, 245–46, 259
    Executive Order 8802, 245–46
    NAACP "Double V" campaign, 245
    women, military participation, *244*
    see also, Discrimination; Fair Employment Practices Committee (FEPC); Military service, African-American Members of Congress; Segregation.
Wright, Jim, 396, 474, 478, 480, 558
Wright, Samuel D., 343, 536
Wynn, Albert R., **746–47**

Y

Young, Andrew Jackson, Jr., *5*, *6*, 6, 10, *264*, 264, 371, *375*, 408n, 448, 452,

458–65, 490, 715, 732
    committee assignments, 404–405n, 448
    legislative interests, 380, 388, 402n, 408n
    pre-congressional political experience, 371, 438
    see also, Georgia, black representation.
Youth Employment Services Act, 570

Z

Zabrosky, Alex, 362